CONTENTS

Social Psychology

DISCARDED

Jim McKnight
Department of Psychology,
University of Western Sydney, Macarthur

Jeanna Sutton
Department of Behavioural Sciences,
University of Sydney, Cumberland

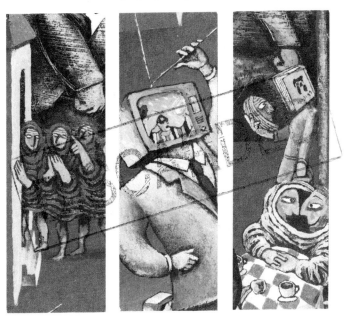

PRENTICE HALL AUSTRALIA

New York London Toronto Sydney Tokyo Singapore

© 1994 by Prentice Hall Australia

Acquisitions Editor: Joy Whitton
Production Editor: Fiona Marcar & Katie Millar
Cover design: Matthew Davidson
Typeset by Keyboard Wizards, Allambie Heights, NSW

Printed in Australia by McPherson's Printing Group. Victoria

1 2 3 4 5 98 97 96 95 94

ISBN 0 7248 1088 9

National Library of Australia
Cataloguing-in-Publication Data

McKnight, Jim.
   Social psychology.

   Bibliography.
   Includes index.
   ISBN 0 7248 1088 9.

   1. Social psychology. I. Sutton, Jeanna. II. Title.

302

Prentice Hall, Inc., *Englewood Cliffs, New Jersey*
Prentice Hall Canada, Inc., *Toronto*
Prentice Hall Hispanoamericana, SA, *Mexico*
Prentice Hall of India Private Ltd, *New Delhi*
Prentice Hall International, Inc., *London*
Prentice Hall of Japan, Inc., *Tokyo*
Prentice Hall of Southeast Asia Pty Ltd, *Singapore*
Editora Prentice Hall do Brasil Ltda, *Rio de Janeiro*

PRENTICE HALL

A division of Simon & Schuster

PREFACE

Prefaces generally allow authors to waffle a bit about the nature of their craft, and if they are in their second or subsequent editions, to apologise for their previous shortcomings. Well we are no different. Have you ever wondered why a couple of otherwise normal people would undertake such an all-consuming task as writing a major introductory text from scratch? Read on . . .

We wrote this book because we were fed up turning our students' American English back into English English and felt the time had come for a comprehensive text with an unashamedly local flavour. New Zealand and Australia have produced several social psychologists of international standing and we wanted our students to see them up there with the rest in an introductory text. We balanced their contributions, outlined in our *profiles* boxes, with many studies by lesser known researchers, who nevertheless are creating an indigenous social psychology. You will notice this text has an Australian flavour and a New Zealand afterglow. Australian studies in our book outnumber those from across the Tasman about six-to-one. This is not an unconscious ethnocentrism on our part. Rather Australian social psychologists outnumber New Zealand ones in that proportion.

We have also tried to raise your consciousness of Asia and Oceania in a modest way. At present psychology is in its infancy in those regions and there are few social psychologists. Those that do practise are more interested in an indigenous psychology which is beyond the scope of our book. Still at the rate that psychology is growing in Asia, we hope to reach a wider audience in another edition. To the extent that we have reached beyond our two countries, it is in studies that compare Australian and New Zealand samples with those of Indonesia, Malaysia, New Guinea, Fiji and Hong Kong. We hope that overseas students reading these studies will feel at home.

In honour of our more Eurocentric tradition of social psychology, we have used straightforward language. Academics who hide brilliant thoughts in totally incomprehensible academic prose are a dead loss, so we adopted a discursive, narrative style and wrote our book as if it were a novel. This might come as a bit of a surprise if you were expecting a stiffer "scientific" style but stick with it, we did not sacrifice intellectual rigour in trying to make our book more readable. We have also paid you the compliment of assuming you have sufficient intellectual and critical capacity to handle social psychology's diverse theoretical perspectives. To emphasise these we have scattered *food-for-thought* pieces throughout. Nor have we tried to hide that social psychology has areas of profound disagreement and that often we, the authors, take opposing positions. After all, this makes us very conscious of our biases and the need for balance. We have let our individual differences speak for themselves and have indicated in the contents section who wrote what. There was really no other way of writing the book.

If you have flipped through the book you will have noticed its decidedly anecdotal tone. This may come as a surprise given some of the stiffer texts around, but any pedagogue will tell you that a short story, providing it is relevant, will make your point more forcefully than just describing theory. Perhaps half of all social psychology texts use this approach and half don't. We are in no doubt which are the more riveting and we have not lost sight of our ultimate audience, social psychology students, who would occasionally enjoy being riveted. The chapter openers are mostly drawn from Jim's rather eclectic experiences.

So who wrote the book?

Ten years ago we both joined what was then a small but cosy college. We discovered we both had worked in gaols and were soon busily swapping war stories. This led to a firm friendship which is just one of the many reasons for this book. Jim used to tease Jeanna about her interest in social psychology, but she left and then he had to teach it himself. Over the years we have had many glorious arguments about the ultimate nature of social reality and managed to disagree almost entirely (which is yet another reason for the book).

Jeanna is currently a lecturer in social psychology in the Faculty of Health Sciences at the University of Sydney. While she quite enjoys lecturing, she really wanted to be a principal ballerina but grew too much. Jeanna holds degrees in psychology and criminology and was formerly senior lecturer in applied psychology at the NSW Police Academy. She also taught at the Macarthur Institute and

Macquarie University. Jeanna has extensive research and consulting experience with various government agencies and community groups, and is an experienced sexual assault, child abuse and domestic violence counsellor. Her academic interests include policing studies, violence against women and children, and psychology and the law. She likes cats, history and the gentle art of conversation. Her dislikes include students who dispute the relevance of acquiring an earful of knowledge; bullies, fundamentalists of any persuasion; economic rationalists; and pretentious intellectuals.

Jim is a senior lecturer in the Psychology Department at the University of Western Sydney (Macarthur). He has degrees in psychology, sociology and the philosophy of knowledge. He has a strong interest in environmental issues and the evolutionary roots of social behaviour. He has hand-built several houses, lived in alternative communes for many years and has published in this area. His last book described how to build wind turbines, and his last article was on the practics of retrofitting washing machines to run on 12 volts. This book is a return to a slightly more academic topic. His likes include meaningful conversations with slightly cracked students, fixing old washing machines, existential philosophy and reading science fiction. He basically dislikes what Jeanna dislikes, which is another reason they are friends.

And now for a few notes on the contents

If you are wondering on what basis we picked or excluded studies, we tried to frame our book so that it covered the high ground of social psychology, while filling in areas of local research which are significant but poorly reported. We had two choices. Social psychology fades into developmental psychology in one direction and into personality theory in the other. We chose to go towards the personality end because there are already a wealth of local developmental texts. Even so, hard decisions had to be taken about content and areas such as emotion, motivation and values were excluded, as were enormous chunks of socio-development. We have sprinkled a few such studies throughout the book but it is large enough already.

We also resisted blandishments from our colleagues to turn our book into a treatise on cross-cultural, or health, or community psychology! Please somebody, write comprehensive introductory texts in these areas.

If you are going to read this text as a book rather than dip into it as a reference, try to read it in chunks. Chapters Two and Three, Four and Five, and Eight, Nine and Ten, should be read as units as they were written interdependently. Chapter Nine was far and away the most difficult to write. We agonised over its structure for months and it is no accident that it is our largest chapter. The sheer size and rapid growth of close relationships research presents a problem for authors writing social psychology texts. There are so many studies on love and attraction that the research base is skewed towards the start of relationships. Equally it is virtually impossible to decide what are social or developmental studies. There is so much material that you have to chop back the content before you become engulfed. You either decide to write several chapters to cover all the material, which gives your book a decidedly developmental flavour, or skim the material doing little justice to it. In desperation we decided on a third course and specialised, concentrating on just a few areas. The price you pay for such a decision is receiving parcels of dead fish through the mail from colleagues whose areas were excluded!

Chapter Eleven, on Gender, was written by Dr Jac Brown, Director of Education for the Marriage Guidance Council of NSW. Rumour has it that we both wanted to write this chapter, to air our own pet theories, and would have entirely disagreed on its approach and content. Jac, a therapist of many years standing, has a special expertise and interest in the area and settled the argument by deciding to write the chapter himself. Much to Jeanna's amazement, Jim has recently been offered a contract to write an evolutionary analysis of feminism, so he is not too put out.

The rest of the book is fairly straightforward

In summary, social psychology is perhaps the most controversial and hotly contested area in psychology. For the last twenty years the discipline has been engaged in a giant dust up (vigorous argument) about its method, its content, and its applicability. As with many adolescences this has been accompanied with much *sturm und drang*. That this storm and stress is basically healthy is seen from the continuing interest of undergraduates, the many students doing their PhDs in social psychology, the collegiate networking of social psychologists on both sides of the Tasman, and numerous publications. That its adolescence has been unduly prolonged is unquestioned, but relative to some areas of psychology that are plodding amiably along social psychology's growth has been explosive. While the controversies are many and the syntheses few, there are more local social psychologists of international stature than in any other area of psychology. We hope that this vitality (and our book) will inspire you to a much wider reading and deeper appreciation of social psychology.

One final comment before we go. As you read you might like to consider that this book is really about you. As an exercise we counted the percentage of studies that used university students as subjects. A content analysis of our book showed that 68 per cent of the research studies we cited used some university students in their samples.

ACKNOWLEDGMENTS

Too many people contributed to this book for us to acknowledge them all. We would like to thank all the people who read bits and pieces, advised, argued and patiently shuffled chapters back and forwards until we got it right. Some wanted to remain anonymous and some didn't mind, but in the event there were just too many to name.

Thanks to the staff at Prentice Hall. We would particularly blame Chris Lowe who was the original genesis of the book and thank her and Mike Page for their confidence and encouragement at the earliest stages of writing. Joy Whitton, our editor, already knows just how much her support made it all happen. Thanks Joy. Our production manager, Fiona Marcar, was patience personified as the photos, etc., straggled in.

Jenni Rice and John Ray deserve a special thanks for reviewing the entire manuscript at short notice. Their detailed reviews and incisive comments did much to shape the final product. Graeme Mitchell and Steve Harris preserved our humour as they penned many cartoon ideas. Tiina Iismaa read the ms word for word several times, a real grind, which she did painstakingly. Thanks Tiina! Finally Barry and Gavin Price, Mathew Munro, Mark Bramley and Chris Simkin's artistic talents are reflected in the many photos which grace this book.

And an extra special thanks to the University of Western Sydney (Macarthur) which provided the time and resources to make it all happen. We would particularly acknowledge the financial support from the Faculty of Arts and Social Science, University of Western Sydney, which made possible the many photos in this book and the equally generous support from The Faculty of Health Sciences, University of Sydney, which took us part of the way in paying the impossible prices demanded by some overseas publishers for permission to reproduce illustrations.

CREDITS

Chapter 1
Box 1.6 The Australian Psychological Society Ltd (1986) CODE OF PROFESSIONAL CONDUCT, Section E, paras 3–7. Reproduced courtesy of the Australian Psychological Society.

Chapter 2
Fig. 2.1 Nesdale A.R. and Dharmalingam S. (1986) Category salience, stereotyping and person memory. AUSTRALIAN JOURNAL OF PSYCHOLOGY, 38, 145–51. Reproduced with permission of the authors and by courtesy of the Australian Psychological Society.

Fig. 2.2 Rosenberg S., Nelson C. and Vivekananthan P.S. (1968) A multidimensional approach to the structure of personality impressions. JOURNAL OF PERSONALITY AND SOCIAL PSYCHOLOGY, 9, 283–94. Copyright (1968) by the American Psychological Association. Every attempt has been made to contact S. Rosenberg, C. Nelson and P.S. Vivekananthan. Would the authors please contact Prentice Hall Australia.

Fig. 2.3 Figure from THE PSYCHOLOGY OF RUMOR by Gordon W. Allport and Leo J. Postman, copyright 1947 and renewed 1975 by Holt, Rinehart and Winston, Inc. Reproduced with permission of the publisher.

Fig. 2.6 Jussim L. (1986) Self-fulfilling prophecies: A theoretical and integrative review. PSYCHOLOGICAL REVIEW, 93, 429–45. Copyright (1986) by the American Psychological Association. Reproduced with permission.

Chapter 3
Fig. 3.2 Forgas J.P. (1992) Affect and perception: Research evidence and an integrative theory. In Stroebe W. and Hewstone M. (eds) EUROPEAN REVIEW OF SOCIAL PSYCHOLOGY (Vol. 3), Wiley, Chichester. Reproduced with permission of John Wiley & Sons Ltd.

Fig. 3.4 Fletcher G.J. and Haig B.D. (1989) An evaluation of the "naive scientist" model in social psychology. In Forgas J.P. and Innes J.M. (eds) RECENT ADVANCES IN SOCIAL PSYCHOLOGY: AN INTERNATIONAL PERSPECTIVE, Elsevier, North-Holland. Reproduced courtesy of Elsevier Science Publishers BV.

Fig. 3.5 Berglas S. and Jones E.E. (1978) Drug choice as a self-handicapping strategy in response to non-contingent success. JOURNAL OF PERSONALITY AND SOCIAL PSYCHOLOGY, 36, 405–17. Copyright (1978) by the American Psychological Association. Reproduced with permission.

Fig. 3.6 Craske M-L. (1988) Learned helplessness, self-worth motivation and attribution retraining for primary school children. BRITISH JOURNAL OF EDUCATIONAL PSYCHOLOGY, 58, 152–64. Reproduced with permission.

Chapter 4
Table 4.1 Feather N.T. (1989) Attitudes towards the high achiever: The fall of the tall poppy. AUSTRALIAN JOURNAL OF PSYCHOLOGY, 141, 239–67. Reproduced with permission of the author and by courtesy of the Australian Psychological Society.

Table 4.2 Lange R. and Tiggemann M. (1980) Changes within the Australian population to more external control beliefs. AUSTRALIAN PSYCHOLOGIST, 15, 495–97. Reproduced with permission of Marika Tiggemann and by courtesy of the Australian Psychological Society.

Fig. 4.6 Lee C. (1989) Perceptions of immunity to disease in adult smokers. JOURNAL OF BEHAVIORAL MEDICINE, 12, 267–77. Reproduced with permission of Plenum Publishing Corp.

Fig. 4.7 Festinger L. and Carlsmith J.M. (1959) Cognitive consequences of forced compliance. JOURNAL OF ABNORMAL AND SOCIAL PSYCHOLOGY, 58, 203–210. Courtesy of the American Psychological Association.

Chapter 5

Table 5.1 Vaughan G.M. (1988) The psychology of intergroup discrimination. NEW ZEALAND JOURNAL OF PSYCHOLOGY, 17, 1–14. Reproduced with permission of the New Zealand Psychological Society Inc.

Table 5.2 Hepworth J.T. and West S.G. (1988) Lynchings and the economy: A time-series reanalysis of Hovland and Sears (1940). JOURNAL OF PERSONALITY AND SOCIAL PSYCHOLOGY, 55, 239–247. Copyright (1988) by the American Psychological Association. Reproduced with permission.

Table 5.3 McConahay J.B. (1986) Modern racism, ambivalence, and the modern racism scale. In Dovidio J.F. and Gaertner S.L. (eds) PREJUDICE, DIS-CRIMINATION AND RACISM, Academic Press, NY. Reproduced with permission of Academic Press. Every attempt has been made to contact J.B. McConahay. Would the author please contact Prentice Hall Australia.

Table 5.4 Brehm Sharon S. and Kassin Saul M. SOCIAL PSYCHOLOGY (1st edn). Copyright ©1990 by Houghton Mifflin Company, Boston. Used with permission.

Fig. 5.1 Marjoribanks K. and Jordan D.F. (1986) Stereotyping among Aboriginal and Anglo-Australians: The uniformity, intensity, direction, and quality of auto- and heterostereotypes. JOURNAL OF CROSS CULTURAL PSYCHOLOGY, 17, 17–28. Copyright © 1986. Reproduced with permission of Sage Publications Inc.

Table 5.5 Ray J.J. (1972) A new balanced F scale and its relation to social class. AUSTRALIAN PSYCHOL-OGIST, 7, 155–66. Reproduced with permission of John Ray and by courtesy of the Australian Psychological Society.

Chapter 6

Opener (p. 258) Pilger J. (1987) HEROES, Jonathan Cape, Lond. Reproduced with permission.

Box 6.1 Cerf C. and Navarsky V. (1984) THE EXPERTS SPEAK, Pantheon Books, N.Y. Copyright 1984. Reproduced courtesy Pantheon Books.

Fig. 6.4 Tanford S. and Penrod S. (1984) Social influence model: A formal integration of research on majority and minority influence processes. PSYCHOLOGICAL BULLETIN, 95, 189–225. Copyright (1984) by the American Psychological Association. Every attempt has been made to contact S. Tanford and S. Penrod. Would the authors please contact Prentice Hall Australia.

Table 6.1 Lovibond S.H., Mithiran and Adams W.G. (1979) The effects of three experimental prison environments on the behaviour of non-convict volunteer subjects. AUSTRALIAN PSYCHOLOGIST, 14, 273–85. Reproduced with permission of the authors and by courtesy of the Australian Psychological Society.

Table 6.2 Hong's Psychological Reactance Scale. Courtesy Sung-Mook Hong.

Quoted material, p. 288. Excerpt from OBEDIENCE TO AUTHORITY by Stanley Milgram. Copyright © 1974 by Stanley Milgram. Reprinted with permission of HarperCollins Publishers.

Table 6.3 Peterson C. (1989) LOOKING FORWARD THROUGH THE LIFESPAN (2nd edn) Prentice Hall, Sydney. Reproduced with permission of Prentice Hall Australia.

Chapter 7

Fig. 7.1 Buss A.H. (1961) THE PSYCHOLOGY OF AGGRESSION, Wiley, NY. Courtesy John Wiley. Reproduced with permission of Arnold Buss.

Fig. 7.3 Gerbner G., Gross L., Signorelli N. and Morgan M. (1986) Television's mean world: Violence profile. Occasional papers 14–15, Annenberg School of Communications, University of Pennsylvania, Philadelphia. Reproduced with permission of the authors.

Table 7.2 Sheehan P.W. (1987) Coping with exposure to aggression: The path from research to practice. AUSTRALIAN PSYCHOLOGIST, 22, 291–311, 239–67. Reproduced with permission of the author and by courtesy of the Australian Psychological Society.

Table 7.3 Reproduced with permission Australian Institute of Criminology, Canberra, from Satyanshu K. Mukherjee and Dianne Dagger (1990) THE SIZE OF THE CRIME PROBLEM IN AUSTRALIA (2nd edn) AIC, Canberra.

Fig. 7.4 Reproduced with permission Australian Institute of Criminology, Canberra, from Strang H. (1992) HOMICIDES IN AUSTRALIA 1990–91, AIC, Canberra.

Fig. 7.5 Reproduced with permission Australian Institute of Criminology, Canberra, from National Committee on Violence (1992), VIOLENCE: DIRECTIONS FOR AUSTRALIA, AIC, Canberra.

Fig. 7.7 NSW Bureau of Crime Statistics and Research (1990) NSW RECORDED CRIME STATISTICS 1989/90. Courtesy NSW Bureau of Crime Statistics and Research, Sydney.

the Office of the Status of Women, Department of the Prime Minister and Cabinet, Canberra. Courtesy Office of the Status of Women.

Fig. 11.3 Bittman M. (1991) JUGGLING TIME. HOW AUSTRALIAN FAMILIES USE TIME. Report from the Office of the Status of Women, Department of the Prime Minister and Cabinet, Canberra. Courtesy Office of the Status of Women.

Box 11.8 Quoted from Dennis W. (1992) HOT AND BOTHERED: WOMEN SEX AND LOVE IN THE 1990S, Penguin Books Aust. Ltd, Ringwood, Vic. Reproduced with permission of Penguin Books.

Chapter 12
Fig. 12.2 Zajonc R.B., Heingartner A. and Herman E. (1969) Social enhancement and impairment of performance in the cockroach. JOURNAL OF PERSON-ALITY AND SOCIAL PSYCHOLOGY, 13, 83–92. Copyright (1969) by the American Psychological Association. Reproduced with permission.

Fig. 12.3 Vaughan G.M. (1988) The psychology of intergroup discrimination. NEW ZEALAND JOURNAL OF PSYCHOLOGY, 17, 1–14. Courtesy New Zealand Psychological Society Inc. Reproduced with permission of the author.

Fig. 12.4 Vaughan G.M. (1986) Social change and racial identity: Issues in the use of picture and doll measures. Special Issue: Contributions to cross-cultural psychology. AUSTRALIAN JOURNAL OF PSYCHOLOGY, 38, 359–70. Reproduced with permission of the author and by courtesy of the Australian Psychological Society.

Fig. 12.5 Tedeschi, Linskold and Rosenfeld (1985) INTRODUCTION TO SOCIAL PSYCHOLOGY, West Publishing Co., p. 351. Every attempt has been made to contact West Publishing Co. Would West Publishing Co. please contact Prentice Hall Australia.

Table 12.1 Ng S-H. and Wilson S. (1989) Self-categorization theory and belief polarization among Christian believers and atheists. BRITISH JOURNAL OF SOCIAL PSYCHOLOGY, 28, 47–56. Reproduced courtesy British Psychological Society and authors.

Chapter 13
Fig. 13.1 Cialdini R.B., Reno R.R. and Kallgren C.A. (1990) A focus theory of normative conduct: Recycling the concept of norms to reduce littering in public places. JOURNAL OF PERSONALITY AND SOCIAL PSYCHOLOGY, 58, 1015–26. Copyright (1990) by the American Psychological Association. Reproduced with permission.

Table 13.2 Brown B.B. and Altman I. (1983) Territoriality, defensible space, and residential burglary: An environmental analysis. JOURNAL OF ENVIRON-MENTAL PSYCHOLOGY, 3, 203–20. Reproduced with permission of Academic Press Ltd.

Chapter 14
p. 666 "Coping with victimisation" section drawn from Bowie V. (1989) COPING WITH VIOLENCE, Karibuni Press, Sydney. Reproduced with permission.

Box. 14.2 Chan J. (1992) POLICING IN A MULTI-CULTURAL SOCIETY: A STUDY OF THE NSW POLICE, Commissioned Report, School of Social Science and Policy Service, University of NSW. Courtesy Julie Chan.

Social Psychology

AN INTRODUCTION TO SOCIAL PSYCHOLOGY

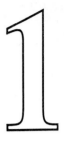

Anti-Vietnam war demonstration late 1960s. (Photo: Mackae/Sydney Morning Herald)

For Jeanna's and my generation the Vietnam War was crucial to our development. No-one could remain neutral and the way you saw the conflict had any number of social consequences. The war deeply polarised our nations and the debate it engendered was bitter and partisan. In some ways the least prepared for the turmoil were young men like myself faced with conscription. In Australia you were chosen by a lottery based on your birth date, so you were denied even the luxury of certainty. The emotional turmoil this created was matched only by the bitterness of those unlucky enough to be chosen while their mates got off scot-free.

Many were uncertain how they should respond and found themselves caught in social riptides. The ANZAC tradition was still very strong and we were bred to a consciousness of the red menace. We also faced strong pressures to follow the example of our fathers who had successfully fought the Japanese and the Germans; a lesson that was drummed into us every ANZAC Day. However, countervailing forces were at work and the great stagnation of the Menzies years bred a feeling that change was overdue. Many thought that our treaty obligations had dragged us into a futile and unwinnable war, and playing handmaiden to American imperialism also stuck in the national craw. None of us wanted to become one of the steadily mounting statistics, so awaiting the conscription lottery was a trying time.

It was against this backdrop that I, a callow youth facing the conscription lottery, found myself watching an anti-war demo, trying to decide where I stood on it all. The demonstration was a beauty and all sides were represented. The marchers were a mixed bag of draft-dodgers, activists, clerics, academics, journalists, students, unionists, mothers and a few disgruntled but high-profile Vietnam veterans. Lining the footpaths behind police barriers were pro-war

The ANZAC tradition is still strong in Australia and New Zealand, a lesson that is reinforced every ANZAC Day.

Vietnam veterans and other activists, a flying squad from the RSL and a strong police contingent. Most onlookers were probably as undecided as myself but had turned out for the show. Scattered among the crowd were a few US servicemen on R and R and their inebriated antics provided a touch of light relief.

The crowd moved off down the road from the marshalling areas in an orderly procession, banners waving. For about half a kilometre all went well until one protester spotted an Australian uniform mixed in with a bunch of American soldiers. Quick as a flash, he stepped out of the line, yelled "killers" and belted the soldier with his sign. Pride stung, the soldier jumped the barricades and broke the marcher's nose. The Americans, showing laudable restraint, clapped politely. The police, surprised by the speed of the assaults, riposted by arresting both and then mayhem broke out as the march degenerated into a brawl.

Chaos reigned! The few police present were overwhelmed. One mewed with pain as an elderly woman on his back tried to pull his hair out. Two clerics were beating another policeman with their signs, while a unionist wearing a tee-shirt

*labelled "Out Now" solicitously rescued the injured officer. A young woman,
clearly incensed, was twisting a policeman's ear off as he tried to handcuff her
boyfriend, a completely innocent bystander! Two old fogies sporting RSL badges
were just as confused, shouting encouragement to the anti-war marchers, while
their horrified mates desperately tried to shut them up! On the sidelines two
middle-aged female spectators were standing toe-to-toe trading blows and
insults, for whatever reason.*

*The melee was over in a few minutes as police reinforcements shovelled the
combatants into paddy-wagons. The onlookers, generally aroused by a good
brawl, chewed it over, labelling the police as "fascists and warmongers" and the
marchers as "poofters, dirty-long-haired-gits, dole-bums, bleeding hearts and
draft-dodgers". The soldiers were studiously ignored.*

An introduction to social psychology

This anecdote from a distant past is a microcosm of the issues social
psychology studies. Why were marchers protesting about violence so ready
to become violent themselves? Why did grannies turn into viragos? What
impact had onlookers on their behaviour? Why were some people prepared
to march and others watch? Why were the police so undiscriminating?
Why did the unionist help his opponent in the midst of battle? What
group dynamics made this situation such a powder keg and was an explosion
inevitable? What stereotypes and prejudices were held by each side? What
attributions of responsibility did each side make? Perhaps most interesting,
why did so many people act out of character? The brawl left me no clearer
in my opinions on the war but it did lead to a lifelong interest in social
psychology!

These questions, history now, have no real answers but hopefully you
will find your own along the way, as such issues are the life-breath of
social psychology. Our reason for postponing their discussion is an
acknowledgment of the old truism—if you don't know where you are
going, you'll end up somewhere else. So to reduce the inevitable confusion
of a novice tackling a new area and to give these questions depth, we will
take some time to build a framework in which you can slot new information.
First we define social psychology and consider its implications. Then we
will look at the various *types* of social psychology and *levels* of explanation.
Next a potted history will give you some feel for its historical context and
evolution. Acknowledging that social psychology has a rambunctious nature
with lots of disputes and controversies, we then map some of the more
recent challenges to traditional mainstream social psychology. Finally we
examine the many ways social psychologists go about collecting data and
the pitfalls they face. Hopefully by the end of this chapter you will have
some feel for the way we approach social behaviour, how the past shapes
present inquiries and how future hopes define present research efforts.

Arthur, the publican across from St Barnabas, has been gently mocking vicar Bob's notices for years. Why? This and other more mundane questions are the meat and drink of social psychology. (Photos: Gavin Price)

Defining social psychology

Social psychology studies social behaviour

This short definition summarises an enormous range of assumptions and a research effort that is one of the largest within psychology. In 1968 Gordon Allport gave what is fairly universally accepted as an all-inclusive definition:

> Social psychology is a discipline in which people attempt to understand, explain, and predict how the thoughts, feelings, and actions of individuals are influenced by the perceived, imagined, or implied thoughts, feelings, and actions of others. (Allport, 1968, p. 3)

It is an obvious truism to say that social psychology's territory is the study of "social" behaviour but what does this mean? You will recall from your introductory psychology days that psychology prides itself as the study of

What is social psychology?

the individual and this was held up as the feature distinguishing it from all other social sciences that took a more collective view. Notwithstanding this individual focus, we are a social species and define ourselves against a social backdrop. So social psychology is that branch of psychology that examines the *individual* in social settings. A moment's reflection on Allport's definition will lead you to conclude that social psychology must also be a study of group behaviour, even if of only two people interacting. Nevertheless, it is still an individual focus that psychology brings to these social interactions. For example, in the street protest described above, the young girl's anger at the injustice of her boyfriend's arrest was evident. A social psychologist would look for a personal motive here, while other "ologists" would no doubt focus on the riot as an entity, attributing her anger to more impersonal social forces.

Saying that social psychology is preoccupied with individuals is in some ways setting up a straw man to be knocked down immediately. As we will see when we consider social theorising, social psychologists give differing explanations to account for social behaviour and the individual perspective is just one of many. The problem with defining social psychology as "the study of social behaviour" is its sheer inclusiveness. Every day, in every way, we judge social niceties to a tee and, in predicting others' behaviour, we tap a vast amount of social mores, personal experience, attribution, stereotypes and use inspired guesswork. Obviously we are not all social psychologists, so what divides the psychologist from the practitioner? Perhaps if nothing else, they both study social behaviour but the psychologist draws extra insights from psychology and other social sciences, and reflects upon them to give more precise accounts of why we act as we do. Put another way, maybe social psychologists work just a little harder at trying to understand us and, given the enormity of social phenomena, they tend to specialise.

What do social psychologists study?

While social psychologists study social behaviour, what is selected for study is a bit of a sore point with critics who can always point to the neglect of their favoured child. As we noted in the preface, social psychology courses and their texts tend to be a smorgasbord of selected areas with few obvious interconnections. In some ways this represents the vastness of social psychology's domain and a consequent retreat into specialisation. This is in sharp contrast to other areas, for example personality, where each theory, no matter how different it is to competing theories, nonetheless purports to be an all-embracing account of human nature. If you skim our contents pages you will see a fairly representative view of the discipline's interests. Yet, like most sciences, social psychology's development has been driven by interest, necessity, money, luck, interesting insights from other areas and the spirit of the times. Put another way, social psychology is an unplanned discipline. Even so there are some discernible patterns.

Approaches to social theorising

How would you explain the young girl's anger at the wrongful arrest of her boyfriend? Was it the instinctive aggression of a woman protecting her mate; or had all her prior contacts with the police been negative? Was it an act of social protest aimed at a stereotypical oppressor; or would you see it as the unfortunate consequences of a simple attribution error? Whatever your viewpoint, and whatever the truth, our differing answers point to many possible explanations of social behaviour. Social psychologists, like all theorists, differ in the interpretations they place on events and this is reflected in their theories. To illustrate the main approaches to social theorising we will consider our riot anecdote from several different perspectives.

Cognitive perspectives

Social cognition, the quickest growing area of social psychology over the last decade, explores how our thoughts, feelings and beliefs help us understand social interactions. Those committed to this perspective focus on our perception of situations and the impact this has on our behaviour. When we face unexpected events, like the young woman at the riot, we quickly sum up what is happening and react. No doubt she immediately identified the policeman as an aggressor and, from a sense of injured pride, took swift retaliatory action. These cognitive processes allow us to swiftly impose order on a complex and often chaotic social world, and that we are able to act so promptly argues we rely on past experience do so. That such impressions are sometimes inappropriate, and often in error, in no way diminishes their importance and, as we will see in Chapter Two, they may literally be lifesaving.

The onlookers' comments at the march illustrate two important principles of social cognition: that we are attracted to those aspects of a situation that stand out (are salient) and that we interpret (explain) and categorise information as we perceive it. Out of a march of over 100 000 people, onlookers at that point along the route will no doubt remember the small riot as its chief feature and their recollections will be influenced by the sheer salience of the violence. No doubt their impressions of an otherwise peaceful demonstration will be skewed by this small incident and they will recall the march as a violent and disorderly event. Such small but highly salient aspects of our environment often exert a disproportionate influence on how we interpret and react in social settings.

In a similar way we almost automatically rely on past learning to interpret new situations and this leads us to assign responsibility (make causal attributions) based on our attitudes and prejudices. The onlookers probably did not realise that their prejudices were on display when they discussed the riot among themselves. Those who held the police responsible showed their prejudices—"fascists and warmongers"—while others' attributions left no doubt about their feelings towards the marchers, or why they thought they were marching—"poofters, dirty-long-haired-gits, dole-bums, bleeding hearts and draft-dodgers". And again, onlookers ignored the soldiers' not insignificant role in the events.

So social cognitive psychologists build theories by examining the ways in which we perceive, interpret and explain social behaviour to ourselves. In a sentence: Social cognition studies how our perception influences our behaviour.

Learning perspectives

Social psychology overlaps other disciplines and perhaps shares most in common with developmental psychology. One of the more obvious explanations of social behaviour is that we have learned to think and feel and act as we do, and developmentalists study how this influences our growth patterns, while social psychologists concentrate on the content of our learning. So you can see there is just a shift in emphasis here and in practice the two disciplines blend into each other and the **social learning theory** of Albert Bandura (1986) is a good example of this intersection.

The learning perspective relies on the principles of learning theory: association and conditioning, reinforcement and reward, and the imitation and modelling on which observational learning relies. These principles will probably need little explanation as you will remember them from your introductory courses but in any case we will return to them throughout the text. Those social psychologists who adopt a learning perspective prefer theories based on overt, observable behaviour which reflects our conditioning histories. Such theories are *how* rather than *why* explanations and are less

social learning theory

We learn by observing others and our actions are shaped via vicarious reinforcement.

Social learning perspectives argue that we acquire social roles by imitating our parents.

interested in internal states or personal motives as influences on behaviour and, on the whole, they tend to minimise cognitive explanations.

So from the learning perspective, the riot would be explained in terms of the individual's prior experience and the environmental factors at work during the riot. The two clergymen's attack on a policeman might reflect a long period of adverse interactions in which they had been the butt of police ridicule? Or perhaps they were spontaneously imitating the other aggressive acts going on around them and were reinforced by some onlookers' shouts of encouragement? The soldier punched the activist because he had been trained to respond aggressively to violence? From a learning perspective many explanations for the riot are possible, ranging from vicarious arousal to direct manipulation of the marchers by an agent provocateur intent on rabble rousing. Whatever the reason, from this perspective explanation will be environmentally driven!

Motivational perspectives

An early approach to social explanation was to posit motivational influences on behaviour. This approach proceeded on the assumption that the best way to understand social behaviour was to ask people what they thought they were doing (Heider, 1958). This simple analysis is fraught with difficulties and too often led to **reification**, simply assigning labels to behaviour and pretending you have explained it. The activist belted the soldier because he had a need to act aggressively. How do we know he had such a need? Because he acted aggressively! This unsatisfactory way of explaining social acts led to the discrediting of need theory in the late 1950s, and its demise was hastened by the simple observation that most people had limited insight into the wellsprings of their behaviour (which is just as well, otherwise there would be little role for social psychologists).

Even so, motivation theory does have a place in social theorising and several needs have stood the test of repeated research. As an example, social psychologists have identified related norms that control our helping behaviour: the norm of **social responsibility** obliges us to help others in distress, and perhaps this is why the unionist helped the battered and bleeding policeman from the fray, despite their traditional antagonism. Equally the **norm of reciprocity** would require that the policeman return the favour if the roles were reversed. These and other related norms serve by their very generality. They are higher level explanations which make general predictions but our actions on the ground are directly influenced by more immediate factors. For example, if the unionist recognised the policeman as one of those who had beaten him up after a previous march, then despite these general norms, he would not only be unlikely to help but might see this as a glorious opportunity to even the score. Put another way, these norms are generally accurate but weak predictors of specific behaviour.

In a more general sense the related theory of drive reduction is of considerable use in social explanation. If you posit a specific need located in a specific context (two middle-aged women who really disliked each other, so that it only took a small thing to lead to fisticuffs) then you can

reification

Explaining by naming; pretending you have explained something by giving it a name; circular explanation.

social responsibility

A social norm requiring us to give help to those who need it.

norm of reciprocity

A learned rule requiring us to pay back others' prosocial acts.

posit an accompanying level of arousal which might lead to a tension-reduction strategy (belting the other woman). There is little doubt that much of our social behaviour is driven by tension reduction but the link to one specific behaviour rather than another is less clear. If indeed the two women found each other's presence so oppressive why didn't one leave?

Ecological perspectives

A newly emergent area which owes a lot to its parent discipline is environmental psychology. There is little doubt that environmental influences contribute to the way we act and that climate and other factors directly affect behaviour. Perhaps the riot started because the activist who triggered it was hot and bothered and was a little crazy due to a lunar tidal influence on his brain! As you will see in Chapter Thirteen, there is a link between temperature and aggression, though the influence of the moon on behaviour is a little more dubious. Other environmental factors have a direct effect on social behaviour—crowding, high density living, climate, noise, pollution, urban and occupational distress and a host of other factors all influence the way we act. Environmental social psychologists would not want to explain social behaviour in entirely environmental terms but instead argue that it is a relatively neglected variable in social research.

Biological perspectives

As we will see in our section on current challenges to social psychology (p. 23), the psychobiological perspective is seriously challenging traditional social psychology. Fuelled by explosive growth in the biological sciences, psychobiologists argue (much like their environmental colleagues) that there has been a relative neglect of biological insights in social theorising. Again they would not want to claim that everything we do is caused by our biological nature, but just remind us that we do have bodies that need to be taken into account when framing theories. Though there are many differing biological insights available to social psychology, the one making the greatest inroads looks to our evolutionary heritage and asks what influence this exerts on us. Perhaps we can explain the explosiveness of the confrontation between marchers and the police partly in terms of crowding, leading to intrusions into the marchers' intimate body space, and the heightening of arousal and discomfort as age-old genetic reactions are tripped.

While there is some evidence that mistrust of strangers is instinctive and that aggression is linked to body-space invasions, this does not necessarily imply the marchers reacted violently because they were crowded. To use that explanation we would have to explain why the onlookers, who were even more crowded, did not also react violently (some did). While heightened arousal and deep-seated genetic potentialities may have contributed to the riot, it is well to remember that they are just that, potentialities. One of our species' finest achievements is our ability to transcend the limits placed on us by our biology. For this reason we must be cautious when viewing social behaviour as biologically based, but we must not neglect its influence either.

Social exchange and equity perspectives

The social exchange and equity perspectives that we consider in Chapter Eight assert that individuals construct society in a relatively hard-nosed way and that most relationships (if not all) are run along tit-for-tat lines. Often when we act, we do so deliberately and rationally and expect to receive rewards and incur costs in proportion to our activities. In other circumstances, our interactions are more unconscious but with the same balancing of costs and rewards. If imbalances occur, then corrective forces will arise. Unlike other perspectives, social exchange takes a mid-point view of relationships, seeing them as dynamic reciprocal interactions, rather than as static, one-sided affairs. The *exchange* in social exchange is this reciprocal anticipation of costs and benefits. When the activist thumped the soldier he anticipated the likely consequences of his actions and thought that they were a fair exchange for the anticipated benefits. Further it is unlikely the activist was acting irrationally when he thumped the soldier; from this perspective it is assumed that he weighed the benefits and costs before wielding the sign.

Cultural perspectives

As with the biological perspective, one of the recent challenges to social psychology has been its neglect of cross-cultural viewpoints in explaining behaviour. We will review this question below but it is often the case that social theorising does not translate well from one culture to another. This variability suggests there are less universal factors underlying social behaviour than we first thought. If this is true then we face a major problem, for we will need a social psychology for each culture. Indeed if we consider the multicultural nature of our society then perhaps we need a set of explanations for each region, ethnic group, race and subculture.

These and many other theoretical viewpoints all contribute to our understanding of social interactions and, in combination, represent the diversity that is social psychology. However, explanation does not end there. Social psychologists also frame their theories at different levels of explanation and these differences in approach may be confusing to a novice.

Levels of explanation in social psychology

We noted in the preface that social psychology is at war with itself. Social psychology is a fractured discipline with a large cleavage right down its middle. On the one hand are those committed to an experimental approach who adapt the methods of the physical sciences to study social phenomena.

experimentalism

Critique of experimental social psychology which suggested that much of what was being tested was trivial, did not reflect real-life behaviour and did not lead to meaningful conceptual advances.

crisis of social psychology

A challenge between 1965 and 1975 to experimentalism and the paucity of conceptual development accompanying experiments.

They argue that social psychology is an experimental science which studies individual social behaviour. On the other are those who derisively call this **experimentalism** and argue that such an approach is too limiting or inappropriate, and that restricting social inquiry to experimental settings limits its scope, trivialises human social interactions and drastically curtails broad conceptual and theoretical development (see Box 1.3). If we examine the differences between these two camps, we find that the former is mostly influenced by North American experimental psychology, while the latter are mainly influenced by European sociological approaches. These differences have led to much contention within social psychology and to a bitter internecine struggle, the **crisis of social psychology**, which we review below. Moreover, it reflects fundamentally different approaches to theory-building.

Social psychology is such a vast subject that it attracts experts from many professions all with unique insights (see Figure 1.1). Differences in training and approach also lead to theories constructed at different levels of meaning. For example, as we have already noted, some psychologists prefer to explain riots from an individual's perspective, but other theorists

Figure 1.1
Social psychology: A hybrid discipline

The distance from the centre equals the degree of contribution each discipline has made to social psychology

prefer more group or cultural-based explanations. This difference in approach is known as **reductionism** or the belief that, while knowledge is knowledge, it may be explained at different levels. Within science, knowledge stretches from elementary particle physics to the most abstract of philosophies. Meaning, therefore, is pitched at different levels of explanation to suit our purpose and audience (Figure 1.2).

reductionism
Belief that all knowledge may be broken down (reduced) to more fundamental explanations.

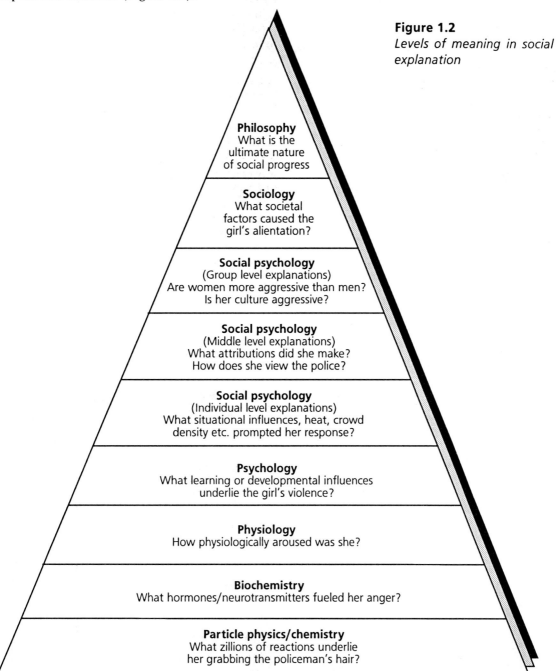

Figure 1.2
Levels of meaning in social explanation

Philosophy
What is the ultimate nature of social progress

Sociology
What societal factors caused the girl's alientation?

Social psychology
(Group level explanations)
Are women more aggressive than men?
Is her culture aggressive?

Social psychology
(Middle level explanations)
What attributions did she make?
How does she view the police?

Social psychology
(Individual level explanations)
What situational influences, heat, crowd density etc. prompted her response?

Psychology
What learning or developmental influences underlie the girl's violence?

Physiology
How physiologically aroused was she?

Biochemistry
What hormones/neurotransmitters fueled her anger?

Particle physics/chemistry
What zillions of reactions underlie her grabbing the policeman's hair?

These explanations are hierarchical, and the further down you go, the more complicated they become (imagine trying to explain a riot using a particle physics explanation). As we move up the hierarchy beyond a simple description, theorising changes from the physical to the social. Psychological explanation is the next step up and asks: why did individuals riot? Social psychologists a little further up might ask: what was the social context of the riot? While sociologists and anthropologists, a little higher still, might query its societal meaning. Finally philosophy, the queen of the sciences topping the hierarchy, asks: what is the ultimate nature of social protest? From this example you can see that social psychology is a mid-range or interpersonal explanation incorporating both the individual and social meanings of an act.

More immediately, social-psychological explanation has its own hierarchy. The perspectives we encountered in the last section are broadly arrayed with *individual* approaches like social cognition and learning at the bottom, *interpersonal* approaches like social exchange midway, and more *sociological* explanations like environmental and cross-cultural views at the top. Such is the range of possible social explanations that there are both sociological and psychological social psychologists and students are often confused by the apparent similarities between the two disciplines. As social psychology lies between psychology and sociology these distinctions are often not easy to make. Kohn (1989) noted that sociological social psychology does not look for causes of social behaviour within individuals and is more concerned with the way society as a whole works, examining the impact of issues such as poverty, crime and the stresses of urban living. It also favours methods that are more group-based such as surveys, field and participant-observation studies and, as we have seen, psychological social psychologists have a more individual focus and prefer methods that allow them to directly manipulate social behaviour. In practice though, the distinctions between these two levels is sometimes blurred and often entirely ignored. We will return to levels of explanation a little later in the chapter.

A *history of social psychology*

In perhaps psychology's most celebrated quote, Hermann Ebbinghaus observed that "Psychology has had a long past but only a short history" (Ebbinghaus, 1908). Psychologists delight in appropriating this quote, claiming antecedents amid the Ancient Greeks and Enlightenment thinkers, and Ebbinghaus' quote is much abused in psychology's historiography. Many areas draw a long bow to claim historical antecedents, for such claims consolidate a discipline's identity and as Carl Graumann (1987) observed, the discovery of ancestors confers prestige and a sense of being in the mainstream of scientific thought. Nevertheless social psychology may justly claim impeccable credentials in antiquity, as it has been in the mainstream of intellectual thought since Plato (427–347 BC).

Antecedents

The Ancient Greeks saw society as an organic whole with divine overtones. In some respects society was an organism, an animal in which all *men* had their respective parts. Though individualism was lauded by certain philosophers, in everyday life it was an exception rather than the rule. Greek society and the social thought it inspired were quite fatalistic and one's destiny was a matter of chance and divine whim. Unlike our stern, remote and rather inflexible Judaeo-Christian God, the Greek deities were a whimsical lot who actively meddled in daily life. So life was a chancy experience which depended on being favoured and able to double-guess divine intentions. Greek thought dwelled on how one might invoke and propitiate the deities— an ancient version of "Man proposes, God disposes". Critical thought on culture and social interaction, therefore, was permeated with an extra dimension of causality, and social explanation had to include this wild

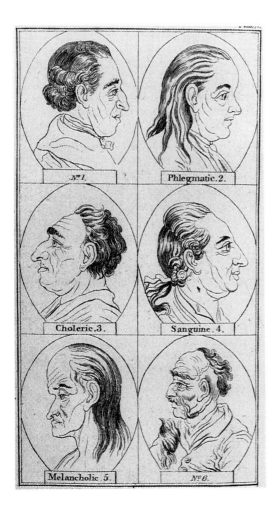

Plate from J. C. Lavater's Physiognomy *(1789). The Enlightenment brought a renewed interest in the link between our physical features and temperament, foreshadowing social Darwinist notions of race.*

card, limiting its predictive ability, which is after all the test of modern science. Individual social behaviour reflected this duality. Plato taught that life is a struggle between our lower and higher natures, and the stress of life is a reflection of our striving to become god-like while subduing our animal appetites. All humanity, Plato asserted, may be viewed in these terms.

This philosophy fitted neatly into the Christian worldview and through the next 1800 years social explanation was largely god-centred. Only with the coming of the Enlightenment in the eighteenth century were social thinkers freed from the necessity to couch their explanations in religious guise and were free to speculate on the *social* causes of social behaviour. As the eighteenth and nineteenth centuries were times of great social upheaval, in which long-established social orders fell and were replaced with newer ideals, most social thought was essentially political, what we would today call political science. The great thinkers of this age were Jean-Jacques Rousseau, Thomas Paine, Jeremy Bentham, James and John Stuart Mill, and Karl Marx. Social thought was essentially reflexive. That is social thinkers were trying to tease out and justify an ideological basis for newer forms of political and economic order, and to justify transferring political power into the hands of elected assemblies. As such there was a shift of theoretical interest, from the private struggle to reach perfection to a study of mass social action. The individual became less important in the theorist's scheme of things.

This essentially sociological tendency was reinforced by the advent of Darwinism. Gone were religious accounts of human existence and now society was evolutionary in aspect. Darwin wrote extensively on the social implications of his biological theories but Francis Galton and Herbert Spencer spelled out the implications of an evolutionary past in contemporary life. Society and social life reflected our remotest antiquity. Women were inferior to men because the evolutionary imperatives of child-bearing assigned them secondary roles; altruism or helping behaviour became nothing more than "intelligent selfishness", and inequality proof of society's ongoing betterment. Spencer's "survival of the fittest" justified the inequalities of Victorian life and became a goad to those arguing for more equitable social order. It was out of a reaction against this **social darwinism** that a more individual approach to social theorising developed.

The rise of modern social psychology

Depending entirely on one's viewpoint, modern social psychology had various beginnings. Whatever event marks the discipline's inception, there is little doubt that its formation reflected the *zeitgeist* or spirit of the times. The late nineteenth century was a period of rich social theorising and from its fertile ground our contemporary social sciences emerged. In social psychology's case much of the credit for its content, if not title, goes to Auguste Comte (1798–1857), the founder of sociology, who also foreshadowed modern social psychology. Comte was a **positivist**, a person who rejected religious or other metaphysical accounts of the world and argued against accepting theories or reasoning based on tradition. Comte

social darwinism
Belief that evolutionary forces shape social differences, particularly those of class or race.

zeitgeist
The "spirit of the times"; the prevailing ideology of the day.

positivist
Person rejecting religious or other metaphysical accounts of the world.

argued the social sciences should only use positive data, obvious to our senses and useful in enhancing mankind's lot. Comte held a three-stage view of the development of knowledge. He believed our remote ancestors felt the rocks and trees had spirits which were capriciously kind or malevolent. As society developed this was replaced with a more formalised theological belief in gods and impersonal occult powers. In Comte's view, both stages precluded social explanation as, ultimately, explanation resided out there in God's territory. Not until the advent of the Enlightenment and the rise of the scientific method was it possible, in his view, to explain anything in terms other than the metaphysical.

Comte was more a philosopher of science than a scientist himself and he was concerned to chart the rise of scientific fields with a view to "reducing confusion to its necessary bounds". As such he took an evolutionary view of scientific achievement. Logic and mathematics were first to arise as they reflected the nature of our minds. Next the physical sciences emerged as applied science (technology) revealed its benefits. Last the **psychics** or "studies of the body" gained in prominence as, man's curiosity satisfied, he turned to consider himself. Comte felt this last area would arise from a study of biology (the most fundamental psychic) and then spawn the study of society (sociology) and in turn a study of the human mind. Curiously Comte rejected the use of the term "psychology" for this last area as he thought its prescientific connotations debased its meaning, preferring instead to call this area *la morale positive*. It is clear from Comte's writings that this new discipline would study much that we would recognise today as social psychology, and Comte therefore foreshadowed both a scientific social psychology and its development as a distinct discipline, separate from philosophy. Comte's insights not only clarified the fields of study but led to an explosive burst of interest in the social sciences and many sociological investigations of social behaviour.

> **psychics**
> Nineteenth century "studies of the body".

Modern social psychology then emerges slowly and indistinctly from this explosion of social thought. The first notice of this new discipline came when Wilhelm Wundt, the "father of modern psychology", somewhat arbitrarily divided his child into experimental and **volkerpsychologie** camps in 1879. The latter does not translate well into English but roughly means "folk" or "cultural" psychology (see Box 1.1). Though Wundt is most famous for his experimental work, he noted the importance of "folk" psychology and virtually devoted the last twenty years of his life to its study. Wundt's study of culture was essentially integrationist, compiling many sources of social information into a grand theory to account for social life, rather than individual social behaviour. His emphasis was on the impact institutions such as schools and churches have on society, rather than individuals. In this he foreshadowed **sociological social psychology**, an approach that explains social behaviour in terms of wider social forces (Stryker, 1989). This approach is still strong in Europe, where the distinctions between psychological and sociologically based social psychology are less strongly drawn than in the English-speaking world.

> **volkerpsychologie**
> Folk or cultural psychology; a nineteenth century precursor of social psychology.

> **sociological social psychology**
> An approach that explains social behaviour in terms of wider (non-individual) social forces.

Some see Wundt and 1879 as the start of social psychology, others view Norman Triplett's 1898 article in the *American Journal of Psychology*

Box 1.1 *Wundt and volkerpsychlogie*

In 1879 Wundt divided psychology into experimental and *volkerpsychologie* camps. Early in his academic life Wundt set himself three tasks: to establish a purely experimental science modelled on the methods of the natural sciences; a scientific metaphysics; and a social psychology which was to be non-experimental (Danziger, 1979). Wundt was quite definite in establishing psychology's bounds. As Robert Farr (1983) elegantly puts it: "Part of our inheritance from Wundt is an experimental psychology which was non-social and a social psychology which was non-experimental." This division followed the Germanic tradition of separating the natural sciences from social studies. Wundt's *volkerpsychologie* was based on three principles:

> Firstly, that experimental psychology could never be more than a part of the science of psychology as a whole; secondly, that it needed to be supplemented by a branch of psychological studies that was devoted to the study of human mental processes in their social aspects; and thirdly, that this latter type of study was able to make use of data that was no less objective than the data of experimental psychology. (Danziger, 1983, p. 307)

Wundt's social psychology was greatly influenced by evolution. "Darwin, with his theory of evolution, had made it scientifically respectable to speculate about the origins of man. Wundt readily accepted that challenge" (Farr, 1983), and *volkerpsychologie* sees human culture as the product of evolutionary and historical change. It was also essentially collective and concerned itself with "the study of language, customs, religion, myth, magic and cognate phenomena" (Farr, 1983), which Wundt felt could never be satisfactorily understood in laboratory studies of individual consciousness. Wundt was strongly anti-reductionist (recall our discussion of levels of explanation) and felt with Durkheim "that

'social facts' cannot be explained in terms of a mere psychology of individuals" (Farr, 1983).

Volkerpsychologie's method was similar to that of anthropology and combined detailed analyses of individual cases, with broad cross-cultural comparisons. Wundt was particularly interested in the structure and content of language and the impact this had on cultural evolution. Much of his ten volumes on *volkerpsychologie*, published between 1900 and 1920, was devoted to comparative studies of the evolution of language and used correlational methods to piece together insights from biology, linguistics, philology, sociology, anthropology and social psychology. His method was essentially interpretative. He left explanation of individual consciousness to the laboratory and interpretation of collective experience to social psychology (Farr, 1983).

Wundt's *volkerpsychologie* had an enormous impact on psychology and the other social sciences. Jung was clearly influenced by Wundt's work on primitive forms of social explanation, myth and magic, and collective understanding, which came together in Jung's theory of the collective unconsciousness. It was also a seminal influence on anthropology and sociology and was acknowledged by all the great social scientists of the early twentieth century, including Freud, de Saussure, Malinowski, G.H. Mead, Durkheim, Thomas and Znaniecki. *Volkerpsychologie* still has a strong influence in European social psychology, particularly sociological social psychology. Its collectivist and integrationist method still has a strong appeal and was resorted to by many leading critics in the crisis of social psychology debate, who used Wundt's work to criticise what they saw as the excessive sterility of much experimentalist social psychology. If you wish to read further on the history and origins of Wundt's *volkerpsychologie*, the *British Journal of Social Psychology* devoted their November 1983 edition to articles on this topic.

as the first empirical social psychology experiment. Triplett was interested in what we now call **social facilitation** or how an actor or athlete's performance is enhanced by the presence of others. He wondered if cyclists rode faster when alone and trying to beat their personal bests, than when competing in races. As you might imagine, competition with others is more stimulating than competing against yourself. Triplett's study was significant in several ways. Not happy with just answering his question, he experimented with other groups to see if his results generalised to other situations (children winding in fishing reels) and used statistics to compare his results. In so doing he was one of the first to apply the scientific method and statistical analysis to social research (Haines & Vaughan, 1979). His paper was also influential in triggering the interest of a number of other American experimenters.

If the emergence of a text signals the formal start of a discipline then the French sociologist Gabriel Tarde's *Studies on Social Psychology* published in 1898 marked social psychology's debut. Tarde's first love was criminology. For many years he was a judge and from curiosity made detailed analyses of the cases he tried. These qualitative analyses eventually led to his heading the Bureau of Statistics in the Ministry of Justice, Paris, and in turn becoming one of the first criminology professors on the Continent. Tarde believed that crime was social in origin, rather than inherited, and in defence of his view wrote at length about social processes in many books, few of which have been translated into English. His 1898 book was well in advance of its time and took a quite modern view of social psychology. He distinguished between sociological and psychological social processes, and argued for a rigorous statistical underpinning to the social sciences as the best method to enhance their scientific credibility (Davis, 1906; Pepitone, 1981).

Other writers favour 1908 as a starting point, a year in which two social psychology texts were published. William McDougall, a British psychologist, published *An Introduction to Social Psychology*, which, despite its title, relied heavily on biological instincts and emotions to explain behaviour and foreshadowed drive theory. Edward Ross, on the other hand, was a sociology professor at the University of Wisconsin and his *Social Psychology* reflected his sociological perspective, concentrating on interpersonal processes and group behaviour. Both pioneering texts seem strange to us today as they were more speculative than "scientific" in content but they signalled that social psychology was on the map and growing.

Social psychology's infancy, 1908–30

Social psychology slowly defined itself over these years and like any new area fought for academic recognition, with courses still being taught from an educational or philosophical perspective. On the applied front however, World War I and the harnessing of psychology to the war effort lifted social psychology's public profile and engaged the interest of social researchers. By 1924 there was sufficient published research to warrant Floyd Allport's *Social Psychology*, which was quite modern in character and contained

social facilitation
How an actor or athlete's performance is enhanced by the presence of others.

many of the distinctive research areas that typify social psychology today. More importantly, it saw social psychology as a legitimate field of scientific inquiry with its own method and agenda; so social psychology had clearly emerged into the light over those few years. This evolution was further acknowledged in 1921 when the *Journal of Abnormal Psychology* changed its title to the *Journal of Abnormal and Social Psychology*, becoming in effect the first social psychology journal.

These were vigorous if slightly unfocused years, with many researchers pursuing their idiosyncratic interests, with little integrative conceptualisation and no **grand theories** emerging. Allport's text reported research into co-action effects, the studies of facial emotions, compliance and conformity studies. Perhaps the major difference from today was that social psychology and personality theory had yet to become separate fields. For example, in 1928 Louis Thurstone published a significant paper, clearly setting out how attitudes could be operationalised and scientifically measured, revolutionising their study in both areas. Modern social psychology's focus on situational factors, and personality theory's interest in individual differences was not yet a distinct difference and remained blurred for the next twenty years. Nevertheless, this was an incredibly fruitful partnership which still continues today, with social psychology sliding imperceptibly into personality theory (Kihlstrom, 1987). If you wish to read further, an account by Gordon Allport (1897–1967), Floyd's younger brother, was published posthumously, covering this period from a participant's perspective (Allport, 1968, 1985).

Childhood and early adolescence, 1930–45

The 1930s were a time of vigorous growth and differentiation within social psychology. Hitler's rise to power caused many social thinkers to emigrate and this infusion of European perspectives stopped British and American psychology becoming too exclusively experimentalist. Chief among these migrants was Kurt Lewin (1890–1947), whose **field theory** and applied social psychology have had an enduring effect on the discipline. Lewin took an **interactionist** approach to social theorising, stressing both the role of individual differences and the social context of behaviour. In other words, a person's behaviour is a function of the interaction between a person and their environment (Lewin, 1936). His field theory also stressed that our actions flow from our highly selective perception and personal motives, emphasising a subjective side to social behaviour. Lewin developed a **topological methodology** or a system of map-like representations of all the psychological factors underlying a person's social behaviour. His methodology continues to influence successive generations of social psychologists who are primarily concerned with the subjective side of social experience.

Lewin's work also stressed the importance of applying social psychology to everyday life. During World War II, Lewin worked for the US Office of Strategic Services, a forerunner of the CIA, developing persuasion techniques to modify public behaviour in ways that would promote the war effort. His work in persuading US housewives to modify family diets to save high

---

grand theories
Comprehensive theories which relate and explain all the research within an area.

field theory
A person's perceptual universe (field) from which social and motivational factors govern behaviour.

interactionist
A belief that behaviour is a function of the interaction between the person and their environment.

topological methodology
A system of map-like representations of psychological factors which underlie a person's social behaviour.

protein foodstuffs for the troops was an important precursor of social influence and compliance research which boomed after the war ended.

This was also a significant time for social psychology's developing scientific methodology. One consequence of a growing groundswell against Freudian psychoanalysis (which many thought was completely speculative and unscientific) was a crisis of confidence within social psychology as theorists struggled with the difficulties of experimenting on complex social forces. Muzafer Sherif's 1935 study of social influence, or how a person's judgment could be influenced by group behaviour, had a profound impact on social psychology around the world. Sherif's experiments demonstrated how complex behaviour could be broken down into small discrete units and then reassembled into rigorous theories, which were both predictive and testable. The coming of World War II proved to be the perfect fillip for a shaky morale as psychologists were snapped up by the armed services and put to work on a variety of social issues. Nothing is surer to enhance one's self-esteem than being desperately needed and the war years were a productive time for psychology. At the war's end social, along with all other areas of psychology, was set for explosive growth.

Early adulthood, 1945–65

If you read through any chapter of this text, with the possible exception of the environmental psychology of Chapter Thirteen, you will see that most current theories are based on fundamental research conducted during these two decades. Gordon Allport's work on prejudice (Chapter Five); Asch's studies of conformity and person perception (Chapter Two); Festinger's work on cognitive dissonance (Chapter Four); Heider's balance theory (Chapter Four); Hovland's work on attitude change (Chapter Five); Kelley's social exchange theory (Chapter Eight); Janis' group polarisation (Chapter Twelve); Milgram's studies of obedience (Chapter Six); Schachter and Singer's two-factor theory of emotion (Chapter Three); Walster and Walster's close relationships research (Chapter Nine); and Zajonc's social facilitation (Chapter Twelve) are just a few of the many powerful theories launched in these decades.

Full of vigour, social psychology's early adulthood was a time of tremendous growth any way you wish to measure it. The weight of knowledge multiplied considerably. Books were written; journals blossomed; universities boasted of their social psychologists' prowess; research funds were plentiful; PhD students anticipated interesting careers; academics strove to apply theory to practice and were the darlings of the media, as well as of considerable influence with policy makers. While much of this heady atmosphere was fuelled by the enormous postwar economic boom, they were still exciting times in their own right. Unfortunately in the cyclical nature of things a bust was imminent.

Social psychology's midlife crisis, 1965–75

It would be an interesting exercise to correlate the history of social psychology with a general history of Western society. The decade stretching from the middle sixties to the middle to late seventies was one of gradual slowing of the postwar boom and of considerable economic and social confusion. Politics was stormy and several unpopular conflicts divided the world into uneasy armed camps as they divided populations at home. It was a time of social protest and of searching reappraisal of taken-for-granted values. In this atmosphere it was unlikely that social psychology could escape being put under the spotlight.

The seeds of a revolt within social psychology had been brewing for some time and gradually researchers' dissatisfactions began to coalesce into a sustained challenge to social psychology's method and its applicability. Unlike other areas of psychology which were vigorously challenged by out-siders, most of social psychology's critics were social psychologists of some standing. This bred a bitter internecine fight which still has some energy in it (e.g. Zajonc, 1989). The challenge was threefold: the validity, applic-ability and ethical nature of social research was studied in some detail (see Box 1.3).

The so-called "crisis of social psychology" started slowly with isolated expressions of concern (e.g. Campbell, 1957) but really took off when an article by Orne (1962) appeared in the *American Psychologist*. Orne challenged the validity of much laboratory-based social experimentation as inevitably setting up subtle expectancies in subjects (demand characteristics) which led subjects to guess the experimental hypotheses and so "cook" their results. This article stirred up a debate about the appropriateness of laboratory research which still continues and which we will review in our "current challenges" section below. Robert Rosenthal (1966), a prominent researcher on the **Pygmalion effect** (that our expectations of others becomes self-fulfilling prophecies), weighed into the debate with a well-documented book on experimenter effects. From this point the debate broadened into a thoroughgoing reconsideration of the appropriateness of social research in the laboratory.

Pygmalion effect
Our expectations become self-fulfilling prophecies.

Allied to this critical scrutiny were concerns that the deception so necessary in much social research was unethical and indeed detrimental to solid theorising (Kelman, 1967; Mixon, 1972) (see Box 1.5). In 1973 Ken Gergen launched a scathing attack on experimentalism, concluding that much of what was being tested was basically historical and of limited applicability (Moscovici, 1989). At the same time, European social psycholo-gists joined the debate en masse, arguing the limitations of American experi-mental research. Partly this was a greater willingness on their part to move beyond laboratory research and theorise on the possible sources of social behaviour, and a cultural difference that was less individualistic and more inclined to develop theories which integrated many differing sources of data, not all of which were experimental in nature. We will return to this debate in a little while. Despite the heat of the debate this period was also highly productive with many fundamental advances in our understanding of social behaviour including Berkowitz on aggression (Chapter Seven); Kelley's attribution theory (Chapter Three); and Latane and Darley's work on altruism (Chapter Ten).

Towards maturity, 1975–90s

As with any struggle, time brings its own resolution of conflict and social psychology has now entered a period of steady growth and consolidation. Nobody really won the past debates but they were healthy enough in retrospect. Though current challenges are no less fierce, there is a less frenetic edge to them and a more considered reflection on issues raised. The attack on experimentalism continues but researchers are more ready to use **multiple act criteria**, preferring many types of data in theory building. The European challenge has led to multi-level explanations that are wide ranging and less tied to traditional social experimentation. In much the same way current challenges have led to a more diverse and less ethnocentric social psychology. Cultural differences are acknowledged and calculating their influences has made the discipline a more international enterprise.

Social psychology is also more interdisciplinary and applied than it once was. Now that the energetic growth of childhood and the doubts of middle age are behind us, social psychologists seem less threatened by collaborative work with other psychologists and other specialists outside the profession. This may be seen in the steady growth of "cross-over" journals like the *Journal of Social and Clinical Psychology*. This view is strengthened by an increased willingness to apply social psychology without worrying about the limitations this might place on the "purity" of pure research. Journals like the *Journal of Applied Social Psychology* reflect this trend, while specialist journals like *Environment and Behavior* combine theory and application without difficulty. As we will see in Chapter Fourteen, applied social psychologists are active in the legal system, examining the validity of eyewitness testimony and the jury system; the health system and researching the social causes of illness; looking at occupational health and safety issues in the workplace and how we might enhance productivity. Social psychologists are also actively engaged in designing more humane environments to better serve humanity.

In summary all these trends have left social psychology a more diversified and responsive area than at any other time. Though predicting the future is an uncertain affair, we believe these trends will continue and as we approach the year 2000, social psychology faces a bright and optimistic future (see Box 1.2) .

multiple act criteria
The more ways you measure behavioural intention, the stronger it is linked to attitudes and behaviour.

Current challenges to mainstream social psychology

As we have already intimated, traditional (experimental) social psychology has any number of critics and faces several sustained challenges from within its own ranks. This does not weaken social psychology, rather it reflects a vigorous growth and is evidence that practitioners are willing to reappraise

Box 1.2 *Social psychology in the Antipodes*

Ernest Beaglehole, the first academic social psychologist in New Zealand (circa 1955). (Photo: courtesy Victoria University of Wellington)

Australian and New Zealand social psychology has always been small beer compared to its American and European counterparts, and this is largely a question of relative size and our small academic community. Nevertheless, we have produced theorists of international stature and they are featured throughout our text.

Psychology developed slowly in New Zealand and Australia (Turtle, 1987) and social psychology even more slowly. The first psychologists were appointed as professors of philosophy and taught part-year courses which had vestiges of social theory within them (Nixon & Taft, 1977). It was not until Henry Tasman Lovell was appointed an Assistant Lecturer in Philosophy at the University of Sydney in 1913, that a recognisable form of social psychology emerged. Lovell introduced psychology into Philosophy 1 and by 1915 half of that subject comprised psychology and included statistics and experimental methods. When Lovell expanded psychology offerings in 1919, he included a senior level course in social psychology which included studies of gregariousness, suggestion, imitation, and the psychology of crowds (O'Neil, 1987). This was the first course in social psychology and used McDougall's *Introduction to Social Psychology* (1908) as a text.

In New Zealand psychology had a much slower evolution, though otherwise its progression was similar to that in Australia (St George, 1990). Sir Thomas Hunter, who pioneered psychology in New Zealand, taught scraps of social psychology at Victoria College, Wellington, from 1904 onwards, using texts by McDougall and later Thouless. Hunter was at heart an experimental physiological psychologist in the tradition of Tichener (Brown & Fuchs, 1969) and included social psychology more for the sake of completeness, than from interest. The few papers or theses set on social psychology topics were sent to England to be marked by Robert Thouless and others. It was not until the arrival of Ernest Beaglehole at Victoria College that social psychology gained more prominence. Beaglehole, Hunter's eventual successor and from 1938 first professor of psychology in New Zealand, taught courses in social relations but his interests were more anthropologic and ethnological than social psychological (Beaglehole, 1949; Beeby, 1979). It was not until the mid-1950s that a recognisably modern form of social psychology appeared.

Social psychology was taught fitfully on either side of the Tasman as a senior level course or thesis topic from 1929 but did not attract any real attention until the arrival in Australia in 1946 of Oscar Oeser, who must rank as the first professional social psychologist in Australia and New Zealand. Oeser, a South African trained at Rhodes, Marburg and Canterbury, was appointed to establish the new Department of Psychology at the University of Melbourne and from its inception in 1946 made social psychology an integral part of the undergraduate programme. Oeser taught a full-year senior level course which required a thorough grounding in non-experimental research methods and much fieldwork. Oeser's interest in intergroup processes within rural communities quickly engendered the interest of several other colleagues and many postgraduate students. Numerous journal articles and two book-length reports followed (O'Neil, 1987) and soon there was a flourishing social psychology community on both sides of the Tasman.

From the early 1950s social psychology grew rapidly with second or third year courses appearing in all undergraduate programmes, and many honours and postgraduate theses were written. In 1969 Leon Mann wrote the first local text, a slim volume on social psychology, for the John Wiley *Basic Topics in Psychology* series, under the general editorship of Professor R.A. Champion of the University of Sydney, marking a milestone in the evolution of a local social psychology. It also signalled a shift of influence from Melbourne to Flinders University, where a partnership of two professorial social psychologists, Mann and Norm Feather, did much to establish a purely indigenous social psychology. Another milestone was the formation in 1972 of a loose network of social psychologists who meet annually to promote their craft. The network also produces an *Australian Social*

Psychologists Directory, now in its sixth edition, compiled by Margaret Foddy and Brian Crabbe (1990). The directory, which also lists many New Zealanders, serves as a reference point for those interested in social psychological research and contains over two hundred contacts.

Social psychology is alive and well and flourishing in Australia and New Zealand. Mary Nixon (1987) estimated that approximately 12 per cent of undergraduate courses in Australian universities were social psychology. Ray Over (1991a) found 11 per cent of members of the Australian Psychological Society identified their primary interest as personality-social psychology. O'Neil (1987) found a similar percentage of PhD theses awarded between 1970 and 1978 were on personality or social psychology topics and our perusal of dissertation abstracts for the period 1987–90 gives a similar percentage for Australia, with a slightly higher proportion (14%) from New Zealand. Academic interest appears stronger than this would suggest and Over (1991b) found 32 per cent of Australian academics saw themselves as personality/social psychologists. From university calenders and publications it appears that over 50 academics have a primary responsibility for teaching social psychology in New Zealand and Australia, and at least that many again publish regularly on related topics. While this is a small number compared to the US and Europe, it is large considering a combined total of a little under 400 psychology academics in our two countries (Commonwealth Universities Year Book, 1991).

their discipline's underlying assumptions. From the froth and ferment of such academic debates new syntheses emerge and such disputes point to the discipline's basic strength. All areas of scientific inquiry have periods of quiet reflection and times of heady dispute; at this point social psychology is alive and well and rapidly expanding. Nevertheless, it does face three sustained challenges.

Social psychology, a North American science?

Many argue that social psychology is an essentially North American science which ignores the rest of the world and as such has limited applicability. There is little doubt that social psychology has been the darling of US

Many critics of American social psychology argue that it is an inappropriate explanation of other cultures. To what extent should we use Western notions of the group to interpret Fijian behaviour?
(Photo: Barry Price)

researchers for many decades and American research has gradually dominated the field. As we review the experimental literature in the following chapters, you will notice that approximately 80 per cent of the studies and most of the conceptual breakthroughs are of North American origin (though it must be acknowledged that much of its early impetus was gained from European émigrés fleeing Hitler's Europe). No doubt this pre-eminence reflects the enormous number of North American social psychologists and their greater access to resources than European or local counterparts. While social psychology has gained greatly from this explosive interest, critics doubt that North American college students, the usual subjects of these experiments, are representative of the wider global community (Triandis, 1989).

This challenge was one of the impetuses for yet another offshoot from social psychology: **cross-cultural psychology** as a corrective to an excessive North Americanism. Cross-cultural psychology has its own theoretical agendas and is only incidentally interested in reforming social psychology. With roots in anthropology and a mandate to make psychology globally representative, this new discipline is fully occupied. Nevertheless, during the eighties cross-cultural studies presented a substantial challenge to traditional social psychology, perhaps culminating in 1988 with Michael Bond's book, *The Cross-cultural Challenge to Social Psychology*. Predictably this led to a strenuous defence by those under attack:

> A typical title in the *Journal of Cross-cultural Psychology* might be "A Cross-Cultural Study of Resource-Allocation Behavior: Bahumphia and Xoma" . . . Perhaps many of these articles are theoretically interesting and methodologically sophisticated, but they don't create the slightest bit of interest for us mainstreamers, and we will not read them. Because

cross-cultural psychology
Comparisons of social and other variables across different cultures.

such comparisons are so common in the *Journal of Cross-Cultural Psychology,* we will not subscribe to that journal. We have never been to these places and know nothing about them. To make good sense of these studies, we would need in-depth knowledge of the cultures, and we simply don't have it and don't have the time or inclination to acquire it. (Wheeler & Reis, 1988, p. 36)

As you can see the debate is vigorous and, in fairness to Wheeler and Reis, they go on to concede the worth of much cross-cultural research, although on fairly limited grounds. The authors acknowledge their position might make others "foam at the mouth and try to bite us" but they defend the vital importance of studying one's own culture exhaustively. Implicit in such defences is the notion that "mainstream" social psychology provides a basis for evaluating the worth of cross-cultural comparisons, and that many such comparisons just raise relatively trivial differences between cultures. Needless to say, these are hotly disputed assumptions and while there is much merit in studying one's own culture exhaustively, critics argue that the sheer volume of American research amounts to yet another form of cultural imperialism (Moghaddam, 1987). Yet, it is the nature of such theoretical debates to blend over time into a synthesis that resolves the dispute. As cross-cultural research gains in strength, the emphasis is less on noting differences between cultures and more on identifying which aspects of Euro-American social psychology have universal applicability and which need to be modified.

While it is still unclear whether there is one global psychology, or several social psychologies, evidence is slowly accumulating that some theories based on American, or even European, studies fail to represent humanity adequately and indeed might even be socially oppressive (Sampson, 1978). We will note such differences as we go along but for now it might be useful to remember social psychology's cultural antecedents and question whether what you are studying adequately represents your own ethnicity.

A surfeit of experiments

The second challenge notes the lack of a grand theory uniting seemingly disparate areas of study within social psychology. Critics point out that, until recently, social psychologists seemed to share a method and an interest in social behaviour and little else (Harre & Secord, 1972; Gergen, 1973; Moscovici, 1969, 1989). The average introductory text was virtually a smorgasbord of interesting areas with little attempt at a synthesis. Much of the blame for this has been attributed to an overwhelming fixation on the experimental paradigm which led Gustav Jahoda (1988) to comment "we know more and more about less and less".

As we have already discussed in our history section, it may be fairly said that there are two (or three, or four) different social psychologies. Much of the dissatisfaction and feelings of lack of progress, which emerged in the early seventies among American social psychologists, were not felt by their European colleagues. Many such took the opportunity to remark that social psychology should always have been primarily a matter of social explanation or conceptual development rather than atomistic social experimentation. Many continental theorists felt American "social science" was so reductionist that you could not help forgetting why you were doing the experiment in the first place:

> The experimenter manipulating independent variables aims at complete control of the processes studied and tends to forget their insertion into a social context very much wider than that of the experimental situation. (Doise, 1982, quoted in Jahoda, 1988, p. 87)

What is at issue here is quite different views of social psychology's fundamental nature. The European experience of social theory, while not averse to social experimentation, is much more "top-down" in nature, stressing field investigations, conceptual synthesis and integration of research findings—an essentially *social studies* approach. As we have discussed, such views argue that much of social psychology's content is irreducible, or not amenable to experimental manipulation. American researchers, and those following their lead, adopt a "bottom-up" view, modelling social psychology on the natural sciences—an essentially *social science* approach. That 70 years of experimentation had led to a narrowing research base and a certain sterility within social psychology, led many American researchers to question where they were going and to doubt their method. Naturally their European colleagues were more than willing to remark that they had known this all along, and it is little wonder that this European critique stirred up the fires of dissatisfaction felt by many Western experimentalists.

Such criticisms led to the so-called crisis of social psychology of the early 1970s, which was a full-on challenge to individualism and experimentalism and the paucity of conceptual development accompanying experimentation (see Box 1.3). The crisis started with the publication of Ken Ring's 1967 paper, "Experimental social psychology: some sober questions about some frivolous values". Ring argued that social experimentation on American college students had dubious generalisability and that, in any case, many such experiments were frivolous and did not increase our understanding of social forces. European critics were not slow to agree but the dispute was largely a European preoccupation until Ken Gergen's 1973 paper, "Social psychology as history". Gergen argued that social psychology was not really a science because it had failed to generate stable generalisable laws of behaviour. Rather it was more akin to history in that experiments dealt "with facts that are largely nonrepeatable and which fluctuate markedly over time". This meant that "such knowledge does not generally transcend its historical boundaries" (Gergen, 1973, p. 310).

While Ring was an outsider, Gergen was one of the inner circle and his paper was interpreted as a massive betrayal of American social psychology (Rijsman & Stroebe, 1989). The controversy and bitterness this article generated still continues (cf Zajonc, 1989). However Gergen's paper was in some ways the high-water mark of the debate and it is the most often cited paper in the history of this controversy. Since that time the debate has waned and, while the two social psychologies are as distinct as ever, there seems a greater willingness on the part of American researchers to

Box 1.3 *Food for thought: Don Mixon—"Getting the science right is the problem, not the solution"*

Don Mixon abandoned his university studies in 1949 and devoted 17 years to acting, and to working in various factories, fields and workshops before attending San Francisco State and obtaining BA and MA degrees in psychology. His PhD thesis at the University of Nevada/Reno was supervised by social psychologist Paul Secord and radical behaviourist Willard Day. Post-doctoral work at Oxford was with philosopher Rom Harre. Mixon taught at three US universities before joining the faculty of the University of Wollongong in 1981. He has published widely and has written a book, Obedience and Civilisation (1989), on conceptual, methodological, theoretical and ethical issues in psychology. Retirement in 1992 freed Don to give time to a book on freedom.
(Photo: courtesy Media Unit, Wollongong University)

As you can see, social psychology suffered a prolonged attack from the mid 1960s and, while this was no doubt a reflection of the times, it was also unexpected, because some of the severest critics were its own leading lights. In comparison with other areas of psychology which were also undergoing review, social psychology was severely trounced. What was it about social psychology which drew such ire?

This is a question that has engaged Associate Professor Don Mixon from Wollongong University and he has written many papers that take a critical look at the theoretical and philosophical underpinnings of social psychology.

Two papers by Mixon provide an analysis of the problem and pose solutions. Both were written for the *Journal for the Theory of Social Behaviour*, which is a forum for those interested in the philosophy of social psychology. His latest paper (Mixon, 1990) looks at the overall condition of psychology but applies equally well to social psychology. Mixon argues that psychology fails "to embrace problems over which it is possible to feel intellectual passion". Many of its most stimulating questions are not really amenable to experimental manipulation but, argues Mixon, psychology has always given first priority to method rather than problem. So often the most

interesting questions are discarded. Mixon suggests that psychology's hunger to be accepted as a hard science has led us to slavishly ape the experimental methods of the physical sciences, often with absurd results. In his view, while psychology might long for scientific status, "compared to the accomplishments of physics and chemistry, much of psychology is scientifically unimpressive and technologically worthless".

Mixon acknowledges that this critique is not new but suggests its perseverance indicates that something is fundamentally wrong in psychology. In a cynical touch of realism, he notes honours students rarely choose topics that really interest them as they "know very well that to gain a high mark on their empirical thesis they must demonstrate a mastery of an approved method of research". However in his view, getting the "science" or the method right is often the problem, not the solution.

All this is very interesting but does not really answer the question, why is this particularly a problem for social psychology? Mixon's 1986 paper directly addresses this issue and argues that social psychology differs from other experimental research in psychology:

> For quite a few years now I have been convinced that a body of research—chiefly

in social psychology—called by practitioners "experiments" are not experiments. The research mimics experimental forms and looks like experiments, but differs in two crucial ways from the work being done in experimental psychology. The nature of the subject matter is different and research practice involves lying to participants. (Mixon, 1986, p. 123)

Mixon argues the move away from asking people why they act as they do has flawed social experimentation. To ensure that the person being studied does not influence the results by their willingness to cooperate, social psychologists use deception techniques to deceive their subjects. Mixon suggests this just underrates the subject's ability to double-guess the real aims of the experiment, and substitute "trained and practised observers with a strong commitment to reliable knowledge" with "untrained and often unwilling participants with a less certain commitment in reliable knowledge and a widely alleged dedication to self-protection and to 'looking good' ".

Mixon believes that subjects *participate* in experiments. The determinism of the experimental method leaves no place for subjects who actively feign behaviour. That subjects choose between alternatives suggests that there are many possible responses to an experiment. Mixon notes that social experimenters either try and control for these effects or ignore them; or even worse pretend it is not a problem. However, the enormous commitment to deception (see Box 1.5) within social research over the last 40 years shows that most experimenters are well aware of the problem, but lying to your subjects is, Mixon argues, ultimately self-defeating.

What is the answer? Mixon argues we should shift social psychology's paradigm from a methods-based to a problems-led discipline. This would make it more realistic. Substituting experimental designs in which subjects are prevented from pretending, or altering demand characteristics so it is not in their interests to do so, will lead to successful experimentation. Where this is not possible, "certainty can only be gained when the behaviour being studied is the exercise of ability, skill, or power". In short, social experimentation needs to take account of volition or the "power to pretend". Mixon (1990) concludes that "doing science" is not sufficient justification for "doing psychology" unless you get it right.

"cross-over" into conceptual articles more reminiscent of their European counterparts. New movements in social psychology, especially social cognition (Adair, 1991), have also somewhat healed the breaches. If you are interested in reading further on this issue the *European Journal of Psychology* in 1989 devoted a whole edition (September/October) to a retrospective to mark the dispute's twentieth anniversary. This edition contains comments and reflections from the leading proponents in the debate.

Social psychology, a biological science?

The third challenge acknowledges psychology's gradual drift towards the biological sciences and argues that social psychology's lack of a grand theory is attributable to a failure to incorporate biological perspectives. Two factors reinforce this third challenge to mainstream social psychology.

First, psychology as a whole is gradually drifting out of the social and into the biological sciences. Biological science is undergoing an enormous theoretical and technical revolution which got underway in the early eighties and, as we write, shows no signs of slowing down. Among the fastest growing biological sciences are neurophysiology and genetic engineering, and in the mid-eighties new technology suddenly swept away conceptual logjams leading to spectacular advances. The intersection of these areas was crucial to many advances within psychology, which in turn have given it a more biological flavour. Psychologists would be less than human if they were not attracted by these successes; however, social psychology seems to be resisting this trend. Why?

The reason is largely historical and explains social psychology's reluctance to entertain biological perspectives. Experimental psychology, as conceived by Wilhelm Wundt, had its roots in physiology and was deliberately modelled on the methodology of the natural sciences (Farr, 1991). Therefore in its infancy, social psychology as an experimental science looked for answers from biology and was disappointed when attempts by McDougall and others failed to demonstrate a concrete link between instincts and behaviour. Similarly, drive theory in the 1940s failed to make this connection and by then the Social Darwinism which underlay much earlier social theorising was morally repugnant. For these reasons, social psychologists now emphasise the social and dodge biological explanations. To challenge this reluctance, critics point to biology's recent successes and ask where are those of social psychology? Rather than attack a view that has worked so well for general psychology, perhaps we should incorporate biological perspectives within social psychology to flush away any theoretical constipation. This incorporation takes several forms.

There has always been a strong connection between developmental and social psychology and when we study the way culture is transmitted the distinctions blur. Developmental research has been given a fillip by recent advances in the biosciences, and a reawakened interest in the genetic components of development has gradually crept into related areas of social psychology. Similarly much of the impetus of cognitive research has come from biological sources and that intersection between cognitive and social psychology, social cognition, has proven receptive to biological insights (Fiske & Taylor, 1991). Yet neither of these biological incursions into the social are anywhere near as violent as the challenges of **sociobiology**.

sociobiology
The study of the evolutionary roots of human social behaviour; innate predispositions.

Sociobiology blends evolutionary theory and psychology and its focus is an interpretation of social phenomena from an evolutionary perspective. Sociobiology sees our behaviour as partly shaped by our biological and genetic heritage. Psychobiologists see the hand of evolution at work in many of the traditional areas of social psychology. Prejudice, sex-roles, romantic attraction, cooperation and altruism, aggression and territorial behaviour, incest and child abuse, are all influenced by natural selection and have an evolutionary logic underlying them (Crawford, 1989). Proponents of this view argue that if psychologists and, in particular, social psychologists wish to understand the true dimensions of social behaviour and indeed culture, they ignore evolutionary theory at their peril.

To say this view is extremely controversial understates the case. Earlier social-evolution theories, crudely modelled on classical darwinism, suggested that sex and class differences reflected one's heredity. The social darwinism of Herbert Spencer was Victorian Europe's answer to the oppression of the

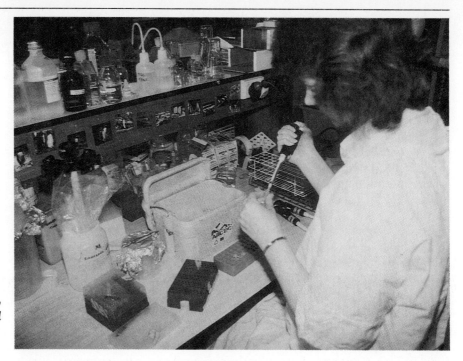

Genetic research may provide insights into how heredity influences social behaviour.
(Photo: Gavin Price)

poor. The poor were poor because they were of poor stock and their situation reflected their abilities (Spencer, 1862). Francis Galton, Darwin's cousin, supported a patriarchal view of women by demonstrating their intellectual inferiority and explaining it in evolutionary terms (Galton, 1869). Galton implicitly assumed a male intellectual superiority that was most likely linked to the masculine gene (Buss, 1976). The crudeness of this early form of sociobiology may be judged from Galton's view of the consequences of inferior intellect on the feminine personality:

> . . . she is capricious and coy and has less straightforwardness than the man . . . Coyness and caprice have in consequence become a heritage of the sex, together with a cohort of allied weaknesses and petty deceits, that men have come to think venial and even amiable in women, but which they would not tolerate among themselves. (Galton, 1883, p. 20)

What early sociobiologists like Galton and Spencer were suggesting was that sex, race and individual differences followed the rule that "ontogeny recapitulates phylogeny" or, freely interpreted, that what one becomes or does is largely a matter of what one is genetically. This rule does not work for any number of reasons we will not pursue here. Modern sociobiologists, while rejecting the rule as too individualistic, would believe that evolution shapes a species' developmental timetable and governs its overall evolution by regulating resource use. Such theorists believe that the discrediting of earlier theories has blinded contemporary psychologists to advances that make the newer version of sociobiology of considerable use (Crawford,

1989). While it is still difficult to demonstrate a direct link between genetics and behaviour, this has not ruled out the other test of this theory's validity, predictive efficiency. As these advances throw new light on social phenomena, social psychology has a lot to gain from this biological insight. As yet the sociobiological challenge to social psychology is piecemeal and confined to specific areas of inquiry, though some conceptual syntheses are emerging (Cosmides & Tooby, 1989). Notwithstanding the piecemeal nature of the challenge, it is vigorous with hundreds of articles and books emerging in the last decade. At present evolutionary theory is biology's most basic concept; it remains to be seen if it will have any impact on social psychology.

Research methods in social psychology

Theorising in social psychology

Personal experience gained from our everyday interactions with others provides us with considerable knowledge about the substance of social psychology. We continually ask ourselves questions about human behaviour. We make observations about ourselves and others, infer motivations and attribute causality to our own and others' social behaviour. Often we believe that our *commonsense* notions about "how the world works" are correct. However, a moment's reflection tells us that our observations and explanations are often unsystematic and unreliable. So social psychology depends on systematic and controlled observations to acquire knowledge about social behaviour. It is this systematic approach that distinguishes social psychological inquiry from commonsense explanations and predictions. "Social psychology may be commonsense but it is organised and tested commonsense" (Penrod, 1986).

What does it mean to say that social psychology is a science? A science is a body of knowledge based upon objective observations and systematic testing. When scientists collect data they follow a series of procedures with established rules and principles. Collectively these procedures and rules are known as the **scientific method**. The process involves systematic observations; the development of theories that attempt to explain data; the application of theory to test predictions; and revision of these theories when research suggests our predictions are inaccurate. This method provides us with an invaluable tool in our search for understanding and knowledge about a particular topic. These information-gathering procedures assist us to achieve the basic objectives of description, explanation, prediction and control.

scientific method
A process involving systematic observations; the development of theories that attempt to explain data; the application of theory to test predictions; and revision of these theories when research suggests our predictions are inaccurate.

How do social psychologists gather information?

Research in social psychology can be divided into two methodological approaches: non-experimental methods and experimental methods. Non-experimental methods, such as *archival research*, *case studies*, *surveys* and *field studies*, make no attempt to influence conditions under which participants respond. With experimental methods such as laboratory and field experiments, the researcher randomly assigns subjects to two or more groups and manipulates a treatment variable (independent variable) to one group and not the other (the control group). The experimenter then measures the effect of such treatment by comparing the groups on some behaviour variable/s (dependent variable). Both these methods involve different approaches to the collection of data.

Non-experimental methods

Archival research

This method of data collection involves the systematic collation of information that has been collected for some other purpose by other researchers. Archival research may include the study of biographies; public registers of births, deaths and marriages; hospital records; crime statistics and other large databases. This method has many advantages: we can examine social behaviour that could not be studied by other means; it allows us to collect a large amount of data quickly, with little effort and is relatively cost-effective; particular populations may be studied over a specific time frame; it highlights gaps in research, assists in generating hypotheses, and signposts ways for future inquiry.

While this method is often a good starting point for research, it also has limitations. A major disadvantage is that researchers are usually unable to obtain a representative sample of behaviour for the period they are studying. Records are compiled for reasons other than your own and your choice of variables is often limited by whatever data are available. Valuable data may be missing or may have been collected in an uncontrolled way and compiled unsystematically. Archival research is only as good as the available database. While this method has the potential to yield valuable information, it must be remembered it does not allow researchers to draw conclusions about causal relationships between the variables being studied, nor does it allow us to test theory in a valid way. To achieve this it is necessary to supplement this approach with other research methods.

Case studies

This method involves in-depth research and analysis of a limited number of cases of interest and may focus on a single individual, a specific event, or representative samples of a group of people, such as a probing interview with a serial killer. This method is often employed to study behaviour that is relatively uncommon and cannot be examined by laboratory experiments or other methods. Its major advantage is that it allows an exhaustive study of a particular behaviour, individual or event. It also enables the study of specific phenomena over time and is useful for generating research ideas and hypotheses. However, findings may not be applicable to other examples of the behaviour and it is open to both researcher and subject bias. Again, as with archival research, it does not permit conclusions about cause and effect.

Surveys

Surveys are very much a part of our culture and abound in market research. They are used to sample voting patterns; predict election outcomes; and provide the basis for TV ratings, just to mention a few examples. Surveys represent systematic ways of asking people how they think, feel and behave on certain issues. While there are a variety of survey techniques, there are two basic types: interviews and questionnaires. An *interview* consists of structured questions presented in a specific order, or open-ended questions intended to elicit more detailed information. In an interview, the researcher asks questions and records respondents' answers. Their weakness is that interviewer bias may influence the course and outcome of an interview as well as the recording and coding of data. Surveys may also take the form of written *questionnaires*, where respondents are asked to provide written responses to open-ended questions; to indicate their agreement or disagreement with a series of statements; or to rank their views on an issue on a predetermined scale. Questionnaires are quite time-efficient. They enable a large amount of data to be collected quickly and relatively inexpensively, and are useful in obtaining data on a wide range of beliefs, values and behaviour that do not lend themselves to direct observation.

However, there are limitations to the survey method. Findings from surveys only provide information about interrelationships among variables. They do not enable us to draw conclusions about whether or not one variable influences another. Also, this method is based on self-reporting, which is open to bias. Questions may be poorly constructed, ambiguous or shape the respondent's answer. People do not always report their feelings and behaviour accurately or honestly. They may have their own ideas about what answers the researcher wants or what a socially appropriate response would be. Often people tend to respond to questions in a systematically biased way. For example, some give *down the middle* answers while others tend to give extreme responses. Some respondents may repeatedly answer yes or no, regardless of the questions.

The advantage of both survey methods is that we can obtain information about a large number of variables relevant to our specific hypotheses. Also, surveys enable researchers to obtain a representative sample of a particular population about which they wish to generalise.

Field studies

In many instances social psychologists want to study how we behave in real-life settings. Field studies enable researchers to observe social behaviour directly in natural settings—they simply observe behaviour without attempting to change or influence it in any way. Data may be recorded on audio or

video tapes or manually coded. There are two basic types of field study—
naturalistic and *participant* observation. In naturalistic observation the researcher
remains unobtrusive and simply observes and records behaviours of interest.
With participant observation the researcher joins and participates in a
particular group being studied in order to better observe their activities,
such as joining a religious sect, bikie gang, or riding with a police patrol.
This is a traditional method of many anthropologists who live with the
people they wish to study.

In a classic participant observation study, Rosenhan et al. (1973) faked
symptoms of mental illness to staff at psychiatric hospitals and were admitted
as patients. After admission, they reverted to normal behaviour and observed
how they were treated by patients and staff. Findings indicated that many
patients immediately realised the researchers were not really mad and
wondered what they were doing in the institution. On the other hand,
staff remained blissfully unaware and continued to interpret these pseudo-
patients' normal behaviour in accordance with their admissions diagnosis.
When the researchers sat by themselves in the ward, they were recorded
as withdrawn. When they made notes on their observations, this was
regarded as abnormal by staff. The studies lasted for periods ranging from
2 weeks to 3 months. When the pseudo-patients concluded their study
and left the hospital they were regarded as being in remission rather than
free of psychiatric illness.

There are advantages and disadvantages with both methods. Naturalistic
observation allows the researcher to observe spontaneously occurring activity
in a real-life setting and can provide valuable and detailed information
about social behaviour that cannot be studied in a laboratory. However,
we can never be sure if the situation we are studying is not somehow
atypical. Our observations may not be random (determined by chance
alone) and not representative of usual behaviour in that setting. For participant

*Social psychologists often
use unobtrusive
participant/observation
strategies to gain
information about the
social groups they study.
In this method they
become part of the
group.
(Photo: Chris Simkin)*

observers, it is even more difficult to remain unbiased while working so closely with people they are studying, as their behaviour may influence the very behaviours they want to observe.

When social psychologists want to research questions of everyday life, the field study is often the method of choice but may be biased by the focus of our study, the particular setting, the individuals who just happen to be present, or the behaviours we have chosen to research. Again, field studies limit the extent to which we can comment on causality and generalise our findings to other settings. While field studies have limitations and may offer a distorted view of reality due to researcher and subject bias, they remain particularly valuable for collecting data about real-life interactions. They provide useful insights into social behaviour in natural environments and are important for formulating hypotheses for further research.

Experimental methods

What distinguishes experimental methods from other forms of data collection is that these methods allow for the study of social variables under more carefully controlled and standardised conditions. Experimental procedures allow researchers to manipulate and control factors being studied so that causal statements can be made about how variables influence each other. These methods include laboratory, field and natural experiments.

Laboratory experiments

Typically, a laboratory experiment involves the random allocation of subjects to two groups (the experimental and control groups). Random assignment of subjects provides a safeguard against characteristics of subjects that may bias results. These two groups receive identical treatment except on the variable manipulated by the experimenter. The experiment is explicitly designed to observe the causal influence of one variable on another. For example, in an experiment designed to test the effects of frustration on aggression, the experimenter manipulates an **independent variable** by either frustrating or not frustrating subjects and then measures the effect of this manipulation on a **dependent variable** or their subsequent aggressive behaviour. Many students get confused between the two; if you are ever in any doubt, ask yourself what is being measured and you have the dependent variable.

Appropriately designed experiments allow researchers to make statements about cause-effect relationships, that is, changes in the dependent variable can be attributed to variations in the independent variable. **Control** is the key consideration here. The primary objective is to hold everything constant, except the independent variable, while controlling or minimising extraneous variables, such as differences in room temperature, family background and so on, which might otherwise affect the results. If these are carefully controlled, a systematic effect may be attributed to the causal influence of the independent variable.

Laboratory experiments have several advantages. They permit a high degree of flexibility and allow the experimenter to control extraneous variables. Also, complex behaviour and interactions can be examined in smaller units. A major advantage of this method is that cause and effect

independent variable
Manipulation of one or more factors in an experiment to see what effect it has on another variable.

dependent variable
That which is being measured in an experiment; the variable influenced by the experimental manipulation.

control
Eliminating or controlling all sources of bias in an experiment which might confound results.

relationships among variables can be established. However, experiments conducted in laboratory settings are subject to limitations. In many instances, it is difficult to generalise findings to real-life settings and not all variables are amenable to manipulation in the experimental context. In addition, it is paramount that researchers in designing such studies attempt to elicit "real" behaviour, that is, that the experimental setting is as natural as possible and not so unusual or atypical that participants may respond in uncharacteristic ways.

Field experiments

Field experiments involve hypothesis testing conducted in real-life settings. These experiments attempt to combine the control and standardisation procedures of the laboratory setting with experiments out in the real world. My students, for example, replicated a study by Dutton and Aron (1974) which we will see in Chapter Nine. They were interested in the impact of autonomic arousal on romantic feelings and interviewed subjects who had just got off the Wild Cat at Wonderland in Sydney. This is a truly awesome ride acknowledged as one of the most hair-raising in the Southern Hemisphere. Students pretended to be doing a market survey and asked young men and women, who were unaccompanied by a partner of the opposite sex, what they thought of Wonderland. The students were not interested in responses to the survey, these were discarded. Their dependent variable was the number of sexual comments, flirtatious behaviours and propositions the very attractive interviewers received as they asked their questions. The independent variable manipulation was being on the ride, contrasted with responses from people waiting for friends to come off it. Their hypothesis, that the ride would arouse subjects and they would be more flirtatious than the onlooker group, was amply confirmed.

A major advantage of field experiments is that they provide social psychologists with many opportunities to examine aspects of social behaviour that are difficult to study under laboratory conditions. Typically, subjects in field experiments are unaware that they are participating in an experiment. A distinct disadvantage of this method is that it is less artificial and more realistic and minimises subjects' reactivity. However, in real-life settings many variables may interact in complex ways. Data obtained from field experiments is often influenced by a myriad of factors not relevant to the behaviour being studied. Also, it becomes much more difficult to control extraneous variables. So results may not be as confidently generalised to other similar contexts, and inferences drawn about cause-effect relationships must be regarded as tentative.

Natural experiments

Natural experiments are *unplanned, post hoc* experiments which occur outside the laboratory. Researchers compare groups after the independent variable is manipulated by nature or by some third party unaware of the researcher's interests. Natural disasters such as floods and earthquakes often provide fortuitous contrasts between groups, which are then measured after the fact by researchers (see Box 1.4). These events provide the researcher with opportunities to conduct comparative studies and often yield valuable information about social behaviour, which in the case of disasters can be used to alleviate future victims' suffering.

Social psychologists would not want to create such events as riots, revolutions and natural disasters. When these events occur spontaneously, the independent variables are manipulated by nature or other people, not the experimenter and, however unfortunate for the victims, are of great interest to researchers. Of course there are limitations to this method. Experimenters must wait for such events to occur, their occurrence cannot be predicted and they occur relatively infrequently.

Correlational studies involve computing the relationships between two or more variables. These studies are usually drawn from pre-existing data in population census or smaller statistical surveys. A correlation coefficient measures the degree to which changes in one variable are related to changes in another. For example, when stress is high, is illness also high, or are stress and illness unrelated? Correlations can range from +1 to –1. A correlation of +1 indicates a perfect positive relationship, stress and illness levels change at the same rate. A negative correlation indicates that as stress increases, illness decreases and vice versa. Unlike the experimental method, correlational studies do not involve random allocation of subjects to groups or manipulation of independent variables by the researcher.

Correlational research

If we are interested in finding out if watching violent programmes on TV is related to subsequent aggressive behaviour in children, we may choose to conduct a correlational study. Obtaining a correlation of +1 indicates that, in every case, frequency of viewing violence would exactly match the frequency of subsequent aggression. A major advantage of this method is that it is an efficient and relatively inexpensive way to investigate associations between many variables. It provides social psychologists with a way to collect a large amount of information and test more relationships than is possible in many experiments. It also allows us to examine many important issues which for practical and ethical reasons could not be researched in the experimental context.

A major limitation of correlational research is how to interpret your findings. Correlational studies that indicate two variables are related reveals little about what causes their relationship. Because two variables are correlated does not mean one causes the other. In our TV example, a finding indicating a relationship between the amount of violent content viewed by children and subsequent aggression only means they are related. We cannot say that viewing violent programmes causes aggression. Other interpretations may be applicable. Children who like to act aggressively may prefer to watch violent programmes. It may be that aggressive parents rear aggressive children and that parental viewing patterns are a factor in their offspring's aggression. Such potential **correlational fallacies** bedevil correlational research.

correlational fallacy
Correlation does not equal causation.

Box 1.4 *The Ash Wednesday bushfires—A natural experiment*

Natural disasters often provide opportunities to conduct unplanned experiments. (Photo: Barry Price)

In the summer of 1983, a series of wet years followed by a very dry season set bushfires raging throughout southern Australia. These culminated in the Ash Wednesday bushfires of 16 February in which 28 people died and 385 homes were lost in the Adelaide Hills and southern Victoria. The human impact of this tragedy was intensively studied in over 140 reported investigations, turning this disaster into one huge natural experiment.

Professor Alex McFarlane, of Flinders University School of Medicine, has intensively studied the 1983 bushfires' impact on the mental health of victims, relief workers and bushfire personnel (McFarlane, 1990). As a researcher interested in the **posttraumatic stress disorder**, McFarlane was presented with an opportunity to conduct a natural experiment to see what impact the fires had on these groups. Over 14 studies, he has reported on the frequency of mental disorder attributable to the disaster; life changes in victims and workers compared with those who were unaffected; a longitudinal investigation of a group of 469 volunteer firefighters who had particularly intense exposure to the fires; and how children in the area coped with its aftermath.

McFarlane started his natural experiment by immediately gathering data from 1526 adults, 808 primary schoolchildren, and 469 firefighters in the disaster area (McFarlane, 1989a). He then structured two longitudinal studies to look at the "predisposing, precipitating and perpetuating factors of the posttraumatic stress disorder". The firefighters were studied at 4, 11 and 29 months after the fires and "completed an inventory of events occurring before and after the disaster, the General Health Questionnaire, and the Eysenck Personality Inventory" (McFarlane, 1989b). McFarlane's experiment was to compare firefighters' responses to those of the general public (his scales' norms). These measures were his dependent variables. The fire provided the "experimental manipulation" by touching some people's lives and not others'. Being involved or not was the

independent variable. McFarlane (1988a) was able to later refine his design by identifying a high-risk group of 50 firefighters whom he followed up over the next 3 years, comparing their posttraumatic stress with a matched sample of 96 other subjects.

In a similar way, McFarlane (1988b) studied the fires' impact on children and their families (McFarlane, 1987). By careful comparisons with those not affected, McFarlane was able to trace the impact of selected aspects of the posttraumatic stress disorder.

What did McFarlane find? The children were fairly robust and their experiences in the fires did not predispose them to being more vulnerable to additional misfortune after the disaster. The trauma they experienced affected them deeply and remained for some time. But McFarlane found that changes in the family dynamic were likely to account for the persistence of their distress. He found that mothers' responses to the fires were better predictors of children's distress than the children's own experiences. Their mothers suffered intrusive memories and flashbacks and this led to changed parenting practices which seemed to account for this prolonged distress. A comparison of 183 families with 497 families that did not suffer through the fires found that disaster-affected families were more con-flict prone, irritable and withdrawn. Mothers were more overprotective and their post- traumatic distress was the major determinant of children's ongoing reactions (McFarlane, 1987).

The firefighters were another story. McFarlane found that personality factors such as neuroticism or prior treatment for a psychological disorder were better predictors of posttraumatic distress and, contrary to his expectations, "the intensity of exposure, the perceived threat, and the losses sustained in the disaster, when considered independently, were not predictors of posttraumatic stress disorder". So for this group at least "vulnerability is a more important factor in breakdown than the degree of stress experienced" (McFarlane, 1989a).

third variable problem
In correlational research, when two variables are related, maybe a third unknown factor causes their relationship.

reverse causality problem
In correlation research, we find that *x* and *y* are related, but which variable is the cause and which is the effect?

The ambiguous nature of cause-effect relationships in correlational studies can be related to two factors. The **third variable problem** notes that when two variables are correlated, it is possible that *x* causes *y*, or the reverse, or a third variable (*z*) influences both *x* and *y*. Returning to our earlier example, it may be that airborne lead toxicity causes both stress and illness. The **reverse causality problem** asks, if we find that *x* and *y* are related, which variable is the cause and which is the effect? We cannot be sure whether *x* causes *y*, or the reverse, that *y* causes *x*. For instance, do aggressive children prefer to watch violent TV programmes, or does viewing violence cause them to behave aggressively? So, remember that "correlation does not imply causation".

Sources of bias in social experimentation

Getting our science right

demand characteristics
Guessing the true purposes of an experiment and altering your behaviour to give the experimenter what you think they want.

experimeter bias
Reactions to the subject's biosocial characteristics; experimenter attributes; and their expectations, all of which potentially bias research.

subject bias
Subject variables (age, sex, expectations etc.) that bias experimental results.

Studying behaviour in experimental contexts is an area worthy of social psychologists' interest as it represents a social interaction in itself. Collecting data and observing behaviour is a social process that affects the behaviour being observed. Subjects participating in experiments do not simply respond passively to stimuli presented to them, they act and react to their environment. Subjects are curious, problem-solving individuals, who are aware that they are being studied and thus actively influence the experiment (Orne, 1962). In social research there are three main problems which may influence the experimental situation: **demand characteristics**, **experimenter bias** and **subject bias**.

Demand characteristics

Subjects have opinions about the experiment, what its aims and objectives are, and in attempting to define the nature of the situation, make use of any available information. Demand characteristics are cues in the experimental setting itself that may influence subjects to respond in a particular way (Orne, 1962). Such cues may include: the experimenter's tone of voice; facial expressions; body posture; arrangement of experimental apparatus; or other cues that provide clues about the research hypotheses. For example, some subjects may see a cue in the experimental setting which they believe indicates the way the experimenter wants them to respond. One way to check on demand characteristics is simply to ask subjects in a post-experimental interview what they thought were the aims of the study. However this may not provide a valid check because of what Orne refers to as "the pact of ignorance" which may exist between experimenter and subject. The subject is aware that if they say they have guessed the purpose of the experiment they may have wasted their time, and data will be excluded. Likewise the experimenter knows that subjects who have guessed the aims of the experiment will have to be discounted. This means testing another subject, time delays, and so on. "Hence neither party to the inquiry wants to dig very deeply" (Orne, 1962). While it is difficult to control for demand characteristics completely, careful design and planning of the experimental situation can do much to minimise their effect on experimental outcome.

Experimenter bias

Experimenters in the course of their research can sometimes subtly influence how subjects respond in the research setting. They are not infallible human beings and sometimes have a vested interest in experimental outcomes. Biases can inadvertently creep in at any stage of the research, including errors in recording data, analysis and interpretation of results. Three main types of experimenter bias have been identified by Rosenberg (1969): biosocial factors, psychological factors and experimenter expectancy effects. **Biosocial factors** include such variables as the experimenters' reaction to the subject's age, gender, ethnicity and physical appearance. Psychological biases include the attributes of the experimenter, for example her authoritarian manner, or outgoing, friendly way of interacting and how this influences the subject. Experimenters formulate hypotheses and hold beliefs or opinions about what will happen. They may act in subtle, unintentional ways which may lead to confirmation of their expectations. This is known as the **experimenter expectancy effect** and is akin to the self-fulfilling prophecy which we will discuss in Chapter Three. Researchers can minimise and often eliminate this bias by designing their study carefully. One way to safeguard against experimenter bias is to standardise experimental procedures as much as possible, so as to treat all participants in the same way. Another useful method is for the experimenter to remain blind to, or to be unaware of, which experimental condition the subject has been assigned.

Subject bias

Humans are naturally curious, so subjects try to work out what the experiment is all about. Subjects' motives are a potential source of bias in the experiment and will be more likely to occur when strong demand characteristics are present. Of course the mere fact that subjects are aware of being studied tends to alter their behaviour somewhat. This is why field experiments are often preferable. Also subjects who guess the experiment's aims may then give correct or socially desirable responses. Again, participants may adopt several roles in the experiment. They may be cooperative and act in accordance with what they think the experimenter wants them to do. They may act negatively and attempt to disrupt the experimenter's aims and disconfirm the hypothesis. Some are "evaluation apprehensive" and avoid being negatively evaluated or being seen as bad subjects (Rosenberg, 1969). Faithful subjects, perhaps from the experimenter's viewpoint, represent the ideal subjects. Faithful subjects follow instructions without attempting to confirm or disconfirm the hypotheses, and endeavour to respond as they would in non-experimental conditions.

Ethics in social research

Beyond deception

Social research often poses ethical dilemmas for social psychologists. Dilemmas occur in how to conduct methodologically sound, unbiased research, while respecting the rights of subjects to be treated ethically. Potential sources of conflict arise when studies involve deception, invasion of privacy and potential risk, harm or distress to participants.

Potential risk, harm or distress

Ethical notions of risk generally refer to situations likely to produce unpleasant consequences to an individual not likely to be experienced in the course of everyday behaviour. Saying that the experiment may be unpleasant provides a safeguard for subjects participating in social experiments. Where procedures involve some potential risk or harm to subjects, it is usual practice for the researcher to obtain their informed consent. This helps to ensure that participation is voluntary. Most subjects are informed of any risks that might influence their decision to participate and that they are free to withdraw from the study at any time.

Deception

The use of deception in social psychology experiments raises another ethical dilemma for researchers. Many studies in social psychology employ varying degrees of deception in order to minimise demand characteristics and subject bias. As previously mentioned, subjects' awareness of the procedures and purposes of the research can invalidate findings. The experimenter's truthfulness may influence the subject to react artificially. For these reasons, social psychology experiments routinely use **deception** (see Box 1.5). For example, many experiments use confederates (**stooges**). It is an important ethical requirement that the use of any deception procedures, and the nature and purpose of the research, be fully explained in a debriefing session at the end of the experiment. This post-experimental session can also be a valuable methodological tool. The experimenter may gain useful insights into subjects' motivations and opinions about the purpose of the experiment. It is important to note that sometimes ethical issues arise due to acts of omission as well as commission.

deception
Misleading, or not informing, subjects of the true purposes of an experiment.

stooges
Experimenter confederates usually used in experiments involving deception procedures.

Right to privacy

Our right to privacy is somewhat taken for granted. This issue is of paramount concern in research involving deception where subjects are unaware of what behaviours are being investigated and in real-life settings where subjects do not know they are participating in a psychological experiment. Another issue relevant to privacy is confidentiality. It is essential that experimenters maintain confidentiality unless they have the subject's permission to divulge information.

Box 1.5 *Deception in social psychology experiments*

Successful research often involves lying to the subject about the experiment's real aims. Deception may be covert where the experimental aims are withheld, or overt where deliberate misdirection is built into the experimental design. The extent of deception within social psychology is rather alarming. Gross and Fleming (1982) assessed the percentage of studies using deception in the well-respected *Journal of Personality* and *Social Psychology* and found that between 1959 and 1969 they rose from 41 to 66 per cent of reported studies.

Figures like this so alarmed critics during the crisis-of-social-psychology decade that deception and experimental ethics became a whipping boy to use against experimentalist factions in social psychology. Many argued that misleading subjects was an invasion of privacy as it "extracted data under false pretences"

(Aronson et al., 1990); or they would be embarrassed by their actions when they learned the true nature of the experiment (Kelman, 1968). It was assumed that actual harm would occur when subjects saw unpalatable insights into their character as in the Milgram obedience to authority experiments (see Chapter Six). When Michael Nash (1975) pointed out in *American Psychologist* that those conducting deception experiments were technically committing offences of negligence, deceit and foreseeability of harm—not to mention invasions of privacy, intent and consent, and the possibility of being sued by subjects—even hardnosed experimentalists began to worry and the codes of most psychological societies were revised to tighten up experimental ethics.

Four strategies were suggested to offset the supposed effects of deception. First,

"DON'T WORRY ITS NOT ALL THAT HARD TO FIGURE OUT WHAT YOU HAVE TO DO TO SHUT THEM UP."

Perhaps even laboratory animals are aware of demand characteristics!
(Cartoonist: Steve Harris)

experimenters were urged to use "non-invasive strategies", that is not use deception. As this is virtually impossible in many areas of social psychology, informed consent, withdrawal options and post-experimental debriefing were suggested as ways of alleviating its adverse effects.

To see if these critiques had any effect, Gross and Fleming surveyed 1188 articles published in four leading social psychology journals (*Journal of Experimental Social Psychology*, *Journal of Personality* and *Social Psychology*, *Journal of Social Psychology*, and *Social Psychology*) between 1959 and 1979. Despite the debate, use of deception did not decrease during this period and remained about 58 per cent of total studies. From my own perusal of recent issues of these journals, percentages continue to be about the same.

More to the point, social experimenters began to question the ready assumption that deception led to subjects being harmed (Baumrind, 1985). Christiansen (1988) in a literature review found that most subjects were not worried about deception when debriefed; some even enjoyed the experience (Smith & Richardson, 1983); and many believed deception was necessary and justified (Fleming, Bruno, Barry & Fost, 1989).

Alternatives to deception have proven impractical. For example, experiments often go in embarrassing directions which neither the experimenter nor informed consent agreements envisaged. Often the degree of consent required would give away the purposes of the experiment. One suggestion to resolve these difficulties proposed a prior general consent plus proxy consent technique. This envisaged a subject giving a general consent and having a friend examine the details of the experiment and decide if it were acceptable! A moment's reflection will show that this idea raises more ethical problems than it fixes (Aronson et al., 1990). To give another example, Trice and Ogden (1987), studying the effects of a withdrawal clause on longitudinal research, found that 52 per cent of their subjects were lost when reminded of their withdrawal option. They argue that this has a potential to bias samples and render them invalid.

To make a final observation, while deception is a technique that does require close scrutiny and care, often ethical concerns are more an artefact of self-conscious reflection by confederates and experimenters than real worries of the subjects (Korn, 1987; Oliansky, 1991). So it seems we will keep on lying to our subjects.

Professional code of ethics

Peer review? No single solution will provide the panacea for ethical issues in social psychological research. Most professional psychological associations have developed strict ethical guidelines for research on human subjects. Box 1.6 provides excerpts from the Australian Psychological Society's Code of Ethics for research with human subjects.

Summary

Social psychology is the study of the individual in group settings. While other disciplines, such as sociology, study social processes from a collective or societal perspective, social psychology examines what the individual does in groups as small as two-person settings. Social psychology has a vast territory as it studies the entirety of social processes. For this reason it specialises in traditional areas.

Box 1.6 *The ethics of experimenting with human subjects*

The following excerpts are from the Australian Psychological Society's *Code of Professional Conduct* (1986) Section E, paras 3–7. Other provisions of this section of the code deal with the general ethics of experimentation, the physical welfare of subjects, confidentiality and animal experimentation.

3. If a research procedure involves participants in significant levels of emotional arousal (e.g. use of fear-evoking stimuli) it is incumbent on the investigator to ensure that no psychologically vulnerable person participates.

4. When a research procedure necessarily involves participants in physical or mental stress, the investigator must conscientiously inform participants of the procedures to be used, and the physical and psychological effects to be expected. No research procedures likely to cause severe distress should be used under any circumstances. If unexpected stress reactions of significance occur, the investigator has the responsibility immediately to alleviate such reactions and to terminate the investigation.

5. When it is necessary for scientific reasons to conduct a study without fully informing participants of its truer purpose, the investigator must ensure that participants do not suffer distress from such a procedure.

6. Investigators must preserve and protect the respect and dignity of all participants. Wherever possible, participants must be fully informed of the nature and purpose of the investigation at an appropriate stage of the investigation.

7. Investigators must endeavour to ensure that participants' consent to be involved in the research is genuinely voluntary. Participants must be advised that they may withdraw from the research project at any time. If informed consent cannot be obtained by reason, for example, of stage of intellectual development of participants, consent must be obtained from the persons who are legally responsible for each participant's welfare.

Source: The Australian Psychological Society Ltd, 1986.

Depending on their theoretical orientation, social psychologists explain social behaviour in different ways. Cognitive approaches concentrate on how we perceive and explain our own and others' actions. Learning approaches examine the environment's influence on our behaviour. Motivational approaches assume we are driven by needs. Ecological and biological approaches infer inherent motivations. Social exchange and equity perspectives see social interactions as trading relationships. Cultural views note the role of societal and cross-cultural forces.

Social psychology is a multidisciplinary area which incorporates insights from many other branches of knowledge. Social explanation proceeds at several levels and individual, interpersonal and sociological perspectives reflect both its multidisciplinary borrowings and scientific reductionism in social psychology.

Social psychology has a long past but short history. Social theorising predates the Ancient Greeks but only since the 1870s has it incorporated a scientific outlook. Auguste Comte is credited with establishing social psychology, Wilhelm Wundt defined its relations to experimental social psychology, and Gabriel Tarde published the first recognisable social psychology text in 1898.

Social psychology's growth has been explosive. From its infancy to the early 1930s growth was haphazard as the new discipline slowly defined itself and produced its own theoreticians, texts, journals and professional support groups. Its adolescence and early adulthood was an applied phase, as it struggled with the twin challenges of the Great Depression and World War II. 1945–65 were social psychology's golden years when most of the basic research that underlies the discipline was done. The decade 1965–75 were years of doubt and indecision as various challenges caused a period of intense self-scrutiny and reflection. Since the mid-1970s social psychology has steadily reasserted itself and found newer, more multidisciplinary, directions.

Social psychology has faced many severe challenges since the mid-1960s. Many argue it is a North American science as most of the research effort with social psychology is concentrated on that continent. A cross-cultural challenge argues social psychology is Western or Eurocentric in outlook. Others argue its over-reliance on laboratory experimentation has led us to know more about less. Others feel social psychology should incorporate more biological insights into its theorising, while others argue it should not pretend to be a science at all. These and other challenges led to a period of intense self-reflection, the so-called "crisis of social psychology" from which the discipline is slowly emerging with renewed confidence.

Because of the diversity of settings in which social behaviour occurs, social psychologists employ many different research strategies to understand behaviour. These are usually grouped as non-experimental methods, experimental methods, and correlational studies. Non-experimental studies are a rich source of insights and hypotheses but usually provide limited control and predictability to the researcher. These methods include archival research, case studies, surveys, interviews and field studies.

Experimental methods, such as laboratory, field and natural experiments, provide a greater degree of control and predictability. Correlational studies are useful for finding variables which co-vary, but they may not be direct influences on each other and may not be causally connected. Even so, correlational studies are very useful pointers to possible cause and effect relationships.

Experiments are designed to maximise an experimenter's chances of predicting cause and effect relationships and to minimise chances that the results are affected by extraneous variables. Control is the key consideration in all social experiments. Variables that may distort or corrupt results include demand characteristics, experimenter and subject bias.

Social psychological research raises ethical issues and concerns. These include potential risk or distress to participants, the use of deception in experiments, the right to privacy, the need for informed consent, and debriefing of research participants.

Recommended reading

Aronson E., Ellsworth P.C., Carlsmith J.M. and Gonzales M.H. (1990) METHODS OF RESEARCH IN SOCIAL PSYCHOLOGY (2nd edn), McGraw-Hill, NY. A very readable and detailed look at the many practical issues faced by social experimenters. Very much a manual for the novice setting up experiments.

Blackler F. (Ed.) (1983) SOCIAL PSYCHOLOGY AND DEVELOPING COUNTRIES, Wiley, NY. Translates the affluent college student based social psychology of the Western world into novel and applied contexts. See particularly Chapter 10 by Michael Bennett and Kepas Watangia on social psychology and primary health care in New Guinea.

Bond M.H. (Ed.) (1988) THE CROSS-CULTURAL CHALLENGE TO SOCIAL PSYCHOLOGY, Sage, Newbury Park, Calif. A very readable book which reviews the place of traditional experimental social psychology in the light of cross-cultural challenges. The chapters are written by the luminaries in the field.

Doise W. (1986) LEVELS OF EXPLANATION IN SOCIAL PSYCHOLOGY, Cambridge University Press, Cambridge. Another challenge to the straight experimentalist tradition noting the many ways in which social phenomena may be studied. A reasonably difficult but worthwhile read.

Hendrick C. and Clark M.S. (eds) (1990) RESEARCH METHODS IN PERSONALITY AND SOCIAL PSYCHOLOGY, Sage, Newbury Park, Calif. Vol. 11 of Sage's series A REVIEW OF PERSONALITY AND SOCIAL PSYCHOLOGY. Simply written introductory primers containing chapters by leading experts in the field.

O'Neil W.M. (1987) A CENTURY OF PSYCHOLOGY IN AUSTRALIA, Sydney University Press, Sydney. A brief survey from Australia's second full-time professor of psychology. Contains many interesting insights into the rise of social psychology.

Patnoe S. (1988) A NARRATIVE HISTORY OF EXPERIMENTAL SOCIAL PSYCHOLOGY: THE LEWIN TRADITION, Springer-Verlag, NY. A tribute to Kurt Lewin. Twenty interviews with leading social psychologists (Festinger, Darley, etc.) who felt Lewin's influence on their work. An interesting biographical insight into some of America's leading social theorists.

SOCIAL KNOWLEDGE

*I*n the early 1970s I used to run encounter groups. In the best Californian tradition, twelve or so optimists would meet on a Friday evening at a motel and spend all weekend raising each other's consciousness. In a hundred or so groups I had many profound experiences but one stands out head and shoulders above all the rest. To this group came eleven rugged individualists with their own idiosyncratic agendas. It went so wrong before it all came together, that the weekend was truly memorable. The previous Saturday, a prime-time TV special had portrayed the turbulent inner workings of an encounter group and the subsequent dramatic changes in participants' lives. My groups, while fairly confronting, were tame by comparison, with no sex, nudity or violence allowed. Unfortunately nine of the group had seen the show and came along fully primed and ready to go!

We started off by swapping expectations. One woman in her early forties set the pace by announcing she was sexually repressed and hoped to find new ways of expressing her sexuality. A man in his mid-forties, recovering from a messy divorce, was trying to put himself back together again. He pursued her for hours until he discovered she was a nun. Another elderly man was a body-language expert and annoyed everybody by constantly interpreting our nonverbal behaviour. His problem was loneliness. Halfway through he turned into a retired psychiatrist, which put a certain dampener on the group. It was definitely a weekend for stereotypes! We also had two young religious brothers, one was panicked by the thought he might be gay; the other was and used the group as a dry-run for his eventual coming out. An extremely attractive young woman, thus encouraged, shared she was a lesbian and a date-rape victim. She had espoused radical separatism and had come to let some men know what she thought of them under controlled conditions. And so it went . . .

With this volatile mix the group quickly developed into a marathon and by eleven next morning we were completely mentally constipated. We weren't going anywhere. One man with a truly hideous problem insisted we weren't being open enough and only through nudity could we achieve mutual vulnerability. Quick as a flash our nun had shed her gear, closely followed by her suitor and the feminist. Despite my protests, within a minute flat I was staring at eleven nudists. Tension built up and up, and suddenly the silliness of it all became apparent and we were roaring with a laughter which bubbled on and on as they dressed. It was a wonderful cathartic experience. For the rest of the weekend we talked as close friends sharing the way we saw the world, each other, our private selves and hopes for the future. All very corny but quite powerful. The group ended wonderfully, with tears and promises to stay in touch. We never did. Years later I saw the radical separatist on a train. She gave me a glorious smile and turned to her children.

Social knowledge

Human beings are social animals whose complex interactions are largely unconscious. As we can see from our anecdote, when exposed they are strikingly intricate and each day we navigate ourselves through a maze of legality, tribal customs, shared expectations and understandings, which are partly the baggage of history and of our own upbringing. Informed by a complex mix of attitudes, values, mores and beliefs, we strive for conformity and, in the act of relating, use our past experience, sensitivity and acuteness to assess what is expected of us. That we do this all so matter-of-factly points to our sheer skill as social beings and our accumulated social wisdom.

The formal study of social knowledge within psychology is called **social cognition** and since the mid-1980s has rapidly emerged as a field of study in its own right. As the title indicates, social psychologists are interested in people's thought processes as they manoeuvre within a complex social world. Although social cognition is firmly rooted in social psychology, it draws equal inspiration from the rapidly expanding cognitive sciences. Social psychology helps us understand the social context in which we think and act, while cognitive research provides a minute dissection of how we conceptualise it. In this chapter we take an *individual* approach to social knowledge, while in Chapter Twelve we consider the *social* context of social knowledge. Psychology's reawakened interest in mental life has deepened our awareness of the essentially schematic nature of social knowledge, in whose mental maps reside our accumulated experiences and enculturation. While this has increased our understanding of social processes, it has also enormously enlarged social psychology's scope.

The more we lift the lid on this area, the more complex our taken-for-granted skills become (Fiske & Taylor, 1991) and social cognition is a rapidly expanding area with many research emphases and new methods for examining social phenomena. Yet this new approach has also reconfirmed and extended our understanding of traditional social psychology, emphasising the discipline's basic strength. This cross-fertilisation has reawakened interest in how we construe the world around us. Social cognition studies how we make sense of our world and how we put it all together. In a sense it is the study of how we think about our thoughts. The research we review in this chapter reconfirms earlier theorists' views that we are active shapers of our social knowledge, engaged in a reciprocal process of **social constructionism**. As we act on our assumptions, so the feedback we receive modifies our worldview and in turn how we see ourselves. Whether we interpret these experiences accurately or not in no way diminishes the power of this process. We see the world around us, interpret it and act on our assumptions—"social cognition automatically involves social explanation" (Fiske & Taylor, 1991).

Similarly we are engaged in a process of **self-construction**. While at this stage of theoretical development, social cognition is still undecided about the ultimate nature of the self, with many differing opinions nevertheless, it acknowledges that the self is socially constructed. Social cognition stresses the self's plasticity and the way we shape our identity. Much of our social knowledge is used in defence of our self-concept. We sum up other people's reactions to us and modify our behaviour accordingly. It is clear from research that we really care how others see us and this is a powerful modifier of our self-image. Our *selves*, or our construction of ourselves, are vulnerable and greatly influence how we react in social encounters. So

social cognition
Study of how people make inferences, attributions and social judgments about themselves and others.

social constructionism
Philosophical perspective that we live in a reality constructed from our subjective experience of social interactions.

self-construction
Belief that the self is socially constructed.

much so it often seems we are more interested in self-presentation than achieving our goals. Whatever the self's ultimate nature, it is a major concern of social cognition.

Nor do we live in splendid isolation. Social psychology is the study of individuals in society. While we are busily trying to think and act appropriately and send out the right signals, others are trying to do the same. Social cognition is in part the study of these interpersonal processes that construct society. At this point there is a division of labour between psychological and sociological social psychologists. For many years, sociologists like Karl Mannheim (1972), Alfred Schutz (1972) and Thomas Luckmann (1983) delved into our common social reality, exploring the social reality that individuals inherit and subsequently modify. Psychologists Kurt Lewin (1951) and George Kelly (1955) in turn examined how individual worldviews are shaped by subjective experience, and others like Fritz Heider (1958) and Thibaut and Kelley (1959) developed methods and theories to account for individual variations over time.

Like any new area of study, social cognition is still in the process of defining itself. Yet some areas have emerged as major concerns and in this chapter we consider person perception, heuristics, salience, schemas, the self and self-presentation; while in Chapter Three we will round off our discussion with an in-depth look at attribution, misattribution, self-perception and self-attribution.

Person perception and social salience

Why would I remember a particular encounter group so vividly after more than twenty years? Surely time should have blurred memory into a composite of all the many groups I ran during those years? What was it about this group that made it so memorable? Perhaps the shortest answer is the sheer unusualness of the people who attended. Most groups were quite ordinary because average, ordinary, people came with ordinary problems. The people in this group, however, were anything but ordinary, their sheer difference so starkly contrasted with the other groups that they will remain forever distinctive.

One benefit of marrying social and cognitive psychology was the application of object perception models to social phenomena. Object perception examines how sensory information is transferred to memory and is particularly interested in those characteristics that influence this process. Our perception of objects is both physical and psychological. Physical cues , such as brightness, saturation and hue, influence how we process colour pictures, while psychological factors, such as closure, similarity and constancy, help us recognise what we are seeing. Some cues are more powerful attention-grabbers than others and have a larger impact on how and what we see. In a similar way, social perception looks at those factors, physical and psychological, that help us to interpret social situations. While person-perception is one

Object perception is a matter of salience and past learning. We rely on cues and similarities to identify unfamiliar objects. What do you think this object is? (Photo: Chris Simkin)

of the more technical areas of social cognition, it is mainly concerned with what makes people, or their context, stand out or become salient.

Salience, or that which is distinctive, is a term borrowed from **gestalt theory** and refers to anything that stands out from its background. When we look around us our attention is captured by a sequence of cues. We are immediately drawn to obvious contrasts, to brightness, movement, noise, unusual or unexpected phenomena (McArthur & Post, 1977). As much as we seem to be hard-wired to attend to dominant cues, we are even more conscious of people in our perceptual field. Fritz Heider (1958) argued that behaviour so engulfs our perceptual field that we are immediately drawn to people. When we enter a room people capture our attention first, their behaviour second, and their surroundings last. When we combine the priority people enjoy with any visually dominant cues, our attention is automatically drawn to those who are perceptually salient. For example, a friend who came to a formal tie and tails nurses' graduation in a sports suit was easily the most salient person at the dinner and ball which followed the ceremony. He even outshone the ladies. In the sober ranks of black-suited men waiting their partners, his light coloured coat literally made him the centre of attention. He was so unexpected and unusual in his context that he stood out and was perceptually salient.

Consistency is also an important perceptual cue. When others defy expectations they become socially salient even if their behaviour is not

salience
That which is distinctive and stands out from its background.

gestalt theory
Argues social psychology should study behaviour and experience as a whole and not as separate categories.

Salience!
(Cartoonist: Steve Harris)

"PERHAPS IT REPRESENTS SOME DEEP SEATED PENIS ENVY OR AUTO-EROTIC FANTASY. ON THE OTHER HAND, PERHAPS IT'S JUST TOO BLOODY OBVIOUS."

unusual in its context. So if we see a friend smoking with others in a smokers' lounge, his behaviour is instantly distinctive if he had been a vociferous anti-smoker in the past, even if smoking is an expected behaviour in that place.

Perceptual salience is often simply a matter of perspective.
(Photo: Mathew Munro)

Social salience

Given that salience captures our attention, we then try to tease out why people act as they do. Apart from contextual factors, people become salient when they breach our expectations. This **social salience** relies on our past experience and the expectations of appropriate behaviour it generates. It is our nature to see people as conscious, deliberate and responsive actors. Whether or not this is true, if they act unexpectedly and stand out we think it must be intentional. Seeing a sport-suited person at a formal ball we immediately start manufacturing reasons for their inappropriate attire. Is he making some sort of statement, or was he unsure of what was expected, or simply forgetful? The process of inferring reasons for another's behaviour, or **attribution**, is the topic of our next chapter, where we will examine the many attributional errors possible; however at this point it is worth noting that if we are unaware of perceptual distortion, we may be adding saliency biases to attributional errors.

social salience
Behaviour that is distinctive or unexpected in its context.

attribution
Making causal inferences about our own or another's behaviour.

Saliency biases and perceptual distortion

The implications of perceptual salience in perceiving people are far-reaching. Taylor and Fiske (1975) suggested that what captures our attention is most likely to be taken as the cause of observable behaviour, which may present a problem if it obscures subtle but real causes. In a series of experiments Taylor (1981) demonstrated that making one member of a group more salient, for instance being the only black in a group of whites, increased others' evaluations of their influence within the group. This bias not only obscures less salient, but possibly more important, people but also obscures environmental factors and leads to skewed and more extreme evaluations (Fiske, Kenny & Taylor, 1982). As perceptually salient people move centre stage, our impressions, possibly badly biased, follow.

The determinants of saliency effects

There are many, many factors that influence salience's dominance over the perceptual field and their study is becoming an increasingly important part of social cognition research. Although it is beyond our scope to review all of these factors, local researchers have made several significant contributions to basic theory. Penny Oakes and John Turner of the Australian National University, Canberra, for example, challenged the belief that novelty has automatic perceptual salience (Oakes & Turner, 1986). They argued that the widely held **distinctiveness hypothesis** (that we are drawn automatically to novel or contextually distinctive stimuli) is not automatic and may be mediated by other variables. They supported their position by showing how high school children sex-stereotyped (socially categorised) a group planning a meeting to warn of the dangers of a proposed nuclear power station. Oakes and Turner found that by directing the children's attention towards individuals, or the collective functioning of the group as a whole, they could manipulate stereotyping. By altering the sex-ratios of the six actors discussing the proposed power station, Turner and Oakes showed that children concentrating on individual actors tended to stereotype when there was only a sole male or female group member, whereas collectively focused subjects only did so in the equal sexes condition. Therefore, task mediated the effects of sex-salience. They concluded that being the novel

distinctiveness hypothesis
We are drawn automatically to novel or contextually distinctive stimuli.

member of a category does not automatically lead to a corresponding perceptual bias (see also Hogg & Turner, 1987; Turner, Hogg, Oakes, Reicher & Wetherell, 1987). As you can imagine this has wide implications for the whole salience debate (see Box 2.1).

Box 2.1 *Profile: Drew Nesdale and category salience: Stereotyping and person memory*

Drew Nesdale, Associate Professor at the University of Western Australia, represents social psychology in the West and has long been interested in social cognition and related issues.
After completing an Honours degree in psychology at the University of New England Drew Nesdale studied for his Masters and PhD degrees at the University of Alberta. His initial research activities focused on aggression and included work on its causes and consequences, as well as on moral judgments of aggressive behaviours. This latter work led to a continuing interest in the area of social cognition and its mediation of social behaviours. Much of this work has centred on the causal attribution process, particularly attributions of success and failure on performance tasks. Most recently, he has worked on social stereotypes concentrating on their relationship with affect and their influence on other cognitive processes such as memory, judgments and decisions. A special focus of his work is how these processes develop in children. (Photo: courtesy Drew Nesdale)

Salience is often a subtle and unconscious process affecting our perceptions. The assumption is, of course, that what is perceptually distinctive at the time captures our attention and is central to recall and subsequent evaluations. It is also assumed that salient features like sex and race increase the probability of stereotyping. To what extent is this true? As we have seen, Taylor (1981) argued that our category **salience** (being the only man in a group of women) increases the probablility of recall, as sex, race or other salient features invoke our stereotypes of that group. That is, we are more likely to stereotype someone if we cannot remember them in detail. As an example, a friend attributed his colleague's sales success to his ethnicity and his wife's even greater success to her sex. Their salience as the only Armenians, or as the only woman, on a large sales team led my friend to invoke stereotypes of Armenians as shrewd traders and women as flirts, to account for their success (see also Forgas, 1983a). So, we are more likely to stereotype someone if they are the sole representative of their sex or race.

However, this is contrary to commonsense expectations. We should expect that as ethnicity, for example, becomes less salient in a mixed group, we would be harder pressed to remember details of each and every member of a minority and, indeed, Taylor et al. (1978) reported as much. Surely we will then have to rely on our stereotypic views of such people to remember them? When a person is distinctive we should be able to remember more about them and rely less on stereotypes.

In the event neither viewpoint seems appropriate. Like so many issues in social psychology, the truth is a lot more complex than either alternative would suggest. Nesdale's interest in this issue was prompted by a careful re-analysis of Taylor et al.'s (1978) results. In an earlier study (reported in Nesdale, Dharmalingam & Kerr, 1987), Nesdale found that "both male and female observers' impressions of male speakers became less stereotyped as the numbers of males in the group increased whereas impressions of females were not influenced by changes in sub-group ratios" (Nesdale &

Dharmalingam, 1986). They concluded that recall was an interactive function of group ratio and the characteristics of the speaker.

In his later study (reported in Nesdale & Dharmalingam, 1986) Nesdale set out to test this possibility. Thirty male and 30 female Introductory Psychology students were randomly assigned to one of three group-ratio conditions: 9 males and 1 female; 5 males and 5 females; and 1 male and 9 females. Subjects were shown nondescript pictures of 10 speakers, whose gender balance reflected group ratios. They then listened to an audio tape cued to a photo of the speaker. While a videotape would have been more naturalistic, the audio tape/photo method was used to reduce the effects of extraneous cues such as dress, and to increase the category salience of gender. The speakers were discussing whether or not "smoking should be banned in public places" and each speaker contributed equal numbers of arguments for and against the proposition. In each of the

three gender-ratio conditions, speaker number 4 was male and speaker number 6 was female. The dependent variables were the numbers of opinions subjects recalled speakers 4 and 6 making in their condition.

When an analysis of variance was performed, Nesdale found three significant results. First, there was a clear category salience effect. Subjects remembered more about speakers who were solo in their groups as opposed to one of five or one of nine. Second, as you can see from Figure 2.1(a) there was a significant speaker's gender by group-ratio interaction. Male speakers' contributions were more often remembered when they were solo than either one of five or one of nine. In contrast there was no significant differences for recall of female speakers' contributions across the conditions. Third, as you will see from Figure 2.1(b) there was a significant subject's gender by group-ratio interaction. Male students recalled more when the speakers were solo irrespective of the

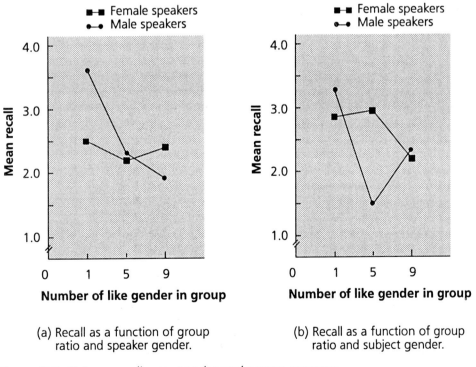

(a) Recall as a function of group ratio and speaker gender.

(b) Recall as a function of group ratio and subject gender.

Figure 2.1 *Category salience, gender and person memory*

Source: Nesdale & Dharmalingam, 1986.

speaker's sex. Female students showed no significant recall differences across the conditions.

How may we interpret these results? There is a clear category salience effect but the interaction effects show that a simple stereotyping-of-minorities explanation as posited by Taylor and others is inadequate to account for the results. Recall is a function of "who the participants are, what they contribute, and by whom they are being observed" (Nesdale & Dharmalingam, 1986). Nesdale suggested that their results reflected gender stereotypes. As the discussion was concerned with a concern for others' welfare, women speakers were within their stereotypically nurturant roles and so the ratio did not affect how they were seen. On the other hand, solo male speakers were more salient as they were acting atypically. When male ratios became more predominant, individual salience declined and recall was more difficult. So salience and person memory interacts variously depending on the person, their contribution and their distinctiveness.

One final comment. Which sex had the better person memory? Looking again at Figure 2.1, as you might expect, women did better than men but only in the equal ratio condition (there were no significant differences between sexes in the other two conditions). Perhaps this reflects sex roles which sensitise women to other people or, as Nesdale suggests, they may have been more motivated in this condition?

Emotion is also salient. Professor Ken Strongman and Peter Russell of Canterbury University, Christchurch, demonstrated that emotion affects our recall much more powerfully than neutral stimuli. Subjects were asked to complete sentences that had either an emotional or animal content in the target word, or sentence; for example, "The high-speed drill slipped from the dentist's grasp and sank directly into the woman's *breast/nipple/face/hand*." Sentences were constructed to have an emotional or neutral impact in the frame or target. Subjects were asked to complete 20 sentences, choosing from the words provided and then to list as many target words as they could remember (Strongman & Russell, 1986). Results from this study and an earlier one by Strongman (1982) show that emotion enhances alertness more so than memory for other material. They speculate that emotion provides a certain mnemonic salience which raises the overall level of performance, enhancing recall.

Salience is also often implicated in personality research where the distinctiveness of certain characteristics is assessed to see how salient they may be in a person's makeup or identity (see, for example, Lancaster & Foddy, 1988).

Although salience is important because it focuses our attention in ways that bias our subsequent recall, nevertheless, we distort *consistently*. If we are enjoying a party and notice someone's extravagant behaviour, we may attribute our enjoyment to their "livening things up". Our recall of this enjoyable event will be consistent with this hypothesis. The scintillating company, music, good food and wine provided by our hosts are forgotten. Indeed we seem to actively distort reality to deal with any discrepant information. Fiske and Taylor (1991) in particular note the ways in which discrepancies are dealt with to provide a consistent whole (pp. 126–32). They also note that expectations may be influenced by our intent and that we pay more attention to those who are of importance to us. The causes of social salience are reviewed in Table 2.1.

A person can be salient relative to the perceiver's:
Immediate context   By being novel (solo person of that race, sex, hair colour, shirt colour)   Be being figural (bright, complex, moving)
Prior knowledge or expectations   By being unusual for that person (e.g. behaving in unexpected ways)   By being unusual for that person's social category (e.g. behaving in out-of-role ways)   By being unusual for people in general (e.g. behaving negatively or extremely)
Other attentional tasks   Being goal-relevant (e.g. being a boss, a date)   By dominating the visual field (e.g. sitting at the head of the table, being on camera more than others)   By the perceiver being instructed to observe the person

Table 2.1
The causes of social salience

Source: Fiske & Taylor, 1991, *Social Cognition* (2nd edn), McGraw-Hill, New York.

Schematic processing

When I was in the Army the importance of giving written orders was rammed home by playing Chinese Whispers. One soldier was told a story, which he then told another, passing it on in turn until eventually the final version was compared with the first. The end-result was so distorted it made a big impression and I have used this game to great effect when demonstrating the finer points of schematic processing. Consider the following story:

Tin Lizzie

A farmer in western Kansas put a tin roof on his barn. Then a small tornado blew the roof off, and when the farmer found it two counties away it was twisted and mangled beyond repair.

A friend and a lawyer advised him that the Ford Motor Company would pay him a good price for the scrap tin, and the farmer decided he would ship the roof up to the company to see how much he could get for it. He crated it up in a very big wooden box and sent it off to

Dearborn Michigan, marking it plainly with his return address so the Ford Company would know where to send the check.

Twelve weeks passed, and the farmer didn't hear from the Ford Company. Finally he was just on the verge of writing them to find out what was the matter, when he received an envelope from them. It said "We don't know what hit your car, mister, but we'll have it fixed for you by the fifteenth of next month." (Johnson & Johnson, 1975, pp. 327–28)

The last time I told this story to a group of five students the final version ended up like this:

A farmer near Wagga was hit by a willy-willy and smashed his car into a shed. He sent it to a local panel-beater who was very slow repairing it.

As you can see the final message is quite distorted though there is still a basic thread left. Each person decided what was important information and discarded anything they thought was irrelevant. Certain points were *sharpened* and others *levelled* and forgotten. Moreover each person did this, so the story shortened dramatically. When it was retold, each person *accommodated* or twisted the message into a more familiar context. In the first retelling, the tornado became a willy-willy and the Ford Company was now in Adelaide. In the second, Kansas became Wagga. Each person filtered the story through their own experience and reconstructed it until it rested comfortably with the way they saw the world. Bartlett (1932) and Allport and Postman (1947) used similar techniques to illustrate how perspective plays such an important role in our interpretation of reality. Their subjects reduced a situation to its essentials and converted it into a form with individual relevance. Impressions became more concise, more stereotypical and more representative of each person's experience, and these are typical processes we use when forming schemas.

What are schemas and what do they do?

schema
Organised collection of ideas, impressions and experiences that form mental representations of external reality.

The word **schema** comes from the Greek and means shape or contour of things. In a similar way we have "boxes" in our minds that contain collections of ideas, impressions and experiences which have coalesced into notions about the way things work. These notions allow us to reduce the complexity of our social world by comparing new experiences with old ones and identifying patterns. Schemas (or more correctly schemata) are the characteristic ways in which we perceive, interpret and organise new information. Every new situation we face is filtered through our existing understanding of the world and categorised in the light of our past experience. These schemas provide us with guides to interpret and understand the world around us.

Schemas then have three main functions: they allow us to identify and categorise new experiences, thus simplifying and reducing cognitive complexity; they allow us to move beyond immediate events by comparing them with past experience and inferring causality; and they allow us to anticipate what will happen next (Fiske & Taylor, 1991). Schemas are essentially personal and idiosyncratic, coming in all shapes and sizes. Any classification system then, despite its usefulness, is really just a theoretical exercise in establishing boundaries. For this reason, there are many different systems in the literature. As an example, Taylor and Crocker (1981) proposed four main social schemas: **person schemas**, used to categorise and describe specific individuals, as when we compare a new workmate's anxious behaviour with our past experience of similar types and conclude he is neurotic; **self-schemas** are the way we see ourselves, or an exercise in self-description; **role schemas** are behaviour patterns we expect certain people to follow. For instance, parents are expected to be caring, nurturant and concerned for the welfare of their children. When we apply role schemas to groups they become stereotypes, such as the old furphy about accountants being anal-retentive obsessives. **Event schemas** on the other hand tell us the behaviours which occur in a situation and the sequence of their occurrence. We all assemble for a lecture at a set time, expect to hear a lecturer talk on the advertised topic, leave at a certain time, and so on. While there are many other types of schema, these are some of those we use to represent our social interactions.

Another way of classifying social schemas is into **implicit personality theories** (Schneider, 1973), which tell us what people are like, and **life-scripts** which tell us how they are destined to react (Abelson, 1976). Both theories are closely related and are more general explanations of schemas than Taylor and Crocker's categories.

Implicit personality theories

Implicit personality theories are your own view of how people tick. They are similar to academic theories in intent but generally lack a scientific basis (Rosenberg et al., 1968). They may include assumptions about core traits and how these interrelate; schematic profiles drawn from personal experience, or cultural stereotypes; and sets of expectations which predict how such people will react. Implicit theories link observed characteristics to implied personality dispositions and are used to infer reasons for others' behaviour. As our memories usually contain a large number of culturally programmed prototypes clustered around certain key traits, if I find a person is thrifty, this may be linked in my mind to other related traits like "stingy" and "mean spirited" and cultural stereotypes like Dickens' Scrooge. It is a short step to inferring similar traits to the thrifty person.

Scripts

Scripts on the other hand are more general sets of expectations about how people and situations should work. For example, the movie "Bob and Carol, Ted and Alice" was on television shortly after it finished its cinema run and attracted a large audience. The movie bred a powerful expectation of an encounter group's internal dynamics in the nine group members of my encounter group who watched it. They expected our group (1) to start

person schema
A social schema used to categorise and describe specific individuals.

self-schema
A social schema; the way we see ourselves, or an exercise in self-description.

role schema
A social schema which describes the behaviour patterns we expect certain people to follow.

event schema
A social schema that tells us how events should unfold.

implicit personality theory
Naive personality theories; the assumptions we make about how traits relate and influence behaviour.

life scripts
A social schema which tells us how our lives should unfold.

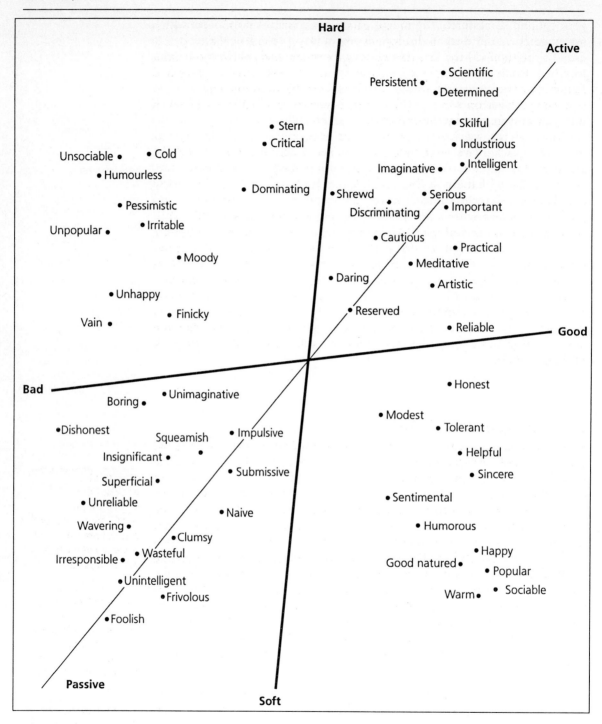

Figure 2.2 *Implicit personality theories*

Source: Rosenberg et al., 1968.

with limited disclosures, (2) to use games to loosen everyone up, which would lead to (3) deeper disclosures and (4) profound insights. If this didn't work then (5) the facilitator and the group would confront reluctant members leading to (6) forced exposure and (7) emotional support and rescuing by the group as a whole. Outcomes for the weekend would be (8) new perspectives on society, (9) personal growth and (10) high levels of intimacy and sharing by the end of the weekend.

Although we reached these outcomes eventually, it was not by this route. Only when we were able to abandon these expectations did the group work itself out. Yet normally we do have scripts for virtually every aspect of life, which are at least as elaborate (Abelson, 1981). On a more mundane level scripts allow us to anticipate expected behaviour and predict outcomes with a high degree of probability (Read, 1987). You walk into a shop and play a ritual of economic exchanges in buying your lunch. You know what to do and so does the shopkeeper, departures from the script would only lead to confusion. So scripts allow us to rely on pre-programmed scenarios and to avoid having to work out our relationships from first principles all the time. Research has shown both that we are able to flesh out incomplete scripts with a high degree of accuracy (Gagnon & Simon, 1973; Bower, Black & Turner, 1979) and that the more experienced we are, the more elaborate our scripts will be (Pryor & Merluzzi, 1985).

George Kelly and the C-P-C cycle

When we combine implicit personality theories and scripts, our schemas become all-embracing and represent the world for us in a fairly deterministic way. This has several implications. George Kelly's (1955) theory of **constructive alternativism** is perhaps the most complete account of how implicit personality theories and expectations intersect. Kelly made this link the cornerstone of his cognitive theory of personality. His **fundamental postulate** states: "A person's processes are psychologically channelized by the ways in which he anticipates events" (Kelly, 1955). In other words, how we anticipate the future determines our present behaviour and we often do so in routine, narrow and pre-emptive (channelized) ways—but not always. Kelly felt we represent the world around us as would a scientist. We build hypotheses about why things work as they do and test them in the light of our on-going experience. Our representations, which he called **personal constructs** (schemas) allow us to predict and control but are often abstractions of reality:

> Man looks at his world through transparent patterns or templates which he creates and then attempts to fit over the realities of which the world is composed. The fit is not always very good. Yet without such patterns the world appears to be such an undifferentiated homogeneity that man is unable to make any sense out of it. (Kelly, 1955, pp. 8–9)

constructive alternativism
A doctrine which asserts that all current theories are subject to revision and change without notice.

fundamental postulate
Our mental processes are psychologically channelled by the ways in which we anticipate events.

personal constructs
Mental representations which allow us to predict and interpret social reality.

propositional constructs
Tentative, exploratory, open-ended and flexible schemas.

predictive efficiency
The test of how close a schema, inference or attribution is to social reality.

C-P-C cycle
Circumspection, pre-emption and control; exploring, forming, testing, modifying and then using social schemas.

Schemas are at a first tentative and exploratory. Kelly called these **propositional constructs** and they are open-ended and flexible. We might have any number of explanations for some observed behaviour or event. As patterns build up we see links to pre-existing constructs, which then leads to classification. In Kelly's terms the test of a schema is its **predictive efficiency**. If we find a construct works for us then it becomes pre-emptive and we will construe all similar events this way unless some necessary change to our construct becomes apparent. Kelly called this process the **C-P-C cycle**—circumspection, pre-emption and control.

Why use schemas and how accurate are they?

In some ways this is a null issue as we cannot help but use schemas, they are the way we work. We naturally generate categories and automatically use them when processing data. Nevertheless, their *structure* and *content* are largely experiential and idiosyncratic, though resting on a large culturally defined base acquired as part of our upbringing. Yet it is possible to become aware of our schemas and assess their usefulness. Schemas have their pros and cons and when we catch ourselves using unreliable schemas we become aware of the many potential hazards of their use. Markus and Zajonc (1985) identified four main roles for schema: they alter our perception and memory of events; and influence the inferences we make and our behaviour. We will use this framework to assess the strengths and weaknesses of schematic processing.

Schemas and perception

There is no questioning the major impact schematic processing has on our perceptions. Schemas help us to evaluate situations quickly and efficiently often from minimal information (Markus & Zajonc, 1985). They are valuable sources of role-consistent cues (Biddle, 1979) and give us packages of condensed information (Forsyth, 1990). If you heard a paper boy was run over by a taxi at an inner-city intersection, you would invoke your schemas for paper boys, taxis and inner-city intersections and fill in the details yourself. We constantly speak this shorthand to each other and rely on shared images to communicate meaning.

Inexperience easily evinces the power of schematic processing (Markus, Smith & Moreland, 1985). At a recent agricultural show I came across a large ambiguous photo without a caption. It looked like an aerial photo and, as I was looking for clues, two men in white coats strolled up and started discussing it. By judiciously eavesdropping I gathered I was looking at a stained pathology section from a cow with Brucellosis! Processing speed also increases if we are familiar with the information or event being portrayed (Markus, 1977).

The downside of schematisation is that we may see what we expect to see rather than what is actually happening. Partly this is simply selective attention, a normal response to the sheer volume of data available, but also it is in part a filtering process which tells us to view information in a certain way. Attention to detail is notoriously fickle and when we are rushed or otherwise stressed we tend to rely more on schematic representations than reality (White & Carlston, 1983). As we saw in our Tin Lizzie example, we assimilate unfamiliar or inconsistent material into schemas which give us the most comfortable representation of the facts presented. In our example, Kansas tornadoes became Australian willy-willys.

This is particularly the case when we rely on stereotypes as shown by Gordon Allport and Leo Postman's study of the effects of rumour transmission and recall. In their book, *The Psychology of Rumor* (1947), Allport and Postman recount how they showed a picture of a well-dressed black man and a white in worker's overalls having an argument in a subway carriage. Both men were standing in the middle of the carriage and the white had an open switchback razor in his left hand and was menacing the black by holding his finger under his nose. When subjects later recalled this scene, some shifted part or all of the salient facts in line with racial stereotypes of the day. The black was now poorly dressed and menacing the white with a razor. Blacks were seen as more argumentative and, as it was inconsistent that blacks should be better dressed than whites, these

How easy do you think it would be for stereotypes to reverse themselves after just a few retellings?

Figure 2.3 *Allport and Postman's stimulus material*
Source: Allport & Postman, 1947.

items were simply shifted, altering the entire scenario. Unfortunately, many other studies have given similar results (Condry & Condry, 1976; Duncan, 1976; Sagar & Schofield, 1980; Gibbons & Kassin, 1987; Stern & Karraker, 1989). It seems our preconceptions let us see what we expect, rather than what we see.

Schemas and memory

In computer jargon, schemas are "memory resident" or readily available in memory, and when in use compare new data to existing memories and make whatever modifications are necessary. At the same time novel information is often highly salient and captures our attention, leading to perseverance in memory and clear recall (Hastie, 1980). When we grapple with new information or behaviour we form new constructs by comparing them to existing schemas and asking: "What is this like? How does it differ? What is it?" (Kelly, 1955). By way of illustration, I once placed a highly suggestive brown object on my desk and waited for student reactions as they returned from lunch. Wrinkled noses, looks of disgust and indelicate comments about cats showed an immediate identification with prior nasty experiences but they were quick to notice an absence of smell and one adventurous lady poked it with her ruler. As it clunked and was much too heavy to fit their initial schema, it was then gingerly passed around and their guesses (a rock, a plaster cast, an amusement store prop, or fossil) showed they were weighing its discrepancies against an ever wider frame of reference. I explained it was a manganese nodule and proceeded to make my point.

It is this weighing of incongruities against existing schema that leads to new constructs and, in trying to understand how schemas are made and modified, many researchers have concentrated on how inconsistencies influence memory. As a general rule you would think we are more likely to remember data that is consistent with our schema, as indeed we do (Cohen, 1981; Higgins & Bargh, 1987). However, Hastie and Kumar (1979) found we

Ambiguous objects are difficult to incorporate within existing schemas because they overlap several categories. As noted in the text this is a manganese nodule but may be several things. What cues would you use to identify this object?
(Photo: Chris Simkin)

also remember inconsistent information at least as well as consistent information, which presents a bit of a puzzle. They gave subjects a list of eight descriptive adjectives to establish a fictitious person's character and then asked them to read a list of twenty short sentences describing their supposed behaviour. Hastie and Kumar found, as they had predicted, that more congruent items were recalled than irrelevant ones, but even more incongruent items were remembered. When they decreased the proportion of incongruent statements, they found the percentage recalled increased relative to congruent descriptions. Put another way, incongruent statements became more salient and more readily recalled.

This was contrary to expectations and led to more research and a revised model of memory and schematic processing (Hastie, 1980; Srull, 1981) (see Figure 2.4). The effect is not always as marked as in the Hastie and Kumar study; for instance Cohen (1981) found memory for consistent data was higher than for inconsistent data but most studies still show a high percentage recall for incongruent material (e.g. Judd & Kulik, 1980; Fiske, Kinder & Larter, 1983).

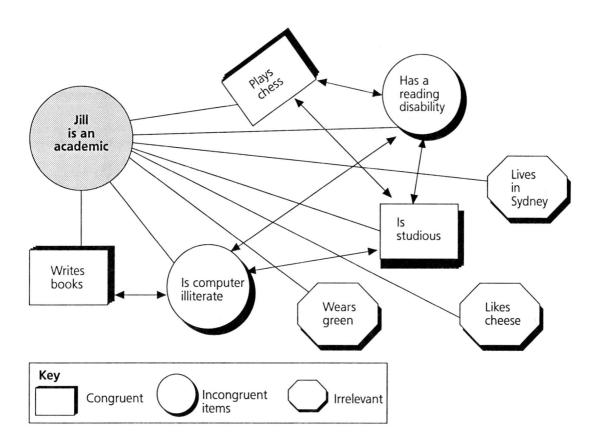

Figure 2.4 *Schematic processing of consistent and inconsistent cognitions: The Srull-Hastie model*

The explanation seems to lie in the degree of processing required. Congruent material requires very little effort and incongruent quite a lot, so both types of data are remembered. If, for example, we return to our encounter group anecdote, one of the features that made this group so unforgettable was the number of people who were other than they seemed at first. An elderly man representing himself as "retired public servant" who was thought to be a clerk perhaps, a bit fussy and pedantically obsessive with his interest in nonverbal behaviour, turned into a senior government medical officer and psychiatrist. Similarly a teacher, a middle-aged maiden-aunt type with sexual problems, turned into a nun; and a demure and stunningly attractive girl-next-door type turned into a radical separatist and lesbian. While these disclosures midway through the group once again taught us the dangers of stereotyping, they also presented challenges to our preconceptions made over the preceding hours. Much of what we knew about these people was consistent with their persona; we processed this congruent information by simply attaching it to existing stereotypes of "retired clerk", "middle-aged unmarried teacher" and "girl-next-door" where it became readily incorporated and readily recalled.

On the other hand, incongruent information by its intrusive nature is harder to square away and it is this extra processing effort which cements it in memory and later makes it easier to recall. When quite a bit of incongruent information was revealed in an honesty session, we had to incorporate these incongruities into our existing schemas. In the nun's case this meant a major modification of an existing cultural stereotype from "spinster, middle-aged sexually repressed teacher" to "teaching sister, middle-aged and vocationally troubled". With the psychiatrist and radical separatist it was harder to fit new schema-inconsistent facts into our existing stereotypes so, after some considerable cognitive reappraisal, new ones emerged. So if we have the time and make the effort to juggle congruent and incongruent data into a consistent whole, we are more likely to remember such material (Hastie, 1984; Srull, 1983). Still, we must be a little cautious with these studies as there are many unanswered questions about specifying precisely what leads one item of information to be remembered on one occasion and another, at another time.

There are obvious dangers with schema-enhanced recall. Regular patterns of life become superimposed on odd events and we find it difficult to remember what we did last Wednesday week. Stop for a minute to consider what you did on that day. If you are like most, you will try to recollect what happened by asking yourself what you do most Wednesdays and trying to recall if that is in fact what happened. Chances are this schema-based memory search will obscure many of the unusual things you did that day unless they were unusually distinctive (Read & Rosson, 1982). While this may seem like a trivial example, consider for a minute the implications of being an expert witness.

One of the more daunting aspects of visiting a health worker is that they always take notes of what we say. Because we live in a litigious society, psychologists, doctors and welfare workers often find themselves in court giving evidence on matters connected with past clients. Certain bits of client information are important to professional judgment and become sharpened in memory, while other information is actively forgotten. Unfortunately, professional perspectives differ and sometimes lawyers ask health workers detailed questions about information they have difficulty recalling. Nor is this just the passage of time and forgetfulness, but often that the material was considered unimportant at the time. Out of hard experience most workers keep detailed case records and this is a wise move because research on casual and eyewitness testimony shows just how flawed schema-based recall is.

Eyewitness testimony

Eyewitness testimony research reveals just how bad we are at accurately recalling what we have seen (Loftus & Palmer, 1974; Wells & Loftus, 1984). In one widely quoted study by Buckhout (1980), after viewing a film of a mugging only 14 per cent of subjects (and less than 20 per cent of those legally trained) were able to pick the criminal from a six-person line-up. Not only do we have poor and biased recall in experimental situations but in real life as well (Wells & Loftus, 1984). It is a pretty depressing picture, particularly when we consider the many miscarriages of justice due to poor witness recall (Brandon & Davies, 1973). Why is recall so deficient?

Part of our problem is that we rarely see things from a complete perspective. Walking down a road and hearing a bang and scream, we turn and see the tail-end of an accident. Recalling the event later, we do not present the facts as we saw them, incomplete and partially understood but rather our reconstruction of what happened. We have to explain the event to ourselves before we can explain it to others and, inevitably, other information intrudes on this process. Elizabeth Loftus (1979), a leading researcher in the area, called this **reconstructive memory** and argued that our initial impressions are added to and modified by other witnesses' testimony, and by police, legal or other interpretations (see Figure 2.5). This has become a fascinating and important academic dispute, with some theorists claiming these reconstructions prove memory has changed (Tversky & Tuchin, 1989);

reconstructive memory
After-the-fact modifications of eyewitness testimony. Initial impressions are often modified by others' recollections.

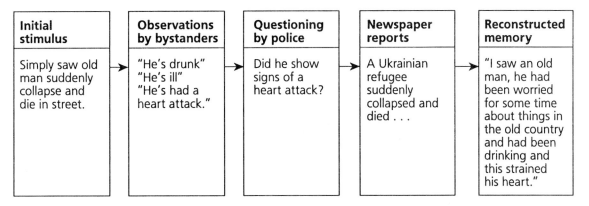

Initial stimulus	Observations by bystanders	Questioning by police	Newspaper reports	Reconstructed memory
Simply saw old man suddenly collapse and die in street.	"He's drunk" "He's ill" "He's had a heart attack."	Did he show signs of a heart attack?	A Ukrainian refugee suddenly collapsed and died . . .	"I saw an old man, he had been worried for some time about things in the old country and had been drinking and this strained his heart."

Figure 2.5 *Reconstructive memory*

and others that factors like suggestion influence but do not actually alter memory (Smith & Ellsworth, 1987; Zaragoza & McCloskey, 1989). Research shows suggestion can influence recall (Wells & Loftus, 1984); that stress and salient effects like focusing on the weapon in a robbery can alter one's perception (Brigham et al., 1983; Loftus, Loftus & Messo, 1987; Tooley et al., 1987); and there are cross-racial identification biases and other problems in identifying someone from outside your group (Platz & Hosch, 1988). For a review see Kassin, Ellsworth and Smith (1989).

The research base is now enormous because if memory is indeed altered after the event, then eyewitness testimony on which the legal system so heavily depends is in question. The debate is not resolved but recall is definitely variable and we use schemas to explain and interpret what we see. The implications of this finding are enormous. For instance, consider the admissibility of children's evidence in sexual abuse cases. Often child-at-risk prosecutions depends on judgments of how well a child recalls the event. Here again the evidence is hotly debated (e.g. Ceci, Ross & Toglia, 1989 versus Goodman, Aman & Hirschman, 1987) but is there sufficient doubt to lead judges to rule this evidence inadmissible and perhaps let the guilty go free?

Box 2.2 *Mr Bubbles, child abuse and preschoolers as eyewitnesses*

Perhaps the most celebrated argument over the accuracy of eyewitness testimony was the Mr Bubbles case. In November 1988, Dawn and Anthony Deren and two assistants, from the Seabeach Kindergarten in Sydney, were charged with over fifty counts of abducting and sexually assaulting 17 preschoolers in their care. The charges led to public outrage and media hyperbole:

> It was every parent's nightmare—a gang of depraved paedophiles operating under the cover of a kindergarten systematically sexually abusing children in their care, forcing them to take part in pornographic movies and devil worshipping rituals. (*Sydney Morning Herald*, 13 February 1990, p. 57)

However, not all was as it seemed. Some of the children had been sexually abused, but where? The children's testimony was insubstantial. In court it was alleged that the mother who first complained to the police had been diagnosed as mentally ill six months prior to her complaint and her two children were found to be "disturbed" (Bowman, 1990). Was she a reliable person? Notwithstanding that her psychiatric diagnosis was in fact five months after her complaint, the media argued the toss as to whether the whole affair was a fantasy, whether she or the children were reliable witnesses, and to what extent the police and prosecution had botched it. In the end the magistrate hearing the case ruled the children were too young to be reliable witnesses and in any case had been questioned by so many people that their evidence was likely to be "contaminated". Without their evidence the case lapsed. This prompted cries of "Outrage" (*New Idea*, 20 January 1990) and calls for a Royal Commission. Television reports that Anthony Deren had sexually molested two girls in New Guinea 17 years before the Mr Bubbles affair added fuel to the fire and prompted the Derens to sue for defamation (Bowman, 1990). Several years later the issue still bubbles along and no one is satisfied with the outcome and suspicions abound: "The tragedy of the whole thing. There really is a Mr. Bubbles—I know who he is" (Tony Deren, quoted in *Sydney Morning Herald*, 26 October 1992).

How reliable would the children's testimony have been?

Whatever the truth of the Mr Bubbles affair, taking eyewitness testimony from very young children is a hazardous affair. A review article by Keith Brooks and Michael Siegal (1991), from the University of Queensland, examined how accurate, suggestible and credible young children's recollections where. While taking evidence from preschoolers is a risky business, Brooks and Siegal concluded their memories are useful in certain circumstances.

Brooks and Siegal's review found that children's memory is generally inferior to that of adults, although when dealing with an area they know well it may be superior to unknowledgeable adults' (Chi, 1983). The younger the children are, the more difficulties they have in acquiring, storing, retaining and recalling information and the more problems they face in rehearsing and using other memory consolidation techniques that adults take for granted. For example, Flin, Markham and Davies (1989) found that younger children had more problems using a Photofit kit to reconstruct faces. Preschoolers also lack a broad knowledge base and their recall is often influenced by situational variables, leading to errors in recall and leaving them open to suggestion from leading questions. Because they do not have a rich store of experience, they are more often faced with unfamiliar situations and their fantasies are ways of attempting to assimilate complex events rather than a failure to distinguish between fact and fantasy (Nurcombe, 1986).

While preschoolers perform more poorly than other children and adults, Brooks and Siegal argue their testimony should not be dismissed. Even though they recall less than adults they *do* recall significant amounts of detail. Moreover they are less likely to be prejudiced, or respond to "subtle semantic nuances which can interfere with accurate recall in adults" (Brooks & Siegal, 1991). While preschoolers remember less, they are also less likely to pass on incorrect information. In short, preschoolers have poorer memories and recall, but if seen as sources of information rather than interpreters of events, they may make a significant contribution.

In the Mr Bubbles case the presiding magistrate refused to hear evidence from the children because he feared it had become contaminated by suggestions and assumptions made by the various police, social workers, parents, defence and prosecution lawyers and expert witnesses, who interviewed them. The magistrate, after hearing expert testimony, assumed that the children were not credible witnesses as their recollections were no longer their own. The sheer repetition of the questioning process and the nature of the questions asked would have shaped the children's recollections, particularly as young children rely on adults to give clues as to correct interpretation. So suggestibility ruled out their testimony.

Brooks and Siegal's review found that preschoolers are very suggestible but that steps can be taken to limit its influence. Australian studies by O'Callaghan and D'Arcy (1989) and Mertin (1989) confirm the overseas research which suggests that using careful questioning and prompts increases accurate recall. Young children become less sure under repeated questioning by many adults and are more likely to guess and concur with the drift of questioning. Repeated questioning shapes recall since children see adults as authority figures. Young children are particularly susceptible to post-event information and this biases their testimony. Any strategy that minimises these effects would enhance the accuracy of preschoolers' recall. Ralph Underwager, the American expert on children's eyewitness testimony who appeared in the Mr Bubbles case, was severely critical of the questioning process and commented that evidence gathering "was conducted by people with the least amount of skill" (Crisp, 1989). Underwager contrasted the Mr Bubbles case with the Israeli system where independent "youth conservators", highly trained developmental psychologists, are the only ones to question children and determine the accuracy of their testimony.

How credible is a preschooler's testimony? Perhaps it is as much a matter of how it is elicited as it is of the child's memory or recall. It would be a mistake to see young children as unintelligent puppets repeating what they are told. Preschoolers are active information-processors who just lack the experience to sift the information they are given. They are actively involved in the testimony process and, however reluctant a witness, nevertheless try to make sense of their experiences. Green (1986) found that children are no less honest than adults and Greene, Flynn and Loftus (1982) found that when children are alerted to the motives of questioners they are less suggestible and less likely to be misled.

There is no doubt that the Mr Bubbles case had a profound impact and focused attention on the psychological aspects of judicial procedure. In part, it led to changes in the laws of evidence in New Zealand, the *Evidence Amendment Act 1989* and the *Summary Proceedings Amendment Acts No. 2 1989* (Henaghan, Taylor & Geddis, 1990); and in Australia, the *Oaths (Children) Amendment Act 1990,* (Rogers, 1991). It also occasioned much discussion in the community and in the legal profession as to whether a competency test for children was appropriate (Cashmore, 1991; Parkinson, 1991). We leave the last word to Brooks and Siegal: "Children of all ages, if adequately prepared and handled in accordance with their experience, are often capable of giving accurate and informed evidence."

All is not lost because we can help eyewitnesses become more reliable (Wells & Luus, 1990) and many of the above effects are not directly connected with schematic processing but are artefacts of the courtroom procedure, line-up instructions and so forth. We will return to a further consideration of this important topic in our last chapter but for now you can see that schematic processing and recall are fallible and we would do well to question our recollections before making a judgment.

Schemas and social inference

The role of schemas in the way we make social inferences is becoming a major debate within social cognition (Jussim, 1991). We cover this topic throughout the following chapter, so we will only briefly cover it here by way of introduction.

Social inference may be summed up as: what we think we see is what we think is happening. We use schemas to predict and infer what the raw facts of experience mean socially. We have seen how perception is selective and partial and how it may influence our judgments. Once we use a schema to interpret reality, it then forecloses how we interpret events. This is particularly the case if there is any ambiguity about what we are seeing. On the whole, the more we know (Pryor & Merluzzi, 1985) and the more complex our schemas (Linville, 1982), the more accurate our inferences will be.

It goes without saying that our inferences will only be as good as the information on which they are based. If our schematic representation is incomplete or ill-informed, then it will not be of much use to us. Culture and socialisation offset inaccurate schemas and provide corrective feedback to children as they develop cognitive competency. Over time, only schemas that have some utility are incorporated into one's culture. Even biased stereotypes like overt racism are purposive and useful, otherwise we would not bother to hold them, as we will see in Chapter Five. Our inferences are also affected by the rules of information processing (heuristics) which we will consider shortly. It seems we use certain cognitive shortcuts in developing schemas and these sometimes lead us into logical errors such as mistaking the base-rate. As individuals we often make wrong inferences and this is partly due to inadequate information and defective schemas and partly to our inherent tendency towards correspondent inference and misattribution. Again we will cover these at length in our following chapter.

Schemas and behaviour

That what we expect is what we get is an obvious truism, so most research on the behaviour-schema link concentrates on our expectations and predicting how we will react in certain circumstances. Kurt Lewin (1951), one of the forefathers of social cognition, made two points about this link. He noted we see the world subjectively, so we must understand how individuals interpret their experience to make accurate predictions. We cannot just extrapolate from diverse and idiosyncratic behaviour. For example, you are introduced to an Arab and immediately act in a formal and overly courteous way. Why? If your stereotypes of Arabs suggest they value politeness, then you are simply being courteous. If you are biased against Arabs then your behaviour may express your disdain for them. From a simple behavioural analysis, who knows what your behaviour means? Lewin also pointed to the difference between cognition and motivation. Knowing how a person perceives and interprets an event still does not allow us to predict their likely response. We need to know what factors motivate them, so predicting behaviour also means knowing a person's goals.

Even so, the cognition–behaviour link is still not that straightforward. Much research has shown one's attitudes and goals do not necessarily determine what one does (Cook M., 1984). For a while it seemed to researchers that individual variability defied meaningful prediction. In Chapter Four we examine the puzzling discrepancy between attitudes and behaviours (Nisbett & Wilson, 1977) and underlying attitudinal shifts (Cook M., 1984). Attitudinal theorists have come up with several theories to resolve this difficulty. Cognitive researchers on the other hand concentrated on identifying situational factors influencing the cognition-behaviour link and which behaviours were more likely to be consistent with schema. Research from this point diverged into a mainly attitudinal analysis of individual differences affecting consistency and our ability to predict others' behaviour.

Confirmatory hypothesis testing

Much of the latter research concentrated on what Fiske and Taylor (1991) called **confirmatory hypothesis testing**. Schemas are used to predict and control our environment and like all useful processes rely on feedback to monitor effectiveness. How accurate is this feedback? Snyder and Swann (1978a) noted we often form impressions of others which our subsequent behaviour then validates. We subtly and often unconsciously select behaviours that will confirm our impressions and there was a classic example of this in my encounter group. The lonely middle-aged divorcee felt the sexually repressed woman was also lonely, had little experience with men and had come to the group to find a mate. As he was interested in her, most of his

confirmatory hypothesis testing Selecting details that confirm our beliefs rather than taking an honest sample.

Priming may be quite deliberate! In the middle 1980s several books hit the market suggesting how women should dress to enhance their careers. Unfortunately, like all fashion advice, it was highly variable.
(Cartoonist: Steve Harris)

"POWER DRESSING MAY HELP, BUT GETTING THE MIX RIGHT IS OFTEN A PROBLEM."

questions supported his presuppositions. He suggested her lack of social experience limited her sexual expression, proposed that intimacy with men was a prerequisite of healthy femininity, ignored her contrary assertions and spent more time with her than other group members. With the benefit of hindsight it is now obvious he was acting on false assumptions, yet it was some time before this link was made and the nun reluctantly disclosed her religious status to warn him off.

This confirmatory bias has quite an impressive track record of manifestations and disregard of contrary evidence (Snyder & Gangestad, 1981). However the effect is not without its critics. Trope and Bassok (1982) noted several methodological difficulties with studies of confirmatory bias and also pointed out instances where the effect was not found. Several other studies have shown we often prefer accurate feedback ahead of self-confirmatory information (see Kruglanski, 1989).

Priming

Trope and Mackie (1987), among others, suggested how information is presented will also influence our behaviour towards others. One such effect is priming. Years ago I acted as a scrutineer in a poll where the opposition's candidate was overwhelmingly elected. At my booth so many ballots supported him that when I finally came across a vote for my candidate I called it for the opposition and was promptly corrected by the electoral officer. The constant votes for the first candidate had created a mental set which made me expect to see just another opposition vote. In a similar way, priming alters our perceptions of others and often our behaviour (Wyer & Carlston, 1979). Priming may be used deliberately to influence our judgment.

For example, equal opportunity principles usually forbid discussion of job applicants until after they have been interviewed, to offset priming effects.

There is substantial research on priming effects and it seems the more often we use a schema, the more likely it will prime us (Wyer & Srull, 1980), often with long-term consequences (Higgins & King, 1981). Simple juxtaposition of the prime and target along classical conditioning lines effectively alters behaviour and Herr (1986), for example, found subjects could be thus primed to act in a hostile, competitive manner towards inoffensive partners. The effect seems to work best when we are unaware of being primed and, when we become aware, our behaviour is much less predictable (Lombardi, Higgins & Bargh, 1987). For a more detailed review of the many priming effects, see Higgins (1989); Fiske and Taylor (1991).

Priming is a very important aspect of schema research because our environment is constantly priming us. Much of our socialisation may be seen as priming. Parents who cleverly associate dentists with subsequent delights are priming their children. Constant exposure to prejudicial stereotypes unconsciously primes our reactions towards members of the stereotyped groups. Our schemas are in part then the result of both deliberate and unconscious priming and this is the stuff of literature. The stereotypical teacher who treats adults like children and the hardnosed cop who thinks all people are corrupt may be overdrawn examples from real life but nevertheless point to people whose careers have primed them to see the world in a certain way. Although priming is an interesting, if specialised, part of social research, the effect has wide application.

Self-fulfilling prophecies

Before leaving schemas we need to acknowledge that some schemas not only predispose others to act in certain ways but may also elicit the very behaviour we expect to see. Self-fulfilling prophecies are really an extension of the confirmatory hypothesis-testing effect, by noticing only behaviour consistent with our impressions. When our expectations are somehow communicated to their target, this may then elicit behaviour confirming our impressions. The music teacher who thinks a young girl is "gifted", and puts this child's interests ahead of the rest of the class, may well find she reciprocates his obvious interest and, if not becoming a prodigy, at least justifies her teacher's expectations by becoming an enthusiastic student (see Figure 2.6).

Sociologist Robert Merton (1948) first brought self-fulfilling prophecies into theoretical prominence and many other theorists, notably Robert Rosenthal and his colleagues (Rosenthal, 1966; Rosenthal & Jacobson, 1968; Rosenthal & Rubin, 1978; Rosenthal, 1985) demonstrated how this powerful schema may change behaviour. In a classic demonstration dubbed the Pygmalion effect, Rosenthal and Jacobson told some San Francisco primary teachers at the start of their school year that certain children were "intellectual bloomers who will show unusual intellectual gain". When the class was assessed several months later, these children had improved academic performance and increased in intelligence up to 30 points, despite

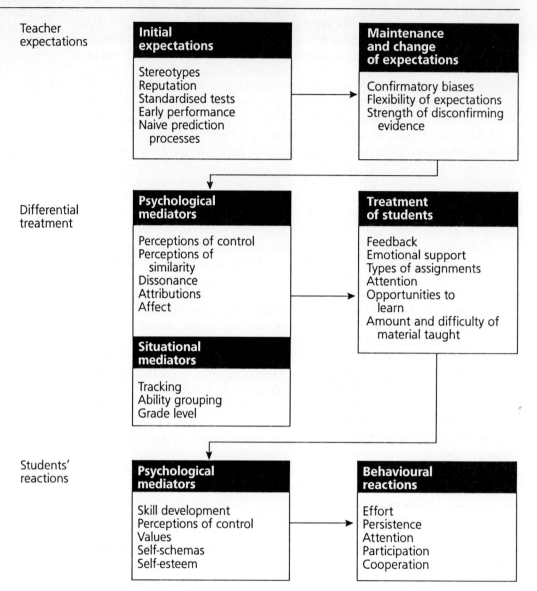

Teacher
expectations

**Initial
expectations**

Stereotypes
Reputation
Standardised tests
Early performance
Naive prediction
   processes

**Maintenance
and change
of expectations**

Confirmatory biases
Flexibility of expectations
Strength of disconfirming
   evidence

Differential
treatment

**Psychological
mediators**

Perceptions of control
Perceptions of
   similarity
Dissonance
Attributions
Affect

**Situational
mediators**

Tracking
Ability grouping
Grade level

**Treatment
of students**

Feedback
Emotional support
Types of assignments
Attention
Opportunities to
   learn
Amount and difficulty of
   material taught

Students'
reactions

**Psychological
mediators**

Skill development
Perceptions of control
Values
Self-schemas
Self-esteem

**Behavioural
reactions**

Effort
Persistence
Attention
Participation
Cooperation

Figure 2.6 *The self-fulfilling prophecy*

Source: Jussim, 1986.

being of the same calibre as their peers at the start of the year. Although
this controversial experiment had many methodological and conceptual
criticisms raised against it (Jensen, 1969; Elashoff & Snow, 1971), on the
whole, later research has confirmed the power of this effect (Rosenthal,
1985; Jussim, 1986, 1989; Chow, 1988).

Harris and Rosenthal (1985) explained these effects in a widely supported
theory. They proposed that our expectations influence the climate, feedback,
input and output the target person receives. Our hypothetical music teacher,

frustrated no doubt with a steady succession of mediocre, disinterested novices, warms to the possibility of someone displaying a minimal interest in his chosen profession. Irrespective of whether the young girl has any real talent (indeed she may have been attracted to the teacher for reasons unconnected with music), this interest is warmly reciprocated, which in turn provides the right climate for an interest in music to develop. She then receives more input, guidance and detailed feedback than her peers, which strengthens her interest and her output steadily improves. While this is a positive example, self-fulfilling prophecies may just as easily have a negative effect. If this teacher feels all his students are disinterested in music, his evident frustration may alienate any interest students may have and fulfil his negative beliefs.

The unconscious power of the self-fulfilling prophecy has been shown by any number of studies and is an important factor in the way we relate to others (Darley & Fazio, 1980). Indeed our lack of awareness of these expectations may often modify our own behaviour as it modifies the behaviour of others (Curtis & Miller, 1986). Mark Snyder in a series of experiments (Snyder & Swann, 1978b; Snyder & Campbell, 1980; Snyder, 1984) demonstrated we unconsciously aid this effect by using leading questions to elicit information and behaviours that support our initial presuppositions. Babad, Bernieri and Rosenthal (1989) noted teachers, who (presumably) were trying to assist children of whom they privately held negative views, nevertheless gave themselves away by their nonverbal behaviour. That this double message and nonverbal leakage is picked up and acted upon by the more sensitive of their charges has been demonstrated in several studies (see Cooper & Hazelrigg, 1988 for a review).

The self-fulfilling prophecy turns up in many guises: Pygmalion effect (Rosenthal & Jacobson, 1968); interpersonal expectancy effect (Brehm, 1985); behavioural confirmation (Snyder & Swann, 1978a); expectancy confirmation sequence (Darley & Fazio, 1980); and is subsumed under the more general area of expectancy effects. In experimental settings this effect becomes one of the most difficult to control for, particularly with human subjects. Rosenthal and Fode (1963), in one of a series of controversial experiments, randomly labelled rats as "maze-bright" and "maze-dull". Student experimenters later found "brighter" animals displayed better performance in a maze than the "duller" rats. Rosenthal and Fode put these differences down to the quality of care and differential expectations of the students who had the care and control of these animals. It seemed the expectation of better performance translated itself into a self-fulfilled fact. Such subject and experimenter expectancy effects, if present, limit our confidence that results are a true reflection of a measure's impact on the dependent variable.

Rosenthal has long been critical of much experimentation in social psychology which ignores the all-too-obvious effects of working with subjects who have the capacity to guess the purposes of the experiment. He has published several times on ways of coping with expectancy effects in social research (see Rosenthal, 1966, for an extended treatment). While the best experiments are those in which subjects are unaware they are participants, this is often difficult to implement for practical reasons and raises the ethical issues we noted in our introduction (Mixon, 1986). For these reasons, double-blind, unobtrusive measures and deception are the preferred ways to control for this effect. For a discussion of the broader area of expectancy effects and prediction dilemmas in the applied behavioural sciences, see Wexler (1990).

Self-fulfilling prophecies, like all social effects, are quite variable and you would be mistaken thinking that we automatically conform to others' expectations. Swann and Ely (1984) were interested in factors limiting this effect and thought that our degree of self-certainty would predict how influential others' expectations might be on our self-concept. In an experiment where one student interviewed another, they first gave them an introversion/extroversion test, assessed how certain they were of their own traits and then gave the interviewer doctored information about whom they were interviewing. Swann and Ely were interested in what happened when an interviewer's information did not coincide with the interviewee's self-perceptions.

Swann and Ely varied the degree of certainty of interviewees' labels. In the high certainty condition, interviewers were told everyone was certain the interviewee was an extrovert (or introvert). In the low certainty condition, an element of doubt was introduced. In no case were two subjects ever likely to be in agreement. Extroverts were assigned to interviewers who thought they were introverts (of varying degree) and so forth. Swann and Ely found if interviewees held strong self-beliefs, then interviewer judgments tended to shift towards the real personality of the interviewee. Only when the interviewer was sure of his subject and the interviewee was unsure of themselves was there any evidence of the self-fulfilling prophecy (behavioural confirmation) at work.

Compatible indus without uncertainty

We will return to this important effect when considering prejudice and the role of social categorisation and stereotyping in Chapter Five and how expectations influence love and attraction in Chapter Nine.

Box 2.3 *Food for thought: What is social about social cognition?*

A decade ago, Joseph Forgas (1983b) wrote a powerful article entitled "What is social about social cognition?" reflecting an emerging preoccupation within social psychology. Forgas, now a Professor at the University of NSW, was worried about the direction that social cognition research was taking and, in particular, its increasing reliance on an information-processing view of humanity. While Forgas was not adverse to a paradigm shift within psychology from behaviourism to cognitivism, he was worried that it was too individualistic

and would de-emphasise the social aspects of behaviour.

Forgas challenged the assumption that all social behaviour could be explained in information-processing terms, arguing that "studies which apply signal detection, reaction time, or recall and recognition techniques" would only lead to a limited number of outcomes and have problems in **model indistinguishability**—data that could have any number of theoretical explanations. He also argued we should not rely on "the essentially individualistic, non-social character of the [information-processing] metaphor" as social psychology is more than just a study of how "isolated, individual information processors manage to make sense of the social stimuli presented to them". He noted that critics' calls for a new form of social theorising stressed the normative, affective and motivational aspects of social behaviour. Forgas felt the information-processing perspective had a potential to limit research on the collective aspects of social behaviour.

His paper then examined the historical and theoretical underpinnings of social social cognition and concluded with an overview of neglected topics in social cognition research a decade ago. We will review his concerns and then estimate how they have been met over the last decade.

Forgas argued that "a comprehensive approach to social cognition must also include a concern with the development of social understanding in children". Such an approach would in his view appreciate "the social nature of acquiring even the simplest skill", in particular language acquisition, and would play "a crucial role in explaining how children, initially 'cognitive aliens', become fully skilled members of our adult universe". This has become a major preoccupation of theorists at the intersection of social cognition and developmental research over the decade since Forgas' article. Researchers have made substantial gains in understanding how children represent their social world and we would mention the work of Sue Spence (1988) at the University of Sydney; and Kay Bussey (1983) at Macquarie University as good examples of this approach.

Another neglected aspect of social cognition research was motivational and emotional influences on social behaviour. Forgas felt the information-processing perspective had a mistaken belief that ordinary people have a "single overriding passion . . . to achieve rational understanding". While we do try to explain the world to ourselves in rational terms, Forgas noted that this process is massively influenced by affective and motivational forces. The last decade has seen a resurgence of interest in motivation and emotion mainly from within

personality theory. We have already reviewed the work of Professor Kenneth Strongman of Canterbury University as an example of this approach and Forgas himself has done significant work exploring affective factors in cognition (Forgas, 1991, 1992) (see Box 3.1 Chapter Three).

Forgas also felt the individualism of the information-processing approach might limit social cognition's ability to represent our collective social world. He agreed with Moscovici (1989) and others that social psychology needed to counterbalance this individualism with a more socially and culturally integrative view of collective social cognitions, such as social norms, morality and commonsense accounts of behaviour. As we saw last chapter, part of the problem in reconciling two very different approaches was Wundt's "historical bifurcation" of the discipline into collective and individual psychologies. Moreover, it is not simply a difference in approach but also a difference in levels of explanation. The information-processing perspective pursues a more individual-level explanation, looking at schemas, decisional rules and heuristics. Forgas felt that while individualism had its place, social psychology should also include more social or middle-range explanations, such as social representations and social norms. Not as much progress has been made over the last decade as Forgas might have wished, as proponents of each perspective are still wedded to their methodological predilections. However, it is no longer an either/or debate and most social researchers are aware that either level of explanation suffices. Even so, there have been attempts to integrate schematic views of social cognition with a more collectivist approach. For a start you might like to read a fascinating paper, "Towards an integration of social representations and social schema theory" by Martha Augoustinos and John Innes (1990), of the University of Adelaide.

So in retrospect the last decade has been a productive one and many of Forgas' concerns have not come to pass. While there are many researchers still vitally interested in reaction times, schematic processing and heuristics, social cognition remains social.

Heuristics

heuristics
Mental rules-of-thumb used to process information quickly by reducing complexity or ambiguity.

availability heuristic
Estimating the probablility of an event on the basis of how many instances you can call to mind.

representativeness heuristic
Judging a person to be typical of a population on the basis of a few representative characteristics shared with those of the larger population.

Schemas play an important role in representing our social world by reducing its complexity. There is so much social information available that we must take steps to limit it (Allison, Worth & King, 1990). In effect we become cognitive misers (Taylor, 1981). Our processing capacity has been extensively studied by cognitive psychologists (Matlin, 1989) and there are physical limits to the amount we can process at any one time, let alone handle the sheer volume of information available. So to reduce it all to manageable chunks we take shortcuts. This is not a random process, rather, it is quite lawful. The rules of thumb we follow in making these precis of reality are called **heuristics**. They allow us to use schemas systematically. If, for example, you conclude a close friend is an alcoholic, it is likely you have carefully studied her behaviour and compared it to your knowledge of alcoholism. Although you have an "alcoholic" schema, its use is governed by how much you know about alcoholism and how closely she fits your stereotype. In so doing you are using the **availability** and **representativeness heuristics**.

Our understanding has grown enormously from the work of Daniel Kahneman and Amos Tversky (1972, 1984) who put heuristics on the map and made them a major part of decision-making theory. Heuristics, as rules of thumb, are usually accurate but as approximations may suffer from

Perceptual set plays an enormous role in schematic processing. How would you interpret this situation? What did this person do to land in goal? What aspects of his environment are significant? Whatever your inference, it is wrong. This is a photo of a visitor and the inmate is on the other side of the bars!
(Photo: Barry Price)

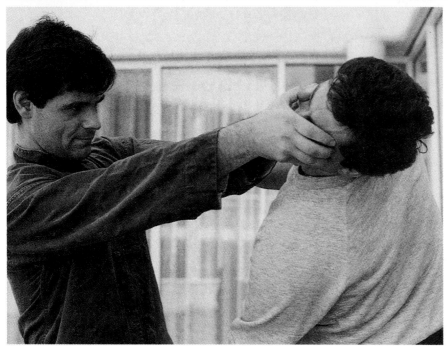

If you decide that this person is a martial arts intructor rather than a mugger, what heuristic are you relying on?
(Photo: Chris Simkin)

several errors, which we consider. Although some theorists have criticised heuristics as **post-hoc (after the fact) reasoning** (Olson, 1976), their usefulness is generally recognised. We use heuristics not in a slap-dash way but often quite deliberately to reach the best social appraisal possible under considerable cognitive overload.

post-hoc reasoning
After the fact reasoning.

The availability heuristic, or judging the likelihood of something from the instances you can readily bring to mind, is a *frequency* estimate. In deciding your friend is an alcoholic, your diagnosis relies on your previous exposure to alcoholics and how common an occurrence you think it is. So the availability heuristic sets a base-rate for alcoholism in the community. Obviously those who have alcoholic family members, or who work with drug dependents, will make better base-rate estimates.

Availability heuristic

While this heuristic is usually accurate within the limits of our experience, it does suffer from **recency, vividness** and **base-rate biases**. For instance, we are more likely to remember sensational multiple slayings like Hoddle Street and Strathfield because of their vividness effects and thus overestimate the incidence of violent murder in our community. The way information is presented is also crucial, as any journalist knows. Consider the following vignettes:

recency bias
We are more likely to remember and be affected by recent rather than distant experiences in our judgment.

vividness bias
We are more likely to remember vivid effects and thus overestimate their incidence.

base-rate bias
Under or overestimating the total population from which a sample is drawn.

Some homeless street kids are as young as six and suffer from hunger and exploitation.

Tim is six and lives in a clothing bin. It's cold but a better home than home was. Tim hadn't eaten in three days and hunger finally drove him out looking for food, though he risked losing his bin to other street kids. A kind man took him in and fed him. The things he did to Tim later were, Tim felt, only a small price to pay for no longer being hungry.

You can see the effects of salience here—the second passage is much more vivid and likely to stick in our minds. When estimating the frequency of events this effect can easily lead to unhealthy bias. Consider that stereotypes are often powerful caricatures which distort our perception of reality. As we will see in Marjoribanks and Jordan's (1986) study in Chapter Five, Anglo-Australian attitudes towards Aborigines were quite negative. One vividly written piece of racist journalism, portraying all Aborigines as shiftless drunks, will powerfully colour your perceptions. If you have no direct experience to offset this racist slur and this is the only information you have to hand, when asked to estimate the incidence of Aboriginal alcoholism, the availability heuristic will readily serve up such examples and bias your answer.

Recent noteworthy events also shape our thinking and behaviour (Higgins, King & Mavin, 1982). Slovic, Fischhoff and Lichtenstein (1982) gave a number of examples of people buying more earthquake insurance after major tremors, or overestimating the incidence of murders, or deaths by fire, after reading graphic portrayals in the media. What these and our example of racist stereotyping have in common is that they all mistake the base-rate.

Please answer the following puzzle before reading on:

There are 100 students in your lecture-room, 30 are studying education, while 70 are science students. Please read the following description and decide what the probability is that Lyn is an education student (from 100%):

Lyn is 19 and comes from a large family. She is interested in children and has worked part-time in a library. She is fairly conservative in outlook but has many friends from her school days and likes to keep in touch. Her hobbies are reading, art and needlepoint.

Probability that Lyn is an education student _____%

(Adapted from Kahneman & Tversky, 1973)

What did you answer for this problem: 30% or 90%? If you guessed 90% then the chances are you recognised a stereotype more like that of a teacher than a mathematician, but how did you make your decision? In a strict mathematical sense the odds are only 30%, yet you probably let the stereotype offset the only sure answer there is (at least 30%). Your reasoning illustrates a good use of base-rate information and social inference. It may

Unexpected disasters like the Newcastle earthquake, lead to sharp increases in insurance sales (which helps to somewhat offset the losses insurance companies have incurred)! This is an example of mistaking the base-rate, or more colloquially, shutting the door after the horse has bolted.
(Photo: courtesy of The Newcastle Herald*)*

well be that Lyn is an education student and in guessing so you used **Bayes' theorem**, which states your decision should be influenced by both base-rate *and* likelihood information. Yet many people completely ignore the base-rate when they make inferences. For example, I once had a client referred with a diagnosis of "multiple-dissociative disorder", more commonly known as multiple personalities, a very rare and unusual condition. I had never seen a case, nor had the referring social worker who completely ignored base-rate information in her diagnosis. The client was schizophrenic, a much more common complaint.

Bayes' theorum
Our estimate of the probability of an event based on statistical and likelihood information.

Another way you might decide your friend is an alcoholic is to compare her behaviour with your image of alcoholism to judge how representative a case she is. Where the availability heuristic helps us assess likelihood or frequency, the representativeness heuristic allows direct comparisons between your schema and the person or situation. So we save ourselves the trouble of making a thorough diagnosis and just call up a prototype of what we

Representativeness heuristic

think is a typical alcoholic and compare her to it. Again, like the availability heuristic, this process, though often accurate, depends on how much you know about alcoholism and also suffers from vividness, recency and base-rate biases, while having its own peculiar difficulties.

Consider the case of Geoff who came from a working-class family and left home at seventeen for a lifetime job with built-in security of employment. A neat, orderly, superfit person, he despises slobs and believes strongly in self-discipline and conservative morality. Would you think he is a librarian, an academic or an army officer? If you find out he lives near a major military base, would this influence your decision? Chances are he is in the Army. However, you now learn he is an ardent conservationist, has spoken at several rallies in defence of rainforests and has helped to organise logging blockades. Is he still likely to be an officer? This increase in uncertainty has been labelled the **dilution effect** (Zukier, 1982).

Perhaps Geoff is an army officer. The additional facts are no more likely to describe a librarian or academic but they do not fit our stereotype of the military. In experimental studies adding additional neutral information (the dilution effect) led to increased uncertainty and more conservative judgments, even though the additions did not suggest another schema (Zukier, 1982; Zukier & Jennings, 1983–84). It was precisely the new material's lack of representativeness that confused a clear picture and led to a discounting of the obvious stereotype, an instance of a negative representativeness heuristic at work. This is not the only error into which the representativeness heuristic leads us. You might like to try the following scale before reading further:

> Please rank the following statements in the order you think most represents Geoff: (1 = most likely).
>
> ___ Geoff is a librarian
> ___ Geoff is a conservationist and an army officer
> ___ Geoff is an academic
> ___ Geoff is an army officer
> ___ Geoff is a conservative voter
> ___ Geoff is an academic conservationist
> ___ Geoff is a gym instructor

dilution effect
The decrease in certainty that accompanies information that does not match our impression of someone.

conjunction error
Violating the conjunction rule; statistically, adding up information reduces the probability of an overall description being accurate, if any element of doubt exists.

It is a safe bet that you have put "Geoff is a conservationist and an army officer" ahead of "Geoff is an army officer" (or if you think he is "an academic conservationist" you have put this ahead of "Geoff is an academic"). If so, you may have fallen into the **conjunction error**. Statistically, adding (conjoining) extra information to his being a conservationist reduces the probability of our overall description being accurate. You have two principles warring against each other here. The representativeness heuristic wants to find the most complete list of traits to typecast Geoff, but simple statistical probability tells you to be cautious. Consider for a moment that we know the probability of his being a conservationist is 100%. Each additional bit of information conjoined increases the probability of the overall description being wrong.

The **conjunction rule** states: "the probability of a conjunction of two events cannot be larger than the probability of its constituent events" (Matlin, 1989). If one element is uncertain the overall probability must be lessened. Only if the probability of Geoff also being an army officer (or academic) is 100% may we conclude that he is an academic-conservationist or whatever. Each new piece of information we add to our description carrying less than 100% certainty must increase its dubiousness. Tversky and Kahneman (1983), who used a similar example, discovered we often fall into this error, yet this is precisely what heuristics are all about, trying to make the most informed estimate despite the odds. We have to return to Bayes' theorem and use both likelihood and base-rate information in our inferences.

conjunction rule
The probability of a conjunction of two events cannot be larger than the probability of its constituent events.

Anchoring and adjustment heuristics

Like the representative and availability heuristics, anchoring is a useful cognitive tool, which gives reasonable approximations when we are asked to estimate some unknown quantity without having to undertake exhaustive processing to reach an answer. We most often use it when we do not have all the facts but can rely on some equivalent known quantity to give us a starting point. Imagine you are trying to predict the percentage of people who will pass a short answer exam in a newly introduced subject. As no one as yet has taken the course we have no real baseline. We do know, however, that the lecturer who will teach the course has a reputation as a hard marker and that 40 per cent of his students did not pass his last exam. Using this as a guide and assuming he will mark as hard in the future, we estimate a similar percentage will fail.

This guess then becomes our anchor and this is where the heuristic sometimes lets us down. Once we have made our estimate, we are "anchored" by it and are reluctant to make even minor adjustments in the light of new information. Tversky and Kahneman (1974) gave a striking demonstration of this effect when they spun a roulette wheel with their subjects watching and then asked them to estimate how far from the chance result various percentages deviated. For example, if they asked what percentage of male Icelanders were smokers and the wheel stopped on 80, they then asked how far the actual percentage differed from this number. Subjects did make adjustments but their "confidence intervals" were clearly anchored by the chance result and were quite small.

In making social judgments our "anchors" are sometimes quite misleading as the information on which we base our assessments is often tenuous (Carlson, 1990; Cervone & Palmer, 1990). To return to our exam example, what you are really trying to assess is the lecturer's expectations of students in the new course and, by implication, his attitudes to assessment. Suppose you now learn his course is introductory, whereas the others were advanced units. You also learn the exam will be "take-home" while the others were unseen. How much will you now adjust your initial estimate? Not much, if research on the anchoring heuristic is any guide (Tversky & Kahneman, 1982).

Again, one's knowledge provides a baseline for this heuristic and the more you know the less likely it is you will fall into this trap. Perhaps if you are an Icelandic anti-smoking campaigner you wouldn't really need to use heuristics for an answer, although even being an expert does not protect you from this bias. There are ample local and overseas studies that suggest it affects even professionally trained clinicians (Pain & Sharpley, 1988; Richards & Wierzbicki, 1990). In any event, when we do use the anchoring heuristic it is very difficult to move us from our initial estimate, which led Nisbett and Ross (1980) to observe:

> . . . once subjects have made a first pass at a problem, the initial judgment may prove remarkably resistant to further information, alternative modes of reasoning, and even logical or evidential challenges. (Matlin, 1989, p. 445)

There are many other heuristics and we have only covered the three major ones that influence schematic processing (for an extended coverage see Nisbett & Ross, 1980). Nor do we use them one-by-one, in practice we would use all three eclectically to decide what Geoff's career is. Nor do we necessarily rely on heuristics entirely in processing new information. Shelly Chaiken (1987) has distinguished between logical or **systematic processing**, where we rationally assess information, and **heuristic processing**, where we are more likely to accept information if it meshes with our existing schema and can be used to simplify an issue to a few quickly processed propositions. For this reason using heuristics is sometimes called **peripheral processing**. While heuristics might lead us to become imperfect processors of information, they are fast and we often use both styles of reasoning to reach a result.

One final comment before we leave heuristics. Up to this point we have assumed that people reason logically but this is often not the case. Social psychologists are always finding people with illogical worldviews, haphazard thought processes and a marked antipathy to logical reasoning

systematic processing
Processing information by deliberate attention to detail.

heuristic or peripheral processing
Using *heuristics* to process information, rather than more time-consuming *systematic processing*.

Heuristic processing takes many forms. Strictly logical processing, such as we use in a chess game, is quite different to that which we use in navigating social settings.
(Photo: Gavin Price)

itself. This prompted Jan Smedslund (1990) to point out that Tversky and Kahneman's and similar research rests on the assumption that faulty reasoning flows from logical inferences drawn from erroneous premises, or to put it colloquially—garbage in, garbage out. There are, however, many different ways of reaching conclusions other than by using logic. Only if we assume that understanding equals logicality can we then see misunderstanding as a logical distortion. Smedslund argues that Tversky and Kahneman fail to appreciate the potential differences between logical fallacies and misunderstanding, and to realise that "what is genuinely illogical cannot be explained and understood". A point worth contemplating.

Self-schemas

The self

Consider these two pieces of information before we start our discussion of self-schemas: first, cognitive scientists tell us we have a limited processing capacity. It is not the vast amount of biographical information we have stored in our long-term memories that determines our *selves* but rather our ability to retrieve and use this information within a strictly limited short-term memory. From an information-processing viewpoint, our consciousness, though rich and variable, is quite transient. Second, the range of roles we adopt moment-by-moment are often so incompatible as to make us doubt

*Whatever the self is, it is a composite!
(Cartoonist: Graeme Mitchell)*

there is a common basis for them all. For example, I watch my ten-year-old getting ready for school as I write these lines. Watching TV he was momentarily a super-hero, two seconds later a snivelling mess as his viewing was cut off mid-cartoon in an attempt to get him out the door; one minute later rationally debating why he should not wait for his younger brother; and within another, acting the parent as he ushered his sibling out the door. Such human variability, coupled with the transience of consciousness, has led some psychologists to disregard the self, considering it to be an **epiphenomenon**, or in Skinner's words "the mist above the stream".

epiphenomenon
Illusory or unsubstantial phenomenon.

Whatever its ultimate nature, there is little doubt the self is socially constructed. In his epic book *The Principles of Psychology* (1890), William James said "a man has as many social selves as there are individuals who recognise him and carry around an image of him in their mind". Researchers have shown how easy it is to manipulate our self-concept and, whatever the self is, it seems to shift around to suit different contexts, which Markus and Nurius (1986) labelled "our possible selves" (Nurius, 1989; Oyserman & Markus, 1990).

Even if we have only one unitary self, for all practical purposes we may as well have many, for our self-knowledge is so vast we can only fit limited amounts of it in our immediate memory and so display differing aspects over time. On the balance of probabilities, it is likely our self-concept is phenomenal, or influenced by our goals and situation, and changes moment-by-moment (Rhodewalt & Agustsdottir, 1986).

Nor are we adequately equipped to explore ourselves. Early in psychology's history, William James (1890) pointed to the dilemma of conscious: the self as knower. We are at once the object of perception and its observer. The *I* observes the *me*. This puts us in an impossible position as we can never independently observe ourselves and the sheer immediacy of experience leaves self-theorising floundering in the wake of ongoing experience. Part of James' answer to this dilemma was to define the self materially:

> In its widest possible sense . . . a man's Self is the sum total of all that he can call his, not only his body and his psychic powers, but his clothes and his house, his wife and children, his ancestors and friends, his reputation and works, his lands and horses, and yacht and bank-account. (James, 1890, p. 188)

James concluded this was only a small part of ourselves, further dividing the self into social, spiritual and pure ego states, all of which impinge on immediate consciousness. From this heady mix, "a certain portion of the stream is abstracted from the rest" and becomes that part around which the other elements accrete. James was confounded in his attempts to observe this inner self because whenever he tried to observe its spontaneity, he was left with just "bodily process, for the most part taking place in the head". He concluded that whatever the self is, it is observable only in its outward manifestations. A century later, social and cognitive psychologists have not moved much beyond this point.

Psychology *has* developed an empirical understanding of the self's antecedents. An enormous body of research has built up within developmental psychology examining the growth of self-consciousness and identity in the young. Another equally large research effort within personality theory has grappled with the question of who we are and has mapped out the self's commonalities and individual differences. Social psychology has played a more modest role, by portraying the social dimensions of the self. It seems we rely in large part on others' direct and indirect feedback to support our self-concept. Cooley (1902) coined the term looking-glass self to describe how we see ourselves through others' eyes, and Mead (1934) extended this idea to include how we evaluate these opinions, our **reflected appraisal**. We are, after all, operating on what we think other people think about us. This has certain methodological difficulties but there is a fair body of research that suggests the self is partially constructed from others' evaluations (Marsh, Barnes & Hocevar, 1985; Felson & Reid, 1986; McGuire & McGuire, 1982).

reflected appraisal
Acting on what we think other people think about us.

Perhaps the best way to picture the self is as a schema with all its constituent elements under one protective umbrella. The self, like other schemas, reduces cognitive complexity and helps us understand ourselves. That is, we have a need, probably intrinsic to our nature, to know who and what we are (Tesser, 1988). The self-schema then acts as a structural framework on which we hang all the information which goes to make up a working self-concept (Markus, 1977) and includes others' feedback, past experiences, memories, personality attributes, habits, self-knowledge, roles, emotional reactions, goals and future hopes, and an encompassing sense of how well these all hang together. The self is an active pastiche of these factors which we constantly monitor and revise, by adding and subtracting bits of our self-image. At any point we are able to "give an account of ourselves", so this process is essentially an evaluative one. This structural view of the self is called **self-representation**, or how we explain ourselves to ourselves.

self-representation
How we explain ourselves to ourselves.

Relying on one's looks may be a shortcut to enhanced self-esteem but only while looks last.
(Photo: Barry Price)

There is little practical difference between the terms self-schema and self-concept, rather just a shade of emphasis (Burke, Kraut & Dworkin, 1984) and we use them interchangeably. The former implies an information-processing aspect to the self and whether this is a formal hierarchy, or just a loose cluster of associated processes, has yet to be determined (Fiske & Taylor, 1991). Nor are we schematic in all aspects of our lives, rather only in areas important to us. We may have elaborate occupational self-schemas and scanty ones for going to the races, and it is clear the more detailed they are, the quicker and more automatic our self-evaluations (Bargh, 1990).

Our self-concept is also intimately bound up with the social inferences we make. Because our self-concept is a most salient aspect of our consciousness, we have ready access to it and this allows a rich and complex conceptualisation of ourselves (Linville, 1982). Information related to ourselves is also more easily processed and recalled (Rogers, Kuiper & Kirker, 1977). It also seems the sheer elaboration of our self-schemas leads to their use in interpreting others' behaviour. For example, while waiting to start an exam you see others walking around staring at the ceiling and muttering to themselves and, as you do this yourself as a way of rehearsing memory, you will assume they are doing likewise. While this is a fair assumption (after all you have little else to go on) it is just one possible interpretation. Perhaps it is our self-schema's immediate accessibility that leads to its use in evaluating others (Higgins & Bargh, 1987). We will return to this interesting question in our discussion of misattribution and the false-consensus effect in the next chapter.

Self-enhancement and self-regulation: Reducing self-discrepancy

Self-verification and enhancement

As we have already seen we are protective of our self-image and most of us view ourselves very favourably indeed (Greenwald, 1980). Given that "there exists a pervasive tendency to see the self as better than others" (Fiske & Taylor, 1991) and as this is a logical impossibility, then we must often hold unrealistic and illusory views of ourselves (Messick et al., 1985; Brown J.D., 1986; Taylor & Brown, 1988). At any rate, this is a problem if you consider that we need accurate feedback and reliable self-schemas to effectively protect our self-esteem. So self-assessment must also be part of our self-schema. This conflict is one of the most interesting aspects of this research and we will return to it after we have considered the various elements underlying it.

Self-verification

We have a powerful need for consistency as nothing detracts more strongly from our self-esteem than discrepant information (Backman, 1988). Similarly (and somewhat paradoxically given the variability of our public persona) we do not want to change our self-image, for to do so would increase our vulnerability and further erode self-consistency. Swann and Read (1981) argue we avoid discrepant information by engaging in **self-verification**. As a general rule, rather than risking accurate feedback, we avoid possible sources of discrepancy and structure our lives to provide the sort of feedback that reinforces our self-image. They suggest we ignore and/or selectively filter information damaging to our viewpoint, and there are parallels to the confirmatory hypothesis-testing bias discussed earlier. Self-verification thus often becomes more an exercise in perceptual distortion than accuracy.

self-verification
Rather than risking accurate feedback, we avoid possible sources of discrepancy and structure our lives to provide the sorts of feedback that reinforce our self-image.

Notwithstanding our need for consistency, we do have a need for accurate information, as self-delusion may be equally risky. How do we reconcile these seemingly incompatible ends?

One way out of the difficulty is to distinguish between cognitive and emotional reactions. We may resolve dissonance at different levels of functioning. Swann et al. (1987) suggested that while self-verification deals with ego-threats cognitively, much of our self-concept is emotional. In a poignant twist to this theory, they found that people with poor self-images prefer to have these reinforced in the interests of cognitive consistency. That is, if you know you are useless, you will prefer to get consistent feedback which supports your low self-concept. At the same time you feel terrible, and while you know this emotional reaction is justified by the facts (after all we should feel terrible if we are so useless), it also provides a powerful incentive towards self-enhancement. In this unusual example you can remain cognitively consistent while being emotionally discrepant. While this may be uncomfortable, we often manage to hold contradictory beliefs (McGuire & Padawer-Singer, 1976).

Swann, Pelham and Krull (1989), however, in three studies examining these potential contradictions, found that even those with low self-schemas would like to be positive and prefer positive self-enhancement even though insisting on accurate negative feedback to self-verify. So whether we self-enhance or self-verify seems to be determined by how positive is our anticipation of the future, rather than our present level of self-esteem. To meet our self-enhancement needs we accent positive and downplay negative emotional experiences, all the while hoping for a better future (Strube & Roemmele, 1985; Swann, 1990).

The degree of certainty is also important in resolving this difficulty. As we have already seen in Swann and Ely's 1984 experiment, if we are sure of the accuracy of our self-image it is remarkably durable and hard to change. The obvious corollary is that when we are less certain, we can entertain discrepant information more readily, which might otherwise threaten our self-concept. The importance (or relevance) of the new material plays a role here too. If the new information is discrepant but unimportant, it is unlikely to trouble us. In Chapter Four we will take this discussion further when we consider Leon Festinger's cognitive dissonance theory and the role of social evaluation in resolving ambiguity.

Self-regulation

Taylor and Brown (1988) in their review verified that much of our self-regulation is aimed at maintaining self-esteem (see also Greenwald, Bellezza & Banaji, 1988). Several studies have shown a **self-reference effect**, that information related to the self is more readily remembered than other material. In one study Rogers, Kuiper and Kirker (1977) showed subjects 40 descriptive adjectives one at a time and then asked them to make one of four judgments on ten items from the list. They were asked if the adjective was in capital letters, if it rhymed with other words, if it had synonyms, and if it applied to themselves (e.g. "Are you kind?"). Obviously the last question was priming the self-referent effect. Subjects were then asked to recall as many adjectives as they could and when their recollections were compared it was clear that self-referent items were better remembered than other categories. From similar studies it is evident that information that readily connects with our self-schemas is more easily processed and recalled because we have better and more elaborate retrieval cues (Brown, Keenan & Potts, 1986; Klein & Loftus, 1988). Does this aid self-enhancement?

Egocentricity is unidirectional. If we easily recall self-enhancing material, Kuiper et al. (1985) found we also have difficulty recollecting things that show us in a bad light. It is clear that the self-referent effect is also a self-serving bias. We will consider these biases at length in the next chapter but for the present we wll assume our unrealistic illusions are clearly tied to self-enhancement. We are much more likely to attribute successes to ourselves and failures to others (Taylor & Koivumaki, 1976; Ross & Fletcher, 1985) and evaluate our performance more favourably than others would (Lewinsohn et al., 1980). This also extends to our belief that we can influence or control chance events such as the roll of a die (Langer, 1975). We may confidently conclude that there is a wealth of evidence showing that we generally have positively biased self-perceptions. Why?

Defensive adaptation

In some respects the world is not a particularly safe place and to ensure that we remain emotionally balanced and able to withstand a constant low level of threat to our egos, it may be in our interests to indulge in the occasional perceptual distortion. Taylor and Brown (1988) argue self-enhancement is a positive adaptation in as much as it allows us to be happy and productive. This is a theme we will return to at length in our next chapter.

The developing self

Whether this self has any real existence or is a creature of our cognitive processes is still an open question in psychology, yet there is no doubt its evolution is social. From birth, if not before, the self-concept is the gradual intertwining of our experiences of the world around and our development of self-awareness, a steady nub of regularly occurring comparisons and feedback which gives us some hope of eventual consistency. As our memory lays down self-schemas, or layers of organised self-knowledge, we strive for a balance between self-enhancement and self-consistency. Only when we are tentatively sure of who we are, will we risk this self on public display.

Self-presentation and impression management

Self-presentation

The mature self is never stable. As a construction it is subject to revision as an ongoing process. Self-presentation, or a public display of the self, is in part a calculated act of revision. We ask for and receive a constant stream of appraisals which, from our subjective perspective, affords us comparisons between others and our own self-perception. This self-monitoring helps us maintain the right level of self-disclosure, consistent with the fragility of our developing selves. Only when we have the security of a workable self are we able to risk it in self-actualisation.

The entirety of our next chapter is on the attributional process that in part ensures our self-concepts are developed, enhanced and protected from threats without and within. Our point of contact with others is our public face and, given a multitude of social roles, this argues a well-developed self-monitoring system which is in tune with the self and evaluates its performance (see Box 2.4). By way of introducing our next chapter we will consider this process. Self-schemas' final product is self-awareness, which is basically protective and, as attack is often the best form of self-defence, we sometimes aggressively manage our public image to ensure the best possible outcomes. Essentially this is a process of regulating the reinforcers of our self-esteem, an area that has an enormous research base.

Impression management

The terms "self-presentation" and "impression management" are not quite synonyms, but rather the ends of a process. We present a self we hope will give the right impression and, as immediate feedback is important, we constantly manage our image to meet others' expectations and reach desired outcomes. If you have ever gone for a job interview, you will be intimately acquainted with this process.

Identity

Irving Goffman (1959), in *The Presentation of Self in Everyday Life*, argued that the self is a facade and our public persona is just a parade of ready-made images which we select according to need. Not only do we present a self consistent with our objectives but we are like actors on a stage portraying "ourselves" complete with props. But to what purpose?

As we are social animals with a powerful need for approval, self-presentation then becomes an exercise in pleasing an audience and an act of self-construction (Baumeister, 1982). We think we know who we are and what will please others and test our self-definition by seeing if others will support and confirm our identity. At the same time we modify our self-schema until it is more closely aligned with our idealised self. The battle we face is to stay in control of our self-construction while still meeting

---

Box 2.4 *Protective self-presentation in Malaysians and Australians*

Despite the recent push to become Asia-conscious, Australians and New Zealanders are still very Eurocentric in attitude. This is not helped by television sitcoms which portray our East Asian neighbours as a homogeneous race of inscrutable, overly polite conformists. Just how limiting these views are is constantly borne out in research which shows the inaccuracy of such stereotypes.

One such example was a pilot study by Jack Schumaker and Robert Barraclough (1989) of the Warrnambool Institute, Victoria, who studied the comparative differences in protective self-presentation of Malaysian and Australian undergraduates. It is part of our folklore that Asians are overly concerned with matters of *face* and avoid doing anything that might cause social disapproval or embarrassment. Schumaker and Barraclough reviewed the literature which suggested that various Asian cultures are concerned with politeness; that Asians were more sensitive to failure and loss of face; were shyer and more introverted; and their self-presentational styles were a consequence of a higher self-monitoring. Protective self-presentation was then aimed at "conformity, compliance, highly modest self-portrayals, and a reluctance to behave out of accordance with perceived social demands".

Schumaker and Barraclough hypothesised that this would not reflect Malaysian self-presentation. Despite the interracial and ethnic differences in Malaysia, Malaysian parents "are typically very gentle, with children being strongly prized and enjoyed". They hypothesised these warm parent-child relationships would lead to different self-presentational styles than those engendered by our own "more harsher power and authority-oriented child-rearing practices". As we experience more criticism in our upbringing it might be expected that this would lead to social anxiety and hence a more protective presentational style. Even so, Schumaker and Barraclough noted that there are forces in Malaysian society "which encourage compliance, passive submission, and a repressive mode of self control" so they were interested to see what actual differences there were between the two cultures.

Schumaker and Barraclough used a Concern for Appropriateness Scale to compare protective self-presentation in 159 Australian undergraduates and 125 Malaysian university students living in Australia. Unfortunately, there were no ethnic Malays in their sample, 93 were of Chinese and 32 were of Indian descent. In line with their hypothesis, their results showed that Australians scored significantly higher than Malaysians on protective self-presentation measures. Indian and Chinese Malaysians did not differ in their responses, there were no significant sex differences, and length of stay in Australia did not affect self-presentational style.

Why was the "stereotypical view that Malaysians are more socially restrained and motivated towards 'appropriateness'" not supported in this study? Perhaps Australians are more concerned with self-presentation? Schumaker and Barraclough explore many reasons for this result in their article. Perhaps a concern for social conformity and appropriateness does not translate into self-defensive self-presentation? Then again, maybe Malaysian students living in Australia are not representative of their society? Perhaps they were changed by the Australian educational process, although the lack of significant length-of-residence effect would seem to rule this out? Whatever the ultimate reasons, and this was just a preliminary study with a small sample from one provincial campus, the direction and magnitude of the differences between the two cultures warns us to be cautious about assuming all Asians are overly concerned with face.

The self is a parade of ready-made images which we select according to need".
(Cartoonist: Graeme Mitchell)

others' expectations. An important part of this process is negotiating different identities for all the roles that make up an adult's life (see Alexander & Rudd, 1981, for a review). Obviously we will most often want to make a good impression, but not always (Baumeister & Hutton, 1987). A lecturer who is warm and approachable in class, yet appears aloof and distant when met socially, is perhaps protecting herself from people-overload. Such variability is normal and automatic.

Power

Impression management involves redressing power imbalances in relationships (Tedeschi, 1981). Edward Jones (1964) believes we are motivated to equalise relationships to protect ourselves from the arbitrary exercise of power. As often we have little real power ourselves, an alternative is to ingratiate ourselves with those who do. To a certain extent, by associating with the powerful we share their power and restrain them from damaging us. Ingratiation is then a self-protective measure and by impression management we achieve this end (Jones, 1964; Jones & Wortman, 1973).

Jones and Pittman (1982) suggest we use several tactics in self-presentation: ingratiation, or figuring out what our audience wants and giving it to them so we will be liked; intimidation, where we create so powerful and competent an image that others feel intimidated; self-promotion, saying we are competent; exemplification, trying so hard that others are shamed into helping; and supplication, in which if all else fails, we acknowledge our shortcomings and ask to be rescued!

ingratiator's dilemma
The less power you have the more you will need to ingratiate yourself to get ahead but then you risk seeming devious to those with power.

Jones has dubbed a difficulty with effective ingratiation the **ingratiator's dilemma**. The less power you have, the more you will need to ingratiate yourself and the more obvious you will become. Those with influence over us will not want sycophants around them and will be alert to obvious attempts at wooing them. The ingratiator is also right up against social norms which denigrate "crawlers". So the potential ingratiator treads a very fine path in equalising power relationships. One way of diminishing this effect is by carefully differing from those we wish to influence but in areas not too important to them (Jones, Gergen & Jones, 1964). Luckily most people like to be liked and, in line with our previous discussion, both parties to the relationship may choose to ignore the more obvious signs of currying favour and accentuate the positive aspects of their relationship.

There are subtler ways of managing one's impression and Cialdini (1985; Cialdini & De Nicholas, 1989) noted that associating ourselves with the influential rubs off. Even trivial connections like sharing a birthday with the famous allows us to bask in the reflected glory of their success and there is some evidence that this may impact on our subsequent careers. In an extreme case, one local politician tipped the balance in a hotly contested preselection for a safe seat by simply following the retiring member around during his last term: standing close they were often photographed together. Although neither politician cared for the other and indeed came from opposing factions within their party, the young candidate managed what seemed to be an endorsement-by-association (and preselection) by basking in the reflected glory of a well-respected representative.

A *final note: The problem of deception*

Perhaps it is only a short step from managing our public image to selectively enhancing it. Perhaps its an even shorter step to an awareness that others might be doing the same. As good as we may be in assessing a person's character in an unguarded moment, deception is a problem of a different order. If others are intent on misleading us, then beyond Shakespeare's advice to watch out for lean and hungry men, what can we do to avoid being duped? Surprisingly, given the heavy emphasis on overt behaviour in the literature, it is often the subtler aspects of behaviour that are the more revealing, and studying nonverbal behaviour has provided some interesting insights.

While there have been many books dedicated to the study of body language, promising all manner of insights into human nature, unfortunately most nonverbal behaviour is so culturally determined and variable as to be

Box 2.5 *How to make a good impression*

Everyone admits how praiseworthy it is in a prince to keep faith, and to live with integrity . . . Nevertheless our experience has been that those princes who have held good faith of little account, and have known how to circumvent the intellect of men by craft, in the end have overcome those who have relied on their word . . . But it is necessary to know well how to disguise this characteristic, and to be a great pretender and dissembler; . . . Therefore it is unnecessary for a prince to have all the good qualities I have enumerated, but it is very necessary to appear to have them. And I shall dare to say this also, that to have them and always to observe them is injurious, and that to appear to have them is useful; to appear merciful, faithful, humane, religious, upright, and to be so but with a mind so framed that should you require not to be so, you may be able and know how to change to the opposite.

(Nicholo Machiavelli, *The Prince*, 1513)

an unreliable guide to intent. Nevertheless, the study of paralinguistics, those vocal and bodily clues accompanying speech, give some hope of spotting deception. DePaulo and Rosenthal (1979) demonstrated that subjects watching videos of actors describing people they liked or disliked were able to pick up instances where the actors' own views were inconsistent with their supposed beliefs. They noted that subjects tuned in to deceptive behaviour, rather than the true feelings of the actors. That is, we are able to spot deception more readily than we can determine the truth. Why?

Several other researchers replicated and extended these findings (DePaulo, Stone & Lassiter, 1985). Ekman and Friesen (1974) showed that we more readily detect deception from bodily cues than from faces. They played videotapes of people being honest or deceptive, showing subjects footage of only body language or facial features and found the body language group were better able to detect deception. Still, this did not entirely explain how these judgments were made and the situation was further muddied by Zuckerman, DePaulo and Rosenthal (1981) who found that people hearing the speaker were as good (or bad) at detecting deception as those who both saw and heard them.

Starkey Duncan's (1972) interest in conversational turn-taking cues led him to develop techniques to note in minute detail the shifts in paralanguage (rhythm, intonation patterns, pitch, stress points, and the like) and the almost microscopic shifts in body language, which signalled conversational changes. This precision inspired several researchers to use similar techniques on deception. Knapp (1978) noticed deceivers use less factual material in their speech and are generally more circumspect in what they say. Ekman and Friesen (1975) and Knapp (1978) noted an increased tendency towards "manipulative gestures" by deceivers: playing with glasses, touching face and the like. Pitch also rises as we lie and there are slips-of-the-tongue and averted eyes too (Zuckerman et al., 1981).

It seems we rely on discrepancies, or "nonverbal-leakage" to detect deception (Ekman & Friesen, 1969) and in deciding we are being deceived we look at all available channels of information to see if they are congruent.

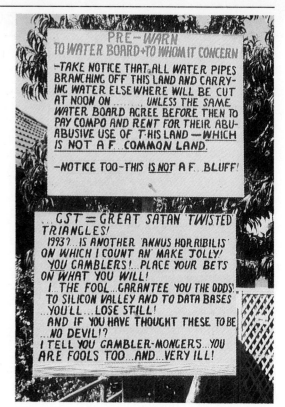

What message do you think this person is trying to communicate? What does it say about his sense of self?
(Photo: Gavin Price)

Incongruities may be micro-expressions, fleeting glimpses of our real feelings before we get "appropriate" expressions on our faces, or minute discrepancies between what we say and what our body language reveals (Brown, 1986). On the whole, the face is a less reliable guide to deception than we may think, as people are generally more conscious of their expressions and keep them under control. In any case, a range of other physical factors, such as stress, may alter facial expression and complicate our analysis. These difficulties led to a proposed controllability-leakage continuum as a guide to the reliability of deception-detectors: from highly controllable words, to facial expressions, to body language, and then to the relatively leaky dead giveaways of paralanguage (see reviews by Ekman & Friesen, 1975; Knapp, 1978).

As you would expect, people differ in their ability to deceive successfully. Highly self-monitoring people, those who pay close attention to themselves, are the least likely to leak (Ekman, 1985). Equally, the socially adept are attuned to others and are more skilled in communicating the appropriate messages (Riggio, Tucker & Throckmorton, 1987). Even if others are trying to be as honest as possible, there is a fair chance we will make inaccurate impressions anyway, if you recall our discussion of eyewitness testimony.

Summary

Humans are social animals whose complex interactions depend on a well-developed social understanding. This social knowledge comprises our enculturation, personal experience and schemas. Social cognition is the formal study of how we acquire social knowledge and is a rapidly expanding field in its own right. Social cognition studies person perception and attention, schematic processing and heuristics, attribution and perceptual bias, and the construction of the self and social reality.

Person perception studies the physical and psychological determinants of salience. Salience, or that which is distinctive, rests on physical characteristics such as contrast, brightness, loudness and movement, and psychological factors like emotion, novelty and meaningfulness. People are more perceptually salient than their backgrounds and, when expectations based on prior knowledge and experience are violated, the person may be said to become socially salient.

Social salience is multifactorial and our own theorists have added substantially to basic theory in the last decade. Studies of distinctiveness have found novelty to be mediated both by task and by the stereotypes held by observers, leading to challenges to the distinctiveness hypothesis. Emotion also plays a role in recall by its arousal effects. Salience, while leading to perceptual distortion, is nevertheless consistent in its subsequent attributions. Links with attribution theory and impression formation are noted.

We use schematic processing to cope with social complexity and avoid sensory overload. We reduce complexity by accommodating new information to existing schemas or building new ones. Schemas are mental maps which allow us to identify and categorise new experiences, thus simplifying and reducing cognitive complexity. They allow us to move beyond immediate events by comparing them with past experience and inferring causality, allowing us to anticipate what will happen next.

Schematic representation is an innate process but its content and structure is culturally defined and idiosyncratic. There are many relatively arbitrary classification systems, though a distinction between person, self, role and event schemas is useful. A broader classification of schemas recognises implicit personality theories and lifescripts as important sources of personal guidance. Kelly's constructive alternativism provides the most elaborate account of their use to date.

Schematic processing has been found a variable and often distorted process. Schemas influence the way we perceive and interpret new information, and studies of recall demonstrate that memory is strongly influenced by existing schemas, sometimes inaccurately. A debate is ongoing as to whether original memory is altered or merely modified at recall by factors like suggestion. This is particularly important in eyewitness testimony which is often inaccurate, leading to inadmissibility of evidence from young children.

Schemas also affect the way we make social inferences and are an important part of attribution and impression-formation research. New information is interpreted in the light of prior experience and upbringing, often leading to distorted inferences. Schemas also alter behaviour, and such is the power of schematic processing that we often ignore contradictory information and resolve dissonance by seeking supporting props—the confirmatory bias effect. Priming and mental sets also distort behaviour and may lead us into self-fulfilling prophecies which promote the very behaviour we expect.

Heuristics are rules of thumb used as mental shortcuts to reduce cognitive complexity and sensory stimulation. The availability heuristic estimates the likelihood of an occurrence from the ease with which similar examples may be recalled from memory. Its accuracy is affected by our experience and vividness and recency effects, which may cause perceptual distortions. A common problem is mistaking the base-rate, under- or over-estimating the frequency of an occurrence. Bayes' theorem specifies that accurate estimates are a function of both statistical and likelihood information.

The representativeness heuristic compares new information with existing schemas to aid an easier identification of new material. Otherwise consistent schemas may be thrown into doubt by the addition of neutral material which reduces our certainty (the dilution effect). A common problem with this heuristic is the tension between statistical probability and judgments based on social inference. Adding additional information to a description often decreases the statistical probability of its accuracy (the conjunction error) even if it strengthens our inferences.

The anchoring heuristic allows us to estimate quantities and probabilities by comparisons with similar situations. The heuristic falls down when we try to revise our estimates in the light of new information, as research has shown that, once "anchored", our estimates defy adjustment.

The self has proven a difficult entity to define empirically. The limited capacity of consciousness and the variability of our self-presentation have led some to see the self as an epiphenomenon. Perhaps the self is best understood as a process that combines our past experiences, current self-reflections and future hopes into a malleable schema. Many attempts have been made to characterise the self, with variable results, but the most successful empirical basis to date concentrates on its social antecedents.

The self-schema provides a framework for our collectected self-attributions and is essentially protective. Research suggests we hold inflated opinions of ourselves and avoid dissonance by providing self-verifying feedback and avoiding contrary evidence. However we do need reliable feedback to avoid potential embarrassment, so we practise cognitive compartmentalisation between our cognitive and emotional experiences. This mild perceptual distortion is a defensive adaptation which protects our ever changing self-concept.

As the world is a relatively unsafe place, we limit incursions against our "selves" by actively managing our public image. Impression management and self-presentation are a continuum of overt behaviours which try to present an image that is a compromise between others' expectations of us and our own interests and, in so doing limit others' power over us. Techniques of ingratiation, intimidation, self-promotion, exemplification and supplication are all tactics used in self-presentation.

While we may be good at impression management, others are too, and this often leads to problems in detecting outright deception, though we can often detect deception even if we are unsure of the truth. Studies of body language and paralinguistics reveal that the face is a relatively poor guide to deceit, while paralanguage (tone intonation patterns and the like) are a better guide, leading to the proposition of a controllability-leakage continuum.

Recommended reading

Fiske S.T. and Taylor S.E. (1991) SOCIAL COGNITION, (2nd edn) McGraw-Hill, NY. To date the most readable and comprehensive general text on social cognition. Our chapter has been structured to permit ready use of Fiske and Taylor as the primary reference in this area.

Forgas J.P. (ed.) (1991) EMOTION AND SOCIAL JUDGMENTS, Pergamon Press, London. A useful collection of articles edited by a leading Australian researcher in the field.

Kahneman D., Slovic P. and Tversky A. (eds.) (1982) JUDGMENT UNDER UNCERTAINTY: HEURISTICS AND BIASES, Cambridge University Press, NY. A primary reference for heuristics, an easy read with many worked examples.

Nisbett R.E. and Ross L. (1980) HUMAN INFERENCE: STRATEGIES AND SHORTCOMINGS OF SOCIAL JUDGMENT, Prentice Hall, NJ. Though dated, this book is a useful overview of how we make social judgments and contains many examples of how we go wrong in our estimates.

Shaver P. (ed.) (1985) SELF, SITUATIONS AND SOCIAL BEHAVIOR, Sage, Newbury Park, Calif. Vol. 6 of Sage's series A REVIEW OF PERSONALITY AND SOCIAL PSYCHOLOGY, simply written introductory primers containing chapters by leading experts in the field.

Tedeschi J.T. (1981) IMPRESSION MANAGEMENT THEORY AND SOCIAL PSYCHOLOGICAL RESEARCH, Academic Press, NY. A wide-ranging primer on all aspects of impression management written at the height of theoretical interest in this topic.

ATTRIBUTION

Y ears ago during the hippy era, a friend applied for a management position in an import/export distributorship. The salary was good, the work interesting and, as the office was less than five minutes from home, Mark was anxious to get the job. On the day of the interview he dressed conservatively, stuffed his resumé and references into a newly purchased briefcase and turned up early to create the right impression. To his dismay the receptionist ushered him into a room where three other similarly dressed men were patiently waiting their turn. As a desultory conversation resumed, Mark found their backgrounds were similar to his own and within twenty minutes another carbon copy turned up. As he later said: "We all looked like Fairy Penguins in a rookery."

Soon an ageing hippy dressed in shorts, sandshoes, beads and plaits ushered out yet another clone. As he collected the next interviewee he paused to introduce himself as the firm's managing director, apologised for the delay and offered refreshments. As it turned out Mark was the only one hungry and walking through the office to the canteen, he noticed most staff seemed to be ready for the beach. Several wore T-shirts and thongs (jandels). One employee sat on a beach towel and another had a surfboard beside his desk. Mark returned to the reception area, told the secretary he was popping out briefly and returned ten minutes later in an open-necked shirt, shorts and sandals.

Mark's gamble paid off. He enjoyed working for the company for many years and his employment interview became his favourite anecdote. He related how the interview committee were all unreconstructed hippies who immediately relaxed when he walked into the room. After cursorily discussing his management experience, they turned to more immediate matters and soon the interview dissolved into an argument about dope, rock concerts and the best surfing beaches. When the owner died and the company was sold, Mark returned to the workaday world of suits, ties and briefcases, regretting that marketing conferences could no longer be held at the beach.

Social inference and attribution

attributional cycle
Social inference starts with observation, and impression formation, then forms inferences and causal attributions and ends in self-reflection and incorporation into existing schemas, before starting again.

In Chapter Two we considered how we saw others and how we filed impressions in our minds. Now we move up a gear and consider the same material on another level and ask what sense we make of it all, or attribution. Where previously we saw how social data is gathered, now we want to understand how we use it. This is an enormous research area and literally thousands of studies, many local, were published over the last decade on attribution theory and its implications—far too many for us to review here, even the local ones. Nevertheless, it is an area with an unusual degree of agreement, by social psychology standards, and the last decade has seen a steady increase in our understanding of this vital social process. We start with a consideration of the **attributional cycle** (see Figure 3.1)

When we form impressions we ask ourselves why others act as they do and then consider what implications this has for us. This process starts

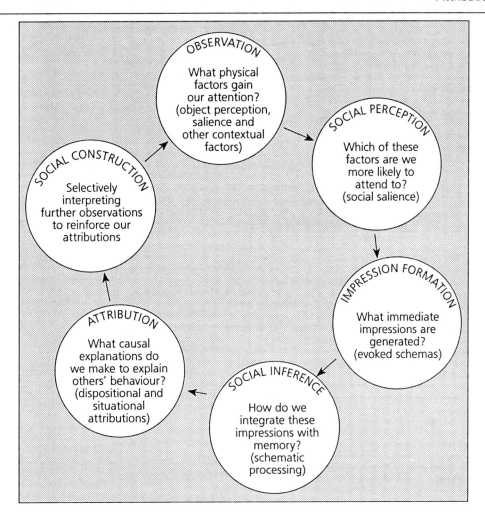

Figure 3.1 *The attributional cycle*

with observation, perception leads to impression formation, moves on through inferences and causal attributions of others' acts, and ends in self-reflection with us incorporating it all into our own schemas, before the whole process starts again. Social inference is then a continuous cycle of construing and re-construing our world. Within this cycle attribution plays a major part. The world is not as it is but rather as we see it. We live in a subjective world constructed from data available to us and interpreted through our past experiences. This does not imply that the world is plastic and, as we will see, reality does shape our attributions, as do the attributional beliefs we learn from our parents (Cashmore & Goodnow, 1986).

As unpredictable as life is, we try to exert some control by predicting what will happen in any given circumstance. Like Mark, we make the best guesses we can on the available information and act on our hunches. Yet these are purely subjective, our reading of situations in which we find ourselves. To predict and control, we read meaning into information. This attribution process is essentially causal; we constantly ask ourselves why is this as it is? In assessing his situation Mark asked himself: why are the managing director and his staff dressed so casually?—and provided his own answers. Right or wrong, Mark was putting his own causal inferences on events as he found them.

Mark's dilemma demonstrates social inference and attribution par excellence. Mark came to his interview blessed with all the cultural baggage that dictates appropriate interview etiquette. Unfortunately reality did not match his expectations, yet armed with a new set of attributions he revised his behaviour and carried off the prize. Similarly, in a world of complex social interactions, we face an ever greater demand to assimilate all the information that a technological society can generate. If we try to work our way through this complexity unaided we will rapidly overload our cognitive capacity and come unstuck. So to remain sane and to chart our way through life, we need to make the kinds of informed assumptions that Mark made, relying on our experience and shared social norms to double-guess our way through it all. So in a way attribution is a form of heuristics.

Impression formation

Understanding strangers

Much of the abundant work on impression formation may be summed up in two words—impressions count. Many new relationships are fatally flawed from the outset because some small thing or preconceived bias is triggered and puts us off. Unfortunately, these hasty first impressions are hard to change. To generalise, we are not good at forming accurate impressions and equally loath to change them. The dimensions of this problem become apparent when police compare eyewitness accounts of accidents and crimes. Often ten witnesses saw different accidents happening at the same time and place. So many people pass through our lives that we need to use mental shortcuts to sum them up and rely on stereotypes to interpret who and what we see. Stereotypes, carefully pre-packaged beliefs about certain types of people, are often oversimplified, narrow and sometimes quite rigid. While useful mental shortcuts, they often limit our accuracy because they foreclose the way we see others. We will return to an extended discussion of stereotyping in Chapter Five.

Impressions are important in other ways too. One of this chapter's consistent themes is our need to predict and control the world around us to make it a safer place. Our ability to "pick" people greatly enhances these efforts. The salesperson summing up a customer with a glance uses the same techniques as a shopper suddenly confronted by a disturbed person outside the supermarket, and asks the same questions: What is significant about this person? What type of person are they? What do they want? What is expected of me? and so on. A Chilean student told my

Attribution is all about summing people up and explaining their behaviour. What type of explanation will you construct to explain this man away?

tutorial group how this ability once helped her avoid serious injury. Walking down a back street in Santiago she was approached by three men who looked like beggars but held knives. She quickly summed them up as thieves and, thinking quickly, she walked up to them and begged for some money to buy her children food. Nonplussed, the men put away their knives and one gave her some pesos. Making accurate impressions then has a survival value attached to it.

The power of single attributes on our impressions

Our ability to develop an integrated overall impression of others based on minimal information has always been of great interest to social psychologists. Often it seems that a few strong salient cues dominate our consciousness and shape the way we see others. Several pioneering efforts in the 1920s and 1930s explored this effect (Lorge, 1936) but the real path breaker was Solomon Asch who in 1946 published twelve studies that convincingly demonstrated a single attribute's hold on our impressions. In one study Asch gave the following descriptive adjectives to students—intelligent, skilful, industrious, warm, determined, practical and cautious—and then asked them to write a short piece on their impression of the person described. A second group received the same list but with the word "cold" instead of "warm". Not only did the groups' impressions differ radically, but Asch found his subjects had no trouble forming a detailed picture of the person from minimal information.

While there was some criticism of Asch's work as being sterile and divorced from reality, more realistic replications confirmed his results (Kelley,

algebraic model
Where we assign weights to various traits and then add them up to form an overall impression.

configural model
Balancing traits to form a unified picture of an individual. Altering traits so they fit together more readily.

primacy effect
Information presented first in a sequence has greater impact on impressions than subsequent data.

law of primacy in persuasion
Initial arguments are more persuasive than subsequent ones.

central traits
Important traits around which others coalesce to form first impressions.

cognitive misers
Using mental shortcuts to process information.

1950). Asch concluded we see people as *wholes* and need to integrate all our disparate impressions into one overall unifying concept. He proposed two models to explain his results. First, an **algebraic model** where we assign weights to the traits and add them up to form an overall impression. For example, you might moderately value "intelligent-skilful-industrious" but be turned off by the word "cautious". You would then sum your weights and reach a relatively negative judgment because "cautious" by itself outweighed the favourable impression made by the first three traits. Second, in the **configural model**, our need to reach a unifying picture of the individual alters the traits' meanings so they fit together more readily. "Industrious" is generally seen as a positive trait, but if it is linked with "cold" our overall impression of the person might change to a more neutral "analytical" or "organised" impression. In this way "industrious" has changed meaning so it will more readily fit (configure) with the other descriptions. For quite a while each model had its supporters but eventually the futility of trying to exclude one or the other theory was acknowledged (Ostrom, 1977). It is now accepted that first impressions use both strategies depending on the context and information available (Fiske & Neuberg, 1990).

In a related experiment, Asch varied the word order with the key trait difference at the beginning of the list. He found his subjects' overall impressions were coloured by this initial stimulus, which he recognised as yet another example of the **primacy effect**, which had long been known to psychologists (e.g. Lund's 1925 **law of primacy in persuasion**). Subsequent research has shown a similar, perhaps even more powerful, recency effect, for material presented last (Hovland et al. 1957). Asch found in another experiment that these effects were sometimes upset by other traits which seemed to carry extra weight in our evaluations. He called these **central traits** and it is partly from this work that implicit personality theories have grown; we will return to this a little later in the chapter.

The effects described by Asch do not always work as he suggested (McKelvie, 1990) and it was partly an analysis of these discrepancies that led to a simpler explanation of the primacy effect itself. Much of the research on the primacy and recency effect had concentrated on the rather obvious time element. For example, Miller and Campbell (1959), looking at the role these effects play in persuasion, built an elaborate theory based on decay rates. Perhaps the sheer obviousness of position and its associated time effects blinded theorists to another interpretation. If primacy works because an initial impression is salient and all subsequent information just modifies it, perhaps we simply pay less attention to the rest of the information, and this leads to the first trait's dominance (Fiske & Taylor, 1991). As **cognitive misers** we are looking for shortcuts.

Yet if the primacy effect is not as powerful as we might expect, perhaps something else dominates our evaluations. Any number of factors may be at work and this is the essential weakness of single factor accounts of impression formation. If you are told a new boss is "fair, careful, even-handed, a moderate risk-taker, attractive and quite masculine", your perspective will determine your response. Primacy effects may give an impression of a good person to work for, but for a sales-team expecting a fire-eater to rescue a dying company, a steady-as-she-goes description will not impress. What they want is not on the list! If you have had bad experiences with male bosses, past experience will make "masculine" dominant, providing a recency effect as all you will remember is he is yet another male. Prior experience, our expectations, context, hidden agendas, the conditions under which information is presented and many other factors vary Asch's effects and our impressions. So on the whole it is better to be cautious about single attribute theories of impression formation.

Factors affecting first impressions

Many factors influence our social judgments and in particular our first impressions. As we saw in Chapter Two, if we are conscious of these variables we can alter our appearance and behaviour to send carefully crafted messages about ourselves. The area of impression formation has so many studies it would be impossible to do more than skim them all. For this reason, we decided to limit our coverage to just a few key areas.

Physical appearance

Sex, age, race or ethnicity, build and facial features are the first and often most durable impressions we gain about a person (McArthur, 1982). Leslie McArthur and her colleagues in a series of studies confirmed the importance of physical appearance in impression formation and offered a biosocial rationale (McArthur & Baron, 1983). They suggest we judge a person's underlying nature from their appearance and, as the Chilean example shows, this has adaptive value. Certain combinations of features become associated through experience with certain outcomes. Although large males with low sloping foreheads are not necessarily dull and brutish, popular stereotypes portray them as such. Irrespective of the veracity of these stereotypes, physique sends warning signals to us, and certain cues are more salient than others. For example, Hansen and Hansen (1988) found that we seemed to be programmed to recognise anger signals in a crowd more readily than other emotions.

Much of the work in this area has concentrated on facial features. Whether or not the eyes are the window of the soul, the biosocial perspective has received support from Paul Ekman's studies which show that interpretations of facial expressions are universal in our species (Ekman, 1971; Ekman & Friesen, 1975; Ekman & Oster, 1979). What this means in terms of underlying emotions is still hotly debated (Hager & Ekman, 1981; Matsumoto, 1987). There are studies (Cacioppo et al., 1986; Fridlund, 1990; Ekman, Davidson & Friesen, 1990) which demonstrate a psychophysical link between emotions, brain activity and facial muscles, yet the problem of deception remains. Method actors, for example, are able to "psych" themselves into intense emotional states in pursuit of their craft. Moreover, feeling emotions and

Some facial expressions are universal!
(Photo: Chris Simkin)

reflecting them facially may say little about one's underlying personality. Yet we act as if it does. A person who looks sad will be seen as a melancholy person, all other things being equal. While our emotional expressions may have evolved so that we can send nonverbal messages of danger or support to one another, it has yet to be demonstrated that they are a sure guide to personality (see also Eckard Hess's work on pupil dilation in Chapter Nine).

McArthur and Apatow (1984) and Berry and McArthur (1985, 1986) explored the link between facial characteristics and the impressions they evoke. Despite a certain lack of agreement about what various features mean, most people will readily make snap personality judgments based on facial features. McArthur and her colleagues found that baby-faced adults were judged to have infantile traits: trusting, child-like, submissive, honest, weaker and generally less capable than others. Notwithstanding the ability or inability of facial expressions to give us deeper readings of character, they do provide powerful clues to a person's present state and are useful guides in forming impressions. A steady gaze may signal liking or friendship (Kleinke, 1986); constant stares on the other hand may signal hostility (Ellsworth & Carlsmith, 1973); while avoiding eye contact is generally perceived as signs of nervousness, shyness or uneasiness.

Overall physical appearance is just as important as our faces. Montepare and Zebrowitz-McArthur (1988) found the way we walk is an important nonverbal signal. Walkers who had a youthful gait (loose-jointed walk and bouncy rhythm) were more positively rated than others, even when many other nonverbal discrepancies were present. Many studies have shown the beneficial effects of attractiveness (Landy & Sigall, 1974; Benson, Karabenick & Lerner, 1976; Maruyama & Miller, 1981) and clearly it is an important part of first impressions. We feel positively about the attractive and drawn to them, a fact often exploited by the unscrupulous. We see

What does this man do for a living? What cues would you use to form a first impression? Age? Sex? Dress? Context? Physical appearance? Expression? Not sure? Barry is a forensic photographer and many of his action shots appear in this book.
(Photo: Barry Price)

the attractive as being more intelligent, personable, capable and friendly and we treat them as if it were so, which then becomes a self-fulfilling prophecy. It is difficult to overestimate the advantages of attractiveness and we pity and stigmatise those born less fortunate. The link between attractiveness and its benefits is explored more fully in Chapter Nine.

Salience

The basic principles of salience are also at work in impression formation. You will recall that people are more salient than their surroundings and this dovetails with the importance we attach to others' appearance. Anyone who departs from average or the expected is immediately distinctive (Roberts & Herman, 1986) and as their saliency increases so does the chance of our inferring personality attributes on that basis. For example, an obese man may be seen as a "glutton and a slob"; a person with a facial twitch as "anxious"; and a thin girl as "anorexic"—despite the possibility that all three suffer from physical complaints beyond their control.

Status factors

Prestige cues are important in making initial impressions. Any number of factors add up to what we perceive as being prestigious; it is really a matter of culture and socialisation and you can make your own list. Most of us are duly impressed with the trappings of power and importance, sometimes with amusing results. In an early Australian study, Paul Wilson (1968) introduced five groups of students to a confederate acting as a guest lecturer and variously described him as: a psychology professor from Cambridge, a senior lecturer, a lecturer, tutor, and a student. He then asked students to estimate his confederate's height. The higher the ascribed status the higher his estimated height, with the Cambridge professor being rated 6 cm taller than he was. That the students were not poor judges of height was ascertained when they were asked to estimate their normal lecturer's height. They did so accurately and with little variation between the five groups. Wilson concluded that status had been ascribed to height, amply demonstrating its importance in the Australian psyche.

Box 3.1 *Profile: Joseph Forgas and the priming effects of mood on our social judgments*

Joseph Forgas, currently Professor of Psychology at the University of NSW, was born in Hungary. He was an undergraduate at Macquarie University, and received his doctorate from the University of Oxford. His work focuses on the study of social interaction, and the influence of affect on social perception and behaviour. He has published seven books and numerous chapters and articles in this field. He held visiting appointments in the USA, Britain and Germany, has been elected Fellow of the Academy of Social Sciences in Australia, and was recently the first Australian psychologist to be awarded the Doctor of Science degree from Oxford.
(Photo: courtesy Joe Forgas)

In Chapter Two and in this chapter there is an often unarticulated clash in social cognition between differing views of information processing. One viewpoint takes a *motivational* approach that assumes that we actively select information that enhances existing schemas. Another viewpoint suggests that new information *primes* or draws out existing schemas, which then interpret, elaborate and to an extent foreclose the way we see others. These two models are by no means exclusive and each contributes to our social judgments. We will consider the former view in Boxes 3.3 and 3.5 and the latter in Joseph Forgas' studies of the role of affect in social judgment.

Forgas has an international reputation for

his research on the impact of mood on impression formation and is one of the most frequently cited theorists in this rapidly expanding area. He is also a prolific researcher and author and his most recent book *Emotion and Social Judgements* (1991) encompasses some of the leading research on the influence that feelings, mood and emotion have on our social perceptions and judgments. As we saw in Chapter Two, person perception is a constructive process in which "expectations, predispositions, and implicit personality theories are sometimes more important than the actual characteristics of the people we judge" (Forgas & Bower, 1987).

Affect is a general term which encompasses both mood and emotion. **Moods** are affective states that gradually arise and fall, without obvious antecedents or conscious reflection. In contrast, **emotions** are short, sharp reactions to experiences and we are usually aware of our emotional reactions. Most of the research on affective states studies "mild non-specific experiences of feeling good or bad" precisely because they are less obvious to us and so we are less likely to notice, and correct, how they bias our perceptions. Intense emotional states like anger and fear are more obvious distortions of perceptual processes (Forgas, 1992).

We have known through the ages that emotions influence the quality of our social judgments but until recently emotion was the neglected stepchild of social cognition research. Over the last decade researchers have come to recognise it as one of the most important influences on social judgment (Forgas & Moylan, 1987). Mood states may bias our initial impressions by selectively influencing what we learn about others, or distort the interpretations and associations we make (Forgas & Bower, 1987). What is clear from such research is that impression formation is a constructive, inferential and elaborative process in which our emotional reactions to others often *precede* and inform our subsequent interpretations (Forgas, 1992). Affect then seems to play a dual role in influencing the kind of information processes we use in our judgments (Forgas, 1983b) and "through its influence on the way social information about another person is attended to, selected, interpreted, learned,

remembered and evaluated in judgments" (Forgas, 1992). How does emotion influence this process?

Affect-priming models argue that our mood may automatically activate existing schemas which we then use to form impressions, or make social judgments. To paraphrase Forgas (1992), it does this in three ways: Affect should facilitate *mood-congruent learning*. We are more likely to notice and better process information that reflects our mood. Affect also aids recall of information in matching rather than non-matching mood states. That is, memory is *mood dependent*. We are more likely to recall positive information about people when we are in a positive mood, similar to that in which we first formed our impressions. Finally, a "superior availability" of mood-consistent schemas should increase *mood-congruent associations* leading to more mood-consistent interpretations of ambiguous social information. So the impressions we make will be primed by associations to existing mood-congruent schemas. These three processes lead to a persistent mood-consistent bias in social judgments (Forgas, 1992).

In some of his earliest experiments, Forgas established that mood does influence the way we see and interpret others' behaviour (Forgas, 1979, 1982). For example, he hypnotically induced happy and sad moods in subjects and asked them to rate positive and negative, skilled and unskilled behaviours of themselves and partner in a previously videotaped interaction. Across four experimental conditions ranging from formal to informal interviews, happy subjects gave themselves and their interviewer more positive and skilled ratings than did sad subjects. Sad subjects deprecated their own performance more than their interviewer's; a consequence of depressive affect and social norms that tells us not to run others down. These experiments also showed an enhanced recall effect. In positive moods subjects recalled more detail in "easy informal episodes", while in negative moods, more about "difficult formal interaction episodes" (Forgas, 1992).

Subsequent experiments found that subjects took longer to process information congruent with their mood states but less time to make mood-consistent judgments (Forgas & Bower,

1987). These results are generally consistent with an affect-priming model. Presumably we take more time to study and process mood-consistent information because it elicits or "triggers" an already extensive "associative base" into which the new information must be encoded (Bower, 1991). As we already have elaborate schemas we can form quicker impressions. In other words: "A richer associative base may lead to the slower and more detailed processing of mood-consistent information in a learning task . . . but the faster recall of mood-consistent details in a judgmental task." (Forgas, 1992).

However, this is not the full story. These experiments found a stronger positive mood effect and a consistent pattern of sad subjects' self-deprecation, which was not explained by an affect-priming model. Research with children gave an insight into the developmental processes underlying these two affects (Forgas, Burnham & Trimboli, 1988). While their impressions were mood-related and reflected adult patterns, children showed a significant negativity bias in recall and judgments of others, contrary to the positivity bias of adults. Perhaps children have "a more restricted repertoire of emotional experiences" and may not have had enough time to internalise fully social norms that limit negativity. These social norms in adults are a countervailing force which is superimposed on to priming effects, limiting negative judgments. Children without the fully internalised norms are freer to be negative. Then again it may be a matter of negative moods requiring more difficult information processing, while positive moods lead to simpler heuristic processing strategies (Forgas, 1992).

Corroborative evidence came from a series of experiments that examined the effect of transient moods on attributions (Forgas, Bower & Moylan, 1990). As we will see a little later in the chapter, attributions are the causal explanations we make about our own and others' behaviour. Contrary to the motivational theories of attribution, which suggest that we should make self-serving attributions to enhance our egos when feeling down, the social cognition perspective argues we are primed to make more negative judgments of ourselves and others (Forgas & Bower, 1988). Results in both experimental and real-life settings showed that happier people make more favourable attributions to self and others and less ego-defensive biases. Unhappy subjects were particularly critical of their own actions in a way that reflected poorly on their own behaviour and personality. However, contrary to motivational and priming theories, unhappy subjects continued to give "credit for success, and no blame for failure when judging others" (Forgas, 1992). Forgas accounts for this self-deprecation in terms similar to the learned-helplessness and self-efficacy models we discuss at the end of the chapter.

There is much more that we might consider when investigating the role of affect on impressions. Forgas has studied the impact of affect on: interpersonal preferences; group versus individual judgments; context effects on processing styles; and mood effects on stereotyping (see Forgas, 1992, for a review). However, from these studies and many others over the last decade, Forgas concludes that affect-priming is one of a number of ways affect impacts on information processing and social judgments. Figure 3.2 gives a schematic of his multi-process model of mood effects on social judgment. To the extent that priming influences our judgments, it does so when information is selectively and thoroughly processed to make a novel judgment about a person.

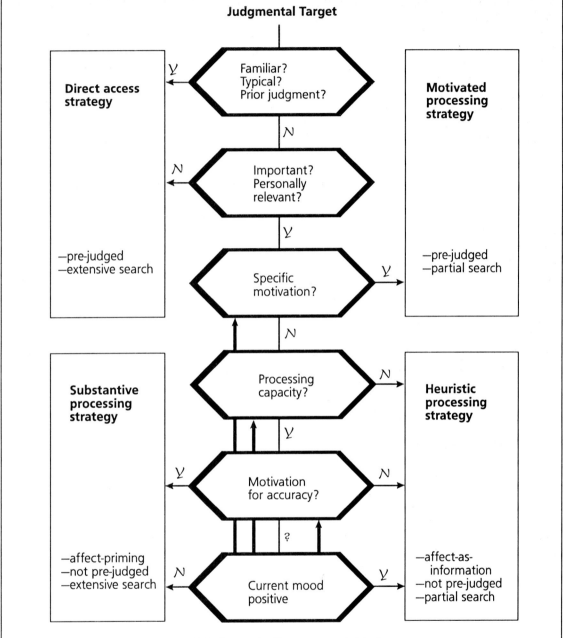

Figure 3.2 *A multi-process model of mood effects on social judgments*

Source: Adapted from Forgas, 1992.

Theories of attribution

Fritz Heider's naive psychology

Fritz Heider (1944, 1958) introduced the concept of attribution to psychology and posed many questions which he left for following researchers to address. Heider, drawing on the work of Brunswik (1956), started with the assumption that we see the world through a "lens" of our past experiences. Heider proposed that all humans need to be able to predict and control their lives to ensure some basic security. If we are able to predict how others will behave, then we are in a better position to influence our own outcomes. As we make successful predictions, we build a body of experience which shapes our future actions. We develop confidence in our ability to interpret events correctly, which over time coalesces into a personal theory about the way the world operates. Heider called this naive psychology, our own idiosyncratic view of human behaviour.

Heider proposed that attributions play a central role in this process. To predict and control we need to know why things happen as they do. Our naive theory of human behaviour relies on an understanding of how things tick. We carefully review our experiences, noting what caused things to happen as they did. We carefully file these away in our mind to guide our actions next time a similar situation occurs. Over time, our experiences start to yield patterns and, as we mull them over, perhaps unconsciously, we start to construct schemas which will determine future actions. This perhaps explains why we pay more attention to unpleasant events (Weiner, 1986).

Heider felt that causal attribution also influences our future behaviour. As we look back at prior experiences, our attributions give rise to expectations that govern our outcomes. A friend Rob, had held several management positions in marketing, saw himself as a competent marketing executive and was confident he would succeed in the future, and indeed he is more likely to do so (Schaufeli, 1988). Although he had been sacked from his previous job, he attributed this to a general downturn in the fast-foods industry, rather than to poor performance. As he had been successful in the past, he attributed his unemployment to external causes and was confident of the future. Weiner (1986) and Weiner et al. (1987) noted our causal attributions also shape our emotional reactions and are important determinants of future behaviour. If Rob felt that his sacking was a vindictive action of his previous employer and unrelated to his performance, then this attribution would give rise to hostility and anger. If he felt he had performed poorly, then this attribution would lead to depression and so on.

locus of control
Whether we believe our actions are controlled by ourselves (internal LOC), or others (external LOC).

Heider stressed the importance of **locus of control** in attribution. He distinguished between internal and external causes of behaviour and this distinction has become the central feature of attribution theory (see Rotter's "Locus of Control Scale" in the next chapter). In assessing our own or someone else's behaviour we have to decide if some internal trait or personality disposition is at work. In this case we have to judge whether this is a conscious or unconscious motivation, a point we will return to in our discussion of intent and responsibility. Perhaps external or situational factors are causing the behaviour? Is Christchurch's famous Wizard driven by some deep inner compulsion to dress up and catechise his audience, or is this just another form of gainful employment? Perhaps he just enjoys an audience and the cut and thrust of debate. Whether we attribute behaviour to internal traits or some environmental cause, or some combination of the two, we act on our attributions as if they were fact.

In an extension of this theory Weiner et al. (1972) proposed that we are also interested in whether observed behaviour in others is stable or unstable as this will affect our ability to form accurate predictions. If we attribute another's behaviour to internal causes, are these stable or unstable? If we judge them to be unstable, then we are less able to predict their future behaviour. If, over time, the person acts consistently, we may attribute this to some relatively stable personality characteristic and make predictions accordingly.

Heider stressed that simple attributions of causality were often inadequate to explain behaviour. Being able to attribute a cause often does not explain why people act as they do. Saying you came to university to gain a degree does not tell us much about your *intent* in becoming qualified. Why do you want a degree? Heider felt that questions of motivation were perhaps the crucial issue in attribution and gave considerable thought to how we attribute responsibility in others' actions. As you can see from Box 3.2, Heider proposed five types of responsibility or intent we commonly attribute to others. As you work through the examples, note the importance the legal system places on attributions of intent in deciding culpability. Considerable collateral work has been done on this important issue (Weiner, 1982; Shaver, 1985; Shaver & Drown, 1986; Karlovac & Darley, 1988).

Harold Kelley's naive scientist

After Heider, arguably Harold Kelley has made the greatest contribution to attribution theory. He has certainly developed the most elaborate framework of causal attribution to date. Kelley's two great contributions to attribution theory were his theory of **covariation**, which is often called the ANOVA model of attribution, specifying how people make attributions of causality based on patterns of behaviour (Kelley, 1967), and his development of attributional schema to explain how we make attributions based on only limited exposure to our subjects (Kelley, 1972).

covariation
Attribution of causal connection based on the conjunction of a situation and some behaviour within it.

If Fritz Heider thought we attributed causality on the basis of our own naive personality theories, Harold Kelley (1967) felt we acted as naive scientists. Kelley believed that, even if we are largely unconscious of our motivations in attributing reasons to behaviour, we nevertheless use logical processes in making attributions and we always look for connections between behaviour and its antecedents. The clue to this causality is covariation, or noticing that some things occur together. If you notice that this textbook is rapidly disappearing from your campus bookshop and it is no longer on the library shelves, you might infer that an exam, or some other assessment

---

Box 3.2 *Who killed whom? Heider's attributions of responsibility*

The following examples were drawn from newspaper accounts of deaths in various countries over the last ten years. The cases illustrate the five types of attributed responsibility proposed by Heider (1958). A brief description of the type is followed by an account of the case and its outcome.

Causal responsibility You caused the act but did not intend nor foresee the outcome. A building worker on a city high-rise accidentally dropped a tool killing a fellow worker below. Coroner recorded a finding of death by misadventure.

Justifiable responsibility You foresaw the outcome but did not intend the act. A pack-rape victim stabbed one of his assailants to death during the rape. Magistrate found he has no case to answer and recorded a finding of justifiable homicide.

Association You neither foresaw nor caused the act but are held accountable for the outcome. An elderly woman was asphyxiated in a nursing

home fire. She had tried to leave the building but found the exit locked. Coroner noted her senile dementia and need to be kept under restraint but found the nursing home director had a case to answer in not exercising due care with regard to fire precautions, and recommended charges of criminal negligence.

Foreseeable responsibility You foresaw the possibility of harm but did not intend the outcome. Police charged a minor drug dealer with murder after she had administered a lethal dose of heroin to a friend. The authorities argued this was an instance of a "hot-shot" aimed at killing a suspected informer. The accused pleaded not guilty of murder but guilty of manslaughter because she knew the heroin was uncut and foresaw the possibility of an overdose. Convicted of manslaughter. Sentenced to four years.

Intentional responsibility You foresaw and intended the outcome. A premeditated gangland killing. Charged and convicted of murder and, after unsuccessful appeal to a higher court, executed.

---

based on the book is imminent. If at the same time you notice that normally happy-go-lucky fellow students seem preoccupied, irritable and distant, you could conclude that they are worried about assessment. In each case you use processes similar to the scientist's. You are looking for a systematic pattern of relationships that infers cause and effect. Observations are carefully compared with conditions that may have caused behaviour to change. If over time you notice that library usage rate correlates (covaries) with the degree of preoccupation and moodiness of the student body, you could conclude that this pattern may mean the variables are related. While we should be cautious, as some third factor may be at work, the more obvious the pattern the more confident we may be that the two variables are related. We may have established an association between cause and effect.

Kelley felt our attempts to explain another's behaviour were influenced by the stimulus, the context and the actors/objects present. Three variables—*distinctiveness*, *consistency* and *consensus* provide us with the tools to assess circumstances and attribute causality. To explain and illustrate their role we will work through a real-life example.

Heider and Kelley argue that we rely on implicit personality theories to explain others' behaviour and predict and control our environment. What personality schemas are evoked by these two men? Despite their appearance they were quite charming when asked for their photograph.
(Photo: Gavin Price)

An inmate in a juvenile correctional facility I once worked in tried to commit suicide while on a weekend home leave. Late one Sunday afternoon, his distraught mother phoned to say that "Bill" refused to return to the institution and had cut his wrists and locked himself in the bathroom. A youthworker and I drove to Bill's home and found he had superficially injured himself. He was clearly very depressed and desperately homesick. After some reassurance he seemed to cheer up and agreed to return with us. Yet all was not well and as we left he asked to go to the toilet, locked himself in again and then severely gouged both wrists. We took the door off its hinges, applied tourniquets and took him to the casualty ward of a local hospital, fortunately only two minutes away. That Bill was serious about his suicide attempt was evident from his struggles on the operating table. He had to be restrained and sedated.

How might we explain Bill's behaviour and to what may we attribute his depression? Consistency asks how we react to similar situations over time. Was Bill's mood a typical reaction when he returned from home leave? While there will be variations in the degree of homesickness and depression, had this mood been observed often and how had Bill handled it? Did he have a history of suicidal behaviour? Was his behaviour consistent? Distinctiveness examines the uniqueness of our acts. Our behaviour is distinctive if we act in a way unlike our normal reactions to similar people or situations. Distinctiveness differs from consistency because it asks: "What is it about this target which is calling forth such an atypical reaction?" Was Bill's act an unusual reaction to returning to the institution that day, or does he react to other stressors in similar, if less drastic, ways? In assessing an act's distinctiveness, variations in one's actions towards different people and situations will give a clue to its uniqueness. Lastly, consensus gives us some form of baseline in assessing the behaviour. How did the other inmates' behaviour compare to Bill's as they returned from home leave?

In Bill's case he had a history of depression and a pattern of self-destructive acts. We had noticed his homesickness increased when given leave, but felt that rebuilding bonds with his family outweighed the disruption caused. His mother reported that he reacted in similar ways to many different situations (living with uncle, family, end of school holidays). By way of contrast, while no one liked returning to our institution, most of Bill's peers were philosophically resigned to it.

So we can attribute Bill's behaviour as highly consistent and low in distinctiveness and consensus. Kelley (1967) predicted that this combination would inevitably lead to dispositional attributions for such behaviour. We would conclude that "Bill" was a disturbed teenager and his behaviour was symptomatic of deeper personality problems. Kelley felt we could make confident predictions of "entity" causality when there was a combination of high distinctiveness, consistency and consensus. In this case we would conclude the institution was such a horrible place to return to that Bill's behaviour was by no means unusual! Similarly, Kelley's covariation model allows a number of explanations depending on the combination of these variables (see Figure 3.3).

Kelley's model was tested by Leslie McArthur (1972) in a pivotal experiment which is often cited in the literature. She provided subjects with a brief description of another's reaction to a comedian—"John laughs at the comedian"—and detailed information about the distinctiveness, consistency and consensus of subjects' responses. Examining attributions her subjects made to various combinations of these three variables led to experimental support for Kelley's predictions. Many other experimenters have found

DISTINCTIVENESS	CONSENSUS	CONSISTENCY	LIKELY ATTRIBUTION
HIGH Bill does not have a history of suicidal behaviour in other situations	**HIGH** Many other inmates have tried to kill themselves rather than return to the institution	**HIGH** Bill's third suicide attempt while in custody	**SITUATIONAL ATTRIBUTION** The institution is a life-threatening place
LOW Bill has tried to kill himself in many other contexts	**LOW** His behaviour is atypical compared to other inmates	**HIGH** Bill's third suicide attempt while in custody	**DISPOSITIONAL ATTRIBUTION** Bill is a disturbed adolescent

Figure 3.3 *A matrix of possible explanations of Bill's behaviour*
Source: Adapted from Kelley, 1967.

similar results (Frieze & Weiner, 1971; Ruble & Feldman, 1976; Major 1980).

Causal schemas

Kelley's other major contribution explains how we make causal attributions when we have only a limited exposure to the target situation. Distinctiveness, consistency and consensus rely on multiple observations over time, yet we often sum up people at a glance and act accordingly. What processes support these one-shot attributions?

Kelley (1972) proposed that we use causal schemas as templates to interpret reality. These schemas are collected patterns of experience which we have mulled over at length and on which we rely to interpret the world around us. They act as a sort of mental shorthand which contains our social knowledge. In an unfamiliar situation, we look for familiar aspects and compare them with our experience. In a way we stereotype situations and behaviour. At this point we ask ourselves how the present situation differs and then make attributions based on a "best guess". The accuracy of these attributions has long been a major preoccupation of social research; we will return to this in our section on misattribution. However, we are usually so cognitively busy that we rely on these schemas to reduce cognitive complexity to a manageable level.

While we often attribute in haste, we do not do so casually. Kelley proposed that such causal attributions are rule bound. We use heuristics to assess how likely our causal attributions are. There has been considerable research into the types of rules we follow and you will remember our discussion of heuristics in our last chapter. In attribution research the **discounting** and **augmentation principles** proposed by Kelley (1972) have received the most theoretical attention.

When we make causal attributions, the discounting principle states we will not settle on any one cause for a behaviour if other likely causes exist. If you discover a person has AIDS, your first reaction is likely to be conditioned by media stereotypes of needle-sharers, promiscuous lovers and homosexuals. However ready you are to accept these explanations, you would have to re-evaluate them if you are subsequently told that while the cause is unknown, he had received many blood transfusions prior to 1985. Research on the discounting principle is mixed and it has sometimes been shown experimentally and sometimes not (Reeder, 1985). One consistent finding is a preference for internal explanations for behaviour while discounting or ignoring situational variants. We will return to this curious finding later.

Kelley suggested that in moving from cause to effect we weigh up the likely checks and balances at work in promoting certain behaviour. Inhibitory causes reduce the possibility of behaviour while facilitative causes enhance its occurrence. When they occur together we have to decide which is the stronger. The augmentation principle suggests that we will make a stronger causal attribution if we see behaviour in a situation that would normally discourage it. Evidence for the augmentation principle is less clear than for the discounting principle. Hansen and Hall (1985) in a study of the

discounting principle
When we are faced with a number of possible causes of an event, we will not settle on any one cause if other likely causes exist.

augmentation principle
We tend to make stronger attributions of causality in the presence of a factor which would normally stop behaviour from occurring.

relative strength of the two principles, concluded that discounting was a stronger factor than augmentation.

Not only do we follow rules in making our attributions but we also establish favoured schema. Kelley (1972) borrowed a concept from the philosophy of science to explain two types of prominent causal schemas. In determining why an event occurs in the natural world, scientists distinguish between **necessary and sufficient conditions** for it to happen. An event will not happen if any one of a series of necessary conditions is absent. The chain reaction in a nuclear reactor is the end of a series of necessary steps, miss one and the reaction will not start. On the other hand, there are likely to be several reasons why you got a good mark for your last essay; you might have put in a lot of work; the competition was minimal; the lecturer was trying to encourage you; and so on. Any one of these reasons on its own is a sufficient cause for your mark. Kelley proposed that we rely on multiple necessary cause schemas to explain complex and difficult events, and choose between multiple sufficient causes to explain less complex events.

necessary and sufficient conditions
If any one of a series of necessary conditions is absent, an event will not happen; for most events there are a number of causes, any of which is sufficient for the event to happen.

Box 3.3 *Food for thought: Naive scientists and scientific realists, or just cognitive misers?*

Kelley's theory of attribution has withstood an enormous number of attacks over the years from social psychologists committed to a social constructionist approach (see Box 3.5). These attacks assume that "rather than being like scientists, laypeople . . . are lazy thinkers more akin to 'cognitive misers' " (Fletcher & Haig, 1989). Supporting this, is a view that laypersons' social judgments are riddled with processing errors (Ross & Fletcher, 1985; Jussim, 1991). This has led many to assume that rather than being naive scientists as Kelley claimed, our attributions and social cognition are a more pragmatic matter of understanding and controlling behaviour while expending the least mental effort. Our self-attributions make us look good and we do not worry too much about the truth. Which view is correct? Are we careful rational people who take care in building theories based on attribution, or just expedient cognitive misers?

Garth Fletcher of Canterbury University, Christchurch, challenged the social constructionist position head-on in a series of articles which assert that we are careful attributers and theory builders when given the chance (Fletcher, 1984; Fletcher & Haig, 1989; Fletcher, 1992). Fletcher, who has studied depth of attributional processing for some time (see profile in Chapter Nine), argues that it is the amount of time we have and how elaborate our attributional schemas are, that will determine if we act as cognitive misers or lay scientists (Fletcher, Bull & Reeder, 1988). The speed and complexity of our attributions will determine the type of theory we build (Fletcher, Reeder & Bull, 1990).

Based on these studies, Fletcher argues a case for **scientific realism**. So, like scientists, laypeople look for hidden unobservable connections that explain phenomena. While the physicist postulates atomic particles as explanations of events, we attribute motivations or personality dispositions to explain behaviour. We cannot see these connections but inferring their existence makes more sense of the world than simply using cognitive miser strategies would. Fletcher argues we do live in a real world and try to build theories to explain it. Even pragmatic attributional processes have to deal with "questions of truth or falsity at some level" (Fletcher & Haig, 1989). Fletcher is not particularly worried by research showing that people are reluctant to abandon suspect theories (see our discussion of prejudice in Chapter Five). All this means in Fletcher's view is that we are adopting a conservative view of "not yet proven". Much of the controversy in social psychology shows that "theory is underdetermined by evidence" (Fletcher & Haig, 1989). There are simply no rules to tell us which theory to connect to what data; and so our lay attributions proceed in a dishevelled fashion.

How plausible is Fletcher's view? As you can see from Figure 3.4, our theories have three components: *aims, epistemic values* and *methodological rules*. Fletcher argues that the aims of the layperson are much the same as those of the scientist and dismisses critics such as White (1984) who suggest we are more caught up in pragmatic concerns like maintaining relationships, rather than "explaining or making psychological inferences about behavior" (Fletcher & Haig, 1989). He asserts that commonsense suggests that building causal explanations also assists everyday pragmatic concerns. "Hence, if laypeople are pragmatists, it does not follow that their aims are not those of the psychologist or scientist—albeit, those of an 'applied scientist' rather than the 'pure scientist' " (Fletcher & Haig, 1989).

Fletcher's main arguments are reserved for the epistemic values of lay attributions. Scientists search for theories that have explanatory depth, unifying power, internal and external coherence, predictive accuracy, fertility, simplicity, and wide applicability. These tests of the usefulness of a theory have been used to discount lay attributions as little more than expediency:

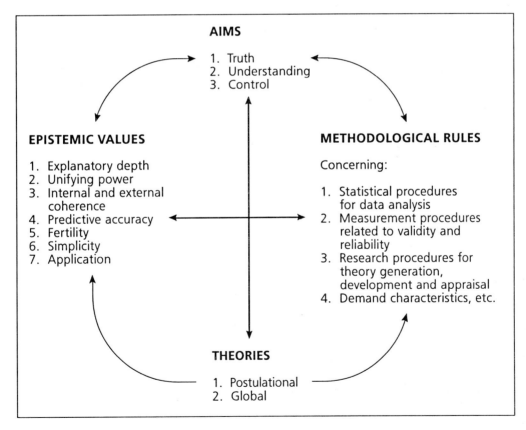

Figure 3.4 *Components of scientific rationality*

Source: Fletcher & Haig, 1989.

Possibly the most serious challenge to the idea that laypeople take these epistemic values seriously, emanates from the view that a prime determinant of human cognition is the need to retain a flattering and positive self-concept. In a recent review, for example, Taylor and Brown (1988) conclude that human cognition is characterized by unrealistically positive views of the self, exaggerated perceptions of personal control, and unrealistic optimism. In the attribution literature there has been a related debate concerning whether certain attributional biases are cognitively or motivationally controlled. (Fletcher & Haig, 1989, p. 122)

Rather than this being an either/or situation, Fletcher and Haig argue that both views are correct. Laypeople are "both rational and rationalizers—at times concerned with explanation, at times with justification". So the motivation for attribution is not really an argument against the naive scientist viewpoint, rather it is more a question of what factors are important in the attributions being made. When we need to protect ourselves we will make self-serving attributions.

We will turn to attributional bias further on; however, that we make mistakes in our attributions does not suggest that we use different methodological rules than scientists. Rather, Fletcher (1992) suggests this reflects differences in our ability and opportunity to make social judgments. The very literature used to damn the "naive scientist" model is an argument for it. Social psychologists differ in ability and insight, so do laypeople. Given sufficient data and opportunity to process it, the differences between the two are minimal.

Attributional biases

The fundamental attribution error

fundamental attribution error
Our preference to over-attribute others' behaviour to dispositional causes and under-attribute it to situational causes.

Research has shown we clearly prefer internal explanations of behaviour and often fail to take account of environmental factors. Ross (1977) styled this tendency the **fundamental attribution error** and noted our preference to over-attribute others' behaviour to dispositional causes and under-attribute to situational causes. This is the grand-daddy of all attributional biases and you will see how it runs as a common thread through all of the remainder of our discussion. Later researchers labelled this the "correspondence bias" and demonstrated its importance in our attributions. There is now an enormous research base which shows we prefer person-centred causal explanations.

For example, Martha Augoustinos (1990), of Adelaide University, was interested in the effects that social class and its perception would make on attributions of academic success or failure. She had secondary school students read short accounts about candidates from differing social classes who were taking an examination. Overall, students significantly favoured internal over external attributions for academic outcomes and this dispositional bias increased with age. This preference for internal over external explanations has been a common finding of several hundred studies. Why?

Salience

Heider (1958) felt we are just naturally people-conscious, leading us to attribute causality to underlying factors rather than to their setting. We are often so cognitively busy that our attention is limited and this may lead to dispositional attributions (Gilbert, Pelham & Krull, 1988). If we are caught up in our own mental life we are less likely to attend to our environment. The principles of salience, which we have already discussed, would then come into play and the most perceptually dominant features of our environment would grab our attention. As people are more salient than often less obvious situational aspects, it is an easy jump to attribute their behaviour to people-based or internal causes. If you reflect for a moment that our attributions are aimed at predicting and controlling our environment, you will see why other people's behaviour is so salient in our attributions.

In a series of experiments, Gilbert, Pelham and Krull (1988) tested the proposition that cognitive overload and salience lead to the fundamental attribution error. In one experiment, subjects watched a series of silent videotaped interactions between two women who had just met. One of the women appeared highly anxious as she talked to the other. One group of subjects was told she was discussing anxiety-raising, embarrassing personal experiences and in the other more neutral topics such as current fashions. Half of each experimental group were then asked to memorise a list of the topics the woman was purportedly discussing to keep them cognitively busy while they watched the tape. At the conclusion each of the four

Attributional bias: Research has shown we prefer internal explanations of behaviour and often fail to take account of environmental factors.

(*Cartoonist: Graeme Mitchell*)

groups in this 2x2 experiment were asked to rate just how anxious a personality the woman was.

Results clearly demonstrated the fundamental attribution error, while at the same time supporting the hypothesis that cognitive overload contributes to a dispositional attribution bias. The cognitively busy subjects saw the woman as an anxious type whether or not she was discussing anxious or relaxing topics. Similarly undistracted subjects who were told she was discussing relaxing topics tended to ignore situational variables and saw her as highly anxious. In contrast, those undistracted subjects who were told she was discussing anxiety-producing material discounted dispositional factors and rated her as a less anxious type. Clearly our cognitive state is important.

We should not discount the role that straight perceptual salience plays in dispositional attribution, and cognitive overload may not always be a factor here. Taylor and Fiske (1975) showed quite clearly how observers' seating arrangements played a large part in the type of causal attributions they made of actors. One's visual orientation brings different people into view and those we see most often become the dominant figures in our explanations.

Similarly we often fail to distinguish between behaviour and its causes, confusing the act and the agent. Once again we are up against the correlational fallacy. Just because a habitually angry man makes some bad decisions at work one day does not necessarily mean that in this case anger impaired his decision-making ability. He may have had the flu, argued with the boss, been distracted by home worries, or found the air-conditioning set too low for comfort.

The fundamental attribution error would lead us to make dispositional attributions about this man's personality. You might think him a derelict, drunk, addicted, indigent, developmentally delayed, or otherwise responsible for his predicament. However, he may just be tired!
(Photo: Gavin Price)

Correspondent inference

While there is a large body of research supporting our preference for dispositional attributions, how do we account for variations? Jones, Davis and Gergen (1961) devised an interesting experiment to show how dispositional attributions are affected by circumstances. In a 2x2 experiment they asked subjects to listen to a tape of an occupational psychologist interviewing people who were purportedly applying for two highly competitive jobs. In actuality they were confederates of the experimenter and followed a prepared script. Half the subjects thought the person was applying to become a submariner and the other half thought they were listening to a potential astronaut. An ideal submariner was described by the experimenter as an outwardly directed person who took account of other people's feelings and was pleasant, cheerful and cooperative. The ideal astronaut by contrast was someone who was self-contained and inner-directed. The other experimental condition varied the behaviour of the applicants. Half acted consistently with their ideal role and the other half inconsistently. The conditions are portrayed in Table 3.1.

Jones et al. were initially interested in role-discrepancy and what inferences subjects would make about the personalities of the interviewees in the four conditions. They asked subjects what they thought the applicants were really like, and then how confident they were of their evaluations. In the two experimental conditions where the applicant/confederate acted consistently with the desired traits of an astronaut or submariner, subjects rated them moderately, midway between inner and outer directedness, but subjects expressed little confidence in their evaluations. In contrast, subjects who listened to out-of-role applicants were definite in their evaluations and made extreme dispositional attributions. Out-of-role astronauts were seen as being extremely gregarious and the out-of-role submariners were seen as quite self-sufficient. Jones et al. concluded their subjects thought that role-discrepant behaviour gave glimpses of the applicants' true nature, while they discounted in-role behaviour as just "presenting well for the interview" and so were less sure of the applicants' real personalities.

These results were subsequently reinterpreted by Jones and Davis (1965) in their theory of **correspondent inferences**. Simply put, when we see someone acting altruistically we make a corresponding inference that their behaviour is caused by an altruistic nature. Within this simple statement is a wealth of assumptions. Jones and Davis start by assuming that we are intentional creatures. We act meaningfully. Our acts are not random but

correspondent inferences
When we see someone acting in a certain way (e.g. altruistically), we make a corresponding inference that their behaviour is caused by an altruistic nature.

Table 3.1 *Submariner or astronaut?*

Behaviour	Role	Role conformity
Inner-directed	Submariner	Out of role
Outer-directed	Submariner	In role
Inner-directed	Astronaut	In role
Outer-directed	Astronaut	Out of role

Source: Adapted from Jones, Davis & Gergen, 1961.

planned for a purpose. If that is so we can discover the intent of another's actions. This automatically biases us towards dispositional reasoning because intent is an internal process. They further assume that we act habitually, that is, our intentions and actions are stable. Jones and Davis assume an element of circularity in our reasoning at this point. If our attributions are made to predict and explain another's behaviour, then we would prefer a stable rather than unstable causality. This would bias us to internal causes because we may assume the actor's underlying personality is reasonably stable, whereas situational causes, by their nature, change from situation to situation. Because we want to see the world as a relatively safe and predictable place, we will prefer to make dispositional, rather than situational, attributions.

This whole process leaves open the question whether the world is indeed unstable, or that our actions are always rational (see Box 3.5). We will return to this point a little later, but for Jones and Davis it is sufficient that we act as if it were so. Their theory, which has enjoyed considerable research support, further assumes an implicit personality theory and a logical approach in our attributions, showing Heider's influence on their thought. Our security in making these attributions comes from our previous experience and rests on a body of personal social knowledge. Ultimately, correspondent inference assumes we believe the actor understands the consequences of their actions.

Jones and Davis' theory is essentially one of expectancies. Things occur in predictable ways. To do the socially desirable thing is normal, so when we see people acting unpredictably we are forced to take notice and explain their atypical behaviour. Thus, unexpected behaviour is more informative and, as in the astronaut and submariner experiment, we are more likely to attribute dispositional causes to such behaviour. To sound just a note of caution to these interpretations, Nesdale (1986) found that distraction altered our reactions to unexpected behaviour and caused more situation-based or indeterminant attributions. It seems that if we are in any doubt about behaviour, despite our expectations, we will make provisional judgments "pending the receipt of further information".

Not only do we form attributions from behaviour but also from the consequences of that behaviour. Jones and Davis pointed out that attribution is a two-way, cause and effect process. We learn as much about a person from what happens to them as we do from their actions. The more striking the effects, the more likely our inferences will be dispositional. They made their point by distinguishing between the different types of commonality. Most of what we do has any number of causes. For observers it is often difficult to make any definite causal attribution but if we act in a distinctive way it is easier to infer causality. Our actions are said to be correspondent. *Common effects* are where different choices lead to the same result; *non-common* effects are where they give different outcomes. Common effects then tell us relatively little about the person or event, whereas non-common effects, by their difference, are more informative. Jones and Davis argue that we make the strongest correspondent inferences when there are only a few, highly distinctive non-common effects.

For example, on two consecutive days in 1992, Sydney had large rallies, first against and then in support of tighter gun laws. At the first rally 30 000 angry people marched on the New South Wales Parliament. Beyond the fact that they were protesting against tougher gun laws, the many groups and viewpoints made any attribution of the marchers' motives for being there difficult, if not impossible, to infer, but they marched to a common effect. However, one elderly man carried a large placard proclaiming "GUNS KILL". It was obvious that he had decided to defy social conventions and stage his protest within the opposing rally. To say he had opted for a non-common effect would be an understatement, yet the marchers tolerated him. Not so pro-gun lobby supporters amid the crowded onlookers. While they cheered, clapped and encouraged the marchers, they booed and jeered the elderly man. Listening to the comments of onlookers gave strong support to Jones and Davis. Onlookers made mixed comments about the marchers, but made extreme dispositional attributions about the old man: "He's mad", "Must be senile—he's got his rallies confused", "He's quite brave to do that". The uniqueness of his behaviour led to striking dispositional attributions.

The theory of correspondent inference suggests that our actions reflect our personality. What could you say about this anti-gun lobbyist's personality?

(Photo: Mark Bramley)

subtractive rule
We subtract from our personality attributions those situational determinants that clearly imply we should act in a dispositional way.

While we favour the dispositional over the situational, we also take into account any situational factors that would imply we should appear to be one type of person or another. We then discount any behaviour which does not "ring true". Trope, Cohen and Moaz (1988) styled this reappraisal the **subtractive rule**: that we should subtract from our personality attributions those situational determinants that clearly imply we should act in a dispositional way. For example, it was clearly in the interests of real potential submariners to present self-sufficiently whether they were or not. In assessing their personalities we should apply the subtractive rule and ask what situational factors may be at work in the applicants' apparent personalities. All may not be as it seems. You will note a curious circularity here which denies and yet confirms the strength of the dispositional bias. While we apparently use situational reasons to discount personality attributions, we are really making a comment about the type of person who would be so calculating in their behaviour.

If we return for a moment to our previous discussion of the discounting and augmentation principles, we can see how the subtractive rule may be used either negatively or positively. Jones and Davis suggested we need to take account of the social desirability of another's behaviour and estimate how calculating they are when we make dispositional attributions. If, for example, I espouse a popular cause like environmentalism, you might judge this to be not a reflection of my deep interest in all things green but rather social pressure to conform. Using the subtractive rule you would discount dispositional reasons for my beliefs which would enhance (augment) a situational explanation of my behaviour. However, a *negative* negative turns into a positive. If I am pro-logging, using the subtractive rule you would conclude that, given the pressures to conform, I should really be an environmentalist. You then ignore (subtract) situational (negative) reasons for holding an unpopular outlook and conclude there must be dispositional reasons for my behaviour, that is, a double negative becomes positive proof of dispositional causes of my beliefs! If you cannot follow the quasi mathematics of the subtractive rule, just remember the next time you use personality attributes to explain another's behaviour, you need to ask yourself, on what basis am I making this judgment?

Before we leave the fundamental attribution error we need to note questions of time and complexity. There is fair bit of evidence that when we have opportunity to process information we do so more accurately. Studies by Fletcher, Bull and Reeder (1988) and Gilbert, Pelham and Krull (1988) show that under favourable conditions we process information at greater depth and make less fundamental attribution errors. We also make better trait attributions when we have more complex attributional schema (Fletcher, Rosanowski, Rhodes & Lange, in press).

The actor/ observer effect

One of the curious aspects of attribution research is our tendency to attribute our own behaviour differently to those around us. Jones and Nisbett (1972), in introducing the actor/observer effect, defined it as "a pervasive tendency for actors to attribute their actions to situational requirements, whereas observers tend to attribute the same actions to stable personal dispositions".

For example, as I write, a student rang and asked why he had failed a joint project. We discussed his lack of effort, failure to follow instructions and generally missing the point. He quickly conceded the fairness of the grade and rationalised by explaining that he had a job and had been pressed for time. In the same breath he attacked his two partners as "lazy, dumb and incompetent". While his own behaviour was situationally determined, his poor partners failed because they were defective!

Research has found that the actor/observer effect is a matter of degree. Watson (1982) in a review of research on the effect, noted we still prefer dispositional explanations for both our own and others' behaviour, but less so for our own. So even if the fundamental attribution error is still at work, we tend to use it less in explaining our own behaviour. Nisbett et al. (1973) demonstrated this effect by asking male students to write a short paragraph explaining why they were attracted to their dates and their academic majors. They were then asked to repeat the exercise as if they were their best friend. When the paragraphs were scored for situational and dispositional reasons, the effect was well demonstrated. The actor/observer effect has become one of the more studied aspects of attribution research (Storms, 1973; Ross, Amabile & Steinmetz, 1977; Goldberg, 1978; Watson 1982; Baxter & Goldberg, 1988).

What is behind this effect? Jones and Nisbett offer two related explanations: first, we have access to different information about our own actions from those we observe. We are more aware of what has happened to us and the influence the environment has on our behaviour. This would naturally predispose us to situational explanations as we are more aware of the variability of our behaviour (White & Younger, 1988). At the same time, all we really have to go on in explaining another's actions is observable behaviour. The fundamental attribution error will bias us towards personality-based attributions at the expense of the environment. Second, we have a different perspective. We are not really observing our own behaviour but rather our surroundings. We are inside ourselves, whereas the actors are out there. When we observe others, salience once again focuses our attention on the person, rather than their surroundings, and this leads us to make

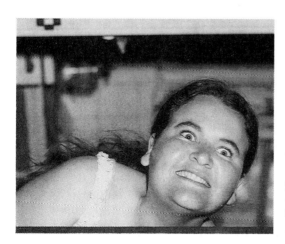

The actor/observer effect suggests that if you observed this person, you might think her a right goog. However, from her perspective, she is merely being humorous.

(Photo: Chris Simkin)

dispositional attributions about them. In our own case, as we look out from ourselves it is the environment that is salient.

You will probably have noticed that both these explanations rely fairly heavily on Kelley's covariation research. We are looking for consistency, consensus and distinctiveness in our attributions and for stable causal connections. We know more about ourselves than about others, so our self-attributions are higher on these dimensions than for those we observe. You will recall from our example of Bill's suicide attempt, this leads to external situational attributions. Conversely, we know relatively less about others and so we make dispositional attributions. Support for this view came from Baxter and Goldberg (1988) who found that when we attribute behaviour to others we are surer it is stable (i.e. dispositional) than when we explain our own actions in situational terms. We know our behaviour is less stable because we can see how it changes from situation to situation.

There is a fair bit of evidence for both of Jones and Nisbett's explanations and the area has been extensively reviewed (Nisbett et al., 1973; Ross, 1977; Kelley & Michela, 1980; Fiske & Taylor, 1991). Michael Storms (1973) demonstrated the importance of perspective in an elegant role-reversal experiment. He asked two subjects to introduce themselves and chat for a while and videotaped them. He asked two other subjects to observe the interaction. Later Storms asked all four subjects to evaluate the interviewees and then scored their attributions and found clear actor/observer effects. He then showed the actors the tape of their interaction and asked them to account for their behaviour. Not surprisingly, when he reversed their perceptual field the two actors, now observers of their own behaviour, gave more dispositional attributions than they had done as actors!

Although the actor/observer effect has been amply demonstrated, it is not as strong a bias, as say, the fundamental attribution error, and later research has shown it to be quite variable (Goldberg, 1981). In a similar way, self-attributed actor/observer effects may be altered or reversed when it is in our interests to do so (Taylor & Koivumaki, 1976). For instance, we are more likely to attribute positive aspects to our character if this reflects well on us. We are bringing flowers to our dear old dying granny, not because we hope for an inheritance, but because we are caring generous people. If we are subsequently disinherited, we can attribute this to situational factors like her drugged state, the lack of time in building a relationship and so forth, and not to her noticing our venality. Often in these situations we will rate ourselves more dispositional (or situationally) than observers would (Chen, Yates & McGinnies, 1988; Fiske & Taylor, 1991). It all depends on whether we want to enhance our image, or dodge the consequences of an unpleasant act.

Similarly, when we are coached to see things as the actor does (Regan & Totten, 1975) or are likely to face similar problems in the future ourselves (Chen, Yates & McGinnies, 1988), our empathy may make our attributions more situationally determined. Active involvement in the actors' problems gives similar results (Chen, Yates & McGinnies, 1988). Yet Fiske and Taylor (1991) caution that "overall, the actor-observer effect is modest in size" and that "the actor may know . . . [what really caused the behaviour] better than the observer and make more competent dispositional attributions". All good reasons to be cautious in our interpretation of this effect.

We like to reward ourselves and limit our failures. As we have just discussed we can alter attributions selectively to protect our egos. Most involve some selective reinterpretation of responsibility. Several related attributional biases work to minimise the damage we might feel from too revealing an encounter with the truth.

Self-defensive biases

Self-defensive attribution

Elaine Walster (1966) long ago showed that rationality often takes a back seat in our attributions. In a simple scenario, Lennie parked his car on a hill, the brakes failed and off it went. Walster varied the amount of damage caused to people and property, in one case the car hit a tree, in another it damaged another car, and in the third version it seriously injured a shopkeeper and a young child. Walster asked her subjects how responsible Lennie was. Not surprisingly the more severe the damage and injury the more they felt Lennie was responsible. At one level this makes sense, the greater the potential consequences, the more we should take care. Although at another level, why should the amount of damage caused determine his culpability? If you consider that the responsibility to keep his car in a roadworthy condition is the same notwithstanding the actual damage caused, why should Lennie be seen as lucky and not really responsible if the damage was slight? Consider that the potential for a disaster was the same despite the actual outcome.

Several studies have shown these types of situation make us uncomfortable and we try to reduce our arousal by distancing ourselves from the consequences. If we can attribute some cause to the actor which makes them responsible for their actions, then we can convince ourselves that is their fault and reassure ourselves it is unlikely to happen to us (Ryan, 1971). We can damn Lennie as a negligent, disorganised, careless person while at the same time congratulating ourselves we are quite different. Unfortunately, the self-defensive attribution bias has a severe downside and one disturbing instance is the **blaming the victim syndrome**. Thornton et al. (1986) reported how female subjects reduced their own anxieties by holding a rape victim responsible for provoking the attack, and there is considerable evidence that this follows through into real life (Brownmiller, 1975; Symonds, 1975) (see Box 3.4).

blaming the victim syndrome
Believing that life is fair and that innocent victims are responsible for their fate.

It would not come as any surprise to you that you often act in ways different to your beliefs and attitudes, but it may be uncomfortable to explore the rationalisations we make to square away the dissonance this causes. Evidence suggests we will go to some lengths to protect ourselves from the vicarious pain of others' misfortune, damning the unfortunates with all sorts of negative attributions (Lerner & Matthews, 1967). More worrying is our overuse of defensive attributions to protect ourselves from the consequences of our actions.

Box 3.4 *The just world hypothesis*

Christianity, like most world religions, is quite specific that we will each get our due rewards and punishment, if not here, then in the next life. Based on this doctrine of just deserts, we vaguely believe something, somewhere, is keeping tabs and dishing out appropriate reinforcements. The notion that we will be rewarded according to our efforts underlies the Western work ethic and is imbibed with our mothers' milk. We have to believe that hard work pays off, our society constantly tells us it does, otherwise why bother? If, for one moment, we admit to ourselves that sheer capricious chance plays a part in our destinies, we are undone.

Melvin Lerner (1980) in his book, *The Belief in a Just World: A Fundamental Delusion,* labelled this "just world thinking". We act as if there were some universal application of the norm of reciprocity at work (see Chapter Eight), that we are owed for keeping faith and working hard. Believing this is so makes our world that bit more secure. If we pay our dues, then everyday justice is the recognition that we deserve our rewards (Lerner, Miller & Holmes, 1976).

If we push this view a bit, perhaps its most frightening manifestation is our belief that good things happen to good people and those suffering from misfortune must have somehow brought it on themselves. After all, if they had been good they should have been rewarded. To think otherwise would engulf us in existential anxiety, the world would no longer be a safe place. There is little doubt that this is an everyday common or garden variety attribution in which we all engage. As I write these lines, a radio talk-show host is blaming the unemployed for their "lack of job-search skills and initiative, and their welfare mentality"—horrible attributions to be making at a time of high structural unemployment, as we will see at the end of the chapter.

To protect our view of a just, orderly world we defensively attribute blame and responsibility to accident and disaster victims, those suffering from incurable diseases like AIDS, rape victims, welfare recipients, the poor and oppressed, the handicapped and mentally ill, and minorities. Blaming the victim can be legitimately justified as their due deserts and we can ignore their plight. If we cannot attribute responsibility to a victim's neglect or oversight of some important external cause, then it can be attributed to some imagined character defect.

The just world hypothesis argues that when we see a beggar we assume they are responsbile for their plight. This protects us from the anxiety of seeing their circumstances as beyond their control and by implication, that it could happen to us.

(Photo: Chris Simkin)

Absurd as this sounds there is unfortunately overwhelming empirical evidence for this effect. As an example of just one of hundreds of such studies, John Connors and Patrick Heaven (1990) of Charles Sturt University, Wagga, asked to what extent are individuals likely to blame AIDS sufferers for their plight? They hypothesised that those who believed in the **just world hypothesis** would be more likely to attribute blame to AIDS sufferers on the basis that "you get what you deserve". They tested 184 humanities and social sciences graduates on the Just World Scale (Rubin & Peplau, 1975) and on an Attitudes towards AIDS Sufferers Scale (Heaven, Connors & Kellehear, 1990). Men were less sympathetic, exhibited greater social distance and greater victimisation and less empathy towards AIDS sufferers than women. Their social distance score positively related to their belief in a just world and negatively correlated with "endorsement of care and research into the disease". Women were less condemnatory and "there was no significant association between just and unjust world beliefs and attitudes toward AIDS sufferers". Connors and Heaven interpret these results as reflecting media stereotypes of AIDS as a homosexual disease, so their male subjects were less sympathetic and possibly more threatened by the disease and its "associated homosexual activity"—a finding many others have made (see Ross, 1988 and Box 5.1 on homophobia in Chapter Five).

Another sinister outworking of this belief is our appalling treatment of rape victims (Brownmiller, 1975). In an adversarial system, it is every accused person's right to try and shake the testimony of their accusers. Unfortunately, Martin Symonds (1975) in his interviews with victims of rapes, assaults and other violent crimes, found they were often treated by the police, and family and friends, as if they had contributed to the offence occurring, and victims often faced preliminary interrogations as vigorous as they would in the courts. Often this experience is unnerving enough for the victim to decline to press charges or take the matter further. Smith, et al. (1976) found this was often the case in rapes where the rapist was unknown to the victim and there was no obvious motive.

All is not lost and there is some evidence that we try to compensate for blatant injustices. Sometimes we give aid to victims and positively discriminate in their favour. If they are victims of crime or abuse, we invoke the norm of reciprocity by trying to punish the perpetrator (Lerner, 1980). All too often though we have to face the uncomfortable reality that there is no real avenue of justice available.

Harvey, Harris and Barnes (1975) used a modified version of the Milgram experiment (see Chapter Six) to assess differences in actors' and observers' attributions of moral responsibility. Subjects in groups of three were brought to a simulated learning experiment and assigned roles of teacher, pupil and observer. As in the Milgram experiment, the teacher had to deliver an electric shock every time the pupil gave a wrong answer. Again, like in the Milgram experiment, the pupil was a confederate primed to simulate varying responses to the supposed shocks. Both teacher and observer were left in no doubt as to the pain caused—they had a meter to tell them so!

Despite the unambiguity of who was shocking whom, and why, when severe shocks were given there was little rationality in the attributions made. Actors and observers differed markedly in their attributions of responsibility. Teachers gave the **Nuremberg defence**: they were not responsible for their actions, were just following orders, and blamed the victims for getting themselves into the situation and for being so dumb. Observers, though, made definite dispositional attributions which squarely sheeted home the responsibility to the teachers and accused them of gutlessness in

Nuremberg defence
"I am not responsible for my actions, I was just following orders"; defence used by Nazis at Nuremberg War Crimes Trials.

not refusing to cooperate and absolved the pupils of all blame. Interestingly, in a confirmation of Walster's (1966) findings, when the shocks were mild actor and observer attributions were basically the same. Still, we have to be cautious in interpreting these types of result because there are many instances in which our attributions of responsibility are rational and logically thought out (Arkkelin, Oakley & Mynatt, 1979).

The self-enhancing biases

self-serving bias
Attributional bias which diminishes our responsiblities for failures and maximises our responsibilities for success.

egocentric bias
Our self-centred belief that we are more important and involved than we really are.

Ross and his colleagues have identified a loose cluster of attributional biases that enhance our self-esteem at the expense of others (Ross 1975; Miller & Ross, 1975; Ross & Sicoly, 1979). Unlike the self-defensive attributional biases which protect us from threat, the **self-serving** and **egocentric biases** are ways we alter attributions of responsibility for our benefit (Marsh, 1986). The self-serving attributional bias is at work when we take undue credit for successes and play down our failures. The egocentric bias is nothing more than our self-centred belief that we are more involved than we really are (Fiske & Taylor, 1991). These biases, like the others we have discussed, usually operate unconsciously and benefit from the passage of time and subtle shifts in memory (Burger, 1986a), sometimes quite amusingly . . .

Years ago my friends and I used to race old sports cars and, as we were impoverished students, our cars were always in a state of disrepair. In one weekend race my co-driver leaned against her door which sprang open and she fell out. Time passes and at a reunion ten years later, a friend, who was always on the periphery of our group, recalled the event and claimed he had organised and won the race—both contrary to fact. It was even more amusing ten years later still, to hear that he had driven the car concerned! In the rosy afterglow of memory he took undue credit for the race and its outcome. You can see that his need to feel included led to self-serving distortions of memory, while the egocentric bias gradually shifted him further centre-stage in his recollections.

Such attributions often are immediate and conscious distortions of reality but you can see from the above anecdote that they play a significant role in how history is shaped and in the development of our self-image. Yet we should not necessarily assume that all such attributions are deliberate distortions of reality (Bradley, 1978). As our own role looms large in our self-perception, we will inevitably see ourselves as critically important in any drama we find ourselves in and give ourselves a starring role. Given that we are the most perceptually salient aspect of our universe, we will almost automatically make egocentric attributions that explain our actions to ourselves and others. This will magnify the self-enhancing effects and minimise others.

Theorists have often argued the purpose of the self-enhancing biases and four reasons are usually advanced: they enhance the ego; protect us from anxiety; reinforce our existing beliefs and stereotypes; and show us in a good light to others. For a while the debate was polarised into those supporting motivational, or ego-enhancing reasons, and theorists supporting

Have you ever noticed that after-dinner speeches inevitably involve self-aggrandisement, ego enhancement, inflated opinions of friends, outright lies and other reality distortions?

cognitive reasons for these biases. While it would be easy to attribute purely motivational roles to these biases (Snyder, Stephan & Rosenfield, 1976), there is also quite a bit of evidence to suggest that cognitive factors are at work (Miller & Ross, 1975; Taylor & Reiss, 1989). Denying responsibility for failures has been a pivotal question in these debates. One initially puzzling finding was that we are more likely to claim successes as our own, than dodge the responsibility for our failures (Miller & Ross, 1975). If these biases are basically self-enhancing why are we relatively more prepared to own our mistakes?

Control is a key issue here. Bradley (1978) suggests that these effects are more prominent when we have some choice in what we are doing, when we become highly involved and are exposed to public scrutiny. If we believe we have some control over our situation, our self-enhancing attributions lead us to claim a greater share in successes and accept more responsibility for failure. If you believe sales bonuses in a part-time job are related to personal effort, you will claim credit despite intensive advertising. Equally, if sales are low but you think it is due to your poor performance, then there is scope for improvement. In either case, our egocentricity accepts that we shape our futures (Miller & Ross, 1975). If you believe that low sales stems from customer disinterest rather than your sales pitch, there is little you can do about it.

Closely allied to control are our expectations. Nothing succeeds like success and if you have been successful in the past, you will expect to do likewise in the future. It is also more likely you will naturally attribute your successes to your own efforts, than minimise your responsibility for failure. This cognitive appraisal of outcomes not only reinforces our self-esteem but also sets us up for success in the future (Taylor & Brown, 1988). Initial self-esteem also plays an important role in these biases. While people with high and low self-esteem both equally claim responsibility for success, those low in self-esteem seem more likely to take responsibility for failure and attribute it to their personality, whereas those with high self-esteem attribute it to external causes. This may ultimately account for differences between our willingness to claim success and our relatively less (but still high) willingness to dodge personal responsibility for failures (Campbell, 1986).

The debate has dimmed with age and the number of studies that support either motivational or cognitive explanations while trying to exclude the other. It is likely that both reasons contribute to these biases and that they are essentially adaptive as well as protective. What is clear from research is their universality and their usefulness in maintaining ethnocentric and other group boundaries (Hewstone, 1989). It is equally clear that we are conscious of, and willing to modify, our attributions and behaviour when we are in the centre of the public gaze (Carlston & Shovar, 1983). It may be that our bias is little more than an egocentric view of covariation, a personal linking of cause and effect in which motivation and cognitive factors both play a large part.

Illusory attributional biases

false consensus bias
A tendency to think that our attitudes and behaviour are more representative of others than they are.

Closely related to the self-enhancing biases are the **illusion of control** and **false consensus bias**. Both help us to alter reality to make it a safer and more orderly place and share or diminish responsibility. The false consensus bias sees our attitudes and behaviour as being typical of others' attributions, and our illusion of being in control allows us to act as if our attributions are reality-based. Both subtly alter our circumstances to make life a little more bearable.

False consensus effect

While we all like to be unique and distinctive, none of us wants to stick our heads out too far ahead of the protection of the herd. One interesting way of managing this impossibility is to believe the herd is a reflection of ourselves and shares our attitudes and behaviour. While the false consensus bias does distort reality, we genuinely believe that others are more like us than they really are. So the false consensus bias is more a cognitive and perceptual error than a deliberate distortion of reality (Mullen et al., 1985). Studies routinely find this effect (Lord, Lepper & Mackie, 1984; Marks & Miller, 1987; Mullen & Hu, 1988). We attribute similar motives and outlook to our own and others' behaviour and see it as both an expected and appropriate response to the situation. Behaviour too diverse to be included is labelled inappropriate and unusual (Ross, Greene & House, 1977).

You will recall that Kelley (1967) drew attention to the underutilisation of the consensus test in making causal attributions. Ross, Greene and House (1977) demonstrated the effect by asking students to walk around their campus for 30 minutes wearing billboards advertising "Eat at Joe's". They were also asked to estimate the percentage of other willing students in the study. Those in agreement thought that 62 per cent would agree, but those refusing felt that 67 per cent would refuse to wear the sign. Clearly students thought others would think as they did and made this attribution without any base-rate data. The power of this effect was demonstrated by Goethals (1986) who found that subjects' self-comparisons ignored information that conflicted with their consensus estimates.

As with the self-enhancing biases, there seems to be no one cause of this effect but rather a combination of motivational and cognitive factors (Wetzel & Walton, 1985), which parallel those of the self-enhancing effect. Ross, Greene and House felt our attributions are structured to avoid potential embarrassment. We predict what others will think of us and attribute similar beliefs to ourselves. This has the effect of making others over in our own image. Marks and Miller (1987) in their review gave two further reasons for the bias. We tend to mix with people who enhance our self-image and over time we will select friends whom we think are most like us. Whether this is true or not, our attributions will be based on this biased sample and over time this effect may become a self-fulfilling prophecy. Equally, because our own beliefs are so perceptually salient, it is difficult to see others as having different opinions to our own. See Fiske and Taylor (1991) for a further discussion of this aspect of the false consensus effect.

This bias also has its antithesis, the **false uniqueness effect** (Marks, 1984). When it is in our interests to be part of the crowd, we see others as ourselves; when we need a lift, it is in our interests to think that few share our positive attributes (Suls & Wan, 1987). Moreover, this effect balances a general finding that the false consensus effect is stronger when we use positive self-attributions to identify with desirable models (Van der Pligt, 1984). Kernis (1984) suggests that we attribute similar opinions to others yet falsely overvalue our skills and accomplishments.

false uniqueness effect
We think that few people share our positive attributes.

Voluminous research has explored the dimensions of the illusory biases and how they work, and the power of these effects and their implications has become apparent (Marks & Miller, 1987). Considerable evidence shows that not only do we attribute consensus overmuch but we often do so inaccurately. Campbell (1986) observed that depressed people tend to see others in a similarly negative light and underestimate the number of positive characteristics they share with normal people. This might militate against their seeking help as they would assume that everyone is as themselves. Harris and Wilshire (1988) noted a similar role for the effect in shyness, perhaps leading to continued loneliness. Drug users, prisoners and abusers may also rationalise their actions and resist treatment. Wallschutzky (1984) noted that convicted tax cheats thought everyone was like themselves and justified their actions accordingly. Fiske and Taylor (1991) hypothesised that "under certain conditions, the false consensus effect may function as a justification for the imposition on others of political, moral and religious beliefs". There is little doubt that this bias has a profound effect beyond just providing a false sense of security and simple reassurance.

Illusion of control bias

Like the false consensus bias the illusion of being in control allows us to distort reality in a self-protective way. One of the major topics of social psychology is the literature on our perceived locus of control which we cover in Chapter Four. You will recall that Rotter (1966) argued that our perceptions of causality were dependent on who we thought was in charge of our lives. Obviously if we believe that we are the masters of our own destiny then we will take a greater proportion of the credit for our successes and a greater share of the responsibility for our defeats, but what if we are really not in control of our lives to the extent we think? In our highly interdependent technological world, we have relatively little control over our lives. For example, just one car broken down on an inner-city expressway during the morning peak hour will delay up to 100 000 workers and has the potential to cause major productivity losses when all the late-arrivals are added up. That our economic system has the flexibility to allow for these hiccups does not lessen their impact.

In a similar way, in our daily interactions we often assume a degree of control that is illusory. One of the subthemes of our chapter so far is our desire to live in a nice orderly, stable, and above all, predictable world. Successful attribution after all assumes this as a basic requirement. So our distortions err in the direction of controllability; we want to be in charge. For example, one of the first demonstrations of this bias was Ellen Langer's (1975) analysis of card games. She observed that student subjects felt they had greater control and made higher bets in a game of high card (cutting cards to see who gets the highest score) when their opponent was nervous rather than confident. This is obviously irrational behaviour, as our personality makes no difference to the game's outcome. Langer coined the phrase, **illusion of control** to emphasise our need for control when rewards are at stake. No doubt you have seen similar behaviour in clubs and discos, where people religiously nurse one poker machine in a belief their increasing investment will eventually return a dividend—it will but not more so than using any other machine! Many other researchers have studied this effect (Wortman, 1975; Burger & Cooper, 1979; Taylor & Brown, 1988).

You will immediately see an obvious parallel with the self-centred bias. The illusion of control rests on our assumption of personal responsibility for what happens around us and, as Ross and Sicoly's (1979) studies illustrated, the importance of this effect is not to be underestimated. In the 1970s I observed an Aboriginal elder each morning walk a little way outside Andamooka township and, facing east, kneel and sing the sun up. He explained that unless someone, somewhere, faithfully sang each morning, the sun would not rise and the world would end. Western conceptions of causality often

illusion of control
Perception that chance events are more controllable than they really are.

assume no less important correlations. For instance Titchener and Kapp (1976) reported how disaster victims often experienced **survivor guilt** and their bereavement was prolonged by pointless attempts to figure out how they could have controlled chance events. Given the illogicality of survivor guilt, it is ironic that some of the most vicious examples of the illusion of control are found in our attributions of responsibility to the victims of chance, as we have already explored in the just world hypothesis.

survivor guilt
Anxiety brought on by survivors' attempts to rationalise how they could have predicted and controlled chance events such as natural disasters.

Suppose you were asked to solve an impossible problem and then given the choice of two drugs: "Actavil" which would boost your intelligence or "Pandocrin" which would retard it. Which would you take? While we would suspect that most would take Actavil, some of the results of Berglas and Jones' (1978) experiment are given in Figure 3.5. Berglas and Jones asked students to solve either an insoluble or solvable problem and then gave both groups feedback that they had done well. The students were then given a choice of drugs that would aid or retard performance. As you can see students faced with a second go at an insoluble problem choose the debilitating drug much more so than their peers faced with a solvable problem. How should we interpret these results?

Often we find ourselves asked to perform at a level that we feel is beyond our capabilities. If you are asked to act as the master of ceremonies at a friend's wedding, yet on the day drink so much that you are incapable

Self-handicapping biases

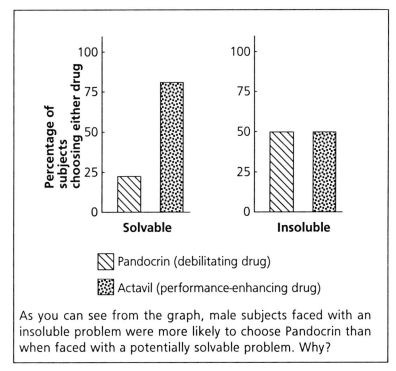

Pandocrin (debilitating drug)

Actavil (performance-enhancing drug)

As you can see from the graph, male subjects faced with an insoluble problem were more likely to choose Pandocrin than when faced with a potentially solvable problem. Why?

Figure 3.5 *Drug attributions and self-handicapping strategy*

Source: Adapted from Berglas & Jones, 1978.

of performing, you have effectively handicapped yourself and avoided the task. Social psychologists like Berglas and Jones see parallels to this behaviour in attributions that are equally self-handicapping. We avoid the pain of failure by finding ways to attribute it to external causes beyond our control. This helps us avoid the embarrassment of taking the responsibility for our failure. Berglas and Jones interpreted their results as an indication of such self-handicapping behaviour. Students asked to have another go at an impossible task attributed their initial success as pure luck and, as they expected to fail the second time round, chose the debilitating drug to give a good reason for their expected failure. We often use such self-handicapping attributions when we face future difficulties. Similar results were obtained by Arkin and Baumgardner (1985), Shepperd and Arkin (1989) and Tice and Baumeister (1990).

Self-handicapping not only helps us rationalise our embarrassment and protects our self-esteem (Kimble, Funk & DaPolito, 1990) but also allows us to substitute more salient reasons for our disability than lack of talent. We are then able to avoid making internal attributions about our lack of competence by having some external source of difficulty to which we can attribute failure (Snyder & Higgins, 1988). In practice we can range far and wide for reasons to avoid this embarrassment. DeGree and Snyder (1985) noted that self-handicapping is a favoured tactic of neurotics who may invent causes for their anxiety not rooted in fact. Self-handicapping has clear links to the self-serving biases' avoidance of responsibility and our excuses may serve to prevent others from attributing blame to us (Snyder, Higgins & Stucky, 1983). In everyday life such self-handicapping ranges from excuses for poor performance to actual behavioural handicapping such as our master of ceremonies example (Baumeister, Kahn & Tice, 1990).

Self-attribution

Up to this point you would be forgiven for thinking that attribution is solely about protecting our egos. In a way it is, but perhaps a more immediate goal is self-awareness. As we saw last chapter, the self is a circular process which relies on feedback from others, as much as on our own perceptions. We construct ourselves from the sum of our experience of others and their experience of us. Self-awareness monitors our self-construct and integrates impressions into a coherent whole. To do this, we use the same processes on ourselves as we do with others and attribute internal and external reasons for the way we act. Still, we also suffer the problems of perspective that William James noted last chapter. As the objects of our own perception, there is always some question as to how accurately we see ourselves. Self-attribution, therefore, is in part a testing of the accuracy of our self-knowledge. So just how well do we know ourselves?

Box 3.5 *Food for thought: Do we live in a real or unreal world?*

By now astute readers will be probably be wondering if we do indeed inhabit a real world. If you review the contents of Chapters Two and Three you will be impressed with our coverage of perceptual distortion and bias. We review saliency biases, base-rate errors, availability, representativeness, anchoring distortions and conjunction fallacies, reconstructive memory, the fundamental attribution error, false consensus effects, defensive attribution, self-serving biases, illusory correlations, self-fulfilling prophecies, hypothesis testing biases, cognitive loafing, primacy and recency effects, levelling, sharpening and accommodation effects, pre-emptive constructs, self-verification and self-enhancement biases; not to mention prejudice, stereotyping and misattribution. It was just such a list which led Lee Jussim of Rutgers University to wonder, with Bertrand Russell, if it were not also true that "if everyday experience is not to be wholly illusory, there must be some relation between appearance and the reality behind it" (quoted in Jussim, 1991, p. 54).

Jussim suggests most theorists over the last 35 years explicitly assumed we live in a socially constructed reality. This social constructionism takes two forms. The strong form argues that "social perception *creates* social reality" as much as it reflects it. The weaker form suggests that this is only sometimes, or partially, the case. Both forms however, either explicitly, or implicitly assume that we do so erroneously, though they both acknowledge that even mistaken perceptions may accurately reflect social reality, especially when they become self-fulfilling prophecies.

Jussim's review found virtually no empirical support for the strong social constructionist position and he suggests this would hardly come as any surprise to you. However, he argues that he was not just creating a straw man by defining a strong form. Social psychology is riddled with the strong constructionist perspective. Whether this is conscious or unconscious, it does not deny the reality that most prominent theorists make strong constructionist statements and their theorising more often suggests that social beliefs create social reality, rather than the other way round. To back up his contention, he quotes several examples which explicitly make strong constructivist claims and concludes with a humorous quote: "If I didn't believe it, I wouldn't have seen it" (p. 55). That social psychology is so interested in error and bias and overlooks studies which suggest accuracy, is nothing less than a major attributional bias within social psychology itself! Jussim goes on to suggest a cure but we will leave you to read that for yourself.

Just as we make inferences about ourselves by monitoring what we do, we also make emotional attributions. We monitor our emotional reactions to events and attribute accordingly. This evaluation is important in monitoring discrepancies between our ideal and experienced selves and in providing feedback on the difference. Self-attribution helps us interpret differences and posits corrective strategies. Just how effectively we label our emotional reactions is another matter.

Stanley Schachter and Jerome Singer (1962) proposed a **two-factor theory of emotion** much like Bem's self-perception process. Their theory suggests we become physically aroused, notice our arousal and then, after monitoring our surroundings, attach an appropriate emotional tag to our arousal. This was not a new idea and harks back to William James' 1884 emotion theory (Winton, 1990). The "two-factor" tag derives first, from

Emotional self-attribution

two-factor theory of emotion
When we become physically aroused, we first notice our arousal and then, after monitoring our surroundings, give it an appropriate emotional tag.

experiencing ambiguous physiological arousal and second, labelling it using situational and other cues. They tested their theory by asking a group of subjects to take part in an experimental trial of a vision-enhancing vitamin, Suproxin. The subjects were then given an injection of adrenalin which has high physiological arousal effects: accelerated pulse, sweating, racing heart, flushed face and heightened alertness, all symptoms experienced in emotional arousal. Given that subjects would not be aware of the effects of this "new" drug, Schachter and Singer hypothesised that the test of their theory would come from the subject's reactions to the drug. They divided them into four groups. One was given accurate information about the arousing side-effects of the drug; another received a placebo and no information; another group was given misleading information; and a final group was left completely ignorant. They were then asked to fill in a very embarrassing, intimate questionnaire. To prime subjects' reactions, in one trial subjects shared a room with a confederate who angrily denounced the questionnaire and the experimenters. In another the confederate acted euphorically. At the conclusion of the experiment they were quizzed about their feelings.

As Schachter and Singer predicted, in the informed group, subjects were aware of the drug's effects and discounted their reactions. In the euphoric condition they were euphoric and in the angry condition angry. In these conditions they would need to find reasons for the way they felt as they did and would use the situational cues presented by the confederate and attribute their emotions accordingly. The placebo group having no drug effects would not need to attribute what they did not experience.

Both the methodology (Marshall & Zimbardo, 1979) and the powerfulness of the effect (Cotton, 1981; Reisenzein, 1983) of these findings were disputed. Through further work (Schachter, 1964, 1971; Schachter & Singer, 1979), we now know situational cues are interpreted a lot more stringently than previously thought. Not only do we try to explain our ambiguous arousal using others' behaviour as a guide but we also use social comparison processes (see Chapter Eight) to set a baseline for our reactions.

Misattribution of emotions

Given the ambiguity involved in this process it would not come as any surprise that we often misattribute our emotions. Not only do we label our arousal after the fact but often quite variably. Most of the studies that have examined the misattribution of emotions use experimental manipulations of the cues on which our self-attributions are based. In an extension of the two-factor theory, Zillmann (1978) proposed that by a process of **excitation transfer**, one emotional state may be misattributed and heighten another. Perhaps the hypertensive effect of consuming too much salt while dining at a Chinese restaurant adds to your feelings of undying love for your dinner partner. If you are aroused it must be love. At a slightly less facetious level, similar effects have been amply demonstrated (see Dutton and Aron's experiment in Chapter Nine).

Is it possible to mistake our arousal or attribute emotions even in the

excitation transfer
One emotional state may be misattributed and then heighten another.

absence of arousal? In a classic and oft reported experiment, Valins (1966) showed male university students slides of nude females and gave them an amplified feedback of their heart-beat. Unknown to them this was a taped recording manipulated by the experimenters. At randomly varied points the heart-rate increased and subjects were later asked to rate the slides for attractiveness. Not surprisingly, the subjects rated pictures accompanying the increased heart-beat as the most attractive, and this was confirmed when they were later offered a parting gift of a slide of their choice and most took the same slide. Fairly obviously the subjects had not only misattributed their ratings to sexual arousal but also had mistaken how aroused they were. In an interesting insight into the power of this effect, in a similar experiment when the subjects were told the real intent of the experiment and then asked whom they really preferred, most stayed with their previous ratings (Valins, 1970).

Applications of emotional misattribution were soon perceived. Nisbett and Schachter (1966) argued that if our worries could be misattributed to neutral or third parties, our anxiety and stress could be reduced. Displacing our fears would allow us to make fewer stable internal attributions for our problems, which would then promote feelings of self-efficacy. Again this was not a new idea and had been formulated as early as 1911 by Freud and used in various therapies since then. Yet Nisbett and Schachter's experiments led to a more precise theoretical underpinning and to empirical validation. In a series of experiments this strategy was used to reduce physical pain (Davidson & Valins, 1969); to reduce guilt (Dienstbier & Munter, 1971); to sleep sounder (Storms & Nisbett, 1970); to relieve shyness (Brodt & Zimbardo, 1981); and to relieve public speaking anxiety (Olson, 1988). The effect is weak and short lived however, and only seems to work well where the source of the arousal is unclear and when the misattribution is to a highly credible alternative source (Olson & Ross, 1988).

The consequences of self-attribution

To make the point that attribution theory is one of the more important areas of social research we will end the chapter with a look at the consequences of negative self-attributions. This is perhaps the most studied aspect of attribution theory and has wide applicability within the social sciences. Our literature search revealed a wealth of local research concentrated mainly in educational (Relich, Debus & Walker, 1986), developmental (Siegal, Waters & Dinwiddy, 1988), sports (Anshel & Hoosima, 1989; Grove, Hanrahan & Stewart, 1990), and clinical areas (Watson, 1986). Researchers are applying the insights of attribution theory to see why people perform differently in various situations. As you might expect, positive self-attributions are correlated with high self-esteem, mental health and productivity, while negative attributions have the opposite effect, and many studies amount to little more than confirmation of this pattern in previously unresearched areas. Nevertheless, there is vigorous research on ways the self-attribution process might be monitored and modified.

Depression and learned helplessness

Possibly the most interesting application of this theory is research on the self-attribution/depression linkage. Many studies have shown that poor self-esteem and its consequent negative self-attributions lead to a vicious cycle which feeds on itself and inevitably produces a whole range of unfortunate consequences. Martin Seligman (1975) proposed that when we face uncontrollable aversive situations, like being trapped in an abusive household, our not being able to rectify or escape the situation eventually leads to depression. He hypothesised that successive failures lead to feelings of not being in control of our life, and to debilitating stress and feelings of discouragement. When we learn it is not possible to effect change in our lives, we start to make negative self-attributions of being incompetent, ineffectual, low in initiative and the like. This cycle eventually breeds learned helplessness, as we give up on any further attempts to alter our situation and lapse into pessimism and depression.

The Seligman model sparked a heated debate within psychology when critics pointed to the variability of responses in learned helplessness experiments (Winefield, 1982). This led to a reformulated theory which stressed the role of the attributions we make in these uncontrollable situations (Abramson, Seligman & Teasdale, 1978). The revised model of learned helplessness examined the attributions made on three continua: internal versus external, global versus specific, and stable versus unstable causality.

When we make internal attributions for failure we usually suffer low self-esteem. People who see their failure at a job interview as unstable and specific, in effect a "one-off" such as feeling ill on the day of the interview, are less likely to give up and may eventually succeed, as they are less likely to make internal attributions about their failure. By contrast, those who saw their failure to get the job as a global and stable, caused by a falling labour market, will see their failure as an indicator of likely future outcomes and become pessimistic and passively resigned to unemployment. Even so this is still an external attribution of causality. Those who make stable, global and internal attributions, such as blaming themselves for being dumb, are condemning themselves to repeated failures and the greatest risk of depression (Dobia & McMurray, 1985). So it is not inevitable that repeated failure leads to depression, rather it is our attributional style that influences outcomes (Peterson, Seligman & Vaillant, 1988).

There has been some considerable debate and many studies about the expectancy–depression link. Over time, repeated failure will reinforce a depressive view of the world and even positive events in such a person's life may be discounted and negatively interpreted. This depressive explanatory style has been shown to lead to learned hopelessness depression (Sweeney, Anderson & Bailey, 1986; Abramson, Metalsky & Alloy, 1990), though there is some question whether the depressive explanatory style precedes depression or is a result of it (Metalsky, Halberstadt & Abramson, 1987). Robbins (1988), reviewing inconsistencies in this area, noted research did not always show a clear link between negative dispositional self-attributions and depression. So, while the research is yet to provide a clear-cut answer, at this point it seems that negative, stable, global attributions are linked with helplessness and depression; while the experience of repeated failure may have many different outcomes.

The learned helplessness theory, whatever its limitations, does show a link between some types of attribution and depression. If we believe the world is an alienating place over which we have little control then our self-esteem will suffer. Our expectation that our world is uncontrollable will lead to (or reinforce) lowered self-efficacy, which will in turn diminish our likelihood of success. Locus of control is once again a key variable in our expectations. Whether or not we attribute our lack of success to internal or external causes, we are both socially and emotionally at risk.

As an example, two Australian studies point to the consequences of this linkage. Love (1988), from La Trobe University, Melbourne, assessed the attributional styles of 91 depressed and non-depressed chronic low-back-pain sufferers to test the revised learned helplessness model of depression. His findings indicated that most but not all depressed patients attributed negative events to internal, stable and global characteristics. While in this respect they differed from non-depressed patients there were no differences in attributional style for positive events. Innes and Thomas (1989), of Adelaide University, examined how 90 high school students' social avoidance and inhibition, views of self-efficacy and their attributions of social success and failure, interrelated. Their results suggested that inhibited, socially avoidant young people attribute their successes and failures to stable internal causes and see themselves as less socially adept.

Unemployment and attribution

As all developed nations battle the problem of fewer meaningful jobs for youth, perceptions of employment have been changing gradually since the full employment of the 1960s. As our society equates self-worth with productivity, the unemployed are missing a substantial plank in their adult identities. For this reason, the study of the social and emotional effects of unemployment is a major research area for social psychologists in most countries.

In Australia, Adelaide is the focus for such studies and two sets of researchers, Marika Tiggemann and Tony Winefield at Adelaide University, and Norman Feather and Gordon O'Brien at Flinders University, have tracked the effects of unemployment, in cohorts first measured during their school years in the early 1980s. In his recent book *The Psychological Impact of Unemployment* (1990b), Feather gave a general review of research showing fairly predictable consequences of unemployment:

> . . . lower self-rated competence, lower positive attitude toward self, lower self-rated activity, higher self-rated depression, lower life satisfaction, higher stress symptoms, lower PE [Protestant Ethic] values, lower employment value, and lower need for a job, for those who became unemployed when compared with those who found jobs. Differences also emerged on selected variables assessed only at school (e.g. lower job expectancies and lower teachers' ratings of academic potential for those who subsequently became unemployed). (Feather, 1990b, p. 182)

Indigenous people often suffer high levels of unemployment due to prejudice. This leads to further stigmatisation as "dole-bums" and increased unemployment; which becomes a self-fulfilling prophesy. Much of the work of units like Naamoro Aboriginal Employment Centre involves reattributional training to break this vicious cycle. (Photo: Gavin Price)

Feather notes these differences occurred "before our subjects attempted to enter the workforce and they were maintained subsequently" and described them as "risk factors" predisposing unemployment. A number of other local researchers also found that unemployment led to personal difficulties and dissatisfaction (Tiggemann & Winefield, 1984; Winefield & Tiggemann, 1990), though a study by Patton and Noller (1984) failed to find differences between the employed and unemployed while still at school. Over time these differences became more pronounced for the unemployed but Feather (1990b) comments that his studies did not show the clear pattern of raised self-esteem and life satisfaction in the employed sample that was found by other researchers. On the whole, these studies give a clear picture of these "risk factors" being a recipe for unemployment. How might we account for these results?

One factor clearly distinguishing the employed and unemployed were changes in their attributions, particularly after leaving school. Those who gained employment were a little less likely to blame youth unemployment on the economic recession, but Feather notes that "in marked contrast, employment appeared to lead to an increased tendency for respondents to blame unemployment on lack of motivation" on the part of the unemployed. Are these attributions correct? Feather found an opposite pattern among the unemployed. They increasingly felt the recession was to blame for their state and were less likely to see lack of motivation as a cause of their condition. This argues that life experiences shaped the attributions of both groups, with the employed's success contributing to a self-enhancing bias that their efforts and initiative gained them employment, while the unemployed protected themselves with self-defensive strategies that favoured external, global reasons for their lack of success.

It may be that the unemployed subjects were less optimistic and less well prepared to gain employment and that the causal attributions made by the employed about them had a measure of truth. Certainly Feather reported significant differences between the two groups on job-need, self-reported activity, Protestant Ethic and other measures before and after leaving school, which would support such a view. Still, we must be cautious in assuming that these differences caused their unemployment. Although there were differences on these measures, Feather notes that measures of job-need, employment value and disappointment were well above the midpoints on these scales, showing a clear commitment to seek and hold employment, on the part of the unemployed. In short, although discouraged, they still wanted jobs.

Feather and O'Brien also found significant gender differences in their longitudinal study (Feather & O'Brien, 1986). Girls more often attributed youth unemployment to the recession, were more stressed and saw themselves as "less in control of their lives, and less powerful and they were less confident about finding employment" (Feather, 1990b). These findings were consistent with other studies (O'Brien & Kabanoff, 1981). Boys were more confident about finding work and felt this was more under their own control.

Another interesting finding to emerge from these longitudinal studies was the differences in satisfaction between those in satisfactory employment and those who found it less fulfilling than they expected (O'Brien & Feather, 1990). "The results of our new analyses showed clearly that the positive benefits of employment for young people depended upon the quality of their employment" (Feather, 1990b). While employment benefited those satisfied with their work, they found negligible differences between the dissatisfied employed and the unemployed. These results parallel those of Winefield, Tiggemann and Goldney (1988) whose data showed the satisfied employed were better adjusted psychologically, while the dissatisfied employed and unemployed did not differ and had much worse self-esteem, more minor psychiatric disturbances and more depressive feelings. Clearly, self-attributions affect the way we see ourselves and this influences our outcomes. In Chapter Four we will return to this topic in our discussion of locus of control.

Efforts have been made to correct this pernicious tendency for some people to damn themselves with faint praise. Reattribution training has taken one of two main paths (Forsterling, 1985). One approach based on Schachter and Singer's two-factor theory of emotion tries to alleviate depression and anxiety by providing external, non-personal reasons for these emotions. This approach assumes that misattributing the causes of arousal will allow people to explain their anxiety as being caused by some neutral cause. It is hoped this "cognitive restructuring" will then break the depressive cycle

Reattributional training

Box 3.6 *Arithmetic and reattributional training*

Self-efficacy training has been much more successful than misattribution therapy and one such example is Dr Marie-Louise Craske's 1988 study. Craske, then at the University of Tasmania, was interested in the relationship between learned helplessness, self-worth and attribution retraining. In a clever study she first assessed 69 primary school children's self-concept and then gave them four sets of age-graded arithmetic sums. Series A, C and D were within the child's previously assessed ability. Children were told to do only as many sums as they wished from each set. Set B was "designed to provide a failure experience". Craske marked this in the children's presence and made sure that at least two-thirds of the sums were wrong. After set B the children were given an attributions-for-failure scale to determine their reasoning for an apparent failure on this set. Set D, though of the same difficulty as the others, had a misleading instruction which told the child the sums were harder than the others. By subtracting set C from set A, a performance-after-failure index was gained.

The elegance of this design becomes apparent when we consider what Craske did next. She was interested in the differences between children who lapsed into learned helplessness and gave up and those who were motivated to protect self-worth and could be expected to try harder when they no longer had to protect their self-esteem. Craske suspected that each group would require different training to make good their failure and this was the ultimate purpose of her experiment. Twenty-nine pupils whose performance deteriorated, that is they did worse on set C than set A, entered the second part of the study. She was able to divide the groups by comparing scores on sets A and D. Those who did better on D, she considered motivated to protect their self-worth; those who did worse, had lapsed into learned helplessness.

These children then entered the reattribution

training stage. Formed into small same-sex groups, the children played an arithmetic game on the blackboard where sums were structured to have one in three designed for failure. Pupils publicly worked out these sums, were given immediate feedback on their correctness and were asked to make an attribution based on the following reasons hung on a wall chart:

I got the sum right because:

- I had good luck
- I tried hard
- It was easy
- I am clever

I got the sum wrong because:

- I had bad luck
- It was too hard
- I didn't try hard enough
- I'm not clever enough

Spontaneous effort attributions were verbally reinforced and minimal experimenter cueing elicited them when they "were not forthcoming". After this retraining period the children completed sets E, F and G, to repeat the initial measures, again completing an attributions-for-failure after set F, the failure experience.

Figure 3.6 shows Craske's results. As you can see the hypothesis that only the learned helplessness group would really benefit from training was supported and this was in line with Craske's earlier findings (Craske, 1985). The learned helplessness group seemed to be "inoculated to the experience of failure", while the self-worth group "did not respond to training". Not only did performance improve but attributional change occurred too. Both groups made increased use of external, lack-of-effort attributions to account for failure and the learned helplessness children made fewer lack-of-ability attributions.

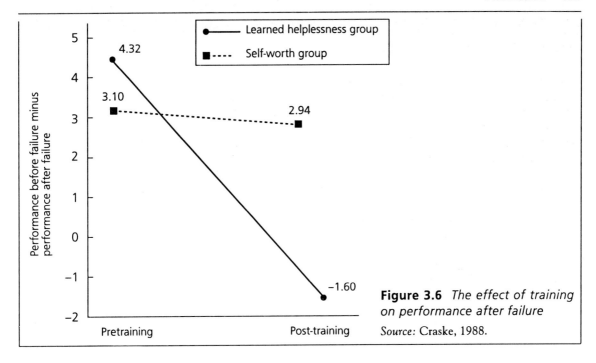

Figure 3.6 *The effect of training on performance after failure*
Source: Craske, 1988.

and lead to improved self-esteem and performance. Unfortunately, neither the effect nor the link between relief of depression and improved performance has been reliably shown, leading one reviewer (Ross & Olson, 1981) to conclude that "widespread application of misattribution therapies should await more encouraging data" (quoted in Forsterling, p. 497).

The other approach is based on Bandura's (1982) **self-efficacy theory.** Unlike misattribution therapy it does not involve arousal and simply assumes the cause of many problems lies in our attributing failure or other outcomes to stable internal factors. Reattribution therapy aims to get people to reattribute their negative state to external or at least unstable causes. This has become a particular concern of educationalists where much of the research has tried to help students experiencing academic failure to shift their attributions from stable internal (I'm stupid) to unstable external (I need to make more effort) beliefs (see Box 3.6).

self-efficacy theory
A theory which assumes the cause of many problems lies in our attributing failure and other difficulties to stable internal factors, rather than circumstances.

Summary

Social inference is a continuous cycle of construing and re-construing our world. The process starts with observation, which leads to impression formation, moves on through inferences and causal attributions of others' acts, and ends in self-reflection with us incorporating social judgments into our schemas, before the whole process starts again.

As a generalisation, research suggests that first impressions are all-important and often wrong, yet they colour our subsequent attributions. Asch noted that often single attributes colour our impressions and these attributes are then summed into algebraic and configural wholes. The order in which we notice features also shape our impressions—the primacy and recency effects.

Many factors affect our first impressions. Physical appearance and the age, sex, race and ethnicity are the first and often most durable impressions we gain of a person. That which is different or salient also captures our attention. Build is important too and taller people are usually assigned a higher status. Much work on facial features shows that our emotional reactions and impressions of others are powerfully influenced by prototypical facial patterns.

Attribution is the interpretations we place on our own and others' behaviour. Fritz Heider argued we make naive causal attributions to explain and predict and control our environment. We judge others' behaviour as either stable or unstable and make attributions about their locus of control. Attributions of responsibility and intent are central to Heider's theory.

Harold Kelley saw attribution as a process of naive scientific theorising. He suggested we look for patterns of covariance and are guided by distinctiveness, consistency and consensus in making attributions of causality. To Kelley, attribution was a process of making and refining predictions about others' behaviour and so attributions are really casual schemas in his view. In making attributions we look at the many necessary and sufficient causes of behaviour.

Our attributions are often incorrect and suffer many biases. The fundamental attribution error, or over-attribution of dispositional factors and under-attribution of situational factors, is *the* major bias. There are many reasons for this bias but salience and cognitive overload underlie most explanations. We also try to infer reasons for behaviour from situational contexts and make correspondent inferences but, as we prefer to see the world as a safe and stable place, our attributions parallel our beliefs and we will see others as acting from stable internal dispositional causes.

The actor/observer is another attributional bias. We are more likely to attribute our behaviour to situational causes and others to dispositional ones. This selective use of the fundamental attribution error shows how self-knowledge and perspective play a role in making attributions. We know more about our ourselves and so are less inclined to see our actions as reflections of our personalities. Yet, the context determines whether the actor/observer effect works and it is often in our interest to make dispositional attributions about our behaviour, so we must be cautious in assuming this effect.

While the attributional biases explain our actions, another group, the self-defensive biases, protects us from adverse evaluations. These biases are self-protective and work by reality distortion and selective perception. Often they are carefully cherished delusions and the just world hypothesis is one example. While we all hold these biases and to a certain extent they are normal, they cause problems when overused, or shift too much responsibility for our actions onto others.

The self-enhancing biases act to enhance our self-esteem at the expense of others. Unlike the self-defensive attributional biases which protect us from threat, these biases are ways we alter attributions of responsibility to our benefit. The self-serving attributional bias is when we take undue credit for successes and play down our failures. The egocentric bias is our self-centred belief that we are more important than we really are. These biases usually operate unconsciously and benefit from the passage of time and subtle shifts in memory.

The illusory attributional biases help us to alter reality to make it a safer and more orderly place and share or diminish responsibility. The false consensus bias sees our attitudes and behaviour as being typical of others, and our illusion of being in control lets us act as if our attributions are reality-based. Both subtly alter our circumstances to make life a little more bearable.

Self-handicapping attributions act in similar ways to self-handicapping behaviour. They allow us to avoid the pain of failure, or to rationalise our actions. Self-handicapping is often implicated with neuroticism and depression.

Attribution is not only about enhancing our egos but also about understanding ourselves, and emotion plays a big role in our attributions. The two-factor theory of emotion argues that we attribute reasons for our emotions after the fact and so understanding our reactions to a person or event is an attributional process.

The ease with which our emotional reactions can be misattributed has been shown by many experiments. Yet such misattribution holds out hope for dealing with many intractable emotional problems. Learned helplessness and depression are often caused by emotional misattribution. Reattributional training has done much to counter these emotional states.

Recommended reading

Bierhoff H.W. (1989) PERSON PERCEPTION AND ATTRIBUTION, Springer Verlag, Berlin. An overview of European research on social perception, impression formation, attribution and stereotyping.

Forsterling F. (1988) ATTRIBUTION THEORY IN CLINICAL PSYCHOLOGY, Wiley, NY. A translation by Jonathan Harrow of a book that has enjoyed tremendous popularity in the German-speaking world. A short monograph and fairly heavy reading but a must for those interested in the intersection of attribution theory and clinical practice.

Furnham A. (1988) LAY THEORIES: EVERYDAY UNDERSTANDING OF PROBLEMS IN SOCIAL SCIENCES, Pergamon Press, Oxford. An interesting alternative view of attribution theory. Furnham, a British researcher, examines how ordinary people construe the same sort of issues that social psychologists tackle scientifically. Interesting sections on the role that belief, doubt and commonsense play in everyday attributions.

Heider F. (1958) THE PSYCHOLOGY OF INTERPERSONAL RELATIONS, Wiley, NY. Reprinted in 1980, this is the classic text on attributional theory from one of its earliest pioneers.

Hewstone M. (1989) CAUSAL ATTRIBUTION: FROM COGNITIVE PROCESSES TO COLLECTIVE BELIEFS, Basil Blackwell, Oxford. An overview of attribution research from a European perspective, from Britain's leading researcher into attribution theory.

Weary G., Stanley M.A. and Harvey J.H. (1989) ATTRIBUTION, Springer Verlag, NY. A basic primer on attribution theory from a North American perspective. Very readable.

ATTITUDES AND BEHAVIOUR

One of the delights of academic life is the richness and challenge of a diverse student body, particularly in the newer universities where we have spent our teaching careers. Every semester brings a new cohort of students whose multiculturalism inevitably challenges the way a couple of Anglo social psychologists see things—and some more so than others. This came to a particularly sharp focus in a course where I ask students to write a 2000 word essay challenging them to explore their worldviews as a way of introducing the whole topic of attitudes and their formation. In ten years I thought I had covered the whole gamut of beliefs (which for the most part are fairly conventional) but one day I met a man who worshipped garden gnomes.

The student, a civil engineer in his early thirties, wrote that the world is full of spiritual forces and even inanimate objects like rocks and trees possess souls. Their influence in human affairs, he asserted, is profound and only the difference in our metabolic rates clouds our consciousness of their power. Trees that live for hundreds of years think and act more slowly than we do. In a similar way, rocks take an almost geologic view of humankind. Nevertheless, they exercise immense power and can act decisively to discipline we ephemerals when we step out of line. Floods, earthquakes and the whole ecological crisis were, in his view, active interventions in human affairs. This view, known in theological circles as primitive animism, was quite surprising coming from a sophisticated Westerner; you are more likely to encounter it in tribal cultures.

How do the gnomes fit in? He argued that gnomes are the symbolic representatives of an awesome slumbering power. Although we have forsaken the gods of our remote antiquity, we still possess some sort of unconscious race memory, and gnomes on our front lawns are an equally unconscious attempt to placate these spiritual forces. He went on to argue in an almost Tolkienesque way that garden gnomes tend to run heavily to trolls, dwarfs, elves and pixies which suggests that we still give some credence to these almost universal human archetypes. Moreover, gnomes themselves have spirits and, as the deity's representatives cast in quasi-human form, they are very powerful and do not slumber like their masters. We mock them at our peril.

I confess that I thought he was fooling me and challenged him. Unfortunately I deeply offended his religious sentiments and he invited me to a gnome worship service. Intrigued, I visited his inner-city house which had a population of over 300 plaster gnomes strategically located in every room: in his bath, bed, oven, cemented to his chimney, and under the floor. He explained that a successful life required their immediate oversight of each human activity. I also noted a great number of gnomes in neighbours' yards, so the gnomes were obviously getting their point across. Thirty people gathered on Wednesday night and adjourned to a room to commune with at least 100 different gnomes. We sang several hymns of praise in their honour and then the gnomes were ceremoniously dusted. We concluded by offering prayers, making requests of them and then leaving money, food and drink offerings. The whole experience was quite unselfconscious and had faintly Buddhist overtones.

Over the next few weeks I plumbed his belief system and the attitudes it entailed. I was curious to see how a civil engineer could square his views with

*the hard science his workaday career required and how he came to hold such
unconventional attitudes. I gradually built up a picture of a person who lived in
two different worlds and who dealt with a discrepant reality by compartmental-
ising his life. In one mental compartment he was a civil engineer and in another
a gnome worshipper. I never did find out how he came by his beliefs as he
dropped out of the course a few weeks later. However, I am in no doubt that he
was as sane as the next person and that he genuinely held his beliefs. My
curiosity will have to wait until the next gnome worshipper comes my way.*

An overview of attitudinal research

Attitude research is one of the oldest and most comprehensively studied
branches of personality and social psychology. Long before modern psychology's
birth, attitudinal theorising was a well-established practice. The ancient
Greeks as acute observers left us many accounts of how fate and upbringing
shape our attitudes and Plato's *Dialogues* stand as a prime example. In turn
Roman, Byzantine, Arabic and Mediaeval scholars continued in this tradition
until Spinoza's epic *Ethics* (1677) marked a turning point towards a more
introspective, research-oriented view. The enlightenment brought a resurgent
interest in attitudes with David Hume's *A Treatise on Human Nature* (1739)
as a high watermark. Modern attitudinal psychology draws its roots from
this tradition and from the rise of a scientific study of humanity in the
nineteenth century. As you read this chapter, be aware that there is a
long tradition behind modern attitudinal research. (For an interesting
review of the history of just one aspect of attitude theory, see Weir, 1983.)

Despite this impressive ancestry, attitude research is clearly on the
wane. This does not mean that research has diminished, rather it continues
to steadily increase. This is not a paradox but rather points to a sharp
division between *process* and *content*. As you will see as you read through
this chapter, research into the nature of attitudes had its heyday in the
1950s and 1960s. It then experienced a brief renaissance in the early
1980s and theoretical interest has fallen sharply since then (Abelson,
1983; McGuire, 1986). However, research into the content of specific
attitudes is still as vigorous as ever.

As you read the literature you will find three types of study. Developmental
psychologists are interested in how we acquire attitudes; personality theorists
measure their structure and content; and social psychologists investigate
how they work. While the developmental material is easy to pick, distinguishing
between the other two is often more difficult. Remember that personality
theorists want to know *what* we think about an issue or its content, for
example our views on racism, and use personality tests and related measures
to find out. Social psychologists on the other hand are less interested in
content but want to know *how* attitudes tick and what are their underlying
processes and functions. The difficulty for students arises because in practice

these two research areas largely overlap, interested researchers studying both issues and using many common research methods.

The distinction is a useful one though. Social psychology students faced with an essay on attitude theory often serve up reams of personality research believing it to be appropriate. Unfortunately this does not tell us much about *how* attitudes develop. This is an easy trap to fall into when you consider the prolific work of personality theorists. For example, in preparing this book, we found that since 1982 there were over 200 Australian and New Zealand attitude articles in psychological journals and as many from other disciplines, mainly in sociology and anthropology. Virtually all of these were personality articles and/or developmental in nature; few drew the sorts of connections between attitude content and underlying processes that would be of interest to a social psychologist. Do not worry unduly about these distinctions, as many local researchers' interests straddle

---

Box 4.1 *The tall poppy syndrome*

Norm Feather is the Foundation Professor of Psychology at the Flinders University of South Australia in Adelaide. He is a graduate of Sydney University and the University of New England and was awarded his doctoral degree from the University of Michigan in 1960. He is past President of the Australian Psychological Society and a Fellow of the Academy of Social Sciences in Australia. His research interests include achievement motivation, attribution theory, the psychology of values, the psychological impact of unemployment, expectancy-value theories, the psychology of justice, and social attitudes in Australia and elsewhere. He is the author or editor of five books that include: A Theory of Achievement Motivation *(1966) (with John Atkinson),* Expectations and Actions: Expectancy-value Models in Psychology *(1982) and* The Psychological Impact of Unemployment *(1990).*
(Photo: courtesy Norm Feather)

A **tall poppy** is someone who is sufficiently successful and in the public eye enough to attract our admiration and/or envy. Feather notes the term goes back to ancient times:

> The Roman historian Livy, refers to the symbolic decapitation of the heads of the tallest poppies by the elder Tarquinius when walking in his garden. This message was conveyed to his son, Sextus Tarquinius, who then rid himself of the chief men of the state of Gabii and thus delivered the state unresisting to the Roman king. (Feather, 1989, p. 265)

We love to criticise our leaders and election campaigns are prime time for lopping tall poppies. However, some leaders seem to thrive on such treatment.
(Photo: Chris Simkin)

Feather's interest in this area flows from his earlier work on achievement motivation. While we know a reasonable amount about how people strive for success, our knowledge of how we regard successful people is "relatively sparse". Feather was not only interested in extending our understanding but was curious about a particularly Australian satisfaction "when tall poppies are cut down to size and suffer a major reverse in status". He speculated that while Australians are taught to value competence, individualism and accomplishment, we are also ambivalent about success and the successful. The reasons for our ambivalence are unclear. Perhaps it is part of a pervasive collectivist streak in the Australian psyche which tells us

"Jack's as good as his mate" and "not to get too full of ourselves"; or simply to "keep our heads down". Still, other cultures have ambivalent attitudes towards the successful, so perhaps it is a simple case of envy? Feather noted research that made a distinction between affection and admiration, and speculated that "we do not necessarily choose as our friends those whom we admire and respect". Perhaps our ambivalence is an extreme case of this distinction. While we admire success, we might see the successful in a slightly self-protective way, as "distant, unsociable unscrupulous and overly competitive". Whatever the reasons for this attitude, Feather was sure it was a multi-variable phenomenon and that "a global approach to understanding how people react to the fall of tall poppies is likely to be unattainable".

To clear the undergrowth a little and initiate a new field of investigation, Feather conducted three studies which he reported in 1989. In the first, he gave a questionnaire and rating scales to 531 Year Eleven Adelaide secondary students, to examine their attitudes and attributions towards the fall of a high and an average achiever. Students were given a classroom scenario where two mythical students fell moderately or disastrously below their usual performance at their final matriculation exam. Feather made four trial hypotheses: that the subjects would have more mixed and ambivalent attitudes towards the fall of the high achiever; that they would be more pleased about their fall than they were about that of the average achiever; that subjects would be more pleased if the high performer's fall was only to the average performance position and not to the bottom of the class; and that those who were more strongly attracted to the high and average performers would be less pleased about their fall. Feather's results met all four hypotheses as far as the fall went but he found his subjects were not initially more negative towards the higher achiever, when compared with the lower achiever. The mix of their ratings differed but average attraction scores were similar. Feather concluded: "We may need to ask more subtle questions to uncover mixed feelings towards a high achiever."

Feather's second study used a similar scenario

with 361 Introductory Psychology students at Flinders University. In this study he gave reasons for the tall poppy's and average performer's fall. His scenario had two mythical university students failing because they were caught cheating in an exam. He hypothesised that his subjects would be more punitive towards the tall poppy because of generalised social norms which put an extra burden of responsibility on those in the public eye, and this allowed subjects to cut the high achiever down to size, making them more like the average person. Equally Feather suggested, subjects might suspect that the high flyer had got there because of similar behaviour in the past and being extra punitive is an appropriate "pay-back". Feather's findings support his hypothesis. Subjects were more punitive and more pleased about the high achiever's fall than that of the average performer, though Feather cautions this might be for different reasons than in his first study.

In the third study, Feather designed a Tall Poppy Scale (see Table 4.1) and administered it to 205 members of Adelaide's general population, along with a values survey and self-esteem measure. In this survey he was interested in comparing value preferences and global self-esteem with the tall poppy syndrome. Feather hypothesised that those with low self-esteem, feelings of relative deprivation or frustration, would suffer by comparing themselves to high achievers. This process of social comparison (see Chapter Eight) would put them in a poor light, particularly when comparing themselves to those with whom they can identify or see some similarity. Subjects could offset this adverse comparison by running down the tall poppies. Feather also speculated that "a desire to bring down a tall poppy will be related to underlying values". Those with more collectivist

Table 4.1 *Feather's tall poppy scale*

Item

1. People who are very successful deserve all the rewards they get for their achievements.
2. It's good to see very successful people fail occasionally.
3. Very successful people often get too big for their boots.
4. People who are successful in what they do are usually friendly and helpful to others.
5. At school it's probably better for students to be near the middle of the class than the very top student.
6. People shouldn't criticise or knock the very successful.
7. Very successful people who fall from the top usually deserve their fall from grace.
8. Those who are very successful ought to come down off their pedestals and be like other people.
9. The very successful person should receive public recognition for his/her accomplishments.
10. People who are "tall poppies" should be cut down to size.
11. One should always respect the person at the top.
12. One ought to be sympathetic to very successful people when they experience failure and fall from their very high positions.
13. Very successful people sometimes need to be brought back a peg or two, even if they have done nothing wrong.
14. Society needs a lot of very high achievers.
15. People who always do a lot better than others need to learn what it's like to fail.
16. People who are right at the top usually deserve their high position.
17. It's very important for society to support and encourage people who are very successful.
18. People who are very successful get too full of their own importance.
19. Very successful people usually succeed at the expense of other people.
20. Very successful people who are at the top of their field are usually fun to be with.

Source: Feather, 1989.

values would be more likely to approve of a tall poppy's fall and those who favour individual achievement and the like, less so. Again in this third study Feather's hypotheses were sustained.

So where are we? Feather's three studies taken as a whole tell us that a tall poppies effect does exist; that an observer's perceived similarity to the high achiever will determine their sympathy for the tall poppy after their fall, unless of course they brought it on themselves by shoddy practice. Our values play an important part in our approval of high flyers. Those who believe in individual effort and initiative will favour them, and those who believe in more egalitarian, collective values will be less approving and more likely to cheer after a high flyer

crashes. Our own self-evaluation also determines our views. Those of us who suffer by comparison with a tall poppy are more likely to be envious and suffer the pangs of jealousy.

Feather was cautious to stress in his conclusion that many other variables influence this attitude and that we are just at the beginning of our study of the tall poppies attitude. He stressed that it was a study into a specific type of attitude and that at this stage he was not going to attempt "to explain the research findings in terms of some universal theory". Indeed he concludes "that could turn out a fruitless exercise". Professor Feather's research is not concluded and he continues to tease out the dimensions of this interesting attitude (Feather, 1991, 1992).

---

all three areas; but it is a useful distinction to keep in mind as you are reading the literature. To reinforce this point, we will look at Feather's study of the **tall poppy syndrome**.

tall poppy syndrome
Prejudice against those who are successful; desire to see them fall from favour.

What are attitudes?

Daryl Bem, whose self-perception theory we will cover later in the chapter, defined attitudes simply as "our likes and dislikes" (Bem, 1970). Attitudes, he felt, were our affinities and aversions to the world around us and have both referent and evaluative components. When we express an opinion we are making a judgment (evaluation) about someone or something (the referent). This one-dimensional theory stresses a social perception approach to attitude research. We are using our social knowledge to interpret and attribute reasons for another's behaviour, and our attitudes are the repository of all our previous schematic processing on the subject. When we say we like Prokofiev's Symphony No. 2 in D Minor, our opinion rests on our prior knowledge of Russian classical music of that period. We have a standard of comparison to justify our belief and may enjoy Prokofiev's intense dramatic quality, in comparison to the livelier, lighter work of his contemporary, Ravel. When attitudes express an opinion, they do so for good, if not necessarily accurate, reasons.

Social psychologists use the term **attitude** in a precise way meaning "our evaluation of an object or person" (Fishbein & Ajzen, 1975). In common usage *attitude* is synonymous with *feelings*, *values*, *beliefs* and *opinions* but there are distinct differences. Our emotions may well be at odds with

An ABC of beliefs

attitude
A relatively stable pattern of beliefs, actions and feelings about an object or person.

our attitudes. For instance, a friend supported Muldoon's 1984 re-election bid because she agreed with his fiscal policies, even though she felt he had the soul of an accountant. She much preferred the ebullient personality of David Lange who, to her regret, succeeded Muldoon as New Zealand's Prime Minister. Nor do our values and beliefs exactly correspond with attitudes. Our beliefs represent our expectations, and our values the importance we assign them, but neither are strictly evaluations. To give another example, many people believe in the stars and eagerly anticipate their destiny (values and beliefs), yet when pressed admit they think astrology is rubbish (attitudes).

Values and beliefs are intimately connected with our attitudes, strengthening and reinforcing each other. Belief connects objects to attributes (Fishbein & Ajzen, 1975) and even the most dismal politicians may be favourably evaluated as statesmen if we believe their policies are apt. Strength of belief and/or values correlates with attitudinal strength (Rokeach, 1973). The more we know about something, the more likely we are to hold definite values and similar attitudes. Beliefs and values, therefore, while not evaluations have strong connections with attitudes. Opinions on the other hand *are* evaluations, yet they lack the cognitive underpinnings of attitudes. In some ways this is a fine distinction but attitudes as viewed by psychologists are reasoned views, while opinions are evaluations without much foundation. When social psychologists use the term "attitudes" they do so in a precise and operationalisable way.

Many people believe in the stars and eagerly read their horoscopes in the weeklies but, when pressed, admit they think astrology is rubbish.
(Photo: Gavin Price)

Attitudes, behaviour and cognition

In contrast to Bem's definition, another approach defining attitudes concentrates on the components that underlie our evaluations—what attitudes are, rather than what they do. This approach, which goes back to the earliest foundations of psychology (Oskamp, 1977), emphasises the affective (emotional), behavioural and cognitive components, or the **ABC theory** of attitudes (Breckler, 1984). When we are attracted to someone, we have positive feelings about them, act positively towards them and tell ourselves why we feel as we do. Attitudes, in this view, are an evaluation and an intention to act, reinforced by the appropriate emotions.

ABC theory
Theory that attitudes are composed of affective (emotional), behavioural and cognitive components.

The ABC account stresses the link between attitudes and behaviour but does not say that one necessarily determines the other. As we will see, there are many discrepancies between what we think, or say, and actually do (LaPiere, 1934). Even so, holding appropriate values, attitudes and beliefs increases the *probability* that we will act in a certain way and we are on reasonably safe ground inferring that attitudes will predispose us to certain kindred behaviours (Fishbein & Ajzen, 1975). This approach is important as it reminds us that attitudes often lead to extreme behaviour and to biased and unrealistic stereotypes. We will return to stereotypes in the next chapter.

Do attitudes determine behaviour?

Do attitudes determine our behaviour? This is perhaps *the* most fundamental question within attitudinal research and in many ways would be "the keys to the kingdom of behaviour change" if it were only so—but is it? Does a belief in spirits of the rocks and forests compel one to become a gnome worshipper? If so, why? We acquire our attitudes as part of our upbringing and from our immediate hands-on knowledge of what works and what does not. This would argue there is a strong attitude-behaviour link, that our attitudes will determine our behaviour. Unfortunately this link has proved anything but deterministic and, as Zanna and Fazio (1982) note in their review, research seems to have gone through three phases in addressing the question.

Once upon a time attitudinal researchers uncritically accepted that attitudes were sure guides to conduct. Then along came a race-relations sociologist, Robert LaPiere (1934), who challenged this cosy assumption and ushered in the first wave of research. LaPiere found strong evidence that attitudes did not necessarily predict related actions. In the midst of the Great Depression, when anti-Asian attitudes were at their height in the United States, LaPiere, accompanied by a young Chinese-American couple, visited 251 hotels and restaurants. Despite the prejudice of the day they were only once refused service. However, he later sent a questionnaire to the same places asking, among other things, "Do you accept members

Robert LaPiere found that racist attitudes towards Asians did not necessarily translate to actual discrimination, shaking our certainty of the attitude–behaviour link.

of the Chinese race as guests in your establishment?" Of the 128 replies, less than 10 per cent were willing to accept Chinese customers! Several studies gave similar results throughout the 1950s and 1960s, leading theorists to conclude that attitudes do not predict behaviour. Alan Wicker (1969), in an influential review of over thirty such studies, concluded there was little evidence for an attitude-behaviour link.

However, the very definiteness of Wicker's conclusions went against the commonsense view that attitudes do change behaviour. This prompted a thoroughgoing re-evaluation of the previous evidence and ushered in a second wave of theorising (Zanna & Fazio, 1982) that found LaPiere's and others' studies were methodologically suspect (Ajzen & Fishbein, 1980). LaPiere, for example, wrote six months after his visits and had no surety that the people replying to his letters were the ones who had served him. Nor was he able to control for the force of habit, or embarrassment, that may have led waiters to serve his companions, even if they did not want to (Dawes & Smith, 1985). The six months that went by before LaPiere wrote to the hoteliers and restaurateurs gave more than enough time for them to change their racist views, and so forth. Flaws like these threw similar findings into question and through the 1970s, theorists again began to ask if attitudes might affect behaviour.

Zanna and Fazio propose that subsequent theorists quickly found that attitudes did lead to behaviour, *though only in some circumstances.* The third wave of theorists are now preoccupied with teasing out the "how" and "why" of the attitude-behaviour link. We will consider the nature of this link before turning to its determinants.

How do attitudes determine behaviour?

At the outset please understand that this is one of the most controversial areas of social psychology and a *direct* relationship between attitudes and subsequent behaviour is almost impossible to prove conclusively. Nevertheless, they are linked, but sorting out the intervening variables has proved a veritable dog's breakfast with any number of factors influencing the result. Several factors complicate a straightforward relationship not the least of which is our inability to measure attitudes directly. At best we are measuring *expressed* attitudes and behavioural intentions, which as we have already seen are weak and unreliable guides to behaviour. Further, attitudes are extremely difficult to define, and personality tests, which are the main way we operationalise attitudes, are among the most disputed aspects of psychological experimentation (Cook M., 1984; McGuire, 1985). Such tests rarely allow us to conclude there is a causal link between attitudes and behaviour (Mischel, 1968). With these caveats in mind, how do attitudes lead to behaviour?

A theory of reasoned action

Fishbein and Ajzen's **theory of reasoned behaviour** provided the conceptual breakthrough that allowed attitudes and behaviour to be theoretically linked. The theory is quite predictive (Ajzen & Fishbein, 1980; Vallerand et al., 1992) and has been used to predict students' academic aspirations and later college attendance (Carpenter & Fleishman, 1987); women taking precautions against cervical cancer (Hennig & Knowles, 1990); individual differences in behavioural intentions (Kashima & Kashima, 1988); and education and AIDS risk behaviour (Ross & Rosser, 1989), to name only a few of the many local studies.

theory of reasoned behaviour
The attitude–behaviour link is partly determined by social norms and our subjective evaluation.

Ajzen and Fishbein argue that earlier studies failed to find a link between attitudes and behaviour because they ignored the **specificity variable**, which suggests that general attitudes are only very loosely related to specific behaviours. If we wish to increase predictive efficiency, we need to specify precisely *which* attitude leads to *what* behaviour. For example, in Chapter Thirteen we will see that general pro-ecological attitudes are poor predictors of recycling behaviour but specific attitudes towards recycling are more likely to predict recycling rates (Oskamp et al., 1991). This is hardly surprising when you consider that the best guide to future behaviour is our past actions (Fazio & Zanna, 1978; Chaiken & Stangor, 1987). Avid recyclers are likely to hold detailed recycling attitudes and just keep on recycling. Ajzen and Fishbein's model would predict, for example, that although recycling was part of a general pro-ecological attitude, it said nothing about recyclers' interests in conserving Leadbeater's possums. Wicker's review, which showed a weak connection between general attitudes and specific behaviours, was therefore to be expected but his conclusions were conceptually flawed.

specificity variable
Being able to precisely specify which of many factors influence behaviour.

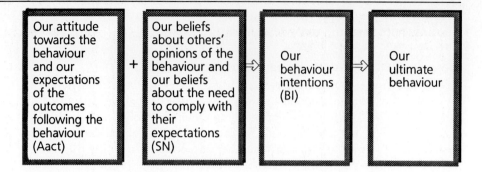

Figure 4.1
A model of reasoned action

Source: Adapted from Fishbein & Ajzen, 1975.

Figure 4.1 sets out the basics of Fishbein and Ajzen's theory. In essence it is a theory of how our subjective evaluation of social norms impacts on our attitudes and behaviour. In their model, our subjective evaluation of a proposed behaviour (Aact) and the social norms (SN) that surround it, combine to influence our behavioural intentions. The relative importance of these two variables in determining behaviour will vary from issue to issue. How we feel about the proposed act and the strength of our beliefs will also have an influence. For example, Grace and Hussein's inter-racial marriage went ahead despite her parents' strenuous objections and the disapproval of her friends, because both parties held very strong beliefs that discounted the objections raised. Even so, from Figure 4.2 you will see that they married for very different reasons.

The reasoned action theory is just that, a theory of *reasoned* action. Ajzen and Fishbein assume we deliberately think through the consequences of our actions and that our attitudes determine our behavioural intentions. That conscious choice is a factor in our behaviour may prove a weakness in their theory. Often we seem to act automatically and our behaviour is not always entirely under our control and has involuntary aspects to it (Ajzen & Madden, 1986). This led Ajzen (1987) to suggest a further modification to their theory, perceived control, to take account of perceived constraints.

The theory of reasoned action is also a composite theory, relying on multiple measures for its accuracy. Fishbein and Ajzen (1975) argue that many attitudes are not single acts but rather classes of behaviour. In LaPiere's study for instance, racism may be found not so much in a refusal of service but in other more subtle behaviours like poor service, cold meals, or giving the worst room. They argue that, in addition, single observation measures like those reported by Wicker are poor approximations of real life. Too many "one-off" factors could influence the result on the day. To test their predictions, Fishbein and Ajzen (1974) correlated religious attitudes with behaviour. Single religious acts correlated poorly with religious attitudes, though when responses to 70 religious behaviours were correlated with religious attitudes, correlations climbed from +.15 to +.70. Zanna, Olson

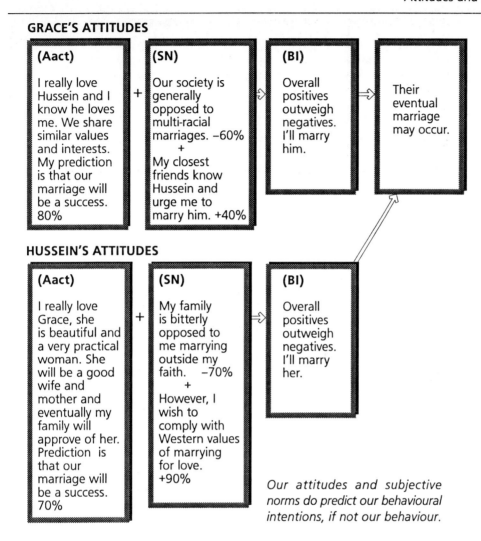

GRACE'S ATTITUDES

(Aact)	(SN)	(BI)	
I really love Hussein and I know he loves me. We share similar values and interests. My prediction is that our marriage will be a success. 80%	+ Our society is generally opposed to multi-racial marriages. –60% + My closest friends know Hussein and urge me to marry him. +40%	Overall positives outweigh negatives. I'll marry him.	Their eventual marriage may occur.

HUSSEIN'S ATTITUDES

(Aact)	(SN)	(BI)
I really love Grace, she is beautiful and a very practical woman. She will be a good wife and mother and eventually my family will approve of her. Prediction is that our marriage will be a success. 70%	+ My family is bitterly opposed to me marrying outside my faith. –70% + However, I wish to comply with Western values of marrying for love. +90%	Overall positives outweigh negatives. I'll marry her.

Our attitudes and subjective norms do predict our behavioural intentions, if not our behaviour.

Figure 4.2
Why did Hussein and Grace marry?

Source: Adapted from Fishbein & Ajzen, 1975.

and Fazio (1980) found a similar result with a composite of 90 religious behaviours. Fishbein and Ajzen argue that a multiple act criterion must be adopted to ensure predictive efficiency. Put simply, the more ways you measure behavioural intention, the more strongly it is linked with attitudes.

Equally, the more precisely and concretely you define attitudes, the more likely they will predict behaviour. In predicting voting trends at the next election, we are less interested in whether people are conservatives, or Labor supporters, than in their current attitudes towards incumbents. Many a supporter has voted their preferred party out of office because they have become disillusioned with its representatives. Fishbein and Ajzen suggest that a way around such difficulties is to measure attitudes towards *behaviours* rather than *objects*. Many studies have shown their model accurately predicts behaviour (Peay, 1980), though several tests of their extended model have raised doubts about its explanatory power (Dickson & Miniard, 1978).

When do attitudes determine behaviour?

Asking "when" of Fishbein and Ajzen's model is rather like asking how long is a piece of string. Figure 4.3 shows just a few of the many intervening variables that influences our behaviour (and see also our section "When Will We Help?" in Chapter Ten). A multitude of factors impinging on our decision decides our behaviour.

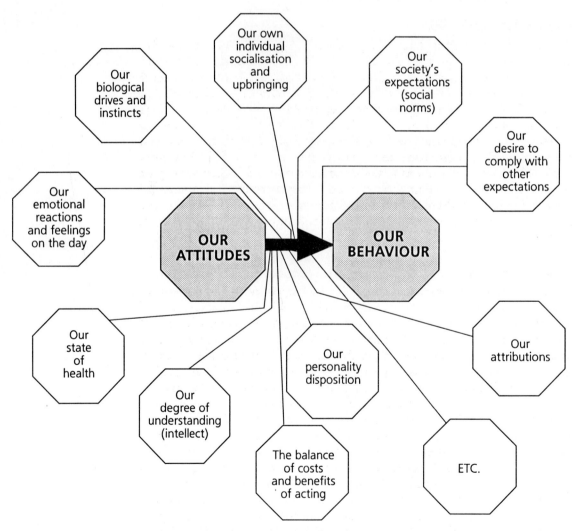

Figure 4.3 *Mediating variables between attitude and behaviour. There are many reasons for not acting in accordance with our attitudes*

Situational factors

Simple situational factors are important mediating variables. The time between an intention and an act is important. Someone may convince you to recycle but any number of things may stymie actual recycling behaviour if three weeks go by before you have a chance to implement your commitment. A recycler may decide to buy only products whose packaging may be reused but is impotent because they do not make the purchasing decisions for their family. Similarly, holding general attitudes may not translate into specific behaviours. Our recycler may decide that an ecological attitude should also include a personal commitment to conserving endangered species, but unfortunately they are so busy recycling they have neither the time nor opportunity to put these good intentions to work (Fishbein & Ajzen, 1975).

Personality variables

Personality is a crucial determinant of the reasoned action theory. For example, our level of self-awareness will affect our actions. High self-monitors, who continually assess their performance in the light of situational factors, will have a greater variability in their behaviour. They are less influenced by their attitudes and will react more to the demands of the moment (Snyder & Swann, 1976). Those who are low self-monitors, by contrast, will have greater insight and be freer from the influence of social norms and will act more consistently with their attitudes (Miller & Grush, 1986). However, this is not as straightforward as it seems. Directing people's attention to the way their attitudes work decreases the consistency of their behaviour, perhaps by forcing them to differentiate between the emotional and cognitive components of their behaviour (Wilson & Dunn, 1986).

Locus of control

Another important determinant of attitude's impact on behaviour is how in control we feel we are. Julian Rotter (1966, 1973, 1975) argued that if we believe that others control our behaviour (external locus of control) then we are more likely to be influenced by our situation and less so by internal factors like attitudes. Rotter's Locus of Control Scale is one of the most intensively studied aspects of social psychology and personality theory (Strickland, 1989). Substantial research has also shown that our locus of control is a very stable trait and our self-attributions are consistent over time (Rotter, 1975). An externally oriented person, when faced with a run of bad luck will attribute their misfortunes to uncontrollable external forces: malign fates, others' interference and to just plain bad luck. Indeed Ray (1980b) has argued that Rotter's scale "is actually measuring belief in luck and its empirical correlates" rather than locus of control itself.

The link between this trait and behavioural intentions is rather obvious. *Internals* take responsibility for their own actions and their behaviour is more closely tied to their attitudes (Rotter, 1975; Strickland, 1988). These people see the connection between their attitudes and circumstances and

Developmental psychology suggests that children have a more external locus of control than adults. Experiences beyond their control shape attitudes in later life, reinforcing an external locus.

actively shape their lives. In short, they are more in control of their lives than *externals*. Literally hundreds of studies have shown this effect. For example, Gordon O'Brien of Flinders University interviewed 300 male and female retirees about their satisfaction with retirement. You would expect internals to be more in charge of their lives and show higher levels of contentment following retirement. O'Brien found just that. Rotter's scale was a significant predictor of retirement satisfaction for men and of life satisfaction for women. While the results for other factors were mixed, on the whole internals were more satisfied with their life and retirement than externals (O'Brien, 1981). Similar results were found by Helen Place from Waikato University. Place gave a life history questionnaire to 130 middle-aged women managers in New Zealand's public and private sectors. Her results showed that the most important predictor of managerial effectiveness was an internal locus of control. She concluded: "The girl who perceives herself as controlling and mastering her adolescent environment is likely to become the woman who succeeds in management" (Place, 1979). Also see Innes and Thomas' (1989) study of attributional style, and the self-efficacy, social avoidance and inhibition of Australian secondary school students.

While locus of control is sometimes a significant predictor of behaviour, we must be cautious in making this link (Parker, 1980). Many factors alter our self-attributions and it is often difficult to show how they influence our behaviour. Rotter (1975) cautioned that locus of control is a multi-attitudinal attribution and that one belief may predispose behaviour while another limits it. For example, you may believe that nothing you do will help you pass your course and that lecturers are totally responsible for your abysmal grades. However, rather than giving up and lapsing into apathy, your awareness that unemployment looms large on the horizon may keep you struggling with the books, and you achieve a grade that

Box 4.2 *Are Australians more externally controlled than Americans?*

Rotter's internal-external locus of control theory attracted much international interest and support. However, the international community was less happy with Rotter's scale, which was normed on 1180 Introductory Psychology students at Ohio State University. Several cross-cultural studies quickly challenged the universal applicability of these norms (McGinnies et al., 1974; Watkins, 1980).

Prue Gorman, Luke Jones and Jacqui Holman of the Australian National University, Canberra, sounded a warning to local researchers. In a short *Australian Psychologist* article, Gorman et al. (1980) reported using Rotter's scale on 159 first year students. They advised that their "results indicated a substantially higher (external) score, for the Canberra population, than that reported by Rotter". They tried to account for this unexpected result in several ways. Perhaps the 15 years between their study and Rotter's

had dated his norms? A second possibility was that differences in university admission procedures between US and Australia may have given two distinctly different groups of students, leading to an apples and pears comparison. Another possibility was that Australian students were genuinely more external than Americans, and they were measuring real cultural differences. A final possibility was that their sample was too small and their results were erroneous. Not knowing the answers but worried, they appealed "to those interested in these results, and having a larger first year population than ours, to replicate".

Their appeal prompted a swift response from Robert Lange and Marika Tiggemann (1980) of Adelaide University who reported several unpublished studies using Rotter's Internal-External Locus of Control Scale on undergraduates and confirmed Gorman's results. They also reviewed

Table 4.2 *External locus of control. Means and standard deviations of introversion and extroversion scores for Australian undergraduate samples*

	N	Sex	Mean	SD
Feather (1967)	31	M	8.90	2.84
	53	F	10.96	4.09
	153	M	9.54	4.22
	46	F	7.67	3.82
McGinnies, Nordholm, Ward and Bhanthumnavin (1974)	105	M	9.92	3.60
	164	F	11.54	3.76
Lange (1977)	104	M	11.13	4.00
	173	F	11.71	4.26
Lange and Tiggemann (1979)	30	M	11.83	4.98
	63	F	12.67	4.52
Lange (1979)	38	M	11.55	3.83
Gorman, Jones and Holman (1980)	65	M	12.12	4.09
	94	F	12.14	4.16

Source: Lange & Tiggemann, 1980.

several other Australian studies (see Table 4.2) and indicated "that over the past decade there has been a gradual shift within the population towards a more external locus of control". Lange and Tiggemann noted that Feather (1967a) had found similar results to Rotter's sample and doubted that more recent studies like Gorman's reflected "true cross-cultural differences in personality or university admissions procedures". They agreed with Gorman and her colleagues that both American and Australian students' attitudes had probably changed since the heady days of the mid-sixties' student protests, and argued that harder economic times had made students more realistic. They concluded that "the norms of the mid-1960s are not suitable for use with Australian populations and serious doubt must exist about their continued use with American populations".

Robert Spillane from Macquarie University took a different approach, arguing there *were* real cultural differences. He compared Australian and American MBA candidates in 1977–78 and found Australians were significantly more external in their orientation and noted similar results for municipal administrators. Spillane also reported eight years' research on 829 Australian managers in the public and private sectors that gave similar results. Commenting on his findings, Spillane argued that differences in the Protestant Ethic may have led Australian managers to being more external. While American managers:

. . . have a high achievement and competence orientation, emphasise . . . profit maximisation, organisational efficiency and high productivity . . . Australian managers tend . . . to be dependent on government; lacking in boldness and initiative; dependent on overseas sources for capital, ideas and techniques; conservative; interested in leisure, social activity and family; non-aggressive; low in Machiavellian characteristics; egalitarian both socially and at the workplace. In sum, it might be predicted that Australian managers would show more of an external orientation than their American counterparts. (Spillane, 1980, p. 498)

So where are we? Do Americans and Australians differ significantly or is it just a problem of dated and/or inappropriate norms? David Watkins, another contributor to the 1980 debate, while noting similar findings to Gorman et al., questioned whether the Rotter scale was the most appropriate instrument to measure locus of control in any case. He noted the multi-dimensional nature of internality-externality and suggested that newer instruments such as Levenson's (1972) scale were more valid measures. Perhaps he was right. Research since 1980 has shown clear international differences in locus of control and the difficulties of adequately measuring this construct.

surprises you. Locus of control is further complicated by situational influences. To a certain extent everyone is controlled by their environment and often our actions are quite independent of our attitudes, however much we might believe otherwise.

Despite the strength of this effect, many studies failed to find clear correlations (Phares, 1976). In addition, several critiques challenge the assumption that Rotter's scale predicts behaviour and as we saw in Box 4.2 Lange and Tiggemann raise serious doubts about the scale's norms. Strickland (1988) argues that not only are the norms suspect but they reflect middle-class attitudes and social values, so are unsuitable for assessing minority worldviews. Ray (1980b) doubts that Rotter's central concept of *controllability* is in fact what is being measured; while Weiner (1986) argues that Rotter's concept confuses our *efforts* which are under our control and our *ability* which is not. Nevertheless, despite these critiques, Rotter's construct has shown a clear link over hundreds of studies. Perhaps this is just another case of "Attitudes do determine behaviour, sometimes".

Attitude strength

As we saw in Chapters Two and Three, a schema's strength and availability increases its usefulness. The more we know about something, the stronger our schemas and the more consistent our attitudes and behaviour will be. Familiarity with the object or person at the sharp end of our attitudes polarises our intentions more so than secondhand experience. Attitudes we acquire directly are more vivid and have greater perseverance than those indirectly acquired. Their power to promote consistent behaviour is obviously strengthened if we hold a range of related attitudes (Fazio & Zanna, 1981). Many people hold racist views with little foundation, while others feel they have good and sufficient reasons for their prejudice, having suffered at the hands of those they despise. Much of the recent debate about Japanese trading policies is still coloured by war experiences of fifty years ago. This led one politician to comment ruefully that a generation needs to die out before we will be really comfortable with the Japanese. As we will see in Chapter Eight, Alex's war experiences were so formative that they still interfere with his everyday life. The corollary of all this, Fazio (1986) reminds us, is the more easily attitudes are called to mind, the more readily they determine behaviour. The more central they are to our make-up, the more powerful they will be. This is a basic principle of personality research, which distinguishes between core and peripheral traits.

One of the longest running debates within psychology, and a major preoccupation of some personality researchers, is how far do **personality traits** control behaviour? Character traits are stable and enduring personality features with attitudinal and behavioural components. Trait theorists believe they do determine behaviour and have long sought distinctive traits to support their view. The extensive enterprise of personality testing rests in part on this assumption but unfortunately research suggests traits are even less accurate predictors than attitudes; or are they?

Many researchers over the years have found traits poorly predict behaviour (see Epstein & O'Brien, 1985, for a review). Such findings led Walter Mischel in his book, *Personality and Assessment* (1968), to make a sustained attack on trait research. Low correlations between traits and behaviour, Mischel argued, show behaviour is "specific to the situation". It was not good enough to argue that a general personality disposition predisposed certain behaviour, rather the real test was if traits did so consistently across similar situations. The crux of his argument is a **consistency paradox:** we believe that personality predicts behaviour, and perhaps it does in a general way, but not consistently. A trait of thriftiness may predict cost-consciousness but does not necessarily predict frugality, or recycling behaviour.

Unfortunately even responses to "highly similar situations often fail to be related". For personality dispositions to be truly predictive they must

Is personality a poor predictor of behaviour?

personality traits
Relatively stable and enduring aspects of personality.

consistency paradox
Personality predicts behaviour, but at too high a level of generality to be useful in predicting specific behaviours.

be stable *and* this stability must show itself in consistent reactions across similar situations. Low cross-situational consistency, Mischel argues, demonstrates that behaviour is "situationally determined" and "the more dissimilar the evoking situations, the less likely they are to lead to similar or consistent responses". Inconsistency means that behaviour is driven by our perception of situational variables; or that *cognition* rather than *personality* is the critical determinant of our responses and "even seemingly trivial situational differences may reduce correlations to zero". Each situation is so different in Mischel's view, that trait explanations cannot begin to predict behaviour.

Mischel's book and subsequent articles (Mischel, 1973) prompted a debate and many critiques. While there were many conceptual attacks, the main pro-trait defence was that Mischel had failed to heed the specificity variable (Epstein, 1979, 1983). As we noted when discussing reasoned action theory, if we carefully specify which attitude leads to what result *and* we aggregate our observations over repeated measures, then correlations may improve and attitudes more adequately predict behaviour. Perhaps if we do the same with traits, we will increase their predictive efficiency also.

Mischel did not agree, and in an even more controversial paper than his 1968 book, reported the results of an intensive study of the traits *conscientiousness* and *friendliness* in students at Carleton College, Minnesota (Mischel & Peake, 1982). Students were given various personality tests and completed self-report measures, while parents and a close friend also assessed their attitudes and behaviour. The researchers then repeatedly compared these measures with actual behaviour over a ten-week period. Despite aggregated and quite specific measures, their results did not support traits as adequate predictors of behaviour.

For example, on the trait conscientiousness, temporal consistency on specific variables like class attendance was reasonably high. That is, we always turn up for class on time. However, cross-situational consistency was quite low; or put another way, punctuality did not lead to neatness. Remember these correlations are for *aggregated* observations. Some individual correlations were reasonably high, and when Mischel and Peake looked at patterns of behaviour they found that lecture attendance, punctuality and getting assignments in on time were all related. The researchers concluded that we pick and choose our behaviour and that "broad cross-situational consistencies remain elusive with reliable measures".

While Mischel defended his position (Mischel & Peake, 1983; Mischel, 1984), his critics continued their attack. Epstein and O'Brien (1985) argued that low aggregated consistency figures reflected Mischel and Peake's poorly defined theory of conscientiousness. If their list of behaviours measuring this trait was both more specific and more representative, it may have led to higher correlations. This is where the debate has stalled, Mischel arguing that poor correlations demonstrate situational determinants and his critics arguing that Mischel's attempt to be specific was not specific enough (Jackson & Paunonen, 1985).

So where are we? To argue that personality, or attitude, does not affect behaviour is counter-intuitive and probably incorrect. On the other hand, the evidence that personality determines behaviour is at best inconclusive. At this stage, perhaps the only conclusion to be drawn is that many factors combine to influence our behaviour. As with many similar situations in psychology, the truth probably lies in an interaction of situational and dispositional variables. Mischel (1986), acknowledging this point and the complexity of the basic issue, concludes we may most fruitfully decide if attitudes determine behaviour by developing a theory of the "personality of situations". The argument continues with Mischel and his colleagues intensively studying children's ability to delay self-gratification as a test case of their position (Shoda, Mischel & Peake, 1990).

As a final comment before leaving the impact of attitudes on behaviour, we need remind ourselves we often believe we are more influential than we really are. Not only do we lack personal control but we are sometimes led a certain way by a complete lack of alternatives. The husband who "makes the best of a bad marriage" may do so less from his religious beliefs, than the reality that no one else will have him. Paul Meehl (1978) noted that unforeseen circumstances often completely derail our best intentions. As an example, at possibly the busiest time of my life, when I least needed to be distracted, a friend asked me to help him hang wallpaper. A casual favour totally altered my life as I found myself hanging wallpaper for my future wife. Such a **random walk** of causality led Meehl to suggest that the link between what we think and what we do is often impossible to predict. Nevertheless, as we shall see in our last section on cognitive consistency and behaviour, we often think otherwise!

random walk
Seemingly arbitrary interaction of two patterns of causality that mimics randomness in a deterministic universe.

Does behaviour determine our attitudes?

In real life we often find ourselves acting contrary to our attitudes and beliefs, so how do we resolve such attitude-discrepant behaviour? Do we change our actions, or attitudes, or just remain discrepant? A fair bit of research suggests that to the extent that attitudes determine behaviour, the reverse is also true. If our behaviour determines what we think then this simple equation has enormous ramifications. If we can change attitudes by forcing others to act in a certain way, then Orwell's apocalyptic vision becomes a little more frightening. For such reasons, this is a widely studied question in social psychology. Attitude change, compliance, persuasion, impression management, self-monitoring, brainwashing, reactance, effort-justification, role-taking, self-perception and cognitive dissonance studies, all have a vested interest in behaviour's impact on attitudes. It is quite clear from this research that in certain circumstances our behaviour does influence attitudes. We will look at role-taking, effort-justification and self-perception before turning to cognitive dissonance and the search for self-consistency.

Role-taking

Back in the mists of time, one of my workmates was conscripted and eventually ended up in Vietnam. Before he went, Ian was part of the counterculture, bright, easy-going, articulate, devil-may-care and quite anti-authoritarian. Two years later, he returned to work with a crewcut and a completely different personality. Ian joined the RSL and several extreme right-wing groups, talked incessantly about the "red tide engulfing Southeast Asia" and joined a rifle club. He wore sober suits, affected military mannerisms, marched to and from work, and his obsessive neatness was quite abnormal to his old friends. This was so unlike the Ian we knew and we all wondered how long it would last. At that point I changed jobs and only caught up with him a year later. He was back to normal and recalled that part of his life as a "horrible aberrance". Ian had been so caught up with playing soldier that it took some time before he could de-role and recover.

Anecdotes such as these show the power of roles to modify our attitudes. As we saw in Chapter Two, all of life's a stage and we are but actors on it.

Military socialisation is considered one of the most powerful shapers of occupational attitudes and professional identity. What attitides will these recruits hold in several years?

(Photo: Barry Price)

The corollary is that our "selves" are not fixed but vary with circumstances as we find them. From this perspective it is not surprising that behaviour will have an impact on attitudes. Daily life requires us to play many roles and a major preoccupation of developmental theory is how we maintain a sense of self amid change. As we go through the impressionable years we expect attitudes to change in line with the many new roles we adopt, but as we settle into adulthood does this continue?

Evidence is mixed. Krosnick and Alwin (1989) found that though attitudes were plastic in adolescence and early adulthood, as we age they become quite stable. Studies of psychological reactance, (Chapter Six) suggest an age-related resistance to attitude change. On the other hand, many studies have found that role-playing leads to changed attitudes. Janis and Mann (1977), for example, review a series of simulation studies where enacting a role led to attitude changes in their subjects. A widely reported field study by Lieberman (1956) traced changes in attitudes of two groups of workers who were either promoted to foreman or became union shop stewards. As you can see from Figure 4.4, after two years foremen's attitudes towards management were much more favourable than shop stewards'.

The importance of roles in shaping attitudes is evident when we think about how our careers shape us and this is a particular concern of developmental and occupational psychologists. We all know people whose identity is so

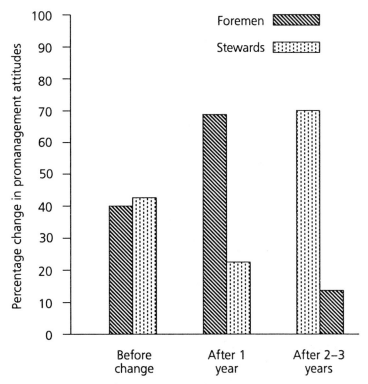

Figure 4.4 *Unionists or foremen, attitudes to management two years on*
Source: Adapted from Lieberman, 1956.

Children often mimic significant adults in their lives. To what extent does this modelling determine adult attitudes?

deformation professionelle
Occupational distortion. Incorporating one's occupational roles into one's everyday persona.

caught up with their vocational image that they cannot leave their job at work. Such **deformation professionelle** or occupational distortion (Moore, 1969) moulds our attitudes in line with the "shop-floor ethos" to the point where it may become damaging and lead to disenchantment, loss of creativity and declining productivity (Hall & Lawler, 1969). Retirees, particularly blue-collar workers, report that retirement cuts off contact with workmates and the loss of roles sometimes seriously impairs our health and well-being (Solem, 1978). Roles are evidently important shapers of attitudes and you can probably think of several examples from your own experience; yet this does not tell us why roles change our attitudes.

Self-perception theory

Daryl Bem proposed a controversial, counter-intuitive theory in 1965 to explain such effects. His self-perception theory argues we do not know who and what we are, nor what we like, but infer these things from our behaviour. This runs counter to the commonsense view that our attitudes determine our actions, but Bem says most of what we do is situationally determined and we look for repetitive patterns when inferring reasons for our behaviour. These patterns become the basis of our attitudes, which are therefore after-the-fact representations of reality. This is another example of self-attribution and, as we discussed in the previous chapter, we have a bias towards dispositional or attitudinal explanations of behaviour. Before making these attributions we carefully discount any external reasons that might explain what we are doing, as situational influences will tell us little about ourselves. As these patterns build up so we refine our self concept.

For example, a student shared in a tutorial how he became a soccer coach. Coming from an academic family his life had been full of learning. Sport, while not frowned upon, was considered a bit declassé. Then Mike dated Karen who was an enthusiastic soccer player. They conducted their romance before, during and after soccer matches. To his amazement he found himself enjoying the sport, listening to radio commentaries and on one memorable occasion going to a match by himself. This quite surprised him and as a psychology major at first interpreted his interest as simple classical conditioning. Mike liked Karen, Karen liked soccer, so liking her rubbed off on soccer too. At this stage he thought his interest was externally determined and discounted this new insight into his personality. Eventually the romance fizzled out but, to his continuing amazement, his attention was still caught by soccer commentaries on the radio, friends discussing matches, and the sight of Saturday afternoon games as he drove home. Depressed and restless, he analysed his emotions and decided it was not breaking up with Karen that was causing his depression, but the thing he missed most was the soccer matches! Mike then decided (inferred) he must have always been "sports minded" and had not realised it, joined a soccer team, recovered, and eventually became a soccer coach to his continuing enjoyment.

There are many ways to end up a Little League coach. One way is to find ourselves involved in football by accident and then after the fact decide we must be interested!

(*Photo: Barry Price*)

Our example demonstrates the basics of Bem's view. Only after Mike was free to choose whether he would go to a match without Karen, could he decide if his interest in soccer was genuine. Such clear self-perception usually occurs when we, like this student, are introduced to novel experiences on which we hold few opinions (Fazio, 1987). Of course once we have gained this insight, we incorporate it into our self-concept and it becomes part of our attitudinal repertoire and will colour our future attributions about sport. Self-perception theory asserts that we learn as much from what we do not do, as from what we do regularly. If our student had been asked to play soccer after the romance had ended and quickly found himself back among his books, he might infer that he disliked sport, or at least was disinterested; although Fazio, Sherman and Herr (1982) found that negative information is a less obvious guide to our attitudes.

While Bem initially concentrated on the behaviour–attribution link (reflecting his behaviourist background), thoughts and feelings are also positive clues to self-perception. We often surprise ourselves by developing interests in things without any direct experience of them. An acquaintance became immensely absorbed in St Brendan's voyages after hearing a report of Tim Severin's re-enactment of the saint's journey from Ireland to Newfoundland. My colleague is not of Irish descent, nor religious, and has little interest in visiting Brendan's ports of call but found this obscure interest shaped his views of modern history. Experimental demonstrations of the cognition/self-perception link have been made with ecological (Chaiken & Baldwin, 1981) and religious attitudes (Andersen, Lazowski & Donisi, 1986).

Despite the power of self-perception theory as an explanation of behaviour-induced attitudes, the theory has obvious limits. It works best when we are unsure what our attitudes are (Chaiken & Baldwin, 1981), or with children whose identity is still developing, or with adults who have a weak sense of self. In our example of Ian's military service, youth and powerful pressures towards conformity in the Army had an impact but his previous attitudes and behaviour did reassert themselves. Obviously, if we have strong attitudes and then find ourselves behaving contrary to our beliefs, we are unlikely to simply infer that our attitudes have changed. Nevertheless, we often do act contrary to our beliefs, so how do we explain this to ourselves?

Effort-justification

One early theory suggested the simple formula that we grow to like that for which we have suffered. Effort-justification predicts that when we find ourselves making undue efforts we will justify or rationalise our behaviour by forming favourable opinions about what has caused us to suffer.

Aronson and Mills (1959) demonstrated effort-justification in a study where college women were invited to participate in a sexual discussion group. As a condition of volunteering they had to pass a screening test to see if they could tolerate being embarrassed by the discussions. One lot of girls was the severe or high-effort condition and read aloud a list of obscene words and an explicit piece of pornography. Another group read a much milder list and passage. To heighten their embarrassment, the girls had to read the list to a male experimenter! Subjects were then asked to listen in on earphones to a group discussing sexual material to give them an idea of what to expect. They then rated how interesting the discussion and participants were and their responses were then compared to a control group who had not been given a "screening test". At this point the experiment was over.

Unbeknown to the subjects, they were not listening to last week's discussion group as they thought but rather a tape designed, in the words of the experimenters, to be "one of the most worthless and uninteresting discussions (of animal sexuality) imaginable". The speakers droned on and on in a completely turgid way and it took a real effort to listen. When Aronson and Mills compared the groups' ratings, they found the controls and mild condition gave similar low interest ratings but the girls who had read aloud a piece of highly obscene pornography found the discussion significantly more interesting! How do we interpret these results?

The severe condition girls did suffer considerable embarrassment, so how did they justify this to themselves? As they had volunteered for the screening test, they were not able to blame the experimenters for their embarrassment. One way out of their dilemma was to distort reality and minimise the effects of the embarrassment, but the experimental situation was too explicit for this to work. The only possible excuse for their suffering was to rationalise their behaviour by thinking the discussion was more interesting than it was. Several other studies report similar effects (Schopler & Bateson, 1962; Zimbardo, 1965; Wicklund & Brehm, 1976; Cooper & Axsom, 1982).

Not all effort-justification is voluntary and in Ian's case being conscripted caused enormous dislocation and suffering; he was in tears the day he was inducted into the Army. In retrospect he rationalised the horrors of combat in Vietnam by saying "the Army made me" and by embracing its attitudes. In his case effort-justification effects did not last and in time he gained a new perspective and revised his opinions. It was likely that the involuntary nature of his commitment, while it led to effort-justification in the short run, led to a diminution of its effects over time. If, however, we voluntarily embrace suffering in pursuit of a goal, then our rationalisations and changed attitudes are more durable (Cooper & Axsom, 1982).

You will notice a certain circularity here, as a voluntary decision presupposes attitudes already in conformity with the changes to be embraced. Notwithstanding this, costs may well exceed what we expected and our new attitudes will justify our efforts. What happens though when we have acted deliberately and then cannot justify the consequences to ourselves? How do we now square our attitudes and behaviour? This problem introduces the fascinating area of attitudinal consistency and cognitive dissonance.

Attitudes, cognitive consistency and dissonance

One of the most pervasive assumptions in social psychology this century is that our attitudes, values and beliefs must square with our actions. Unless we "practise what we preach", we will become uneasy and take steps to reduce this discrepancy. Early attitudinal research in the 1920s and 1930s fairly uncritically assumed a drive toward cognitive consistency but ignored the many instances where we remain comfortably discrepant or change our attitudes rather than our actions. This drive for mental balance seemed so obvious that it was not until the early 1940s that Fritz Heider started to explore how it worked, and it was not until the 1950s that this uncritical assumption of cognitive consistency theory was really challenged. Heider's theory was not a new idea, having philosophical antecedents dating back to Hume and Spinoza. Still, it was a major turning point in social psychology and, as Weir (1983) notes in his article on the prehistory of cognitive balance theory, it brought together "many diverse lines of thought, such as theories of sentiments and interpersonal relations, the analysis of emotions, conflict theory, personality development, and the association principle".

As we have seen, interest in certain types of attitudinal research has waned since the late 1960s and nothing could be more true of this than the sad case of consistency theory. Consistency theory has had its day in social psychology. However, this does not mean that we have plumbed its depths, or that it is unimportant. As we will see in our discussion of cognitive dissonance, several issues are still unresolved. Why interest waned when it did is one of the curiosities of science. As Robert Abelson noted: " . . . vanished from psychology is the central theme that cognitive inconsistency is intrinsically disturbing and demanding of resolution. We have here an intriguing mystery—something that perhaps should be referred to the missing concepts bureau." Whatever cognitive consistency theory's fate, it was still a giant leap forward in understanding how attitudes and behaviour interact (Abelson, 1983).

Cognitive balance theory

Fritz Heider (1944, 1958) made many contributions to social psychology not the least of which was his attribution theory that we reviewed last chapter. Heider was also a ground breaker in the field of cognitive dissonance with his balance theory, which specifies the conditions for consistency in relationships. Heider's starting assumption was that people were basically logical and would modify their attitudes in the interests of maintaining cognitive consistency. As we will see when we turn to Festinger's theory of cognitive dissonance, which stresses our illogicality, this assumption is the point of departure between the two theories. Heider argues that how we think about each other is governed by how we feel about each other. If two people like and care for each other, the quality of their relationship is determined in part by the consistency (or balance) of their attitudes towards important objects and themes in their lives. If they hold similar or balanced attitudes they will have fewer difficulties than if they disagree on key issues. Unbalanced relationships are dissonant because we like the person concerned (and they like us in return) but we disagree with them. This dissonance causes psychological stress and discomfort which motivates behaviour aimed at reducing the gap between the two sets of attitudes and finding consistency.

Figure 4.5(a) shows the fundamentals of Heider's theory. Boy meets girl, they fall in love and agree on important issues like children, careers and where and how they will live. Figure 4.5(b) shows an unbalanced relationship. Boy still loves girl, but despite all their areas of mutual agreement, they cannot decide where they should live. She wants to live in the country and he likes the beach and they experience dissonance on this key issue. No matter how good their relationship is in other areas, this imbalance will have to be resolved before the relationship becomes truly mutual. As you can see from Figure 4.5(c), balance theory works just as well when people differ from each other. However, they then would need to disagree on most key variables, otherwise dissonance (Figure 4.5(d)) would cause them to doubt their dislike of the other and cause them to re-evaluate their view.

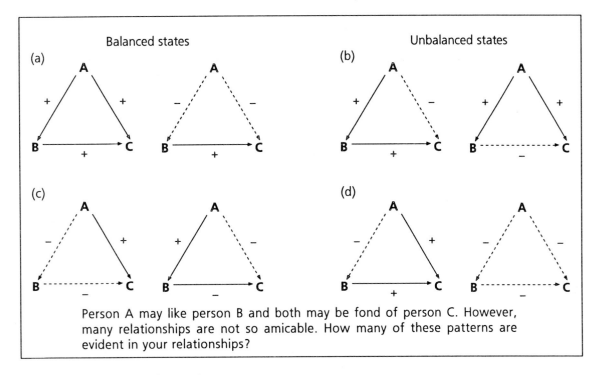

Figure 4.5 *Heider's Balance Theory*
Source: Adapted from Heider, 1958.

For example, a friend had a colleague who was obnoxious and took great delight in undermining her and they had many violent clashes over the years. Their relationship was strained at best and they were eventually put into separate teams by their supervisor in the interests of harmony. Unfortunately this did not work because they were very similar in outlook and their many shared interests constantly brought them into contact. The imbalance was resolved when my friend left for another academic position and commented as she left that it was a pity X was such a pain as he was a good teacher and held all the right attitudes! Clearly the personal chemistry between the two was more powerful than their shared interests and areas of agreement.

Balance theory will seem so obvious that you will wonder why it was such an important theoretical breakthrough. Some of the interest it attracted was due to its pioneering status, opening up new areas within social psychology and as a forerunner of Festinger's more elaborate cognitive dissonance theory. Despite its apparent simplicity, balance theory contains a number of subtleties. Heider was the first to point out that although close relationships are generally balanced, we may use perceptual distortion to paper over disagreements that might otherwise ruin the relationship. Balance theory predicts, therefore, that dissonance will lead to attitude and/or behaviour change. The direction of change is determined by the relative costs of the action required and this is where the theory becomes more complicated but quite predictive (Abelson et al., 1968; Cacioppo & Petty, 1981). Heider argued that dissonance will be reduced through the least costly avenue. If both cannot bear to live other than where they desire, then a compromise is not possible and the relationship will probably flounder; but it is more likely that a compromise will be found and attitudes will be modified accordingly. If one partner holds stronger desires than the other, then balance theory will predict the direction and type of outcome, and so forth.

Balance theory, for all its seeming simplicity, prompted much research into the complex interplay between inconsistent attitudes (Insko, 1984). Heider, although noting the potential for perceptual distortion, did not specify in any detail how we might regain cognitive consistency but subsequent research found six main avenues:

1. *Compromise*
When our couple argues over living at the beach or in the bush, they may resolve their conflict formally with a compromise, by agreeing to live in an acceptable but less favoured location. They restore the balance by both agreeing to a positive alternative.

2. *Give in*
An alternative is one partner giving in and changing their mind about the object. They would then need to resolve the stress induced by changing their attitudes.

3. *Give up*
If the issue of where to live is too important to one or other's well-

being, then the unbalanced relationship will be very stressful and may eventually be resolved by the partners starting to actively dislike each other.

4. *Devalue the object*
One partner might change their mind about living on the beach. This can be done rationally, or by some form of psychological defence.

5. *Cognitive compartmentalisation*
One partner might keep the relationship intact, by divorcing where they live from how they feel about each other. This defensive adaptation takes considerable emotional effort to keep the two issues separate.

6. *Perceptual distortion*
If all else fails and you find yourself living in the bush and hating it, you can convince yourself that you are only doing it for a short while and will soon assert your rights. Tomorrow!

Balance theory is not without its limitations. Olson and Zanna (1983) summed up its difficulties by noting that its apparent simplicity was really at the expense of a more thoroughgoing analysis. Heider stopped short of specifying the determinants of change, promoting consistency and how balance might be restored. He also neglected the degrees of liking for the object and other, which motivate us. An equally important criticism is that few relationships are equally balanced. As we will see in Chapters Eight and Nine, most of us recognise and accept such differences without attempting to change them. Indeed we often cherish them, preferring a degree of inconsistency to add a bit of spice to life (Zajonc, 1968b). Despite these justified critiques, balance theory prompted much valuable research (Feather, 1967b). It has also proved useful in predicting the nature of relationships (Thompson, 1989; Lassiter & Briggs, 1990) and set the stage for a comprehensive look at cognitive dissonance. Its simplicity and intuitiveness still ensures it a place with attitudinal research.

Cognitive dissonance theory

As we have noted, Heider's assumption that we try logically to reduce inconsistencies did not reflect what Leon Festinger (1957) saw in the field. Often people cope with discrepancies between what they do and what they think, by using bizarre and illogical cognitive strategies to reduce dissonance. As an example, we will see in Chapter Eight how a disturbed prisoner rationalised away his cell mate's vicious assaults on him, not as evidence of a very real hatred but rather as an inability to control frustration. Instead of changing cells to avoid being beaten, he offered himself as a sacrifice to show his love for his assailant. Such perceptual distortions are everyday commonplaces and Festinger proposed his theory of cognitive dissonance to take account of the cognitive strategies that let us live with such impossible distortions.

Festinger's theory, like Heider's, is in essence a **drive-reduction theory**. When we experience a discrepancy between our attitudes and behaviour we are physiologically aroused—a negative drive state. This unpleasant

drive-reduction theory. Behaviour that reduces unpleasant physiological arousal.

Box 4.3 *Profile: Christina Lee and why smokers continue to kill themselves. A study in cognitive dissonance*

Dr Christina Lee studied at the University of Adelaide, completing a PhD on aspects of self-efficacy theory in 1983. She is currently a Senior Lecturer in Psychology at the University of Newcastle. Her theoretical studies focus on the relationships between cognition and behaviour, and her applied work is particularly concerned with the role of psychology in health. In recent years she has focused on the role of psychological theories in the promotion of health-related exercise, with a particular emphasis on women.
(Photo: courtesy Christina Lee)

An estimated 16 000 Australians die from smoking-related illnesses each year, despite the millions of dollars invested in anti-smoking campaigns (Armstrong, 1987). Given the vigorous push to encourage smokers to quit, it is unlikely anyone is unaware of the dangers of smoking and every packet of cigarettes carries a blunt warning. Yet an estimated 1.2 million Australians still smoke. Why do they continue this slow suicide?

This conundrum led Christina Lee (1989) from the University of Newcastle, NSW, to examine adult smokers' perceptions of immunity to smoking-related disease.

Lee was fairly sure that smokers must practise some heavy denial to avoid facing the risks they took and in the light of cognitive dissonance theory she framed the following hypotheses:

• Smokers' rating of their own risk would be higher than non-smokers' ratings of their own risk, reflecting smokers' acceptance of the risk they faced.
• Smokers' ratings of the risk to the average Australian smoker would be lower than non-smokers' ratings; reflecting a generalised denial.

• Smokers' ratings of their own risk would be lower than their ratings of the risk to the average Australian smoker, reflecting a sense of personal immunity.
• Younger smokers would perceive a lower risk than older smokers.
• Smokers who do not want to quit would perceive a lower risk than those who did (Lee, 1989, p. 269).

Lee tested her hypotheses on 97 smokers and 95 non-smokers of either sex, aged between 15 and 65. Smokers smoked an average of 17.3 cigarettes per day and had been regular smokers for an average 14.7 years. Respondents rated the risk to themselves and to an average Australian smoker of contracting three smoking-related diseases: lung cancer, heart disease, and chronic lung disease, on a 100 point scale designed for the exercise.

As you will see from Figure 4.6, "smokers' ratings of the risk to the average smoker were lower than non-smokers' ratings, and smokers' ratings of their own risk were lower still". In line with Lee's hypotheses this effect was more pronounced for younger adult smokers than it was among older smokers. While there were

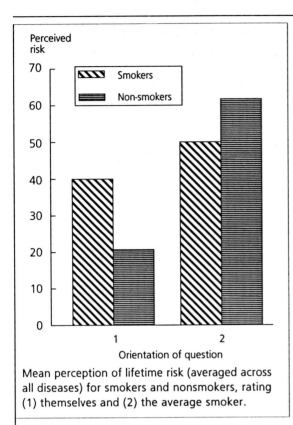

Mean perception of lifetime risk (averaged across all diseases) for smokers and nonsmokers, rating (1) themselves and (2) the average smoker.

Figure 4.6 *Smokers' and non-smokers' ratings of health risk to themselves and to the average smoker*

Source: Lee, 1989.

no differences for age, women rated the risk of disease for themselves and the average Australian smoker higher than did men. The only one of Lee's hypotheses not supported by her study was her last one. It seems that those who want to quit and those who do not are equally aware of the dangers of continuing to smoke.

Lee concludes: "Denial or minimization of risk may well help smokers to deal with the cognitive dissonance arising from their smoking" but it also interferes with efforts to reduce smoking rates. She argues that such denial of risk can only be overcome by carefully targeted campaigns which confront smokers with hard evidence of their own mortality but notes that "people who deny or minimize their own risk of disease may be unlikely to attend stop-smoking programs".

dissonance motivates us to reduce stress by somehow resolving the discrepancy. Heider's balance theory would have us rationally resolve our difficulty but this is often more difficult to do than putting up with the pain of our dissonance. Festinger invokes the **principle of least effort**, that is, we will move in the direction of the easiest change and this is often via perceptual distortion, rather than any fundamental change of attitudes or behaviour (see Box 4.4). As we saw in our list of possible accommodations to discrepancy above, the last three options fall into this category. For example, many science teachers teach evolution and believe in religious creationism. They do not bother to reconcile these opposing beliefs but just keep them in separate mental compartments.

Ultimately, such conflicts are either resolved by changing behaviour or attitudes and the main thrust of Festinger's theory is to look at "normal" accommodations to dissonance, rather than perceptual distortions. Every day we make decisions that force us to choose between alternatives and this causes dissonance. The act of deciding nearly always causes us to re-

principle of least effort
Resolving attitude–behaviour discrepancies by easiest means, often via perceptual distortion.

evaluate the pros and cons of our decision. As we abandon the benefits of one alternative in favour of another, we still have to face the negative consequences that go with our choice. Do we buy a Toyota or a Holden? Both cars are about equal when we compare their features. If we opt for the Holden as a lower cost local product, we miss out on the Toyota's elegant styling and better fuel economy. We resolve such dissonance by enhancing our evaluation of the Holden (more reliable, solid construction, locally made and parts readily available), while decreasing our estimate of the Toyota (imported, tinny, horrible colour and soon to be outdated). As a rule, the more equally weighted the alternatives, the greater the dissonance to be resolved. Changing our attitudes after the fact to reduce dissonance is therefore a normal everyday occurrence, though it may take unusual turns.

Box 4.4 *Mrs Krech, the planet Clarion and the end of the world*

Competing alternatives aside, what happens when our single-minded pursuit of just one alternative comes unstuck? Though dissonance theory has produced some of the most colourful experiments in social psychology, perhaps the most bizarre instances of cognitive reappraisal come from field studies of prophecies that fail the test of real life. In their book *When Prophesy Fails* (1956), Leon Festinger, Henry Riecken and Stanley Schachter report the consequences of a failed doomsday prophecy and the way adherents coped with the dissonance that resulted.

In 1955, Mrs "Marion Krech", an American housewife, announced the world would end on 21 December 1955. As news was a bit slow that week newspaper headlines announced: "IT'LL SWAMP US ON DEC. 21, OUTER SPACE TELLS SUBURBANITE" and "PROPHESY FROM PLANET CLARION—CALL TO CITY: FLEE THAT FLOOD!" Such headlines attracted investigators who descended on Mrs Krech and her group *en masse*. Apparently super-intelligent beings from the planet Clarion had contacted her and via automatic writing, predicted that a giant earthquake and flood would destroy her city and submerge much of the two Americas. However inter-stellar "Guardians" would rescue those who heeded Clarion's call, pick up Earthlings seven hours prior to the catastrophe and whisk

them off to safety in their flying saucer. So there was a definite prophecy and a definite date.

Mrs Krech's bold announcement encouraged a small group, including Festinger, Riecken and Schachter, to meet in her living room to discuss the coming catastrophe and prepare for rescue. Dr "Armstrong", a local college professor with strong interests in the occult and cosmology, brought some of his students along and soon they became firm believers. Mrs Krech and her assistant, Mrs Blatsky, continued to receive messages of encouragement from Clarion with specific instructions on how to prepare for the day. So convinced was the group that they vigorously prepared for the end of the world. Some quit college or jobs, settled their affairs and encouraged others to do likewise. The preparations were very costly to these true believers and ruined marriages when spouses rejected Clarion's call. As predicted by dissonance theory, the stronger the dissonance experienced, the greater the efforts to defend belief. Dr Armstrong was so vehement that his embarrassed university sacked him! So the group had a lot invested in the prophecy being fulfilled.

Festinger and his colleagues predicted that before the event, the group would be self-legitimating and tight-knit as it battled others' derision. By excluding dissenters they would avoid dissonance, and support and encourage each other's belief. Such was the case, and Festinger and his colleagues had difficulty joining and had to pretend to believe in Mrs Krech's prophecy to gain admittance to the group which, after experiencing a media circus, now refused to make further comment. If the world did not end, they predicted the group would reduce its dissonance by reinterpreting beliefs to accommodate reality, rather than acknowledge the error of their ways. Their beliefs were so costly that rejecting them would cause massive cognitive dissonance. Specifically, they predicted the group would seek social support by opening up and actively encouraging others to believe as they do. This would then reduce the dissonance within the group by gaining external legitimation of their beliefs. As Festinger put it: "If more and more people can be persuaded that the belief system is correct, then clearly it must after all be correct"—a time-honoured religious practice.

On the night of the impending catastrophe, Festinger, Riecken and Schachter and two assistants, Dr Armstrong and some of his students, and Mrs Krech's friends, all assembled in her living room to wait being spirited away at midnight. The sixteen assembled seekers had to take elaborate precautions including removing metal objects from their clothing. Anxiety mounted and when Festinger was found, at 11.30 p.m., to have a metal zipper, they panicked and Dr Armstrong performed some rough and ready surgery with a razor blade to ensure that Festinger was not left behind!

Midnight came and went. At 12.05 on the 22nd they were "completely stunned" and momentary relief was gained when someone noticed one of the clocks was running slowly and maybe it was not yet midnight. At that point Mrs Blatsky received a message saying: "There will be a slight delay, just a slight delay." By 4.00 a.m. the prophecy was looking a little wilted, yet rather than admitting their erroneous

"THE GUARDIANS FROM PLANET CLARION
WILL BE HERE AT MIDNIGHT TO RESCUE US."

(Cartoonist: Steve Harris)

beliefs, they chose to believe that the Guardians had abandoned them for some unknown reason. Mrs Krech was distraught and began to cry. The group were desperately needing social support and when one of the researchers stepped out for some air, Dr Armstrong sprang up encouraging him to return, thinking he was deserting:

> I've given up about everything. I've cut every tie. I've burned every bridge. I've turned my back on the world. I can't afford to doubt. I have to believe . . . and I don't care what happens tonight. I can't afford to doubt. I won't doubt even if we have to make an announcement to the press

tomorrow and admit we were wrong. You're having your period of doubt now, but hang on, boy, hang on. (p. 168)

The investigators' predictions were then fulfilled. Just as the tension became unbearable, Mrs Krech had another message saying that due to the group's sincerity and goodness the catastrophe was averted! Much relieved by their salvation and happy to have saved the world, the group called a news conference to take credit for staving off global calamity.

This classic example of cognitive dissonance and its resolution has many parallels in field research (Russell & Jones, 1980; Van Fossen, 1988).

Forced compliance and dissonance

induced compliance
Where we are forced to act contrary to our attitudes and beliefs.

just world hypothesis
Our belief that we get what we deserve.

Blaming the victim

Although cognitive dissonance is a simple theory, it has profound consequences, most of which stem from **induced compliance**, or where we are forced to act contrary to our attitudes and beliefs. Considerable evidence has accumulated that when we behave poorly to others with little justification, we then blame the victim to reduce our dissonance (Davis & Jones, 1960; Lerner, 1977, 1980). You will recall from Chapter Three how the **just world hypothesis** led to our denigrating innocent victims of aggression. In our desire to avoid seeing ourselves in a bad light, it is all too easy to reduce dissonance by adopting a just world attitude and blaming the victim. We will consider how this particularly pernicious process may be combated in the next chapter. Because forced compliance produces powerful effects, it has become a favourite research tool in examining dissonance and several studies have had interesting findings.

Insufficient justification effects

In an early test of cognitive dissonance Festinger and Carlsmith (1959) found that insufficient incentive often leads to more powerful attitude changes, than to requests for more appropriate rewards. Festinger and Carlsmith asked students to participate in an extremely boring manual task where they spent a long time packing and repacking spools and twisting pegs around a quarter of a turn a time. Afterwards subjects were told they were part of a study looking at the effects of mental set on a subject's performance and were in the control group, as they had received no encouragement to twist their pegs. The experimenter then commented that his assistant was late in arriving and rather than hold up the next subject, asked if they would mind acting as the person providing the encouragement and offered to pay them to do so.

Unbeknown to the subjects this was a tissue of lies. The next subject was an accomplice of the experimenter and the real agenda was to see how incentives influence the dissonance between behaviour and attitudes. Some subjects were given $1 and others $20 to convince the stooge how exciting it all was. At the conclusion of the experiment they were paid and asked to rate how interesting the manual tasks were. Festinger and Carlsmith's findings supported their predictions. Subjects paid $20 (a very generous amount in 1958) had more than enough external incentive to justify lying to the next subject. They experienced little dissonance. Poorly paid subjects were in an entirely different boat. They had spent half an hour being thoroughly bored, then had to lie to another subject. They had good reasons to feel dissonance, as $1 was insufficient justification for lying to the next victim. As you can see from Figure 4.7 they escaped this predicament by convincing themselves that peg twiddling was intrinsically interesting and rated the boring task more favourably than their well-paid peers.

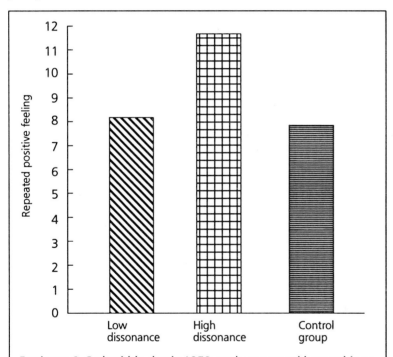

Festinger & Carlsmith's classic 1959 study measured how subjects felt about a boring job after telling another subject how interesting it was. Subjects in the low dissonance group (those paid $20) had little reason to change how they felt about the task. Those in the high dissonance group (only paid $1) experienced dissonance between their actions (lying to other subjects) and their attitudes (a really boring job). As you can see they shifted their attitudes and rated the task more positively.

Figure 4.7 *The price of twiddling*

Source: Festinger & Carlsmith, 1959.

Several now classic experiments replicated and extended our understanding of this effect. Cohen (1962) paid students to write pro-police essays after a riot at Yale University was violently suppressed by police, an act by the authorities that incensed the student body. He found the *degree* of self-justification was commensurate with the *amount* paid. Noting the effect of

---

Box 4.5 *Altered realities: Attitudinal or situational change? The paths to Australian Christian community*

As we have seen, one possible response to cognitive dissonance is changing our attitudes to bring them into line with our behaviour, but what happens when both your behaviour and attitudes are out of step with the rest of the world? One possible response to avoid changing your beliefs is to construct a new reality.

Phenomenologists Alfred Schutz (1970), and Peter Berger and Thomas Luckmann (1967) have explored what happens when such a discrepancy arises. Many options are possible from perceptual distortion through to sublime indifference, but you face a major problem if your attitudes need to be reinforced by some external source of legitimation. This is particularly so when religious belief crashes head-on into the indifference of an uncaring secular world. If you believe in an all-powerful being, you need to see some evidence for your beliefs, or at the very least mix with like-minded people. Churches then are mutual-reinforcement agencies but what do you do if you find your church is just as indifferent as everyone else?

Join another church! Unfortunately, the Church's lot is an unhappy one in a secular age and many troubled souls find their new church just as indifferent. Such was the lot of 4000 unhappy middle-class Australians who took a bizarre route out of their cognitive and social dissonance, moving into communes to prevent it happening again.

McKnight (1990) noticed while researching countercultural groups that the most rapidly growing Australian communes were full of conservative, straight-laced, middle-class Christians—the most unlikely people you would expect to find living in a commune. It was quickly apparent that they were a severely marginalised group who had formed communities to offset the spiritual indifference of their home churches and the massive cognitive dissonance this engendered.

McKnight found that most communards followed a definite path into communal life. Most were very active church members, many having become converts as adults. They were deeply spiritual and among the most conservative and literally minded of their congregations. As such they saw their churches as the primary legitimation of their beliefs. Unfortunately, some personal crisis caused them to test their congregation's religious commitment and found it lacking. After an angry period of trying to get the congregation to enact its beliefs, they tried other churches and found a similar indifference. Now facing a major psychological crisis as their primary source of personal legitimation was found wanting, many had breakdowns; lapsed into unbelief; sought solace in eastern religions; or joined cults. Even these alternatives were found wanting, so gradually they returned to their faith and moved into a communal life as a way of guaranteeing a context for the full expression of their beliefs.

But why communes? Partly this was a belief that communes were the closest present-day form of the early Church, and more importantly, a mini-reality that could be defended against ungodliness. Most communes were highly contractual and prospective members were required to sign covenants binding themselves to certain forms of religious expression. Though communes differed widely, they were without exception ways in which massive cognitive dissonance could be resolved, not by altering beliefs, or even behaviour as such, but rather the world in which it arose.

low pay on counter-attitudinal behaviour, Cohen named this the **insufficient-justification effect**. Feelings also are incentives as Zimbardo et al. (1965) found when they induced military personnel to eat grasshoppers, ostensibly as a "bush-tucker" experiment! If the experimenter was friendly when asking you to try a fried grasshopper, you had some reason to agree. However, if the experimenter was cold and abrupt in his approach, you had little reason for complying; but if you did, how would you justify it to yourself? By convincing yourself that fried grasshoppers were a delicacy and rating them more highly than soldiers in the "friendly" condition. Note that in all these situations you cannot reverse your behaviour, all you can do is change your opinion.

As with balance theory, Festinger's cognitive dissonance theory has several weaknesses. As it stood it was hard to determine actual dissonance levels and adequately predict what types of cognitive change we use to reduce dissonance. For example, the most popular couple on your social touch footie team is letting the side down by not taking training seriously. Which variables do we measure to understand why their dereliction causes greater dissonance for you than other team members? Perhaps even more important, what predicts how you will reduce the dissonance of liking those who are letting you down? Will you change your attitude: "I don't like them anymore"; change your perceptions of their behaviour; "It's not really important"; distort reality; "They are better players than I and need less practice"; or just dodge the responsibility; "It's the coach's problem anyway".

Such individual differences, and measurement and prediction problems, led to many modifications of Festinger's original theory. Most critics accept his basic premises and challenge only aspects of his theory, and over time a new model of cognitive dissonance gradually evolved. Cooper and Fazio (1984) in their review of these changes noted that both antecedent variables and arousal modify our perceptions of dissonance and proposed the model in shown in Figure 4.8. We will consider these extensions first. Other critics challenged Festinger's basic premises and proposed alternative theories. We will consider their challenges as the final section of this chapter.

Unpleasant and unwanted consequences

It seems to go without saying that dissonance only arises if our actions have unpleasant consequences; but is this so?

First, unexpected and unwanted consequences may also cause dissonance. In the Festinger and Carlsmith experiment, subjects lied to fellow students and their reactions were explained by their different rewards. Another way of interpreting these results is that some students *wanted* to lie to their peers and others did not. Those paid well experienced little dissonance. One of the criticisms that may be made of the Festinger and Carlsmith study is that subjects were forewarned and were then able to adjust their thoughts ahead of their discrepant behaviour. Such **forewarning effects** play an important part in how we resist persuasion; they also have a large role in maintaining consistent attitudes (Petty & Cacioppo, 1981). Forced

insufficient-justification effect Evaluating an otherwise attitude-descrepant behaviour more favourably because we have insufficient rewards or excuses for our behaviour.

Factors influencing cognitive dissonance

forewarning effects When forewarned we are able to adjust our thoughts ahead of attitude-discrepant behaviour.

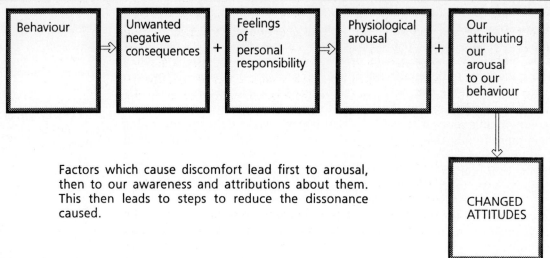

Factors which cause discomfort lead first to arousal, then to our awareness and attributions about them. This then leads to steps to reduce the dissonance caused.

Figure 4.8 *A new look at dissonance theory*
Source: Adapted from Cooper & Fazio, 1984.

compliance studies show this clearly. When we cannot foresee the consequences of our actions, we experience little dissonance (Goethals, Cooper & Naficy, 1979; Petty & Cacioppo, 1986). Equally when we do not foresee the consequences but should have, we feel more responsibility and greater dissonance.

Second, we often *intend* the consequences of our negative actions and would only experience dissonance if the harm we caused was unintentional. While theorists have found that most of us would not deliberately harm someone else, in some settings we will hurt others if we think it is in our, or their, best interest. As we will see in our discussion of Milgram's obedience-to-authority experiments in Chapter Six, cognitive dissonance may be minimised depending on how we evaluate our actions. Some subjects excused themselves by displacing responsibility on to the experimenter. They complied with his directions to shock other subjects, fully intending the consequences of their actions. While few subjects escaped feeling some remorse in this experiment, its extent depended on their feelings of responsibility for harming the other. Our degree of intent determines our responsibility and, in turn, our dissonance.

Responsibility and dissonance

For a while one of the most controversial issues in attitudinal research was the induced compliance controversy (Olson & Zanna, 1983). While this debate was principally a clash of competing explanations of attitude change, a key issue was: did being responsible for our predicament increase our dissonance? As we saw with effort-justification, free choice is an important variable determining the extent of our dissonance. If we have volunteered, we are responsible for our plight and are more likely to experience dissonance and attitude changes (Aronson & Mills, 1959). The reverse is also true. Linder, Cooper and Jones (1967) forced some students to write an essay contrary to their views and compared the extent of attitude change with those who were led to believe their response was voluntary. Clearly a sense of personal responsibility led to greater dissonance and attitude change. Note, it is our self-attributions that cause dissonance, not the actual degree of control we have.

Commitment and dissonance

Commitment also causes greater dissonance and, as we saw in our analysis of post-decisional attitudinal change, once we have freely chosen between alternatives our attitudes swing round to reinforce our choice. Most of the studies that have linked responsibility and commitment have been of this type. Brehm (1956) compared women's ratings of appliances when they were allowed to choose a gift, compared to having one chosen for them. Knox and Inkster (1968) compared attitudes of punters at a racetrack before and after placing a bet. In both cases, having a choice, and then making a commitment, led to a greater post-decisional justification of the alternative chosen.

Arousal, attribution and dissonance

The other half of Cooper and Fazio's extended model is necessarily circular. Not only must our dissonance be arousing but we must also make correct attributions about why we are aroused. When Zanna and Cooper (1974) gave their subjects a drug and told them it would alter their behaviour, they attributed their arousal to the drug and were not disturbed by their discrepant behaviour. No attitude changes were then necessary. The role of attribution in dissonance studies is relatively straightforward, but that of arousal is a little less clear. As we saw, explanations of attitude change, like Bem's (1972) self-perception theory, argue that attitudes flow from an appraisal of behaviour and so they have little use for arousal-based explanations.

What is the role of arousal in dissonance? This is an area that has attracted much research of late. One explicit assumption of Festinger's theory is that cognitive dissonance causes feelings of discomfort. There is no doubt that dissonance and discomfort are linked but is this discomfort psychological or physiological? The question is of more than academic interest, as it will govern how we implement social-change strategies. If we want to modify Australian attitudes towards Aborigines, we need to introduce dissonance into current stereotypes. Hopefully this will lead to improved attitudes and behaviour, but how might this be best achieved? If the unpleasant effects are caused by perceptual or psychological dissonance, then we might consider educational or other cognitive strategies to effect change. If our evaluations are after the fact, as Schachter and Singer (1962) suggest, then the simplest strategy might be to develop a pill that leads to profound discomfort and then tell racists their discomfort is caused by their prejudices! We could then use reattribution training to change attitudes.

contact hypothesis
Intergroup prejudice will be reduced by the dissonance caused by realistic close contact between groups.

This is not as far-fetched an idea as it may seem. One of the common findings of research on racism is that bigots often know little about the objects of their prejudice. If this is so, then the easiest way to deal with racism might be to skip trying to re-educate racists and force them to live and work with those they despise and so confront the absurdity of their prejudices. Although this **contact hypothesis** has had a mixed press (Furnham & Bochner, 1982; Stephan, 1987), if it works, the initial discomfort (arousal) caused by dissonance could then be gently steered towards less prejudicial attitudes. We will see how sensible this idea is in Chapter Five.

Clearly attitude-discrepant behaviour may cause physiological arousal. Croyle and Cooper (1983) wired up their subjects and took direct physiological measures of arousal in a counter-attitudinal essay-writing study and showed that higher dissonance subjects became *more* aroused (see also Elkin & Leippe, 1986). Although it is more a matter of faith than science to decide that arousal leads to cognitive dissonance, rather than the reverse, Croyle and Cooper's results support a commonsense interpretation. We become dissonant and then become aroused. However, Claude Steele and his associates argued that alcohol may relax the arousal caused by counter-attitudinal essay writing thus reducing arousal but not the dissonance (Steele et al., 1981). So perhaps discomfort is both physical and psychological.

So in summary, for attitude change to result from cognitive dissonance, we need to act contrary to our attitudes; then feel responsible for the unintended and unforeseen consequences; be aroused by the resulting

The ultimate results of unresolved cognitive dissonance!
(Photo: Chris Simkin)

dissonance; and then attribute its source correctly. Note that Cooper and Fazio's model is really one of antecedent conditions and dissonance. It still does not account for the variability of our reactions, or predict how we might rationalise our dissonance. Such research as there is concentrates on one-off factors, so when considering these studies *en masse*, all we see is a confused pattern of individual differences influencing reactions. Cognitive dissonance theory has yet to generate a model to account for this end of the dissonance process and such explanations as we have come from competing theories like impression management and self-perception theory.

Towards a synthesis of attitudes and behaviour

There have been many challenges to dissonance theory and most take the simple line that a "cognitive dissonance" construct is an unnecessary complication in explaining attitude discrepant behaviour (Bem, 1967). As we saw earlier, Bem's self-perception theory argues that we simply attribute reasons (attitudes) to our behaviour after the fact. As rational observers of ourselves, we do not experience discomfort when our attitudes are discrepant, we simply bring them into line with our behaviour. While there has been considerable support for this theory, it has the obvious difficulty of explaining away mutually contradictory attitudes, and the arousal which does flow from dissonant behaviour (Croyle & Cooper, 1983).

Other challengers assert that what Festinger and his interpreters see as the motivational effects of dissonance are really just another example of incentives at work (Rosenberg, 1965). There are many reasons why we might want to change our attitudes, and critics argue that attitude change is easily explained by identifying the underlying incentives. Impression management theory (Chapter Two) for example, argues that attitudes are relatively plastic (Cialdini et al., 1976) and we have a strong incentive to present ourselves in the best possible light. Such critics argue that the attitudinal changes of induced compliance studies need not be explained by "dissonance reduction" but rather as simply "saying what pleases" (Tedeschi, Schlenker & Bonoma, 1971).

Another variant **self-affirmation theory** was put forward by Steele and his associates (1981, 1983, 1988). While Steele accepts the cognitive dissonance perspective as one possible explanation among many for attitude change, he believes that people are often less concerned with dissonance and more concerned with their own self-image. Dissonant cognitions therefore are often less important in altering our attitudes (and behaviour) than simply our avoiding self-embarrassment. The test of his theory, Steele asserts, is that discrepant behaviour does not always lead to cognitive consistency, and if we have other ways of reinforcing our self-esteem we do not have to change our attitudes. His viewpoint has received some

self-affirmation theory
Behaviour that reinforces our view of ourselves rather than reducing dissonance.

experimental support (Steele & Lui, 1981). One implication of his research is that alcoholism may well be an alternative way of coping with dissonance (Steele, Southwick & Critchlow, 1981). Alcohol is a sedative whose first effects are behavioural relaxation. When faced with a gap between our hopes and our expectations, rather than revising our attitudes and lifestyle, we may reduce our dissonance with alcohol. Over time this pattern may become chronic.

Where do these theories leave us? As with most controversies in social psychology the true position probably involves all explanations and several attempts have been made to integrate differing perspectives (Paulhus, 1982; Tetlock & Manstead, 1985; Tesser & Shaffer, 1990).

Several theorists have linked self-perception and cognitive dissonance theories. For example, Fazio, Zanna and Cooper (1977) suggested that the *degree* of discrepancy determined whether attitude changes were mediated by one or other theory. Highly attitude-discrepant behaviour was arousing and led to cognitive dissonance, while only mildly discrepant behaviour led to self-perceptual change. To test these hypotheses students wrote counter-attitudinal essays and both mildly and very discrepant conditions led to attitude change. To test whether cognitive dissonance accounted for the highly discrepant group's attitude change, Fazio, Zanna and Cooper then varied their subjects' degree of arousal. Some subjects in both the high and low discrepancy conditions were led to believe the experimental setting was causing their discomfort. As with similar misattribution studies, Fazio and his colleagues reasoned that these subjects would attribute their arousal to their setting rather than the essay and would not change their attitudes. However, only the highly discrepant group did this and the researchers concluded that only marked discomfort was alleviated by misattribution. Where we experience disturbing dissonance, we use cognitive strategies and where it is slight we use self-perception processes to deal with attitude discrepant behaviour. The only moderating factor would seem to be the relative strength of our existing attitudes.

Links have also been made between impression management and cognitive dissonance. Baumeister and Tice (1984), for example, linked these two theories. They manipulated public and private behaviour, and high and low choice conditions, to see how these variables caused dissonance and impacted on attitudes. They found that behaviour, contrary to the subjects' attitudes but done in private and not in the public eye, led to high levels of dissonance and attitude change, but only when subjects had a choice about how they acted. Public counter-attitudinal behaviour changed attitudes in both the high and low choice groups. Baumeister and Tice interpret their results as support for both theories. In the private condition, impression management would not be an issue, while in the public condition, attitude change in both high and low-choice groups would seem to rule out dissonance as a reason for attitude change.

So where are we? Dissonance theory has been very controversial but has stood the test of time, albeit with modifications. Festinger's challengers have also had their day and their theories have also proved durable, though relatively narrow in application. At this stage of attitudinal research it seems that dissonant cognitions produce arousal and attitude change, unless our beliefs are weak, or we can reduce tension by other means. Our self-concept and public image are important modifiers of our attitudes, which have proved fairly elastic, and we often modify our beliefs to suit the occasion. The main focus of attitudinal research through the 1990s is likely to be how attributional and self-representational processes shape the way we see ourselves and our world.

Summary

Attitudes are perhaps the most studied aspects of social psychology, with commentaries stretching back to the ancient Greeks. Attitudinal research is divided into developmental studies, which examine how we acquire attitudes; process studies, which look at the nature of attitudes; and content studies, which examine specific attitudes such as envy or jealousy. While research on specific attitudes is booming, process research had its heyday in the 1960s and 1970s and has been languishing since.

Attitudes may be defined as "our likes and dislikes" or "our evaluation of an object or person". Attitudes are composed of affective (emotional), behavioural and cognitive components, and are related to values, feelings, beliefs and opinions, but are not synonyms for these. Attitudes are linked to behaviour but whether they determine it is still a major question.

Do attitudes lead to behaviour? Maybe. Many factors influence the attitude-behaviour link. Research at first uncritically accepted it did; then after LaPiere's studies in the 1930s fairly uncritically accepted it did not. Revisions in the 1960s and 1970s criticised the methodology of earlier studies and current research looks at what influences the attitude-behaviour link.

How do attitudes determine behaviour? A direct link is hard to show as attitude scales are, at best, measures of behavioural intention or self-reports. Behavioural intention is a weak and unreliable guide to subsequent behaviour.

Fishbein and Ajzen's theory of reasoned behaviour showed how social norms (SN) and our subjective evaluation of proposed behaviour (Aact) influence behavioural intention. Their theory relies on a multiple act criterion to ensure predictive efficiency. While their theory has been challenged and modified, it is reasonably predictive.

Our intention to act is influenced by situational and personality variables, and attitudinal strength. Situational variability makes the attitude-behaviour link a tenuous one; personality differences likewise are a poor predictor of behaviour. However, the stronger and more entrenched the attitude, the more likely an appropriate behaviour.

Our perception of being in control of our lives or as controlled by others, influences our behaviour. Rotter's locus of control construct suggests that internals' actions are more closely tied to their attitudes, while externals are affected by their situation and so their attitudes are less predictive of behaviour. Rotter's scale has proven a useful and quite predictive tool, though many studies have questioned the applicability of his norms.

Does behaviour determine our attitudes? Inconsistencies in our behaviour often alter our attitudes. Role-taking, effort justification and self-perception theories all suggest we alter our attitudes after the fact to square with our actions. However, these theories do not adequately explain our continuing to hold inconsistent attitudes and/or behaviour.

One of the most pervasive assumptions in social psychology this century is that our attitudes, values and beliefs must square with our actions. Cognitive consistency theory argues that discrepancies between our attitudes and actions must be resolved. Heider's balance theory specifies how unequal relationships may be brought into balance but has several major limitations, not the least of which is our often stable, but unbalanced, state.

Festinger's cognitive dissonance theory does acknowledge that our actions are often at odds with our attitudes. We are often dissonant and remain so, but Festinger concentrated on the ways in which we resolve dissonance. We may change our attitudes, change our actions, alter our perceptions, blame someone else or use psychological defences or mental compartmentalisation, to reduce the tension dissonance brings. Festinger found that insufficient justification or incentives often produced profound attitude changes and sometimes people construct new realities to externalise dissonance.

Festinger's theory has limitations and does not predict which course of action we will follow beyond invoking the least effort principle. Cooper and Fazio have extended Festinger's theory to take account of antecedent conditions such as arousal, commitment, responsibility, forewarning effects, and the like. Several critics have argued that a cognitive dissonance construct is unnecessary and we can explain attitude change after the fact, but these theories have difficulty accounting for continuing inconsistencies in our attitudes and behaviour.

Recommended reading

Ajzen I. and Fishbein M. (1980) UNDERSTANDING ATTITUDES AND PREDICTING SOCIAL BEHAVIOUR, Prentice Hall, Engelwood Cliffs, NJ. A thorough review of attitudinal research with a detailed coverage of the reasoned action theory, before its major modification.

Cooper J. and Fazio R.H. (1984) "A new look at dissonance theory". In Berkowitz L. (ed.) ADVANCES IN EXPERIMENTAL PSYCHOLOGY, Vol. 17, Academic Press, NY. Probably the best overview of modifications to dissonance theory.

McGuire W.J. (1986) "The vicissitudes of attitudes and similar representational constructs in twentieth century psychology", EUROPEAN JOURNAL OF SOCIAL PSYCHOLOGY, 16, 89–130. A short but useful history of attitudinal research since 1920.

Robinson J.P., Shaver P.R. and Wrightsman L.S. (eds) (1991) MEASURES OF PERSONALITY AND SOCIAL PSYCHOLOGICAL ATTITUDES, Academic Press, San Diego. An update of an immensely popular book on the measurement of attitudes first published 20 years ago. Contains detailed information on over 150 of the most commonly used personality and attitudinal scales.

Van Fossen T. (1988) "How do movements survive failures of prophecy?" RESEARCH IN SOCIAL MOVEMENTS, CONFLICT AND CHANGE, 10, 193–212. A fascinating insight into how messianic movements survive failures of prophecy by Tony Van Fossen of Griffith University. His article on the French messianic cult of Georges Roux reviews the major theories of the ways in which the dissonance of a failed prophecy is dealt with.

PREJUDICE, DISCRIMINATION AND ATTITUDE CHANGE

My most amusing experience occurred in the most depressing place I have ever worked—Parramatta Gaol. The Gaol at that point was home to several hundred long-term recidivist prisoners, many doing life sentences. One of my tasks was to interview prisoners applying for changes in classification or transfer to other gaols. One day I interviewed "Bob" who was by far the greatest bigot I have ever met.

Bob was an Anglo-Australian in his middle-thirties, convicted of a violent offence and had already served six years. He was requesting reclassification to medium security to further his education and "for personal reasons". The classification committee were happy enough with his conduct. He had done more than enough time to warrant a shift to a lower security gaol but Bob's refusal to explain his "personal reasons" worried us and they held over his application pending my advice.

When I interviewed him, he quickly decided to be more forthcoming. After asking whether I was Jewish, he said he wanted to leave Parramatta to avoid the "Jewish filth" he was forced to mix with daily. Several prisoners in his wing were Jews and he suspected that some of the custodial officers were too. He explained he was worried about the contagious effects of too close a contact with Jews and wanted to move to a country gaol to avoid them. He also wanted easier access to letter-writing privileges to further his growing interest in genealogy.

Despite my growing incredulity, he explained he believed in ethnic superiority, racial purification and the non-violent separation of the races. He supported the Australian Nazi Party and believed that when they came to power all Jews would be required to emigrate. He could quote Julius Streicher and Hitler at length on

Orthodox Jews suffer inordinately because their distinctive dress makes them highly visible targets.
(Photo: Gavin Price)

the subject, though he deplored their final solution as a heavy-handed approach. All that was necessary he explained was to concentrate world Jewry into Israel; cut off US aid and let them stagnate.

His racial bigotry extended beyond anti-Semitism. He disliked Slavs, particularly Poles, and "Coloureds". He acknowledged Aborigines' rights to their land but felt this was best exercised in Bantustans organised along South African lines.

Despite his racial obsessions he was otherwise normal, with a good gaol record. So with some misgivings I recommended a transfer to medium security. That Bob was basically sane was evident several months later when I visited X-Wing Bathurst. When I asked how his genealogical studies were going, he shamefacedly admitted his views had undergone somewhat of a change after discovering he was the great-grandson of a Polish rabbi!

The nature of prejudice

As we can see it is rather hard holding racist views when you suddenly find yourself one of the despised minority. Yet this anecdote revisits the three most interesting questions in attitudinal research we considered last chapter: Why do we hold the attitudes we do? Do our views translate themselves into behaviour? How do we square discrepancies between attitudes and behaviour? I spent about fifteen hours talking with Bob and gained a fascinating insight into the complex way belief and reality interact. Bob had virtually no experience with Jews, came from a family without strong beliefs, racial or otherwise, and was not personally disadvantaged by Israel's (or Poland's) existence. Nevertheless, he held some extreme attitudes. Why did he hold these strange beliefs and what maintained them? We will see as we go along, however, life seldom rewards you as much as it did in Bob's case and I had a front-row seat as his bigoted attitudes met an uncomfortable reality.

And we need hardly mention how important this research is, nor the urgent need for new ways to combat such prejudice. As I write, our world is facing a resurgence of ethnic tensions that had been repressed by the Superpower conflicts. With the death of Communism and the end of the Cold War, nationalism has again shifted centre stage. Unfortunately national aspirations usually draw sharp boundaries, alienating friends and neighbours and fostering prejudice. Language and culture become the tools promoting a resurgent national consciousness but often at the expense of creating an "us and them" attitude. The power of nationalist sentiment as a breeding ground of prejudice is hard to underestimate. Eastern Europe is changing at a staggering speed and so is the re-emergence of ethnic hatreds and grudges that have their roots in antiquity. The ultimate cost of such prejudice is worth remembering with a conservatively estimated 60 000 000 people having lost their lives in intercommunal violence this century (see Table 5.1).

Table 5.1 *Deaths in "bushfire" wars since 1946*

War	Period	Deaths
Afghanistan	1982–	130 000
Algeria	1954–62	115 000
Angola	1961–	25 000
Arab–Israeli conflicts	1946–	38 000
Argentina	1978–86	45 000
Armenia–Azerbaijan	1989–	36 000
Bengali Wars	1971–73	1 010 000
Bosnia Croatia Serbia etc.	1989–	45 000
Burma	1948–	17 000
Cambodia	1975–	2 750 000
China	1945–49	12 000
China–Taiwan	1949–69	5000
Cyprus	1955–	3000
Egypt	1948–59	8000
El Salvador	1980–88	52 000
Eritrea	1961–92	78 000
Guinea Bissau–Portugal	1961–74	17 000
Honduras–El Salvador	1969	2000
Hungary	1956	39 000
India	1946–	1 200 000
Indochina	1946–54	105 000
Iran	1978–79	7000
Iraq–Kuwait	1990–91	110 000
Kashmir	1947–	19 000
Kenya	1950–56	13 000
Korea	1950–53	3 000 000
Kurdistan	1948–	176 000
Laos	1953–73	10 000
Lebanon	1958–	110 000
Libya–Chad	1983–87	2000
Madagascar	1947–49	11 000
Malaya	1948–60	10 000
Mozambique	1960–	100 000
Nigeria	1967–70	1 500 000
Palestine	1948–49	16 000
Sinai	1956	4000
Sino–Indian Wars	1962–63	5000
Somalia	1988–	55 000
Sri Lanka	1987–	13 000
Sudan	1963	550 000
Tibet	1956–	70 000
Tigre	1974–92	238 000
Vietnam	1961–75	1 000 000
Western Sahara	1976–	11 000
Yugoslavia	1946–48	45 000
Zaire	1960–65	30 000
Zanzibar	1961–64	5000
Zimbabwe	1965–80	45 000

To put this somewhat daunting list in perspective, it includes only 50 of the estimated 356 inter-communal or intra-communal conflicts that have killed more than 1000 people since 1945. It is also drawn from the most conservative estimates of deaths available.

Source: Adapted from Vaughan, 1988.

We need to understand such prejudices and develop new ways of dealing with bigotry, sexism, racism, ageism, and the like. Last chapter we considered how all attitudes are formed and how they influence behaviour. Here we will continue that discussion by concentrating on prejudice, or negative attitudes, looking at the various types and their expression in active discrimination. As we noted, there is a distinct difference between research on attitude formation and research on specific attitudes, or the difference between process and content. In this chapter we will emphasise how prejudicial attitudes are formed, what sustains them and how we may combat them. Although we will use examples of specific types of prejudice to illustrate these processes (see Box 5.1) we will leave our coverage of specific prejudices to later chapters.

Box 5.1 *The anatomy of a prejudice: Homophobia*

Most research on prejudice covers the stigmatisation of "acceptable" minorities: women, migrants, the disabled and Aborigines, but homosexuals still excite more fear and loathing than any other group in Australia (with the possible exception of AIDS sufferers, who are usually seen as homosexuals anyway). In a recent survey of 80 of my social psychology students' attitudes, homosexuality was placed second last in a rank ordering of 40 "acceptable and unacceptable behaviours", neatly bracketed by child molesting and murder. Ray (1983a) found that TV stereotypes adversely portrayed gays and led to negative attitudes, particularly in the less well educated. Gay bashing is a great Australian sport but in 1990, eight people lost their lives when the game went too far. Why are we so homophobic?

There is much speculation but not much empirical research on this question. Many writers see homophobia and heterosexism as an irrational fear but Miller and Romanelli (1991) argue it is a well-defined ethic, deeply embedded in Western civilisation. Heterosexuality is seen as a biological norm; after all, if everyone were homosexual, it would mean the end of the human race! They also argue sex for pleasure, rather than producing offspring, has always upset the Church as it distracts the mind from higher things and weakens the Church's authority (Clark, Brown & Hochstein, 1989; Edwards, 1989-90). For these reasons homosexuality violates the moral order.

Related to this analysis is a collection of explanations of homophobia which straddle the leftist/feminist political divide (Gould, 1985; Queen, 1987; Connell, 1990). This approach argues homophobia is partly "hegemonic heterosexual masculinity" or that men are trapped in sex roles that are not biological but rather reflect a male-dominated society. Such theorists argue that masculinity and heterosexuality are not politically neutral, rather they support a social order that encourages male rivalry "and the exploitation and violent subordination of women and homosexuals" (Frank, 1987). Homosexuality by its very existence is seen as a challenge to this male hegemony. Homosexuals' struggle for equal rights is seen as a threat to a male-dominated society and heterosexual privilege. Homophobia is then a reaction against this perceived threat (Lewis, 1978) and may be seen as a device to keep men within the boundaries of traditionally defined roles (Morin & Garfinkle, 1978). Similar explanations account for lesbianism.

Following the Freudian formulation that homosexuality is an arrested stage of psychosexual development, Reiter (1991) argues that homophobia originates in the breaking of a pre-Oedipal attachment to a mother figure. The process of gaining a male gender identity for boys, and attachment to a heterosexual love object for girls "represent early points of vulnerability". Johnson (1981) agrees and argues "becoming heterosexual, for both sexes, involves

Stereotypes of homosexuals obscure the fact that many gays form enduring relationships based on mutual caring and trust.
(Photo: Gavin Price)

establishing a relationship with a father figure . . . and the Oedipal period may be understood as the time when the father's power, representing the system of male dominance, is substituted for the power of the mother". Reiter argues that these early developmental origins "later interact with cultural factors" and account for the persistence of the prejudice". Similar accounts of "difficulties" in the Electra period are used by Freudian theorists to explain lesbianism. As you evaluate these assertions, it is well worth remembering that one of the unstated assump-

tions of Freudian interpretation is that extreme homophobia is a defensive rejection of one's own fear of being gay.

There is also no doubt that the AIDS epidemic has reinforced homophobia and given it fresh impetus (Fisher, 1985; Poirier, 1988). Anagrams like "AIDS is an Anally Inserted Death Sentence", while clever, inaccurately stigmatise AIDS sufferers (and homosexuals) and tragically worsens their plight, by reducing public sympathy; and unfortunately AIDS sufferers already suffer enough public indifference (Tindall & Tillett, 1990). Many researchers have found evidence of irrational fears of catching AIDS from casual contacts with gays, particularly in young males (Cochran & Peplau, 1991).

What can we make of these theories? In a review of the literature, Siegel (1979) suggests that the best predictor of anti-gay prejudice is **sex-role rigidity**, or a "need to keep women in their place". Most of the research Siegel argues can be summarised as "men are more prejudiced against gays than are women; gay men elicit more negative reactions than do lesbians; and effeminate gay men are less threatening to most non-gays than are their 'macho' counterparts". This suggests that homophobia is a learned reaction against threats to traditional male roles. Collateral support comes from a number of cross-cultural studies by Professor Michael Ross of the University of New South Wales (Ross, Paulsen & Stalstrom, 1988) which show no common international reactions to homosexuality; this argues that homophobia is socially constructed.

Whatever the origins of this pernicious prejudice, there is evidence that with appropriate interventions it is relatively easily reduced (Morin & Garfinkle, 1978; Pagtolun-An & Clair, 1986). Hopefully in time it will disappear altogether.

The nature of prejudice and discrimination

prejudice
An attitude or belief about someone based solely on our stereotypes.

As we can see from our opener, prejudice need not be enacted and most of us hold prejudices that we would not dream of airing. This illustrates the difference between **prejudice**, an attitude or belief about someone based solely on our stereotypes, and **discrimination**, an active outworking of these beliefs. For example, Bob's views found only mild expression and on the whole his contacts with Jews, although distasteful, were peaceful. He even shared a cell with a Jew for two months and suffered no ill effects! This points to a crucial difference we explored at length last chapter: attitudes do not necessarily determine our behaviour and in a similar way prejudice does not necessarily lead to discrimination.

Another important characteristic of prejudice is that it relies on **social categorisation** or assigning characteristics to a person based on group stereotypes. So prejudice is essentially schema driven and, as we have seen in Chapter Two, schemas are shorthand ways of categorising people based on their sex, age, nationality, class or other social characteristics. The nature of prejudice is that we superimpose our view on to a person and process data in a way consistent with our beliefs (Fiske & Taylor, 1991). As we saw in Chapter Two, we tend to ignore discrepant information and only process data that confirms our impressions. Bob thought Jews were devious and underhanded, and so looked for these characteristics while ignoring contrary evidence (and that in a gaol he was hardly likely to find a representative sample of Jewry). In this way schematic processing confirms our prejudice and is a convenient way of pigeonholing people without the inconvenience of really getting to know them. Unfortunately, this type of processing quickly leads to self-fulfilling prophecies.

Prejudice also assumes that social categorisation reflects reality. In essence it sees individuals as somehow *representative* of their group and that they will think and react in predictable ways. These stereotypes are often entirely erroneous and it is an assumption of prejudice research that we cannot assign attitudes and behaviour solely on the basis of social characteristics. This is a hotly debated point, as we will see when we contrast prejudice and realistic intergroup conflict later in the chapter.

While we are defining terms it is also important to note that prejudice is usually, but not always, a negative attitude. As with the Pygmalion effect we discussed last chapter, we may often view certain groups in an unrealistically favourable light and so create self-fulfilling prophecies. In some ways favourable prejudices are the flip side to negative beliefs; for every outgroup there must be a positive ingroup as a counterbalance or baseline. It will come as no surprise that our favourable prejudices are directed at those who are most like us, or groups we want to join (Rosenthal, 1966). We turn now to consider the active expression of prejudice—discrimination.

discrimination
Actual harm to another caused by our prejudical beliefs.

social categorisation
A pervasive tendency to divide the world up into us and them categories on some characteristic.

Discrimination

Enacting prejudice

Discrimination is influencing another's interests based on our beliefs about that person. Most discrimination is negative, though as mentioned we may positively discriminate in someone's favour. It is not inevitable that prejudice will lead to discrimination and as we saw last chapter there is a big gap between our attitudes and our actions. Just because we hold an attitude does not mean our behaviour will be determined by it. As we will see it is almost impossible to avoid prejudice as we are all hostages of our time and place and upbringing. Our attitudes reflect those of our culture but this does not mean we necessarily enact these views and indeed in times of rapid social change, our beliefs quickly date and we may choose to act contrary to them. For instance, many men bred to a traditional view of women may embrace new ways of behaving, while still regretting changing sex roles. Unfortunately, this is seldom the case and we often actively discriminate against others, sometimes unknowingly (Cowlishaw, 1986, 1988).

Discrimination is widespread and pernicious and comes in many forms, some not so obvious. Active discrimination may range from mild slander through to violence and murder, but while a knife in the back is fairly obvious, much modern discrimination is covert. The liberalisation of community attitudes and the various consciousness-raising and affirmative action programmes have driven much discrimination underground and it is no longer acceptable to be overtly prejudiced (Dovidio & Gaertner, 1986). Subtle discrimination occurs in three main ways: failure to act, tokenism, and reverse discrimination.

Failure to act

The easiest way to discriminate without being labelled racist, sexist, or whatever, is to refuse to act when the situation calls for it. In the early 1970s a young woman was appointed as a graduate entrant in a Federal Government insurance agency for which I worked. Like all new entrants she rotated through most sections, before being permanently assigned a post. She started in Underwriting and, as the first woman appointed to such a post, she was something of a novelty and a threat to the elderly men who comprised the section. I worked in another area but even from a distance it was obvious that she was not getting the same treatment that young men serving their obligatory six months would get. She was treated with courtesy and respect but none of the men offered the informal advice and correction automatically given to her male peers. Whether this was due to awkwardness or an active discrimination is an open question but she had a rough time of it. This form of discrimination is almost impossible to pin down when it happens but shows up readily enough when we examine the statistics for disadvantaged groups. Many theorists have commented on the variables underlying our failure to act and we will return to this in Chapter Ten when we consider at length the question: "When will we help?"

Tokenism

An even more subtle form of discrimination is assisting someone *because* of their race, sex or age. The woman employed as a graduate entrant was left in no doubt that her appointment was solely to satisfy new Federal Government Equal Employment Opportunity (EEO) requirements. If she was in any doubt, she was cited in the annual return, by name, as evidence that they were complying! You can guess what this does for the token person's confidence and self-esteem. This woman had an economics degree and had joined the organisation to enter the insurance industry, but after her first year was permanently assigned to Personnel, as befitted a woman! Disgusted, she soon resigned.

Tokenism hurts in a number of ways. Not only does it victimise the individual but it also masks the unfair practices of many organisations. Tokenism sends confused messages to employees. Only gradually do they become aware of hidden agendas in the workplace. Even those people who believe they are acting appropriately may send out contrary nonverbal signals that reveal their basic insincerity. The **nonverbal leakage hypothesis** (Ekman & Friesen, 1974) argues that we tune in to subtle nonverbal cues that give away a person's real attitudes, allowing us to spot phonies. The problem with tokenism is that it usually takes some time for the person to realise the basic insincerity of others' attitudes, leading to a sense of betrayal and bitterness at their wasted efforts within the organisation. Even then some tokens will continue to deny this reality and strive for acceptance (Wright, Taylor & Moghaddam, 1990). Being a token also means you are more obvious and whatever mistakes you make will be more obvious too (Yoder, 1991).

Tokenism is also poor use of resources. Chacko (1982) surveyed young women managers to evaluate their job satisfaction. Those women who felt they had obtained their positions through affirmative action, or their gender, were significantly less satisfied with their jobs, though there is some evidence that this applies more to women than men (Heilman et al., 1987). Work performance can only decline under such circumstances, particularly when your employers do not expect much of you anyway. In short a fairly impossible situation that Pettigrew and Martin (1987) called **triple jeopardy**.

Reverse discrimination

The essence of discrimination is not treating a person just as you would any other. Many targets of prejudice are acutely sensitised to the subtle ways we alter our behaviour when they are around. So it is as hurtful to *overreact positively* to another, as it is to be overtly discriminating. This somewhat paradoxical form of discrimination arises from changing community attitudes which make overt discrimination unacceptable. People who hold prejudicial attitudes may react too favourably as a way of showing they are not prejudiced but give out exactly the opposite message. Canadian psychologist Dutton in a number of studies demonstrated this effect (Dutton, 1971, 1973; Dutton & Lake, 1973). In one experiment men not wearing ties tried to gain admission to restaurants with strict dress codes. More than twice as many blacks gained admission as whites, which Dutton felt showed management were eager to appear non-discriminatory and so were overly lenient to blacks (Dutton, 1973).

Why does reverse discrimination occur? On the face of it the people who are overreacting are trying to combat prejudice; why are their actions still prejudiced? Part of the answer is the changing nature of prejudice and the patterns of discrimination it gives rise to. Gone are the days when

nonverbal leakage hypothesis
We tune in to subtle nonverbal cues that give away a person's real attitudes.

triple jeopardy
Being appointed as a token minority-group employee means you are highly visible, people do not expect much of you and these factors predispose you to fail.

overt prejudice was fashionable, but social change has been so fast that community attitudes lag behind social practice. Many people find themselves trapped between two sets of values. Their childhood values tell them to be cautious with minority groups, while the newer affirmative action values stress active engagement and tolerance. One way of resolving this cognitive dissonance is to be tolerant in relatively unimportant situations, while maintaining our prejudicial attitudes in more personal situations. Unfortunately, as with tokenism, these nominal acts allow us to avoid genuine change as we can delude ourselves that we are really quite tolerant (Dutton & Lennox, 1974).

For example, Gaertner and Dovidio (1986), in their review of racial discrimination, argue that old fashioned overt racism has been replaced by **aversive racism**, a subtle blend of ambivalence, egalitarian attitudes and old-time racist beliefs. Middle-class whites, caught up in rapid social change, are thrust into more immediate contact with the objects of their prejudice. This causes an aversive reaction as longstanding prejudices are triggered, and ambivalence as they confront the negative aspects of minority life, poverty, disease, etcetera. At the same time they believe they should be more tolerant and give the other a fair go. This conflict leaves whites feeling uneasy but also ashamed of their repugnance. They are in conflict between the new, more liberal, attitudes and their upbringing. To avoid the pain of confronting and dealing with their true prejudices, they practise

aversive racism
A subtle blend of ambivalence, egalitarian attitudes and old-time racist beliefs.

A lifetime of suffering subtle discrimination may instil a powerful motivation to succeed. Peter Walker overcame many impediments to become a university graduate, teacher, role-model and leader of his people. (Photo: courtesy Peter Walker)

trivial acceptance, while emotionally distancing themselves from objects of their prejudice. Pettigrew (1985) found that such racial discrimination showed up in marked behavioural leakage. Whites spoke faster and more abruptly with blacks, had less eye contact, kept a greater interpersonal distance, stumbled and had more slips of the tongue, and on the whole were less friendly than with whites. Similar findings were reported by Word, Zanna and Cooper (1974).

Before we move on, it is worth noting that discrimination may be positive, though **positive discrimination** has proven a mixed blessing. One of the ways we have tried to combat prejudice is to give special advantages to minorities, to break the cycle of disempowerment. Such affirmative action strategies have created special training courses, admission quotas in schools and universities, special hiring practices in the workplace, and differential health, housing and welfare funding to disadvantaged groups. Since 1990 in Australia, organisations above 100 employees have had to report their progress towards equal opportunity to Federal Parliament. How successful have these schemes been?

positive discrimination
Selectively advantaging minorities to overcome longstanding inequalities.

Box 5.2 *Getting equal: Women, work and affirmative action*

With a revision of community attitudes the traditional sexual division of labour is now viewed as sexism, and equality in employment has been government policy since the early 1970s. Many laws, regulations and affirmative action schemes have been put in place to implement equality of employment, but how successful are they?

Equality in employment is measured by equal pay for equal work, hours worked per week, the ratio of male/female unemployment, participation rates, occupational segregation, workforce stratification and the numbers of highly paid women in senior positions. Over the last decade the average female hourly earnings were 85 per cent of male earnings. Female participation rates were approaching male levels in some professions and the overall female participation rate had increased by over 25 per cent since 1975. However, most of this growth were in "low paid, part-time, casual or otherwise marginal work" (O'Donnell & Hall, 1988). While more men were looking for work than women, the proportion of women seeking work was steadily increasing; and the proportion of women gaining senior positions continued to improve slowly. This mixed bag shows some

progress towards equality, but when women's limited access to superannuation, childcare, education and training are taken into account, we have still a long way to go.

Since the 1972 National Wage and Equal Pay Case, legislation for equity in employment has been progressively introduced. However, the Australian system has favoured equality of opportunity rather than positive discrimination strategies so as to uphold the merit principle (O'Donnell & Hall, 1988). While this deals adequately with direct discrimination, it does not easily handle indirect discrimination, particularly that associated with lifecycle changes such as childbearing and rearing. To this end the *Affirmative Action (Equal Opportunity for Women) Act* was introduced in 1986 requiring employers with over 1000 employees to implement affirmative action targets and report to the Director of Affirmative Action. From 1990 this legislation covers employers with over 100 employees. Although this Act is written so that it appears a positive discrimination strategy requiring employers to set employment targets, in practice it has no powers to enforce compliance.

To date the legislation has had limited impact, as it only requires companies to report on their equal employment record but does not require them to implement any affirmative action measures. The Act was first trialled as a pilot study in 1986 in universities and colleges, but has not resulted in many significant changes as many factors, including the merit principle explicit in academic advancement, is contrary to the target-based nature of affirmative action (Thornton, 1989; Allen, 1990). The Act pleased no one when it was introduced. Private companies argued it was expensive and time consuming to compile the required information. Women's groups argued its exemption of smaller employers denied coverage to a sector in which the majority of the most marginal and exploited women worked, and that the Act was toothless (the only sanction under the Act is being named for non-compliance in Federal Parliament, hardly a serious penalty). A recent evaluation of the reporting process suggests that it is no longer seen as an onerous imposition, but 83 per cent of employers found its format inappropriate and 70 per cent would prefer much longer reporting intervals, if at all. Only 21 per cent gave the Act as the primary reason for implementing affirmative action initiatives and most cited "good management practices" as their main reason; an optimistic sign (Affirmative Action Agency, 1992)

So while affirmative action strategies appear to be in place in Australia, the fact that they do not have mandatory quotas, limits their effectiveness. Yet there seems to be a general resistance to imposing quotas, even among prominent feminists:

> [Quotas] would be an unacceptable departure from the government's insistence that merit should be the criterion on which people are selected to fill jobs . . . Quotas would be counterproductive for women and business. (Anne Summers, former head of the Office for the Status of Women, quoted in O'Donnell & Hall, 1988, p. 92)

Many commentators also make the point that the way affirmative action legislation is framed makes it difficult for potential complainants to use (Thornton, 1986). So at this stage affirmative action legislation may be of some use in educating the public at large and good for shaming employers into more equitable practices, but we still have the most segregated workforce in the OECD.

Critics of such schemes argue that positive discrimination is just another form of reverse discrimination and that special preference schemes actually *disadvantage* recipients by unnecessarily labelling them and downgrading their efforts (Glazer, 1988). Equally, other members of the community may feel cheated, that one group is being unfairly advantaged and does not deserve the special treatment (Cowlishaw, 1986). Minorities are particularly sensitive to such charges. For instance, Aboriginal students at my university were outraged when admission to their Associate Diploma was closed to all but black students, feeling that this would turn it into "a Mickey Mouse black degree". Whether "positive" equals "reverse" discrimination depends on how level a playing field exists. If it does, then all things being equal, minorities can now succeed on their own merits. Whether a level playing field can exist without government intervention and positive discrimination policies, is a hotly contested point (Katz & Taylor, 1988). As we saw with Chacko's 1988 study, the beneficiaries of affirmative action schemes are less happy with their lot than those who have unambiguously made it on their merits.

Why are we prejudiced?

The sad fact is that most, if not all, of us are prejudiced in some way. Why? What are the roots of prejudice and how does this most pernicious of social failings arise? These are some of the most closely studied questions in social psychology with an enormous base in applied areas like racism and sexism research. As we explore the nature of prejudice it seems likely that its major wellsprings lie outside our individual psyches, being part of the structures of our society. Gordon Allport (1954) in his classic contribution, *The Nature of Prejudice*, identified a number of causes and stressed the importance of historical, economic and sociocultural factors underlying prejudice. We will consider these before turning to more individual reasons.

Historical and economic explanations

The first of Allport's categories reminds us that human beings are not stupid, or always irrational, and that if prejudice is prevalent it is there for a reason. Allport noted that conceptions of the other are part of the historical baggage of a culture—we believe what our society tells us to believe and this is shaped by a culture's history. If, for example, we consider the appalling treatment of indigenous peoples worldwide, perhaps a large part of the explanation may be found in past attitudes of European colonists. Part of the reason Aboriginal Australians fare so poorly in our society may reflect the views of the first European explorers and settlers, which we in turn perpetuate (Cowlishaw, 1986, 1988). In some ways our Aboriginal cousins are unlucky as European views of indigenous peoples were in flux in the late eighteenth century, alternating between Rousseau's "noble savages" and the more economically expedient line that they were "brutes in human guise".

Robert Hughes in his book *The Fatal Shore* (1986), a history of the transportation of convicts to the antipodes, quotes a representative passage from William Dampier's account of his meeting in 1688 with Western Australian Aborigines, "the ignoble savage, orphan of nature" (Hughes, p. 48):

> The inhabitants of this country are the most miserable people in the world. The Hodmadods [the Hottentotts of Southern Africa] . . . though a nasty People, yet for Wealth are Gentlemen to these . . . and setting aside their humane shape, they differ but little from brutes. (Dampier, quoted in Hughes, p. 48)

Fashions change, and by the time of Cook, Rousseau's "noble savage" view was in vogue. Cook disagreed with Dampier but gave an equally unrealistic, if utopian vision:

> They may appear to some to be the most wretched people upon Earth, but in reality they are far happier than we Europeans; being wholly

unacquainted not only with the superfluous but the necessary Conveniences so much sought after in Europe, they are happy in not knowing the use of them. They live in Tranquillity which is not disturb'd by the Inequality of Condition. (Cook, quoted in Hughes, p. 54)

Fashions change again, and Dampier's view was once more current when Phillip sailed into Botany Bay in 1788, though he noted that, on the whole, the inhabitants were peaceable enough. It is one of the ironies of history that much of the prejudice and racism endured over two centuries of colonisation is partly attributable to the very lack of prejudice and the accepting attitudes of indigenous Australians. If, like the British, they were xenophobic and warlike, they may have enjoyed more respect and less prejudice. There is ample historical evidence that the Maoris' defiant defence of their territory won the colonists' respect and prompted a cautious attitude. "I suppose they live intirely on fish, dogs, and enemies", noted Joseph Banks, Cook's botanist. This led to a more favourable view of the Maori and ultimately the Waitangi Treaty (1840) which, in theory at least, saw the Maoris and colonists as equals.

Allport, in an American context, notes a similar pattern for black–white relations rooted in slavery. Racial prejudice flows from historical realities, blacks were an underclass and continue to be seen as such. The problem with assigning historical reasons for prejudice is it pushes explanations back into the past. We may well ask why were our cultural forebears so racist?

Realistic conflict theory

realistic conflict theory
Argues prejudice is ultimately a question of conflict over scarce resources.

Allport linked historical reasons with economics and the latter has enjoyed considerable theoretical interest within and without psychology. The **realistic conflict theory** argues that prejudice is ultimately a question of economics and scarcity of resources (Levine & Campbell, 1972). It is a basic principle of ecology that the greatest conflict will occur over the resource in shortest supply. If we live in a finite world and believe that we must grab our share, then conflict for scarce resources is inevitable. The bottom line of this theory is *inter-group competition* (Taylor & Moghaddam, 1987). Prejudice from this view is not irrational but rather a belief that one's quality of life is being eroded by the competing demands of another group. Stigmatisation is then a reaction to the cut and thrust of the competitive struggle; the winners are "spoilers and exploiters" and the losers "whingers and bludgers".

Many theorists see prejudice as a natural part of conflicts (White, 1977; Olzak & Nagel, 1986) and discrimination as a corrective to perceived economic advantage of one group over another (Bobo, 1988). That prejudice underlies extreme intracommunal violence was shown by Hovland and Sears in 1940, linking racial murders in America's Deep South with economic conditions. Hovland and Sears argued that racial prejudices were fuelled by adverse economic conditions. They correlated various economic indicators like cotton prices with lynchings of blacks in fourteen states between 1882 and 1930 to test their theory. The results confirmed their hypothesis. When economic conditions were bad, the incidence of lynchings and violence escalated, declining when conditions improved (see Table 5.2).

Table 5.2 *Lynchings and the economy: Correlations between lynchings and economic indexes*

Category	White lynchings	Total lynchings	General economics index	Acre value	Farm value
Black lynchings	−.36	.67***	−.28	−.50**	−.75***
White lynchings		.54**	−.42*	.41*	.34
Total lynchings			−.65***	−.13	−.24
General economic index				.32	.33
Acre value					1.36***
*p<.10. **P<.05. *** p<.01.					

Source: Adapted from Hepworth & West, 1988.

Hovland and Sears argued that whites were displacing their frustration over poor economic conditions on to blacks—in effect, using them as scapegoats. We will return to displacement when we consider the frustration/ aggression hypothesis in later chapters, however, in this instance, hard times were attributed to the black community who became the target of extreme discrimination. Though we must be cautious because correlation does not equal causation, a more sophisticated statistical analysis recently reconfirmed Hovland and Sears' results (Hepworth & West, 1988).

What follows from studies like Hovland and Sears' is that Southern whites' prejudice led them to see blacks as responsible for the economic downturn. Violence against blacks was therefore retaliatory. While it seems absurd that the price of cotton, largely governed by the international market, should be attributed to the black community, you must remember that cotton at that time was labour intensive and the bulk of the black community worked in the cotton industry. Any disruption, demand for relief from the appalling conditions in the cotton mills, or fields, would be savagely repressed. Racial prejudice was "realistic" in as much as the wages and conditions of the black workers was one of the few factors under white farmers' control. In the struggle to compete, black needs were indeed "competitive" with white attempts to exploit them. Racial prejudice was a useful excuse to lower wages and conditions of the black community and to savagely repress dissent. After all, if you saw your workers as subhuman brutes, discrimination could be justified. You might like to consider similar prejudicial attacks on workers as the Western industrial nations deal with the worst recession since the Great Depression.

There is considerable conflicting evidence for and against the realistic conflict hypothesis and several studies by Sears show little evidence for it (Kinder & Sears, 1981; Sears & Allen, 1984; Sears & Kinder, 1985; Sears,

Racism is often less a matter of the shape of your nose or skin colour, than competition for scarce resources driven by historical necessity.
(Photo: Chris Simkin)

modern racism
Espousing equality but believing minorities are taking too great an advantage of liberal attitudes and receiving unfairly preferential treatment.

1988). What seems to be at work is not so much economic competition but some *perceived* economic disadvantage (Olson et al. 1986). Prejudice is linked to our perception that someone is doing better than us and our fear that the status quo is under attack. Prejudicial stereotyping then justifies discrimination and, like all attributions, need not necessarily be accurate to be effective. What *is* important is our feeling that someone is doing *relatively* better than we are (Crosby, 1982). For example, racism has changed its shape over the years and **modern racism** (Sears, 1988) asserts that minority groups, while free to compete equally in society, nevertheless are pushing too hard, taking too great an advantage of liberal attitudes, and are receiving unfairly preferential treatment from a society eager to avoid being seen as racist (McConahay, 1986) (see Table 5.3). So what ultimately drives the realistic conflict theory is not relative economic advantage but rather the *perception* of relative advantage.

Genetic similarity hypothesis

genetic similarity hypothesis
We will recognise and be attracted to those whose genetic makeup is closest to our own.

Next we look at a related insight from sociobiology. You will recall from our first chapter that sociobiology is a science concerning itself with the genetic predispositions underlying social behaviour. Sociobiologists argue that *part* of our social nature has evolutionary roots and, in one of the most hotly contested contributions to attitudinal research, argues that prejudice is normal, has a biological basis and is part of our genetic makeup (Rushton, 1989). The **genetic similarity hypothesis** suggests that we will favour those whose genetic makeup is closest to our own, as this provides the strongest opportunity to pass on our genes; what is known as "maximising **inclusive fitness**". Settled communities within a species share a reservoir of closely related genes, even if individuals are not directly related. The theory suggests we use both physical and behavioural similarity as guides to genetic similarity, a fairly basic genetic proposition (Wilson, 1975; Rushton, Russell & Wells, 1984; Reynolds et al., 1987; Russell & Wells, 1991).

Table 5.3 *Old-fashioned versus modern racism: The modern racism scale*

Old-fashioned racism items

I favor laws that permit black persons to rent or purchase housing even when the person offering the property for sale or rent does not wish to rent or sell it to blacks. (Disagree Strongly = 5)

Generally speaking, I favor full racial integration. (Disagree Strongly = 5)

I am opposed to open or fair housing laws. (Agree Strongly = 5)

It is a bad idea for blacks and whites to marry one another. (Agree Strongly = 5)

Black people are generally not as smart as whites. (Strongly Agree = 5)

If a black family with about the same income and education as I have moved next door, I would mind it a great deal. (Strongly Agree = 5)

It was wrong for the United States Supreme Court to outlaw segregation in its 1954 decision. (Strongly Agree = 5)

Modern racism items

Over the past few years, the government and news media have shown more respect to blacks than they deserve. (Strongly Agree = 5)

It is easy to understand the anger of black people in America. (Strongly Disagree = 5)

Discrimination against blacks is no longer a problem in the United States. (Strongly Agree = 5)

Over the past few years, blacks have gotten more economically than they deserve. (Strongly Agree = 5)

Blacks have more influence upon school desegregation plans than they ought to have. (Strongly Agree = 5)

Blacks are getting too demanding in their push for equal rights. (Strongly Agree = 5)

Blacks should not push themselves where they are not wanted. (Strongly Agree = 5)

Source: McConahay, 1986.

Prejudice and discrimination, then, are basically a matter of ingroup favouritism and outgroup derogation which we will discuss later. Sociobiology just offers another view of why this bias arises. The genetic similarity theory makes several predictions which have quite a deal of support:

- First, we will befriend and marry those with similar physical, attitudinal and behavioural characteristics as this maximises reproductive similarity (Rushton, 1991). Chapter Nine, Close Relationships, reviews the supporting evidence.

The genetic similarity hypothesis argues that we favour those with whom we share a common genetic inheritance and reject those unlike us. This theory works best in the large extended family of yesteryear. The smaller nuclear family of today and social mobility provide less support for this view.
(Photo: Chris Simkin)

- Second, we will show ingroup favouritism to those who share a common genetic message as this maximises our resource pool and facilitates natural selection. In Chapter Ten, Prosocial Behaviour, we review supporting research on kin and group selection and reciprocal altruism.
- Third, we will show hostility towards those dissimilar to ourselves. In Chapter Seven, Aggression, and Chapter Eight, Social Exchange, we consider how dissimilarity leads to resource competition and aggression.

xenophobia
An irrational fear of strangers, or those different to ourselves.

Support also comes from comparative studies that show that **xenophobia** or fear of strangers has many parallels in the animal kingdom (Hebb & Thompson, 1968; Rushton, 1989) and that young children have an instinctive fear of strangers (Berkowitz, 1962). E.O. Wilson, the father of sociobiology, agrees and argues that recognising this is the first step towards combating prejudice:

> Part of man's problem (xenophobia) is that his intergroup responses are still crude and primitive, and inadequate for the extended relationships that civilization has thrust upon him . . . [So] Xenophobia becomes a political virtue. (Wilson, 1975, p. 575)

Critics like Anderson (1989), Dunbar (1989) and Cunningham and Barbee (1991) argue that sociobiologists ignore the social determinants of behaviour (a much rejected criticism) and that prejudice and discrimination do not reflect genetic dissimilarity as we have few reliable ways of determining who is genetically related to us. They also point out that the end product

Box 5.3 *Is sociobiology racist?*

Perhaps by now you are wondering if sociobiology isn't just an attempt to give prejudice a scientific veneer. Many social theorists would see the proposition that ethnocentrism has genetic roots as tantamount to racism (Allen, et al., 1976, 1977). Unfortunately, the great ethologist and Nobel Prize winner, Konrad Lorenz, *was* racist and his support of Hitler's racial eugenics gave critics free rein. Is sociobiology inherently racist? Michael Ruse in his critical review, *Sociobiology: Sense or Nonsense?*, tackles this head on:

> Taken at its most immediate level, this criticism strikes me as being intemperate to the point of unfairness—cruel even . . . Let it be stated categorically: the sociobiologists are not racists. There is no suggestion at all in their writings that (for instance) blacks are inferior because of their genes. Even less is there suggestion that we might properly embark on a wholesale eugenics programme to eliminate genes of certain racial types, like blacks or Jews. I do not know the political views of the sociobiologists but they are certainly not neo-Nazis. (Ruse, 1979, p. 75)

So sociobiologists are not racists, but is their theory? How can they argue that prejudice is part of our evolution and escape charges of racism?

The first defence might take the moral high ground and argue that banning any area of scientific inquiry is morally indefensible. What if xenophobia is part of our genetic makeup? Surely we need to know this if we are to construct a more equal society?

Allied to this is the old philosophical **two rights problem**. We may only build a fairer world by treating all humanity equally, but it is patently obvious that human beings are not all equal. We differ sexually, racially, intellectually, physically, and so forth. Whether these differences, in sum, disadvantage any one group of humans over another is problematic, however, we need to know what these differences are to take account of them in building a fairer society—which may mean positive discrimination programmes.

In any case there is no suggestion that xenophobia is stronger in any one group of humans than another (Trivers, 1971; Lewontin, 1972; Alexander, 1974; Wilson, 1975; Cosmides and Tooby, 1989; Crawford, 1989). Sociobiology's ultimate defence against critics' charges of racism is that it favours no one portion of humanity. As Ruse (1979) states: "sociobiologists are affirming the unity of humankind". If all of humanity is inherently racist, then sociobiologists are not racist for saying so.

of ingroup favouritism from this perspective would be inbreeding and racial extinction. Rushton and others acknowledge these difficulties but offer much collateral research supporting their position (see Rushton, 1989, for a review).

This controversial theory argues that prejudice has primeval roots in mistrust of those who are different from us and who, in competing for scarce resources, pose a threat to our survival. Prejudice is therefore a normal biological reaction to outgroups. However it is worth remembering that most sociobiologists do not take an extreme view of biological determinism, and recognise that our evolutionary past and genetic makeup only set up behavioural predispositions from which all the other factors we have discussed make their own contribution to human prejudice.

Social identity theory

Explanations of prejudice based on social cognition suggest we define ourselves and create our social identity by a process of social comparison that involves stereotyping and social categorisation. An inevitable part of this process is categorising others unfavourably (Tajfel, 1982; Messick & Mackie, 1989). As we define those with whom we share similar traits and experiences, we will also exclude those who are different from us. This leads to prejudice. A number of related theories bear on this important phenomenon and we will consider them in turn.

Intergroup conflict, ingroup favouritism and outgroup bias

Closely allied to realistic conflict theory is a large body of work suggesting that competition leads to intergroup hostility.

This effect was shown by Carolyn and Muzafer Sherif in a number of similar experiments run over 14 years. The first of these was conducted at a summer camp at Robbers Cave, Oklahoma, in 1954. Twenty-two average, middle-class, white, eleven- and twelve-year-old boys participated unknowingly in what became one of social psychology's classic field experiments (Sherif et al., 1961; Sherif, 1966). Sherif was interested in the effects of intergroup cooperation and competition and obtained permission from the boys' parents to introduce a few surprises into their lives. Sherif divided the boys into two eleven-member groups, the Rattlers and the Eagles, and for a week the two groups did the usual summer camp activities such as swimming, canoeing, bushwalking and sports, not knowing that the other group existed. The boys were given activities that encouraged cooperation and mutuality. Sherif and his colleagues noted that the groups quickly grew their own cooperative cultures. They named themselves, shook down into leaders and followers, and appropriately rewarded each boy's contribution to the group. Sherif then threw the two groups into competitive contact.

The boys played tug-of-war games, football and other team sports. They were rewarded for camp neatness and overtly encouraged to measure their performance against the other group's. Not surprisingly, a hostile culture quickly developed, and the boys began to tease the other group calling them "cowards", "sissies", "bums", "sneaky" and "smart alecks". This quickly escalated to verbal abuse, fights, raids and damage to the other group's cabins and a riotous food fight. Sherif remarked that an outsider with no knowledge of the experiment would see the boys as "wicked, disturbed and vicious bunches of youngsters" (Sherif, 1966, p. 85) and we might add highly prejudiced!

Having set up the two groups to become enemies, the researchers then altered conditions to promote cooperation, not easy given the hostility and mistrust built up over the two weeks. At first they increased the two groups' contact, believing this would lead to more realistic interactions and friendship, but quite the opposite happened and if anything, increased contact gave more chances to score off the other group. The experimenters then tried sermonising, among other things stressing the benefits of cooperation and goodwill during weekly religious services, to little effect. Finally Sherif and his colleagues hit on the happy strategy of joint cooperation towards mutually desired goals. They sabotaged the camp's water main and the boys had to track down the blockage and restore the water supply. They teamed together to push start the food truck and later pooled their money to rent a movie. By these devices the experimenters imposed **superordinate goals** on the two groups, goals that required both groups to cooperate so that all would benefit.

By these devices Sherif was able to turn the boys' attitudes around and return them to their parents in a reasonable state of mind. By the end of the camp the two groups were on good terms, and the victorious group on the points competition shared their spoils with the losers. Both groups left for Oklahoma City on the same bus, best of mates. While Sherif's study has a wider application to intergroup conflict and cooperation, it also sheds considerable light on the nature of prejudice.

superordinate goals
Group goals that require hostile groups to cooperate on a joint task so that all will benefit.

Minimal group situation

How might we explain Sherif's results? At the simplest level competition is a game in which some win and others lose. We strongly identify with those sharing the same goals as ourselves and try to beat our opponents. Competition involves tension; tension leads to intergroup prejudice. However, while this seems rather obvious, it is another example where the obvious explanation is not the whole answer. Henri Tajfel suggested in the early 1970s that it was not necessarily competition but the simple fact of being placed in a group which led to ingroup favouritism and outgroup bias. Perhaps the Rattlers and Eagles were hostile to each other simply because they had been placed in different groups.

Tajfel tested this hypothesis in a series of simple experiments. In one he asked British schoolboys to estimate the number of dots on a series of slides; ostensibly a visual perception experiment (Tajfel et al., 1971). They were then randomly assigned to groups but supposedly on the basis of their under or overestimation of the number of dots. The boys were told that neither group was better than the other at estimating, only different. In the next unrelated task, they could differentially reward each other by giving each boy points that could later be redeemed for cash. It must be stressed that the groups were designed to be only trivially different, yet the boys chose to reward their own group, a clear case of ingroup favouritism. When they were given the choice of either increasing their group's take, or maximising the difference between the groups, they chose the latter at the expense of their group's overall profit (Tajfel, 1970, 1972). In a later experiment, even being openly randomly assigned to a group by the flip of a coin still gave the same result (Billig & Tajfel, 1973). Clearly, random assignment to groups produced competitive effects and ingroup favouritism. This ingroup favouritism which comes from simply being assigned to a group was called the **minimal group situation** (Tajfel & Turner, 1986) to reflect the minimal differences which led to this intergroup discrimination.

Many other experiments have confirmed this effect and extended our knowledge of its power. The effect is international and ignores age and sex differences (Brewer, 1979; Messick & Mackie, 1989), though the effect is heightened in individualistic cultures (Gudykunst, 1989). Members rate each other as more attractive (Brewer & Silver, 1978), more likable (Turner,

minimal group situation
An experimental design which shows that trivial differences of themselves lead to intergroup hostility.

1978) and their performance higher (Ferguson & Kelley, 1964) than the outgroup. They are more tolerant towards their own group (Howard & Rothbart, 1980). They are also more competitive collectively than they would be as individuals (McCullum et al., 1985; Brown, 1988) all of which amounts to a classic case of prejudice. How is it then that simply being put into a different group produces these effects?

Henri Tajfel and his colleague John Turner (see Chapter Twelve) proposed the **social identity theory** to explain these effects (Tajfel & Turner, 1986; Turner 1987, 1991). Their theory argues that our sense of self has both personal and social elements. Our self-esteem derives from both our own efforts and our identification with the groups to which we belong. Our social identity then derives from the groups with which we are affiliated. Anything that reflects favourably on them will reflect favourably on us. It is then natural for us to support and enhance these groups. In a nutshell, ingroup favouritism overvalues the groups to which we belong and so inflates our self-esteem.

social identity theory
Aspects of our identity based on the groups and social categories to which we belong.

An example will illustrate this process. Shortly before the Seoul Olympics, a fairly disturbed student joined one of my classes. Evidently he had a poor self-image and, without wanting to be too Freudian about it, was into guns as a compensation for whatever was missing in his life. He was a real nuisance; no matter what the topic, guns crept into our discussions. He habitually wore a flak jacket and ammunition pouches, continually distributed pro-gun literature in class, and almost drove us silly with his fund-raising support of the Olympic pistol team. This all came to a head the day he produced a gun in class. The rest of the students rounded on him in no uncertain terms and told him to shove his guns and the Olympics! In tears, and not very coherently, he invoked his membership of gun clubs, praising the other members, pointing out they were "all rich, famous people, managing directors (and academics!), successes in life". In the same breath he disparaged all the other students' affiliations, belittling their achievements. He was obviously on shaky ground and the students compassionately backed off. The next week, when one of his fellow gun-club members won a medal at the Games, he was ecstatic. Her achievement was his also.

Social identity theory predicts that when our personal identity is threatened we will overvalue the social group to which we belong to bolster our self-esteem (Crocker et al., 1987; Abrams & Hogg, 1988). In this somewhat extreme example, the young man obviously had a poor personal image and drew most of his self-esteem from his affiliation with the gun clubs. His social identity was the larger part of his sense of self. Accordingly, he invested most of his energy in supporting the gun clubs and their Olympic effort. In so doing he was really supporting his own identity. In his estimation the champions of his club became super heroes and his view of them was quite unrealistic. The point is that his self-esteem depended heavily on *how he evaluated* the groups he was affiliated with, not necessarily on their real strengths. It was fortunate that his clubmate did so well, as he basked in her reflected glory.

Considerable research supports the basics of this theory and its premises, though we will note some problems with the link between self-esteem and group polarisation when we consider self-categorisation theory in Chapter Twelve. Cialdini found an increased tendency to bask in the reflected glory of a successful ingroup when subjects' self-esteem had been threatened (Cialdini et al., 1976). Meindl and Lerner (1985) humiliated subjects, reducing their self-esteem and found they then rated outgroup members more negatively. Oakes and Turner (1980) ran a minimal group experiment and then had subjects complete a self-esteem test. As predicted, both ingroup favouritism and self-esteem were higher than for the control group. Lemyre and Smith (1985) found that when you restrict ingroup favouritism, self-esteem does not rise, and so forth. However, such research does not tell us why enhancing our social identities leads to prejudice towards others. Two other parts of the puzzle are missing: stereotyping and social learning.

Stereotyping and negative attribution

To this point we have been considering theories of causation, or how people come to be prejudiced, but we have yet to consider the nature of their prejudice. Without wanting to examine the individual *content* of prejudices, which was the approach up to the early 1970s (Brigham, 1971), we turn now to the *process* of stereotyping others. From 1975 social psychologists have seen prejudice as an integral part of a unified cognitive process underlying all attitudes (Fiske & Taylor, 1991). Not all stereotypes are prejudicial but all attitudes have a stereotypic component. What are stereotypes and why do they sometimes lead us into prejudice?

Stereotyping is an integral part of human information processing. A stereotype is a preconceived image of an individual or group based on a few representative characteristics. There is a fair bit of argument whether prejudicial stereotypes have any real basis in fact—the **kernel of truth hypothesis** (Levine & Campbell, 1972)—but all theorists agree that they are exaggerated distortions of the targeted group. Stereotyping research looks at how we form collections of beliefs about people into coherent wholes to simplify our understanding them. They are based on abbreviated and often inaccurate information and, as you can see from Box 5.5, stereotypes usually favour our own group at the expense of those different from us. Stereotypes are not necessarily prejudicial but are often based on limited information, leading to perceptual distortion. If I introduce you to another person at the beach and say he is an accountant, you immediately call up your mental schema of accountants and overlay that on the person lying on the sand next to you. Though you have no other clues to go on other than age and sex, you assume he is conscientious, a little overprecise and fussy, has a good head for figures, is a materialist, and probably has poor people skills. In your mind his image is overlaid with visions of pinstripes. Stereotypes are a form of social shorthand, they allow us to weigh up others quickly and react appropriately but at the expense of accuracy and individuality.

kernel of truth hypothesis
A belief that at the root of every prejudice is a kernel of truth.

NO MATTER HOW FAR YOU RUN,
YOU'LL ALWAYS BE AN ACCOUNTANT.

(*Cartoonist: Steve Harris*)

We will consider the nature of stereotypes before moving on to consider how they are formed; how they lead to prejudice; and what the consequences are of prejudicial stereotypes.

The nature of stereotypes

Stereotype is a French term for a printing process where a metal plate is cast from a plaster mould of set-up type and used instead of the type itself. By this method many exact reprints can be made without the slight imperfections and variations that come from printing directly from type. While this process gave a better product, and was both time and energy saving, it did not allow the printer to make corrections or variations. The word was first used in its modern sense by the English social commentator Prescott in 1868, when he used it to convey the many identical images of himself held by friends which permitted no variations and hence little accuracy. Stereotypes are by their nature rigid and oversimplified images. When we meet someone for the first time we immediately use salient information—their context, dress, sex, race, age, or vocation—to *typecast* them, yet another printing allusion which conveys the other aspect of stereotyping—once we have made a judgment it pre-empts all further judgments. Stereotypes are prejudicial to the extent that they unfairly typecast others.

One of the earliest studies of ethnic stereotyping was undertaken in 1932 by Katz and Braly (1933). They asked 100 white male undergraduates from Princeton University to rate Italians, Americans, Chinese, English,

Table 5.4 *The changing nature of racial stereotypes*

	For Negroes (1933, 1951, 1967) or black Americans (1982)				Percentage who rate traits as typical	For Americans (1933, 1951, 1967) or white Americans (1982)			
	1933	1951	1967	1982		1933	1951	1967	1982
Superstitious	84	41	13	6	Industrious	48	30	23	21
Lazy	75	31	26	13	Intelligent	47	32	20	10
Happy-go-lucky	38	17	27	15	Materialistic	33	37	67	65
Ignorant	38	24	11	10	Ambitious	33	21	42	35
Musical	26	33	47	29	Progressive	27	5	17	9
Ostentatious	26	11	25	5	Pleasure-loving	26	27	28	45
Very religious	24	17	8	23	Alert	23	7	7	2
Stupid	22	10	4	1	Efficient	21	9	15	8
Physically dirty	17	—	3	0	Aggressive	20	8	15	11
Naive	14	—	4	4	Straightforward	19	—	9	7
Slovenly	13	—	5	2	Practical	10	—	12	14
Unreliable	12	—	6	2	Sportsmanlike	19	—	9	6
Pleasure-loving	—	19	26	20	Individualistic	—	26	15	14
Sensitive	—	—	17	13	Conventional	—	—	17	20
Gregarious	—	—	17	4	Scientifically-minded	—	—	15	4
Talkative	—	—	14	5	Ostentatious	—	—	15	6
Imitative	—	—	13	9	Conservative	—	—	—	15
Aggressive	—	—	—	19	Stubborn	—	—	—	20
Materialistic	—	—	—	19	Tradition-loving	—	—	—	19
Loyal to family	—	—	—	39					
Arrogant	—	—	—	14					
Ambitious	—	—	—	13					
Tradition-loving	—	—	—	13					

Attitudes of university students towards black and white Americans have changed over the years and generally in a less prejudiced direction.

Source: Brehm & Kassin, 1990.

Germans, the Irish, Jews, Japanese, Negroes and Turks from a list of 84 descriptive adjectives. From these ratings they compiled ethnic images which they felt reflected not only undergraduate stereotypes but also those of the wider community. Some of their results are shown in Table 5.4 contrasted with follow-up studies in 1950 (Gilbert, 1951), 1967 (Karlins, Coffman & Walters 1969) and 1982 (Dovidio & Gaertner, 1986). As you can see stereotypes not only diminished in percentage terms but also became more positive over the years though the same general patterns continued.

Box 5.4 *Measuring stereotypes: A little fading and a little faking*

How accurate are these studies of changing stereotypes? Is racial prejudice declining or is it merely going underground? Sigall and Page (1971) suspected that a decline of "old fashioned racism" had led to racist comments becoming socially unacceptable. They reasoned that current students were perhaps as prejudiced as those in Katz and Braly's original study but socially conditioned to appear more accepting and less prejudiced. To test their hypothesis that racism had gone underground they devised an interesting bogus pipeline experiment.

Students were divided into two groups and asked to rate the traits of white and black Americans. Half just filled in the questionnaire but the other half were wired up to an impressive lie detector and told it would measure their true feelings. The machine did nothing of the sort, it was just a way of bluffing students into giving more honest responses.

The results partly confirmed their hypothesis. While they found that students hooked up to a "lie detector" were less prejudiced than the 1932 sample, they were more prejudiced than the control group. Sigall and Page interpreted their results as indicating a shift towards less overt and more subtle racism, with students wanting to appear less prejudiced and more socially acceptable. They concluded that American college students' prejudices were undergoing "a little fading and faking".

The formation of stereotypes: Social categorisation

We gain stereotypes through learning and social categorisation. We have already seen in Chapter Two that we automatically process information about people using ready made schemas. It is natural for us to label and categorise people by age, sex, race, class, the way they dress, their social context and any other information that is salient about them. Much of the information we extract from observing others is *implicit*. That is, we rely on past learning and stereotypes to assign meaning to those being observed. We see a poorly dressed woman going through a garbage bin and immediately use the stereotype "derelict" to categorise and explain her condition. However, we are also using this information to draw a line between her and ourselves. Part of our evaluation is asking ourselves, "is she like me and how does she differ?" This pervasive tendency to divide the world up into *us* and *them* categories is known as social categorisation (Turner et al., 1987).

It needs to be stressed that social categorisation is automatic, natural and an inevitable process. As we saw in Chapter Two, the sheer amount of information available in our environment (and inside our heads) makes schematic processing necessary to reduce information overload. So social categorisation allows us to make rapid judgments by using *category-based* rather than *attribute-based* processing (Fiske & Taylor, 1991). As we have seen, this allows a lot of information to be used quickly, if at the expense of accuracy. The most *salient* characteristics of an individual trigger appropriate stereotypes. So to label other people we automatically look for differences to sort them into categories. Any salient difference will do (Hamilton & Trollier, 1986).

Prejudice is often a matter of fairly illusory ingroup and outgroup categorisations as this cartoon suggests.
(Cartoonist: Graeme Mitchell)

It is a short step from social categorisation to prejudice. Ingroup favouritism inevitably leads to outsiders' feeling less valued, but this is still not prejudice. If, however, we enhance ourselves by affiliation, then it follows we will also protect ourselves by dissociation (Snyder et al., 1986). When our self-esteem is threatened by too close an identification with failure, we remove ourselves to avoid a negative impact on our social identity. We avoid too close a contact with minority groups as we do not want to be identified with them and have some of their negative image rub off on us. After all we are known by the company we keep! However, this is a little more active that just avoidance. Part of the process of dissociation is actively looking for those aspects of the outgroup that will stigmatise and thus reinforce our decision to dissociate (Rosenbaum, 1986). Basically we want to draw sharp boundaries between ourselves and others (Wilder, 1986; Schaller & Maass, 1989).

Our feelings of superiority then are elevated by finding reasons to contrast ourselves and others but this inevitably leads to conflict with outgroups who have the same desire. Tajfel called this process **social competition** to distinguish it from a more realistic conflict over resources (Tajfel, 1982), though in practice the two conflicts are usually inseparable. As a general rule the more threatened we feel, the more likely we are to draw sharper boundaries. Yet as Gaertner et al. (1989) noted, when the boundaries are

social competition
Intergroup competition based on perceived differences rather than a realistic conflict.

shifted to include formerly despised groups, we see just how ingrained, but arbitrary, the process of social categorisation really is.

This effect is not straightforward and many other variables influence our reaction, and we must be cautious in interpreting these results. For example Tesser et al. (1988) found that while we usually enjoy another ingroup member's triumph, we will dissociate ourselves if it puts us in a particularly bad light. This also applies to members of our ingroup who fail and weaken the group's credibility. Marques and Yzerbyt (1988) found that subjects listening to taped speeches by other students showed ingroup favouritism when the speeches were of equally high quality but more harshly underrated a poor-quality speech by an ingroup member than one from an outgroup. These studies suggest that we not only dissociate ourselves from those unlike us but also from our peers who are letting the side, or ourselves, down.

We will return to an extended coverage of social categorisation, social identification, and self-categorisation and group polarisation effects in Chapter Twelve. We turn now to consider how the self-attributional biases we discussed in Chapter Three reinforce ingroup favouritism and outgroup stereotyping.

Stereotypes and misattribution

As we saw in Chapter Three we attribute characteristics to ourselves and others based on perceptually dominant (salient) characteristics. We also saw that this is a flawed process with many biases and perceptual errors leading us into constant misattributions. The attribution process drives our stereotypical notions of others, serving up a biased and perceptually distorted picture of them in what is in effect a vicious circle. Our bias distorts our perception, which then reinforces our biases, leading to self-perpetuating stereotypes (Skrypnek & Snyder, 1982). The ultimate nature of prejudice therefore might be this tendency to see ourselves as perfectly representative examples of our favoured groups, and to lump all others together, as somehow different and inevitably inferior to ourselves.

outgroup homogeneity effect
Any member of a minority becomes a stereotypical representative of the whole and less differentiated than members of our ingroup.

One of the more distinctive biases is the **outgroup homogeneity effect** (Park & Rothbart, 1982) which suggests we see all minority group members alike and differences become an indistinct blur. Any one member of a minority becomes a stereotypical representative of the whole. "All Asians look the same to me" is a classic example of the effect (Bothwell, Brigham & Malpass, 1989). Personality and other variables blur as we assume that all group members will think, feel and react in the same way. Our lack of perception homogenises individual differences so we assume that the bad behaviour of one individual is a representative sample, and on that basis unfairly stigmatise the whole group. The flip side to this is that we will see our own ingroup members as individuals; more distinct, more complex and more diverse (Linville & Jones, 1980; Linville, 1982; Linville, Salovey & Fischer, 1986). This is not unexpected if you consider that we spend more time with them and naturally would know them better.

Thomas Pettigrew (1979, 1985) extended this analysis with his **ultimate**

One view of animal liberationists sees them as fuzzy-minded bleeding hearts engaging in unwarranted anthropomorphism. Nevertheless, animal liberationists come in all shapes and sizes. Seeing them as all the same is yet another example of the outgroup homogeneity effect. (Photo: Gavin Price)

attribution error hypothesis. If we see all outgroup members as an homogeneous whole and the actions of one as somehow representative of the whole, then we risk making a fundamental attribution error and applying it too indiscriminately. Pettigrew argued that while we see our actions as a consequence of our environment, in stereotyping the outgroup we blame them for their mistakes and minimise their successes. This tendency to use inherent personality defects to explain outgroup behaviour is an "ultimate error" (Pettigrew, 1985).

Another bias associated with social categorisation is the **assumed similarity effect**. As we have seen, we assume that those who like us are like us. Believing that your ingroup reflects your beliefs polarises differences between them and others. This leads to prejudice because making this assumption masks differences that would otherwise make our ingroup seem more diverse and thus more like the outgroup. For example, Bob, our Jew-hater, assured me that "most crims here hate Jews" and went on to justify his belief by saying that "most are Christians like myself and so must think as I do". He assured me that the Jews in the gaol were "foreign thinkers and non-Australian". In reality, the few Jewish inmates came from almost identical backgrounds as the rest of the gaol population. By focusing on religious affiliation alone, Bob saw too much similarity in his own group and too few similarities in the outgroup.

ultimate attribution error hypothesis
Assuming the actions of one outgroup member are representative of the whole group.

assumed similarity effect
The belief that all members of an outgroup are the same.

Another problem related to stereotyping is sampling errors. Many of us hold elaborate stereotypes without ever consciously mixing with the objects of our prejudice (Allport & Kramer, 1946; Ray, 1983c; Quattrone, 1986). During the Cold War we were taught to hate communists aka Russians and Vietnamese, yet few of us had ever met one. We held a firm belief based on a flawed sample. Media stereotypes portrayed the average Russian as a twisted devotee of Marx, brainwashed into an unthinking hatred of the West, and offered us a few highly vocal Red Brigade members as **archetypes** of "the evil empire". This carefully constructed and packaged illusion completely ignored that over 90 per cent of Russians were not communists and that the Communist Party was overwhelmingly despised within the former Soviet Union. On a more mundane level we often mistake the base rate (Chapter Two). My mate's firmly held conviction that all elderly "hat drivers" should be required to take a 120 kph spin around a racetrack before an annual licence renewal, shows a similar sampling bias. Try as I might, I cannot convince him that he only notices slow drivers who wear hats (and not the fast ones wearing hats or the rest of humanity ambling along) and this unfairly stigmatises the elderly as slow (poor) drivers.

archetype
A cultural stereotype which typifies a class of people, ideals or objects.

Box 5.5 *Stereotyping among Aboriginal and Anglo-Australians*

How do Aboriginal and Anglo-Australians view each other? Over the years several studies have asked this question (Callan and St John, 1984). In 1986 Professor Kevin Marjoribanks and Dr Deidre Jordan of Adelaide University reported the results of a study they undertook with 90 Aboriginal and 260 Anglo-Australian secondary students drawn from two rural and two urban schools in South Australia.

Marjoribanks and Jordan were curious about the content students would assign to stereotypes of their own and to the other's race. After extensive discussions with both communities they selected nineteen attributes, which they formed into seven-point, bipolar rating scales. Each student was then asked to rate Aboriginal Australians on these scales and then asked to do the same for Anglo-Australians. These two sets of ratings formed the four schedules the researchers used in their analysis: how Anglos rated themselves and Aboriginals; and how Aboriginals rated Anglos and themselves. You should note the students were not asked for individual self-assessments but rather how they saw the communities as a whole, and these

results should be interpreted in that light. Though the study had roughly even numbers of each sex from both groups, the data was not analysed for sex differences.

The mean attribute scores for each community are given in Figure 5.1. The data was later factor analysed to see what descriptors underlay each group's attributions and gave worrying results. On the whole, both communities saw Anglo-Australians favourably and Aboriginal Australians less so.

Analysing Aboriginal views of their community led to the following factors: "well-socialised, go-getting, good citizens and socially accep-table". By way of contrast, Anglos rated Aboriginals on attributes like "untrustworthy, concern for money rather than for occupational status, poor providers, aggressive, often in trouble with the police, often in debt, unmotivated, dirty, unreliable, quick tempered, and don't know when to stop drinking alcohol"—which factor the researchers labelled "poorly socialised citizens".

Anglo patterns of attributes led to the following descriptors of their own community:

"well-socialised, go-getting and good citizens". Aborigines agreed Anglos were "well-socialised and good citizens"; adding they were "law-abiding, motivated and caring, and socially acceptable".

These are worrying findings indeed. Looking at the relative magnitude of these four images, the outstanding finding was the negative view held by the Anglo students towards the Aboriginal community. It was a uniformly intense and unfavourable stereotype. One of the study's ironies was that Aboriginal students did not reciprocate these feelings and indeed held "extremely favourable" views of Anglo-Australians.

For themselves, the Aboriginal sample saw their community in only moderately favourable terms. This inversion of stereotypes by minorities has been found by other researchers. Lynskey, Ward and Fletcher (1991) in a study of outgroup attributions and stereotypes found that Pakeha adolescents showed a self-serving bias in stereotypes and attributions, while Maoris demonstrated a weak tendency to favour Pakehas rather than their own race. One may only speculate on the morale of the minorities that leads to such findings. We will return to this issue in Chapter Twelve.

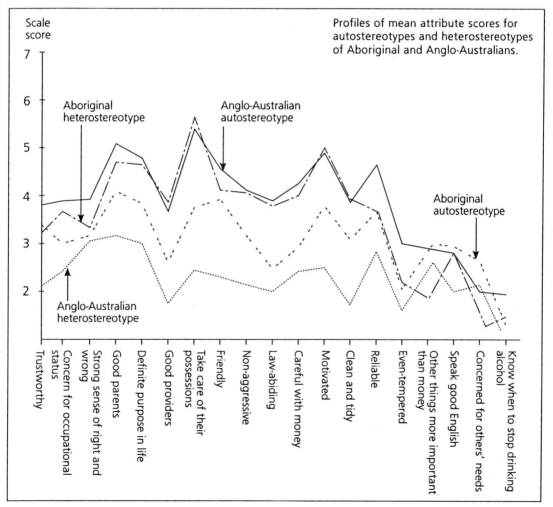

Figure 5.1 *Aboriginal and white Australians views of themselves and each other*
Source: Marjoribanks & Jordan, 1986.

illusory correlations
Attributing non-existent causal connections between variables.

Allied to this are **illusory correlations** (Chapman, 1967). In the above example, my friend has firmly linked fashion to a negative stereotype. He has correlated a predilection for hats with driving skill and perhaps fallen into an ageist prejudice. Given that there are an enormous number of slow drivers, it is only the salience of wearing hats while driving that has captured his attention. His linking hats, age and driving skill is probably an illusory correlation but awaits a doctoral study to definitively decide the issue. Nevertheless, there is a serious underlying issue. As negative actions are less common than other events, why do we link these with minorities?

Hamilton and Gifford (1976) pondered this point and hypothesised that frequency of occurrence might itself be salient. They asked a group of their students to read short descriptive statements about two anonymous groups labelled "A" and "B". Despite the fact that the proportion of negative statements was the same for each group and that twice as many statements overall were positive, the students judged the minority group more negatively. Although there was no correlation the subjects saw one. Why? Hamilton and Gifford suggested the only link was a *shared distinctiveness*. Negative statements and descriptive comments about the minority were relatively less frequent and so became linked in the subjects' minds. This is a great worry if you consider that we are quick to make these connections and slow to forget them (Hamilton & Sherman, 1989); it is even worse when you consider we might even manufacture evidence to support the stereotype (Slusher & Anderson, 1987) once it is established and terrible if you consider it may well become a self-fulfilling prophecy.

The consequences of prejudicial stereotypes

As we saw in the last chapter, attitudes do not necessarily determine behaviour, and so it is with prejudicial stereotypes—they do not always lead to discrimination. We may also add another caveat—the distinction between *knowing* a prejudicial stereotype and *accepting* it (Devine, 1989). As we have already discussed, the changing face of prejudice has thrown old attitudes on the scrap heap; it is no longer fashionable to be openly sexist or racist. Improving race relations, for example, has brought many to acknowledge the social discrimination inherent in their upbringing and to attempt to deal with it. We cannot help the way we were brought up, we can only question it as adults.

Where are we though? Is a greater consciousness of social discrimination changing stereotypes? As we saw at the beginning of the chapter, attitudes are changing, however slowly. Education plays an important role in reducing the mindless acceptance of stereotypical views of the other (Ray, 1983c). The more we know about another the less we will rely on stereotypes (Krueger & Rothbart, 1988). We will return to this theme in the final section of our chapter.

There is also much ambivalence in our attitudes. As we saw in our section on discrimination, we are often unsure of appropriate social etiquette and avoid minorities to resolve our dilemma. While this feels like discrimination to those affected, it is often just simple ignorance and embarrassment. As a colleague recently returned from Perth observed, academics tiptoe through a semantic minefield when lecturing on race as the use of "Koories" is inappropriate or a deadly insult to some Aborigines, while being called "blacks" or "Aborigines" is a sure sign of racial chauvinism to others. This difficulty is made even worse by the real ambivalence many people feel towards minorities. As Katz and Hass (1988) noted, many Americans see their blacks as both *disadvantaged* and *deviant*. They found there is still a great reluctance to admit that cultural difference does not equal deviance; and this is not all one sided, as an old in-joke among Maoris that they should rename New Zealand "The land of the wrong white crowd" demonstrates! On a more serious note, in Australia and New Zealand there is an ongoing debate about how far we should recognise Islamic law as part of our legal system. Many educated citizens, while fully supportive of multiculturalism, nevertheless consider many Islamic practices barbaric—a difficulty not helped by tabloids serving a steady diet of imagined atrocities: child kidnappings, female circumcisions, ritual floggings and decapitations.

At this point we leave psychology and enter the realms of speculative ethics. When is an act right or wrong, and when is our setting our face against it moral indignation or simple prejudice? So summing up, it seems that prejudiced people still hold and enjoy their stereotypes while the rest of us muddle along trying to sort out how we feel about minorities from first principles. We turn now to consider how stereotypes are learned.

Learning to be prejudiced

It goes without saying that virtually all social behaviour has a hefty learned component and prejudice is no exception. We learn to be bigots in much the same way we learn to become members of our society, it is all part and parcel of growing up. We will reflect whatever prejudices are current with our parents, peers, teachers, media, political leaders and other socialising agents. Sad to say, few of us are really aware of the extent of our prejudices as we have seen many are quite subtle (Devine, 1989). The real test is how we react when our consciousness is raised.

Prejudice is acquired formally, informally and by vicarious reinforcement. Consider the following advice to schoolchildren from Alfred Rosenberg, the editor of the *Volkischer Beobachter*, the official Nazi daily:

> Children of the Reich it is a holy duty to resist the sly attacks of the Jew. Be vigilant! His cunning and treachery are a national illness. Keep Germany pure and unsullied. Avoid the Jewish disease . . . do not associate with lesser peoples. Beware the hidden Jew. Your parents may not see through his disguise but they are weak. You are the vigilant hope of our future. Sniff out the Jew, expose him! (*Volkischer Beobachter*, 13 May 1936)

The implication of this piece of blatant racial vilification is obvious. German children are invited to play "spot the Jew", a modern form of sniffing out witches. The article goes on to alert children to the sentimentality of their parents towards Jewish neighbours and friends, and cautions them to expose them as a patriotic duty. From reports of the time, young girls in the German League of Young Maidens were given silhouette charts of "Jewish profiles" to aid them, in much the same way that Boy Scouts across the channel were given aircraft recognition silhouettes to aid coastal defence. Neither group thought their behaviour odd and were probably thrilled to be helping out the national cause.

Learning views of prejudice stress the importance of early experience in the formation of attitudes (Bishop, 1976; Bandura, 1986). Goodman (1952, 1964) found that children as young as three were aware of racial differences, and a quarter of his four-year-old sample expressed racist attitudes. Katz (1976) demonstrated that children as young as four were able to make elaborate conceptual differentiations between blacks and whites based on racial cues such as skin colour and facial features. How do we learn to become prejudiced at such a young age?

Classical conditioning

Simple association often shapes the young mind. An Islander trying to be friendly pokes a face at a baby in a stroller, sets it screaming and starts a lifetime's distrust of Polynesians. Our parents' avoidance of an Arab neighbour teaches us to avoid Arabs. TV images of black-skinned men rioting in Johannesburg are linked with profoundly disturbing images of violence, teaching us that blacks are dangerously violent. Neighbours refusing to shop in an Asian grocery because "they are dirty" associates dirt and Asians in general. Often this simple association is quite unconscious; the linking of an unconditioned response like being frightened, with an object of prejudice, creates an adverse reaction, the first step to racial hatred.

Modelling

Similarly, much of our early learning is observational. We see important models—parents and relatives, friends, teachers and figures of public importance—acting in prejudicial ways and being rewarded. As we identify with these models we emulate their behaviour. The essence of this social learning is the vicarious thrill (reinforcement) we experience as we see others benefiting from prejudicial behaviour and we want to also. The young girl, who hears her elder brother telling a derogatory joke about "wogs" and getting all his mates laughing, is inspired to repeat it to her friends hoping for a similar result (although she first might have to explain what wogs are). The young boy who sees his father treating his mother as an intellectual lightweight and sex object ("don't trouble your pretty little head dear") is learning sexism, and so forth. The process is insidious because neither the observer nor the model is usually aware that learning is going on. Modelling and observational learning are also extremely powerful; our actions (or lack of them) speak louder than words.

instrumental conditioning
Using reinforcement to shape behaviour.

Operant conditioning

Perhaps a more active form of learning, operant or **instrumental conditioning**, uses reinforcement to shape behaviour. Any behaviour that is immediately followed by reinforcement will be strengthened (or weakened). When a mother, discussing who her daughter should play with for the afternoon, selectively praises a local child over a recent immigrant, she shapes her daughter's choice. When her daughter agrees and the mother praises her, the mother is reinforcing similar preferences in the future *and* ethnic selectivity. This works the other way too. A child giving cheek to an elderly couple on a bus stop, who gets a clip on the ear from a passerby for his trouble, is well on the way to having his ageist prejudices extinguished.

In practice these three forms of learning are artificial divisions and they are interwoven in everyday life. What is important to remember is that such learning rapidly builds up a culture of prejudice and these attitudes become social norms, or accepted ways of behaving. What is easily learned is often hard to unlearn (Perlman & Oskamp, 1971).

Social conformity

Tom Pettigrew (1958) picked up on this point and argued that prejudice is not so much a matter of hate but of social inertia. As social norms, including prejudice, are passed from one generation to another, it is easier to accept the status quo than to learn new ways of behaving. All of us are powerfully constrained by our culture's social norms. If we want to be liked and accepted, we conform. If you add the sheer unconsciousness of most of our attitudes, then Pettigrew argues prejudice is more likely to be a matter of social conformity than thought-out bigotry (Pettigrew, 1980). We learn to be prejudiced, never give it a second (or first) thought and simply conform.

Several studies of racial attitudes in America's Deep South confirm Pettigrew's hypothesis. Pettigrew (1958) pointed out that several earlier studies demonstrated a selective racial inequality, arguing it reflected social norms rather than any deep-seated racial hatred. For example, he cited Minard's (1952) study of the Pocohontas coalminers of West Virginia— blacks and whites worked shoulder-to-shoulder in the mines and skill alone was rewarded. However, above ground, West Virginian society was strictly segregated and workmates lived in different parts of the town, shopped separately, attended different churches and schools and rarely mixed. When questioned, miners "allowed as they had never thought about it before". You should remember that this study was before the civil rights movement of the 1960s and it would be a different matter today.

Pettigrew also argued that those who were the culture bearers were more likely to be prejudiced as they had the responsibility for carrying forward social norms and ensuring social stability. He predicted that churchgoers, women (particularly mothers) and those who were upwardly mobile were more likely to be prejudiced, and in a series of studies in America and South Africa found just that; those who were most concerned with conformity were the most prejudiced (Pettigrew, 1958, 1959, 1961). Another prediction was also borne out. Pettigrew felt that those who were less concerned with social norms would be less prejudiced, but he also noted the social costs of non-conformity (Campbell & Pettigrew, 1959). We will return to conformity in an extended treatment in Chapter Six.

The prejudiced personality

As we have just seen, the *content* of prejudice is acquired through learning and socialisation, but are some individuals more prone to prejudice than others? This is an area in which Australian social psychologists have made enormous contributions.

Research started after World War II, when several researchers worked collaboratively, under the aegis of the American Jewish Committee, to determine why anti-Semitism led to the horrors of the Holocaust. In our next chapter we review the work of Stanley Milgram on compliance and social control, which also has much to say about the nature of prejudice. However, it was one of Milgram's colleagues, Adorno, who was particularly interested in the link between political conservatism, the authoritarian personality and prejudice, and published his results in a monumental work, *The Authoritarian Personality* (Adorno et al., 1950). Adorno hypothesised that authoritarianism was a root cause of the rapid rise of anti-Semitism during the Nazi era, somewhat surprising given Germany's relatively liberal attitudes by prewar standards. Adorno speculated that the German national consciousness favoured political and economic conservatism: right-wing politics, conventionality, strong national leadership, ethnocentrism, defensive aggression and hostility, rejection of dissent, a stereotypical and superstitious worldview, and a generally conservative morality. They dubbed these characteristics **authoritarianism**.

authoritarianism
Personality trait favouring political and economic conservatism, conventionality, strong leadership, ethnocentrism, and a conservative morality.

Adorno and his colleagues then set out to test their hypothesis by designing four Likert scales measuring ethnocentrism, anti-Semitism, political conservatism and totalitarianism. They gave these to a large number of Californian volunteers and gradually refined their test items after assessing each for reliability and validity. The final scale they dubbed the **Californian F Scale** (F for fascism). Though the F Scale dated quickly, in its many reincarnations it has proven a useful tool over the years, and has been widely used by John Ray and his colleagues in local studies (see Box 5.6).

Californian F scale
Measurement of *authoritarianism*.

What did the F Scale find? As expected the scale found clear patterns of prejudice. Those who scored high on one scale generally scored high on another. Whites who despised blacks also despised Hispanics, Jews and other minorities. Clear correlations emerged between totalitarianism, political conservatism and high levels of prejudice. Adorno concluded that authoritarianism clearly was linked to prejudice, but why?

The next step in their research was to interview a number of highly prejudiced and non-prejudiced subjects. After intensive interviewing, Adorno and his colleagues felt they were both able to characterise the authoritarian personality and give a good account of how it developed. Highly authoritarian

Box 5.6 *Profile: John Ray and authoritarianism*

John Ray was born in Queensland in 1943 and some of his ancestors were in fact early convict settlers. He grew up in a highly multicultural environment and attributes his interest in intergroup relations and its allegedly related phenomena to this. He took his BA in psychology from the University of Queensland in 1968, his MA from Sydney University in 1969 and his PhD from Macquarie University in 1974. He taught in the School of Sociology at the University of NSW until 1983, when he took an early retirement. (Photo: courtesy John Ray)

Authoritarianism is a construct which has engaged social psychologists since it first came into theoretical prominence in the early 1950s and has caught the interest of many local researchers. Although it is a topic of only occasional interest overseas, Australia has the distinction of having three of the leading luminaries in this area: Patrick Heaven, John Ray and Ken Rigby. By far the most prominent in this area is Dr John Ray, formerly of the University of NSW.

Ray has long been interested in authoritarianism and related concepts: **ethnocentrism** (holding one's race or ethnic group to be inherently superior), **conservatism** (valuing long established institutions and ways of behaving) and prejudice. He has published in excess of 100 papers on authoritarianism alone and many others on Australian neo-Nazis, anti-Semitism, militarism, religious conservatism and dogmatism, White attitudes to Aborigines, Afrikaner attitudes, Scottish nationalism, and antisocial attitudes.

As we have noted, Adorno et al.'s F scale assumes among other things that authoritarianism and right-wing conservative attitudes are closely linked. Ray has always been somewhat sceptical of this assumption and argues that the F Scale "inextricably confounded" the relationship between authoritarianism and conservatism and other related variables (Ray, 1989). He is particularly scathing about Adorno et al. (1950) and Altemeyer's (1981, 1988) attempts to define it as a right-wing attribute (Ray, 1985, 1990a) and notes "Right-wing is hardly the commonest description of Joseph Stalin!" (Ray, 1989). Rather he argues that authoritarianism is multivariate and at its core has more to do with dominance and submission relationships than political ideology. The authoritarian in his view is one who is submissive to superiors and the prevailing ideology, and dominant and aggressive towards subordinates.

Ray has a particular interest in psychometric aspects of studying authoritarianism. His early concern about the limitations of the F Scale— its ambiguities, datedness and assumption that authoritarianism was in effect right-wing conservatism—led him at first to attempt to rework the F Scale (Ray, 1970, 1972, 1976; see Table 5.5). However, as our understanding of authoritarianism grew, in 1976 Ray introduced his *Directiveness Scale* which measured "the desire or tendency to impose one's own will on others" (Ray, 1989). This, Ray felt, was the core of authoritarianism. Both Heaven (1987) and Rigby (1987a) were not so sure, arguing that the Directiveness Scale was too narrow a definition of authoritarianism, and in turn produced their own multitrait scales. Heaven (1985) would argue that authoritarianism should include an element of conformity through achievement motivation, while Rigby (1984) is more concerned with attitudes to authority, directiveness and rebelliousness. While the ultimate nature of authoritarianism is still unclear (see Ray, 1989, for a review), the ongoing debate about its nature owes much to these three Australian researchers.

Table 5.5 *Ray's balanced F scale*

The first 14 items are scored 1 to 5 for "Strongly Agree" to "Strongly Disagree". The last 14 are scored 5 to 1.

1. The rebellious ideas of young people are often a constructive source of change for the better.
2. Homosexuality between consenting adults may be distasteful but it should not be regarded as a crime.
3. Many of the radical ideas of today will become the accepted beliefs and practices of tomorrow.
4. Familiarity does not breed contempt.
5. People who want to whip or imprison sex criminals are themselves sick.
6. What a youth needs most is to be free to make up his own mind, to be flexible and to work and fight for what he considers right personally, even though it might not be best for his family and country.
7. Many good people honestly could never bring themselves round to feeling much love, gratitude or respect for their parents.
8. You need to get out and rub elbows with all kinds of people to get new ideas and broaden your understanding of life.
9. There are times when it is necessary to probe into even the most personal and private matters.
10. It's all right for people to raise questions about even the most personal and private matters.
11. Insults to our honour are not always important enough to bother about.
12. Sex crimes such as rape and attacks on children, are signs of mental illness; such people belong in hospitals rather than in prison.
13. Most honest people admit to themselves that they have sometimes hated their parents.
14. Disobedience to the government is sometimes justified.
15. If people would talk less and work more, everybody would be better off.
16. The business man and the manufacturer are much more important to society than the artist and the professor.
17. Every person should have complete faith in some supernatural power whose decisions he obeys without question.
18. No sane, normal, decent person would ever think of hurting a close friend or relative.
19. Young people sometimes get rebellious ideas but as they grow up they ought to get over them and settle down.
20. An insult to our honour should always be punished.
21. Sex crimes, such as rape and attacks on children deserve more than mere imprisonment; such criminals ought to be publicly whipped or worse.
22. Obedience and respect for authority are the most important virtues children should learn.
23. Most of our social problems would be solved if we could somehow get rid of the immoral, crooked and feeble-minded people.
24. People can divide into two distinct classes: the weak and the strong.
25. What the youth needs most is strict discipline, rugged determination, and the will to work and fight for family and country.
26. Familiarity breeds contempt.
27. There is hardly anything lower than a person who does not feel great love, gratitude and respect for his parents.
28. Homosexuals are hardly better than criminals and ought to be severely punished.

Source: Ray, 1972.

people were quite prejudiced, ethnocentric, status conscious, were sexually repressed, had rigid inflexible worldviews, did not tolerate dissent, were punitive, preferred to see issues in black and white terms, and on the whole were cynical and highly conventional personalities. What was more striking was their upbringing. Most lived in cold unloving homes in an atmosphere of diffuse hostility. They had aloof parents, who insisted on self-discipline and submission to parental authority; controlled their children by withdrawing affection; and who set high standards for them to achieve. Adorno argued that this led to considerable frustration for the children as they sought parental love and approval, which was usually withheld. Children dealt with this by venting their frustrations on scapegoats, generally stereotypical representatives of the groups despised by their parents. In essence Adorno's theory is fairly psychodynamic; children displace their aggression onto scapegoats to avoid risking conflict with their parents.

Adorno's theory has attracted much support over the years though the original study was not without a fair amount of mainly methodological criticism about the F Scale and what it purported to measure (Christie & Jahoda, 1954; Kirscht & Dillehay, 1967; Cherry & Byrne, 1977; Snyder & Ickes, 1985; Ray, 89). Much of the arguments surround the exact nature of authoritarianism and how it might be defined. Ray (1989), in a review article, explores the limitation of Adorno's conceptualisation of authoritarianism as right-wing connservatism and traces the attempts of Patrick Heaven, John Rigby and himself to define it more precisely and to build better measuring instruments (see Box 5.6). Critics have also argued that while the link between authoritarianism and prejudice was established, Adorno and his colleagues mistook the reasons for this link. Challenges to their psychodynamic interpretation include: not controlling for social class and education (Hyman & Sheatsley, 1954); intelligence (Kornhauser et al., 1956) and cultural differences (Brown, 1965). However, literally hundreds of studies have shown a link between authoritarian personalities and prejudice (Bierly, 1985; Heaven & Furnham, 1987; Rigby, 1988a, c; Altemeyer, 1988).

Altemeyer (1981, 1988) constructed an updated version of the F Scale, the *Right-wing Authoritarianism Scale* which attracted savage criticism about its inability to adequately define what "right-wing" meant (see Ray, 1990). However, Altemeyer did confirm Adorno's views of the development of authoritarianism. He found that given their conventionality, authoritarian parents usually feel themselves smugly morally superior to those they despise. This self-righteous superiority though is coupled with a fear of the outgroup and they communicate to their children that the world is an unsafe place, with many deviates wanting to challenge "right-thinking". Their children, therefore, grow up believing they are in conflict with the rest of the world and fearing moral contamination by too close a contact with outgroups. Their parents provide them with ready-made scapegoats for their frustrations and it is only a short step to prejudice and discrimination.

Box 5.7 *Authoritarianism and attitudes to Vietnamese Australians*

The last decade has seen an acrimonious debate over Asian immigration in Australia. This is perhaps best typified by Professor Geoffrey Blainey's *For All Australia* (1984) which, though hardly a racist commentary, expressed a concern that Indochinese migrants were so different culturally that they might prove indigestible to the Australian way of life and possibly pose a threat to it (Blainey 1984; Brown, 1986a). Nevertheless, several researchers have found that Australians generally favour multiculturalism, even if still a little uncertain about who should be admitted (Ho, 1987, 1990). Given this debate, John Morris of the Australian National University and Patrick Heaven of Charles Sturt University (Wagga) thought it was time to investigate Australian attitudes and behaviour towards the Vietnamese.

Morris and Heaven (1986) hypothesised that a number of factors might underlie the debate and any overt racism. From reviewing research they felt that economic disadvantage might fuel racist attitudes, a finding supported by

(Photo: Chris Simkin)

Taft et al. (1970) who found that poorer whites were the most prejudiced toward Aborigines. Among other possible explanations they felt that prejudice might "serve the unconscious" by "cover[ing] up severe feelings of inferiority, resolve guilt feelings, or act as a displacement of frustration"—much along the lines of Adorno's psychodynamic authoritarianism theory.

To test this theory and look for a possible contrast, Morris and Heaven surveyed Canberrans, who they assumed were more highly educated than the Australian average; and following up Thomas' (1974) suggestion that Queenslanders were more racist than other Australians, also surveyed in Toowoomba. Altogether 83 people returned a questionnaire, which had items measuring self-esteem, conformity, authoritarianism, perceived economic deprivation and attitudes towards the Vietnamese. Most of the questionnaire was drawn from various scales developed by John Ray. Demographic data was also gathered to compare with the questionnaire responses.

They found that several variables failed to support previous research:

> With regard to racial attitudes and racist behavioral intent, the results for both samples failed to support the hypotheses that racists are more likely to be male than female, to be older than younger, to have spent most of their lives in urban rather than rural areas, to have low social status in the community, to be upwardly or downwardly mobile in social status, and to have no equal-status contact with Vietnamese refugees. (p. 518)

They found the best single predictor of racist attitudes and behaviour for both samples was authoritarian attitudes—fully supporting Adorno's theory. Racists were also less well educated, saw themselves as economically deprived, and were more conforming. Canberra respondents who held median (below degree) level qualifications were more racially prejudiced in attitudes and behaviour than their peers. The authors explained this surprising result in terms of social comparison theory:

> Given the extraordinarily large percentage of the Canberra population who hold degrees, and given the importance placed upon qualifications for promotion and status in the Australian Public Service . . . those with an educational attainment slightly below degree standard may feel inferior and resentful and consequently displace these feelings through prejudicial attitudes and behavior onto ethnic groups. (p. 518)

The hypothesis that low self-esteem was an important predictor of prejudice was not supported, a point we will return to later in the chapter.

Scapegoating

One immediate implication of Adorno's theory is that certain groups encounter prejudice and discrimination because they are the victims of **displaced aggression** rather than a real threat to the bigot (Allport, 1954). The Freudian concept of displaced aggression suggests that everyday frustrations are redirected towards safer targets because we are blocked from venting our feelings on more appropriate targets. We have already noted Hovland and Sears' study of economic conditions and black lynching, and the displacements of the children of authoritarian parents; several related studies suggest that often victimised minorities encounter prejudice because they are just "convenient targets" (Allport, 1954).

> **displaced aggression**
> A Freudian concept; everyday frustrations are redirected towards safer targets because we are blocked from venting our feelings on more appropriate ones.

Leon Berkowitz (1962) followed up this idea in his analysis of racism, proposing the **scapegoat hypothesis** to identify the characteristics of a "convenient target". Berkowitz felt that victims of prejudice had four common characteristics:

> **scapegoat hypothesis**
> Victims of prejudice are chosen because they are available, obvious, different and unable to retaliate.

Safeness
We rarely pick on those who can give a good account of themselves. Victims of prejudice are easy targets who are unable to retaliate. Successful discrimination encourages the notion that they are "stupid" and "weak" and legitimises and reinforces further discrimination.

Visibility
Targets of discrimination must be obvious and available victims. Their characteristics must be salient. Racism thrives because differences in skin colour, facial features and body type immediately identify them as a member of the minority group.

Strangeness
Similarly, the victims must be salient because they are unusual and different. Berkowitz argued that we have an instinctive mistrust of strangers and that ethnocentrism is an evolutionary imperative.

Prior victimisation
We learn who to discriminate against and prior victimisation further legitimises prejudice. If you grow up in a society that treats its minorities in a certain way, you are likely to do likewise.

You will see the obvious parallels to our discussion of the self-perpetuating nature of stereotyping and social categorisation in Berkowitz's theory. We turn now to the tricky question: "Is prejudice a natural part of our makeup?" and also to a consideration of how we might combat this most pernicious human failing.

Box 5.8 *Are Christians less prejudiced than the rest of us?*

Unfortunately the answer seems to be no and, if research is any guide, active church membership is correlated with greater levels of prejudice than in the general community (Pettigrew, 1959; Allport & Ross, 1967; Batson et al., 1985; Gorsuch, 1988).

Batson and Ventis (1982), in their book *The Religious Experience: A Social Psychological Perspective*, review a wealth of studies which show that religiosity is negatively correlated with tolerance: "religion is not associated with increased love and acceptance but with increased intolerance, prejudice and bigotry". On the face of it this would seem contradictory given that Christianity stresses love and tolerance of others.

Does Christianity attract bigots or is something else at work here?

Batson, in a series of studies (Batson & Gray, 1981; Batson & Ventis, 1982; Batson et al., 1989), has identified three different types of religiousness: Some are *intrinsically religious*, their beliefs are caught up with their identity and these people suffer great dislocation when their beliefs are challenged (McKnight, 1990). Others are *extrinsically religious*, their beliefs serve to locate them socially and serve other than religious ends, social acceptance, civic advancement and so on. A final but numerically much smaller group are *existentially religious*. These people see religion as a quest for meaning

Are strong religious beliefs indicative of authoritarianism and a prejudiced personality? Many researchers feel this is so.
(Photo: courtesy John Buchner)

and an open ended struggle to resolve the basic existential question: "What's it all about?" It is in these differences of religious orientation, Batson believes, that the links between religious belief and prejudice may be found.

Intrinsically religious people are often quite rigid in their beliefs and, as their identity is bound up with a dogmatic acceptance of the tenets of their faith, challenges to their beliefs are basic destabilisers of their core identity. This group shares much in common with the authoritarian personality type. The very existence of groups that think and act differently is a direct ego threat and so they must be *ungodly*, a short step to prejudice. Extrinsically religious people are less caught up with dogma and define themselves more conventionally. They go along with the mores of their society, including church membership. If they live in a racist society they will be racist also. Religious belief is therefore

incidental to being prejudiced. Batson, Naifeh and Pate (1978) found that while attitudinal surveys found the latter to be more prejudiced, behavioural measures found little difference between the two groups.

The existential group were neither attitudinally nor behaviourally prejudiced (Batson et al., 1986). These people were unsure that they had the final answer and so were quite accepting of others' beliefs. They eagerly entered into interdenominational and interfaith dialogues as a way of testing and extending their faith. The very open-endedness of their quest ensured their tolerance.

So it seems that the way you hold religious belief determines whether you are prejudiced or not, and lest you think we are picking on Christians, similar results occur across all religions (Batson & Ventis, 1982).

Attacking prejudice

How malleable are we? Is it possible to combat prejudicial attitudes and change behaviour? Yes and no. As we saw in our opener, Bob's prejudices changed overnight when he discovered his Jewish ancestry and an uncomfortable reality intruded on his fantastic beliefs. Further, as we saw in the last three chapters, attitudes and behaviour *are* changeable and we are not necessarily condemned to mirror our culture and upbringing. Unfortunately few of us do change and we seem generally to be content to accept and perpetuate the beliefs that sustain our time and place's milieu.

The intergroup contact hypothesis

One of the earliest theories of combating prejudice was the **intergroup contact hypothesis** of Gordon Allport (1954). Though Allport was not the first to suggest it, his work brought this theory into prominence (Miller & Brewer, 1984). This theory saw that prejudice was only possible when we maintain a social and cognitive distance from the object of our prejudice. Allport proposed that bringing the object of prejudice and the prejudicial person into close and continuing contact would show how inaccurate most stereotypes are. The resultant cognitive dissonance would break down the stereotypes that sustain bigoted beliefs. As we have already seen, stereotypes are only sustainable when we are at a remove from the objects of our prejudice. Allport proposed that such contacts would reduce intergroup

intergroup contact hypothesis
Contact between the prejudiced and the object of their prejudice will lead to more realistic attitudes.

hostility and lead to more realistic attitudes. However, simple contact is not enough to combat prejudice. Germany had one of Europe's largest prewar Jewish populations and, though mildly anti-Semitic, was quite liberal by European standards. Jews were well integrated and occupied positions of respect and power throughout German society. Yet under the influence of Nazism, average, ordinary Germans quickly lapsed into rabid anti-Semitism, and actively or passively condemned their Jewish neighbours, whom they had probably known all their lives, to the horrors of the Holocaust. Simple contact therefore is not insurance against prejudice.

Allport was well aware that simple contact was not by itself enough to combat prejudice and proposed four conditions for its effectiveness. First the contact must be *sustained* and involve close interaction. Most of the work on the contact hypothesis was done in the United States on racial integration. Analyses of Southern communities showed that many multiracial societies were segregated and the actual degree of meaningful contact was minimal between blacks and whites despite their close proximity (Brewer & Miller, 1984). Ray found a similar situation in Australia (Ray, 1983c). Without sustained and meaningful contact, both sides can hide behind their prejudices. Only close individual contacts will promote the cognitive dissonance which eventually weakens stereotypes.

Second, the interaction must produce *cooperative interdependence*. Multiracial societies, like Israel, have long used military conscription as a pressure-cooker way of promoting integration. Not only is contact close within a platoon structure but the soldiers must rely on each other to survive. Prejudice has little room to grow when you are counting on the other to literally "watch my back".

The intergroup contact hypothesis suggests that cultural exchanges such as this between Australian and Indonesian students will reduce prejudice.
(Photo: Chris Simkin)

Third, the contact must promote *equality*. If you are thrust into close and even interdependent contact which is still unequal, such as the classic master and servant routines of racial inequality, your prejudices will be reinforced, not changed.

Fourth, Allport noted two important aspects of equality—that people meet as equals and that their interaction is in *an atmosphere favouring equality*. The social norms must reflect the new view of the other. Little will be gained if the other three conditions are met but the prejudicial views are still being reinforced by their wider community. Much research has shown that forced racial integration and desegregation has still not reduced racial prejudice as the wider community is not in favour of the changes and resists them. For this reason most of the successful contact programmes involve a complete break from one's home and the creation of a new environment where the authorities carefully construct *and model* the new beliefs (Amir, 1976; Aronson et al., 1978).

The contact hypothesis has had a strong press and many social psychologists have used these factors experimentally to reduce prejudice (Pagtolun-An & Clair 1986), particularly in educational settings (Slavin, 1983; Aronson & Gonzales, 1988). However, these conditions rarely prevail in real life and many studies have shown its limitations (Ray, 1983c). For example, a study by Wagner, Hewstone and Machleit (1989) examined patterns of inter-ethnic contact between Turkish and German school students and found that only quality leisure time interactions lessened ethnic Germans' prejudice towards Turks, in all other interactions prejudices were unchanged. This confirms the work of Amir (1969) and others that intergroup contact works best when it is intimate, relaxed, pleasurable and non-competitive.

The problem with the contact hypothesis, like many social phenomena, is the sheer number of variables that influence its effectiveness (Amir, 1969). Rothbart and John (1985), for example, propose three factors important in disconfirming prejudicial stereotypes: First, the contact must present clear and unambiguous behaviours which disconfirm the stereotype. Rothbart and John found that some aspects of prejudicial stereotypes are hard to operationalise and hence disconfirm. For instance, how would you begin to disconfirm "racial inferiority"? Other traits like "uncooperative" and "surly" are much easier to observe and comment on.

Second, it may take many months to disconfirm a trait and yet only a few instances to reconfirm it. Rothbart and John comment on the perniciousness of this aspect of prejudice, noting that the more unfavourable a trait the greater the effort we must make to disconfirm it and that a few exceptions will quickly re-establish the prejudice. Equally, favourable stereotypes are "difficult to acquire but easy to lose". This frustrates those on the wrong end of stereotypes as they must be continually on their best behaviour.

Third, Rothbart and John also re-emphasised the importance of the setting in which intergroup contacts occur. Prejudices are hardly likely to change unless the setting gives scope for new behaviour to be observed. Much of the prejudice against Aborigines as "lazy, shiftless and indigent dole bludgers" simply reflects a depressed rural life in which employment opportunities are non-existent. Prejudices will not change unless they are

Many Aboriginal people have joined work-for-the-dole schemes on useful community projects rather than be stigmatised as "dole bums"
(Photo: Gavin Price)

seen as productive citizens. For this reason 40 000 rural Aborigines have joined work-for-the-dole schemes, surrendering their entitlements for the dignity of employment.

As Stuart Cook (1984) and others noted, even if we come into close, prolonged and positive contact with the other, all that might change is our attitudes towards the individual and not the group. Unfortunately, changed attitudes do not readily generalise to other members of the outgroup. Allport (1954) called this **re-fencing** and noted that if we form positive views of the other we may the reduce the dissonance caused by seeing them as somehow atypical of the group they represent—perhaps they are "an exception to the rule" (Weber & Crocker, 1983). As you will recall from our discussion of social cognition and cognitive dissonance, we are reluctant to abandon existing stereotypes and, as cognitive misers, we prefer to invent subcategories to contain dissonant information (Fiske & Taylor, 1991).

re-fencing
Altering our prejudices to accommodate discrepant facts which would otherwise weaken them.

Cognitive interventions

As someone to whom Rugby League is a deep and incalculable mystery, I am always surprised at the hero worship of players and the loyalty of fans for their clubs. I've attended several games and still think it's a complete waste of time. My prejudices aside, what I did notice was the ease with which fans transfered loyalty from game to game. This was obvious when a Kiwi friend took it upon himself to re-educate me. At a premiership round, my host came close to blows with another fan after roundly condemning a player on the opposing team. Four nights later he was cheering and supporting him at a State of Origin game and argued with a Queenslander about the relative merits of this player. The unsubtle irony was that to defend the player, he used exactly the opposite arguments he had used four days previously! This was rammed home several weeks later at an international match where my friend cheered the All Blacks to yet another victory over Australia, now again disparaging the player who was part of the Australian team. When I pointed out his inconsistency he gave me a pitying smile and I've not been invited to any matches since.

What may we conclude from this? Apart from the obvious interpretation that all rugby fans are addled, it demonstrates the ease with which we can redraw cognitive boundaries. Recently interest has turned to cognitive remedies for prejudice, and several studies of redrawing the boundaries between them and us have emerged. Is it possible that this **recategorisation** of ingroup and outgroup boundaries may be used to reduce prejudice?

recategorisation
Redrawing ingroup boundaries to include outgroup members to reduce prejudice.

In an experimental demonstration Gaertner et al. (1989) used a variant of the old survival-at-sea exercise to get in- and outgroup prejudice going. Groups of six subjects were divided into two teams and then had to decide what they would salvage from their aircraft that had crashed in a remote forest. The exercise was then repeated but the groups were divided up differently. In one condition the two groups were retained, in another they worked individually and in the third as a whole group. After each trial subjects reported back to the whole group and then rated each other on an adjective checklist. These ratings were compared and Gaertner and his colleagues predicted that intergroup bias would be higher for the two-group condition than for the individual and whole-group conditions. Their results confirmed this. Two-group members rated each other higher and overall this condition had a higher intergroup bias than the other conditions.

Box 5.9 *"Gubbin": A racist town?*

Gillian Cowlishaw's (1986) study of "Gubbin", a composite of four towns in western NSW, analyses racism against an Australian backdrop. Her excellent article is not only a penetrating look at racism but also a summation of the theories covered in this chapter. We will conclude with a look at her study as a chapter summary.

"Gubbin" is a play on "Gubb" or "Gubbo", the Aborigines' slang term for whites, deriving from "governor"—a cynical comment on white attitudes. While Cowlishaw's position is that "race" is a socially constructed ideology, she critiques three theories of racism that implicitly assume biological racial differentiation. Her study examines how "racism as prejudice, racism as natural and racism as justifying ideology in a colonial situation" work out in Gubbin.

The first notable finding is that there are no racists in Gubbin, at least not in the old up-front prejudicial sense. Rather, Cowlishaw found that Gubbin has made a transition, similar to that described by McConahay (1986), from the old-fashioned to symbolic/modern racism:

There are few people in Gubbin who are racists in the classic sense. Many others show overt or covert hostility to Aborigines yet deny they are racists. There are also many who conform to anti-racist liberal beliefs while agreeing with the former groups about the racial problems with which they are confronted. (Cowlishaw, 1986, p. 7)

Kevin Brown from Monash University noted

that often discrimination occurs even when we do not intend it and argued that such **non-racist racism** was well entrenched in Australia (Brown, 1986b). It certainly was in Gubbin:

> And there are those few who are actively engaged in supporting Aboriginal interests but who nevertheless adhere to values that, in the final analysis, work against the interests of those they claim to help. Thus my argument is that in a racially divided town all become racists if they accept the definitions and processes that surround them. (p. 7)

Cowlishaw also rejects the second explanation or "natural racism" theory which in her account is basically the genetic similarity hypothesis, with a few realistic conflict theory overtones. Given the disproportionate numbers of European men and few white women in the colonial era, **miscegenation**, or racial interbreeding, was the rule throughout the Western Division. The genetic similarity hypothesis would argue that parents should favour their mixed-race offspring given the closeness of their genes. Cowlishaw notes this was the exception rather than the rule in the past. "The virulence of racism among the white population increased rather than decreased with the increase in genetic relatedness", an empirical observation at odds with predictions of the genetic similarity hypothesis. Cowlishaw also notes that at present people of "mixed blood" who "crossed the divide" did so at the expense of rejecting their former kith and kin. To the extent that mixed-race relationships work in Gubbin, it is only where the white partner crosses the divide and becomes accepted as part of the black community, and their children "are not recognised as warranting membership of the white community, unless, as occasionally happens, they repudiate their black kin. Even then their status is tenuous."

Cowlishaw favours "racism as a justificatory ideology" though she notes several problems with this view. Nevertheless the history and sociopolitics of Gubbin reflect a European view of Aborigines as inherently inferior and their dispossession as a historical necessity. Being "Aboriginal" in this context is just "looking different enough". Cowlishaw traces the evolution of these views but their modern expression is all too obvious in Gubbin.

Aborigines in Gubbin live on the margin. "The level of capital accumulation by Aborigines is virtually nil. None own businesses or pastoral properties." Unemployment is endemic. One consequence is that a small proportion of Aboriginals meet on the street near the town's supermarket, spending their day sitting, drinking and talking. The whites are quite clear what this says about the Aboriginal community:

> There are clear status meanings among whites attached to this behaviour. For most it would be a difficult thing to do, mainly because of a recognition that either abnormality or destitution is implied by sitting or drinking in the street. (p. 18)

The shire council's response was to remove the seats because, as one councillor said: "Aborigines sat on them." This explanation was amended to: "Too many sat on them, lounged all over them. It didn't look nice for the tourists." This overt racism echoes complaints about delinquency, crime and public drunkenness. Whites explain away these consequences of poverty as an inherent part of Aboriginal makeup, another example of blaming the victim and the ultimate attribution error. That this is a clear case of racist prejudice is shown in white anger over affirmative action policies trying to break this cycle. It's unfair, they say, that they have to pay for their kids to go on an excursion, while Aborigines go for free. Other policies, such as equal pay, housing assistance and unemployment benefits, are undeserved and in their view squandered.

Cowlishaw also found clear examples of outgroup homogeneity effects:

> What makes this a racist ideology is not the content of the beliefs . . . Rather it is the direction of the complaints, the objectification and homogenisation of Aborigines which is most clearly evident in the constant discussions of *them* . . . This defining of Aborigines as *them* as opposed to *us* has many correlates in social life. (p. 18)

The perniciousness of this effect is seen in the whites' recognition that not all fit the mould. However:

> . . . the fact that not all Aborigines show the alleged depravity becomes another weapon against those that do. For if some Aborigines behave well why can't they all? (p. 19)

In most other respects the lot of Aborigines in Gubbin is appalling and distressingly similar in many small country towns. Perhaps we can conclude our discussion of prejudice with one final quote which neatly encapsulates the problem:

> While the Gubbs would like to emphasise that it is the *behaviour* of the Aborigines which is a problem, it is their identification of the behaviour of the *Aborigines* that becomes the Aborigines' problem. (p. 19)

While this study could be criticised for the seating arrangements during the report-back sessions, which went a fair way towards giving away the purposes of the experiment, nevertheless, the results show that physically reshuffling group boundaries will reduce bias. You will recall from our discussion of ingroup favouritism that getting competing teams to work on a superordinate task will reduce conflict. What Gaertner's study suggests is that redefining the group boundaries will enhance this process and other studies agree (Vanbeselaere, 1987; Neuberg, 1989). What these and several other optimistic studies suggest is that if we can readily shift the boundaries then prejudice can be reduced.

Summary

Prejudice is an extreme attitude based on our beliefs about another. It relies on schema-based stereotypes and cognitive distortions which categorise individuals according to salient features such as age, sex, race or ethnicity. We attribute personality and other characteristics to these representative others and ignore or distort information that disconfirms our prejudices. Prejudice may be positive, when we view those with whom we identify as superior, but it is usually negative and has contributed to at least 60 000 000 deaths through intra-communal violence this century.

Discrimination is not prejudice but rather the active outworking of our beliefs. Like prejudicial attitudes discrimination may be positive but is invariably negative. With the changing social attitudes this century discrimination has changed from overt to more subtle forms. Rather than exclude women and minorities from employment we discriminate by failing to act, or appear to help by using tokenism and reverse discrimination as subtle discrimination. Even positive discrimination or equal opportunity programmes have been condemned as ultimately further disadvantaging minorities.

There are many reasons for our prejudice and some are not psychological. We are captives of our history and culture, and our attitudes and prejudices will reflect those of our forebears. The history of European colonisation, for example, was marked by changing views of indigenous peoples and this historical accident colours present attitudes to Maoris and Aborigines. Prejudice may also be fuelled by realistic intergroup conflicts over scarce resources, though these shortages are sometimes more imagined than real.

The genetic similarity hypothesis argues that there is a genetic basis to prejudice and that we are able to recognise and favour those who share similar genes to ourselves. The mainspring of this theory is that we wish to reproduce with those who will perpetuate our genetic message as closely as possible. This inevitably leads to dissimilar others being excluded and stigmatised. Although there is some evidence for this theory, it is highly contentious, with critics arguing it represents genetic determinism.

Social identity accounts argue that prejudice arises from an antithetical process of excluding those who are not part of your ingroup. Tajfel argued we define ourselves by excluding others and this inevitably leads to intergroup competition, stigmatisation and outgroup derogation. Evidence for this view comes from minimal group paradigms where the sole difference leading to conflict is being placed in a different group.

While we are prejudiced for varying reasons, the content of our prejudices reflects the schema-based way we see the world, as we discussed in Chapter Two. Stereotypes are attribute-based schemas and salient characteristics of the other, such as age, sex, race and ethnicity, trigger cultural stereotypes acquired as part of our socialisation. While the derivation of the word *stereotype* implies a certain rigidity and resistance to change, recent research indicates that community attitudes are slowly changing toward less prejudicial views.

We gain stereotypes through learning and social categorisation. Placing others into *us* and *them* boxes allows us to use a much faster category-based, rather than attribute-based, processing. However, an inevitable consequence is that our attributions are less accurate, as the many attributional errors—such as the outgroup homogeneity illusion, the ultimate attribution error, the assumed similarity effect, archetypal processing and illusory correlations—suggest.

That we hold stereotypes does not mean that we have to accept them, yet in a multicultural society it is sometimes difficult to accept that difference does not equal deviance, and this is not helped by disagreements within minorities as to what constitutes prejudice. Stereotypes are learned by classical and instrumental conditioning and acquired directly through modelling, social conformity and vicarious reinforcement. The power of stereotypes derives in part from their sheer taken-for-grantedness.

Many have questioned whether a prejudiced personality type exists. Early psychodynamic work by Adorno identified authoritarian personalities as being more prone to certain types of prejudice related to their conservative worldviews. Research has generally confirmed Adorno's observations, though his theory accounts for only a small portion of prejudicial attitudes.

Prejudice may be combated through education, though such strategies are weak and require prolonged application. More direct approaches are favoured and it is argued that intergroup contact on favourable terms is effective in reducing prejudice. Intergroup contacts must be sustained; operate on a non-trivial level; allow the groups to meet as equals; and foster mutual interdependency, for an effective reduction of prejudice. However, many theorists argue that such schemes are not long-lasting and only produce changes that establish the outgroup as "exceptions to the rule". Cognitive recategorisation strategies may be more effective but relatively little work has been done on them.

Recommended reading

Aboud F. (1988) CHILDREN AND PREJUDICE, Basil Blackwell, Oxford. An intriguing look at the developmental origins of intolerance.

Allport G.W. (1954) THE NATURE OF PREJUDICE, Addison-Wesley, Reading, Mass. The classic text on prejudice which summarises all of the early research work. Still well worth a read.

Altemeyer B. (1988) THE ENEMIES OF FREEDOM: UNDERSTANDING RIGHT-WING AUTHORITARIANISM, Jossey-Bass, San Francisco. An eminently readable introduction to the authoritarian personality and how it develops.

Dovidio J.F. and Gaertner S.L. (eds) (1986) PREJUDICE, DISCRIMINATION AND RACISM, Academic Press, Orlando, Florida. A collection of articles by the leading researchers in the field.

O'Donnell C. and Hall P. (1988) GETTING EQUAL, LABOUR MARKET REGULATION AND WOMEN'S WORK, Allen & Unwin, Sydney. A comprehensive look at women's position in the Australian labour market and the various Acts and Regulations that address gender inequity.

Stone W.F., Lederer G. and Christie R. (eds) (1992) STRENGTH AND WEAKNESS: THE AUTHORITARIAN PERSONALITY TODAY, Springer-Verlag, NY. A collection of articles that give a comprehensive overview of 40 years of research on authoritarianism.

Taylor D.M. and Moghaddam F.M. (1987) THEORIES OF INTERGROUP RELATIONS: INTERNATIONAL SOCIAL PSYCHOLOGICAL PERSPECT-IVES, Praeger, NY. An overview of the major theories that explain differing types of prejudice and discrimination.

SOCIAL POWER, INFLUENCE AND CHANGE

M y father fought five bloody and exhausting years in World War II as a gunner. Unlike most who were immediately demobbed at the war's end, a natural linguist, he spent another three years in occupied Germany processing displaced persons and was actively involved in the de-Nazification programmes. Although he bitterly regretted the extra years the Army stole from his life, at least he always felt he had the satisfaction of ensuring that never again would the horrors of the Holocaust arise. I'm glad that he was long dead before Pol Pot's crimes against humanity in Cambodia surfaced. The following excerpt from journalist John Pilger's book Heroes demonstrates the extent of human suffering resulting from crimes of obedience:

> Two months earlier Eric Piper and I had followed Pope John Paul on his return to Poland, where we had seen Auschwitz for the first time. Now, in South-East Asia, we saw it again. On a clear, sunny day with flocks of tiny swifts, the bravest of birds, rising and falling almost to the ground, we drove along a narrow dirt road at the end of which was a former primary school, called Tuol Sleng. During the Pol Pot years this school was run by Khmer Gestapo, "S-21", which divided the classrooms into an "interrogation unit" and a "torture and massacre unit". People were mutilated on iron beds and we found their blood and tufts of their hair still on the floor. Between December 1975 and June 1978 at least 12 000 people died slow deaths here: a fact not difficult to confirm because the killers, like the Nazis, were pedantic in their sadism. They photographed their victims before and after they tortured and killed them and horrific images now looked at us from walls; some had tried to smile for the photographer, as if he might take pity on them and save them. Names, and ages, even height and weight, were

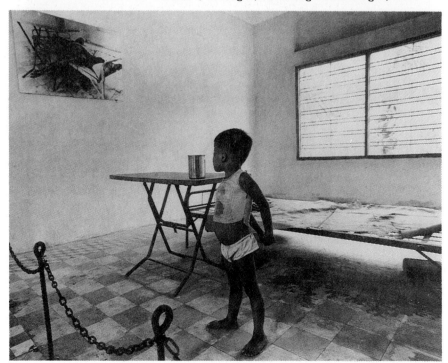

The horrors of Sol Sleng. Notice the picture on the wall. (Photo: Sygma/Austral International)

recorded. We found, as at Auschwitz, one room filled to the ceiling with victims' clothes and shoes, including those of many children.

However, unlike Auschwitz, Tuol Sleng was primarily a political death centre. Leading members of the Khmer Rouge Army, including those who formed an early resistance to Pol Pot, were murdered here, usually after "confessing" that they had worked for the CIA, the KGB or Hanoi. Whatever its historical model, if any, the demonic nature of Tuol Sleng was its devotion to human suffering. Whole families were confined in small cells, fettered to a single iron bar. They were kept naked and slept on the stone floor, without blanket or mat, and on the wall was a school blackboard, on which was written:

1. Speaking is forbidden
2. Before doing something, the authorisation of the wardens must be obtained.

"Doing something" might mean only changing position in the cell, but without authorisation the prisoner would receive twenty to thirty strokes with a whip. (Pilger, 1987, p. 383)

Social power, influence and change

In Germany the Nazis came for the Communists and I didn't speak up because I was not a Communist. Then they came for the Jews and I didn't speak up because I was not Jew. Then they came for the trade unionists and I didn't speak up because I was not a trade unionist. Then they came for the Catholics and I was a Protestant so I didn't speak up. Then they came for me . . . By that time there was no-one to speak up for anyone. (Niemoller, cited in Pepper, 1989, p. 229)

The quote from Pilger and this quote from the German theologian Martin Niemoller, imprisoned by the Nazis in a concentration camp for his support of the Jews, remind us just how far we will go when pushed by social forces. In this chapter we examine one of the most powerful and yet hidden social forces: the extent to which our behaviour is shaped and controlled by others. Most of us are unaware of how powerful and all pervasive these forces are in our everyday lives. Social influences shape our thoughts, feelings and actions to an extent that would horrify us, if we only knew. According to Turner (1991) what conformity, compliance, persuasion and obedience all have in common is the problem of normative social similarities and differences:

> The key idea in understanding what researchers mean by social influence is the concept of a social norm. Influence relates to the processes whereby people agree or disagree about appropriate behaviour, form, maintain or change social norms, the social conditions that give rise to, and the effects of, such norms. (Turner, 1991, p. 2)

Power

Ultimately social influence and control is about power. The word power comes from the Latin *posse* meaning "to be able". Power's original meaning was more akin to "self-realisation" or "self-actualisation" rather than the modern day usage of "competitive power" (May, 1972). If we think about it, much of our existence can be viewed as the interplay or conflict between power, or our ability to effectively influence others and their feelings of powerlessness. Often we deny or avoid reflecting on the issue of power. Close examination of power and its connotations often exacerbates our sense of powerlessness.

> Majority rule for which people have struggled for centuries has produced a situation in which we are more impotent, more powerless to inform governments than 150 years ago. The juggernaut of the state grinds on with no attention paid to you or me. (Morgenthau, cited in May, 1972, p. 21)

How are we to define power? For psychologists, social power means our potential or ability to affect, influence or change other people. Rollo May (1972) provides us with an interesting outline of five different types of power:

1. Exploitative power

According to May this is the simplest and most destructive form of power. It identifies power with force and always presupposes violence or the threat of violence. With this oppressive form of power, for example slavery, there is little choice or opportunity for those subjected to it.

2. Manipulative power

This type of power occurs when we influence another, often relying on the other's vulnerability or anxiety. May comments that the state of economic hardship, helplessness and anxiety about the future, experienced by the German people prior to 1933, enabled Hitler to exert such manipulative power and influence.

3. Competitive power

In its negative form this type of power enables a person to gain an advantage at the expense of others. There are many examples of this in our capitalist society: for example, our dog-eat-dog businesses and our competitive classrooms. Of course competitive power is not always negative. As with sport it can often be constructive and provide us with incentives to realise our potential. Perhaps it is not competition itself that is negative but only the forms it takes.

4. Nutrient power

This type of power is typified by caring for others such as effective parenting. Obviously the exercise of this power can be positive and constructive in our social relations such as those with friends and loved ones.

5. Integrative power

This form of power "abets my neighbour's power". Consider Gandhi's policy of militant non-violence, which was effective in exerting considerable psychological and spiritual power over the British in India, as an example of integrative power. "The whole British Empire creaked and groaned as it moved to find new ways of dealing with this little brown man who knew how to turn his suffering to constructive uses" (May, 1972).

In our everyday life we experience all five types of power at different times. We may exercise manipulative or competitive power in the workplace and likewise act as nurturers in our families. For May the significant question is not power as such but a moral concern with the proportion of each kind of power in a person's personality.

May's summary of the types of power available to us is complemented by French and Raven's (1959) six bases of social power. They spell out the attributes or characteristics that enable a person to exercise the powers May outlined.

The bases of social power

Reward power

Social power often relies on an ability to reward. Someone who is able to control the rewards we receive is able to exert powerful influence over us. The employer who controls our wages not only specifies the tasks to be performed but also expects acceptance of their conditions and social approval. While rewards enable another to exercise social power, it is not a particularly efficient way of controlling behaviour. To be effective it requires constant monitoring of our behaviour. Reward power may also foster social dependence. It may cause compliance, a change in overt behaviour, but not change our attitudes and beliefs (Raven & Rubin, 1983).

Expert power

The effectiveness of this form of power rests on a person's ability to demonstrate a special expertise. Expert social power may influence people's attitudes and beliefs and in certain circumstances may lead to permanent changes in behaviour such as the highly effective anti-smoking campaigns. This type of power is more efficient than reward or coercive power. Surveillance is not required, nor does the person influenced fear threats or punishment. All that is required is our belief that a particular person is an expert on a specific topic and therefore knows more than we do (see Box 6.1).

Expert power may also have negative influences. If we suspect a person of using knowledge to influence us for selfish motives, we will ignore that person's advice. Also if we perceive a lack of credibility, or feel we are unable to trust them, we will be less likely to be influenced.

In a revision of their original model of social power, Raven and Kruglanski (1970) distinguished between expert and informational social power:

Box 6.1 *The experts speak*

While commonsense tells us that it is in our best interest to follow the advice of experts, they are not always infallible. In their book *The Experts Speak,* Cerf and Navarsky (1984) cite expert judgments which in hindsight would have been wiser to ignore. For example:

"Forget it, Louis. No Civil War picture ever made a nickel." A production executive at Metro Goldwyn Mayer movie studio advising the president of the studio not to buy the film rights to the novel *Gone With The Wind* (1936).

"[He] doesn't have the presidential look." An executive at United Artists movie studio explaining why he did not select Ronald Reagan for a role in a movie (1964).

"You ain't going nowhere . . . son. You ought to go back to drivin' a truck." The manager of the Grand Ole Opry, explaining to Elvis Presley why Presley was being fired after one performance (1964).

"The singer will have to go." An early manager of the Rolling Stones evaluating Mick Jagger's value to the group (1963).

"How can he call it a wonderful success when everyone acquainted with the subject will recognise it as a conspicuous failure?" A professor of physics evaluating Thomas Edison's invention, the electric light bulb (1879).

"I think there is a world market for about five computers." The chairman of the board of International Business Machines (IBM), commenting on the future of computers (1943).

"The boy will come to nothing." Jakob Freud predicting the future of his son, Sigmund (1864).

Source: Cerf & Navarsky, 1984.

Informational power

A person's influence is often based on the perceived correctness of the information being communicated. With informational power the message's content is the critical factor and the significant characteristic of such influence is cognitive change, or perceiving a problem in a different light. This type of influence is not socially dependent and does not depend on the attributes or characteristics of another person.

Referent power

Referent power refers to a person's ability to exert influence and control because we like, respect or admire them. Studies of reference groups have demonstrated how powerful this type of influence is when we compare ourselves to others to evaluate our opinions, beliefs and behaviour. The powerful influence of peer groups on adolescent behaviour is one such example. This type of power does not require monitoring by the influencing agent as it is socially dependent, as are reward and coercive power. Moreover this type of influence is akin to a process called **identification** and persists only as long as we identify with the influencing person or group. Referent power may also have a negative effect. I'm sure you can remember times when you decided to disassociate yourself from someone by adopting a different attitude or behaving in a different way based on your dislike of that person.

identification
Identifying with the standards, beliefs and roles of an influencing person or group.

accepts | Shuttle grounded, strategy launched

Most of us think we read newspapers to be entertained or informed. Rarely do we consider the informational power they exert on us. (Photo: Armen Deushian/Macarthur Advertiser)

Legitimate power

Legitimate power relies on our belief that others have the right to influence us. In our society, people who occupy positions of authority are legitimate social influences: politicians, police, judges, the military. Generally, legitimate power is more efficient than reward, coercive or referent power. I do as someone asks me, because they have a right to ask and I am therefore obliged to comply. A legitimate power relationship is signified by such words as *should, ought* and *oblige*.

Coercive power

Social power sometimes rests on a person's ability to punish. There are many examples of coercive power in our daily lives, which may be either explicit or implicit threats for non-compliance. For example, students required to submit assignments on time; traffic offences; withdrawing affection, approval or love; or threat of rejection. In many instances coercive power proves difficult to maintain as it usually requires constant surveillance to be effective, such as random breath testing and the like. Often in such cases we dislike those who use this type of influence and try to conceal our non-compliance in order to avoid punishment.

Attempts to integrate the varying effects of the six bases of social power have proven complicated. Obviously several may be operating at the same time and in some instances an increase in the effectiveness of one form of power may decrease or even negate another. The exercise of coercive power may lead us to display public compliance but cause us to dislike the influencing agent so that privately we are non-compliant (Raven & Rubin, 1983)

Coercive power comes in many forms. Whether it is also legitimate power is often a matter of which end of the leash you are on. (Photo: Barry Price)

Social conformity, compliance and obedience

The study of social influence has primarily focused on three kinds of process: conformity, compliance and obedience. We will spend the majority of our chapter considering each in detail but by way of introduction will quickly define each and review their differences.

We **conform** when we adhere to, or change our attitudes, beliefs and behaviour to be consistent with the standards of a group or society. All societies require degrees of conformity and there is usually widespread acceptance of rules indicating how we should behave in certain situations. Of course many social norms are implicit—staring at people is considered rude as are poor table manners. There are good reasons for our tendency to conform and in many situations conformity serves an important function. Imagine no traffic regulations in our big cities, no queuing in shops, or at bus stops—it would be pretty chaotic. While a certain amount of conformity is needed to maintain social order, giving in to social pressure is not always useful or constructive. We will return to this aspect later in the chapter.

Earlier this century many social theorists believed that our strong tendency to conform was instinctive. Psychologists such as William James and William McDougall believed the motive to imitate others was an integral part of human nature. However, this has had little appeal for most psychologists since the 1920s, due to limitations associated with an instinctual view of social motivation (see Chapter Seven).

As with conformity, we continually experience situations where we have to comply when we get direct requests from friends, lovers, family or employers. **Compliance** involves the use of direct or indirect strategies and techniques by others to influence us to change our attitudes or behaviours (by using certain products!). The list is endless. **Obedience**, like conformity and compliance, is widespread and occurs when we follow a direct command from another person. We obey when we perceive the person issuing the command to be a legitimate authority, such as a police officer.

Social psychologists typically seek to identify and examine the processes involved in these various kinds of social influence and ask such questions as: When are we more likely to conform, comply and obey? Under what circumstances are we more likely to resist such social influence? To what extent is social influence able to control our individual thoughts and actions?

compliance
Involves the use of direct or indirect strategies and techniques by others to influence us to change our attitudes or behaviours.

obedience
Following a direct command from another person; we obey when we perceive the person issuing the command to be a legitimate authority, such as police officers.

Conformity

One of the first systematic series of studies of how social pressure influences an individual's perceptual judgments was reported by Sherif (1935) whose experiments made use of a perceptual illusion called the **autokinetic effect**. In a completely darkened room, subjects were introduced to a stationary pinpoint of light. Under these conditions the light appeared to move. Subjects were asked to estimate the distance the point of light appeared to move. Sherif reported that when subjects shared their estimates with other group members their judgments converged in successive trials (see Figure 6.1).

This procedure was modified by Jacobs and Campbell (1961). Single subjects made judgments with three confederates of the experimenter. When the confederates made extreme judgments regarding the apparent movement of the light, subjects tended to conform and their guesses were almost as extreme as those of the confederates. Sherif proposed that in ambiguous situations, where we have no previous experience, others' judgments establish a norm—a standard we tend to adhere to. In other words we come to believe the group's consensus.

autokinetic effect
A perceptual illusion; as we stare at a stationary pinpoint of light, the light will appear to move.

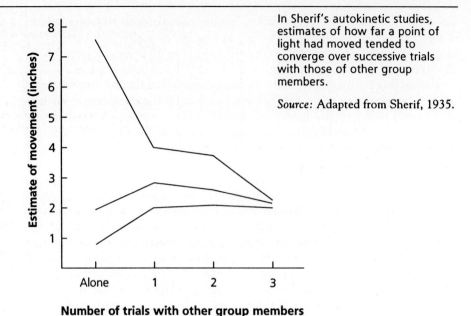

In Sherif's autokinetic studies, estimates of how far a point of light had moved tended to converge over successive trials with those of other group members.

Source: Adapted from Sherif, 1935.

Figure 6.1 *Group conformity in perceptual judgments*

Like Sherif, Solomon Asch was also concerned with the pervasive effects of group pressure on decision-making and carried out a series of experiments that expanded our knowledge of this important social phenomenon. Asch (1955) placed subjects in a room with 7-9 other people, who were confederates, and told them they were participating in an experiment on visual perception. They were asked to examine three lines of different lengths drawn on a white card and judge which was equal in length to a standard line presented on another card. They were asked to make 18 assessments during the experiment and were required to give their answers aloud to the rest of the group. As you can see from Figure 6.2, the correct answer is quite obvious and on the first two trials subjects gave the correct response. On the third trial, however, the first stooge gave an incorrect answer and, as the experiment continued, confederates gave incorrect answers on 12 of the 18 trials. The results of Asch's classic experiment indicated that of 123 subjects, 94 (78%) conformed at least once and on average they conformed more than a third of the time (4 out of the 12 critical trials).

An interesting question posed by these results is whether or not the subjects actually believed their incorrect answers. Asch reported that generally this was not the case. When subjects were asked to write their estimates instead of sharing them with others in the group, conformity rates dropped to about one third of that obtained in the original experiment. Does this result surprise you? Why did so many conform, preserving unanimity by making obviously incorrect judgments?

Perhaps they felt pressured by the "majority is always right norm" and did not want to appear "one out" and risk rejection. There are many instances when we refer to a group for guidelines and psychologists call

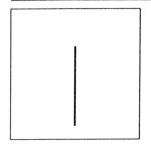 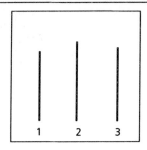

Similar stimulus material has been widely used to assess the extent of social conformity. Subjects have to decide which line in the box on the right is equal to that on the left. When confederates posing as other group members give wrong answers, the fun begins.

Source: Asch, "Opinions and social pressure", *Scientific American*, 1955, November. Copyright © 1955 by Scientific American, Inc. All rights reserved.

Figure 6.2 *The Asch-type lines*

this **informational social influence**. Other times we conform to obtain some reward or perhaps to avoid punishment or disapproval from a group, or **normative social influence**. Research evidence supports both these notions. We conform to groups to be liked and accepted (normative) and to be correct (informative) (Insko, Drenan, Solomon, Smith & Wade, 1983; Insko, Smith, Alicke, Wade & Taylor, 1985). For example, is Lenin orange or red? Moscovici (1991) conducted an experiment on imagery and social influence in which 30 female subjects viewed four slides that progressively drew a portrait of Lenin against an orange-red background. In a second experiment, 54 female subjects were shown just one complete portrait of Lenin against either background. Moscovici's findings suggest that the girls, when faced by a majority opinion, compared their responses with others when asked what colour Lenin was, and were concerned to agree with the group. When faced with a minority asserting something unbelievable or unseen, the girls attempted to validate this response by comparing it with reality. According to Moscovici, during this process individuals inadvertently changed their opinion.

We all conform to various standards or norms set by various groups in which we interact: family, friends, workmates, church members. So maybe we should not be surprised at the extent of such behaviour reported by various psychological experiments. We do not always conform do we? Asch's experiments demonstrated that even in laboratory settings a significant number of subjects were able to resist a unanimous majority. Indeed he reported that 25 per cent did not yield at all, despite the presence of group pressure. What factors determine the extent to which we will respond to pressure to conform? While many variables may play a part in this process, social psychologists have given special attention to the following:

informational social influence
Using a group for guidelines for correct behaviour.

normative social influence
When we conform to obtain some reward or perhaps to avoid punishment or disapproval from a group.

The person

Are some people more conforming than others? Is there such a thing as a conforming personality? Research evidence suggests that although there may be specific traits such as ego strength and authoritarianism, which may be related to degrees of conformity, correlations are usually very small. Also, different personality characteristics may predict different sorts of conformity. Again the degree of conformity is inconsistent and varies across situations.

True extroverts often make us feel uncomfortable, perhaps providing an insight into just how conformist we really are. (Photo: Mark Bramley)

For example, McDavid and Sistrunk (1964) found that making the task on an Asch-type perceptual experiment either easy or difficult gave different results depending on the sex and personality characteristics of the rater, and greatly influenced subsequent conformity. If the task was clear-cut, timid subjects with a high need for approval, conformed, while sex, trust, suspiciousness and similar variables affected conformity when making difficult judgments. McDavid and Sistrunk concluded that there were many reasons why we conform, and a personality profile allowing us to predict conformity was unlikely to be found.

Gender

Crutchfield (1955) reported that women generally are more susceptible to pressure to conform than men, but these reported differences vary across studies and have been challenged (Eagly, 1987). Several authors argue that classic studies on conformity were flawed because they often involved tasks and materials that are subtly biased in favour of males (Sistrunk & McDavid, 1971). Eagly and Chrvala (1986) investigated status and gender role explanations of the tendency for women to conform more than men under group pressure. In a deception paradigm, 91 male and female university students were led to believe that they were assigned to a group of two males and two females. After the subjects gave their opinions, group members then gave differing opinions. Subjects were then asked to express their opinion in one of two settings: one in which group members monitored their opinion, and a non-surveillance condition. Subjects' impressions of group members' likability or expertise were then analysed. Findings suggest that, for 19 years and older, females conformed more in the surveillance condition than when unobserved. Surveillance did not influence male conformity and, with increasing age, females were more conforming than men. Eagly's (1987) social role theory proposes that women conform more than men because they often occupy different and lower-status roles in our society. Traditionally, women occupy lower-status positions, such as nurturers and homemakers. It remains to be seen if conformity rates decrease as women achieve higher social status and traditional sex-roles change.

Group size

How do situational factors influence the degree of conformity we will display? Is our tendency to conform to group pressure dependent on the number of people in the influencing group? Asch (1955) reported that when the number of confederates varied from one to 15, conformity peaked in groups of three to four. Asch's results indicated that in the largest groups conformity declined. From these findings and other experiments (Rosenberg, 1961) it appears that our conformity will increase as group size grows from one to four other people. However, further increases, from four upwards, will not increase our conformity (see Figure 6.3).

How do we explain these effects on our tendency to conform? Several authors (Wilder, 1977; Insko et al., 1985) have proposed some reasons for this effect. They argue that when groups are larger than four people, individuals may begin to be suspicious of the degree of unanimity they observe. That is, they begin to suspect collusion and may also doubt the independence of a large group displaying unanimous wrong decisions. Wilder (1977) found that when judgments are perceived to be independent, more conformity is likely to result. So, as Wilder suggests, the central issue is probably not

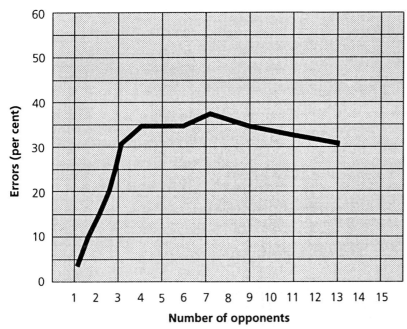

Figure 6.3 *Does conformity increase with group size?*

Size of majority which opposed them had an effect on the subjects. With a single opponent the subject erred only 3.6 per cent of the time; with two opponents he erred 13.6 per cent; three, 31.8 per cent; four, 35.1 per cent; six, 35.2 per cent; seven, 37.1 per cent; nine, 35.1 per cent; 15, 31.2 per cent.

Source: Adapted from Asch, 1955.

the size of the group as such but rather how the subjects perceive each other.

Several researchers have attempted to delineate the amount of social influence that groups of varying size exert on individual members, by developing quasi-mathematical models (see Figure 6.4) (Latane, 1981; Latane & Wolf, 1981; Tanford & Penrod, 1984). The **social influence model** (Tanford & Penrod, 1984) implies that social influence increases rapidly with each additional member of the influencing groups but levels off after a point. As in Asch's experiments, influence increases as group size increases to about four people and then levels off. As the group increases the curves get flatter, that is each additional member adds less and less to the group's influence on an individual until additional members add no further influence.

While there is considerable support for the predictive validity of this model, it does not tell us *why* variables are related, only *how* they are related.

social influence model
Model which implies that social influence increases rapidly with each additional member added to a group but levels off after a point.

Group cohesiveness and attractiveness

Everyday experience tells us that we are more likely to conform to groups we find attractive and this is supported by several research studies (Newcomb, 1943; Festinger, Schachter & Back, 1950; Lott & Lott, 1961; Sakurai, 1975). Generally, when all members are highly attracted to each other we call such a group *cohesive*. On average, when group cohesiveness is high,

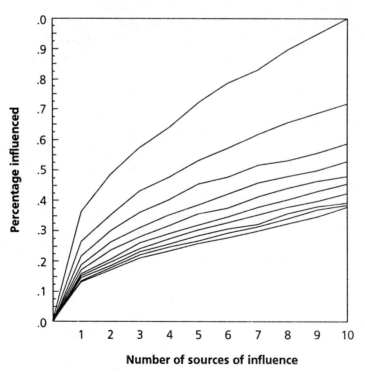

As you can see, initially adding extra members to a group increases social influence but you quickly get to a point of diminishing returns.

Figure 6.4 *The social influence model*
Source: Tanford & Penrod, 1984.

that is, when we are strongly attracted to a group and want to be approved and accepted by its members, we are more likely to respond to pressure to conform, than when cohesiveness is low.

Social support

What happens when we find ourselves in situations where others break away from group unanimity? Are we less likely to conform to social influence?

In the Asch experiments, when an ally supported a subject's judgments, group pressure to conform was reduced. The presence of an ally allows us to share the possibility of disapproval or rejection by the group. In these situations, conformity will decrease only as long as the ally continues to deviate from the majority view. While it appears that the presence of support will reduce pressure to conform in perceptual judgments, what happens in the wider social context? Allen and Levine (1968, 1969) found that the presence of social support will reduce conformity only when it agrees with our opinion, but not when allies' opinions are more extreme than that of the majority.

Status and commitment

Evidence confirms that we are more likely to conform to groups to which we are attracted, but what happens when groups are attracted to us? Do we tend to conform even more? Earlier research (Dittes & Kelley, 1956; Hollander, 1958) on perceptions of status in a group reported that high-status individuals felt more secure in their position and did not feel as much pressure to conform, whereas people who saw themselves in a low-status position felt rejected and were therefore less attracted to the group.

Harvey and Conslavi (1960) studied friendship cliques among delinquent boys. In this conformity experiment the researchers observed that middle-status boys (measured by peer ratings) conformed more than high- or low-status boys. This is commonsense. High-status people (movie and rock stars) and low-status individuals (minorities) often appear to conform less to social conventions than average middle-class people, because they have less to gain from doing so.

Degree of commitment also influences conformity. The more we non-conform, the more we are likely to resist group pressure (Deutsch & Gerard, 1955). It appears that if we are asked to commit ourselves in writing, or to publicly express dissent, this is likely to strengthen our resolve in resisting influence from a majority who may disagree with us (Kiesler, 1971; Kerr & MacCoun, 1985).

Minority influence

Many social psychologists interested in social influence have focused their attention on factors influencing a minority to conform to the majority view. It has been suggested that part of the reason for this focus is historical. At the time of the classic studies of Asch and others, there was deep concern about the effectiveness of majority influence in suppressing minority

*One dissenting voice in a group is
often sufficient to reduce social
conformity.*
(Photo: Mark Bramley)

dissent. The 1940s and 1950s witnessed much debate as events in Nazi
Germany and McCarthyism in the US provided an impetus for such concerns.

While majority influence on the minority is a valid phenomenon, it is
only one kind of social influence operating in a group. In real-life settings
all group members interact and can influence and be influenced whether
they belong to the majority or minority (Moscovici, 1976, 1980). In many
instances members of a minority are able to influence the majority and
resist group pressure (Wolf, 1985). Under what conditions is this likely to
occur? To examine this issue, Moscovici and Faucheux (1972) designed
an experiment where four subjects and one confederate were required to
identify shared characteristics of a series of subjects. The confederate consistently
gave incorrect answers. The experiments compared the majority's answer
in this group to that of a control group without a non-conformist confederate.
They found that if the confederate was highly consistent in his judgment,
the majority tended to be influenced by his consistency and regarded him
as having confidence in his judgment. Thus the minority of one was able
to exert a considerable influence.

In later studies (Moscovici, 1980) subjects were confronted with opinions
on social issues that were either moderate and reasonable (car manufacturers
should include pollution control devices in new cars) or unreasonable and
extreme (governments should close down any industry that causes pollution).
These positions were allocated to a majority or to a minority group. Subjects
were then asked to indicate whether or not they agreed with a series of
statements representing the positions they had just heard. Subjects were
retested three weeks later on the same series of statements. Results indicated

that in the initial experiment the reasonable majority exerted more influence on subjects. However, findings at the retest suggested that unreasonable minority positions had the greatest influence on a subject's views. In interpreting these findings, Moscovici suggested that the reasonable majority had reduced compliance, whereas the unreasonable minority position had converted others to its position.

Moscovici's findings have been supported by other research studies (Mugny, 1982; Maass & Clark, 1984; Bray, Johnston & Chilstrom, 1982). This research evidence suggests that minorities who consistently voice their dissenting opinions, and thus are perceived to be more committed to and confident of their position, are able to influence a majority position. Consistency is a significant factor contributing to both majority and minority influence. How consistency is interpreted in any given situation is also important, as are the psychological meanings attributed to it (Turner, 1991). Maass, Clark and Haberkorn (1982) suggest that a minority group may exert the greatest influence when its position reinforces prevailing societal values and cultural norms. For instance, were the opinions expressed by the women's movement in the 1970s reinforced by changing patterns and trends in the traditional roles of women?

However, Maass and Clark (1984) suggest that double minority groups, those that differ both in opinion and in other obvious ways from a majority, will impact less than members of a single minority group. Research by Maass and Clark indicated that a minority group perceived to be gay and supporting gay rights had less influence on a heterosexual majority view, than a heterosexual minority which supported gay rights. So the following factors are important contributors to minority influence:

1. Members of minority groups must demonstrate committed consistency in their opposition to majority views.
2. Minority groups should not appear to be rigid and dogmatic (Mugny, 1975).
3. Single minority groups that differ with respect to beliefs or attitudes have more impact than double minorities (differing in both beliefs and attitudes, and group membership).
4. The wider social context in which the minority group operates is important in determining the outcome of the influence on the majority (Moscovici, 1985).

Is there a particular strategy that we should follow if we are trying to influence a large number of people who believe they hold the correct view?

Two proposed models (Moscovici, 1980 and Hollander, 1964) argue that a minority group can reduce a majority's opposition to their position. However, they differ on the issue of timing, or when is the most appropriate time for the minority to challenge the majority position. Moscovici (1980) believes that in order to exert influence on the majority it is crucial that the minority dissent from the beginning and continue consistently to challenge the majority position. According to his model, over time the minority's commitment and consistency will lead to a greater acceptance of its point of view. Hollander (1964), however, proposed that members of a minority group should display initial conformity to the majority opinion in order to gain acceptance and status, and demonstrate commitment towards group goals.

Both these approaches may provide the basis for effective influence, although in some instances choosing the Moscovici strategy may result in minority members being labelled as extremist, radical fringe, or crackpots, more than individuals who choose the approach suggested by Hollander (initial conformity followed by later opposition to majority position). Research on minority influence has important social implications and warrants more attention. Many social movements begin with a small group who dissent from the majority viewpoint. Research of this nature can provide useful insights and increase our understanding of why some of these movements succeed and others fail.

Majority and minority social influence: An integrated approach

Two theoretical perspectives have attempted to integrate minority and majority influence into a single framework. These are the social impact theory and the social influence model.

Social impact theory

Proponents of the social impact theory (Latane, 1981) believe that social influence has a multiplier effect. The more sources of influence, the more rapidly credibility grows. Effectiveness is dependent on: strength, or the agent's power, status and/or knowledge; immediacy, or the proximity of the sender and receiver; and group size. According to this theory, majority influence has more impact due to larger numbers, and members of a minority group can only succeed if they can demonstrate consistent argument to compensate for their lack of numbers. While this approach predicts a levelling of influence with increasing numbers in a group, no ceiling effect (where influence ceases to exist) is envisaged. Evidence for the role of strength and immediacy has been questioned by some research (Mullen, 1985) as being weak and inconsistent. However, in response, Jackson (1987) has questioned the types of studies reviewed in making conclusions about the basic tenets of this theory.

Social influence model

Tanford and Penrod's (1984) social influence model, as we have seen, involves the use of computer-simulated groups to assess minority and majority social influence. Akin to social impact theory this approach predicts that as group size increases, influence will increase. According to this model, the second and third confederates exercise more influence towards conformity than the first confederate, and their influence levels off after this. Also consistent with much research, minorities are more likely to exert influence on small majority groups (six or less), especially when there is a minority of two.

Both these models suggest that the size of the minority and majority group affect the level of social influence. These two approaches offer useful insights as to how we positively or negatively influence each other in group settings.

So far we have seen that many factors influence the nature and extent of our conformity. Moreover, our tendency to conform is very strong and all too commonplace. We conform to others' expectations, societal standards and group norms most of the time but what do we get out of conformity?

Why do we conform?

Insko et al. (1985) maintains that while many factors impact on our tendency to conform, two basic human motives underlie conformity: our desire to be liked and our desire to be right. The Stanford Prison experiment by Zimbardo, Haney, Banks and Jaffe (1972) is a dramatic example of the compelling nature of conformity to social roles and group norms.

In 1972 Philip Zimbardo and his colleagues recruited 24 normal college-age males by newspaper advertisement to be subjects in his simulated prison experiment. Subjects were informed of the general purpose of the experiment and were paid $15.00 a day to participate. Subjects were randomly allocated to the role of either prisoner or guard. Subjects allocated to be prison guards were given a general briefing about the dangers of such a position but received no specific instructions on how to behave. It was up to them to establish the prison's rule and regulations.

The study began with the "prisoners" being picked up unexpectedly at their homes and taken to the local police station where they were charged and fingerprinted. They were then taken to a mock prison in the basement of the Psychology Department at Stanford University. Prisoners were stripped, searched, deloused and issued uniforms (uncomfortable shapeless garments and tight nylon caps) with numbers on them and shown the cells where they were to spend the next two weeks. "Prison guards" were given identical uniforms and reflective sunglasses which made eye contact impossible. They also carried badges of authority such as batons and whistles.

The primary aim of this study was to ascertain whether subjects would behave like "real" prison guards and inmates, and to what extent both implicit and explicit social norms would guide their behaviour. After six days the two-week study was terminated. In just a few days major changes had occurred in both prisoners' and guards' behaviour. Many guards became increasingly brutal in their treatment of prisoners. They constantly harassed and forced inmates to harangue one another and gave them tedious, senseless tasks such as carrying boxes back and forth between closets.

Initially, prisoners resisted and even attempted to take over the prison. This failed and they became increasingly servile, depressed and dehumanised. They appeared to lose their sense of personal identity and social responsibility. They called each other by their numbers and on one occasion let a fellow prisoner spend all night in a small closet rather than give up their blankets. Several began to show signs of emotional disturbance (outbursts of crying and screaming). Subjects in this experiment had come to act more and more like prisoners and guards in an actual prison. Why? Zimbardo suggested

The Zimbardo studies showed the powerful influence of roles on inmates and guards alike. Resistance by inmates was often followed by depression. (Photo: Barry Price)

that labelling subjects "prisoners" or "guards" and placing them in a context where these labels are relevant, exerted a very powerful influence, producing the pathological behaviour observed.

> The prison situation as presently arranged is guaranteed to generate severe enough pathological reactions in both prisoners and guards as to debase their humanity, lower their feelings of self worth and make it difficult for them to be part of a society outside of their prison. (Zimbardo, et al., 1972, p. 164)

The Stanford Prison Study stirred up a controversy within social psychology. Critics focused attention on the subjects' awareness that they were volunteers in a psychological experiment. They commented that observed changes in subjects' behaviour may have been due to beliefs about how prisoners and guards should behave (demand characteristics), rather than the environmental effects of a simulated prison (Banuazizi & Movahedi, 1975). Supporters replied that even if this were the case, subjects were no different from those who take on these roles in real prisons. Real prison officers and prisoners carry expectations regarding what is appropriate role behaviour and attempt to adhere to these in practice (Thayer & Saarni, 1975). Regardless of the controversy surrounding research such as Zimbardo's and his colleagues, the pressure to yield to social norms can be extremely powerful (see Box 6.2).

Box 6.2 *Four more days*

Zimbardo's Stanford Prison Experiment was extended by Lovibond, Mithiran and Adams in 1979 at the University of NSW. Their study examined how different instructions and settings would create differing prison regimes. They compared three experimental prison environments. The first regime, the *standard custodial condition*, was modelled on a medium-high security prison in Australia. In the *individualised custodial condition*, in which the setting was identical to the first, guards were told that the individuality of the prisoners was to be respected and they were to be addressed as Mr rather than by number. The third regime, the *participatory custodial condition*, encouraged constructive and responsible behaviour wherever possible. In this last condition the need to get to know the prisoners and to involve them in decision-making was emphasised in the guards' initial instructions.

A mock prison, similar to Zimbardo's was erected in the basement of the School of Psychology at the University of NSW. Sixty men, aged 18-45 years, were selected from responses to newspaper ads and screened by psychological testing before being randomly assigned to either 24 prison officer or 36 prisoner roles. Prisoners and officers were then issued standard prison uniforms, except in the participatory condition where officers wore civilian clothes. With minimal further intervention the officers settled down to run their gaols. A review panel

of independent professional observers (which included Jeanna) monitored the experiment.

The results indicated marked differences between the three regimes, both in the general atmosphere and quality of prisoner–officer interactions. In the participatory condition there was minimal overt hostility between officers and inmates. In the standard custodial group, there was a constant undercurrent of hostility between prisoners and officers, while in the individualised custodial regime, a "formal paternalistic atmosphere" developed with little overt hostility: "In general the individualised custodial groups were characterised by a certain routine flatness" (Lovibond, Mithiran & Adams, 1979).

Comparing their results with Zimbardo's, the authors found some significant differences in procedures between the two studies (see Figure 6.5). Subjects in the UNSW experiment were subjected to much tighter behavioural controls than in the Stanford experiment, and the experiment was "literal, rather than symbolic or functional". Inmates' behaviour was less extreme in the Australian study than at Stanford but the UNSW experimenters suggest that their results support the wider conclusion of Zimbardo's that:

. . . hostile affrontive relations in prisons result primarily from the nature of the prison regime, rather than the personal characteristics of inmates and officers. (Lovibond, Mithiran & Adams, 1979, pp. 283–85)

Table 6.1 *Comparison of UNSW and Stanford prison studies*

Comparison of UNSW and Stanford Prison Studies	
Conduct of Investigation	
Stanford	*UNSW*
One group, exploratory study	6 groups, 3 conditions of replication.
Paid volunteer student subjects.	Paid volunteer "representative subjects".
No training of guards.	Training of guards with training manual.
Symbolic, functional simulation (smocks, stockings, caps, chains on ankles for prisoners, reflective sunglasses, billy sticks for guards).	In baseline (standard custodial) group, literal representation of prison (standard uniforms, officer training, daily activities, rules), no weapons for guards.

(continued)

Table 6.1 *Comparison of UNSW and Stanford Prison Studies (continued)*

Conduct of Investigation

Stanford	UNSW
Consent of subjects "to be harassed and have civil rights curtailed". Physical abuse prohibited.	Harassment and physical abuse prohibited. Demand characteristics minimised by "awesome Consent Form" and use of non-student subjects.
Arrest procedure, suggesting possibility of change in rules.	No arrest procedure. No question of change in rules.
Communication between Superintendent and guards not specified.	Communication between Superintendent and guards rigidly controlled.
Duration 6 days.	Duration 4 days (each of 6 groups).

Results

Stanford	UNSW Standard Custodial
Pathological reactions: Extreme sadistic harassment by guards. Negative, hostile, affrontive relations between officers and prisoners. Gross emotional reactions in prisoners (depression, crying, rage and acute anxiety). Reality transformation.	Constant undercurrent of hostility between officers and prisoners. Some hostile exchanges and examples of arbitrary control and harassment. Attempts by prisoners to oustsmart, belittle and frustrate guards. Very lengthy searches. No reality transformation. Participants simultaneously prisoners for officers and experimental subjects.

Stanford and UNSW Standard Custodial

Meals treated as "privileges".

Prison authorities regarded by officers as siding with prisoners.

Offers by guards to work overtime without pay.

Inappropriate carry-over of role behaviours.

Behaviour under surveillance consistent with behaviour when believed unobserved.

Spontaneous assumption of leadership roles by the most hostile guards.

UNSW Individualised Custodial	UNSW Participatory
Paternalistic atmosphere. Officer–prisoner relations distant and formal. Form of address (if any) usually Mr. Authority of officers accepted. Little overt hostility. Very few incidents or reports. Searches thorough but rapid.	After initial period of suspiciousness, general atmosphere of tolerance and co-operation. Form of address first names on reciprocal basis. Virtually no overt hostility. Prison regarded as "living quarters", "commune". Authority existed outside group. The few conflicts resolved within group. Perfunctory searches. Some tendency to slackness in relation to cleaning and routines.

Source: Lovibond & Mithiran, 1979.

Compliance

Every day in our interactions with others we engage in compliant behaviour. Acceding to others' requests is a common occurrence. In such situations we comply with direct requests to change aspects of our behaviour; to buy something; or to donate money. These requests come from many sources: advertisers, employers, friends, family, lovers, colleagues, the media. Social psychologists have termed this form of social influence "compliance", and are interested in studying what encourages effective compliance. Given that we like to be liked, recognising that others also want to be liked provides the baseline for strategies employed to gain compliance. Researchers have studied the various techniques and strategies which we use to gain compliance with our requests. Let us briefly examine some of these.

Ingratiation

Ingratiation refers to efforts by other people to make themselves more attractive, to increase our willingness to comply with their requests, by using praise or flattery, or by agreeing with us. Research suggests that because of our desire to be liked by others, using ingratiation may be a

Advertisers often use attractive people to induce favourable attitudes towards their products and to promote unconscious compliance with their wishes.
(Photo: Mark Bramley)

powerful step towards compliance. Arvey and Campion (1982) found that employment applicants who were appropriately dressed and who demonstrated positive nonverbal cues, such as maintaining eye contact and smiling frequently, tended to receive higher ratings than those not exhibiting such behaviour in an interview. Also Schlenker and Leary (1982) noted that in many instances, if we perceive others to be gullible, we are more likely to use ingratiation in our attempts to influence them. However, if we suspect that we are being deceived and believe that there is an ulterior motive for such techniques we will often avoid interaction with those trying to influence us (Liden & Mitchell, 1988).

Saying no, but meaning yes: Token resistance

We often believe that when others offer initial resistance they are not really serious and that they really want to comply with our requests. Traditional beliefs about appropriate sexual behaviour are a good example of this kind of technique. The belief that women should initially resist the sexual advance of men is a widely held sex-role stereotype in our culture. By way of example, Muehlenhard and Holloabaugh (1988), in a study of college women, found that subjects who engaged in token resistance to sexual advances by men held more traditional sex-role beliefs than those women who did not use such strategies. Also, those subjects who used techniques of token refusals viewed male–female interactions as adversarial and saw verbal persuasion and even physical force by men as acceptable in sexual encounters.

Stereotyped ideas like these often cause problems. Believing that refusal is only token resistance leads to misunderstanding and poor communication between the sexes, and in some cases to sexual violence against women.

Multiple-request techniques

Compliance techniques take many forms, some as old as the hills. If you have ever caught yourself coming out of a shop with a dearer product than you wanted to buy, then it is a moral certainty that you not only encountered a super-salesperson but probably fell foul of a multiple-request technique! Not only psychologists play these games, beware!

The foot-in-the-door technique

This strategy is based on a simple principle—if you can get them to agree to a small thing, they are more likely to agree to a larger request. The foot-in-the-door technique has been found to be effective in producing compliant behaviour in a wide range of situations (Freedman & Fraser, 1966; Katzev & Johnson, 1984).

Why do we tend to comply with a larger second request after agreeing to an initial one? Perhaps the **norm of reciprocity** (Chapter Ten) helps explain this tendency. This norm maintains that we are obliged to return favours in our social relations (Gouldner, 1960). Many successful sales strategies are based on reciprocity. Companies give away "freebies" in

norm of reciprocity
A learned rule requiring us to pay back others' prosocial acts.

supermarkets, and samples of products are often placed in letter boxes and magazines.

Beaman et al. (1983) doubt this is an effective technique. In a review of over 120 foot-in-the-door experiments, they reported that in nearly half compliance was not increased, and may even decline when this technique is employed. For this strategy to be effective it appears that a number of conditions must be met. Time must pass between the two requests in order to reinforce compliance to the second request. The effectiveness is reduced when the second request is perceived as too demanding or too large. If individuals were promised money to comply with the first request, they are less likely to comply with the second larger request (Zuckerman, Lazzaro & Waldgeir, 1979). One possible explanation is that those who are paid to comply fail to develop the necessary altruistic motivation that will foster a favourable response to the second request.

The door-in-the-face technique

This strategy is the opposite of the foot-in-the-door technique and consists of a large request followed by a more modest reasonable one. Cialdini and colleagues (1975) in a study of university students initially asked subjects to spend two hours per week for two years as voluntary counsellors to juvenile delinquents. Most refused this commitment. When a more modest second request was made (to act as chaperone for a group of juvenile delinquents on a short trip to the zoo), half the students complied. Only 17 per cent of students in a control group, those who were not asked to be counsellors, agreed to this request.

This technique is often effective, because we see the shift from a larger to more reasonable request as a concession to us. The reciprocity principle then requires us to meet them halfway by complying with the smaller request. This strategy also enables us to see ourselves as helpful and cooperative.

That's-not-all technique

Again the norm of reciprocity influences our compliance to the use of this technique. The that's-not-all technique consists of offering a person a product at a high price and before they have time to respond, the influencer "sweetens" the offer by lowering the price or by including something extra with the original product. Research indicates that people are more likely to accept the second offer than the initial one as they need to reciprocate the concession made by the salesperson (Burger, 1986b). This strategy differs from the door-in-the-face technique as the person is not given time to consider or refuse the initial offer.

The low-ball procedure

This widespread technique also relies on initial compliance to increase a subsequent commitment. For example, we commit ourselves to the purchase of a new car, thinking we have just struck a great deal. Then we discover that the initial price does not include certain features we assumed were included (tape deck, air conditioning and power steering). Research suggests that in this instance many of us will still proceed with the sale because we feel strongly committed to the purchase.

Cialdini and his co-researchers (1978) demonstrated the effectiveness of this technique in a series of studies. Two groups of Introductory Psychology students were scheduled to participate in an experiment. In the experimental condition (using the low-ball technique) subjects were informed after they had agreed to take part that the study was at 7 a.m. The control group were informed of the 7 a.m. starting time before they were asked to participate. Fifty-six per cent of the subjects agreed to take part in the experiment in the low-ball condition, while only 31 per cent in the control condition agreed to participate. Also 53 per cent of subjects in the experimental situation turned up at the appointed time (7 a.m.) whereas only 24 per cent from the control group showed up.

Why is this procedure so effective? One explanation suggests we comply not because we want to but because we feel a sense of personal responsibility to the person making the request. Also if subjects are unable to meet an initial request they are more likely to comply with the second offer. The low-ball technique fails to produce the required effect only when a different person (not the initial requester) subsequently increases the cost to the recipient (Burger & Petty, 1981).

A study by Joule (1987) compared the effectiveness of low-ball and foot-in-the-door techniques. The low-ball condition involved subjects agreeing to complete an experiment, and then, before the experiment, being informed that they would be required not to smoke for 18 hours. In one of the foot-in-the-door conditions, students completed a short questionnaire, then were asked to give up smoking for 18 hours. Findings suggested that variations of low-ball technique were more effective. It appears individuals may experience a greater degree of cognitive commitment to behave in a certain way when they have already decided to pursue a particular course.

Psychological reactance and compliance

reverse psychology
Exerting influence by telling someone that they cannot have, or are unable to do, something which causes them to do it.

The general notion of psychological reactance is often loosely referred to as **reverse psychology**. Sometimes people exert influence on us by telling us that we cannot have something or we are unable to do something, and this gets our back up and causes the very behaviour they want (compliance). A customer immediately buys a certain product when informed it is the last one, a man proposes marriage when told his long-term girlfriend has found a new lover—why does this type of influence spur us to action? Is it forbidden fruit? The theory of psychological reactance (Brehm, 1966; Brehm & Brehm, 1981) proposes that when we perceive that our freedom to choose is under threat, we feel unpleasantly aroused. This negative arousal motivates us to restore personal freedom (see Box 6.3).

Non-compliance

Non-compliance is the term used to describe many patients' resistance to therapeutic regimes, whether diet, exercises or medications prescribed for them by their medical practitioners (Cotton & Antill, 1984). A major

Box 6.3 *Measuring psychological reactance*

Our understanding of psychological reactance is hindered by the paucity of suitable ways of measuring it. Brehm (1966), the originator of the concept, devised a scale but this and other similar instruments have suffered from cross-cultural and methodological difficulties (Tucker & Byers, 1987). There have been many attempts to redress these difficulties which have tried to replicate Brehm's findings using local samples. In Australia, Sung-Mook Hong from the University of Western Sydney (Macarthur) has devised a reactance scale as part of a larger measure, which has a clearly defined four-factor structure of psychological reactance with acceptable reliabilities (Hong & Page, 1989).

Items on Hong's Psychological Reactance Scale are shown in Table 6.2. Raters indicate on a five point scale their degree of agreement or disagreement. Factor 1 (items 4, 6, 8 and 10) relates to freedom of choice in decisions and behaviour. Factor 2 (items 1, 2 and 3) reflects a common theme of **conformity reactance** or objection to following rules. Factor 3 (items 11, 12, 13 and 14) represents **behavioural freedom**, a need for freedom from the control of others. Factor 4 (items 5, 7, and 9) refers to reactance to others' advice and recommendations. Hong and Page comment that the scale is quite robust but could be improved still further given psychological reactance's applicability across a broad range of behaviours and situations.

Hong has used his scale to some effect in a number of studies. Psychological reactance is a robust concept little affected by sex or other variables. Hong (1990) reported the effects of sex and church attendance on psychological reactance. Two hundred and fifty-three undergraduates at the University of Western Sydney (Macarthur) completed his scale and indicated whether they attended church regularly, occasionally or never. When the results were analysed there were no sex differences and, although Hong expected to find "an inverse relationship . . . between church attendance and the level of psychological reactance given the presumed religious discipline and practice among regular churchgoers", no significant difference was found between the three groups on church attendance.

Psychological reactance?
(Photo:Mathew Munro)

Table 6.2 *Hong's psychological reactance*

1. Regulations trigger a sense of resistance in me.
2. I find contradicting others stimulating.
3. When something is prohibited, I usually think "that's exactly what I am going to do".
4. The thought of being dependent on others aggravates me.
5. I consider advice from others to be an intrusion.
6. I become frustrated when I am unable to make free and independent decisions.
7. It irritates me when someone points out things which are obvious to me.
8. I become angry when my freedom of choice is restricted.
9. Advice and recommendations ususally induce me to do just the opposite.
10. I am contented only when I am acting of my own free will.
11. I resist the attempts of others to influence me.
12. It makes me angry when another person is held up as a model for me to follow.
13. When someone forces me to do something, I feel like doing the opposite.
14. It disappoints me to see others submitting to society's standards and rules.

Source: Hong, 1989.

area of study concerns patients not taking prescribed medication. Most researchers suggest that between 25 and 60 per cent of patients make errors in taking medication and in 35 per cent of such people this is sufficient to endanger their health (Maddock, 1967; Stewart & Cluff, 1973; Jellett, 1975).

Many research studies have tried to identify factors underlying this non-compliance but with mixed success: non-compliance increases with the number of medications taken and with the complexity of the regime (Ayd, 1974; Porter, 1969). The doctor–patient relationship is an important variable. When there is good rapport and effective communication between doctor and patient, and instructions and explanations are clear and simple, patient satisfaction and compliance have increased (Blackwell, 1974; Ley, 1978). Philip Ley (1986) of Sydney University proposes that patients' understanding of and memory for information given to them by doctors can affect compliance and patient satisfaction. According to Ley, if doctors use written instructions this will enhance understanding and recall, improving rates of patient compliance. Also, our attitudes and opinions about taking medication have been suggested as a significant factor influencing patient compliance (Stimson, 1974; Stimson & Webb, 1975). However, studies attempting to investigate these issues have been inconclusive and mostly confined to psychiatric patients (Raskin, 1961; Davis, 1968).

Personality characteristics of patients have also been studied. Researchers have identified non-compliers as being hostile and aggressive, obstructive and demanding (Richards, 1964; Davis, 1968). Locus of control, specifically external control, or believing that one is powerless to change what happens to oneself, is also linked to non-compliance in studies of alcoholic patients (Schofield, 1978). Notwithstanding, research results overall are again inconclusive and most researchers now feel that non-compliance is a multidimensional phenomenon. It was against this backdrop that Sandra Cotton and John Antill (1984) from Macquarie University studied non-compliance as a function of medical/pharmacological variables, doctor–patient relationships and patients' attitudes and personality using a multivariate approach (see Box 6.4).

Box 6.4 *Non-compliance: Medical and psychological aspects*

Subjects in Cotton and Antill's study were 109 adults ranging in age from 23 to 80 years, recruited at two pharmacies in an outer western suburb of Sydney. For each medication taken, subjects were asked the name, dosage, how long they had been taking it and whether they had ever varied the dosage and for what reasons. Subjects were asked about the clarity of their doctor's explanations and instruction, doubts about their doctor's diagnosis or treatment prescribed, satisfaction with doctor's consultations and so forth. Their attitude to medication items and opinions about taking medication were surveyed. Demographic data was collated and Rotter's (1966) Internal-External Locus of Control Questionnaire (IEC) (see Chapter Four) was administered.

Contrary to the researchers' expectations, the more drugs a person took and the more complicated the pattern in which they had to be taken, the more compliant the patient (Cotton &

Antill, 1984). The compliant and non-compliant groups differed significantly on their view of taking medication and on their locus of control scores. Non-compliers had a much greater sense of being in control of their lives and this seemed to account for their reluctance to take medication. Cotton and Antill suggest that non-compliers wanted to "do it alone rather than some external agent being responsible for health or their recovery".

While this study failed to substantiate previous research on non-compliance and medication, it provided support for the multidimensional nature of this issue. Results also indicated that attitudes and personality are important determiners of non-compliance, particularly patients' opinions of having to take the medication. Doctors need to be more aware that individuals have definite beliefs and opinions about taking medication and that these will affect their behaviour.

Research suggests that compliance with prescription recommendations is low. However, Cotton and Antill found that the more complicated the drug regime and the more medications that patients took, the more compliant they were. (Photo: Rob Pozo/Macarthur Advertiser)

Obedience to authority

One of the most powerful and basic elements of social influence is obedience to legitimate authority. Obedience is an integral part of *authority* and our experience tells us that some system of social control is necessary in all societies. Obedience is rooted in our culture, religions and in the shared values of our Western tradition. While it is usually an implicit rather than a spelled out value, in some contexts, like the monastic life, the military or police forces, obedience is demanded and codified within the rules of the organisation.

> Under orders from an authority it appears that many normal people respond with obedience despite their own scruples and discomfort about actions that they and others would usually regard as illegal, immoral or even unthinkable. (Kelman & Hamilton, 1989, p. 23)

Obedience differs from conformity and compliance. Conformity often occurs beneath the surface, while compliance is more obvious, such as adherence to a direct request. Pressure to obey is usually more explicit and occurs when we are commanded to do something, typically by some authority we perceive to be legitimate and who usually occupies a position of higher status or authority.

When will we obey and when will we disobey? This subject raises profound issues for us as individuals. Obedience to those in authority sometimes has extreme consequences—and what serves political ends often does so at the expense of moral and ethical considerations. For example,

Enthusiasm for the Third Reich led to destructive obedience and the Holocaust.
(Photo: Sygma/Austral International)

the Holocaust led to millions of innocent people being systematically slaughtered, but without the willingness of large numbers of people to obey the commands of others, atrocities such as those committed under Hitler, Stalin and Pol Pot would not have occurred.

A dramatic illustration of the willingness of some to follow orders is the case of Adolf Eichmann, the former Nazi held responsible for the murder of millions of people. In 1961 Eichmann was tried in Jerusalem for war crimes committed during World War II. In his defence Eichmann maintained that he was not personally responsible and was merely following orders from those in authority, who had led him to believe his actions were lawful and patriotic (Arendt, 1963). He was convicted and hanged.

The following exchange between the prosecutor, Hausner, and Eichmann, demonstrates the classic Nuremberg defence—orders are orders:

Hausner: "Then you admit that you were an accomplice to the murder of millions of Jews?"

Eichmann: "That I cannot admit. I ask myself whether I am guilty as an accomplice from the human point of view. But I do not consider myself guilty from the legal point of view. I received orders and I executed orders. If the deportations which I carried out—the ones in which I had a part—led to death of some of these Jews, then the legal questions must be examined as to whether I am guilty in terms of responsibility. (Pearlman, 1963, p. 467)

When will people obey an unethical or immoral command from an authority? Stanley Milgram (1963, 1974), in a series of famous experiments sought to determine whether people would obey commands to inflict pain on another person. Milgram's experiments were designed in an attempt to understand why the Nazi Holocaust systematically killed millions of innocent people. Why were these orders obeyed? Milgram's subjects were paid recruits from the community in New Haven, Connecticut. The men were informed they were participating in a study to assess the effect of punishment on learning. The experimenter ordered the subject to deliver electric shocks to another person each time they gave an incorrect response to a simple learning task. Subjects were told to increase the level of shock each time an incorrect response was given. The labels on the equipment varied from a mild 15 volts, through 390 volts (labelled "danger—severe shock"), to a maximum of 450 volts (labelled "XXXX"). In reality the learner was a confederate of the experimenter and was not actually receiving shocks (see Figure 6.5).

During the experiment the confederate (learner) gave many incorrect responses (about 75 per cent of the time). Subjects then had to decide whether they would continue to deliver increasingly painful shocks or disobey the experimenter. When subjects appeared tentative the experimenter issued a series of graded prods ranging from "Please go on" to "It's absolutely essential that you continue", and finally, "You have no other choice; you must go on." As the experimenter ordered the subject to continue and as the shocks increased in severity, the learner (confederate) displayed increasing

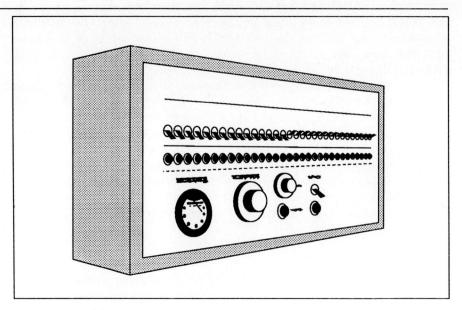

Figure 6.5 *Milgram's experimental apparatus*
Source: Milgram, 1974.

pain and responded with screams of protest, pounding on the wall and screaming "Let me out of here" and, in one version of the study, indicated they had a heart condition.

Given that all the participants were volunteers and paid in advance, what outcome would you have predicted? After all this was just an experiment, and surely subjects would refuse to obey the experimenter's orders? Indeed Milgram expected most subjects to either refuse to deliver any shocks at all, or to cease as soon as the confederate expressed discomfort. This was not the case. No subject disobeyed before delivering at least 135 volts. Seventy-five per cent of subjects gave 300 volts and 65 per cent or 26 of the 40 subjects went all the way and delivered the maximum of 450 volts.

While subjects in Milgram's experiment obeyed the experimenter it was clear they did not wish to inflict pain on another person, or enjoyed administering shocks.

> There were striking reactions of tension and emotional strain. One observer related "I observed a mature and initially poised businessman enter the laboratory smiling and confident. Within 20 minutes he was reduced to a twitching stuttering wreck, who was rapidly approaching a point of nervous collapse. He constantly pulled on his earlobe and twisted his hands. At one point he pushed his fists into his forehead and muttered 'Oh God, let's stop it', and yet he continued to respond to every word of the experimenter and obeyed to the end" . . . Subjects were observed to sweat, tremble, stutter, bite their lips, groan and dig their fingernails into their flesh. These were characteristic rather than exceptional responses to the experiment. (Milgram, 1963, p. 377)

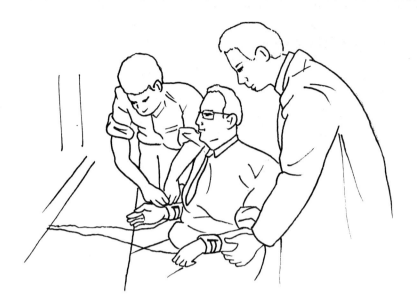

Despite his expectations, Milgram found that most of his subjects obeyed commands to inflict pain on another person.
Source: Milgram, 1974.

Other factors influenced obedience:

Proximity

Sixty-five per cent of subjects obeyed the experimenter when the learner was in another room. Obedience declined to 40 per cent when the learner was in the same room as the subject, and when the subject was required to force the learner's hand on a shock plate only 30 per cent of subjects obeyed completely. Milgram's results suggest that the greater the distance between the experimenter (authority figure) and the subject, the less the obedience. When the experimenter issued orders by telephone, obedience declined to 21 per cent.

Institutional setting

Initial experiments were conducted at Yale, a highly prestigious university. To examine the possible effect of the institution's status on obedience, Milgram conducted similar experiments in a run-down office building in a nearby city. Results indicated that obedience declined only slightly to 48 per cent.

Milgram's results were replicated in several studies. Levels of obedience similar to that of Milgram's original study have been reported for various samples in the United States (Bock & Warren, 1972; Costanzo, 1977; Rosenhan, 1969), in Spain (Miranda, Caballero, Gomez & Zamorano, 1981), in Germany (Mantell, 1971), in Japan (Shanab & Yahya, 1977, 1978), in Australia (Kilham & Mann, 1974) and in Italy (Meeus & Raaijmakers, 1986).

For example, in 1974 Kilham and Mann conducted a modified study at the University of Sydney based on the Milgram obedience paradigm. The subjects were 63 male and 62 female first year Psychology students at Sydney University. The researchers found that subjects were more obedient when required to communicate an order to inflict pain on another (transmitter condition) than when they were ordered to implement that order (executant order). While the general level of obedience in the executant condition (40%) was lower than reported by Milgram (45%), interestingly, female subjects were less obedient than males, especially when required to carry out orders. Kilham and Mann (1974) suggest possible explanations for this result. When females are expected to act aggressively against another female, they may face greater reactance. They may seek to form an alliance with the female victim in order to oppose the demands of a male experimenter perceived as unreasonably aggressive and may also demonstrate a concern for the vulnerability of the female victim.

Other studies have reported destructive obedience in different settings. Hofling, Brotzman, Dalrymple, Graves and Pierce (1966) found that nurses will deliver dangerous levels of medication if ordered to do so by a doctor. In a study conducted by Sheridan and King (1972), subjects delivered real electric shocks to puppies, at greater levels of obedience than subjects in Milgram's studies.

Milgram's research findings and similar results obtained from other studies are alarming. The question remains why did subjects in these various experiments and many others in real-life situations readily obey the orders of authority figures? Several factors appear to contribute to why we so willingly obey. Milgram's experiments are outlined in his book *Obedience to Authority* (1974).

Individual responsibility

In many real-life situations authority figures relieve those who obey and carry out their orders of any personal responsibility for their actions. The Nuremberg defence of "I was only following orders" is offered by many engaging in destructive acts of obedience. This transfer of responsibility may be implicit or explicit. Subjects in Milgram's experiments were explicitly informed they would not be held responsible for the learner's well-being. However, when responsibility is shifted to the subject, obedience declines markedly and fewer people will deliver higher levels of shock (Mantell, 1971; Milgram, 1974). "A man feels responsible to the authority directing him but feels no responsibility for the content of the actions that the authority prescribes" (Milgram, 1974).

Symbols of authority, power and status

Many authority figures display outward signs of their authority—uniforms, badges and titles, play an important role in eliciting obedience to the police, military and the judiciary.

Gradation of commands

In many situations, initial orders may be relatively small and reasonable. Later, commands may escalate until they require individuals to engage in behaviour that is immoral, dangerous or unethical. This is akin to the foot-in-the-door technique mentioned previously. In the Milgram studies, subjects obeyed the experimenter's requests to administer low levels of shock and later proceeded to inflict more and more severe shocks.

While research evidence suggests that levels of obedience are a consistent and cross-cultural phenomenon, Milgram's paradigm has evoked much debate, praise and criticism. Some critics questioned the ethics of exposing individuals to such experimental procedures. Baumrind comments:

> Because of the anxiety and passivity generated by the setting, the subject is more prone to behave in an obedient, suggestible manner in the laboratory than elsewhere. Therefore the laboratory is not the place to study degrees of obedience or suggestibility as a function of a particular experiential condition, since the base line for those phenomena as found in the laboratory is probably much higher than in most settings. (Baumrind, 1964, p. 422)

Several critics argued there were conflicting cues in Milgram's experiential scenario. The meaning of the labels on the shock equipment was unambiguous—the labels clearly indicated serious outcomes (Danger; Severe shock; XXXX) and silence followed after 345 volts had been administered. However, the experimenter contradicts this interpretation, both non-verbally and verbally: "Although the shocks may be powerful there is no permanent tissue damage so please go on." Yet the experimenter's behaviour suggests the learner is not suffering harm and cannot suffer harm, in fact he is assuring the subject that these shocks are not dangerous.

> Their extreme emotional reactions were not due to the certain knowledge that they were inflicting serious harm but to the fact that they could not be certain. The evidence of their senses told them they were, but background expectations and the expert responsible told them they were not. (Mixon, 1979, p. 170)

Thus subjects found themselves in an ambiguous situation. Two options were available to them: continue to trust the experimenter and assume the learner is in no danger; or rely on the learner's behaviour and presume that he is suffering and in danger of being severely injured. In Meeus and Raaijmakers' (1986) view, the first reaction is the most plausible one. "Considering the ambiguity of the situation it is quite natural that subjects allowed themselves to be influenced by the experimenter. Ambiguous stimuli lead to greater conformity" (Meeus, Quinten & Raaijmakers, 1986). Mixon's comment is worth noting:

> From the range of work done in the social psychology of the psychological experiment we know that for many years now people have been making a number of (correct) assumptions about the experimental context—in particular that things are not always what they appear to be and that safety precautions protect participants from harm. Because of these assumptions about safety any conceivable experimental command will appear legitimate. (Mixon, 1979, p. 169)

Several critics have maintained that subjects derived no benefit from participating in such experiments. Milgram (1974) refutes this and comments:

> By their statements and actions, subjects indicated that they had learned a good deal. A year after his participation in the study one subject wrote "This experiment has strengthened my belief that man should avoid harm to his fellow man even at the risk of violating authority. (Milgram, 1974, p. 196)

Milgram's studies also attracted widespread support. Enham comments:

> That [Milgram's] pioneer work in this field is attacked as being unethical, unjustifiable, uninformative or any other derogative dismissal is to be expected simply because people like to shut their eyes to undesirable behavior, preferring to investigate memory and forgetting of nonsense syllables. (Enham, 1968, cited in Milgram, 1974, p. 201)

Perhaps Milgram's conclusion is worth some reflection. He comments that often it is not so much the kind of people we are as the kinds of situation in which we find ourselves, that determines how we will behave. Milgram in the epilogue of his book comments: "Every generation comes to learn about the problem of obedience through its own historical experience." The catalogue of crimes of obedience has been well documented throughout history and in more recent times, we have been confronted with many atrocities committed in the name of obedience. The Nazi Holocaust, the massacre at My Lai, the Argentinean Dirty War (1976-83), Pol Pot's atrocities in Cambodia, and the current internecine murder in Eastern Europe are just a few examples of this deadly game. Indeed as you read this page somewhere in the world people are being systematically tortured and killed by those who are "only following orders".

> To the psychologist these do not appear as impersonal historical events, but rather as actions carried out by men just like ourselves who have been transformed by authority and thus have relinquished all sense of individual responsibility for their actions. (Milgram, 1974, p. 180)

Moral reasoning and moral conduct

Lest you leave Milgram's studies feeling depressed about humanity, it is well to remember that many of his subjects refused point blank to comply and many dropped out as the study proceeded. The implied connection between an individual's behaviour and their inability to put themselves in the place of the victim, highlights the entire issue of morality and moral conduct. Remember that our decision to act in a certain way is determined not only by our moral reasoning but also by others' behaviour and by the standards and morality of our society. How these factors work themselves out for any given individual is probably developmental in origin, although early learning and moral training can only account for part of our decision in any given situation, situational pressures also play their part as we have seen. Inconsistencies in our moral behaviour suggest that the link between our moral reasoning and behaviour is a tenuous one. This is not surprising, given that moral choices involve resolving powerful and often conflicting pressures. Mischel (1986) suggests that knowing another's moral stance would only allow us to predict their behaviour in 10 per cent of situations. However, as we will see in Chapter Ten, early moral training does determine behaviour to a degree. For example, many of the people who hid Jews during the Nazi era risked their lives because of their strong moral convictions, even though pressured by family and friends not to become involved. So it is worth considering what role moral reasoning plays in our decision to resist immoral pressures.

Those of you who have already studied developmental psychology will be familiar with the work of Lawrence Kohlberg. Kohlberg (1963, 1969) extended Piaget's studies of moral reasoning by studying how adults and children resolve moral dilemmas. Like many theories in developmental psychology, Kohlberg's theory is one of stages. It suggests we gradually develop more abstract ways of reasoning and these are age related. Not everyone reaches the most abstract levels of moral reasoning, nor do we reason at this level most of the time. However, when faced with a dilemma that energises us we will then consider it at the level of our moral capabilities. How we resolve these issues depends on many factors other than reasoning alone. Table 6.3 sets out the basics of Kohlberg's theory.

You might like to consider how at each stage of Milgram's experiment a subject may have reacted to his requests to hurt another human being. According to Kohlberg it is *how* an individual thinks, rather than what they decide or whether they implement their decisions, that is important. People at the highest level of reasoning may have decided to comply with Milgram's request because they felt that doing so was in the best interests of humanity or some other **universal ethical absolute**. In later revisions of his work, Kohlberg (1976, 1978, 1981) proposed that two types of reasoning occur at each stage of moral development. Type A reasoning reflects literal interpretations of moral ethical issues. Type B reasoning stresses the intent of the norm, rule or standard used in reasoning. Kohlberg states that Type B reasoning is the more advanced form and he now considers stage six to be an extension of stage five reasoning rather than a stage in itself (Schell & Hall, 1983).

universal ethical absolute
Belief in moral principles which transcend culture, time and place (e.g. thou shalt not kill).

Crimes of obedience and denial of responsibility

The world is a sad place. As I give this chapter a final review before sending it to our publishers, TV news updates are full of images of Serbian death camps. These are not a new invention. The British invented "concentration" camps during the Boer War and "accidentally" killed thousands of innocent women and children in them. The Soviet gulags killed an estimated 4 000 000 people this century. Even more died in Nazi extermination camps during World War II and, as we saw at the head of the chapter, Pol Pot continued a longstanding custom in Cambodia. As sad as these camps are, the majority of the staff employed in them were not the deranged sadists portrayed by the media, but ordinary people obeying orders and drawing a pay cheque each week. The image of the torturer kissing his wife and kids goodbye and going off to work with his lunch in a brown

Table 6.3 *Kohlberg's stages of moral reasoning*

Level and stage	Content of answers		Basic philosophy
	What is right?	*Why do right?*	
Level 1: Stage 1: Heteronomous morality	Avoid breaking laws or rules. Obey laws blindly because they are there. Avoid being punished.	Authorities will get even with those who break their rules even if they do so unknowingly or for humanitarian reasons.	No coherent moral theory; can't relate multiple viewpoints; can't separate abstract questions of right and wrong from concrete displays of power or punishment.
Level 1: Stage 2: Instrumental hedonism	Follow rules if you stand to gain by doing so. Allow and expect others to do the same. Keep bargains with others so they will keep theirs with you.	To serve your own interests best, you have to recognise systems which help everyone gain the most.	Right and wrong are relative to one's own immediate gain. No abstract moral values transcend "enlightened" self-interest.
Level 2 Stage 3: Conformity (or: "good boy/good girl" focus)	"Being good" means having good motives and showing concern for others. Live up to other people's rules about how you should act, even if you don't gain materially by doing so.	The need to be liked and to be a good person in your own eyes means you have to behave according to everyone's stereotype of what "goodness" consists of.	Can consider the Golden Rule ("Do unto others . . .") at a concrete level. Is aware that feelings and expectations of others take primacy over self-interest. But has no ability to abstract beyond the values of other known people to consider an abstract or impersonal ethical code.
Level 2: Stage 4: Conformity to the social system (or: "law-and-order" focus)	The most important guide to how to act is the legal rule book. If in conflict, abide by the rule rather than own or others' individual need.	To keep the "system" (country, religion, etc.) going just as it is, you must obey all laws just as they are.	Is now able to distinguish the social system from individual personal relationships, but cannot go beyond existing sets of laws or rules to choose or formulate a more just and and encompassing set of moral values
Level 3: Stage 5: Principled morality	Follow universal rules like "life and liberty for all" regardless of majority opinion.	One's "social contract" as a human being is to make and abide by rules which serve the welfare of all people and promote the "greatest good for the greatest number".	Recognises conflicts between legal and humanistic or ethical viewpoints and strives to go beyond existing rules to integrate them. Will now view rule-abiding behaviour as immoral if it interferes with basic human needs.

Note: Kohlberg's (1969) original model included a sixth stage of 'universal ethical principles'. This was dropped from the new theory 'because none of the interviews in the longitudinal sample seemed intuitively to be Stage 6' using the new scoring scheme. (Colby, Kohlberg, Gibbs & Lieberman, 1983, p. 5)

Source: Adapted from Colby et al., 1983, Table 1, pp. 3–4.

The power of ethnic hatred evokes even distant echoes in peaceful communities on the other side of the world. (Photos: Gavin Price)

paper bag is much nearer the mark. Why do these ordinary people act so routinely in such extraordinarily inhumane ways?

After World War II, Nazi war criminals were prosecuted and executed on the grounds that individuals are personally responsible for the crimes they commit against humanity, even though they argued that they were ordered to do so by their superiors. While orders to kill people should be disobeyed on ethical grounds, in practice it is all too easy as Box 6.5 dramatically illustrates.

Box 6.5 *My Lai massacre, South Vietnam, 16 March 1968*

The nature of the war in Vietnam made it extremely difficult to identify who was the enemy. As well as young men, women, children and the elderly were engaged in the fighting. Villagers working in rice paddies during the day often became guerrilla fighters by night.

The men from Company C (Charlie Company), US Army, believed that the objectives of the operation at Sin My was to occupy an enemy village at My Lai. By the time the operation was over the men of C company had killed an estimated 450 to 500 non-combatants including infants, women and old people. "And by nightfall," as Hersch reported, "the Viet Cong were back in My Lai helping the survivors bury the dead. It took five days. Bat was not a communist at the time of the massacre, but the incident changed his mind. 'After the

shooting' he said 'all the villagers became communist' " (1970, p. 74).

Some atrocities that occurred towards the end of the operation were part of an almost casual "mopping up", for which it was impossible to attribute responsibility since by that time all US soldiers would look alike to the Vietnamese.

Nineteen-year-old Nguyen Thi Ngoc Tuyet watched a baby trying to open her slain mother's blouse to nurse. A soldier shot the infant while it was struggling with the blouse, and then slashed it with his bayonet. Tuyet also said she saw another baby hacked to death by GIs wielding their bayonets. "Le Tong, a twenty-eight-year-old rice farmer, reported seeing one woman raped after GIs killed her children. Nguyen Khoa, a thirty-seven-year-old peasant, told of a thirteen-year-old girl who was raped before being killed.

GIs then attacked Khoa's wife, tearing off her clothes. Before they could rape her, however, Khoa said, their six-year-old son, riddled with bullets, fell and saturated her with blood. The GIs left her alone" (Hersch, 1970, p.72). All of Company C were implicated in a pattern of death and destruction throughout the hamlet, much of which seemingly lacked rhyme or reason. (cited in Kelman & Hamilton, 1989, p. 5)

The following excerpt is from an interview a CBS News journalist had with a participant in the My Lai massacre and reproduced in the *New York Times,* 25 November 1968.

A: And Lieutenant Calley told me, he said, "Soldier, we got another job to do." And so he walked over to the people, and he started pushing them off and started shooting . . .

Q: Started pushing them off into the ravine?

A: Off into the ravine. It was a ditch. And so we started pushing them off, and we started shooting them, so all together we just pushed them all off, and just started using automatics on them. And then . . .

Q: Again—men, women, and children?

A: Men, women, and children.

Q: And babies?

A: And babies. And so we started shooting them and somebody told us to switch over to single shot so that we could save ammo. So we switched off to single shot, and shot a few more rounds . . .

Q: Why did you do it?

A: Why did I do it? Because I felt like I was ordered to do it, and it seemed like that, at the time I felt like I was doing the right thing, because, like I said, I lost buddies. I lost a damn good buddy, Bobby Wilson, and it was on my conscience. So, after I done it, I felt good, but later on that day, it was getting to me . . .

Q: But these civilians were lined up and shot? They weren't killed by cross fire?

A: They weren't lined up . . . They [were] just pushed in a ravine, or just sitting, squatting . . . and shot.

Q: What did these civilians—particularly the women and children, and old men—what did they do? What did they say to you?

A: They weren't saying much to them. They [were] just being pushed and they were doing what they was told to do.

Q: They weren't begging, or saying, "No . . . no", or . . .

A: Right. They were begging and saying, "No, no". And the mothers was hugging their children, and . . . but they kept right on firing. Well, we kept right on firing. They was waving their arms and begging, . . .

(cited in Milgram, 1974, pp. 185–86)

Lieutenant William Calley was tried and convicted for his actions at My Lai. He served three years of a life sentence and was then paroled. In his defence Calley claimed that he was simply following orders. While other soldiers, both higher ranking and subordinate to Calley, were prosecuted and brought to trial, he was the only one convicted for the crimes at My Lai.

Milgram's analysis of these and similar incidents reveal recurring themes:

- People carrying out their jobs are dominated by an administrative rather than moral outlook.

- Individuals distinguish between killing others as a matter of duty and the expression of personal feeling.

- The individual's sense of loyalty, duty and discipline derive from the organisational needs of the hierarchy.

- Euphemisms come to dominate language—as a means of guarding the person against the moral implications of his acts.

- In the mind of the subordinate responsibility shifts upwards. Often there are repeated requests for authorisation perhaps indicating at some level that moral transgression is involved.

- Actions are almost always justified in terms of a higher ideological goal, such as the final solution to the Jewish problem started as a hygienic process against supposed "Jewish vermin".

Milgram concludes:

> Obedience does not take the form of a dramatic confrontation of opposed wills or philosophies but is embedded in a larger atmosphere where social relationships, career aspirations, and technical routines set the dominant tone. Typically, we do not find a heroic figure struggling with conscience, nor a pathologically aggressive man ruthlessly exploiting a position of power, but a functionary who has been given a job to do and who strives to create an impression of competence in his work. (Milgram, 1974, p. 187)

It is interesting to note that during the operation at My Lai some soldiers avoided Calley's orders and more than one directly refused to obey them.

Resisting destructive obedience: The choice to disobey?

> No, I just stood there. Meadlo turned to me after a couple of minutes and said "Shoot! Why don't you shoot! Why don't you fire?" He was crying and yelling. I said "I can't, I can't". (Kelman and Hamilton, 1989, p. 7)

An interesting example of resistance to authority came from US Army helicopter pilot, Chief Warrant Officer Hugh Thompson, who witnessed the massacre from the air. While evacuating wounded, Thompson noticed some villagers hiding in a bush.

> Protecting the Vietnamese with his own body Thompson ordered his men to train their guns on the Americans and to open fire if the Americans fired on the Vietnamese. He then radioed for additional rescue helicopters and stood between the Vietnamese and the Americans under Calley's command until the Vietnamese could be evacuated. (Kelman & Hamilton, 1989, p. 8)

We have discussed some of the variables that influence our tendency to obey authority figures. However, a central question remains: How can we resist destructive forms of social influence? How can we promote and enhance independent judgment when faced with such influence?

Kelman and Hamilton (1989) in their book *Crimes of Obedience* discuss the role of **binding forces**, "those elements of the situation that psychologically tie the individual to the authority's definition of the situation" and create subservience and obedience. These forces are strengthened by situational factors such as surveillance; the consequences of disobeying (punishment, embarrassment); the power of hierarchical structures; the presence of symbols of authority; and observing the obedience of others. Also they suggest

binding forces
Those elements that psychologically tie an individual to the authority's definition of a situation and create subservience and obedience.

rule orientation
Conformity to the expectations of social norms which tend to bind individuals to an authority's definition of a situation.

that an individual's **rule,** or **role, orientation** tends to bind the individual to an authority's definition of a situation:

> Each orientation for its own reason leads to an impairment of critical judgement, a denial of personal responsibility and a tendency to act without question according to the authority's definition of the situation. (Kelman & Hamilton, 1989, p. 322)

Rule orientation

Rule orientation increases ties to the authority out of a sense of powerlessness. More rule-bound individuals are less able to challenge the authority figure's interpretation of the situation. According to Kelman and Hamilton, to counteract these effects it is necessary to bring the individual and their superior closer together. This will increase familiarity and they will see themselves as more capable of interpreting and analysing the authority's orders or commands. This would entail changes in social structures: dispersal of authority within society; better education; and group support which will promote a sense of individual power and foster a sense of personal efficacy.

Role orientation

Role orientation binds the individual out of a sense of obligation as they do not feel they have a right to question orders or challenge superiors. These individuals could challenge authority, but lack the will to do so. To counteract "entrapment in the authority's framework", it is necessary to *increase* the individual's distance from authority so they can gain an independent perspective on their orders. Again, to be effective, this strategy requires structural changes to expose individuals to perspectives external to, or independent of, hierarchical authority. This would allow a greater psychological distance from authority and allow us to evaluate demands or orders, with a greater sense of independence. Also, this may heighten an awareness of an obligation to disobey in some instances (Kelman & Hamilton, 1989).

Outlined below is a brief overview of several strategies which may help us resist the tendency to obey without questioning and foster independence of judgment and action when faced with unethical or immoral demands from authority figures.

- Take individual responsibility for our actions. If we are subject to commands from authority figures we can remind ourselves that it is not the authorities, but we who are personally responsible for the consequences of our actions. Several researchers (Hamilton, 1978; Kilham & Mann, 1974) have found that our tendency to obey is generally reduced under these circumstances.
- Remember that unquestioning submission is always inappropriate. We can reduce the tendency to obey by making it clear to individuals that blind obedience to commands, without questioning, is inappropriate. For example, exposing individuals to people who disobey the commands

While social morality usually means conformity, occasionally our conscience compels us to contest unjust laws.
(Photo: courtesy Macarthur Advertiser*)*

of an authority figure can lessen the degree of obedience (Milgram, 1965; Powers & Geen, 1972).

- Always question the expertise and motives of authority figures. By posing such questions as: Why are they issuing such commands? What are the underlying motives? Are they in a position to make such a demand?, we may find reasons to disobey the command. Findings from research studies indicate that the presence of social support can enable us to resist social pressure to conform or obey.

- Be aware of the power of authority figures to elicit obedience. When people become aware of social psychological research this may increase their awareness and influence them to modify their behaviour to incorporate this knowledge. Perhaps knowing about the nature of obedience can enhance our ability to resist. By being informed and constantly aware of the nature and power of social influence we can resist it when it is unethical and immoral.

Summary

This chapter has examined various aspects of social influence, broadly defined as attempts to change our attitudes, beliefs or behaviour.

Social power refers to our ability or potential to influence other people. There are six bases of social power: reward power, expert power, informative power, referent power, legitimate power and coercive power. These bases of social power are not mutually exclusive. Several may operate at the same time in some instances and an increase in the effectiveness of one form of power may decrease or even negate another.

Conformity refers to our tendency to "go along" with certain social norms or expectations acquired during our upbringing. Our tendency to conform is influenced by many factors including our personality; our attraction to a particular group; gender; the presence of an ally; and the size of the group attempting to influence us.

Compliance—in everyday life we comply with direct requests from many people. There are several strategies that may enhance our tendency to comply. These include ingratiation, foot-in-the-door and door-in-the-face techniques and low-balling.

An extreme form of compliance is obedience. The extent of an authority's power and influence is demonstrated by many obedience studies and a sorry history of torture and murder. Our willingness to obey authority figures usually occurs within a hierarchical setting, where we feel that the person in authority has a legitimate request to expect such behaviour.

Conformity and obedience both involve the transfer of initiative to another person but, as Milgram (1974) noted, they differ in terms of hierarchy, imitation and explicitness. Conformity regulates behaviour among equals, whereas obedience involves obeying orders from perceived superiors.

Unlike conformity, obedience does not involve imitation. Pressure to conform leads us to change our attitudes or behaviour to be more like others. When we obey we yield without imitating the influencing agent. With conformity, the pressure to conform may be explicit but often remains implicit. With obedience the prescription for action is always explicit.

Several strategies may help us to resist the tendency to obey without questioning when faced with unethical or immoral demands from authority figures. These include individual responsibility for our actions; questioning the expertise and motives of authority figures; exposure to people who disobey authority figures; the presence of social support; and awareness and vigilance regarding the power of authority figures to elicit obedience.

Recommended reading

Cialdini R.B. (1988) INFLUENCE, SCIENCE AND PRACTICE (2nd edn) Scott, Foresman, Little and Brown, Glenview, Illinois. A general review of social influence. Has a major section on resisting social influence.

Kelman H.C. and Hamilton V.L. (1989) CRIMES OF OBEDIENCE: TOWARD A SOCIAL PSYCHOLOGY OF AUTHORITY AND RESPONSIBILITY, Yale University Press, New Haven. A social psychological and sociological analysis of some of the major crimes of obedience to authority and the public's reaction to them. Fairly American in tone.

Milgram S. (1974) OBEDIENCE TO AUTHORITY, Harper and Row, NY. A classic work; contains most of Milgram's work and a rebuttal of some of the criticisms of his study.

Ng S.H. (1980) THE SOCIAL PSYCHOLOGY OF POWER, Academic Press, London. A scholarly read from a leading New Zealand social psychologist.

Staub E. (1989) ROOTS OF EVIL: THE PSYCHOLOGICAL AND CULTURAL SOURCES OF GENOCIDE, Cambridge University Press, New York. An insight into the mind of the torturer and how authority may corrupt innocent people to do its work. A disturbing book, powerfully written.

Turner J.C. (1991) SOCIAL INFLUENCE, Open University Press, Milton Keynes. A comprehensive overview of social influence and group processes by an Australian scholar who has an international reputation in this area.

AGGRESSION AND VIOLENCE

Maximum security gaols are quite violent places and tensions usually run fairly high. Because prisoners must live cheek by jowl and work out live-and-let-live compromises, they are also, paradoxically, very polite places. Gaols have their own cultures and, to the chagrin of the custodial staff, peace inside the walls is often more a matter of a "heavy" imposing his will on the institution than any efforts on their part. Often these heavies are the only ones to use violence, to enforce their authority. In a curious way such violence is tolerated by the rest of the inmates, who otherwise avoid giving offence. The combination of overcrowding and desperation makes for an explosive mix and few inmates would risk being violent, as the results are often unpredictable.

During my tenure as the resident psychologist of a maximum security gaol, an ageing heavy and his cohorts kept the peace by judicious use of violence. Occasionally when tensions rose or someone was stepping out of line, this heavy would administer a ritual beating as a salutary reminder of the perils of challenging his authority. Usually this was enough and only when there was a real sense of grievance throughout the gaol would wholesale violence erupt.

One day the Superintendent called me to his office and, when I arrived, I found that he was trying to convince a scared but highly truculent remand prisoner that he should accept an immediate transfer to a country gaol for his continued good health. The prisoner having been in gaol for one day, flatly refused and insisted on remaining close to his family. In disgust the Superintendent gave me the bare facts and turned him over to me.

It seemed that the young man had committed several heinous offences against gaol culture within a few hours of his imprisonment. Placed in a yard, he had sat on a chair while awaiting his turn with the welfare officer. He was politely asked to move by a middle-aged balding man, who explained it was his spot. The remand prisoner, not realising who this other prisoner was, refused. When told bluntly to push off, he replied colourfully. Several spectators immediately gathered to see how the reigning heavy would deal with this whippersnapper.

Unfortunately, the young man realised too late that he had committed a major faux pas and compounded his error by interpreting the gathering crowd as a lynch mob. Scared out of his wits, he launched a pre-emptive strike on the heavy and, before the crowd could intervene, a brawl erupted. Although he had never fought before, the young man was convinced he was going to die and in desperation decided to take a few with him. To the consternation of the onlookers he rapidly outclassed the heavy and inflicted telling injuries. Seeing an approaching guard he added insult to injury by racing up to him and dobbing the heavy in. No worse a crime could be committed within a gaol than to be a "dog", turning in another inmate. The crowd was ominously quiet.

I took him to my office and explained in words of one syllable where he stood and the enormity of his offence. However, despite my best efforts I could not get him to agree to a transfer. So we locked him in protective custody over the weekend and luckily the Court released him on a recognisance on the following Monday. The heavy never got over his humiliating defeat and by the time he was released from hospital, a series of bloody power struggles had thrown up a new cock of the walk. That this is not an extreme example of human behaviour is evident from the following quote:

In general, the orientation of a culture, or the shared beliefs within a subculture help define the limits of tolerable behaviour. To the extent that a society values violence, attaches prestige to violent conduct, or defines violence as normal or legitimate or functional behaviour, the values of individuals within that society will develop accordingly. (National Committee on Violence, Australia, 1990, p. 61)

Living in a violent world

We live in a violent world. War abroad and violence at home leave an uneasy undercurrent of anxiety in our national psyche. How are we to begin to comprehend these blatant acts of aggression and violence? Each day the media confront us with human tragedy and suffering resulting from various acts of human aggression.

- In August 1991, Wade Frankum, a 33-year-old taxi driver opened fire at Sydney's Strathfield Shopping Plaza, killing 7 people before turning his SKK semi-automatic rifle on himself.
- In October 1991, a man stopped to help a woman when her car broke down on an isolated road in suburban Sydney. He demanded payment after fixing her car and then raped her at knife point when she refused.
- In October 1992, a 40-year-old man shot and killed seven family members and their friends on the Central Coast of NSW.
- As we write, Sydney's Homicide Squad are piecing together several carefully dismembered human limbs that floated in on the tide in Botany Bay and wondering if they belong to a limbless torso discovered a few weeks previously on the South Coast.

These are fairly worrying incidents for those of us who live in Sydney but they are just a few of the awful acts that occur all too regularly in any part of our two nations. They lead us to ask a fundamental question: How is it that aggression and violence are so interwoven into the fabric of our social relations? Little wonder that many of us take a pessimistic view of human nature and are tempted by simplistic explanations of such behaviour. This is easily done given that violence has been well documented from our remotest antiquity. Often this is offered as causal evidence and how often have you heard people make comments like: "We are aggressive by nature; it's in our genes; it's universal and inevitable; that's just the way we are, it will never change."

Social psychologists, however, seriously question these views, believing that such behaviour is not inevitable and that our violent history may be more a description of the problem rather than an adequate explanation for it. So social psychologists ask themselves: Is aggression "naturally and inevitably human" or do we learn the "how and when" of such behaviour? What situations foster the development of aggression? What precipitating

We live in a violent world as depicted by this gangland slaying of a drug courier who tried to shortchange his syndicate. His body was found in Sydney's southwest with $50 000 stuffed in his underpants; obviously as a warning to others who might try to rip off organised crime. (Photo: Barry Price)

factors influence people to commit violent acts? How might we reduce and control aggression and violence? While we assume that most of us generally disapprove of such behaviour, violence continues unabated. Perhaps a more relevant question is: Do we only condemn certain types of aggression and sanction others?

In our society much violence is tacitly condoned. This acceptance is influenced by a number of factors both at the individual and group level. In our everyday language *aggression* is a commonplace word and is used in a variety of ways. Many in the corporate world praise sharp business practices, and aggression is widely accepted. In many instances aggression may be indirect: sarcasm, subtle putdowns of others and one-up-manship games. All of us have differing views on what is fair, and how we justify aggression is influenced by our cultural norms. Although these are often unwritten, they are acquired with little effort and are reinforced either directly or indirectly in our everyday interactions with others.

"All human social groups condemn violence and attempt to control it, but not all violence at all times" (Gergen & Gergen, 1981). Many authors note that we sanction aggression and violence in certain situations, ignoring the means to reach ends that are perceived to be important. For example, we expect military personnel in combat situations to act violently. We tolerate and legitimise levels of aggression from police and government officials. Atrocities committed during the Nazi Holocaust, at My Lai during the Vietnam war and in Cambodia under Pol Pot, were all politically sanctioned. While these acts of violence often occur during revolutions and wars, and may not be approved of by conventional values or institutions, they are sanctioned and justified at the time as "matters of necessity". Unfortunately, by this logic violence sometimes ends up on our doorstep. For example, some terrorist groups and indeed many governments believe they have a right to engage in systematic acts of brutality to achieve their goals.

USEF AND HIS BROTHERS COULD NOT LOAD THE STRANGE NEW WEAPON.

To what extent is violence between nations a consequence of how others are portrayed?
(Cartoonist: Steve Harris)

Box 7.1 *Justifying acts of aggression*

Our reaction when someone kills or seriously hurts another depends on how we perceive the aggressor. Clarence Darrow, the famous US defense lawyer, noted: "Juries seldom convict a person they like or acquit one they dislike. The main work of a defence lawyer is to make a jury like their client or at least feel sympathy towards them; facts regarding the case are relatively unimportant" (cited in Sutherland, 1966). Rule et al. (1975) and Shepherd and Bagley (1970), in mock jury studies, found that *unlikable* people convicted of aggressive acts receive longer sentences than those seen as *likable*. Also, the aggressor's apparent motives play an important part in influencing the decision. The extent of harm caused may be the same but whether their motive is perceived as acceptable or not will influence the outcome (Nesdale & Rule, 1974).

Much research suggests victim characteristics are influential in courtroom proceedings. "The best defence in a murder case is the fact that the deceased should have been killed regardless of how it happened" (Forman, cited in Smith, 1966). Similarly, in mock rape trials, offenders are more likely to receive longer sentences if the victim is seen as being "respectable" and shorter sentences if the woman is perceived as not "respectable" (Jones & Aronson, 1973; Gergen & Gergen, 1981). This has obvious parallels to **blaming the victim** and the **just world hypothesis** we discussed in Chapter Three.

We are often outraged by the many atrocities that others see as acceptable sanctioned violence, and often find it difficult to comprehend how such things are possible. Consider the Nazi Holocaust. It is estimated that six million Jews were murdered during World War II. Adding gypsies and "undesirables" raises this figure to 10–12 million (Gergen & Gergen, 1981). Reports from Amnesty International indicate that the use of systematic torture and execution of political prisoners is widespread and that hundreds of thousands of men, women and children are imprisoned throughout the world for their political beliefs. Rollo May comments:

> We have a tendency to label an act as aggressive and therefore to be condemned when performed by those out of power and to label the exact same act as good when performed by those in power or vice versa. (May, 1972, p. 149)

"The range of speculation about aggressive behaviour is unusually intense and diverse and this is probably an indication both of our ignorance and of our concern" (Johnson, 1972). In our society, aggression is usually referred to with negative connotations. Is there a positive side to aggression? and if so why have we tended to emphasise the negative side? For Rollo May:

> One obvious reason is that we have been terrified of aggression and we assume, delusion though it is, that we can better control it if we centre all our attention on its destructive aspects as though that's all there is. The truth is that practically everything we do is a mixture of positive and negative forms of aggression. (May, 1972, p. 151)

We tend to use the term *aggression* generically and it has taken on many different usages. Important contributions to our understanding of this topic have come from many disciplines such as biology, physiology, medicine, psychology, sociology, anthropology, criminology and political science. Aggression is not a simple phenomenon. To treat it thus, narrows and limits our understanding and our attempts to predict, control and reduce its destructive aspects. These limitations become apparent in the following section where we attempt to define aggression.

When is behaviour aggressive?

Defining aggression

The word aggression comes from the Latin root, *aggredi*, which means: "to go forward, to approach" in the sense of approaching someone for counsel or advice. Also it means to move against or to move with intent to hurt. May (1972) has described this as the Janus-faced nature of aggression, an allusion to the Roman god of human enterprise, whose two faces looked forward and backwards. In essence the origin of the word is a reaching out, or making contact, and in May's view the opposite of aggression is not "love, peace or friendship but isolation, the state of no contact at all". If we follow *aggredi's* original meaning when we define aggression, many things come to mind. Aggression may then be a personality attribute, a learned response, an emotion or feeling, and/or an underlying biological process.

Box 7.2 *How good are you at defining aggression?*

Most of us think we know aggression when we see it but a closer look suggests that our commonsense views are often ambiguous and misleading. We have given you some examples drawn from Kaufmann (1970) and Johnson (1972) who give more extensive lists. Before reading on, which of the following behaviours would you consider as examples of aggression?

- A cat stalks and eventually kills a mouse, then discards it.
- A politician evades legislation which would fix an environmental problem.
- A hunter kills an animal and mounts it as a trophy.
- A child fantasises about beating up the school bully.

- A gossip maliciously slanders someone.
- A tennis player smashes his racquet after missing an important shot.
- A bomb planted by a terrorist fails to explode.
- A boxer throws a punch and seriously injures his opponent.
- A women subjected to years of physical abuse by her husband dreams of killing him.
- A firing squad executes a prisoner.
- A woman commits suicide.
- Police trying to stop a riot injure someone.
- A bomber pilot presses a button and kills thousands below.

(Adapted from Johnson, 1972)

These examples appear to have little in common except that they all have to do with aggression.

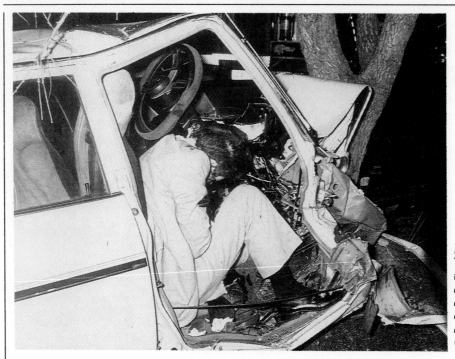

Is suicide aggressive? This man drove his car into a tree at considerable speed. The coroner returned an open verdict. Is suicide aggression?
(Photo: Barry Price)

Nevertheless, you will see elements of contradiction in this list and problems of how far we should extend our definition. As Kaufmann states:

> It would simply enlarge our category beyond all useful bounds if we were to consider the eating of a fly by a spider, or the killing of a mouse by a cat as aggressive behaviour. There is little purpose in considering as aggressive the enormous amount of interspecies mayhem that occurs in the animal world. (Kaufmann, 1970, p. 5)

Of course we may simply define aggression as any behaviour that causes harm to others. This definition is defective as it does not take *intent* into account. If we fail to include the intention of an act, some behaviour would not be defined as aggression because no harm occurred. Although the terrorist intended to inflict damage, the bomb failed to explode but surely this is aggression. Also, ignoring a person's intent may lead to inappropriate judgments, as, for example, it would be wrong to consider a doctor's injection as an aggressive act. Thus it is important when discussing definitions to distinguish behavioural intent from actual harm or injury. We also need to consider how such behaviour is perceived by others.

Thus we face an initial problem in studying "aggression"—how to define it? Whether an act is considered aggressive or not depends on our definition. If we include physical injury taking place then the police and the bomber pilot, among others, aggress. The daydreaming child and the gossip are excluded because they have not caused physical injury. The tennis player only causes damage to inanimate objects. If we widen the meaning to include psychological injury, we can include ridicule and belittling, bigotry and maybe suicide, which all hurt others in some way. Then what about acts of omission? Do we label the politician's behaviour aggressive, even though he insists he has not hurt anyone by his inaction? As you juggle these issues one against another you will come to appreciate that defining aggression is not a simple matter. So spare a thought for poor experimenters who have to try and operationalise it!

Perhaps a satisfactory "operational definition" is that proposed by Johnson (1972): "Aggression is behaviour directed against another living being that is intended to harm or injure." While this allows for the inclusion of psychological as well as physical injury, applying this definition can prove difficult. It does not primarily depend on observable behaviour and in many instances when we infer intent, our attributions are biased and inaccurate as aggression is not a unitary process. What about hostile feelings and anger? Many individuals experience anger yet refrain from hurting or injuring others. Likewise, some are capable of acts of extreme brutality without displaying any emotional involvement (Johnson, 1972).

Aggression and violence

Is it useful to distinguish between aggression and violence? By violence we usually mean overt physical aggression and we have traditionally defined it as an intentional use of force (though in our domestic violence section we broaden this to include psychological aspects). Social psychologists identify two main forms of human aggression; hostile and instrumental aggression (Sears, Maccoby & Levin, 1957; Buss, 1961, 1971; Feshbach, 1970; Baron, 1977; Zillmann, 1979). **Hostile aggression** is usually triggered by pain or distress, it is an emotional response and its primary aim is to inflict harm. Hostile aggression is usually considered a more "pure" form of aggression. **Instrumental aggression** is not necessarily triggered by anger or emotion, yet it involves intentional injury. The main aim is to achieve some non-aggressive goal, such as the hired assassin's financial reward. A child who hits another to obtain a toy, or a professional boxer, may be engaging in instrumental aggression. Of course an act may sometimes combine both hostile and instrumental aggression.

> **hostile aggression**
> An emotional response to pain or hurt; its primary aim is to retaliate, inflict harm.

> **instrumental aggression**
> Dispassionate aggression which is not triggered by anger or emotion, yet involves intentional injury.

Why make this distinction? First, the reasons and motivations for engaging in such behaviours vary enormously. Hostile aggression may be provoked by psychological stimuli that we find painful or offensive (being put down, insulted), or reinforced by physical stimuli that increase emotional arousal. Second, hostile feelings in the presence of environmental cues, such as a weapon, may lead to hostile behaviour. Hostile and instrumental aggression can also be controlled and reduced in different ways. For example, if we intervene, defuse or distract a person who is extremely angry or emotionally distressed, we may be able to avoid tragic consequences of hostile aggression. However, we are more likely to inhibit instrumental aggression by altering the environmental reinforcers that encourage it.

Researchers measure aggression in a number of different ways:

Measuring aggression

Verbal measures

Early studies attempted to use verbal measures as indicators of aggression (McClelland & Apicella, 1945; Davitz, 1952). In these studies, subjects were provoked or frustrated in some way and then asked to rate another individual on certain characteristics. Negative ratings were assumed to demonstrate aggressive behaviour. Unfortunately, one limitation with verbal ratings is they have no direct link to aggression. Experimenters attempting to overcome this problem often deceive subjects into believing their verbal rating would actually cause some harm to another individual. For example, in a study conducted by Worchel (1974) subjects became frustrated when the experimenters failed to honour a promise to give them some prizes. Subjects then rated the experimenters' competence, believing their ratings would be influential in the decision to rehire the researcher.

Behavioural measures

A common research tactic is measuring an individual's level of aggression before and after some activity to see whether this increases or decreases aggressive responses. For instance, this may involve watching a film depicting violent or non-violent incidents (Berkowitz, 1964; Parke et al., 1977; Donnerstein, 1980; Donnerstein & Berkowitz, 1981). A variant of this approach is to measure a person's aggression levels over time, to see what lasting effect such material has (Olweus, 1979).

The weapons effect

Several studies suggest that environmental cues are likely to increase the probability of aggression. Berkowitz and LePage (1967) provoked their subjects and compared their responses when either a racquet or gun was placed close by. They reported more aggressive responses from subjects who saw the gun and suggested that in certain instances the presence of cueing effects may be important in prompting later aggression. Although these findings have been replicated by several authors, other studies have failed to find a weapons effect (Page & Scheidt, 1971; Buss, Booker & Buss, 1972); so the presence of weapons does not always lead to heightened aggression. Whether or not we respond in an aggressive manner depends on how an event is interpreted, the meaning we give it and our state of arousal.

Social learning

Albert Bandura has spent a lifetime exploring the influence of social learning and modelling on aggression (Bandura, Ross & Ross, 1961; Bandura, 1965). In his classic Bobo doll experiment, children observed adult models who either played aggressively with or ignored a blow-up doll. Children who had watched aggressive models were more aggressive in their subsequent play, punching and kicking the dolls, than children exposed to non-aggressive adult models. In the laboratory setting, investigators researching aggression often make use of a Buss Aggression Machine (Buss, 1961) (see Figure 7.1).

To measure aggression in a quantifiable way, Buss developed an electronic device with an ominous array of switches. Subjects are informed they are participating in a learning experiment. They are then asked to administer an electric shock whenever a learner, in reality an accomplice of the experimenter, responds incorrectly. These shocks range in intensity from

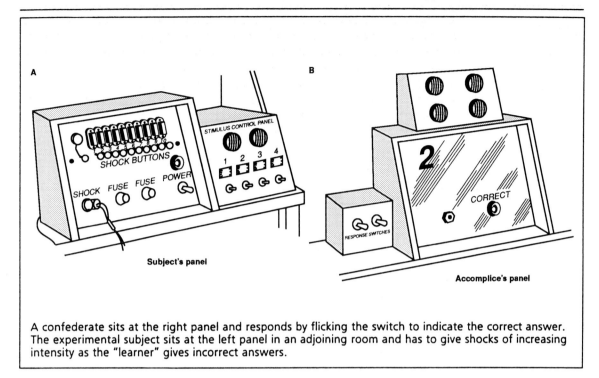

A confederate sits at the right panel and responds by flicking the switch to indicate the correct answer. The experimental subject sits at the left panel in an adjoining room and has to give shocks of increasing intensity as the "learner" gives incorrect answers.

Figure 7.1 *The Buss aggression machine*

Source: Buss, 1961.

mild to quite painful but deception is at work and no electric shocks are actually received by the learner. Figure 7.1(a) displays the subject's side and 7.1(b) the accomplice's side.

These experiments are usually portrayed as a study of effects of punishment on learning. In reality no shocks are delivered, rather the frequency, duration and intensity of shocks given by subjects are used as indicators of aggression. Because such responses are easily quantified, this is an attractive research method, yet these procedures have been criticised on a number of grounds. First, these measures may not be an expression of the subject's real aggressive tendencies but rather their compliance with the perceived characteristics of the experimental situation (demand characteristics). Also it appears that this technique is neither very reliable, nor a direct measure of aggression (Baron & Eggleston, 1972). Further, this approach raises ethical issues of inducing people to deliver electric shocks. These procedures have been seriously questioned, especially when modified versions of Buss' device are used to deliver real, though mild, shocks.

Several authors were critical of such experimental attempts to measure aggression and doubted that they reflect reality (Krebs & Miller, 1985). A review by Berkowitz and Donnerstein (1982) indicates there *is* a significant relationship between laboratory measures and real-life aggressive behaviour, despite difficulties in generalising from the experimental situation (Lippa, 1990). These considerations may make experimental measures slightly less credible but nevertheless, the high levels of aggression obtained are impressive (Berkowitz & Donnerstein, 1982).

Direct measures of aggression include simply observing and recording behaviour as in Bandura's experiments. Other observational studies include simulations of aggression such as shooting rubber bands at people (Diener, 1976), or playing war games (Zillmann, Johnson & Day, 1974).

Determinants of aggression

What causes aggression? In this section we will examine various theoretical approaches to the nature and origins of aggressive behaviour.

Theories of aggression

Instinct and biological theories

It is frequently suggested human beings behave in aggressive and violent ways because we are somehow biologically programmed for such behaviour; that we possess a natural and universal instinct for aggression. On the surface the concept of an innate tendency to violence is very appealing and it is the oldest and perhaps most publicised explanation of human aggression.

An early proponent of this approach was Sigmund Freud who believed that aggression stems from primitive biological impulses. In 1920, partly as an attempt to account for the vast cruelty and destructiveness of World War I, Freud proposed that a death instinct **thanatos**, common to all individuals, underlay aggression. Freud felt another instinct, **eros**, the life instinct, was concerned with pleasure and procreation, and was opposed to thanatos. Accordingly, human motivation is an admixture of these conflicting impulses. Several theorists have noted this concept's influence on contemporary research and the relationship between sex and aggression (Malamuth & Donnerstein, 1982; Scully, 1990).

A similar view was later presented by the ethologist Konrad Lorenz (1966, 1974). Lorenz suggested human beings, like animals, have an innate capacity for aggressive behaviour. These aggressive impulses have their origins in an inherited fighting instinct, common to all species. He proposed that this unlearned biological drive developed during the course of evolution and indeed was adaptive and necessary for survival. As Kaufmann (1970) notes:

> Survival and evolution could not occur if organisms had no provision for protecting their territory against intrusion, for defending their young, and for engaging in contests in order to select the strongest specimen for procreating. (Kaufmann, 1970, p. 15)

According to Lorenz, evolution led animals to develop ritualistic ways to limit aggression among their own species. Often the primary function of intra-species aggression is not to kill or injure but to reinforce dominance

thanatos
A Freudian term; the death instinct, held to underlie all aggression.

eros
A Freudian term; the love instinct, concerned with pleasure and procreation.

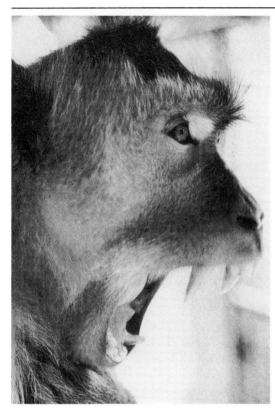

Ethologists argue that aggressive behaviour is innate and they use animal–human studies to reinforce their point.
(Photo: Chris Simkin)

hierarchies (Montague, 1976). As outlined in Table 7.1, animals have evolved elaborate ways of reducing conflict and aggression.

Lorenz further argued that human social evolution has weakened such inhibitory signals and cites as an example modern long-range warfare which makes it difficult for human beings to communicate submission signals.

Table 7.1 *Inhibition of aggression in animals*

1. Keeping one's distance from the antagonist.
2. Making a non-competitive response, such as a sexual display so the antagonist is distracted.
3. Avoiding others' provocation and not fighting back.
4. Producing rapid familiarity. This includes making one's own smell, taste, sight, and sound as familiar as possible to the other animals with whom one must remain in close contact. Animals are less likely to attack "friends" than "strangers". Animals sprayed with deodorants, for example, are attacked by normally friendly members of their group.
5. Diverting attack elsewhere. A victim might attack a third animal and have his own attacker then become an aggressive partner. Such coalitions are found among both human and non-human primates. Lorenz has repeatedly claimed that defeated wolves inhibit further aggression by baring their throats to their victors. However, other authors such as Scott (1958) strongly dispute this claim.

Source: Beck, 1978, p. 291.

Sociobiological approaches

The sociobiological approach (Wilson, 1975; Rushton, 1989) adopts a similar position. Sociobiologists suggest all social behaviour has evolutionary roots. Aggression, according to this viewpoint, is partly innate and may be explained in terms of its adaptive role in evolutionary development. Sociobiologists assert that much of our behaviour can be understood in terms of reproductive success. Genetically determined behaviour has evolved by the natural selection of particular sets of genes and, if a particular trait predisposes us to behave in a certain way, such as aggressively, and if this trait aids the survival of the species, this gene will be passed on to the next generation. According to sociobiologists, aggressive behaviour is valuable for human survival and over time has become part of our inherited biological nature.

The views proposed by Freud, Lorenz and the sociobiologists, while fostering much debate, helped to popularise the notion of aggressive and violent behaviour as an inherited universal characteristic common to both human and animal species. This is perhaps *the* most controversial question in social psychology and the debate has been vigorous. The sociobiological approach has been questioned by some social scientists who argue this perspective is scientifically unsatisfactory and based on faulty logic. To accept this idea *in toto* would assume that a biological mechanism determines aggressive and violent behaviour, and that such behaviour is inevitable. The explanation for such behaviour then becomes somewhat circular in their view: aggression and violence are universal and inevitable. Why are human beings aggressive and violent? Because they possess biologically inherited tendencies. How do we know individuals are biologically programmed? Because they engage in aggressive and violent behaviour.

However, others like Rushton (1988) and Crawford (1989) argue such criticisms show that critics do not understand sociobiology and instead are

Modern long-range warfare allows us to avoid the consequences of violence and makes it less likely that we will receive submission signals from our victims.
(Photo: Barry Price)

relying on a strict darwinism, which is at least 120 years out of date and ignores recent advances in genetics. They also rebut the criticism that sociobiological explanation limits scientific inquiry. While critics argue that labelling a behaviour as "instinctual" or "inherited" forecloses on a search for further explanations and ways of predicting and preventing such behaviour, sociobiologists do not claim that human aggression is inevitable and biologically determined, rather, that it has biological roots from which social learning builds.

Findings from several research studies have only increased the controversy. Cross-cultural data together with anthropological evidence suggest that human aggression is endemic, though levels vary considerably across societies and over time (Buss, 1988). That learning plays a strong role in shaping our responses is evident: "When aggressive behaviour is strongly discouraged as among the Hutterites and Amish, the Hopi and Zuni Indians, it is practically unknown" (Montague, 1976). Nevertheless, many societies are quite violent. For example, more murders are committed each year in some US cities than in European and Asian nations with 10 times greater populations.

Some writers quote **Lloyd Morgan's canon**—"Do not make animals men"—and question the usefulness and validity of generalising from animal studies to complex human behaviour:

> The critical issue is that human beings are different from animals. Man creates symbols and bases his cultures upon them; the flag and patriotism are examples as are states, religion and language. This capacity to create and deal with symbols actually is a superb achievement and also accounts for the fact that we are the cruelest species on the planet. We kill not out of necessity but out of allegiance to such symbols as the flag and the fatherland, we kill on principle. Thus our aggression occurs on a different level from that of animals and not much can be learned from animals about this distinctive human form of aggression. (May, 1972, p. 156)

Lloyd Morgan's canon
"Do not make animals men"; questioning the usefulness and validity of generalising from animal studies to more complex human behaviour.

Instinctual theories of aggression are still one of the most controversial topics in social psychology and, while most social psychologists favour learning approaches, many acknowledge that biology does influence social behaviour. It is possible to reject an instinctual viewpoint and still take a biological approach in studying aggression and violence. Many social scientists propose that the brain and endocrine systems have structures that significantly influence violent, aggressive behaviour. This interesting line of inquiry originated from research on brain stimulation in animals, and recent findings suggest that many violent outbursts are triggered by neurological disorders which may predispose certain individuals to behave aggressively (Mednick, Brennan & Kandel, 1988). Several studies (Denno, 1982; Baker & Mednick, 1984) suggest that individuals who commit violent crimes are likely to have sustained mild neurological damage during the prenatal period, or to suffer from tumours.

A dramatic example is the case of Charles Whitman. Whitman, aged 25 years, had spoken to psychiatrists about his periodic uncontrollable violent impulses and complained of severe headaches. After killing his mother and his wife, he barricaded himself on the observation tower of the University of Texas with a high powered hunting rifle. For 90 minutes he shot at anything moving. By the time he was killed he had shot 38 people, killing 14. A post-mortem examination of his brain revealed a highly malignant tumour in the area of the amygdaloid nucleus. This may have contributed to his violent behaviour (cited in Johnson, 1972).

Several studies suggest a relationship between hormones and violent behaviour, and it has been suggested that male androgens influence aggressiveness. The male sex hormone testosterone has been suggested as a factor in accounting for sex differences in aggression which are relatively stable across cultures (Maccoby & Jacklin, 1974, 1980; Olweus, 1986). Olweus (1988) reported a positive correlation between levels of testosterone and responses to threats and provocations. A smaller positive correlation was also found between testosterone levels and unprovoked physical and verbal aggression. However, a review by Denno (1988), while finding a relationship, gave inconclusive causal mechanisms for hormonal influences on aggressive behaviour. Although hormones play a role in sexual differentiation, by building up different patterns of energy usage, muscles and physique, the exact link with aggression is still unclear.

Certain chemical imbalances and brain sites have also been linked with aggression. Lidberg et al. (1985) reported low levels of inhibitory neurotransmitters such as serotonin and gamma-aminobutyric acid (GABA) and related substances in aggressive patients and violent offenders. Mednick et al. (1982) have observed that some individuals, described as aggressive when reacting to threatening situations, display different physiological reactions than normal subjects, with diminished pulse rates, arousal levels, blood pressure and galvanic skin responses. Brain electrical abnormality is also linked to aggression. Mednick et al. (1982) concluded in their review that various studies show abnormal electroencephalograph (EEG) patterns

---

Box 7.3 *Supermales and violence*

Females have two X chromosomes (XX) and males have a Y (XY). The Y chromosome carries male characteristics. It is estimated that one in 3000 males is born with an extra Y chromosome (XYY). A review by Jacobs, Brunton and Melville (1965) found the incidence of males with XYY chromosomes was higher in maximum security prisons and hospitals in Edinburgh, Scotland, than in the general population. Hook (1973) and Jarvik, Klodin and Matsuyama (1973) also reported high incidence of males with XYY chromosomes in a prison population.

However, later research findings propose another explanation for these figures. In a study of male prisoners in Denmark, Witkin et al. (1976) found that XYY prisoners had committed far less violent crimes than the general prison population. It was also found that XYY males tended to score lower on standardised intelligence tests. Perhaps we can conclude these males are not more violent as such, only less clever and therefore more likely to get caught? While heredity may influence human aggression, there does not appear to be a significant relationship between the presence of XYY chromosomes in men and subsequent aggressive behaviour (Raven & Rubin, 1983).

between 25 and 50 per cent of violent offenders. Again, we have difficulties in interpreting what these findings mean. While hormones and structural characteristics of the brain may predispose certain individuals to respond in aggressive ways, this does not infer that biology is destiny. We will consider the role cognition and social learning play later in this section.

Drive theories of aggression

Suppose you conducted a survey asking people what they thought was the most important cause of aggression. Would you be surprised if many of your respondents named frustration as a significant factor? Yet from your own experience you can possibly recall instances in your life where frustration did not lead to aggression, such as when you failed an assignment you thought you did quite well; or when you were running late for an appointment and your car wouldn't start. The view that aggression often results from frustration, or thwarted efforts to achieve some goal, still enjoys considerable support. Indeed many of my students favour this view when asked to evaluate theoretical approaches to aggression.

This view suggests that the blocking of our goals arouses a drive which precipitates an aggressive response towards the cause of our frustration. Alternatively, it results in some displaced activity if the cause of our frustration is unavailable, or if we fear to retaliate. We may then engage in some less direct action and displace our aggression to a substitute target. For instance, you experience frustration with a particular lecturer but feel it would be unwise to aggress against this person. Instead you go home and "get stroppy" with your family. The most influential of these drive theories is the frustration/aggression hypothesis.

Frustration/aggression hypothesis

This hypothesis was first proposed by Dollard, Doob, Miller, Mowrer and Sears in 1939 and since then has provoked much debate and attention by researchers:

Box 7.4 *Death from helplessness*

Bettleheim describes how some prisoners in Nazi concentration camps, soon after their captivity, "gave up", stopped eating, sat mute and motionless and finally died without an apparent physical cause.

Prisoners who came to believe the repeated statements of the guards—that there was no hope for them, that they would never leave the camps except as a corpse—who came to feel that their environment was one over which they could exercise no influence whatsoever, these prisoners were in a literal sense, walking corpses. In the camps they were called "muslems" (Muselmann) because of what was erroneously viewed as a fatalistic surrender to the environment . . . They were people who were deprived of affect, self-esteem and every form of stimulation, so totally exhausted, both physically and emotionally, that they had given the environment total power over them. (Bettleheim, cited in Seligman, 1975, p. 184)

Occurrences of aggressive behaviour always presupposes the existence of frustration and contrawise the existence of frustration always leads to some form of aggression. (Dollard et al., 1939, p. 1)

Such aggression includes physical, verbal, implied and fantasy forms. Frustration was defined as "a condition which exists when a goal response suffers interference" (Dollard et al., 1939). In many instances frustration may trigger some form of aggressive response. Nevertheless, frustration does not inevitably lead to aggression and many other factors precipitate aggression—consider military personnel responding to orders, or the sport of boxing. In these instances factors other than frustration may be responsible. There are numerous responses to frustration. For example, frustration can lead some to increase striving to overcome the frustration, while other individuals become resigned, depressed, withdrawn or inactive when frustrated and unable to act effectively (Seligman, 1975).

Many studies have demonstrated an important relationship between social attribution and the frustration/aggression effect. Worchel (1974), Baron (1977) and Kulik and Brown (1979) have argued that strong, arbitrary frustrations induce aggressive responses, whereas milder frustrations, or those that are perceived to be fair, are less likely to trigger aggression. Of course this implies that all aggression is negative and that if we could envisage a society with limited frustration then aggression would be at a minimal level. However, frustration is part of everyday life and unavoidable. Given these shortcomings, the authors recast their frustration/aggression hypothesis, arguing that frustration acts as "an instigation to aggression" and that aggression sometimes follows (Miller, 1941). This reformulation appears to be quite acceptable. Of course we are then left with the question: Under what conditions does frustration lead to aggression?

Cognitive neo-associationist approach

This approach examines the relationship between unpleasant feelings and overt aggression (Berkowitz, 1984, 1988). This theory suggests that when we experience aversive events negative feelings are aroused, which in turn activate aggression and/or flight responses and the physiological and mental reactions related to such experiences. Whether we express aggression overtly then depends on the significance of the event, our needs and mediating cognitive processes, to name just a few factors. There is considerable support for this view. Recall when you last responded aggressively. You probably first felt some kind of negative emotion: hurt, annoyance, rejection, betrayal or anger.

Evidence suggests that individuals who are exposed to a greater range of nasty experiences tend to act more aggressively than others (Berkowitz, 1989). Also negative emotions, variously triggered, encourage aggressive thoughts and memories (Rule, Taylor & Dobbs, 1987). While this view contributes to our understanding of what precipitates aggression, remember we are constantly faced with unpleasant events and their associated negative emotions in our everyday interactions yet do not always act aggressively (Baron & Byrne, 1991) (see Figure 7.2).

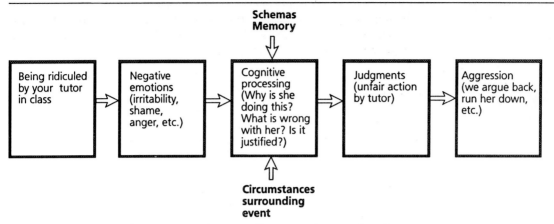

Figure 7.2 *How unpleasant experiences affect emotions and actions*

Learning theory has always been important to the study of human behaviour. Likewise in the search for the nature and origins of human aggression and violence, the learning approach provides a general framework in which to analyse the various forms of aggressive behaviour. It maintains that aggression and violence, like much social behaviour, is acquired or learned. Accordingly, we learn when, how, and against whom, it is appropriate to aggress. We are not born with a repertoire of aggressive responses but acquire these in the course of our social development, either through direct or vicarious experience. Bandura (1973) proposed that we learn to be aggressive or non-aggressive through either instrumental conditioning or observational learning.

Aggression as a learned behaviour

Instrumental conditioning

Learning theorists argue that social behaviour reflects the reinforcers we receive. Instrumental conditioning's basic tenet is that if aggressive behaviour is rewarded it is likely to be maintained or increase. If we respond aggressively and are rewarded for this behaviour, we will aggress again. Human beings are reinforced in many ways. Primary reinforcers (unlearned) such as food and drink may influence our behaviour as well as numerous secondary reinforcers (learned), such as money, possessions, status, success or approval. Many studies support this viewpoint (Bandura, Ross & Ross, 1963a,b; Bandura & Walters, 1963; Bandura, 1973). Research also suggests that when individuals are angry and inflict pain, this acts as a reinforcer (Baron, 1974; Feshbach, Stiles & Bitter, 1967).

Observational learning

Human beings do not just act in a willy-nilly fashion to achieve reinforcement, or rewards for their behaviour. Much of our learning takes place by observing others and imitating their behaviour. By observing others, we learn which particular behaviours are rewarded and reinforced and what behaviours are punished. By observing others acting in aggressive ways we overcome our inhibitions when we see that this behaviour is sanctioned and acceptable.

For example, in a series of experiments Bandura, Rossand Ross (1963a, b)

Box 7.5 *Profile: Ken Rigby and bullying*

Associate Professor Ken Rigby, PhD (Adelaide), is a social psychologist with an academic background in Economics, Education and Psychology. After teaching in secondary schools for ten years in England and Australia, he worked as Guidance Officer in South Australia and then as a Lecturer in Psychology and Research Methods at the University of South Australia where he is currently Director of the Institute of Social Research. He has conducted research and published papers primarily in the areas of attitude to authority, social aspects of AIDS, and bullying in schools. He is married with four children.
(Photo: courtesy Ken Rigby)

Over the last decade there has been increasing interest in the topic of bullying in our schools (Olweus, 1978, 1984; Perry, Kusel & Perry, 1988; Stephenson & Smith, 1989). Research from these studies has identified bullying as a significant problem for at least 10 per cent of children in primary schools, who are victims of other children's aggression. The figure is somewhat lower in secondary schools (Rigby & Slee, 1991). It has often been argued that the school environment itself may provide an ethos in which tough-minded, insensitive attitudes to others are shaped and fostered by processes of social learning. According to Askew (1989) the norms and rules to be emulated in this context are often stereotypical notions of *maleness*. Dominance, competitiveness, ambition, independence and aggression are viewed as admirable qualities, with expressions of emotion such as crying seen as weakness, or "being a wimp". "With children's increased exposure to such normative pressure, unsympathetic attitudes towards bullying would be expected to become increasingly common among children as they become older" (Rigby & Slee, 1991).

As a former teacher and guidance officer,

Ken Rigby has long been interested in the social aspects and consequences of bullying, a practice which makes so many children's lives a misery. As part of ongoing research in the area, Rigby and Philip Slee in 1991 reported the extent of bullying among Australian schoolchildren and attitudes towards victims in a survey of 685 schoolchildren aged 6 to 16 years, and of 32 of their teachers. Their results suggest that approximately 10 per cent of the children in the sample were commonly subjected to bullying by other children. Although teachers noted that bullying was a problem in their schools, their responses indicated lower estimates of its occurrence than was actually the case.

Boys in the sample reported being bullied more often than girls, who tended to be more supportive of victims. There was a slight decline in bullying as the children's age increased. However, this was offset by increasingly more insensitive and less supportive attitudes among older children. Factor analysis of children's responses to attitudes towards victims of bullying yielded three main attitudes: a tendency to despise the victims of bullies; general admiration for school bullies; and avowed support for intervention to assist the victim. Rigby and Slee conclude: "On the available evidence it appears that the incidence of bullying among Australian schoolchildren is similar to that reported in the more extensive Scandinavian studies by Olweus (1991)."

Even gentle people such as Private Edward Brophy 7RAR may learn to act aggressively when forced to by circumstances. Many like Ted paid the supreme sacrifice in Vietnam.

found that children learned to play aggressively by watching aggressive models. Some nursery school children watched an adult punch and kick a doll while making aggressive comments such as "sock him in the nose" and "hit him down". Other children watched the adult play peacefully. Subsequently all children were allowed to play freely with the toys. Children who were exposed to aggressive models significantly displayed more aggression, often imitating the adults. Also children imitated the aggressive models more when the adult model's aggression was rewarded and less when it was not reinforced (Bandura, 1965). According to social learning theory, whether we behave aggressively in any given situation is influenced by

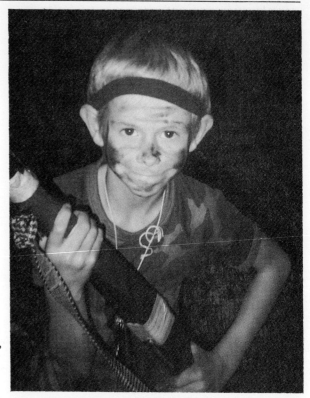

How do boys learn to be aggressive? One explanation, social learning, is that they model adults. Who do you think Jaan identifies with?

many factors, including our past experiences, the meaning and significance of the event, the possible rewards, and our assessment of the potential consequences of such behaviour.

Social learning theory has been very influential and has contributed much to our understanding of human aggression and violence. Most social psychologists accept this viewpoint as an important explanation of aggression. It is also appealing and more optimistic than theories based on innate tendencies. If human beings learn to act in aggressive and violent ways, then it should be possible to predict, modify or change such behaviour by applying principles of social learning.

In summary, aggression like many social behaviours is influenced by a complex web of factors: our biological processes, prior learning, physiological differences, our thoughts, environment and societal norms all decide when aggression occurs. Given the difficulty in specifying just what causes aggression, social psychologists with an applied bent usually focus on the triggers of aggressive behaviour. We turn now to a consideration of these factors.

Gender and aggressive behaviour

In our society men are ten times more likely to be charged with violent offences (National Committee on Violence, 1990). What does this differential mean? Does this reflect real sex-based differences? According to Maccoby and Jacklin (1974), information from virtually all societies shows men more aggressive than women. Their research indicates that gender differences

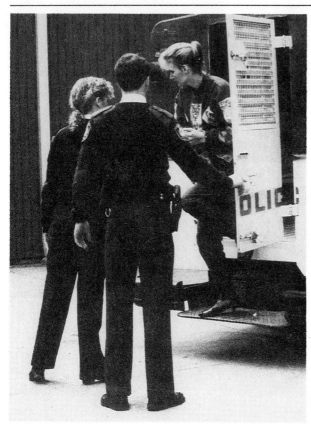

Men are more violent than women but even women may deliberately kill as did this woman who murdered the boy who delivered her pizza.
(Photo: Barry Price)

in temperament and aggression are present very early in human development and social learning accounts only give an incomplete explanation of such differences. Yet this does not mean that men are predestined or biologically programmed to be more aggressive than women. Research suggests that such sex differences are more evident in children than adults, leading Eagly and Steffen (1986) to comment that sociocultural factors may become paramount as children develop. Men and women respond differently to aggressive cues and provocation, and what may produce anxiety in women may be anger-inducing for men. Frodi, Macauley and Thome (1977) found that when women saw aggression as being justified, or prosocial, they behaved as aggressively as their male counterparts.

Eagly and Steffen (1986) reviewed 63 studies in a meta-analysis of sex differences and aggression (see Eagly's research in Box 11.4 in Chapter Eleven). While they report that men were more aggressive across the board than women, men were also more physically aggressive, causing pain and injury, rather than aggression causing psychological or social harm. Women, more than men, were aware of the consequences of their aggression and the harm it caused, and were more likely to suffer guilt and anxiety as a result. Eagly and Steffen conclude that sex differences in aggression may in part be a function of how we perceive its consequences. While the evidence suggests that men are more innately aggressive, it also

Box 7.6 *Profile: Sue Kippax "Emotion and Gender"—The experience of anger*

Susan Kippax is a social psychologist—of the sociological social psychologist variety. Her undergraduate and early post-graduate years were spent at the University of Sydney where she obtained a BA (Hons I) and PhD. Apart from two years at Oxford (1971–72) as the first woman to become a Rhodes Fellow, she has spent the rest of her career in the School of Behavioural Sciences at Macquarie University in Sydney. In the main, her research interests have been in areas of applied social research although she has a strong interest in the social production of practice and the social construction of emotions with special reference to the role of gender. She has worked and published in the following applied research areas: television and its impact on children and adults; the meanings of the arts to its audiences; and the social aspects of the prevention of HIV. She is currently Deputy Director of the National Centre for HIV Social Research.
(Photo: courtesy Susan Kippax)

Kippax and colleagues—Crawford, Onyx, Gault & Benton—have been involved in ongoing collective research on the social construction of emotions. These authors consider that emotions, while complex and difficult to separate from one another, are socially constructed. Theoretically, their approach suggests that significant events that are remembered and the way we subsequently construct them play a major role in the construction of the self (Kippax et. al, 1988).

The co-researchers employed a method of inquiry known as memory-work which uses written memories and collective theorising of them as source material. This method focuses on the construction or reconstruction of past experiences. Memories are collected and analysed according to certain rules. The aim is to reveal the source meaning in the written description of past events. In order to understand the processes involved in the construction of emotions, memories about particular events are analysed in a cross-sectional manner to identify common patterns and features (Kippax et. al, 1988).

Much research on emotion has focused on anger and its relationship to aggression/violence. Despite this, our understanding of the experience and expression of anger remains problematic. Anger and its expression have often been described as an emotion that presents difficulties for women. Kippax et. al, (1988, 1990, 1992) believe that women's experience of anger is likely to be different from that of men. Their analysis suggests that anger is construed as a negative emotion by women and that their experience of anger is different than that of men because it provokes different responses. These authors suggest that the social representation of anger differs between the sexes and that this difference possibly reflects differences in social power (1990). They identify at least two aspects of anger associated with sex differences: differences existing in the social representation of anger dependent on the sex of the angry person and a consideration of power in relation to anger. They suggest that power considerations may underlie differences in social representation if such exist and therefore these two aspects are related (1990, p. 346).

From their analysis, these authors suggest that the connection between anger and aggression, characteristic of much of men's anger, is more likely to be found in anger directed towards inferiors (social or physical), while women's anger is related to powerlessness and assumes an out-of-control ineffective character. This anger is more often directed against more powerful others or possibly peers and has a strong component of victimisation. The expression of this anger in many instances is viewed as a challenge to the other's power and is likely to provoke angry reactions. "This may well be why women are characterised as both more emotional and less violent" (1992, p. 183). Interestingly, analysis revealed few successful experiences of women's anger. The authors comment: "The memories are not dependent on our understanding of what anger is, but rather anger emerges from memories of diverse episodes" (1992, p. 184).

suggests that the way we express aggression is a matter of learning, and gender and social roles, rather than biological differences as such. We will return to this topic in Chapter Eleven where we consider the work of Eagly in some depth.

An interesting aspect related to this question is how our society's social construction of *maleness* and masculinity is synonymous with aggression. Morgan (1989) and Connell (1992) both argue *masculinity* itself is a multifaceted sex-role with quite diverse patterns of expression. Therefore, masculine aggression is not a unitary dimension and may express itself in many ways. Connell (1992) comments that unlike other categories of social analysis such as class or race, gender is designed to divide the sexes and perhaps aggressive sex differences are ultimately socially constructed.

Psychologists are interested in identifying factors that trigger or restrain individual acts of aggression, and a particular focus is the way in which characteristics of both the aggressor and the victim can modify our reaction to an aggressive act. Research has consistently demonstrated that human beings respond to aggression in kind (Dengerink & Myers, 1977; Ohbucki & Kambara, 1985). Many reasons explain this tendency and may include principles of equity and exchange—violence begets violence; as we do so shall we receive (see Chapter Eight). Also, when attacked, we become angry and aroused and this state tends to generate hostile responses. Why is this so?

Situational determinants of aggression

Temperature and aggression

Many authors have reported a tendency for people to react more aggressively as temperatures increase. Of course this relationship does not always hold, especially when heat becomes so oppressive that we lack energy to engage in such behaviour (Baron & Bell, 1975; Bell & Baron, 1977). Similarly, there seems to be a relationship between high rates of violent crime in cities experiencing higher temperature and humidity (Cotton, 1986; Anderson & Anderson, 1984; Anderson, 1987; Harries & Stadler, 1988). We will return to this in more detail in Chapter Thirteen.

Aggression and physical pain

While physical pain does not inevitably lead to aggression, several researchers have observed a relationship. Although the link between pain and aggression may be automatic and reflexive and not learned, pain-induced aggression can be reduced by reinforcement and the reverse—a decrease in pain due to expressed aggression. For example, individuals may become more hostile when exposed to unpleasant odours (Rotton, Barry, Frey & Soler, 1978) and cigarette smoke (Jones & Bogat, 1978).

Crowding and aggression

Several researchers have demonstrated that crowding may enhance aggressive behaviour (Freedman, 1975). The impetus for research on crowding and aggression has its origins in animal studies which suggest that crowding triggers physiological and behavioural effects in mice and other mammals (Calhoun, 1962; Davis, 1971). For example, rats in a crowded environment tend to fight and cannibalise each other and may eventually fail to procreate. Dubos (1965) also suggests that crowding makes many animals more susceptible to stress and disease (see Chapter Thirteen).

It is reasonable to assume that people become irritable, stressed and uncomfortable when crowded. Of course, individual reactions will differ under such conditions. Some may feel trapped and closed-in by crowds, or irritated and frustrated while waiting in a long queue, or during the mayhem of bargain sales. On the other hand, a crowded open-air concert can foster feelings of excitement, exhilaration and togetherness (Worchel & Teddlie, 1976). While not a direct cause of aggressive behaviour, it appears crowding sometimes enhances aggressive responses, especially when individuals are feeling angry and hostile (Freedman, 1975).

Media violence

The media's impact on aggressive and violent behaviour has long been the subject of controversy and debate.

> It is hard to believe that the constant vicarious relentless portrayal of violence at all levels at all times of the day in the most popular medium for young people does not in some way shape perceptions and reflect social and cultural values. What is any young person to make of an advertisement for a daytime TV series which has as its constant message "Here's a character you would love to hate. She's a bitch, a slut". There is no context, no justification, no framework under which these aberrations are displayed. (Peter Garrett, lead singer of the rock group Midnight Oil, 1990, cited in National Committee on Violence Report, 1990)

While the relationship between television violence and subsequent aggressive or violent behaviour has been intensively researched since the 1950s, a direct cause–effect relationship has yet to be established. Nevertheless, the National Committee on Violence publication, *Violence in Australia* (1990) noted: "Almost every household in Australia owns a TV. By 1986 almost half of all Australian households owned or rented a video recorder."

The National Health and Medical Research Council estimates that Australian children watch between 3 and 5 hours of television daily. In the United States, Gerbner and his colleagues analysed the amount of violent content programmed in prime time and weekend daytime television since the 1960s (Gerbner, Gross, Signorelli & Morgan, 1986; see Figure 7.3). Their findings suggest the level of violence portrayed has remained at a constantly high level since that time. The authors are particularly concerned at the level of violence in children's cartoons, observing that the average TV cartoon portrays an aggressive act once every three minutes.

A study conducted by McCann and Sheehan (1985) analysed 80 Australian TV programmes with a wide variety of content. Their study focused on the display of aggression or violence defined as "the overt expression of physical force (with or without a weapon, against the self or other)". Programmes were rated according to this definition. Table 7.2 indicates an overall rate of four violent episodes per programme and 5.4 violent episodes per broadcast hour. When popular fictional programmes are analysed this rate rises. These findings are comparable to those found in New Zealand, higher than Canada, but lower than the US (Haines, 1983). McCann and Sheehan comment that the frequency of violent episodes indicates the presence of substantial violence on Australian TV.

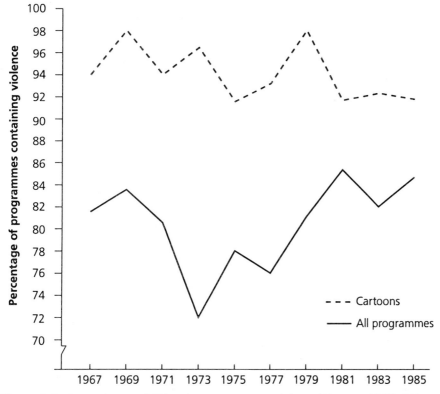

Figure 7.3 *Percentage of TV programmes containing violence, 1967–85*
Source: Gerbner, Gross, Signorelli & Morgan, 1986.

Table 7.2 *Indices of perceived violence for different programme categories*

Programme category	No. of programmes	No. of hours	% of programmes violent	% of hours of programmes containing violence	No. of violent episodes per programme	No. of violent episodes per hour
Cartoons	7	3.5	85.7	78.6	5.1	10.2
Fiction	51	38.5	66.7	72.6	5.4	7.2
Crime	15	14.0	96.7	96.4	8.5	9.2
Western	1	1.0	50.0	50.0	3.5	3.5
Action	19	14.5	73.7	75.9	6.4	8.4
Comedy	16	9.0	31.3	30.6	1.5	2.7
Non-fiction	22	17.0	4.6	4.4	0.3	0.4
Variety	13	9.0	3.9	2.3	0.2	0.3
Documentary	5	5.0	10.0	10.0	0.7	0.7
Educational	4	3.0	0.0	0.0	0.0	0.0
Total	80	59.0	51.3	53.0	4.0	5.4

Source: Sheehan, 1987.

TV violence and children's aggressive behaviour

Many studies suggest TV violence alters children's behaviour (Friedrich-Cofer & Huston, 1986; Hearold, 1986). Liebert, Sprafkin and Davidson (1989) comment that young children are particularly influenced by violence on TV. This would come as no surprise, considering children's social development and the powerful influence of role models such as sporting heroes, movie idols, rock stars and peers on their behaviour. Liebert and Baron (1972) found many children engage in more aggressive play immediately after watching violent programmes, and Liefer and Roberts (1972) found they are then more likely to opt for aggressive solutions when solving problems. Findings from a cross-cultural study of 1505 children conducted by Huesmann, Lagerspetz and Eron (1984) in the US, Finland, Poland and Australia, suggested a small but consistent relationship between TV viewing and aggressive behaviour in children.

Peter Ling and David Thomas (1986) from Waikato University studied the effects on play of viewing TV aggression among 52 Maori and Pakeha children aged 8. The children watched videotapes of boys' aggressive and non-aggressive play. The boys portrayed in the tape were similar in age, ethnicity and socioeconomic status, and Ling and Thomas were interested in how viewing either tape would affect the children's play during a 10 minute break after the videos. Watching a video increased overall levels of activity but only increased aggressive play in those children who had watched the aggressive video. Ling and Thomas found no race or sex differences.

Joy, Kimball and Zabrack (1986) conducted a study in three Canadian towns of television viewing and children's physical and verbally aggressive behaviour. One town had no television until 1974, a second town received broadcasts only from one network (CBC) and the third received both

CBC broadcasts and programmes from three commercial US channels. The results indicated that children with no TV reception until 1974 demonstrated larger increases in aggressiveness than did children from the other towns. The researchers attributed this increase primarily to the introduction of TV into their community. Incidentally, Murray and Kippax (1977) interviewed 282 families with children under 12 years in three Australian towns. They found marked differences in patterns of adult activity and perception depending on the availabilty or non-availability of television.

However, Huesmann et al. (1984) comment that a relationship between viewing violent material and aggressive behaviour in children depends on how much they see as well as the extent of the violence. They suggest a bi-directional relationship between TV violence and subsequent behaviour. Watching TV violence gives rise to aggression, while aggression fosters the viewing of TV violence.

Other factors may influence this relationship. A literature review by Waters (1989) suggests that other correlates, including parental preference for television violence, and the levels of expressed hostility and violence in families, significantly impact on children's aggressive behaviour. These findings receive considerable support from Australian research. Sheehan (1987) concludes that parents' viewing patterns are a more reliable predictor of children's aggressive behaviour than the habits of children themselves (National Committee on Violence, 1990).

Of vital concern is the possible long-term effect of exposure to constant TV violence and how this may impact on our values, attitudes and behaviour. Research evidence is inconclusive on this issue. Findings from a study conducted by Phillips (1978, 1982) suggest that there may be a tendency in the short term for some people to imitate violence (copycat crimes) but

Does watching violence on television inevitably lead to aggressive acts? (Photo: Chris Simkin)

Baron and Reiss (1985) criticise these findings on methodological grounds. Gerbner et al. (1986) and Huesmann and Eron (1986) suggest that exposure to frequent media violence may influence long-term attitudes, levels of aggression and violence in society. Compared to others who do not have this exposure, individuals overestimate the occurrence of violence in society, the number of law enforcement personnel employed and the possibility of becoming a victim of violence (Gerber, Gross, Signorelli & Morgan, 1986).

Several research studies suggest that exposure to violent television desensitises, or habituates individuals to violence in everyday life (Bandura, 1983). According to these findings such exposure lowers inhibitions towards behaving in aggressive ways and encourages apathy or indifference towards others' aggression and violence. The effects of TV violence and subsequent aggressive and violent behaviour remain a public concern:

> As a matter of personal observation the one subject more than any other that people volunteered to me in conversation as I travel around Australia in this job is their concern with TV violence. (Bill Hayden, Governor-General, National Committee on Violence, 1990)

If the majority of Australians generally regard television content as too violent, does this mean they wish to see a reduction in such content? Quinn believes this to be the case and asks: "Why is there no response to the preferences clearly indicated in surveys by the mainstream of the Australian viewing public that they want less violence?" (Quinn, 1990, cited in National Committee on Violence Report, 1990). Of course the relationship between TV violence and behaviour may be mediated by a number of factors. These may include whether the violence depicted appears to be realistic, whether it is perceived to be legitimate, and many other situational variables (National Committee on Violence, 1990).

> It seems unlikely that TV plays more than a minor role in producing violence and violent crime directly when compared to many other social forces. At the same time it is partly conceded that the viewing of TV violence may produce attitude change, provide justification for violence and suggest that problems can be solved through aggressive behaviour. (Huesmann et al., 1984, p. 82)

third-person effect
Our belief that the media or some other influence is more likely to affect others than it would us.

Innes and Zeitz (1988) examined the hypothesis that there is a pervasive **third-person effect** where people feel the media is more likely to affect others than themselves. They asked 171 Australian adults to rate the likely impact of a political campaign, the influence of media violence and a drink-driving advertising campaign. Their findings suggest that the issue was important as their subjects reported being less influenced by media violence and the political campaign than they were by the drink-driving advertising. However, Innes and Zeitz observed that in all cases their subjects felt they were less influenced by these media influences than other people would be! This has interesting parallels to the self-attributional biases we discussed in Chapter Three.

Media and sexual violence

An intense and controversial debate concerns the link between exposure to sexually explicit and violent material and subsequent aggressive and violent behaviour. Defining aggressive and violent pornographic material as distinct from erotica has proved difficult. The word *pornography* is derived from the ancient Greek word *porne*, the lowest class of prostitute, available to all male citizens, and *graphos* meaning writing, or describing something. For the purposes of our discussion, aggressive pornography refers to portrayals of sex that would be considered overtly coercive. Generally these are depictions in which force, both physical and psychological, is used or threatened, to coerce a person to engage in sexual acts (Malamuth & Donnerstein, 1982).

As an example of what we might be heading towards, the pornographic industry in the United States is estimated to be worth $4-6 billion, with child pornography estimated at 7 per cent of this market. According to one estimate, this industry is larger than the commercial movie and recording industries combined (Lederer, 1980). In the US 20 million pornographic magazines are sold each month and more than 75 million pornographic videos are rented each year. Well over half the videos rented in the US are pornographic (Malamuth & Donnerstein, 1982).

According to a study conducted by the US Attorney General in 1986 only a very small proportion of this pornographic material is non-degrading, or could be labelled as non-violent. According to their report, most material was either sexually violent, or non-violent but portraying humiliation, subordination, dominance or degradation, with abuse of women predominant.

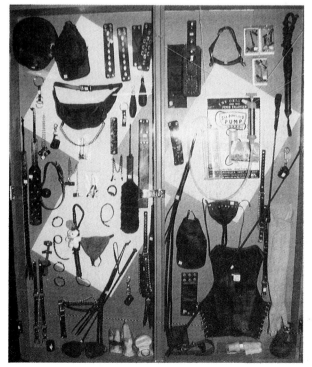

Why are sex and violence so often linked together? Is such a linkage valid? Are there gender differences in how we like our sex? (Photo: Gavin Price)

Several authors suggest that pornographic material has become both more violent and more accessible over the last 20 years (Linz, Donnerstein & Penrod, 1987). Several studies, including those conducted by the South Australian Council for Children's Films and Television, indicate that young people under 18 have increasing access to explicit and violent sexual material in the R and X rated videos (National Committee on Violence, 1990).

What does the psychological literature reveal about this relationship? Of particular concern is the reported increase and availability of child pornography. Defined as "any visual representations of the sexual abuse of children" (Schoettle, 1980), this is clearly on the increase. Lanning (1987) states: "The only way you can produce child pornography is to molest a child." Pornographic material involving children has never been sanctioned and legitimated as adult pornography has, and most countries prohibit the production and sale of such material. Child sexual abuse is not a new crime but what is disturbing is the realisation that there is such a large market for this material (Bennett, 1991).

Earlier studies conducted in Denmark appeared to suggest that liberalisation of laws regarding sexually explicit media had no antisocial consequences and may even be beneficial (Ben-Veniste, 1971). However, Court (1984) criticised these studies on a number of methodological grounds. He contends that measuring sexual offences is fraught with difficulties and conflicting interpretations. Inherent problems include the well-documented under-reporting of such offences and failure to distinguish between different categories of sexual offences (voyeurism, exhibitionism and crimes involving no violence, as opposed to those involving elements of violence like rape). Different categories of crime do not necessarily correlate well. For example, from a review of relevant research, Court (1984) concludes there has been a decline in the reporting of minor sexual offences over the previous 10 years, whereas reporting of more serious offences such as rape has increased. The increased reporting of violent sexual crimes such as rape is influenced by many factors, including an increasing community awareness, the breaking down of myths about rape and better policing methods, but seems to have come at the expense of a more tolerant attitude to the exploitation of women and children.

According to Court (1984) such social trends are exacerbated by easy access to sexual violence and pornography in the mass media. Malamuth and Check (1985) found that viewing sexually violent movies reinforced and increased false beliefs (myths) about rape, particularly in men who already have negative attitudes to women. Several studies demonstrate that stereotypical beliefs result in narrow and limited definitions of rape; denial of perceived injury and suffering of victims; not guilty verdicts in mock rape trials; blaming victims for the crime; and predicted self-reported probability of engaging in such behaviour (Jones & Aronson, 1973; Calhoun et al., 1976; Burt & Albin, 1981). (See also Chapters Three and Fourteen.)

Perhaps it is not sexual content as such but rather aggressive and violent media depictions (in pornography in particular) that contributes to aggressive behaviour towards women:

Of concern to many is not the sexual explicitness but rather the profusion of degrading images of women as well as the amount and degree of violence that has appeared in pornography since the 1970s. Not only is sex increasingly fused with violence but equally alarming contemporary depictions often suggest sexual violence has a positive outcome. (Scully, 1990, p. 55)

Scully cites a study by Smith (1976) where 428 adults-only paperback books were analysed. A major theme was the use of force and violence on women who initially resist. Finally, regardless of the amount of force inflicted, the victim becomes sexually aroused and responds physically. These pornographic images of women and rape seriously distort the crime and our views of male and female sexuality, reinforcing messages such as: women want to be raped and in fact enjoy it; the use of violence and force is acceptable; and rape is a minor crime—all of which trivialises sexual assault.

Linz, Donnerstein and Penrod (1984) found that prolonged exposure to media violence lowers our ability to empathise with victims of violence and decreases our sensitivity to violence in other contexts. They also suggest that violent portrayals in the media can produce attitude change that may indirectly affect subsequent aggressive behaviour. Similarly, Wilson and Nugent (1987) suggest there is a considerable amount of support (though inconclusive) that sexually violent media content and even popular songs may play an important role in the psychology of offenders who commit certain types of violent crime, such as serial killings of children.

The nature of this problem and the research methodologies available at the moment make this topic a difficult one to investigate, and we need to exercise caution in assuming a direct cause–effect relationship.

The link between pornography and sexual violence is a well-established, if controversial, one. (Photo: Gavin Price)

At the very least we can posit an indirect relationship, i.e. the more cultural support in forms like violent pornography that exist in a society for hostile and aggressive acts towards women, the more likely it is that such acts will occur and be sanctioned in that society. (Scully, 1990, p. 58)

The impact of alcohol and illicit drugs on violent behaviour

Alcohol

Numerous studies have suggested there is a strong link between alcohol consumption and violent behaviour. Although the exact nature of this relationship remains unclear, it is reasonable to assume that alcohol plays a significant role in violent behaviour in Australian society and police records bear this out (National Committee on Violence, 1990). In a study conducted by the NSW Bureau of Crime, Statistics and Research, Wallace (1986) reported that over one-third of suspected homicide offenders had consumed alcohol prior to the offence, in many instances to excess. A study of sexual assault conducted by Coid (1986) suggests that in many instances alcohol can influence an offender's attitude and subsequent behaviour towards the victim; enhancing the potential for increased violence and humiliation.

Alcohol is often cited as a predominant factor in domestic violence. While alcohol use may provide a "trigger" in many of these incidents, this does not suggest a direct cause–effect relationship, and many researchers deny that the issue of alcohol consumption has any valuable contribution

Often alcohol impairs our judgment and leads us to act impulsively as did these adolescents who drove a car through a shop window because they felt like some fruit!
(Photo: Barry Price)

to make to our explanation and understanding of this crime. Nonetheless, several studies suggest that alcohol can trigger and/or enhance aggressive behaviour, particularly when individuals under the influence of alcohol perceive a situation as provocative or threatening or are placed in such situations (Taylor et al., 1976; Straus, 1984).

A study conducted by Robyn Norton and Marsha Morgan (1989), from the University of Auckland School of Medicine, examined the role of alcohol in mortality and morbidity stemming from interpersonal violence. Findings from 29 descriptive studies indicated that persons who consume alcohol are at greater risk of perpetrating violence and victimisation than those who do not consume alcohol. However, this is not the full story, as the authors comment that the proportion of interpersonal violence caused by alcohol, and the levels of alcohol consumption that would be needed to significantly increase your risk of involvement in interpersonal violence, could not be predicted with any success from their study.

Research attempting to establish a causal link between alcohol and aggression has covered the whole gamut of research methods we discussed in Chapter One, including experiments in laboratory and field settings, naturalistic observation, analysis of police records, case histories and interviews with offenders. On the whole these studies have given inconsistent results. In part these equivocal results may be more the result of methodological difficulties in defining violence and aggression, variability in consumption and reactions to alcohol, and inherent difficulties in delineating the relative contribution of alcohol to violence from a whole host of other factors (National Committee on Violence, 1990).

While alcohol does lower our inhibitions, our reactions are influenced by sociocultural rules and expectations, and violence is only one reaction among many. It may be that in our culture we expect aggressive behaviour to be elicited from those under the influence of alcohol. Indeed Hull and Bond (1986) demonstrated that an individual's belief that they had consumed alcohol influenced their behaviour to the same extent as if they had in fact consumed alcohol. Our expectation that alcohol lowers inhibitions and leads to violence also provides us with a rationalisation or justification of aggressive behaviour and, in our legal systems, alcohol intoxication is accepted as a grounds for pleading diminished responsibility to violent acts.

While it is obvious that alcohol consumption is implicated in much aggressive and violent behaviour, the exact nature of this relationship remains unclear. The association of aggression and violence with alcohol is a result of highly variable interactions, and includes what expectations the person brings to the situation, their personality characteristics and the nature of the situation itself. As nice as it would be to conclude that alcohol causes violence, while they are linked, there are few direct connections.

Illicit drugs

Similar to alcohol consumption, the relationship between illicit drug use and violent behaviour is indirect. A review of aggressive and violent behaviour linked to drug abuse indicates that with the exception of PCP (Angel

Dust), amphetamines and the combination of certain tranquillisers with alcohol, little evidence exists to suggest that commonly abused illicit drugs lead to aggressive or violent behaviour (National Committee on Violence, 1990). Many drugs such as heroin produce an opposite effect as they relax the person. Yet there is an indirect link between drugs and violence. Aggression and violence play a large part in the drug culture, having to do with the economics of supply and demand of the illicit drugs. In Australia and New Zealand, competition between rivals in the drug trade has led to many instances of violence and homicide. Also, many drug users may resort to robbery with violence in order to obtain money and drugs to support their habit (National Committee on Violence, 1990).

Violence against the person

familial violence
Violence that occurs in the home, or between relatives or close associates.

Our chapter now changes gear as we consider the impact of violence in our society. We are conditioned to view violence in terms of crime statistics which feature murders, armed robberies and serious assaults. However, as you will see, as serious as these crimes of aggression are, they are perhaps only a reflection of a greater problem in our homes. While local psychologists, with the exception of Sheehan and Rigby, have made relatively few contributions to the fundamental theories of aggression, there is an enormous applied research base. For these reasons the second half of our chapter concentrates on **familial violence**, that which mainly occurs in the home or between close associates. We will examine the incidence and attitudes towards domestic violence, sexual assault and child abuse while featuring a very small part of the enormous local research base, before turning to our final topic, the reduction of violence.

Social psychology leaves the bounds of general psychology when it attempts to examine the causes of social behaviour with societal rather than individual origins. When we try to examine attitudes to violence against individuals we quickly find ourselves in the nether reaches of criminology, sociology and policing practice. Nevertheless, as a crossover discipline, social psychology has gained many insights from such studies. In this section we look at just a few of the many areas of violence against individuals in which social psychologists have made contributions. From the range of hidden abuse in our society we have chosen domestic violence, sexual assault and child abuse as vehicles to examine public attitudes to what are serious and prevalent crimes, but ones our community by-and-large is resistant to dealing with. Why is this so? What maintains these attitudes of public apathy and indifference? While our reading in preparing this section revealed that changes are occurring in community attitudes, it also showed we have a long way to go. We start our discussion of these areas by asking, just how violent a society are we?

> Australia is a less violent place today than it was during the period from its establishment as a penal colony until Federation. However it is more violent than it was before the Second World War. (National Committee on Violence, 1990, p. xxvii)

Any international comparison of violence usually compares rates of homicide and serious assault. By contemporary world standards the incidence of homicide in Australia is relatively low (Mukherjee, 1981; Grabosky, 1983) (see Table 7.3 and Figure 7.5). Australian studies indicate men are likely to be perpetrators, and women are more likely to be victims of homicide (Bonney, 1987). Most homicides are committed by family members (43%), or by friends and acquaintances of the victims (20%). A minority of homicides are committed by strangers (18%). Children under 10 years of age contribute to 10 per cent of the homicide victims, with infants between birth and 12 months exposed to the greatest risk (Wallace, 1986; Bonney, 1987). In New South Wales during the period 1968–86, 48 per cent of women killed (but only 9 per cent of men) were murdered by their spouse or de facto.

> The vast majority of homicides which take place within the framework of relationships which are of a sexually intimate character, appear to be the result of possessiveness on the part of males. Confrontational homicides are exclusively male and imply the existence of a set of norms regarding "honour" or "face" which are acted upon in such a way as to lead down an interactional path to homicide. (Polk & Ranson, 1989, p. 54)

Substantial increases in the rates of reported serious assault and sexual assault have occurred during the 1980s (see Figure 7.6(b)). So it is against this background that we examine two areas of serious assault.

Domestic violence

> The family situation holds the greatest potential for homicide and the greatest potential for prevention strategies. (Wallace, 1986, p. 83)

Traditionally there has been a conspiracy of silence about domestic violence. As late as 1975 there was no published research in Australia specifically devoted to this crime (O'Donnell & Saville, 1982). It is only recently that domestic violence has received significant attention from governments, researchers and practitioners. The social and individual costs of this violence have now become evident and currently are an issue of major concern. Sherman (1992) commented: "Domestic conflict is the largest single cause of violence in United States." Mugford (1989) adds: "The behaviour is widespread almost to the point of being a normal expected behaviour pattern in many homes." Domestic violence in its broadest sense includes violence between different types of family and household members, but research indicates the vast majority of victims/survivors are women abused by their partners (Smith, 1989). Indeed, Stubbs and Powell (1989) comment that some authors prefer such terms as *wife abuse* or *wife beating* because they feel that using a gender-neutral term like **domestic violence** masks this important point (Matka, 1991). However, in our discussion we will

domestic violence
The gender-neutral term which focuses on violence between males and females in domestic relationships.

Table 7.3 *Number of homicides in Australia per 100 000 of population, 1973–91*

State		1973 -74	1974 -75	1975 -76	1976 -77	1977 -78	1978 -79	1979 -80	1980 -81	1981 -82	1982 -83	1983 -84	1984 -85	1985 -86	1986 -87	1987 -88	1988 -89	1989 -90	1990 -91
New South Wales	N	116	79	104	103	108	115	109	110	122	124	122	112	112	110	117	120	99	127
	R	2.40	1.62	2.12	2.08	2.16	2.26	2.12	2.10	2.30	2.32	2.26	2.05	2.02	1.96	2.05	2.08	1.70	2.15
Victoria	N	62	67	49	54	68	51	90	56	68	71	68	79	71	77	109	79	80	81
	R	1.69	1.80	1.31	1.43	1.78	1.32	2.32	1.42	1.70	1.76	1.67	1.92	1.71	1.83	2.56	1.83	1.83	1.83
Queensland	N	49	42	53	61	43	42	40	40	42	46	53	44	76	63	75	68	71	60
	R	2.39	2.02	2.51	2.85	1.98	1.91	1.78	1.71	1.73	1.85	2.10	1.71	2.90	2.35	2.73	2.40	2.44	2.02
Western Australia	N	23	27	18	32	19	33	26	20	27	20	29	30	29	26	30	31	28	24
	R	2.06	2.35	1.54	2.67	1.55	2.66	2.06	1.54	2.02	1.46	2.08	2.11	1.99	1.74	1.94	1.95	1.71	1.44
South Australia	N	31	30	32	31	37	27	30	16	23	19	21	18	20	14	13	18	21	25
	R	2.51	2.40	2.54	2.43	2.86	2.09	2.31	1.21	1.73	1.41	1.54	1.31	1.45	1.00	0.92	1.26	1.46	1.72
Tasmania	N	2	6	7	9	8	6	9	7	5	9	6	5	16	6	6	1	7	5
	R	0.50	1.48	1.72	2.19	1.93	1.44	2.13	1.64	1.16	2.08	1.37	1.13	3.58	1.34	1.34	0.22	1.53	1.09
Northern Territory	N	11	14	22	24	20	9	19	16	16	27	24	18	18	25	25	28	23	31
	R	10.54	15.66	21.70	22.74	17.94	7.76	15.66	13.05	12.28	19.87	16.88	12.12	11.66	15.78	16.05	17.93	14.62	19.52
Australian Capital	N	—	—	1	3	3	2	—	n/a	2	2	9	2	2	3	4	5	0	3
	R	—	—	0.49	1.44	1.40	0.90	—	n/a	0.86	0.84	3.67	0.80	0.77	1.14	1.46	1.80	0.00	1.02
Australia	N	294	265	286	317	306	285	323	265	305	318	332	308	344	324	379	350	329	356
	R	2.16	1.92	2.06	2.25	2.15	1.98	2.21	1.78	2.01	2.07	2.13	1.95	2.15	1.99	2.29	2.08	1.93	2.05

Source: Mukherjee & Dagger, 1990.

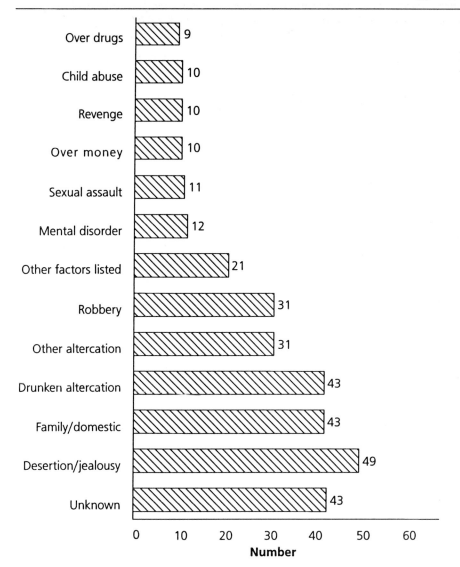

Figure 7.4 *Primary precipitating factors in homicide in Australia between 1990 and 1991*

Source: Strang, 1992.

adopt the gender-neutral term and focus on violence between males and females in domestic relationships.

Domestic violence is a crime in Australia but is seriously under-reported. Research indicates that up to a third of the population may be involved, yet the public perception is that it is an infrequent crime most often committed by the lower classes. The reality is otherwise. Although current statistics do not yet accurately reflect the distribution of domestic violence, it is widespread within society. To the extent that statistics show that many women do come from low-income families, this is more likely to

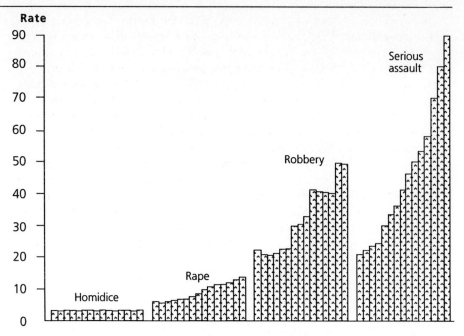

Figure 7.5 *Violent crime rate per 100 000 of population between 1973 and 1988 in Australia*

Source: Mukherjee & Dagger, 1990.

reflect that poorer women have less resources and come to the notice of various agencies by requiring financial assistance. Research evidence suggests that domestic violence occurs equally in all socioeconomic and ethnic groups.

Domestic violence defined

Domestic violence includes physical assault, emotional and psychological abuse, sexual assault, financial and economic abuse, and social abuse. It has always been extremely difficult to establish the extent of domestic violence in our society. Most authors agree that data from conventional sources is likely to underestimate the extent of the problem.

> There are no accurate figures on how widespread the problem may be in Australia. Overseas research has suggested that from 1 in 3 to 1 in 10 partnerships involve violence at some point. (Matka, 1991, p. 11)

Research by Wallace (1986) indicated that 42.5 per cent of all reported homicides in NSW between 1968 and 1981 occurred within the family. Spouse killings accounted for almost one in four of all killings in NSW, 73 per cent of these being committed by men on their wives. These findings also indicated that prior incidents of domestic violence had occurred in at least half of these homicide cases. An update by Bonney (1987) to 1986 gave virtually the same results.

Many people still regard violence that occurs within the home as somehow less serious than other forms of violence. The results of a recent Federal Government survey (Office of the Status of Women, 1988) into community attitudes on domestic violence indicate the extent to which this crime is apparently accepted by the community. Of the 1504 men and women surveyed, 17 per cent of women and 22 per cent of men believed that the use of physical force by a man against his wife is acceptable under some circumstances. One in three people surveyed believed domestic violence is a private matter, and nearly half the respondents knew either a victim or a perpetrator personally. While domestic violence is finally being recognised as a crime by our society, in many instances emotional violence still remains hidden. Whereas physical injuries are visible, the effects of emotional abuse are not clearly visible. "There are indeed many abused women whose partners never hit them. The majority of these women fail to recognise that they are the victims of domestic abuse" (Condonis, Paroissien & Aldrich, 1989).

The cycle of violence

In many violent relationships, a particular dynamic, termed the **cycle of violence**, appears to operate (Walker, 1979). This cycle is represented in Figure 7.6 and consists of a number of phases:

The *build-up phase* is characterised by an increase in tension within the relationship. For many reasons, in a violent relationship this tension is unable to be satisfactorily resolved. The tension may be intrapersonal and/or interpersonal and may be unrelated to relationship difficulties. In

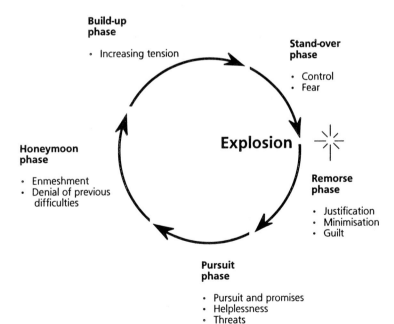

Figure 7.6 *The cycle of violence*
Source: Adapted from Walker, 1979.

response to the tension, the male moves into the *stand-over phase*. In this phase he may use threats of physical violence and verbal attacks in an effort to undermine the woman's self-esteem and autonomy. This behaviour increases the tension and continues until it results in an assault on the woman (explosion). Following the assault, which in many instances is rationalised in self-righteous terms, the perpetrator becomes *remorseful*. He may feel ashamed of his behaviour and fearful of its consequences (will she leave me?) and his response is usually verbal, accompanied by denial and minimisation of the attack, such as: "She knows I get angry when she behaves like that" or "I only pushed her". Often the woman will collude with these statements because the alternative, admitting the violent nature of the relationship, is too painful. In the *pursuit phase* (buy-back phase) the man attempts to avoid the consequences of his behaviour in order to maintain the relationship (flowers and promises). If these buy-back strategies fail, the man is likely to resort to threats and more violent attacks.

During the *honeymoon phase*, the relationship achieves a high degree of intimacy and mutual support. However, because the underlying difficulties have not been resolved, the cycle usually recommences as tension increases over time. It is important to note that not all violent domestic relationships conform to this pattern (Queensland Domestic Violence Task Force Report, 1988).

There are striking similarities in many of the behaviours displayed in domestic violence to tactics used to brainwash prisoners of war. While perhaps not as systematic, both are about gaining control and power, and both result in the victim experiencing feelings of fear, helplessness and hopelessness (Condonis, Paroissien & Aldrich, 1989).

Attitudes and attributions about domestic violence

Many people in our society adhere to stereotypic notions about domestic violence. These attitudes are not helpful, in many instances reinforcing notions of **blaming the victim** and shifting responsibility from the perpetrator, as we saw in Chapter Three. There is also a tendency for these attitudes to become taken for granted and stand as *truths* in the public mind. Even worse, they may become self-fulfilling prophecies, engendering the exact behaviour we wish to avoid. What is the reality of domestic violence? The following summary is drawn from Walker (1979) and the Domestic Violence Action Group (1989).

Causal attributions abound. Many see alcohol as the main cause of domestic violence, but while many incidents can be said to be alcohol-related, or that alcohol serves as a "trigger", there is no evidence that alcohol actually *causes* domestic violence. There is an abundance of research literature to indicate that violence occurs without alcohol being involved (Walker, 1979). Equally pernicious is the belief that women must have done something to deserve the violence and that a woman's nagging or other unreasonable behaviour provokes male violence. However, the decision to be violent has more to do with the man's than the woman's behaviour. Even if people act unreasonably there is no excuse or justification for the use of violence. Nevertheless, another causal attribution which ties in

blaming the victim
Believing that life is fair and that innocent victims are responsible for their fate.

with this belief is that violent men cannot control themselves. Male perpetrators often believe this. Unfortunately this self-serving attributional bias enables many violent men to continue to avoid accepting responsibility for their violent behaviour.

Nor are victims of domestic violence masochists who enjoy being abused. Many do not understand why victims do not leave the perpetrator and reason that they must enjoy the abuse. There are many reasons for remaining in a violent relationship but acceptance and enjoyment of violence are not among these. Many factors may influence a woman to stay: economic dependence; perceived needs of the children; self blame; perceptions of being a wife and mother; emotional attachment to the perpetrator; hopes he will change; fear of retaliation; and inadequate outside assistance. Many violent men are loving and sensitive partners much of the time and it is this fact that often makes it difficult for women to disclose the violence and induces them to remain in the relationship. Unfortunately, violent relationships are stubbornly resistant to change and this behaviour is unlikely to cease spontaneously. Even with specific intervention, change is usually a slow and difficult process (Domestic Violence Action Group, 1989).

Sexual assault is a violent crime, all too pervasive in our society: "Sexual assault is an attack on a person's body, senses, emotion and whole self. It is an attempt by one person or a group to humiliate, hurt and destroy another human being" (NSW Department of Health, 1988). Both males and females, from infants to the elderly, from all socioeconomic groups, rural and urban areas, are the victims and/or survivors of sexual assault. Notwithstanding, the majority of child and adult sexual assault victims are female and the vast majority of sexual offences are committed by males. Groth (1985) suggests there are multiple motivations for sexual assault:

Sexual assault

> Regardless of the pattern of the assault, rape is a complex act that serves a number of retaliatory and compensating aims in the psychological functioning of the offender. It is an effort to discharge his anger, contempt and hostility toward women—to hurt, degrade and humiliate. It is an effort to counteract feelings of vulnerability and inadequacy in himself and to assert his strength and power—to control and exploit sexuality is not the only, nor the primary, motive underlying rape. It is, however, the means through which conflicts surrounding issues of anger and power become discharged. (Groth, 1985, p. 13)

As one instance, Asha Yourell and Marita McCabe (1988), from Macquarie University, examined the motivations of rapists and related these to various forms of rape using Bandura's (1986) social learning theory. Their motivations for raping included: sexual gratification; aggression; and an enacting of an exaggerated view of the traditional male sex-role. Findings suggested that the use of force was the main factor in six different types of rape: random and specific blitz; pack or ceremonial rape; white collar rape; date rape; and sexual assault by a family member or relative. The researchers found their study supports a social learning approach to rape. That is, rape is a learned pseudosexual behaviour that is motivated primarily by aggression.

Estimates of prevalence vary greatly. They appear to reflect major differences in the criteria used to identify rape or sexual assault. As the degree of force and threat of injury increases, the perceived seriousness of an act increases and so too does its probability of being reported to police (Easteal, 1992). Because the majority of sexual assaults and attempts occur among persons who are acquainted, such rape has a low probability of being reported to police. Sexual assaults with the greatest probability of being reported to police are those which involve violent attacks by strangers. Sexual assaults by strangers are also more likely to be taken seriously by police, courts and juries than sexual assault by acquaintances (Russell, 1987).

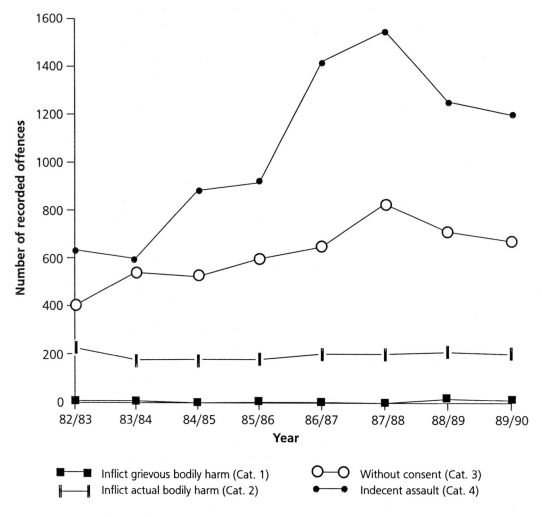

Figure 7.7 *Reported sexual assaults 1982–83 to 1989–90*
Source: NSW Bureau of Crime Statistics and Research.

Data from a study conducted by the NSW Bureau of Crime Statistics and Research (Bonney, 1985) indicated that sexual assault committed by a stranger accounted for only 25 per cent of reported incidents. In nearly half the cases the relationship between the victim and offender was classified as family, friend/acquaintance, or neighbour:

> Despite the seriousness of the offence, few systematic studies of Sexual Assault have been conducted in Australia. Because of the nature of the offence, the majority of victims are reluctant to disclose the fact that they have been assaulted. The dark figure of Sexual Assault is thus substantial and our knowledge of both its victims and its perpetrators is fragmentary. (National Committee on Violence, 1990, p. 29)

Nicola Gavey, from the University of Auckland, conducted a survey of the prevalence of sexual violence and victimisation experiences by 347 New Zealand undergraduates. Of the female students 51.6 per cent reported experiencing some form of sexual victimisation in their lives and 25.3 per cent had been a victim of either rape or an attempted rape. Gavey commented that her data was almost identical to that of a national sample of US university women undergraduates studied, using the same survey. However, the men in the New Zealand sample engaged in considerably less sexual aggression than their US counterparts. Virtually all of the sexual victimisation was within heterosexual relationships.

Societal reaction and attitudes

Society's perception of sexual assault or rape is strongly influenced by a mixture of emotions, prejudice, credence and voyeuristic curiosity (Burgess, 1988). No other crime attaches social stigma as much as rape or sexual assault. Several factors may account for this further victimisation of the victim. It may be a lack of knowledge and fear of sexuality within the society; or misinformation about factors that promote or contribute to violence. Wanting to deny the high incidence of violence against women and children may reflect community attitudes towards women and children which negate their right to control their own lives. Because of the above factors, victims often feel they are to blame for the violence and therefore will remain silent (NSW Department of Health, 1988).

People's reactions to the topic of sexual assault vary from an intuitive or gut response to the victim's trauma, to subjective reactions that are based on myths and stereotypes. Either type of reaction impacts on the victim/survivor of sexual assault. Not only does the victim suffer the incident itself, but is also subjected to various reactions from others, often negative reactions based on false beliefs and stereotypes that have been perpetrated about this serious crime. A national survey on beliefs about rape conducted by Easteal (1992) indicated that stereotypical attitudes and beliefs about sexual assault are still prevalent in our community. While the vast majority of men surveyed believe that rape was never justified by a women's behaviour, 24 per cent of men either disagreed or strongly disagreed with this. A further 15 per cent were undecided. Fifteen per cent of women sampled

Box 7.7 *The myths of rape*

The Myths of Rape were compiled by the Rape Crisis Centre, Sydney, and the statistics are taken from the NSW Bureau of Crime Statistics and Research studies into the *Crimes (Sexual Assault) Amendment Act,* 1981.

- *Women enjoy being raped.* Rape is a frightening and humiliating experience during which the woman has no control over what happens. No one enjoys an experience like this.
- *Nice girls don't get raped. Some women are safe.* All kinds of women are raped. Age and attractiveness are often unimportant. Being morally upright will not exempt a woman from an attack. The only requirement is that the victim is a female.
- *It is impossible for one man to rape a woman unless he has a gun or knife.* It is often quite easy for a rapist to terrify a victim into submission with threats and some force or roughness. A large amount of violence is often unnecessary, most victims are in fear of their lives, or of very serious physical injury. A majority of assaults (77.6%) do not involve the use of a weapon. Verbal threats are present in 70.5 per cent of sexual assaults.
- *A woman who did not scream or resist was not really raped.* Many women who have been raped did not scream or struggle. They have usually been threatened and become paralysed with fear. Most women have no idea how to resist an attack. They may be so frightened they are unable to scream, or afraid the attacker will use violence if they do scream; 57.5 per cent of women offer some form of physical resistance and 68.4 per cent some form of verbal resistance.
- *Men can't help themselves.* Rape occurs when a man is sexually frustrated and becomes so excited he can't control himself.

Studies have shown that a large proportion of rapes (about 70%) are premeditated and planned. Many rapists state that they could have had sex elsewhere but preferred to rape an unwilling woman. In many cases the rapists do not achieve orgasm. It seems that sex is used as the most effective way of degrading the victim but the motive has more to do with power than with sex.

- *Women provoke rape by the way they dress or act.* Almost anything a woman does can be construed as being an invitation to rape, or asking for rape. Women are supposed to be attractive but if they are raped they are told they provoked the attack by dressing attractively. Women are supposedly free and equal but if they act that way they are then told they are asking to be raped.
- *All rapists are strangers.* Approximately 72 per cent of rapists are known to the victim e.g. father, relative, husband, acquaintance, friend, boyfriend, neighbour or boss. Bureau of Crime Statistics indicates 28 per cent were total strangers.
- *All rapes occur at night on a dark street or in a park.* Many rapes occur during the day. Almost half the rapes reported take place either in the victim's home or the rapist's home, with less than 3 per cent occurring in well-lit streets.
- *Rapists are psychopaths (sick).* Nearly all rapists are "normal" men. Every rapist is someone's father, brother, son or husband.
- *Having sex with your wife or girlfriend when she doesn't want to is not rape.* Forcing a woman to have sex when she doesn't want to is rape. Coercion does not have to be physical. There are many ways men put pressure on women to have sex when they know the woman is unwilling. Forced sex is what rape is all about.

Source: Sydney Rape Crisis Centre, 1990.

also thought there were cases where a woman's behaviour could justify rape. One man in 20 believed that *nice* women did not get raped, and 16 per cent of the men sampled agreed or were undecided that a woman does not really mean it when she says "No!" Also some 28 per cent of men agree or are undecided that most charges of rape were unfounded. For women, this figure was 15 per cent. It is against this background that some false beliefs about rape are outlined in Box 7.7.

Violence against children: A vicious cycle

By now you are probably wondering why we live in such a violent society. Why are we so brutal to our near and dear? As we have seen in our sections on domestic violence and rape, familial assault is so prevalent in our society that it challenges the very nature of relationships between men and women. As we indicated in the introduction to this chapter most of the applied research we have looked at over the last two sections applies equally well to too many other areas in our society. Attitudes and aggression towards homosexuals (Box 5.1) and AIDS victims (Box 3.4) parallels research on aggression within families and our attitudes to victims of familial assault. So to return to our question, why are our homes as violent as they are?

Perhaps part of the answer lies in the early experiences of the perpetrators themselves. While it would be too simplistic to just argue that abusers were abused themselves, extensive research supports a view that early child abuse plays a part in perpetuating the cycle of abuse. Criminal statistics suggest, all too often, instances in which those victimised as children become criminals and/or abusers as adults. Such studies suggest that as many as 85 per cent of convicted criminals experienced abuse as children (Oates, 1990). Straus, Gelles and Steinmetz (1980) argue that early experience reflects later behaviour and report studies in which abused children, or even those who only view domestic violence, are more likely to abuse their own children, who in turn become abusers too. Straus and his colleagues called this "the self-perpetuating **cycle of family violence**". While early neglect does not excuse familial abuse, it may help explain it. We conclude our study of violence with a look at child abuse from the perspective of the victim and perpetrator.

cycle of family violence
The process whereby abused children become abusers themselves.

Child abuse, which includes physical abuse and neglect, sexual abuse and emotional maltreatment, is not a recent phenomenon. What is new is the professional and community recognition of this crime. Child abuse has a long history and occurs throughout the world and across all social classes. Violence against children is well documented throughout our history and authors who have examined the history of child abuse reveal incidences of violence and infanticide dating back to biblical times. Infanticide, mutilation and other forms of violence have persisted from ancient times, often with the legal mandate and consent of ruling religious and political forces in society.

Oates (1990) comments that sexual prohibitions were becoming stringent by the time the New World had been settled. He cites a case of incest recorded in Connecticut in 1772. In this instance the court ruled that the daughter be whipped and the father executed. While, in this case, the seriousness of the offence was recognised, the victim was also blamed—an attitude still prevalent today. All too often society refused to acknowledge the gravity of these offences, and nor were the early therapists immune from these pressures: "Even Sigmund Freud recognised the extent and significance of child sexual assault, particularly intra-familial abuse, before pressure from his colleagues made him review his theory" (Oates, 1990). There are many reasons why child abuse has only been recognised as a serious problem in recent times. Among these are:

- Historically, children have always been regarded as the property of their parents. So how children were treated was to a large degree the parents' prerogative.
- Religious and legal systems have supported seeing children as property with little concern and attention given to their rights.
- Historically, children were often viewed as an economic cost to their families, especially when birth control methods were inadequate and therefore the number of unwanted children might be high. In many instances exploitation of child labour or child prostitution were viewed as acceptable means of family survival.
- During periods when large families were exposed to disease, poverty or famine, bonds of affection and concern for children often diminished.

The incidence of child abuse

Attempting to assess the extent of child abuse in our society remains problematic. Definitional problems, different methods of gathering information and statistics, and differences in sample populations contribute to variations in reported incidence. During the last few years there has been a steady increase in the number of reported cases. It remains difficult to assess whether this tendency reflects an actual increase in the number of children being maltreated; an increase in community awareness; an increase in the number of people willing to report abuse; or some combination of these factors.

Table 7.4 *Total notifications confirmed by type of abuse 1987–91*

Date	Physical	Sexual	Emotional	Neglect	Unknown	Total
1987	3376	3606	2302	4335		13 619
1988	3065	3533	2023	3939		12 560
1989	2563	2503	2220	2674		9960
1990	2303	2383	2144	1721		8551
1991	2534	2843	3433	2505	(4)	11 315
1992	2702	3271	3473	2232	(7)	11 685

These figures are based on the number of children notified for the first time to the NSW Department of Community Services.

Source: NSW Department of Community Services.

Child physical abuse and neglect

A NSW study of reported cases of child maltreatment (Young & Brooks, 1988) estimated that one in 11 children born in a given year will be confirmed as abuse cases at some stage during childhood (under 16 years). Of course, actual incidence is likely to be higher, as Young and Brooks' research is based on reported cases only (NSW Child Protection Council, 1990). Children of all ages from birth to adolescence may be physically abused or neglected. Moreover, research indicates that infants and very young children are most vulnerable to physical abuse and neglect. Young and Brooks (1988) found that children of both sexes, under one year of age, show the highest incidence of reported physical abuse and neglect.

Child sexual assault

Female children are more likely than males to be sexually abused. A review by Finkelhor (1984) suggests that among all victims, 71 per cent are female and 29 per cent male. It is the view of many researchers and practitioners that abuse of boys is under-reported (Watkins & Bentovim, 1992). Male children may be reluctant to disclose due to expectations of masculinity and the homosexual nature of most abuse on male children (cultural denial). Also media and public stereotypes have tended to focus attention on the risk to female children. This may have resulted in parents and professionals being less able to identify abuse to males (NSW Child Protection Council, 1990). Such studies suggest children are more at risk in the pre-adolescent period between 8 and 12, with an increasing vulnerability at ages 6 and 7. Of course children are vulnerable to sexual assault from birth to 16 (as many reported cases indicate). However, lower reported rates for very young children may indicate that early memories of sexual assault are repressed or forgotten.

Characteristics of perpetrators

Most representative surveys of child sexual abuse have discounted any relationship between child sexual assault and socioeconomic status of the family in which victims grew up. Also the notion that child sexual assault is more common in rural areas is not substantiated by research evidence. For physical abuse and neglect, carers or parents who abuse their children are males and females who represent the broad spectrum of our society, coming from all socioeconomic levels, geographic areas, religious affiliations and all ethnic and cultural groups. Perpetrators include biological and foster parents, siblings, relatives and friends of the family and, sadly, many instances in which professional carers (childcare centres, institutions, hospitals, residential care and kindergartens) have allegedly abused their trust (see Box 2.2, Chapter Two). Unfortunately, all too often the perpetrators are well known to the child.

Are perpetrators mentally ill? Quite the contrary. Again from figures quoted by Oates (1990) and others, perpetrators reflect the wider community and only 5–10 per cent are psychologically disturbed, about the population average. Perhaps abusers are more the victims of their own abuse as children, as we noted above, and child abuse may be more developmental in origins than a matter of psychological disturbance. At present there are no convincing figures to demonstrate conclusively that this is the case.

As a final comment before we turn to consider how we might reduce aggression, you might like to reflect on the role of women as abusers. At present most studies suggest that child abuse is an almost exclusively male activity, with about 98 per cent of all reports of sexual abuse involving male perpetrators (Briggs, 1987). However, just as in the 1950s and 1960s society denied that child sexual assault existed, now perhaps we are starting to grapple with the disbelief that a mother may sexually abuse her child. Reports already suggest that women are as likely to physically abuse and neglect children as men (Straus, Gelles & Steinmetz, 1980), so perhaps reported instances of physical and emotional abuse by men only provides a partial picture. Banning (1988) suggested that the incidence of child sexual assault by female perpetrators may be considerably underestimated— "perhaps due to a culturally biased unwillingness to believe that women commit such acts"—and that social changes in the roles of men and women may lead to an increase in such assault.

Reducing aggression and violence

It is unrealistically cowardly and in all probability incorrect to assign our present desperate dilemmas to "human nature". We do not know what human nature is and therefore cannot plead this alibi for a failure to examine the problems with which we must in the course of our lives come to grips. (Kaufmann, 1970, p. 142)

It is apparent from our discussion that aggression and violence are not unitary phenomena. Their origin and nature are complex, with many factors contributing to such behaviour, and consequently we must not be seduced by simplistic solutions. It is doubtful that any one simple programme or policy will provide a panacea to reduce or eliminate aggressive behaviour in the short or long term. The many influences on such behaviour do not occur in a vacuum but interact with other factors in the wider social context. While it is acknowledged that not all forms of human aggression are maladaptive, it is vital that we find effective ways of reducing its destructive aspects within our interpersonal relationships, and within the broader social context. In this section we will briefly discuss some possible ways of reducing levels of aggression and violence in our society.

Catharsis

Sigmund Freud's notion of aggression was based on a kind of hydraulic model. He hypothesised that aggressive acts may help "drain the reservoir of aggressive energy". His catharsis hypothesis states that the experience of acting aggressively tends to reduce an individual's internal state, therefore lessening the likelihood of future aggression. This tension-reduction model suggests that if we are permitted to engage in aggressive actions like certain sports, or if we are exposed to media violence (vicarious experience), we will subsequently be less likely to act in aggressive ways. Over the years this view has enjoyed popularity and attracted much research attention. The catharsis notion appeals to our commonsense view: "getting it out of your system", "getting it off your chest", "letting off steam", are all familiar expressions. However, research suggests that catharsis may reduce aggression in some instances while in many other cases it may stimulate or enhance aggressive behaviour.

Engaging in physical activity as a means of "letting it out", via strenuous exercise and sport, has been shown to offer little support for the catharsis theory (Geen & Quanty, 1977). As we have seen already, research by Patterson (1974) found that high school football players displayed more aggressive behaviour after a session of football than before it. Similarly, findings from experimental studies suggest that verbal aggression does not consistently lower subsequent aggression. Under certain conditions it may actually encourage increased aggression (Wheeler & Caggiula, 1966).

As we have also noted, several researchers (Berkowitz & Geen, 1967; Ebbesen, Duncan & Konecni, 1975) found that when people are permitted to engage in direct aggression against a target who has angered them, they subsequently displayed more aggression and punishment towards the target. Many psychologists have been critical of catharsis as a model for reducing aggression. Generally, research evidence offers little support for the catharsis hypothesis as an effective method of reducing aggression. Instead, most studies suggest that catharsis is more likely to have a disinhibiting effect on aggression and is more likely to increase, rather than decrease, aggressive behaviour (Feshbach, 1986).

Social learning and the reduction of aggression

According to principles of social learning, early experience influences how and when we will express aggressive behaviour. The social learning framework provides us with a foundation for reducing aggression and violence. Because this viewpoint assumes that many forms of aggression are learned and influenced by positive and negative reinforcement, the principles of learning can be used to reduce such behaviour. We can also alter the social and economic rewards for aggressive and violent behaviours. We can reward prosocial values and behaviour incompatible with aggression, and withhold rewards when aggression occurs. Research studies have demonstrated how the power of modelling influences various forms of social behaviour. Socialisation begins early in childhood, and during our development society provides us with many negative models of social behaviour. Many authors have stated that we need to focus our attention on this early developmental process and use positive modelling strategies in order to offset these negative models, as well as encouraging behaviour incompatible with aggression.

It is important that we are able to express negative emotions, but we can be encouraged to express anger and hostility without acting aggressively. We can foster learning to express anger in a variety of ways more constructive and incompatible with aggression and violence.

Punishment

In our society, notions of punishment and punishing consequences have a long history; they are embedded in our value system and influence how we react to aggression and violence. In its extreme form punishment becomes retribution or "an eye for an eye". How effective is punishment in modifying or reducing aggressive behaviour?

It appears that punishment may temporarily suppress aggression. Nevertheless, punishment for such behaviour does not encourage or develop prosocial responses. It is important to note that punishment is itself a form of aggression and may provide another trigger to the arousal of aggression. Several research studies suggest that inflicting physical punishment on children can provide a modelling effect, which may encourage or increase the likelihood of subsequent aggressive behaviour (Rollins & Thomas, 1979; Olweus, 1980; Stevenson-Hinde, Hinde & Simpson, 1986). Baron (1983) has argued that the threat of punishment for instrumental aggression is more likely to be effective when: such threats are made when a person is not angry or hostile; the punishment administered is quite severe; it is applied quickly and consistently after the inappropriate behaviour; and the punishment outweighs any positive outcomes achieved by the aggressive behaviour.

The use of punishment to reduce aggressive behaviour involves certain limitations. Punishment may provide individuals with an aggressive model. In the long term they may learn when and how to act aggressively (Baron, 1977). Punishment may be appropriate, but the person may see this behaviour as an aggressive act and therefore punishment may arouse rather than inhibit aggressive responses (Zillmann, 1978). If punishment suppresses aggression but fails to address the source of the person's anger, it may lead to subsequent aggression. Long-term effects on aggressive behaviour will only be achieved when punishment is administered regularly and predictably (Fantino, 1973).

Developing responses incompatible with aggression

Responses that are incompatible with aggression may serve an important function in defusing and often reducing aggression. The use of humour, empathy, mild sexual arousal and distraction are some techniques that may discourage certain forms of aggression (Baron, 1983; Ramirez, Bryant & Zillmann, 1983). Of course in certain situations attempts to use these responses may enhance another individual's anger and lead to counter-aggression.

Cognitive strategies

Research studies suggest that in many instances aggression can be modified and reduced by altering the individual's perception of a frustrating, hostile or threatening incident (Feshbach, 1986). Effective cognitive strategies to reduce aggression can be learned. These include conflict resolution and negotiation strategies, effective interpersonal communication skills, and techniques to enable us to deal with frustration and stress (Baron, 1983).

Social sanctions

In Western society there appears to be a high level of acceptance of various forms of violence and many local sources have noted that gender inequalities are embedded in Australian society. Both domestic violence and sexual assault can be viewed as violent expressions of this cultural mode. We need to place more emphasis on fostering social attitudes and values that do not condone or idealise violence. Also we need to develop and encourage active participation, both at the individual and group level, in speaking out and condemning such behaviour.

> Experiences of childhood, infancy and of the family are paramount in determining whether or not an individual becomes violent in his or her behaviour. We acknowledge that biological and personality factors may predispose individuals to violence but evidence suggests that a loving and secure environment can overcome such predispositions. Likewise, although alcohol, media, peers and school may exert their influence, what children observe and learn in their home, what they come to recognise as norms of behaviour will largely determine their reactions to these influences. (National Committee on Violence, 1990, p. 103)

Now with agents of mass destruction, the consequences of sanctioned violence are too horrible to contemplate. We need to find a better way. If we need any reminder, the huge numbers of war cemeteries in every nation should act as a salutary reminder.
(Photo: Chris Simkin)

Summary

Aggression is defined as behaviour directed against another person that is intended to harm or hurt. Defining violence is difficult because any one definition by nature excludes other definitions. For example, is all aggression violence? Social psychologists measure aggression via verbal rating, behavioural measures and by physiological indicators.

Various biological perspectives attempt to account for the nature and origins of aggression and violence. Trait theorists argue we have a universal instinct for aggression. Sociobiologists would argue it has evolutionary roots. Physiological psychologists would argue it is a hormonal reaction, a brain mechanism, a genetic pattern; or some combination. However, innate influences are indirect and are overlaid by sociocultural factors.

Drive theories such as the frustration–aggression hypothesis suggest that aggression arises from arousal over some blocked goal, which is then reduced by direct aggression, or is displaced onto some other object. The cognitive neo-associationist approach examines the relationships between unpleasant feelings and overt aggression, and sees aggression as a reaction to aversive experiences, negative cognitions and the like. Social learning theorists argue that it is a learned social behaviour.

While the relationship between media violence and subsequent aggressive behaviour has been extensively researched, a direct cause and effect relationship has yet to be established. Some argue that frequent media violence may change attitudes, desensitise and habituate people to aggression in everyday life. Media violence also suggests that violence may be justified as a way of solving problems.

Considerable evidence suggests exposure to violent pornography may contribute to increased aggression against females. While this influence may be indirect, it is influential. Pornography gives a distorted view of sexuality, helps shape and reinforce negative attitudes to women, and legitimates sexual abuse of women and children.

Violence against women and children is a continuing concern for our society. Domestic violence, sexual assault and child abuse usually reflect the perpetrator's needs to exert power, to dominate, manipulate and control those in less powerful positions. Many individuals adhere to stereotypic attitudes about such abuse and these myths reinforce notions of blaming the victim and the just world hypothesis.

Numerous studies have suggested a strong association between alcohol and aggression. Although the exact nature of this relationship remains unclear, it is reasonable to assume that alcohol plays a significant role in aggressive and violent behaviour in our society and some illicit drugs play a similar role.

Aggression is not a unitary phenomenon so we must not be seduced by simplistic solutions. Catharsis may reduce aggression but is more likely to have a direct disinhibitory effect and foster aggression. Social learning theorists suggest we should learn less violent ways of coping with problems. Punishment (itself a form of aggression) may temporarily suppress aggression but provides those punished with aggressive models.

Learning responses that are incompatible with aggression may defuse and often reduce aggression by increasing empathy with the victim, and humour and distraction also play a role. In many instances aggression may be reduced or changed by cognitive strategies such as altering an individual's perception of a particular event. Other strategies include conflict resolution strategies and communication skills.

Disregarding social sanctions, we need to place more emphasis on fostering attitudes and values that do not condone or idealise violence, and to develop and encourage active participation in condemning such behaviour.

Recommended reading

Bandura A. (1973) AGGRESSION: A SOCIAL LEARNING ANALYSIS, Prentice Hall, NJ. A classic that gives a definitive account of how we acquire patterns of aggression through imitating others. Well worth a read if you can find it.

Baron R.A. and Richardson D.R. (1991) HUMAN AGGRESSION (2nd edn), Plenum Press, NY. A revision of a popular text first produced in 1977. Gives an overview of the biological, social, environmental and personal determinants of human aggression. A comprehensive and readable book. Start with this one.

Easteal, P. (1993) KILLING THE BELOVED: HOMICIDE BETWEEN ADULT SEXUAL INTIMATES, Australian Institute of Criminology, Canberra. A recent book which provides an in-depth analysis of domestic killings in Australia.

May R. (1972) POWER AND INNOCENCE: A SEARCH FOR THE SOURCES OF VIOLENCE, Norton, NY. A noted existentialist psychologist takes a look at the roots of aggression in Western society. A powerful and disturbing book but quite readable.

National Committee on Violence (1990) VIOLENCE: DIRECTIONS FOR AUSTRALIA, Australian Institute of Criminology, Canberra. A good source book for many of the local studies quoted in this chapter.

Oskamp S. (ed.) (1988) TELEVISION AS A SOCIAL ISSUE, Sage, Newbury Park, Ca. An edited collection of articles from both academics and media executives which looks at how television and films shape social learning. A very good insight into how we construe reality.

Zillmann D. and Bryant J. (eds) (1989) PORNOGRAPHY: RESEARCH ADVANCES AND POLICY CONSIDERATIONS, Erlbaum, Hillsdale, NJ. Although this book is a general review, it does address pornography's impact on violence. A review of recent research and applications by leading experts. A moderately hard read.

SOCIAL INTERDEPENDENCE

*I*n the 1960s I once worked with a tradesman Alex, who was one of the most miserable people I have known. He was physically repulsive. His grey skin, florid acne, dermatitis and decaying teeth spoke volumes about his lack of personal hygiene. He stank, lacked any social graces and hated everyone impartially. Dagos, boongs, bosses, poms, unionists, commos, Jehovah's Witnesses and lesser god-botherers, politicians, queers and women, all had a place in Alex's pantheon of hate and got the rough edge of his tongue. And he hated us passionately too. He delighted in setting pitfalls for his workmates and several suffered minor injuries at his hands. If all this wasn't enough he was fixated on his war experiences and every day we had reruns of the Malayan campaign. Nasty and brutal, Addled Alex was an object of derision.

You would expect Alex to be a pariah and to be excluded from the give-and-take of the workroom but, perversely, no one really minded him; he was too pathetic to take seriously and had become the factory pet. Despite his shortcomings Alex was a magnificent toolmaker and this redeeming feature kept him employed. The relationship this least gregarious man had with his fellows illustrates the basics of social exchange and our interdependency. Although no one liked him, he belonged and was a fixture in the foundry. He was tolerated for his skills and on that basis accepted as part of the workaday tribe. In a curious way Alex only took as much as he gave.

On the nature of human social interdependency

Humans are social animals but since we came down from the trees, self-interested individualism has been at the cutting edge of human evolution. In our heart of hearts, we all want to get on. Yet in the long run, this urge to get ahead and stand out from the pack benefits us all. That we have prospered from the cultural and scientific advances of exceptional men and women is self-evident. Yet our evolution owes as much to the cooperative effort that built the pyramids, as it does to individual achievement. So at the heart of society lies a tension between our competitive and cooperative natures and perhaps the most fundamental question for social psychology is: just what are the ties that bind?

If the last few chapters have placed a rather gloomy emphasis on the human condition, the next three sound a lighter note as we consider topics like affiliation, social exchange, cooperation, friendship, attraction, love, altruism and prosocial behaviour. Underlying these topics is the assumption that our species has grown through mutual interdependence: that in some ways we have evolved from a stock that has painfully learned the benefits of cooperation and selected for prosocial behaviour. This assumption rests on the uneasy balance between our cultural evolution and those more primitive aspects of our nature which continually drag us backward: hostility, aggression, discrimination, prejudice and envy. While we have yet to decide our species' future, we stand to gain an enormous amount from knowing as much as we can about human interdependence.

We start with the question: "Why is our species gregarious?" At the outset, we predict that two separate yet intertwined needs underlie our gregariousness: the need to belong and the need to be liked. Our next two chapters cover the positive aspects of relationships but, as we can see from Alex's story, to belong does not mean we are necessarily liked and this chapter explores our interdependency at its most basic level. To highlight the importance of these two needs, we look at what it is like to be lonely, before considering our gregariousness. The chapter ends with a detailed look at affiliation, the first step towards that most profound of all human emotions, love. Chapter Nine is an extended coverage of research into close relationships, the underlying factors and consequences—attraction, friendship, love and marriage. Chapter Ten concludes this section with a look at the social lubricant of relationships—helping or prosocial behaviour.

Loneliness and social deprivation

Dear Jim

I'm sorry I missed the tut but I've dropped social psych. I enjoyed your class but I've deferred because I'm really lonely. I'm going home. I wanted to make new friends when I came here . . . but in the first weeks everybody paired up and I was left on my own. I haven't been able to make friends and I've been really depressed and even my flat-mate is sick of me. I've really enjoyed uni. but can't stand the misery anymore. I always thought I could make friends easily but not here. I'll come back when I'm a little more together.

Sorry
K . . . . . .

This note from a student, shoved into my assignment box to explain a missed tutorial presentation, is a sad reminder of the value of friends. Without a doubt the strongest social need we have is to belong to someone special. In all its many forms this need recurs throughout the lifespan. Children want to be loved by their parents, adolescents need their peers, adults seek intimacy with a spouse and the elderly the comfort of children and grandchildren, and we all value close friends. There is no more powerful confirmation of this essential human need than the research on the consequences of social deprivation and loneliness.

We have all been lonely, yet for some it may well mean a lifetime of intense misery (Peplau & Perlman, 1982) and causes many suicides. Often

*We've all experienced feelings of loneliness.
However, sometimes they are all-pervasive
and lead us to feel we are no longer part of the
herd.
(Photo: Rob Pozo/Macarthur Advertiser)*

misunderstood, loneliness is a subjective state, which reflects how we see
our lives unfolding. Lonely people describing their condition report they
are depressed; feel trapped and suffocated by the boring pointlessness of it
all; live lives of quiet desperation; and self-deprecatingly blame themselves
for their state (Rubenstein & Shaver, 1982). These interrelated emotions
are all indicative of having missed out in some way. If loneliness is such a
debilitating state, what are the lonely missing?

Robert Weiss (1974) saw six basic needs being met by close relationships.
As you read through these needs, consider how the lonely are marginalised
by their condition:

- *Attachment:* We all need to feel we belong to someone and, in bonding,
  experience intimacy and security.
- *Social integration:* Like attachment, we need to share attitudes and interests
  and take our place in society. Friendships in social groups, sport, work
  and church help us bond to the wider community.
- *Reassurance of worth:* Friendships reinforce our sense of being a useful
  member of society.
- *A sense of reliable alliance:* Close friends care. In times of crisis we are
  secure knowing there is someone who will come to our aid.
- *Guidance:* Friends provide us with resources to enrich our lives. Our
  contacts provide us with a rich source of advice, information, guidance
  and support.

- *Nurturance:* As we receive the nurturance and support of others, so in turn we have the opportunity to nurture. This provides us with a sense of personal satisfaction and reinforces the above needs.

How do we become lonely? From Weiss' list it is evident we are dealing with basic developmental issues here and research has suggested loneliness is learned from childhood. At the outset it is important to distinguish between *state* and *trait loneliness*. We all experience state loneliness when we leave home, change jobs, lose friends or loved ones; such loneliness is usually temporary. Yet some are lonely by nature and report loneliness throughout their lives, despite many friendships. So trait loneliness seems to be a stable enduring personality characteristic marked by low self-esteem, self-deprecation, depression, inappropriate levels of self-disclosure and poor social skills (Jones, Freeman & Goswick, 1981; Peplau, Miceli & Morasch, 1982; Solano, Batten & Parish, 1982; Hill 1989).

Box 8.1 *Profile: Gabrielle Maxwell and patterns of loneliness in a New Zealand population*

Gabrielle Maxwell is currently at Victoria University of Wellington. She was previously in the Department of Psychology at the University of Otago where she led a research programme focusing on interpersonal relationships and social skills. Latterly she has moved to applied research examining the impact of counselling in the New Zealand Family Court and evaluating the effectiveness of a new family-based decision-making model of youth justice. A book Kids in Trouble, *stemming from the latter research, is being published by Daphne Brasell Associates. Her next study will evaluate the New Zealand family-based model of intervention for children who are the victims of abuse and neglect. (Photo: courtesy Gabrielle Maxwell)*

Gabrielle Maxwell has contributed much to both sides of close relationships research. In this chapter we feature her work on loneliness and in Chapter Nine we mention her study of the behaviour of lovers.

Loneliness is certainly a damaging state and, to better understand its antecedents, Gabrielle Maxwell and Branko Coebergh (1986) of Otago University surveyed 243 residents of Dunedin to identify prevailing patterns of loneliness. The researchers were interested in measuring rates of loneliness and estimating its periodicity to identify vulnerable periods within the lifecycle. In line with US research, they were particularly interested in the attributions the lonely gave for their state; the amount and quality of contact residents had with a close confidant; and how this offset loneliness.

Raw scores indicated that a little less than a third of their respondents reported chronic loneliness. Maxwell and Coebergh then distributed their data into four categories from "least lonely" to "often lonely". Their data showed that while 12 per cent fell in the latter category, only 2 per cent of the "most lonely" reported severe loneliness. Adolescence was perhaps the loneliest time, but other points throughout the lifecycle led to loneliness, usually at major life changes. While almost everyone reported *state* loneliness when close relationships were disrupted, 50 per cent of their sample also attributed "the sort of person I am" as part of the reason for their loneliness.

When they compared the "least" and "most often lonely" categories, demographic variables like sex, education and socioeconomic status were relatively unimportant determinants of loneliness although "the married, the employed, and people in midlife were less likely to be lonely". As US research would predict, having a close confidant offset loneliness, though the quality of such contacts was more important than having many acquaintances: "The four most important predictors of loneliness were: how close the person was to the closest person in their life, how many close friends they had, how satisfied they were with their relationships, and whether they had contact with others during the working day."

Maxwell and Coebergh concluded that while their study gave little support to stereotypical views of the lonely as old or desperate, it was likely that our highly mobile lifestyles lead to increased social disruption and the loss of close relationships. Part of the price we pay for our affluence is severed relationships and those who are less socially competent will experience greater loneliness as they move around.

The truism "that to have friends you need to be a friend" points to a fundamental source of loneliness. We are rarely formally trained in friendship acquisition skills during childhood and if we miss the opportunity to acquire appropriate social skills we are handicapped in our later learning. Early failure quickly compounds to become an entrenched personality disposition. Brennan (1982) stressed the importance of learning friendship skills before adolescents make the transition from the family to the peer group, as this becomes the platform on which the teenager's subsequent adult identity is based. Bruch, Gorsky, Collins and Berger (1989), in a multi-component analysis of shyness and sociability, found that not only do lonely people have few interpersonal skills, they are unable to use the social graces they do possess appropriately. In experimental situations this alienated them from others as their essential passivity was interpreted as disinterest (Jones, Hobbs & Hockenbury, 1982).

Not only is being lonely an unpleasant experience it also perpetuates itself. Mike Powling and Bill Hopes (1988) examined the aspirations, self-characterisation and acquaintanceship patterns of 30 psychology students at the University of New South Wales, who responded to a loneliness survey and then volunteered to take part in a small group study. "Subjects were asked to write and video-record character sketches of themselves which were then evaluated for desirability of acquaintanceship by members of other groups." Although the literature supports the view that lonely people evaluate themselves more negatively than others would, Powling and Hope's results showed the contrary. While the lonely were eager for relationships, others were not interested. Factors like unattractiveness and lack of outgoingness played a part but the lonely were also handicapping themselves:

> The present results show that the lonely are socially discriminated against, and that they presumably transmit information which allows others to make this discrimination. Some of that information is contained in the content of their self-characterizations. (Powling & Hopes, 1988, p. 50)

Robert Weiss (1973) identified two kinds of loneliness: a social loneliness, or lack of social outlets we are all familiar with, and the emotional isolation we may experience even though bonded to others. Weiss argued that neither type of loneliness is worse than the other, though there is evidence that we are more lonely when we have lost close emotional ties (Stokes, 1985). Rubenstein and Shaver (1982), in a major survey, found loneliness was much more prevalent among widows, the divorced and the unmarried. Knowing we have the emotional backup of a close friend when needed seems to help, but simply having close friends or a spouse does not guarantee we are exempt from loneliness (see Box 8.2). Weiss argued we cannot substitute one type of relationship for another to reduce these feelings and we may well experience compartmentalised loneliness in our lives. A teenager with close family ties may suffer from not having a peer group, a wife with intimate friendships may feel lost in an emotionally barren marriage, and so on. This is evident when we watch bereaved friends fight loneliness despite the support of many close friends.

It is interesting to see attribution and locus of control theory at work in Box 8.2. There is considerable evidence that it influences our degree of loneliness and others' reactions to us. Anne Peplau and her colleagues developed a self-report loneliness scale to assess how student self-attributions affected their behaviour. Russell, Peplau and Cutrona (1980) first examined students' causal attributions. Some students saw their loneliness as a personality defect and attributed it to their shyness, lack of social skills, or fear of rejection; their loneliness sprang from internal sources. Others felt it was external: the university was too large, the student body too busy, the social opportunities too few, and their time too precious to make time for friends. A second dimension assessed whether loneliness was a stable or unstable condition.

As you can see from Figure 8.1, these two dimensions are combined in a matrix with probable behavioural outcomes. Students who saw their loneliness as internal and unstable felt they needed to "make more effort to get out", "meet people", or "attend assertiveness classes". Students who saw loneliness as their fault and as a condition of life were unlikely to modify their behaviour, and so on. Peplau, Russell and Helm (1979) noted that lonely people are not immune from the fundamental attribution error and tend to overestimate the dispositional causes of their problem and minimise environmental causes. In simple terms: "that's just the way I am, nothing will ever change."

As a final comment before we move on, we should note the difference between loneliness and aloneness. Simple absence of relationships does

---

Box 8.2 *The experience of loneliness in religious women and other mature Australian women: Tracing patterns of causation*

Although there are many reasons for loneliness, they are mainly situational, or bound up with some aspect of our personalities. Powling and Hope's study suggests that cognitive variables, or the way we characterise ourselves, may also play a part in sustaining loneliness. An interesting study explored how these variables influenced the lives of women in religious orders and compared their responses with an equivalent sample of married Catholic women.

Margaret Smith and Ann Knowles (1991) from Swinburne University of Technology, Melbourne, were interested in the relative contributions of personality, extent of social networks and cognitive processes on loneliness. They were concerned that many studies of loneliness were conducted on young adults who were usually university students. They decided to test the relative contributions of these variables to loneliness on a group of mature women who might be expected to be more vulnerable than most.

Smith and Knowles' review of the literature suggested that nuns are particularly vulnerable to changes within the Church and as a group had high levels of geographic mobility which fragmented their social networks. Surveys had indicated that many religious were leaving their orders because they were lonely and lacked the intimacy and social support enjoyed by the wider community. As our society idealises romance and passion, perhaps women religious might also feel a loss of the close relationships that marriage may bring. For these reasons, the researchers surveyed 70 women religious, whose mean age was 51 years; and compared their responses to those of 83 women (mean age 50) who were practising Catholics drawn from four parishes in Melbourne. The two groups were then comprehensively surveyed on "the UCLA Loneliness Scale, the Marlowe-Crowne Social Desirability Scale, an Inventory of Socially Supportive Behaviours, a Social Networks list, cognitive measures, measures of social and

Smith and Knowles found that older religious women may often suffer greater social isolation than their married peers but that patterns of loneliness are similar.
(Photo: Rob Pozo/Macarthur Advertiser)

emotional loneliness and the Eysenck Personality Questionnaire".

To test if social desirability was contributing to loneliness and confounding their results, they analysed its impact on the UCLA Loneliness Scale but this only accounted for .001% of the variance. So the women were not lonely because they were socially undesirable. With this concern out of the way, they compared the two groups on the other measures.

There was a large difference between both groups on the Social Network List, with the religious having far fewer confidants, relatives or other social supports but this did not influence loneliness scores. While there were a few methodological difficulties in completing this section of the booklet, it was clear that the religious were not lonely because they had fewer contacts. Were they lonelier then?

Loneliness scales' scores did indicate that the religious were lonelier but the differences, while significant, were small. To determine which type of loneliness accounted for the effect, Smith and Knowles performed a discriminant analysis and found that emotional loneliness was a greater discriminant of differences between the two groups than UCLA scale and social loneliness scores, but even these differences were small. As emotional loneliness was the major discriminant between the two groups this was then used as the basis for comparisons with the remaining variables.

Testing what impact extroversion, neuroticism, socially supportive behaviours, intimacy of existing relationships, satisfaction with social networks and desire for new relationships had on the religious women's emotional loneliness, gave clear results. Personality variables like neuroticism and extroversion had no significant impact on the women's emotional loneliness, while cognitive variables and social support accounted for much of the variation between the two groups.

This elegant study shows that the experience of loneliness for both groups of women was similar. Women in religious life were more lonely than their married peers in the parish but differences between the two groups were small. Situational or personality factors did not account for differences between the two groups, though they may have influenced the overall levels of loneliness of the combined sample. Where the women did differ, it was not so much differences in their situation or social networks but rather cognitive variables, or how they saw their relationships, that accounted for differences in emotional loneliness: "Women religious who feel that their most important relationships do not provide high levels of intimacy feel emotionally lonely"—a finding corroborated by many other local studies of lonely people (Henderson, Scott & Kay, 1986; Hamid, 1989; Boldero & Moore, 1990).

So the differences in loneliness between the groups were small but we must note that the women are similar in many ways and perhaps a comparison to a wider, more diverse sample of mature women may give sharper contrasts. Then again, Smith and Knowles make the point that, although the religious have reasons for their loneliness which are peculiar to religious life, "perhaps other equally important factors [lead] to loneliness in women who are married, single, widowed, or separated".

not mean we are lonely. At times in our lives we may value time alone, particularly during periods of high stress when being alone may be quite therapeutic (Rubin, 1973). Rubenstein and Shaver's survey found that people who choose to live alone are no more likely to be lonely than others. Many people—hermits, mystics, artists, those in contemplative orders and outback workers—choose lifestyles that would be debilitating to the majority of society, yet experience many rewards from solitude without psychological disturbance (Suedfeld, 1982). It is clear that how we see our relationships plays a large part in our emotional well-being.

	Stable	**Unstable**
INTERNAL	My totally unattractive personality and lack of good looks.	I have not made enough effort to get to know people
EXTERNAL	People do not like my ethnic group.	I've been too busy but that will change soon.

Figure 8.1 *How students explain their loneliness*

Source: Adapted from Russell, Peplau & Cutrona, 1980.

Gregariousness

Human beings are social; at heart we are herd or colony animals. Human gregariousness is such an obvious part of our nature that we accept it without comment and few researchers have made it their area (Rubin & Lewicki, 1973). Yet we spend a large part of our day with others. Larson, Csikszentmihalyi and Graef (1982) found that we spend on average 72 per cent of our waking hours with other people. Nor is this social interaction all that conscious. One of the under-developed areas of social psychology is mapping complex casual social interactions.

Perhaps at heart we are a herd species.
(Photo: Chris Simkin)

To ram home the sheer taken-for-grantedness of human interaction, consider for a moment the complexity of a casual conversation with your friends as you stand in a cafeteria line at lunch time. Did you carefully consider the social etiquette of queues before joining the line? How did you know where to stand? What minimal attention are you paying to the gradual shuffle towards the food bar? When is someone in the queue or not and how do you act if they are standing in an ambiguous position? How's your queue? Queues have variable spacing depending on their purpose (Hall, 1966). What is the queue's ambience? Is it fast or slow, long or short, impatient or peaceful? What collective behaviours is the queue indulging in to speed up service or undecided purchasers? What about your friends? Why did you decide to stand the way you are? What rules of social interaction are you following? Who is dominant and how do they enforce their hold over the group? At what level are you attuned to your friends' body language? These are just some aspects of cafeteria queue ecology and note we haven't yet got to your conversation. (If you wish to read further on the fascinating ecology of queues, see Mann, 1970, 1977).

We could go on an infinite analysis but the point is made. Most of our waking moments are meshed in a complex ritual dance with others. We know the moves but we do not think about them. To do so would probably raise our self-consciousness to the point where it would impair our performance. The subtleties of our social interaction are eclipsed by the sheer unconscious coordination required for it to work successfully. This coordination may be either cooperative or competitive but it is mutual. Even when we are trying to cut someone off and take over a conversation, it is a joint activity. This unconscious interdependence argues a long evolution of cooperative behaviour and raises several interesting issues which are the bones of our chapter: Are we a cooperative species, or does our cooperation mask something much more self-interested? What rewards does cooperation bring and what standards of comparison do we use to see if we are getting a good deal? Working on the assumption that cooperative behaviour is more than an instinctive end in itself, how do we maximise these benefits and what social cement holds it all together? In our following chapters, we raise the equally fascinating issues of why we like and help each other and debate whether we are a truly altruistic species. If, however, you are now convinced that human interdependency is important, we will dissect the four interpretations social psychology places on it.

Are we gregarious by nature?

Is gregariousness programmed into our genes? From a biosocial perspective, species that use cooperative strategies are more likely to have evolved at a faster rate than others. This is a hotly debated point and highly cooperative species like ants could hardly be considered top of the evolutionary pile. Indeed Alexander (1971) argues that aggression has had the most to do with the growth of intellect and our rapid evolution. At the heart of the argument we have to decide where we stand on natural selection. Is "the survival of the fittest" best accomplished by individual initiative or group action? Crudely, if we favour individual selection then that which gives individuals a competitive advantage allows them greater reproductive opportunity and should lead to intraspecific competition (Lewontin, 1970). If we favour group selection then individuals will benefit from both individual and group selective pressures and have a double advantage in the evolutionary stakes. Obviously we can see many species that follow either pattern and, equally obviously, our species is gregarious, but is it cooperative or does it just look like it is? Is cooperation a by-product of our need to rub along together in some sort of harmony, or is it calculated self-interest? The acid test of this argument is self-sacrificing altruism, which we will look at in some detail in Chapter 10.

Darwin and Wallace, the co-discoverers of natural selection, differed on this question with Darwin coming down solidly for individual selection:

> However valuable something might be for the group, if it is not also of value, directly or indirectly, to the individual, it just will not get passed on. Selection works first on the individual, and if a characteristic is to be preserved, it must make its case there. (Darwin, cited in Ruse, 1979, p. 16)

At present the balance of evidence seems to favour individual selection, though the argument is by no means over. Rephrasing the issue, perhaps behaviours that look cooperative are really just ultimately self-serving. Perhaps for this reason some psychologists regard human social behaviour as an end in itself, an instinctive, basic drive which has long since evolved past its evolutionary purposes. However, most concede it is unlikely we would remain social without some continuing adaptive advantage.

Have we learned to be gregarious?

Learning theory in the narrowest behaviourist sense has been largely silent on human interdependency, preferring to see it as an obvious given. For example, B.F. Skinner in his provocative book, *Beyond Freedom and Dignity*, devotes two chapters to the evolution and design of human culture (Skinner, 1971). A close reading of these chapters leads us to little more than his belief that culture is a product of our biological and environmental evolution and that circumstances (reinforcers) will determine the shape and outcomes of any society. Cooperation and competition then are products of historical processes and whether a society is gregarious or hostile will depend on the benefits derived from these differing social structures. This immediately raises the often voiced criticism that behaviourism explains "how" but not "why" things are as they are. This is not a problem for Skinner as these are synonymous questions in his view.

Reward theory

Nevertheless Lott and Lott (1961, 1985), in periodic reviews over 25 years, have shown that learning theory can play a role in expanding our understanding of interpersonal influence. Byrne and Clore (1970) were able to show experimentally that conditioning influences our responses to others and, when positively reinforced, leads to attraction. They proposed a reward–affect model which suggests our emotional reactions to places and events are conditioned, and that relationships and their development can be accounted for by learning theory. Griffitt in several studies has explored a number of conditioning variables that influence our attraction to others. In one experiment, room temperature and humidity were varied to influence subjects' evaluations of others (Griffitt, 1970). In another, good and bad news in radio broadcasts influenced how subjects felt about others (Veitch & Griffitt, 1976).

From this theoretical perspective, relationship development is uncomplicated. If you are accidentally knocked over going out to the shops one night for some milk, it is possible that you may associate this unpleasant experience with milk and milk-bar proprietors and avoid both in the future. The arousal of strong feelings becomes associated with the context in which they were aroused. The poor shopkeeper, as an innocent bystander, becomes the inadvertent victim of simple classical conditioning (Griffitt & Guay, 1969). Unfortunately for the elegance of this theory, the sheer number of variables at work in determining the outcome often means it is just as likely you will shrug it all off, buy your milk, and go home.

The content-free approach of learning theory, while leading to an enviable simplicity in explaining human gregariousness—"If you positively reinforce me, it is likely I will become your friend"—also leaves little room for more symbolic or cognitive interpretations of behaviour. This is not to say that learning theory is unimportant, rather, that it often offers too detailed and fundamental a level of explanation to be usefully employed across a range of social phenomena. The test of reward theory's explanatory power was readily apparent when I was planning this section of the book. In reviewing fifteen other social psychology texts' coverage of learning theory and interpersonal attraction, it averaged out about half a page, which is what we have given it.

Before we move on it is worth mentioning that gregariousness has also been extensively studied by anthropologists and both cross-cultural and developmental psychologists, whose perspective assumes it to be both an innate and a learned behaviour. We will review the developmental position briefly in our discussion of altruism in Chapter Ten.

At the heart of social interdependency lies a great paradox: we are at once competitive and cooperative. Are we at war with ourselves, or are these seemingly contradictory behaviours really different sides of the same coin? Most of the research reviewed in this chapter clearly suggests individual actions by and large are self-interested. Life is a game of maximising our returns for the least effort. To evaluate our performance we use neighbours and friends as a competitive baseline. Nevertheless, whatever the motivation behind our striving to succeed, we are sometimes embarrassingly cooperative. Why?

Is it more profitable to be gregarious?

As hard and unpalatable as it may seem, research suggests we deliberately exchange material and psychological commodities within relationships to ensure their equity and durability (Blau, 1964). Put another way we calculate the costs and benefits of our alliances and make sure they are balanced. Relationships that are relatively rewarding deepen, and those that are costly or unrewarding tend to fail. This trading is a conscious process of choice between alternatives, mediated by the value we place on commodities given and received. We affiliate, then, on the basis of greatest benefit.

social exchange theory
A model of relationship development based on the rewards and costs to each party.

It will come as little surprise that **social exchange theory** has its roots in economics (Von Neumann & Morgenstern, 1944). It has also been very influential in the growth of both sociology and social psychology (Homans, 1961; Adams, 1963). John Thibaut and Harold Kelley (1959) developed a most influential and elaborate version of this theory, proposing that people are intrinsically hedonistic, seeking the greatest possible benefit for themselves. Although we do not go through life with a checklist, we are finely attuned to the costs and benefits we derive from relationships and, as we are attracted to those who reward us, to a large measure this regulates our affiliative behaviour. Foa and Foa (1974), in their widely quoted book *Societal Structures of the Mind*, identify six interpersonal benefits we exchange in our relationships: goods, services, money, status, information and love. Obviously different types of commodities are bartered in differing relationships. We make entirely different exchanges with the corner greengrocer than we do with intimate friends. However informal these exchanges are, one of the most consistent findings of relationship research is the extent that we use them to assess the costs of continued cooperation. As we have all been on the wrong end

Cynically speaking, perhaps romantic love is merely a matter of trading commodities!
(Photo: Mark Bramley)

of one-way relationships, evidence suggests we have finely tuned skills in assessing just how equitable our relationships are.

Foa and Foa suggest rewards may be either specific (particular) or concrete (see Figure 8.2). Obviously benefits are commensurate with the nature of our relationships, and Foa and Foa feel we are less particular about exchanges within intimate relationships. Conversely, less intimate social exchanges work best when equivalent resources are being exchanged (Brinberg & Castell, 1982). On one dimension we would value (and expect) a greater degree of trust and commitment in intimate relationships, so status and love exchanges are more specifically attached to a chosen individual. In contrast, we are less choosy from whom we will accept money, information, goods and some services. The other dimension, concreteness, deals with the tangibility of the rewards we seek from our relationships.

It is worth pointing out that what is rewarding to one may well be a cost to another. Social exchange theory is largely silent on why something is rewarding. Naturally the benefit derived is as specific to the individual as it is intrinsic to the reward itself. You might really enjoy hugs and so are willing to accept them from any number of people, while I might see hugs as intimate behaviour and restrict them to close friends. Money on the other hand is quite unambiguous. The value and symbolism of rewards then depends on who is giving what to whom, and the interpretations we place on it all. Thibaut and Kelley's theory, while clearly hedonistic, is only uncaring at first glance. They stress that while we assess our exchanges,

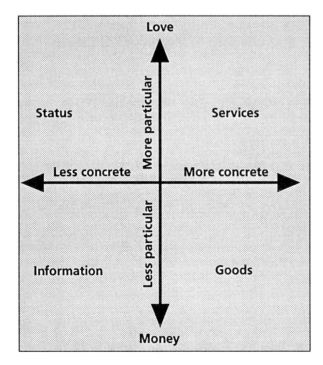

Figure 8.2 *Trading commodities in interpersonal relationships*
Source: Adapted from Foa & Foa, 1974.

we are not necessarily selfish. We may well enjoy giving. Philanthropists are clearly concerned with humanity and derive great personal satisfaction from giving to others. In a similar way Thibaut and Kelley suggest that some may have a need to nurture and may structure satisfying relationships around caring for others.

As an explanation of the factors promoting human cooperativeness and affiliation, social exchange theory relies on three related processes (Nye, 1979): cost/benefit analysis, comparison level, and comparison level for alternatives.

Cost/benefit analysis

Relationships stand or fall on the balance between costs and benefits. Costs are essentially any negative factor perceived by participants in a relationship. As they are subjective they may be actual or imagined. Thibaut and Kelley stressed that benefits forgone were as much a cost as actual expenditures of time or money. A colleague, to the great consternation of family and friends, ended a marriage of some fifteen years, because her spouse would not agree to move from Christchurch to Auckland to further her career. Costs and benefits are then both subjective and relative. While Thibaut and Kelley felt we valued relationships more if our cost/benefit ratio was in profit, later equity research suggests we are equally uncomfortable if we are over-benefited (Sprecher, 1986).

Comparison level

Not only do we strike a rough balance of profit and losses but we also compare our relationships with others to assess how well we are doing. The level of satisfaction these comparisons engender determines their health. We may well have an excellent relationship but feel dissatisfied because others seem to be doing even better. This has many parallels to relative deprivation theory (Crosby, 1976). The same New Zealand colleague pointed out that many Cook Islanders felt themselves to be the real underclass in New Zealand today, but in absolute terms, social welfare, income levels and employment they were doing much better than in Rarotonga. However, despite their relative affluence, they compared themselves to their Maori cousins and Pakeha and felt hard done by. In moving to New Zealand they had also adopted a new comparison level. Kelley and Thibaut (1978) further proposed that we evaluate our relationships against what we feel we deserve. This standard is a compound of our past experiences, our perception of similar relationships around us, and our implicit belief as to our own sense of worth. A friend's intense romance of some months ended uproariously when she was unfavourably compared with Madonna! She concluded that her lover was:

> (a) Unrealistic in his expectations
> (b) Enacting his fantasies at her expense
> (c) Setting too high a value on himself
> (d) All the above

Whatever the answer to this quiz is, she concluded his comparison level surpassed hers, and departed laughing.

Comparison level for alternatives

Implicit in any exchange view of relationships is our constant evaluation of alternatives with a view to maximising our chances by moving on. The stability of our alliances is then dependent on our belief that we have few real alternatives. Obviously sometimes costs outweigh benefits to the extent that social isolation is preferable, a situation too many battered wives find themselves in. While many factors militate against our leaving old alliances—loyalty to an organisation, religious views of marriage, or the familiarity of a rut—these are all part of our comparison of alternatives. Our decision to move on is a complex one involving several related factors. If our relationship is unsatisfactory, what are our alternatives? When we compare other options available to us, we have to weigh the risks and benefits of leaving our current relationship and moving to a new one. Equally, many people stay in boring jobs, have mundane friends and face limited prospects because they feel unsure of doing better. When our comparisons tell us the pasture is definitely greener somewhere else, we will move on regardless.

Social exchange seems a relatively simple theory but quickly becomes quite complex when we try to use it to make predictions. One of the complicating factors is the time element. We often forgo present benefits in the hope that we will gain a relatively greater advantage in the future. For example, you are engaged in an opportunity cost equation right now. While studying for a degree is undoubtedly stimulating, you are forgoing several years' income and considerable socialising, in the hope that you will have better opportunities in the future. In the same way we often enter one-sided relationships because we believe they will improve over time (as demonstrated by the old cliché that many brides choose unsuitable marriage partners according to the formula "aisle altar hymn"). Also, what may seem like one-sided exchanges may be one partner's belief that the other will have a greater capacity to reward them in the future, as when a wife works to put her husband through university.

Lifespan considerations also play a large role in the timing of our relationship satisfactions (McCulloch, 1990). Many teenagers will date anyone rather than be left on the shelf. Several years ago I eavesdropped on a Nursing Mothers' meeting in my home. The women were discussing their husbands' callous indifference to the plight of motherhood. After an hour's vitriolic roasting of their men, they cheerfully concluded it would all get a lot better when the children were out of nappies. Similarly, Nye suggested that when immediate outcomes are likely to be equal, we choose more promising long-term alternatives; when the reverse is true and long-term outcomes are seen as being equal, we opt for immediate benefits (Callan & Noller, 1987). Such time factors make it difficult to strike an easy equation for social exchanges.

Social exchange theory underwent considerable modification over the years, mainly in improving outcomes analysis. So far we have discussed

Be it ever so humble, it's a matter of our comparison level for alternatives!
(Photos: Barry Price; Chris Simkin)

social exchange as if it were a unitary one-person process; however Kelley and Thibaut's 1978 revised theory had its greatest interest in the coordination of outcomes so that all the parties to a relationship could gain the greatest possible benefit. If I want to go camping in Tasmania next holidays and my wife wants to stay home and spin, our conflicts of interest will lead to tension unless we coordinate our outcomes in some way. Perhaps we can compromise, splitting our holiday, spending one week at home and the other camping at Catamaran. Thibaut and Kelley predicted couples with similar (correspondent) interests and attitudes would have more satisfying relationships as they had less difficulty coordinating outcomes; as subsequent

"RELATIONSHIP SATISFACTION DEPENDS ON
OUR COMPARISION LEVEL FOR ALTERNATIVES".

(Cartoonist: Steve Harris)

Box 8.3 *Are we all tax cheats or just social exchangers?*

Associate Professor Ian Wallschutzky, from the University of Newcastle, set out to determine the possible causes of tax evasion. He guessed that three determinants—the exchange value, or what we thought we were getting for our tax dollars in social services received; social class and our understanding of the tax system; and our estimates of our chances of successful evasion—would determine our liability to cheat. These hypotheses were tested with approximately 200 convicted tax evaders and 200 members of the general population "who completed a questionnaire assessing their attitudes toward taxes and why they thought taxpayers felt justified in evading tax" (Wallschutzky, 1984).

Wallschutzky's study gave some interesting, if predictable results, which support a social exchange view of taxpayers' attitudes towards taxation. Both groups said that taxes were too high; they were not getting value for money; and the government was not spending tax dollars wisely. Both groups felt the tax laws as they stood were unsatisfactory. From their comments, both groups felt the burden of taxes fell on low income and salary earners, who unfortunately had less chance of avoiding paying tax! This allowed the self-employed and the rich to avoid taxes. Taxpayers who complained about government waste had a little list of:

> . . . public servants who were paid too much for doing too little, and who received excessive superannuation payments on retirement; too many "freeloaders" on social security pensions; too many other abuses of social welfare schemes and too much spent on "useless armaments". (Wallschutzky, 1984, p. 381)

While Wallschutzky found no significant social exchange differences between the two groups, evaders "tended to be older, to be self-employed, to have slightly higher incomes and to be more often born outside Australia". Evaders also knew more evaders than did non-evaders, but Wallschutzky was surprised by the high numbers of people in the general population who thought they knew tax evaders! As expected, those who had been caught were least satisfied with the taxation system.

Because Wallschutzy's comparisons between the two groups showed no statistical differences, his first reaction was to conclude that "the exchange relationship hypothesis did not explain why evaders evaded tax", but the comments they made suggested otherwise. After some reflection, Wallschutzky decided that there were as many evaders in his general population sample and this meant "that one would expect little difference in responses from the two groups".

research has shown. In our following chapter we will discuss at length the role of similarity in promoting closer relationships.

This brings us closer to resolving our paradox. If we are essentially self-interested exchangers, intent on exploiting our relationships, then we will quickly run into what biologists call the Law of Limiting Factors, that growth is limited by the commodity in the shortest supply. In social exchange this may well be an intangible or symbolic lack, but if the relationship is competitive then this point is quickly reached. To gain the greatest possible individual return, each person must coordinate their desires to reach mutually agreed upon outcomes. In this way competitive systems become cooperative. Unfortunately there are many obstacles to this transformation.

Distributive justice

At the heart of human gregariousness is the sad fact that we live in an unfair world and we are forced to legislate for fairness to ensure some order out of the chaos of life's lottery. Some of us are born into families of wealth and privilege, some into abject poverty; others are born without arms or legs, and some of us are the wrong sex or colour. Some nations are more favoured than others and it is unlikely that you would be studying social psychology now if you were born in the hinterland of Burkina Faso twenty years ago. Some of us seem destined by force of character, intellect or good looks, to rise to the top of the pile, others get there by sheer determination and bloody-mindedness, while the majority of us wonder how they did it. Nor is good looks, guts, intellect and position any guarantee of a fair deal. One wonders what the rich and powerful felt in their last moments as the great Lisbon earthquake of 1755 dropped 30 000 holiday makers below the waters of the Tagus.

It is precisely because the world is such an unfair place that we have evolved intricate moralities, social codes, legal systems, bills of rights and other such elaborate structures to ensure fairness for all, and it is in this sense that we have been forced to become gregarious. This is not a new idea. Plato and other ancient Greeks wrote on the subject and it probably reached its fullest expression in the social contract ideals of Thomas Hobbes, who saw government as vulnerable people subordinating their interests to a sovereign to gain some minimal protection from each other and the savage competition in an otherwise lawless state of nature:

> For the laws of nature, as justice, equity, modesty, mercy and in sum, doing to others as we would be done to, of themselves without the terror of some power to cause them to be observed, are contrary to our natural passions, that carry us to partiality, pride, revenge, and the like. And covenants without the sword, are but words and of no strength to secure a man at all. Therefore, notwithstanding the laws of nature, . . . if there be no power erected, or not great enough for our security, every man will and may lawfully rely on his own strength and art for caution against all other men. (Hobbes, 1651, p. 99)

While Hobbes' quote in its narrowest interpretation is strictly an issue of social exchange, it highlights the two rights problem, which has been disturbing the peace throughout the ages. To ensure a just society we must treat everyone equally yet, as Hobbes points out, it is patently obvious that people start unequally. Unfortunately, disparity between the favoured and the less well off has always been a major check to a peaceful life and a cooperative society (Greenberg & Cohen, 1982). The limitations of social exchange theory became apparent when conflicting definitions of fairness were applied to social problems. What was fair for some, disadvantaged others. So social psychologists in the 1960s became interested in the various ways we construe fairness, or **distributive justice**.

distributive justice
Decisional rules for allocating resources.

It is not enough to treat people equally for them to feel equitably treated, a lesson we learned at some cost in the 1970s as we implemented anti-discrimination policies. The dimensions of the problem will become apparent if you consider a conversation I overheard on the train one morning, between two obviously well-educated migrant women in their early thirties:

> "It's unfair that Aborigines get free housing, cheap home loans, reduced taxes, free health care, legal aid, cars [!], special entry into university [and she had a much longer list]. It's not fair. No one gives me those things. Why am I forced to pay for them from my taxes?"

> Her friend: "But they've been thrown off their land and oppressed for two hundred years etc."

> "But I didn't do it to them! I've only been here ten years! Why should I have to pay for someone else's cruelty? I started with nothing. I've really worked hard for what I've got! They can too. Treat them fairly, give everybody a fair go, but not an unfair go. It's me that's being discriminated against."

You can see that different definitions of fairness are being used here. Deutsch (1975) identified three differing interpretations: equality, need and equity.

Equality

The first lady forcefully asserts that everyone should have equal slices of the common wealth—"Give everybody a fair go, not an unfair go." Unfortunately this formula may further increase inequality. Spreading hospital beds evenly throughout the country on a per capita basis, while fair in one sense, may deprive disadvantaged areas of the beds they need, while adding superfluous beds to more healthy areas. An equal-lots formula works best with strangers whom we cannot trust yet but wish to develop a relationship with (Deutsch, 1975); or with children who cannot understand more elaborate notions of distributive justice (Piaget, 1965; Hook & Cook, 1979).

Need

Unfortunately, the lot of indigenous people everywhere has not been easy. The other lady is obviously appealing to a notion of differing needs (Crosby, 1976). She wants to redress relative deprivation—"they have been oppressed for two hundred years." She wants to ensure that Aborigines get positive discrimination programmes aimed at making up lost ground. Equality's view of fairness involves a level playing field approach to rewards; we should be rewarded equally but some start way off-field. Need-based formulas aim at varying rewards to put everyone on an equal footing. The problem with advantaging some in the short term, as we saw in Chapter Five, is you may have to disadvantage others to do so, and they may well be innocent third parties as the first lady vigorously insists she is.

Distributive justice. The level of benefits provided to the physically disabled is higher than for most recipients. While this is an unequal distribution of society's resources, it is justified in terms of their greater need.
(Photo: Rob Pozo/Macarthur Advertiser)

Equity

Neither view of fairness takes account of effort, that we should be rewarded according to our efforts (Adams, 1965). The Cultural Revolution in China during the 1960s abolished salary differentials, attacked intellectuals, closed universities and sent educated Chinese to the country to learn humility and grassroots wisdom from the peasants. This had the effect of wiping out a decade or more of China's progress and led many Chinese to doubt the benefits of higher education. After all, why bother making all the extra effort to acquire a degree when at the end you get the same (or less) than everyone else? So the equity (proportionality) approach argues that people should be rewarded according to their relative efforts. The more you do, the more you expect.

Deutsch (1985) and many others have argued that the greatest limitation of early accounts of social exchange theory was its relative neglect of investments in relationships. They saw a need to focus on contributions made, as well as costs and benefits. **Equity theory**, an extension of social exchange theory, arose to explore the consequences of unfair exchanges. While there is quite an intellectual debate about how to operationalise it (Alessio, 1980, 1990), equity theory differs from exchange theory in the emphasis it places on needs and contributions being acknowledged in relationships, rather than just balancing costs and benefits. The essential difference between the two is that equity does not require equality of outcomes for fairness to exist.

> *Equity versus social exchange theory*
>
> **equity theory**
> The ratio of net rewards to investments.

For example, the bane of an academic's life is students complaining about their marks. There are basically two ways of assessing and passing students. Set an objective standard like a multiple-choice test and require 50 per cent for a pass, where equality of outcome gains the same grade. However, this takes no account of effort; extremely bright students, or at least those with a retentive memory, will pass easily for little effort, while others, perhaps from less favoured academic backgrounds, will have to slog to reach a similar standard. Setting a subjective task like an essay allows you to assess the effort a student puts in and reward them accordingly. But which is the fairer method of assessment? Needless to say, this assessment question is a hot topic of academic debate.

While perceived equity is important, ultimately it is the ratio of inputs to outcomes that determines if relationships are fair or not, and comparable worth seems to be the final test employed (Lowe & Wittig, 1989). Equally, there is little doubt that equity is a major factor in how alliances progress (Leventhal, 1979; Harris, 1980; Sprecher, 1988; Greenberg, 1990). For example, Hatfield et al. (1985) found that if marriages are seen as being equitable, partners are less likely to have extra-marital sexual adventures.

It is clear that equity and depth of commitment are related but the relationship is unclear. Caryl Rusbult has studied inequity for over a decade and, in a comparison of social exchange and equity factors in college dating, she concluded that social exchange factors were the best indicators of satisfaction (Rusbult, 1980). Depth of commitment on the other hand was related to both satisfaction and investment in the relationship. However, Van-Yperen and Buunk (1990), in a major longitudinal study of dating and the relationship between intimacy and equity, found only equivocal evidence that equity was related to satisfaction. Rather, they found that satisfaction was based more on commitment within the relationship. Rusbult also noted that commitment was strengthened by a lack of perceived alternatives, a finding replicated by Jemmott et al. (1989). In a later study Rusbult modified her position a little when she found that deeply committed lovers may disparage viable alternative partners as a means of resisting temptation and strengthening commitment (Johnson & Rusbult, 1989).

From Figure 8.3 you can see that Rusbult believes we have active and passive ways of dealing with inequity, which may be either constructive or destructive. There is a time element involved as well. Cate, Lloyd and Long (1988) found that couples' concern with equity issues declined over time, and this is consistent with both the investment hypothesis, and the gradual change from exchange to communal relationships which we will explore next chapter.

A final note before we leave our comparison of equity and equality. Many theorists have noted that how we perceive others in our exchanges influences which type of outcome we prefer (Feather & O'Driscoll, 1980); see Leventhal, 1976, for a review). Allocation of rewards in group settings tends towards the equality norm as this promotes cooperation and group morale irrespective of input, whereas more intimate relationships take more account of equity and need in allocating resources. However, how

While equity is clearly a factor in how relationships develop, with the deeply committed this relationship is less clear.
(Photo: Mark Bramley)

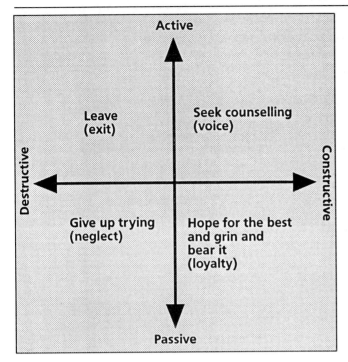

Figure 8.3 *Dealing with relationship inequity*

Source: Adapted from Rusbult & Zembrodt, 1983.

we see the allocator also bears on our preferences for distributive justice. Our feelings of being treated fairly reflect our estimation of the fairness of the allocator. Personality, situational and cultural variables all influence our preference. For example, Feather and O'Driscoll (1980), in their study of observer reactions to an equal or equitable allocator, noted that: "Protestant ethic values, competence values, and the value assigned to wisdom also influenced reactions to the allocator, as did an Australian concern with 'mateship' ". So it seems that many variables influence what we think is fair (see also Feather, 1983, 1990a; and Walker & Mann, 1989, for an overview of local research; and Siegal & Shwalb, 1985; Mann, Radford & Kanagawa, 1985; Kashima, Siegal, Tanaka & Isaka, 1988, for crosscultural comparisons).

Promoting equity

Equitable relationships are relatively conflict free, so learning how to promote equity is prudent social insurance. Research has followed two paths towards promoting equity. Researchers like McClintock (1988) have concentrated on the allocation strategies used to promote interdependence, and others like Argyle and Henderson (1985) are more interested in the rules we generate to ensure a fair go for all. Any relationship, be it a casual friendship or a lifetime devotion to a religious order, stands or falls on the problems encountered in maintaining one's commitment (Verdieck, Shields & Hoge, 1988). Problems occur in coordinating outcomes and in living with the personal foibles of others as much as with imbalanced cost/benefit analyses. To cope with these difficulties and remain committed takes some doing, and conflict is a feature of all relationships, however humble. Interestingly, the deeper the commitment the more potential there is for conflict (Braiker & Kelley, 1979). To survive such conflict often takes some doing if our divorce figures are any indication.

The need for equity in social exchanges becomes acute when you consider the powerful holdover effect of traditional sex roles on present-day marriages. Although these were once reciprocal and balanced (and maybe even equitable), time has moved on and they are no longer so. While newer, more egalitarian roles are being hammered out on the anvil of social change, we pay a price. Developmental psychologists tell us that most Australian marriages still are fairly imbalanced, though slowly changing to become more equitable. For example, Candi Peterson, of the University of Queensland, surveyed husbands' and wives' perceptions of marital fairness across the family lifecycle. Husbands felt their marital equity declined when children came along and improved after the children's departure. Wives' perceptions were fairly constant but only a slender majority saw their marriages as equitable, and both sexes agreed that when equity was imbalanced it was most likely at the wife's expense (Peterson, 1990). This does not bode well for the health of our marriages. Peterson has undertaken other studies to compare perceptions of equity across the generations and some of these are reported in Box 8.4.

Box 8.4 *Need, equity and equality in the family*

As we will see in Chapter Nine, the development of close relationships proceeds from initial attraction and casual acquaintanceship to mutual interdependence. The factors that are important in initial attraction have a calculated reciprocity about them which is reminiscent of an equity approach to distributive justice, with each partner ensuring they are appropriately rewarded for their efforts (Deutsch, 1975). However, longer term relationships such as those within a family seem more interdependent and mutual. While we would expect parents to care selflessly for young children, and considerably over-benefit the child, does this continue into the child's adult years, or would the parents expect some reciprocal recompense? Candi Peterson, Reader

at the University of Queensland, undertook two studies to determine what type of distributive justice governs the relationships between parents and their adult children.

Her first was a modification of Greenberg's (1983) study of the inferences subjects made about how couples decided to share a restaurant bill. Peterson (1987) presented 90 female university students with one of three identical stories but with different conclusions.

All involved a low income widow who ordered a $5.50 lunch, while her professional daughter's lunch cost $19.50. The equity conclusion had each woman pay for her own, equality had them halve the bill, and need had the daughter pay for both meals. (Peterson, 1987, p. 543)

Students rated the mother–daughter pair on liking, intimacy, degree of contact, and how hostile their relationship was. Predictably the endings that used *need* to settle the bill were seen as closer and more intimate than the equality and equity outcomes, which did not differ significantly. Similarly, an equitable division was seen as indicating a more hostile mother–daughter relationship, than need and equality outcomes. Peterson felt students saw equity outcomes as a colder approach to working out the bill and "disruptive of social respect".

She concluded by agreeing with Deutsch that families took little account of the relative contributions of members and would not want to allocate rewards on the basis of equity or equality.

Her follow-on study (Peterson & Peterson, 1988) examined how equitable older men and women's relationships really were with adult kin. Research had suggested that the elderly seemed to have inequities in their relationships with others, but difficulties in measuring all the benefits the elderly felt they received threw these studies into question. Peterson wanted to assess the *entirety* of the costs and benefits the elderly thought they received. She recruited

Peterson found that the elderly saw their marriages as either strictly equitable or, if not, they felt they were over-benefited.
(Photo: Chris Simkin)

62 adults over 55 years of age and compared their relationship satisfaction with those of 45 younger adults aged between 18 and 45 years. Her subjects listed all their relatives over the age of 18, and how often they saw them. Subjects were then asked:

> Now we would like you to think about each of your target relationships in turn *as a total package*. Consider everything that

you put into this relationship, and everything you get out of it. Then consider everything the other person puts into it and everything he or she gets out of it. How does your relationship with [ ] *stack up?* (Peterson and Peterson, 1988, p. 223–24)

Her results are shown in Table 8.1. As you can see the majority of the elderly felt their marriages were "strictly equitable" and of the

Table 8.1 *Equity within the family*

	Respondents													
	Older men (n = 31)							Older women (n = 31)						
			Equitability category							Equitability category				
			E		O		U			E		O		U
Relationship type	Total	Mean	n	%	n	%	n	%	Total	Mean	n	%	n	%	n	%
Marriage	27	.70	14	52	10	37	3	11	17	.66	11	65	5	29	1	6
Parent of an adult child	31	–.32	20	64	4	13	7	23	31	.05	21	68	6	19	4	15
Child of an aged parent	12	–.33	9	75	1	8	2	17	7	.00	7	100	0	0	0	0

E = Strict equity; O = Self over-benefited; U = Self under-benefited.

	Respondents													
	Younger men (n = 15)							Younger women (n = 30)						
			Equitability category							Equitability category				
			E		O		U			E		O		U
Relationship type	Total	Mean	n	%	n	%	n	%	Total	Mean	n	%	n	%	n	%
Marriage	6	.33	5	83	1	17	0	0	10	–.30	7	70	1	10	2	20
Offspring of mother	14	1.14	8	57	6	43	0	0	30	.80	19	63	10	33	1	13
Offspring of father	14	.93	8	57	6	43	0	0	26	.77	17	65	8	31	1	14
Grandchild	5	.60	4	80	1	20	0	0	11	0	11	100	0	0	0	0

E = Strict equity; O = Self over-benefited; U = Self under-benefited.

Source: Peterson, 1988.

43 per cent who felt they were inequitably treated 79 per cent felt they were over-benefited! The elderly also felt the same way about their adult children, though the 34 per cent minority, who saw their relationships as inequitable, "were as likely to feel under- and over-benefited". Younger adults felt much the same way about their own marriages and saw themselves as "significantly over-benefited" in their relationships with their parents. As the majority of younger respondents were university students you might expect them to be over-benefited, as many would be supported by parents. Peterson tested for differences between students and the employed, and married and single younger adults but found no significant differences between these groups. All felt over-benefited.

These are surprising findings as you would not expect longstanding relationships to be as concerned with equity as they were. Intuitively, it may be that the Petersons' sample felt a good marriage should be an equitable one

and responded that way. Perhaps they also felt that parents should still care for their children and not count the cost. That most who were not in strictly equitable relationships felt there was a significant degree of over-benefit in their relationships, says as much. Unfortunately, Petersons' study did not test actual parent and child combinations, and respondents were unrelated to each other. For this reason we must treat these results a little cautiously, but even so it is clear that each group thought they were doing all right out of their relationships. Equally, it would have been interesting to have some specific measures of marital and/or parent–child relationship satisfaction, to compare with the global equity measures. Such a comparison might have told us more about just what "getting a better deal" meant for each group. Even so, the Petersons note that the absence of a significantly under-benefited group means that someone's perceptions must be one-sided!

To keep our relationships together we sometimes need advanced conflict-resolution skills but having to negotiate our way through life would be extremely tedious. All alliances therefore generate formal and informal rules as a way of shortcircuiting questions of who does what. The rules may be societal, "one husband per marriage"; or domestic, "you put out the garbage". They may be as explicit as "employees should not spend more than five minutes in this ablutions block", or quite implicit "only lovers know". Rules guide correct conduct and warn of the consequences of inappropriate behaviour, and so act to anticipate and reduce conflict. They also regulate our expectations and set clear conditions on what are rewarding interactions (Argyle & Henderson, 1985). Our rules are both distributive and procedural (who gets what and how) and clearly reflect the types of equity outcomes we wish to see promoted in our social exchanges (Thibaut & Walker, 1975).

Rules for inter-dependence

Power

Relationships are about power. In harmonious relationships, particularly of the intimate kind, we are not too concerned with equity because the power balance struck is something the partners can live with (Grauerholz, 1987). However, troubled relationships usually have serious power sharing problems and Blau (1964) felt the inequitable exchange of material and psychological resources lay at the heart of most power struggles. He predicted that the partner with less resources to contribute would have the least power. In this way the relative balance between resources and power determines our ability to influence another's actions, thoughts or feelings (Bacharach & Lawler, 1981; Huston, 1983). Few relationships are equally balanced, yet some manage to survive without too much conflict. Molm (1985, 1988) suggests that, in these cases, one partner is usually more dependent, needing more from the relationship and this extra commitment balances out other inequities. Nevertheless, when inequity is too great, conflict follows.

Trust

Trust is also a major factor in both equity and exchange relationships. We invest resources in relationships against their anticipated return. If we feel we cannot trust our partners to reciprocate, we are less open to equitable relationships and face higher competitive pressures to get as much as possible for ourselves. We will return to the role of trust and defectors shortly.

Responses to inequity

Responses to inequity vary. Much of the research has been done in the industrial arena where costs and benefits may be more easily quantified than in more intimate relationships. Inequity occurs when workers feel

Okay, okay, take the bottle!

Troubled relationships usually have serious power-sharing problems . . .
(Cartoonist: Graeme Mitchell)

their pay and conditions are somehow inappropriate. If their pay inadequately reflects their skills and qualifications, then they are under-rewarded. Equally, they may feel they are being overpaid or over-rewarded.

Responses to over-reward and under-reward

There is much more research on the consequences of under-reward as it is more easily quantified. When we feel exploited, we become dissatisfied, angry, frustrated, and the greater the perceived inequity the greater our disgruntlement. We have four possible responses, which reflect our comparison level of alternatives:

Table 8.2 *Dealing with inequity*

When under-rewarded we will . . .	When over-rewarded we will . . .
• Reduce our outputs which will . . . • Decrease our partner's outcomes . . .	Increase our outputs to . . . Increase our partner's outcomes . . .
• Increase our outcomes by . . . • Increasing our partner's input . . .	Decrease our outcomes by . . . Reducing our partner's input . . .

Source: Peterson, 1988.

If we feel we have few alternatives we may either passively or actively resist by decreasing our inputs. This has been the bane of industrial relations. Workers who feel they are under-rewarded, yet have few real alternatives, usually suffer declining morale and become apathetic about company goals (Greenberg, 1989). This expresses itself in increased absenteeism, lower productivity and poorer quality control. Under-rewarded workers also suffer burnout, and feelings of inequity are significantly related to elevated occupational stress (McKenna, 1987). Most people usually prefer to take direct action, and when alternatives are few, strikes, confrontation, industrial sabotage and go-slow tactics are favoured. Szwajkowski (1989) suggested that many employees' "illegal and unethical behaviours may be more a reaction to work-place inequities and ineffective justice, than character defects". Many employee misconduct behaviours, like thieving or "production deviance", may be interpreted as self-help mechanisms attempting to redress perceived grievances. A related tactic with underpaid pieceworkers paid by output is to reduce the quality of each item produced to increase output and pay (Lawler & O'Gara, 1967). Evidence supporting these observations comes from two studies by Eisenberger, Fasolo and Davis-LaMastro (1990) who report how employees' perceptions of being valued by their firms led to conscientiousness, reciprocal feelings of affirmation, involvement, and innovation on behalf of the organisation, all without anticipating any extra rewards or recognition.

Responses to over-reward are more mixed. We are less troubled by overpayment and we may selectively reinterpret our worth on the assumption that we must be worth what we are paid (see Box 8.5). In some situations though, particularly when colleagues doing the same work are less well paid, we become disturbed by over-reward and feel guilty and indebted. As with under-reward, we prefer to actively redress inequity, though again research suggests we are less likely to fully redistribute resources to promote complete equity (Leventhal, Weiss & Long, 1969).

Nevertheless, we often strive to reduce inequity by increasing outputs to a level we feel is commensurate with our rewards. In a much quoted, classic study, Adams and Jacobsen (1964) demonstrated how students would go to some lengths to redress inequity. They hired students to work as proofreaders and, after assessing their skills, divided them into three conditions. In the over-reward condition they were told that though they were relatively unskilled compared to professional proofreaders, they would be paid a full rate of 30 cents per page. In another, students were given a reduced payment

---

Box 8.5 *Are academics paid too much?*

Whether we feel we are paid enough is a perennial research topic. Most of the tests of pay satisfaction rely on either equity theory (or being rewarded for what we put in) or social comparison theory (which we will discuss at the end of our chapter) if we are being paid comparably to others doing the same job. Therefore, our sense of being fairly paid is a mix of equity and equality considerations, and how much we know about conditions in similar jobs. Lawler (1971) combined these considerations into a scale for measuring pay satisfaction, and Christopher Orpen and Josef Bonnici (1987, 1990), of Deakin University's Department of Management (Victoria), used a derivation of his scale to examine perceptions of pay level and equity, personal input, job demands, other rewards, and pay satisfaction of 101 Australian academics.

Orpen and Bonnici's subjects gave their annual salary, estimated how their pay compared to others doing similar work in non-university settings and within their universities. To establish a baseline, academics were also asked to rate their performance, and what their job demanded of them. Given that academics are notoriously other-directed, they also rated whether they received many non-financial rewards from their jobs. They were then asked to rate their actual satisfaction with their job, their internal motivation to do their job well, and how adequate they thought their pay was.

Orpen and Bonnici's results were an eye-opener. When they correlated academic expectations with pay satisfaction, four of the independent variables "were highly significant and two nonsignificant". Academics felt they were fairly paid when they were getting comparable pay to other academics and outsiders, and when their jobs gave them more non-financial rewards and more pay. Personal effort and job demands were unrelated to pay satisfaction. Correlations between pay satisfaction and outcomes was only significant for work satisfaction. Performance, job involvement and internal motivation were not related to pay satisfaction.

You could sum up these results by saying that academics: are happy with their jobs the more they are paid; when they receive greater non-financial rewards; and when they feel they are paid at least as well as other people. Their pay satisfaction was unrelated to what they did, what was expected of them, their motivation, or performance. You might like to speculate on what these findings mean.

of 20 cents per page and this was justified given their lack of experience. In the third condition students were told they had sufficient skills and experience to receive the professional rate. Adams and Jacobsen reported that over-rewarded students caught many more errors than the equitably paid and their conscientiousness was such that they often queried correct material.

Not all our ways of coping with inequity involve revising our input/ output levels. Often we are forced to selectively reinterpret reality to reduce frustration. We are often caught by a sheer lack of alternatives and the inequity of our exchanges is offset by psychological means. We may alter our comparison level and, rather than using well-benefited friends, may choose to compare our lot with the less well off (a much loved tactic of parents trying to get their disgruntled children to eat their vegetables). We may also use perceptual distortion to remain sane. Any number of clinical studies would attest to the defence mechanisms people use to reduce the anxiety they feel in unfair relationships. By way of example, I once had a prisoner client whose reality distortions left him quite disturbed. He was emphatic that his cell mate loved him despite evidence to the contrary and several vicious assaults. He explained this away by insisting that his cell mate had emotional problems and was only relieving the stresses of gaol by beating him up. Further he was happy to help him reduce his frustrations by being a willing victim! Unfortunately this is an all too common occurrence in abusive relationships.

This type of reality distortion does nothing to resolve real resource inequities and often leads to psychological disturbance, particularly depression. Schafer and Keith (1980) surveyed 333 married couples to identify role inequity in being a parent, cook, housekeeper, companion and breadwinner. The greater the perceived over- or under-reward, the more partners reported loss of appetite, sleep disturbances, boredom, decreased sexual libido, loneliness and other symptoms of depression. Schafer (1988) found the degree of psychological distress experienced in inequitable relationships depended on one's self-image, and positive self-esteem went some way towards mitigating the effects of inequity. Unfortunately, perceptual distortion can also have its rewards. Gergen, in a number of studies, found that over-rewarded partners may alleviate guilt associated with overcompensation by simply concluding that their partners' performance is inadequate (Gergen, Morse & Bode, 1974).

One final comment before we leave inequity. Assessing fairness is a subjective process, so our perceptions are the all-important factor in our feeling satisfied or otherwise. Folger (1986) has emphasised that it is the basis on which these judgments are made that determines our feelings. Our knowledge of procedures used in reaching a decision is as important as the outcomes reached. In dividing up the proceeds of a successful business venture, friends are more likely to be happy with their share (whatever it is) if they feel the procedure used to divide the resources was fair. Thus, procedural justice is as important as distributive justice (Cropanzano & Folger, 1989; Kabanoff, 1991). Distributive justice is a major factor in determining whether we will abide by the rules of a relationship or defect.

Dilemmas and defectors

Defections from the social contract

So far we have explored how perceptions of equity can alter the way relationships grow or deteriorate. However, the end of many inequitable relationships reflects the hard fact that not all people are intrinsically fair-minded. Withdrawing from inequitable relationships is not always possible, particularly in competitive work relationships where we may find ourselves stuck with defectors, people who for whatever reason decide to put their own self-interest ahead of the group's welfare. Defection has serious consequences for relationships and has been much studied over the years. Luce and Raiffa (1957) aroused enormous psychological interest with a simple game they called the **prisoner's dilemma**. The game mimics real-life dilemmas where we have to decide whether to cooperate or compete, and proved a useful tool in unravelling factors influencing defections from the social contract. This in turn shed much light on why inequity flourishes in relationships and why they fail. The game goes like this:

prisoner's dilemma
A game for modelling real-life dilemmas where choosing an individual benefit may spell collective disaster.

Two men are arrested by the police shortly after a robbery. The evidence is insufficient to convict either man, and by a clever stratagem the police decide to try for a confession by entering into some apparent plea-bargaining with each, but all is not what it seems! Each suspect is isolated and told that his partner will be asked to "dob him in" in return for immunity from prosecution. The prisoner is told that if this happens he will get eight years on the robbery charge. To avoid this he is asked to confess and is offered a reduced sentence of four years. As an added inducement he is told that even if his mate does not squeal, the police have sufficient evidence to try him on a minor charge which will guarantee a six months' sentence.

The poor suspect is told to hurry up as his partner will probably agree to become Queen's Evidence and testify against him. He is then left to think it over and faces the following choices: Assume his mate will tell all, and confess, or hope he remains silent, and do the same. The full outcomes are set out in the matrix of Figure 8.4. The outcome will depend on the nature of the prisoners' relationship prior to the offence and how much they trust each other. If each stay silent, six months is the maximum they will get. If they cheat on each other hoping the other will stay silent, they stand to get off free and away; however it is more likely that they will both confess and get four years each, the outcome the police are looking for.

Sad as it may be, the most likely outcome is that both prisoners will betray each other. You might like to try this game with some friends and see what outcomes you get and then reflect on what factors influenced the outcomes. For a relatively simple game, the results are often surprising. The complexity of factors underlying an individual's choice are diabolically complicated and there is a vast literature surveying the various motives at work. Rubin and Brown (1975), in an extensive review, found several

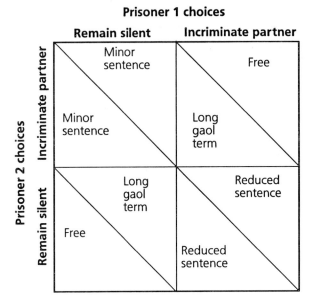

Prisoner 1 choices

Figure 8.4 *Prisoner's dilemma outcomes matrix*

hundred studies looking at various factors and their implications. If my computer search on Psychlit when preparing this chapter is any guide, these studies are probably in their thousands by now.

The sheer complexity of the variables underlying the Prisoners' Dilemma led to a waning theoretical interest until Garrett Hardin (1968) recast it into an environmental context. In one of those rare papers that literally turn scientific inquiry around on its ear, Hardin's "The Tragedy of the Commons" married dilemma games to public morality and environmentalism. Using the old English commons system of grazing cattle on public land as a model, he showed how for individual gain, people would ruin the environment by overgrazing the commons. "Each man is locked into a system that compels him to increase his herd without limit—in a world which is limited. Ruin is the destination toward which all men rush, each pursuing his own best interest." In much the same way, we are destroying our environment because we see resources like air and water as free goods to be exploited by all. The thrust of his article is that an obsolete morality has led us to overbreed. This he sees as the root of all our problems and feels that population growth must be forcefully curtailed. This will never be achieved voluntarily so we need "mutual coercion mutually agreed upon", a modern recasting of Hobbes' formula. He concludes: "The morality of an act is a function of the state of the system at the time it is performed."

Hardin's article aroused enormous interest because why people endanger their own long-term interests in the pursuit of short-term gains had always been a bit of a puzzle to social psychologists. It often seemed as if we were being forced into unproductive behaviour. Extending Hardin's analysis, Robyn Dawes (1973) labelled these situations **commons dilemmas** and

commons dilemmas
Actions which benefit an individual but when added collectively spell ruin to all.

The problem in resolving commons dilemmas is that no one feels responsible for that which everybody owns. This Indonesian hillside is severely eroded precisely because it is common property.
(Photo: Chris Simkin)

social traps
Immediate gains which promote long-term resource depletion.

individual good, collective bad social trap
As in overgrazing where each person's additional cow has just a small extra impact but in sum the environment is ruined.

self social traps
Where the immediate pleasure obscures the long-term harm (as in smoking).

missing hero social trap
We refust to act because no one else does.

John Platt (1973) coined the term **social traps** to identify the factors underlying them. They found **individual good, collective bad traps,** as in overgrazing where each person's additional cow has just a small extra impact but in sum the environment is ruined; **self social traps** where the pleasure of just one more piece of chocolate masks the possibility of future heart disease; and **missing hero social traps** where we fail to act because no one else does. Platt's analysis was crucial in our understanding of dilemmas by pointing out that the timing of reinforcements was their central problem. There is a positive or negative outcome to all these interactions but these have become separated in time some way. For instance, our pleasure in eating chocolate is immediate and overshadows future negative consequences, however horrible. In the overgrazing case our net gain is individual but the collective harm is diluted over the group and offset into the future. In the missing hero situation, we refuse to act because the immediate consequences seem more adverse than some remote future gain. In similar ways, the pleasure of taking small rewards at our partner's expense often obscures the greater long-term damage done to the relationship.

It follows that our attitudes to resource allocation are critical to the health of our relationships, and understanding why people defect would help us promote more cooperative attitudes. Deutsch (1960) in a related study suggested we follow three different patterns: cooperators who maximise joint outcomes; competitors whose outcomes are win–lose; and individualists who maximise their own gains without worrying about others' outcomes. The critical point here was that each personality type saw others as behaving the same way and their outlook became a self-fulfilling prophecy. Many theorists have extended Deutsch's analysis and, unfortunately, it is clear that some people are more likely to defect from the social contract, however it is framed. A number of studies have identified a so-called Machiavellian personality who mimics cooperative behaviour as a way of cheating the group (Christie & Geis, 1970). Other obviously uncooperative defectors are those economists call **free-riders** (Marwell & Ames, 1979; Kerr & Bruun, 1983) and those who enjoy power for its own sake. Even so, most people hold cooperative values as we will see in Chapter Ten.

Why do ordinary people defect? As you can see from Box 8.6 and the Prisoners' Dilemma Game, low-trust individuals have their own individual justifications for defecting (Sato, 1988). Conversely, Robyn Dawes (1980) found that friendship is positively related to both trust and increasing cooperative behaviour. He suggested that temptation and fear were two main reasons for a lack of trust. When we see a way to gain an advantage, we realise others will too, and we act impulsively to pre-empt their taking advantage of us. After all, resources are limited and we want to make sure of our share. In other words, we have to get in first to avoid being taken down; a result confirmed by Bruins, Liebrand and Wilke (1989).

Julian Edney (1979) demonstrated just how widespread this attitude was with his simulated commons dilemma, the **nuts game**. A group of subjects was told that any resources left in a bowl placed in their midst would be replenished at ten second intervals, doubling what was left. Edney said the object of the game was to gain as many resources for themselves as possible and invited them to help themselves anytime after the game had started. Obviously the best strategy was cooperatively to refrain from taking any nuts until the experimenters had exhausted their supply and then divide the spoils. However, in 65 per cent of trials there were no resources left after the first ten seconds. In a test of this result, my students obtained even worse figures with kindergartners; and adults left a few chocolate almonds on only two of twenty trials. Even though we

free-riders
Defectors; those who mimic cooperation to gain its rewards, without contributing.

nuts game
A declining resources simulation game.

The individual good, collective bad social trap argues that we litter because it is easier than disposing of our rubbish thoughtfully. However, if everyone does this the environment will be ruined.
(Photo: Mark Norman)

Box 8.6 *Profile: Margaret Foddy: Trust and the consumption of a declining resource*

Margaret Foddy (BA University of Saskatchewan, PhD University of British Columbia) did her academic training in small groups sociology, and now works in the Department of Psychology at La Trobe University. "I first became interested in the study of social dilemmas when Peter Brann did his Honours and Masters research on the role of trust and social values in resource conservation. I have continued to study the ways in which individual differences in social motives (cooperativeness, competitiveness, altruism interact with structural variables) (e.g. scarcity of resources, communication, information) to influence cooperation. My other research interests include children's self-perceptions of cooperativeness/competitiveness, double standards in the evaluation of ability, and social comparison processes." (Photo: courtesy Margaret Foddy)

Many theorists have argued that the tragedy of the commons is ultimately our generalised expectation that others will act irresponsibly. To pre-empt being ripped off, we make a pre-emptive strike against the resource pool and so create the very conditions that lead others to mistrust us. Our expectation of others' non-reciprocation induces defensive behaviour and non-cooperation, and sets up a spiral of negative reinforcement. How soon this spiralling resource depletion starts depends on the initial levels of trust among those who share the resource. When we trust, we rely on others to act responsibly and, though uncertain of the outcome, we risk something in the expectation that we will benefit from their trust and cooperation. So our expectations are central to trusting others.

This question was just one of the many issues in social psychology which engaged Dr Margaret Foddy. Brann and Foddy (1987) were curious about the impact of generalised expectations on interpersonal trust and resource consumption. They constructed a resource depletion game, a sheep farm managed by five farmers. Each player could remove sheep to sell for their own benefit, but the more that were taken out, the less sheep there were to breed in the next lambing season. Their subjects were tested for trust and then assigned to high and low trust conditions. The two independent variables were feedback (four different rates of resource depletion) and time (number of lambing seasons). Although subjects thought they were playing with four others, in fact deception was used and they were playing against a predetermined computer script. The subjects were randomly allocated to one of four depletion rates and then played five trials over four lambing seasons (20 trials). After each regeneration, subjects were asked "How many sheep do you expect there to be after the next breeding season is over?" Their withdrawal rates and their predictions of others' behaviour were two of the dependent variables measured. A third variable was a post-game readministration of the trust scale to see if trust had altered. Their results are shown in Figure 8.5.

All subjects responded predictably by

consuming more in an optimum regeneration condition, but increased depletion led to lower consumption. When the resource rapidly depleted, high-trust subjects consumed significantly less than low-trust ones, but low-trust subjects were unaffected by the rate of resource depletion and their consumption rates remained the same across all feedback conditions. Comments post-game "elicited answers that reflected the condition they were in". As you would expect, the more severe the depletion rates the less satisfied the respondents: "I tried to sacrifice some of my own sales, the bastards all bought more at my own and the farm's expense."

The important role of trust as a minimal basis for any equitable relationship has been noted by many researchers, and was once again demonstrated in this study. Brann and Foddy's results were as expected, except that the two trust groups' consumption patterns differed when resource depletion was minimal. Brann and Foddy guessed that the low-trust subjects felt they were unable to affect others' behaviour, so their consumption rates did not vary as the resource declined. As their consumption rates were the same across all conditions, this tends to support their explanation. High-trust subjects, who initially consumed more, "could afford to

increase their own consumption, assuming that they, and others, would act responsibly if the circumstances changed". Given that their consumption rates declined markedly in the high depletion condition, it is likely that the high trust subjects were cutting back their usage to "a level that, if others were to follow suit, would be sufficient to permit the resource to be sustained at an optimum level".

Brann and Foddy concluded that both groups' comments at the end of the game indicated an awareness of the commons dilemma, but they differed in how they responded to it. The low-trust subjects kept their consumption rates constant at a level only slightly higher than optimum depletion levels across all conditions. This is the type of response you would expect from those concerned about a problem but feeling able only to control their own behaviour. The high trusters displayed an inverse pattern. They assumed everyone else would be responsible and, when they were proven wrong, chopped back their consumption to compensate and maintain the balance. Unfortunately, extrapolating from Brann and Foddy's data, the combination of responses would have eventually led to no more sheep.

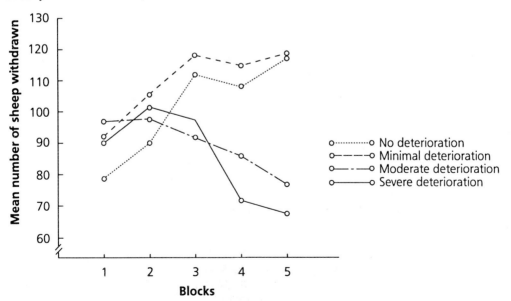

Figure 8.5 *Trust and consumption in a declining commons*

Source: Brann & Foddy, 1987.

Overconsumption of resources is often a matter of a sheer lack of trust
(Photo: Chris Simkin)

repeatedly spelled out the benefits of waiting, similar results were obtained in subsequent trials. It seems we are an untrusting lot.

Edney (1980) cautions that although this is a striking result, individuals differ and many other factors like age, sex, the number of times the game is played, the nature of the reward, the prompts given by the experimenter and amount of communication, all influence our relationships when it comes to allocating scarce resources. Various studies have shown that cooperative behaviour decreases as the value of a resource increases (Mintz, 1951; Kelley et al., 1965). Dawes (1980) also found that as the numbers involved in a dilemma increase, self-interest becomes more dominant and cooperation decreases. Theorists studying groups have noticed a similar effect which they call **social loafing** (Harkins & Szymanski, 1989). As group size increases we feel less responsible for group outcomes and are less likely to worry about our level of cooperation, as we feel we have little real control over outcomes (Kerr, 1989). We will return to this effect in Chapter Twelve but Gifford (1987) suggests that other reasons prompt our defection. As the numbers in a relationship increase, the damage caused by defection is spread ever more thinly and defectors become less visible. Conversely, the harm done becomes less visible to the defectors. It becomes harder to detect and deal with defectors, making it more likely they will get away with their defection; a finding generally supported by Yamagishi's (1988) study of the effects of sanctioning and cooperative behaviour in social dilemmas.

Age also plays a role. Young children have not developed to the stage where they can reason past their own egocentricity. They cannot see the

social loafing
Diffusion of individual responsibility for group task as numbers increase.

benefits of giving up immediate rewards for longer term gains and prefer to get what they can for themselves in simulation games (McClintock, Moskowitz & McClintock, 1977). As age increases there is a slight tendency towards more cooperative behaviour, though this decreases towards adulthood (Gifford, 1982).

In a similar way, the role of sex differences in cooperative behaviour is quite confused. Vinacke et al. (1974) found females to be much more cooperative than males, but Caldwell (1976) found no such difference. Interestingly, Stockard, Van de Kragt and Dodge (1988) found that women were only slightly more cooperative than men and concluded that other experimental variables were more important influences than gender. However, they found that irrespective of whether or not women cooperated, they were more likely than men to see themselves as being helpful and principled and they stressed harmonious group relations, pointing once again to the real differences between our attitudes and actions.

Box 8.7 *Profile: Leon Mann and children's decision-making*

Leon Mann was born in 1937 and educated at the University of Melbourne where he received his Bachelor of Arts (1961) and Masters of Arts (1962), and the Diploma of Social Studies (1961). He gained his PhD from Yale University in 1965 during which time he held the Carl I. Hovland Memorial Fellowship. He was elected a Fellow of the Australian Academy of Social Sciences in 1975.

Following his doctoral studies Leon Mann returned to Melbourne University in 1965 as a lecturer in the Department of Psychology. In 1968 he was appointed Assistant Professor of Social Psychology at Harvard University and, on his return to Australia in 1971, he became a senior lecturer at Sydney University before accepting a Readership at Flinders University in 1972. He was Professor of Psychology at Flinders from 1973 to 1990. He currently holds the Chair of Organisational Behaviour and Decision Making in the Graduate School of Management, University of Melbourne.

Professor Mann is a major international figure in the study of decision behaviour and his book Decision Making: A Psychological Analysis of Conflict, Choice and Commitment *(with Irving Janis) was a milestone publication and is still widely used by researchers and teachers. His publications include over fifty journal articles, ten book chapters and three books. Professor Mann has pioneered the teaching of decision-making skills to adolescents and his GOFER course has been adopted in a number of schools. He is also in the forefront of research on the improvement of decision-making practices of professionals and others.*

He was editor of the Australian Journal of Psychology *from 1981 to 1986 and is presently on the editorial boards of five international psychology journals.*
(Photo: courtesy The Mercury, Hobart)

Chapter Four showed that our beliefs are often not matched by our actions. Yet social psychology relies to a large part on self-report measures to understand attitudes and predict behaviour. Using "hypotheticals" is another way of estimating our reactions to a given situation; but if our predicted behaviour often differs in real life, how useful are self-reported intentions? In 1985, an interesting insight to this question was reported by Professor Leon Mann and Mark Radford from Flinders University, and Chie Kanagawa of Osaka University.

Mann and his colleagues were interested in how collectivist and individualist cultures differ in the ways they achieve distributive justice in group decision-making. In a cross-cultural comparison of Japanese and Australian children, they tested whether children would differ in the rules they used to divide up chocolate rewards between a minority and majority in a classroom. Mann hypothesised that collectivist cultures, like Japan, would use decision rules which protect the interests of all members and predicted children would use taking turns, or a similar decision rule, to effect a compromise between majority and minority. Australian children, brought up in an individualistic culture, would use decision rules that favour themselves or, when they have no personal interest, would favour the majority rule.

Mann and his colleagues proposed to test responses to a real-life problem and felt that individual and collectivist differences would be found in line with their hypothesis. Yet they also wanted to explore how attitudes impacted on behaviour in both real-life and hypothetical situations. By contrasting the two, the researchers would be able to determine if Australian and Japanese children's responses differed when "actual rewards and self-interest were at stake". If there were differences in the rules, then this would enhance our understanding of socialisation and self-interest. Although they made no direct hypotheses about such differences, to ensure maximum insight into factors which might arise they used a social attitudes questionnaire to measure "group loyalty and personal interests, acceptance of various decision rules for resolving competing interests in the group and beliefs about people's willingness to be helpful and altruistic".

They then devised a classroom decision game for primary schools. Twelve-year-olds in Osaka and Adelaide were randomly assigned to a large group (14 children), a small group (7 children), or as observers (the remainder). Students were told only one of the groups, either large or small, would get a chocolate reward on each trial. "The children were asked to indicate how many chances (out of 6 trials) each group should have to obtain the rewards." They first played the game hypothetically and then for real. At the end of the experiment the children were rewarded with two chocolates each for cooperating.

The results were interesting. Group values showed that Japanese children held strong collectivist values while Australians were roughly equally divided between collectivism and individualism. In the hypothetical game both groups of children distributed chances equally between the majority and minority, though the researchers noted a "quite pronounced favoritism to the minority, especially among Australian children" had skewed the results. In contrast, the real-life game gave expected results. From Table 8.3 you will see that both Japanese majorities and minorities followed the collectivist rule, distributing chances equally. The Australian majority clearly were self-interested while a minority split chances equally. A comparison between hypothetical and real-life conditions showed Japanese children to be consistently collective, while in contrast Australians were quite inconsistent.

How may we interpret these results? While clearly Japanese children are collective in attitude and action, the behaviour of Australian children takes some explaining. The elegance of Mann's study becomes apparent when we see all the possible comparisons available to interpret the results. The observers' roles give us some clues. Australian observers, with nothing to lose, favoured an equal say for all in real life. Perhaps Australian children will profess equality as long as they do not risk anything by it. Comparing responses to collectivist values in the questionnaire—"Class (or group) is more important than the individual"—with the decisions they made, further strengthens this view. "When

Australian children endorsed the collectivist value they were less likely to distribute chances equally than children who rejected the value." Mann et al. feel these comparisons show each nationality views group primacy differently. Approximately half the Australian children accept group primacy, yet for them this belief is as much linked to majority rule as to equality. They conclude that these results suggest "that Australian cultural values pertaining to the relationship between person and group may be ambiguous, diffuse or weakly internalised".

If you are wondering if boys and girls differed in their responses, Mann and his colleagues checked for gender differences and there were none in both hypothetical and real-life situations!

Table 8.3 *Use of the "equal-say" decision rule by 12-year-olds in a hypothetical and real decision game*

Sample	Hypothetical decision game % using "equal-say" rule	Real decision game	
		Experimental condition	% using "equal-say" rule
Australia (n = 162)	56%	majority (n = 83)	37%
		minority (n = 41)	49%
		observers (n = 37)	68%
Japan (n = 149)	65%	majority (n = 55)	73%
		minority (n = 28)	86%
		observers (n = 65)	75%

Source: Mann & Greenbaum, 1987.

It is quite clear that our decision to cooperate or defect in simulation games is multifactorial and relatively difficult to predict and yet, if anything, we are competitive. The studies we have reviewed are mostly Western and we have not considered multicultural differences. Perhaps we are among the competitive peoples of the world, bred to strive for achievement. These findings are supported by cross-cultural research. Shubik (1986) compared Australian, Indian and US university students' opinions on how gains from a cooperative game should be divided. Bearing in mind that equality, rather than equity, is indicative of low trust and competition, Shubik found Australians were "significantly more biased toward the equal-split solution than were the other students".

The limits of equity theory

While equity theory has done much to explore why we form the types of relationships we do, it is not without its critics. The evidence is mixed (Clark & Reis, 1988) and some studies show few equity effects. Our next chapter explores the differences between exchange and communal relationships (Clark & Mills, 1979). In communal relationships, where couples are less likely to keep track of relationship benefits, it seems that as trust builds up, they become less concerned with equity. While it is clear that equity is a factor in some relationships and less so in others (Hays, 1989), this is not the only difference. Berg has shown that equity is not necessarily a good predictor of future relationship outcomes. College roommates' feelings of equity did not predict how satisfied they were with each other at the end of the year (Berg, 1984). Similarly, dating couples were surveyed early in their relationship and at a four-month follow-up. Even though those still involved reported deeper commitment, equity did not predict which couples would still be together (Berg & McQuinn, 1986).

Affiliation

affiliation
The need to belong, as distinct from the need to be liked.

attraction
The need to be with others we like.

Abraham Maslow (1971) suggested that on the scale of human motives we have a more powerful need to belong than to be liked. This distinction is reinforced by studies on close relationships. Psychologists distinguish between **affiliation**, the need to belong, and **attraction**, the need to be with others we like (Schachter, 1959). In a model of how close relationships evolve, the first stage may well be the need to affiliate. Human beings form unions to promote their mutual well-being and often relationships do not develop beyond a grudging cooperation. We have all had the experience of working closely with someone we respect but do not like. Perhaps affiliation is the platform on which all relationships close or otherwise are built.

Why do we affiliate?

Beyond stating the obvious that we need each other, social psychology has raised a number of explanations which broadly follow the major theories within psychology.

Biological models

Crook (1981) stressed the evolutionary significance of affiliation strategies which aid group survival. It is clear that affiliation brings its own rewards. Our species has evolved elaborate social codes for promoting cooperative behaviours in the face of individual self-interest. For example, going hungry to share limited food supplies during famines has the longer term benefit of group survival: greater numbers means easier defence, a wider choice of mates, more efficient hunting, and so on. To promote mutuality and self-denial we have had to learn to live together and have probably selected for affiliative behaviours (Wilson, 1975). Research on intra-species violence has thrown interesting sidelights on the limits of aggression and shown the affiliative strategies used to avoid going too far (Lorenz, 1966). While primate work at first threw doubt on an instinctive basis for these behaviours, de Waal's (1989) more recent work gives strong support for well-developed primate affiliative behaviour, including friendship networks, conflict resolution strategies, mediation rituals and primate "marriage". Anthropologists have described the ritualistic formulas used between warring tribes for bride exchanges, third-party trading and limiting hostilities—traits all found in modern international diplomacy. Tribal structures permit people to live together without necessarily enjoying each other's company.

The sociobiological perspective suggests that human evolution has selected for affiliative behaviour. This "herd instinct" and the wider question of group selection underlying it have been vigorously debated since the controversial exchanges in the 1960s between the naturalists V.C. Wynne-Edwards (1962) and G.C. Williams (1966). As yet we have not resolved whether there is an affiliative instinct, but in the first half of this century much research was carried out to determine if there was a dispositional basis to affiliation.

Trait approaches

Henry Murray (1938) is generally credited with putting affiliation on the map as a research area. Though it is only one of his 20 identified needs, along with the need for achievement, it has attracted enormous research interest (Shipley & Veroff, 1952; Schachter, 1959; McClelland, 1975). While Murray rejects traits as such, he proposed that needs are "brain states" which are "caused by arousal" and which lead to "instability". Needs, then, are tension-reduction mechanisms which seek to resolve this unstable state. Needs can be provoked by either internal or environmental factors and may be a combination of both. Along with needs he proposed *press*, the environmental condition that triggers or contributes to their existence. The need to affiliate then is a felt tension and its corresponding environmental press. A lack of friends or a negative press may combine with the positive

Identification with one's team also promotes social cohesion with one's mates.
(Photo: *Rob Pozo*/Macarthur Advertiser)

press of meeting a congenial person, to provoke affiliative behaviour to reduce a felt tension.

Murray speculated that the need to affiliate might arise from the anxiety associated with childhood socialisation to be liked and part of the group, and drew attention to the particular importance of *belonging* to adolescents (Murray, 1938), which Erik Erikson later called affiliative anxiety (Erikson, 1968). Murray is also credited with assigning a hierarchy to felt needs (Murray, 1951). The need to affiliate may well combine with similar needs, such as the need for nurturance, and become an all-powerful motive. Equally, it may be subordinated to other needs which require more immediate satisfaction, as when we reject potential friends after being hurt by a thoughtless comment. Affiliation may also fuse with other needs, such as the need for achievement or order, to produce a person who becomes a joiner of clubs and organisations. Murray's seminal work has had its critics but his insight that anxiety is a major factor in promoting affiliation has spurred further research and given us a good understanding of the fundamental basis of human relationships.

Social comparison processes

social comparison
Comparing our behaviour with others when situations are ambiguous or unclear.

Our understanding of affiliation has been extended considerably by a series of experiments that showed the power of social appraisal as a behavioural influence. Leon Festinger (1954) coined the term **social comparison** to explain why we use other people to judge the adequacy of our own behaviour. He postulated that we all have a need to feel we hold the correct attitudes, are performing adequately and have an accurate perception of reality. Though this is in essence quite subjective, we try to use as many objective measures as possible to ensure we are seeing things accurately. For example, if in preparing for an exam, you are unsure what social comparison theory is, you might write out your understanding and then look it up in a psychological dictionary to see if you have it right. You are using an outside objective measure to measure your understanding. Yet this is only half the answer you need. As a student you are also interested in how well your peers understand the term. That is, you are interested in both an objective understanding and some performance baseline. Obviously you can only get this baseline by social comparison, that is, by being with other people.

Festinger's theory underwent many modifications. An early change was to extend social comparison to include feelings. He felt it would be a powerful modifier of behaviour and emotions and a major factor promoting social conformity. Here social comparison acts to level out our emotional responses. We do not want to over-react and so keep our feelings within the group range. The most important point for our immediate interest is that we are very careful to pick appropriate people to act as our baseline. We want them to be comparable to ourselves. To return to our exam analogy, you wouldn't want to compare your understanding of social comparison theory to that of your local greengrocer's, nor your lecturer's, since neither provides a true standard of comparison.

Anxiety and affiliation

To test the notion that anxiety promotes affiliation, Stanley Schachter (1959), a colleague of Festinger's, conducted an elegantly simple experiment that has become one of the most widely quoted, argued about (and replicated) in the literature. Schachter asked female undergraduate students at the University of Minnesota to participate in an experiment on the effects of electric shock. Each student was individually interviewed by a colleague masquerading as "Dr Gregor Zilstein" of the Medical School's Department of Neurology and Psychiatry, and was randomly assigned to either a high or low fear condition. Equipped with all the forbidding paraphernalia of the medical profession—white coat, glasses, stethoscope, pens and clipboard—and surrounded by ominous electrical equipment, "Dr Zilstein" told the girls in the high fear condition:

> We would like to give each of you a series of electric shocks. Now, I feel I must be completely honest with you and tell you exactly what you are in for. These shocks will hurt; they will be painful . . . What we will do is put an electrode on your hand, hook you into apparatus such as this . . . give you a series of electrical shocks, and take various measures such as your pulse rate, blood pressure, and so on. Again, I do want to be honest with you and tell you that these shocks will be quite painful but, of course, they will do no permanent damage. (p. 13)

In contrast girls in the low fear condition were told:

> I have asked you all to come today in order to serve as subjects in an experiment concerned with the effects of electrical shock. I hasten to add, do not let the word "shock" trouble you; I am sure that you will enjoy the experiment. What we will ask each of you to do is very simple. We would like to give each of you a series of very mild electrical shocks. I assure you that what you feel will not in any way be painful. It will resemble more a tickle or a tingle than anything unpleasant. We will put an electrode on your hand, give you a series of very mild electric shocks, and measure such things as your pulse rate, blood pressure, measures with which I am sure you are all familiar from your visits to your family doctor. (pp. 13–14)

Both experimental conditions were then told it would take ten minutes to set up the rooms for the experiment and they were asked if they preferred to wait by themselves in a comfortably furnished room or to wait together in a common room. Their choice acted as the dependent variable. Schachter predicted that girls in the high fear condition would choose to affiliate more than girls in the low fear condition; that is "misery loves company". The girls were asked to specify their choice or lack of a preference on a form and were then told (to their relief) that the experiment was over, no shocks would be given and they were then debriefed. Schachter's hypothesis was confirmed: 63 per cent of the high fear condition chose to affiliate whereas only 33 per cent did so in the low fear condition. Schachter concluded that people stressed or anxious would affiliate. The mere presence of others is, in itself, reassuring.

Why? There have been various challenges to Schachter's hypothesis and he modified his experiment to clarify this question. What did the girls gain from each other's presence? There are any number of possible explanations. Perhaps the girls sought the company of others being shocked to share experiences and to form a basis for social comparison; or were they just seeking distraction from their anxiety and social support in each other's company? The critical test of these explanations would be when the girls were given the choice to affiliate with fellow sufferers or others. In a subsequent experiment, Schachter exposed two groups to a high fear condition and gave them the choice of either waiting alone, or with other girls who were to be shocked; or with girls who were waiting to see an academic advisor.

His results were unambiguous. Girls given the choice to share a room with others in the same predicament chose to do so. All the girls not given this choice, wanted to wait alone. Schachter concluded that distraction was not the answer, rather, the girls preferred to share their common misery (Schachter, 1959). Though Schachter ruled out distraction as a reason for affiliation, Sarnoff and Zimbardo (1961) questioned whether it was fear or anxiety causing this result. While in a replication of Schachter's experiment with undergraduate men they got similar results, their data led them to question whether anxiety of itself led to affiliation.

Sarnoff and Zimbardo argued that Schachter's results were both affiliation responses. Girls in the high-anxiety condition were experiencing fear and so chose to affiliate. In contrast, girls in the low-fear condition were experiencing anxiety and to avoid their embarrassment chose not to affiliate. They hypothesised that we deal with anxiety by an avoidance, which allows us to reduce our embarrassment and regain self-control.

To test their hypothesis they designed a truly pythonesque modification of Schachter's experiment! Young men in the high-anxiety condition were told they were taking part in a psychophysiological study. They were asked to suck a range of objects "commonly associated with infantile oral behaviour" for two minutes and then be measured. They were shown a range of objects including lollipops, sticks, large nipples, nursing mothers' breast shields, and other similarly embarrassing items. The low-anxiety group were shown pipes, toy whistles, balloons and other innocuous items, no mention was made of sucking, and they were only to place the items in their mouths for ten seconds.

The results confirmed Sarnoff's and Zimbardo's expectations and further replications showed conclusively that when we are asked to do something embarrassing we prefer privacy, particularly when others are watching (Fish, Karabenick & Heath, 1968). We can conclude from Schachter, and from Sarnoff and Zimbardo, that affiliation is not the only way we deal with our problems. Shaver and Klinnert (1982), in a review of the developmental implications of Schachter's work, suggested the group provides a way of clarifying the experiences we jointly share. We turn to others to assess appropriate reactions to the difficulties we face and for emotional support. Shared misery has then both informative and social support functions and this essential social comparison has been demonstrated by many other researchers (Suls & Miller, 1977; Rofe, 1984; Cohen & Wills, 1985; Cutrona, 1986).

Summary

Our species benefits as much from cooperative action as it does from individualism. The tension between these two mainsprings of human endeavour is a key feature of evolutionary theory and of practical social research. Whether our gregariousness and desire to affiliate are essentially selfish or prosocial is addressed in later chapters, but there is no doubt that we have a powerful need to belong.

Human interdependency at its most basic level implies that we have a need to belong which is more fundamental than a desire to be liked. Studies of scapegoating and loneliness illustrate how powerful a need affiliation is. The lonely miss out on the bonding, attachment, social integration, reassurance of worth, sense of reliable alliance, guidance and nurturance which relationships bring. Loneliness may be a state and we all experience periods of loneliness throughout the life cycle, but for some people early social deprivation becomes a trait.

Human gregariousness is built on a platform of intricate interactions which show just how interdependent we really are. Some social psychologists argue that gregariousness is an evolutionary outcome and having learned to cooperate for our mutual benefit we have become a herd species. Learning theorists are relatively silent on gregariousness, arguing that it is merely an outcome of differential reinforcement, though reward theorists have applied basic principles of classical and operant conditioning to model how it might be acquired.

A more fruitful approach to gregariousness concentrates on the benefits to be gained from cooperation. Social exchange theory suggests relationships are finely calculated profit and loss statements. Those that reward us deepen and those that are costly or unrewarding fail. What may be a cost to one may be a benefit to another, and often we exchange reciprocal commodities in the form of goods and services, money, status, information and love. Our relationship's strength is dependent on how satisfied we feel with the exchanges we make and we constantly engage in a cost/benefit analysis to reassure ourselves. This involves our comparison level and what we have in the way of alternatives.

Another explanation of gregariousness suggests we were forced to become gregarious to offset inequalities in the human condition. Here we face the two-rights problem. To live satisfying lives we have to be treated as equals but were not born that way. This leads us into the quagmire of competing claims of equity, equality and fairness. Critics have charged that social exchange theory is limited as it does not take enough account of inputs into exchanges. Equity theory, a modification of social exchange theory, tries to balance the demands of equality, equity and distributive justice.

Promoting equitable relationships is complex. Most relationships work out complex procedural and distributive rules for exchanges. The relative levels of power and trust of each participant alter the balance of the exchange. Partners who see themselves as unworthy may be prepared to accept inequitable exchanges as their due. However, being over- or under-benefited will cause problems in the long term.

Unfortunately, equitable relationships are often a matter of whether we trust others enough to cooperate. Too many cheat and defect from the social contract for us to be comfortable with strangers. The prisoner's dilemma game was set up to model defection and has economic and environmental social parallels in real life. Hardin's commons dilemma was modified by theorists to analyse the conditions of reinforcement which underlie the individual good and collective bad, the self and missing hero social traps. Repeated commons dilemma games have shown us how group size, social loafing, age, sex and nationality variables influence cooperation or competition.

The first stage in the evolution of close relationships is affiliation. Psychologists distinguish between affiliation, the need to belong, and attraction, the need to be with others we like. We can work with someone we respect but do not like, which argues separate etiologies.

There are several theories of why we need to affiliate. Sociobiologists argue it is an evolutionary adaptation which facilitates group and individual survival. Related trait approaches argue that all humans have a need to affiliate which is stronger in some than others.

Theorists interested in social comparison processes take a different tack and argue that we need others to model appropriate behaviour and to provide us with a standard of comparison. The mere presence of others is rewarding of itself and studies show that anxiety increases our need to affiliate.

Recommended reading

Blau P.M. (1986) EXCHANGE AND POWER IN SOCIAL LIFE, Transaction Books, New Brunswick. An examination of how social exchange influences social structures, economics and power relations within groups.

Burgess R.L. and Huston T.L. (eds) (1979) SOCIAL EXCHANGE IN DEVELOPING RELATIONSHIPS, Academic Press, NY. A classic with many articles by leading experts on exchange theory. Papers analyse each stage of relationships from an exchange perspective.

Cook K.S. (1987) SOCIAL EXCHANGE THEORY, Sage, Beverly Hills, Ca. An easily readable treatment of social exchange theory from a sociological perspective.

Daniels N. (1988) AM I MY PARENTS' KEEPER?, Oxford University Press, NY. Subtitled "An essay on justice between the young and old", it is a provocative read on equity, equality and power relations across the generations.

Folger R. (ed.) (1984) THE SENSE OF INJUSTICE: SOCIAL PSYCHOLOGICAL PERSPECTIVES, Plenum Press, NY. See in particular Reis' article on the multidimensionality of justice.

Rubel P.G. and Rosman A. (1978) "YOUR OWN PIGS YOU MAY NOT EAT": A COMPARATIVE STUDY OF NEW GUINEA SOCIETIES, Australian National University Press, Canberra. An anthropological account of social life and customs in one of the most social-exchange conscious of indigenous cultures. Well worth a read if you can find it.

Walster E., Walster G.W. and Berscheid E. (1978) EQUITY: THEORY AND RESEARCH, Allyn & Bacon, Boston, Ma. Another classic which relates equity theory to relationships.

ATTRACTION AND CLOSE RELATIONSHIPS

9

As a young psychologist one of my first jobs was in a clinic for social isolates. These clients, generally in their late twenties or early thirties, had woken up one morning and discovered the opposite sex. Unfortunately, as late developers they had missed out on the kissy-cuddly-fumbly experiences most of us go through in our teens. When they looked around, most other singles were experienced players in the dating game. As social isolates are shy and retiring people with little self-confidence and fewer social skills, finding a mate was quite trying. After a few disasters and with crushed egos they ended up at our clinic.

As we will see, the last person you want to go out with is someone as desperate and inexperienced as yourself. So we doled out equal dollops of confidence and social skills, and returned our clients to practise in the real world. This was usually enough to get them over the hump but one client really gave me my comeuppance! A very short, roly-poly 29-year-old clerk had fallen madly in love with a young typist in his office. He was sure she wouldn't be interested in him and nerved himself up for weeks before finally asking her out. He was so agitated when he asked her, that she freaked out and hid in the Ladies. Crushed and rejected, he became depressed and after three weeks of sick leave was referred to our clinic.

After sorting out his depression and pumping him full of self-confidence, I used a tactic called systematic desensitisation, to overcome his anxieties about using his new-found skills. I asked him to imagine the worst thing that could happen on a date. After thinking about it he said that it would be terrible to take a girl home and on her doorstep not be able to "read" her body language. Did she want to be kissed or not? So real was this dilemma that he was shaking with anxiety as he imagined the embarrassment of not knowing the right moves. I then asked what was the least, but still embarrassing, thing that could happen to him. He thought it would be having a pretty stranger smile at him and not be able to smile back. We then constructed a hierarchy between these extremes and in imagination I took him through each step, visualising the situation and then using relaxation strategies to deal with his anxiety. After several weeks he could face the prospect of reading the signals wrongly and it was time to venture into the real world.

At our Friday afternoon session, I set him homework for the next week. Each lunchtime he was to go down to the plaza outside his office and get eye-contact with two pretty girls and just smile at them, nothing more. After we rehearsed his self-relaxation routines one last time, I sent him off to conquer the world. All Friday night he doubted, all Saturday he worried, all Sunday he panicked and come Monday he was so wound up that he almost needed hospitalisation. Nevertheless, he was determined to succeed and come lunchtime he screwed up his courage and descended to the plaza. Incredibly anxious and shaking with fright he awaited his first opportunity. A poor girl went past and he gave her a death's head grin and leered at her! She scurried off before he could get satisfactory eye-contact and despondent but resolute he tried again and again. The whole plaza was now watching and one victim decided to do something about this strange man. On the opposite side of the plaza was a police station and she hurried in and asked the desk sergeant to pop outside. After a quick glance, he scooped my client up and took him into the station.

The sergeant asked what he thought he was up to and he explained he was told to do it by his shrink! He was then given a phone and told to get his shrink to come and bail him out! Unfortunately I was home at the time and had to go to the station and explain the finer points of behaviour therapy to an increasingly incredulous officer. Much chastened after a stern ticking off, he released us with a warning and we left.

Now you could excuse my client if he called it a day and got a better therapist, but to my surprise he only asked what next? What next indeed! I decided new tactics were required and paid an attractive colleague to be an escort. We three met, carefully scripted a typical date and rehearsed the necessary social skills including a good-night kiss. The next Friday, he rang her up, asked her out, wined and dined her, took her to the movies and then home, and kissed her good night; completely confident it would all go well. It did and half an hour after dropping her off, we all met to discuss the evening and de-role. My colleague was quite frank but also quite complimentary.

Well like all good romances, this tale has a happy ending. Buoyed by his success he apologised to the typist, explained his previous embarrassment and asked her out. Six months later they were married and if that wasn't success enough, they named their first child after me. For years afterwards, I would occasionally meet them coming down the street, he with his arm firmly in hers, smiling proudly as she towered over him.

An overview of close relationships research

This anecdote, while a mark of my embarrassment and his triumph, is also a salutary reminder of love's importance. If love is a many-splendoured thing for poets, it's also a difficult thing for social psychologists to tackle scientifically (Berscheid, 1985). Until relatively recently, love was thought to be best experienced, rather than dissected, and a number of economic, political and religious factors actively hindered research (Clark & Reis, 1988). Even now research on close relationships is not as developed as other comparable areas of social psychology (Maxwell, 1985).

There are many different types of close relationships and from the outset there has been a debate whether friendships are of a similar nature to intimate relationships and what these have in common with family ties. Are all relationships the same at a process level? Do we become bonded in the same way? Is attraction, liking and love a continuum? The scientific study of these questions has yet to fully address the many relationships we are capable of making. Most of the research we review in this chapter has concentrated on romantic/intimate relationships as these dominate the literature. Unfortunately this obscures research into other types of unions. As an area of social theory that only came to some prominence in the middle 1970s, its rapid expansion has led to haphazard growth, making a balanced overview that much more difficult.

One line of inquiry grew out of attitudinal theory and examined those aspects that attract people to each other and predispose them to affiliate; their shared beliefs and attitudes, common experiences and the ties of similarity. Other theorists took a more biological perspective and analysed physical attraction, assortative mating and sex ratios. As Ellen Berscheid (1985) noted, this all led to a concentration of research on the early stages of friendship, rather than the longer term. This research encounters the problems we discussed in Chapter One—social processes are not often readily experimentally manipulated. For this reason it is easier to influence the beginning of relationships, examining the causal factors that promote attraction, while we rely on surveys and longitudinal studies to map the longer term. So we know a great deal about falling in love and relatively little about staying that way.

That marriage as an institution is clearly in trouble in the Western world has focused attention on the other end of romance. Local divorce rates parallel those of Europe and America, and much applied research has tried to identify and prevent problems that destabilise marriage. While it is not inevitable that romance always ends messily, it is clear from research

A perennial question!
(Photo: Armen Deushian/
Macarthur Advertiser)

that satisfactory relationships need a great deal of work over the years (Levinger, 1983). We are starting to see the results of longitudinal studies which give us a clearer picture of healthy long-term relationships (Kelley et al., 1983; Caspi, Herbener & Ozer, 1992) and hopefully this will translate into strategies to ensure their continued health.

So we are left with an unbalanced rapidly growing area of research that is dominated by studies of romantic attachment and divorce and separation. We know relatively little about the processes that keep relationships healthy over the long haul, very little about companionate relationships, virtually nothing of homosexual unions, and have only just begun to seriously study loneliness. As we start our examination of liking, loving and close relationships, it is well to keep this is mind.

The evolution of close relationships

Close relationships research shares much in common with developmental psychology and many researchers are more interested in its developmental aspects than in teasing out its social processes. If you have studied lifespan development, you will recognise many theorists covered in this chapter. Indeed, the boundary between developmental and social psychology blurs at this point, and many prominent Australian and New Zealand social psychologists are also active researchers on the developmental side. We would in particular mention the work of researchers at the University of Queensland as examples of cross-over research. Patricia Noller and Victor Callan's work on families and marital communication (Noller, 1984; Callan & Noller, 1987) and Judith Feeney's work on childhood attachment styles as a predictor of how close relationships develop in later life (Feeney, 1990; Feeney & Noller, 1990, 1991, 1992) are two examples of this type of developmental research.

Reflecting the influence of developmental psychology, one very widely quoted theory is George Levinger's (1980) ABCDE model of relationship development. Levinger proposes five stages of relationship evolution: attraction, building, continuation, deterioration and ending. Obviously not all relationships deteriorate before they end with the death of a partner, but they do change over time.

Gabrielle Maxwell of Otago University developed a model of close relationships' evolution (Figure 9.1) that owes much to the earlier work of Levinger and others (Levinger & Snoek, 1972; Murstein, 1976). Her model emphasises the importance of shared experiences and support as relationships develop. Initial feelings of attraction gradually lead to commitment and then to mutual dependence. Maxwell's model arose from four studies that assessed behavioural indicators of closeness in same-sex friendships, between mothers and their adult children, in young married couples and between couples who had been married for over 20 years. Maxwell developed a

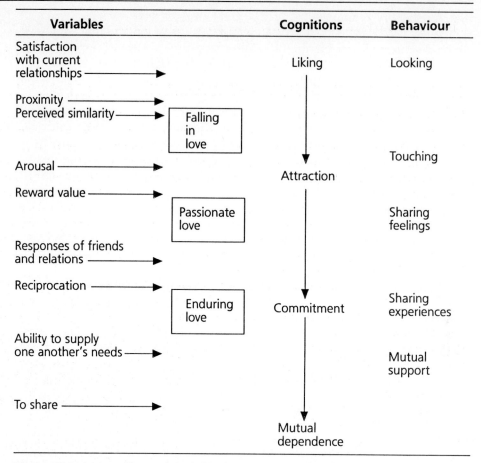

| Variables | Cognitions | Behaviour |

Satisfaction with current relationships ⟶   Liking   Looking

Proximity ⟶
Perceived similarity ⟶   **Falling in love**

Arousal ⟶   ↓
                          Attraction   Touching

Reward value ⟶   **Passionate love**   Sharing feelings

Responses of friends and relations ⟶

Reciprocation ⟶   **Enduring love**   ↓
                          Commitment   Sharing experiences

Ability to supply one another's needs ⟶   Mutual support

To share ⟶   ↓
                          Mutual dependence

Figure 9.1 *Maxwell's model of the development of love*
Source: Maxwell, 1985.

Close Relationships Scale to assess closeness measures such as touching, separation distress, levels of self-disclosure, naturalness within the relationship, attitudinal and behaviour similarity, giving and receiving help, and other variables. Her results showed that "behaviour important for marital satisfaction is virtually identical with the behaviour that is related to the closeness of friendships and the closeness of young adult children and their mothers". This argues that all close relationships have a common behavioural base and that they develop in much the same way though at differing speeds depending on the type of relationship. A mother and child may achieve mutual dependence at the child's birth, while friends may take years to reach similar levels of commitment.

We will return to the progression from attraction to dependence when we consider **interdependent love** later in the chapter. However, we will start at the beginning of Maxwell's model and consider what leads us to become attracted to another.

interdependent love
Love which has become more mutual over time.

Attraction

Box 9.1 *Friends at university*

Try this quiz. Take a piece of paper and list all the friends you have at university. Now read the following and make rough notes on the questions posed.

If you remember back to your first day at uni., chances were you did not know anyone. Hopefully by now you will have made some close friends who will probably last your lifetime. It might be interesting to pause and ask yourself what led to these friendships. Note, you may have made four different types of friends at university: mentors, workmates, close friends and perhaps a romantic liaison or two. The reasons you were attracted to each may differ. For a moment consider why your friends were attractive to you. You might also ask why they were attracted to you.

For whatever reason, certain lecturers will have a greater impact on you and often, particularly in smaller faculties, you will form strong bonds. Did mutual interests bring you together over several subjects, or just the lecturer's warm and caring personality? Perhaps you took hard courses and you were delighted to find him entirely approachable? Or if you admire scholarship, was she the source of all wisdom?

Students mostly stay together throughout their degrees and familiarity leads to friendship. Even so, you may have two sets of friends— those you enjoy and friends with whom you like to work—and there is a difference. What attracted you to your friends—common interests, similar backgrounds, their manner, or did they choose you? What role did physical appearance play? A common tactic for lonely new students is to start up temporary friendships with anybody, and later decide whom you like. Did you? How have your friendships changed?

It is a sexist joke that men go to university to afford a family and women go to start one. Nevertheless, given that we marry people like ourselves, whom we know well, it's hardly surprising that students of marriageable age choose mates from among their peers. As our student population ages, with many more mature-age students at university, perhaps it will decline as a marriage market. Still, if you are romancing a fellow student, or just someone special, you

Going to university is a new experience. New faces may become firm friends and research suggests that some will remain significant throughout our lives.
(Photo: Chris Simkin)

might consider why. How did you meet? What was the context? Who asked whom out? How good is your relationship? What factors attract and repel you? Would you marry this person?

Look over your notes and try to identify common factors that all your friends share. What are you looking for in a friendship? What special features do you want from different types of relationships? You might like to compare your answers with those of this chapter.

Last chapter we considered why you might choose to affiliate and the various needs you met by so doing. In a general way affiliation is the basis of all relationships but sometimes it is a long step from affiliation to friendship. We are often repelled by people who we nevertheless respect and with whom we are affiliated in business or work but would not mix with socially. So what are the parameters we choose within when we select a friend or a mate? The processes of initial attraction are one of the most intensively studied areas of social psychology and had an enormous research following in the 1960s and early 1970s. From this research seven factors stand out as major contributors to another person's attractiveness:

- sheer proximity
- physical attractiveness
- similar beliefs and attitudes
- similar background to ourselves
- reciprocity
- complementarity
- exogamic relief

Propinquity

Friendship equals opportunity. All things being equal we will become attracted to those people we meet most often. Office romances are no less the stuff of legend than "boy meets girl" through a shared circle of friends. As you review your answers to Box 9.1, note how repeated exposure and opportunity played a role in forming your friendships. Geographic closeness (propinquity) is an often unrecognised yet major player in the friendship stakes. In 1987 some of my students surveyed 100 of their peers to see how they had met their paramours. Propinquity certainly played a role. The majority (79%) knew their special friend for some months before dating and 83 per cent met them in familiar settings, at university, through friendship circles, other social groups, work and church. One lucky soul shared a one-hour ride on a commuter train from Gosford to Sydney for six months with the girl of his dreams, whom he subsequently married! Only 6 per cent had met their partners through casual encounters, blind dates or pick-ups. The remaining 11 per cent were waiting for good offers.

These figures are certainly supported by a wealth of research. Anthropologists have led the way with an often quoted study by Bossard (1931) who compared couples' addresses on 5000 Philadelphia marriage licence applications and found proportions decreased markedly the further partners had lived from each other. Festinger, Schachter and Back (1950), in another classic experiment, analysed the friendship patterns of married students at Massachusetts Institute of Technology. Graduate students and their families were randomly housed within one of seventeen, two-storey apartment blocks in such a way as to minimise the effects of previous friendships. Later they were asked to nominate who they were friendly with in the housing estate. Two-thirds nominated friends within their block and of those, a further two-thirds lived on the same floor. An interesting result was the correlation between relationships and the functional distance between friends. Distance also included accessibility, and architecture imposed its own logic. Students who lived at the ends of the floor were less likely to be nominated than those who lived in the middle, or near the staircases. So functional, as well as physical, distance was an important variable.

This result has been echoed by any number of studies that have extended our understanding of propinquity. Priest and Sawyer (1967) measured the distance between rooms in a university dormitory and derived a positive relationship between proximity and friendship; Nahemow and Lawton (1975) found a similar relationship among the elderly in a senior citizens' housing complex; and Schutte and Light (1978) in business offices. Hays (1985) was able to add a predictive note by asking students to nominate two potential friends and then three months later correlated their depth of friendship with how far apart they lived. Byrne (1961) and Segal (1974) found a similar relationship between students seated alphabetically in a classroom and so on.

Why does propinquity lead us to affiliate? A number of theories have been suggested:

Sheer familiarity

Perhaps it is as simple as sheer familiarity reducing interpersonal anxiety and fear of rejection. Having a relationship on a work-a-day basis rubs off any rough edges and gives a comforting sense of involvement that may lead to attraction (Davis, 1982).

The mere exposure effect

Robert Zajonc (1968a) suggested that repeated exposure to any stimulus makes it more appealing, a fact that had been known to advertisers for several centuries. He named this phenomenon the **mere exposure effect**. He demonstrated its power by giving subjects a series of photographs of male graduating students drawn from the Michigan State University yearbook and established a clear correlation between extent of exposure and liking. In a related experiment (Moreland & Zajonc, 1982) showed that it is the mere exposure to stimuli, not the type of stimulus, that increases our liking. Zajonc (1980) stresses that we hold these likes or dislikes in the absence of any meaningful opinion on the stimulus. It is simply continual perceptual exposure increasing our familiarity and hence positive feelings, a factor remorselessly pursued by the advertising industry.

mere exposure effect
Repeated exposure to any stimulus makes it more appealing over time.

Zajonc's findings have been widely replicated (Harrison, 1977; Saegert, Swap & Zajonc, 1973). Mita, Dermer and Knight (1977) hypothesised that we would react more favourably to our own face as we see it in the mirror, not as it is seen by our friends. You will see in the photo on p. 420

(Cartoonist:
Graeme Mitchell)

Which photo do you like best? The one you see every morning in the mirror, or the face your friends see?

that we see a mirror reversed picture of ourselves and this accentuates certain aspects of our profile that are not as obvious to our friends who see us from a different angle. To test their hypothesis, they asked college women to bring along a close friend and then photographed the women. Mita and his colleagues' guess was confirmed. Women shown their photo in normal and mirror reversed perspectives preferred the latter by 68 to 32 per cent. Their friends, however, shown the same pictures, opted for the former, the view they knew best, by 61 to 39 per cent. This lends support to Zajonc's view that repeated exposure, or familiarity, leads to liking.

Similarity

Moreland and Zajonc (1982) also suggested that proximity leads to seeing others as similar to ourselves. This may be as simple as the gradual accumulation of shared experiences that over time binds people together, or may be explained by our desire for cognitive consistency. Festinger (1957) proposed that one of the ways we reconcile dissonance is by rationalising our inconsistent attitudes to reduce the tension between our actions and our attitudes. This may account for our gradual adjustment to situations we find ourselves in. If we move to a new suburb we may find our neighbours trite and unappealing. Even so, they are neighbours and we must develop an accommodation with them. As we don't want to spend time with those we do not enjoy, we gradually modify our attitudes and come to see them as more like ourselves. Tyler and Sears (1977) have shown that even obnoxious people gradually become more appealing if we must live with them. Finally, Darley and Berscheid (1967) found that simply anticipating that we must work with someone increases the prospect of our liking them.

The downside of proximity

While all these points suggest that proximity is a powerful force in promoting attraction, it is not infallible, and the combination of factors at work determines whether it leads to affiliation or revulsion. Swap (1977) showed that familiarity does indeed breed contempt if our initial unfavourable impression of a disagreeable person is reinforced by repeated unpleasant experiences. Larson and Bell (1988) reminded us of our variable need for privacy. High-privacy people can become overwhelmed by the sheer intrusiveness of another person's presence, and repeated exposure may well lead to decreased interpersonal attraction and interaction on their part.

Beauty in the eye of the beholder

Physical attraction

As you will see from Box 9.2, beauty is definitely in the eye of the beholder. It may well be true. Hess (1975) speculated that perhaps the only universal beauty feature is dilated (enlarged) pupils. Hess (1965) retouched one of a pair of otherwise identical photos of an attractive female enlarging her pupils. Most of his subjects, while not being able to spot the difference, were more attracted to the dilated pupils photograph. It has been folk wisdom for several millennia that the juice of certain types of datura leaves when rubbed in the eyes enlarged pupils and increased attractiveness. The ancient Egyptians and Romans used a preparation of the plant, deadly nightshade, in this way and it is still a widespread practice today (Julien, 1985). Actresses in the 1960s used similar preparations to enhance their beauty, which is one of the reasons why films of this period favour close-in shots of the female lead (and the induced myopia probably accounts for their seeming lack of coordination). The active ingredient of these plants, atropine, a neurotransmitter inhibitor, has been a favourite poison of antiquity. The dual uses of the drug are reflected in deadly nightshade's botanical name, *Atropa Belladonna*—*Atropos*, the goddess who numbers our days, and *bella donna*, beautiful woman.

Physiology tells us that pupil dilation is a response to low light and stress conditions, where in both cases it improves visual acuity by letting more light on to the retina. As a stress response, there are interesting ties to research we review later in the chapter that shows that anxious subjects were more likely to attribute their arousal to the presence of an attractive woman and label their feelings love. Gazing at your partner's dilated pupils might lead to misattribute their arousal and to your feeling more positive towards them. Perhaps this indicates why dimly lit restaurants are romantic and why girls with glasses seem to have an advantage over their clearer-sighted sisters; although from an evolutionary perspective this would seem to be selecting for myopia, hardly a great leap forward for the species!

Hess (1975) also found that our pupils dilate in response to things that interest us, and contract for subjects of little interest. Women's pupils

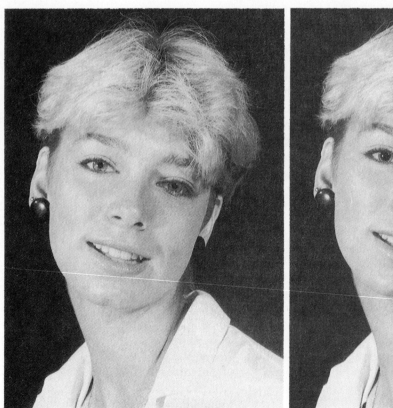

Beauty is in the eye of the beholder. Which of these photos is the most attractive?
(Photos: Chris Simkin)

Box 9.2 *How beautiful you are, my love!*

The old saying that beauty is in the eye of the beholder is certainly true. The following is a selection of quotations from the hundreds I found while preparing this chapter. I have included a diverse spread to show just how broad definitions of love (or at least attraction) really are.

> Thou art beautiful, O my love, as Tizah, comely as Jerusalem, terrible as an army with banners. Turn thine eyes from me, for they have overcome me: thy hair is as a flock of goats that appear from Gilead. Thy teeth are as a flock of sheep which go up from the washing, whereof every one beareth twins, and there is not one barren among them. As a piece of pomegranate are thy temples within thy locks . . . My dove, my undefiled one is but one . . . the joints of thy thighs are like jewels, the work of the hands of a cunning workman. Thy navel is like a round goblet which wanteth not liquor; Thy belly is like a heap of wheat set about with lilies. Thy two breasts are like two young roes that are twins. Thy neck is as a tower of ivory; Thine eyes like the fishpools in Hesbon, by the gate of Bath-rabbim: thy nose is as the tower of Lebanon, which looketh towards Damascus . . . How fair and how pleasant are thou, O love, for delights!" (The Song of Songs, Old Testament, 5th century BC)

Socrates was discussing aesthetics with Critias when Charmides, a great beauty, walked in:

> Now you know, my friend, that I'm not sure of anything, least of all beauty . . . for almost all youngsters appear beautiful to me. But when I saw Charmides coming, I confess I was astonished by his beauty . . . That grown men like us were affected was not surprising, but I observed the same feeling among the boys . . . Now my friend, I was beginning to feel awkward . . . and at that moment his garments opened and I saw his private parts and I was inflamed

> and could no longer contain myself. I thought how well Cydias understood love, when speaking of youth, he warned "Do not let the fawn be seen by the lion or he will be devoured" for I was overcome by a sort of wild-beast appetite. (Plato, c.428–348 BC, *Charmides*)

> Beauty, unlike greatness, we regard as absolute and as a quality; "More beautiful" as the relative. Yet even the term "beautiful" may be attached to something which in a given relation may appear ugly: the beauty of man, for example is ugliness when compared with that of the gods . . . Nonetheless, a thing is beautiful in itself; as related to something else it is either more or less beautiful. (Plotinus, 205–270, *Sixth Ennead*)

> For there is no corporeal beauty, whether in the condition of a body, as a figure, or in its movement, as in music, of which it is not the mind that judges. But this could never have been had there not existed in the mind itself a superior form of these things . . . But even in respect of these things, had the mind not been mutable, it would not have been possible for one to judge better than another. (Augustine, 354–430, *The City of God*)

> Tis likely we do not well know what beauty is in nature and in general, since to human and our own beauty we give so many diverse forms . . . Indians paint it black and tawny, with great swollen lips, big flat noses, and load the cartilage betwixt the nostrils with great rings of gold to make it hang down to the mouth. . . . In Peru, the greatest ears are the most beautiful, and they stretch them out as far as they can by art. . . . There are, elsewhere, nations that take great care to blacken their teeth, and hate to see them white: elsewhere people paint them red . . . The Mexicans esteem a low forehead a great beauty . . . and have great breasts

in such reputation, that they make boast to give their children suck over their shoulders: we should paint deformity so. The Italians fashion beauty gross and massive, the Spaniards, gaunt and slender: and amongst us, one makes it white, another brown: one soft and delicate, another strong and vigorous. (Michel De Montaigne, 1513–92, *Essays II,* "Apology for Raimond de Sebonde")

It is well known that with many Hottentot women the posterior part of the body projects in a wonderful manner . . . and Sir Andrew Smith is certain that this peculiarity is greatly admired by the men. He once saw a woman who was considered a great beauty, and she was so immensely developed behind, that when seated on level ground she could not rise, and had to push herself along until she came to a slope. Some of the women in various negro tribes have the same peculiarity; and according to Burton the Somal men "are said to choose their wives by ranging them in a line, and by picking her out who projects farthest *a tergo.* Nothing can be more hateful to a negro than the opposite form. (Charles Darwin, 1809–82, *The Descent of Man*)

"OFTEN NOTIONS OF BEAUTY ARE MORE THAN JUST IN THE EYE OF THE BEHOLDER".

(Cartoonist: Steve Harris)

dilated when shown pictures of nude men and babies, men on the other hand showed similar responses to photos of nude women. He concluded the eyes were indeed the mirror of the soul and reflected a person's thoughts and emotions. Hess' conclusions have been controversial. Kassarjian (1982), for example, while supporting Hess' findings on pleasant emotions, has found little support for constriction of the pupils when exposed to unpleasant stimuli. However, the weight of research to date supports Hess' findings that enlarged pupils are an attraction to both sexes.

Is there a Western stereotype of beauty?

Despite differences in cultural conceptions of beauty, when we review the research evidence it seems there is a definite Western stereotype, though much of the research still concentrates on female attractiveness, a holdover from the less gender conscious 1960s and early 1970s. In the West it does seem there is a converging view of what is beautiful if recent movies are any guide. Weight is a definite problem, obese people are much less attractive than their slimmer peers, and ideal body size has declined markedly over the last decade (Lerner & Gellert, 1969; Franzoi & Herzog, 1987). Wiggins, Wiggins and Conger (1968) found there was an ideal female body shape. Most men preferred a torso with average bust, medium waist and hips, and small buttocks, and Beck, Ward-Hull and McLear (1976) found a corresponding male stereotype for women. Lavrakas (1975) noted women prefer a V-shaped male with broad shoulders tapering to a petite bottom!

Cunningham (1986) explored female facial attractiveness with male students. Using a combination of yearbook and Miss Universe contestant photographs, he found two preferred profiles. Men substantially agreed that the so-called "child-like" profile of large eyes, small nose and chin were more appealing than small eyes and large nose and chin. They also responded favourably to a more mature profile. Male profiles were judged attractive if they expressed dominance, clear small eyes, square jaw, thrusting chin and so forth (Keating, 1985; Cunningham 1986). Women find tall men (over 175 cm) more attractive than shorter men (Graziano, Brothen & Berscheid, 1978). Unfortunately, the same is not true for women. Shepperd and Strathman (1989) found a strong male bias towards short women and their research confirmed that shorter women had more dates than their taller sisters. Age was important too. In a study of a commercial video-dating service, Woll (1986) confirmed these results and noted that men preferred younger women, while women selected men older than themselves.

These findings would come as no surprise to you. Traditional Western sex-roles have always seen *attraction* as a female task and concentrated efforts on improving what nature bestowed, while male physical attributes are less important in attracting a mate. However, we must be a little cautious in accepting these results at face value. Marika Tiggemann (1992) of Adelaide University, for example, noted that women are usually portrayed as dissatisfied with their body sizes, and as we have noted, what constitutes ideal female beauty has become more anorexic of late. Tiggemann presented 338 young female undergraduates with 9 silhouettes ranging from very thin to very fat, and found that "these women rated their current figure as significantly larger than their ideal and attractive figures, whereas there was no difference in ratings for young men". However, only for older women (over 21) was body dissatisfaction correlated with lower self-esteem. Tiggemann concluded that body weight may carry different meanings for women of different ages. Still, there is much evidence linking beauty with popularity and Berscheid, Dion and Walster (1971) found this link was much stronger for women than men. Further, Donovan, Hill and Jankowiak (1989) showed there is considerably less agreement on what constitutes male beauty, than on female beauty. While this is culturally determined (and there are many cultures where the opposite is true) the reasons why the West sees women as the attractors and the men as the attracted are still speculative.

Are these results due to gender, or sexual orientation? Donovan, Hill and Jankowiak suggest their results are partly due to heterosexual and homosexual men's differing views of what constitutes male beauty. While the determinants of beauty for the gay community are still unclear, Brehm (1985) suggests close homosexual relationships basically develop along heterosexual lines. An interesting study by Deaux and Hanna (1984) threw some light on this question and is reviewed in Box 9.3. While their results confirm the gender–physical attraction link, sexuality was quite important for gay males seeking a mate, more so than for heterosexual men and women, and lesbians.

Box 9.3 *Gay courtship and media mating*

What do gays look for in a mate? Lumby (1978) assessed what homosexual men sought and offered when they placed contact advertisements in the gay media and found a striking interest in physical traits; though Laner and Kamel (1977) in a similar study noted this was less so than for heterosexual men. Both Laner and Kamel, and Lumby, found these ads to be quite specific about anticipated outcomes, usually openly seeking a sexual encounter. In comparison, Laner (1978) assessed lesbian ads, finding that gay women were less likely to offer appearance and more concerned with personality, recreational interests, occupation and intelligence issues, though less so than heterosexual women.

To assess whether this is primarily due to sexual orientation or gender, Kay Deaux and Randel Hanna (1984) assessed 800 ads equally distributed between each gender and sexual orientation. Their findings in large part confirmed Laner and Lumby's studies. While homosexuals and heterosexuals did differ in a few respects, their gender seemed a more important variable. Both gay and straight men were more interested in physical characteristics and attractiveness, while women of either orientation "were more interested in the psychological aspects of a potential relationship", confirming previous research on interpersonal attraction.

Comparisons between heterosexual men and women gave similar findings to research on heterosexual advertisements (Harrison & Saeed, 1977). Men sought youth and beauty and offered security; women sought security and offered beauty in return (though they were less likely than the other three groups to offer their age). Comparisons between homosexual men and women were also in line with Lumby and Laner's research. Homosexual men were less interested in psychological characteristics and more concerned with sexuality than the other three groups, though Deaux and Hanna caution against "overestimating the importance of sexuality to this group". Gay men also stressed physical characteristics and were less concerned with status issues. Gay women, however, stressed hobbies, interests and sincerity, and the authors concluded they had slipped the bonds of sex-role stereotypes and were freer to build relationships on interests and psychological compatibility.

Deaux and Hanna conclude that, irrespective of sexual orientation, gender still plays an important role in mate selection, reinforcing the research we have already reviewed. Nevertheless, sexual orientation also shows some striking features, with gays having differing expectations based on their unique needs. We must remember, though, that people who advertise for a mate may well be an unrepresentative sample of the gay community, though field research has tended to confirm these results (Steinman, 1990).

In a word, everything. There is an enormous amount of research that shows clearly and categorically the sheer unfairness of life's lottery, and again demonstrates the gap between belief and actions. All available research shows the beautiful to be the chosen few. Indeed, their few problems are more related to our envying them, than to their beauty. The irony is that we all realise that beauty is skin deep and, when surveyed, invariably put more sober attributes ahead of beauty on our shopping list for a mate. For example, Wakil (1973) asked 300 Canadian students what they would look for in a marriage partner. Men ranked "attractive, good-looking" 12th, and women 22nd out of a 32 trait list. Several other researchers had similar results (Hudson & Hoyt, 1981; Buss & Barnes, 1986). The problem is research suggests we do not practise what we preach.

What does being attractive do for you?

In one of those studies that seem to trigger an avalanche of follow-on research, Walster, Aronson, Abrahams and Rottman (1966) used a student dance to assess over 700 first-year university students' attitudes towards their partners. On the pretext of computer-matching them with suitable dates, the researchers first gave each student a thorough battery of psychological tests to evaluate their personalities, attitudes and scholastic aptitude. When they arrived for the dance, each student's physical attractiveness was assessed by four independent student researchers, and they were then introduced to their "computer dates" (who in reality had been randomly assigned to them, with the sole exception that the man was always taller than his partner). After two and a half hours, during a break, students were asked to fill out a questionnaire assessing their partner. Some months later the students were followed up to see if they had had any further contact with their dates.

The significant finding from this research is that we clearly prefer attractiveness. The more attractive you were, the more you were liked and asked out again. This was a striking result with a very high correlation between the judges' independent valuations of attractiveness and the students' positive feelings towards each other. We must be cautious in extrapolating from the factors at work in such a short-term relationship to the longer term, but at least in the initial stages of a relationship, it seems, academic competence, maturity, intellect, courtesy, femininity, masculinity, introversion or extroversion, had little to do with your partner's attractiveness. Green, Buchanan and Heuer (1984) studied a commercial dating service which used, among other techniques, a photo matching service to help their clients find a date. The investigators found yet again that physical attraction was a major factor in whom we would choose to date.

Any number of other studies show a similar result. Clearly, all other things being equal, we prefer the beautiful. Indeed it is a particularly unequal contest. The physically attractive not only look good but seem to enjoy an unfair social advantage. Dion (1972) noted adults reacted more leniently to naughty attractive children than unattractive children. Dion, Berscheid and Walster (1972), Langlois and Stephan (1981), Brigham (1980), Moore, Graziano and Millar (1987) and Feingold (1990) between them suggested we see the attractive as altogether happier, as well as being alluring, interesting, well adjusted, sexy, independent, assertive, dominant, together, socially adept and more successful than us mere mortals. Dipboye, Arvey and Terpstra (1977) found the attractive are more likely to be hired. Teachers often rate attractive kids as more popular and intelligent than plainer children with the same academic record. Landy and Sigall (1974) found that attractive college students' poor essays were given a higher grade than the unattractive. Though these are important studies, they pale into insignificance compared to the work of Sudnow (1967) and Landy and Aronson (1969).

In a study reported by Raven and Rubin (1983) Sudnow studied the decision-making processes in a casualty ward for accident cases brought in dead on arrival:

> The most common death in an emergency ward is DOA (dead on arrival). Yet the pronouncement of DOA requires a judgment first by an ambulance driver and then by a physician. Sudnow observed that one patient "was brought into the emergency room with no registering heartbeat, respiration, or pulse—the standard signs of death", but a large team of doctors and nurses, applying heart stimulation and resuscitation, managed to revive an apparent corpse. Yet another patient with the same physical signs and no discernible difference in skin color or warmth was pronounced DOA and sent off to the county morgue. What was the difference? Sudnow observed that doctors were less inclined to make a DOA pronouncement if the patient was younger, well-to-do, nicely dressed, clean, and without the smell of alcohol—generally of pleasing appearance! (Raven & Rubin, 1983, p. 226)

Although this disturbing study did not deal directly with physical attractiveness and how we are treated, it prompted considerable research which did (Efran, 1974; Sigall & Ostrove, 1975; Deseran & Chung, 1979), establishing direct links to attractiveness.

Why do we like the beautiful?

Why do we invest so much in physical beauty and why is it such a powerful factor in whom we choose to relate to? Given that we are all relatively sane, it seems odd that a factor over which we have so little control should occupy so much of our time. Given the billions we invest each year in the fashion and cosmetics industry, it is clearly of some considerable importance. Beyond the obvious that we need to attract friends and a mate, what drives this phenomenon?

When you boil down the research, three factors stand out: we think being with the beautiful somehow rubs off onto us; we feel more self-assured in their presence; and the beautiful may well have something we lack. Dion and Dion (1987) suggest we form our stereotypes on the basis of the just world hypothesis (Chapter Three); the good get what they deserve and the bad, the bad. They suggest we think, somewhat circularly, that attractiveness equals goodness and the beautiful people are getting their just deserts as good people should. By association we hope a little of their image rubs off (Wedell, Parducci & Geiselman, 1987) and indeed, it does seem to. Kernis and Wheeler (1981) have shown that we are more

Why do we seek the company of the beautiful? Do these friends of a successful beauty contestant bask in her reflected glory? Or are simpler factors at work?
(Photo: Barry Price)

positively evaluated when we are accompanied by physically attractive partners, though Bar-Tal and Saxe (1976) demonstrated this works better for men than women.

There is more than an element of circularity in this whole process. We mix with the physically attractive because we perceive them to be socially adept, successful and so on; and because they are perceived that way perhaps they become so; after all, nothing succeeds like success. If everyone is wanting your attention and you seem to be surrounded by beautiful people, then it is likely you will develop a healthy self-concept and go on to acquire the social graces and self-confidence to become a success (Goldman & Lewis, 1977; Dion & Stein, 1978). Langlois and Downs (1979) and Stephan and Langlois (1984) found this process starts early and continues throughout life.

This may become a self-fulfilling prophecy (Chapter Two). Reis, Nezlek and Wheeler (1980) asked students to keep detailed records of their socialising over several months and found strong links between their degree of physical attractiveness, dating behaviour and enjoyment. In a follow-up study, they examined their patterns of interaction, contrasting with those of the less attractive (Reis et al., 1982). Attractive men were more assertive, had a wider circle of female friends, were less fearful of being rejected, and their

Are the beautiful different?

enjoyment of these relationships increased over time. For women, they found no relationship between degree of beauty and social interaction. Attractive women, though less likely to initiate relationships, had just as many friends as their less attractive peers but enjoyed their relationships more. This suggests a complementarity between the sexes which is reinforced by their good looks. Attractive women, though not initiating relationships, are sought after and may enjoy themselves more given their evident popularity. Attractive men likewise seem to be reinforced by their dating assertiveness. It seems that beauty generates its own rewards.

The consequences of being beautiful

It is not all good news for the attractive and a little envy creeps in along the way. Dermer and Thiel (1975) and Cash and Duncan (1984) found we stereotype beautiful women as: conceited, vain, empty-headed materialists and promiscuous; while Bar-Tal and Saxe (1976) found we see attractive men as less intelligent than most; an interesting, if sexist, contrast. Beautiful women may find they have few girlfriends who would wish to suffer by comparison (Krebs & Adinolfi, 1975). In the Sigall and Ostrove study mentioned above, defendants who had used their looks to swindle others received harsher sentences from student jurors. Sigelman, Thomas, Sigelman and Robich (1986) showed that beauty is a handicap for women politicians, "the dumb-blonde phenomenon", and extreme beauty generally carries occupational and other penalties (Hatfield & Sprecher, 1986) (see Box 9.4).

Feingold (1990), in a wide-ranging analysis, found the physically attractive, though socially adept and popular, do not fit the rest of the stereotype we hold of them. This is cause for some concern to the beautiful as there is a fair bit of research that points to the dangers of being continually valued for your looks, rather than more meaningful characteristics (Maruyama & Miller, 1981; Major, Carrington & Carnevale, 1984).

The matching principle

One final comment before we leave physical attraction. Berscheid et al. (1971) suggest we are attracted to those who are of a similar physical beauty and avoid those either more or less attractive than ourselves. They coined the term the **matching principle** to explain this phenomenon and suggested that social comparison (which we discussed in the context of affiliation) is at work in our choice of partners. While the matching principle has attracted its fair share of criticism (Huston, 1973; Curran & Lippold, 1975), many other researchers have found that we choose partners similar in appearance to ourselves (Murstein, 1972; Cash & Derlega, 1978; Price & Vandenberg, 1979). Various explanations have been advanced. The most favoured, which relies on social comparison, suggests we fear rejection by more attractive partners and select according to our estimation of our own attractiveness (Shanteau & Nagy, 1979; Bernstein et al., 1983). Kalick and Hamilton (1986) suggest that assortative mating (see Box 9.5) narrows our choices anyway: the least attractive in our society are left to choose from what is left after everyone else has had their choice, and so on. It

matching principle
We are attracted to those who are of a similar level of physical beauty as ourselves.

Box 9.4 *The downside of being attractive*

You would be forgiven for thinking that the beautiful are blessed but, as we will see in Chapter Fourteen, physical beauty does have a downside. Several studies show that while we usually favour the beautiful, we are more severe in our judgments if we think they have used their beauty to defraud or influence us (Sigall & Ostrove, 1975). Often subtle nonverbal signals such as a smile will influence our initial impressions and subsequent attributions. How we interpret these signals will determine whether we make positive or negative judgments, and these subtle messages may be of profound importance in job interviews, presentations, jury trials and the like.

Professor Joseph Forgas of the University of NSW investigated the interaction of these subtle messages and female beauty on our judgments of culpability. While smiling and physical attractiveness should result in a positive evaluation, would they do so if a woman was suspected of cheating in an exam? Forgas had pictures of an attractive and unattractive woman altered by a graphic artist so that the expressions were happy, smiling or neutral. One hundred and seventy-five psychology students and 248 adult volunteers were then given one of the six pictures and a detailed narrative, including a personal description and the information that "she is suspected of cheating at an exam by allegedly copying the answers of another student". Subjects then rated their impressions on ten general personality traits which previous research found influenced judgments of nonverbal behaviour (Forgas, O'Connor & Morris, 1983). The subjects were also asked three questions: "How likely is it that the target was guilty of cheating?" "How likely is it that the target would cheat in the future?" and "What sort of punishment would you recommend as most appropriate in this case?"

Forgas hypothesised that the main effects of physical attractiveness and facial expression would follow previous research, and they did. Physically attractive targets were viewed more positively across all three facial conditions and were judged more leniently than the unattractive woman. Even a positive facial expression gave similar results. However, the interaction effects for physical attraction and nonverbal expression told another story. For the attractive person smiling made little difference in judgments of self-confidence but a smile on an unattractive woman was seen as signalling submissiveness and under-confidence and was markedly less favourably evaluated than a neutral expression. Attributions of responsibility showed similar effects.

> Once again, we found that smiling had little influence on the degree of responsibility attributed to an attractive target for the alleged cheating incident. In fact, smiling targets were judged to be somewhat more responsible and punishable for the transgression than were non-smiling targets. (Forgas, 1987, p. 484)

Expression was much more important in the unattractive conditions and a positive expression led to markedly more lenient treatment for the unattractive target.

Forgas' results indicate that subtle nonverbal signals are often powerful modifiers of first impressions, and that physical beauty is not always a plus, and highlight the often paradoxical effects of physical attractiveness. Subjects seemed to interpret the interaction between smiling and physical attractiveness as signs of over-confidence, unrepentance and an apparent lack of humility. As Forgas put it: "It is almost as if being good-looking *and* smiling after committing a transgression may be almost too much of a good thing."

Box 9.5 *Assortative mating and Australian patterns of exogamy*

The term **assortative mating** as used by population biologists and geneticists means breeding with a partner selected for similar genetic characteristics. When sociologists and social psychologists use the term, they do so in a less precise way and generally mean choosing a like marriage partner with the intention of starting a family. However, in both usages the term implies that we select a partner on some set of criteria which ensures we end up with someone like ourselves. Assortative mating practices, therefore, are important determinants of marriage and even sex-roles as we will see later in the chapter and incidentally provides us with a test of the matching principle and related theories.

Ken Dyer is a social biologist at Adelaide University with an interest in the biology of racial integration. In 1988 he published a paper on the changing patterns of marriage, marriage choice and mating within different Australian ethnic groups. While the thrust of his paper was to challenge estimates of exogamy (marrying outside your ethnic group) his paper also gives us an insight into who is marrying whom and a test of theory. If the similarity hypothesis is correct then Australians should be marrying those of similar ethnic background to themselves. As you can see from column A of Table 9.1 this is a decreasing trend and on the face of it a rejection of the matching principle at least as far as ethnicity is concerned. However, as

Table 9.1 *The departure from endogamy in Australia*

Year	(A) Australian and UK born treated as a single entity	(B) Australian states and UK constituents treated separately
1961	.510	.642
1962	.507	.639
1963	.503	.638
1964	.491	.629
1965	.482	.620
1966	.466	.616
1967	.449	.604
1968	.412	.597
1969	.398	.589
1970	.375	.581
1971	.360	.376
1972	.349	.563
1973	.331	.552
1974	.325	.540
1976	.312	.527
1978	.296	.515
1980	.295	.506
1982	.278	.492

Source: Dyer, 1988.

The observed number of marriages in which bride and groom are from the same country is compared with the number which would be expected if chance alone determined marriages. The statistic 895–660/1000–660 = 0.69 measures the departure from endogamy. The statistic can vary from 0, an exact match of observed and expected mating, to +1, a total absence of expected matings. During the four post war decades the degree of endogamy in Australia as measured by this statistic has declined steadily.

you can see from column B, the trend is not as simple as it first appears.

Analysing the figures, Dyer concedes there is an Australia-wide trend towards exogamous marriage but it is not as great as other researchers have concluded. His analysis revealed that other studies had confounded country of birth with ethnicity and thus gave higher rates of exogamy than were warranted. For example, a marriage between an Australian-born ethnic Italian and an Italian-born ethnic Italian may reflect nationalism, but hardly exogamy. As you can see from column B, when we adjust for region of birth, assortative mating rates increase markedly.

Dyer found several clear trends in Australian marriage patterns. While the levels of out-marriage increased across all communities, this trend was slower for Italian, Greek and Yugoslav Australians than for Northern European Australians. In the early 1950s out-marriages among men were higher than for women, but by the middle 1970s this was no longer true for Dutch, German, Polish and British Australians but remained so for Southern European Australians. Levels of exogamy for all Australian women, except those of Greek ethnicity, have increased and on this basis Dyer concludes that "women's freedom and opportunities have increased in all groups migrating to Australia", though he cautions against reading too much into these trends.

What may we conclude from this analysis? Certainly in multicultural Australia, assimilation is alive and well as we marry outside our ethnic origins, so to that extent the matching, similarity and familiarity factors of attraction are cast into some doubt. However, Dyer's study was not a social survey, so reasons for this trend are unclear. Assortative mating also works on any number of levels and it may well be that we still choose partners who look, think and act like us, even if they are ethnically dissimilar.

What processes led these two impaired people to marry? Was it simply availability, or the matching hypothesis at work? (Photo: Barry Price)

may also be that we are attracted to those shaped by similar environments as ourselves and research by McKillip and Reidel (1983), Zajonc, et al. (1987) and Hinsz (1989) has shown that couples grow to look more like each other over the years, although a recent study by Caspi, Herbener and Ozer (1992) has cast doubt on this finding.

While there are exceptions to the matching principle and some dissenting research, it is usually explained away using equity theory which we discussed last chapter. For instance, ugly partners married to attractive spouses were thought to offer other compensations to make up for their perceived deficits.

Similarity: Birds of a feather flock together

The term *homogamy*, literally "self-marriage", was borrowed from botany and is used to describe the benefits we derive from affiliating with like members of the flock. Indeed this is almost incestuous as research suggests similarity's greatest rewards come from reinforcing our existing worldview and lifestyle. If we recall the original meaning of homogamy, where it is the study of self-fertilising plants, the implication is plain enough. The norm of appropriateness specifies that we should seek out those similar to us in personality, attitudes, beliefs, religious values, educational level, ethnicity, geographic, political and national affiliations, socioeconomic class, age, background and appearance; which research clearly shows we do (Kerchkoff, 1974; Kandel, 1978; Murstein, 1980; Buss, 1985, 1988; Russell & Wells, 1991). Similarity occurs in two main ways: similarity of attitudes and beliefs and similarity of backgrounds. We look for people who will meet our needs and reflect our upbringing. Like seeks like, and in so doing reinforces itself.

As we can see from the marriage of these two gypsies, we marry those who reflect our own social class, ethnicity and outlook.
(Photo: Barry Price)

Why is similarity important?

There are many reasons why similarity is important, but choosing similar partners rewards us. Our discussion of attraction will have given you a few clues as to why this may be so. Perhaps the major reason for seeking someone similar is that we are less likely to have difficulties if they share our worldview.

Again we see the importance of cognitive consistency and social comparison. Similar people are likely to become friends, as they reinforce our self-concept. We're okay, so if they think the same way they must be okay too and should be friends, otherwise something is out of step. In the same way they provide a standard of comparison for us to measure ourselves against. If I think the world is flat, it's reassuring to find several million other people thinking the same way. In the absence of objective standards, we use other people as a guide for our behaviour, to give us norms of acceptable conduct or social comparison. This leads us to affiliate and, as these people have similar needs, it is likely they will want to too. So similarity breeds a tight circle of self-sustaining rewards. We need them, they need us; we do the same things, so they must be okay; so we should approve of their actions and support them; and we hope they will do the same for us. All things being equal, we cannot help becoming friends.

Attitudinal similarity

Research has established a clear link between attitudinal similarity and attraction (Neimeyer & Mitchell, 1988). Theodore Newcomb (1961), in a pioneering study, gave University of Michigan students free accommodation in exchange for filling out a series of questionnaires, intensively studying how their friendships developed. After assessing their political, racial, vocational, social, sporting and other attitudes, he was able to predict how perfect strangers at the start of the semester would affiliate on the basis of attitudinal similarity. Donn Byrne reviewed years of similar findings in his book *The Attraction Paradigm* (1971). Even when experimenters were using deception, only leading people to think there was some similarity, subjects reported attraction commensurate with the degree of purported similarity (Byrne & Nelson, 1965).

As you would predict, not only is the degree of shared attitudes significant but also the *importance* of those attitudes to the people concerned. For example, it is little use having most values in common while being massively at odds on religion or politics (Clore & Baldridge, 1968). Touhey (1972) demonstrated this effect by assigning couples in a computer-dating simulation on matched religious and sexual beliefs. He predicted that as the degree of similarity increased, so would eventual attraction. His results agreed but there were interesting gender differences. Although the degree of similarity on both variables predicted attraction, men emphasised sexual attitudes, while women felt religious beliefs to be more vital. Still, his results indicated that attitude similarities do lead to attraction provided they are significant ones.

While similarity of attitudes clearly leads to attraction, it does so to increase our potential rewards and minimise conflict. In this light, similarity

---

Box 9.6 *Attitudinal similarity and marital satisfaction*

Attitudinal similarity leads us to select our partners, but is it important in ongoing relationships? Alan Craddock, of the University of Sydney, has long been interested in this issue and in 1991 reported on how similar religious beliefs and role expectations influence marital satisfaction.

Craddock surveyed 100 married and de facto couples that were part of a larger group participating in a marriage enrichment programme. His subjects were aged between 17 and 63 years, had been married an average of 8.5 years and, though hardly a representative sample of Australian couples, were nevertheless a broad sample that included "highly satisfied and highly dissatisfied couples". From previous research (Craddock, 1980, 1983, 1988; Antill, Cotton & Tindale, 1983), Craddock hypothesised that highly religious couples and those sharing equalitarian attitudes towards marital roles would be more satisfied with their marriages than those with dissimilar attitudes.

Craddock was also curious about how marriage structure interacted with attitudinal similarity. Earlier research suggested that marital cohesion and adaptability influenced marital satisfaction (Olson & McCubbin, 1990). He predicted that couples in "balanced" relationships, that were moderately cohesive and adaptable, would be more satisfied than those at either end of these two dimensions. Although Craddock made no predictions about the interaction of balanced cohesion and adaptability and attitudinal similarity on marital satisfaction, his analysis related these two dimensions.

His subjects were administered a 125-item questionnaire which is part of ENRICH, a marriage enrichment programme with a religious basis. The scale measures attitudinal similarity and marital structure on the above dimensions and has nine measures of marital satisfaction. Craddock's results met some of his predictions but also gave a few surprises. He found positive though relatively weak correlations indicating that similar religious orientations were associated with higher levels of couple satisfaction. This finding must be treated cautiously because his sample did not include any highly congruent non-religious couples, as his respondents were participating in what was essentially a religious programme. Craddock was therefore only comparing "couples with similar highly religious orientations to couples with incongruent religious orientations" and it would be interesting to compare these with highly congruent non-religious couples.

As predicted, he found that couples who were very similar in their attitudes towards equalitarian marital roles were more satisfied than those with dissimilar views. Unfortunately his sample had "too few congruent traditionalist couples to examine the differences between them and congruent equalitarian couples", which was surprising given the source of his sample. Also as predicted, "couples whose relationships were balanced on adaptability were more satisfied on all satisfaction dimensions relative to more rigid or more chaotic couples". However, contrary to predictions, balanced cohesion was not related to couple satisfaction, rather "high levels of satisfaction were reported by couples who were highly cohesive and also balanced on adaptability". Craddock speculated that perhaps extremely high levels of cohesion were not dysfunctional when relationships were characterised by flexibility rather than rigidity or randomness.

And how does marital structure intercorrelate with attitudinal similarity as a measure of satisfaction? Well-balanced adaptability and equalitarian-roles similarity correlated positively with marital satisfaction. His analysis indicated that balanced adaptability "is by far the more salient factor" and this accords with the view that shared roles is a characteristic of adaptability. All the other intercorrelations were not significant.

What does this all mean? It seems that Craddock's sample had two groups of highly satisfied people. One group shared highly congruent religious orientations and the other held equalitarian views and felt that their marriage was adaptable and flexible. That there were few correlations between the two groups suggests that religious attitudinal similarity and marital adaptability are not related and that there is more than one reason for a happy marriage.

may well decrease attraction if we feel the comparison is unfavourable. If the person with whom we share similarities is otherwise obnoxious (Cooper & Jones, 1969); a psychiatric patient (Lerner & Agar, 1972); or of low social status (Karuza & Brickman, 1981) then we are less likely to like or affiliate with them. These studies emphasise the importance of perception in social comparison. Byrne (1971) noted several studies where imagined attitudinal similarities were less than couples thought they were. In one study Byrne and Blaylock (1963) assessed attitudinal similarity and found it increased markedly when the marriage partners were asked to predict each other's attitudes!

Does similarity really attract?

Milton Rosenbaum (1986) argued that rather than being attracted by similarity, we are really repelled by dissimilar people and we develop relationships with alike people by default. That is, we discard unlikely friendship prospects and are only left with similar people to choose from. Attraction is thus a negative, rather than positive, process. To test his hypothesis he asked students in an attraction experiment to rate strangers and varied the amount of information he gave them about similarity of attitudes. In one condition strangers were presented as having similar attitudes, in another, dissimilar, and in another, no information about attitudes was given at all. Rosenbaum hypothesised that if it was similarity causing attraction, then there would be little difference between the no-information and dissimilar conditions, the similar stranger would be the most attractive. If, however, dissimilarity causes repulsion, then the dissimilar stranger would be the least liked. While Rosenbaum's data gave some support for his hypothesis, his interpretation was questioned by the research community. Byrne, Clore and Smeaton (1986) inferred that attraction was a two-stage process; first we "weed out" unlikely prospects and then, on the basis of positive factors, choose our friends.

Not only do we seek similarity in attitudes but, just as obviously, in shared backgrounds. Our history moulds our interests such that anyone with a similar background is likely to share the same preferences, live near us, attend the same church, enjoy similar hobbies and so on; all factors that increase the chances of our becoming friends. As obvious as this is, however, it does raise an important point: is similarity of attitudes more important than similarity of interests? Denise Kandel (1978) surveyed nearly 1900 high school children on a variety of issues and found that while attitude similarity was important in forming friendships, shared activities were at least as important, a finding confirmed by Werner and Parmalee (1979).

No doubt similarity plays a very large part in selecting a friend and the literature has hundreds of studies supporting its centrality. Nonetheless, there is also a truism that opposites attract and we all know unlikely couples who seem to be making a go of it. Why are they not repelled by their differences? So far we have emphasised, over and again, that similarity

Complement-arity

reduces conflict and promotes affiliation. Why then would we seek people different from ourselves? Surely this would only increase sources of potential conflict?

At this point we should differentiate between *need compatibility* and *need complementarity*. Some human needs are universal, such as friendship or security, and some relationships are built on shared needs and interests. A couple may find satisfaction in their shared love of hockey and the theatre. Their needs are compatible and this is how similarity works. Other people may have needs that require reciprocal roles. The born organiser needs to organise and the muddled, presumably, needs organising. Their needs are opposite and complementary. Perhaps this is the basis of uneven relationships.

While intuitively it makes sense that all human relationships are some compound of these needs, there is quite an argument about the importance of need complementarity (Winch 1958; Levinger, 1964; Murstein, 1972; Antill, 1983; Strong et al., 1988). Meyer and Pepper (1977) tested married couples on a number of needs and discovered little evidence of needs complementarity, while finding a correlation between marital adjustment and similarity. Better adjusted couples were higher on needs compatibility and apparently suffered less conflict. However, Kerckhoff and Davis (1962) conducted a longitudinal study of dating couples, interviewing them over a seven-month period and did find needs complementarity at work. Couples who became more seriously involved over that time were assessed to determine which factors were leading towards permanence. Couples who had only been together a short time were more likely to be attracted by similar attitudes and behaviour, while longer term couples seemed to rely more on complementarity. The verdict is not in yet but it seems attraction relies on both needs compatibility and complementarity, even if we have more evidence for the former.

Games shows, such as Perfect Match, clearly believe there should be a balance between similarity and complementarity in romantic relationships. Winch's 1958 book, *Mate-selection: A Study of Complementary Needs,* showed how couples consciously sought spouses who they thought had complementary attributes, even when this was not the case. This sometimes imagined complementarity suggests we attach considerable importance to balancing both skills and needs within marriage, though the evidence suggests that complementarity does not in itself guarantee a happier relationship (Katz, Glucksberg & Krauss, 1960; Meyer & Pepper 1977). Nonetheless, we desire both similarity and complementarity as the following ads show:

> I am a 30 year old attractive lady, slim and sexy, 5'8", n/s, no kids, sense of humour, into organic gardening and yoga, seeking soul-mate. Must be 35–45, healthy, not overweight, non-smoker and no kids (no slobs please). Write to Claire c/- P.O. Box . . .

> Are you passionate, able to trust yourself beyond the rules, with a commitment to honesty and adventure? AC/DC o.k. but must be a non-smoker, Anonymous, Box . . .

I am 39, single with 2 kids, 6 and 9 and desperately lonely. Would provide a warm, financially secure life for the right woman (25–35). Please reply (with photo) to Box . . .

Although these ads are fictitious, they closely resemble those found in the personal columns of our newspapers and selected contact magazines. With the exception of "Anonymous" who is clearly more adventurous than most, these ads show a strong support for complementarity as a factor in our choice of partner. Koestner and Wheeler (1988) studied 400 ads from two weekly newspapers and concluded that each sex had strong complementary agendas in their search for a mate. Women sought older mates who would provide financial security and in exchange emphasised their physical attributes. Men sought physically attractive younger women and offered financial and emotional security as an inducement. These results confirm those of Harrison and Saeed (1977), Cameron et al. (1977), Deaux and Hanna (1984), Lynn and Bolig (1985) and Davis (1990), all of whom studied similar advertisements.

If you check the contacts sections of these papers, several aspects of complementarity become obvious. Western stereotypes of physical beauty are well to the fore. Height and weight play a major part. Lynn and Shurgot (1984) found that males who mentioned tallness got more replies than those who did not. In looking over a year's recent editions of *Grassroots* (a local self-sufficiency magazine which, among other things, provides a contact service for alternative lifestyle devotees), I found women describing themselves as: "active, slim, young 30s (40, 50, 60), sexy, attractive, good-looking, blue-eyed and cute". Men reciprocated with what they thought their prospective partners would desire: "professional, financially secure, own home, good job". In accord with all the studies cited above, there was a curious symmetry between what one gave and expected in return. Slim women sought tall men, who in turn sought slim petite women (with photo please); landholders sought homemakers; and fathers, mothers for their children; which demonstrates yet another example of the matching principle at work.

The irony of these ads was in the curious reversal of sex-roles between what each sex wanted and offered, and how they presented themselves. While each wanted fairly traditional things in their prospective partner, they also decided to have "two-bob each way" and give the opposite sex what they felt the new-age person wanted. Men obviously felt women were seeking expressive mates and described themselves as: "sincere, gentle, caring, quiet, stable home-bodies, empathetic and loving". Women felt they needed to be fairly instrumental: "creative, intelligent, decisive, efficient, professional and competent". If you appreciate that these advertisers are trying to attract a mate and were projecting what they hope is appealing, it is interesting to note their gender expectations and the double guessing involved in getting your image right. It is poignant that in one breath women wanted to touch traditional bases and yet appear liberated; while in another, men needed to be seen as nurturant, while still asserting their ability as providers. These general comments agree with both Koestner and Harrison's studies and reflect both complementarity and a shrewd appreciation of universal human needs.

Although on the face of it these ads show a complementarity, the last thing advertisers want to do is meet another advertiser! Darden and Koski (1988) found that placing an ad in the contacts column is still regarded by embarrassed advertisers as a deviant behaviour. Reading through contact ads you come away with a sense of the genteel desperation of lonely people, who have exhausted the opportunities where they live and are hoping to broaden their horizons through the media. Cameron et al. (1977) noted that men in their sample were on average 39 years of age and sought women who were 7 years younger; women, on the other hand, were on average 41 years and sought men about 3 years older. They concluded: "since the average age of the women advertisers was over 9 years older than that desired by male advertisers, a serious problem of matching is evident" (quoted in Kenrick & Trost, 1989, p. 98). This led Bolig, Stein and McKenry (1984) to the conclusion that men and women who placed such ads were not looking for each other! So while you might be desperate enough to use the contacts section yourself, you certainly would not want to meet anyone that desperate!

Reciprocity

We all like to be liked and we are attracted to those who like us. This is so obvious that it has fostered little psychological research in the attraction area. We can see immediately that attraction relies on reciprocity and the psychological processes that sustain it are those we have already commented on at length in our previous chapters:

- Learning theory suggests we will become attracted to those who positively reinforce us and repelled by those who punish us.
- Balance theory promotes attraction. If you like me I will like you in return.
- Cognitive consistency theory indicates we adjust our attitudes to reflect the situation we find ourselves in.
- Equity theory predicts reciprocity in calculating the rewards and costs of a relationship.
- Interdependence theory stresses the mutuality of social comparison.

There is a vast overlap between these theories and they all show the importance of reciprocity (Hays, 1984; Curtis & Miller, 1986; Condon & Crano, 1988). An early study by Backman and Secord (1959) demonstrated that when we are told another group member likes or dislikes us, we are more likely to like or dislike in return, though they found this effect declines over time. Aronson and Cope (1968) showed how a mutual enemy will promote friendship and in-group solidarity (which we discuss in Chapters Five and Twelve). Clark & Mills (1979) detailed the asymmetrical rewards we give and expect from each other underlying various social exchange relationships. And flattery promotes mutuality, even if it is obvious and clumsy (Drachman, deCarufel & Insko, 1978).

Margaret Clark has long distinguished between strictly exchange

Maybe love is simply a matter of liking those who like us.
(Photo: Armen Deushian/ Macarthur Advertiser)

relationships and those more communal friendships in which mutual concern is present (Clark & Mills, 1979). In a series of studies she showed that reciprocity is more than just the hard-nosed give and take of social exchange. That it often leads to genuine friendship was demonstrated in an intriguing experiment by Clark (1984). She paired her subjects with a friend or a stranger and gave them an ostensibly visual recognition task, looking for number sequences. They then took turns looking for and circling sets. She provided them with two different coloured pens and offered a joint reward which they could divide if they wanted on the basis of individual effort. The dependent variable was the use of a red or black pen as a way of record-keeping. Clark reasoned that friends would act communally and use the same pen. Strangers on the other hand would be more interested in individual effort and would use separate pens to record individual contributions, thus demonstrating a more hard-nosed social exchange relationship. Her hypothesis was confirmed, showing that reciprocity is more a matter of concern for your friends, than equity. These results have been confirmed and elaborated in subsequent experiments (Clark, Mills & Powell, 1986; Clark, Mills & Corcoran, 1989).

Exogamic relief

As we end our study of attraction we need to realise that not all people are attracted by the near and dear. Some of us (however few) are attracted by the lure of distant places and exotic people. Indeed it is part of our romantic literature that our fate compels us to fall for the someone who at first repels us. Yet eventually destiny (and/or biology) strikes and we fall madly in love and live happily ever after (for a while at least). Is there anything underlying this so-called Mills and Boon effect?

From a biosocial perspective Kenrick and Trost (1987) have noted that we are attracted to people who are similar to us, and they speculated on the adaptive nature of that similarity. They also noted that we do not choose people exactly like ourselves, for to do so would defeat the evolutionary purposes of natural selection. Human evolution is in part a conscious process. A short woman may marry a tall man in the hope that this will produce children who are taller than herself. This sexual selection ensures the evolutionary pot is kept bubbling and offsets pressures we would otherwise face towards incestuous marriage. Long experience has taught us the dangers of in-breeding and our cultural patterns probably reflect an unconscious exogamy (out-breeding).

At a psychological level it seems we want to "marry the boy or girl next door" but to do so would be slightly incestuous, we know them too well. Though there is a large amount of developmental research into the whys and wherefores of mixed marriages, the extent to which we consciously seek this "exogamic relief" and the role it plays in attraction is more a matter of anthropology and sociobiology than social psychology.

Close relationships: The evolution of the Western romantic tradition

Romantic love is an ideal with a limited history in the West and is not shared by most cultures on our planet (Ford & Beach, 1951). The ancient Greeks, though held to be the source of our modern ideals of romantic love, disdained close emotional relationships with women and saw family life as a duty and little more. Day-to-day life for Greek women was hardly romantic. To the Romans must go some credit for liberalising male–female relations, though this was a more sexual, than romantic, equality. With the advent of Christianity within the Roman world, women's social position rose further, but following the Augustinian view, romance and sexuality were seen as distractions limiting a purer spiritual love. This notion lasted some 800 years and saw sex and marriage as duties performed by those unable to pursue a higher way.

It was the rise of Islam from the seventh century onwards that gave us a new view of the romantic ideal and some of the greatest love poetry and romance epics of the Western world. The great poet, Umar ibn Abi Rabiah of Mecca (died c. 712), freed up a ponderous pre-Islamic style and started a romping, vigorous, amorous love poetry, which still has a contemporary flavour. At the same time the **Medina Circle** was writing idealised love poetry with a more courtly aspect, that later had an enormous impact on the West. As it developed over the next few centuries, the *Udhrah* style was chivalrous, the lover seeking an unattainable beloved, a pure and mystical love object. For example, the Persian *Vis o-Ramin* epic (c. 1035) foreshadows *Tristan and Iseult*, the great romantic epic of mediaeval Europe. There is little doubt that these two strains of Arabic love poetry have profoundly influenced the way we see romantic love. The diffusion of Islamic love poetry through Moorish Spain is yet another intellectual debt we owe the Arab world.

Medina circle
Seventh century Islamic love poets who wrote in a romantic style later popular in the West.

The courtly romances of twelfth century Europe eventually shook Augustinian attitudes towards sexuality, though the courtly ideal was equally chaste and only of concern to the nobility. It did, however, invest women with desirable qualities that had to be sought after (and withheld). Equally it gave women a revised status as sex objects. In addition to their economic and familial value, they became male adornments. From the fifteenth century attractive women begin to feature as important props to male status, whereas before their beauty was seen as an added plus to an otherwise pragmatic relationship. By the Renaissance, increased leisure brought on by rising affluence gradually led to attitudes towards love and sex similar to those of our "traditional" sex-roles.

Since the middle seventeenth century, the West has cycled through periods of relatively liberal attitudes towards romance and sexuality, interspersed with more puritanical times. The Renaissance led to the Calvinism of the Puritans, followed by the relative prurience of the Enlightenment, and in turn the purism of the Victorian era and its twentieth century abreaction. An interesting view of these periodic changes in Western attitudes towards women, romance and sexuality, was put forward by Marcia Guttentag and Paul Secord (1983) who suggest it has to do with sex ratios and availability of marriage partners (see Box 9.7).

Despite these fluctuations we have a clear idea of romantic love. Lantz, Keyes and Schultz (1975) suggested that five ideals typify the Western romantic tradition and in their original and follow-up studies (Lantz, Schultz & O'Hara, 1977) found a steady increase in these themes in American magazines between 1741 and 1865:

- Love at first sight.
- We will only ever have one true love.
- True love will conquer all.
- There is a perfect match for us.
- We must be true to our hearts rather than our heads.

However unsatisfactory these beliefs are as a basis of mate selection, and whatever the reasons for changing views of Western romance, there is no doubt that it is all quite odd by world standards (Dion & Dion, 1988). In most cultures, marriage is a hard-nosed affair with little room for the frivolity of romance, and arranged marriages are the rule.

Box 9.7 *Too many women?*

William Novak in his book, *The Great Man Shortage* (1981), first publicised the strictly mathematical problems many women face in finding a mate. Ours is an essentially female species and tends to produce slightly more female live births. Glick (1977) pointed out that, given this imbalance and other social factors, approximately 7 per cent of all women remain single and this proportion has stayed fairly constant over this century. If you subtract the higher proportion of gay males than lesbians, this man shortage just gets worse, and the available stock less and less appealing. As one 37-year-old woman commented to Novak, "I'm no longer waiting for a man on a white horse. Now I'd settle for the horse" (quoted in Santrock, 1986, p. 426).

Marcia Guttentag and Paul Secord (1983) in their book, *Too Many Women: The Sex-Ratio Question*, set the cat among the pigeons by suggesting that women's roles were linked to their relative availability. Although we produce roughly even numbers of both sexes, the relative balance may be disrupted by disease, famine, war, migration, deaths in childbirth, infanticide and many other physical and cultural variations. They suggested that when women are in oversupply society becomes more permissive, and men's commitment to love, marriage or indeed to any one woman through life would be lessened. As a compensation for a shortage of men, cultural mores will become more tolerant of extra-marital affairs, and divorce will become more easily available. Women's sex-roles will become more egalitarian as was seen in an extreme case during World War II, when many Australian women worked in heavy industry as welders, riveters, boilermakers and foundry-hands.

In contrast, when the ratio is the other way, as during the Victorian period when women were scarce, sex-roles will reverse as women will become a valuable commodity. Romantic love and motherhood will be idealised and femininity encouraged. Women are valued as sex objects and eagerly sought as mates. Society would emphasise marital commitment and women would be protected and encouraged to remain in the home. During extreme shortages, in some cultures they may become tradable commodities

Guttentag and Secord tested their hypothesis against data from the ancient Greeks to the modern day, across many cultures and found much historical support for their theory. They speculated that because men hold dominant positions in most societies they will be able to control the economic and political structures and dictate the shape of close relationships. Given the continuing oversupply of women since the last war, Guttentag and Secord suggest that women are again devalued and the sharp rise of postwar feminism is a reaction to male indifference and women's feelings of powerlessness and being taken for granted. As yet little research has tested this theory, but it is an intriguing insight into male–female relationships (see Secord, 1983, and South & Trent, 1988, for a further study of sex ratios and women's roles).

Romantic love: Liking or loving?

Intuitively we feel we must like someone before we fall in love with them, but is this so? Is loving just a more intense form of liking, or are they qualitatively different experiences? Rubin, a pioneer researcher in this area, thought they were related, but different, attitudes. He felt lovers were more intimate, attached and caring than close friends. Rubin (1970, 1973) tested his hypothesis by compiling a list of statements that spoke of either love or liking. He then asked several hundred students to rate their feelings towards their amours and a close non-romantic friend of the opposite

---

Box 9.8 *Attitudes to romantic love: An Australian perspective*

A moment's glance through your neighbourhood newsagency will confirm the strength of the Western romantic ideal, but is it real for us? Sung-Mook Hong and Cathryn Bartley (1986) at the Darling Downs Institute in Queensland set out to find out. They surveyed 587 rural Queenslanders aged between 20 and 30 on a variant of Dion and Dion's (1973) Romantic Love Scale and compared their scores with their sex, marital status, education level and the duration of their longest love affair, to see how each influenced romantic love.

Overseas studies suggest that romantic love diminishes over time as couples become disillusioned, or their relationship makes the transition towards a more mature companionate love. Hong and Bartley, to their surprise, found that "duration of love proved to be the best predictor of romantic love attitudes", or put another way, the longer they were in love the more romantic they were. They interpreted this unexpected result as evidence of a greater pragmatism towards love: "Perhaps, then, Australian young adults are more inclined to believe in romantic ideals when a relationship based on romantic love has been successful."

As we will see in Box 9.9, in some respects men are more romantic than women and so it was in this study. Males were found to have significantly higher love scores than females. Hong and Bartley attribute this to changing sex-roles which gave women more flexibility and the chance to "adopt more practical attitudes towards love while men retain more traditional attitudes".

Education also predicted one's attitude to romantic love, with the results confirming overseas studies showing that the more educated you are, the less idealistic you become. You might like to reflect on Hong and Bartley's explanation for their result: "This can probably be accounted for by the pragmatic emphasis of higher education and the cynical attitudes adopted by many tertiary students."

Finally, neither age nor marital status was significantly correlated with romance. Hong and Bartley suggest that their respondents' limited age range may explain this result. Given their age, most had not been married for long and so "were unlikely . . . to have changed their romantic attitudes"—yet?

---

sex. If love and liking were separate states, then the lists would differ and so they did, leading Rubin to conclude that, at the very least, these close relationships evolve differently.

Rubin extended his research by developing written liking and loving scales, using descriptive statements like, "Most people would react favorably to . . . after a brief acquaintance" (liking statement); or "I would do almost anything for . . ." (loving statement). He gave these to each member of 182 dating couples at the University of Michigan who had been going out for an average of one year. The scales measured each person's perception of their partner or friend's personal adjustment, maturity, responsibility, likability, attachment, intimacy and caring. Rubin predicted that his subjects would have high scores on both liking and loving scales for couples, and a high liking but low loving score for just close friends. The results confirmed his predictions, suggesting they were measuring different emotional states.

The scales gave several interesting results. As you would expect, there was a strong correlation between saying you are in love and a high loving-scale score. When high scorers on *love* and *romantic idealism* were followed up six months later, the scales successfully predicted more intense relationships and eventual marriages (Rubin, 1973). Liking scores on the other hand were less predictive of eventual marriage. In an interesting sidelight Rubin found some distinct gender differences. Men and women reported liking their same-sex friends equally but women said they loved them significantly more than men said they did. While there were no differences in the amount each sex said they loved each other, women were less liked by their dates! Rubin concluded women's friendships were closer, more intimate and expressive than those of men's, who reserved their love for sexual relationships, a point supported in a follow-up study by Dermer and Pyszczynski (1978). Rubin's predictions were further confirmed in the laboratory, where traditional predictors of attraction like eye contact and closeness were stronger for high scorers than lower scorers. We will return to this distinction a little later.

What is love?

Who knows? Some argue it is a grand passion; others that it is a gentle drift from sex to satisfaction; while many feel it is all a matter of commitment and interdependency. We will examine these views in turn but it seems there are many more dictionary definitions and several psychological theories of love waiting in the wings. In an exhaustive coverage of its forms, the American sociologist John Lee (1973) carefully studied films, pulp romances and the serious literature, love poetry, philosophical insights, and how lovers saw themselves, before deriving the six types of love shown in Figure 9.2. The first three, **eros**, **ludus** and **storge** are primary love styles and Lee argued that we are rarely just one type of lover and our loving displays a mixed style with these predominating.

eros love
Erotic, intense passionate love.

Ludus love
Non-serious, flirting, uncommitted love.

storge love
Platonic, friendship-based love style.

pragma love
Pragmatic love style.

mania love
Possessive and obsessive, fixated love.

agape love
Altruistic, selfless love.

game-playing love
Non-serious, flirting love style.

Hendrick and Hendrick (1986) devised a questionnaire to assess Lee's styles of love and found some empirical support. Hendrick and Hendrick found the sexes differed in their love mixtures, men were more eros and ludus, while women were more **pragma** and storge. Irrespective of sex, there was a tendency to move from eros to storge and/or pragma love, as you would expect given a gradual waning of passion and a shift to a more companionate style of loving as the relationship matures. In a further test, Hendrick, Hendrick and Adler (1988) found students were similar in their love styles and several combinations were predictors of relationship satisfaction. Couples high on eros (and for women storge) were more satisfied with their relationships, while **game-playing** style was a predictor of relationship difficulties.

In another approach to typifying love styles, Sternberg proposed the triangular model shown in Figure 9.3. Sternberg was interested in the interactions between various types of love and argued that three factors, intimacy, commitment and passion, are in a dynamic tension. The growth of relationships can be modelled by varying the axes to represent degree of commitment (Figure 9.3(a)). The total overlap of a couples' triangles represents the state of their relationship (Figure 9.3(b)) and by combining triangles we can predict how congruent partners are (Sternberg & Barnes, 1985). While this is a persuasive theory, it is little more than a tool for visualising relationship dynamics at this stage.

Figure 9.2
Lee's six styles of love
(*Cartoonist: Steve Harris*)

The grand passion

The experience of being in love has long been the stuff of literature and poetry. Each generation seems to feel a need to publicly declare (and intimately describe) their love for each other. Even with the coming of records, radio, television and videos, this urge still appears to be unsatisfied,

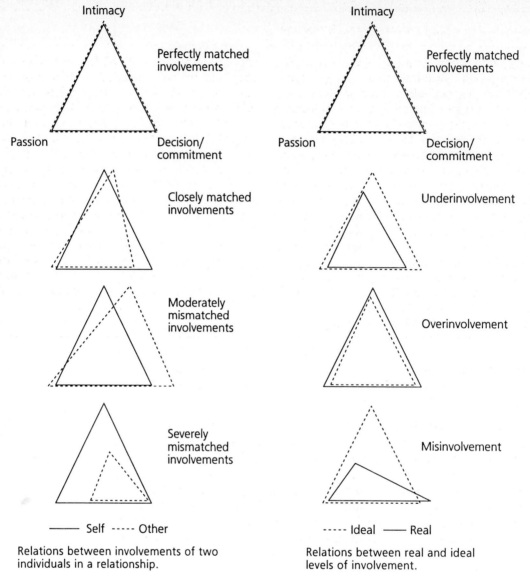

Figure 9.3 *A triangular theory of love*

Source: Sternberg, 1986.

though we are no longer in any doubt about what love is all about. If purple prose is any guide, falling in love is a passionate affair, as this safely anonymous piece suggests:

The Poet grasped her hand and gazed into her eyes. Startled she drew back. Now? Was this the right time? Was he the one? She felt her blood heat as he challenged her womanhood. She trembled. He looked again. A mad desire to fling herself into his arms, to abandon and

Box 9.9 *Are women more romantic than men?*

Contrary to popular stereotypes, in some ways men are more romantic than women. Rubin (1973), as one example of many similar studies, found that men completing a scale measuring the romantic ideal, agreed that strong emotions were a good guide to love's intensity; that you should marry whomever you loved regardless of their background; and that love conquers all. Women were more cautious. Sung-Mook Hong (1986), of the University of Western Sydney, found that young Australian women had significantly less idealistic views of romance than men, though they did not differ on a pragmatic view of romantic love.

Yet women report greater subjective feelings of being in love (Dion & Dion, 1973), while Hill, Rubin and Peplau (1976) found that women were more likely to end unsatisfactory relationships, and Fletcher (1983a) found that women coped better with separation than men and saw themselves as less responsible for the relationship's end. What does this confusing picture mean? Rubin (1973) suggested that ultimately mate selection is the crucial factor in these sex differences. Woman's relative vulnerability in the mating game suggests she needs to be fairly clear-eyed and pragmatic about her options and what she is getting herself into. Once the decision is made however, it is an all or nothing commitment. In this light, you might like to speculate why the single best-selling item in Australian and New Zealand publishing over the last few years was romantic fiction, closely followed by cookbooks, both sold almost exclusively to women.

abase herself grew until she quit the path to madness and fled thru the sun-dappled grass. The Poet cried "Stay!" and she felt her heart would burst with love, but on she ran.

Well might the poet burn with an unquenchable desire for his beloved. Various researchers have noted this temporary derangement (Berscheid & Walster, 1974; Walster & Walster, 1978; Hatfield, 1988) and attributed it to a high state of autonomic arousal, analogous to the stress response. You will recall Schachter and Singer's two-factor theory of emotion (Chapter Three) which suggests that emotions are simply high arousal states to which we attach appropriate labels. When we become aware we are physically aroused, we look to see what is causing it and then attribute our arousal to an emotional source in our environment. Is this what is happening when we fall in love?

There is a fair amount of research that supports Berscheid and Walster's (1978) belief that passionate love (as distinct from other sorts) may well be an attribution made in a state of high arousal, when we are also in the presence of a "species-specific sex object" at the appropriate time in our development (Ruse, 1979). Unfortunately, there is little psychological research on the triggers and timing of passionate arousal, and what few studies we have are mainly developmental. We do have some clues, however, from misattribution research. Dutton and Aron (1974) performed several studies that support an arousal-attribution view of love. In one experiment they asked men who were anticipating receiving electric shocks how attracted they were to a pretty female experimenter. Their responses were compared to other men in a low-anxiety condition. The highly anxious men were

Is it necessary to believe you are in love to be in love? (Photo: Mathew Munro)

much more interested in dating her, pointing to a link between arousal and romantic interest.

In what became a classic experiment of social psychology, Dutton and Aron stationed an attractive female researcher near a narrow, swaying, 120-metre long suspension bridge over a deep ravine on the Capilano River in Canada. She asked young men, who were unaccompanied by female companions, to help with some research after they had crossed the bridge. They were given an ambiguous drawing of a woman and asked to write a short story about it. After they complied, she gave her phone number and asked them to ring her if they wanted further information on the study. The measures were the amount of sexual content in the stories and how many phoned her later. Their responses were compared to those of a control group who crossed a sturdy bridge over a shallow drop in the same park. Dutton and Aron correctly predicted that men in the high-anxiety condition would be more sexually aroused, and this would show in story content and subsequent phone contacts, than responses in the low-fear condition, or when approached by male experimenters. In later replications women subjects reacted in the same way to male researchers.

Dutton and Aron argued their subjects misattributed their fear of the bridge for sexual attraction towards the pretty experimenter. This study has its critics. Kenrick and Cialdini (1977) argued that such experiments were more about reinforcement than attribution. They argued that Schachter and Singer's work showed the source of the arousal must be unclear if misattribution is to occur, and backed this up with a series of experiments showing that misattribution does not occur if the fear stimulus is obvious (Kenrick, Cialdini & Linder, 1979). In Dutton and Aron's experiment they suggested that, the presence of an unruffled experimenter (who presumably had already crossed the bridge) had a calming, reinforcing effect, and any arousal felt would have been correctly attributed to the bridge. Unfortunately, this does not entirely explain away the differences in romantic attraction between conditions. Conversely, it may be another instance of "misery loves company", fear promoting affiliation which then reduces anxiety. These explanations, while probably contributory, are unlikely to be the whole story as an experiment by White, Fishbein and Rutstein (1981) showed.

White and his colleagues were interested in assessing the effects of various forms of male arousal and two-factor attribution on potential romantic partners. Male subjects were aroused by running on the spot, or watching comedies or violent movies. They were supervised by either an attractive or unattractive female confederate and later rated her attractiveness. The results showed that all the arousal conditions found the pretty woman more attractive, and her plainer colleague less attractive, than the ratings of an un-aroused control group. Similar results from Valins (1966), Stephan, Berscheid and Walster (1971), Carducci, Cozby and Ward (1978) and White and Knight (1984) suggest a role for two-factor theory and romantic attribution, as in many of these experiments there was little fear associated with the arousal, yet increased romantic interest occurred. So Kenrick and Cialdini's reinforcement theory cannot be the sole explanation, a point they acknowledge.

From sex to intimacy

George Levinger's theory, which we introduced at the start of the chapter, proposes a gradual evolution of relationships from first contact to their eventual dissolution. The movement from attraction towards a deeper relationship has many causes but three—self-disclosure, intimacy and a gradual build-up of trust—predominate in the literature and are deeply intertwined.

Altman and Taylor's (1973) theory of **social penetration** argues that one of the important determinants of a healthy and developing relationship is reciprocal self-disclosure. Apart from the **intimate-stranger effect**, which suggests we will freely disclose our most intimate details to perfect strangers we will never see again (Jourard, 1968), we rarely share private information with people we hardly know. Notwithstanding our hesitancy, if we share personal information with strangers, we will gradually reveal ever more intimate details and, if they reciprocate, the relationship becomes more intimate (Hendrick, 1981). The deciding factors are the rate and depth of disclosure. Too much too soon and we are repelled, too little too late and we feel our friend is cold and disinterested (Derlega, 1984). Davis (1976) found that as subjects spent more time together, reciprocity and intimate

social penetration
Progressive reciprocal self-disclosure leading to a more intimate relationship.

intimate-stranger effect
Disclosing our most intimate details to perfect strangers because we will never see them again.

Box 9.10 *Profile: Garth Fletcher: Attribution in close relationships*

From my undergraduate days onwards I have been fascinated with the idea that laypeople, just like social psychologists, develop their own theories to explain, predict and control social behaviour. Indeed, all my subsequent research and theorising, in the US and New Zealand, has been directed towards trying to understand the nature of such naive theories and the role they play in social judgment and behaviour. I have been especially interested in investigating social cognition, including attribution processes in close relationships, partly because such settings represent real world, complex social contexts, chock full of cognition, affect and social interaction. Such research holds the promise of informing our understanding of both basic social cognitive processes and the way in which relationships function in the real world.
(Photo: courtesy Garth Fletcher)

Garth Fletcher teaches social psychology at Canterbury University, Christchurch and has an international reputation based on many studies of attribution in close relationships:

As we saw in the Dutton and Aron experiments, attribution plays an important role in initial attraction and its influence penetrates every aspect of our lives. The way we see our partners influences the degree of satisfaction we feel and, perhaps more importantly, the way we understand our relationships. As Fletcher et al. so elegantly put it:

> Love and intimate relationships are of central importance in people's lives. Hence it is hardly surprising that on occasions we invest considerable cognitive activity in evaluating the personalities of our prospective partners, predicting the future of our relationships, trying to understand why they are deteriorating or becoming more successful, and so on. (Fletcher, Fincham, Cramer & Heron, 1987, p. 481)

While this may seem obvious, Fletcher and Fincham (1991) remind us that the obvious often masks important questions. As we saw in Chapter Three, attributions may serve different purposes, so in their 1987 study Fletcher, Fincham and colleagues explored the timing and precise nature of the attributions we make in close relationships. Students at Illinois State University, who were in heterosexual dating relationships, completed a multifaceted questionnaire which probed several aspects of their relationship. As expected, more attributions were made when relationships were in their early stages, when subjects spent time analysing just what the relationship meant to them. Attributional activity was also greater "when important choice points or changes were occurring" such as considering whether to commit oneself, or marry. Equally, when the relationships were going sour, or were unstable, more time was spent analysing what was going wrong and deciding whether to end the relationship.

As predicted, the type of attributions made determined how one saw the relationship. Students who "were happier, more committed, and in love", also tended to see the relationship in more interpersonal terms, to rate each person's inputs as equal, and to make fewer external attributions for relationship maintenance. Students who saw their partners as doing most of the work in maintaining the relationship were less happy, committed and in love. Unrequited lovers who saw themselves as doing all the work in keeping the relationship afloat "reported high levels of love, moderate levels of commitment, and low levels of happiness".

Attributions also influence outcomes. In following studies, Fletcher found that attributions for relationship maintenance are causally related to relationship happiness. In a study of spontaneous attributions in happy and unhappy dating relationships, his results suggest that happy partners make causal attributions that enhance the relationship, "whereas people in unhappy relationships produce attributions that are more likely to maintain their current levels of unhappiness" (Grigg, Fletcher & Fitness, 1989).

Happy partners made external locus of control assumptions about their partner's negative behaviour and saw it as "more a function of outside circumstances, less intentional, less global, less stable and less controlled by partners". These attributions, the reverse of those made by unhappy partners, let them excuse negative behaviour and take a more optimistic view of the relationship. A further study replicated these results and found that depression, or general explanatory style, was unrelated to the link between the types of causal attributions and levels of happiness in close relationships (Fletcher, Fitness & Blampied, 1990).

In summary, Fletcher's studies show that responsibility and causal attributions clearly influence the degree of commitment, love and satisfaction we feel in relationships and these in turn influence how relationships grow, or decline (Fletcher, 1983a, b).

self-disclosure increased, but Altman (1973), Morton (1978) and Won-Doornink (1985) noted that at a certain level of friendship it decreased. This suggests that as trust develops, close friends become less worried and hence less concerned about tit-for-tat disclosure. You might like to reflect on this when we discuss Cunningham and Antill's findings on the evolution of marital satisfaction a little later in the chapter.

There is a large volume of research following on from Altman and Taylor (1973), which bears on the link between self-disclosure, reciprocity, the growth of intimacy, and liking. Self-disclosure of itself does not create intimacy, rather it engenders feelings that you are valued, appreciated, trusted and cared for (Reis & Shaver, 1988). We will return to this point and the reciprocity norm in our discussion of prosocial behaviour in Chapter Ten.

It is a truism that the closer the friendship or marriage the more intimate it becomes; yet the link between intimacy and closeness is not as automatic as you might think. Several models of this link provide little agreement but the major decision points are clear enough. Secord and Backman (1974) and later Backman (1981) proposed a four-stage model. First comes the exploration or discovery stage, where large amounts of information are gradually exchanged and the costs and benefits of the relationship are evaluated. Next we enter the bargaining stage, where we try out the relationship and establish its rules. This is a time of trial and error as we find out what works in the friendship. If the benefits seem to outweigh the costs, we move to a commitment and interdependency. Finally we reach the institutionalisation stage, in which the relationship becomes exclusive, mutual and forward-looking.

Trust is another factor promoting closer relationships. Larzelere and Huston (1980) developed an interpersonal trust scale and surveyed more than 300 university students, recently married couples, and random selections from a phone book. Figure 9.4 shows the results for seven different types of heterosexual relationships. Rempel, Holmes and Zanna (1985) also gave couples scales that measured several factors promoting trust and intimacy. They found that as trust increased, so did love. Other related factors, such as predictability, dependability and faith, were also positively correlated, indicating that being in an on-going relationship breeds security based on experience and a considerable personal investment.

Companionate love

Obviously not all love is passionate and it would be wrong to conclude that the gradual waning of passion in a relationship signals it is heading for the rocks. Rather it may well be a natural and healthy adaptation. Walster and Walster (1978) distinguished between passionate love and compassionate love, a deep abiding attachment felt in close relationships and not only by lovers. In 1981, Jane Traupmann and Elaine Hatfield (formerly Walster) outlined a transition from the early stages of an intimate relationship, to a more companionate love that featured less sheer emotion and sexuality but a more deeply felt trust, intimacy, mutuality and companionship. Perhaps after the intensities of a full-on romantic period,

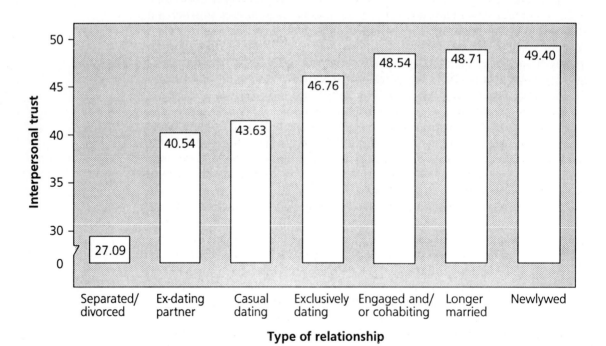

Figure 9.4 *Interpersonal trust scores for seven types of relationships*

Source: Adapted from Larzelere & Huston, 1980.

The passage of time often leads to companionate love based more on shared experience than romantic attachment. (Photo: Mark Bramley)

couples settle down for the long haul and in so doing discover another side to themselves and become friends in much the same way that any close relationship develops. This makes some sense when you consider that the sheer self-absorption of the romantic period leaves little room for much else.

Traupmann and Hatfield felt that equity theory accounted for the development of companionate love. They traced the married lives of 400 women aged from 50 to 92 years through several decades of marriage. They focused their research on the reciprocal balance between husband and wife, assessing the costs and benefits for each. In virtually all cases complete equity or balance was the norm. In 52 per cent of cases women reported complete equity throughout their married lives and most others had only minor hiccups along the way.

However, do we go through life calculating the pluses and minuses of our partners? An intriguing theory from Macquarie University researchers, John Cunningham and John Antill (1981), suggests otherwise. In what virtually amounts to an extra step from companionate to interdependent love, they suggest that as partners experience the tension between a concern for themselves and a concern for the other, they gradually discover and resolve obvious, and hidden, incongruities in their relationship and an interdependence grows which replaces equity with mutuality. As the couple shake down together over time, they increasingly identify as a couple and this mutual identity becomes the focus of the partners' concerns. The relationship is no longer concerned with equity or even really equality but rather identity:

"Equality", undoubtedly a prerequisite for friendship, is not quite the proper term, as it implies that the pie is divided into halves and each partner takes his/her own half away. "Identity" is a preferable choice: love implies that the satisfaction of the pie-eater can be savoured just as much as by the pieless partner. This contrasts sharply with the marketplace metaphor, where the tit-for-tat swap of one resource for another means that each trader loses what he had initially but acquires sole possession of the new resource. In love, both delight in one's gain and both grieve at one's loss. The loved one's pleasure and pain become one's own. (Cunningham & Antill, 1981, p. 32)

Mate selection

Now we grasp the nettle and try to sort out the thorny issue of whether we are dealing with learned preferences or biological sex differences in human courtship practices. We will cover the wider theoretical issues in Chapter Eleven, but at this point we face several immediate questions about this most intimate relationship. We need to note distinct gender differences in how we choose a mate and what sexuality means within intimate relationships. We also seem to follow different reproductive strategies and whether this is cultural, or biological, or some mix of the two, is unclear. What is clear is the bitterness of the debate between those who support either the biosocial or experimentalist learning perspectives.

Right at the sharp end of the battle between the experimentalist and biosocial camps within social psychology, which we discussed in Chapter One, are divisions over human reproductive behaviour, its origins and purposes. On a global basis the following facts are quite clear. Despite the infinite variety of cultural overlays, in every society men and women mate, bond and live in families (Daly & Wilson, 1979). Women equate sex with bonding (though not necessarily marriage), while men on the other hand distinguish between marriage and sex (Hinde, 1984; Kenrick & Trost, 1989). Throughout the world women prefer mates with strong bread-winning credentials, while men seek physically attractive mates. Men look for younger women, while women are attracted towards the maturity and experience that comes with age (Buss, 1989). Women also have a much greater interest in child rearing; and there are several universal courtship practices (Eibl-Eibesfeldt, 1975). From the biosocial perspective these studies suggest human mate selection and reproductive strategies start from an innate base and reflect our evolutionary history. This has not been a popular outlook and has faced substantial challenges, but the debate continues.

From a learning perspective, these are all acquired behaviours based on principles of reciprocity, equity, social exchange and mutual reinforcement. Although the biological bases of behaviour are acknowledged in passing, human mate selection and marital behaviour, in this view, are largely learned. We are moulded by our culture. It tells us who are acceptable mates and what courtship practices are allowed; it controls marriage and sets sex-roles. Unfortunately, this perspective has a continual problem with the sheer diversity of human experience and changing social and sexual values and behaviour, which necessitates new mini-theories almost weekly to keep abreast of changes in the human condition! This has led more than one theorist to suggest that social psychology desperately lacks an underlying unifying theory (Harre, 1979) and led Kenrick and Trost to comment facetiously:

> As social psychologists tuned to proximate environmental variations, we have often been frustrated when our carefully manipulated situations seem to produce effects that can only be detected with the aid of a square root transformation on a special contrast performed under an electron microscope on Windsorised data. In that context, we have often been impressed with how differently males and females have acted in our studies of attraction and sexuality, even when we did not expect them to . . . If one stays within the bounds of the traditional social psychological explanations, each sex difference is explained as due to another arbitrary norm thrown onto the heap of random historical accidents that need to be drummed into the heads of the next generation by rote. (Kenrick & Trost, 1989, pp. 112–13)

It is clear the battle-lines are drawn though, as we will see, Kenrick and Trost suggest a model that embraces both perspectives. We will now review the sociobiology of mate selection which, though hotly contested, at least has the coherence of having been tried in the fire. The sociobiology of courtship rests on four assumptions:

- We have inherited sexual selection tendencies.
- Our aim is the broadest distribution of our genes.
- Women have less reproductive chances than men.
- Each sex follows different reproductive strategies.

We are the products of countless generations of successful reproducers. Whether their success is incorporated into our genes is the most controversial aspect of evolutionary biology. If we accept for the sake of argument that having many children equals reproductive success, then certain things follow.

Women have more biological limits than men in passing on their genes. Given lengthy gestation periods, high infant dependency and the limited time between menarche and menopause, women have fewer chances to pass their genes to offspring. As conclusive genetic success is having your offspring reproduce in turn, women will have a higher investment per child than men, who have many chances to reproduce. Men are fertile throughout their adult years and reproductive success is limited only by the availability of sexual partners. This leads to either male monogamy, or competitive promiscuity. While men are also interested in maximising their reproductive success, they face a choice of strategy not shared by women. Should they play the odds and father as many children as possible, or increase their investment in a lesser number, whom they will then support until puberty? Obviously our culture has organised all of its social supports and sanctions to promote the latter course. From the sociobiological viewpoint it is *because* they have this choice, that gender differences arise.

So, from a biosocial view, women have only one reproductive strategy available to them. They have to follow what biologists call a K-strategy, seeking mates who will share a high investment in a small number of children. Men on the other hand have both K and R strategies (lower investment, higher fecundity and promiscuity) available to them (Rushton, 1987). Although sexual practices in all cultures recognise female vulnerability and organise social norms to enforce K strategies, behavioural differences between the sexes ultimately may be traced to men having two evolutionary alternatives.

We may take this further and see what it suggests for sex-roles and social organisation. Because males are constrained to adopt K-strategies, they will want to ensure that any offspring they protect are their own and this, together with women's reproductive vulnerability, will promote male dominance. Precisely because women have less reproductive chances they will be more interested in child nurturance to ensure their own genetic destiny, and so child-rearing is a biologically programmed female behaviour. One of the poignant sidelights of this theory is that the very forces in society enhancing women's options—equal opportunity, career expectations, sexual freedom and contraception—all lead to smaller families, which further limit women's reproductive chances, perhaps accounting for some of the anxiety many liberated women feel.

The biosocial perspective argues that love is intimately tied to reproduction. In our species the K strategy suggests we place many resources in few offspring. (Photo: Armen Deushian/Macarthur Advertiser)

Critiques of the biosocial perspective

We will return to this theory in our next chapter when we consider the role it plays in reciprocal altruism and critique it in our discussion of gender (Chapter Eleven). You can see why this theory is as controversial as it is and why it was rejected by many theorists. For example, Rom Harre (1979), an influential European social psychologist, while lamenting the limitations of social psychology and calling for a new unifying theory of social processes, starts his book with a considered attack on sociobiology to ensure that it does not command the high ground in the subsequent debate. Critics reject this theory out of hand as either too simplistic or as latent sexism. Yet a more considered view points out that human social evolution has been one continual struggle to transcend the limits our biology imposes on us. As we were not designed with wings we invented aeroplanes, so in much the same way, even if the biosocial view is correct this does not mean we have to organise society that way, only recognise our nature for what it is.

If we turn to social exchange theory for an understanding of mate selection, as possibly the most credible alternative to the biosocial perspective, we are still left with the suggestion that romantic alliances are basically self-gratifying, perhaps even longstanding communal relationships where we have simply learned to trust our partners and take equity for granted. All have rules based on reciprocity and equity. The experimental tradition has proposed any number of mini-theories to explain mate selection from this perspective. When we look for Mr or Ms Right, we are also seeking an equitable exchange of resources and mutual reinforcement (Dermer & Pyszczynski, 1978).

As noted above, it's quite a problem aligning all these theories into a coherent whole. For example, I reviewed 12 differing accounts in preparing the "What is Love" section, before just deciding I liked John Lee's theory best. Perhaps one way of rescuing social psychology from this mild academic anarchy is to adopt Kenrick's suggestion that the social exchange and biosocial views be combined into one **reproductive exchange model**. He argues that taken at face value they appear contradictory but similarities in their underlying assumptions provide differing but complementary levels of meaning (Kenrick & Trost, 1987, 1989). Does the evidence agree? We will venture an answer by looking at some of the more puzzling aspects of mate selection.

reproductive exchange model
A model of mating and partner choice which combines sociobiological and social exchange perspectives.

An ideal mate

Our ideal mate is someone just like ourselves, as we discovered while exploring attraction. While we are not after clones of ourselves, by assortative mating we shuffle through the available stock for a best fit and make the best of whatever opportunities present themselves (Buss, 1984). Although this is all very predictable, there are a few surprises when we view the data from the biosocial perspective. In this penultimate section, we will review two of Kenrick's mate selection studies which have come up with a few surprising results.

(Cartoonist:
Graeme Mitchell)

Sexuality

Sex is a key component of romantic relationships though sexual activity declines as we age (Blumstein & Schwartz, 1983). Without a doubt the sexual revolution has changed our attitudes to premarital sex and it is now the expected norm. For example, Christopher and Cate (1985), in just one of many studies of university students' sexuality, found that 83 per cent of their sample were sexually intimate. In another major study of intimate relationships, Peplau, Rubin and Hill (1977) surveyed 200 dating college couples and found that 80 per cent believed premarital sex was completely acceptable for those who love each other. Eighty-two per cent had slept with their partner and roughly 40 per cent had done so in their first month together. Fairly casual sexual encounters are clearly part of getting to know your partner, but what do they mean for each sex?

The biosocial perspective predicts there would be distinct differences between men and women's attitudes toward sexual activity. Presumably in monogamous societies, where a high premium is placed on female virginity, courtships are longer as men risk more in selecting a mate and need time to study their prospective spouse (Barash, 1977). In contrast, permissive societies like our own would give men a number of opportunities to test sexual compatibility and so sex would be less important as a factor in mate selection. While in permissive societies females would have as many opportunities for sexual intercourse as men, they also have more at stake in choosing the right mate. So sexual relations would be less of a casual matter to them, a factor found by Peplau and her colleagues and in a number of other surveys (Hendrick et al., 1985; Buss & Barnes, 1986).

Kenrick, Trost, Groth and Sadalla (1988) tested this hypothesis by asking college men and women about their minimum acceptable standards for a partner's intelligence and other traits as a relationship developed through a first date, to sexual relations, a steady dating and marriage. The results of their study and a replication are shown in Figure 9.5 for the intelligence variable. As you can see men were quite happy to have sex with someone who did not meet the minimum requirements for a first date, while females steadily increased their minimum demands as the relationship became more serious.

Age

In our discussion of complementarity, we examined personal column ads to find out what we were looking for in a mate and such ads are a powerful source of psychological insight into mate selection. Still, we must be a little cautious with this material, as by definition these advertisers are so far unsuccessful in the mating stakes and perhaps they are a self-selected and unrepresentative sample of the entire romantic population. With this reservation in mind, it was clear that women sought older men, who in turn sought younger women. Why? We can explain this by saying it is the norm in our society for women to seek older men but this is just a circular explanation. After all, our evidence for this theory is that the statistics show it to be so!

The biosocial perspective suggests that women will select mates who in prospect can make a greater investment in their children and research has clearly shown this to be the rule across all cultures (Buss, 1989). Obviously there is a correlation between age and material wealth, so women should choose mates who have higher educational qualifications, job security

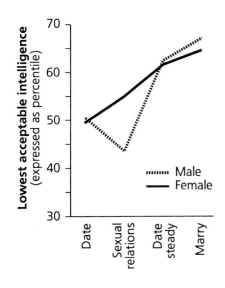

Figure 9.5

Minimum percentile intelligence required by males and females at different levels of relationship

Source: Kenrick & Trost, 1989.

and seniority, and other age-related aspects of maturity. Yet, the social-exchange perspective can just as easily explain this as a simple exchange of resources. When we bring the two perspectives together they become a much more powerful theoretical tool.

While clearly women seek older men, and the reverse, this does not tell us much. To expand our understanding of age effects in mate selection, Kenrick and Keefe (quoted in Kenrick & Trost, 1989) examined contact advertisements where the advertiser's age and a preferred maximum and minimum for a partner were specified. The results are shown in Figure 9.6 and yield striking support for the biosocial perspective. As you can see there was a big difference between the sexes. Women's preferences remained fairly constant from the twenties to the sixties. They sought a mate up to a decade older than themselves. Men's preferences on the other hand changed markedly. Younger men were less worried about their partner's age, preferring someone within 5 years either way of their own. As they aged however, their stated preferences clearly were for younger women until men in their sixties were advertising for women up to 15 years younger than themselves.

This study shows that simple exchange equations are less revealing than they might be. Using the researchers' reproductive exchange theory, the results become more revealing. Kenrick says the results may be "explained parsimoniously":

> . . . by assuming that reproductive value weighs heavily, and by noting that older females have increasingly fewer years left. (Kenrick & Trost, 1989, p. 112)

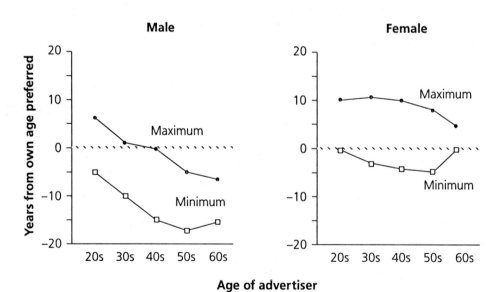

Figure 9.6 *Minimum and maximum age preferences specified by males and females in singles advertisements*

Source: Kenrick & Trost, 1989.

Endings

As we close our discussion of close relationships, we end with a word or two about falling out of love. Obviously from the divorce statistics that turn up weekly in our media, we have a problem keeping it all together. So now we close with the observation that expectations of relationships rarely consider their ending.

Somewhere between the clichés "Till death do us part" and "The course of true love never runs smooth" lies a truth. Levinger (1980) suggested the end of all relationships is deterioration and decline. The death of a spouse or close friend has a sharp focus and grieving finalises our relationship. In many others, internal problems gradually weaken "the ties that bind". Levinger (1976) saw the termination of unsatisfactory alliances involved a fine calculation of benefits and costs, the possibility of alternatives, and impediments to dissolution. Many relationships continue uneasily poised between the joys of ending and costs of continuing on, with neglect the final outcome. Rubin, Peplau and Hill (1981) noted men suffer more from the end of romantic alliances and suggest this is related to their relative insensitivity to problems within the relationship. The time you have been together is correlated with the degree of disruption experienced when you break up, which prompted the researchers to remark, "The best divorce is one you get before you get married" (Hill et al., 1976).

While research into the termination of intimate relationships is still in its infancy, clearly we still need whatever joys such relationships brings. Over 43 per cent of Australians and New Zealanders who divorce will remarry within three years.

Summary

Research on close relationships is relatively new to social psychology and only really started in the early 1970s. Most theoretical interest has been on love and we are only slowly starting to understand the differences between close friendships, family bonds and intimate relationships. Research is quite patchy and we know a fair bit about the beginnings of close relationships but little about their evolution over the longer term and how they end.

Levinger proposed a model of relationship development that starts with attraction and progresses through building, continuation, deterioration to ending. Attraction involves proximity, similarity, reciprocity, physical beauty and complementarity variables. Proximity or propinquity leads us to like others because they become familiar and the mere exposure effect guarantees that will make them more attractive. Proximity also interacts with similarity to increase liking.

Physical attractiveness is a very important factor in forming relationships. It is more important to males than females in our culture, though this is not the case everywhere, arguing it is a socially acquired characteristic. However, gay and heterosexual men show more interest in the physical beauty of their partner than gay and heterosexual women, arguing an innate sex difference. Whatever the reason, a clear stereotype of Western beauty is emerging.

The beautiful are especially favoured and are seen as more competent, mature and more desirable than their less favoured peers; and this often becomes a self-fulfilling prophecy. Our obsession with beauty sometimes leads to clear discrimination in their favour and research suggests we think being with the beautiful rubs off on to us somehow; we feel more self-assured in their presence; and the beautiful may well have something we lack. The matching principle says we choose friends and partners who are as attractive as ourselves. Being beautiful is a positive experience unless others think we are exploiting our looks.

Similarity is also important in attraction. Homogamy suggests we try to reinforce our self-image by finding identical partners, who will mirror us. Processes of cognitive dissonance reduction and social comparison enhance our search for the similar other and reduce potential sources of conflict within the relationship. Similarity on major attitudes is important in attraction, although some research suggests that it is attitude dissimilarity which leads to attraction but it is more likely that we first reject those who are unsuitable and then choose friends from the remainder.

Complementarity seems opposed to similarity as a factor in attraction but theorists distinguish between needs-compatibility, or similarity, and needs-complementarity. Most theorists would argue that close relationships combine both elements though the research evidence is mixed.

Reciprocity argues that we will be attracted to those who reward us. This point was covered in detail last chapter and several theories (learning, balance, cognitive consistency, equity and interdependence theory) explain how reciprocity leads to affiliation and friendship.

Exogamic relief, or out-breeding, suggests we would be attracted to dissimilar partners as this would minimise the deleterious effects of in-breeding. However, there is little research on psychology of exogamic relief at this stage.

Marrying for love is a peculiarly Western phenomenon. The Western romantic tradition has slowly evolved over the last 2000 years and is still foreign to most non-Western cultures. Roman liberalism, Arabic love poetry and mediaeval courtly lays all contributed to its evolution but it was not until the Enlightenment that economics and changing social roles ushered in modern love. Sex-ratio imbalances may have contributed to the historical waxing and waning of romantic sentiments and to changes in women's roles, but this is still somewhat speculative.

Defining love is difficult. There are many definitions and Lee in an exhaustive review found six major styles of love: storge, pragma, eros, ludus, mania and agape. Several theorists argue that romantic love is nothing more than missattributed arousal; others suggest it is a reciprocal reinforcement process; and some that it is a gradual shift from passion to intimacy, commitment and companionate love. Whatever the nature of love, it is clear that women take a more realistic view of it than men.

Human mate selection practices show many common features, which argues they are innate. However, the biosocial view of courtship, stressing the innateness of sex differences, has been attacked as sexist but nevertheless flourishes. The biosocial view argues that we have inherited sexual selection tendencies; that our aim is the broadest distribution of our genes; that women have less reproductive chances than men; and that each sex therefore follows different reproductive strategies.

While some critics make ideological attacks on the biosocial viewpoint, a more considered view asserts that we are a species that strives to transcend its biological limits. A model of reproductive exchange relationships tries to resolve these differences by marrying the biosocial and social exchange perspectives.

Recommended reading

Anyone interested in the interface between developmental and social psychology in close relationships research should start with the JOURNAL OF SOCIAL AND PERSONAL RELATIONSHIPS which caters for this area.

Brehm S. (1985) INTIMATE RELATIONSHIPS, Random House, NY. A fairly readable if highly American account of research into close relationships. Recommended as a rigorous overview of experimental research.

Fletcher G.J. and Fincham F.D. (eds) (1991) COGNITION IN CLOSE RELATIONSHIPS, Erlbaum, Hillsdale, NJ. A collection of articles on the social cognition of close relationships, that includes several chapters by local researchers.

Hendrick C. (ed.) (1989) CLOSE RELATIONSHIPS, Sage, Newbury Park, Ca. A simply written introductory primer containing chapters by leading experts.

Nunnally E.W., Chilman C.S. and Cox F.M. (eds) (1988) TROUBLED RELATIONSHIPS, Sage, London. A collection of eminently readable articles on the pressures that cause family relationships to unravel.

Patzer G.L. (1985) THE PHYSICAL ATTRACTIVENESS PHENOMENA, Plenum Press, NY. A comprehensive look at why beauty counts.

Perlman D. and Duck S. (eds) (1987) INTIMATE RELATIONSHIPS: DEVELOPMENT, DYNAMICS AND DETERIORATION, Sage, Newbury Park, Ca. An easy to read collection of articles on the development and decline of intimate relationships.

Sternberg R.J. and Barnes M. (eds) (1988) THE PSYCHOLOGY OF LOVE, Yale University Press, New Haven. A collection of papers by leading theorists written in an entertaining style.

ALTRUISM AND PROSOCIAL BEHAVIOUR

I live out on Sydney's fringe in a semi-rural area which, among other things, hosts a speedway. The surrounding country roads are an absolute joy for local teenagers who zoom around the back roads pretending they are inside on the circuit. It's also an ideal area for our more enterprising citizens to dump and incinerate stolen cars, keeping our local police constantly employed.

I was driving home from a late lecture one night and, coming over the hill by the speedway, I vaguely noticed an upside-down Torana XU1 on the verge. Such sights are not uncommon and it was only several hundred metres further on that it occurred to me that someone was hanging upside down in the driver's seat. A minute later I was helping a concussed eighteen-year-old out of a full racing harness that had probably saved his life, even if it had contributed to broken collarbones and a rather unpleasant twenty minutes upside down. While I was negotiating him out of his car, he vented his feelings on several motorists who had subsequently stopped to watch, accusing them of being among other things vultures and parasites. Although the road is rural it is busy enough and it seems thirty or so motorists had slowed down to have a good look before I got to him. No one had stopped to help before I did, yet now there were a dozen or so onlookers.

I took him to our local hospital. The right way up he was rapidly recovering and, though in great pain, cheerfully admitted he'd had about one hundred and ten "real live miles per hour out of her" before he lost control on the bend by the speedway. He was sublimely indifferent to the fate of his car and next morning it was gone. Well, I have my suspicions, as when I last saw him he was sitting in the casualty ward foyer anxiously arguing with the night clerk about ringing his mates to come and collect him. I wondered as I drove to work the next day why it was that no one had stopped to help and why it was that when I stopped, others did too. Was it because the road was dark and lonely, or late at night, and what were those passers-by thinking? I thought to myself that if I ever wrote a social psychology text it would make a great introduction to the fascinating puzzle of altruism.

Altruism and prosocial behaviour

One of the great paradoxes of human behaviour is why some people care an enormous amount for perfect strangers, while most restrict helping to family and friends. Observations of those rare members of our species, who selflessly serve others, can only be contrasted with the tale of woe found in any afternoon paper. Too many times we read outrageous reports of desperate people calling out for help to passers-by who avert their gaze and hurry away. It seems we are a callous lot and yet the prevailing Christian ethic is to do unto others as we would have them do in return. Altruism seems to be an international ethic (Schwartz & Bilsky, 1990) and the helping professions continue to attract people expressing altruistic beliefs (Feather, 1982a), nevertheless, it seems we interpret the rule passively. All we want from others is to be left alone and not bothered. Is this a justification for not extending a helping hand?

Uncomplicated altruism
(Photo: Armen Deushian/
Macarthur Advertiser)

This is not the only question of importance. While there are many examples of generous people who spend themselves unstintingly for "the cause", or another's benefit, many question why they care. Is it because they are genuinely superior human beings whom we should emulate, or are they more than amply rewarded by the praise they enjoy? These two aspects of human nature present some fascinating paradoxes and are two of the great questions of antiquity which philosophers and theologians have considered at length. Social psychologists and other kindred researchers are only recent arrivals on this scene (Sorrentino & Rushton, 1981). It is a little unclear just how far they have advanced our understanding beyond the parable of the Good Samaritan, as similar questions are still being debated. Nor are we sure that the insights we have gained are being translated into action. Or if our culture has advanced as a result—after all the Samaritan was only the third person on the scene when he gave the required help. In biblical times it seems they were a lot more helpful than recent reports show us to be:

> Fear of rape haunts every woman who ever walked a city street alone after dark. Her senses alive to every footstep, every laneway every bush and every man in the proximity.
>
> But no woman expects to be sexually assaulted in a night club with onlookers cheering as allegedly happened in the Cadillac Night Club in Melbourne last week. A young woman was grabbed as she left the toilets. One man reportedly stood on her hands as another attempted to rape her. Other men stood around cheering. Apparently none of the 500 patrons heard and none helped. (Adele Horin, *Sydney Morning Herald*, 5 March 1991, p. 14)

No one would doubt society has a few problems that an increase in altruism would go a long way towards fixing, yet we seem to enjoy indifference and apathy if our viewing tastes are any guide. Many current box office successes portray society as an unfeeling jungle in which urban predators selfishly stalk their prey. As I write these lines on a Saturday evening, our local television channels are offering the following examples of American "art": a group of young businessmen believe greed is good and are ripping off the system; a framed cop is on the run, everyone knows he is innocent but even the heroine is reluctant to do anything about it; and the struggles of a little Negro match-girl over general indifference. In the end Truth, Justice and the American way prevail in these three movies but it is hard to avoid being cynical, even if the hero wins in the end. Nor is the serious media immune. At the height of tragedies like the Ash Wednesday fires or the Nyngan floods, when we experience genuine outpourings of national generosity, the media still seems to focus on those few exploiting the relief agencies.

Daniel Batson is one psychologist whose work is dedicated to answering these questions and he firmly believes that we may selflessly care for others. He argued that as much as we need to nurture the fragile flower of altruistic caring, it is much more important to believe that it exists in the first place (Batson, 1990). So we will start our exploration of the fascinating subject of altruism by asking whether it is exists and, if it does, is it part of our nature, or something we acquire?

Prosocial behaviour

prosocial behaviour
Behaviour that benefits another irrespective of whether it benefits the giver.

altruism
Behaviour that benefits another without any desire for a reciprocal benefit to the giver.

Psychologists have helped to tease out the puzzle a little by distinguishing between **prosocial behaviour** and **altruism**. Prosocial behaviour is that which benefits the other and is a broad category including helping acts motivated by a desire for some reward in return, as well as selfless altruism. Altruism is restricted to helping behaviour that is selfless, or its own reward. Over the last decade the use of *prosocial* has drifted quite a bit from its precise meaning and has become a synonym for altruism. Prosocial now covers a range of activities that are not strictly altruistic such as cooperative play; standing for public office; thinking nice thoughts about your neighbour; indeed anything that is positive rather than anti-social. In my literature search for this chapter I found that most "prosocial" articles were in developmental journals and were concerned with training the young to become citizens. The difference is now one of emphasis.

Krebs and Miller (1985) further refined our understanding of the term prosocial by contrasting these behaviours with those that are anti-social. In this sense we are speaking of behaviour that strengthens the social bond. Strictly defined, prosocial means acts that benefit others or society as a whole and does not bother with an examination of the helpers' motives. A student who offers to promote a lecturer's poorly selling monograph may well be hoping for a reward in return—more favourable grades or admission to a competitive course. Note that prosocial behaviours may be both selfish or selfless. This is not just an arbitrary academic distinction but points to a fundamental shift in the way we understand helping behaviour, and has led some theorists to argue that perhaps all altruistic acts are ultimately selfish.

This is perhaps the most hotly contested aspect of prosocial theory and divides theorists like Batson (1990) who argue that selfless altruism does exist and those like Trivers (1985) who argue that even seemingly selfless behaviours are ultimately self-serving. The central issue seems to be whether prosocial behaviour is part of our biological make-up, or whether it is part of our upbringing. If helping is entirely learned, obviously a better understanding of how it is acquired should help us fashion a more humane society. If, as Wilson (1984), Alexander (1975) and Bierhoff and Klein (1988) argue, prosocial behaviour is innate and self-serving, then perhaps we are fighting the logic of our biological nature in seeking selfless altruism. No one has won the debate yet, but it has led to much vigorous research and has raised several fascinating questions that we will address. At this point we will consider the major theories of prosocial behaviour and start with the controversial sociobiological position that gave such an impetus to the field in the 1970s as social psychologists tried to decredit it.

The sociobiology of prosocial behaviour

The study of prosocial behaviour is the area in which the sociobiological viewpoint has made its greatest impact on social psychology. More theoretical articles and research reports investigate the origins of altruism than any other area of social behaviour. As we have seen, sociobiologists believe that the roots of human behaviour may be traced back to our evolutionary heritage and have innate origins. They would argue that human society is based on a platform of instinctive behaviours that we share with our co-evolutionists, the rest of the animal kingdom. They rely on the comparative approach, extrapolating a case for innate human behaviours from the observations of simpler animals. You will be aware, if you have studied introductory research methods, that this approach has several questionable assumptions, not the least of which is how far we can generalise these findings to humans. Nevertheless, it is a fruitful approach, stimulating much diverse research. As with most novel insights there are those who would take the position to its extremes and state that *all* human behaviour is innate. More commonly, sociobiologists like E.O. Wilson would only assert that heredity provides a basis from which culture and experience moulds us.

Charles Darwin was the first theorist to recast the prosocial paradox into biological terms when in *The Descent of Man* (1871) he observed that an altruistic animal loses by its prosocial act and breaches the basic law of the survival of the fittest. In the extreme case, any animal that sacrifices itself for the group would have lost the struggle to survive and as Wallace, Darwin's contemporary, noted, altruism would seem to lead us down an evolutionary dead end. Nevertheless, Darwin agreed that many naturalists had observed prosocial acts of animals at all levels of the phylogenetic tree. For example, in *The Descent* (1871) he reported Brehm's observations of a pack of baboons. When a young baboon was surrounded by a pack of dogs, an older baboon calmly came down from safety, coaxed the youngster to move and led him through the astonished dogs to safety. These acts led Darwin to propose what came to be called group natural selection:

> With mankind, selfishness, experience and imitation, probably add to the power of sympathy: for we are led by the hope of receiving good in return to perform acts of sympathetic kindness to others: and such sympathy is much strengthened by habit. In however complex a manner this feeling may have originated, as it is of high importance to all those animals which aid and defend one another; it will have increased through natural selection: for those communities, which included the greatest number of the most sympathetic members, would flourish best, and rear the greatest number of offspring. (Darwin, 1871, p. 309)

So altruistic acts increase the likelihood of the species as a whole prospering and, by the same logic, allow the greatest possible number of individuals to survive. This is the notion of inclusive fitness. A cooperative social species thus maximises its members' benefits and it is a tenet of sociobiological theory that altruism, as a successful behaviour, will become incorporated into such species' genetic endowment. Even species that require members to die for the greater good (and Darwin instances honeybees defending the hive) nevertheless gain a benefit for themselves in ensuring the passing on of similar (family) genes to their own. Sociobiologists believe that species that do not have these prosocial tendencies tend to die out.

In the century since Darwin's epic, cooperation has been a bit of an embarrassment to naturalists as it did not fit in with a view of "nature red in tooth and claw". For almost a century evolutionary theory ignored cooperative behaviour, preferring to talk about natural selection occurring at a population level rather than with individual animals. However, this misreading of Darwin's original theory came to an end in the early 1960s when the advent of the genetics revolution focused attention back on to individual animals (Axelrod & Hamilton, 1981). Cooperation was back on the agenda and needed to be explained in the face of a resurgent individualism in natural selection theory. Two accounts emerged to square away this embarrassment. Evolutionary theory was extended to incorporate modern genetics and gave rise to kin selection theory which saw cooperation as a matter of gene survival. Also **reciprocation theory** arose to explain cooperation as a social strategy. We will consider these two theories in turn:

reciprocation theory
Sociobiological term; explains cooperation as a social strategy aimed at maximising individual resources.

Kin selection theory

In modern evolutionary theory, the work of Dawkins (1976) and his colleague Ridley (Ridley & Dawkins, 1981) converts the classical Darwinian notion of an individual's struggle to survive into genetic survival. In *The Selfish Gene* (1976), Dawkins proposes we are merely vehicles for transmitting

Sociobiologists argue that we help those who are genetically the most closely related to us.
(Photo: Mark Bramley)

our genetic potential and that species survival depends on the diversity and penetrance of an accumulated gene pool. Individuals are less important than their genes, and evolutionary success is a matter of passing on our genetic message to future generations. Having offspring is only one way to ensure your genes survive. Animals who act altruistically towards blood relatives maximise their common genetic heritage. Prosocial activity then serves the dual purposes of passing on your genes and assuring group survival. Therefore natural selection should favour social species that act altruistically towards their kin and ensure that prosocial acts gain them an evolutionary edge. For an example, see the analysis of lower primate prosocial activity by Anne Goldizen (1990) of the University of Tasmania.

Selfless altruism may then be explained as a hard-nosed protection of one's genetic investment, and Wilson (1975) sees its extrapolation as the central theoretical problem of sociobiology. Alexander (1971, 1975, 1977), Dawkins (1988), Trivers (1971, 1983) and Wilson (1975, 1984), between them have blended the concepts of kin selection, parental investment and reciprocal altruism into a plausible system accounting for many of the intriguing effects in prosocial research. Wilson, among others, reminds us that this is only a model built to expose human culture's biological basis, which he asserts is "jerrybuilt on the Pleistocene".

If genetic survival is the basis of human altruism, then it is entirely probable that we will be most favorably disposed towards blood relatives and human culture should show a strong leaning towards kinship. The closer the blood tie, the more likely it is that we would help kin. Alexander (1971) in a series of studies argues this is the case and that in pre-literate societies: "Man is aware to an extraordinary degree of the differences in his relationship to the other men with whom he lives." This is certainly the case in Aboriginal societies where one is always aware of the paramount importance of kinship. While this theory was challenged by many, notably the anthropologist Marshall Sahlins in his book, *The Use and Abuse of Biology* (1976), Dawkins' more recent work, *The Blind Watchmaker* (1988), shows the debate is still vigorous. Indeed Alexander's work in the early 1970s is still a convincing rebuttal of most criticisms (too often repeated since) and demonstrated a clear correlation between degree of kinship and strength of helping behaviour. For an interesting sidelight on this issue, see the controversy that blew up in the journal, *Ethology and Sociobiology*, on reciprocal altruism, kin selection and beneficent behaviour between Donald Symons (1989) and Steve Rothstein and Ray Pierotti (1988, 1989).

If the test of selfless altruism is constantly caring for another individual, then in our species the clearest example is **parental investment** in their children. Yet kin selection explains why this bond is as strong as it is. Parents have a double investment in their offspring, passing on their own genes and ensuring their children reach their reproductive years, as it is no use producing children only to have them die without issue. What is at stake here is not selfless altruism but reproductive self-interest, and this theory suggests a reason for the eternal willingness of parents to cope with their adolescents' pique.

parental investment
The investment parents make to ensure their children reach their reproductive years and, in turn, reproduce the parents' genes.

(Cartoonist:
Graeme Mitchell)

The weakness of evolutionary modelling is that empirical proof will take millennia to work itself out. Thus scientific inquiry in sociobiology is generally *post hoc*, based on assumptions that the theorist first has to make to explain his or her observations. The primatologist sees a successful ape colony engaging in prosocial behaviour and then concludes that altruism has led to their evolutionary success. This reasoning has more than a little circularity in it. The test of such a theory would seem to be the number of predictions the theorist can then verify in the field. And the conclusions are really only as good as the first assumption (that evolution has selected for altruism), which you must grant to follow the subsequent reasoning. This is why there is so much controversy in this area, as few critics are willing to take this first step. This is never more evident than in the study of reciprocal altruism.

Reciprocal altruism

One of the main challenges to kin selection accounts of altruism is the commonplace observation that unrelated people do help each other. Trivers would ask us to accept the assumption that such a common behaviour must also have an evolutionary basis and be of mutual benefit. That is, it is reciprocal and what we give to others is a cost to be recovered somewhere along the way.

> There is no direct evidence regarding the degree of reciprocal altruism practised during human evolution nor its genetic basis today, but given the universal and nearly daily practice of reciprocal altruism among humans today, it is reasonable to assume that it has been an important factor in recent human evolution and that the underlying emotional dispositions affecting altruistic behaviour have important genetic components. (Trivers, 1971, p. 48)

Accepting this assumption we can then follow the sociobiologists' chain of reasoning to account for seemingly selfless altruism. As you read through the latter parts of this chapter, ask yourself how plausible this assumption is in the light of various theorists' empirical research. If you are interested in the social outworking of this theory in human populations, see Rushton (1989) for an overview and detailed commentaries.

Consider what happens if we reject the notion of selfless altruism. People are then prosocial for what they can get out of it. They are altruistic only to the degree they cannot get away with cheating and gaining an individual advantage. We will punish cheaters severely as they weaken the fragile system of favours on which society is built. As Trivers (1971) says: "This sets up a selection pressure for a protective mechanism." So we all are quite sensitive to others ripping us off. Friendship is then based on mutual advantage. We are most likely to be attracted to those who are altruistic to us and we return the favour, being more generous to friends than enemies. It also suggests that we should select for a sense of obligation and a willingness to pay back favours—"I owe you one."

Trivers goes on to argue that we have each developed a very well-honed sense of the costs of altruism and this leads to some unconscious calculations about the amount of altruistic effort we put out for benefits received. It also suggests why we should readily help others in emergencies. Their need is immense relative to what we are asked to give and so they are then really in our debt. Unfortunately the work of Latane and Darley (1970), reviewed later, suggests that this calculation is a little more complicated than Trivers might imagine.

Notwithstanding all the above assumptions, a society that has evolved by selecting for traits of cooperation and reciprocity must still explain away the other side of our paradox, why people sometimes do not help. If we return to Trivers' assumption that we would cheat if only we could get away with it (see Box 10.1); then the next best thing is to pretend to be altruistic, "so that we can influence the behaviour of others to our advantage" (1971). This also explains why we are so suspicious of secondhand car dealers. An ability to spot phonies is a selection pressure counterbalancing the all too obvious benefits of insincerity.

Box 10.1 *Food for thought: The evolution of cooperation*

Helping is closely linked to cooperation. As we have seen in this section, reciprocal altruism is in essence a selfish theory—we help because it is in our interests to do so. In animals lower down the phylogenetic tree, cooperative behaviour is instinctive and the honeybee worker stinging an intruder has no choice about sacrificing its life in defence of the hive. However, humans do have a choice and, whatever the instinctual roots of cooperation, we may choose to help or not to help. Thus, if the nature of human relationships is an exchange of commodities, it may well be in our interests to mimic cooperation to gain rewards without much effort. Such defectors weaken cooperative strategies, so to avoid being exploited we are suspicious of strangers and have an ability to spot phonies. Still exploitation occurs all the time. Given this climate of selfish self-interest how can cooperation evolve?

This question limped along theoretically, until an article published in *Science* in 1981 by Robert Axelrod and David Hamilton, entitled "The evolution of cooperation", shifted the issue centre stage. Their paper borrowed the Prisoner's Dilemma Game concept (reviewed in Chapter Eight) to model the evolution of cooperative strategies *from a baseline of mutual distrust*.

You will recall that the original game involved two suspected thieves in police custody, independently chewing over an offer of a light sentence in return for a confession and acting as witness against the other. The prisoners had to balance the probability of the other not being tempted to defect and accept a light sentence, against remaining silent and hoping the other would too. If both defected, neither would benefit. As Axelrod and Hamilton observe "The Prisoner's Dilemma Game is an elegant embodiment of the problems of achieving mutual cooperation".

Axelrod and Hamilton's analysis of the dilemma suggested that "no matter what the other does, the selfish choice of defection yields a higher payoff than cooperation", and you can see their reasoning in Figure 10.1. So in an evolutionary sense we should defect (cheat) rather than cooperate, despite the lesser benefits it brings. However, "cutting and running" only holds good if we do not meet the other person again. If we do then their recollection of our last interaction will influence how they interact with us. Axelrod and Hamilton note that when we repeatedly interact with others, whether we continue to defect or choose to cooperate is a function of our estimates of the likelihood

Player B

Player A	C Cooperation	D Defection
C **Cooperation**	R = 3 Reward for mutual cooperation	S = 0 Sucker's payoff
D **Defection**	T = 5 Temptation to defect	P = 1 Punishment for mutual defection

The payoff to player A is shown with illustratrive numerical values. The game is defined by $T > R > P > S$ and $R > (S + T)/2$. If the other player cooperates, there is a choice between cooperation which yields R (the reward for mutual cooperation) or defection which yields T (the temptation to defect). By assumption $T > R$, so that it pays to defect if the other player cooperates. On the other hand, if the other player defects, there is a choice between cooperation which yields S (the sucker's payoff) or defection which yields P (the punishment for mutual defection). By assumption $P > S$, so it pays to defect if the other player defects. Thus, no matter what the other player does, it pays to defect. But if both defect, both get P rather than the larger value of R that they both could have gotten had both cooperated. Hence the dilemma." (Axelrod and Hamilton, 1981, p. 1391)

Figure 10.1 *Prisoner's dilemma matrix*

Source: Axelrod & Hamilton, 1981.

of further interactions. Somewhat paradoxically, if there are only a fixed number of interactions we will still cheat as "defection on the last interaction would be optimal for both sides, and consequently so would defection in the next-to-last interaction, and so on back to the first interaction". However, when the probability of meeting again is uncertain, new possibilities arise.

If we are unsure of the number of future interactions, it would be in our interests to test the other's willingness to cooperate by risking resources in an act of initial cooperation on our part. If the other defects, we reply in kind on the next interaction. This tit-for-tat strategy may then become an *all defects* strategy which is evolutionarily stable just like the finite interactions strategy. If, however, our reprisal warns the other party that we will not tolerate further defection, they may decide to cooperate on their next move. All that is needed for a stable cooperative strategy to evolve is our willingness to "forgive" the initial defection and reset the game to the beginning. That the tit-

for-tat game is an enormously robust and stable evolutionary strategy was tested by Robert Axelrod (1980) in an international competition in which 62 entrants from six countries tried to devise rules that would beat the tit-for-tat strategy in a computer tournament. After 3 million moves, the impressive robustness of this strategy in overcoming all opponents was found to rest on three simple rules: "It was never the first to defect, it was provocable into retaliation by a defection of the other, and it was forgiving after just one act of retaliation" (Axelrod & Hamilton, 1981).

Still, this does not address how such a strategy might first arise in an atmosphere of mutual distrust and selfishness. Axelrod and Hamilton argue that the benefits of inclusive fitness and kin selection we discussed earlier alter the payoffs in games with relatives. Punishing a relative by defecting also hurts yourself. Axelrod and Hamilton suggest that cooperation may have evolved in groups of closely related individuals and then gradually generalised to more and more distant relatives, and eventually to unrelated members of the tribe and beyond. This is likely given that "promiscuous fatherhood and events at ill-defined group margins will always lead to uncertain relatedness among potential interactants".

So according to Axelrod and Hamilton's theory, mutual defection is the "primeval state" and stable until either it generalises from cooperation among relatives or through "a mutant strategy which prompts members of a group to start cooperating and then devolves into the tit-for-tat rules". The balance of their paper spelled out how this strategy might work for even single-cell organisms. This was certainly a controversial theory, although most of its impact was felt beyond social psychology. However, there has been a vigorous debate within psychology and many tests of its efficacy (Bartholdi, Butler & Trick, 1986; McGinnis, 1986; Boyd & Lorberbaum, 1987; Boyd, 1988; Milinski, 1990).

This intriguing theory also explains the puzzling tendency we sometimes have of being quite altruistic to complete strangers while neglecting proven friends. It would be in our interests to expand our possible range of benefactors and a little altruism towards new faces may well encourage a new person to give us their resources. Obviously for this theory to work it must involve multi-party transactions in which we help people who will never be able to help us, as we hope that someone will do the same for us one day. Thus in the final instance selfless altruistic acts are really bread cast on the waters.

Learned altruism

norm of equity
That all members of society should be treated equitably.

norm of social justice
Learned norm that requires us to protect the rights of others.

norm of reciprocity
A learned rule requiring us to pay back others' prosocial acts.

norm of social responsibility
A learned rule requiring us to protect those less fortunate than ourselves.

One of the influential critics of the sociobiological position, Donald Campbell (1975), argued that what the sociobiologists saw as innate behaviour potentials was in fact learned behaviour regulated by a complex set of social norms. Campbell, while not entirely dismissing a biological basis for altruism, emphasised its social evolution. The limits of our biology were always a factor that humans have tried to overcome with improved social organisation and technology. If we hear poorly, we design hearing aids; if we cannot fly, we design planes; and so on. At the heart of this social evolution is the ability of human beings to cooperate and to share the benefits it brings. As Rushton (1980) points out, these two positions are really differences of emphasis in the relative importance of our biological nature. There may well be a melding of biological and learning perspectives in the near future as psychology continues to reap the benefits of the rapid advances in biological science.

The American sociologist, Alvin Gouldner, in 1960 proposed that altruism was learned and coined the term prosocial reciprocity. His minimum conditions for reciprocity were (1) we will help those who help us and (2) we do not attack those who have helped us. Helm, Bonoma and Tedeschi (1972) pointed out there was much experimental support for the first assumption and little for the latter. Similar analyses developed different norms to account for significant variations in helping behaviour—the so-called altruistic **norms of social justice, reciprocity, equity** and **social responsibility**.

Box 10.2 *Does political affiliation influence altruism?*

Political affiliation is a learned behaviour, most often acquired in childhood as part of the package of attitudes and beliefs we get from our parents. To what extent do these political attitudes influence our helping behaviours? In an interesting study, Ray and Najman (1988) surveyed 209 Brisbane voters shortly after the 1983 elections ended the National–Liberal alliance and swept Sir Johannes Bjelke-Petersen's Nationals to power in a single-party government. Ray and Najman were interested in using the sharply polarised political allegiances that resulted from this election to test Milbrath's (1984) assertion that leftist parties with their environmental consciousness are more altruistically compassionate than conservative parties.

Ray and Najman tested voters on achievement motivation and altruistic compassion. They predicted that National Party voters would score higher on achievement motivation and lower on altruistic compassion than Labor voters, if Milbrath's assertions—"Environmentalists, much more than non-environmentalists, have a generalised sense of compassion . . . In contrast, the competitive market system . . . urges us to look out for ourselves first"—held true. Ray and Najman thought this an eminently testable

proposition and that the sharply polarised debate of the 1983 elections would provide a good test of Milbrath's hypothesis. Although Milbrath was a little coy about who were capitalists and environmentalists, Ray and Najman thought they were on safe ground contrasting the conservative parties and Labor, given the rhetoric of their electioneering.

In the event, Nationals did score as Milbrath predicted but the differences were only marginally significant at the .05 level. Interestingly, Liberal Party voters scored similarly to Labor voters. Ray and Najman concluded that Milbrath's assertion was an over-generalisation:

> Altruistic compassion is less prevalent among enthusiastic supporters of capitalism but only by a whisker . . . And more moderate conservatives are every bit as compassionate as those who vote for (Labor) . . . Milbrath may believe that the competitive market system urges us to look out for ourselves first but it seems that those who favour the competitive market system have not heard it that way. Alternatively they are pretty good at not letting it affect them. (Ray & Najman, 1988, p. 432)

Moreover social learning theorists like Bandura (1986) suggest that prosocial behaviour reinforces these beneficial norms that all cultures have as part of their social control mechanisms.

There is a substantial amount of research that has given wide experimental support for all four altruistic norms. For instance, Berkowitz (1968a) and Wilke and Lanzetta (1970) showed support for the norm of reciprocity by demonstrating that people are more likely to help those who have already helped them. Regan (1968), in an often cited study, tested pairs of college students in a purported perceptual experiment. Unknown to the subjects one of the pair was an experimental stooge. Subjects were divided into three groups and, at a rest break in the middle of the experiment, one group was given Cokes by the experimenter. In another group, Regan's confederate left the room and brought a Coke back for his partner. A little later in the experiment the confederate tried to sell his partner raffle tickets. The dependent variable was the number of raffle tickets sold and results were compared to a third no-Coke control group. As predicted there was little difference in the mean number of tickets sold to the no-Coke (.92) and experimenter-Coke (1.08) groups, while the confederate-Coke group (1.73) was substantially different.

Further research has looked at the determinants of reciprocity. This norm works strongly in most cultures (Gergen et al., 1975). There is also a sense of comparison and equity involved in reciprocity. Greenberg (1980) found we tend to help those who have really gone out of their way for us, rather than just returning casual favours. Goranson and Berkowitz (1966) showed we tend to be quite discriminating in returning favours to a specific person who has previously helped us. McCorkle and Korn (1954) found that prisoners manipulate the norm in their own interests, and so on. There is a wealth of similar research supporting the other three altruistic norms.

Most Commonwealth countries share the old English common law, which enshrines these norms in our social code and reflects them in such documents as the Magna Carta of 1215. For example, Article 40, the social justice norm, states: "To no one will we sell, to no one will we refuse the right of justice." To the extent that we see these norms as being of universal benefit, we will socialise our young to support them and penalise breaches accordingly. Nevertheless, they may be broken to our advantage, which takes us back to the paradox with which we started this chapter.

Two psychological theories underlie these norms and expand our understanding of learned prosocial behaviour.

Exchange theory (see Chapter Eight) proposed by the sociologist George Homans (1958, 1961, 1974) assumes that altruistic norms are rooted in a sense of reasonable exchange. Though Homans uses economic language, this translates equally well to social psychology. If we see someone getting away with outrageous demands on another who is their social equal, we immediately assume the relationship must be balanced in some other way. The actor who tyrannises his director and upsets the cast is humoured by all because of his immense artistic talent and the expectation of future profits from a great film. Both the director and the artist feel the relationship is in balance, even if it does not appear so to outsiders.

Exchange theory works well to explain altruistic behaviour. Homans speculated that these altruistic norms work because the more past activities are rewarded, the more likely they are to occur in the present and be copied by others to be similarly rewarded. So we have an expectation of a reasonable reward for our actions. If this is not met, we feel ripped off and the norms operate to reinstitute a reasonable exchange. This process intensifies if we see others being rewarded for the same behaviours when we are not. As Thibaut and Kelley (1959) point out, the important point here is not just comparison but comparison to some standard dictated by social norms or our experience.

In much the same way, equity theory (Chapter Eight) looks at the perceived equity of these exchanges. Experimenters such as Adams (1963), Walster, Walster and Berscheid (1978), Messe and Watts (1983), Messick and Sentis (1979) and Simpson (1987) have all shown that we bring an expectation to our relationships based on past commitment and expectation of future rewards. We need to feel that our rewards are commensurate with both our input and what we expect of others. If not, we are less likely to continue contributing to the relationship. Helping, therefore, will not continue if we feel it is all one-way.

As useful as the normative approach is in understanding prosocial behaviour, critics have noted its substantial shortcomings (Schwartz, 1977; Latane & Darley, 1970). In some ways it repeats an earlier trend in social psychology of explaining everything by proposing a need and giving it a name. This process of reification (explaining by naming) was repeatedly challenged over the years and, as Krebs (1970) points out, is not only circular but often contradictory. The norm of social responsibility may ask you to support Maori land rights, while the norm of reciprocity asks what's in it for you. The altruistic norms may even contradict other, more powerful, personal beliefs as we may believe that Maori advancement is best served by assimilation into white society. We may find ourselves in an approach/ avoidance gradient between the conflicting norms of social justice and our socialisation towards individual self-reliance and respect for others' privacy.

Perhaps the very generality of these norms leaves them open to wide interpretation and leave us unsure how to act in specific situations. Nor do the norms really explain differences in individual helping behaviour and why we sometimes simply refuse to help. A substantial critique was mounted by Berkowitz (1972) who conducted a series of experiments in which people gave aid anonymously to strangers with no expectation of reward. While this may be seen as an example of the norm of social responsibility, it may also be interpreted as altruism for its own sake. Schwartz and his colleagues (1973, 1977, 1981, 1982) have proposed a partial answer to these criticisms. He suggests that we have personal norms that are compounded from our experiences, our attributions or values based on those experiences, our socialisation including altruistic norms and our specific emotional reactions on the day. These personal norms are powerful motivators and Schwartz feels that we gain most from living up to our own intrinsic standards.

So far we have sketched the two main theoretical positions underlying the prosocial field. We turn now to a consideration of the major research areas which Bierhoff (1988) has identified as empirical concerns in prosocial behaviour: how do we acquire altruistic responses in everyday life? what are the processes underlying altruism? what are the determinants of altruistic behaviour in specific situations; and how do we respond to being helped?

The role of empathy

If we accept that prosocial behaviour has biological and environmental determinants, then psychologists will immediately try to understand how altruism develops in the very young and what the critical factors are in promoting prosocial personalities. Unfortunately the research evidence is inconclusive. It is clear from the work of Hoffman (1977, 1981) and

Learning to be altruists

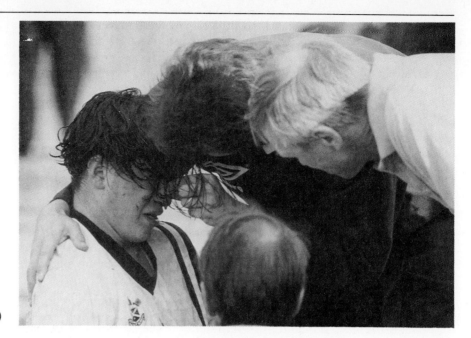

Is empathy with another's distress an essential part of our capacity to care for others?
(Photo: Mark Bramley)

Zahn-Waxler, Radke-Yarrow and King (1979) that empathy is a key building block in becoming altruistic. However, other researchers have found that global measures of empathy do not predict prosocial behaviour (Bandura, 1986). Again we face the perennial problem that attitudes do not necessarily lead to similar behaviour, which we discussed in Chapter Four. Empathy may even restrict altruism as the empathiser avoids the emotional distress of involvement with those in need. Clearly the acquisition of prosocial attitudes is a multifactorial process.

The development of empathy

Zahn-Waxler et al. (1979) demonstrated that empathic responding is a crucial determinant in learning to help others. From careful behavioural measurement, it would seem that **vicarious arousal**, or letting another's predicament affect you, is the first stage in empathy building. Very young children from two to four start to empathise with a hurt child, even if they do nothing, or act inappropriately. It seems that as children enter the preconceptual state of development and begin to differentiate themselves from others, they also experience spontaneous vicariousness (Bandura, 1986). This leads them to develop the further skills of **role-** and **perspective-taking** and to put themselves in the place of the hurt child (Strayer & Roberts, 1989). At this stage, helping behaviour may well be primarily aimed at reducing the helper's own discomfort. By eight they have mastered complex role-taking skills and their empathy aims not only at helping others but understanding the source of another's discomfort (Flavell et al., 1968; Lourenco, 1990). A recent four-nation study by Klaus Boehnke et al. (1989), of the Free University of Berlin, quantified these developmental variables and added that gender differences in empathy onset about age twelve.

vicarious arousal
Being aroused by another's predicament; social learning concept.

role-taking
Assuming or incorporating another's behaviour into our own social repertoire; as opposed to role-playing.

perspective-taking
Being able to see things from another's perspective; Piagetian concept.

It seems clear then that early altruistic behaviour changes from an egocentric need to reduce one's own discomfort to a more rational attempt to meet another's needs. Rubin and Schneider (1973) demonstrated that the degree of role-taking skills the children had led to greater prosocial acts. Iannotti (1978) was able to train six-year-olds in role-taking skills and then found they were much more spontaneously prosocial than controls. Radke-Yarrow and Zahn-Waxler (1984) conclusively demonstrated that family values play a critical role in reinforcing altruistic behaviour. They suggested that not only was parental modelling of altruism important but also the child's experience of parental nurturing, which was their primary exposure to altruism (see also Rehberg & Richman, 1989). As the child becomes an adolescent, education, peers and other cultural factors and the development of an independent abstract reasoning capacity, increasingly determine whether the person remains an altruist (Mussen & Eisenberg-Berg, 1977).

Vicarious arousal and helping

Tests with adults have conceded a place for empathy as a powerful motivator of prosocial behaviour. Lazarus et al. (1962) showed movies of painful circumcision rites to subjects and found clear evidence that they were emotionally aroused; Berger (1962) noted his subjects' evident emotional distress after watching stooges supposedly receiving electric shocks; and Paul Amato (1986) found that the horrific scenes of the Ash Wednesday bushfires prompted helping in line with the degree of arousal engendered. Piliavin and her colleagues (1981) concluded there was sufficient evidence to show that seeing others hurt caused arousal in the observer—but does this lead them to help?

Coke, Batson and McDavis (1978) established that vicarious arousal may lead to empathy and, in turn, to helping behaviour. In the first of a series of experiments they used false feedback techniques to tell subjects they were physiologically aroused when hearing of another's misfortune. Compared to a control group, these misinformed subjects not only were more empathic but also more likely to help. Coke et al. reasoned that arousal was a necessary precursor of helping and tested this by varying the attributions given to their subjects. Coke and his colleagues then divided subjects into two groups that were either asked to observe or empathise with a person crying for help. They then gave some subjects a placebo and led them to believe that it would mimic feelings of arousal similar to empathy. Coke reasoned that only those who were asked to empathise and who were not misdirected by attributing arousal to the pill would help. As you can see from Table 10.1 their predictions were confirmed. Clearly how we interpret our arousal has an important bearing on whether we help.

Is empathic helping altruistic or merely prosocial? Jane Piliavin (1981) developed a cost-analysis model of helping which we will examine in the context of emergency interventions. She suggested that far from empathic helping being a selfless concern for the other's plight, we act primarily to

Table 10.1 *Helping, empathy and misattribution*

	Anticipated side effect of norephren	
Observational set	*Relaxation*	*Arousal*
Imagine her	2.60	.68
Observe broadcast techniques	1.27	.68

(a) Mean amount of help volunteered by subjects in each condition of experiment 1

	False arousal feedback condition		
	High arousal (n = 17)	*Low arousal (n = 16)*	*t*
Measure			
Empathic concern index	4.56	3.38	2.80***
Individual empathic emotions			
Empathic	4.18	2.81	2.17*
Concerned	5.29	4.19	2.21*
Warm	4.00	2.69	2.63**
Softhearted	4.82	3.56	2.40*
Compassion	4.53	3.63	1.62
Personal distress index	2.53	1.98	1.22
Individual distress emotions			
Upset	2.53	1.81	1.47
Troubled	2.82	2.13	1.13
Alarmed	2.24	2.00	.54

(b) Subjects' mean ratings of emotions in experiment 2

Subjects rated the extent to which they experienced each emotion on a scale ranging from 1 (not at all) to 7 (extremely). The incidences of empathic concern and personal distress were coded on the same 1-to-7 scale.

* $p < .050$. ** $p < .02$. *** $p < .01$.

Source: Coke, Batson & McDavis, 1978.

reduce our own feelings of discomfort rather than alleviate the other's distress. It is also possible to avoid uncomfortable experiences but, as Piliavin notes, the costs of not helping are either empathic (guilt), or social (loss of esteem or social disapproval). In either case altruism is an essentially egoistic act. Rushton (1981), however, after reviewing the developmental work on prosocial behaviour concludes that some people are genuine altruists and Batson and Coke (1981) agree.

Batson and his colleagues in a variant of the earlier Berger experiment had subjects watch a woman confederate being electrically shocked. The dependent variable was whether the subjects would accept shocks themselves to relieve the woman's pain. The experimenters allowed some subjects to leave the experiment and others had to remain. They reasoned that those who reported high empathy would choose to help, whether they could leave or not. Their results confirmed their hypothesis. Batson et al. (1983) concluded that there are clearly differences between egoistic and altruistic types of empathy.

A prosocial personality type?

If altruism is as complex a phenomenon as it seems, then it is unlikely there will be a simple altruistic trait (Mussen & Eisenberg-Berg, 1977; Krebs, 1978). This opinion is based on the conflicting evidence for a purely disinterested altruism that goes back to the work of Hartshorne and May (1928), and the problems that normative explanations pose. At any rate, the sociobiological position suggests we should expect to find some evidence of an innate characteristic that is perhaps submerged under the weight of cultural overlays. Rushton (1981, 1984) argues the search for such a characteristic is perhaps a little misguided and we should instead look for the multiple helping behaviours that make up practical altruism. From this perspective a composite picture of multiple helping behaviours emerges and is supported by his more recent research on altruism in identical and non-identical twins (Rushton et al., 1986).

What, then, is the inside of a good Samaritan's head like? We are not sure. Latane and Darley (1970) spent a considerable time trying to devise a predictive test to identify altruists and found the only distinguishing feature was the size of the town the person came from! Ten years later, Bibb Latane concluded ruefully that the search for a predictive description had failed (Latane, 1981). Perhaps the problem in identifying an altruistic

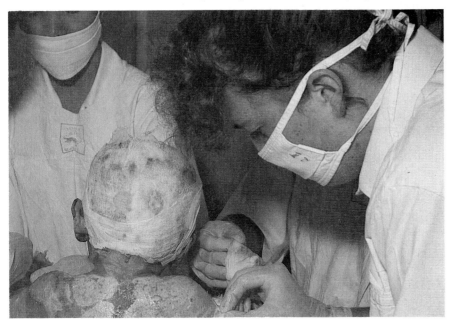

Is there a prosocial personality type? Do nursing and other helping professions attract those with a greater capacity for caring?
(Photo: Mark Norman)

personality is that we all have altruistic tendencies and perhaps the search is a matter of degrees. While we can all identify Mother Teresas after the fact, how do we predict whether little Jaan will emulate them? Some factors are linked to increased prosocial behaviour and we review these below, but at the moment the best predictor of a helpful person is past behaviour.

Clearly if you had parents who were good models of prosocial behaviour and who value other people, you are more likely to become an altruist. It would seem that religious belief coupled with a concern for others increases this possibility. London (1970), in a much quoted study, interviewed people who risked their lives hiding Jews and others in occupied Europe during World War II. He found a common theme of having identified with a parent who, usually from religious convictions, had high moral standards, the ability to empathise and the capacity to translate this into practical action. Interestingly, many who defied the Nazis had an adventurous streak, were non-conformers and risk-takers. Not surprisingly, they also reported feeling a little removed from their peers (see also Fogelman & Wiener, 1985; Oliner & Oliner, 1988). It would seem that early social learning would account for a fair part of our subsequent prosocial behaviour.

Personality factors are a somewhat more limited guide. Rushton (1984) identified highly developed morality and sense of social responsibility as critical factors. Staub (1974), Eisenberg-Berg (1979), Blasi (1980), Erkut, Jaquette and Staub (1981) and Levine (1987) all argued a greater capacity to reason abstractly led to a greater understanding of complex ethical issues and a willingness to help. Altruists are capable of empathy and putting themselves in another's situation (Underwood & Moore, 1982). Further they have an ability to understand the emotional, cognitive and ethical attributions of others (Batson et al., 1986). Perhaps the most interesting finding was that altruists do not tend to adopt stereotyped sex-roles (Tice & Baumeister, 1985; Siem & Spence, 1986). While this list is not exclusive and has little predictive efficiency, because many people who possess these attributes are not particularly helpful, there are interesting correlations to Abraham Maslow's (1971) portrait of a fully self-actualised person.

When will we help? The personal and situational determinants of helping behaviour

Cognitive variables

Perhaps a better way of predicting altruism is to try for an extensional definition and ask why, or more practically, when do people help? We can work backwards from actual situations and examine motives for helping. Immediately we encounter a major difficulty as most of the work in this area has dealt with emergency interventions. As Eagly (1987) points out this skews our research efforts away from the majority of non-heroic, daily prosocial acts. Even so this is a fascinating area of research that has produced three cognitive, decision-based models of helping: Latane and Darley (1970), Piliavin et al. (1981) (which we will review), and Schwartz's process model of altruism (see Schwartz, 1977).

(Photo: Chris Simkin)

Bystander intervention calculus

If prosocial research has thrown up a colossus that commands the high ground of student interest, this would have to be the work of Bibb Latane and John Darley who ran a series of imaginative experiments in the 1960s and 1970s, which are classics of the literature and are often repeated.

Latane and Darley's interests were stimulated by the brutal attempted rape, and then murder, of New Yorker, Kitty Genovese, in March 1964. Though 38 of her neighbours heard her as she fought off her attacker for over 30 minutes, repeatedly calling for help, not one came to her assistance, or rang the police. It would be hard to underestimate the impact this murder had on American consciences, nor the subsequent worldwide attention it received. Many wild theories were thrown about why her neighbours did not help and they in turn became some of the most intensively studied people in the history of psychology. Newspaper headlines speculated on the dehumanising impact of city living; the brutalising conformity that led to a supposed callous indifference on the part of her neighbours; and the apathy of it all, as this quotation from the reporter who broke the story, shows:

> It can be assumed . . . that their apathy was indeed one of the big-city variety. It is almost a matter of psychological survival, if one is surrounded and pressed by millions of people, to prevent them from constantly impinging on you, and the only way to do this is to ignore them as often as possible. Indifference to one's neighbor and his troubles is a conditioned reflex in life in New York as it is in other big cities. (Rosenthal, 1964, p. 146)

Yet her neighbours were not completely indifferent to her plight and many experienced considerable anguish over their inaction for some years (Latane & Darley, 1970). So why didn't they help? Many similar situations, in which bystanders looked on as other people died, led Latane and Darley to propose the bystander effect. They hypothesised that as the number of people involved increased, so individual responsibility declined and help became less likely. The group as a whole suffered a diffusion of responsibility. You are much more likely to receive aid if only one person is looking on. We will return to this phenomenon in later chapters when we consider the role of social loafing in group dynamics.

To test their theory, they invited students to fill out a questionnaire on urban living. As the experiment proceeded, smoke was introduced into the room through a wall vent. Half of the subjects in the room by themselves immediately reacted when they noticed the smoke, examined the vent and within four minutes had gone for help, and over three-quarters did so within the six minutes the experiment ran. Students in groups of three reacted quite differently, covertly examining each other to see who would make the first move, and only one of the 24 subjects reacted within four minutes. To confirm their surprising results, Latane and Darley introduced two confederates into the room with the experimental subject and they were instructed not to react to the smoke at all. As you can see from Figure 10.2 their results were equally dramatic.

A weakness of these interesting experiments was that the subjects were unsure whether they were facing a real emergency, and the ambiguity seemed a major factor in delaying their responses. To more closely approximate an unambiguous emergency, Latane and Darley set up another experiment where students were invited to join in a discussion of adjustment to campus life, talking to other students over an intercom system to ensure privacy. However, subjects were really listening to a taped sequence (see quote) in which a student explains his loneliness and adjustment problems, then admits to an epileptic condition and after a few minutes has a seizure. One of the variables manipulated was the numbers of students supposedly talking to each other. As Darley and Latane (1968) predicted, subjects

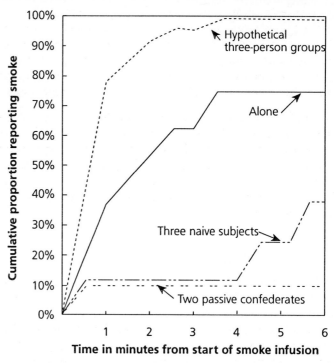

Figure 10.2 *Is it an emergency? The influence of group size*
Source: Latane & Darley, 1968.

As crowd size increases, our feelings of being obliged to help decreases. (Photo: Chris Simkin)

who thought they were talking in a one-to-one situation responded almost immediately to their companion's seizure. As the group size increased, however, subjects hesitated for up to three minutes before taking action, and it should not be supposed that subjects in the larger group were any the less concerned about their companion. All displayed considerable anxiety and if anything their predicament was made worse by not knowing which of their supposed companions would take charge of the emergency.

> I-er-um-I think I-I need-er-if-if could-er-somebody er-er-er-er-er-er- give me a little-er-give me a little help here because-er-I-er-I'm-er-er-h-h-having a-a-a real problem-er-right now and I-er-if somebody could help me out it would-it would-er-er-s-s-sure be-good . . . because-er-there-er-er-a cause I-er-I-uh-I've got a-a one of the-er-sei . . . . er-er-things coming on and-and-and I could really-er-use some help. (Darley & Latane, 1968, p. 379)

The mere presence of others

Latane and Darley reported several replications of these experiments in their book, *The Unresponsive Bystander* (1970). Eleven years later, Latane and Nida (1981) reviewed 56 other studies of emergencies, which showed this phenomenon to be remarkably consistent. They postulated that the mere presence of others led to a diffusion of responsibility that was debilitating. Only 22 per cent of those in groups helped, while over half of the sole bystanders intervened. In interviewing onlookers it became clear that they were worried about appearing "right googs" and putting their foot in it,

evaluation apprehension
Wanting to avoid a negative social evaluation; performance anxiety.

what Latane and Darley called **evaluation apprehension**, as much as they were affected by diminished responsibility. In the Kitty Genovese case, neighbours were sure others had already rung the police and were unwilling to be yet another person reporting the attack. In the event everyone thought the same and no one called.

From their experiments Latane and Darley proposed a cognitive model of bystander intervention (see Figure 10.3) to account for these and related effects that has become known as bystander calculus. Notice that after becoming aware of the emergency and before they act, bystanders engage in a complicated decision-making process, and at each step along the way they may refuse to help. In their experiments, bystanders often experienced severe approach-avoidance conflicts. They wanted to help but did not think they had the skills, feared ridicule, and so on.

With even as robust a model as this, there are many intervening variables that may alter our helping behaviour either way. For instance, the presence

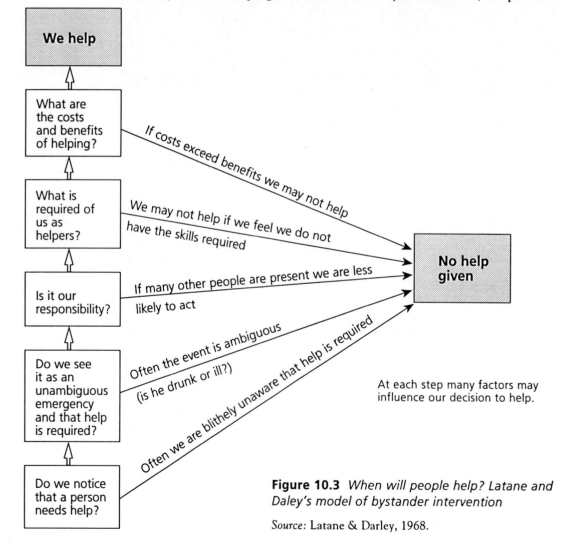

At each step many factors may influence our decision to help.

Figure 10.3 *When will people help? Latane and Daley's model of bystander intervention*

Source: Latane & Darley, 1968.

Expertise greatly increases our willingness to help.
(Photo: Armen Deushian/Macarthur Advertiser)

of a recognised leader, or person in a position of authority, will quickly motivate a group to action (Firestone et al., 1975). Similarly, Yinon et al. (1982) have shown that when the group has a strong norm of social responsibility, the addition of others will increase the probability of altruism. Schwartz and Clausen (1970) found the presence of trained onlookers— police, medical personnel, ambulance workers—inhibited helping, while Huston et al. (1981) interviewed men who had intervened and found that most had some emergency training and felt more competent to assist than other onlookers. Clearly the skills and attitudes of onlookers are crucial.

Ambiguity

As emergencies are usually sudden and unexpected there is always an element of ambiguity and confusion present, and this can lead to tragedy. If an elderly gent collapses in front of you on a busy street you are likely to be startled and take some time to collect your thoughts. If you are unsure whether he is drunk or ill, you will take your cue for appropriate action from other onlookers. If we all are startled and checking each other out to see what is happening, this hesitancy may well lead us to conclude it is not an emergency, and this ambiguity means he might die before we help. Darley, Teger and Lewis (1973) noted that cries of alarm and other signs of a clear emergency lower our inhibitions and the time it takes to respond. If it is unambiguously an emergency, or if the victim defines it that way for us—by clutching his chest saying "my heart, my heart!"—it is more likely we will respond immediately (Shotland & Heinold, 1985).

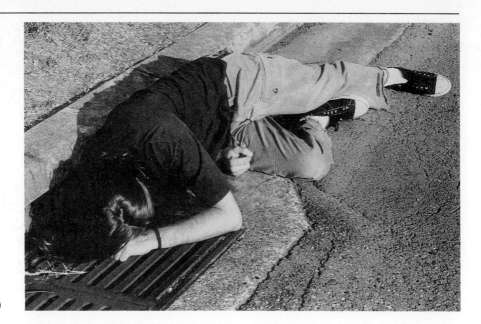

Is this an emergency? Ambiguity reduces helping behaviour. (Photo: Chris Simkin)

Diffusion of responsibility

The more people there are, the less likely we are to help. In a classic study, the French agronomist Max Ringelmann (1913) used a spring balance in a tug-of-war game to measure the force each person applied as team sizes increased. He found that with increasing numbers individual effort decreased. It seemed each man decided they had less individual responsibility, or their efforts became less coordinated as numbers increased. Perhaps similar effects are at work in deciding whether to help? Latane speculated that in emergencies we either are unsure or feel less accountable as group size expands (Latane, Williams & Harkins, 1979). Evaluation apprehension is at work too. Cacioppo, Petty and Losch (1986) suggested that increased numbers of onlookers *increase* a potential helper's concern to act appropriately and avoid further injury to the victim. Paradoxically, wanting to do the best for the victim might stop you acting. No one wants to be centre stage, unrehearsed, without a script and worried that an expert might be in the audience. We hesitate to assume this extra accountability to onlookers as well as to the victim and so are less likely to help.

Social loafing increases with group size. The last thing you want is to be the only other late night commuter when the person across the aisle has a seizure—then it is your emergency too! However, it is hard to feel much responsibility as just one of 500 onlookers on the platform. We can walk away or look on with impunity and suffer no future guilt. This diffusion of responsibility can often become a fine emotional calculation. Bickman (1972) found that if we think we are more experienced than others we feel bound to assist. Yet Ross and Braband (1973) found we are less likely to help when we think other people are equally able. So perhaps there is an element of egoism in our practical altruism, which brings us to the fascinating work of Jane Piliavin.

A cost/benefit analysis of helping

As we move up Latane and Darley's cognitive model, we become more conscious of the costs of helping and weigh these against the rewards (if any). Jane Piliavin has spent fifteen years examining the situational variables that influence our decision to help. One of her earlier contributions (Piliavin & Piliavin, 1972) focused on the helper's autonomic arousal in emergencies. Her model complements Latane and Darley's work and looks at the emotional side of helping. Selye (1976) has detailed the stress-related changes we go through when faced with a sudden alarm, and many researchers have shown these are all present in bystanders confronted with an unexpected trial (Gaertner & Dovidio, 1977; Sterling & Gaertner, 1984).

As you can see from Figure 10.4 there are costs for both helping and not helping, and distinguishing the *nature* of the costs alters the decision-making process. Piliavin, like many altruism theorists who see prosocial behaviour as ultimately self-serving, sees a role for innate helping behaviours, but these are modified by culture and the demands of the moment. The type of situation we face will in part determine the costs of helping, and in turn, our response. By working through the sectors of Figure 10.4 you will see how arousal may influence your actions. When faced with the prospect of relieving your host's embarrassment by taking a noisy friend home from a barbecue and you then find she is harmlessly drunk and can be easily jollied along to get in the taxi, you're in a win-win situation. There is a high cost in staying (your host's disapproval) and everything to gain in going (gaining praise as a good Samaritan). You experience little anxiety and so decide to help quickly. This is a high not-helping, low helping-cost scenario.

However, if you find your friend viciously drunk and swinging a broken bottle to emphasise her point, you are in a real bind. You have everything to lose, as the potential costs of not helping, or helping, are arousing in the extreme. When faced with a vicious drunk, few of us have well-developed bouncers' skills, and tend to dither safely out of reach. In this type of

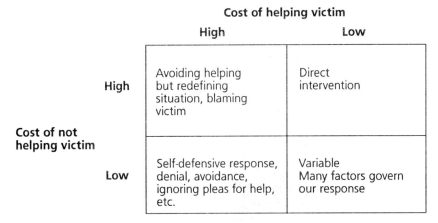

Figure 10.4 *The costs of helping and not helping*

Source: Adapted from Piliavin, Piliavin & Rodin, 1975.

situation Piliavin found people help in safe but indirect ways, or distort reality to avoid the dilemma. In our example this would amount to offering her coffee, while assuring your host she's not a problem and will calm down in a moment. The arousal in these situations can be quite debilitating for bystanders, and would explain the high anxiety experienced by subjects in Latane's seizure experiment discussed earlier. They were caught in precisely this type of dilemma.

If your host asks you to take your friend home because she is drunk and abusive, you are in a dilemma until you discover she is unknown to you. In this example the costs are high if you intervene but, as you are in no way responsible, the costs of not helping are minimal. In this situation you may experience high arousal but this is easily dealt with by avoiding the responsibility. You explain you don't know her and offer to ask around to see who does.

Up to this point Piliavin's model is elegantly simple and quite predictive (Piliavin, Dovidio, Gaertner & Clark, 1981) but its real strength comes from explaining those situations in which people have differing reactions to the same circumstances. What happens if the costs of not helping and the costs of helping are both low? The drunk is harmless and you don't know her. Here there is little arousal and few costs. Whether we will help or not depends entirely on the range of norms, number of people present, ambiguity of the situation; the age, gender, race and nationality of the victim; the squeamishness, competency and empathy of the helper and other situational variables that we will go on to consider in the remainder of this section.

Piliavin et al. (1981) have constructed a more elaborate emergency intervention model (see Figure 10.5). Although comprehensive, faithfully portraying the real nature of the prosocial act, it is quite complex and lacks the predictive clarity of her earlier model, so reminiscent of the approach/avoidance gradients of the early drive theorists.

Race, sex and ethnicity of the victim

An enormous number of comparison studies have looked at the question of race and ethnicity in helping behaviour; yet the results are inconclusive. Hindus and Moslems live peaceably together in Fiji and Bali, while killing each other in India. It seems there are too many variables to take into account to make any predictions beyond stating that we tend to help those people who are similar to ourselves—a general rule in social psychology that perceived similarity leads to ingroup favouritism (Krebs, 1975).

Inter-racial helping has an equally baffling research record. Piliavin et al. (1981) report a number of American intercommunal studies in which every possible combination of helping and non-helping behaviour between black and whites was observed, with variable results. Katz (1981) noted there is an ambivalent attitude between races and while most whites do not wish to be seen as prejudiced, they are hesitant in their relationships with blacks, because they hold negative attitudes based on community stereotypes. This sometimes leads to reverse discrimination where whites go out of their way to help blacks, much to the disgust of blacks who feel

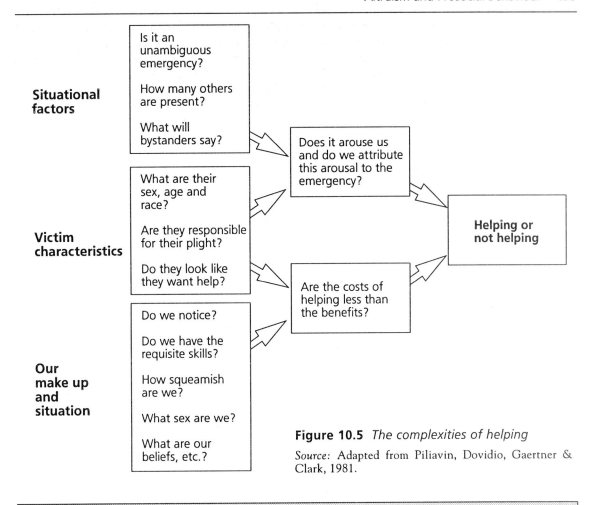

Figure 10.5 *The complexities of helping*

Source: Adapted from Piliavin, Dovidio, Gaertner & Clark, 1981.

Box 10.3 *How do Australians rate as altruists?*

An earlier study by Ralph Turner (1975) compared the responses of 1008 Los Angeles adults with samples drawn from two Australian universities and one each from the US and Britain. Turner was interested in the quest for identity traditionally achieved through altruism and work, which some theorists felt had been displaced by intimacy as a means of self-discovery. While his survey gave mixed findings, there was little difference in his samples on altruism, which all groups rated most frequently as the way to self-discovery.

In a more recent study (Johnson et al., 1989), Associate Professor Stephen Bochner of the University of NSW was one of an international team in a cross-cultural comparison of altruism and its correlates. The study surveyed university populations in Australia, Egypt, Yugoslavia, Taiwan, Korea and two US samples, Hawaii and Missouri. Although the Australian samples were small, the survey was a major undertaking with measures of: altruism; giving and receiving help and valuing it; extrinsic and intrinsic religiosity; lie and shame scales; and three personality measures—psychoticism, extroversion and neuroticism.

Their results showed a consistent response pattern across all countries. Altruism was "positively correlated with guilt, extroversion, and intrinsic religiosity; shame was negatively correlated with giving and receiving help but positively correlated with the rated importance of helping". Australia came out middle-ranked on altruism measures with the US samples highest and the Asian countries lowest, though on the scale "rated importance of helping" Australia was second lowest, just ahead of Taiwan. While an analysis of the results showed significant differences between countries on mean helping measures, correlating each item's frequency for the three altruism measures across groups gave Australia a similar pattern of helping to the two US samples (median correlation r = 0.93).

Though there were differences in mean altruism scores, the authors emphasise the similarities across the samples. Women are less likely to help than men (except in Taiwan), particularly in situations involving pain, or physical and psychological harm. There is "a positive association of guilt and a negative association of shame with giving help", for both sexes.

The authors noted: "The most striking correlations (across all groups) are those across the three altruism measures. Those who give help are those who get help, both within and across groups. These results strongly support Trivers' (1971) sociobiological theory of reciprocal altruism." They conclude by pointing out that their sample is very similar in background and values, despite nationality, and this may well account for the marked similarity in response patterns.

patronised. The motivation here is essentially self-serving, to avoid being seen as racist and if whites, or blacks for that matter, can avoid helping, without appearing racist, they are less likely to help. The nature of the emergency is also important, as are attributions of responsibility for the dilemma. Gaertner and Dovidio (1977) found that helping rates were identical in unambiguous emergencies but from a further study (Frey & Gaertner, 1986) it was clear that the onlooker's feeling about the victim's degree of responsibility for their predicament played a large part in whether they helped the other race.

Again race may often be a barrier to helping because we suffer evaluation apprehension. Many people feel uncomfortable helping those of another race, not because of prejudice but because they fear saying or doing something inappropriate. Although we were unable to find any local research on this subject, at my university (which has one of Australia's largest on-campus Aboriginal programmes), Koorie students were so upset at this inter-racial hesitancy, that they held a "Come Join With Us Day" to break down the barriers.

Gender plays a much less ambiguous role. While it is generally conceded that women are socialised to be more compassionate than men (Hoffman, 1975; Hesketh, 1982; Currie, 1982), many studies have shown that they are less likely to help (Gruder & Cook, 1971; West et al., 1975; Latane & Dabbs, 1975; Forsyth, 1978; Austin, 1979; Mills et al., 1989). It seems that the traditional practice of socialising girls towards nurturance and prosocial behaviour is also tempered with an equally socialised caution towards strangers.

In a classic study, James Bryan and Anne Test (1967) attempted to measure the influence of gender on helping behaviour. They positioned a stranded motorist at the side of a freeway and observed who would stop to help. Just up the road was another stranded motorist being helped by a confederate acting as a role model. People were much more likely to stop if they saw a model than no model. In any event, in both conditions more

The sex, age, race or ethnicity of the person in need influence our helping behaviour. Bryan and Test found that male drivers were more likely to stop for an attractive female motorist. (Photo: Chris Simkin)

men stopped than women and even more men stopped if the stranded motorist was female. While this pioneering study had a clear result, its design made it hard to determine the exact variable promoting helping behaviour. Were men stopping because they were genuinely altruistic, or were they attracted to a pretty female, or felt that women were less likely to have mechanical skills? Conversely were women genuinely less altruistic, or not stopping because they had few mechanical skills, or was it because we socialise our daughters to be cautious in these sorts of situations?

There were many variations of this experiment to tease out the relationship between helping and gender, and it seems that male sexual arousal is one operative variable. Bryan and Test (1967) dressed their women in two styles, short dress and bikini top, and sloppy college dress. Men were much more likely to stop for revealing, rather than more sedate, dress. West, Whitney and Schnedler (1975), Benson et al. (1976) and West and Brown (1975) varied the attractiveness of their female confederates with similar results, and Snyder et al. (1983) found that those most likely to stop are young lone males.

To directly test the hypothesis that sexual arousal increases helping behaviour, Przybyla (1985) showed erotic films to male and female college students, and then measured how much they helped a stranger. There were three conditions—a sexually explicit video, a non-erotic video and a control group with no film. As the students left the film, a male or female accomplice accidentally knocked over a pile of questionnaires. The dependent variables were the percentage of each sex helping to retrieve the pile and how long they took. Ninety per cent of males in the erotic condition helped and, predictably, spent twelve times longer helping female confederates than helping men.

These results are not conclusive given differences in male and female arousal patterns. It may take different material, or strategies, to sexually arouse women and take longer than males. There are many other considerations to take into account before we conclude that men are more likely to help women than the other way round (Deaux, 1976). We must also remember Eagly's (1987) caution that studies of gender and prosocial behaviour probably are biased in the way they construe helping situations. Women may be more helpful in situations different than that that contrived by Przybyla.

Living in the city

Another factor deciding if you will help is the size of your home town (House & Wolf, 1978). Paul Amato (see Box 10.4) conducted several studies on population density and helping behaviour and found that the larger the town you come from the less you will help. In 1983 he measured various helping tasks in 55 Queensland and New South Wales towns ranging in size from hamlets to major cities. His tasks were simple requests: to give a donation to the Multiple Sclerosis Society; a student asking pedestrians to write down their favourite colour for a school project; dropping envelopes in front of a letterbox; correcting wrongly given directions in a store; and helping up a man with an injured leg after he had fallen. The results of this elegantly simple experiment are shown in Figure 10.6. Only the dropped envelopes attracted less helping in smaller towns—though as you can see it brought little help even in the cities.

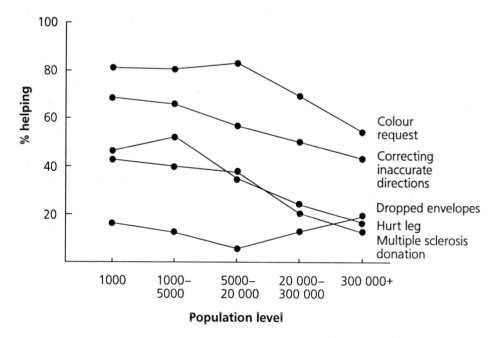

Figure 10.6 *Helping as a function of city size*
Source: Amato, 1983a.

Box 10.4 *Profile: Paul Amato and predicting helping behaviour*

Paul R. Amato was a tutor in the Department of Behavioural Sciences at James Cook University of North Queensland between 1977 and 1982. After obtaining his PhD there, he spent four years as a research fellow at the Australian Institute of Family Studies in Melbourne. He returned to the United States in 1987 and is now an associate professor of sociology at the University of Nebraska-Lincoln. Although he maintains an interest in prosocial behaviour, most of his research these days is concerned with families. In his spare time, he enjoys playing classical guitar and synthesiser.
(Photo: courtesy Paul Amato)

As you can see from the dates of studies reviewed in this chapter, the 1960s and 1970s were the halcyon years of altruism research. In the local arena, we were little interested in altruism until the advent of Paul Amato, who from 1979 began a burst of publishing, stimulating local interest.

Amato was interested in the situational determinants of helping behaviour and in particular the impact of population density (Amato, 1980, 1981, 1983a). Nevertheless, his interests were catholic and included: cross-cultural helping behaviour (Amato, 1981a, 1983b); a taxonomy of helping behaviours (Pearce & Amato, 1980; Smithson & Amato, 1982); urban-rural differences (Amato, 1981b/c, 1983a); helping after the Ash Wednesday bushfires (Amato, 1984, 1986); and planned helping behaviour (Amato, 1985). Much of this research was featured in a book he co-authored with Mike Smithson and Philip Pearce in 1983, *Dimensions of Helping Behaviour*. More recently Amato's interests have included studies of planned helping behaviour (1985) and the role that

personality and social networks involvement plays (1990).

So far we have considered two approaches to understanding helping. Most studies examine situational variables: age and sex of the helper, age and sex of the victim, the number of onlookers, and so on. An alternative is to try to find some individual difference in personality underlying rates of helping. Most of the studies we review are laboratory based and most examined spontaneous helping of strangers in simulated emergencies, the so-called **bystander effect**. Amato (1990) notes that these approaches have little to do with the bulk of real-life helping: "most everyday assistance involves people . . . who are known to the helper (and) helping is usually not an isolated event but is embedded in long-term social relationships". We help not because of a personality trait or "momentary situational variables" but because our social network demands we do. "Helping is simply part and parcel of what it means to occupy certain roles." This also argues most of our helping is planned, not spontaneous, and is reciprocal in nature—we help our friends, they help us.

This does not mean that the bulk of research we have examined so far in the chapter is useless. As Amato (1990) notes, the point is not that individual personality differences or whatever are irrelevant to helping but that researchers may have spent too much time studying the wrong differences. Amato's previous research suggested that social network involvement may possibly be a better predictor of helping behaviour than personality or other individual differences (Amato, 1985). Studies by Pearce and Amato (1980) and Smithson, Amato and Pearce (1982) suggested that most subjects made a major distinction between planned and spontaneous helping. Would these two variables predict helping behaviour? Amato set out to test two hypotheses:

> Social network variables, such as the number of regular social contacts and the frequency of social interaction, are associated positively with the frequency of help provided in everyday life . . . Individual characteristics (including both intrapsychic and social network variables) are better predictors of planned

helping than of spontaneous helping. (Amato, 1990, pp. 32–3)

In three studies, Amato (1990) examined helping behaviour in a total of 558 university students and 127 non-student adults. His first study, a simple checklist of helping behaviours and situations, showed as predicted that most everyday helping occurred between friends, family members, and other familiar individuals; providing assistance to strangers was less common (see Table 10.2). Much of the help given to familiar others was planned, whereas help given to strangers was almost always spontaneous. Amato used these results to construct a self-report questionnaire of helping behaviours, which included personality measures of social responsibility, empathy, interpersonal trust, mastery, helping efficacy, authoritarianism, Machiavellianism and locus of control (all factors we have already discussed in preceding chapters). Amato also included a test of social desirability to see if subjects were likely to give socially appropriate responses. A multidimensional scaling analysis revealed three types of helping: planned formal, planned informal, and spontaneous. In his final study Amato used this scale and

Table 10.2 *Percentage of everyday spontaneous and planned helping episodes*

Recipients	Percentage of episodes		Percent planned	
	Students	Non-students	Students	Non-students
Friends	35.1	22.9	36.5	43.7
Family	20.2	27.4	34.2	52.5
Co-workers	7.9	10.7	20.9	40.0
Roommates	7.3	1.4	17.5	—
Classmates	6.1	0.5	13.3	—
Neighbours	2.1	4.8	33.3	57.1
Acquaintances	2.9	3.3	13.3	25.0
Organisations	4.4	11.4	77.8	61.5
Customers/clients	2.9	8.8	16.7	26.3
Strangers	10.8	8.8	2.9	2.7
N of episodes	793	420		
N of subjects	192	142		

Source: Amato, 1990.

found that characteristics of individuals were related more strongly to planned forms of helping, than to spontaneous forms of helping and that social network variables were better predictors of self-reported helping behaviour than were traditional personality variables.

Amato's results are not surprising but only obvious in hindsight. Formal planned helping for students and non-students was associated with social network variables like the number of friends they had, the length of time they had lived in a neighbourhood and the number of clubs and other social organisations they belonged to. Spontaneous helping was associated only with the amount of help received. This suggests that reciprocity or exchange issues (see Chapter Eight) underlay one's willingness to help spontaneously, although greater levels of this type of helping were associated with higher levels of help received from friends and family, suggesting that being often helped makes one more generous in return. Students showed only a few very weak correlations between

personality and helping, and non-students none at all. This suggests that traditional personality approaches, which study social responsibility, empathy, interpersonal trust, locus of control and the like, are missing the point as these measures have little relation to self-reported helping.

While Amato's study gave strong and clear results using conservative tests of significance, they are still only self-report measures and, as we have seen in this chapter so far, if there is an area of social psychology where the rule "don't do as I do, do as I say" applies, it is in helping. Nevertheless, Amato is confident these results reflect real-life helping as they are intuitively plausible, and because errors of subject bias (like wanting to appear a helpful person) should have shown up equally across all categories of helping and did not. Amato concludes: "The 'helpful' individual may turn out to be the person who plays a relatively large number of social roles with a relatively large number of people."

Sensory overload

How do we interpret these results? Wirth suggested in 1938 that urban dwellers are not necessarily ruder or less helpful than country people but are subject to greater stimulation. This was examined by many other researchers (Simmel, 1957; Milgram, 1970; Cohen, 1978; Korte, 1981); see in particular Steblay's 1987 meta-analysis of all the statistical research on the subject). In 1970 Stanley Milgram proposed a sensory overload theory to account for this difference. City people face greater stimulation and so have higher basal stress levels. One of the many ways we cope in cities is to reduce the amount of information we process, indeed this may not even be a voluntary action (Schmidt & Keating, 1979). Crowding may overwhelm city dwellers' capacity to process information and their decisional control is probably impaired.

Nor must we forget what a singularly unobservant lot we are. City dwellers may be less observant, rather than less helpful, than rural dwellers. One of the consequences of the overstimulation thesis is that city dwellers reduce the amount of sensory input they attend to. So often they do not get beyond step one of Latane and Darley's process and fail to notice the need for aid. In addition, the number of aid requests might contribute to the city size/helping gradient. We have to rank our sensory inputs and filter out those that are background constants. As Gifford suggested:

> The reason city dwellers sometimes walk past persons who are collapsed on the street is not because they are less kind, but because they are forced to rank order their social priorities to manage the extremely

heavy amount of stimulation they face each day. Unfortunately, there are many needy individuals on the streets of large cities; most individuals could not manage a normal life if they attended to the needs of every needy person they encountered. (Gifford, 1987, p. 192)

An interesting sidelight on this theory is Witt's (1989) research with students administered the Just World and Rotter's Locus of Control scales. His results suggest that city dwellers were less likely to believe it was a just world, had encountered more controlling forces, and felt they had less control of their lives. If you believe you have less than total control of your actions, you will feel less responsible for not helping. Perhaps this feeling of diminished responsibility lessens urban dwellers' responsiveness to others' needs.

Although there are many reasons for this city/rural difference, clearly city dwellers are less likely to help, but there are significant qualifications from an environmental perspective. Environmental psychologists have pursued the stress-adaptation theory with some vigour in their studies of crowding (see Chapter Thirteen) with varying results. Richard Kammann, Richard Thompson and Robyn Irwin (1979) of Otago University suggest that immediate pedestrian density, and the consequent diffusion of responsibility, is a more important variable than city size in helping behaviour. Steblay's (1987) statistical analysis further demonstrated that city or rural differences had more to do with the male sex of the victim and then only when the help requested was trivial, or an unambiguous emergency. Urban crime rates and density were another factor leading to decreased altruism, which suggests people have learned when it is inadvisable to help (House & Wolf, 1978). These and many other studies (Weiner, 1976; Hannson & Slade, 1977; Amato, 1981b) all suggest that environmental factors are crucial, if variable, in determining helping behaviour.

Amato's 1983 experiments dealt with assisting strangers and considerable research has looked at helping those we know. Form and Nosow (1958) noted that in the wake of American Midwest tornadoes and other disasters, people first help family, then friends and acquaintances and then strangers. This may ultimately come back to in-group/out-group differences (Hornstein, 1976), which we will discuss at length in Chapter Twelve. Latane and Darley (1970) and Queensland researcher Philip Pearce (1980) demonstrated that even a short acquaintanceship increases future helping.

Time pressures

Living in the city is not only stressful, it is rushed. Bornstein (1979), by measuring the mean walking speeds in various countries, was able to show that the pace of life accelerates as population density increases. In Limerick, Eire (population in 1979, 57 161), mean walking speed was 1.27 metres per second (m/s); in Edinburgh, Scotland (population 470 085) it was 1.51 m/s, and in 1989 in Sydney my students measured mean speeds at 1.63 m/s (see also Walmsley & Lewis, 1989). Recalling Gifford's comments quoted earlier, city dwellers are less likely to be observant as the pressures build up and are even less likely to be observant as their walking pace accelerates (Newman & McCauley, 1977).

Darley and Batson (1973) tried to assess how situational determinants interfered with moral principles. While they were unsuccessful in showing that one's religiosity influenced helping, they found their situational variable, time pressure, was highly significant. Darley and Batson asked twenty theological students at Princeton University Seminary to give an impromptu talk on vocational careers for seminary graduates, and another twenty to speak about the parable of the Good Samaritan. The tasks were presented as a test of their ability to think on their feet and they were asked to walk over to another building and give their talk. As they left they passed an alley-way in which a confederate was slumped over, obviously ill and groaning loudly as they passed. Some students literally had to step over the person to continue. The dependent variable was the number helping and the experimental conditions varied the time limits imposed on the students. Some were told they were late and holding things up and to hurry over; others were told that they were on and should go over; and in the low-rush condition students were told they had a few minutes yet but should head over.

Results were as tragic as they were significant. There were no significant differences between topics! The high-rush students had a low 10 per cent helping rate, the moderate-rush 45 per cent and the low-rush, 63 per cent, averaging to an overall helping rate of 40 per cent. Those who noticed the confederate later revealed their conflict of interest between the needs of their audience and those of the victim. While everyone has commented on the theological students' failure to enact their supposed empathy and Christian principles, perhaps the more profound finding was the sheer conflict and preoccupation caused by time pressures. If you are interested in reading about the role of religious belief as it affects altruism, see Chen (1988), Batson et al. (1989), Bernt (1989) and Chau et al. (1990). For an interesting view of how Australian Protestant clergy are caught between radical social action and more traditional forms of altruism, see Norm Blaikie's 1974 article.

Mood and helping

We have already considered the role of empathy in promoting helping behaviour, but how about your psychological state on the day? If you have just had a terrible fight with your boss and then yet another psychology student approaches you for a donation, you are hardly likely to be altruistic. Isen (1970) in a series of tests measured this phenomenon. In her first series, she assigned teachers and students to one of three experimental conditions to do a series of paper and pencil tests, and gave them varying levels of praise on their performance. She then measured their willingness to help a woman struggling with a heavy pile of books and compared their responses to a control group who had not done the tests. As expected the more successful students were more prosocial, but is helping due to a "warm rosy glow" after success, or are there happy and altruistic personalities? To test this she gave biscuits to half the students waiting for an experiment in which they had alternatively to help or hinder a learner. As expected those students who received the free biscuits were more helpful than the controls, moreover they were less likely to distract learners (Isen & Levin 1972). Isen concluded that the happier we are the more benevolent we become. Any further praise or success amplifies helping by setting up "a loop of positive cognitions" (Isen & Simmonds, 1978).

If being in a good mood increases altruism, what does being down in the dumps do? The situation is not as straightforward as when feeling good. Quite a bit of conflicting evidence over the last few decades suggests a bad mood may either increase or decrease helping (Barden et al., 1981; Dovidio, 1984; Amato, 1986). For example, Soames Job of the University of Sydney (1987) measured the return-rate of "lost" letters placed on the cars of supporters of the winning and losing rugby teams after a major match in Sydney. Significantly more letters were returned by supporters of the losing team, suggesting that their negative mood increased helping behaviour, in comparison to the cheerful mood and low return rates of the winning team's supporters.

negative-state relief model
Helping others, to assuage vicarious guilt over a victim's trouble and reducing our empathic distress.

It seems from these studies that whether feeling good or bad, we help more than if in a neutral mood. This led Robert Cialdini to propose the **negative-state relief model** (Cialdini et al., 1973). Cialdini's model is a variant of the classic tension-reduction theories of early psychology. A person who witnesses or causes harm to another becomes uneasy; to reduce this uneasiness they may increase their helping to "pay back" someone, even if not to the original victim. But this is not the only way they deal with their feelings. Cialdini et al. also found that if the negative experience is followed by a positive one there is a cancelling that reduces future

(Cartoonist: Graeme Mitchell)

helping. Perhaps this is further evidence supporting the view that altruism is egoistic and all we are interested in is feeling better (Manucia, Baumann & Cialdini, 1984; Batson et al. 1989).

Several theorists have added interesting insights to this puzzle. Cunningham et al. (1980) convincingly showed that arousing guilt increases helping. Freedman, Wallington and Bless (1967) told subjects the importance of not double-guessing an experiment, while half were casually told about the test by a confederate and their evident consequent increase in guilt promoted increased helping. Again it seems that equity theory is at work here (Walster, Walster & Berscheid, 1978). Our emotional state needs to be in balance and if we are either too much or too little rewarded, we adjust our actions accordingly. According to Lerner, in his book *The Belief in a Just world: A Fundamental Delusion* (1980), we act as we wish the world to be. So when we are faced with guilt, we try to balance out our activities on the scales of divine justice. This can be taken metaphorically as in the study by Carlsmith et al. (1968), where subjects "accidentally" ruined another's thesis, or literally in the study of Catholics before and after confession, by Harris, Benson and Hall (1975). In both studies subjects who had confessed were less helpful than those who had not.

Many other factors influence the way we help when emotionally aroused and it is not possible to give a complete list here (see Bierhoff & Klein, 1988, for a European perspective). From the developmental side, guilt

Lerner found that those who regularly attended emergencies were less likely to believe in a just world.
(Photo: Barry Price)

only works as a behavioural lever after the child has left the egocentric stage of cognitive development and can put themselves in someone else's shoes (Cialdini & Kenrick, 1976). Further, children only respond positively to induced guilt when they are reinforced for their actions, or at a minimum, noticed (Kenrick et al., 1979). Mayer et al. (1985) suggested that focus seems to be the crucial point. If a person is concentrating on their own misery, egocentric helping to reduce their own emotional upset becomes a matter of whether they notice another's needs. Thompson and Hoffman (1980) suggest that if we can displace responsibility for our negative mood on to another, we are more likely to help them, particularly if, as Rogers et al. (1982) noted, we otherwise have to blame ourselves for our poor state. Nor does the negative-state relief model cover the possibility of a positive-relief state. Kyle Smith et al. (1989) found that as well as egoistic sadness reduction, many of their subjects experienced a burst of "vicarious joy at the resolution of the victim's needs". This raises the more general point that helping may be an enjoyable, as well as a costly, process.

Before leaving this section on the personal and situational variables that affect helping, we must note once again the importance of attribution, though we have covered this topic at length (Chapter Three). Our attributions play an enormous role in whether we will help. If we think the victim is a lazy, shiftless indigent, we are hardly likely to help (see Furnham, 1984, for a review of British and Australian research on public attributions about the young unemployed).

Being helped

So far we have almost exclusively dealt with helpers, but what about the other side of altruism? All human interactions are reciprocal at one level or another, and our next turn as a helper will be governed in part by our experience of either being helped, or of someone's reaction to our last reincarnation as the Good Samaritan. We have all felt like idiots as we have sat in class realising we have missed something important and yet squirm around uneasily not wanting to display our inattention to our peers. Research would confirm your commonsense impressions that as much as we might need help, we are uncomfortable receiving it (Broll, Gross & Piliavin, 1974) and feel we are less competent if we require it (DePaulo & Fisher, 1980). As with helpers, equity theory explains our discomfort. We feel embarrassed and wonder if we are really worthy of the help offered (Wilke & Lanzetta, 1970). Equally, the norm of reciprocity is at work, and the saying "I owe you one" sums up our dilemma: how can we ever repay our debt? (Greenberg, 1980).

As we discussed in our section on reciprocal altruism, we are shrewd judges of helpers' motives and feel put upon if we think helpers are responding to meet their own needs. Empathic carers are less likely to cause resentment than those who expect our gratitude, or whom we feel are only helping to fulfil some sort of civic duty (Rosen et al., 1986). Perversely, although we much prefer to be helped by friends, we feel much more threatened by their help and it comes at great expense to our self-esteem (DePaulo et al., 1981); particularly if it reflects poorly on our own intellect (Baumeister, 1982; Nadler et al., 1983). This seeming paradox is resolved if you consider that friends are less likely to be keeping tally of the times they have helped us and less inclined to want immediate reciprocity (Clark & Mills, 1979; Clark, 1984). On the other hand, kin selection and reciprocal altruism imply a much stronger debt to one's "tribe" than to strangers. So the experience of being helped is an uneasy one and sometimes our gratitude slips a little, particularly if we think the help received is inappropriate (Ventimiglia, 1982). It seems then that the important factor in receiving help gracefully is how responsible we are for our dilemma. This is often confirmed by accounts of the philosophical resignation and cheerfulness of survivors of disasters like the Bay of Islands Ferry sinking and Cyclone Tracy. We are more likely to feel comfortable accepting help when the situation was beyond our control.

Fisher, Nadler and DePaulo in their book *New Directions in Helping* (1983), which reviews much of the early research covered in this chapter, also draw parallels to helping on the international scene. Australians were much put out in 1990 when a former Papua New Guinea Prime Minister, Rabbie Namaliu, commented unfavourably on Australia's aid policy towards his country. As Papua New Guinea's major aid donor, giving some 50 per cent of their Government's revenue, commentators thought this was a little like looking the gift-horse in the mouth. Although it is generally easier to accept international aid from a friendly country, like Australia, there are times when it may be damaging. Brehm in 1966 coined the term "psychological reactance" to mark the universal reaction against perceived threats to freedom of choice. While it is acceptable for a medium-ranked country like Australia, with a relatively non-interventionist world stance, to offer aid and assistance, it is another thing to interfere in New Guinea's internal affairs. Perhaps Mr Namaliu was reacting to our press coverage of the Western Mining debacle and New Guinea's handling of the Bougainville secession?

While it is always a bit speculative to translate individual psychological reactions on to the world stage, some interesting experiments have offered intriguing insights.

To test the hypothesis that helping may sometimes do more harm than good, Ken Gergen set up an international experiment to test the effects of aid-giving (Gergen et al., 1975). Students from Japan, Sweden and the US were formed into groups of six and given an equal stake so they could play a game of chance. Unfortunately the game was rigged so subjects would lose their money. Aid was then received from a confederate who gave the loser enough money to continue and eventually win the game. Subjects were divided into different experimental conditions according to the type of aid given. In one trial, donors lent the money with a note attached saying it could be repaid later; in another it was largess from a winner with a big pile; in yet another the donor was a modest winner. The results met Gergen's expectations that aid was most gratefully received as a loan and less so as a gift. Results were similar for all nationalities and it was clear that poorer donors were more likely to be respected and appreciated than richer donors (Fisher & Nadler, 1976).

Perhaps this explains why major aid donors like the United States are so resented internationally. If aid is unconditional and at some considerable expense to the donor, we feel we are being assisted and by implication respected. If aid is pin-money to the donor, then by implication the recipient is an unimportant afterthought. Perhaps the moral in avoiding giving offence to our aid recipients is to help until it hurts.

Box 10.5 *Food for thought: Ecology and altruism*

You will have noticed that all of our examples dealt narrowly with humans giving aid to another human, however removed, and perhaps this reflects our preoccupations as psychologists. Obviously altruism can take many other forms. Every summer holiday as we head off on our long Christmas vacation to the beach and bush, we abandon pets in their hundreds of thousands—nor are we any less cruel to our fauna. Rob O'Neil, past State President of the NSW RSPCA commented recently that the best training helping professionals could get would be in an animal pound and there is considerable wisdom in his remark. Only slowly are we beginning to realise our interdependence with, and the enormous toll we have imposed on, our co-evolutionists. Each species we extinguish is one less chance for our survival and yet we rarely hear about the need for a little altruism towards slugs and slime moulds.

And altruism will start to take quite unusual forms in the next few decades, at least from twentieth century perspectives, as ecology strikes back, nor am I alone in thinking it is a sobering future we face. Garrett Hardin's 1977 book, *The Limits to Altruism: An Ecologist's View of Survival*, is required reading. As we start to realise just how many of us are crammed into our small world, we will have to frame and enforce public policies for human survival quite punishing of individuals and yet prosocial in the broadest sense. Take the human population

A little altruism goes a long way. Pups like these are often abandoned and have to be destroyed. (Photo: Armen Deushian/Macarthur Advertiser)

explosion as an example. Humans are considered *the* most successful species because we have experienced few limits to our breeding potential. As we start to face these limits globally, we will do so by insisting on enforced contraception, compulsory termination of unallocated pregnancies, birth quotas and taxes, and compulsory sterilisations. This will promote a market for genetic materials, birth rights and a black-market in babies; not to mention a wholesale modification of our current religious attitudes to sexuality; and these will be the very least of the changes we will experience as we try to rein in our population explosion. As we have to bail ever faster in a sinking lifeboat, the greatest good for the greatest number may make the public coercion of individuals a prosocial act in its deepest sense.

Why should we help anyway? One of the saddest conclusions of the international resources market is that an oversupply drives the value of the goods down. As constant famine and our paltry relief efforts show, if all you have is an oversupply of people, then life is cheap. In a secular age, when few of us feel obliged to obey divine writ to love one another, we need to develop a morality of expediency to face the coming ecological catastrophe and start using the world's resources equitably. As we realise just how interconnected we all are, sharing and caring should be our highest moral imperative. As the ethicist Peter Singer of Monash University argues, in support of the starving millions, "if it is in our power to prevent something bad happening, without thereby sacrificing anything of comparable moral importance, we ought, morally to do it" (Singer, 1987).

Summary

Altruism is one of the paradoxes of human behaviour. Why is it that some people selflessly help others, often at great personal cost, while research shows most of us are indifferent to others' plight? We believe that we should help, and believe we will, but in practice don't, as much research and many accounts of public indifference demonstrate. So why do some people help, and is their reward some intrinsic satisfaction, or the praise they receive?

Prosocial research is less ambiguous. It does not concern itself with motive but teases out the determinants of helping, and a major concern is whether it is innate or learned. Sociobiologists argue helping is innate with evolutionary benefits in promoting group natural selection, through parental investment and kin selection. Ultimately we help because we expect to be rewarded in the future—reciprocal altruism.

Critics argue helping is an acquired behaviour, part of the package of prosocial norms we are socialised to support. Norms of social justice, equity, reciprocity and social responsibility are part of each culture's social exchange processes and part of their social control mechanisms. Some research, however, has found these norms may conflict with more personal and deeply held beliefs, diminishing their effect. We learn to become altruists as part of our development. Vicarious arousal and empathy with another's plight are necessary building blocks of altruism.

The bulk of altruism research has explored the determinants of helping behaviour. "When will we help?" has proved a complex multifactorial problem. Cognitive theories, such as bystander intervention calculus, predict that as group size increases personal responsibility to act diminishes. We will help if we feel capable and understand what is required. If the situation is ambiguous or helping is likely to be costly, we are less likely to help. The victim's sex, race, age, ethnicity, and several other factors, all influence whether we will help.

Environmental theories stress the role of social stressors and sensory overload in limiting helping behaviour. If you live in a densely populated area you are more likely to suffer over-stimulation and role overload and are less likely to help. City people are not less caring, but more pressured, and possibly less observant, than their rural counterparts.

Mood also determines whether we will help. The negative-state relief model predicts that helping leads to tension reduction and emotional relief. Arousing guilt in the potential helper is a powerful inducement to feel better by helping and many onlookers experience vicarious relief when a victim is helped.

Being helped is an uncomfortable experience. It reflects adversely on our competence and leaves us feeling indebted to helpers as equity theory would predict. We are resentful of institutional and uncaring aid, and react best as victims when we are clearly not responsible for our state, or when we are able to return the favour. Paradoxically we are less likely to enjoy being helped by a friend than a complete stranger.

Altruistic behaviour is likely to become less individualistic and more societal, as we put the needs of the group ahead of the needs of individuals. As we face the major social changes needed to cope with population pressures and environmental degradation, prosocial behaviour will take some novel turns from a twentieth century perspective.

Recommended reading

Clark M.S. (ed.) (1990) PROSOCIAL BEHAVIOR, Sage, Newbury Park, Ca. Vol 12 of Sage's series A REVIEW OF PERSONALITY AND SOCIAL PSYCHOLOGY, simply written introductory primers containing chapters by leading experts in the field.

Dawkins R. (1976) THE SELFISH GENE, Oxford University Press, Lond. An account of altruistic behaviour from a sociobiological perspective.

Eisenberg N. (1986) ALTRUISTIC EMOTION, COGNITION AND BEHAVIOR, Erlbaum, Hillsdale, NJ. A general review of altruistic research from an emotion and social cognitive perspective.

Hardin G. (1977) THE LIMITS TO ALTRUISM: AN ECOLOGIST'S VIEW OF SURVIVAL, Indiana University Press, Bloomington. A foremost ecologist reviews the tragedy of the commons and the limits to our current prosocial behaviour.

Smithson M., Amato P.R. and Pearce P.L. (1983) DIMENSIONS OF HELPING BEHAVIOUR, Pergamon Press, Sydney, 1983. A review of prosocial research by Paul Amato and two Australian-based authors.

GENDER

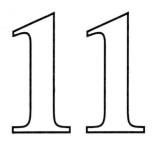

*T*here are two ways of looking at the sex-role revolution this century.
Either we are moving from one set of roles to another or, as some
percipient commentators suggest, we are abandoning gender roles
altogether and discovering the freedom of just being people. Whatever the case,
there is little doubt the current situation is confused and even the enlightened
may go astray. Many men are finding it increasingly difficult to know how to
behave around women. If we talk too much about our feelings we are too
sensitive, out of control and too emotional. If we don't talk about them enough,
we are too insensitive, controlling and too cognitive. If we hold back from
sexual advances, we are not masculine enough and if we make an advance too
quickly, we are acting "just like a man who only has one thing on his mind".
Over the past few years I have had a number of experiences that have only
made the situation more confusing for me.

A number of years ago, a friend from university whom I hadn't seen for a
couple of years rang to arrange to go out to dinner to discuss some problems
she was having with her husband. At the end of the evening, the bill arrived
which I picked up. She made no attempt to pay, expecting that, as a man, I
should pick up the tab for a meeting that she arranged. I met her a few months
later for lunch and I assumed that it was her turn to pay. When we discussed
this at the end of the meal, she angrily threw enough money for her meal onto
the table and clearly stated that she certainly would not pay for me. This
became an interesting game between the two of us for the next few years as
we each tried to convince the other of the validity of our views. I thought we
should split the bill while she thought men should pay at restaurants and that
women should return this favour by cooking meals at home and inviting them
over.

Even simple actions are often loaded with meaning. I was travelling with a
female friend in India. We were sharing expenses and were having trouble
keeping our money sorted out when going to restaurants and using public
transport. To help simplify the procedure, we kept a common purse that we
contributed equal amounts of money to at regular intervals. Initially, I took
charge of the purse. After a short time, my friend stated very clearly that she
would like to be the person paying from the common purse. I enjoyed the luxury
of not having to worry about paying for things and simply left this up to her.
She saw it as an issue of control and privilege while I saw it as an issue of
tedious responsibility.

You have to watch your language too! I was at a coffee shop with a couple
of female friends. In the course of the conversation, I used the term "ladies"
to refer to them. I was immediately attacked and told that they were not ladies
but women and I would do well to remember it! I spent the next few months
monitoring most of my speech, scanning it for sexist language before allowing
words out of my mouth.

In my current employment, I am working in an organisation largely
composed of women. I frequently approach a door at the same time as one
of my colleagues. Sometimes I stand back or open a door and am clearly
instructed to go first as the woman grabs the door to hold it for me. At other
times, my behaviour is treated as a courteous gesture. At other times, I simply
walk through first, assuming that the woman will hold the door for me. It is

*very hard for me to predict what I should do as it seems situation-specific and
not person-specific. Thus, gender becomes an issue in many situations that are
difficult to decipher.*

Gender identity

Why has the gender that gave us the Sistine Chapel brought us to the
edge of cosmocide? . . . men are systematically conditioned to endure
pain, to kill, and to die in the service of the tribe, nation or state. The
male psyche is, first and foremost, the warrior psyche. Nothing shapes,
informs, and moulds us so much as society's demand that we become
specialists in the use of power and violence, or as we euphemistically
say, "defence". Historically, the major difference between men and
women is that men have always been expected to be able to resort to
violence when necessary. The capacity and willingness for violence
has been central to our self-definition. (Keen, 1991, p. 36–7)

The human animal is divided into two genders, not really very different
from one another until one is taught from birth how to be Masculine
and the other is taught how to be Feminine. Most people have been
taught their gender stereotype so well that they don't remember learning
it and assume it is inherent and innate, as if they came into the world
wrapped in either a pink or blue blanket, and everything flowed naturally
from there. (Pittman, 1985, p. 24)

In this chapter, we explore issues of sex and gender and how these affect
our feelings and behaviour, and the way we understand each other. As
Pittman suggests, we rarely think about being programmed to be male or
female. Yet, how much of our behaviour is a direct result of a classification
made at birth? Keen (1991) suggests the main difference between men
and women is their capacity for violence. Can gender differences be distilled
to just one difference? Infants look virtually identical except for the genitalia.
On the basis of this one piece of information, a whole set of expectations
is set up, and the programming begins.

While it is usually easy to classify a newborn infant's sex, occasionally
this is difficult because of underdeveloped or ambiguous genitalia. Sometimes
it is discovered that an incorrect sex was assigned at birth. Many such
problems are corrected surgically, and Money and Tucker (1975) investigated
what happens when sex is assigned in an arbitrary manner. They concluded
that prior to two and a half years, the sex of an infant can be reassigned
without any readjustment difficulties for the child. Past that age, however,
serious problems are often apparent. With modern methods of chromosome
analysis, it is now possible to make more accurate assessments of sex when
it is ambiguous at birth. These findings demonstrate just how strong the
effects of the environment are on gender-role behaviour and how similar
infants are before the assignment of gender has an opportunity to take
effect.

Learning to be male and female

As we learn to be male or female, we also learn there are sanctions for failing to follow the prescribed gender roles. Why is society so concerned that gender roles are followed? What other factors contribute to the socialisation and maintenance of female and male behaviour? Perhaps it is helpful to consider these questions from different levels of analysis, by looking through various lenses. The concept of lenses is interesting as it suggests that when we view something through a lens, we are restricted in what we see. Thus, only certain information passes through the lens, only that which reflect its nature. In this sense lenses are censors of information. For example, when we look through a red lens, other rays of light are not permitted through and we only see a red world. For the purposes of this chapter, let us consider three very different lenses through which gender issues may be viewed.

Learning to become men and women rather than people starts at an early age. To what extent are these children already in entrenched gender roles?

Biological perspectives

The first lens is *biological*. This is one of the most fundamental ways of considering differences in gender behaviour. This can be further categorised into biological constitution and physical appearance. Physical appearance can indirectly influence behaviour. Size differences between females and males may be influential in the way we behave. It is probably much easier to comply with the wishes of someone who is 2 metres tall than of someone who is only 1.3 metres tall. Thus, size may present certain demand characteristics influencing the behaviour of those around large or small people. They in turn will influence each other's behaviour. All of this mutual influencing may begin with a basic biological difference related to size. Many examples of other physical attributes related to gender could be used to show how influence might occur between people.

Apart from biological appearance, there are obvious differences in the biological constitution of males and females. There are differences in the amounts and types of hormones and other chemicals present. How big an influence do these differences have on behaviour? Studies of neurotransmitters have been linked to differences in behaviour, suggesting that chemicals can influence behaviour (see Box 11.1).

Box 11.1 *Brain sex: Are men and women different?*

Brain sex is a term that was popularised by Moir and Jessel (1989), a psychologist and a journalist, who teamed up to consider the evidence for a biological explanation of gender differences. They note a number of reported gender differences that we discuss later in the chapter. For example, men perform better on tests of mathematics, hand–eye coordination and spatial abilities, while women perform better on tests of verbal ability and hearing. They present a number of case studies that show the absence of the male hormone **testosterone** at crucial stages of early development predisposed men towards more female behaviour, and the

Man the hunter? A masculine construct?

presence of this hormone predisposed women towards more male behaviour. Thus, the evidence suggests that the more male hormone present, the more likely the adult behaviour will be male-oriented. The converse also follows: the less male hormone present, the more likely adult behaviour will be female-oriented.

Moir and Jessel cite evidence from autopsies, which suggests that the **corpus callosum** is much larger in women than in men. The corpus callosum connects the left and right hemispheres of the brain. There is some evidence to suggest that damage to similar parts of the brain is less incapacitating in women than in men, as the greater number of connections between the hemispheres allows women to use the undamaged side of the brain for a particular function located in the damaged area. Thus, the authors suggest that the male brain is more specialised while the female brain is more generalised in terms of function. From this information, they conclude that women are more general thinkers while men are more specialised in their thinking. The argument from this biological base is then extended to encompass all observed differences in male and female behaviour. Men are more orderly and organised in their thinking while women are more intuitive. Men are more logical while women are more emotional. Men are more promiscuous wanting sex, while women want relationships, and so forth.

The authors conclude that their book, *Brain Sex: The Real Differences Between Men and Women*, was not written to justify a conservative view or to maintain the status quo, but with the "hope that men and women will be more honest about how they actually feel, and happier to be themselves". In their view, men and women are not created equal. As the book so aptly points out in reference to the women's movement, "science has set at naught their hard-won struggle towards equality". The implications of this conclusion are best expressed in their own words: "marriage is profoundly unnatural to the biology of the male" and "the roles of father and mother are not interchangeable". With these differences scientifically established "beyond speculation, beyond prejudice and beyond reasonable doubt", at least for the authors, they conclude that it is time for men and women to begin to appreciate the value of domestic labour. It is also obviously time for bumper stickers that unashamedly proclaim "Women do it better!"

This argument points to the importance of biological aspects of behaviour. Psychologists have always acknowledged the interplay between nature and nurture. Some of the evidence cited in Moir and Jessel (1989) is correlational and may not support the causal claims made by them. As we saw in Chapter One, correlation does not equal causation. Moir and Jessel clearly extrapolate beyond anatomical differences between males and females, to areas such as cognition, division of labour, sexuality and relationships. They fail to state adequately how the social constructions of gender are accounted for by their biological evidence. (At this point you might like to review our discussion of mating in Chapter Ten for an alternative view.)

Thus, while accepting the validity of biological influences on behaviour, we must not underestimate the powerful effects the environment plays in conditioning gender roles. As a general rule, as we move up the phylogenetic scale in terms of greater brain power, the influence of biology over behaviour is less and less significant. Thus, human beings with the power to think are able to moderate the biological impact on their behaviour in most situations. As we have already noted, even if there are real biological sex differences, our society does not have to perpetuate them.

While the biological lens may explain some differences, it is only one of many factors underlying gender. This nature–nurture controversy is the history of psychology and the sort of research required to unravel this question is often unethical. Even the concentration camp experiments in Hitler's Germany were unable to sort out this issue! As a student of behaviour, you will need to be aware of biology's influence, but its limited scope and the far-reaching implications of its acceptance make it only an inadequate explanation of the gender issues commented upon in this chapter.

Interactional or systemic perspectives

The second lens is *interactional* or *systemic* and moves the focus of analysis from within the individual onto relationships between people. This lens views behaviour as a product of reciprocal feedback within a system (Bateson, 1979). Groups are mutual. We interpret others' behaviour, they do the same to us. The feedback we receive, as well as our beliefs about how we should behave, determines our behaviour. If a man believes that he should be more active, or in charge of a situation, it is likely that he will take that role. Likewise, if a woman believes that she should be passive if a man is present, her actions will allow him to take charge. It follows that as the woman is passive, the man may feel that he *should* take charge and thus becomes more active. The woman's behaviour feeds into the response of the man, forming a cycle. In situations involving power, as a man takes more power, a woman takes less power or becomes more submissive, and he becomes more dominant. When we analyse situations from an interactional perspective, we notice there is no beginning or end to the cycle of behaviour set up between two people. Thus, no cause or effect may be attributed to either person, as their interaction becomes a system operating on behavioural feedback between each member of the interaction. Ultimately, this analysis leads to statements suggesting power does not exist, or is only a product of the interaction. One person is more powerful only because the other is more submissive.

While this lens may be useful for understanding some behaviour, it concentrates at the process or interactional level and ignores the content of the interaction. Power does exist and is of primary importance when discussing issues of gender. If males are more powerful in certain interactions, it is difficult to say this is simply because females are more submissive. A powerful man is powerful because of the domination he holds over another person, in this case a woman. The issue of domination, or greater amounts of power to enforce compliance, limits other responses from the woman in the interaction. Once power has been established, submission is the most practical response. Thus, it is ludicrous to speak of submissive behaviour as allowing powerful behaviour to occur. This line of argument is similar to suggesting that slaves allow their masters to be more powerful through their submissive behaviour! While this is true at one level, it is too simplistic an analysis. Much more fundamental processes ensure their enslavement.

While the interactional lens has limitations, its analysis may be useful in situations where power is not an issue, as in the first example describing active and passive behaviour. It may also be an appropriate analysis in the initial stages where a balance of power is being established between two people. I once had a neighbour whose husband had been violent to her on one occasion. She lived in Adelaide at the time and, following his violent display of power, she immediately moved to Melbourne for a year to be with her family. At the end of the year, she returned to her husband and never had another incident of violence in the relationship. Her display of power at the time surpassed her husband's, changing the dynamics of their relationship. Had she been submissive on that occasion, she probably would have ended up in a dominant–submissive relationship. Research suggests that when violence is punished very early, the chances of a violent relationship are reduced. When we consider issues of gender, power is a very significant factor, making the interactional lens of limited utility in providing a satisfactory analysis, unless as in this example it is applied at the very start of the problem behaviour.

Sociopolitical perspectives

The third lens is sociopolitical. This is the broadest level of analysis as it argues that societal structures support gender differences. It sees power as fundamental to the structure of our patriarchal society which by definition oppresses women (James, 1984). Power is clearly related to the acquisition of money and other valuable resources. Most of the wealth in New Zealand and Australia is controlled by men, who occupy most of the positions of power where wealth may be accumulated. The laws and rules of society favour men. For example, a current debate in Australia relates to the ordination of women in the Anglican Church. As women are now being ordained and will move into influential positions within the Church hierarchy, we are likely to see challenges to some of the beliefs the Church considers fundamental to its doctrine. Similarly, property settlements after divorces often leave women in a state of poverty, holding out their hands to their ex-partners for money to support their family. Our society has decided what is valuable in terms of human effort and does not see child-rearing or household duties as sufficiently valuable to reward them financially in the same way that other effort is rewarded. All of these factors point to a significant bias towards men, helping to create a patriarchal culture. Some argue that this is hardly surprising, as men decide what we value and have created the rules about how we reward the things we value. At this point you might like to consider why men are as powerful as they are and how they first acquired their power.

Whether men like it or not, they are born into very powerful positions and often unthinkingly use this power in the way they act with each other and with women. Even though they may argue this is an accident of birth and they are powerless to act against the system, they continue to play the role and perpetuate the existing hierarchical arrangement. Feminists argue that men have no motivation to change a system that favours them and that the dominant culture punishes men who try to challenge its rules. In fairness, some men do attempt to change a stressful system that provides little opportunity to show vulnerability as men strive to be competitive, influential and dominant. However, change is always slow, particularly when the dominant view is embraced by both men and women. We must also recognise that the rewards are too great for those who would have to sacrifice their power to create a truly egalitarian society not based on gender differences.

The sociopolitical lens accounts for power differences in gender relations, but fails to deal adequately with biological and interactional perspectives. In their analysis of the conflict between the sociopolitical and interactional

Patriarchal science? This dedicated scientist has forstalled marriage and children in trying to succeed in her profession. Even at this level of sacrifice, many women still do not succeed. (Photo: Gavin Price)

perspectives, James and McIntyre (1989) argue for a "double description" that validates both ways of understanding male and female relations. Thus, both views are valid at different levels of analysis. However, when the special issue of power is considered, the interactional lens is inadequate because it assumes equality of participants to an interaction. I would extend this argument, and suggest that all three lenses are appropriate until they reach the limitation of dealing with power differences. It is possible that gender power relations may even encourage interactional or biological interpretations. Gender is a very sensitive issue and many opinions use all three interpretations and go far beyond the scientific evidence. While I acknowledge the usefulness of each lens, the problem of power in gender differences requires special attention. Therefore, the sociopolitical lens will be the predominant perspective through which gender will be interpreted in this chapter.

Defining sex and gender

Gender is a term that is increasingly used in the literature, where sex would have been used in the past. This reminds me of a story of a family who had recently moved to a new house. As the father was outside, getting to know a neighbour, his eight-year-old daughter shouted from the upstairs window, "Daddy, what is sex?" The father was embarrassed and fumbled for words as he tried to think of an appropriate answer. In the ensuing silence, his daughter explained that she was attempting to fill out a play application for a driver's licence. Relieved, the father answered, "write female".

gender
A term used to denote differences between men and women that are learned not biological in nature.

Sex is now used to refer to a biological differentiation. Thus, we refer to maleness and femaleness as a way of indicating biological distinctions relating to genitalia, chromosomes or reproductive hormones. Gender, on the other hand, has been used to refer to the social results, or the environmental effects, of the classification of sex. Thus, it represents the interaction between the biological and social aspects associated with the labelling process. As we are predominantly interested in the social aspects of behaviour, this chapter will concern itself predominantly with issues of gender.

sex
A term used to denote differences between men and women that are biological in nature.

So from the day we are born, we are classified by sex and forced to learn different behaviours; emotions and ways of expressing feelings; different attitudes; and differing ways of seeing the world. These gender differences are closely linked to inequities of power and control in our hierarchical society. Of course this classification has enormous implications for our development, including our self-concept, and comes complete with expectations and opportunities that will influence the decisions we make about our lives.

Imagine what would happen if one day you woke up and people began to respond as though you were the other gender. If you had been male and were now arbitrarily female, you might not be able to be out by yourself at night in a city like Melbourne or Auckland. You might have to change your career, as it might now be an embarrassing occupation for a woman. You now have to be concerned about the shape of your body and the way you present it in public. You might also have to be less forward in talking to men and might even have to pretend you do not enjoy sex as much as your partner. On the other hand, if you had been female and woke up male, you might have to pretend that you didn't have any feelings about the hurtful comments that people made to you. You might suddenly have freedom to go wherever you wished at any time of day. You might have to initiate contact with women who interested you and be prepared to face their rejection. You are now free to age and be seen as more desirable rather than less desirable, while your facial lines now reflect character rather than simply age. You might also have to perform sexually whether you were interested or not because it was expected of you. Thus, far-reaching ramifications become apparent that reflect our sexual classification. As you can see, there are some pluses to being a different gender, but do you think the advantages outweigh the disadvantages? From your brief sex change, you were able to see some of the implications of gender in our society. In this chapter we will explore the following areas and associated questions:

- *Gender stereotypes:* What expectations does society place on males and females? How are these expectations conveyed? What are the sanctions from society for failing to live up to the expectations?
- *Gender differences in behaviour:* Do stereotypes really affect the behaviour of females and males? Are there differences in behaviour between men and women? What does the research say? Are there more similarities or differences in behaviour? Is it more useful to highlight similarities or differences across gender?
- *Gender roles:* How do stereotypes and behaviour interact to produce gender roles? How widespread are these roles locally? In what ways are gender roles changing?

Gender stereotypes

As indicated in our starting quotation from Frank Pittman, one of the most significant differentiating gender features in infants is the colour of their clothes and blankets. While the infant is behaviourally undifferentiated at birth, the first question that parents and other people ask relates to the sex of the child. Have you ever wondered why we are so clearly oriented towards sex differences? Would we really not know how to treat an infant whose sex we did not know? Would we be confused about what to say to the parents of a child without knowing its sex? It seems that we all have a strong, perhaps unconscious, interest in maintaining stereotypes based on gender. It is common for parents to relate the sex of the child to appropriate characteristics far before they would be able to see such behaviour. Rubin, Provenzano and Luria (1974) interviewed parents of sons and daughters within twenty-four hours of birth. Parents saw their sons as resembling their fathers and their daughters as resembling their mothers. Although the infants did not differ in length, weight or physical activity, parents described females as being softer, smaller, finer-featured and less attentive than their male children.

With expectations based on gender from such a young age, it is little wonder that we grow up to fit the roles expected of us. As gender stereotypes are so widely accepted and actively promoted, with sanctions for those who stray, it is easy for parents to do their part in ensuring they are fulfilled. Parents are assisted by other family members, family friends and eventually the wider society to ensure that the stereotypes have been adequately applied; and this starts from the moment of birth. Lewis (1972) found female babies were looked at and talked to more than male babies. This may be related to the expectations that parents have regarding the dependency of their daughters and the support that female babies may require. These seemingly insignificant differences in handling infants can have powerful effects in the final behaviour of men and women.

Antill, Cunningham, Russell and Thompson (1981) developed an Australian list of male and female characteristics that were balanced for social desirability and social undesirability. The traits seem to fit a similar pattern to those described by American researchers (Broverman, et al., 1972). In both the American and Australian studies, traits seemed to fall into two clusters: instrumental (masculine characteristics) and warmth-expressiveness (feminine traits). It is interesting that our patriarchal capitalist society has defined instrumental behaviour as masculine, and warmth and expressiveness as feminine. As our society values productivity and sees maximum growth through competition, thinking logically and rationally, and actively taking control of all situations, it is not surprising that these instrumental characteristics are expected and cultivated in males. The stereotypes become the models for gender development and the criteria against which successful growth and maturity is measured. So we seem to define maturity at least partially on the basis of whether or not behaviour is appropriately male or female? How do you rate on this definition of maturity?

Appropriate behaviour is modelled by those of one's sex, but expectations are established by both genders. Thus, males are taught by observing males and females by observing females. This behaviour is reinforced by the expectations that females have of males and that males have of females. The world famous case in Ayers Rock, where Lindy Chamberlain was charged with killing her baby while on a family holiday, provides an interesting study of female stereotypes. Following an extremely sensational trial where a case was made for a dingo having taken her baby, she was convicted of the murder of her child. Some of the more subtle bits of evidence involved stereotypes of how a mother should respond to the loss of a child. Lindy was not perceived as emotional, excitable or submissive in portrayals by the media and in court. Very soon after the death, she began negotiations for the sale of a book about the incident. This was clearly not seen as appropriate female behaviour, increasing the suspicion of her guilt. We may well ask how much her failure to fit the stereotype was responsible for her eventual conviction. It was only after serving time in gaol and the discovery of an important piece of evidence, the child's jacket, that she was acquitted. There is still considerable debate about whether or not she committed the crime (see Chapter Fourteen).

The power of these stereotypes was seen in an Australian study that asked subjects to comment on the success of postgraduate students' work in nursing, teaching and medicine, where the postgraduates were described only by name (Feather & Simon, 1973). The success of the postgraduates with male-sounding names was explained in terms of superior talent, while the success of females was explained as postgraduates having taken easy courses, having cheated or having had lots of good luck. Men are often rated higher on traits such as competence, objectivity and independence, while women are rated higher on traits such as warmth, expressiveness, gentleness and awareness of feelings of others (Rosenkrantz, et al., 1968).

In recent times, we have had to deal with not only the expectations of family and friends, but also the invasion of our homes with government approved propaganda regarding appropriate male and female behaviour, values and attitudes. Media stereotypes have long been thought to exert a subtle influence on the way attitudes and behaviour are maintained in society and no doubt reinforce gender roles too. For instance, students watched commercials where gender roles were traditional, with men portrayed as authorities and women as sex objects, or in domestic roles (Jennings,

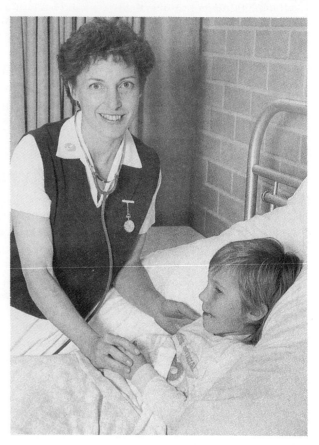

Gender stereotypes.
Why is the nurse always
female?
(Photo: Chris Simkin)

Geis & Brown, 1980). In a second set of commercials, the roles were reversed with women as authorities and men as sex objects. Participants subsequently were given a task to complete. Women who had watched the traditional version of the commercials conformed more and showed less self-confidence than women who watched the non-traditional commercials. With results like this in a one-off experiment, we can only surmise that the effect is more pronounced given the media barrage with which we are confronted. You might like to look for this when you next watch your favourite programme, and in particular during commercials, which are noted for their extreme stereotypes (see Box 11.2).

Box 11.2 *A show for sensitive new-age men and women?*

The problem of stereotypes is not restricted to commercials. I recently watched a television show called "Stud", which for feminists and sensitive new-age men must have resulted in frequent bouts of nausea if they endured an entire programme. It seemed the object was to find willing males and females who would appear on the show to discuss their dates that were previously arranged for them by the television station. The women were required to provide their reactions to the events surrounding the date, which were generally pithy statements with sexual innuendoes and double meanings. These statements were flashed on the screen and the men were required to guess which woman made the statement about them. If they were successful, they were given a heart to pin on their clothing. The compere then asked the men which one of them would be more likely to do various things such as buy sexy underwear for a partner or carve initials into a tree. After the men had made their decision, the women were required to make a unanimous decision as to which man would perform the particular behaviour. When there was agreement between the men and the women, the particular man was awarded a heart. Finally, the men were required to say with which woman they would like to have a holiday. The women had previously recorded the man with whom they would like a holiday.

If their answers matched, they were given the holiday.

It is interesting to note that there were two men and three women, meaning that at best one woman would be left out and that both men would get a holiday. Men were portrayed as being in charge in that they were given the hearts as points. The women were required to expose their thoughts about the men, but men were not required to engage in this level of self-exposure. Finally, the men selected the woman they desired for a holiday which was granted if the woman agreed. The stereotypes of male control, greater chances and opportunities for men, logical thinking in determining which woman made which comment, and female lack of control, greater self-disclosure and fewer opportunities were reinforced at the level of a supposedly humorous television game. Appropriate gender behaviour is not only modelled, but financially rewarded, and the message is transmitted at a subtle level, where the frivolity of the moment ensures that no one questions the underlying values. Needless to say, all participants were young and physically attractive. With such a consistent campaign, we must ask who is the author of the pervasive plot to maintain gender stereotypes? Is it simply that men, worldwide, control our media and are interested in maintaining power and control over women? I will leave you to speculate on this.

Changing stereotypes?

In 1979 Australian children were asked what they would like to be when they grow up (Russell & Smith, 1979). They found the responses of 7- and 15-year-old Sydney children were very stereotypical. Boys wanted to enter trades, armed forces, the police and male-dominated professions, and girls wanted to become nurses, teachers, secretaries and to marry and have children. In a large study of appropriate roles for men and women, more egalitarian responses were obtained in 1982 than in 1971 (Glezer, 1984). She concludes that domestic role-sharing is now taken for granted and the role of motherhood is seen as less central to the definition of self by young married women. With the 1981 sample, young married men also answered the questions. There were no overall differences between the male and female responses. Similar findings between males and females were obtained in another study where husbands and wives rated traditional and egalitarian role statements (Antill, Cotton & Tindale, 1983). They also noted that if husbands were more egalitarian, they tended to share more tasks than if only the wives were egalitarian.

Thus, it appears that some of the stereotypes regarding behaviour surrounding domestic roles is beginning to change. Change has also been noted in the attitudes of female students entering the health professions in Sydney. Surveys in 1976 and 1986 examined change associated with self perceptions, career and study ambitions (Westbrook & Nordholm, 1987). The results indicated the 1986 sample of women was more ambitious, more committed to career (even if there were small children) and had more egalitarian attitudes towards women's roles. This is of course a very middle-class sample which restricts its generalisability. It is not surprising that the data suggests that women are more prepared for change than are most men, as

Gender roles are slowly changing, leading to a greater acceptance of atypical roles for men and women.
(Photo: Rob Pozo/
Macarthur Advertiser)

it is the oppressed in any society who agitate for change. The powerful are comfortable remaining in that position, even though it may be to their own detriment from a psychological point of view.

As we saw in Chapter Five, prejudice is often subtle and unconscious, even among professionals. A sample of therapists was divided into three; one group was asked to describe a "mature, healthy, socially competent adult man"; a second group was asked to describe a "mature, healthy, socially competent adult woman"; while a third group was asked to describe a "mature, healthy, socially competent adult person" (Broverman, et al., 1970). The description of the healthy male was similar to the healthy adult. When compared to the healthy man, a healthy woman was seen as less independent, adventuresome, objective or competitive, but more emotional, excitable and submissive. If professionals in our health services, who are normally seen as an enlightened sector of society, believe that maleness is equated to maturity, then we have a measure of the extent to which stereotypes are active in our culture. While these attitudes are characteristic of health workers in the 1970s, there is still a disturbing trend in today's stereotypes. There has been strong feminist criticism about the failure to address these issues from a sociological perspective of power differentials between men and women (Avis, 1987; Bogard, 1984; Imber-Black, 1986). This feminist critique has resulted in a recent emphasis on gender-sensitive therapy (Brooks, 1991; Philpot, 1991, see Box 11.7).

In an attempt to deal rationally with gender stereotypes, Sandra Bem (1974) proposed a model of mental health based on a concept of **psychological androgyny**. The central premise of her model is that masculinity and femininity were not ends of a continuum but rather separate patterns of behaviour. It was her feeling that healthy individuals, regardless of their gender, should have traditionally defined masculine and feminine traits as part of their behavioural repertoire to use as each situation warranted.

psychological androgyny
People who incorporate both masculine and feminine traits into their self-concepts.

"PERHAPS WE OUGHT TO ENCOURAGE HER TO BECOME ANDROGYNOUS." (Cartoonist: Steve Harris)

Thus, androgynous individuals should be able to be logical, independent and active as well as gentle, nurturing and emotional. She developed the Bem Sex-Role Inventory which was based on her assumption that masculine and feminine traits were not opposite ends of the same dimension. The scale identified four groups of people: *masculine*, those high on traditional masculine traits; *feminine*, those high on traditional feminine traits; *androgynous*, those high on both masculine and feminine traits; and *undifferentiated*, those low on both masculine and feminine traits (see Figure 11.1).

The implication of this model is that psychologically healthy individuals are those who have a mixture of traits that go beyond gender stereotypes. This has occasioned a fair bit of debate but the point has generally been conceded that androgynous people are more flexible and less concerned with others' perceptions of them (Edwards & Spence, 1987). Whether this equates to psychological health is another matter, but Bem's model does have implications that are important and have stood the test of time. Bem proposed that people who score high on masculine and feminine gender role traits are **gender schematic**, that is, they perceive themselves in terms of traditional roles and have personal schemas that incorporate these traits. Put another way they are *trying* to be masculine or feminine. Those who are **gender aschematic** do not rely as much on gender traits for social comparison and are more interested in other aspects of identity (Bem, 1981). You will recall from Chapter Two that schematic processing is linked to personal identity and that the content of our schemas both reflects and reconstructs the ways we see others. Gender schemas then reflect the emphasis we give them. We will return to this point in a little while.

gender schematic
People who perceive themselves in terms of traditional roles and have personal schemas that incorporate these traits.

gender aschematic
People who do not rely on gender traits for social comparison and are more interested in other aspects of identity.

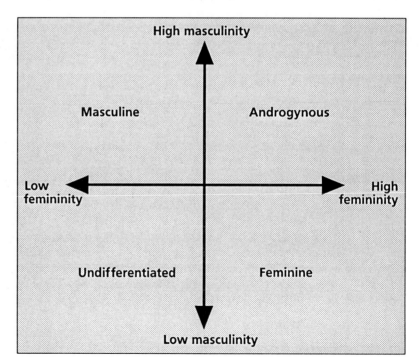

Figure 11.1
A two-dimensional model of androgyny

Bem's model was influential in understanding gender self-stereotypes but her scale did not travel well. Due to the methodological difficulties of using American scales in different cultures, a new scale was developed in Australia called the Personal Description Questionnaire (Antill et al., 1981). This scale has both positive and negative traditional male and female characteristics, an advance on the Bem Sex-Role Inventory. One interesting finding of this scale was to confirm overseas reports that males and females classified as having masculine traits had higher self-esteem than those with a more feminine identification (Russell & Antill, 1984). Other Australian studies found self-esteem positively related to masculinity and unrelated to femininity (Feather, 1985; Antill & Cunningham, 1979, 1980). Self-esteem is not masculine in nature but leads to greater feelings of self-worth in cultures like our own which value traits traditionally seen as masculine. Thus, having masculine traits is empirically more strongly associated with believing oneself to be acceptable than having feminine traits which are less valued (Rice, 1992).

This is not the full story, however. Androgynous styles aside, femininity makes for marital happiness (Antill, 1983; see Box 11.3). Marital happiness scores were positively related to both partners scoring high on femininity but not on masculinity. Traditional feminine traits and a warm, caring and nurturant style by both partners enhances satisfaction. In a laboratory study for example, Rosenthal and Harding (1983) found both males and females preferred androgynous and feminine members of the other sex, while those with only masculine qualities were not preferred. The qualities of traditional male and female behaviour are important, but in different contexts. Thus, it seems that while many studies show that masculine

In a patriarchical society men are not supposed to be interested in babies and women do not pump iron. Despite these beliefs, we often enjoy acting aschematically.
(Photo: Peter Watkins)

Box 11.3 *Profile: John Antill and sex roles*

John Antill is an associate professor of psychology at Macquarie University, Sydney where he has taught since 1973. He was educated at the University of Sydney, where he majored in mathematical statistics and at Oxford University where, as a Rhodes Scholar, he studied philosophy and psychology. He completed his PhD at the University of Michigan on the work of Eysenck under the direction of Melvin Manis and Richard Nisbett. Since then his major research interest is sex-roles: their nature, measurement, antecedents and consequences. This work has involved the development of sex-role scales and their application to interpersonal relationships and the division of labour within families. Of particular interest are the beliefs parents hold regarding the origins of sex differences, sex-roles and sexuality, and the transmission of this information from parent to child.
(Photo: courtesy Macquarie University Media Unit)

By now you will have noted the name Antill cropping up frequently in this and preceding chapters (see Chapter Six). John Antill is perhaps Australia's leading researcher on the methodology of measuring sex-roles, a vitally important part of the ongoing debate of this chapter. His Australian Sex Roles Inventory has been widely used to measure changing attitudes towards sex-roles and is often cited in local and overseas research.

John is also interested in applying psychological knowledge. To this end he has recently been involved in the development of Macquarie's Master of Applied Psychology programme and the focus of his teaching has been on psychological measurement and assessment, survey research and research design. He has also conducted several large-scale surveys of the behaviour, knowledge and attitudes of teenagers regarding road safety issues in order to evaluate the effectiveness of road safety education programmes.

qualities are linked with self-esteem, happiness and feminine qualities are linked in close relationships, pointing to the advantages of androgynous development, or having it both ways.

However, it must be pointed out that by continuing to identify the traits associated with male and female behaviour, we are perpetuating the differences between the genders, one of the reasons for which androgyny was originally hypothesised. Nor is androgyny a goal in itself. We may wish to create a society with newer, sharper and more rational gender differences, or none at all—only time will tell. As cultural norms change, the concept of typical masculine and feminine behaviour will also change; these changes may or may not be in the direction of androgyny. Perhaps it is more important to think about how we as a society define and encourage self-esteem in ourselves and others. If we as a society continue to devalue feminine traits, then the problem of gender differences in self-esteem will continue.

It seems ironical to me that we have defined self-esteem, which is strongly related to our relationships to others, in terms of the perceived masculine qualities that detract from the relationships. We have all experienced the good feelings that emerge from good friendships and relationships. Yet, why do we continue to relate "real" self-esteem to gender traits that create barriers, such as logical thought processes and competition, rather than bridges between people?

Thus stereotypes have had an oppressive effect on both males and females in our society. Many people say that stereotypes have had a negative effect on females, which of course only supports patriarchal ideas about masculine supremacy and preference. We have seen that the stereotypes begin to operate at first through family and friends, and continue through the attitudes of society as portrayed through avenues such as education, careers and personal therapy. The media then entertains us with further propaganda to support the stereotypes we have condoned. All of society's institutions and the media reflect the attitudes of the wider society, making any substantial change desired by a minority very remote. We have examined these stereotypes and will now turn to consider the actual behavioural differences that have been studied.

Sex and gender differences

To support his family, the man has to be distant, away hunting or fighting wars. To be tender, he must be tough enough to fend off enemies. To be generous, he must be selfish enough to amass goods, often by defeating other men. To be gentle, he must first be strong, even ruthless in confronting enemies. To love, he must be aggressive enough to court, seduce, and "win a wife". (Gilmore, 1990, p. 230)

Why do we try to find differences between men and women? It is easy to find perceived differences if we try, but surely it would be more productive for us to focus on commonalities between the sexes? When we act differently towards a group of people because our actions are based on race, age or gender beliefs, it is important to try to understand why we do so. Williams (1984) suggests we think of our own gender as the favoured ingroup and the other gender as the outgroup (see Chapters Five and Twelve). The outgroup suffers in comparison with our gender and is often rejected, or seen as inferior. Men may despise women simply because they are women and identifiably different. On the other hand, women may envy men's power and wealth and may wish to join this group or at least identify with it. Thus, differences tend to create unconscious processes of identification confirming the existence of differences that define either gender as inferior or superior.

The question of gender differences has been studied extensively over the years. Most studies involving humans automatically use gender as an independent variable, and this has created copious quantities of data that is unmanageable simply by its sheer volume. It is impossible to review all of the gender differences reported and reviewers select what they consider to be the main studies to review—but are there biases in the studies they select to review? The quality of the research also differs significantly between studies. While many studies report gender differences, others find no such difference. By this stage of the book you will have discovered that inconsistency of results over many repeated studies is one of the problems that bedevil social research. How can we make sense of such a complex situation? Fortunately, psychologists have developed a new technique called meta-analysis to evaluate such data. This technique uses statistical procedures to pool information from many studies to ascertain any overall trend. Meta-analyses have been used extensively to tease out gender versus sex differences (Hall, 1984; Eagly & Steffen, 1986; Hyde & Linn, 1988) (see Box 11.5). We will now review the major differences in gender that have been noted in the literature.

Cognitive abilities

Prior to the use of meta-analysis, one of the major works on gender differences was that of Maccoby and Jacklin (1974) who considered many studies, systematically excluding those with weaknesses and including only those where findings were replicated over a number of research articles. They did not find any difference between men and women on overall intelligence or achievement motivation, but when they considered the components that make up intelligence, they noted that women seemed to be superior on verbal abilities and men were superior on mathematics and visual–spatial abilities.

Differences in moral reasoning

Differences in thought processes were studied by Kohlberg (1963) in his theory of moral development (see Chapter Six). His theory proposes that, as human beings develop, they progress through various stages of moral reasoning until they reach a final stage represented by a level of reasoning emphasising abstract principles. He devised ways of testing this and found a greater proportion of men than women reached this most advanced level. In a critique of his work, Gilligan (1977) discovered that moral reasoning seemed to be based on interdependence among individuals as well as responsibility and caring for individuals. Whereas Kohlberg's theory suggested that advanced stages of moral reasoning were abstract in that they ignored time and place as important elements, Gilligan found that advanced moral reasoning was concrete, focusing on relationships that extended over time. When Gilligan tested subjects, she found men were more likely to reason following abstract principles, while women were more likely to reason in a concrete way where relationships were emphasised as important. Her work has seriously called into question the uni-dimensional concept of moral reasoning proposed by Kohlberg. She concluded that both the abstract and concrete principles were important in moral development.

Controversies such as these surrounding gender differences in cognitive abilities are now being considered, prompting researchers to ask searching questions about the nature of their research. For example, what does the narrowing of verbal abilities between men and women really mean? Possibly the gap between males and females is actually becoming smaller, as the research indicates, but maybe researchers' expectations of how males or females should perform have also changed over the years? This could be reflected in the type of tasks selected, as in the Kohlberg study, as some cognitive ability tasks may be biased, inadvertently favouring one gender. Another explanation may be that low-ability males are dropping out of school earlier than previously and are no longer available for testing, causing an increase in the overall male scores on these tests of ability. Yet another explanation may be the changes in the social environment in which males and females grow up. One study found mothers talked more to their female infants than to their male infants (Cherry & Lewis, 1976). This would mean that females would have greater amounts of practice with verbal skills than would males, providing them with a distinct advantage on tests of verbal abilities. Finally, Waber (1977) pointed out that females mature earlier than males, which could also account for the difference in results. Moral reasoning has been shown to be influenced by how it is conceptualised, so all research findings need to be questioned in terms of their methodology. Alternative explanations of the results should be considered, before reaching definite conclusions. From my own review of the literature, all we can say at this stage is that the reason for cognitive differences between males and females is ambiguous, and may be due to any number of other factors in addition to those mentioned above.

Aggression

In the literature the strongest gender difference on record is that men are more aggressive than women (Hyde, 1986). If we look throughout the world today, we see men are more likely to be directly involved in war than women, there is much more male crime than female crime and, in particular, men are much more likely to assault or kill another person than are women. We have only to look at the serial killers and multiple shootings that are increasingly common in our countries to verify this. We rarely see women involved in mass killings. Meta-analyses of studies of aggression have found men are more aggressive in verbal and physical manifestations than women. For verbal aggression, the gender difference was smaller than for physical aggression (Hyde, 1984; Eagly & Steffen, 1986). They found men were more likely to engage in spontaneous aggression, which society condones in males but not in females. In a more recent study, the anticipated consequences of aggressive acts were elicited from boys and girls (Perry, Perry & Weiss, 1989). Girls anticipated more parental disapproval and expected to feel more guilt than boys. It is possible that anticipated guilt and societal disapproval may be one of the influencing factors that restrains women from being as aggressive as men.

Men are also stronger than women and differences in physical size no doubt offers further deterrent. Considering the odds, it is unlikely that you would consciously fight with someone larger than yourself as the chances of ending up in a mess would significantly increase. However, there are situations where women are just as aggressive as men. Consider the reports of torture where women are the perpetrators and also situations where women commit murder. There are many individual differences in aggression, as with any other behaviour: Not all men are aggressive and not all women are passive. However, the research, as well as our knowledge of the world, indicates that men as a group are more aggressive than women (see Box 11. 4).

Box 11.4 *Men and aggression: An innate difference?*

Men are undoubtedly more aggressive than women but is this difference innate? In the 1960s this was one of the most hotly debated issues of gender and had enormous implications for relations between the sexes. While men are much more aggressive than women, as we have noted, women are also aggressive in given circumstances. As one example, we reviewed the crime statistics for homicide in New Zealand and Australia from 1985 to 1990. While the vast majority of homicides were committed by men (93%), you were eight times more likely to be killed by your mother if you were an infant. So gender differences in aggression is just as vexed an issue as in other areas. How do we decide if aggression is an innate or socialised sex difference?

Eleanor Maccoby and Carol Jacklin, two American developmental researchers, tackled this issue in their definitive work *The Psychology of Sex Differences* (1974). The authors established four tests for deciding if a sex difference was innate or learned:

- Are differences obvious in very young children shortly after birth? The early onset of a behaviour suggests that learning has had little opportunity to alter innate behaviours.
- Are there consistent sex differences across cultures? If women are much more aggressive than men in some cultures and not in others,

this argues the behaviour is learned rather than innate.
- Are similar sex differences obvious in other species? If such differences occur in our near relatives, the primates, particularly at an early onset, this argues the difference has an evolutionary (innate) base.
- Is there a physiological basis for the sex difference? If we can find a brain site or some hormonal difference between men and women, then this argues the difference is innate.

None of these tests by itself is definitive; however if we combine all four, this increases the probability that a behaviour is either innate, or learned. What does the evidence say about sex differences in aggression? Maccoby and Jacklin (1974, 1980) conclude that the evidence across all four tests shows men are innately more aggressive than women. Their own studies of young children show that from birth boys are more aggressive than girls, and it is unlikely that a newborn is consciously deciding to use aggression. By age two the differences are stark (Maccoby, 1980) but decline over age (Hyde, 1986). This suggests that male aggression is innate and that socialisation processes moderate these differences as boys grow. The anthropological evidence is also overwhelming. Maccoby and Jacklin report many cross-cultural studies of sex differences in aggression and in very few cultures are women more aggressive than men and then only in restricted areas (Whiting & Edwards, 1973; Whiting & Whiting, 1975). The *Journal of Primatology* and *Ethology and Sociobiology* contain many articles which demonstrate that male primates, particularly the Great Apes, are as aggressive as their human cousins. Sex differences in primate aggression have an early onset too (Moyer, 1976). While there are no definitive brain site differences between men and women triggering aggression, there are clear hormonal differences that do (Olweus, 1986). At this point you might like to review our discussion of testosterone and male aggression in Chapter Seven.

As you can see from the dates of our citations, this topic was of major interest in the 1960s and 1970s, but by the early 1980s it was generally conceded that men are innately more aggressive than women. However, at the risk of repeating ourselves, even if this is true, men do not have to act aggressively. Human beings have many more strategies to achieve their ends than do their evolutionary cousins.

Depression

There is a higher incidence of clinical depression among women than among men (Dohrenwend & Dohrenwend, 1977; Gove, 1978). There are many reasons why this may be the case. Certainly married women seem to be more depressed than unmarried women or men in general (Gove, 1972). Married women have less control over their lives than men, rendering them somewhat powerless. Seligman (1975) has developed a theory of depression around the concept of **learned helplessness** (see Chapter Three). People feel depressed when they feel they are unable to do anything about their situation. Many married women will identify strongly with this. In

learned helplessness People feel depressed when they learn they are unable to do anything about their situation.

Is aggression an innate male behaviour, or is this dust-up a socialised response to frustration? (Photo: Rob Pozo)

considering the causes of their own behaviour, women tend to make more external than internal attributions, thus seeing the external environment as the factor responsible for their behaviour (Frieze et al., 1978). This is a powerless position, which encourages depression. Furthermore, women are encouraged to be passive in our society, which again may be associated with depression. So women are more depressed than men and, in a patriarchal society where men are defined as dominant and women defined as submissive, it is not surprising that men are more aggressive or act out their anger, and women are more depressed and turn their anger in on themselves.

Power

As we have seen already, power is interactional in that we give power to others by our deference to them and take power when we stand up to other people. However, there are structures and situations where the physical power differential is substantial and can hardly be called interactional. It is clear that there are relative differences in power between men and women, based on the patriarchal society in which we live, where men have made the rules and set up the structures of society that prevent women from taking more control. There are a number of different types of power, discussed elsewhere in this book (see Chapter Six) so we will not define the various forms of power here.

Given the power structures in our society, what forms of power do men and women use to exert some control over their lives? In a series of studies, Johnson (1974) considered how gender and control are linked in hypothetical situations where one person attempts to influence another. Subjects were presented with hypothetical situations where different forms of power were used and they were then asked to guess the gender of the influencing person. Referent power, legitimate power of helplessness, and indirect informational power were attributed to females, while expert power, formal legitimate power and direct informational power (see Chapter Six) were attributed to males. In a follow-up study, Johnson found that both females and males were more likely to use the forms of power attributed to them than other forms of power. Subjects reported greater feelings of competence when they had influenced others in a laboratory setting. In another study of the successful influence of another, Johnson found women were likely to use indirect information, manipulation and emotions to influence others, while men were more likely to report using more direct strategies. These results suggest that there are power differences between men and women, which reflect gender stereotypes. Men are more likely to use active, direct methods of power, while women are more likely to use passive, indirect methods in influencing another.

Conformity

Given the research considered so far, we would expect males and females to differ on their degree of conformity. In a meta-analysis of many studies conducted on conformity and gender, there appears to be a small tendency for women to conform more than men (Eagly, 1987) but these results are conflicting. Women tend to conform more when they know very little about the task. Many of the studies used male-oriented topics where women were not as familiar with the content and thus more likely to defer to male opinion. Eagly (1981) also found male investigators were more likely to find differences in levels of conformity than female researchers, hence more female conformity, and presumably this reflects an unconscious bias. The difficulties in examining the literature on this topic are highlighted in a study by Sistrunk and McDavid (1971). They asked students to answer a questionnaire about facts and opinions about male topics (sports cars, politics and mathematics) and female topics (cooking, sewing and cosmetics). The possibility for conformity was provided by each question indicating how a group of other people had responded to the questions. In their research they found males tended to conform on items that were defined as feminine and females tended to conform on items that were defined as masculine. Thus, conformity may be based on familiarity with the situation rather than on gender. However, we must also acknowledge the societal norm of men being in more powerful, higher status and influential positions. This raises the expectation that women will conform to their wishes and directions (Eagly & Wood, 1982). While both men and women tend to conform when they are unfamiliar with a situation, because our society is designed by and for men, there is a greater tendency for women to conform to what men think.

Box 11.5 *What are the differences between men and women?*

In this section we have used a sociopolitical perspective to reflect the great social edifice of gender roles we have built upon very small sex differences. Nevertheless, there are sex differences and to provide some balance we will consider them now. Alice Eagly (1987), whose meta-analysis *Sex Differences in Social Behavior* we have referred to throughout the chapter, concluded that there was strong support for three main sex differences:

- Men are more aggressive than women.
- Women have greater verbal ability than men and outperform them on measures of reading and verbal fluency, verbal comprehension and vocabulary.
- Men have greater spatial and mathematical ability.

Eagly's list restated Maccoby and Jacklin's (1974) work which did much to sort out the real distinction between sex and gender differences. In a careful review of the literature they debunked

many "commonsense" notions of men's and women's abilities, revealing them to be just gender stereotypes. Women were no less intelligent than men, nor did their ability to process complex higher-level material differ. Eagly's book, among other things, reviewed the controversy that Maccoby and Jacklin (1974, 1980) stirred up. What does her research tell us about sex differences?

We have already considered aggression. Clearly men are more aggressive than women. Eagly and Steffen (1986) took this one step further. In a review of 64 studies of sex and aggression they found that, while men were more aggressive than women on most measures, they were particularly more *physically* aggressive than on measures of verbal or instrumental aggression. We will leave our discussion of sex and aggression here (see also Chapter Seven).

Evidence is inconclusive on verbal cognitive abilities. Maccoby and Jacklin and Eagly found that women have greater verbal ability than men and outperform them on measures of reading and verbal fluency, verbal comprehension and vocabulary. Hall's (1984) meta-analysis, for example, found that women had better decoding skills and greater verbal fluency, while men scored less well and relied more on what linguists call **filled pauses**—"ums" and "ahs"—and so-called **null signals**—"you know," "I mean"—and so on in communication. However, the conclusion that women are more verbally skilled was challenged by an exhaustive meta-analysis of 165 studies that sampled approximately 1.5 million subjects (Hyde & Linn, 1988). The authors concluded that gender differences in verbal ability are narrowing over time, to the extent that soon they may no longer be of any real significance. Diane Halpern (1989) questioned this finding, claiming that differences continue to favour females and that testing procedures may have underestimated the true size of this difference.

The situation is a little clearer in boys' maths and visual–spatial ability, and meta-analyses continue to show moderately high sex differences (Hyde, 1986). However, all is not clear developmentally and research has shown that girls may surpass boys in maths ability in the earlier stages of their education. Maccoby (1980) attributes this to girls' greater developmental maturity during the primary school years, and argues that when this is taken into account boys perform better than girls. Certainly by age 11 boys regain the lead in these two areas and rapidly outstrip girls (Hyde, 1986). Still, the gap between boys and girls is narrowing (Feingold, 1988, 1992) and what this means in terms of sex differences has caused some controversy (Kimball, 1989). So where are we?

Probably small sex differences exist on measures of maths, visual–spatial and verbal ability. It is certainly the case that Australian and New Zealand matriculation results reflect those of students in America and Europe with a narrowing gap on mathematical ability. However, we need to be aware that individual differences are such that *most* boys do as well as *most* girls on any measure, and it is only at the very extremes of genius that these differences really make themselves felt. For most of us, even if nature has handicapped us a little in some area, the differences are small enough to be overtaken by an extra effort.

Prosocial behaviour

As we saw in Chapter Ten there are gender differences in helping behaviour. Eagly and Crowley (1986) in a meta-analysis found strong support for men offering more assistance than women. They concluded that men are less likely to be deterred by the consequences of helping, while women were more likely to be cautious even though their sex-roles stress nurturance and caring. Much of the research on gender differences is conducted on bystander apathy, where someone in distress waits for assistance from those standing around. In these situations it would be more likely for men to assist as it is a societal expectation that, in a dangerous situation, men are stronger; know more about the situation through previous experience; and would be better equipped to help. For example, it is common for men to know more about starting a stalled car than do women. Men are also more likely to help when the person in the predicament is female, when there is an audience, or when women perceive the situation as dangerous (see Chapter Ten). A few studies in the meta-analysis found women to be more likely than men to do favours and provide advice about personal problems. Another study found women's ability to empathise was greater than men's (Hoffman, 1977). Perhaps there are many different types of prosocial behaviour that lend themselves to a variety of skills, some of which are present in men and some in women. When these effects are adequately controlled for, it may be that there are different gender patterns of prosocial behaviour.

Nonverbal communication

Understanding what is happening in a situation can be facilitated by the ability to read nonverbal cues. Traditionally women have been thought to have a greater ability to do this. Possibly this is because they are socialised to express emotion more readily, which often relies on nonverbal cues. A common research strategy involves subjects viewing video clips where the voices are distorted to eliminate emotional cues. Subjects are then asked to describe the emotion being expressed in the video. In a meta-analysis of studies conducted, Hall (1984) found women were better able to decode nonverbal cues than were men. The gender difference was greatest for reading facial expression, next for body cues and least for voice tone.

These differences have been found across all ages and cultures and reflect women's ability to express emotion, and their greater experience in dealing with others' emotion in their role as nurturers, a role encouraged in women and discouraged in men. Women's additional experience thus increases their ability to understand nonverbal communication. In her analysis, Henley (1977) comments on the similarities between the nonverbal behaviours of superiors and subordinates and of men and women. Those in superior positions tend to relax and show less emotion than those in subordinate positions. Consequently, women in more subordinate positions need to develop more skills in interpreting men's nonverbal cues as fewer cues are given. These factors may account for the gender differences noted in nonverbal communication.

As seen from the above range of gender differences, there are possibilities for many biases to influence the results. The question we must ask ourselves is why were the particular characteristics selected for investigation in the first place? What was the agenda of the researchers? How did they choose to measure the characteristics? What was the experimenter's bias in rating subject performance on tasks selected? Were the subjects free to go against the stereotypic norm when doing the rated task? Were the test items and tasks selected gender-free, or deliberately masked to disguise gender? If they were not gender-free, were the items counterbalanced to provide as many opportunities for masculine or feminine responses? What do the findings actually mean in terms of gender? Do they reflect a significant difference or are they merely confirming cultural stereotypes and social conditioning? In what way is it helpful to note the differences?

As an example, often experimental differences are statistically significant, but do they reflect real differences? Figure 11.2 shows the scores on a test of spatial skills for males and females (Frieze et al., 1978). While there are significant differences on the test, the drawing clearly shows more similarities than differences between men and women when you look at the common area under the curve. This reflects Sandra Bem's (1987) comment after two decades of researching sex differences, that while there may well be biological sex differences these are small in comparison to our commonalities.

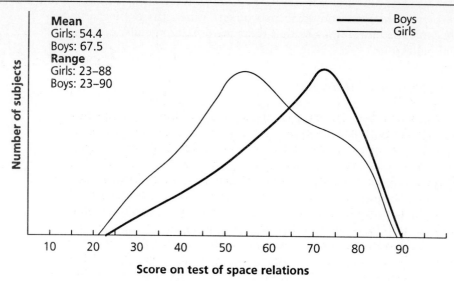

Figure 11.2 *Sex differences and spatial skills*

Source: Sherman, 1974.

Connell (1987), an Australian sociologist, notes that although many years of research have found more gender similarities than differences, this has not stopped the search for more differences!

Box 11.6 *Food for thought? So where are we with sex differences?*

Whether there are any real *sex* versus *gender* differences underlying behaviour, is one of the most controversial areas in social psychology and the debate has hotted up recently after a long period of quiescence. In this chapter I have taken a critical perspective which doubts there are any real sex differences beyond those of menstruation, gestation, lactation and impregnation. Nevertheless, as we saw in Boxes 11.4 and 11.5, others disagree. I believe that one of the difficulties of discussing differences in male and female behaviour is that of attributing them to biological causes. While there are some important biological differences between women and men, they are not responsible for the differences in behaviour reported in the literature (Money & Tucker, 1975).

As we have noted throughout our chapters, biology is not destiny. Most of the difference appears to be more related to stereotypes and expectations that society encourages for men and women. Behind these stereotypes is a patriarchal culture that is clearly designed to promote the dominance of men who subscribe to a capitalist society and the subordination of women. The system is in place despite efforts of men and women to change it. I think that other differences disappear when appropriate gender-free measures and controls are implemented. It is quite possible that the research could lead to lots of interesting party conversation. However, you must be prepared for the inevitable consequences, depending on whether you are talking to males or females. It seems to me that sex differences research has not been helpful in increasing our understanding of men and women, but has merely confirmed the social construction of gender.

What do you think?

We turn now to consider how gender and society are organised in relation to gender roles.

Gender roles

Division of labour

The division of labour between married couples is one of the most frequently discussed inequalities that is observed in Australian homes and the focus of much gender role research. A recent study asked 93 Melbourne couples who completes various tasks at home (Findlay & Lawrence, 1991). The results of this survey indicate that women engage in more tasks than men and that these jobs are those traditionally viewed as female household chores, which reflects traditional sex-roles, and confirms previous research (Antill & Cotton, 1988). In the Findlay and Lawrence study, it is interesting to note that in about one-third of the cases, the couples did not agree with each other's responses to individual items. It may also have been important in this survey to ask who has responsibility for each task, rather than simply who performs each of the tasks. Often it is the responsibility for the task rather than the actual completion of it that proves to be onerous.

Craddock (1974) found with a sample of couples that males tended to specialise in jobs such as repairing things around the house and putting out the garbage, while women were more likely to engage in tasks such as washing dishes and keeping in touch with family. Ten years later, Glezer (1984) obtained similar findings which suggested that women take responsibility for most of the traditional chores seen as women's household jobs. A further study in Adelaide randomly surveyed adults on shopping and food preparation, and noted a change with younger couples (Worsley, 1988).

(Cartoonist: Graeme Mitchell)

There are increasing numbers of young men interested in cooking, and also an increasing number of men over forty who are helping their partners with the shopping and food preparation. However, women often report that their male partners do the exotic cooking while the major responsibility for food preparation still rests with them. While the Findlay and Lawrence (1991) study mentioned above found women still performed more household tasks than men, the couples reported that they were less traditional in their division of labour than their own parents had been. However, the reported distribution of tasks did not differ from the reported literature over the past fifteen years.

Although women often receive some help for the performance of traditional household and childcare tasks from their partners, they continue to be the one responsible for their completion. Russell (1987) notes, after talking with fathers, that they perceive themselves more as financial providers for the family than as being responsible for childcare or other tasks at home. Thus, they often wait to be invited to become involved in childcare. Consequently, children ask them to play with them, a demand that is often met. As both men and women tend to support the traditional division of labour by their behaviour and often their beliefs, change continues to be slow. It should be noted that the psychological burden of the financial maintenance of a family falls mainly on the male partner. Often this side of the picture is minimised because men are paid more for the work they do. Somehow being paid for work outside the home is seen to lessen the psychological burden.

The above findings are seemingly in contradiction with many studies that report egalitarian relationships between men and women in relationships. These studies often consider family power as reflected in decision-making at home. A study of participation in decision-making was conducted in South Australia where adolescents and their parents were asked to rate parental involvement in decisions made at home (Brown & Mann, 1988, 1989). Mothers, fathers and adolescents agreed that the pattern of decision-making was egalitarian, with both parents involved to a similar degree in most family decisions. However, decision-making is an executive function in that the decision-maker is often not involved in actually doing the work involved in implementation of the decision. Most managers make decisions but are never actually involved in the execution of them. It is the whole question of chiefs and Indians that emerges with alarming regularity throughout society. In integrating division of labour and decision-making literature, it seems there is involvement by males and females in that men are involved in deciding what to do and women involved in actually carrying out the decisions—a strange sort of egalitarianism!

The scenario does not change to any great extent when both partners are in paid employment. A recent study completed by the Australian Institute of Family Studies shows very little change as the wife moves from unemployment to full-time paid employment (Glezer, 1991). She is still expected to complete housework and cook meals. As wives increase their level of paid employment, husbands tend to engage in more maintenance and spend more time with the children, but the effect is minimal compared with the input required by their female partners. Table 11.1 shows how tasks are divided between partners when wives are in paid employment. This finding was also noted in a study by Presland and Antill (1987), where wives were found to be spending four times as much time as their

Table 11.1 *Division of household tasks when both spouses are in full-time employment*

	Wife not working %	*Wife working part-time* %	*Wife working full-time* %	*All couples* %
Housework				
Doing the laundry				
Husband more	1	2	7	3
Both equally	5	5	16	9
Wife more	94	93	77	88
Cleaning the bathroom				
Husband more	3	3	9	5
Both equally	7	7	11	9
Wife more	90	90	80	86
Vacuuming the carpets				
Husband more	5	5	12	7
Both equally	12	11	21	15
Wife more	83	84	67	78
Meals				
Cooking the evening meal				
Husband more	3	4	10	6
Both equally	8	12	19	13
Wife more	89	84	71	81
Doing the grocery shopping				
Husband more	3	5	8	5
Both equally	21	15	27	22
Wife more	76	80	65	73
Doing the dishes				
Husband more	6	8	12	9
Both equally	23	30	32	28
Wife more	71	62	56	63
Maintenance				
Taking out rubbish				
Husband more	51	54	60	55
Both equally	24	28	24	25
Wife more	25	18	16	20
Taking care of the lawn				
Husband more	69	74	80	74
Both equally	21	15	14	17
Wife more	10	11	6	9

(continued)

	Wife not working %	Wife working part-time %	Wife working full-time %	All couples %
Repairing things around the house				
Husband more	83	78	81	81
Both equally	12	13	13	12
Wife more	5	9	6	7
Children				
Taking the children to their activities and appointments				
Husband more	5	4	7	5
Both equally	30	31	47	35
Wife more	65	65	46	60
Playing with the children				
Husband more	6	10	9	8
Both equally	71	68	71	70
Wife more	23	22	20	22
Punishing the children				
Husband more	7	10	12	9
Both equally	68	65	72	68
Wife more	25	25	16	23

Source: Australian Family Formation Project (Stage Two) 1990–91, Australian Institute of Family Studies.

partners working on traditional tasks while husbands were more likely to share childcare rather than household tasks. Often the husbands' involvement with the children was confined to play, including weekend activities and outings for the children. As wives obtained paid employment, they still did most of the household tasks. Other studies confirm a slight increase in male involvement in household tasks; however, the female partner tends to maintain her pre-employment level of involvement or pick up the majority of the extra work when she is in paid employment (Bryson, 1983; Russell, 1982).

There also appears to be little change when both partners are retired. A survey of older couples indicated that they still maintain very traditional gender roles (Healy, 1988). However if there is some physical disability or if both partners were in paid employment, there is a greater flexibility in the division of labour. With ethnic couples, there was less flexibility in the division of labour following retirement. Thus, it appears that paid employment does little to lighten the burden of household responsibilities for women in Australian homes, as they seem to take on extra tasks through the paid employment while continuing to maintain their partner and children by washing, cooking and cleaning at home.

The relationship between paid and unpaid work was analysed in a report by the Office of the Status of Women. They re-worked data from the Australian Bureau of Statistics, where a pilot survey of time use in Sydney homes was completed in 1987 (Bittman, 1991). Their report found that women performed 70 per cent of all unpaid work but noted that such work is ignored as it is not taken into consideration in calculating the gross domestic product. The report cites the example of a minister of religion marrying his housekeeper, where the work that she now does is done for love rather than for money and is consequently no longer reflected in the gross domestic product.

It has been estimated that unpaid housework accounts for between 52 and 62 per cent of the gross domestic product and indicates men are becoming less involved in paid employment while women are becoming more involved in paid work over time. Less paid work for men is distributed in more leisure, more personal time and more unpaid work, composed mainly of cooking, shopping and laundry. Women, on the other hand, are involved more in paid employment with a corresponding drop in unpaid employment as well as a slight decrease in leisure time. As with other studies, when women are more involved in paid work, their unpaid work drops slightly, but never to the same extent as men with similar paid work commitments. Table 11.2 compares changing time use of males and females aged 20 to 59, between the years 1974 and 1987.

Table 11.2 *Changing patterns of time use for men and women between 1974 and 1987*

	Women			Men		
	1974	*1987*	*Change*	*1974*	*1987*	*Change*
Paid work	17.3	21.7	+4.4	49.6	44.0	−5.6
Unpaid work	39.9	36.0	−3.9	12.0	14.4	+2.4
Personal needs	74.2	74.3	+0.17	0.0	71.6	+1.6
Free time	36.4	35.9	−0.5	36.2	37.9	+1.7
Total week	**168**	**168**		**168**	**168**	
Components of unpaid work						
Cooking	12.0	10.1	−1.9	1.3	3.0	+1.7
Home chores	7.5	4.5	−3.0	0.7	0.4	−0.3
Laundry	5.5	5.0	−0.5	0.2	0.9	+0.7
Garden	2.3	1.4	−0.9	2.6	1.7	−0.9
Shopping	5.2	5.9	+0.7	2.5	3.5	+1.0
Other house	0.4	1.3	+0.9	3.2	2.8	−0.4
Child care own & others'	7.0	7.6	+0.6	1.6	2.1	+0.5
Selected components of leisure						
Television	10.0	11.6	+1.6	11.4	13.0	+1.6
Read	3.0	2.2	−0.8	3.2	2.4	−0.8
Social	8.1	6.5	−1.6	8.8	6.4	−2.4
Conversation	2.6	3.2	+0.6	1.9	1.8	−0.1
Active sports	0.9	1.5	+0.6	1.5	2.5	+1.0
Entertainrnent	0.6	0.9	+0.3	1.1	0.6	−0.5
Resting	1.4	1.7	+0.3	0.6	1.8	+1.2
Other leisure	3.6	1.4	−2.2	1.8	0.7	−1.1
Total leisure	*33.5*	*32.3*	*−1.2*	*33.8*	*33.5*	*−0.3*

Source: Bittman, 1991.

In a regression analysis, the study indicates that as women take on an extra hour of paid employment, they decrease their unpaid employment by 26 minutes. The analysis, if extended, indicates that if a woman worked for 95 hours in paid employment, she would do no unpaid work. For men, the paid to unpaid work trade-off is virtually one for one, with one hour more paid employment resulting in one hour less of unpaid work. A comparison of unpaid work for males and females, and how time is divided into various activities, appear in Figure 11.3. As you can see, significant proportions of women's unpaid work time is involved in cooking, laundry, cleaning, childcare and shopping. For men, significant proportions of time are involved in outdoor activities and travel, cooking and shopping. While there is overlap with cooking and shopping, the majority of male unpaid work

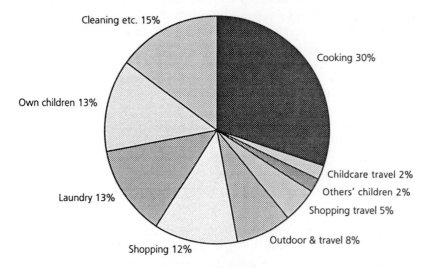

(a) Proportion of all women's unpaid work time spent on various tasks

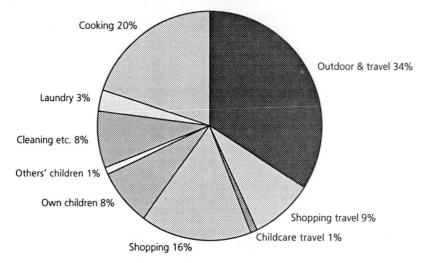

Figure 11.3
Proportions of all unpaid work time spent on various tasks by sex

Source: Bittman, 1991.

(b) Proportion of all men's unpaid work time spent on various tasks

time is involved in outdoor activities, a finding supported by studies previously considered.

As with the previous study, this analysis of data also concentrated on stage of the lifecycle, but also extended the analysis, comparing those with children, sharing houses, those living alone and childless couples. Women consistently are more involved in unpaid employment than men, with the largest increase evident when in a couple relationship. The regression analysis indicated that the most powerful predictor of paid and unpaid work for women was marriage. With the advent of children, the picture changes for women, but not significantly for men. Comparing male and female involvement in unpaid work with children at various ages, for men, there is little change regardless of the presence or age of children while there is a substantial increase in unpaid work for women, particularly with younger children. It could be argued that men are spending significant amounts of time in paid employment, reducing the available time for involvement in unpaid employment during this stage. However, the analysis compared retired couples and continues to show significantly greater amounts of time spent by women in unpaid work even when the couple retires. It is only when males and females are retired and living alone that the amount of time spent on unpaid employment is equal. This data confirms other findings that indicate women are more involved in unpaid work than men, increasingly with the presence of children and retirement. From an interactional perspective, it seems that as women are more involved in unpaid work, men are less involved. The message seems clear, if you want a truly egalitarian relationship, live by yourself!

Gender role development

Recently, on an ordinary afternoon, I watched an early stage of the education of a warrior in my side yard. Two boys, four and six years old, were swinging on a rope that hung from a tall limb of an old cottonwood tree. For a while they took turns in an orderly way, but then the bigger boy seized power and began to hog the swing. The little boy protested, "it's my turn," and went over and tried to take the rope. "Bug off" shouted the big boy, and pushed the little boy roughly to the ground. The man-child struggled to his feet, jaw quivering, fighting to hold back his tears, and said defiantly, "That didn't hurt." (Keen, 1991, p. 41)

From the moment of birth, infants are labelled by sex and the process of appropriate conditioning is begun. Perry and Bussey (1984) define sex-role development or **sex typing** as "the process whereby children come to acquire the behaviours, attitudes, interests, emotional reactions and motives that are culturally defined as appropriate for members of their sex". As suggested by our quotation from Pittman earlier in the chapter, this process is subtle in the sense that it happens often without conscious awareness. Keen's example of the denial of emotional expression, starting in childhood, outlines how males may help condition other males in establishing appropriate male behaviour, as defined by the wider society.

Antill, Bussey and Cunningham (1985) note that some Australian

sex typing
Process whereby children come to acquire the behaviours, attitudes, interests, emotional reactions and motivations appropriate to their sex.

parents are becoming more aware of traditional gender typing and are trying to raise their children in egalitarian ways. However the effects of the sexism in Australian culture on these children have not been investigated. The processes of identification with a same-gender parent and modelling of other same-gender children and adults are significant in the development of behaviour. Children identify with same-gender parents because they perceive them to be powerful and loving; they are also strongly attached due to the intensity and duration of their relationship together. On the other hand, children tend to model or imitate other people outside the family because they are seen as powerful or because they observe the rewards these other people obtain through their behaviour. Sex typing becomes more apparent with age when children are asked their preference regarding a variety of toys and activities (Barry, 1978). Usually, by the age of three, children have developed a gender identity. This develops further between the ages of four and seven, when gender is seen as constant (Kohlberg & Ullian, 1974).

In the literature, there appears to be a stronger preference for male sex typing than for female sex typing (Nadelman, 1974). One of the factors influencing this finding may be the discrepancies in the punishment imposed for inappropriate cross-gender modelling. A study by Fagot (1977) found boys were criticised more by peers than girls for modelling cross-gender behaviour. Bussey and Perry (1982) explored the effect of same-gender acceptance of models and cross-gender rejection of models on the process of imitation. Children in Brisbane were allowed to see the choices of same- and other-gender models and were then able to make their own choice. They found boys accepted same-gender models while rejecting cross-gender models. For girls, same-gender modelling was also accepted, but cross-gender modelling was not rejected to the same extent. In a follow-up study, this process was noted at five years of age, but not at three years of age, where there were no differences between acceptance and rejection of same- and cross-gender models (Bussey, 1983). Bussey (1981, cited in Antill et al., 1985) notes that children must negotiate a number of cognitive tasks in order for their gender-role behaviour to be influenced by others:

- They must distinguish between males and females.
- They must be aware of their membership of one sex.
- They must be able to associate certain behaviours
  with a particular sex.
- They must be motivated to model their own sex.

This is a complex range of cognitive tasks, requiring a degree of sophistication not present in small children. Consequently, it is not surprising that children appear to reach this level of development only by five years of age. What motivates children to model their own sex is probably the most complex aspect to understand and is probably related to their past experience with both parents, other adults and children. The influence of emotions engendered by these experiences could easily influence the child's motivation to model one or other sex.

Power has also been seen to have an unexpected effect on boys. In a further study, Bussey and Bandura (1984) observed that boys would model females to the same extent as male models if they were seen as powerful. These findings may be interpreted in different ways. Through an interactional or systemic lens, the powerful are powerful through the submissive behaviours of other people. In an interaction, as one person becomes more submissive, the other becomes more powerful, resulting in greater submission. This becomes a cycle that eventually has no beginning or end. Thus in normal society, men are powerful as women are submissive. As women become more submissive, men become more powerful. It would not take very long for this cycle to create a set of expectations regarding male and female behaviour that would operate in conjunction with the cyclical interaction. In the situation above, where boys model powerful women, they would see the effects of the power on other people and thus acquire the powerful manner of operating to enhance their own sense of control. Thus, with the expectation of male power and female submission, boys would use any opportunity to develop further a sense of power.

Through a sociopolitical lens, it could be argued that male modelling of power may reflect a male identification with the power base that is present in our patriarchal society (see Box 11.7). Thus, the effects of modelling appear to be more pronounced with males than with females. Boys are socialised into the male culture of dominance and will imitate appropriate dominant roles even if the powerful behaviour is presented by female models. However, submissive behaviour is not modelled by males if it is observed in women. The research suggests that punishment for inappropriate modelling of cross-gender behaviour is more pronounced with males than with females. Why would this be the situation? Many would suggest that the dominant male gender does not wish to risk any challenge to its authority and will resist this even to the extent of punishing inappropriate gender behaviour in non-conforming male members. The irrational hostility and resentment directed towards gay men in our Australian culture provides further evidence of the effects of attacking the patriarchy through inappropriate gender behaviour (see Box 5.1, Chapter Five). In effect, gay men are perceived to be acting in a relatively female role, having rejected traditional masculinity. This may be perceived at an unconscious level as being a traitor to masculinity by an identification with the traditional feminine behaviour of loving men instead of women. Thus, two views may account for the same gender behaviour. I leave it to you to decide which view best explains these findings.

Apart from modelling, parents and other powerful figures in the child's life appear to have different expectations for males and females. In a study by Antill (1984), parents reported that they encouraged girls more than boys to develop female interests, behaviour and occupational choices. Boys were encouraged to be more independent than girls. Support for differential treatment by fathers comes from a study by Noller (1978), where she found fathers spent more time hugging and kissing their female children than their male children when they were left at a day-care centre. This finding was not noted with mothers, who spent the same amount of time

Box 11.7 *Gender-sensitive therapy*

Theorists are beginning to reject the idea that some gender roles are more mature than others. This view has encouraged clinicians to focus on gender issues in therapy. Traditional gender assumptions often provide difficulties for couples in their relationships, making them fruitful areas for exploration by therapists. Clients' beliefs are often reflected in their behaviour and Brooks (1991) highlights some of the traditional male beliefs that may disempower women. These may often need to be challenged in therapy:

1. *Men are entitled to use coercive control and intimidation when dealing with their partner.* Physical intimidation is now seen as a reason for intervening in relationships. Brooks points out that coercive tactics relying on financial control and fear are also intimidating.
2. *Men, who provide the main source of income for their family, should not be responsible for household tasks and childcare.* Some men try to gain a better deal for themselves by offering a less egalitarian relationship which emphasises the provider role. In this role finances are used to balance an imbalance in power in the division of labour. A man may offer holidays to his partner in an attempt to keep division of labour issues from being addressed.
3. *Men are logical and women are irrational.* The man may attempt to convince his partner that she is going through a period of confusion when she expresses a new feminist awareness. In this situation, men sometimes develop a pattern of unpredictable behaviour which may disorient their partner.
4. *Men have a right to female nurturing and may use guilt to obtain it.* When a man recognises the futility of using power to elicit traditional feminine nurturing, he may use guilt to obtain what he feels he needs from his partner. This may involve attempting suicide, abusing drugs or alcohol, or neglecting self care.
5. *Men do not have vulnerable or nurturing*

feelings, or at least do not need to express them if they do exist. Men are often unaware of their feelings or feel uncomfortable, unsafe or out of control when expressing them to others. They may feel their partner will take advantage of them if they express feelings.

The above views are commonly held by men and often supported by women and are counterproductive to egalitarian relationships. In my experience as a therapist, I have noted that women also hold reciprocal views that are as disempowering in their relationships. These may also need to be challenged in therapy:

1. *Women should take responsibility for the behaviour and feelings of others and especially of the men in their lives.* Women very easily slip into the role of feeling responsible if their partner or children have difficulties. They handle the problem by providing support, guessing what the other is feeling, trying to elicit the feeling from the other person, or even experiencing the feeling for them.
2. *Women are ultimately responsible for traditional areas of the division of labour involving cooking, cleaning and childcare even if they are in full-time paid employment.* They often see their partner as providing help but never taking responsibility for these areas. When these tasks are left undone at home, women may feel guilty and feel that they have failed as women. This view is commonly reinforced by other women, men, and society.
3. *Women are responsible for nurturing and maintaining the relationship.* If the relationship fails, it is seen as the woman's fault. If their partner is not communicating, women tend to draw out the problem and in a sense become the therapist for their partner. Women often change their behaviour to accommodate their male partner as a means of eliminating any distress.
4. *Women are incompetent and dependent and should show this, particularly when men*

are around. Women often feel that they cannot take control of their lives because they do not know how to obtain paid employment and are not in the habit of doing the things that they want to do. To make their male partners feel better, they may choose to act in an incompetent manner, even if they are able to act differently.

5. *Women should protect their partner by not standing up to them or by holding back feelings that might prove to be distressing for their partner to handle*. They often put up with lack of communication and large periods that the partner is away at work or with friends in order to keep the peace or because they feel that their partner would not be able to handle an emotional scene.

6. *The needs of women should be met mainly by their partner*. They often feel that their partner is going to meet all of their emotional needs and thus do not look elsewhere for some of them to be met. They may feel that it is unfair to have good friends where they have needs met that their partners are unable to meet. Sometimes they feel that they should not have emotional needs if their partner apparently does not have them.

Many of these views by men and women are accepted through the reinforcement of family and endorsement of society and are thus never questioned. You might like to consider to what extent they have been part of your socialisation.

Research would have us believe that women are better at interpreting social interactions. You might like to discuss this photo with a friend of the opposite sex.

on each child. The effects of these different expectations and parental reactions feed into the stereotypes around masculinity and femininity, and thus influence gender differences in expressing feelings. The message communicated by parental models is that women may express their feelings to males and females, while men may express feelings only to women. The more subtle message is that females are more dependent and thus require additional support from males when they are about to be left on their own. Boys are very quick to receive the corresponding message that they indeed are very independent, and thus do not need extra support when their fathers leave them alone. It does not take much imagination to see the connection between independence and the suppression of emotion in males from scenarios such as the one described above.

handyman factor
Sex-role socialisation where boys become more competent on traditional male skills than girls.

Thus, different expectations due to gender may result in competencies on different tasks at relatively young ages. In a Sydney sample of 9- and 11-year-olds, boys tended to outperform girls on what was called the **handyman factor** while girls were more competent on domesticity and maturity factors (Burns & Homel, 1989). Expectations tend to have a self-fulfilling element that is related to actual competencies on gender appropriate activities.

Classroom observations have noted that teachers interact more with boys than with girls (Evans, 1988). When girls interact with teachers, it is often at their initiation. The more significant studies of the influence of teachers on students have been conducted in America. From observing over 400 children in the classroom, it was concluded that there are gender differences for expectations on children, with girls having lower expectations than boys (Parsons, Kaczala & Meece, 1982). The teachers' expectation of the boys' success led to more praise for their efforts. For girls, there was no relationship between teacher expectancy and the amount of praise the girls received. As with parents, teachers may influence and be influenced by stereotypes, and consequently have an impact on gender-role development. This often reported finding does not seem to have impacted on new teachers attitudes. An Australian study of female pre-school teacher trainees indicated that their attitudes to four-year-old males and females is consistent with traditional gender-role stereotypes (Rodd, 1986). Perhaps the persistence of one-gender schools in New Zealand and Australia may be related to the lack of comparison and different expectations between males and females. Some evidence suggests that girls are more successful in single-gender schools than are boys.

Children's literature provides another piece of evidence to support the insidious indoctrination of society-approved sex-roles. An analysis of Australian books for children concluded that girls were encouraged, through the stories, to give up any aspirations for a career in favour of living in a dream home in a state of marital bliss (Lees & Senyard, 1985). With such aspirations continuously reinforced through recreational reading from an early age, it is hardly surprising that the myth of the dependent, happy housewife, cooking, cleaning and taking care of the children and waiting for her man to come home so that she can attend to his every need is rarely questioned until it is too late. The plight of women being caught at home without the necessary skills to change their lot, because a career was never seen as important, coupled with the guilt that society provides to any mother who dares to create a career for herself, "at the expense of the children", is often sufficient disincentive to keep women at home.

While this scenario is devastating for women, we rarely consider what this conditioning does for men. Men have never been given the choice of whether of not they would prefer to stay home with the children or pursue leisure interests while their partner pursued a career that provided them with financial support. While women are portrayed as living at home, men are presented as going out and responsibly providing for the family, regardless of personal wishes. While going out for paid employment appears to provide more freedom and certainly provides a greater sense of financial independence, it also provides a lot of stress, where stretched budgets and rising unemployment provide pressures that men must bear. This is exacerbated by society's holding men responsible for providing for their families. Thus, both men and women are caught in an oppressive set of limiting circumstances that prevent much freedom of choice for either gender, an idea that is rarely challenged in children's or adults' literature.

While there are many forces at work supporting a traditional gender-role development, there are some signs of change. A national Australian sample of 2268 students in grades one to six indicated that girls are less satisfied with their gender role than are boys (Burns & Homel, 1986). This trend was shown to increase with increasing age as older girls were less satisfied than younger girls. The basis of this dissatisfaction was more restriction on sporting opportunities for girls than for boys. This lack of perceived fairness obviously increases over age until women find themselves caught with several small children in the suburbs without a career. A career seems to be the important factor, as this is the most common way for people to develop some sense of independence and opportunity for choice in our society. It appears that greater change may occur only with greater inequalities being noted at earlier ages, highlighting the necessity of career choices that maximise the range of choices for future life. Unfortunately, we only seem to change when there is sufficient pain to make our current situation unbearable. The research suggests that the pain comes too late to effect any great change in gender roles. However, I am preaching to the converted, as the mere fact that you are reading this text suggests that you are on the path of increasing your career options!

Requiring children to participate in all household activities encourages the development of non-sexist adults.

Gender differences and their usefulness

We have used a good deal of space to consider gender differences from the psychological literature. Many of these differences highlight the inadequacies in the methodology used in the studies, as well as verifying the different socialisation between males and females with regard to behaviour. The gender stereotypes tend to obliterate individual differences and mask the commonality between men and women. Connell (1987) states that gender roles do not allow for a discussion of power differences. The differences between men and women are perceived to be much greater than they actually are (Deaux, 1984). Hare-Mustin (1987) argues that male and female are not opposite, meaning that traits that are perceived to be associated with one gender may be equally available to the other gender. The model of opposites implies that this is not the case. As we saw above, mental health is closely associated with the male gender role. One of the consequences of rigidly defined gender roles is over-conformity to the role, which is particularly true for the male role: its definition implies continued existence because of its connection with perceived mental health (Hare-Mustin, 1987). Society has also clearly provided sanctions for men who do not fit the prescribed role. Thus, both men and women suffer from the stereotypes that are promulgated by society (Ganley, 1990). The perpetuation of the concept of opposite sex maintains a form of hierarchy, and by inference, power differences between men and women (Hare-Mustin, 1987). Emotional behaviour is not the opposite of intellectual or rational behaviour. Human beings are complex and as such are capable of a wide range of behaviours, depending on the situation. Autonomy and relatedness are not mutually exclusive and thus can be seen in men and women. When we conceive gender differences as opposite, we infer hierarchy and power, and when we minimise gender differences and see them as equal, we ignore inequalities.

Is it then useful to discuss gender differences? Most of the psychological research points to minor differences supporting differences in the processes of socialisation. A number of writers have questioned the advantages in continuing to consider these perceived differences, when they are so small. Continuing to focus on differences has the effect of ignoring the power inequalities. It also has the effect of emphasising possible biological differences as uncontrollable explanations for gender differences. Perhaps it would be more appropriate to consider starting from a stance of similarities rather than differences, leaving the issue of power inequalities to be considered in its own right. As long as patriarchy is the dominant factor in shaping society, the inequality will continue to exist. Men are reluctant to give up this role and in fact are even quite restrained from noticing that the inequalities even exist (Neal & Slobidnik, 1990). Through a systemic or interactional lens, Australian women also support this role through submissive female conditioning. However, it is difficult to tell a group of people who are more powerful that they are not more powerful, which women would have to do if they were to challenge the dominant cultural view.

Gender differences may usefully be construed if we do not think of them as opposites, if we realise that the differences within males and

There are many different ways of being male, as these participants at a recent men's festival discovered!

females can be greater than the differences between them, and if we keep the issue of power differences foremost in our minds. Just how does the concept of differences become useful? A recent study compared married men and women on health factors (Hafner, 1989). He found women were almost twice as likely to have psychiatric disorders while they have only half the annual mortality rate of men. Findings such as these suggest differences between men and women that have important ramifications. A search for the basis of these differences, primarily due to patterns of socialisation, could potentially increase longevity. Changing socialisation of males and females can most probably occur through changes in the existing power structure. When we highlight gender differences we tend unconsciously to emphasise biological differences in people's minds, which does not appear to be useful in challenging stereotypes. This approach accents power inequalities by justifying them with a biological argument, preventing appropriate consideration of changes to Australian and New Zealand society.

Box 11.8 *Why are women confused?*

This chapter has taken an uncompromisingly strong view of gender inequities and examined their psychological underpinnings. To end the chapter I will leave you with a piece taken from Wendy Dennis' *Hot and Bothered: Women. Sex and Love in the 1990s* (1992), to indicate just how far we still have to go:

In those heady days, feminism was making women an offer they couldn't refuse—the chance to have sexual equality with men plus a crack at having it all—and women practically trampled one another rushing to get in on this extraordinary deal. Now women could have everything men had always had: carefree casual sex, fulfilling work, supportive mates and adoring kids. The twin notions that women might be equal to men and have it all gripped my female contemporaries with an unrelenting, almost mystical force. Certainly I believed in the possibility too.

In their enthusiasm to sign on the dotted line, few women took time to read the fine print. By the late seventies, however, the fine print was a lot more noticeable. There were, as it turned out, a few kickers to this bargain. By this time, disenchantment had surfaced and women were grumbling that maybe they had been taken.

By then women were pulling their weight in previously "male" domains—like the workplace—but men weren't exactly picking up the slack in "female" spheres—like the home. In *Heartburn,* for instance, Nora Ephron observed that during the seventies women all over America nagged their husbands to do some housework, with the result that their husbands agreed to clear the table, acted "as if they deserved a medal" and then prayed the women's movement would disappear. And it did. The women's movement went away, and so, in many cases, did their wives. Their wives went out into the world, free at last, single again, and discovered the horrible truth: that they were sellers in a buyers' market, and that the major concrete achievement of the women's movement in 1970 was the Dutch treat.

Indeed, by the eighties, any woman with even one functional brain cell had discovered that the realistic possibility of achieving her goals was a whole lot of crapola; you could hire a nanny for the kids, but nanny was not exactly going to parent them. You could convince your boss to agree to part-time work at home, but you'd kiss the fast track goodbye. You could become a Fortune 500 CEO, but you would die a lonely woman with cats. You could hold out for a "supportive" man, but you would wind up having a meaningful relationship with your VCR. You could put all kinds of gluey emotional energy into your relationship, but it wouldn't necessarily stick. You could become an accomplished, successful, well-rounded human being—but your husband would dump you for a gum-popping bimbette named Bethany. (Dennis, 1992, pp. 20–1)

Summary

Gender may be understood from three different perspectives or lenses: biological, interactional or sociopolitical. The biological lens accounts for gender differences on the basis of the different biological constitution of males and females. The interactional lens accounts for gender differences on the basis of how males and females relate to each other and expectations around complementary roles. The sociopolitical lens accounts for gender differences on the basis of different levels of power in a patriarchal culture.

There is a difference between sex and gender. Sex refers to biological differentiation between males and females while gender refers to the different social roles and expectations for males and females.

Parents and others tend to classify infants within minutes of birth and begin to respond to them according to a gender appropriate stereotype. The stereotype associates instrumental characteristics with men and warmth and expressive characteristics with women. The stereotypes are not only supported in interpersonal interactions, but also in the media and other groups such as helping professionals.

Bem developed a model of mental health around the concept of androgyny. She concluded that androgynous individuals were able to be logical and independent as well as nurturing and emotional. The Personal Description Questionnaire, developed in Australia, was designed to measure androgyny and was balanced for positive and negative male and female characteristics. Research with this instrument has failed to substantiate androgyny. The concept of androgyny is highly correlated with self-esteem.

While there are no overall gender differences in cognitive abilities, there appear to be some differences in that women perform better on verbal tasks and men perform better on mathematics and visual–spatial tasks.

In terms of emotion, men tend to be more aggressive than women. On the other hand, women have a higher incidence of clinical depression. With regard to power, men are more likely to use direct methods of power while women are more likely to use indirect methods of power. This analysis fits well with a sociopolitical view in that men wield power openly while women, being less powerful, are required to use indirect means.

While it appears that women conform more than men, when the familiarity with the particular situation is controlled, there are no significant differences between them. As prosocial behaviour appears in many forms and context, it is difficult to determine the differences based on gender. In some situations men show more prosocial behaviour, while women show more such behaviour in other situations.

Women appear to be better able to read nonverbal cues than men. This finding fits well with a sociopolitical analysis, that less powerful women are required to read the cues of the more powerful men, as there are fewer cues provided.

Women engage in more unpaid household and childcare tasks than men, even if they have similar hours of paid employment to their male partners. Men are more likely to help out at home rather than actually taking responsibility for household tasks. When women enter the paid workforce, they continue to complete most of the household tasks associated with cleaning, cooking and childcare. This continues throughout the lifecycle and seems to change only when males and females live alone.

Gender-role development occurs as children identify with the same gender parents who they see as being powerful. Children tend to model or imitate those in society who are perceived as the most powerful. Thus, if a cross-gender parent is perceived as more powerful, the child will tend to model that parent.

Gender-role development is further reinforced by experience at school. Teachers tend to interact more with boys than with girls and generally reinforce the expectations around gender that are held by society. Children's literature also reinforce the stereotypes regarding gender that are present in society.

Many professionals are now questioning the usefulness of discussing gender differences, as they view the power differences in Australian society as the main factor accounting for the differences. They suggest that we should focus more on the similarities between males and females rather than their differences.

Recommended reading

Basow S.A. (1986) GENDER STEREOTYPES: TRADITIONS AND ALTERNATIVES (2nd edn), Brooks/Cole, Pacific Grove, Ca. An interdisciplinary examination of sex-role stereotyping and their origins.

Dennis W. (1992) HOT AND BOTHERED: WOMEN, SEX AND LOVE IN THE 1990'S, Penguin, Ringwood, Victoria. A look at where women are in the 1990s.

Eagly A.H. (1987) SEX DIFFERENCES IN SOCIAL BEHAVIOR: A SOCIAL ROLE EXPLANATION, Erlbaum, Hillsdale, NJ. Alice Eagly is one of America's foremost researchers on the psychosocial aspects of sex-role development. Her book is essentially an exhaustive review of how men and women differ.

Maccoby E.E. and Jacklin C.N. (1974) THE PSYCHOLOGY OF SEX DIFFERENCES, Stanford University Press, Stanford, Ca. The classic treatment of sex differences. Although dated, most of the research covered in their book was fundamental to more recent research.

Money J.B. and Tucker P. (1975) SEXUAL SIGNATURES: ON BEING A MAN OR A WOMAN, Little Brown, Boston. The primary source for a lot of fascinating material on sexual reassignment surgery and the variability of gender identity.

Shaver P. and Hendrick C. (eds) (1987) SEX AND GENDER, Sage, Newbury Park, Ca. An easy to read primer written by leading experts in the field. The starting reference if you are new to the topic.

Tavris C. and Wade C. (1984) THE LONGEST WAR: SEX DIFFERENCES IN PERSPECTIVE (2nd edn), Harcourt Brace Jovanovich, San Diego. An eminently readable text on the politics and the evidence underpinning the gender debate. Has an excellent critique of the biology of gender.

SELF-CATEGORISATION, GROUPS AND GROUP INFLUENCE

*I*n 1980 I visited China, shortly after it opened its borders to tourists. The visit was a rushed affair, squeezed in on our way to London and was even shorter when our hydrofoil broke down in the middle of a stormy South China Sea! Two hour later, quite seasick, we landed in Macau and quickly hopped on a bus heading for Guangzhou. Because of the lateness of our arrival the itinerary had collapsed and harried officials scurried around trying to devise alternatives. Our bus driver, at a loss as to what to do with these foreigners for two hours, in the end just took us to his home village.

This unexpected insight into an ordinary Chinese community showed a culture enforcing group cohesiveness by consciously promoting social identity. Everything was organised collectively and the Chinese were exceptionally proud of their group accomplishments. Everyone wanted to show us the new pump, their clinic, the fish-farm, and so forth. I noticed everyone used the plural pronoun, our clothes, our pump, our future. This collective identity made conversations take unusual turns. I fell into a conversation with some men in their mid-thirties, one of whom spoke fluent English. I asked how he viewed the trickle of tourists starting to wander through old Canton. He made a few vague noises of collective appreciation, so I asked him again how he felt. Nonplussed, he scratched his head and said he didn't know and would ask his friends to tell him how he should feel about us; and did!

This collective consciousness extended from the trivial, like the "People's Republic of China Hygiene Facilitator No 6" badge on a washroom attendant in Guangzhou, to the very fabric of society. Visiting a new restaurant complex developed for tourists, another man spoke eloquently about "our building", "the struggle we had to get enough concrete to complete it on time" and "the sacrifices we made". I assumed him to be one of the workers but it turned out he was a technical translator on holiday from his home in Shenyang 860 km up the coast and had just arrived that morning! Not only was their consciousness collective, but so were their work practices. Catching a local bus, our ticket was taken by a uniformed collector who handed it to another, who wrote in a ledger, handed it to a third to be cancelled and then back to the first, who after consulting his colleagues, smiled and returned it to us. Not even a policy of full employment could account for the seriousness of this casual transaction! Neat queues patiently waited for the next bus as we left. I vowed to return to see what impact an open-door, modernisation policy would make.

As it happens I have yet to return to China, but Jeanna recently spent 10 days there recovering from our effort to get this book together. Either she visited another country entirely, or things have changed since my visit. Gone were the neat queues as everyone shoved to catch a train or buy an evening meal. While the traditional Chinese cohesiveness was still quite evident, a policy of openness has certainly made many changes.

Groups

As you can see, human beings are social animals—we are all part of the herd—and our activities are governed by the herd's direction. Our daily lives are a rich and unconscious tapestry of the many interconnecting groups to which we all belong. Some groups are formal, when we consciously join a club and agree to abide by its rules; some are informal, groups formed for the moment as when one half of the family challenges the other to a Scrabble game; and some are notional, calling ourselves Westerners, Christians, Papuans, freethinkers or whatever. As students reading this text you are probably members of a social psychology course group. Groups have a profound impact on how we think and feel about things, and how we act and react in our social environment. Membership of various groups exposes us to a wide range of social influences, direct and indirect.

As you read this chapter you will sense yet another level of social psychological theorising, that of seeing social behaviour from a collectivist viewpoint. That is, researchers study the *social* in social psychology, or how the group affects behaviour; a sharp contrast from the individualism of social cognition, which looks at social behaviour from within a person's head. For a long time these two areas within social psychology were seen as ends of a continuum. However, as you will see from this chapter, rather than being a continuum, they are circular in nature reinforcing one another. This bridging of the gap between the individualism of social cognition and groups was initiated in Bristol by Henri Tajfel and is continued by a group of local researchers some of whom were Tajfel's colleagues. As you read through the chapter you will notice that we have more boxes featuring prominent local social psychologists than in any other chapter. This reflects the importance of our contributions in this area. We will start by defining groups.

What are groups?

Groups define us. I am a university student, member of a drama club, part of a political party and so forth. Who we are and how we relate to others is largely determined by the groups to which we feel we belong. Group membership affects our social identity, provides us with rules and expectations about appropriate attitudes and behaviour, and prescribes how we should act towards others. In many instances, identifying the groups to which people belong provides us with valuable information and insight into their attitudes and what they regard as important and meaningful. For example, if you discover a fellow student is a neo-Nazi you are sure to make some definite attributions about their personality, attitudes and behaviour!

Groups consist of two or more people who share common beliefs, goals and social norms. This chapter explores group processes and how they affect our behaviour. We begin by considering how just mixing with others influences our actions. Next we discuss how the group context influences our notions of self and social identity. The nature and function of groups is outlined, followed by an examination of the processes of group interaction, such as decision-making in groups. We conclude with an examination of leadership and its influence on group processes and performance.

Social facilitation

The social facilitation effect

How does the mere presence of others influence an individual's task performance? As we have seen, it sometimes has a powerful effect. The term "social facilitation" is used by social psychologists to explain how such performance is enhanced or impaired by another's presence. The drive theory of social facilitation proposed by Zajonc (1965) postulates that the mere presence of others arouses us. This arousal then facilitates dominant well-learned habits or responses but inhibits non-dominant or poorly learned habits or responses (see Figure 12.1).

Findings from many experimental studies on animals and humans have offered support for the social facilitation effect (Zajonc & Sales, 1966; Matlin & Zajonc, 1968; Bond & Titus, 1983; Guerin, 1986, 1989; Schmitt et al., 1986; de Castro, 1991). An example of the social facilitation effect in action is Zajonc, Heingartner and Herman's (1969) ingenious study of cockroach behaviour. The researchers had cockroaches run through easy or difficult mazes to avoid a bright light. Compared to solo cockroaches, those who ran in groups, ran faster in the easy maze and slower in the difficult maze. So did those running in the presence of spectator cockroaches in audience boxes (see Figure 12.2).

Schmitt et al. (1986) conducted a study where subjects performed either a simple task (typing their names into a computer), or a more complex unfamiliar task (typing their name, backwards). Subjects performed these tasks either with just an experimenter present (evaluation apprehension condition), or in the presence of another subject who wore ear-plugs and was blindfolded (mere presence condition). Findings indicated that subjects' performance on the simple task was enhanced by the presence of others but impaired on the more complex task. de Castro (1991) investigated whether social facilitation could account for a correlation between the amount of food eaten during meals and the number of people present.

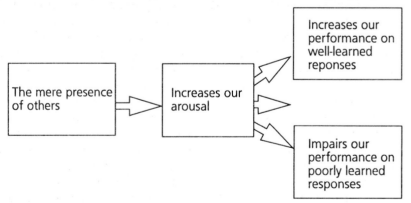

Figure 12.1 *Social facilitation*

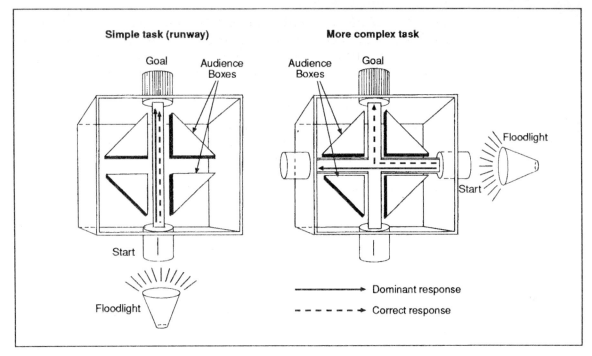

Figure 12.2 *Social facilitation in cockroaches*

Source: Zajonc et al., 1969.

Three hundred and fifteen adults aged 18 to 75 years kept seven-day diaries, recording what, when and where they ate, the amount consumed and number of other people present during the meal. His findings suggested a social facilitation of eating effect. On weekends larger meals were eaten in the presence of more people than during the week suggesting a true social facilitation effect between meal size and food consumed.

Evaluation apprehension

How do we explain this influence? While Zajonc argues that the mere presence of others is arousing and that it is this arousal that automatically affects our performance, more research suggests that other factors may also play a role. Is it just the mere physical presence of others that affects our performance, or does concern that others are evaluating us, **evaluation apprehension,** influence the outcome (Rosenberg, 1969)? For example, Bernard Guerin, at James Cook University of Northern Queensland, in a review of the literature on social facilitation, examined the effects of the mere presence of another person (Guerin, 1986). He suggests these effects are seen only when there is some uncertainty in the behaviour of the person present. He also found mere presence effects influence a tendency to conform to standards or norms, which as we saw in Chapter Six relate to the controlling influence of social approval and disapproval.

Several studies indicate other factors affect social facilitation. Cottrell et al. (1968) and Bond (1982) found the effect occurred only when individuals

evaluation apprehension
Wanting to avoid a negative social evaluation; performance anxiety.

Social facilitation theory suggests that the presence of others and the degree of lecturer expertise equals the degree of arousal.
(Photo: Chris Simkin)

felt their performance was being observed and evaluated by others. Sanna and Shotland (1990) found that when subjects expected a positive evaluation from an audience, they performed better on a memory task. When they anticipated a negative evaluation from the presence of others, their performance was impaired. However, subjects working alone performed better than those who worked in the presence of others. The researchers suggest that it is the direction of expected evaluation, not merely the anticipated evaluation by others, that plays a significant role in social facilitation.

Schmitt et al. (1986) found that in the presence of others individuals performed a simple task quickly but a complex task more slowly. However, individuals who were observed by the experimenter (evaluation apprehension condition) performed the simple task the fastest, compared to all other conditions. The researchers argue that while the mere presence of others arouses us, the anticipation of being evaluated increases that arousal. As a result, they proposed that social facilitation occurs as a consequence of evaluation apprehension; or from related issues such as concern for how we present in front of others; or from competitive feelings. Therefore it may be these factors that determine the impact of another's presence on our task performance.

Guerin (1989) examined the impact of mere presence effects on evaluation apprehension in a sample of 48 Australian undergraduates, who were required to complete a simple copying task. The students were allocated to four groups: alone, with no observer; a condition in which an observer was unable to view the subject but was present; a condition in which the observer sat behind the subject at a desk; and one where the observer sat behind the subject but without a desk. Subjects were led to believe that the observer was just a timekeeper. Guerin found clear effects between the first two conditions and the latter two where the observer could not be seen by the subject. Guerin interprets his findings as clear support for a monitoring view of social facilitation.

So, while research evidence generally supports the idea that the presence of others increases our motivation or drive, there is an ongoing debate about the nature of this motivation (Geen & Bushman, 1987; Geen, 1988). For Zajonc the social facilitation effect stems from an innate tendency or drive to become aroused in the presence of others:

> The problem centres on the concept of drive. It is unclear what drive is and how it can be measured. Glaser (1982) argues that drive is "merely a mathematical construct . . . What is missing is any appreciation of the fact that most 'presence' is social in nature". This has implications for the context and not just the level of performance. It follows that most performance is also social—serving functions for interpersonal relationships, self-definition, communication and so on. Efforts to recognise this have only gone a little way towards "socialising" performance research. (Hogg & Abrams, 1988, p. 121)

Another viewpoint argues that the presence of others may influence our performance because it is cognitively distracting (Baron, 1986). Imagine you are in a group performing a relatively simple task such as putting letters in envelopes, or collating and stapling material. Most of us, if we tried, could probably perform better on such tasks, though then we may find the presence of others somewhat distracting. However, suppose you are working at a highly complex task such as a difficult statistical problem. In such a situation the distraction created by the presence of others would more likely than not result in impaired performance. Baron (1986) extended this basic idea into his **distraction-conflict model**. Briefly, this model proposes that the presence of others is arousing because it leads to a conflict between two basic tendencies, whether to pay attention to the presence of others, or concentrate on the task at hand. This conflict results in increased arousal, which either facilitates or inhibits our performance.

In this section we have discussed several explanations of the social facilitation effect. It is important to remember that these explanations may not necessarily be viewed as mutually exclusive. Depending on the situation and particular task it is possible that all these processes may work together to affect our performance.

distraction-conflict model
Others' presence is arousing because it causes conflict between two basic tendencies, whether to pay attention to them or concentrate on the task at hand.

Social loafing

The social facilitation effect demonstrates that the presence of others can often motivate us to increase our performance in particular tasks. However, the opposite effect has also been identified by social psychologists. This effect, known as social loafing, suggests that sometimes we don't work as hard in the presence of others as we would alone, especially if our behaviour is not under surveillance. Whether we can accomplish more by working

Social loafing theory predicts that the more people pulling, the more each person loafs! (Photo: Chris Simkin)

with others or by working alone appears to depend largely on the particular task being performed.

Social loafing often occurs in group contexts where activities involve members working on additive tasks, that is, when the total product is the sum of all individual effort, for example, tug-of-war. In a study of tug-of-war games, Ringelmann (1913) found that individuals pulled twice as hard when alone than when in a team of 8 members. Support for the social loafing effect has been found in many studies. In an experiment conducted by Williams, Harkins and Latane (1981), groups of subjects were asked to clap or cheer as loudly as they could. Subjects were told the experiment was to ascertain how much noise people made in social situations. Subjects clapped and cheered in several conditions: alone and in groups of 2, 4 or 6. Findings indicated that as group size increased, the amount of noise made by each subject decreased. However, when subjects in groups were informed that their individual effort was being monitored by the researchers, the effect of social loafing was eliminated (Williams, Harkins & Latane, 1981). Other research findings suggest that social loafing occurs in many group situations, in both males and females, in different cultures and over a wide variety of work settings (Harkins, 1987; Harkins & Petty, 1982).

Social psychologists have identified a number of factors that may contribute to social loafing. A significant factor appears to be social evaluation. Often our individual performance is anonymous in additive group tasks. It is, the group performance that is being monitored not our individual effort. Thus in many instances this leads us to reduce our effort, as no one will know how well we perform and we cannot be held responsible for our individual actions. This effect is akin to diffusion of responsibility discussed in Chapter Ten, that is, being just one of a group decreases our individual sense of responsibility. Also when in group settings we may assume that other individuals will not give their optimum performance and likewise we tend to do the same (Jackson & Harkins, 1985). Equally, we may not be as aroused or motivated in a group, as when we are working alone (Jackson & Williams, 1985).

Reducing social loafing

If we are in the game of improving performance (lifting productivity), one way of reducing social loafing may be to identify the output or effort of each individual. For example, where groups of people are performing collective tasks, such as workers on a building site, giving each individual sub-tasks may help eliminate social loafing. Several studies suggest that asking individuals to evaluate their individual contribution, or the output of their group relative to other groups, will reduce social loafing (Harkins & Szymanski, 1988). These authors also suggest that providing individuals with some standard against which they can evaluate their own performance, or that of their group, may be sufficient to increase performance. Intrinsic interest in a complex, challenging task may increase our motivation and commitment to group goals. While it has been found that social loafing occurs in simple or additive tasks, the effect has not been demonstrated when the task is interesting or complex, or when individuals perform unique sub-tasks.

The presence of others can lead to either social facilitation or to social loafing. The key factor determining which effect occurs appears to be the complexity of the task being performed. It also depends on whether the presence of others increases or decreases our concerns about their evaluating our individual performance.

Social impact theory

We have asked when and under what conditions does the presence of others affect our performance, but there still remains the question of what determines the extent of such influence. Social impact theory attempts to address this general issue. Latane and Nida (1981) define social impact as "the changes in physiological states and subjective feelings, motives and emotions, cognitions and beliefs, values and behavior that occur in an individual as a result of the real, implied or imagined presence or actions of other individuals". Latane (1981) suggests the impact of others' presence on individual performance is a function of three basic principles. First, as the number of observers (group members) increases, so does their influence on our performance. The second factor is the observers' *strength* or characteristics such as their perceived power, age or status and what these mean to the person being observed. A third factor determining others' impact is the immediacy of the audience, that is, their proximity to the individuals in time or space. There is a multiplier effect among these three factors and they may strengthen or weaken each other depending on how the individual evaluates them.

Latane suggests that social impact theory can explain how individual behaviour is affected by the presence of others and why it sometimes results in social facilitation and at other times leads to social loafing. Latane's model has attracted mixed support. As we saw in Chapter Ten, research supports claims that group size influences individual responsibility and performance. However, research on the importance of strength and immediacy factors is somewhat inconsistent and requires further clarification. Social impact theory is still relatively underdeveloped and requires further research to substantiate its predictions (Mullen, 1985; Jackson, 1987).

Social categorisation

How does social categorisation fit into a chapter on groups? In this chapter we draw together many theorists whose work we have already examined in previous chapters. Whereas once a such a chapter would have contained sections on how social groups are structured and then gone on to investigate group processes in some depth, the cognitive revolution that is sweeping through social psychology has brought new, more individual, ways of seeing groups. Although we will give the earlier studies their due place, the central idea intriguing social psychologists these days is how groups provide informational and normative guides to behaviour, and how group salience becomes incorporated into our personal identities. This essentially cognitive view of groups incorporates the work on salience, self-schemas and impression formation we discussed in Chapter Two; the role of attribution and self-attribution discussed in Chapter Three; the powerful role of behaviour in shaping our attitudes and sense of self which we discussed in Chapter Four; ingroup and outgroup polarisation and social identity theory we discussed in Chapter Five; and virtually the entirety of our discussion of social influence in Chapter Six. So you can see that this is an important topic and its key is social categorisation.

As we saw in our discussion of social categorisation theory in Chapter Five, when we interact with others, we tend automatically to view them as members of a particular social category, or *group*. While we may come to know people intimately, in most cases we tend to perceive others not as individuals but in terms of social categories to which they belong. For example, when meeting someone for the first time we would not evaluate their individuality but rather their ethnicity, sex, social class, and so forth. As Hogg and Abrams (1988) noted, social categories do not exist in isolation. For example, the social category of "Maori" is meaningful because it serves to differentiate between those who are and those who are not Polynesian.

Of course these categories are not objective. We all belong to many social groups and have a highly idiosyncratic construction of the social order that divides us into *us* and *them* categories: ingroups, to which we belong, and outgroups, to which we do not belong. Our behaviour in a given context depends on the schemas we hold of ourselves and others. When we belong to a particular group, our membership of the group may determine the way we see and interact with outgroups (Messick & Mackie, 1989). Often members of other groups are perceived to be more like one another than members of our own group, that is, we tend to maximise distinctions between individual members of our ingroup and to maximise the differences between our group and a largely homogeneous outgroup. This process is termed the outgroup homogeneity effect and occurs because we tend to see members of our group as individuals as we know more about them. However, it is unlikely we will have the same information about members of other groups and therefore we tend to perceive them as being more similar to each other than they are.

As we saw in Chapter Five, this somewhat arbitrary division into us and them is a fact of life. When we are frequently exposed to these ingroup/outgroup categorisations we tend to develop set ways of behaving towards outgroups. We then fall into habits, acting competitively, or rejecting outgroup members, irrespective of the particular individual or the context of the interaction. Tajfel (1970) suggests that because of this stereotypic view we discriminate against outgroups even when such discrimination does nothing for our own self-interest. According to Tajfel such discrimination may arise in the absence of pre-existing hostility towards an outgroup. This approach suggests that generally we are prepared to discriminate more or less automatically against outgroups and to favour our own ingroup. For example, Stangor, Lynch, Duan and Glas (1992) conducted a series of experiments to examine how people use immediately apparent features of others as a basis of social categorisation. Findings indicate that most subjects were more likely to categorise by sex than race, but used both simultaneously; racially prejudiced people used race as a category to a greater extent than unprejudiced subjects. Of course this tendency is the result of our socialisation which has indirectly and subtly reinforced ingroup/outgroup discrimination. This takes some curious turns when we are part of the outgroup (see Box 12.1).

Social identity theory

As noted in Chapter Five, we have both *personal* and *social* identities. Several theorists maintain that our group affiliations come to form part of our self-concept, or a social identity (Tajfel & Turner, 1979; Tajfel, 1982; Turner et al., 1987). We constantly evaluate ourselves by social comparison processes, comparing ourselves to the groups to which we belong and contrasting these with outgroups. Therefore social identity refers to those aspects of our self-concept or image that are based on group schemas. We are constantly categorising ourselves in everyday encounters and, depending on the situation, you might see yourself as a social psychology student, member of a drama club or a certain political party, a resident of Australia or New Zealand, and so on. This process of defining ourselves in relation to other people is referred to as **social identification**.

social identification
The process of defining ourselves in relation to other people.

Box 12.1 *Profile: Graham Vaughan and the psychology of intergroup discrimination*

Graham Vaughan has studied the shifting patterns of ethnic awareness and social identities of Maoris in a series of studies since the early 1960s. Professor Vaughan studied at the Universities of Auckland and Canterbury, before gaining his PhD at Victoria University of Wellington, in 1962. Since 1985 he has been Professor of Psychology at the University of Auckland. A Fellow of the New Zealand Psychological Society, Professor Vaughan has had a distinguished career as a social psychologist and is the recipient of many scholarships and international awards including Fulbright Research Scholar, 1966 and Directeur d'Etudes, Maison des Science de l'Homme, 1981. In 1988–89 he was Visiting Senior Fellow at the National University of Singapore. In addition to his years as Editor of the New Zealand Journal of Psychology, he has served on the editorial boards of several journals including the Journal of Intercultural Studies. He is the author of over 50 publications, many in the areas of ethnic awareness and interracial attitudes.
(Photo: courtesy Graham Vaughan)

In Chapter Five and in our discussions here we have examined social categorisation from an ingroup perspective. How does an outgroup member deal with social categorisation effects when they are aware that they are part of an outgroup?

In Graham Vaughan's earliest work which predates social categorisation theory, Vaughan (1963, 1964) found that in tests of ethnic self-awareness and difference, Maori children identified with their own group four years later than did Pakeha children (see Figure 12.3) Vaughan argued that his tests were ultimately a measure of ethnic attitudes and that cognitive processing of ethnic differences and affective processes were intertwined. Maori children's responses reflected an awareness of Pakeha privilege and a reluctance to identify with an outgroup; this delayed their self-identification as Maoris. The strength of this process was seen in three tests of ethnic preference:

Pakeha children consistently favoured their own group on these tests. This trend peaked at six years, at which age there was a nearly total rejection of Maori figures. By 12 years, own-group choices were still clear, but a process of stereotype differentiation had commenced so that the Maori may be "lazier", but also "kinder" . . . The Maori results were nearly a mirror image. Preference for Pakeha figures was strongest at six years of age, whereas at twelve, ingroup preference was detected for the first time. (Vaughan, 1988, p. 10)

As we have seen it is natural to classify people according to their salient characteristics, and race and ethnicity is a key variable in so doing. Part of the process of gaining a positive self-image is identifying with the characteristics others use to categorise us. Race and ethnicity are inescapable consequences of this process of social comparison. Healthy identities "are critically dependent on the degree to which the attributes of membership [of our ingroup] are positively perceived" (Vaughan, 1988). Gaining satisfactory self-images and social identities is then dependent on the ease with which we can form and use social categories that allow us to identify with our ingroup and mark ourselves off from the wider community. Vaughan's early

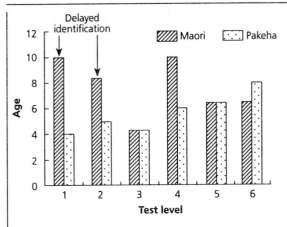

Figure 12.3
Delayed ingroup identification in Maori and Pakeha children

Source: Vaughan, 1986.

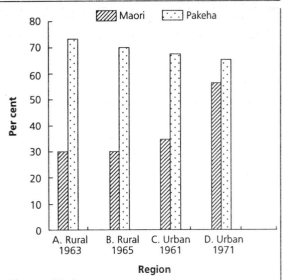

Figure 12.4
Ingroup preference by New Zealand Maori and Pakeha children as a function of social change

Source: Vaughan, 1986.

work suggests that Maori children have an impaired ability to do this as their awareness that they are part of an marginalised outgroup hinders the process of social categorisation. This was reinforced by their inability to influence a social system which devalues their social group. So Maori children identified with the Pakeha, until the consequences of their own ethnicity became inescapable.

Times change and the emergence of the Brown Power Movement, and other social forces seeking to redress the social inequities of New Zealand society, alters the boundaries of the social groups. Vaughan (1978, 1986) in a continuing series of studies of social change and intergroup preferences found that Maori children show a shift away from outgroup preference as a function of urbanisation and of time (Vaughan, 1978). In rural studies Maori children favoured Pakehas and perhaps this reflects the security of a traditional Maori identity which offsets some of the disadvantages of being an outgroup member. However, with the wholesale flight to the cities and increasing urbanisation, traditional social supports are weakened and competition for jobs and education "reveals Maori/Pakeha social inequity for what it is" (Vaughan, 1978). This trend accelerated with the rise of a worldwide minority self-conscious-ness, leading Maoris to become more ingroup-oriented, particularly in older children. Figure 12.4 shows the gradual change in Maori ingroup preferences.

As you can see from Figure 12.4 this process of social change has also led to a diminution of blatant ingroup preference by Pakeha children and perhaps the two communities are more tolerant of each other. If so then the process of forming positive social identities by appropriate self-categorisation will be enhanced. Vaughan (1978) noted this process but warned that the realities of realistic intergroup competition and an increasing Maori militancy might reverse the trend. It will be interesting to see if the current economic downturn will offset more positive attitudes towards Maoris among the Pakeha community.

The social identity approach rests upon certain assumptions concerning the nature of people and society and their interrelationships. Specifically it maintains that society comprises social categories which stand in power and status relations to one another. (Hogg & Abrams, 1988, p. 14)

Social identification is essentially group-based and works in three ways. First, social categorisation, or how we see ourselves and others, is a process of intergroup comparison. Second, the ingroup's norms, attitudes and actions exert a profound influence on our behaviour. Third, our tendency to conform to and enact our ingroup's stereotypes reinforces both our social identity and the social categorisations to which our ingroup subscribes (Turner, 1982, 1985). To see ourselves favourably, we evaluate our ingroups more positively than other groups (Tajfel & Turner, 1979). The social identity approach focuses on these psychological processes and attempts to create psychological reality from a social reality. While many social psychologists are concerned with studying the individual in a group, social identity theory highlights the group in the individual.

It considers identity and self-definition to mediate between social categories as statistical or historical entities and individual behaviour. As a social psychological approach it explains the psychological processes involved in translating social categories into human groups. These processes create identity and generate behaviour which have a characteristic and distinctive form, that of groups behaviour. (Hogg & Abrams, 1988, p. 17)

Self-categorisation theory

The exact nature of the relationship between the individual and the group has provoked much debate in social psychology. We are individuals but when in groups we take on collective characteristics. How does individuality and group conformity coexist? Turner (1991; see Box 12.2) argues that over the last 30 years theorists assumed that normative social influence, or conforming to your ingroup's dictates to gain their approval, was a group process; whereas informational social influence, or using others as a reference point for correct behaviour, was purely private. While the former is power-based compliance, the latter is "true influence" because we have to agree with the information provided before we will incorporate it into our self-identity and repertoire (Turner, 1991). Perhaps this is an artificial distinction, which sees society as being alien and external to the individual and compelling behaviour, while seeing the individual as an asocial cognitive information processor. However, as we have seen, informational influence is socially mediated. It was these insights that led John Turner to explore the way we self-categorise ourselves.

According to Turner and Oakes (1986) we gain part of our sense of self by locating ourselves within existing social categories and this process of self-categorisation provides a means of developing and strengthening our social identity. Self-categorisation theory (Turner & Oakes, 1986; Turner et al., 1987) analyses the self and the relationships between self, social norms and the social context. It highlights the idea that our social

Box 12.2 *Profile: John Turner and self-categorisation theory*

John C. Turner, *whose work is extensively reviewed in this section, is Professor of Psychology at the Australian National University and a Fellow of the Australian Academy of Social Sciences. He obtained his PhD in social psychology at the University of Bristol (UK) where he was also research fellow and lecturer from 1974 to 1982. He spent 1982–83 at the Princeton Institute for Advanced Study and 1983–90 at Macquarie University. He collaborated in the 1970s with the late Henri Tajfel in the development of the social identity theory of group relations and during the 1980s formulated self-categorisation theory as a general account of group processes. He is currently applying these perspectives to the analysis of the self and its relationship to cognition and social influence. Professor Turner is the author of many journal articles, book chapters and books, the latest of which is* Social Influence *(1991) from the Open University Press.*
(Photo: *courtesy John Turner*)

identity encompasses a private self and social norms that "define and shape the activity of the private self and vice versa" (Turner, 1991). This approach also provides us with a general theory of group behaviour. Turner proposes that group behaviour can be understood as individuals enacting a shared identity rather than as just isolated individuals.

Our self-concept can be viewed as a form of self-categorisation. As we saw in our discussion of social identity theory, we categorise ourselves by noting the similarities between us and others according to some ingroup membership, and further refine this by contrasting it in opposition to an outgroup. This notion of ingroup–outgroup membership is also a self-categorisation which is more extensive than notions of a personal self:

> Categories form in such a way as to ensure that the differences between categories are larger than the differences within categories . . . A full exploration of how we categorize people must also take into account the social meaning of the similarities and differences between them (i.e. category content, which is related to normative fit) and the relationship of social categories to the values, needs and goal of the perceiver (their relative accessibility). (Turner, 1991, p. 156)

Self-categorisation theory is thus an extension of social identity theory. It is essentially an examination of the cognitive strategies we use to categorise ourselves in building our self-schema. Part of the process of self-categorisation is using ingroups to test that our perceptions of the world around us, and of ourselves, are accurate. As we saw in Chapters

The problem with being famous is that you have many imitators. To what extent is social identity a simple matter of imitation?
(Photo: Barry Price)

consensual validation
Something is valid because we all agree it is.

Two and Three, the subjective nature of schematic processing unfortunately leads to many errors of judgment. As an alternative, we can test social reality by asking what our ingroup believes, which is in essence a process of **consensual validation** (something is valid because we all agree it is) and social comparison (see Chapter Eight). These are both group-oriented but only to a particular kind of group:

> If the right people (similar, relevant others) agree with our point of view, then we are confident of its correctness and, by extension, any message that embodies an ingroup consensus tends to be perceived as valid. The agreed, shared, consensual attitude of a reference group that a certain way of thinking or acting is correct, appropriate, proper (and therefore desirable) constitutes a social norm. (Turner, 1991, p. 157)

This brings us to the starting point of Turner's thesis:

> Consensual validation is therefore *normative validation* and social reality is the process of finding normative support for subjective validity . . . Thus informational influence and social comparison (social reality testing) go hand in hand. Indeed, the latter is the basis of the former . . . *informational influence is normative influence.* (Turner, 1991, p. 148)

goodness of fit
In self-categorisation theory the degree of correspondence between our subjective reality testing and group based consensual validation.

Self-categorisation may proceed on any number of levels from the cosmic to the mundane. We may see ourselves as *individuals,* or compare ourselves to *humanity,* or to the Whangarei Touch Football Social Club, but what is important is that we make *valid* comparisons and so **goodness of fit** is of central importance to self-categorisation theory (Oakes, 1987). Fit proceeds on two levels: **comparative fit** or that "categories form in such a way as to ensure that the differences between categories are larger than the differences within categories" (Turner, 1991); and **normative fit**, that our stereotypes of a category or group actually reflect the behaviour being represented.

Oakes, Turner and Haslam (1991) conducted a study to examine whether our perceptions of others become salient when their attitudes fit our social categorisation of them. The researchers invoked typical student stereotypes to determine their impact on social categorisation and comparative and normative fit. Fifty-one male and 39 female undergraduates watched a group, which they were told comprised three arts and three science students arguing about "whether university was important for social life or academic work". You can guess what stereotypes the experimenters were trying to evoke!

> In the "consensus" conditions, there was complete agreement in the stimulus group. In the "conflict" conditions, the three arts students took one view and the three science students took an opposite view. In the "deviance" conditions, one arts student disagreed with the five other students (who agreed among themselves). (Turner, 1991, p. 158)

The subjects then rated a target woman and the group as a whole:

> The main findings were that the target person's attitudes were explained more in terms of her arts *social category membership* ("she is an arts student") in the consistent-conflict condition, her *personality* in the inconsistent-deviance condition, and *externally* in the consensus conditions. (Turner, 1991, p. 158)

As self-categorisation theory would have predicted, the stereotyping of arts students as favouring social development and the science students as hard-working were the most salient when both normative and comparative fit were most pronounced (when three arts students disagreed with three science students in the expected directions). The results of this experiment support the hypothesis that "perceived category membership of others becomes salient as a description and explanation of their behaviour, where their attitudes 'fit' the social categorization" (Turner, 1991).

comparative fit
Social categories form in such a way as to ensure that differences between categories are larger than the difference within categories, allowing us to define ourselves in contrast to the outgroup.

normative fit
That our stereotypes of a social category or group actually reflect the behaviour being represented.

Group processes

In this section we will discuss why we as individuals form groups, what they do for us, and some of the important characteristics and processes involved in group functioning. As previously discussed, once we join a group we are subjected to a wide range of influences, Our membership in a particular group can influence and often change our attitudes, beliefs and behaviour directly and in many subtle ways.

As you read this section, think about the various groups to which you belong. Why did you join them, what factors influence you to stay in them

*Groups may be formal
or informal.
(Photos: Barry Price)*

and what do you get out of being a member? While we spend much of our time with others, not all crowds can be viewed as groups. A group is more than just a collection of individuals who happen to be in the same place at the same time but are not involved in a purposeful relationship with one another. Being part of an audience at a concert is not the same as belonging to a specific group such as a university drama club.

Most social psychologists define a group as a collection of individuals who frequently interact and communicate with one another over time; who share common goals; are sometimes interdependent; and see themselves as part of a group (Paulus, 1989). Research suggests our feelings of belonging to a group do develop from conditions similar to those outlined by our definition (Insko et al., 1988). We will feel we belong to a functioning group only when we have the opportunity to interact frequently; feel that others need us; and share common goals and work towards achieving them. When these conditions are met, the group exerts its influence and we tend to act differently than we would as individuals working alone. Of course these processes are not independent, they form complex links and bonds.

Group formation

We join groups for a variety of reasons: some groups may help us fulfil psychological and/or social needs such as belonging; others a similarity of interests and attitudes; while others fulfil a need for approval and attention. Groups may assist us in achieving important goals and often enable us to gain information and knowledge that is otherwise unavailable. Our group memberships also help us develop a positive social identity, which becomes part of our self-image or concept.

Groups come in all shapes and sizes and meet many purposes. The smallest is a couple or **dyad** and most social psychological research has focused on groups smaller than 20 individuals. Groups differ in values such as political groups, religious groups and debating groups. They also vary in duration and function. Jury members may come together for a relatively short period to reach a verdict in a particular case, whereas families may continue for many generations. Groups vary in their scope of activities. For example, some groups focus on a single issue such as fundraising for AIDS research, whereas a family is a wider ranging group.

Group structure

Groups do not just appear fully formed. At first a group may appear as a loose collection of individuals, each member contributing equally to the group. As the group develops and endures over time, members' contributions may change and their influence in the group becomes differentiated. Tuckman and Jensen (1977) suggest that groups appear to progress through several stages of development. The key steps in this process are: *forming*, where the group begins to develop, basic rules are established and the members get to know each other; *storming*, a stage of competition among members for position and roles in the group; *norming*, where they begin to develop ground rules and attachment to the group becomes stronger; *performing*, the stage at which the group gets down to work, becomes task oriented and moves towards shared goals; and *adjourning* where, the task completed, the members drift apart, or decide that other, particularly social, goals remain.

These stages represent a general pattern applicable to many groups. While this model is useful in helping us to understand how groups develop in their early stages, not all groups conform to this model. Given their uniqueness and diversity, many factors will influence whether a particular group conforms to this general pattern and, in any case, groups are fluid and usually change over time. Group structure is defined by such characteristics as roles, norms, status and communication patterns. By studying these components, social psychologists are able to identify patterns, describe relationships among members and differentiate one group from another.

Group formation and structure

dyad
The smallest social group: two people.

Roles

task-oriented role
Where the emphasis is on getting the job done. People adopting this role direct, coordinate and organise group behaviour towards group goals.

relations-oriented roles
Attending to relationships within the group, focusing on maintaining group harmony and morale.

Role theory suggests our behaviour can be understood in terms of the everyday roles we play in our group memberships (reference). What happens in the groups to which you belong? Do all members act in the same way and carry out the same functions? Odds are that each fulfils different roles. These may be formally assigned, for example, individuals chosen to be leader, secretary, treasurer and so on, or we may gradually acquire them without formal procedure. The role of leader often emerges in this way.

Psychologists have identified three distinct group roles. First, there is a **task-oriented role** where the emphasis is on getting the job done. People adopting this role direct, coordinate and organise group behaviour towards group goals. People who adopt **relations-oriented roles** attend to relationships within the group, focusing on maintaining group harmony and morale.

Successful groups are often less a matter of the task at hand (task orientation) than getting the ambience right (group relations)!
(Cartoonist: Steve Harris)

The third role is termed self-oriented. Those individuals who adopt a **self-oriented role** are primarily concerned about themselves and indifferent to group purposes. They may try to undermine and subvert the efforts of those who are task- or relations-oriented if their own interests conflict with group directions.

We sometimes find ourselves holding several different roles within a group and this may lead to **role conflict**, where two or more roles compete for our time and attention. As a result of role conflict, problems may arise for both an individual as well as the group. Conflicting demands imposed on individuals can lead to emotional tension and strain, dissatisfaction with the group and/or the individual and poor task performance.

Norms

Norms are expectations, or explicit or implicit rules developed by groups to regulate the conduct of all members. Irrespective of their position or role in the group, prescriptive norms control group members' behaviour. Continued violation of group norms often results in peer pressure being placed upon individuals to conform or comply. If such pressure fails to achieve compliance, the member may be ostracised and excluded from the group.

Status

Status refers to an individual's prestige within a group. Not all roles are equal and differences in relative social standing implies an evaluation of

self-oriented roles
People who are primarily concerned about themselves and indifferent to group purposes. They may try to undermine and subvert the efforts of those who are task- or relations-oriented if group interests conflict with their own.

role conflict
Where two or more roles compete for our time and attention, causing problems for both individuals and their group.

Some hierarchical groups are more obvious than others!

people—how much influence they exert and how favourable their position is in the group. Generally positions in social systems differ in social status. This prestige or ranking can result from people's position or roles within a group, from their characteristics, or from their achievements such as the leader role which is usually held in high esteem.

Patterns of group communication

Another structural characteristic that affects groups is the communication patterns among members. Centralisation and decentralisation patterns are two concepts used by researchers to describe communication networks. Centralisation refers to some members' greater access to information and communication, whereas decentralisation describes communication where interaction between members is more equal (see Figure 12.5)

The wheel network is highly centralised and requires all communication to be channelled through one member. The next most centralised is the Y structure where communication is directed to either of two members. The chain and the circle networks are less centralised than the wheel, and access to communication is more equal but more centralised than the all-

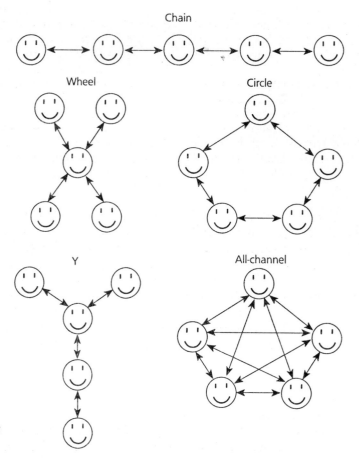

Figure 12.5 *Social networks*
Source: Tedeschi et al., 1985.

Box 12.3 *Profile: Michael Hogg and group cohesiveness*

A University of Birmingham graduate, Michael Hogg received his PhD from the University of Bristol in 1983, where he lectured for three years before moving to Australia in 1985 to take up a postdoctoral fellowship at Macquarie University. In 1986 he moved to a lectureship in Psychology in Melbourne, and then after a sabbatical appointment in 1990 as a visiting scholar at the University of California, Los Angeles, moved to the University of Queensland, where he is currently Reader in Psychology. Michael Hogg is an experimental social psychologist whose research interest is in intergroup relations and group processes. He is involved in the development of social identity and self-categorisation theory, and has published seven books and edited collections, including three with his long-time collaborator Dominic Abrams: Social Identification (1988); Social Identity Theory (1990); and Group Motivation (forthcoming); and over 50 articles and chapters.
(Photo: courtesy Michael Hogg)

Another name which occurs frequently in this chapter is that of Dr Michael Hogg of Queensland University, part of the vital group which coalesced around Henri Tajfel in Bristol University in the early 1970s.

Michael recently released *The Social Psychology of Group Cohesiveness* (1992) an advanced level text which analyses how social psychology conceptualises group cohesiveness and solidarity as interpersonal processes among small interactive groups. In the first part of his book Hogg outlines the development of group cohesiveness theory since the 1950s, critiquing the reductionism in social psychology which that ultimately saw group cohesiveness as just another example of interpersonal attraction. In opposing this perspective, Hogg argues for a group level view of group cohesiveness using the social identity and self-categorisation perspectives we have discussed in this chapter. From this position he analyses concepts such as groupthink, social loafing and group performance; and considers the implications of a social identity view of group cohesiveness.

channel network, where each member can communicate directly with any member of the group. Communication networks such as these are essential to group activities and affect the quality of group problem-solving. Generally with more complex tasks, such as mathematical problems, decentralised networks are more effective, whereas centralised networks are more effective when performing simple problem-solving such as finding a common symbol (Shaw, 1964). Also, patterns of communication significantly affect the morale of a group. In general, the more freedom individuals have to communicate and the more access to information they have, the more satisfied they are.

Group cohesiveness

Group cohesiveness refers to the sum total of forces both positive and negative that influence members to remain part of a particular group (Festinger, 1950). As such it is a characteristic of a group as a whole and is something that develops over time. Researchers suggest there are several key factors which create and enhance group cohesiveness:

- In cost/benefit terms, the greater the initial cost of joining a group, the more we are attracted to it.
- The esteem of each individual for the group contributes to the formation of social identity.
- Groups that have a history of success are in general more cohesive than those that do not (Shaw, 1981).
- Groups are generally higher in cohesiveness when they are faced with some external threat, pressure or serious competition (Sherif et al., 1961).
- Relatively small groups tend to be more cohesive than larger groups (Hogg, 1992).

Cohesiveness has important implications for the behaviour of a group. Members of a cohesive group tend to be highly motivated to remain in the group. Groups that are cohesive also tend to exhibit strong norms and require compliance to the norms, to ensure group continuation. Of course cohesiveness may impose limitations. In some instances members of highly cohesive groups may fail to adopt a critical and questioning approach to the group's perspective, activities and decisions.

Decision-making in groups

Decision-making is a vital part of our everyday interactions. Who we are as decision-makers is just as complex as who we are as people. Many factors influence the process of our decision-making: our parents, education, social status, cultural background and so on. In addition many other variables, such as our tendency towards stereotyping, our prejudices and biases, our willingness to take risks, our fear of failure and rejection, all contribute to the how, what and why of decision-making.

In the social context the decision-making process is extremely important. Society, to a large extent, depends on decisions made by groups, not individuals. Most of our law, economic and business practices, education, health and welfare policies that govern our everyday lives are determined by committees, various boards and similar groups. Our commonsense suggests that groups are more likely to make better decisions than individuals. We tend to believe that a group is likely to be more informed, possess more expertise which can be shared, make fewer errors, is better able to examine all sides of an issue, and is able to avoid hasty or extreme decisions. Is this the case? Are groups actually able to make better and more accurate decisions than individuals?

Social psychological research suggests that our commonsense notions may be a misrepresentation of the true picture of group decision-making, and that groups do not necessarily make better decisions. In their study of group decision-making processes, social psychologists have focused on several related themes: the processes involved and social forces affecting group decisions; differences between decisions determined by groups and individuals; and factors that account for faulty and sometimes disastrous decisions reached by groups. This section will briefly examine these closely related topics. If we can increase our understanding and knowledge of the processes involved in group decision-making we may be more perceptive and aware of what is taking place in group interactions. This knowledge may help us to function more effectively in group situations.

Social decision schemes

Think of the various groups to which you belong. In general, when a group forms and begins to discuss some issue, or plan a course of action, rarely do we reach a unanimous agreement. Usually there is support for different views and perspectives and considerable "to-ing and fro-ing" over different courses of action. Usually after some discussion we manage to reach a decision. Of course this is not always the case, and many groups may reach an impasse or become deadlocked, as with hung juries and so forth.

Kerr and MacCoun (1985) suggest that we can often predict the final decision reached by a group by applying relatively simple rules. These are described as **social decision schemes**. These rules pertain to initial information about group members' opinions and attitudes about the group's final decision. Of course different rules may be more applicable in certain situations. In many instances we will tend to adopt the position initially preferred by the majority. With this **majority-win rule**, the main purpose of group discussion is to strengthen or affirm the most popular view. It appears this rule is most applicable in situations where judgment, or matters of opinion, are involved. A scheme adopted by many juries is a **two-thirds majority rule**. Here a conviction or acquittal depends on the decision reached by two-thirds of the jurors (Davis et al., 1984). The **truth-wins rule** suggests there is a *correct* decision and this will eventually emerge and be recognised by group members. This rule seems to be most successful in situations where intellectual tasks are involved (correct answers or solutions; Kirchler & Davis, 1986). Some groups tend to opt for a decision that is consistent with the direction of the first shift in opinion adopted by any member of the group. This is know as the **first-shift rule**.

Are group decisions more conservative, or are they riskier than those made by an individual? In 1961 Stoner observed that decisions reached by groups were riskier than initial opinions held by individual group members. This finding was described as the **risky shift effect** and occurs when group discussion makes individuals' opinions riskier than they were. A typical study would ask subjects to read a number of complex situations (e.g. a dilemma from the Choice Dilemmas Questionnaire, Kogan & Wallach, 1964; see below). For each situation several alternatives with varying degrees of risk are presented (very high to very low risk). All the reasons for this effect have already been covered in the text so far, and we will only briefly review them for the sake of completeness.

---

social decision schemes
Simple decision-making rules which determine how a group will reach its final decision.

majority-win rule
The main purpose of group discussion is to strengthen or affirm the most popular view.

two-thirds majority rule
An absolute majority; here a course of action depends on the agreement reached by two-thirds of a group.

truth-wins rule
Suggests there is a correct decision and this will eventually emerge and be recognised by group members.

first-shift rule
Reaching a decision consistent with the direction of the first shift in opinion adopted by any member of a group.

Group versus individual decisions

risky shift effect
Group decisions are often riskier than the initial opinions held by individuals because group processes polarise their opinions.

" *A pensioner with a chronic and moderately debilitating ailment could possibly be cured by an operation, but the operation could also prove fatal.*" *What would you choose?*
(Photo: Mark Bramley)

- An electrical engineer must weigh the advantages of giving up a modest but secure job for a much more attractive position with no long-term security.
- A pensioner with a chronic and moderately debilitating ailment could possibly be cured by an operation, but the operation could also prove fatal.
- A small investor could invest in stock that might realise a huge profit or fail completely, or could choose stock with a safe but modest return. (Kogan & Wallach, 1964)

After considering each situation, subjects are required to indicate their preferred choice from available alternatives. Subjects decide individually and are unaware that they will be asked to discuss their decision in a group. Subjects are then asked to discuss each dilemma. Generally these studies report a strong tendency for the group decision to involve greater risk than the average of the decision reached by individuals.

Group polarisation

Findings from many research studies conducted since the 1960s suggest that group discussion polarises individuals' judgment, that is, discussion results in more extreme decisions, not necessarily riskier decisions. This effect is know as **group polarisation effect** (Myers & Lamm, 1976). Research has indicated strong support for this polarising effect and findings suggest that, when initial opinions of group members tend to be risky, discussion leads toward even greater risks. Similarly, when group members' opinions are less conservative, subsequent group discussion results in individuals shifting towards more extreme conservatism (see Figure 12.6)

Several studies have examined self-categorisation and group polarisation. Group polarisation tends to occur more when people are categorised as a group and when group membership is salient (Turner et al., 1989). According to self-categorisation theory "polarisation is simply convergence within a special kind of intergroup context". Polarisation is thus moving toward the mean of the group in order to minimise differences within the group and maximise contrasts between groups, maximising comparative fit (Turner, 1991).

Identification with an ingroup increases polarisation of beliefs and behaviour but in what direction? Hogg, Turner and Davidson (1990) predicted on the basis of self-categorisation theory and goodness of fit considerations that an ingroup confronted with a risky or threatening outgroup will polarise towards caution. An ingroup confronted by a cautious outgroup will polarise towards risk, and when confronted by both risky and cautious outgroups will converge on its present mean. They tested their hypotheses on 62 undergraduates who as individuals and as a group had to give recommendations on three dilemmas scenarios (see risky shift). Subjects gave pre- and post-test and group consensus recommendations on three scenarios involving increasing risk. Their results reflected their hypotheses and the predictions of self-categorisation theory. Comparing pre- and post-test positions the students tended to polarise toward what they thought was the ingroup consensus or norm. There was also some evidence of their behaviour also converging on the mean and the subjects' estimation of degree of group consensus was partly a function of the degree to which they identified with the group (Hogg, Turner & Davidson, 1990). See Box 12.4 for an example.

group polarisation effect
Finding that group discussion polarises individual's judgment; that discussion results in more extreme decisions not necessarily riskier decisions.

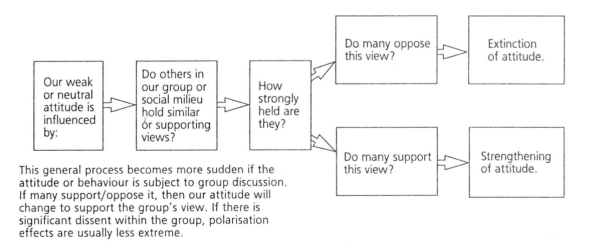

This general process becomes more sudden if the attitude or behaviour is subject to group discussion. If many support/oppose it, then our attitude will change to support the group's view. If there is significant dissent within the group, polarisation effects are usually less extreme.

Figure 12.6 *Group polarisation effects*

Box 12.4 *Profile: Sik Hung Ng and belief polarisation in Christians and atheists*

After completing his psychology and sociology degrees in Hong Kong, Sik Hung Ng carried out doctoral research in social psychology with Henri Tajfel at Bristol. He picked social psychology because it seemed most promising for understanding the relationships between mind, self and society. A recurrent theme of his research is power: How the power concept has been formulated for answering a range of philosophical, sociological and psychological questions; mechanisms of changing the power distance between individuals; majority/minority relations; the power dimension of intergroup bias; and more recently language and discourse processes that enact, recreate or subvert social influence and control. He is the author of The Social Psychology of Power *and* Power in Language *(with James Bradac).*
(Photo: courtesy Sik Hung Ng)

As we have seen our social identity is group-based and our self-concept incorporates group values. Our desire to identify with an ingroup leads to belief polarisation as we have seen. Beliefs, however, do not stand in isolation and are defined in reference to both ingroups and outgroups. That is, our desire to identify with those like us also involves drawing a line between those who think as we do and those who do not. To what extent do outgroups lead to belief polarisation?

This question intrigued Professor Sik Hung Ng of the University of Otago. He started with the assumption that social identity leads to perceptual extremitisation of the ingroup norm and to belief polarisation.

When group membership is made salient (e.g. through intergroup comparison) social identity is heightened and group members infer the ingroup norm from the most representative or prototypical ingroup position, resulting in perceptual extremitization of the ingroup norm. Next they attribute this extremitized ingroup norm to themselves and in so doing adopt a more extreme or

polarized position. In the case where the group norm relates to group beliefs, the end product is belief polarization. (Ng & Wilson, 1989, p. 48)

Reviewing the literature Ng found that the role of outgroup comparison in belief polarisation was unclear. To this end Ng and Shelley Wilson (1989) examined in- and outgroup belief polarisation of students to judge the relative effects of such comparisons in our self-categorisation. To contrast two groups with strong beliefs, Ng and Wilson gave 51 believers drawn from the Christian Union and Catholic Society and 52 nonbelievers drawn from the Atheist Society and Youth for Antichrist, a questionnaire of 16 belief items (see Table 12.1). Their procedure had two parts. First they mentioned two groups "Christians" and "Atheists" and then asked their subjects to estimate the "typical beliefs of either the ingroup (ingroup comparison condition), or the outgroup (outgroup comparison condition), or simply to give their own beliefs (self condition)". Subjects in the self condition were asked to give their own responses without reference to either group and "provided a baseline for ingroup norm extremitization" (Ng & Wilson, 1989).

Next they were asked to rate their own responses on the same form. This was used to test polarisation due to intergroup comparison, by contrasting the self condition with the ingroup and outgroup conditions. Ng and Wilson predicted that ingroup comparison would lead to belief polarisation and it did; the outgroup comparison was non-significant. Christians had higher extremity scores than atheists "indicating their more extreme beliefs and disbeliefs" (Ng, 1989). However, there was an interesting result when examining the direction of Christian belief. "As predicted, the polarization was mediated by the extremitization of the ingroup norms among atheists" (Ng & Wilson, 1989) but among believers it went the other way. Their ingroup estimation was less extreme than their self mean, suggesting their subsequent belief polarisation "must be due to processes other than ingroup extremitization" (Ng, 1989).

What does this all mean? Ng (1989) suggests that atheists have a rough time of it because their beliefs are ultimately only a negation of Christianity. Moreover, atheistic belief is "less clearly articulated" than Christianity, so they suffered in comparison to believers. Precisely because an atheistic social identity is so much harder to achieve, they extremitised their ingroup's beliefs "to achieve group distinctiveness, and through this to enhance their self-concepts" (Ng, 1989). In comparison, Christians are secure in a well-defined social identity and do not have to use ingroup extremitisation for self-categorisation. For this reason Ng argues they are more caught up with developing the other side of their self-concept—personal identity—leading to an individualistic desire to be better than their ingroup in pleasing God, and in this way enhanced their personal identity. Thus, Ng argues, both groups show ingroup polarisation, but for completely different reasons.

Table 12.1 *Christian and atheist belief items*

1. Life ends at death (a: 12/17)
2. A person is only answerable to society and oneself for his or her actions (a: 15/16)
3. Through faith in Christ God offers salvation (c: 15/18)
4. The Bible reveals the truth about God (c: 15/18)
5. The world develops without God (a: 9/16)
6. Sin is a state of separation from God (c: 15/19)
7. The world will end according to God's plan (c: 13/18)
8. The spirits of persons who have died can sometimes communicate with the living (c: 7/10)
9. It is important to lead a good and ethical life respecting one's fellow beings, but religious belief is not necessary for this (a: 18/5)
10. God does not exist (a: 12/17)
11. A person can communicate with God through prayer (c: 17/18)
12. Jesus Christ is the son of God and through him a person can know God (c: 17/17)
13. Science can answer all our questions (a: 6/16)
14. Mankind has evolved from lower forms of life (a: 19/11)
15. The only reality is the reality which can be experienced in this world (a: 10/16)
16. Through belief in the Trinity, resurrection and eternal life are possible (c: 14/18)

Key. (a: 15/16) = an atheist item believed by 15 atheists and disbelieved by 16 believers; (c: 15/18) = Christian item believed by 15 believers and disbelieved by 18 atheists.

Source: Ng & Wilson, 1989.

Why group polarisation?

How do we explain this phenomenon? Why does it occur and what factors influence us to intensify our initial views and opinion, and shift to exceed the group average? Several different interpretations have been proposed (Myers & Lamm, 1976). Among these are social comparison processes, persuasive argument, social identification and diffusion of responsibility.

Social comparison

This approach (Sanders & Baron, 1977) assumes we attempt to present ourselves to others in the most desirable way. As a result of group deliberation we may observe that other group members have similar views and that some even have more extreme views than we do. Our desire to be seen in a favourable way by others influences us to shift toward even more extreme positions, that is, we are trying to perform better than the average.

Persuasive arguments

This interpretation (Burnstein & Vinokur, 1977; Lamm, 1988) focuses on the cognitive aspects of novel and persuasive arguments and maintains that it is actually group discussion that results in polarisation. In theory, discussions expose individuals to arguments for and against a particular position. This process enables them to access new information and, depending on the number and persuasiveness of arguments supporting a particular view, the more likely they are to opt for that decision. As well as encouraging members to think about various perspectives and commit themselves to a position, information gained from discussion may convince us of the accuracy of our initial viewpoint and this results in more extreme opinions. That is, if novel and persuasive arguments affect individual members, a group shift will occur.

Social identification

The process of social identification describes how we compare and define ourselves with respect to others and behave according to norms associated with a particular group. This model of polarisation is based on individuals conforming to a perceived group norm. According to this approach we tend to focus on identifying with the group norms. This leads us to a more stereotypical view of the group and we tend to see it as more extreme than it actually is. As we have already seen, comparative fit and **referent informational influence** increase group polarisation through "conformity through self-categorisation to a local ingroup norm that is polarised as a result of the ingroup being located towards an extreme of the salient comparative context or social frame of reference" (Turner, 1991). In other words, we feel pressure to adhere to this stereotypical notion and shift our opinion to conform with the perceived norm. Our decisions in groups become more extreme because of our expectations.

referent informational influence
The power that an ingroup has to promote conformity, because it acts as a social frame of reference, or a guide to what is expected behaviour.

Diffusion of responsibility

In many group situations people may reach risky decisions because of diffusion of responsibility (recall our discussion of altruism in Chapter Ten). In groups, individuals may feel less personally responsible for their decisions. Some authors (Kogan & Wallach, 1967) have suggested that risk-taking is positively valued in our Western society and consequently this factor may contribute to riskier decisions.

Research has offered support for each of the approaches outlined above. However, at present we are unable to ascertain with any certainty which model is best, and the effectiveness of each approach will, to a large extent, be dependent on the particular situation and/or characteristics of those individuals involved in the group decision-making process. Suffice to say that they all may play a role (sometimes simultaneously) in inducing group polarisation.

Groupthink

Groups, like individuals, have limitations. Examples are continually being cited where groups of apparently intelligent, mature individuals have made faulty decisions, resulting in disasters. This may be explained by certain social processes that develop in cohesive groups. Irving Janis (1982) describes this faulty decision-making process as **groupthink**. Groupthink is "a deterioration of mental efficiency, reality testing and moral judgment that results from ingroup pressure". He defines groupthink as "a mode of thinking that people engage in when they are deeply involved in a cohesive ingroup, when the members' striving for unanimity overrides their motivation to realistically appraise alternative courses of action" (Janis, 1982). Janis based his hypothesis on analyses of a series of important group decisions

groupthink
A deterioration of mental efficiency, reality testing and moral judgment that results from ingroup pressure.

An example of an ill-fated group decision (Photo: Ben Motu/New Zealand Herald)

Box 12.5 *Some examples of ill-fated group decisions*

The British Expeditionary Force to Europe, 1939. The Chamberlain cabinet and War Office completely ignored the advice of strategic analysts that the German army had learned the value of rapid deployment and would not use tactics similar to WW I. This led to the annihilation of the French and British armies and to Dunkirk.

Pearl Harbour, 1941. The decision by US military personnel to ignore warnings of an imminent Japanese attack and their complacency resulted in the destruction of the US Pacific Fleet.

Bay of Pigs, 1961. The decision by US President Kennedy and his advisors to secretly land a small group of Cuban exiles at the Bay of Pigs, Cuba, with the aim of overthrowing the Castro regime resulted in failure. All the invaders were captured or killed by Fidel Castro's forces.

The Vietnam War, 1964–67. Policy decisions taken by US President Johnson and his advisors in the mid 1960s to escalate the war in Vietnam resulted in tragic consequences for both Vietnam and the US.

Watergate cover-up, early 1970s. The decision by US President Nixon and his advisors to attempt a cover-up of illegal actions connected with the Watergate burglary at the Headquarters of the US Democratic Party in 1972.

Iran-Contra Affair, early 1980s. The decision by the Reagan administration to exchange arms for hostages led to the Iran-Contra scandal. The idea that culpability for illegal actions could be avoided by channelling arms through the Israelis, proved to be a false rationalisation.

The decision to sink the Rainbow Warrior. This debacle in Auckland Harbour occurred because the French security forces had an illusion of invulnerability and were dismissive of New Zealand's power to retaliate. The ensuing scandals led to the resignation of two cabinet ministers and almost brought down the French government.

Launch of the Space Shuttle Challenger, 1986. The decision by NASA officials to launch the space shuttle despite warnings of serious design faults and poor weather conditions. This decision ended in tragedy with the loss of seven lives.

The Tricontinental Loans Affair. Financial mismanagement at Tricontinental through the late 1980s eventually brought the State of Victoria to the edge of bankruptcy, to an international downgrading of its credit rating, a rescue by the Federal Government; and to the biggest landslide majority in an opposition election win ever. The commission of inquiry found that corporate decision-making practices and delusions of an ever-expanding market contributed to record Australian losses.

---

made by government policy makers and military officials. See Box 12.5 for some of these famous historical blunders.

Janis' analyses of several similar big policy decisions found a common thread. His case studies revealed an inability of decision-making groups to consider alternatives systematically. Their maintenance of a narrow focus, and their inability to foresee how their chosen courses of action would threaten and subvert the principles and objectives of the group, polarised their decisions.

Symptoms of groupthink

Janis (1982) identified eight symptoms which, if present, signal that groupthink may be operating.

1. *Illusion of invulnerability:* It is important in decision-making groups that there is a feeling of power and authority. However if a group believes that any decision they make will be successful, they have become influenced by an illusion of invulnerability. This creates excessive optimism and may encourage extreme risk-taking.

2. *Belief in the inherent morality of the group:* We all like to believe that we are acting in the best interests of our group and that our choices are the correct ones. The extreme example of this symptom is "God is on our side". Such notions help us abdicate responsibility for accounting for our decisions rationally and are a self-protective mechanism.

3. *Rationalisation:* Of course it is quite normal for individuals to play down limitations and pitfalls of a chosen course of action. A problem arises in groups where members, raising legitimate objections, are discounted because of a perceived negative reaction to any member disagreeing with the group.

4. *Stereotypes of outgroups:* Often groups tend to characterise outgroups in stereotypical ways and make decisions based upon false stereotypes. The result of such "us" and "them" thinking is that groups can become less receptive to constructive criticisms from sources outside the group.

5. *Self-censorship:* The most common form of censorship is that which we impose on ourselves. In this process our reasons may be linked to group loyalty, organisational policy, or *esprit de corps*.

6. *Direct pressure:* Group pressure on individuals to conform can take many forms. In many groups, members are conditioned to remain silent if they have opposing views. What becomes apparent is that expressed dissent against the group's argument is contrary to the interests of the group, or even perceived as being disloyal.

7. *Mindguards:* Mindguards are typically self-appointed and are not a part of the group itself. They deliberately keep facts, opinion, data and other information, which may have direct relevance to the group's decision-making process, away from the group. Often these individuals

When several people in a cohesive group make a decision, the more likely it is that they will be exposed to groupthink.
(Photo: Chris Simkin)

justify their actions by arguing a time factor, that the material is not relevant for the group, or that a decision has already been reached.

8. *Illusion of unanimity:* Finally the group makes a decision. Pitfalls are understated and the inevitability of the chosen course of action is reinforced. Often members who initially have misgivings about the decision come to believe these were perhaps unwarranted.

Janis also argues that a number of other factors that together with cohesiveness may promote groupthink. These include a highly insulated group with limited access to external feedback; a stressful decision-making context (such as a crisis); external threats or pressure; and a recent history of setbacks.

Preventing groupthink

Most of us who are part of decision-making groups are potentially exposed to groupthink. Can you recall instances where decisions have resulted in less than successful outcomes and interpret these in the light of groupthink? While the potential pitfalls of the decision-making process may result in serious implications, a number of positive techniques are effective in reducing groupthink and enhancing group decision-making. These proposals are designed to help ensure that the group considers all relevant information, examines all available alternatives, and avoids a false illusion of consensus.

Strategies for avoiding groupthink

There are a number of techniques that can be used to minimise groupthink. Janis (1982) suggests that leaders should encourage an open-leadership style. This fosters free discussion, non-judgmental attitudes and acceptance of divergent thinking. Avoiding the isolation of the group is also helpful. Decision-makers should be encouraged to frame the problem requiring a decision in a number of ways to examine how stable preferred opinions are. It may be valuable to invite outsiders to participate and provide critical comments and challenge the group's view. This helps to prevent the group being totally isolated. Assigning members the role of critical evaluator stops mind sets and at each meeting at least one person should be allocated the role of devil's advocate in order to question the group's ideas. Leaders should also avoid being too directive. An important strategy is for the leader to be deliberately absent from one or more meetings and allow other members to facilitate group discussion. This is to ensure and guard against the leader exerting undue influence on the group. Also the leader should initially remain impartial in group decision-making, stating their opinions only after group members have expressed their views.

> With these considerations in mind, I suggest that awareness of the shared illusions, rationalisation and other symptoms fostered by the interaction of members of small groups may curtail the influence of groupthink in policy making groups. Here is another place where we can apply George Santayana's well known adage: "Those who cannot remember the past are condemned to repeat it." (Janis, 1982, p. 276)

Leadership: In search of a person for all seasons

Most of us have been fascinated by the lives of people who have had tremendous historical influence over events. Think of someone whom you admire as a leader. What is it about this person that makes them a leader? Are they more intelligent, ambitious, committed, personable, charismatic, or just luckier than others? Or are they just in the right place at the right time? A group's success often depends on its leader and how effective that leader is in planning, organising and directing its activities. Indeed it appears that some form of leadership exists in all groups (Hollander, 1985).

It is obvious that leadership is a complex process and may involve some or all of the features described in the definitions in Box 12.6. However, for social psychologists the key attribute of leadership is social influence. It is the leader and their view of social reality that provides the how, what, when and why of group activities. Most definitions assume that leader-ship is an ability or characteristic that enables an individual to influence others, either by their expertise, information power, or communication, to achieve group objectives (Yukl, 1981). This process of social influence is in part determined by the characteristics of the leader, the group and its context.

Box 12.6 *Problems with defining leadership*

What is leadership? Think of a situation where you have a leadership role or where you had observed someone in that position. How would you define this process? Most of us would probably say we recognise leadership when we see it but find it difficult to define in any clear and concise way. Several definitions are summarised below along with the inherent difficulties of each definition.

- *Centre of attention:* A problem is that groups often focus attention on a deviate or weak member.
- *Moves group towards goals:* The goal is not always obvious and a strong leader may divert group from its original goal.

- *Acquires label as leader:* The actual leader may be someone else.
- *Most influential:* A person may influence a group by causing members to react negatively to all suggestions.
- *Clarifies, decides, suggests alternatives:* Usually these behaviours are carried out by several group members and not just one person.
- *Appointed by a higher authority:* May be given a title but may not win acceptance or legitimation of members.

Source: Tedeschi et al., 1985, p. 353.

Leadership structure

The unique pattern of leadership within groups is referred to as the leadership structure. Groups vary according to this dimension. While in some groups, for example, a small business, the leadership structure is relatively simple, in others, such as a large, diversified transnational corporation, it is much more complex. Leadership structure may be formal or informal. Consider large business corporations or government bureaucracies. Many have formal organisational charts depicting a hierarchical chain of command and guidelines to do with allocation of responsibilities and patterns of decision-making. Some smaller groups simply have designated or elected leaders with specific responsibilities. Of course the person chosen to be the formal head of a group may not be the actual leader, and as we have already seen, there are different types of leadership roles. In addition there are many groups with no formal leaders, such as collectives and friendship groups. It is important to note that even groups without nominated formal leaders still exhibit patterns of informal leadership. I'm sure you have observed this process in various groups to which you belong. For example, in a particular group discussion one person may be more dominant or persuasive than others and may have more influence on decision-making.

There are several ways we become leaders of a group. Some are designated or appointed, as in the military, police and other hierarchical organisations. In many other situations individuals are elected, for example in political parties, unions and various clubs and organisations. A third process is what is referred to as **emergent leadership,** where a group member gradually becomes a leader. We have all observed instances where a friend emerges as an informal leader in our group and, while they are not officially recognised as such, we will generally agree they play a leadership role. Outside observers are often able to identify an emergent leader by observing such things as who is the most talkative in discussions and whose opinions are influential in group decision-making (Mullen, Salas & Driskell, 1989).

emergent leadership
Group dynamic where, in a leaderless group, one member gradually becomes a leader.

Leadership activities

Generally there are two broad types of activity that leaders are involved in and these parallel our previous discussion of role orientation. The first is task-oriented leadership which concerns the achievement of group goals and objectives. In task-oriented activities the leader is involved in offering suggestions, providing information and knowledge, organising, structuring, controlling, directing and monitoring the group activities. Socially oriented leadership centres on the interpersonal and emotional aspects of group relationships. Here the leader focuses on the smooth functioning of the group, fosters positive relations, attempts to minimise conflict and tension, and promotes group cohesiveness. Research has found that both these activities, task and social leadership, are important to effective group functioning (Bales, 1970; Burke, 1971). Rush and Russell (1988) suggest that we are easily able to identify the behaviour patterns of effective and ineffective leaders along four main dimensions: initiating structure so followers should know exactly what is expected of them; care and concern for followers;

assuming roles or being active in exercising their role; and a production emphasis, or pressure to achieve outcomes and "get the job done".

Characteristics of leaders: Are leaders born or made?

The course of human history has been shaped by many great leaders: Lenin, Gandhi, Hitler, Mao-Tse-Tung, Churchill, Franklin Roosevelt, Stalin, Tito, Fidel Castro, Gorbachev and Ruhollah Khomeini, to name a few. What is it that makes prominent leaders so different from the rest of us ordinary folk? Are they extraordinary people, or thrust into prominence by historical necessity? Psychologists have been arguing about this for many years. Two main viewpoints have emerged. The first emphasises the unique personal characteristics possessed by such people, and the second perspective focuses on the situational forces operating at a particular time. A more recent view has tried to integrate these two approaches, maintaining that both personal characteristics and situational influences are important in determining who becomes a leader. These three approaches are discussed below.

The great person (trait) theory

One of the earliest approaches to leadership is the **great person theory**. According to this view some individuals possess key personality characteristics and other unique traits that distinguish them from us "mere mortals" and they are destined to lead. Also, it is assumed that these characteristics remain constant over time and that all great leaders share certain qualities and characteristics regardless of the era or place in which they live. However, research gives little support to these broad claims and has failed to agree on a list of characteristics shared by leaders (Yukl, 1981). While research suggests that generally leaders do not differ from followers in significant and consistent ways, a few findings indicate that personal characteristics can play a limited role in leadership under certain circumstances. The following factors appear to be associated with leadership:

great person theory
According to this view some individuals possess key personality characteristics and other unique traits that destine them to lead the masses.

- The ability to adapt to changing circumstances has been found to promote leadership (Kenney & Zaccaro, 1983).
- Leaders tend to excel in more activities relevant to achievement of group goals. In many situations intelligence correlates with leadership (Fiedler, 1986) while in others, leadership may be associated with other skills or expertise relevant to group activities.
- Power motivation (need for prominence and recognition) appears to be an important characteristic (Foder & Smith, 1982). Leaders tend to be more ambitious, have high needs for achievement and affiliation, and be more willing to assume responsibility (Sorrentino & Field, 1986). Research by McClelland (1985) has suggested that effective leaders display a socialised power orientation and are more interested in enhancing the organisation rather than their own position. Also research suggests that individuals with certain patterns of motives (a high need for power coupled with high degree of self control) are more successful business leaders (McClelland & Boyatzis, 1982).

Churchill, Roosevelt and Stalin divide the world at the Yalta conference in February 1945, near the end of the European phase of World War II. (Photo: Sipa/Austral International)

- Leaders tend to have interpersonal qualities that foster successful interaction. They are articulate, well-organised and interpersonally sensitive. The ability to perceive and respond to the needs of the group is also viewed as an important characteristic (Ellis, 1988).
- Constantini and Craik (1980) found that Californian politicians scored higher than average in self-confidence, need for achievement and dominance, but below average on nurturance, deference and self-abasement.

Situational characteristics

This approach emphasises situational factors in determining who emerges as a leader and is based on the notion that different situations require different kinds of leaders. Many researchers have noted that strong leaders are more likely to emerge and have more influence when a group is facing some crisis, external threat or pressure. Consider leaders such as Lenin, Winston Churchill and Adolf Hitler. Russia in 1917 was experiencing World War I, massive poverty, Czarist oppression and ignorance. These situational factors contributed to the popularising of Bolshevism and the rise of Lenin. During World War II, Churchill emerged as one of England's greatest leaders during their "darkest hour". During the 1920s and 1930s the German people were suffering from the Depression, economic disaster, a recent military defeat and the humiliating treaty of Versailles. These factors no doubt contributed to the rise and popularity of the Nazi Führer, Adolf Hitler.

Our commonsense should tell us that this approach is more applicable than the trait theory. It does not maintain that a good leader in one situation or set of circumstances will be effective in all situations. For example, Winston Churchill was a great war leader but a mediocre postwar prime minister. However, the situational approach has its own limitations. It bypasses factors such as the reaction of followers and varying styles of leadership which may be related to personal qualities. Leaders direct, guide and motivate their followers, but followers form the other half of the equation. They also influence leaders and an effective leader takes into account the expectations and needs of group members. As such we should regard leadership as an interaction of both personal qualities and situational factors, that picks the right person for the job.

Transactional approaches

The two approaches to leadership discussed above give little consideration to the role played by followers in determining who becomes a leader. Transactional approaches attempt to remedy this and propose that the interaction between the leader and followers is bi-directional (works both ways). Hollander (1985) suggests that leadership involves a transaction between group members and the leader. In part, the beliefs, expectations, perceptions and attributes of followers determine who emerges as a leader. On the other hand, leaders monitor and are influenced by their followers' views, and may shift or modify their behaviour in response to group feedback. This transaction is a process of social exchange, and group members' willingness to accept and comply with a leader's influence depends on the social exchange processes we discussed in Chapter Eight.

Can you think of a leader whom you would define as charismatic? The term charisma was first used in a theoretical context by Weber in 1947 (*charisma* is Greek for "divine gift"). Weber believed charisma was an exceptional quality (extraordinary powers) enabling a person to draw a large number of followers. This type of leadership is distinguished by an intense personal relationship and commitment between the leader and followers. The charismatic leader is able to inspire and gain unquestioning obedience, loyalty, commitment and devotion from followers (Howell & Frost, 1989).

Charismatic leadership

We can all think of leaders who exhibit these kind of larger-than-life qualities. Perhaps leaders such as Mohandas Gandhi, Martin Luther King, Adolf Hitler, Eva Peron, Salvador Allende could be viewed as charismatic. Conger and Kanungo (1988) suggest that charisma may be a real phenomenon that can be explained in social psychological terms. Charismatic leadership appears to be characterised by specific patterns of behaviour. These are summarised in Box 12.7

Many researchers have attempted to classify styles of leadership to determine which are more effective for successful group functioning. Early pioneering research assumed that the democratic style was more effective and several classic studies of leadership style found it was more effective than autocratic

Leadership styles

Box 12.7 *The nature of charismatic leadership*

The nature of charismatic leadership is hard to define. For this reason we list below some of the major distinguishing characteristics with illustrative examples drawn from the lives of great leaders. Quotations are drawn from *Profiles of Power* (Murray-Brown, 1979), and the *Oxford Dictionary of Quotations.*

Charismatic leaders are able to put forward compelling arguments condemning certain conditions within an organisation or society and suggest that the situation is intolerable and demand decisive remedies. Franklin Delano Roosevelt rescued America and probably the world from the grips of the Great Depression with his New Deal. Although critics charged that aspects of his programme were confiscatory and anti-American, and that his plan would give him the powers of a dictator, Roosevelt in his Inaugural Address from the steps of the Capitol in Washington did not pull any punches in his famous "Action and Action Now" speech on 4 March 1933:

> I am prepared under my constitutional duty to recommend measures that a stricken nation in the midst of a stricken world may require . . . but in the event that the national emergency is still critical, I shall not evade the clear course of duty that will then confront me. I shall ask Congress for the one remaining instrument to meet the crisis—broad executive power, to wage a war against the emergency as great as the power that would be given to me if we were in fact invaded by a foreign foe.

Charismatic leaders emotionally espouse a vision of another far better state of affairs. David Ben-Gurion, first Prime Minister of Israel and a powerful charismatic figure, recalled:

> I always sought to tell my people that in our lives, and in the society we wish to build in our regained homeland, we must make everything noble, useful, true and beautiful that we can find, both in the

treasury of the past and in human accomplishments in our own day . . . We are rebuilding the ruins of our ancient land. We are building a state which will serve, as I believe, as a model to the peoples of the Middle East by its social and spiritual values, its democratic regime and its reverence for the dignity of man.

They display a strong conviction of the moral righteousness of their beliefs and opinions. As Gandhi said at the conclusion of his trial for exciting sedition in 1922:

> I wanted to avoid violence, but I had to make my choice. I either had to submit to a system which I considered had done irreparable harm to my country or incur the risk of the mad fury of my people bursting forth when they understood the truth from my lips. I know that my people have sometimes gone mad. I am deeply sorry for it, and I am, therefore, here to submit not to a light penalty but to the highest penalty. I do not ask for mercy or plead any extenuating act.
>
> I am here, therefore, to invite and cheerfully submit to the highest penalty that can be inflicted upon me for what in law is a deliberate crime, and what appears to me the highest duty of a citizen.

By the time he died Gandhi had spent 2338 days in British gaols.

House (1977) suggests that in some situations these leaders may not actually believe in the espoused ideology but are good manipulators and are acting a part in order to influence and gain compliance from their followers. Recall the cult leader, Jim Jones, of the People's Temple, who led his followers to mass suicide in 1978. Also Jimmy Baker, presently serving a gaol sentence for misappropriation of church funds in 1987.

These leaders have extremely high levels of self-confidence and dominance (strong desire to influence others) and great levels of personal courage (House, 1977). Charles de Gaulle in 1940 was a rebellious General who refused to acknowledge France's legitimate surrender to the Germans. Technically a traitor to France, he set up a government in exile in Britain and proclaimed himself leader of the "Free French". His speeches to his homeland left little doubt of his towering self-confidence:

> Whatever happens, the flame of French resistance must not and shall not die . . . I am responsible for the interests and destiny of France . . . and will take France upon myself.

After the war, de Gaulle wrote that: "The deep root of action by the best and strongest of men is the desire to acquire power . . . The statesman must concentrate all his efforts at captivating men's minds . . . He must outbid his rivals in self-confidence." That he embodied his own philosophy was evident during his triumphal march through Paris on 26 August 1944. As the victory procession with de Gaulle out in front approached Notre Dame, the marchers were fired upon. While others scurried for cover, de Gaulle did not flinch nor take any notice and marched on alone into history.

They are willing to take risks and adopt radical and unconventional means to achieve their objectives: Gandhi often deliberately provoked the British by non-violent but incredibly confrontational tactics like the great Salt March of March 1930. He also was a master tactician, whose brilliant strategies made their point at the expense of his opponents. For example, in 1913 during the South African racial passes dispute, Gandhi found himself with 5000 eager followers he could neither house nor feed. The authorities informed him they would not tolerate his entering the Transvaal from Natal Province and would arrest anyone who tried. Gandhi solved two problems at once by promptly sending the authorities advance notice (and detailed route map) of his proposed march to the border. Gandhi and his supporters were gaoled and the problem of feeding and housing his followers was solved! As thousands more Indians and "coloureds" joined in the spirit of the tactic and were arrested and gaoled, the South African authorities' race laws became an international farce and for a while the pass laws were abolished.

Essential characteristics of charismatic leaders are personal qualities such as strong personal style, originality, charm and language fluency (Sashkin, 1977). Consider the following hyperbole from Winston Churchill:

> Hitler knows that he will have to break us in this island or lose the war. If we can stand up to him, all Europe may be free, and the life of the world may move forward into broad sunlit uplands. But if we fail, then the whole world will sink into the abyss of a new dark age. Let us therefore brace ourselves to our duty, so bear ourselves that if the British Commonwealth and its Empire last for a thousand years men will still say "This was their finest hour".

These leaders usually have a powerful message and their objectives are often expressed in moral rhetoric and slogans (House, 1977). Consider the following examples:

Lenin: "Bread, Peace and Land."

Winston Churchill: "We shall never surrender."

J.F. Kennedy: "Ask not what your country can do for you but what you can do for your country."

Martin Luther King: "I have a dream."

Gandhi's message to the British: "Quit India."

Hitler: "A Thousand Year Reich."

"For mother Russia."—Stalin eliciting the commitment of the Russian people during the German invasion in World War II.

Box 12.8 *Profile: Ming Singer and attribution and leadership style*

Ming Singer, a senior lecturer in Psychology at Canterbury University, has long had an interest in leadership styles and how it impacts on staff selection, and organisational and social justice. Dr Singer holds a PhD in cognitive psychology from the University of New England. Since then she has worked at Victoria University and New Zealand Police College. She is author of Fairness In Selection: An Organizational Justice Perspective. *Her articles appear in journals including* Journal of Applied Psychology, British Journal of Psychology, International Journal of Psychology, Current Psychology: Research and Reviews, Applied Psychology: An International Review, *and* Social Justice Research. *Her current research interests include selection decision making, and issues related to organisational and social justice.*
(Photo: courtesy Ming Singer)

Singer and Singer (1986) examined the relationships between subordinates' personality traits and their preference for transformative (charismatic, intellectual, stimulating and treating each person as an individual) versus transactional leadership styles. Eighty-seven male undergraduates were asked to imagine an ideal manager in a work situation and then complete a multifactorial leadership questionnaire to describe their ideal leader's behaviour. They then completed sub-scales of the Edwards Personal Preference Schedule (an inventory of personal needs) and a conformity scale, to measure personality variables. Their results indicated a significant relationship between affiliation needs and preference for charisma, being treated as an individual and an overall transformational leadership style. Findings also suggested that non-conformers prefer leaders who are intellectually stimulating. Overall, subjects' preference was for leaders who were more transformative than transactional.

But was there any reality underlying these preferences? Singer and Beardsley (1990) followed up with a study investigating the attributions made about effective leadership and patterns of actual leader behaviour. Ninety

supervisors and 135 of their subordinates completed measures of these two variables. Both supervisors and subordinates emphasised the importance of dispositional over situational attributes for effective leadership. Subordinates consistently rated leadership attributes more highly than their supervisors did. Supervisors saw themselves as more charismatic, intellectually stimulating and concerned for individuals, and more likely to reward on the basis of effort, than their subordinates thought they were.

These findings may be starting to sound a little familiar to you and have much to do with the attributional styles we discussed in Chapter Three. Singer's (1990) research on implicit leadership theory suggests that where we are in hierarchies may determine our views of leadership style. In a comparison of undergraduates and middle managers' ratings of dispositional variables (personality, intellect and competence) and situational variables (support of subordinates, organisational characteristics and factors beyond the manager's control), undergraduates stressed more external locus of control factors than managers did for leadership effectiveness. This suggests that how you view leadership style reflects your position in society.

or laissez-faire forms in promoting group morale and quality of group outcomes (Lewin, Lippitt & White, 1939; Kahn & Katz, 1953). Could it be, however, that the impact of a particular style depends on circumstance? For example, in a combat situation it is doubtful whether a democratic style of leadership would be effective.

Gender and leadership style

What does social psychology tell us about gender and leadership? Are there differences between male and female leaders? Alice Eagly and her associates have recently conducted a number of literature reviews on this issue. Eagly and Johnson (1990), in a review of research studies comparing male and female leaders, found mixed evidence for gender differences. Contrary to the gender stereotype that woman leaders would have more interpersonal skills, while men would be more task-oriented, no such differences emerged. However, experimental studies gave more gender stereotypical results than studies of organisations. In all cases, women emerged as more democratic leaders with a less autocratic and more participatory style than men. This gender difference *is* consistent with stereotypic gender differences, and the authors interpret their findings in terms of social sex-role theory, which we discussed in Chapter Eleven.

In a review of the emergence of leaders in leaderless groups, Eagly and Karav (1991) found that in laboratory studies men took the initiative more than women. Male leadership was more likely in short-term groups and groups concerned with tasks that did not require complex social interaction, whereas women emerged as social leaders slightly more than men. All this is what you would expect given the sex-roles in our society, and the authors interpret their findings again in the light of socialised sex-roles.

How are men and women evaluated as leaders? Eagly, Makhijani and Klonsky (1992) reviewed the literature to see if we are more biased against women leaders. While their findings suggested that, overall, women were only slightly less favourably evaluated as leaders and managers, this bias was more marked under certain conditions. For example, women leaders were devalued relative to their male counterparts when the women were perceived to be adopting a masculine leadership style (being autocratic and directive). Women were also less well thought of when they were leaders in traditional male occupations, particularly when evaluated by men!

Leadership style may also be analysed in terms of the six bases of social power described by French and Raven (1959). Recall our previous discussion of the different kinds of power in Chapter Six. There is coercive power, expert power, reward power, referent power, legitimate power and informative power. Of course these are not mutually exclusive, and a leader may rely on several types of power simultaneously. Are there different consequences for group members depending on the different types of social power? Outlined below are several examples. Can you think of others?

- Coercive power requires surveillance. Leaders relying on coercive power tend to induce compliance in followers so long as they are present.

- Referent power may promote a closer relationship between leaders and members of a group but in certain instances this may have an impact on leadership skills and effectiveness.
- If a leader can present information in a thorough and persuasive way, this may have an effective influence on group members. However, when immediate action is required this may be impractical (time constraints).
- The use of expert power by a leader may enable effective influence but may also lead to increasing social distance from followers.

Fiedler's contingency model

contingency model of leadership effectiveness
Whether a leader is task- or relations-oriented, their effectiveness is contingent upon leader–follower relations, task structure and power position of the leader.

There appears to be general agreement among social psychologists that the performance of a group is affected by the interplay between leadership style and the particular circumstances of the group, and leadership is contingent on the unique characteristics of the group itself.

One perspective on this issue is Fiedler's **contingency model of leadership effectiveness** (1978, 1981). Using a simple rating scale, Fiedler categorised leaders as task-oriented (directive) or relationship-oriented (group-centred). Respondents were asked to rate their least preferred co-worker on this scale (LPC). Fiedler assumed that task-oriented leaders would rate their least preferred co-worker in a more negative way because their main focus was on production outcomes (getting the job done). Again he assumed that relationship-oriented people would rate their least preferred co-worker in a more positive light than those displaying task-orientation. A high score on the LPC (more favourable evaluation) indicated a relationship orientation and a low LPC score (very unfavourable evaluation) indicated a task-oriented leader. In Fiedler's schema, whether a leader is task- or relationship-oriented, their effectiveness is contingent upon three situational factors:

1. *Leader–follower relations:* this concerns the extent to which the group is loyal and supportive of the leader.
2. *Task structure:* this is linked to the extent to which the task is well defined and structured.
3. *Power position of the leader:* this is associated with the extent to which the leader's position enables them to exert influence and control over available resources.

Each of these situational determinants can provide a favourable or unfavourable climate for a leader (see Figure 12.7). Fiedler's contingency theory delineates which kind of leader will be most effective in each of these possible situations. There is considerable support for Fiedler's contingency model. His findings demonstrate that task-oriented leaders are most effective in extremely difficult and extremely easy situations (high and low control situations). On the other hand, relationship-oriented leaders perform more effectively in moderate situations, or moderate control, where leader–group relations are good but the task is complex, or when the leader is disliked by members but task is clear cut (Fiedler, 1978, 1981). It is important to

	Leadership situation		
	Very favourable	Moderately favourable	Very unfavourable
Leader most likely to succeed	Low LPC	High LPC	Low LPC

Low LPC = Task-oriented leader
High LPC = Relationship-oriented leader
LPC = Least preferred co-worker

Figure 12.7 *Fiedler's contingency theory, effectiveness of leadership style*

Source: Heard, 1993. Personal communication.

note that the effect of either style of leadership will shift if there is a change in situational control. Perhaps the point to be made is that no particular style of leadership is effective in all situations. Ultimately the most successful leader may be the one who displays flexibility and openness to change, and is able to adjust their leadership style to a particular situation. A rare human being?

Summary

The presence of others influences our performance on various tasks. This influence may lead to social facilitation or social loafing and is dependent on the nature of the task (simple or complex).

Social impact theory attempts to describe the strength of this effect. The impact of the presence of others on individual performances is a function of three principles: strength of the observers (those influencing), their number, and immediacy.

We all belong to many social categories and our construction of the social order divides people into groups: categories to which we belong (ingroups) and categories to which we do not belong (outgroups). The social identity approach maintains that our social world is made up of social categories that are enmeshed in power and status relations to each other.

Self-categorisation theory highlights the idea that our social identity extends to our private selves and that social norms define and shape the way we construct our identities and vice versa.

Groups are collections of individuals who frequently interact and communicate with one another, share common goals, are sometimes interdependent and perceive themselves to be part of a group. Group structure is defined by such characteristics as roles, norms, status and communication networks. Group cohesiveness refers to the sum total of positive and negative forces which influence members to remain part of a particular group.

Decision-making is a vital part of group interaction. Groups do not necessarily make better decisions than individuals. In certain situations, social decision schemes may enable us to predict group decisions by applying simple rules such as the majority-win rule, truth-wins rule, and the first-shift rule.

Research suggests that group discussion polarises individuals' judgment, resulting in more extreme decisions, the group polarisation effect. Proposed explanations for this phenomenon include social comparison processes, persuasive argumentation, social identification and diffusion of responsibility.

Highly cohesive groups often engage in a process of faulty decision-making known as groupthink. This phenomenon occurs when the members' concern for unanimity overrides their motivation to appraise alternative courses of action realistically.

Leaders exert influence on group members. They typically provide a framework for the group, initiate action, coordinate and monitor activities, and motivate the group to achieve goals and objectives. The central issue of leadership is social influence.

Three main approaches have been proposed to account for the emergence of leaders. The great person theory emphasises the unique personal characteristics of the leader, while the second approach emphasises situational forces impacting on the group. The third approach, the interactional (contingency) perspective, analyses leadership as a function of both personal and situational factors.

Charismatic leadership is characterised by an intense relationship between leader and followers, and these types of leaders typically display specific patterns of behaviour.

Fiedler's contingency model of leadership maintains that the effectiveness of a particular leader depends both on their style of leadership and the situation. This model suggests that task-oriented leaders tend to be more effective than relationship-oriented leaders in very favourable or unfavourable situations, whereas relation-oriented leaders tend to more effective than task-oriented leaders in moderately favourable settings.

Recommended reading

Conger J.A. and Kanungo R.N. (ed.) (1988) CHARISMATIC LEADERSHIP, Jossey Bass, San Francisco. An edited compendium of articles which cover the broad range of charismatic behaviour. Excellent case studies.

Fiedler F.E. and Garcia J.E. (1987) NEW APPROACHES TO EFFECTIVE LEADERSHIP: COGNITIVE RESOURCES AND ORGANIZATIONAL EFFECTIVENESS, John Wiley, NY. The latest word from Fiedler.

Guerin B. (1991) SOCIAL FACILITATION, Cambridge University Press, Cambridge. A broader review of the whole area of social influence and social facilitation effects by Bernard Guerin of James Cook University. The book is good as a background to many of the theories we discuss in this and Chapter Six.

Hogg M.A. and Abrams D. (1988) SOCIAL IDENTIFICATION: A SOCIAL PSYCHOLOGY OF INTERGROUP RELATIONS AND GROUP PROCESSES, Routledge, London. An interesting overview from two Australian authors of much of the material we covered in the first part of the chapter. A medium-heavy read.

Janis I.L. (1982) GROUPTHINK: PSYCHOLOGICAL STUDIES OF POLICY DECISIONS AND FIASCOES, Houghton Mifflin, Boston. The definitive word on decision-makers' illusions of vulnerability. A very readable book.

Paulus P.B. (1989) PSYCHOLOGY OF GROUP INFLUENCE (2nd edn) Erlbaum, Hillsdale, NJ. An overview of group psychology from a fairly traditional perspective. Offers good insights on social facilitation, polarisation and group influence. Very readable.

Turner J.C. (1991) SOCIAL INFLUENCE, Open University Press, Milton Keynes. A fairly technical monograph by John Turner of ANU. However, the most informative source on social identity and self-categorisation theory and an interesting read for someone prepared to handle the relatively difficult concepts.

ENVIRONMENTAL PSYCHOLOGY

13

A little while ago I took my environmental psychology students on a field trip to the Tantawangelo and Coolangooba forests near Eden. As the name Eden implies, this is an area of spectacular beauty, with some of the most rugged, inaccessible and untouched coastal forests in New South Wales. Yet for the last sixteen years the southeast forests have been the centre of a bitter confrontation between environmentalists seeking World Heritage listing and loggers defending Diashowa's chip mill. We were interested in assessing the area's conservation values for ourselves and so an early Sunday morning found us following a local conservationist down the rugged course of Devil's Creek towards its junction with the spectacularly beautiful Tantawangelo river.

Needless to say it was pouring. The track was steep, slippery and washed out in sections and we found ourselves crawling on hands and knees in some places and sliding on our backsides in others. When we reached the confluence of the two rivers we were wet, muddy and had had a definite hands-on experience. While the rivers were undoubtedly beautiful and worthy of conservation, we were happy enough to crawl back up Devil's Creek for some lunch and dry clothes. As our bus loomed in the distance, conversation turned to the lyrebirds we had flushed out, the numerous wombat holes we had jumped over, the recent discovery of koalas by the Southeast Forests Alliance and the finer points of battling the Forestry Commission. The fauna, we decided, was a definite plus and a National Park should be declared forthwith!

Pristine environments such as the Tantawangelo are all too few.
(Photo: Chris Simkin)

This euphoria lasted as long as it took to discover the first representative of the genus Philaemon which had attached itself to a student ankle. Screams multiplied as the true extent of this invasion became apparent. Leeches had secreted themselves with diabolical cunning and, vastly distended, were still being found several hours later. Given their numbers, either university students are extremely tasty, or word of our visit had circulated for some weeks and the leeches had been congregating in anticipation.

Though I lectured in vain on the essential place of leeches in the ecological scheme of things, their uses and evident functional beauty, general opinion had swung round to regard the Tantawangelo as "the pits" and a good place to avoid. This emphasises the vital importance of attitudes in the environmental debate and the unfortunate fickleness of public opinion which sees beauty from a decidedly human perspective. No doubt leeches view each other with a certain satisfaction, though as hermaphrodites they would probably have a more pragmatic view of beauty than we do. In debriefing my students, this leech-eyed view of the world was of considerable benefit in reinforcing the need for a wholistic approach to environmental psychology.

Defining environmental psychology

Social psychology has spawned a number of offspring this century, some of which have become independent disciplines. Environmental psychology is quickly approaching its majority having grown strongly since the first stirrings of interest in the late 1950s. A vigorous research base and the steady emergence of texts, such as Gifford (1987), the third edition of Bell, Fisher, Baum and Greene (1990), Stokols and Altman's mammoth *Handbook of Environmental Psychology* (1987), and the journals *Environment and Behavior* and *Journal of Environmental Psychology*, all point to the health of a discipline which has been taught locally for less than a decade. Nevertheless, it is a vigorously growing area with a definite view of how psychology should be done and a clear agenda: to integrate an environmental awareness into the wider psychological debate and change public attitudes. Towards this end, environmental psychology adopts a three-pronged approach.

Emphasising the physical

Stokols and Altman (1987) define environmental psychology as "the study of human behavior and well-being in relation to the sociophysical environment"—a view that emphasises the reciprocal interaction of environment and behaviour. Environmental psychology is first and foremost a study of *physical* factors in this interaction, for while psychology has always acknowledged the environment's crucial importance in shaping human behaviour, this has more often than not been equated with other people's influence on us. You can readily see this view at work within any developmental text where *environmental influence* is almost synonymous

In cities we often live in environments which are completely man-made and in which the natural is not obvious.
(Photo: Chris Simkin)

with *social influence*. While not rejecting people as environmental factors, environmental psychologists stress the physical aspects shaping human behaviour and their work is partly a response to an overly human-centred view of the environment. Studies of the effects of noise, weather, climate, architectural and interior design, isolation, crowding, urban stressors, disasters, environmental degradation and pollution, all emphasise the importance of the physical environment on human behaviour.

Attitudinal awareness

Environmental psychology also studies our *environmental awareness*. Environmentalism has become trendy but public attitudes are notoriously fickle. Real-life ecology is not only about trees and whales but often a defence of less glamorous citizens, as our opener shows. An environmental consciousness is easily gained but hard to practise and often involves considering what we would rather forget (as a visit to a sewerage works demonstrated to this same group of students). Nor do new attitudes necessarily change behaviour. One of the most worrying aspects of environmental research is the big gap between what we think and what we do. Changing attitudes is relatively easy, but considering the sacrifices we will have to make, it is a lot harder to change our behaviour. While we have covered this question in Chapters Four and Five, it returns with a vengeance in the ecological debate and is a major preoccupation of environmental researchers.

Researchers have intensively studied the content and context of attitudes towards the environment, the gradual evolution towards an environmental consciousness, the rate at which it modifies behaviour, and the social traps and dilemmas which hinder an ecological worldview.

Applying an ecological focus

Perhaps environmental psychology's most potent contribution to the ecological debate is its concern to apply effectively pro-environmental insights. If there is any area that strongly reflects this new discipline's social psychology antecedents, it is its reliance on attitudinal and behavioural change research to achieve this end. However, this is by no means the least of its applied focus. One strength has been environmental psychology's willingness to move across traditional theoretical boundaries both within and without psychology to borrow insights. Another has been a willingness to work in interdisciplinary teams to effect change. Environmental psychologists using insights drawn from physiological and developmental psychology have helped other professionals understand stress and related problems of high density living, crowding in prisons, poor urban design and congested roads. The same psychologists have drawn from architecture, town planning, sociology and the health sciences to create better environments to alleviate these problems. Perhaps it is because environmental psychology is so concerned with the reciprocal nature of human–environment interactions, that it makes so few distinctions between theory and practice, and has such an applied focus (Bell et al., 1990) but whatever the cause this has been a very fruitful and creative amalgam.

Attitudinal and behavioural change: Saving the planet

There is little doubt that the planet is imperilled, and our future has become problematic. Resource depletion, unchecked population growth, declining fertility and environmental damage have become so obvious that we can all see the dangers of continuing our wasteful lifestyles. This is not a new concern. Thomas Malthus in his *Essay on Population* (1798) predicted explosive population growth and forewarned of despoliation and famines like those we have seen in Ethiopia and Bangladesh, while William Cobbett's *Rural Rides* (1821) alerted his generation to the damage the industrial revolution was doing to the countryside. However, our modern environmental consciousness began with Rachael Carson's *Silent Spring* (1962), a warning that indiscriminant use of pesticides was threatening global genocide. A masterly blend of science and speculation, Carson's best-selling book synthesised a burgeoning scientific literature which reflected

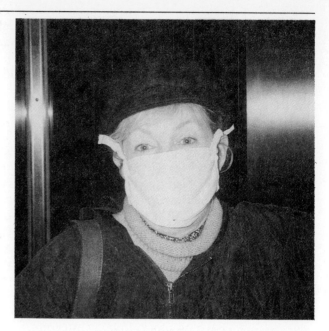

How long will it be before we reach Beijing's level of air pollution? Visitors such as Jeanna had to don surgical masks to avoid respiratory distress caused by excessive pollution during winter temperature inversions.

the growing alarm of biological scientists and presented it in a form that captured public attention and galvanised environmental action.

Environmental education: The weak path to changing behaviour?

Over the last few years we have all been bombarded by a wealth of environmental messages through the media. Few of us by now remain unaware of holes in the ozone layer, the dangers of pouring oil down the sink, sewage disposal, the precariousness of petrol supplies, and the need to conserve resources. The assumption underlying these campaigns is that educating the public will lead to environmental awareness and attitude change (Oskamp et al., 1991) but does this pro-ecological awareness translate into environmental activism? Technological research and simple commonsense provide many readily adoptable solutions to environmental problems, but the evidence is mixed that we are beginning to adopt them. As we have seen in Chapter Four, holding certain attitudes does not necessarily translate itself into action. Indeed research has shown that the congruence between environmental attitudes and behaviour is "far from perfect" (Oskamp et al., 1991). Many municipal kerbside recycling programmes have achieved less than 40 per cent compliance rates (NSW EPA, 1992) and research into adoption rates of domestic solar technology, like solar hot water systems, showed less than 4 per cent market penetrance. Many studies show a similar gap between awareness and action. So what role does education play?

Unfortunately it seems that environmental education is relatively ineffective and programmes aimed at encouraging pro-ecological behaviour show disappointing results. Public awareness of the urgent need to modify our behaviour, and even our knowing how to do so, is only modestly related to actual behavioural change. While early researchers found there was a lack of environmental awareness (Towler & Swan, 1972), this can hardly be the case today.

Maloney, Ward and Braucht (1975), in an early investigation of this issue, found that ecological awareness did not significantly correlate with either verbal or actual commitment, nor with the way people felt towards the environment. Studies since then have reported a mixed relationship between awareness and action (Dispoto, 1977; Vining & Ebreo, 1990). Even acknowledging our personal responsibility to act does not guarantee results. Bickman (1972), for example, found that while 94 per cent of his subjects endorsed the statement, "It should be everyone's responsibility to pick up litter when they see it", only 1.4 per cent of his subjects actually picked up litter afterwards (cited in Bell et al., 1990). Nor does espousing a commitment guarantee effective action, as McGuire (1984) found when he examined garbage discarded by higher-income households claiming high recycling rates. Similar results were obtained from a CSIRO study of energy conservation in Western Australia, which found that self-reported behavioural change and number of requests for additional conservation information were not reliable indicators of actual conservation behaviour (Kantola, Syme & Campbell, 1984). From many other studies it is clear that the link between environmental awareness and action is indeed a weak one. Why is behaviour so hard to change?

Complexity

One of the first insights into the difficulty of changing behaviour was the sheer complexity of contextual factors which determine environmental actions. Kline (1988), while examining attitude-discrepant behaviour in energy conservation practices, summed up the importance of contextual factors this way:

> We would not expect individuals to engage in conservation behavior when . . . personal action is not felt to contribute to the amelioration of a social problem, when the expected behavior is regarded as cumbersome, inconvenient and ineffective, or when others who are similarly expected to conserve are perceived as not doing so. (quoted in Oskamp et al., 1991, p. 497)

Self-interest

A sustainable future will be marked by global equity in resource allocation, control of over-consumption and much central regulation. As we are what our culture shapes us to be, it is a little much to expect members of an individualistic culture to embrace cooperative actions towards a sustainable future that will not be reached in our lifetimes. Many Westerners are still firmly wedded to individual ownership of resources, acquiring material wealth and the idea that economic growth will enhance our futures; which Dunlap and Van Liere (1984) found was antithetical to environmentalism. Economics has a powerful role too. As the beneficiaries of centuries of third-world exploitation, the West has a vested interest in preserving an economic system based on growth economics. Small wonder then that being told to reduce consumption, conserve resources and plan for someone else's future has a limited appeal, as we clearly saw during the Earth Summit in Brazil in 1992.

Defectors and social traps

Behavioural change becomes even more unlikely if we recall Chapter Eight's discussion of social dilemmas and the negative impact of defectors. If we see that what we are doing is not supported by others, or even worse is benefiting them at our expense, we are unlikely to continue as environmentalists. For example, if you are convinced of the need to conserve petrol and limit your trips and car-pool, you are unlikely to continue if you are aware that all you are doing is helping to hold down the price of petrol (scarcity = price), making it cheaper for others to waste what you have saved.

Why do we defect? We have already considered the crucial role of trust in Chapter Eight where we saw that low-trust individuals have their own individual justifications for defecting (Sato, 1988). Robyn Dawes (1980) suggested that temptation and fear were two main reasons for a lack of trust. Resources are limited and in a competitive society we want to ensure our share (Bruins, Liebrand & Wilke, 1989). The sheer size of the environmental problem also encourages social loafing. Dawes noted that as the number of people involved increases, self-interest becomes more dominant and cooperation decreases. We feel less responsible for environmental damage and are less likely to worry as we feel we have little real control over outcomes (Kerr, 1989). When problems are societal, defection's effects are harder to detect and defectors are less visible, making it more likely they will get away with their defection. Similarly, the harm done is less visible to defectors, making it more likely they will be unaware of the consequences of their defection. Simply put, even if we are aware of the problem of environmental damage, its sheer scale and our relative powerlessness to do anything about it makes it easy to ignore.

Social traps amplify this effect. Hardin (1968) argued we are ruining our environment because we see the Earth's resources as free goods to be exploited by all but owned by no one. As you will recall from Chapter Eight, Hardin's theory aroused enormous interest because it explained why people endanger their future by failing to take necessary corrective steps in the short term. Platt (1973) coined this the self **social trap**, where the convenience of driving to the shop hastens the day oil supplies run out. Equally the **individual good, collective bad trap** where throwing your litter on the footpath to avoid the inconvenience of having to find a bin is to your advantage, but if everyone does likewise the environment is ruined. Platt's analysis pointed out that the timing of reinforcement is crucial in modifying behaviour and we will return to this point in our next section.

Self-interest, combined with the social dilemmas and traps to which scarcity of resources makes us prone, explains why people might be aware of environmental issues and support change but resist modifying their

social trap
Adverse reinforcement which promotes resource depletion.

individual good, collective bad social trap
As in overgrazing where each person's additional cow has just a small impact but in sum the environment is ruined.

behaviour. Unfortunately the pay-offs of defection only work if a few of us defect.

Limited processing

O'Riordan (1976) added an extra dimension to the debate by challenging some of the assumptions on which environmental education rests. O'Riordan's analysis questions the inevitability of the attitude–behaviour link promoted by Fishbein and Ajzen (1975) and others, who believed that behavioural intentions and behaviour are related. Promoting an environmental awareness is not, O'Riordan argues, a guarantee of supplanting existing attitudes, nor of behavioural change. Research on attitudinal change (Chapter Five) shows just how resistant habitual behaviour is; while cognitive dissonance research (Chapter Four) shows we are able to hold contradictory beliefs (and actions) without discomfort. O'Riordan also challenges the assumption we always act rationally and that we can be persuaded by information and argument to act in our own long-term interest. On the contrary, much of our behaviour is, on the surface at least, irrational and contradictory (Dawes, 1980). Nor are we particularly consistent. An environmentalist concerned with saving endangered species may enjoy building furniture out of rainforest timbers and pro-ecological attitudes in one area have been found to be poor indicators of a more general ecological activism (Oskamp et al., 1991).

Questioning the attitude–behaviour link

Still another challenge to the efficacy of environmental education comes from theorists who hold the belief that attitudes follow from our behaviour and not the other way round (recall Bem's social perception in Chapter Three and Festinger's social comparison in Chapter Eight). From this perspective, education, while serving a useful interpretive function, is not really a behavioural change agent; to believe so is putting the cart before the horse (Geller, Winett & Everett, 1982). Pro-environmental attitudes are likely to be associated with antecedent variables like the rewards offered (Geller et al., 1982); being caught up with friends' and neighbours' enthusiasm for local recycling (McCaul & Kopp, 1982); and being required to comply with community norms—though O'Riordan once again points out that just because we choose a car fitted with emission-control devices does not mean that our attitudes to air pollution are changing (Bell et al., 1990).

Still it is too soon to dismiss environmental education as a lost cause. There is still a lot of consciousness raising required as environmental awareness is far from complete, and many people hold a partial or skewed understanding of the issues (Olsen, 1981). Stern & Oskamp (1987) and Oskamp et al. (1991) argue this is particularly true of those who implement ill-conceived public education programmes which often fail to appreciate the complex reasons why people act in environmentally unresponsive ways. Perhaps more importantly, Asch and Shore (1975) found that children exposed to environmental issues over a two-year period were much more responsive to environmental concerns than a control group. So perhaps the true place for education as a behavioural-change agent is with the very young, before they too have been socialised to become wastrels.

Changing behaviour to save the planet

The slogans, "Think globally, act locally", "Live simply so others may simply live" and "Every little bit helps every little thing", sum up the environmental agenda. It is almost a credo of the environmental movement that individual effort is more important than government action, for public policies will only be effective when the hearts and minds of ordinary people have been won. Modifying our own lifestyles is the first step towards global behavioural change. Environmentalists believe incremental change is an ultimately effective solution.

Unfortunately this has its problems, relying in large part on public education campaigns to inform and cajole people into environmental responsibility, and as we have seen there is a gap between awareness and action. There are so many conflicting opinions and strategies that ordinary people are just confused (Halford & Sheehan, 1991). Nor does it take into account the urgency of the problem and the sheer inertia of our wasteful lifestyles. Now is not a time for a steady-as-she-goes policy. Further, the emerging environmental consensus is a fragile flower and easily damaged. Defectors and widespread inaction are disincentives to the more socially responsible in our community to persevere in their efforts towards a sustainable future, and thoughtful conservationists are now beginning to warn of the dangers of green issues becoming just another passing fad. Moreover, we are a conforming lot and see environmental problems as a collective issue, more properly the responsibility of the government (Stern, Deitz & Black, 1986). These and other concerns have led environmental activists to pursue the three Rs policy: Reminders, Reinforcements and Rules.

Reminders

It is clear there is a rising environmental consciousness and that most people would prefer a clean and healthy environment. People now need to be encouraged to enact these beliefs. As most of the grass-roots environmental decisions are taken far from the public eye, reminders have to be omnipresent, persuasive and yet subtle enough to avoid giving offence, a very tricky combination to achieve. For this reason much research has focused on the role of **behavioural prompts** (Geller, Winett & Everett, 1982). Prompts are salient, strategically placed reminders to act environmentally. They may be as simple as a message on your milk container, "Please dispose of this package thoughtfully"; amusing signs like "Please don't feed the bears, they're fat enough already"; or physical reminders like bottle-banks at a hotel. Prompts are **antecedent behavioural change strategies**, they try to elicit and influence the direction behaviour will take before it occurs. Prompts work on the assumption that anti-ecological acts are due to thoughtlessness, or limited processing of the consequences of our actions. As such they try to capture our attention, raise our awareness of our behaviour and its consequences, suggest alternatives and reinforce appropriate behaviour.

behavioural prompts
Salient, strategically placed reminders to encourage behaviour.

antecedent behavioural change strategies
Strategies to elicit and influence the direction behaviour will take before it occurs.

REDFERN ABORIGINAL
COMMUNITY
WELCOME TO ALL VISITORS!
PLEASE RESPECT THE PRIVACY
OF RESIDENTS BY REDUCING
NOISE AND ENSURING RUBBISH
IS NOT LEFT LYING AROUND
THANK YOU

Prompts are antecedent behaviour change strategies. They ask us to engage in appropriate behaviour. (Photo: Gavin Price)

Prompts may be positive and negative, deliberate or inadvertent. Modelling is an important prompt (Stern & Oskamp, 1987) and parents who throw out their garbage, making no attempt at recycling, are acting as negative and inadvertent prompts for their children's future resource wastage.

Designing effective prompts is an art. We do not like to be told what to do and officious warnings are likely to provoke psychological reactance (Chapter Six) and reinforce what you are trying to discourage (Reich & Robertson, 1979). So the wording of prompts must be encouraging, thought-provoking and constructive. Geller, Witmer and Orebaugh (1976) suggest the following rules for an effective message:

- Ask for help, don't demand it.
- Make your message specific to the individual: "Would you please" rather than "would all". Such messages help people own their behaviour.
- Suggest appropriate responses: "Take your litter to the recycling bins out front."
- Finally reinforce compliance. "Thanks for recycling your litter in the bins out front, your thoughtfulness helps keep prices down" works a lot better than: "Would all patrons dispose of their litter in the bins provided", as a study of cafeteria littering by Durdan, Reeder and Hecht (1985) confirmed.

Prompts do not need to be written or verbal messages. Sometimes the environment can be a powerful prompt. My four-year-old became an instant convert after a garbage bin chased him down a shopping mall, asking him to pick up some litter he had dropped. The Talking Litter Bin campaign run by the Environment Protection Authority in New South Wales is a clever interactive, but expensive, prompt.

More subtle approaches manipulate the environment to encourage appropriate behaviour. One of the clear findings of environmental research is that compliance is greater if we make it easier for people to comply (Oskamp et al., 1991). Strategic location of garbage bins helps reduce litter, but so does a litter-free environment (Geller, Witmer & Tuso, 1977). It seems a clean environment acts as a powerful reminder to avoid littering. Cialdini, Reno and Kallgren (1990) took this reasoning one step further.

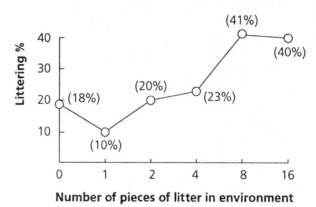

One of the most effective strategies of the NSW Litter Reduction Campaign was the Talking Bin. Countless shoppers got the fright of their lives when a bin chased them, yelling at them to pick up their litter!
(Photo: courtesy Environment Protection Authority)

Cialdini and his colleagues reasoned that if no litter is an effective prompt, would a little litter be more so than none at all? They tested their hypothesis by varying the amount of litter around from 0 to 16 pieces and then handing out flyers and observing what people did with them. Their hypothesis was confirmed. When there was no litter, 18 per cent littered, but only 10 per cent littered when there was one piece. As the litter increased so did littering. The researchers explained their results in terms of the salience of prompts. While a litter-free environment is salient, encouraging cleanliness, an environment with only one violation of this norm makes it that more salient by the sheer contrast it provides. As litter increases, salience decreases and littering becomes less remarkable (see Figure 13.1).

Figure 13.1 *Is a little litter better than no litter at all?*
Source: Cialdini, Reno & Kallgren, 1990.

Geller et al. (1982) and many other researchers have found that prompts and other behavioural manipulations work much better when desired behaviour is made *contingent* on some reinforcement. Unlike prompts which precede behaviour, most reinforcement is consequent, or after the fact. When we act pro-ecologically, positive reinforcement encourages similar actions, while negative reinforcement encourages us to abandon behaviour that is costly. Both of these techniques are in essence feedback on our behaviour, and should be differentiated from punishment, which is counterproductive, causing reactance and avoidance.

Reinforcers

Positive reinforcement

Money talks. Endless studies have shown the power of financial incentives to modify behaviour. In South Australia, deposit legislation introduced in 1975 ensures a return rate between 84 and 95 per cent on beverage containers, whereas in the rest of Australia it averages 34 per cent (Friends of the Earth, 1993). Witmer and Geller (1976) found that by selective use of monetary rewards and prompts, student paper recycling was enhanced in college residences and continued after they were withdrawn. In a similar way many schemes have been introduced to reward pro-ecological behaviour, Alcoa's (Comalco) Cash-in-a-Can scheme as an example.

Some people have always been recyclers—for example, Mark, Jim's favourite scrapmetal dealer. (Photo: Gavin Price)

Unfortunately the use of monetary reinforcers is often self-defeating because whatever the long-term benefits of your campaign, the immediate cost is often greater than any savings made (Winkler & Winett, 1982). Many resources, unlike aluminium, have little intrinsic value so any reward placed on their recycling has to be incorporated as a cost in their reuse (and many resources have no productive uses at this stage but still have to be taken out of the waste stream). Often recycling of marginal resources like paper has to be subsidised by government in the interests of the long-term conservation of the resource. However, careful use of incentives may be cost-effective (Winett, Neale & Grier, 1979), particularly if we use only intermittent reinforcement such as litter-lottery tickets sprinkled amid the garbage (Hayes, Johnson & Cone, 1975). With a little careful planning, sometimes costs can be transferred to the consumer, as with South Australia's deposit legislation.

Positive reinforcement comes in many other forms including encouragement, praise, public recognition and a sense of satisfaction (Geller et al., 1982). de Young (1986) found that recyclers cited frugality, self-sufficiency and self-efficacy, while conserving resources was cited as an important source of satisfaction to be gained from recycling. Unfortunately these intrinsic sources of positive reinforcement have a limited impact on the uncommitted, and many studies have shown that financial rewards are the most effective part of pro-ecological strategies (Cone & Hayes, 1980) and that when they are withdrawn positive action dwindles and stops (Geller et al., 1982).

Negative reinforcement

Negative reinforcers have been widely applied to limit over-consumption of resources. Financial disincentives are relatively easily built into tariffs charged by utilities providing essential services. Increasing the rate per kilowatt after a certain amount of electricity has been consumed provides a disincentive and has the added benefit of placing a higher value on the resource, while funding further conservation measures. Evidence of the effectiveness of this form of disincentive is mixed (Geller et al., 1982), with some studies showing only a minimal decrease of consumption (Stern & Gardner, 1981). It seems that regular feedback of resource usage (placing electricity meters on the kitchen wall) is as important in reducing consumption, as price structures (Stern & Oskamp, 1987).

Like positive reinforcement, negative reinforcers come in all shapes and sizes, limited only by the imagination of their creators. There are several general techniques though.

- Exclusion, where you limit or make a behaviour more difficult. The introduction of anti-smoking policies has limited smoking in the workplace, making a casual smoke much more difficult.
- Thresholds, where an act is restricted unless it complies with an acceptable standard. The Concorde aircraft is not allowed to land in Australia because it cannot comply with noise regulation standards.

- Quotas are a very useful technique where a scarce resource is rapidly declining. Cooperative agreements between New Zealand and Australia, over fishing in the Tasman Sea, have encouraged fisheries to substitute less depleted species for more endangered ones, by varying quotas.
- Threats and sanctions are the other side of the carrot-and-stick approach to environmental management. As long as people and companies know in advance that they are subject to penalties if they act irresponsibly and can act appropriately, then this acts as a negative reinforcer shaping behaviour.

There is considerable evidence that positive and negative reinforcement are powerful shapers of pro-ecological action (Geller, 1989) but their differential effects have yet to be systematically assessed.

Regulation

Given the magnitude of the problems we face and public apathy, legislating for environmental protection is an important global strategy. National and international agreements, like the Montreal Protocols limiting ozone depleting emissions, are major steps in large-scale change, yet local governments have as big a role to play in shaping everyday eco-behaviour. As you can see most of the negative reinforcers discussed above rely on a degree of government regulation. While many studies show the effectiveness of legislation as a change agent, there are few psychological studies reporting reactions to specific environmental laws and regulations.

Yet from studies of other mandated changes, it is likely that people will come to accept them over time as a study by Kahle and Beatty demonstrated. Often legislating for behavioural change pays dividends in altering public consciousness, however reluctantly they are adopted initially. Lynn Kahle and Sharon Beatty (1987) reported on the impact of Oregon's Bottle Bill, one of the first to be adopted in the US over two decades ago. They were interested in changes in recycling attitudes and behaviour brought about by legislation and what impact this had on community norms. In a longitudinal study they found the Bottle Bill had led to changed behaviour, which over time became habitual. This in turn led to a favourable view of the legislation, and new ecological attitudes then generalised to other pro-ecological behaviour (see Figure 13.2). This process reflects the shifts we make to maintain cognitive consistency, as we discussed in Chapter Four. Kahle and Beatty found the reinforcing effects of the legislation led their Oregon subjects to have greater pro-ecological attitudes than subjects in neighbouring states.

Figure 13.2 *Legislating for attitude change*
Source: Adapted from Kahle & Beatty, 1987.

Recycling

So far we have covered the roles of environmental awareness, education, prompts, behavioural manipulation, reinforcement and government regulation in changing behaviour, but how do all of these factors work together? To answer this question we will consider saving the planet by recycling its capital.

As we saw in Chapter Five, one of the mainsprings of prejudice and aggression is resource scarcity. When we face shortages of essential commodities we have limited options. We can:

1. reduce our consumption;
2. substitute other resources;
3. steal them off someone else; or
4. use what we have more wisely.

The history of our species has been one of reluctance to reduce living standards and of human desires outstripping technological advance. Unfortunately this has almost inevitably led to option 3 and indirectly to option 1, as wars of economic readjustment always mean reducing someone else's consumption (and the numbers of consumers). With a rising eco-consciousness, perhaps humanity has at last come of age and is deciding to use option 4 and live within its means. One of the key features of **steady state economics**, the belief that we should only use what may be replaced, is efficient resource recycling. Our planet is a rich one and at present suffers more from bad management than resource deficiency. If we were able to encourage each person to use only what they need, recycle by-products and achieve global zero population growth, we will be able to reach a sustainable future.

The good news is that recycling is gradually becoming respectable. Although we are yet to effectively recycle intractable (and unattractive) wastes, we are at least aware of the need and most of us are pro-recycling. For instance, Williams (1991) surveyed 237 university students on their knowledge and attitudes toward recycling and found that 81 per cent were at least aware of the issues. Two-thirds were recycling returnable bottles and cans, and nearly three-quarters indicated they might recycle non-returnable containers if facilities were available. Similar results are widely reported. To encourage a wider recycling base, diverting more material from the waste stream, we need integrated programmes which use "measures of actual behavior and actual energy usage, long-term longitudinal approaches, realistic field settings, and cost-effective procedures" (Oskamp, 1983).

Much of this work is underway. Jacobs, Bailey and Crews (1984) conducted five studies over a ten-month period to evaluate specific procedures encouraging residential recycling. To paraphrase their results: A decision to participate was frequently closely related to family values and one's outlook; weekly recycling pick-ups coinciding with garbage collection days resulted in higher levels of participation than pick-ups at other times; directly notifying homes through door-to-door brochures was a much more effective way of soliciting participation than through newspaper ads; distributing

steady state economics
A belief that we should only use what may be replaced.

containers to help residents separate recyclable from non-recyclable material was an effective procedure, particularly when combined with frequent prompting; while prompting alone did not have much effect; and the things which promoted the greatest participation were not always cost effective. They concluded that combining "these procedures into a package program resulted in high levels of neighborhood participation that were cost-effective and maintained over a six month period." Similar studies gave similar results (Burn & Oskamp, 1986)

Before concluding our discussion of pro-ecological attitudinal change, we must stress the role of commitment. Many people go the extra distance in recycling even the smallest amounts of personal waste and, though often discouraged by public indifference, their example has potentially far-reaching consequences. Cialdini, Reno and Kallgren (1990) argue that despite the bad press they have received as behavioural change agents, social norms are still important, if only we distinguish between what they tell us to believe and they what tell us to do. Minorities are often the leading edge of societal change. It may well be that most of us wholeheartedly support the minority green movement even if we, and society generally, are not yet ready to wholeheartedly embrace their lifestyle. Nevertheless, their commitment is significant and several studies have shown the importance of modelling and commitment in prompting others to change their behaviour (Wang & Katzev, 1990). It is fortunate for the well-being of this dedicated minority that several other studies have found that recycling is an intrinsically rewarding activity (Shama & Wisenblit, 1984; de Young, 1986; Vining & Ebreo 1990).

Box 13.1 *What are greenies really like?*

Some less charitable cartoonists portray conservationists as half-starved skinny lunatics crouched in trees, but what are they really like? This question was pursued by John Ray, of the University of New South Wales. Ray (1980a) surveyed 4600 Australians to determine how environmentalists differed from the wider community. Although there were minor differences, the only strong difference between them and the general public was a well-developed consumer-consciousness. Ray found environmentalists were just as likely to be conservatives or radicals, and as likely to vary on sociability or misanthropy.

In follow-up studies Ray (1981a, 1987) investi-gated whether greenies came from a distinct social class. Both studies found they were from a broad spectrum of social class and occupations, indistinguishable from the wider community. In another study, Ray and Lovejoy (1984) investigated whether one's attitude to the environment correlated with one's biophilia or emotional commitment to life. Tests of biophilia and environmentalist attitudes were given to university students, unemployed youth and young conservative activists. Ray and Lovejoy found emotionalism played little part in green attitudes and the three groups were as biophilic as each other. It would seem then that greenies are just like you and I.

Our physical environment: Weather and behaviour

As environmental psychology broadened its reach, many pioneering studies gave an impetus to examining the physical environment's impact on behaviour (Russell, 1978). For example, Hans Selye's study of stress (1956) was fundamental to understanding environmental stressors such as pollution (Rotton & Frey, 1985a); noise (Cohen, Glass & Singer, 1973); and atmospheric disturbances (Rotton & Frey, 1985b). In like manner, many other aspects of social psychology helped us understand how physical factors such as architecture (Sommer, 1976) and environmental degradation (Pilisuk & Acredolo, 1988) affect us psychologically and, in turn, heightened our consciousness of their physical impact on us. As we do not have the space to comment at length on this diverse area, we will review climate and behaviour as an example of non-spatial environmental effects, before turning to a major section on the most serious physical impact on our planet—too many people.

Without wanting to anthropomorphise the planet, environmental change is now imperilling our species, leading some of the more fanciful in the environmental movement to say that Mother Earth is purging herself of an indigestible meal—ourselves. Whether or not the planet is striking back against environmental abuse, current climatic change does show we are part of a closed ecology and for every action there is a reaction. Even the smallest act has its impact, and our behaviour does make a difference, however minute, in the global scheme of things.

To what extent do atmospheric disturbances cause marked changes in behaviour?
(Photo: Chris Simkin)

One of the most widely discussed consequences of our actions is global warming and, as we face major climatic upheaval, it is well to consider how weather patterns currently affect our behaviour. As the Earth gradually heats up under the **greenhouse effect**, only a few degrees Celsius will bring enormous physical changes. Climatic changes will not only alter geographical patterns, but also disrupt world economic patterns, threatening agriculture and species' extinction. These changes are crucially important in our region, given that many of our Pacific neighbours inhabit low-lying island chains that are threatened with inundation as the polar ice caps melt and sea levels rise. Nor should we neglect the skin cancer and other health threats faced by southern populations close to the Antarctic ozone hole. What these changes will mean for our psychological and social well-being is no less important to our continued survival, adding a certain urgency to climatic research.

greenhouse effect
Climatic changes brought on by the gradual warming of the planet.

Climate and national character

The belief that climate determines national character is an ancient one, widespread throughout all human cultures. Sommers and Moos (1976) in their review of ancient writings note that most emergent cultures attributed their superiority in part to the influence of climate on the national character, but there is little evidence to support this belief. Perhaps it was so obvious that we didn't bother to confirm our suppositions. However, like most obvious facts, in the hard light of scientific scrutiny they turn out to be less obvious than we would suppose. While there is much evidence showing *weather* variations influence behaviour (heatwaves produce lethargy), there is little evidence that the cumulative average of these variations, or *climate*, affects national characteristics or productivity. Though Sommers and Moos review the work of many theorists who would so argue, it seems most fall into the trap of *post hoc* reasoning, arguing that because civilisations have arisen in certain climatic zones, it is climate that has caused them to arise. This **environmental determinism**, Bell et al. (1990) argue, ignores many other variables that influence national fortunes. That two cultures share similar climates yet have different prospects would point to the fallacy of attributing character to climate (see Ray, 1982a,b, 1983b) for an examination of this question from an Australian perspective).

environmental determinism
Belief that national characteristics and the like are caused by the environment. A circular argument.

Yet climate is important and while climate does not determine behaviour it may well influence it and also set boundaries to what is possible. Obviously the activities characteristic of an area are determined by climate. Several months of snow each year influences Canadian attitudes to work, recreation and leisure differently to Australians and New Zealanders. To what extent climatic possibilities become behavioural probabilities we will explore but, put simply, surfing is less central to the Canadian psyche than it is to ours.

Temperature

Despite our mammalian imperative to maintain a steady core temperature of 37°C, human beings are very adaptable and have evolved to tolerate a wide range of ambient temperatures. The Central Australian Desert Aborigine, for example, can tolerate daily variations from a midday high of 50–55°C

Does climate mould national character? To what extent does five months of snow lead to a less easy-going character than a more clement climate?

to nights which might plummet to minus 10°C. To withstand such daily variations, these Centralians have several physiological adaptations, including dropping core temperature rather than shivering, as a way of conserving energy at night. Similarly the Inuit and Yakutes who live above the Arctic Circle can withstand average daily temperatures of minus 30°C without discomfort and are similarly adapted to their environment (LeBlanc, 1975). While such variations are profound, the available evidence suggests that we quickly acclimatise to changed environments, usually within two weeks and sometimes only a few days. Studies of the acclimatisation of Australians on an Antarctic expedition (Budd, 1973), for example, found that expeditioners quickly reduced their shivering rates as they became adapted to the Antarctic cold. Moreover, human variability is such that what is a cold day for one would be a prostrating heatwave for another. So what is important in temperature–behaviour research is not temperature as such but rather variations from one's average seasonal temperature.

Heat and behaviour

The physiological effects of high temperature are quite well researched. As ambient temperature rises far beyond our adaptive limits, we experience heat stress as our cardiovascular system struggles to maintain core temperature. We pant, sweat and experience increased peripheral vasodilation as surface blood vessels expand to carry more heat to our skins to be released. All these mechanisms lose body water, and dehydration is always a complicating factor in heat stress. If these regulatory mechanisms fail, we suffer heat exhaustion, characterised by headaches and visual disturbances, dizziness and nausea, hot, flushed and dry skin, muscle cramps, fever and cessation of sweating. As conditions worsen we suffer heat stroke, sudden loss of consciousness accompanied by a weak, rapid or irregular pulse, and/or heart attacks; potentially fatal disruptions of the cardiovascular system particularly in the elderly, those with circulatory problems, or those who are unacclimatised to hot weather (Brunner & Suddarth, 1980)

Research on the psychological effects of high temperature are less clear. Many studies have found a link between high temperatures and aggression, and there is clear evidence linking heat with negative side-effects (Goranson & King, 1970; Rotton & Frey, 1985b; Kenrick & McFarlane, 1986; Anderson, 1989; Simpson & Perry, 1990). Baron & Bell (1976) found that as temperature increased beyond a certain point negative behaviour declined. They argued that eventually it became too hot to be bothered and speculated that minimising heat stress became more important than ventilating one's frustrations. While this is intuitively plausible (after all, beyond a certain point you would drop from heat exhaustion), many studies have only found a linear relationship (the hotter it was the more violent you became) and there was some controversy over Baron's studies and interpretation (Carlsmith & Anderson, 1979). At present the weight of evidence supports a linear relationship between heat stress and aggression (Anderson, 1987).

The effects of heat on performance are much less controversial. As the temperature rises our performance drops and eventually we do too. Most studies examining this relationship have had an educational focus, and performance on basic learning skills like memory, comprehension, reaction time, vigilance, concentration and tracking, all decline as it hots up (Provins & Bell, 1970). More complicated skills dependent on these abilities are equally impaired, resulting in lowered reasoning and mathematical ability. For this reason, in non-airconditioned State schools in Australia, when temperatures exceed 38°C children are diverted into non-educational activities and many schools in the Western Division start a few weeks later to miss the worst of the summer heat. Many other studies have shown a corresponding relationship between heat and lowered performance in other settings: lowered productivity in industry (Link & Pepler, 1970), offices (Sundstrom, 1986), and among unacclimatised combat troops (Adam, 1967, cited in Bell et al., 1990).

Human variability influences reactions to temperature rises and many studies have shown an initial improvement in performance in some subjects and increased variability in others. For instance, Pepler (1972) studied the effects of temperature rise in a non-airconditioned classroom, compared to an airconditioned room and found that in the former, performance variability increased, while performance of those in airconditioned rooms was not better but more consistent. Heat therefore affected consistency rather than performance (see Bell, 1981, for a review). However, the basic correlation between temperature rise and decreased performance is maintained if we take individual variation into account, and the speed with which individuals acclimatise themselves to temperature rises. For some subjects,

Watering holes are welcome in the desert.

increased temperature may cause increased arousal and heightened performance, at least until fatigue effects start to take their toll. In a related finding, Bell (1978) found subjects performed better on core tasks when heat-stressed but at the expense of secondary tasks, arguing a narrowing of concentration to avoid the overloading effects of temperature rise. Obviously temperature rise is related to a baseline, and raising the temperature of frozen subjects will increase the likelihood of their performing, as Cunningham (1979) found when asking subjects to help others in mid-winter!

Cold and behaviour

The effects of cold weather are similar to that of heat stress. Performance drops, we become aware of our physiological distress and mental processes focus on defending against the cold. The body becomes increasingly preoccupied with avoiding freezing, and concentration narrows as attention becomes overloaded by the demands of staying warm (Fox, 1967). As our core temperature drops (**hypothermia**) we constrict our peripheral blood vessels and start shivering to generate heat, and this makes heavy demands on our physiology and psychological reserves to the point where little else may be accomplished. One of the intermediate effects of hypothermia is an impairing of consciousness as physiological activity slows, and this often leaves the victims unaware that they are cold stressed—so hypothermia is often more fatal than heat stress.

Unlike heat stress, it is possible to rug up against cold weather and, with suitable clothing and shelter, even extreme temperatures may be endured without ill-effect. For example, several studies have shown that adverse mental effects of over-wintering in the Antarctic (if any) are

hypothermia
Illness caused by a drop of the body's core temperature.

more related to isolation and other factors than climate (Taylor & Duncum, 1987; Rothblum, 1990).

Sunlight

Sol is the motor which keeps our planet trudging along, and its radiant energy provides Earth with an enormous number of physical benefits, including heating, light and power, as well as photosynthesis, the ultimate basis of all life on Earth. Undoubtedly the Sun also has positive psychological benefits as our sun-worship and paeans of praise would indicate—but what does sunshine do for us?

Researchers believe that dusk and dawn provide cues which regulate or entrain our daily sleeping and activity cycles. Sunlight's duration and intensity appears to elevate moods (Cunningham, 1979) and alertness (Rosenthal et al., 1984). Most of the evidence for these effects comes from depression research. Goodwin, Wirz-Justice and Wehr (1982) proposed that depression is a disturbance in our daily or **circadian rhythms**. Our brains have several biological clocks regulating sleep, arousal, temperature and so on, which are coordinated and entrained by environmental cues. These circadian rhythms are linked with light by a biological mechanism which is not yet fully understood. It is thought that a photosensitive hormone, **melatonin**, secreted by the pineal gland in the brain, provides feedback on the intensity and duration of light. While such an effect has been shown in hibernating animals, the results remain unclear for humans (Wehr et al., 1986). Goodwin et al. (1982) suggested that depressives' clocks become desynchronised and out of phase with each other and, as they free-wheel, cause cyclical bouts of depression. Sunlight then acts a **zeitgeber** (time-giver) bringing these clocks into harmony, elevating mood and arousal.

Supporting evidence comes from observations that certain depressives are worse during winter months and even worse in the high latitudes where winter daylight is short or non-existent. That such a phenomenon was clearly related to latitude was shown when sufferers moved south and their symptoms diminished (Pande, 1985). In 1982, Lewy, Kern, Rosenthal and Wehr demonstrated that extending short winter days with a bright artificial light relieved depression. This **seasonal affective disorder** (SAD) (Rosenthal et al., 1984) became a focus of much theoretical interest. Several studies showed that daily exposure to a light intensity of 2500 lux for about 6 hours relieved the condition (Wehr et al., 1986) but exposure to a dim light did not (Rosenthal et al., 1985). It certainly seemed that light was implicated with mood.

Czeisler et al. (1986) added another piece to the puzzle by showing light therapy altered depressives' basal temperature. Part of our daily rhythm is a slight variation in body temperature. It appears that we have at least two internal clocks, one associated with temperature and one with sleep/ activity cycles. Normally these are in tandem, with higher temperatures associated with wakefulness and activity. For unknown reasons some (but not all) depressives have temperature rhythms of less than 24 hours. This

circadian rhythms
Daily cycles; brain-based "biological clocks" regulate sleep, arousal and temperature cycles.

melatonin
Photosensitive hormone secreted by the pineal gland, provides feedback on the intensity and duration of light.

zeitgeber
"Time-giver"; cues which synchronise or entrain our biological clocks.

seasonal affective disorder
Depression caused by lack of daylight during short winter months.

puts their activity cycle out of step with their temperature rhythm. Because the depressed person's body temperature rises and falls several hours too early, when they go to sleep their body temperature is rising rather than falling and this leads to sleep disruption and insomnia. Light therapy entrains these rhythms, bringing them back into line, synchronising mood and activity levels (Kalat, 1988).

So it seems sunlight governs our internal rhythms. In the absence of light some people, for reasons not yet fully understood, shift out of phase and become depressed. For most of us this effect is mild but probably sufficient to ensure that a burst of sunlight into the gloom will lift our spirits. The corollaries are evident. If we wish to promote mental health, sunlight is a factor often overlooked, and often underutilised (Eastman, 1990). By way of contrast, Box 13.2 covers the effects of that other celestial luminary, the moon.

Box 13.2 *Lunacy and the effects of a full moon*

One of the longest running and most hotly contested debates is the influence of the moon on behaviour. During the 1980s correspondence to various journals grew so convoluted, with replies to replies, and charges and counter-charges of statistical incompetence, that manuscript titles were amended by journals to include Roman numerals, indicating the place the authors took in the ongoing debate. The belief in the influence of the phases of the moon on humans or lunar synodic behaviour is as old as humanity and is a strong plank of religion and social practice. As an instance, most Commonwealth countries have mental health Acts whose precedents are the *Lunacy Laws* of Great Britain, which as their title suggests, once made such a connection. Many mechanisms for these supposed lunar effects have been advanced, including ozone, moonlight, gravity, tidal force, weather, ions, geomagnetism and extremely low-frequency electromagnetic waves (Culver, Rotton & Kelly, 1988).

Many occupational groups hold lunar-related beliefs. Police officers believe the full moon promotes craziness and influences criminal activity (Rotton, Kelly & Elortegui, 1986); crisis workers hold it triggers personal crises (Wilson & Tobacyk, 1990); correctional officers feel that psychiatric inmates become more disturbed (Little, Bowers & Little, 1987); nursing home staff think it disturbs elderly patients (Cohen, Marx & Werner, 1989); and maternity nurses believe it influences the time of birth (Nalepka, Jones and Jones, 1983). Are these views superstitious or is some factor at work? Unfortunately for the workers concerned, all these studies found no relationship between lunar phases and their supposed effects but the academic controversy rolls on. So why does the debate continue?

To answer this question we must review a little of the debate's history. In the 1970s several studies emerged, some with impressive sample sizes, supporting any number of lunar-influenced human and animal behaviours (Lieber & Sherin, 1972; Blackman & Catalina, 1973; Tasso & Miller, 1976). However, in the late 1970s reviews by Campbell and Beets (1978) and Frey, Rotton and Barry (1979) surveyed research and concluded that while there was some evidence of a lunar tidal effect on simple animals, there was no influence on human behaviour. These reviews concluded that studies reporting a lunar influence were methodologically flawed; or chance results unsupported by replications; or did not take account of confounding variables.

Supporters of the lunar theory riposted with several studies in the early 1980s supporting their view. For example, Templer, Veleber and Brooner (1982) plotted 291 939 Californian traffic accident injuries in 1980 against the phases of the moon and found a significant correlation between injuries during the full and new moons at night, but either a deficit or no effect during daylight hours. They suggested the light-sensing pineal gland might play a role in explaining their results. Another study by Criss and Marcum (1981) analysed 1968 New York City birth records, in search of a link between lunar influences and human fertility. They found births varied systematically over the lunar cycle and peaked in the third quarter. The effect was small, but robust when analysed a number of ways. As in Templer's study they proposed a light sensitive explanation to link lunar illumination to the timing of ovulation and hence births.

This sparked the controversy which continues to the present. Kelly and Rotton (1983) challenged Templar's methodology, arguing that the claim is based on trivial differences, inaccurate data, probable statistical difficulties and a failure to consider other confounding variables. Templer replied with a further analysis of his data (Templer, Brooner & Corgiat, 1983) and then a plethora of studies appeared demonstrating the absence of a lunar-behaviour effect (Kelly, Saklofske & Culver, 1990; Martens, Kelly & Saklofske, 1988; Tobacyk & Wilson, 1988; Wagner & Almeida, 1987; Durm, Terry & Hammonds, 1986; Russell & de-Graaf, 1985; Startup & Russell, 1985; Rotton & Kelly, 1985a).

From the mid 1980s so many problems had been found with studies supporting a lunar-behaviour link, that theoretical interests changed to measuring correlations with other "superstitious" beliefs. Rotton and Kelly (1985b) devised such a scale and duly found strong correlations with a belief in paranormal phenomena. As negative studies continued to be published, the principal theorists were reduced to arguing about the best way to properly detect a supposed lunar effect, even if there was little further scientific support for this hypothesis (Cyr & Kalpin, 1987; Rotton & Kelly, 1987; Cyr & Kalpin, 1988).

To a certain extent the debate now continues as an academic end in itself, irrespective of any lunar effect. Even so, it was still a valuable debate. Stubborn researchers, trying to prove their pet theories, grapple with measurement problems and in the end often resolve methodological issues which have a wider applicability. Whether the moon influences behaviour is resolved in the negative for the present, however much it remains part of common folklore.

Weather: A multifactorial approach

Many other climatic factors influence our behaviour including wind speed, ozone, atmospheric ionisation, precipitation, humidity, barometric pressure and electromagnetic effects. Over the last twenty years single variable studies were often criticised for ignoring other factors which critics saw as possible confounding variables. To avoid these charges the 1980s saw many multifactorial studies which, despite the complexities of measurement, correlated social indices like suicide or traffic accidents against the overall weather pattern. What did these studies show?

The results are a mixed bag. Studies of atmospheric factors' influence on suicidal behaviour show a pattern one would expect from our previous discussion, where sunlight and temperature are linked with depression. For example, differences in regional suicide rates in France between the years 1975 and 1983 were significantly associated with ambient temperature and sunlight duration (Souetre et al., 1990). Such results, however, differ from those of attempted suicides. As an example, Leo Chiu (1988), in a study of 307 attempted suicide cases in Hong Kong, found no significant correlation between the number of attempts and temperature, humidity, rainfall, or amount of sunshine. Such studies must be interpreted cautiously because of national and other sociocultural differences.

Studies of weather and violence show similar mixed results. Atlas (1984) in a four-prison study found little to indicate that temperature, seasons or moon phase have direct influences on inmate behaviour or violence. However, Rotton and Frey (1985a) found a link between air pollution, weather, family disturbances and violent crimes in the general public, by examining police call-outs over a two-year period. More disturbances were reported when ozone levels were high and their analysis indicated that high temperatures and low winds preceded violent episodes, which occurred more often on dry than humid days.

Notwithstanding the ambiguity of these studies, two significant variables do link weather and behaviour. Humidity and barometric pressure often interact to predict mood and change in behaviour

Humidity

Humidity's influence on mood and behaviour usually correlates with temperature and to a lesser extent wind speed (Tromp, 1980). Its uncomfortable effect is due to the inability of fully saturated air to absorb perspiration and further cool the body. As temperature rises, we perspire more, and with humidity approaching 100 per cent our cooling systems are impaired and we overheat and feel clammy as sweat accumulates on our skin. In low wind speeds this discomfort is heightened as the wind usually aids evaporation and convection currents over the skin surface, reducing perspiration effects. Howarth and Hoffman (1984) measured 24 male university students' mood over 11 days on variables: concentration, cooperation, anxiety, potency, aggression, depression, sleepiness, scepticism, control and optimism; and in a multidimensional analysis compared these against hours of sunshine, precipitation, temperature, wind direction and velocity, humidity, changes in barometric pressure, and absolute barometric pressure. Humidity was the most significant predictor of mood change, though temperature and hours of sunshine were also important. High humidity reduced concentration while increasing sleepiness. Rising temperatures lowered anxiety and scepticism mood scores. Similar results were found by Sanders and Brizzolara (1982) where high humidity caused general enervation.

Barometric pressure

Barometric pressure and particularly sudden changes are also quite significant predictors of well-being. Some of the discomfort we face is due to pressure imbalance in the inner ear, changes in our blood's nitrogen/oxygen balance, and breathing difficulties. All of these are minor for healthy people and are usually only subliminal sources of discomfort. Sunlight factors are also implicated as low pressure is associated with stormy overcast weather. Yet it is quite clear that sudden decreases in barometric pressure reduce feelings of health and well-being (Whitton, Kramer & Eastwood, 1982); bring bodily aches and pains, headaches and bowel distress in children (Scagliotta, 1983); causes arthritic sufferers increased discomfort (Laborde, Dando & Powers, 1986); and effects are felt in more industrial accidents (Persinger & Nolan, 1984) and psychiatric emergency-room visits (Briere, Downes & Spensley, 1983). In all these multivariate analyses, humidity was also a significant factor.

To summarise, weather is a noticeable environmental influence. Temperature, sunlight, humidity and barometric pressure all combine to influence well-being and health. While there is quite a controversy about causes, these variables affect mood and behaviour, even if the case is less clear for others like lunar influence, geomagnetic effects or negative ions. Still, we need to be cautious about the weather's ultimate impact, as non-atmospheric factors may prove to be more significant determinants of behaviour. We turn now to a consideration of just one of these factors—personal space

Human spatial behaviour

We live on a crowded planet. The dimensions of this problem become apparent when you consider that more than half of all the human beings born since the first *Homo sapiens* are alive now. World population stands at approximately 5 450 000 000 people and is growing at about 1.7 per cent annually. This equates with 88.4 million more people each year, or about 3 babies per second (World Watch, 1991). While there is some optimism that the growth rate is slowing from a high of 2.06 per cent per annum in 1970, we have a long way to go before we reach a stable (and hopefully declining) world population. Barring global catastrophe, even moderate estimates (Turk & Turk, 1988) see a nearly doubled world population of 9500 million by the year 2020, when most of you will be only mid-way through your careers. You might like to consider what it will be like when you retire.

Unless we limit our population, there is little point to conservation! (Photo: Gavin Price)

As we consider humanity's impact, it is worth remembering that these new mouths crammed onto a small overcrowded planet mean we are living at social densities never before experienced by our species. What this means in terms of our psychological and social adjustment makes spatial behaviour potentially the most important applied research area in social and environmental psychology. We need to determine if we can withstand the stresses of population pressure and its impact on our future evolution. Nor is our relatively underpopulated region exempt. Fiji and Papua New Guinea will double their populations within 30 years and, while Australia and New Zealand have much longer doubling times, our rapid urbanisation will lead us to experience similar pressures in our urban microcosms, despite our relatively sparsely settled interiors. What impact this will have is still being determined, and became a major theoretical preoccupation from the 1970s when the dimensions of the problem first became apparent. No one knows what a well-managed planet's carrying capacity is, but there can be no doubt that studies of human territorial behaviour and our responses to high density living are vital as we face a crowded future.

Human territorial behaviour

Our long history of territorial aggression demonstrates that like many social animals we are territorial in nature. Yet every year we crowd ever more densely into larger and larger cities, paradoxically limiting the amount of personal territory we can claim and defend. Whether territoriality is part of our genetic programming or a learned behaviour is uncertain. Some theorists like Richard Ardrey (1966) and Konrad Lorenz (1966) argue we have an innate drive to mark and claim territory, which inevitably leads us into conflict over scarce resources (Freedman, 1972). Others like Gifford (1987) argue that evidence of an innate territorial drive may be as easily explained from a learning perspective and is thus more readily experimentally manipulated. While most environmental psychologists would adopt the latter position, the argument is not resolved, and even our acceptance of instinctive territoriality in animals is increasingly questioned (Brown, 1987). Whether a human territorial drive translates into an optimum population density is unknown, although there is qualified support (Balling & Falk, 1982; Kaplan, 1987) for the theory that we have an innate preference for the open (and by implication thinly populated) grasslands, reflecting our evolutionary origins as hunter-gatherers on the savannas of East Africa (see Box 13.3).

Status

Whether instinctive, or acquired, or some combination of both, territoriality plays an enormously important role in human spatial relations. All cultures have detailed codes governing land and property allocation, and these rights are some of the most fundamental in our common law. Property and territoriality are so inextricably linked in some cultures that ownership extends to intangible assets like reputation (lawsuits for "invading" another's privacy by defaming them). As the link between survival and owning productive territory is less immediate for humans than animals, given an

---

Box 13.3 *Hunter-gatherer territoriality: An Australian perspective*

Whether or not human territoriality is acquired or innate is a longstanding debate (Thompson, 1910) and is probably not resolvable. While our outlook is clearly territorial, the way we cram into mega-cities makes territory hard to defend and territoriality hard for researchers to define. For this reason there has been much interest in thinly scattered hunter-gatherer cultures. Anthropologist Nicholas Peterson, from the Australian National University, weighed into this debate in 1975 with a consideration of Aboriginal spacing mechanisms. Peterson argues that whether or not territoriality is innate or a learned behaviour is less important than having effective spacing mechanism to control population. He proposed that the land required by a hunter-gatherer society precludes rigorous physical territorial defence, and so Aboriginal society controls access to an area and its resources socially, via greeting ceremonies.

The problem of optimum populations for any one area is always a tricky balancing act for those living as close to nature as the hunter-gatherers. Population must be controlled to ensure the land is not exhausted. That pre-industrial man limited population by infanticide, abortion, senilicide and abstinence, Peterson argues, shows that they were well enough aware of the need to maintain an optimum population, but the important question is "How did the people know when and at what level of intensity to apply these regulations in the absence of bureaus of statistics and national perspectives?" If they were completely nomadic,

how would they distinguish between a poor yield due to drought or seasonal variation, or as a consequence of overpopulating an area? The answer is fixed territories and a body of local knowledge that provides a baseline of past experience against which to make this judgment. The group living within the territory must be strongly cohesive to offset personal inefficiencies in food gathering and to provide sufficient reserves to support the elderly as custodians of this vital knowledge.

As hunter-gatherers need much land to support a small group, limited numbers makes physical surveillance and protection of the territory impossible as each man, woman and child would have too large an area to protect, and anyway they are more preoccupied with the daily tasks of survival. Nevertheless, there is a need to restrict "unfettered wandering" from one area to another. "An alternative strategy for defending the land is to make acceptance into the local land-using group a preliminary requirement for using the resources in its territory; that is, by defending the boundaries of the social group rather than the perimeter of the territory itself" (Peterson, 1975). They do this via greeting ceremonies, which provide a ritualised way of incorporating visitors within the group and restricting their access to the land.

Limiting local knowledge to only those who are approved, Peterson argues, provides an appropriate control mechanism. Perhaps this is not so different in complex societies if you consider the ultimate ends of your current studies.

---

elaborate system of economic exchange, we use territoriality for more "higher-order needs" like image-management or self-enhancement (Gold, 1982). Ownership of land and related assets often equals social recognition, while the right to exclusive use of a common territory is one of our oldest status symbols. I was somewhat amused for instance to discover on my first day as a junior in the Commonwealth Public Service, that Grade 1 clerks had 1.4 metre desks; Grade 4's had 1.6 metre desks and swivel chairs; Grade 6's hid behind desk partitions; 8's lived in waist-high glass-topped cubicles; while 9's enjoyed real offices. Our betters occupied suites in

(Photos: Gavin Price)

another part of the building entirely, far from the *hoi polloi* and had scenic views commensurate with their status! It seemed the degree of territorial closure, and the privacy thus engendered, led to a sense of self-satisfaction, a finding Eric Sundstrom has explored in a number of studies (Sundstrom, Burt & Kamp, 1980; Sundstrom, Herbert & Brown, 1982; Sundstrom, Town, Brown, et al., 1982).

Predictability

On a more serious note, as we saw in Box 13.3, territory provides a framework through which we can ensure a certain predictability in our lives (Edney, 1975). Being able to claim territory as our own ensures we meet others on our terms, and defines acceptable behaviour. Similarly, what our culture recognises as territorial rights identifies the types of social interaction permitted (Taylor, 1978) and acts as a form of social control. Public territories like libraries limit social interaction, and seating and spatial arrangements act as interpersonal distancing mechanisms; while town planners design new suburbs to promote social cohesion; and inner-city ethnic concentrations are a more informal way of defining in- and outgroups. In the suburbs similar mechanisms are at work. The various *Boundary and Dividing Fences Acts* not only aid privacy but also regulate potential disputes. Within the home each family member has their own "turf" and uses personal property to mark the boundaries of personal space, and so on.

Privacy

These considerations led Irwin Altman (1975) to develop a **privacy regulation model** which proposes we use territoriality to control desired levels of intimacy. In some ways privacy is the opposite of crowding (Sundstrom, 1988) and by limiting others' territorial access (shutting your bedroom door) you reduce stress and overstimulation. Leaving it open signals your desire for company. Altman's theory combines territoriality and our use of personal space to account for the extreme variability of human territorial behaviour. Whatever the factors influencing us, feeling ill, lonely or overstimulated, the difference between our desired and experienced privacy governs our spatial behaviour. Table 13.1 sets out territorial behaviours underlying Altman's theory. As you can see, varying levels of personal control is the key feature differentiating primary, secondary and public territories.

privacy regulation model
Proposes we set territories to control desired levels of intimacy.

Table 13.1 *Altman's territorial behaviours*

	Extent of perceived ownership by self	*Reactions to violations of territory*
Primary territory (homes, car, desk at office)	Very high. Ownership reinforced by full sanctions of law. Absolute right to territory.	Vigorous defence. Territory is extensively personalised and an intrusion (burglary) may be a psychological as well as a territorial invasion.
Secondary territory (regular seat on bus)	Moderate. Limited rights based on regularity of use. Owned to the extent that others acknowledge right to use territory.	Moderate defence based on support of other users in territory. Strength of of defence is partially governed by social norms and the strength of the perceived threat.
Public territory (patch of grass at a rock concert)	Low. Few rights as person is just one of many possible users of the territory.	Little defence but occupiers of public territory may react to perceived invasions of body space.

Source: Adapted from Altman, 1975.

Territorial invasion

We are thoroughly protective of our primary territory and vigorously repel invasions, usually with the full force of the law. Secondary territory is not owned but becomes "ours" through repeated usage. At my university, rapid growth has led to a shortage of space where students can meet. Predictably parts of the common areas have become each faculty's turf, where students congregate. Invasions are resented and on several occasions hapless intruders were summarily ejected by irate students who indignantly warned them off. That such ownership is episodic and of short duration is evident from the same areas being claimed by different faculties' students throughout the day. While we are usually less forceful defending secondary territory (Becker & Mayo, 1971), we do resort to a whole range of intimidation tactics, muttered insults, glares and other body language to scare away potential intruders. Because we feel these territories are ours but do not own them, the potential for conflict is greater than in the other two types of territories (Brown & Altman, 1983). Table 13.2 reviews the major features of our reactions in each territory.

While primary territory is owned and secondary territory is ours through regular usage, our grip on public territory is more tenuous. A seat on a train is ours because we have a ticket to ride but, unless we have a reserved seat, we sit where we can. Public territories are therefore the most ambiguous and least controllable, and hold the greatest potential for conflict. For this reason many researchers have studied how we defend ourselves by using space and boundary markers in public territories.

Sommer (1966) found that we evenly space ourselves from other people in libraries, on park benches and in trains. If space is limited we prefer to

Table 13.2 *Public, secondary and primary territories*

Dimension	Public	Secondary	Primary
Duration	Short	Short, but regular usage common	Long
Centrality	Not central	Somewhat central	Very central
Marking intentions	Intentionally claiming territory	Often claiming territory	Usually personalising or decorating
Marking range	Few physical markers or barriers; much bodily and verbal marking	Some reliance on physical markers; bodily and verbal marking common	Heavy reliance on a wide range of markers and barriers; bodily and verbal marking usually not necessary
Responses to invasion	Can relocate or use immediate bodily and verbal markers	Can often relocate, use immediate bodily and verbal markers, as well as some reemphasis of physical markers	Cannot relocate easily, can use legal recourse, reestablishment of physical markers and barriers, as well as bodily and verbal markers

Source: Brown & Altman, 1983.

sit as far away from others as possible. These two factors combine in a form of **territorial calculus** which is readily seen if you ride an empty train, or bus, and watch the seating pattern as others enter. Each person scans the carriage and then sits equidistantly from others. As the carriage fills, the mean distance between each person shrinks but people continue to sit as far apart as possible. While friends and family are obvious exceptions, as are those who through long familiarity regard a certain seat as a secondary territory, for most this pattern will continue until everyone is standing shoulder-to-shoulder. Once we have chosen a seat, the length of time we occupy it determines how strongly we will defend against intrusions. Sommer (1969) noted how long people had sat in a cafeteria, and then had a confederate approach them asking for "their seat back". Those who had sat the longest were the least likely to apologise and move on.

In another experiment, Sommer and Becker (1969) used territorial markers to personalise empty seats in a study room. We use markers—personal possessions—to protect ourselves and our territories from intrusions. The researchers left scattered journals; orderly piles of journals; a coat; a notebook and coat; and a text, coat and notebook on a chair in a heavily used area. Compared to an empty chair (the control condition), scattered journals were insufficient personalisation to resist usage, but orderly journals were more effective, and the text, coat and notebook combination was sufficient to reserve a chair all night. Claiming possession is not the only use of markers, they may also signal our desire for privacy, as when we put our bag on a seat next to us; or as psychological defences, as when we hide behind our newspapers in an overcrowded tram.

As you can see, control is a key issue underlying territoriality. Knapp (1978) saw territorial markers as a request to others to observe and comply

territorial calculus
The pattern of defensive spacing observed as a space becomes crowded.

We often defend ourselves and our territory by use of markers and/or spacing mechanisms.
(Photo: Chris Simkin)

with our desire for privacy. We exert little real control in public spaces beyond setting markers and hoping others will honour them. They are essentially preventive. Our reactions to intrusions will be determined by their nature. If it is a casual violation, as when somebody bumps us in a crowd, we are unlikely to react; if however it is a deliberate *invasion*, then we are more likely to act defensively. Lyman and Scott (1967) note the difficulties we face in dealing with a third form of intrusion, *contamination*, where the intrusion is obvious (graffiti, vandalism) but the perpetrator is not. This form of territorial violation is the hardest to deal with emotionally and leads to the greatest defensive efforts.

defensible space
Changes we make in our environments to protect us from intrusions.

Newman (1972, 1980) developed a theory of **defensible space** to account for the changes we make in our environments to protect ourselves from intrusions. Newman was interested in the accommodations people make when they fear residential crime. He proposed that we use real or symbolic barriers to mark off our primary territories from public areas as much as possible and redesign our homes to increase our sense of security. Defensible spaces are those in which we can anticipate and reduce threat. Newman (1980), for example, found that certain streets in St Louis were more defensible after they had been converted to restrict traffic flow, and gates and fences and the general street-scape all provided a sense of defensible space. In these streets residents were more likely to use their front yards and build up community ties and so enjoy a greater sense of security. It must be stressed that we are dealing with residents' perceptions of security rather than actual defensibility, as this is difficult to determine experimentally. Most studies, however, do suggest some positive effects from defensible spaces (Taylor, 1982).

Before we leave territoriality to consider crowding, it is worth noting once again the importance of attribution on our behaviour. How we perceive others will influence our spatial behaviour. If we interpret another's behaviour as a threat, we are more likely to flee or fight, than if it is seen as innocuous (Sundstrom & Sundstrom, 1977). Konecni et al. (1975) had helpers crowd persons waiting to cross a street. These "space invaders" were evidently seen as a threat and people reacted by ducking across the street faster than they would have otherwise. However, a number of factors may make us defend ourselves. For example, Art Veno, an Australian community psychologist, was interested in the effects of sex and body size on our reactions when encountering a perceived threat. He noted lone passengers' reactions when entering a trolley tunnel and encountering a tall heavily built male staring and walking slowly towards them. Veno rated his subjects as being bigger, smaller, or the same size as his confederate. Veno hypothesised that smaller subjects would be more likely to avoid the situation and act submissively, while those closer in size would counter the threat more aggressively. As hypothesised, smaller people were more submissive, particularly women. Males who were the same size, or bigger, reacted aggressively; young men were aggressive, middle-aged men were more aggressive, while as you would expect older men were submissive (Veno, 1976).

Overcrowding: Close encounters of the worst kind?

Since the time of the historian Herodotus (c. 484–425 BC) theorists and philosophers have linked overcrowding with insanity and social disruption. Too many people living off too few resources gave ready evidence for the adverse effects of overpopulation. This view was supported by animal studies showing a clear link between overcrowding and abnormal behaviour. There have been many studies of animal territoriality and spatial intrusion, but the classic demonstration of adverse consequences when an animal-to-space ratio was too high was reported by John Calhoun in 1962. Calhoun designed a 300 x 420 cm "rat universe" which is depicted in Figure 13.3. Into this spatially restricted environment he placed 48 male and female Norway rats and allowed them to breed freely, providing unrestricted food and nesting material. Calhoun then sat back to see what would happen as the rat population increased beyond an optimum of 48 rats.

Animal overcrowding

For a while the rats acted normally. The males chose mates and moved into the breeding boxes with a number of females, and marked out and defended territories. Females were soon occupied with building nests and producing numerous litters. While space was not a problem, rat behaviour was quite decorous. Other males respected territory, did not try to mate with other females and fighting was rare, but as population pressure built up and space became restricted, social behaviour deteriorated sharply. As you can see from Figure 13.3 the universe was divided into four pens, and access into pens 1 and 4 was controlled by providing only a single entrance. Into these pens moved the most dominant males and their harems, and a semblance of normal rat behaviour continued, even though the males were constantly vigilant in protecting their threatened territories.

However, in pens 2 and 3, a "behavioural sink" emerged. In these pens, which had two entrances and were harder to defend, the remaining rats lived in totally overcrowded conditions. Life for these rats was appalling and social behaviour quickly broke down. None of the rats acted normally and the most striking manifestation of the pathological effects of overcrowding was their altered sexual behaviour. Estrous females were constantly pack-raped by gangs of roving males. Other females were completely cowed, did not respond to sexual advances and huddled indiscriminately with similarly cowed males. Other males were equally aberrant. Some, which Calhoun called "the beautiful ones", were sexually confused and tried to mate with females who were not in the estrous phase of their reproductive cycle. Other males called "probers" were vicious, aggressive, sexually overactive and often homosexual. With these aberrances, reproductive behaviour was

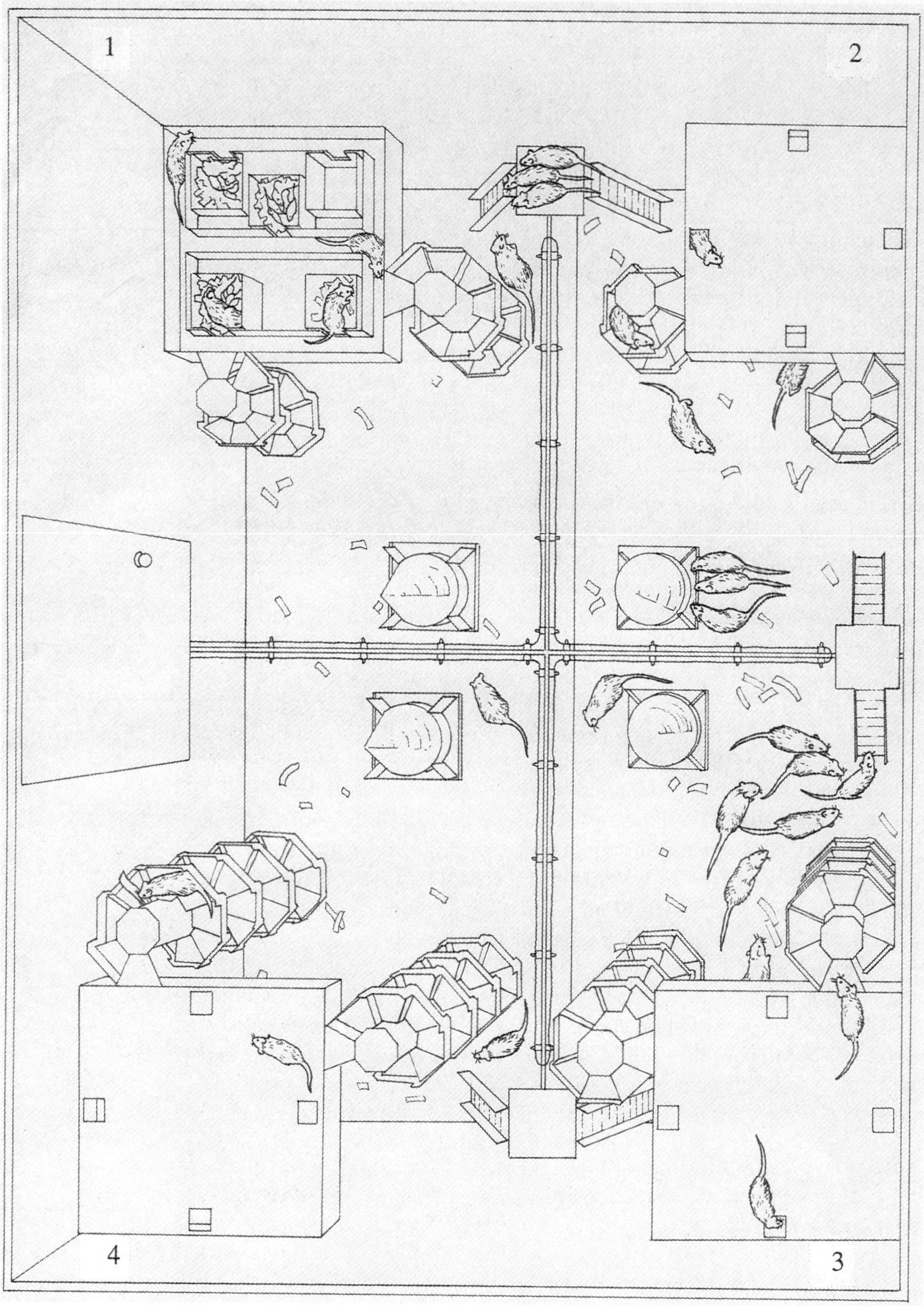

Figure 13.3 *Density and social pathology. A rat's paradise?*

Source: Calhoun, "Population density and social pathology", *Scientific American*, 206, 139–48. Copyright © 1962 by Scientific American, Inc. All rights reserved.

completely disrupted. Female rats were poor nest builders and neglected their young. While fewer females in the behavioural sink mated or success-fully carried to term, up to 90 per cent of all the pups produced died before weaning. Females who reproduced in the behavioural sink were racked by disease and worn out from constant sexual abuse. On autopsy they were found to have enlarged adrenal glands, a sign of prolonged stress, a feature observed in related studies (Christian, Flyger & Davis, 1960; Freedman, 1975).

Aggression and fights were constant and unremitting. Some rats tried to take and defend territory but were unable to do so given the layout of the pens and became the victims of constant attacks from other rats. Many rats were injured and killed because aggressors ignored in-built submission signals which normally limit injury. Other rats were confused and tried to escape this appalling reality by an apathetic and submissive withdrawal from social life (recall our discussion of learned helplessness in Chapter Three). Life was so vicious that some rats became cannibals.

Calhoun's study was as much a manipulation of territoriality as it was of population pressure. Rats in the wild adjust population by moving on when density increases. In this sense, critics suggested that Calhoun's universe was an unreal situation which showed effects unlikely to be found in the wild, though others have shown equally aberrant behaviour in various species facing natural overcrowding (Dubos, 1965; Christian, 1963; Lorenz, 1966). Calhoun (1970) refined his notion of a behavioural sink in which normal behaviours do not apply, by proposing a theory of optimum group size. He theorised that each species has developed an optimal social unit which provides for an individual's needs, while leaving enough space and privacy from other group members, to offset the inevitable irritations of living together. As population increases, however, the safety valve of time alone is eroded by more contact with other animals. He hypothesised that as populations reach twice their optimum size, the ratio of positive and negative interactions is so tilted towards the negative that the presence of any members of one's species becomes aversive, and leads to an abandonment of the rules of normal intra-species behaviour and the type of activities found in his behavioural sink.

Collateral evidence supporting Calhoun's conclusions came from a wide spectrum of international research detailing the effects of crowding on animal behaviour and physiology. Hemsworth, Barnett, Hansen and Winfield (1986) of the Animal Research Institute at Werribee, Victoria, found that pigs raised in crowded pens exhibited a chronic stress response with marked hormone imbalances and a consequent impairment of sexual activity. The implications this has for animal welfare were reported in a follow-up study (Barnett & Hemsworth, 1990). Lesley Syme of the Raukura Animal Research Station, Hamilton, New Zealand, investigated the effects of putting female New Zealand black and white hooded rats either in isolation or in crowded conditions, and subsequently tested them for open field activity. Results showed that socially crowded rats were much less active in the open than those raised in isolation (Syme, 1973).

Still, we must be cautious about such research because it runs into the perennial problem of comparative studies—to what extent may their conclusions be applied to humans? Nieuwenhuijsen and de-Waal (1982), for example, showed that crowding chimpanzees into a small cage in Arnhem Zoo in the Netherlands did not lead to effects similar to Calhoun. The apes established quite an elaborate hierarchy and followed equally elaborate social codes to avoid conflict. There was even an increase in socially constructive behaviours like grooming each other. The researchers concluded we must be cautious applying findings from simple animals like rats to more complex and flexible animals like the great apes and man. This cautious approach has intensified as even our acceptance of instinctive territoriality in lower animals is increasingly questioned (Brown, 1987). While Calhoun's and other studies demonstrate that some animal behaviour is markedly affected by crowding, we need to ask ourselves whether this applies to our species.

Human overcrowding

frustration-aggression theory
Theory that frustration leads to aggression.

social overload theory
Certain environments (urban) are too perceptually stimulating, causing social withdrawal.

psychosocial pathology theory
Proposed that high-density living causes disease, crime, civil unrest and social disruption.

Over the last 10 000 years the history of human evolution has been one of increasing urbanisation. For much of social psychology's years, urbanisation was viewed with alarm, as many studies reported positive correlations between high-density living and all manner of social ills (Winsborough, 1965). Although many causes were offered as explanations, gradually the **frustration-aggression** (Chapter Seven) and **social overload** (Chapter Ten) hypotheses blended into the **psychosocial pathology theory** which proposed that high-density living *caused* disease, crime, civil unrest and social disruption. In the absence of any solid historical data we should be cautious in assuming that, in our highly urbanised world, life is any more stressful than in the past (Burvill, 1982). Even present day comparisons do not support this belief.

For example, rates of attempted suicide in Hong Kong, the most densely populated city in the world, were unrelated to housing density (Chiu, 1988). Even city–rural comparisons which show aversive higher-density effects have been challenged, and it looks as if this assumption is just one more example of the correlation fallacy at work. When later studies were controlled for the effects of poverty and other variables, little if any relationship remained between density and social pathology (Freedman, 1975; Galle & Gove, 1979). It seems that, as with the re-evaluation of animal density studies, we need to be cautious in assuming high-density living causes social disruption. Rather, if there is any overall synthesis emerging, it seems the link between density and social disruption reflects the impact of some third factor such as poverty, low education, social oppression, or poor mental health. Put simply, the poor and insane cannot afford luxury mansions and therefore live crowded lives.

It is certainly true that many believe inner-city, high-density living is aversive, and there is considerable prejudice that sees relatively high population concentrations in publicly funded housing estates as breeding grounds for delinquency:

Newspaper reports reinforce the popular image of public housing projects as huge nests of crime and delinquency . . . and as the domicile of unregenerate and undeserving families whose children urinate only in the elevators. (Gans, 1968, quoted in Mullins & Robb, 1977, p. 575)

Residents often think differently (Bryson & Thompson, 1972; Amerigo & Aragones, 1990). A study of residents' assessment of a New Zealand public-housing estate, Porirua, outside Wellington, found little social pathology. The study, conducted by Patrick Mullins of Queensland University and Professor J.H. Robb of Victoria University, Wellington, found: "In contrast with both popular opinion and the findings of much research (notably American), residents responded to their dwelling and residential environment in a largely positive way." A home of your own, contact with neighbours, with family and friends close by, were all sources of satisfaction. While they did find that residents sharing multiple occupancy dwellings were less satisfied than those in single-family units, this had more to do with the prevailing ethic of single-family dwelling than space invasion, and on the whole residents viewed their town of some 30 000 with some satisfaction (Mullins & Robb, 1977).

Notwithstanding similar findings, other studies have shown that increased spatial density is clearly aversive. To interpret this apparent contradiction we will first need to reiterate the role of other factors like poverty (Kraus, 1975) and distinguish between density and crowding, and then consider, once again, the important role of social perception. As you read on, note that the remaining discussion revolves around two issues: that our reaction to any population density depends on our circumstances, and how we feel about it.

Density and perceived overcrowding

Unlike animals, social perception plays a major part in our experience of high density and we need to distinguish between it and crowding (Stokols, 1972; Paulus, 1980; Peay & Peay, 1983). *Density* is the number of people in a given space and *crowding* is our emotional reaction to that density. Stokols emphasised that simply increasing social density does not automatically increase crowding. In many situations, high density increases our pleasure, as at a rock concert, where it leads to a sense of community and involvement as anonymity decreases accountability (Westin, 1967), while in other situations of equal density, such as packed peak-hour trains, we feel overcrowded. Many factors combine in deciding if high density equals overcrowding.

Basic theories of overcrowding

As you will notice from the references, the 1970s was a decade of vigorous research on the effects of crowding and gave an impetus to the emergence of environmental psychology. The hundreds of published studies are impossible to review here but Daniel Stokols (1976) noted seven theoretical perspectives emerged to explain crowding's effects. We will briefly review these in lieu of a more detailed consideration and if you are interested in reading further,

As we have seen, many high-density estates are relatively tranquil. However, popular wisdom would have us believe that high density and low income inevitably lead to vandalism and residential decay. These inner-city terraces are part of an area extensively vandalised and gutted by fire. How do you account for these differences? (Photo: Gavin Price)

environmental load theory
Broad environmental factors which lead to increased autonomic arousal, overload and escape behaviours.

arousal theory
We are automatically aroused by others' presence.

mere presence
The more people present, the more aroused we will become, a biological rather than a psychological process; simply adding people will arouse us.

start with Baum and Epstein (1978). Most of the research reviewed by Stokols (1976) has the following underlying assumptions: overcrowding causes some form of behaviour constraint which leads to increased autonomic arousal, overload and escape behaviours. This explanation has a much broader environmental focus and has been developed into a major model by several theorists, perhaps most notably Cohen's 1978 **environmental load theory**.

Arousal theory (Evans, 1978) is perhaps the linchpin in understanding crowding. As we noted in Chapter Two, people are perceptually salient and we cannot avoid noticing them. However, their **mere presence** also has arousing effects on us which are unrelated to their actions. So the more people present, the more aroused we will become. This is a biological, rather than a psychological process; simply adding people will arouse us (Guerin, 1986; Geen & Bushman, 1989). Increasing density has an impact on our autonomic nervous system, causing heart rate, blood pressure, respiration and adrenalin secretions to increase, a classic stress reaction (Broadbent, 1971). The critical factor in how we interpret our arousal is the attributions we make. As we noted in Chapter Three, we prefer dispositional attributions and, when overcrowded, may mistakenly attribute our arousal to another's personality and behaviour rather than their mere presence. While this may explain our feelings, it does little to reduce our arousal, and if we make correct attributions this may lead to more appropriate coping responses (Worchel & Teddie, 1976; Aiello, Thompson & Brodzinsky, 1983).

Perceived control is also a factor in how we experience crowding. As we saw in Chapter Three, if we feel we are in control of our lives, we are less likely to experience negative emotions and to make inappropriate attributions. If high density is experienced as being aversive, or we are uncomfortably aroused, we will either try to reduce or avoid the perceived stressors. Several related theories support this approach. Social overload theory (Milgram, 1970) suggests crowding causes excessive stimulation which we then avoid. To reduce this excess stimulation we selectively process information, ignore social cues, or limit our social interaction. Two related approaches, privacy regulation (Altman, 1975) and excessive interaction (Baum & Valins, 1977), both emphasise avoidance and altering our social obligations to limit our exposure. If you are interested in reading further on the role of privacy regulation in limiting excessive interaction, see Finighan (1980) for a report on how over 200 Melburnians used the home as a means of social control and of achieving individual and family privacy.

Intent seems to play a role too. Being thwarted from acting as we wish, because there are too many people present, may easily lead to frustration and feeling overcrowded. If population density stops us achieving our goals, then these behavioural constraints (Schopler & Stockdale, 1977) or perceived interferences (Sundstrom, 1978) will be interpreted as limits to our personal freedom and as threats to the self. As such they are potentially dangerous and often lead to misattributions and aggressive behaviour towards innocent bystanders, as research into overcrowded prisons shows (Cox, Paulus & McCain, 1984).

In contrast to these psychological models, ecological factors (Barker, 1968) also shape how we see density. Too many people trying to share too few resources is a powerful disincentive towards large-scale social cohesion. Here perceptions do not relate to population density but rather the potential division of resources. Desiring an inequitable share may lead you to feel overcrowded, though in reality this is not the case. For instance, I recently heard a right-wing Afrikaner on Radio National defending proposals to repatriate South Africa's migrant guest workers as a measure to reduce population pressure and "ensure a fairer share of resources among real black South Africans and maintain our current lifestyle". This denies the reality that South Africa is a rich country with a modest population density (26.1 per sq. km) relative to its resource base. Resource pressures ensure powerful defence of territory and exclusion of those not considered part of your primary group (Wicker, 1979).

Density perceptions largely determine how we view population pressures and there is much evidence showing how variable this may be. In some cultures high density is not an entirely negative experience (Baum & Paulus, 1987) and there are substantial cultural differences (Gillis, Richard & Hagan, 1986). It seems our perceptions are governed in part by our upbringing which sets a base rate expectation for personal space. Feeling overcrowded then seems an essentially psychological process. Baum and Valins (1977) made a valuable contribution to our understanding by distinguishing between the effects of spatial and social density. If we double the number of people in a room we are manipulating **social density**. If we put the original number in a room half the size as the one they were in, we have altered **spatial density**. In both cases density has doubled but we are more disturbed by the former than the latter (Paulus, 1980).

Why are additional people more aversive than less space? After all the

social density
The number of people in a given space.

spatial density
The amount of space a set number of people occupy.

distance between people is the same. The reasons are not entirely clear but probably have to do with the arousing effects of others' mere presence. Baum and Valins (1979) suggest it is a combination of behavioural constraints, interference and social salience. People are more immediately aware of others and the problems their presence brings. We are less able to ignore their needs and right to share resources. We cannot avoid them and have to plan our interactions taking them into account. This limits opportunities and increases frustration at a greater rate than a lack of space does. For instance, Ruback and Carr (1984) found that prisoners sharing cells were more stressed and felt more out of control than those in smaller but single accommodation. Baum and Paulus (1987) remind us that high spatial density also has its problems but it is clear that they are less onerous than the effects of high social density.

Density or intensity?

As we have seen, overcrowding is a psychological process rather than just a reaction to a lack of space. The sheer variability of our responses led Freedman (1975) to argue that rather than density causing adverse reactions, it merely intensifies our reaction to the situations we find ourselves in. If these are positive, like a rally, crowded conditions would heighten our enjoyment; if we are in a crowded commuter train, each additional person intensifies our discomfort. Freedman's theory predicts that a bad reaction to a crowded train is basically a response to an adverse situation rather than a reaction to density as such. In his view, density intensifies an effect, it does not cause it.

density-intensity model
How we perceive social density determines our reaction to it. Also known as perceived density.

Freedman's **density-intensity model** caused some debate within environmental psychology and, while some studies found evidence to support his effect, others found instances where it did not apply (Prerost, 1981; Nieuwenhuijsen & de-Waal, 1982). This led Freedman to modify his model and acknowledge that density may also cause effects in its own right and these may be additive to his density-intensification model (Freedman & Perlick, 1979). What did emerge from this debate was a clear indication that density and the nature of our reactions were often quite disparate. For example, Gordon O'Brien and Michael Pembroke, of Flinders University, contrasted the job satisfaction of 195 clerical workers in the South Australian Public Service, with their perceived crowding. After controlling for actual physical density and other variables, they found that feeling crowded had little to do with being satisfied with your job, and that skills utilisation was a much greater predictor of job satisfaction. Density and crowding related to quite different aspects of job satisfaction (O'Brien & Pembroke, 1982).

perceived density
How we perceive social density determines our reaction to it.

Whether we feel crowded or not is further confused by our est*imates* of density. Rapoport (1975) called this **perceived density** and offered it as a further explanation of our variable responses. If we think we are crowded we will react as if we are. Our base rate for comparison is also important and would explain the many differences in density preferences found in cross-cultural studies. If you are accustomed to high-density living, you will feel less crowded.

Density or proximity?

Feeling crowded is more than just living in a densely populated area. The space you have in your primary territory may be more influential on your perceptions than the density of your locality. Eric Knowles would go further and suggest it is rather others' proximity than even the amount of space you have, or the actual population density, that is the major factor influencing your judgment (Knowles, 1979, 1983). Hong Kong, for example, has the highest population density of any state (5440 per sq. km) but many of the richer residents living on The Peak have as much space as any in the Western world, and some elderly people are socially isolated and rarely see others, in a town where the average dwelling unit is a single room for nine people and more than 30 per cent sleep three or more to a bed (Turk & Turk, 1988).

Nor is it simply a question of proximity since the actual space we enjoy may be illusory. Apartment dwellers in some major cities may live at site densities approaching that of an average Hong Kong resident but experience little discomfort, because their high-rises, though housing more people per hectare, are designed to minimise exposure to other residents. Architecture plays a big part in how we use our environment (Beattie, 1980) and in limiting our perception of others' closeness (Sommer, 1969). Further support

Many people in the West live at site densities equivalent to those of Asian cities. What is important is the quality of the space, not how much we have.
(Photo: Gavin Price)

for this distinction comes from a New Zealand study of pedestrians' helping behaviour as influenced by city size and immediate pedestrian density. If you recall our discussion of helping behaviour in Chapter Ten, the overload theory proposed that as city size increases helping behaviour decreases. However, this has often been difficult to confirm experimentally. Kammann, Thompson and Irwin (1979) of Otago University replicated the retrieval of lost letters study and found that immediate pedestrian density was a more important indicator of helping than general population density. While the researchers were interested in the diffusion-of-responsibility effects on helping behaviour, the results also illustrate the effects of proximity.

Proxemics

Support for the view, that it is another's proximity rather than actual density that disturbs us, also derives from the work of cultural anthropologist, Edward Hall (1959, 1963, 1966), who found that we have body space zones into which we restrict others' access. Hall found that while all societies had similar rules for how close they would allow certain people to come, the actual distances differed depending on culture and the individual. The more intimate we are, the closer we allow others. Hall concluded that both culture and experience modified a basic genetic potential to be wary of strangers and it is likely this is a factor in our perception of crowding. People who move too close to us are threatening and intrusive. Hall found that when we are in high density situations which force us into close contact with strangers, we act defensively in much the same ways as we cope with overcrowding (Smith & Knowles, 1979).

proxemics
The study of body-space zones.

Hall called his study of these zones **proxemics** and found we surround ourselves with envelopes of space which we regard as extensions of ourselves, and regulate access depending on the type of relationship we have (or desire). The *intimate zone* extends 0–450 cm and we only permit lovers, our children and the very dear into this zone: friends and everyday acquaintances are permitted into our *personal zone* (300–1200 cm). The *social zone* (1–3 m) regulates our contacts with strangers; while we reserve a special distance, the *public zones* (beyond 3 m) for formal occasions like lecturing, where this distance serves a number of social purposes, such as enhancing status (see Figure 13.4). Age and sex play a part in varying the distances we set for these zones as does culture. For example, Jenny Noesjirwan (1978), using Hall's proxemic notation system, found Indonesians had smaller interpersonal distances than Australians and were less inhibited about bodily contact, though after allowing for similar cultural variations, these zones are common across all cultures (Hall, 1966).

Obviously these zones are only for deliberate interactions, as we constantly permit brief violations of our intimate zones as part of the give-and-take of everyday life, as when we walk down a crowded street. Notwithstanding their casualness, Hall maintains they are intrusions which have an impact and are only tolerable because they are governed by rules specific to each time and place. It is permissible for instance to push into a crowded bus and stand physically crushed against a complete stranger for some distance, causing a gross and extended penetration of intimate space; however eye

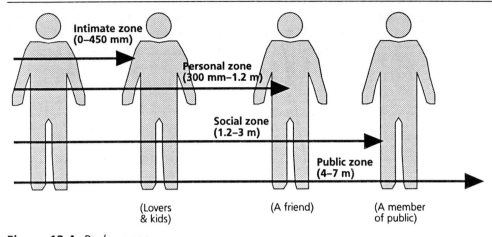

Figure 13.4 *Body zones*

Source: Adapted from Hall, 1966.

contact or any other acknowledgment, beyond a muttered apology, violates the polite fiction of pretending you are not intruding into their space. Riding a packed bus or train and observing these unspoken pacts is always a salutary reminder of the power of a culture's unwritten rules.

These zones act as buffers, preventing unwanted intrusions from becoming unmanageable. Unlike territories, which are fixed and defended, personal space zones change as our social context varies. As such they are often revealing, and our reactions to space invasions may often reveal how each person really feels about the other, or the intimacy of their interaction—

(Cartoonist: Graeme Mitchell)

but not always (Baker & Shaw, 1980). Culture and other factors again vary responses to intrusions. At a consular reception many years ago I observed a tall, elderly European in elegant evening dress talking animatedly in fluent French to a very diminutive and equally dapper Asian. For over thirty minutes I watched them gradually shuffle backwards around the reception hall, as the Asian gentleman backpedalled, distancing himself from the other. They were obviously friends and quite unconsciously backed up over 15 metres or more, as each attempted without success to reach a comfortable interpersonal distance. Such effects can be deliberately manipulated as door-to-door salesmen know all too well. Apart from cultural factors, several Australian studies have shown that situationally induced anxiety (Brady & Walker, 1978); neuroticism and extroversion (Katsikitis & Brebner, 1981; Khew & Brebner, 1985); and conservatism (Ray, 1984), all increase our need for larger body zones (see Box 13.4). Clearly there are many factors that influence our personal space needs and how we react to population pressures.

Box 13.4 *Predicting violence using a measure of preferred interpersonal distance of imprisoned offenders*

Many theorists have identified a relationship between a larger interpersonal preferred distance (IPD) and a potential for violence. Explanations have ranged from alarm reactions and arousal, to territorial defence (Ardrey, 1966). Whatever the reason, the simple observation that violent people prefer a larger interpersonal distance would, on the face of it, have enormous predictive value, but how do we measure this accurately? If we use this observation to treat people differently, we may abuse their civil liberties.

A number of theorists have grappled with the problem of measurement with mixed success, and over time four main methods have developed. Field studies have observed IPD in seating arrangements and the like in natural settings, but suffer from difficulties of making unobserved measurements and gave conflicting results (Aiello & Jones, 1971). Physiological measures like galvanic skin responses and other measures of arousal are cumbersome and time consuming to obtain. Simulation techniques, usually paper and pencil scales, ask the subject to imagine and rate how uncomfortable they would be as their IPD is invaded. While partially successful, they are underdeveloped psychometrically and again show conflicting results and weak

correlations. Experimental manipulations of IPD, like asking subjects to approach targets until they reach their IPD, or telling the experimenter when someone has moved too close, have been the preferred method, but suffer a number of methodological difficulties including problems of control, consistency across subjects, and sorting out the effects that other variables, like the characteristics of the person being approached, have on the IPD measure.

These were the reasons advanced by Frank Walkey and Ross Gilmour of Victoria University, Wellington, for developing a videotaped measure of interpersonal distance to offset some of these methodological difficulties (Walkey & Gilmour, 1979). Their measure consisted of a taped sequence of a male actor, dressed casually, approaching another similarly dressed stationary actor. There were five sequences where the stationary actor could be approached from the front, back, side, or at two 45° front or back approaches. In each case the approaching actor stopped at distances from 150 to 15 centimetres. Combining two variables, first the angle of approach, and second, the distance from the target, gave 35 possible combinations of IPD. These sequences were presented twice in a random order. Subjects were asked to imagine they were the person being approached and after each sequence record how comfortable they felt. This measure standardised the approaches made by others, as all subjects saw the same films, making it much easier to control for other variables. The measure had the added advantage of being economical to use and could be given in groups.

Althought the test was designed as a measure of predicting violence from IPD, it was first given to 50 male volunteer university students whose ratings were compared with their scores on four other IPD measures, to see how it would correlate with existing measures. Three of the measures were paper-and-pencil tests and the fourth was a controlled real-life situation in which a confederate actually approached the subject. Results were comparable with the controlled real-life situation and indicated that the videotaped measure was superior to pencil and paper techniques. They concluded:

> The video may be considered superior in a number of important respects to the other techniques examined. It overcomes the methodological problems associated with other techniques, it is reliable, valid, and is simple to use both with individuals and with groups. (Walkey & Gilmour, 1979, p. 579)

The next step was to test the measure with convicted prisoners to see if it could identify violent offenders by their larger IPD (Gilmour & Walkey, 1981). Seventy-three inmates at Wi Tako Prison volunteered to complete a videotaped measure of IPD. After this measure was taken, records were searched to classify each man as either violent or non-violent and for data on 17 other background variables the researchers thought might relate to IPD. Statistical analysis identified seven variables: current offence, group offence, IPD, family background, height, number of previous convictions and whether alcohol was involved in their offence, as the best combination to discriminate between violent and non-violent offenders, with 92 per cent of the subjects correctly identified as either violent or non-violent. A second analysis omitting the variable "current offence", showed that greater IPD was the next best discriminator. Though it was not possible to distinguish between these two groups on IPD alone, the results showed a clear and positive relationship between preferred IPD and violence. In combination then with the other variables, IPD would be a useful measure to predict which inmates were prone to further violence.

Having established that the IPD video measure was a useful tool in identifying violent offenders, the next step was to test its predictive capacity. Walkey and Gilmour (1984) followed up their 73 prison inmates twelve months later to see if those who had been involved in fights had significantly higher IPD scores. After they had divided these inmates into aggressors and victims, the researchers found a group of previously violent aggressors with very high IPD scores and a group of non-violent victims with very low IPD scores. Further statistical analysis indicated that IPD scores best predicted prison violence and gave a measure with which it was possible to predict fighting with a 71 per cent success rate.

Summary

Environmental psychology is a new disciplinary offshoot relying heavily on mainstream social psychology. It may be defined as the study of human behaviour and well-being in relation to the sociophysical environment. Environmental psychology emphasises our physical surroundings and the reciprocal interaction between behaviour and the environment. It has an applied and multidisciplinary focus.

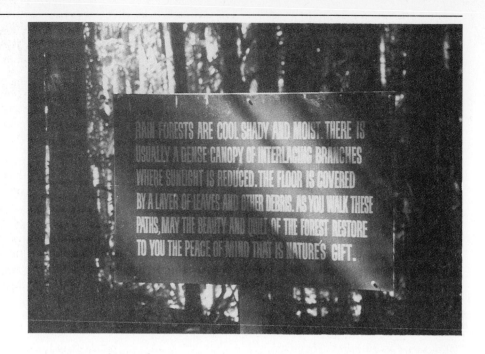

A major concern since its inception is encouraging pro-ecological attitudes and behaviour. Unfortunately people may have an environmental consciousness without changing their wasteful behaviour. Environmental education has proven a weak path to behavioural change as people are put off by the personal costs, the complexities of eco-degradation, discouraged by defections and limited by social traps. Many theorists have questioned whether attitudes change behaviour and this has been the case with environmental attitudes. There is some concern that environmentalism is becoming another passing fad.

Many environmentalists advocate reminders, reinforcements and legislation as a stronger path to pro-ecological change and all have proven effective. When using prompts as antecedent behaviour strategies, care needs to be taken to avoid psychological reactance. Positive reinforcement is often too expensive and not long lasting. Government regulation and the use of negative reinforcers has enforced pro-ecological behaviour, but there are few studies assessing its psychological impact.

The physical environment and humanity interact reciprocally. With an increasing consciousness of our surrounding's impact on psychological functioning, many studies have explored the relationship between the environment and behaviour. From a diverse field we have chosen weather and human spatial behaviour as illustrative examples.

Climate has a direct effect on behaviour though it is unlikely to directly affect national character. Rather, it sets potentials and influences our activities. With the climatic changes of the greenhouse effect, weather has become more important. Hot weather has been linked with increased suicides, and aggression and decreased performance, though both human variability and the effects of cognitive arousal need to be taken into account. Cold weather has similar effects, though they may be more insidious given clouding of consciousness.

Sunlight has a definite psychological effect of elevating mood. Most supporting evidence comes from research on depressives, who are thought to have an imbalance between temperature and sleep/waking circadian rhythms, leading to sleep disorders and depression. Sunlight entrains these rhythms, elevating mood and activity levels. There is no corresponding lunar influence. Multifactorial analyses of weather's influence on mood and behaviour have also found humidity and barometric pressure changes are correlated with the effects of temperature and sunlight.

Global population is increasing by three babies per second, making spatial behaviour potentially the most important aspect of applied environmental research. More people equals less space. There is little clear evidence for an innate human territorial drive, and studying hunter-gatherers suggests that territoriality is socially maintained. Territory is important as a status symbol, as a form of social control, regulates social behaviour, allows privacy and permits predictability in our lives. Spacing mechanisms like territorial calculus limit environmental stress.

Animal experiments on overcrowding and territorial intrusion have given mixed effects. Rat and pig studies have shown marked increases in physiological stress in crowded conditions and markedly aberrant behaviour. However such studies have been criticised as not reflecting natural mechanisms which in the wild control overpopulation. Moreover ape studies found that crowding increases positive social behaviour, casting doubt on the extent to which less complex animal behaviour may be applied to humans.

Urbanisation and human overcrowding has long been accepted as the cause of social disruption. The psychosocial pathology theory, a combination of the social overload and frustration-aggression hypotheses, saw high-density living as a major environmental stressor. More recent studies challenge this view, seeing it as another example of the correlational fallacy. They propose that earlier evidence may be explained by a third factor such as poverty or mental illness linking density and social disruption.

The negative effects of human overcrowding are seen as essentially perceptual and subjective. Whether we feel crowded depends on the level of environmental load we experience. Negative reactions to density have been explained by arousal and social overload, excessive stimulation and interference, privacy needs, behavioural constraints and ecological factors. The subjective nature of feeling crowded is further reinforced by social and spatial density distinctions, estimates of perceived density, density-intensity effects and the role of proximity.

Further evidence on the negative effects of crowding comes from the study of preferred interpersonal distances which predicts prison violence. Proxemics, the study of body space, illustrates the subjective effects of deliberate and casual intrusions into our personal zones.

Recommended reading

Bell P.A., Fisher J.D., Baum A. and Greene J.E. (1990) ENVIRONMENTAL PSYCHOLOGY (3rd edn) Holt, Rinehart and Winston, NY. By far the most comprehensive general environmental psychology text to date. Our chapter was structured to facilitate use of Bell as a primary reference in your further reading.

ENVIRONMENT AND BEHAVIOR published by Sage Publications. Very much the "trade" journal of environmental psychology. Recommended as your first port-of-call for a quick browse of recent environmental issues as Sage's editorial policy seems to favour readability.

Gifford R. (1987) ENVIRONMENTAL PSYCHOLOGY: PRINCIPLES AND PRACTICE, Allyn and Bacon, Boston. Dated and not as comprehensive as Bell, but does extend their coverage into areas not adequately covered. See Chapter 11, Working and Travelling and Chapter 13, Managing the Commons.

Stokols D. and Altman I. (eds) (1987) HANDBOOK OF ENVIRONMENTAL PSYCHOLOGY, Wiley, New York. A two-volume edited compendium of the leading environmental theorists, with a wide coverage of environmental psychology. A short-cut to journal publications prior to 1986.

SOCIAL PSYCHOLOGY AND THE LAW

14

A colleague reported ruefully that he had just caused a district court trial to be aborted and was glad it happened. My colleague, who is not a psychologist, received a jury summons and found himself empanelled on a rape trial. When he was called into the court he found the defendant to be a slight, heavily tattooed young man, who was accused of raping a former girlfriend. My friend admitted, with the benefit of hindsight, that he must have unconsciously recognised the defendant but at the time he just thought he reminded him of someone and wasn't sure whom. The defendant gave no indication that he knew my colleague and his name was a common one.

The trial was messy and the evidence far from satisfactory. The defendant admitted having sex with the woman and claimed she had consented. She denied this, though admitted she had approached the defendant with a view to resurrecting their relationship. Alcohol and violence were involved, both had been drinking heavily before they returned to the defendant's flat. The event was a little fuzzy in both parties' minds, but she had objected to the violence which was the deciding factor in going to the police. The defendant argued that most of her injuries were self-inflicted after the event, and that in any case a bit of violence had always been part of their love-making. The Crown relied on forensic evidence and the defence on trying to smear the woman's reputation. After three days of evidence, my friend didn't have the faintest idea what had actually happened and indeed doubted if either party did.

Not so the rest of the jury! During their rest periods the case was a hot topic, despite having been warned not to discuss it outside the jury room. The majority of women were sure the defendant was guilty. The minority of men were less definite but inclined to the view that the woman's reputation was suspect and her actions provocative. The defendant had several unfortunate mannerisms, and these, together with a slight disability and the tattoos, were sufficient to damn him in everyone's eyes. One male juror observed that even if he wasn't guilty, it would "teach his sort a bit of a lesson to do some time"! Another man argued that they should gaol the girl as she was "obviously a tart", turning up to give evidence dressed to kill, and further opined she had only got what "she really asked for". Unanimously the rest of the jury, which ran heavily to the retired and unemployed, observed it was quite interesting anyway!

My colleague was amazed and horrified that so important a decision could be treated in such a casual way and on such flimsy and spurious grounds. He complained to the jury foreman, an experienced juryman, and was told that, "It would be all right, every jury acts like that until they have to decide the case." My friend wasn't sure when he noted the vindictive gleams in some of their eyes. Anyway it was with mingled shock and relief when a piece of background evidence led him to recognise the defendant as a distant relative whom he had last seen when he was ten! The judge, who didn't appear at all happy with the case, gladly aborted the trial. My colleague observed that the experience was a real eye-opener and that this was just the sort of thing social psychologists should get around to studying.

Social psychology and the law

Social psychology offers us the opportunity to explore two worlds. On the one hand it is firmly based on the scientific method and employs rigorous empiricism to develop theories of human social behaviour. As well, many social psychologists are concerned with applying their theories to social problems in the real world, or practising their science. Social psychological knowledge has application to a wide variety of social issues and has often been described as a discipline with a scientific mind and a humanistic heart.

Social problems, however, are always influenced by a myriad of economic, political and social factors, so it is often impossible for social psychologists to explore a social issue or problem in its entirety. However, by focusing on the psychological aspects, they are often able to make important contributions to social change. Their knowledge may be applied in several ways: focusing attention on questions related to important social issues, such as the effects of unemployment; by applying theories and research evidence to design and implement intervention strategies and programmes; by providing information and advice to policy makers; and by evaluating outcomes of programmes and policies (Roden, 1985).

Our behaviour is shaped by both our physical and social environment. Many social psychologists study social interaction in applied settings such as the workplace, classroom or family. Studies conducted in real-life settings pose certain problems, and the more complex the situation being studied, the less control researchers have over variables that may influence outcomes. In these instances we have to exercise caution in making generalisations from such research. Nevertheless, remember there is nothing as practical as a good theory! (Lewin, 1951).

Given social psychology's applicability, virtually all social psychologists are also practitioners at some level, and having an applied emphasis is also a two-way street. Knowledge gained from the field in turn informs theory, and so many applied areas have become research fields in their own right. This process is not a stagnant one, many new areas are emerging from under social psychology's aegis. Social psychologists are making major contributions in community development, health care, tourism, environmental and urban design, policing, politics, education, organisational behaviour and management.

In our Preface we mentioned some of these offshoots but it would be impossible to cover them all in any real depth. So, rather than try a smorgasbord approach, we decided to take an in-depth look at just two areas. As practitioners who have come to social psychology from the field, we decided we would each write a chapter in our area of interest. While throughout this book we have cited many brief examples of applying social psychology, in the last chapter we explored environmental psychology at length. In this final chapter we will focus on the practice of applying social psychology to the law and justice.

The power of a state (and Law) is constituted not through the "power" exerted by a legal regime, but in its capacity to persuade people that the world described in its images and categories is the only attainable world. (Gordon, 1986, cited in Voyce, 1991, p. 24)

It is a myth of liberal legalism that the law is neutral or autonomous. The law is the central mechanism in our society for transmitting and legitimising values and in every age law has been shaped by the general characteristics of the civilisation of which it is part. (Gilmore, 1963, cited in Thornton, 1991, p. 28)

The Law's power rests in many symbols.
(Photos: Chris Simkin; Armen Deushian/ Macarthur Advertiser)

The law is not autonomous from society or neutral and the legal system does not provide an impartial arena in which contestants may resolve differences. (Starr & Collier, 1989, cited in Voyce, 1991, p. 17)

Today there is a greater intrusion of the law into every level of the social process and our legal tradition operates within a social, economic, political and intellectual context which reinforces the dominant social paradigm: "The law is not neutral and upholds the capitalist imperative and the dominance of white Anglo-Celtic maleness" (Thornton, 1991). As we can see from the three quotations, those who hold such views argue that the law is neither impartial nor fair and does much to shape the nature of social relationships. Alternatively, the law itself may be just a reflection of society and its social mores. Voyce (1991) argues these two views are not mutually exclusive and may in fact sustain each other in a mutually interactive way. The law changes as society changes but also contributes to such changes. Whatever the case, the fact that such views are debated demonstrates that there are inherent tensions in our legal system. As Graycar (1991) observed: "People's lives do not fit readily into legal categories." Yet this has not been reflected in a legal system which fragments its treatment of individuals' problems.

Furthermore, the law changes slowly and social change proceeds apace, often leaving the law floundering in the wake of social subtleties. Even hallowed notions of "equality before the law" and "justice for all" are being seriously questioned and can no longer be abstracted from the social, economic and political context. Attempting to administer equal treatment to "unequals" does not lead to equality of outcome, does it?

The legal system and the law itself provide a fruitful domain of study for social psychologists and over the last decade there has been increased interest in the interface between psychology and the law. This topic is now recognised as a major applied area in social psychology. Many of the fundamental assumptions underlying law-making and the legal process are psychological and reflect a social construction of our world and human action. Social psychologists study how we interact with the legal system and, in particular, researchers have focused on aspects of criminal law and the criminal justice process including: the causes of crime and criminal behaviour; victims/survivors of crime; police and policing; eyewitness testimony; assessment issues such as predicting dangerousness; jury decision-making processes; sentencing procedures; attitudes to capital punishment, and so on.

The operation of the Criminal Justice system cannot be understood by examining laws, policies and procedural guidelines, mainly because the actual operation of the system consists of the various behaviours of the participants and in most cases these behaviours are highly discretionary, and thus only loosely constrained by the rule of law. (Konecni & Ebbeson, 1982, p. 5)

Many observers have noted a widening gap between what the law purports to do and what actually happens in practice. They argue that applying social psychology will make an important contribution to understanding why this is happening. For example, it can help us understand and interpret the framework within which the law and legal system operates, how well the law works, who rules, and for whom, and to evaluate various procedures and propose models for reform and change. In this final chapter it is not possible to examine every aspect of the criminal justice process. We have chosen to focus on several areas where social psychologists have been active: raising issues of gender equity; the plight of victims; the nature of police and policing; and a close look at practices within the courtroom. We turn now to the first of these areas, gender and the law.

Gender and the law

Evatt (1991) noted that the law remains permeated with patriarchial values and as the state has always been patriarchial in nature, this is an important determinant of how we construct and understand our social relations. Graycar (1991) notes the entrenched maleness of the law and its often implicit gender assumptions. Ideas of property and private ownership pre-suppose a public/private dichotomy and this is reflected in legal regulation, which is traditionally resistant towards the more human-centred and caring values of private life. Traditionally, men own property and women look after it for them. So notions of ownership significantly reinforce patriarchial assumptions about how we should structure our relationships and this becomes entrenched in the law. Graycar and other authors argue the private–public concept is oppressive, relegating women to a private sphere which is not the law's concern. "The more the courts subscribe to 'legal objectivity' through procedure the more effectively patriarchial they become; the norm of 'legal objectivity' thus institutionalising men's interests." (McKinnon, 1983, cited in Voyce, 1991)

Whether this is an adequate reflection of reality depends on your viewpoint, however, it is clear that women have fared less well before the courts than men. The law's treatment of women has a long history and the ways in which women have been characterised is obvious from legal discourse and has been well documented. Traditionally, the law sees women in terms of their relationships with others: as dependants of men; as wives, lovers and mothers; and women with "reproductive capacities" (Graycar & Morgan, 1990). While this has in the past given women lenient sentences, such as "not guilty by virtue of her sex" (of unsound mind), on the whole it has worked to limit women's opportunities before the law. As Smart notes:

> Where women resort to law their status is always imbued with specific meanings arising out of their gender. They go to law as mothers, wives, sexual objects, pregnant women, deserted mothers, single mothers and so on. They are not simply women . . . and they are most definitely not ungendered persons. (Smart, 1990, p. 7)

What are the consequences for women in the legal system? Smart (1990) argues that while there are areas of the law which specifically

As women gradually become more senior in the criminal justice system, will this change gender attitudes? (Photo: courtesy Superintendent Christine Nixon)

identify women with their childbearing role, gender neutral areas of legal doctrine, such as contract and torts, are rarely perceived as being relevant to women. Of course to see the law as the panacea of gender inequities is perhaps misguided and may lead to heavy-handed legal solutions which often have unpredictable consequences. Yet many authors argue the law should at least recognise and deal with its traditional view of women. As we saw in Chapter Eleven, gender expectations are self-perpetuating unless challenged.

Perhaps part of the answer is to reform the legal system and, in particular, the heavily male judiciary itself. It was not until well into the twentieth century that women were permitted to practise law in Australia and New Zealand, so it is not surprising that despite large increases in numbers of women graduates, women are still in minimal numbers in the judiciary and the more rarefied echelons of the legal profession (Weisbrot, 1990).

Victims and survivors of crime

It is often said that victims gets victimised twice, once by the offender and then again by the criminal justice process. Traditionally, the community, police and other agents of the criminal justice system have focused attention on crime per se and offenders, and have tended to neglect the needs of victims/survivors of crime. It is only since the 1970s that the needs and rights of victims and their position in the criminal justice process have been given increasing attention and recognition.

It is often held that as the criminal justice system has evolved, community interests and the interests of the state have been predominant over the interests of the individual. The whole community may therefore be said to be victimised by the commission of a crime. (NSW Task Force on Services for Victims of Crime, 1987, p. 1)

As we saw in Chapter Three, society's reactions to victims of violent crime is often to blame the victim for the offence. Victims and/or survivors of crime not only have to deal with their own difficulties, but also with society's views which in many instances are less than helpful. Symonds (1975) noted several reactions to the victims of violent crime and identifies three typical response patterns: assumptions about the victim provoking or stimulating an attack; isolating the victim after an attack; and indifference to the plight of victims.

Non-victims often feel that they differ from victims of crime in some way (Bard & Sangrey, 1986). Stigmatising the victim as somehow different allows us to say, "I'm not like that" and "it won't happen to me". Most of us would like to believe in the illusion of a just world, where good is rewarded and evil is punished, but this belief is constantly contradicted by reality. Innocent people suffer and are injured or killed every day. In order to reconcile this contradiction many consciously or unconsciously believe

In 1992, nine-year-old Ebony Simpson was brutally murdered. Those close to her share in her victimisation.
(Photo: Rob Pozo/Macarthur Advertiser)

that somehow victims must have "done something to deserve it". As we saw in our previous discussion of attribution processes in Chapter Three, research suggests that a belief in a just world leads to an uncomfortable cognitive dissonance which makes us feel vulnerable and powerless. Consequently, many people search for someone to blame. Social problems that resist solutions need a scapegoat:

> The most logical scapegoat is the one who makes us feel guilty—the victim . . . In Ancient times the messenger who brought bad news was sometimes punished or killed. Today our reaction to the bearer of bad tidings may be less overt, but the punishing intention of stigmatisation reflects a similar unwillingness to face the truth. (Bard & Sangrey, 1986, p. 90)

Before we can address the very real problems of victims, we need to understand its impact. In Australia, this information is gathered by the police and by the Australian Bureau of Statistics (ABS). Two victim surveys were conducted by the ABS in 1975 and 1983 and gave similar findings to overseas studies. Many victims chose not to compound their difficulties by involving the police. Approximately 60 per cent of the crimes listed in the survey were not reported and, for example, the 1983 survey of 3500 respondents found that only 25 per cent of sexual assaults but 94 per cent of motor vehicle thefts were reported to the police, which underscores the dilemmas victims of violence face. The survey found that victims of threatened or actual violence were more likely to have been assaulted before, and often by the same assailant, who was known to them before the assault (NSW Task Force, 1987).

Statistics and crime victim surveys

In 1989 the Australian Institute of Criminology conducted a phone survey of 2012 Australians over the age of 16, and found that approximately 5 per cent had been a victim of crime in the preceding 12 months. Again, violent crimes were less likely to be reported than robbery or theft, and 63.8 per cent of victims of threatened or actual assault did not notify the police. What crime does to victims and why reporting rates are so low will become obvious shortly. While such survey information is useful it has its limitations:

- Surveys by their nature tend to under-report, or report offences by categories which may give a false impression of the true extent of crime.
- Classification of offences is based on respondents' perceptions of various offences and does not always correspond with legal or police definitions.
- Specific types of crime are likely to be under-reported. These include the more intimate types of violent crime such as domestic violence, sexual assault and child abuse which we discussed in Chapter Seven.
- Such surveys tell us little about the nature of the victim or provide much data about the actual offence.
- Fraud and white collar crimes are not as detectable by the victims and are often not reported to avoid embarrassment.

- Memory of respondents is not infallible and may be influenced by a number of factors which we will discuss in our section on eyewitness testimony.

The media

There is ongoing debate about the extent of media influence on our perceptions of crime. While the electronic and print media's coverage of victims' suffering has increased public awareness of a previously neglected area, victims have also been exploited by the media (Grabosky, 1989). Several researchers have noted how homicides and crimes of sexual violence are over-represented and over-reported in proportion to their actual incidence. Newsworthy or not, this tends to create a level of fear in the community which is both unjustified and unrealistic. Sensational reporting of violent crime distorts the reality of the crime and in many instances leads to an intrusion on victims'/families' dignity and privacy. Also, such reporting might prejudice a fair trial and is a cause for continuing concern.

A report by the NSW Sexual Assault Committee (1985–87) outlined some effects that may result from sensational media practices. These may encourage: a fear of crime; the non-reporting of further offences modelled upon those reported in the media (copycat offences); insensitive and intrusive scrutiny of victims and their families; and distortion of the nature of the crime, particularly emphasis on **stranger-danger**, whereas most victims know the offender. Such coverage often seems to reinforce and perpetuate myths and stereotypes about crimes such as sexual assault and inappropriately focus on victims' behaviour, such as what they were wearing and what they had been doing prior to the offence; or once again blaming the victim (see Box 14.1).

stranger-danger
A child's fear of strangers induced by parents to protect their children.

(Photo: Chris Simkin)

The victim's perspective

Without the voices of those who are violated, without their courage in speaking out about their experience, we are unable to establish what is truth. Their courage is in speaking out the truth of violence. The truth which is the experience of the victim and not the fabrication of the

---

Box 14.1 *Trial by media: Chamberlain revisited*

Australia's most famous and controversial trial involved the disappearance of baby Azaria Chamberlain from a tent at Ayers Rock in 1980. While at first it was thought that a dingo had taken the child, her mother Lindy Chamberlain was eventually convicted of killing her daughter and gaoled. Subsequently, the trial and the evidence were examined exhaustively in several appeals and informally throughout the nation. Lindy Chamberlain was eventually released and then pardoned by the Northern Territory Government. Many argued the media had aborted any chance of Lindy having a fair trial.

Howe (1989) provides an interesting analysis of the media in an article entitled "Chamberlain revisited: The case against the media". Howe argues: "It was a witch-hunt, a media orchestrated witch-hunt in which the question of Lindy's criminality and guilt was predetermined by the Australian media." Howe notes the media seemed obsessed with Lindy's appearance at the original inquest rather than the evidence. They reported she was dressed "in a fairly sexy sort of way", and during the second inquest "wore a different dress every day". On one day, a journalist commented "she would look like a schoolgirl . . . and on the next she would look like a

filmstar with a black dress, red lips, shoes and handbag". Her pregnancy fuelled more media-instigated rumours. Was her pregnancy a play for sympathy? Who would convict a pregnant woman? Headlines began to characterise her and she ceased being an ordinary woman and became The Guilty Mother, Azaria's Mother, The young mother with far away eyes, and The Dingo Baby Mother (Howe, 1989, cited in Graycar & Morgan, 1990).

Accompanying these reports was also detailed information which focused on her "weird, unnatural and non-stereotypical behaviour". Howe argues her portrayal as "unnaturally impassive and lacking emotion" convinced Australians and women in particular that she was guilty. They interpreted media reports of her dress and manner as "her flaunting, during the trial, of her tanned shoulder and her wardrobe. Their logic was that a woman interested in looking attractive at such a time must be a bad woman and everyone knows that a bad woman cannot be a good mother" (Goldsworthy, 1986, cited in Howe, 1989). Given these factors, it was impossible, many commentators argued, for the Chamberlains to have a fair trial.

---

perpetrator. This truth which comes from receiving violence as compared to initiat-ing violence, this truth has held a mirror to our community. In it we have seen reflected a new and sharpened image of ourselves. (Gilmore, 1989, p. 6)

There are many factors that influence the reactions of victims of crime, and of course, "every crime against a person is an act of violation" (Bard & Sangrey, 1986). In part, victims' reactions will depend on their personality and the severity of the offence. Research with victims of violent crime and other traumatic events suggests that there are many similarities in victims'/survivors' reactions and often these tend to follow a predictable pattern. These responses include immediate, short-term and long-term reactions. The following is drawn from Bowie's *Coping with Violence* (1989).

Initial reactions

Immediate reactions are often characterised by numbness, or disorientation, denial, disbelief, feelings of vulnerability, and loneliness and powerlessness.

frozen fright
A pseudo-calm detachment in crime victims which may last days; anxiety and sleep disturbance are the most common initial responses and other physiological reactions such as headaches may occur with associated psychosomatic symptoms.

Victims may also experience hyperactivity or **frozen fright**, that is a pseudo-calm detachment lasting from hours to days. Anxiety and sleep disturbance are the most common initial responses and other physiological reactions such as headaches may occur with associated psychosomatic symptoms.

Short-term reactions

This stage may last from three to eight months and includes emotional reactions which may alternate between fear and anger, sadness and elation, and self-pity to guilt and self-blame. Victims may experience a loss of identity, self-respect and many feel an erosion of trust and autonomy, and rejection by others. Symptoms associated with post-traumatic stress may be experienced such as insomnia, restlessness, agitation, uncontrollable crying, fear and avoidance behaviour, and intrusive and persistent thoughts about the event.

Long-term reactions

In many instances victims eventually reach a stage of acceptance or resolution by developing more effective or different coping strategies, or reversing attitudes and values. However, victims/survivors of violent crime may continue to experience reactions which continue long-term.

Coping with victimisation

For many victims and survivors, traumatic incidents are accompanied by a number of losses and a re-evaluation of beliefs and attitudes. These may include: a loss of control over one's present and future; lack of trust in God and other people; feeling it is no longer a just world; diminished self-esteem; and feelings of vulnerability and mortality (Bowie, 1989). Janoff-Bulman (1983) has suggested there are two main types of coping strategies which victims may employ to adjust to these losses: intrapsychic/cognitive responses, such as self-blame or redefining the event, and direct behavioural responses such as reporting the offence, initiating legal action, improving security, moving location, seeking professional assistance and establishing support networks.

Bowie (1989) suggests that the process of adjustment and recovery involves the following issues:

* Making sense of or redefining the event.
* Re-establishing a sense of control over one's life.
* Restoring a feeling of self-esteem and trust in others.
* Re-establishing meaning or purpose.
* Re-establishing balance and planning for the future.

One further point before we move on. Taylor (1989) notes that the term *victim* should also be extended to include others, such as family, friends, and police and health workers, who are also affected by their support of victims of violent crimes.

Police and policing

Academic study and research into police and policing has aroused much interest in the law, criminology, sociology and social psychology. The effectiveness of society's legal response depends upon police practice and procedure and their perception of their role in the criminal justice process. Policing is an increasingly difficult profession, which operates in a complex sociopolitical context. It involves the prevention of crime; the detection, investigation and apprehension of offenders; and the preservation of peace and order. Policing the community involves working with a variety of groups differing in language, socioeconomic status and different cultural backgrounds. In many instances these groups are in conflict or at least in tension (Moir & Moir, 1992). As such the police are expected to "hold the line, to piece together the parts of a fragile and sometimes fragmentary social consensus . . . In short the police are being asked to assume more responsibility at a time when difficult social circumstances exist" (Wilson, 1989).

Perception of the police is critical to their effectiveness. Recent initiatives in community-based policing seek to reduce the distance between police and civilians. (Photo: Armen Deushian/ Macarthur Advertiser)

"Civilians have seldom understood the real danger inherent in police work. It has never been particularly hazardous to the body. This line of work has always been a threat to the spirit" (Wambaugh, 1987). The nature of policing is inherently psychological and "police work entails a privileged vantage point in the affairs of society" (McGrath, 1983). Police decision-making can have a profound effect on who and what is policed and, ultimately, who is convicted. The role of the police forms an integral part of enforcement of justice in our society and we live in a society where the social order is constantly in a state of flux and change:

> One aspect of the myriad unintended consequences of such social change has been a reduction in our collective and structural capacity for self-control and self-maintenance. Increasingly we rely upon specialised institutions and agencies to perform tasks previously undertaken by individuals or by local and less formal agencies. In short we have become harder to police and in greater need of the services of the modern institution of police. We have come to enjoy more and more freedoms, and yet that freedom has become more vulnerable to encroachment and abuse as it depends upon the activities of specialised and bureaucratically organised state and other agencies. (Bradley & Cioccorelli, 1989, p. 2)

Who and what are the police? How would you define them? Consider the following definitions:

> The police are an agency of government which enforces law and keeps the peace.

> The police are a weapon the state uses to oppress the working classes, the poor and minorities.

> The police are the people who drive police cars.

(Klockars, 1985, p. 7)

All three definitions are what social psychologists label as norm-derivative. They are based on beliefs about what police "are on about" or the purposes or ends of policing (Klockars, 1985). Klockars argues that a definition of police should be based on means rather than ends and suggests that the means that distinguish police is coercive force. "No police anywhere has ever existed, nor is it possible to conceive of a genuine police ever existing that does not claim a right to compel other people forcibly to do something". Klockars proposes the following definition of police: "Police are institutions or individuals given the general right to use coercive force by the state within the state's domestic territory" (p. 12).

Recall our discussion of the bases of social power in Chapter Six. Ker Muir (1977), in his book entitled *Police: Streetcorner Politicians*, developed the **extortionate transaction model** to help us appreciate the nature of coercive power. His model is an abstract representation of all coercive relationships. An extortionate transaction exists whenever a threat is made by the "victimiser" to injure the "hostage" (something the victim values

extortionate transaction model
A model of coercive power in which a threat is made to injure a "hostage" (something the victim values) unless the victim pays a ransom (something they will give up to save the hostage from harm).

very much) unless the victim will pay a ransom (something they prefer to give up to save the hostage from harm) (Ker Muir, 1977). Ker Muir sees "four paradoxes of coercive power" which limit the police's coercive capabilities.

1. *The paradox of dispossession:* "The less one has, the less one has to lose." All of our valuable possessions, friendships, occupations, reputations and position in the community appear to give us power to resist coercion but may have the opposite effect, that is, make us weaker. For example, we pay our parking tickets and traffic fines, and most of us would not wish to be arrested but consider those who are different from us. Those without jobs, property or social standing, have little to lose. To coerce the truly dispossessed, police have to threaten their limited freedom, or their physical being.

2. *The paradox of detachment:* "The less the victim cares about preserving something, the less the victimiser cares about taking it hostage." This paradox concerns the meaning and values of a person's possessions. Police often confront incidents in which people are detached from things they would normally value, such as in a domestic violence situation, where an offender may injure others, smash possessions, damage property, and so on.

3. *The paradox of irrationality:* "The more delirious the threatener, the more serious the threat: the more delirious the victim, the less serious the threat." This paradox has to do with the element of the threat, the capacity of the victim to appreciate it and the willingness of the victimiser to enforce it. Police encounter many people who are affected by alcohol or drugs, are traumatised, psychiatrically disturbed or extremely angry. If people are so irrational that they cannot understand a threat, they cannot be made to comply, except by the use of coercive force.

4. *The paradox of face:* "The nastier one's reputation, the less nasty one has to be." For force to be an effective threat, the victim must believe that it will be carried out. Klockars (1985) suggests that if we wish to reduce the police's use of coercion, one way to achieve this may be for the police to develop a reputation for violence, but would we be willing to allow our police to engage in activities that would gain them such a reputation? We might end up in a vicious cycle of violence begets violence. The effect of such a reputation would inevitably shape the type of operational policing followed.

Ker Muir's model of the extortionate transaction and the four paradoxes of coercive power present police with choices about how to respond to the challenges of coercive power and have implications for various styles of operational policing.

Policing does not occur in a vacuum, so remember that analyses of police and policing cannot be understood apart from the political and social context in which they occur. Police bureaucracies have often been described as quasi-military bureaucratic structures which are rule-based and command-

Occupational identity: The police culture

driven. For social psychologists an understanding of how police view the world, and their role in it, is vital to analysing what they actually do.

> All organisations develop ideologies to defend their prerequisites, rationalise their errors and fallibilities, spin out myths of sacredness and self-righteousness and transform all that the practitioner sees and does. (Manning, 1977, cited in Findlay & Hogg, 1988, p. 146)

While to some extent occupational groups may develop a subculture, the structure and nature of police organisations and police work lends itself to a more pervasive subculture than in other occupations. The concept of occupational culture may be extended by arguing that there may be several police subcultures: patrol-car culture, detective culture, street culture, management culture, and so forth. Many researchers have attempted to identify and delineate characteristics of the police culture (Lundman, 1980; McGrath, 1983; Skolnick, 1985; Brogden, Jefferson & Walklate, 1988; Fielding, 1989). For many, the concept of a "police culture" conjures up negative images. These include:

- Insularity of police organisations.
- Negative views of human nature: no one is to be trusted.
- Notions of "us" and "them".
- Codes of silence, or pressure not to "blow the whistle" on colleagues who engage in unethical conduct.
- Emotional hardening: defensiveness.
- Cynicism: the NRMA syndrome (nothing really matters anymore), "You can't do the job and play the game at the same time."

Yet there may be advantages in affiliating with the culture, such as a sense of belonging, camaraderie, support from colleagues, or pride in the job (recall our discussion on cohesive groups in Chapter Twelve).

Although it is difficult to define or to describe how the police culture operates, it rests on a set of beliefs about the nature of police work itself.

> There has been an almost universal notion that police duties were mainly a matter of mayhem and violence, and that the police role was a never ending series of life and death confrontations with armed criminals, desperate fugitives and thrill-seeking psychopaths. Like so many heroic images out of our past this one will not stand up to examination. (Sherman, 1973, p. 390)

Recent evidence suggests that this image is incorrect as most police time is spent in non-criminal or service activity.

Smith and Gray (1983) wryly observed that the police's dominant values are still in many ways those of an all-male institution such as a rugby club or a boy's school. These attitudes and values include: an emphasis on remaining dominant in any encounter and not losing face; the importance placed on masculine solidarity; the importance given to physical courage; and the glamour attached to violence. Traditionally the values, norms and perspectives of the "cult of masculinity" structured by police for policing have acted as a powerful socialisation process. Many facets of this socialisation process that influence and shape masculine role definitions and attitudes are implicit in the experience of policing (Policy Studies Institute, 1983).

"It is the implicit, rather than the explicit, that is often the basic force of socialisation and social control" (Arkin & Dobrofsky, 1978). There is a strong relationship between policing and what several authors have referred to as the **masculine mystique** (Komisar, 1976). Traditionally policing has equated with the archetype of the masculine-warrior and, for many police, much of this ethos has become internalised. A community emphasis on "boys being boys" has a special place in street policing where, police believe, the masculinity archetype is best demonstrated, and a steady diet of Hollywood fantasies does nothing to detract from this notion. The politics of masculinity emphasise among other things: "Courage, endurance and toughness, lack of squeamishness when confronted with shocking or distasteful stimuli, avoidance of display of weakness in general, reticence about emotional or idealistic matters and sexual competency" (Stouffer, et al., cited in Arkin & Dobrofsky, 1978).

Many attitudes and behaviours have been used to stereotype police. While social scientists no longer characterise police as a discrete personality category, Reiner's (1985) summary of key characteristics of the police subculture supports stereotypical notions of masculinity. According to Reiner these core characteristics can be summarised as follows: mission (action), cynicism, pessimism, suspicion/solidarity, conservatism, machismo, prejudice and pragmatism. "These characteristics equip officers with a day-to-day attitudinal and behavioural framework for their activities" (Brogden, Jefferson & Walklate, 1988). For example, Lester et al. (1982) examined job satisfaction, cynicism and belief in an external locus of control in police samples from

masculine mystique
An *archetype* that encourages: courage, endurance and toughness, lack of squeamishness when confronted with shocking or distasteful stimuli, avoidance of display of weakness in general, reticence about emotional or idealistic matters, and sexual competency.

Police identity is carefully shaped by extended training and the on-the-job socialisation.

Australia, Canada, England and America. Findings indicated that job satisfaction is higher in police officers who hold less cynical attitudes and have some belief in an internal locus of control.

Becoming a police officer

For most novitiates formal police training commences in a quasi-military police academy. Into this relatively closed and carefully controlled environment come the student police officers, full of ideas of what police and policing are about: "locking up crooks, serving the community, being one of the boys" and so forth. While they are being equipped with a professional identity and policing skills, these images are modified and reinforced by their peers and instructor role models. When they start their on-the-job training, these ideas are further modified as the novice officer "takes it to the street" to be transformed into a "working cop". This socialisation process continues as the commonsense recipes of the police subculture are absorbed and the officer becomes "streetwise".

While it is recognised that to some extent organisational socialisation occurs at all stages of one's career, it is during this initial period that an organisation will be most persuasive and make the greatest impact on an officer's worldview. Several studies found that early organisational learning was a major determinant of one's later vocational attitudes and actions (Lortie, 1968; Van Maanen, 1972). Schein (1971) suggests that this process forms a psychological contract linking the goals of the individual to those of the organisation. "In a sense this psychological contract is actually a 'modus vivendi' between the person and the organisation representing the outcome of the socialisation process" (Van Maanen, 1985). Findings from research studies on police selection and training have identified a pattern which includes a liberalising effect on recruits during the early phases of training. This is then dissipated by the experience of "real police work" and exposure to the operational "street" culture and job related cynicism (Phillips, 1991). Fielding (1988) argues an initial idealistic approach to policing is followed by an instrumental, pragmatic phase, which replaces idealism with a sense of policing becoming "just a job". So it is crucial for an understanding of how police and policing operate not only to understand the formal law and police procedure but also the informal norms and values of the police subculture (Brogden, Jefferson & Walklate, 1988). Several authors have commented that the "cult of masculinity" fails to accord policewomen equal status and is therefore a "major obstacle to ideological integration" (Smith & Gray, 1983).

The police subculture is neither static nor universal. Informal rules and agendas are often not clearly defined and there are many variations in organisational styles and outlook depending on time and place. Moreover:

> The cop culture has developed as a patterned set of understandings which help the officer to cope with and adjust to the pressures and tensions which confront the police. Successive generations are socialised into it, but not as passive or manipulated learners. The culture survives because of its "elective affinity", its psychological fit, with the demands of the rank-and-file cop condition. (Reiner, 1985, p. 2)

Policework seems to be an occupation characterised by a very "they can't understand" sub-cultural element. It is an occupation which evades understanding by an outsider and denies communication of the understanding by an insider. It's an occupation which may entail a resocialisation. (McGrath, 1983, p. 134)

Media images of the police

Whether Hollywood-style media portrayals of police reflect or help create attitudes towards the police is problematic. Clearly there is an association but the relationship is unclear. Traditionally media images of police have portrayed officers as crime fighters:

We see a body of men who never rest, who are continually swooping at dawn on the hideaways of villains and terrorists, who are constantly threatened with sawn-off shotguns, who link arms every Sunday to protect our democratic institutions from intolerant demonstrators. (Chibnall, 1977, cited in Morrison, 1984, p. 175)

In many instances these images conform to a cult of masculinity. The crime fighter is an exceptional mortal, male, strong, brave, handsome and sexually attractive to women. Of course most men lack these qualities. Such images of policing are stereotypes constructed for their newsworthiness. They emphasise action, drama and the simplicity of knowing who the villains really are (Morrison, 1984). Such stereotypes as we saw in Chapter Five are simplistic interpretations of reality and often distorted. In actuality, much police work is routine, mundane and basically administrative. Nevertheless it is stressful, we will return to this in a moment.

Policing in a multicultural society

Our discussion of ingroup favouritism and outgroup stigmatisation (Chapter Five) comes into particular focus when we consider the attitudes of police towards minorities. As our countries are ethnically diverse, multicultural policing is a necessity. However the evidence suggests that prejudice is endemic within our police forces (see Box 14.2). Why is this so? Chan (1992) suggests that policing "visible minorities" raises many difficulties which not only reflect the attitudes of the officers themselves but also reflect the difficulties of the police structures themselves. Several inquiries have raised concern about the ability of our legal system and the police in particular to cope with the cultural diversity of Australian society.

In their inquiry into multiculturalism and the law, the Australian Law Reform Commission (ALRC, 1991, 1992) identified the following problems: certain cultures lack an understanding of the police role; there is a lack of understanding of the rights and limits of police powers; public perceptions of unsympathetic attitudes towards victims of crime; police assumptions

Box 14.2 *"Cop it sweet"*

In March 1992, a television documentary, Cop It Sweet and clips from an amateur video tape from a bad-taste party broadcast to Australia and the rest of the world that New South Wales police officers were racist, unprofessional and oppressive towards Aboriginal people. Even though many police officers publicly expressed abhorrence and disgust at the behaviours of their colleagues and vehemently dissociated themselves from the images conveyed by these media reports, critics of the police saw the media coverage as a scathing indictment of police racism and a vindication of their longstanding criticisms of police practices in Aboriginal communities. Some blamed the wider Australian culture as the basis for racist attitudes among police officers. Others were impatient with the lack of progress in police reforms, advocating immediate action and more drastic measures to be taken. Yet the public debates generated by these events seemed to have an air of resignation and pessimism about them. It was as if police organisations were pathological and impossible to change, or that white man's law is always loaded against indigenous people. Even though the Prime Minister Paul Keating had asked that this be a "turning point" for Australian attitudes, many are skeptical about the elimination of racism in the wider community. (Chan, 1992, p. 4)

These problems cut both ways. Chan found that most officers thought they were not prejudiced against minorities (68%), nor Aborigines (66%). However, the officers thought these groups were prejudiced against them and indicated four areas of concern: attitudes of minorities towards the police (minorities are self-interested, prejudiced, disinterested, disrespectful and hostile to police); the lifestyle and behaviour of minority groups (alcohol abuse, refusal to integrate with Australian culture, and refusing to learn English as problems); immigration and multiculturalism (questioning the Government's immigration and multiculturalism policies); and that minorities should take more responsibility to learn English and fit into the wider community. Chan reports a survey that indicates police saw language difficulties as the greatest problem they faced. However, the survey also found that police felt minorities were: ignorant of the law (85%); distrusted police (76%); were unwilling to report crime (71%); were basically uncooperative (70%); were hostile toward police (64%); were unwilling to testify in court (61%); and unwilling to give statements (59%) (Chan, 1992, p. 19). One officer described his experiences of policing domestic violence in minority communities:

We have had a lot of problems with domestics over the years, where people have been suffering dreadful domestic violence, and they have been ashamed to involve police in their family problems, and as a result, I did one job where the whole family was murdered by a boyfriend, and there was seven of them killed, shot to death, and he then shot himself. And one of the survivors told me that they thought about ringing the police, but they weren't sure if they should, and that was within a few hours of them all being killed. (Chan, 1992, p. 22)

Deciding if police attitudes shape these reactions, or if police are merely reflecting them is a bit like the chicken and egg problem—which came first? Trying to decide this issue is probably unprofitable; however, it is likely that both groups' attitudes contribute to a self-fulfilling prophecy as we discussed in Chapter Five. The evident prejudice on both sides of the equation probably has some kernel of truth but becomes its own logic. Employing police from ethnic backgrounds similar to those they police may be part of the answer to redressing these shortcomings, but it is a major problem in ensuring adequate policing.

Source: Chan, 1992.

about certain communities and their propensity towards crime; selectivity in use of police powers; police insensitivity to cultural differences; communication barriers and need for interpreters; and problems in describing suspects (Chan, 1992). You might like to reflect on this list in the light of social categorisation theory which we discussed in Chapter Twelve. Obviously cultural differences between the police and those they police are causing what amounts to outgroup homogeneity and stigmatisation effects.

There has been an enormous amount written on "stress" and it is generally accepted that some occupations are prone to stress-related illnesses and disorders. Many researchers have suggested that police work is one such occupation (O'Brian & Resnick, 1988). Of course the term "stress" is vague and elusive, and there appears to be little agreement as to its precise meaning. However as Selye (1978) suggests: "It is quite clear that stress is usually a matter of perception and that being the case the body can be instructed to react at a proper level of educating the mind." There are four types of stressor impinging on policework:

Occupational stress

1. External—includes frustration with the courts and the media as well as negative community attitudes.
2. Organisational—includes salary, excessive paperwork, inadequate training and equipment, shiftwork, limited promotional opportunities.
3. Task-related—includes continuous exposure to tragedy and suffering as well as fear, danger and boredom in the job.
4. Personal—includes concern about individual success and failure, peer group pressure, health, marital concerns and alcoholism.

(Wexler & Logan, 1983, p. 46)

O'Brian and Resnick (1988) conducted a risk-prevalence study of health and lifestyle factors among 1051 male and female officers in the NSW Police Service. This survey data was analysed using a National Heart Foundation (NHF) 1983 occupational sample as a baseline, and a measure on the General Health Questionnaire to ascertain symptoms of psychological disturbance such as minor emotional distress and related physical complaints. Compared to NHF subjects, the percentage of male and female officers with high/severe impairment was greater across all ages and most marked in younger age groups (25–39 years). Police officers recorded a high score on such items as: inability to concentrate, feeling useless, incapable of decision-making, constantly under strain and unable to enjoy life. It is interesting to note that women among both the NHF subjects and police sample had a higher percentage of significant responses than males.

Stress as imbalance

McGrath (1970) suggested that, "one is not threatened by demands which are not received or by demands which cannot be handled . . . one is threatened by the anticipation that perceived demands cannot be handled . . . whether these perceived demands are real or not". This definition

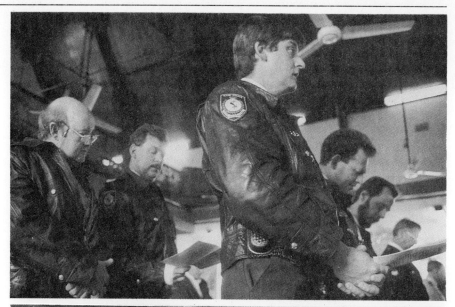

Police suffer a much higher incidence of job-related stress than most occupations. Some pay more dearly than others. (Photos: Armen Deushian/ Macarthur Advertiser; Barry Price)

focuses on how we perceive and appraise our surrounding environment. Violante (1982) maintains that "the police organisation is generally a quasi-military bureaucratic styled organisation designed to exert systematic control over members. The police structure has a built-in imbalance—through strong socialisation processes and strict enforcement of rules, the organisation puts officers in a position of minimal response capability."

A concurrent theme in stress research is this notion of perceived imbalance between individual and environmental forces. This is an interactive problem, where both individuals and the social environment affect stress levels. Remember our discussion of attribution in Chapter Three. How we perceive causes and attribute blame has important consequences for how we act. If we attribute the cause to an inadequacy or weakness in ourselves we will choose to act in certain ways. If we view the causes as largely a function of the situation, then we may choose to act differently, for example, attempt to change the situation or at least make it more tolerable. Why do police officers come to view their relationship with the "system" as one of imbalance? For Violante there are three major forces in the police organisation that exacerbate stress:

1. *Police organisational structure:* One key aspect of police culture is an emphasis on rules. The police structure is a punitive one and rule violations lead to being disciplined by superiors. This obedience to rules is both a major strength and a major weakness of policing. Hierarchies, while ensuring clear chains of authority and swift action, also erode individual initiative and leave one vulnerable to one's superiors.

2. *The criminal justice system:* This factor is a powerful environmental focus influencing perception of imbalance. Kirkham (1981) cited in Violante (1982) concludes that the justice system allows law to be turned into a mockery of justice. "The criminal justice system undermines police idealism and legitimisation of law. Officers cannot effectively contend with the judiciary on an individual basis, they have no viable recourse" (Violante, 1982).

3. *Prevalence of crime and expectations of the police:* The ability of police to control crime is limited and perhaps our society demands too much from its police. "A great deal of our modern difficulty in seeing what police are, derives from false and exaggerated images and expectations of what they can be" (Klockars, 1983). Many officers feel powerless when faced with unrealistic demands and expectations. The social causes of crime are beyond their control and they feel the policing task is "imbalanced by overpowering social factors". While these social factors are not the only ones impacting on police, in general they are indicative of the way police see their task and working environment. Violante proposes the following definition of police stress: "Police stress is a perceived imbalance between occupational demands and the police officer's capability to effectively respond under conditions where failure always has important consequences."

Social psychology in the courts

Unfortunately the truth is not always in the eye of the beholder and, as we saw in Chapter Two, our observations and subsequent reports of events are often inaccurate and biased. In a courtroom, forensic exhibits such as bloodstains, fingerprints or a weapon, can provide compelling evidence.

Eyewitness testimony

However, much apparently convincing evidence is often provided by an eyewitness account of an offence, by someone who describes what took place and who can identify the offender (Wolf & Bugaj, 1990). Even if an eyewitness is attempting to give a truthful and accurate account, other factors must be taken into consideration in appraising the reliability of such testimony (Wells & Murray, 1983). How accurate are eyewitness accounts and what factors lead to error or bias in this type of testimony? Some common misconceptions about eyewitness testimony are described in Box 14.3.

Eyewitness accuracy

Social psychologists have found that eyewitness testimony is often inconsistent and unreliable and have identified and described perceptual and memory processes which may influence these accounts.

Time: the longer a person has to observe an event the more details they will attend to and the more effective their recall. Also the significance and meaning of salient aspects of the environment (such as faces, car registration numbers, features of a landscape) will influence attention and accuracy of recall. Stress also plays a role and alters perception, memory and recall. Krafka and Penrod (1981) report that both low and very high levels of stress in an eyewitness detract from the encoding of relevant information, whereas intermediate levels of stress contribute to this process. Research by Yarmey and Jones (1983) and Tooley et al. (1987) indicate that people tend to focus their attention on unusual or highly significant objects such as a gun or other weapons. This may detract their attention from the face and other salient characteristics of the perpetrator.

In general, people who witness crimes wish to be helpful and offer valuable information. In some instances they will be influenced by the demand characteristics of the situation (recall our discussion of these subtle effects in Chapter One). For example, they may feel pressured to identify someone, yet memory declines over time and can be altered or influenced by new information. Also, recall of relevant information can be affected by the way in which the information is elicited, such as leading questions

---

Box 14.3 *Misconceptions about eyewitness testimony*

- *Eyewitnesses typically underestimate the duration of the offence.* Eyewitnesses usually estimate that a crime takes longer than it actually does. This bias tends to increase as the degree of violence or stress increases.
- *Eyewitnesses remember details of a violent crime more accurately than a non-violent offence.* The opposite is true. Stress and anxiety produced by violence distorts and biases perception and recall.
- *The more confident an eyewitness is the*

more accurate their report of a crime. No relationship has been demonstrated between confidence and accuracy.
- *Witnesses are better at identifying a criminal than remembering the details of an offence.* In general the reverse appears to be the case. Witnesses are better at remembering the details of a crime than identifying the offender (Yuille & Cutshall, 1986).

Source: Loftus, 1984, pp. 22–6.

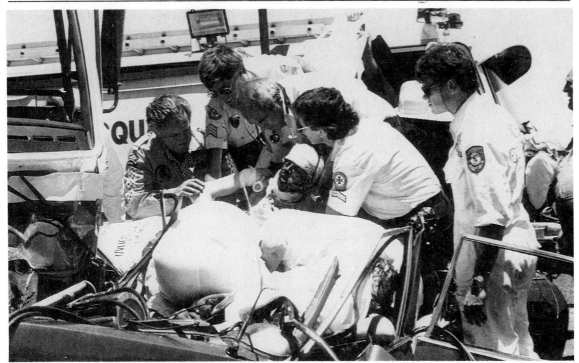

The literature on eyewitness testimony suggests that reconstructive memory differs from person to person. If you saw this accident, chances are your recollections will differ from other eyewitness accounts.
(Photo: Barry Price)

(Lindsay & Johnson, 1989). A classic study conducted by Loftus (1975) demonstrates this effect. Subjects were shown a film of a car accident. One group of subjects was asked how fast a sports car was travelling when it passed a barn. The other group was asked how fast the car was travelling (no mention of the barn). Indeed there was no barn in the film. All subjects were then asked if they had seen the barn. In the first group, 17 per cent said they had, while only 3 per cent in the second group reported seeing a barn.

It appears that as eyewitnesses we often report inaccuracies. For example, Loftus' (1979) findings from a series of experiments where subjects acted as eyewitnesses to portrayals of a crime indicated wide variation in subjects' estimates of characteristics of the offender: hair colour (83% incorrect), age (average error 8 years) and estimates of height (average error 20%). Nor are eyewitnesses any better at identifying offenders from police photographs (mugshots), or assisting police artists in composing identikit photos. And even if they were accurate, evidence suggests it would be of little further use! Buckhout (1980), for instance, conducted a rather ingenious experiment to demonstrate this. An assault was staged and presented on a US television news programme, followed by a six-person line-up. Viewers were asked to identify the perpetrator and to phone in their responses. Only 14.1 per cent of over 2100 calls correctly identified the assailant. Guesswork would have produced better results!

In general there are five criteria that need to be taken into account when assessing the reliability of eyewitness testimony:

1. The time between the offence and subsequent identification.
2. The extent to which the witness attended to the incident.
3. The extent to which the eyewitness was able to closely observe the offender at the time and place of the offence.
4. The extent to which the witness is convinced in their mind.
5. The accuracy of the witness' description of the perpetrator before seeing the suspect again.

Yarmey (1986) conducted a study to examine several of these criteria. In this experiment subjects were asked to imagine they were eyewitnesses to a crime in which a man assaulted and apparently raped a woman. Subjects were then shown a sequence of 60 colour slides depicting various times of day: broad daylight, early or late twilight, and night. Results indicated support for only one of the criteria listed above—criterion 3. Subjects were able to recall more details with greater accuracy in the broad daylight and early twilight conditions. However, no relationship was found between recall prior to seeing the suspect and later identification of the perpetrator in a line-up or voice identification. Also, subjects who felt certain about their choice were no more accurate than those who were less certain about their selection.

The jury

In Australia and New Zealand jurors determine a very small proportion of criminal cases. While the vast majority of criminal cases are heard in the lower courts (Local Courts or Courts of Petty Sessions) the juror system continues to be invoked as a symbol of democracy and a guarantee of fairness in Australian and New Zealand criminal justice systems (Wilkie, 1987). According to Macaulay (1981-82), "A jury representing many of the groups in society operates to offset individual biases and further to guarantee that a range of biases and experience will bear on the facts of the case." Is this so?

Many factors have an impact on jurors and the decision-making process (Pennington & Hastie, 1990). Like all of us, members of juries have implicit theories of human nature and opinions of how the world works. Commonsense tells us that the behaviour of juries is affected by their personalities and expectations, as well as the mix of a particular group. Research indicates this may not be the case. Studies indicate minimal support for a relationship between personality factors and subsequent jurors' opinions (Nemeth, 1981). Several studies were conducted to examine the relationship between characteristics of jurors and prediction of trial verdicts (Penrod, 1986; Hepburn, 1980). Findings suggest that little of the variance in decision-making by jurors can be explained by their personal characteristics. The Fishbein and Ajzen model of attitudes and behaviour discussed in Chapter Four would suggest that perhaps the most accurate predictor of jurors' behaviour would be their specific opinions and attitudes about such factors

(*Cartoonist: Steve Harris*)

as the credibility of witnesses, the particular offence, the defendant, the evidence and so on, rather than their general characteristics, attitudes or values. Hans and Vidmar (1982) suggest that if we were able to measure these more specific attitudes, values and the like, our ability to predict these relationships would be enhanced.

Influence of prior jury service

Are people who have had prior experience as a member of a jury more likely to convict than inexperienced jurors? It is often said that prosecutors prefer jurors who have reached a conviction in a previous trial (Bailey & Rothsblatt, 1971). Research findings on this question have been inconsistent. Nagao and Davis (1980) reported a small relationship between prior experience and decision to convict. Kassin and Juhnke (1983) conducted a series of laboratory studies where student subjects acting as jurors were required to reach a series of verdicts in mock trials. Results indicated no relationship between a "seasoning effect" and consequent jury decisions. Werner, Strube, Cole and Kagehiro (1985) conducted a study of actual jurors in 206 criminal trials in the US. Again results indicated no significant relationship between these two variables. However, Dillehay and Nietzel (1985) report a significant, albeit small, effect for prior experience on jury verdicts. Their findings suggest that as the number of experienced jurors in a jury increases the likelihood that the jury would convict also increases. Werner et al. (1985) in an analysis of actual trials found a small jury comprised of a large proportion of experienced jurors is more likely to convict the defendant. It would appear from research evidence that prior jury service may influence subsequent decision-making but this relationship is a tenuous one.

Characteristics of the defendant

Research suggests that many factors may affect jury deliberations including the defendant's characteristics. Dane and Wrightsman (1982), in a review of the literature, categorised defendant characteristics into six groups:

1. *Gender:* The effect of gender seems to differ, depending on the particular offence.
2. *Socioeconomic status:* No consistent relationship has been reported.
3. *Attractiveness:* Attractive defendants (both physical and interpersonal) evoke more leniency, except where they used this attribute to help commit the crime.
4. *Moral character:* Although knowledge of prior criminal history is not admissible, this is often deduced by jurors. This factor appears to increase the likelihood of a conviction. Also the more repentant a defendant appears, the less likely a conviction.
5. *Attitude similarity:* Members of juries appear to be more lenient towards defendants who hold similar attitudes to their own.
6. *Race:* Jurors are less likely to convict defendants of the same race.

Evidence for the role played by defendant characteristics was reported by a study conducted by MacRae and Shepherd (1989). In this study subjects were shown pairs of photos, previously rated as being high or low on honesty and aggression. Subjects were asked to select which persons they thought were responsible for each of a series of crimes. Findings suggested that subjects tended to select photos with facial features stereotypically linked to the crimes (even after discounting the effects of physical attractiveness). These results indicate that jurors may be influenced in cases where the defendant resembles their stereotype of a criminal. In addition, baby-faced adults, or adults with features such as large eyes or short noses, tend to be convicted of offences involving negligence, but are less likely to be convicted of charges related to criminal intent (Berry &, Zebrowitz-McArthur, 1988).

leniency bias
In many instances jurors are biased in favour of the defendant, because of shared backgrounds, sympahty or reluctance to convict.

In a study by Esses and Webster (1988) subjects were shown photographs of persons identified as sex offenders. Subjects rated the least attractive offenders as more likely to be dangerous and to commit further crimes. Research also suggests that in many instances jurors are biased in favour of the defendant, a **leniency bias** (MacCoun & Kerr, 1988).

The jury decision-making process

What other factors influence juries in reaching their decision? Can we identify patterns of behaviour in these deliberation procedures? We are all familiar with various media portrayals of courtroom dramas, for example, the film *Twelve Angry Men*, where a particular juror "goes it alone" and finally manages to persuade the rest of the jurors to his point of view. This does not usually happen in reality. Our study of conformity in Chapter Six suggests that more often than not it is the majority that pressures the minority to conform to their views. Many researchers have attempted to examine the processes involved in jury deliberations and have developed various models to simulate the jury decision-making process.

Recall our discussion of group polarisation in Chapter Twelve. Group polarisation occurs when members of a group shift their opinion in the direction of their initial preference. In a simulation study of group polarisation in student juries, Myers and Kaplan (1976) found that during the deliberation process, subjects shifted toward guilty verdicts in "high guilt" cases (where evidence was compelling for defendant's guilt) and toward acquittal in "low guilt" cases. Of course, in some instances members *do* dissent and "hold out" and manage to persuade the majority. and research suggests that these dissenters can be influential when they adhere to their opinion consistently throughout the deliberation process (Wolf, 1979). However, Tanford and Penrod (1983) suggest that a minority's influence may be limited to juries of fewer than six members and is less likely to be effective in larger juries, where the influence of the majority is extremely strong.

The psychology of the courtroom

As well as factors discussed above, other factors may play a role in influencing members of a jury before their deliberations. Those of you who have observed a criminal trial will agree that the courtroom can be an intimidating place, with its imposing atmosphere, rituals and procedures. Many aspects of the trial itself may influence and prejudice jurors. These include a presumption of innocence, the order in which evidence is presented, the judge's decision on admissible evidence, and the format of the judge's instructions. Also consider the effect of pretrial publicity! Remember the Lindy Chamberlain case? It is a basic tenet of our Western legal tradition that jurors must presume that a defendant is "innocent until proven guilty". Also that a defendant's guilt must be established "beyond a reasonable doubt". Research suggests that jurors may not always adhere to these assumptions prescribed by law. Kagehiro and Stanton's (1985) research findings suggest that jurors in mock trial experiments often experience difficulty in meeting legal standards of proof. Several studies that surveyed actual jurors indicate that many initially presume guilt rather than innocence (Buckhout & Baker, 1977). Some TV courtroom dramas tend to reinforce this, and as with our opener I often get the impression that the defendant is guilty until proven innocent!

Judges' instructions

Before the jury retires to deliberate, trial judges, in their summing up of a case, instruct members of the jury and explain matters of law, such as presumption of innocence and burden of proof, the meaning of "beyond reasonable doubt" and the need to disregard evidence that may be prejudicial. Are members of a jury always able to understand and interpret judges' instructions? Findings from several studies (Sales, Elwork & Alfini, 1977; Kagehiro & Stanton, 1985) indicate that jurors often experience difficulties in understanding instructions. As a result of this evidence, several researchers have attempted to devise instructions that contain less "legalese" and can be more easily understood by lay people. Timing also seems to influence the effectiveness of instructions. Kassin and Wrightsman (1979) found that judges' instructions on matters of law appear to be more effective when they are given before the commencement of a trial. Research evidence appears to indicate the need for ongoing evaluation of the effectiveness of judges' instructions and other related procedural matters, in order to reduce bias and to ensure fairness, openness and accountability. We have discussed several factors which affect the decision-making process in the courtroom. There is an increasing amount of research literature which attempts to examine these aspects from the characteristics of the witnesses, defendants, the interplay between lawyers and judges, the decision-making in juries, the criteria, and so forth, as the following experience of a South Australian woman demonstrates.

> A woman whose rape-in-marriage case has set off a national furore yesterday demanded an apology from the judge, Justice Derek Bollen.
> "Justice Bollen's attitudes are from the dark ages and barbaric", said Mandy Johns, whose husband was acquitted of five counts of rape.
> "Jury members looked to the judge for guidance", she said, "and his comments might have led them to believe some violence in marriage was acceptable".
> Justice Bollen had told the jury: "There is of course nothing wrong with a husband, faced with his wife's initial refusal to engage in intercourse, in attempting in an acceptable way, to persuade her to change her mind, and that may involve a measure of rougher than usual handling". (*Telegraph Mirror*, 13 January 1993, p. 1)

To give a few examples: Mugford and Gronfors (1978) conducted a study to determine if Maoris commit more serious offences or receive more serious sentences than Europeans. Their findings revealed a serious bias in the way the court system treats minorities and those of a lower socioeconomic status (SES), even though minorities committed fewer crimes. The authors conclude that the New Zealand court system reflected entrenched class interests in the legal system. However, Douglas (1989) examined differences in city and rural sentencing patterns in magistrates' courts in Victoria, comparing sentence length with SES. Douglas found only a slight difference and concluded that SES factors were interpreted differently by different magistrates. While there is no basis to compare these two studies, it does show the variability of this type of factors.

Lawrence (1988) interviewed a sample of stipendiary magistrates in Australia, in order to examine their use of information and decision criteria in sentencing. The magistrates were sorted into two groups on the basis of their previous sentencing of shoplifters. They were asked to comment on the seriousness of shoplifting as an offence and their sentencing objectives, and then sort six cases in order of seriousness. Analysis of the results revealed differences in classification criteria used by tough or lenient judges, and three prevalent themes underlay the differences: *greed, need* and *troubled*. Tough magistrates followed the greed schema more than lenient magistrates and failed to consider the need schema at all. Lenient magistrates followed the troubled schemas more frequently than tough magistrates. Lawrence concluded that "accounts of everyday and professional justice should not be limited to narrow concerns with moral judgment structures but should be opened to include information exchanges and the schematised cues and rules that impose meaning on information".

Methodological considerations

It is not permissible for social psychologists to conduct studies in actual criminal trials. Therefore most psychological studies of courtroom processes are simulated, for example, mock juries, or videotaped re-creations. Results of these simulations are then used to interpret observations of real trials. As you are aware from our discussion of research methodologies in Chapter One, laboratory experiments have their limitations. These settings are artificial and are weak in external validity. In many instances we are not able to generalise to real courtrooms. However, simulations are useful as they enable researchers to isolate and control for variables they wish to examine, for instance, the effect of jurors' gender on decision-making in rape trials. This section has highlighted some aspects of applied social psychology and the law. Much of the research has been concerned with aspects of the criminal justice process, such as influences on jury decision-making. Of course the law has a pervasive influence on our everyday life and social psychologists are expanding their knowledge and research activities in many law-related fields outside the courtroom. This knowledge will continue to contribute to our understanding of the law and justice as these relate to human behaviour.

Summary

Many of the fundamental assumptions underlying law making and the legal process are psychological and reflect a social construction of our world and social action. The law is the control mechanism in our society for transmitting and legitimating values and as such is not autonomous from society nor neutral or value free. The law impacts on the way our social relations are structured, and social attitudes, beliefs and behaviours are reflected in our legal arrangements which are often quite patriarchal.

Traditionally the legal system has focused on crime and neglected the needs of victims. Society's reaction to victims of violent crime is often to blame the victims for their plight. They are often seen as provoking or stimulating an attack, and are often isolated and treated with indifference, leading to a double victimisation.

There is an ongoing debate about the media's influence on perceptions of crime. Sensational media practices encourage fear of crime, the non-reporting of offences, insensitive and intrusive scrutiny of victims and their families; and distortions of the true extent and nature of crime.

Many factors influence victims' and survivors' reactions to crime. The process of recovery involves making sense of the crime; re-establishing control over one's life and a sense of self-esteem and trust in others. Victims also have to re-establish a sense of purpose and forward directions.

The effectiveness of a society's social control depends on its policing methods. Policing is ultimately a coercive act and tends to estrange police from the rest of society. For this reason police have a strong subculture which gives an informal and flexible set of understandings which allows them to cope with the pressures and tensions that confront them.

Policing is a stressful occupation and police are prone to organisational, external, task-related and personal stressors. Police are trapped between the expectations of the public, the bureaucratic structures of the legal system and the sheer volume of crime in society.

Our interpretation and recall of events are often inaccurate and biased. There are many misconceptions about eyewitness testimony which is often unreliable and inconclusive. Factors that limit accuracy of recall include time and meaning of the event, perceptual and memory processing limitations, and stress.

Within the court system jury decision-making is highly variable and influenced by prior jury experience; characteristics of the defendant; witness testimony; the order in which information is presented; group polarisation effects; the size of the jury; judges' instructions; and pretrial publicity.

Social psychologists are unable to conduct actual experiments during criminal trials. As such most psychological studies of courtroom process are simulated by mock juries or videotaped recreations. Such research methodologies have shortcomings.

Recommended reading

Bowie V. (1989) COPING WITH VIOLENCE: A GUIDE FOR THE HUMAN SERVICES, Karibuni Press, Sydney. A useful and practical guide from a Sydney social worker on the costs and strategies for coping with occupational stress and violence.

Graycar R. and Morgan J. (1990) THE HIDDEN GENDER OF THE LAW, Federation Press, Annandale, Sydney. A feminist analysis of the Australian legal system.

Kassin S.M. and Wrightsman L.S. (1988) THE AMERICAN JURY ON TRIAL: PSYCHOLOGICAL PERSPECTIVES, Hemisphere Books, NY. Although quite American and inappropriate in parts, is nevertheless a very useful insight into the limitations of jury decision-making.

Moir P.J. and Eichmann H.S. (eds) (1992) POLICING AUSTRALIA: OLD ISSUES, NEW PERSPECTIVES, MacMillan, Melbourne. An edited collection of readable "think-pieces" on policing.

GLOSSARY

ABC theory of attitudes Theory that attitudes are composed of affective (emotional), behavioural and cognitive components.

accommodation Altering or twisting information into a more familiar form so that it will fit existing schemas.

affect A general term that encompasses both *mood* and *emotion*.

affect-priming model Theory that our moods may automatically activate existing schemas which we then use to form impressions, or make social judgments.

affiliation The need to belong, as distinct from the need to be liked. *See attraction*.

affirmative action Programmes that set targets/agendas to benefit the socially disadvantaged.

agape love Altruistic, selfless love.

algebraic model Where we assign weights to various traits and then add them up to form an overall impression.

altruism Behaviour that benefits another without any desire for a reciprocal benefit to the giver. *See prosocial behaviour*.

anchoring heuristic We guess a first approximation for an event and then use this as an anchor of additional information. *See heuristics*.

antecedent behavioural change strategies Strategies to elicit and influence the direction behaviour will take before it occurs. *See prompts*.

anthropology The study of human physical characteristics, cultures and races.

archetypes A cultural stereotype which typifies a class of people, ideals or objects. *See stereotype*.

archival research Non-experimental method that uses censuses and other statistics, biographical and other sources of data.

arousal theory We are automatically aroused by others' presence.

assortative mating Choosing a mate on similar genetic or social background as ourselves.

assumed similarity effect The belief that all members of an outgroup are the same.

attitude A relatively stable pattern of beliefs, actions and feelings about an object or person.

attraction The need to be with others we like.

attribution Making causal inferences about our own or another's behaviour.

attributional cycle Social inference starts with observation, and impression formation, then forms inferences and causal attributions and ends in self-reflection and incorporation into existing schemas, before starting again.

augmentation principle We tend to make stronger attributions of causality in the presence of a factor that would normally stop behaviour from occurring.

authoritarianism Personality trait favouring political and economic conservatism, conventionality, strong leadership, ethnocentrism, and a conservative morality.

autokinetic effect A perceptual illusion; as we stare at a stationary pinpoint of light, the light will appear to move.

availability heuristic Estimating the probability of an event on the basis of how many instances you can call to mind. *See heuristics*.

aversive racism A subtle blend of ambivalence, egalitarian attitudes and old-time racist beliefs.

base-rate bias Under or overestimating the total population from which a sample is drawn.

bayes theorem When estimating how representative an event is your decision should be influenced by both base-rate and likelihood information.

behavioural confirmation *See self-fulfilling prophecies*.

behavioural freedom A felt need for freedom from the control of others. *See psychological reactance.*

behavioural prompts Salient, strategically placed reminders to encourage behaviour. *See antecedent behavioural change strategies.*

binding forces Those elements that psychologically tie an individual to the authority's definition of a situation and create subservience and obedience.

biophilia An emotional commitment to all living things.

biosocial factors Biological foundations of social behaviour.

blaming the victim Believing that life is fair and that innocent victims are responsible for their fate. *See just world hypothesis.*

brain sex Popular term for biological-based explanations of gender differences.

bystander effect Diffusion of individual responsibility to help, as number of onlookers increases. *See social loafing.*

Californian F scale Measure of *authoritarianism.*

case studies Non-experimental method which uses in-depth interviews of a limited number of subjects as data.

category salience Being distinctive because you are the only man in a group of women, or whatever.

central traits Important traits around which others coalesce to form first impressions.

charisma A type of leadership distinguished by an intense personal relationship and commitment between the leader and followers; charismatic leaders are able to inspire unquestioning obedience, loyalty, commitment and devotion from followers.

circadian rhythms Daily cycles; brain-based "biological clocks" regulate sleep, arousal and temperature cycles.

co-action effects Another's presence enhances performance on simple tasks and decreases it on complex ones. *See social facilitation effects.*

cognitive misers Using mental shortcuts to process information. *See heuristics.*

commons dilemmas Actions that benefit an individual but when added collectively spell ruin to all. *See The tragedy of the commons.*

comparative fit Social categories form in such a way as to ensure that differences between categories are larger than the differences within categories, allowing us to define ourselves in contrast to the outgroup.

compliance Involves the use of direct or indirect strategies and techniques by others to influence us to change our attitudes or behaviours.

configural model Balancing traits to form a unified picture of an individual; altering traits so they fit together more readily.

confirmatory hypothesis testing Selecting details that confirm our beliefs rather than taking an honest sample.

conformity When we adhere to or change our attitudes, beliefs and behaviour to be consistent with the standards of a group or society.

conformity reactance Objecting to following the rules set by others, in particular of authority figures. *See psychological reactance.*

conjunction error Violating the *conjunction rule;* statistically, adding up information reduces the probability of an overall description being accurate, if any element of doubt exists.

conjunction rule The probability of a conjunction of two events cannot be larger than the probability of its constituent events.

consensual validation Something is valid because we all agree it is.

conservatism Overvaluing long established institutions and ways of behaving. *See authoritarianism.*

consistency paradox Personality predicts behaviour, but at too high a level of generality to be useful in predicting specific behaviours.

constructive alternativism A doctrine that asserts that all current theories are subject to revision and change without notice.

contact hypothesis Intergroup prejudice will be reduced by the dissonance caused by positive close contact between groups.

contingency model of leadership effectiveness Whether a leader is *task-* or *relations-oriented,* their effectiveness is contingent upon leader–follower relations, task structure, and power position of the leader.

control Eliminating or controlling all sources of bias in an experiment that might confound results.

corpus callosum Connective tissue between the two hemispheres of the human brain.

correlational fallacy Correlation does not equal causation.

correspondent inferences, theory of When we see someone acting in a certain way (e.g. altruistically), we make a corresponding inference that their behaviour is caused by an altruistic nature.

covariation theory Attributions of causal connection based on the conjunction of a situation and some behaviour within it.

C-P-C cycle Circumspection, pre-emption and control; exploring, forming, testing, modifying and then using social schemas.

crisis in social psychology A challenge between 1965 and 1975 to experimentalism and the paucity of conceptual development accompanying experiments. *See experimentalism.*

cross-cultural psychology Comparisons of social and other variables across different cultures.

crowding Our emotional reaction to the number of people present. *See social density, spatial density.*

cycle of violence The process whereby abused children become abusers themselves.

deception Misleading, or not informing, subjects of the true purposes of an experiment.

defensible space Changes we make in our environments to protect us from intrusions.

deformation professionelle Occupational distortion; incorporating one's occupational roles into one's everyday persona.

demand characteristics Guessing the true purposes of an experiment and altering your behaviour to give the experimenter what you think they want.

density-intensity model How we perceive social density determines our reaction to it. Also known as perceived density.

dependent variable That which is being measured in an experiment; the variable influenced by the experi-mental manipulation. *See independent variable.*

determinism A philosophical position that everything is caused by a prior event; the opposite of freewill.

dilution effect The decrease in certainty that accompanies information that does not match our impression of someone.

discounting principle When we are faced with a number of possible causes of an event, we will not settle on any one cause if other likely causes exist.

discrimination Actual harm to another caused by our prejudicial beliefs.

displaced aggression A Freudian concept; everyday frustrations are redirected towards safer targets because we are blocked from venting our feelings on more appropriate ones.

distinctiveness hypothesis We are drawn automatically to novel or contextually distinctive stimuli.

distraction-conflict model Others' presence is arousing because it causes conflict between two basic tendencies, whether to pay attention to them, or concentrate on the task at hand.

distributive justice Decisional rules for allocating resources. *See equity, equality* and *need.*

domestic violence The gender-neutral term that focuses on violence between males and females in domestic relationships.

drive-reduction theory Behaviour that reduces unpleasant physiological arousal. *See negative-state relief model.*

dyad The smallest social group: two people.

egocentric bias Attributional bias is our self-centred belief that we are more important and involved than we really are.

emergent leadership Group dynamic where, in a leader-less group, one member gradually becomes a leader.

emotion Short, sharp affective reactions to experiences that we are usually aware of and can attribute causes to. *See mood.*

environmental determinism Belief that national characteristics and the like are caused by the environment; a circular argument.

environmental load theory Broad environmental factors that lead to increased autonomic arousal, overload and escape behaviours.

epiphenomena Illusory or unsubstantial phenomena.

equality A norm requiring us to minimise social distance by allocating resources equally. *See distributive justice.*

equity A social norm requiring that others be rewarded commensurate with their efforts. *See distributive justice.*

equity theory The ratio of net rewards to investments. *See social exchange theory.*

eros A Freudian term; the love instinct, concerned with pleasure and procreation.

eros love Erotic, intense passionate love.

ethnocentrism Holding one's race or ethnic group to be inherently superior to other groups. *See authoritarianism.*

ethnology The comparative study of human races.

evaluation apprehension Wanting to avoid a negative social evaluation; performance anxiety.

event schemas A social schema that tells us how events should unfold. *See life-scripts.*

excitation transfer One emotional state may be misattributed and then heighten another.

expectancy confirmation sequence *See self-fulfilling prophecies.*

expectancy effects *See self-fulfilling prophecies.*

experimentalism A critique of experimental social psychology which suggested that much of what was being tested was trivial, did not reflect real-life behaviour and did not lead to meaningful conceptual advances. *See crisis in social psychology.*

experimenter expectancy effects Unintentional experimenter influence on subjects that biases results towards expectations.

extortionate transaction model A model of coercive power in which a threat is made to injure a "hostage" (something the victim values) unless the victim pays a ransom (something they will give up to save the hostage from harm).

false consensus bias A tendency to think that our attitudes and behaviour are more representative of others than they are.

false uniqueness effect We think that few people share our positive attributes.

familial violence Violence that occurs in the home, or between relatives or close associates.

field experiments Experiments conducted in real-life settings.

field studies Non-experimental methods. *See naturalistic* and *participant observation.*

field theory A person's perceptual universe (field) from which social and motivational factors govern behaviour.

filled pauses Meaningless noises in conversation ("um" and "ahs") which provide time to gather. *See null signals.*

first-shift rule Reaching a decision consistent with the direction of the first shift in opinion adopted by any member of a group.

forewarning effects When forewarned we are able to adjust our thoughts ahead of attitude-discrepant behaviour.

free-riders Defectors; those who mimic cooperation to gain its rewards, without contributing. *See commons dilemma.*

frozen fright A pseudo-calm detachment in crime victims which may last days; anxiety and sleep disturbance are the most common initial responses and other physiological reactions such as headaches may occur with associated psychosomatic symptoms.

frustration-aggression hypothesis Theory that frustration leads to aggression.

fundamental attribution error Our preference to over-attribute others' behaviour to dispositional causes and under-attribute it to situational causes.

fundamental postulate Our mental processes are psychologically channelled by the ways in which we anticipate events.

game-playing love Non-serious, flirting love style. *See ludus.*

gender A term used to denote differences between men and women that are learned not biological in nature. *See sex.*

gender aschematic People who do not rely as much on gender traits for social comparison and are more interested in other aspects of identity. *See gender schematic.*

gender schematic People who perceive themselves in terms of traditional roles and have personal schemas that incorporate these traits. *See gender aschematic.*

genetic similarity hypothesis We will recognise and be attracted to those whose genetic makeup is closest to our own.

Gestalt theory Argues social psychology should study behaviour and experience as a whole and not as separate categories.

goodness of fit In self-categorisation theory the degree of correspondence between our subjective reality testing and group-based *consensual validation.*

grand theories Comprehensive theories which relate and explain all the research within an area.

great person theory According to this view some individuals possess key personality characteristics and other unique traits that destine them to lead the masses.

greenhouse effect Climatic changes brought on by the gradual warming of the planet.

group polarisation effect Finding that group discussion polarises individual's judgment; that discussion results in more extreme decisions not necessarily riskier decisions. *See risky shift effect.*

groupthink A deterioration of mental efficiency, reality testing and moral judgment that results from ingroup pressure.

handyman factor Sex-role socialisation where boys become more competent on traditional male skills than girls.

heuristics Mental rules-of-thumb used to process information quickly by reducing complexity, or ambiguity.

homophobia Irrational fear of homosexuals.

hostile aggression An emotional response to pain or hurt and its primary aim is to retaliate inflict harm.

hypothermia Illness caused by a drop of the body's core temperature.

identification Identifying with the standards, beliefs and roles of an influencing person or group.

illusion of control Perception that chance events are more controllable than they really are.

illusory correlations Attributing non-existent causal connections between variables.

implicit personality theory Naive personality theories; the assumptions we make about how traits relate and influence behaviour.

inclusive fitness Behaviour that allows the greatest possible number of our genes, including those carried by relatives, to be passed on to the next generation; sociobiological concept.

independent variable Manipulation of one or more factors in an experiment to see what effect it has on another variable. *See dependent variable.*

individual good, collective bad social trap As in overgrazing where each person's additional cow has just a small extra impact but in sum the environment is ruined. *See commons dilemma.*

induced compliance Where we are forced to act contrary to our attitudes and beliefs.

informational social influence Using a group for guidelines for correct behaviour.

informed consent Telling subjects enough about an experiment for them to give an informed consent to their participation in it.

ingratiator's dilemma The less power you have the more you will need to ingratiate yourself to get ahead but then you risk seeming devious to those with power.

instrumental aggression Dispassionate aggression not triggered by anger or emotion, yet involves intentional injury.

instrumental conditioning Using reinforcement to shape behaviour.

insufficient-justification effect Evaluating an otherwise attitude-discrepant behaviour more favourably because we have insufficient rewards or excuses for our behaviour.

interactionism Theory that a person's behaviour is a function of the interaction between the person and their environment.

interdependent love Love that has become more mutual over time.

intergroup contact hypothesis *See contact hypothesis.*

interpersonal expectancy effect *See self-fulfilling prophecies.*

intimate-stranger effect Disclosing our most intimate details to perfect strangers because we will never see them again.

just world hypothesis Our belief that we get what we deserve. *See blaming the victim.*

kernel of truth hypothesis A belief that at the root of every prejudice is a kernel of truth.

kin selection theory Our preference for cooperating with relatives aids their survival and ensures a pool of closely related genes. *See inclusive fitness.*

kinship theory Sociobiological term; explains cooperation as a biological strategy aimed at maximising *inclusive fitness. See reciprocation theory, reciprocal altruism.*

law of primacy in persuasion Initial arguments are more persuasive than subsequent ones. *See primacy effect.*

learned helplessness People feel depressed when they learn they are unable to do anything about their situation.

leniency bias In many instances jurors are biased in favour of the defendant, because of shared backgrounds, sympathy or reluctance to convict.

life-scripts A social schema which tells us how our lives should unfold. *See event schemas.*

Lloyd Morgan's canon "Do not make animals men"; questioning the usefulness and validity of generalising from animal studies to more complex human behaviour.

locus of control Whether we believe our actions are controlled by ourselves (internal LOC), or others (external LOC).

looking-glass self Seeing ourselves through others' eyes.

ludus love Non-serious, flirting, uncommitted love. *See game-playing love.*

lunar synodic behaviour A belief that lunar cycles influence behaviour.

majority-win rule The main purpose of group discussion is to strengthen or affirm the most popular view. *See social decision schemes.*

mania love Possessive and obsessive, fixated love.

masculine mystique An *archetype* that encourages: courage, endurance and toughness, lack of squeamishness when confronted with shocking or distasteful stimuli, avoidance of display of weakness in general, reticence about emotional or idealistic matters, and sexual competency.

matching principle We are attracted to those who are of a similar level of physical beauty as ourselves.

medina circle Seventh century Islamic love poets who wrote in a romantic style later popular in the West.

melatonin Photosensitive hormone secreted by the pineal gland, provides feedback on the intensity and duration of light.

mere exposure effect Repeated exposure to any stimulus makes it more appealing over time.

mere presence effect The more people present, the more aroused we will become, a biological rather than a psychological process; simply adding people will arouse us.

meta-analysis Statistical procedure that pools information from many studies together to ascertain any overall trend.

minimal group situation An experimental design which shows that trivial differences of themselves lead to intergroup hostility.

miscegenation Racial interbreeding.

missing hero social traps We refuse to act because no one else is. *See commons dilemma.*

model indistinguishability Levels of social explanation too general to permit tests of competing causative theories.

modern racism Espousing equality but believing minorities are taking too great an advantage of liberal attitudes and receiving unfairly preferential treatment.

mood An affective state that gradually rises and falls without obvious antecedents or conscious reflection. *See emotion.*

multiple act criterion The more ways you measure behavioural intention, the stronger it is linked to attitudes and behaviour.

naturalistic observation A non-experimental research method; the researcher remains unobtrusive and simply observes behaviours of interest.

necessary and sufficient conditions If any one of a series of necessary conditions is absent an event will not happen; for most events there are a number of causes, any of which is sufficient for the event to happen.

need A social norm requiring us to allocate resources according to need. *See distributive justice.*

negative-state relief model Helping others, to assuage vicarious guilt over a victim's trouble and reducing our empathetic distress.

non-racist racism Unintentional racism caused by uncons-cious use of racist language and social categorisation.

nonverbal leakage hypothesis We tune in to subtle nonverbal cues that give away a person's real attitudes.

normative fit That our stereotypes of a social category or group actually reflect the behaviour being represented.

normative social influence When we conform to obtain some reward or perhaps to avoid punishment or disapproval from a group.

norm of reciprocity A learned rule requiring us to pay back others' prosocial acts.

null signals Meaningless phrases in conversation ("you know" or "I mean") which provide time to gather thoughts. *See filled pauses.*

Nuremberg defence "I am not responsible for my actions,

I was just following orders"; defence used by Nazis at Nuremberg War Crimes Trials.

nuts·game A declining resources simulation game. *See commons dilemma.*

obedience Following a direct command from another person; we obey when we perceive the person issuing the command to be a legitimate authority, such as police officers.

outgroup homogeneity effect Any member of a minority becomes a stereotypical representative of the whole and less differentiated than members of our ingroup.

paralinguistics Vocal clues accompanying speech such as intonation pattern, pitch, hestitations, etc.

parental investment The investment parents make to ensure their children reach their reproductive years and, in turn, reproduce the parents' genes.

participant observation A non-experimental research method, the experimenter becomes a part of the group being studied.

perceived density *See density-intensity model.*

peripheral processing Using *heuristics* to process information, rather than more time-consuming *systematic processing.*

personal constructs Mental representations which allow us to predict and interpret social reality. *See schema.*

personality (character) traits Relatively stable and enduring aspects of personality.

person schema A social schema used to categorise and describe specific individuals.

perspective-taking Being able to see things from another's perspective; piagetian concept.

positive discrimination Selectively advantaging minorities to overcome longstanding inequalities.

positivism Rejects religious or other metaphysical accounts of the world, or reasoning based on tradition; knowledge should be based on direct experience.

possible selves All of the available alternatives open to us in our construction of ourselves and our self-presentation.

post-experimental debriefing Feedback and debriefing after an experiment to ensure subjects are not unduly disturbed by it.

post-hoc reasoning After the fact reasoning.

posttraumatic stress disorder A pattern of stress reactions manifested after trauma, particularly after natural disasters.

pragma love Pragmatic love style.

predictive efficiency The test of how close a schema, inference, or attribution, is to social reality.

pre-emptive construct A closed schema which determines the way we see others and their behaviour.

prejudice An attitude or belief about someone based solely on our stereotypes.

primacy effect Information presented first in a sequence has greater impact on impressions than subsequent data. *See law of primacy in persuasion.*

principle of least effort Resolving attitude-behaviour discrepancies by easiest means, often via perceptual distortion.

prior general consent plus proxy consent technique A subject gives a general consent and then has a friend decide for them if participation in an experiment is acceptable.

prisoner's dilemma A game for modelling real-life dilemmas where choosing an individual benefit may spell collective disaster. *See commons dilemma.*

privacy regulation model Proposes we set territories to control desired levels of intimacy.

propositional constructs Tentative, exploratory, open-ended and flexible schemas. *See pre-emptive constructs.*

prosocial behaviour Behaviour that benefits another irrespective of whether it benefits the giver also. *See altruism.*

prosocial reciprocity *See norm of reciprocity.*

proxemics The study of body-space zones.

psychics Nineteenth century "studies of the body".

psychobiology Biological psychology, includes evolutionary comparative and physiological psychology, and related areas.

psychological androgyny People who incorporate both masculine and feminine traits into their self-concept.

psychological reactance Refusing to comply as a reaction to perceived threats to freedom of choice, or action.

psychosocial pathology theory Proposes that high-density living causes disease, crime, civil unrest and social disruption.

pygmalion effect *See self-fulfilling prophecies.*

random walk Seemingly arbitrary interaction of two patterns of causality that mimics randomness in a deterministic universe.

realistic conflict theory Argues prejudice is ultimately a question of conflict over scarce resources.

recategorisation Redrawing ingroup boundaries to include outgroup members to reduce prejudice.

recency effect Material presented last in a sequence is remembered more readily.

reciprocal altruism Prosocial behaviour given with an expectation of some future reward in return.

reciprocation theory Sociobiological term; explains cooperation as a social strategy aimed at maximising resources. *See kinship theory, reciprocal altruism.*

reconstructive memory After-the-fact modifications of eyewitness testimony. Initial impressions are often modified by others' recollections.

reductionism Belief that all knowledge may be broken down (reduced) to more fundamental explanations.

re-fencing Altering our prejudices to accommodate discrepant facts which would otherwise weaken them.

referent informational influence The power that an ingroup has to promote conformity, because it acts as a social frame of reference, or a guide to what is expected behaviour.

reflected appraisal Acting on what we think other people think about us.

reification Explaining by naming; pretending you have explained something by giving it a name; circular explanation.

relations-oriented roles Attending to relationships within the group, focusing on maintaining group harmony and morale.

representativeness heuristics Judging a sample population to be likely on the basis of similarity or random-looking appearance. *See heuristics.*

reproductive exchange model A model of mating and partner choice which combines sociobiological and social exchange perspectives.

reverse causality problem In correlation research, we find that x and y are related, but which variable is the cause and which is the effect?

reverse psychology Exerting influence by telling someone that they cannot have, or are unable to do, something, which causes them to do it. *See psychological reactance* and *compliance.*

risky shift effect Group decisions are often riskier than the initial opinions held by individuals because group processes polarises their opinions. *See group polarisation effect.*

role conflict Where two or more roles compete for our time and attention, causing problems for both individuals and their group.

role orientation Conformity to the expectations of social roles which tends to bind the individual to an authority's definition of a situation.

role-playing Modelling another's behaviour without incorporating it into our social repertoire; as opposed to *role-taking.*

role schemas A social schema which describes the behaviour patterns we expect certain people to follow.

role-taking Assuming or incorporating another's behaviour into our own social repertoire; as opposed to *role-playing.*

rule orientation Conformity to the expectations of social norms which tend to bind the individual to an authority's definition of a situation.

salience That which is distinctive and stands out from its background.

scapegoat hypothesis Victims of prejudice are chosen because they are available, obvious, different and unable to retaliate.

schema Organised collection of ideas, impressions and experiences that form mental representations of external reality.

scientific method A process involving systematic observations; the development of theories that attempt to explain data; the application of theory to test predictions; and revision of these theories when research suggests our predictions are inaccurate.

scientific realism The belief that we live in a real world and that we can understand and explain things we cannot see.

seasonal affective disorder (sad) Depression caused by lack of daylight during short winter months.

self-affirmation theory Behaviour that reinforces our view of ourselves rather than reducing dissonance.

self-construction Belief that the self is socially constructed.

self-efficacy theory A theory that assumes the cause of many problems lies in our attributing failure and other difficulties to stable internal factors, rather than circumstances.

self-fulfilling prophecies Confirming our expectations of the future by our present actions, while not realising that we are creating the very effects we expect.

self-oriented role People who are primarily concerned about themselves and indifferent to group purposes; they may try to undermine and subvert the efforts of those who are *task* or *relations-oriented* if group interests conflict with their own.

self-reference effect Information related to the self is more readily remembered than other material.

self-representation How we explain ourselves to ourselves.

self-schemas A social schema; the way we see ourselves, or an exercise in self-description.

self-serving bias Attributional bias which diminishes our responsibilities for failures and maximises our responsibility for successes.

self social trap Where the immediate pleasure obscures the long-term harm (as in smoking). *See commons dilemma.*

self-verification Rather than risking accurate feedback, we avoid possible sources of discrepancy and structure our lives to provide the sorts of feedback that reinforce our self-image.

sex A term used to denote differences between men and women that are biological in nature. *See gender.*

sex-role rigidity Slavishly adhering to (usually traditional) sex-roles.

sex typing Process whereby children come to acquire the behaviours, attitudes, interests, emotional reactions and motivations appropriate to their sex.

social categorisation A pervasive tendency to divide the world up into us and them categories on some characteristic.

social cognition Study of how people make inferences, attributions and social judgments about themselves and others.

social comparison Comparing our behaviour with others when situations are ambiguous or unclear.

social competition Intergroup competition based on perceived differences rather than a realistic conflict.

social constructionism Philosophical perspective that we live in a reality constructed from our subjective experience of social interactions.

social darwinism Belief that evolutionary forces shape social differences, particularly those of class or race.

social decision schemes Simple decision-making rules

which determine how a group will reach its final decision.

social density The number of people in a given space. *See crowding.*

social exchange theory A model of relationship development based on the rewards and costs to each party.

social facilitation How an actor's or athlete's performance is enhanced by the presence of others. *See co-action effects.*

social identification The process of defining ourselves in relation to other people.

social identity theory Aspects of our identity based on the groups and social categories to which we belong.

social impact theory The belief that social influence has a multiplier effect; effectiveness is dependent on: strength, or the agent's power, status and/or knowledge; immediacy, or the proximity of the sender and receiver; and group size.

social influence model Model that implies that social influence increases rapidly with each additional member added to a group but levels off after a point.

social justice norm Learned social rule requiring us to act to promote a just world. *See equity.*

social learning theory We learn by observing others and our actions are shaped via vicarious reinforcement.

social loafing Diffusion of individual responsibility for group task as numbers increase. *See bystander effect.*

social overload hypothesis Certain environments (urban) are too perceptually stimulating, causing social withdrawal.

social penetration theory Progressive reciprocal self-disclosure leading to a more intimate relationship.

social perception We react towards others as we perceive them to be, not as they actually are.

social responsibility A social norm requiring us to give help to those who need it. *See need.*

social salience Behaviour that is distinctive or unexpected in its context.

social traps Adverse reinforcement which promotes resource depletion. *See commons dilemma.*

sociobiology The study of the evolutionary roots of human social behaviour; innate predispositions.

sociological social psychology An approach that explains social behaviour in terms of wider (non-individual) social forces.

spatial density The amount of space a set number of people occupy. *See crowding, social density.*

specificity variable Being able to precisely specify which of many factors influences behaviour.

steady-state economics A belief that we should only use what may be replaced.

stereotype A preconceived image of an individual or group based on a few representative characteristics.

stooges Experimenter confederates usually used in experiments involving deception procedures.

storge love Platonic, friendship-based love style.

stranger-danger A child's fear of strangers induced by parents to protect their children.

subject bias Subject variables (age, sex, expectations, etc.) that bias experimental results.

subtractive rule We subtract from our personality attributions of those situational determinants that clearly imply we should act in a dispositional way.

superordinate goals Group goals that require hostile groups to cooperate on a joint task so that all will benefit.

surveys Non-experimental method that uses interviews and questionnaires as sources of data.

survivor guilt Anxiety brought on by survivor's attempts to rationalise how they could have predicted and controlled chance events such as natural disasters.

systematic processing Processing information by deliberate attention to detail. *See peripheral processing.*

tall poppy syndrome Prejudice against those who are successful; desire to see them fall from favour.

task-oriented role Where the emphasis is on getting the job done; people adopting this role direct, coordinate and organise group behaviour towards group goals.

territorial calculus The pattern of defensive spacing observed as a space becomes crowded.

territorial markers Possessions and other items used to indicate personal territory and to protect ourselves from intrusions.

testosterone The male sex hormone implicated in differences in aggression and crucial in early stages of neonatal development.

thanatos A Freudian term; the death instinct, held to underlie all aggression.

theory of reasoned behaviour The attitude-behaviour link is partly determined by social norms and our subjective evaluation.

third-person effect Our belief that the media or some other influence is more likely to affect others than it would us.

third variable problem In correlational research, when two variables are related, maybe a third unknown factor causes their relationship.

tokenism Being employed because of your race or sex, rather than your ability.

topological methodology A system of map-like representations of psychological factors which underlie a person's social behaviour.

tragedy of the commons Actions that benefit the individual but when added collectively spell ruin to all. *See commons dilemmas.*

triple jeopardy Being appointed as a token minority-group employee means you are highly visible, people do not expect much of you and these factors predispose you to fail. *See tokenism.*

truth-wins rule Suggests there is a correct decision and this will eventually emerge and be recognised by group members. *See social decision schemes.*

two-factor theory of emotion When we become physically aroused, we first notice our arousal and then, after monitoring our surroundings, give it an appropriate emotional tag.

two-rights problem A philosophical problem; we must treat everyone equally, but it is obvious that people are born unequal.

two-thirds majority rule An absolute majority; here a course of action depends on the agreement reached by two-thirds of a group. *See social decision schemes.*

ultimate attribution error Assuming the actions of one outgroup member as being representative of the whole group.

universal ethical absolutes Belief in moral principles that transcend culture, time and place (e.g. thou shalt not kill).

vicarious arousal Being aroused by another's predicament; social learning concept.

vividness bias We are more likely to remember vivid effects and thus overestimate their incidence.

volition Human will, or capacity to choose.

volkerpsychologie Folk or cultural psychology; a nineteenth century precursor of social psychology.

withdrawal options Ethical safeguard allowing subjects to withdraw at any time from an experiment.

xenophobia An irrational fear of strangers, or those different to ourselves.

zeitgeber "Time-giver"; cues that synchronise or entrain our biological clocks. *See circadian rhythms.*

zeitgeist The "spirit of the times"; the prevailing ideology of the day.

BIBLIOGRAPHY

Abelson R.P. (1976) Script processing in attitude formation and decision making. In Carroll J.S. and Payne J.W. (eds) COGNITION AND SOCIAL BEHAVIOR, Erlbaum, Hillsdale, NJ

Abelson R.P. (1981) The psychological status of the script concept. AMERICAN PSYCHOLOGIST, 36, 715–729

Abelson R.P. (1983) Whatever became of consistency theory? PERSONALITY AND SOCIAL PSYCHOLOGY BULLETIN, 9, 37–64

Abelson R.P., Aronson E., McGuire W.J., et al. (eds) (1968) THEORIES OF COGNITIVE CONSISTENCY: A SOURCE BOOK, Rand McNally, Chicago

Abrams D. and Hogg M.A. (1988) Comments on the motivational status of self-esteem in social identity and intergroup discrimination. EUROPEAN JOURNAL OF SOCIAL PSYCHOLOGY, 18, 317–334

Abrams D. and Hogg M.A. (eds) (1990) SOCIAL IDENTITY THEORY: CONSTRUCTIVE AND CRITICAL ADVANCES, Harvester Wheatsheaf, Lond.

Abramson L.Y., Metalsky G.I. and Alloy L.B. (1990) The hopelessness theory of depression: Does the research test the theory? In Abramson L.Y. (ed.) SOCIAL COGNITION AND CLINICAL PSYCHOLOGY: A SYNTHESIS, Guilford Press, NY

Abramson L.Y., Seligman M.E.P. and Teasdale J. (1978) Learned helplessness in humans: Critique and reformulation. JOURNAL OF ABNORMAL PSYCHOLOGY, 87, 49–74

Adair J.G. (1991) Social cognition, artifact and the passing of the so-called crisis in social psychology. CANADIAN PSYCHOLOGY, 32, 445–450

Adams J.S. (1963) Toward an understanding of inequity. JOURNAL OF ABNORMAL AND SOCIAL PSYCHOLOGY, 67, 422–436

Adams J.S. (1965) Inequity in social exchange. In Berkowitz L. (ed.) ADVANCES IN EXPERIMENTAL SOCIAL PSYCHOLOGY (Vol. 2), Academic Press, NY

Adams J.S. and Jacobsen P.R. (1964) Effects of wage inequities on work quality. JOURNAL OF ABNORMAL AND SOCIAL PSYCHOLOGY, 69, 19–25

Adorno T.W., Frenkel-Brunswik E., Levinson D.J. and Sanford R.N. (1950) THE AUTHORITARIAN PERSONALITY, Harper and Row, NY

Affirmative Action Agency (1992) PROGRAM DEVELOPMENT AND REPORTING: EMPLOYERS' VIEWS, Affirmative Action Agency, Sydney

Aiellio J.R. and Jones S.E (1971) Field study of the proxemic behavior of young school children in three subcultural groups. JOURNAL OF PERSONALITY AND SOCIAL PSYCHOLOGY, 19, 351–356

Aiello J.R., Thompson D.E. and Brodzinsky D.M. (1983) How funny is crowding anyway? Effects of room size, group size and the introduction of humor. BASIC AND APPLIED SOCIAL PSYCHOLOGY, 4, 193–207

Ajzen I. (1987) Attitudes, traits and actions: Dispositional prediction of behavior in personality and social psychology. In Berkowitz L. (ed.) ADVANCES IN EXPERIMENTAL SOCIAL PSYCHOLOGY (Vol. 20), Academic Press, San Diego

Ajzen I. and Fishbein M. (1980) UNDERSTANDING ATTITUDES AND PREDICTING SOCIAL BEHAVIOR, Prentice Hall, Englewood Cliffs, NJ

Ajzen I. and Madden T.J. (1986) Prediction of goal-directed behavior: Attitudes, intentions, and perceived behavioral control. JOURNAL OF EXPERIMENTAL SOCIAL PSYCHOLOGY, 22, 453–474

Alessio J.C. (1980) Another folly for equity theory. SOCIAL PSYCHOLOGY QUARTERLY, 43, 336–340

Alessio J.C. (1990) A synthesis and formalization of Heiderian balance theory and social exchange theory. SOCIAL FORCES, 68, 1267–1286

Alexander C.N. and Rudd J. (1981) Situated identities and response variables. In Tedeschi J.T. (ed.) IMPRESSION MANAGEMENT THEORY AND SOCIAL PSYCHOLOGICAL RESEARCH, Academic Press, NY

Alexander R.D. (1971) The search for an evolutionary philosophy. PROCEEDINGS OF THE ROYAL SOCIETY, 84, 99–120, Melbourne

Alexander R.D. (1974) The evolution of social behavior. ANNUAL REVIEW OF ECOLOGY AND SYSTEMATICS, 5, 325–384

Alexander R.D. (1975) The search for a general theory of behavior. BEHAVIORAL SCIENCE, 20, 77–100

Alexander R.D. (1977) Natural selection and the analysis of human sociality. In Goulden C.E. (ed.) CHANGING SCENES IN NATURAL SCIENCES, Philadelphia Academy of Natural Sciences, Philadelphia

Allen E., et al. (1976) Sociobiology: Another biological determinism. BIOSCIENCE 26, 182–186

Allen E., et al. (1977) Sociobiology: A new biological determinism. In Sociobiology Study Group of Boston (eds) BIOLOGY AS A SOCIAL WEAPON, Burgess, Minneapolis

Allen F. (1990) ACADEMIC WOMEN IN AUSTRALIAN UNIVERSITIES, Affirmative Action Agency, Sydney

Allen V.L. and Levine J.M. (1968) Social support, dissent and conformity. SOCIOMETRY, 31, 138–149

Allen V.L. and Levine J.M. (1969) Consensus and conformity. JOURNAL OF EXPERIMENTAL PSYCHOLOGY, 5, 389–399

Allison S.T., Worth L.T. and King M.C. (1990) Group decisions as social inference heuristics. JOURNAL OF PERSONALITY AND SOCIAL PSYCHOLOGY, 58, 801–811

Allport F.H. (1924) SOCIAL PSYCHOLOGY, Houghton Mifflin, Boston

Allport G.W. (1954) THE NATURE OF PREJUDICE, Addison Wesley, Reading, Mass.

Allport G.W. (1968) The historical background of social psychology. In Lindzey G. and Aronson E. (eds) THE HANDBOOK OF SOCIAL PSYCHOLOGY (Vol. 1), (2nd edn), Addison-Wesley, Reading, Ma.

Allport G.W. (1985) The historical background of social psychology. In Lindzey G. and Aronson E. (eds) HANDBOOK OF SOCIAL PSYCHOLOGY (Vol. 1), (3rd edn), Random House, NY

Allport G.W. and Kramer B.M. (1946) Some roots of prejudice. JOURNAL OF PSYCHOLOGY, 22, 9–39

Allport G.W. and Postman L. (1947) THE PSYCHOLOGY OF RUMOR, Holt, Rinehart and Winston, NY

Allport G.W. and Ross J.M. (1967) Personal religious orientation and prejudice. JOURNAL OF PERSONALITY AND SOCIAL PSYCHOLOGY, 5, 432–443

Altemeyer B. (1981) RIGHT-WING AUTHORITARIANISM, University of Manitoba Press, Winnipeg

Altemeyer B. (1988) THE ENEMIES OF FREEDOM: UNDERSTANDING RIGHT-WING AUTHORITARIANISM, Jossey Bass, San Francisco

Altman I. (1973) Reciprocity of interpersonal exchange. JOURNAL OF THE THEORY OF SOCIAL BEHAVIOR, 3, 249–261

Altman I. (1975) THE ENVIRONMENT AND SOCIAL BEHAVIOR, Brooks/Cole, Monterey, Ca.

Altman I. and Taylor D. (1973) SOCIAL PENETRATION: THE DEVELOPMENT OF INTERPERSONAL RELATIONSHIPS, Holt, Rinehart and Winston, NY

Amato P.R. (1980) City size, sidewalk density, and friendliness toward strangers. JOURNAL OF SOCIAL PSYCHOLOGY, 111, 151–152

Amato P.R. (1981a) Urban-rural differences in helping: Behavior in Australia and the United States. JOURNAL OF SOCIAL PSYCHOLOGY, 114, 289–290

Amato P.R. (1981b) The impact of the built environment on prosocial and affiliative behaviour: A field study of the Townsville City Mall. AUSTRALIAN JOURNAL OF PSYCHOLOGY, 33, 297–303

Amato P.R. (1981c) The effects of environmental complexity and pleasantness on prosocial behaviour: A field study. AUSTRALIAN JOURNAL OF PSYCHOLOGY, 33, 285–295

Amato P.R. (1983a) Helping behavior in urban and rural environments: Field studies based on a taxonomic organisation of helping episodes. JOURNAL OF PERSONALITY AND SOCIAL PSYCHOLOGY 45, 571–586

Amato P.R. (1983b) The effects of urbanisation on interpersonal behavior: Field studies in Papua New Guinea. JOURNAL OF CROSS-CULTURAL PSYCHOLOGY, 14, 353–367

Amato P.R. (1984) Responsibility attribution and helping behaviour in the Ash Wednesday bushfires. AUSTRALIAN JOURNAL OF PSYCHOLOGY, 36, 191–203

Amato P.R. (1985) An investigation of planned helping behavior. JOURNAL OF RESEARCH IN PERSONALITY, 19, 232–252

Amato P.R. (1986) Emotional arousal and helping behavior in a real-life emergency. JOURNAL OF APPLIED SOCIAL PSYCHOLOGY, 16, 633–641

Amato P.R. (1990) Personality and social network involvement as predictors of helping behavior in everyday life. SOCIAL PSYCHOLOGY QUARTERLY, 53, 31–43

Amerigo M. and Aragones J. (1990) Residential satisfaction in council housing. JOURNAL OF ENVIRONMENTAL PSYCHOLOGY, 10, 313–325

Amir Y. (1969) Contact hypothesis in ethnic relations. PSYCHOLOGICAL BULLETIN, 71, 319–342

Amir Y. (1976) The role of intergroup contact in change of prejudice and ethnic relations. In Katz P. (ed.) TOWARD THE ELIMINATION OF RACISM, Pergamon Press, NY

Andersen S.M., Lazowski L.E. and Donisi M. (1986) Salience and the self-inference: The role of biased recollections in self-inference processes. SOCIAL COGNITION, 4, 75–95

Anderson C.A. (1987) Temperature and aggression: Effects on quarterly, yearly and city rates of violent and non-violent crime. JOURNAL OF PERSONALITY AND SOCIAL PSYCHOLOGY, 52, 1161–1173

Anderson C.A. (1989) Temperature and aggression: The ubiquitous effects of heat on the occurrence of human violence. PSYCHOLOGICAL BULLETIN, 106, 74–96

Anderson C.A. and Anderson D.C. (1984) Ambient temperature and violent crime: Tests of the linear and curvilinear hypothesis. JOURNAL OF PERSONALITY AND SOCIAL PSYCHOLOGY, 46, 91–97

Anderson J.L. (1989) A methodological critique of the evidence for genetic similarity detection. BEHAVIORAL AND BRAIN SCIENCES, 12, 518–519

Anshel M.H. and Hoosima D.E. (1989) The effect of positive and negative feedback on causal attributions and motor performance as a function of gender and athletic participation. JOURNAL OF SPORT BEHAVIOR, 12, 119–130

Antill J.K. (1983) Sex-role complementarity versus similarity in married couples. JOURNAL OF PERSONALITY AND SOCIAL PSYCHOLOGY, 45, 145–155

Antill J.K. (1984) Parental beliefs and practices concerning sex differences, sex-role stereotyping and cross-sex interests and behaviour. Unpublished manuscript, Macquarie University, Sydney

Antill J.K., Bussey, K. and Cunningham J.D. (1985) Sex roles: A psychological perspective. In Feather N.T. (ed.) AUSTRALIAN PSYCHOLOGY REVIEW OF RESEARCH, Allen and Unwin, Sydney

Antill J.K. and Cotton S. (1987) Self-disclosure between husbands and wives: Its relationship to sex roles and marital happiness. AUSTRALIAN JOURNAL OF PSYCHOLOGY, 39, 11–24

Antill J.K. and Cotton S. (1988) Factors affecting the division of labour in households. SEX ROLES, 18, 531–553

Antill J.K., Cotton S. and Tindale S. (1983) Egalitarian or traditional: Correlates of the perception of an ideal marriage. AUSTRALIAN JOURNAL OF PSYCHOLOGY, 35, 245–257

Antill J.K. and Cunningham J.D. (1979) Self-esteem as a function of masculinity in both sexes. JOURNAL OF CONSULTING AND CLINICAL PSYCHOLOGY, 47, 783–785

Antill J.K. and Cunningham J.D. (1980) The relationship of masculinity, femininity and androgyny to self-esteem. AUSTRALIAN JOURNAL OF PSYCHOLOGY, 32, 195–207

Antill J.K., Cunningham J. D., Russell G. and Thompson N.L. (1981) An Australian sex-role scale. AUSTRALIAN JOURNAL OF PSYCHOLOGY, 33, 169–183

Ardrey R. (1966) THE TERRITORIAL IMPERATIVE, Atheneum, NY

Arendt H. (1963) EICHMANN IN JERUSALEM: A REPORT ON THE BANALITY OF EVIL, Viking, NY

Argyle M. and Henderson M. (1985) The rules of relationships. In Duck S. and Perlman D. (eds) (1985) UNDERSTANDING RELATIONSHIPS, Sage, Beverly Hills

Arkin R.M. and Baumgardner A.H. (1985) Self-handicapping. In Harvey J.H. and Weary C. (eds) ATTRIBUTION: BASIC ISSUES AND APPLICATIONS, Academic Press, NY

Arkin W. and Dobrofsky L. (1978) Military socialisation and masculinity. JOURNAL OF SOCIAL SCIENCES, 34, 151–168

Arkkelin D., Oakley T. and Mynatt C. (1979) Effects of controllable versus uncontrollable factors on responsibility attributions: A single subject approach. JOURNAL OF PERSONALITY AND SOCIAL PSYCHOLOGY, 37, 110–115

Armstrong B.K. (1987) Commentary: Passive smoking and lung cancer. COMMUNITY HEALTH STUDIES, 11, 6–8

Aronson E. and Cope V. (1968) My enemy's enemy is my friend. JOURNAL OF

PERSONALITY AND SOCIAL PSYCHOLOGY, 8, 8–12

Aronson E., Ellsworth P.C., Carlsmith J.M. and Gonzales M.H. (1990) METHODS OF RESEARCH IN SOCIAL PSYCHOLOGY (2nd edn) McGraw-Hill, NY

Aronson E. and Gonzales A. (1988) Desegregation, jigsaw, and the Mexican-American experience. In Katz P.A. and Taylor D.A. (eds) ELIMINATING RACISM: PROFILES IN CONTROVERSY, Plenum, NY

Aronson E. and Mills J. (1959) The effects of severity of initiation on liking for a group. JOURNAL OF ABNORMAL AND SOCIAL PSYCHOLOGY, 59, 177–181

Aronson E., Stephan C., Sikes J., Blaney N. and Snapp M. (1978) THE JIGSAW CLASSROOM, Sage, Beverly Hills

Arvey R.D. and Campion J.E. (1982) The employment interview: A summary and review of recent research. PERSONAL PSYCHOLOGY, 35, 281–322

Asch J. and Shore B.M. (1975) Conservation behavior as the outcome of environmental education. JOURNAL OF ENVIRONMENTAL EDUCATION, 6, 25–33

Asch S.E. (1946) Forming impressions of personality. JOURNAL OF ABNORMAL AND SOCIAL PSYCHOLOGY, 41, 258–290

Asch S.E. (1955) Opinions and social pressure. SCIENTIFIC AMERICAN, November, 31–35

Askew S. (1989) Aggressive behaviour in boys: To what extent is it institutionalised? In Tattum D.P. and Lane D.A. (eds) BULLYING IN SCHOOLS, Trentham Books, Stoke-on-Trent, Staff.

Atkinson J.W. and Feather N.T. (eds) (1966) A THEORY OF ACHIEVEMENT MOTIVATION, Wiley, NY

Atlas R. (1984) Violence in prison: Environmental influences. ENVIRONMENT AND BEHAVIOR, 16, 275–306

Augoustinos M. (1990) The mediating role of representations on causal attributions in the social world. SOCIAL BEHAVIOUR, 5, 49–62

Augoustinos M. and Innes J.M. (1990) Towards an integration of social representations and social schema theory. BRITISH JOURNAL OF SOCIAL PSYCHOLOGY, 29, 213–231

Austin W. (1979) Sex differences in bystander intervention in a theft. JOURNAL OF PERSONALITY AND SOCIAL PSYCHOLOGY, 37, 2110–2120

Australian Law Reform Commission (1991) MULTICULTURALISM: CRIMINAL LAW, Discussion Paper No. 48, AGPS, Canberra

Australian Law Reform Commission (1992) MULTICULTURALISM AND THE LAW, Report No. 57, AGPS, Canberra

Australian Psychological Society (1986) CODE OF PROFESSIONAL CONDUCT, Australian Psychological Society, Ringwood, Victoria

Avis J. (1987) A deepening awareness: A private study guide to feminism and family therapy. JOURNAL OF PSYCHOTHERAPY AND THE FAMILY, 3, 15–46

Axelrod R. (1980) Effective choice in the prisoner's dilemma. JOURNAL OF CONFLICT RESOLUTION, 24, 3–26

Axelrod R. and Hamilton W.D. (1981) The evolution of cooperation. SCIENCE, 211, 1390–1397

Ayd F.J. (1974) Single daily dose of antidepressant. JOURNAL OF AMERICAN MEDICAL ASSOCIATION, 230, 263

Babad E., Bernieri F. and Rosenthal R. (1989) Nonverbal communication and leakage in the behavior of biased and unbiased teachers. JOURNAL OF PERSONALITY AND SOCIAL PSYCHOLOGY, 56, 89–94

Bacharach S.B. and Lawler E.J. (1981) BARGAINING, Jossey-Bass, San Francisco

Backman C.W. (1981) Attraction in interpersonal relationships. In Rosenberg M. and Turner R. (eds) SOCIAL PSYCHOLOGY: SOCIOLOGICAL PERSPECTIVES, Basic Books, NY

Backman C.W. (1988) The self: A dialectical approach. In Berkowitz L. (ed.) ADVANCES IN EXPERIMENTAL SOCIAL PSYCHOLOGY (Vol. 21), Academic Press, NY

Backman C.W. and Secord P.F. (1959) The effect of perceived liking on interpersonal attraction. HUMAN RELATIONS, 12, 379–384

Bailey F. and Rothsblatt H.B. (1971) SUCCESSFUL TECHNIQUES FOR CRIMINAL TRIALS, Lawyers Cooperative Publishing Company, NY

Baker E. and Shaw M.E. (1980) Reactions to interperson distance and topic intimacy: A comparison of strangers and friends. JOURNAL OF NONVERBAL BEHAVIOR, 5, 80–91

Baker R.L. and Mednick B.R. (1984) INFLUENCES ON HUMAN DEVELOPMENT: A LONGITUDINAL PERSPECTIVE, Kluwew-Nijhoff, Boston

Bales R.F. (1970) PERSONALITY AND INTERPERSONAL BEHAVIOR, Holt Rinehart and Winston, NY

Balling J.D. and Falk J.H. (1982) Development of visual preference for natural environments. ENVIRONMENT AND BEHAVIOR, 14, 5–28

Bandura A. (1965) Influence of a model's reinforcement contingencies on the acquisition of imitative responses. JOURNAL OF PERSONALITY AND SOCIAL PSYCHOLOGY, 1, 589–595

Bandura A. (1973) AGGRESSION: A SOCIAL LEARNING ANALYSIS, Prentice Hall, Englewood Cliffs, NJ

Bandura A. (1982) Self-efficacy mechanism in human agency. AMERICAN PSYCHOLOGIST, 37, 122–147

Bandura A. (1983) Psychological mechanisms of aggression. In Geen R.J. and Donnerstein E. (eds) AGGRESSION: THEORETICAL AND EMPIRICAL REVIEWS, Academic Press, NY

Bandura A. (1986) SOCIAL FOUNDATIONS OF THOUGHT AND ACTION: A SOCIAL COGNITIVE THEORY, Prentice Hall, Englewood Cliffs, NJ

Bandura A., Ross D. and Ross S.A. (1961) Transmission of aggression through imitation of aggressive models. JOURNAL OF ABNORMAL AND SOCIAL PSYCHOLOGY, 63, 575–582

Bandura A., Ross D. and Ross S.A. (1963a) Vicarious reinforcement and imitative learning. JOURNAL OF ABNORMAL AND SOCIAL PSYCHOLOGY, 67, 601–607

Bandura A., Ross D. and Ross S.A. (1963b) Imitation of film-mediated aggressive models. JOURNAL OF ABNORMAL AND SOCIAL PSYCHOLOGY, 66, 3–11

Bandura A. and Walters R. (1963) SOCIAL LEARNING AND PERSONALITY DEVELOPMENT, Holt Rinehart and Winston, NY

Banning A. (1988) Mother-son incest: Confronting a prejudice. Royal Australian and New Zealand College of Psychiatry, Faculty of Child Psychiatry Annual General Meeting, Adelaide

Banuazizi A. and Movahedi S. (1975) Interpersonal dynamics in a simulated prison: A methodological analysis. AMERICAN PSYCHOLOGIST, 30, 152–161

Barash D.P. (1977) SOCIOBIOLOGY AND BEHAVIOR, Elsevier, NY

Bard M. and Sangrey D. (1986) "DENYING THE VICTIM": THE CRIME VICTIM'S BOOK, Brenner/Mazels, NY

Barden R.C., Garber J., Duncan S.W., et al. (1981) Cumulative effects of induced states in Children: Accentuation, inoculation and remediation. JOURNAL OF PERSONALITY AND SOCIAL PSYCHOLOGY, 40, 750–760

Bargh J.A. (1990) Auto-motives: Preconscious determinants of social interaction. In Higgins E.T. and Sorrentino R.M. (eds) HANDBOOK OF MOTIVATION AND COGNITION: FOUNDATIONS OF SOCIAL BEHAVIOR (Vol. 2), Guilford Press, NY

Barker R.G. (1968) ECOLOGICAL PSYCHOLOGY: CONCEPTS AND METHODS FOR STUDYING THE ENVIRONMENT OF HUMAN BEHAVIOR, Stanford University Press, Stanford, Ca.

Barnett J.L. and Hemsworth P.H. (1990) The validity of physiological and behavioural measures of animal welfare. APPLIED ANIMAL BEHAVIOUR SCIENCE, 25, 177–187

Baron J.N. and Reiss P.C. (1985) Same time next year: Aggregate analysis of the mass media and violent behavior. AMERICAN SOCIOLOGICAL REVIEW, 50, 347–363

Baron R.A. (1974) Aggression as a function of victims' pain cues, level of prior anger arousal and exposure to an aggressive model.

JOURNAL OF PERSONALITY AND SOCIAL PSYCHOLOGY, 24, 117–124

Baron R.A. (1977) HUMAN AGGRESSION, Plenum Press, NY

Baron R.A. (1983) The control of human aggression: An optimistic perspective. JOURNAL OF SOCIAL AND CLINICAL PSYCHOLOGY, 1, 97–119

Baron R.A (1986) Distraction-conflict theory: Progress and problems. In Berkowitz L. (ed.) ADVANCES IN EXPERIMENTAL SOCIAL PSYCHOLOGY, Academic Press, Orlando, Florida

Baron R.A. and Bell P.A. (1975) Aggression and heat: Mediating effects of prior provocation and exposure to an aggressive model. JOURNAL OF PERSONALITY AND SOCIAL PSYCHOLOGY, 31, 825–832

Baron R.A. and Bell P.A. (1976) Aggression and heat: The influence of ambient temperature, negative affect, and a cooling drink on physical aggression. JOURNAL OF PERSONALITY AND SOCIAL PSYCHOLOGY, 33, 245–255

Baron R.A. and Byrne D. (1991) SOCIAL PSYCHOLOGY: UNDERSTANDING HUMAN BEHAVIOR (6th edn), Allyn and Bacon, Boston

Baron R.A. and Eggleston R.J. (1972) Performance on the "aggression machine": Motivation to help or harm? PSYCHONOMIC SCIENCE, 26, 321–322

Barry R.J. (1978) Development of sex-role stereotyping in rural aboriginal children. PSYCHOLOGICAL REPORTS, 43, 412–414

Bar-Tal D., Graumann C.F., Kruglanski A.W. and Strobe W. (eds) (1989) STEREOTYP-ING AND PREJUDICE: CHANGING CONCEPTIONS, Springer-Verlag, NY

Bar-Tal D. and Saxe L. (1976) Perceptions of similarly and dissimilarly attractive couples and individuals. JOURNAL OF PERSON-ALITY AND SOCIAL PSYCHOLOGY, 33, 772–781

Bartholdi J.J., Butler C.A. and Trick M.A. (1986) More on the evolution of coopera-tion. JOURNAL OF CONFLICT RESOLUTION, 30, 129–140

Bartlett F.C. (1932) REMEMBERING: A STUDY IN EXPERIMENTAL AND SOCIAL PSYCHOLOGY, Cambridge University Press, Cambridge, UK

Bateson G. (1979) MIND AND NATURE: A NECESSARY UNITY, E.P. Dutton, NY

Batson C.D. (1990) How social an animal?: The human capacity for caring. AMERICAN PSYCHOLOGIST, 45, 336–346

Batson C.D., Batson J.G., Griffitt C.A., et al. (1989) Negative-state relief and the empathy-altruism hypothesis. JOURNAL OF PERSONALITY AND SOCIAL PSYCHOLOGY, 56, 922–933

Batson C.D. and Coke J.S. (1981) Empathy: A source of altruistic motivation for helping? In Rushton J.P. and Sorrentino R.M. (eds) ALTRUISM AND HELPING BEHAVIOR, Erlbaum, Hillsdale, NJ

Batson C.D., Flink C.H., Schoenrade P.A., Fultz J. and Pych V. (1986) Religious orientation and overt versus covert racial prejudice. JOURNAL OF PERSONALITY AND SOCIAL PSYCHOLOGY, 50, 175–181

Batson C.D. and Gray R.A. (1981) Religious orientation and helping behavior: Responding to one's own or the victim's needs. JOURNAL OF PERSONALITY AND SOCIAL PSYCHOLOGY, 40, 511–520

Batson C.D., Naifeh S.J. and Pate S. (1978) Social desirability, religious orientation, and racial prejudice. JOURNAL FOR THE SCIENTIFIC STUDY OF RELIGION, 17, 31–41

Batson C.D., O'Quin K., Fultz J., et al. (1983) Self-reported distress and empathy and egoistic versus altruistic motivation for helping. JOURNAL OF PERSONALITY AND SOCIAL PSYCHOLOGY, 45, 706–718

Batson C.D., Oleson K.C., Weeks J.L., et al. (1989) Religious prosocial motivation: Is it altruistic or egoistic? JOURNAL OF PERSONALITY AND SOCIAL PSYCHOLOGY, 57, 873–884

Batson C.D., Schoenrade P.A. and Pych V. (1985) Brotherly love or self-concern? Behavioural consequences of religion. In Brown L.B. (ed.) ADVANCES IN THE PSYCHOLOGY OF RELIGION, Pergamon Press, Oxford

Batson C.D. and Ventis W.L. (1982) THE RELIGIOUS EXPERIENCE: A SOCIAL PSYCHOLOGICAL PERSPECTIVE, Oxford University Press, NY

Baum A. and Epstein Y. (1978) HUMAN RESPONSE TO CROWDING, Erlbaum, Hillsdale, NJ

Baum A. and Paulus P.B. (1987) Crowding. HANDBOOK OF ENVIRONMENTAL PSYCHOLOGY (Vol. 1), Wiley Interscience, NY

Baum A. and Valins S. (1977) ARCHITEC-TURE AND SOCIAL BEHAVIOR: PSYCHOLOGICAL STUDIES OF SOCIAL DENSITY, Erlbaum, Hillsdale, NJ

Baum A. and Valins S. (1979) Architectural mediation of residential density and control: Crowding and the regulation of social contact. In Berkowitz L. (ed.) ADVANCES IN EXPERIMENTAL SOCIAL PSYCHOLOGY (Vol. 12), Academic Press, NY

Baumeister R.F. (1982) A self-presentation view of social phenomena. PSYCHOLOGI-CAL BULLETIN, 91, 3–26

Baumeister R.F. and Hutton D.G. (1987) Self-presentation theory: Self-construction and audience pleasing. In Mullen B. and Goethals G.R. (eds) THEORIES OF GROUP BEHAVIOR, Springer-Verlag, NY

Baumeister R.F., Hutton D.G. and Tice D.M. (1989) Cognitive processes during deliberate self-presentation: How self-presenters alter and misinterpret the behavior of their interaction partners. JOURNAL OF EXPERIMENTAL SOCIAL PSYCHOLOGY, 25, 59–78

Baumeister R.F., Kahn J. and Tice D.M. (1990) Obesity as a self-handicapping strategy: Personality, selective attribution of problems, and weight loss. JOURNAL OF SOCIAL PSYCHOLOGY, 130, 121–123

Baumeister R.F. and Scher S.J. (1988) Self-defeating behavior patterns among normal individuals: Review and analysis of common self-destructive tendencies. PSYCHO-LOGICAL BULLETIN, 104, 3–22

Baumeister R.F. and Tice D.M. (1984) Role of self-presentation and choice in cognitive dissonance under forced compliance: Necessary or sufficient causes? JOURNAL OF PERSONALITY AND SOCIAL PSYCHOLOGY, 46, 5–13

Baumeister R.F., Tice D.M. and Hutton D.G. (1989) Self-presentational motivations and personality differences in self-esteem. JOURNAL OF PERSONALITY, 57, 547–579

Baumrind D. (1964) Some thoughts on ethics of research: After reading Milgram's behavioral study of obedience. AMERICAN PSYCHOLOGIST, 19, 421–423

Baumrind D. (1985) Research using intentional deception: Ethical issues revisited. AMERICAN PSYCHOLOGIST, 19, 421–423

Baxter J. (1988) The sexual division of labour in Australian families. AUSTRALIAN JOURNAL OF SEX, MARRIAGE AND FAMILY, 9, 87–93

Baxter T.L. and Goldberg L.R. (1988) Perceived behavioral consistency underlying trait attributions to oneself and another: An extension of the actor-observer effect. PERSONALITY AND SOCIAL PSYCHOLOGY BULLETIN, 13, 437–447

Bayley D.H. (1989) Community policing in Australia: An appraisal. In Chappell D. and Wilson P. (eds) AUSTRALIAN POLIC-ING: CONTEMPORARY ISSUES, Butterworths, Sydney

Beaglehole J.C. (1949) VICTORIA UNIVER-SITY COLLEGE, New Zealand University Press, Wellington

Beaman A.L., Cole C.M., Preston M., Klentz B. and Steblay N.M. (1983) Fifteen years of foot-in-the-door research: A meta-analysis. PERSONALITY AND SOCIAL PSYCHOLOGY BULLETIN, 9, 181–196

Beattie N. (1980) A review of undergraduate work in man-environment systems at Deakin University. MAN ENVIRONMENT SYSTEMS, 10, 128–130

Beck R.C. (1978) MOTIVATION: THEORY AND PRINCIPLES, Prentice Hall, NJ

Beck S.B., Ward-Hull C.I. and McLear P.M. (1976) Variables related to women's somatic preferences of the male and female body. JOURNAL OF PERSONALITY AND SOCIAL PSYCHOLOGY, 34, 1200–1210

Becker F.D. and Mayo C. (1971) Delineating personal distance and territoriality. ENVIRONMENT AND BEHAVIOR, 3, 375–381

Beeby C.E. (1979) Psychology in New Zealand fifty years ago. In St. George R. (ed.) DELTA RESEARCH MONOGRAPHS, 2, 1–6

Bell P.A. (1978) Effects of heat and noise stress on primary and subsidiary task performance. HUMAN FACTORS, 20, 749–752

Bell P.A. (1981) Physiological, comfort, performance, and social effects of heat stress. JOURNAL OF SOCIAL ISSUES, 37, 71–94

Bell P.A. and Baron R.A. (1977) Aggression and ambient temperature: The facilitating and inhibiting effect of hot and cold environments. BULLETIN OF THE PSYCHONOMIC SOCIETY, 9, 443–445

Bell P.A., Fisher J.D., Baum A. and Greene T.E. (1990) ENVIRONMENTAL PSYCHOLOGY (3rd edn), Holt, Rinehart and Winston, NY

Bem D.J. (1965) An experimental analysis of self-persuasion. JOURNAL OF EXPERIMENTAL SOCIAL PSYCHOLOGY, 1, 199–218

Bem D.J. (1967) Self-perception: An alternative interpretation of cognitive dissonance phenomena. PSYCHOLOGICAL REVIEW, 74, 183–200

Bem D.J. (1970) BELIEFS, ATTITUDES AND HUMAN AFFAIRS, Brooks/Cole, Belmont, Ca.

Bem D.J. (1972) Self-perception theory. In Berkowitz L. (ed.) ADVANCES IN EXPERIMENTAL SOCIAL PSYCHOLOGY (Vol. 6), Academic Press, NY

Bem S.L. (1974) The measurement of psychological androgyny. JOURNAL OF CONSULTING AND CLINICAL PSYCHOLOGY, 42, 155–162

Bem S.L. (1981) Gender schema theory: A cognitive account of sex typing. PSYCHOLOGICAL REVIEW, 88, 354–364

Bem S.L. (1987) Masculinity and femininity exist only in the mind of the perceiver. In Reinisch J.M., Rosenbaum L.A. and Sanders S.A. (eds) MASCULINITY/FEMININITY: BASIC PERSPECTIVES, Oxford University Press, NY

Bennett R. (1991) The relationship between pornography and extrafamilial child sexual abuse. POLICE CHIEF, February, 128–131

Benson P.L., Karabenick S.A. and Lerner R.M. (1976) Pretty pleases: The effects of attractiveness, race and sex on receiving help. JOURNAL OF EXPERIMENTAL SOCIAL PSYCHOLOGY, 12, 409–415

Ben-Veniste R. (1971) Pornography and sex crime: The Danish experience. In TECHNICAL REPORTS OF THE COMMISSION ON OBSCENITY AND PORNOGRAPHY (Vol. 8), Government Printing Office, Washington DC

Berg J.H. (1984) Development of friendship between roommates. JOURNAL OF PERSONALITY AND SOCIAL PSYCHOLOGY, 46, 346–356

Berg J.H. and McQuinn R.D. (1986) Attraction and exchange in continuing and noncontinuing dating relationships. JOURNAL OF PERSONALITY AND SOCIAL PSYCHOLOGY, 50, 942–952

Berger P.L. and Luckmann T. (1967) THE SOCIAL CONSTRUCTION OF REALITY, Anchor Books, NY

Berger S.M. (1962) Conditioning through vicarious instigation. PSYCHOLOGICAL REVIEW, 69, 450–466

Berglas S. and Jones E.E. (1978) Drug choice as a self-handicapping strategy in response to noncontingent success. JOURNAL OF PERSONALITY AND SOCIAL PSYCHOLOGY, 36, 405–417

Berkowitz L. (1962) AGGRESSION: A SOCIAL PSYCHOLOGICAL ANALYSIS, McGraw-Hill, NY

Berkowitz L. (1964) Aggressive cues in aggressive behavior and hostility catharsis. PSYCHOLOGICAL REVIEW, 71, 104–122

Berkowitz L. (1968a) Responsibility, reciprocity, and social distance in help-giving: An experimental investigation of English social class differences. JOURNAL OF EXPERIMENTAL SOCIAL PSYCHOLOGY, 4, 46–63

Berkowitz L. (1968b) Impulse, aggression, and the gun. PSYCHOLOGY TODAY, 2, 18–22

Berkowitz L. (1972) Social norms, feelings and other factors affecting helping behavior and altruism. In Berkowitz L. (ed.) ADVANCES IN EXPERIMENTAL SOCIAL PSYCHOLOGY (Vol. 6), Academic Press, NY

Berkowitz L. (1984) Some effects of thought on anti and pre-social influence of media events. A cognitive-neoassociation analysis. PSYCHOLOGICAL BULLETIN, 95, 410–427

Berkowitz L. (1988) Frustrations appraisals and aversively stimulatred aggressions. AGGRESSIVE BEHAVIOR 14, 3–11

Berkowitz L. (1989) Frustration aggression hypothesis: Examination and reformulation. PSYCHOLOGICAL BULLETIN, 106, 59–73

Berkowitz L. and Donnerstein E. (1982) External validity is more than skin deep. Some answers to criticisms of laboratory experiments (with special reference to research on aggression). AMERICAN PSYCHOLOGIST, 37, 245–257

Berkowitz L. and Geen R.G. (1966) Film violence and the cue properties of available targets. JOURNAL OF PERSONALITY AND SOCIAL PSYCHOLOGY, 3, 525–530

Berkowitz L. and Geen R.G. (1967) Stimulus qualities of the target of aggression: A further study. JOURNAL OF PERSONALITY AND SOCIAL PSYCHOLOGY, 5, 364–368

Berkowitz L. and LePage A. (1967) Weapons as aggression-eliciting stimuli. JOURNAL OF PERSONALITY AND SOCIAL PSYCHOLOGY, 11, 202–207

Bernstein W.M., et al. (1983) Causal ambiguity and heterosexual affiliation. JOURNAL OF EXPERIMENTAL SOCIAL PSYCHOLOGY, 19, 78–92

Bernt F.M. (1989) Being religious and being altruistic: A study of college service volunteers. PERSONALITY AND INDIVIDUAL DIFFERENCES, 10, 663–669

Berry D.S. and McArthur L.Z. (1985) Some components and consequences of a babyface. JOURNAL OF PERSONALITY AND SOCIAL PSYCHOLOGY, 48, 312–323

Berry D.S. and McArthur L.Z. (1986) Perceiving character in faces: The impact of age-related craniofacial changes on social perception. PSYCHOLOGICAL BULLETIN, 100, 3–18

Berry D.S. and Zebrowitz-MacArthur L.Z. (1988) What's in a face: Facial maturity and attribution of legal responsibility. PERSONALITY AND SOCIAL PSYCHOLOGY BULLETIN, 14, 23–33

Berscheid E. (1985) Interpersonal attraction. In Lindzey G. and Aronson E. (eds) HANDBOOK OF SOCIAL PSYCHOLOGY (Vol. 11), (3rd edn), Random House, NY

Berscheid E., Dion K. and Walster E. (1971) Physical attractiveness and dating choice: A test of the matching hypothesis. JOURNAL OF EXPERIMENTAL SOCIAL PSYCHOLOGY, 7, 173–189

Berscheid E. and Walster E. (1974) A little bit about love. In Huston T. (ed.) FOUNDATIONS OF INTERPERSONAL ATTRACTION, Academic Press, NY

Berscheid E. and Walster E. (1978) INTERPERSONAL ATTRACTION, (2nd edn), Addison-Wesley, Ma.

Bickman L. (1972) Social influence and diffusion of responsibility in an emergency. JOURNAL OF EXPERIMENTAL SOCIAL PSYCHOLOGY, 8, 438–445

Biddle B.J. (1979) ROLE THEORY: EXPECTATIONS, IDENTITIES, AND BEHAVIORS, Academic Press, NY

Bierhoff H.W. (1988) Affect, cognition, and prosocial behaviour. In Fiedler K. and Forgas J. (eds) AFFECT, COGNITION, AND SOCIAL BEHAVIOUR, Hogrefe, Toronto

Bierhoff H.W. and Klein R. (1988) Prosocial behaviour. In Hewstone M., et al. (eds) INTRODUCTION TO SOCIAL PSYCHOLOGY: A EUROPEAN PERSPECTIVE, Basil Blackwell, Oxford

Bierly M.M. (1985) Prejudice toward contemporary outgroups as a generalized attitude. JOURNAL OF APPLIED SOCIAL PSYCHOLOGY, 15, 189–199

Billig M. and Tajfel H. (1973) Social categorization and similarity in intergroup behavior. EUROPEAN JOURNAL OF SOCIAL PSYCHOLOGY, 3, 27–52

Bishop B. (1976) Learning prejudice in school. TOPICS IN CULTURE LEARNING, 4, 6–8

Bittman M. (1991) JUGGLING TIME. HOW AUSTRALIAN FAMILIES USE TIME. Office of the Status of Women, Department of the Prime Minister and Cabinet, Canberra

Blackler F. (1983) (ed.) SOCIAL PSYCHOLOGY AND DEVELOPING COUNTRIES, Wiley, NY

Blackman S. and Catalina D. (1973) The moon and the emergency room. PERCEPTUAL AND MOTOR SKILLS, 37, 624–626

Blackwell B. (1974) Patient compliance. NEW

ENGLAND JOURNAL OF MEDICINE, 289, 249–252

Blaikie N.W. (1974) Altruism in the professions: The case of the clergy. AUSTRALIA AND NEW ZEALAND JOURNAL OF SOCIOLOGY, 10, 84–89

Blainey G. (1984) FOR ALL AUSTRALIA, Methuen, Sydney

Blasi A. (1980) Bridging moral cognition and moral action: A critical review of the literature. PSYCHOLOGICAL BULLETIN, 88, 1–45

Blau P. (1964) EXCHANGE AND POWER IN SOCIAL LIFE, Wiley, NY

Blumstein P.W. and Schwartz P. (1983) AMERICAN COUPLES, Morrow, NY

Bobo L. (1988) Group conflict, prejudice, and the paradox of contemporary racial attitudes. In Katz P.E. and Taylor D.A. (eds) ELIMINATING RACISM: PROFILES IN CONTROVERSY, Plenum, NY

Bochner S. (ed.) (1982) CULTURES IN CONTACT: STUDIES IN CROSS-CULTURAL INTERACTION, Pergamon Press, Oxford

Bock D.C. and Warren N. (1972) Religious belief as a factor in obedience to destructive commands. REVIEW OF RELIGIOUS RESEARCH, 13, 185–191

Boehnke, K., Silbereisen, R.K., Eisenberg, N., et al. (1989) Developmental pattern of prosocial motivation: A cross-national study. JOURNAL OF CROSS-CULTURAL PSYCHOLOGY, 20, 219–243

Bogard M. (1984) Family systems approaches to wife battering: A feminist critique. AMERICAN JOURNAL OF ORTHOPSYCHIATRY, 54, 558–568

Boldero J. and Moore S. (1990) An evaluation of de Jong-Giervald's loneliness model with Australian adolescents. JOURNAL OF YOUTH AND ADOLESCENCE, 19, 133–147

Bolig R., Stein P.J. and McKenry P.C. (1984) The self-advertisement approach to dating: Male-female differences. FAMILY RELATIONS, 33, 587–592

Bond C.F. (1982) Social facilitation: A self-presentational view. JOURNAL OF PERSONALITY AND SOCIAL PSYCHOLOGY, 42, 1042–1050

Bond C.F. and Titus L.J. (1983) Social facilitation: A meta-analysis of 241 studies. PSYCHOLOGICAL BULLETIN, 94, 265–292

Bond M.H. (ed.) (1988) THE CROSS-CULTURAL CHALLENGE TO SOCIAL PSYCHOLOGY, Sage, Newbury Park, Ca.

Bonney R. (1985) CRIMES (SEXUAL ASSAULT) AMENDMENT ACT, 1981: MONITORING AND EVALUATION, NSW Bureau of Crime Statistics and Research, Sydney

Bonney R. (1987) HOMICIDE II, NSW Bureau of Crime Statistics and Research, Sydney

Bornstein M.H. (1979) The pace of life revisited. INTERNATIONAL JOURNAL OF PSYCHOLOGY, 14, 83–90

Bossard J.H. (1931) Residential propinquity as a factor in marriage selection. AMERICAN JOURNAL OF SOCIOLOGY, 38, 219–224

Bothwell R.K., Brigham J.C. and Malpass R.S. (1989) Cross-cultural racial identification. PERSONALITY AND SOCIAL PSYCHOLOGY BULLETIN, 15, 19–25

Bower G.H. (1991) Mood congruity of social judgments. In Forgas J.P. (ed.) EMOTION AND SOCIAL JUDGEMENTS, Pergamon, Oxford

Bower G.H., Black J. and Turner T. (1979) Scripts in text comprehension and memory. COGNITIVE PSYCHOLOGY, 11, 177–220

Bowie V. (1989) COPING WITH VIOLENCE: A GUIDE FOR THE HUMAN SERVICES, Karibuni Press, Sydney

Bowman D. (1990) Pride wrestles with the truth. AUSTRALIAN SOCIETY, 9, 12–13

Boyd R. (1988) Is the repeated prisoner's dilemma a good model of reciprocal altruism? ETHOLOGY AND SOCIOBIOLOGY, 9, 211–222

Boyd R. and Lorberbaum J.P. (1987) No pure strategy is evolutionarily stable in the repeated prisoner's dilemma game. NATURE, 327, 58–59

Bradley D. and Cioccorelli P. (1989) Chasing Vollmer's fancy: Current developments in police education. In Chappell D. and Wilson P. (eds) AUSTRALIAN POLICING: CONTEMPORARY ISSUES, Butterworths, Sydney

Bradley G.W. (1978) Self-serving biases in the attribution process: A reexamination of the fact or fiction question. JOURNAL OF PERSONALITY AND SOCIAL PSYCHOLOGY, 36, 56–71

Brady A.T. and Walker M.B. (1978) Interpersonal distance as a function of situationally induced anxiety. BRITISH JOURNAL OF SOCIAL PSYCHOLOGY, 17, 127–133

Braiker H.B. and Kelley H.H. (1979) Conflict in the development of close relationships. In Burgess R.L. and Huston T.L. (eds) SOCIAL EXCHANGE IN DEVELOPING RELATIONSHIPS, Academic Press, NY

Brandon R. and Davies C. (1973) WRONGFUL IMPRISONMENT, Allen and Unwin, Lond.

Brann P. and Foddy M. (1987) Trust and the consumption of a deteriorating common resource. JOURNAL OF CONFLICT RESOLUTION, 31, 615–630

Bray R.M., Johnston D. and Chilstrom J.T. (1982) Social influence by group members with minority opinions: A comparison of Hollander and Moscovici. JOURNAL OF PERSONALITY AND SOCIAL PSYCHOLOGY, 43, 78–88

Breckler S.J. (1984) Empirical validation of affect, behavior, and cognition as distinct components of attitude. JOURNAL OF PERSONALITY AND SOCIAL PSYCHOLOGY, 47, 1191–1205

Brehm J.W. (1956) Post-decision changes in desirability of alternatives. JOURNAL OF ABNORMAL AND SOCIAL PSYCHOLOGY, 52, 384–389

Brehm J.W. (1966) A THEORY OF PSYCHOLOGICAL REACTANCE, Academic Press, NY

Brehm S.S. (1985) INTIMATE RELATIONSHIPS, Random House, NY

Brehm S.S. and Brehm J.W. (1981) PSYCHOLOGICAL REACTANCE, Academic Press, NY

Brehm S.S. and Kassin S.M. (1990) SOCIAL PSYCHOLOGY, Houghton Mifflin, Boston

Brennan T. (1982) Loneliness at adolescence. In Peplau L.A. and Perlman D. (eds) LONELINESS: A SOURCEBOOK OF CURRENT THEORY, RESEARCH AND THERAPY, Wiley, NY

Brewer M.B. (1979) Ingroup bias in the minimal intergroup situation: A cognitive-motivational analysis. PSYCHOLOGICAL BULLETIN, 86, 307–324

Brewer M.B. and Miller N. (1984) Beyond the contact hypothesis: Theoretical perspectives on desegregation. In Miller N. and Brewer M.B. (eds) GROUPS IN CONTACT: THE PSYCHOLOGY OF DESEGREGATION, Academic Press, NY

Brewer M.B. and Silver M. (1978) Ingroup bias as a function of task characteristics. EUROPEAN JOURNAL OF SOCIAL PSYCHOLOGY, 8, 393–400

Briere J., Downes A. and Spensley J. (1983) Summer in the city: Weather conditions and psychiatric emergency-room visits. JOURNAL OF ABNORMAL PSYCHOLOGY, 92, 77–80

Briggs F. (1987) CHILD SEXUAL ASSAULT: CONFRONTING THE PROBLEM, Pitman, Melbourne

Brigham J.C. (1971) Ethnic stereotypes. PSYCHOLOGICAL BULLETIN, 76, 15–38

Brigham J.C. (1980) Limiting conditions of the "physical attractiveness stereotype": Attributions about divorce. JOURNAL OF RESEARCH IN PERSONALITY, 14, 365–375

Brigham J.C., Maass A., Snyder L.S. and Spaulding K. (1983) The effect of arousal on facial recognition. BASIC AND APPLIED SOCIAL PSYCHOLOGY, 4, 279–293

Brinberg D. and Castell P. (1982) A resource exchange theory approach to interpersonal interactions: A test of Foa's theory. JOURNAL OF PERSONALITY AND SOCIAL PSYCHOLOGY, 43, 260–269

Broadbent D.E. (1971) DECISION AND STRESS, Academic Press, NY

Brodt S.E. and Zimbardo P.G. (1981) Modifying shyness-related social behavior through symptom misattribution. JOURNAL OF PERSONALITY AND SOCIAL PSYCHOLOGY, 41, 437–444

Brogden M., Jefferson T. and Walklate S. (1988) BECOMING A POLICE OFFICER. INTRODUCING POLICE WORK, Unwins Hyman, Lond.

Broll L., Gross A.E. and Piliavin I.M. (1974) Effects of offered and requested help on help-seeking and reactions to being helped. JOURNAL OF APPLIED SOCIAL PSYCHOLOGY, 4, 244–258

Brooks G.R. (1991) Traditional men in marital and family therapy. JOURNAL OF FEMINIST FAMILY THERAPY, 2, 51–74

Brooks K. and Siegal M. (1991) Children as eyewitnesses: Memory, suggestibility and credibility. AUSTRALIAN PSYCHOLOGIST, 26, 84–88

Brooks R. and Young L. (1988) THE PROFILE OF CHILD ABUSE IN NSW, Department of Family and Community Services, Sydney

Broverman I.K., Broverman D.M., Clarkson F.E., Rosenkrantz P.S. and Vogel S.R. (1970) Sex-role stereotypes and clinical judgments in mental health. JOURNAL OF CONSULTING AND CLINICAL PSYCHOLOGY, 34, 1–7

Broverman I.K., Vogel S.R., Broverman D.M., Clarkson F.E. and Rosenkrantz P.S. (1972) Sex-role stereotypes: A current appraisal. JOURNAL OF SOCIAL ISSUES, 28, 59–78

Brown B. (1987) Territoriality. In Stokols D. and Altman I. (eds) HANDBOOK OF ENVIRONMENTAL PSYCHOLOGY, Wiley-Interscience, NY

Brown B.B. and Altman I. (1983) Territoriality, defensible space, and residential burglary: An environmental analysis. JOURNAL OF ENVIRONMENTAL PSYCHOLOGY, 3, 203–220

Brown J.D. (1986) Evaluations of self and others: Self-enhancement biases in social judgments. SOCIAL COGNITION, 4, 353–376

Brown J.E. and Mann L. (1988) Effects of family structure and parental involvement on adolescent participation in family decisions. AUSTRALIAN JOURNAL OF SEX, MARRIAGE AND FAMILY, 9, 74–86

Brown J.E. and Mann L. (1989) Parents' and adolescents' perceptions of participation in family decisions. AUSTRALIAN JOURNAL OF SEX, MARRIAGE AND FAMILY, 10, 65–73

Brown K.M. (1986a) Establishing difference: Culture, "Race", ethnicity and the production of ideology. AUSTRALIAN AND NEW ZEALAND JOURNAL OF SOCIOLOGY, 22, 175–186

Brown K.M. (1986b) Keeping their distance: The cultural production and reproduction of "racist" non-racism. AUSTRALIAN AND NEW ZEALAND JOURNAL OF SOCIOLOGY, 22, 387–398

Brown L.B. and Fuchs A.H. (1969) THE LETTERS BETWEEN SIR THOMAS HUNTER AND E.B. TICHENER, Publications in Psychology No. 23, University of Wellington, Wellington

Brown P., Keenan J.K. and Potts G.R. (1986) The self-reference effect with imagery encoding. JOURNAL OF PERSONALITY AND SOCIAL PSYCHOLOGY, 51, 897–906

Brown R. (1965) SOCIAL PSYCHOLOGY, Free Press, NY

Brown R. (1986) SOCIAL PSYCHOLOGY (2nd edn), Free Press, NY

Brown R. (1988) GROUP PROCESS: DYNAMICS WITHIN AND BETWEEN GROUPS, Basil Blackwell, Oxford

Brownmiller S. (1975) AGAINST OUR WILL: MEN, WOMEN AND RAPE, Simon and Schuster, NY

Bruch M.A., Gorsky J.M., Collins TM. and Berger P.A. (1989) Shyness and sociability reexamined: A multicomponent analysis. JOURNAL OF PERSONALITY AND SOCIAL PSYCHOLOGY, 57, 904–915

Bruins J.J., Liebrand W. and Wilke H.A. (1989) About the saliency of fear and greed in social dilemmas. EUROPEAN JOURNAL OF SOCIAL PSYCHOLOGY, 19, 155–161

Brunner L.S. and Suddarth D.S. (eds) (1980) LIPPINCOTT MANUAL OF NURSING PRACTICE (2nd edn), Australia and New Zealand Book Company, Sydney

Brunswik E. (1956) PERCEPTION AND THE REPRESENTATIVE DESIGN OF PSYCHOLOGICAL EXPERIMENTS (2nd edn), University of California Press, Berkeley

Bryan J.H. and Test M.A. (1967) Naturalistic studies in aiding behavior. JOURNAL OF PERSONALITY AND SOCIAL PSYCHOLOGY, 6, 400–407

Bryant J. and Zillmann D. (1979) Effect of intensification of annoyance through unrelated residual excitation on substantially delayed hostile behavior. JOURNAL OF EXPERIMENTAL SOCIAL PSYCHOLOGY, 15, 470–480

Bryson L. (1983) Thirty years of research on the division of labour in Australian families. AUSTRALIAN JOURNAL OF SEX, MARRIAGE AND FAMILY, 4, 125–132

Bryson L. and Thompson F. (1972) AN AUSTRALIAN NEWTOWN: LIFE AND LEADERSHIP IN A NEW HOUSING SUBURB, Penguin, Harmondsworth

Buckhout R. (1980) Nearly 2000 witnesses can be wrong. BULLETIN OF THE PSYCHONOMIC SOCIETY, 16, 307–310

Buckhout R. and Baker E. (1977) Surveying the attitudes of seated jurors. SOCIAL ACTION AND THE LAW, 4, 98–101

Budd G.M. (1973) Australian physiological research in the Antarctic and Subarctic, with special reference to thermal stress and acclimatization. In Edholm O.G. and Gunderson E.K. (eds) POLAR HUMAN BIOLOGY, Heineman, Lond.

Burger J.M. (1986a) Temporal effects on attributions: Actor and observer differences. SOCIAL COGNITION, 4, 377–387

Burger J.M. (1986b) Increasing compliance by improving the deal: The that's-not-all technique. JOURNAL OF PERSONALITY AND SOCIAL PSYCHOLOGY, 51, 277–283

Burger J.M. and Cooper H.M. (1979) The desirability of control. MOTIVATION AND EMOTION, 3, 381–393

Burger J.M. and Petty R.E. (1981) The low-ball compliance technique: Task or person commitment? JOURNAL OF PERSONALITY AND SOCIAL PSYCHOLOGY, 40, 492–500

Burgess A.W. (ed.) (1985) RAPE AND SEXUAL ASSAULT: A RESEARCH HANDBOOK, Cartland, NY

Burgess A.W. (ed.) (1988) RAPE AND SEXUAL ASSAULT II, Garland Publishing, NY

Burgess A.W. and Holmstrom L. (1974) RAPE: VICTIMS OF CRISIS, Prentice Hall, Englewood Cliffs, NJ

Burgess A.W. and Holmstrom L. (1974) Rape trauma syndrome. AMERICAN JOURNAL OF PSYCHIATRY, 131, 980–986

Burke P.A., Kraut R.E. and Dworkin R.H. (1984) Traits, consistency, and self-schemata: What do our methods measure? JOURNAL OF PERSONALITY AND SOCIAL PSYCHOLOGY, 47, 568–579

Burke P.J. (1971) Task and social-emotional leadership role performance. SOCIOMETRY, 34, 22–40

Burns A. and Homel R. (1986) Sex role satisfaction among Australian children: Same sex, age and cultural group comparisons. PSYCHOLOGY OF WOMEN QUARTERLY, 10, 285–296

Burns A. and Homel R. (1989) Gender division of tasks by parents and their children. PSYCHOLOGY OF WOMEN QUARTERLY, 13, 113–125

Burn S.M. and Oskamp S. (1986) Increasing community recycling with persuasive communication and public commitment. JOURNAL OF APPLIED SOCIAL PSYCHOLOGY, 16, 29–41

Burnstein E. and Vinokur A. (1977) Persuasive argumentation and social comparison as determinants of attitude polarisation. JOURNAL OF EXPERIMENTAL PSYCHOLOGY, 13, 315–322

Burt M. and Albin R. (1981) Rape myths, rape definitions and probability of conviction. JOURNAL OF APPLIED SOCIAL PSYCHOLOGY, 11, 212–230

Burvill P.W. (1982) The epidemiology of psychiatric illness in industrialised society. AUSTRALIAN AND NEW ZEALAND JOURNAL OF PSYCHIATRY, 16, 144–151

Buss A.H. (1961) THE PSYCHOLOGY OF AGGRESSION, Wiley, NY

Buss A.H. (1971) Aggression pays. In Singer J.L. (ed.) THE CONTROL OF AGGRESSION AND VIOLENCE, Academic Press, NY

Buss A.H., Booker A. and Buss E. (1972) Firing a weapon and aggression. JOURNAL OF PERSONALITY AND SOCIAL PSYCHOLOGY, 22, 296–302

Buss A.R. (1976) Galton and sex differences: An historical note. JOURNAL OF THE HISTORY OF THE BEHAVIORAL SCIENCES, 12, 283–285

Buss D.M. (1984) Toward a psychology of person-environment (PE) correlation: The role of spouse selection. JOURNAL OF PERSONALITY AND SOCIAL PSYCHOLOGY, 47, 361–377

Buss D.M. (1985) Human mate selection. AMERICAN SCIENTIST, 73, 47–51

Buss D.M. (1988) The evolution of human intrasexual competition: Tactics of mate selection. JOURNAL OF PERSONALITY AND SOCIAL PSYCHOLOGY, 54, 616–628

Buss D.M. (1989) Sex differences in human mate preferences: Evolutionary hypotheses tested in 37 cultures. BEHAVIORAL AND BRAIN SCIENCES, 12, 1–49

Buss D.M. and Barnes M. (1986) Preferences in human mate selection. JOURNAL OF PERSONALITY AND SOCIAL PSYCHOLOGY, 50, 559–570

Bussey K. (1981) The role of beliefs about self and others in the sex-typing process. Paper presented at the Meeting of the Society for Research in Child Development, Boston

Bussey K. (1983) A social-cognitive appraisal of sex-role development. AUSTRALIAN JOURNAL OF PSYCHOLOGY, 35, 135–143

Bussey K. and Bandura A. (1984) The influence of gender constancy and social power and sex linked-modelling. JOURNAL OF PERSONALITY AND SOCIAL PSYCHOLOGY, 47, 1292–1302

Bussey K. and Perry D.G. (1982) Same-sex imitation: The avoidance of cross-sex models or the acceptance of same-sex models? SEX ROLES, 8, 773–784

Byrne D. (1961) The influence of propinquity and opportunities for interaction on classroom relationships. HUMAN RELATIONS, 14, 63–70

Byrne D. (1971) THE ATTRACTION PARADIGM, Academic Press, NY

Byrne D. and Blaylock B. (1963) Similarity and assumed similarity of attitudes between husbands and wives. JOURNAL OF ABNORMAL AND SOCIAL PSYCHOLOGY, 67, 636–640

Byrne D. and Clore G.L. (1970) A reinforcement model of evaluative responses. PERSONALITY: AN INTERNATIONAL JOURNAL, 1, 102–128

Byrne D., Clore G.L. and Smeaton G. (1986) The attraction hypothesis: Do similar attitudes affect anything? JOURNAL OF PERSONALITY AND SOCIAL PSYCHOLOGY, 51, 1167–1170

Byrne D. and Kelley K. (1984) PORNOGRAPHY AND SEXUAL AGGRESSION, Academic Press, Orlando, Florida

Byrne D. and Nelson D. (1965) Attraction as a linear proportion of positive reinforcements. JOURNAL OF PERSONALITY AND SOCIAL PSYCHOLOGY, 1, 659–663

Cacioppo J.T., Martzke J.S., Petty R.E. and Tassinary L.G. (1988) Specific forms of facial EMG response index emotions during an interview: From Darwin to the continuous flow hypothesis of affect-laden information processing. JOURNAL OF PERSONALITY AND SOCIAL PSYCHOLOGY, 54, 552–604

Cacioppo J.T. and Petty R.E. (1981) Effects of extent of thought on the pleasantness rating of P-O-X triads: Evidence for three judgmental tendencies in evaluating social situations. JOURNAL OF PERSONALITY AND SOCIAL PSYCHOLOGY, 40, 1000–1009

Cacioppo J.T., Petty R.E. and Losch M.E. (1986) Attributions of responsibility for helping and doing harm: Evidence for confusion of responsibility. JOURNAL OF PERSONALITY AND SOCIAL PSYCHOLOGY 50, 100–105

Caldwell M.D. (1976) Communication and sex effects in a five-person prisoner's dilemma game. JOURNAL OF PERSONALITY AND SOCIAL PSYCHOLOGY, 33, 273–280

Calhoun J.B. (1962) Population density and social pathology. SCIENTIFIC AMERICAN, 206, 139–148

Calhoun J.B. (1970) Space and the strategy of life. EKISTICS, 29, 425–437

Calhoun L., Selby J. and Warring L. (1976) Social perception of the victim's causal role in rape: An explanatory examination of four factors. HUMAN RELATIONS, 29, 517–526

Callan V.J., Gallois C., Noller P. and Kashima Y. (1991) SOCIAL PSYCHOLOGY, Harcourt Brace Jovanovich, Sydney

Callan V.J. and Noller P. (1987) MARRIAGE AND THE FAMILY, Methuen, Sydney

Callan V.J. and St John D. (1984) Self and other perceptions of urban and rural Australian aboriginal and white youth. JOURNAL OF SOCIAL PSYCHOLOGY, 123, 179–187

Cameron C., Oskamp S. and Sparks W. (1977) Courtship American style: Newspaper ads. FAMILY COORDINATOR, 26, 27–30

Campbell D.E. and Beets J.L. (1978) Lunacy and the moon. PSYCHOLOGICAL BULLETIN, 85, 1123–1129

Campbell D.T. (1957) Factors relevant to the validity of experiments in social settings. PSYCHOLOGICAL BULLETIN, 54, 297–312

Campbell D.T. (1975) On the conflicts between biological and social evolution and between psychology and moral tradition. AMERICAN PSYCHOLOGIST, 30, 1103–1126

Campbell D.T. and Pettigrew T.F. (1959) Racial and moral crisis: The role of Little Rock ministers. AMERICAN JOURNAL OF SOCIOLOGY, 64, 509–516

Campbell J.D. (1986) Similarity and uniqueness: The effects of attribute type, relevance and individual differences in self-esteem and depression. JOURNAL OF PERSONALITY AND SOCIAL PSYCHOLOGY, 50, 281–294

Carducci B.J., Cozby P.C. and Ward C.D. (1978) Sexual arousal and interpersonal evaluations. JOURNAL OF EXPERIMENTAL SOCIAL PSYCHOLOGY, 14, 449–457

Carlsmith J.M. and Anderson C.A. (1979) Ambient temperature and the occurrence of collective violence: A new analysis. JOURNAL OF PERSONALITY AND SOCIAL PSYCHOLOGY, 37, 337–344

Carlsmith J.M., Ellsworth P. and Whiteside J. (1968) Guilt, confession and compliance. Unpublished manuscript

Carlson B.W. (1990) Anchoring and adjustment in judgments under risk. JOURNAL OF EXPERIMENTAL PSYCHOLOGY, LEARNING, MEMORY AND COGNITION, 16, 665–676

Carlston D.E. and Shovar N. (1983) Effects of performance attributions on others' perceptions of attribution. JOURNAL OF PERSONALITY AND SOCIAL PSYCHOLOGY, 44, 515–525

Carpenter P.G. and Fleishman J.A. (1987) Linking intentions and behavior: Australian students' college plans and college attendance. AMERICAN EDUCATIONAL RESEARCH JOURNAL, 24, 79–105

Carson R. (1962) SILENT SPRING, Houghton Mifflin, Boston

Carver C.S. and Scheier M.F. (1981) ATTENTION AND SELF-REGULATION: A CONTROL THEORY APPROACH TO HUMAN BEHAVIOR, Springer-Verlag, NY

Cash T.F. and Derlega V.J. (1978) The matching hypothesis: Physical attractiveness among same-sexed friends. PERSONALITY AND SOCIAL PSYCHOLOGY BULLETIN, 4, 240–243

Cash T.F. and Duncan N.C. (1984) Physical attractiveness stereotyping among black American college students. JOURNAL OF SOCIAL PSYCHOLOGY, 122, 71–77

Cashmore J.A (1991) The reliability and credibility of children's evidence. Paper to the CHILD AS WITNESS SEMINAR, February, University of Wollongong, Wollongong

Cashmore J.A. and Goodnow J.J. (1986) Parent-child agreement on attributional beliefs. INTERNATIONAL JOURNAL OF BEHAVIORAL DEVELOPMENT, 9, 191–204

Caspi A., Herbener E.S. and Ozer D.J. (1992) Shared experience and the similarity of personalities: A longitudinal study of married couples. JOURNAL OF PERSONALITY AND SOCIAL PSYCHOLOGY, 62, 281–291

Cate R.M., Lloyd S.A. and Long E. (1988) The role of rewards and fairness in developing premarital relationships. JOURNAL OF MARRIAGE AND THE FAMILY, 50, 443–452

Ceci S., Ross D. and Toglia M. (eds) (1989) NEW DIRECTIONS IN CHILD WITNESS RESEARCH, Springer-Verlag, NY

Centre for Police Studies (1988) Roles of women in the police in Scotland. University of Strathclyde, Scotland

Cerf C. and Navarsky V. (1984) THE EXPERTS SPEAK, Pantheon Books, NY

Cervone D. and Palmer B.W. (1990) Anchoring biases and the perseverance of self-efficacy beliefs. COGNITIVE THERAPY AND RESEARCH, 14, 401–416

Chacko T.I. (1982) Women and equal employment opportunity: Some unintended effects. JOURNAL OF APPLIED PSYCHOLOGY, 67, 119–123

Chaiken S. (1987) The heuristic model of persuasion. In Zanna M.P., Olson J.M. and Herman C.P. (eds) SOCIAL INFLUENCE: THE ONTARIO SYMPOSIUM (Vol. 5), Erlbaum, Hillsdale, NJ

Chaiken S. and Baldwin M.W. (1981) Affective-cognitive consistency and the effect of salient behavioral information on the self-perception of attitudes. JOURNAL OF PERSONALITY AND SOCIAL PSYCHOLOGY, 41, 1–12

Chaiken S. and Stangor C. (1987) Attitudes and attitude change. ANNUAL REVIEW OF PSYCHOLOGY, 38, 575–630

Chan J. (1992) POLICING IN A MULTICULTURAL SOCIETY: A STUDY OF THE NSW POLICE, Commissioned Report, School of Social Science and Policy Service, University of NSW

Chapman L.J. (1967) Illusory correlation in observational report. JOURNAL OF VERBAL LEARNING AND VERBAL BEHAVIOR, 6, 151–155

Chau L.L., Johnson R.C., Bowers J.K., et al. (1990) Intrinsic and extrinsic religiosity as related to conscience, adjustment and altruism. PERSONALITY AND INDIVIDUAL DIFFERENCES, 11, 397–400

Chen H., Yates B.T. and McGinnies E. (1988) Effects of involvement on observers' estimates of consensus, distinctiveness and consistency. PERSONALITY AND SOCIAL PSYCHOLOGY BULLETIN, 14, 468–478

Chen T.H. (1988) Saving faith to serving faith: A model to facilitate altruistic behavior in Christians. JOURNAL OF PSYCHOLOGY AND CHRISTIANITY, 7, 45–55

Cherry F. and Byrne D. (1977) Authoritarianism. In Blass T. (ed.) PERSONALITY VARIABLES IN SOCIAL BEHAVIOR, Erlbaum, Hillsdale, NJ

Cherry L. and Lewis M. (1976) Mothers and two-year-olds: A study of sex differentiated aspects of verbal interaction. DEVELOPMENTAL PSYCHOLOGY, 12, 278–282

Chi M.T. (1983) TRENDS IN MEMORY DEVELOPMENT RESEARCH, Karger, Basel

Chibnall S. (1989) Law and order news: An analysis of crime reporting in the British press. MEDIA AND POLICE, 14, 257

Chiu L.P. (1988) Do weather, day of the week, and address affect the rate of attempted suicide in Hong Kong? SOCIAL PSYCHIATRY AND PSYCHIATRIC EPIDEMIOLOGY, 23, 229–235

Choderow N. (1978) THE REPRODUCTION OF MOTHERING: PSYCHOANALYSIS AND THE SOCIOLOGY OF GENDER, University of California Press, Berkeley

Chow S.L. (1988) An examination of Jussim's (1986) three-stage model of self-fulfilling prophecies. JOURNAL OF PSYCHOLOGY, 122, 95–99

Christensen L. (1988) Deception in psychological research: When is its use justified? PERSONALITY AND SOCIAL PSYCHOLOGY BULLETIN, 14, 664–675

Christian J.J. (1963) Pathology of overpopulation. MILITARY MEDICINE, 128, 571–603

Christian J.J., Flyger V. and Davis D.E. (1960) Factors in the mass mortality of a herd of Sika deer, *Cervus Nippon*. CHESAPEAKE SCIENCE, 1, 79–95

Christie R. and Geis F.L. (eds) (1970) STUDIES IN MACHIAVELLIANISM, Academic Press, NY

Christie R. and Jahoda M. (eds) (1954) STUDIES IN THE SCOPE AND METHOD OF THE AUTHORITARIAN PERSONALITY, Free Press, NY

Christopher F.S. and Cate R.M. (1985) Premarital sexual pathways and relationship development. JOURNAL OF SOCIAL AND PERSONAL RELATIONSHIPS, 2, 271–288

Cialdini R.B. (1985) INFLUENCE: SCIENCE AND PRACTICE, Scott-Foresman, Glenview, Ill.

Cialdini R.B., Borden R.J., Thorne A., et al. (1976) Basking in reflected glory: Three (football) field studies. JOURNAL OF PERSONALITY AND SOCIAL PSYCHOLOGY, 34, 366–375

Cialdini R.B., Cacioppo J.T., Bassett R. and Miller J.A. (1978) Low-ball procedure for producing compliance: commitment then cost. JOURNAL OF PERSONALITY AND SOCIAL PSYCHOLOGY, 36, 463–476

Cialdini R.B., Darby B.L. and Vincent J.E. (1973) Transgression and altruism: A case for hedonism. JOURNAL OF EXPERIMENTAL SOCIAL PSYCHOLOGY, 9, 502–516

Cialdini R.B. and De Nicholas M.E. (1989) Self-presentation by association. JOURNAL OF PERSONALITY AND SOCIAL PSYCHOLOGY, 57, 626–631

Cialdini R.B. and Kenrick D.T. (1976) Altruism as hedonism: A social developmental perspective on the relationship of negative mood state and helping. JOURNAL OF PERSONALITY AND SOCIAL PSYCHOLOGY, 34, 907–914

Cialdini R.B., Levy A., Herman P., et al. (1976) Elastic shifts of opinion: Determinants of direction and durability. JOURNAL OF PERSONALITY AND SOCIAL PSYCHOLOGY, 34, 663–672

Cialdini R.B., Reno R.R. and Kallgren C.A. (1990) A focus theory of normative conduct: Recycling the concept of norms to reduce littering in public places. JOURNAL OF PERSONALITY AND SOCIAL PSYCHOLOGY, 58, 1015–1026

Cialdini R.D., Vinart J.E., Lewis S.K., Catalan J., Wheeler D. and Darby B.L. (1975) Reciprocal concessions procedure for evidencing compliance: The foot-in-the-door technique. JOURNAL OF PERSONALITY AND SOCIAL PSYCHOLOGY, 31, 206–215

Clark J.M., Brown J.C. and Hochstein L.M. (1989) Institutional religion and gay/lesbian oppression. MARRIAGE AND FAMILY REVIEW, 14, 265–284

Clark M.S. (1984) Record keeping in two types

of relationships. JOURNAL OF PERSONALITY AND SOCIAL PSYCHOLOGY, 47, 549–557

Clark M.S. and Mills J. (1979) Interpersonal attraction in exchange and communal relationships. JOURNAL OF PERSONALITY AND SOCIAL PSYCHOLOGY, 37, 12–24

Clark M.S., Mills J. and Corcoran D.M. (1989) Keeping track of needs and inputs of friends and strangers. PERSONALITY AND SOCIAL PSYCHOLOGY BULLETIN, 15, 533–542

Clark M.S., Mills J. and Powell M.C. (1986) Keeping track of needs in communal and exchange relationships. JOURNAL OF PERSONALITY AND SOCIAL PSYCHOLOGY, 52, 333–338

Clark M.S. and Reis H.T. (1988) Interpersonal processes in close relationships. ANNUAL REVIEW OF PSYCHOLOGY, 39, 609–672.

Clore G.L. and Baldridge B. (1968) Interpersonal attraction: The role of agreement and topic interest. JOURNAL OF PERSONALITY AND SOCIAL PSYCHOLOGY, 9, 340–346

Cobbett W. (1821) RURAL RIDES, (Edited and introduced by G. Woodcock, 1967), Penguin, Harmondsworth

Cochran S.D. and Peplau L.A. (1991) Sexual risk reduction behaviors among young heterosexual adults. SOCIAL SCIENCE AND MEDICINE, 33, 25–36

Cohen A. (1962) An experiment on small rewards for discrepant compliance and attitude change. In Brehm J.W. and Cohen A.R. (eds) EXPLORATIONS IN COGNITIVE DISSONANCE, Wiley, NY

Cohen C.E. (1981) Person categories and social perception: Testing some boundaries of the processing effects of prior knowledge. JOURNAL OF PERSONALITY AND SOCIAL PSYCHOLOGY, 40, 441–452

Cohen M.J., Marx M.S. and Werner P. (1989) Full moon: Does it influence agitated nursing home residents? JOURNAL OF CLINICAL PSYCHOLOGY, 45, 611–614

Cohen S. (1978) Environmental load and the allocation of attention. In Baum A., et al. (eds) ADVANCES IN ENVIRONMENTAL PSYCHOLOGY (Vol. 1), Erlbaum, Hillsdale, NJ

Cohen S. and Wills T.A. (1985) Stress, social support and the buffering hypothesis. PSYCHOLOGICAL BULLETIN, 98, 310–357

Cohen S., Glass D.C. and Singer J.E. (1973) Apartment noise, auditory discrimination, and reading ability in children. JOURNAL OF EXPERIMENTAL SOCIAL PSYCHOLOGY, 9, 407–422

Cohn N.B. and Strassberg D.S. (1983) Self-disclosure reciprocity among preadolescents. PERSONALITY AND SOCIAL PSYCHOLOGY BULLETIN, 9, 97–102

Coid J. (1986) Socio-cultural factors in alcohol related aggression. In Brain P.F. (ed.) ALCOHOL AND AGGRESSION, Croom Helm, Lond.

Coke J.S., Batson C.D. and McDavis K. (1978) Empathic mediation of helping: A two-stage model. JOURNAL OF PERSONALITY AND SOCIAL PSYCHOLOGY, 36, 752–766

Colby A., Kohlberg L., Gibbs J. and Lieberman M. (1983) A longitudinal study of moral judgment. MONOGRAPHS OF THE SOCIETY FOR RESEARCH IN CHILD DEVELOPMENT, 49, 200

Coleman D.H. and Straus M.A. (1983) Alcohol abuse and family violence. In Gottheil E., Druley K.A., Skoloda T.E. and Waxman H.M. (eds) DRUG ABUSE AND AGGRESSION, Charles C. Thomas, Springfield, Illinois

Condon J.W. and Crano W.D. (1988) Inferred evaluation and the relation between attitude similarity and interpersonal attraction. JOURNAL OF PERSONALITY AND SOCIAL PSYCHOLOGY, 54, 789–797

Condonis M., Paroission K. and Aldrich B. (1989) THE MUTUAL HELP GROUP. A THERAPEUTIC PROGRAM FOR WOMEN WHO HAVE BEEN ABUSED, A REFERENCE MANUAL, Cider Press, Wollongong

Condry J. and Condry S. (1976) Sex differences: A study in the eye of the beholder. CHILD DEVELOPMENT, 47, 812–819

Cone J.D. and Hayes S.C. (1980) ENVIRON-MENTAL PROBLEMS/BEHAVIORAL SOLUTIONS, Brooks/Cole, Monterey, Ca.

Conger J.A. and Kanungo R.N. (eds) (1988) CHARISMATIC LEADERSHIP, Jossey-Bass, San Francisco

Connell R.W. (1987) GENDER AND POWER SOCIETY, THE PERSON AND SEXUAL POLITICS, Allen and Unwin, Sydney

Connell R.W. (1990) The state, gender, and sexual politics: Theory and appraisal. THEORY AND SOCIETY, 19, 507–544

Connell R.W. (1992) Masculinity, violence and war. In Kimmel M. and Messner M. (eds) MEN'S LIVES (2nd edn), MacMillan, NY

Connors J.R. and Heaven P.C. (1990) Belief in a just world and attitudes toward AIDS sufferers. JOURNAL OF SOCIAL PSYCHOLOGY, 130, 559–560

Constantini E. and Craik K.H. (1980) Personality and politicians: California party leaders. JOURNAL OF PERSONALITY AND SOCIAL PSYCHOLOGY, 38, 641–646

Cook M. (1984) LEVELS OF PERSONALITY, Holt, Rinehart and Winston, NY

Cook S.W. (1984) The 1954 Social Science Statement and school desegregation: A reply to Gerard. AMERICAN PSYCHOLOGIST, 39, 819–832

Cooley C.H. (1902) HUMAN NATURE AND THE SOCIAL ORDER, (Rev. edn 1922), Scriner's, NY

Cooper H. and Hazelrigg P. (1988) Personal moderators of interpersonal expectancy effects: An integrative research review. JOURNAL OF PERSONALITY AND SOCIAL PSYCHOLOGY, 55, 937–949

Cooper J. and Axsom D. (1982) Effort

justification in psychotherapy. In Weary G. and Mirels H. (eds) INTEGRATIONS OF CLINICAL AND SOCIAL PSYCHOL-OGY, Oxford University Press, NY

Cooper J. and Fazio R.H. (1984) A new look at dissonance theory. In Berkowitz L. (ed.) ADVANCES IN EXPERIMENTAL SOCIAL PSYCHOLOGY (Vol. 17), Academic Press, NY

Cooper J. and Jones E.E. (1969) Opinion divergence as a strategy to avoid being miscast. JOURNAL OF PERSONALITY AND SOCIAL PSYCHOLOGY, 13, 23–30

Cosmides L. and Tooby J. (1989) Evolutionary psychology and the generation of culture, Part II. Case study: A computational theory of social exchange. ETHOLOGY AND SOCIOBIOLOGY, 10, 51–97

Costanzo I.M. (1977) The effect of probable retaliation and sex related variables on obedience. DISSERTATION AB-STRACTS INTERNATIONAL 25:4214B, University Microfilms, Ann Arbor

Cotton J.L. (1981) A review of research on Schachter's theory of emotion and the misattribution of arousal. EUROPEAN JOURNAL OF SOCIAL PSYCHOLOGY, 11, 365–397

Cotton J.L. (1986) Ambient temperature and violent crime. JOURNAL OF APPLIED SOCIAL PSYCHOLOGY, 16, 786–801

Cotton S. and Antill J.K. (1984) Noncom-pliance: Medical and psychological aspects. AUSTRALIAN PSYCHOLOGIST, 19, 193–203

Cottrell N.B., Wack K.L., Sekerak G.J. and Rittle R. (1968) Social facilitation of dominant responses by the presence of an audience and the mere presence of others. JOURNAL OF PERSONALITY AND SOCIAL PSYCHOLOGY, 9, 245–250

Court J.H. (1984) Sex and violence: A ripple effect. In Malamuth N.M. and Donnerstein E. (eds) PORNOGRAPHY AND SEXUAL AGGRESSION, Academic Press, NY

Cowlishaw G. (1986) Race for exclusion. AUSTRALIAN AND NEW ZEALAND JOURNAL OF SOCIOLOGY, 22, 3–24

Cowlishaw G. (1988) BLACK, WHITE OR BRINDLE: RACE IN RURAL AUSTRALIA, Cambridge University Press, Sydney

Cox V.C., Paulus P.B. and McCain G. (1984) Prison crowding research: The relevance for prison housing standards and a general approach regarding crowding phenomena. AMERICAN PSYCHOLOGIST, 39, 1148–1160

Craddock A.E. (1974) Task and emotional behaviour in the marital dyad. AUSTRALIAN JOURNAL OF PSYCHOLOGY, 26, 15–23

Craddock A.E. (1980) The effect of incongru-ent marital role expectations upon couples' degree of role consensus in the first year of marriage. AUSTRALIAN JOURNAL OF PSYCHOLOGY, 32, 117–125

Craddock A.E. (1983) Correlations between marital role expectations and relationship

satisfaction among engaged couples. AUSTRALIAN JOURNAL OF SEX, MARRIAGE AND FAMILY, 4, 33–46

Craddock A.E. (1988) Marital role expectations and premarital satisfaction among Australian couples: 1979–80 versus 1987. AUSTRALIAN JOURNAL OF SEX, MARRIAGE AND FAMILY, 9, 159–168

Craddock A.E. (1991) Relationships between attitudinal similarity, couple structure, and couple satisfaction within married and defacto couples. AUSTRALIAN JOURNAL OF PSYCHOLOGY, 43, 11–16

Craske M-L. (1985) Improving persistence through observational learning and attribution retraining. BRITISH JOURNAL OF EDUCATIONAL PSYCHOLOGY, 55, 138–147

Craske M-L. (1988) Learned helplessness, self-worth motivation and attribution retraining for primary school children. BRITISH JOURNAL OF EDUCATIONAL PSYCHOLOGY, 58, 152–164

Crawford C.B. (1989) The theory of evolution: Of what value to psychology? JOURNAL OF COMPARATIVE PSYCHOLOGY, 103, 4–22

Crawford J., Kippax S., Onyx J., Gault U. and Benton P. (1990) Women theorising their experiences of anger: A study using memory-work. AUSTRALIAN PSYCHOLOGIST, Vol. 25, No. 3, November

Crawford J., Kippax S., Onyx J., Gault U. and Benton P. (1992) EMOTION AND GENDER: CONSTRUCTING MEANING FROM MEMORY, Sage Publications, London

Crisp L. (1989) When a child's word is the only evidence. THE BULLETIN, 111, (No. 5697), 140–144

Criss T.B. and Marcum J.P. (1981) A lunar effect on fertility. SOCIAL BIOLOGY, 28, 75–80

Crocker J., Thompson L.L., McGraw K.M. and Ingerman C. (1987) Downward comparison, prejudice, and evaluations of others: Effects of self-esteem and threat. JOURNAL OF PERSONALITY AND SOCIAL PSYCHOLOGY, 52, 907–916

Cromwell P.F., Marks A., Olson J.N. and Avary D.W. (1991) Group effects on decision-making by burglars. PSYCHOLOGICAL REPORTS, 69, 579–588

Crook J.H. (1981) The evolutionary ethology of social processes in man. In Kellerman H. (ed.) GROUP COHESION, Grune and Stratton, NY

Cropanzano R. and Folger R. (1989) Referent cognitions and task decision autonomy: Beyond equity theory. JOURNAL OF APPLIED PSYCHOLOGY, 74, 293–299

Crosby F. (1976) A model of egoistic relative deprivation. PSYCHOLOGICAL REVIEW, 83, 85–113

Crosby F. (1982) RELATIVE DEPRIVATION AND WORKING WOMEN, Oxford University Press, NY

Croyle R. and Cooper J. (1983) Dissonance arousal: Physiological evidence. JOURNAL

OF PERSONALITY AND SOCIAL PSYCHOLOGY, 45, 782–791

Crutchfield R.S. (1955) Conformity and character. AMERICAN PSYCHOLOGIST, 10, 191–199

Culver R., Rotton J. and Kelly I.W. (1988) Geophysical variables and behavior: XLIX. Moon mechanisms and myths: A critical appraisal of explanations of purported lunar effects on human behavior. PSYCHOLOGICAL REPORTS, 62, 683–710

Cunningham J.D. and Antill J.K. (1981) Love in developing relationships. In Duck S. and Gilmour R. (eds) PERSONAL RELATION-SHIPS 2: DEVELOPING PERSONAL RELATIONSHIPS, Academic Press, NY

Cunningham M.R. (1979) Weather, mood, and helping behavior: Quasi experiments with the sunshine Samaritan. JOURNAL OF PERSONALITY AND SOCIAL PSYCHOLOGY, 37, 1947–1956

Cunningham M.R. (1986) Measuring the physical in physical attractiveness: Quasi-experiments on the sociobiology of female facial beauty. JOURNAL OF PERSONAL-ITY AND SOCIAL PSYCHOLOGY, 50, 925–935

Cunningham M.R. and Barbee A.P. (1991) Differential K-selection versus ecological determinants of race differences in sexual behavior. JOURNAL OF RESEARCH IN PERSONALITY, 25, 205–217

Cunningham M.R., Steinberg J. and Grev R. (1980) Wanting to and having to help: Separate motivations for positive mood and guilt-induced helping. JOURNAL OF PERSONALITY AND SOCIAL PSYCHOLOGY, 38, 181–192

Curran J.P. and Lippold S. (1975) The effects of physical attraction and attitude similarity on attraction in dating dyads. JOURNAL OF PERSONALITY, 43, 528–539

Currie A. (1982) The sex factor in occupational choice. AUSTRALIAN AND NEW ZEALAND JOURNAL OF SOCIOLOGY, 18, 180–195

Curtis R.C. and Miller K. (1986) Believing another likes or dislikes you: Behavior making the beliefs come true. JOURNAL OF PERSONALITY AND SOCIAL PSYCHOLOGY, 51, 284–290

Cutrona C.E. (1986) Behavioral investigations of social support: A microanalytic investigation. JOURNAL OF PERSONAL-ITY AND SOCIAL PSYCHOLOGY, 51, 201–208

Cyr J.J. and Kalpin R.A. (1987) Geophysical variables and behavior: XLVI. The lunar-lunacy relationship: A poorly evaluated hypothesis. PSYCHOLOGICAL REPORTS, 61, 391–400

Cyr J.J. and Kalpin R.A. (1988) Investigating the lunar-lunacy relationship: A reply to Rotton and Kelly. PSYCHOLOGICAL REPORTS, 62, 319–322

Czeisler C.A., Allan J.S., Strogatz S.H., et al. (1986) Bright light resets the human

circadian pacemaker independent of the timing of the sleep-wake cycle. SCIENCE, 233, 667–671

Daly M. and Wilson M. (1979) SEX, EVOLUTION AND BEHAVIOR: ADAPTATIONS FOR REPRODUCTION, Duxbury, Ma.

Dane F. and Wrightsman L. (1982) Effects of defendants and victim's characteristics on jurors' verdicts. In Kerr N.L. and Bray R.M. (eds) THE PSYCHOLOGY OF THE COURTROOM, Academic Press, NY

Danziger K. (1979) The positivist repudiation of Wundt. JOURNAL OF THE HISTORY OF THE BEHAVIOURAL SCIENCES, 15, 205–230

Danziger K. (1983) Origins and basic principles of Wundt's Volkerpsychologie. BRITISH JOURNAL OF SOCIAL PSYCHOLOGY, 22, 303–313

Darden D.K. and Koski P.R. (1988) Using the personal ads: A deviant activity? DEVIANT BEHAVIOR, 9, 383–400

Darley J.M. and Batson C.D. (1973) From Jerusalem to Jericho: A study of situational and dispositional variables in helping behavior. JOURNAL OF PERSONALITY AND SOCIAL PSYCHOLOGY, 27, 100–108

Darley J.M. and Berscheid E. (1967) Increased liking as a result of anticipation of personal contact. HUMAN RELATIONS, 20, 29–39

Darley J.M. and Fazio J.M. (1980) Expectancy and confirmation processes arising in the social interaction sequence. AMERICAN PSYCHOLOGIST, 35, 867–881

Darley J.M. and Latane B. (1968) Bystander intervention in emergencies: Diffusion of responsibility. JOURNAL OF PERSONALITY AND SOCIAL PSYCHOLOGY, 8, 377–383

Darley J.M., Teger A.I. and Lewis L.D. (1973) Do groups always inhibit individual's response to potential emergencies? JOURNAL OF PERSONALITY AND SOCIAL PSYCHOLOGY, 26, 395–399

Darwin C. (1871) THE DESCENT OF MAN AND SELECTION IN RELATION TO SEX, Great Books (Vol. 49), Encyclopaedia Britannica, Chicago

Davidson G.C. and Valins S. (1969) Mainte-nance of self-attributed and drug-attributed behavior change. JOURNAL OF PERSONALITY AND SOCIAL PSYCHOLOGY, 11, 25–33

Davis D. (1982) Determinants of responsiveness in dyadic interactions. In Ickes W. and Knowles E.S. (eds) PERSONALITY, ROLES AND SOCIAL BEHAVIOR, Springer-Verlag, NY

Davis D.E. (1971) Physiological effects of continued crowding. In Esser A.A. (ed.) BEHAVIOR AND ENVIRONMENT, Plenum Press, NY

Davis J.D. (1976) Self-disclosure in an acquaintance exercise: Responsibility for level of intimacy. JOURNAL OF PERSONALITY AND SOCIAL PSYCHOLOGY, 33, 787–792

Davis J.H. (1969) GROUP PERFORMANCE, Addison-Wesley, Reading, MA

Davis, J.H. (1989) Psychology and the law: The last 15 years. JOURNAL OF APPLIED SOCIAL PSYCHOLOGY, 19, 119–230

Davis J.H., Tindale R.S., Nagao D.H., et al. (1984) Effects in multiple decisions by groups: A demonstration with mock juries and trial procedures. JOURNAL OF PERSONALITY AND SOCIAL PSYCHOLOGY, 47, 1003–1012

Davis K.E. and Jones E.E. (1960) Changes in interpersonal perception as a means of reducing cognitive dissonance. JOURNAL OF ABNORMAL AND SOCIAL PSYCHOLOGY, 61, 402–410

Davis M.M. (1906) GABRIEL TARDE, Columbia University Press, NY

Davis M.S. (1968) Physiological, psychological and demographic factors in patient compliance with doctors' orders. MEDICAL CARE, 6, 115–6122

Davis S. (1990) Men as success objects and women as sex objects: A study of personal advertisements. SEX ROLES, 23, 43–50

Davitz J.R. (1952) The effects of previous training on post-frustration behavior. JOURNAL OF ABNORMAL AND SOCIAL PSYCHOLOGY, 47, 309–315

Dawes R.M. (1973) The commons dilemma game: An N-person mixed-motive game with a dominating strategy for defection. ORI. RESEARCH BULLETIN, 13, 1–12

Dawes R.M. (1980) Social dilemmas. ANNUAL REVIEW OF PSYCHOLOGY, 31, 169–193

Dawes R.M. and Smith T.L. (1985) Attitude and opinion measurement. In Lindzey G. and Aronson E. (eds) HANDBOOK OF SOCIAL PSYCHOLOGY (Vol. 1), (3rd edn) Random House, NY

Dawkins R. (1976) THE SELFISH GENE, Oxford University Press, NY

Dawkins R. (1988) THE BLIND WATCH-MAKER, Penguin Books, Lond.

Deaux K. (1976) THE BEHAVIOR OF WOMEN AND MEN, Brooks/Cole, Ca.

Deaux K. (1984) From individual differences to social categories: Analysis of a decade's research on gender. AMERICAN PSYCHOLOGIST, 39, 105–116

Deaux K. and Hanna R. (1984) Courtship in the personals column: The influence of gender and sexual orientation. SEX ROLES, 11, 363–375

de Castro J.M. (1991) Social facilitation of spontaneous meal sizes of humans occurs on both weekdays and weekends. PHYSIOL-OGY AND BEHAVIOR, 49, 1289–1291

DeGree C.E. and Snyder C.R. (1985) Adler's psychology today: Personal history of traumatic life events as a self-handicapping strategy. JOURNAL OF PERSONALITY AND SOCIAL PSYCHOLOGY, 48, 1512–1519

Dengerink H.A. and Myers J.D. (1977) The effects of failure and depression on subsequent aggression. JOURNAL OF

PERSONALITY AND SOCIAL
PSYCHOLOGY, 35, 88–96

Dengerink H.A., Schnedler R.W. and Covey
M.K. (1978) Role of avoidance in aggressive
response to attack and no attack. JOURNAL
OF PERSONALITY AND SOCIAL
PSYCHOLOGY, 36, 1044–1053

Dennis W. (1992) HOT AND BOTHERED:
WOMEN SEX AND LOVE IN THE 1990S,
Penguin, Ringwood, Vic.

Denno D.J. (1982) Sex differences in cognition
and crime: Early developmental, biological
and social correlates. Unpublished Doctoral
dissertation, University of Pennsylvannia,
Phil.

Denno D.J. (1988) Human biology and criminal
responsibility: Free will or free ride?
UNIVERSITY OF PENNSYLVANIA LAW
REVIEW, 137, 615–671

DePaulo B.M., Brown P.L., Ishii S. and Fisher
J.D. (1981) Help that works: The effects of
aid on subsequent task performance.
JOURNAL OF PERSONALITY AND
SOCIAL PSYCHOLOGY, 41, 478–487

DePaulo B.M. and Fisher J.D. (1980) The costs
of asking for help. BASIC AND APPLIED
SOCIAL PSYCHOLOGY, 1, 23–35

DePaulo B.M. and Rosenthal R. (1979) Telling
lies. JOURNAL OF PERSONALITY AND
SOCIAL PSYCHOLOGY, 37, 1713–1722

DePaulo B.M., Stone J.L. and Lassiter G.D.
(1985) Deceiving and detecting deceit. In
Schlenker B.R. (ed.) THE SELF AND
SOCIAL LIFE, McGraw-Hill, NY

Derlega V.J. (ed.) (1984) COMMUNICA-
TION, INTIMACY AND CLOSE
RELATIONSHIPS, Academic Press, NY

Dermer M. and Pyszczynski T.A. (1978) The
effects of erotica on men's loving and liking
responses for the women they love.
JOURNAL OF PERSONALITY AND
SOCIAL PSYCHOLOGY, 36, 1306–1309

Dermer M. and Thiel D.L. (1975) When beauty
may fail. JOURNAL OF PERSONALITY
AND SOCIAL PSYCHOLOGY, 31,
1168–1176

Deseran F.A. and Chung C.S. (1979)
Appearance, role-taking and reactions to
deviance: Some experimental findings.
SOCIAL PSYCHOLOGY QUARTERLY,
42, 426–430

Deutsch J.H. and Gerard H.B. (1955) A study of
normative and informational social
influences upon individual judgement.
JOURNAL OF ABNORMAL
PSYCHOLOGY, 51, 629–636

Deutsch M. (1960) The effect of motivational
orientation upon trust and suspicion.
HUMAN RELATIONS, 13, 123–139

Deutsch M. (1975) Equity, equality and need:
What determines which value will be used as
the basis of distributive justice? JOURNAL
OF SOCIAL ISSUES, 31, 137–149

Deutsch M. (1985) DISTRIBUTIVE JUSTICE:
A SOCIAL PSYCHOLOGICAL
PERSPECTIVE, Yale University Press, New
Haven

Devine P.G. (1989) Stereotypes and prejudice:
Their automatic and controlled

components. JOURNAL OF PERSONAL-
ITY AND SOCIAL PSYCHOLOGY, 56,
5–18

de Waal F.B. (1989) PEACEMAKING
AMONG PRIMATES, Harvard University
Press, Cambridge, Ma.

de-Young R. (1986) Some psychological aspects
of recycling: The structure of conservation
satisfactions. ENVIRONMENT AND
BEHAVIOR, 18, 435–449

Dickson P.R. and Miniard P.W. (1978) A
further examination of two laboratory tests of
the extended Fishbein attitude model.
JOURNAL OF CONSUMER RESEARCH,
4, 261–266

Diener E. (1976) Effects of prior destructive
behavior anonymity and group presence on
deindividuation and aggression. JOURNAL
OF PERSONALITY AND SOCIAL
PSYCHOLOGY, 33, 497–507

Dienhart A. and Myers-Avis J. (1990) Men in
therapy: Exploring feminist-informed
alternatives. JOURNAL OF FEMINIST
FAMILY THERAPY, 2, 25–49

Dienstbier R.A. and Munter P.O. (1971)
Cheating as a function of the labeling of
natural arousal. JOURNAL OF PERSON-
ALITY AND SOCIAL PSYCHOLOGY, 17,
208–213

Dillehay R. and Nietzel M. (1985) Juror
experience and jury verdicts. LAW AND
HUMAN BEHAVIOUR, 9, 2, 179–191

Dion K.K. (1972) Physical attractiveness and
evaluations of children's transgressions.
JOURNAL OF PERSONALITY AND
SOCIAL PSYCHOLOGY, 24, 285–290

Dion K.K., Berscheid E. and Walster E. (1972)
What is beautiful is good. JOURNAL OF
PERSONALITY AND SOCIAL
PSYCHOLOGY, 24, 285–290

Dion K.K. and Stein S. (1978) Physical
attractiveness and interpersonal influence.
JOURNAL OF EXPERIMENTAL SOCIAL
PSYCHOLOGY, 14, 97–108

Dion K.L. and Dion K.K. (1973) Correlates of
romantic love. JOURNAL OF
CONSULTING AND CLINICAL
PSYCHOLOGY, 41, 51–56

Dion K.L. and Dion K.K. (1987) Belief in a just
world and physical attractiveness
stereotyping. JOURNAL OF PERSONAL-
ITY AND SOCIAL PSYCHOLOGY, 52,
775–780

Dion K.L. and Dion K.K. (1988) Romantic love:
Individual and cultural perspectives. In
Sternberg R.J. and Barnes M.L. (eds) THE
PSYCHOLOGY OF LOVE, Yale University
Press, New Haven, Conn.

Dipboye R.L., Arvey R.D. and Terpstra D.E.
(1977) Sex and physical attractiveness of
raters and applicants as determinants of
resume evaluations. JOURNAL OF
APPLIED PSYCHOLOGY, 62, 288–294

Dispoto R.G. (1977) Interrelationships among
measures of environmental activity,
emotionality, and knowledge. EDUCA-
TIONAL AND PSYCHOLOGICAL
MEASUREMENT, 37, 451–459

Dittes J.E. and Kelley H.H. (1956) Effects of

different conditions of acceptance upon
conformity to group norms. JOURNAL OF
ABNORMAL AND SOCIAL PSYCHOL-
OGY, 53, 100–107

Dobia B. and McMurray N.E. (1985)
Applicability of learned helplessness to
depressed women undergoing assertion
training. AUSTRALIAN JOURNAL OF
PSYCHOLOGY, 37, 71–80

Dohrenwend B. and Dohrenwend B.S. (1977)
Sex differences in mental illness: A reply to
Gove and Tudor. AMERICAN JOURNAL
OF SOCIOLOGY, 81, 1447–1454

Dollard J., Doob J., Miller N., Mowrer D. and
Sears R. (1939) FRUSTRATION AND
AGGRESSION, Yale University Press, New
Haven, Conn.

Domestic Violence Action Group (1989)
WORKSHOP MANUAL FOR
COUNSELLORS, HEALTH AND
WELFARE WORKERS, (6th Edn)
Adelaide, South Australia

Donnerstein E. (1980) Aggressive erotica and
violence against women. JOURNAL OF
PERSONALITY AND SOCIAL
PSYCHOLOGY, 39, 269–277

Donnerstein E. and Berkowitz L. (1981)
Victim's reactions in aggressive erotic films
as a factor in violence against women.
JOURNAL OF PERSONALITY AND
SOCIAL PSYCHOLOGY, 41, 710–724

Donnerstein E., Linz D. and Penrod S. (eds)
(1987) THE QUESTION OF PORN-
OGRAPHY: RESEARCH FINDINGS
AND POLICY IMPLICATIONS, Free
Press, NY

Donovan J.M., Hill E. and Jankowiak W.R.
(1989) Gender, sexual orientation, and
truth-of-consensus in studies of physical
attractiveness. JOURNAL OF SEX
RESEARCH, 26, 264–271

Douglas R. (1989) A matter of small importance: Socioeconomic and magistrates court
outcomes. AUSTRALIAN AND NEW
ZEALAND JOURNAL OF SOCIOLOGY,
25, 66–84

Dovidio J.F. (1984) Helping behavior and
altruism: An empirical and conceptual
overview. In Berkowitz L. (ed.) AD-
VANCES IN EXPERIMENTAL SOCIAL
PSYCHOLOGY (Vol. 17), Academic Press,
Orlando

Dovidio J. and Gaertner S.L. (eds) (1986)
PREJUDICE, DISCRIMINATION, AND
RACISM, Academic Press, NY

Doyle J.A. (1983) THE MALE EXPERIENCE,
W.C. Brown, Dubuque, Iowa

Drachman D., de Carufel A. and Insko C.A.
(1978) The extra credit effect in interpersonal attraction. JOURNAL OF
EXPERIMENTAL SOCIAL
PSYCHOLOGY, 14, 458–465

Dubos R. (1965) MAN ADAPTING, Yale
University Press, New Haven

Duck S. and Gilmour R. (eds) (1981)
PERSONAL RELATIONSHIPS 2:
DEVELOPING PERSONAL RELATION-
SHIPS, Academic Press, Lond.

Duck S. and Perlman D. (eds) (1985)

UNDERSTANDING RELATIONSHIPS Sage, Beverley Hills, Ca.

Dunbar R.I. (1989) Genetic similarity theory needs more development. BEHAVIORAL AND BRAIN SCIENCES, 12, 520–521

Duncan B.L. (1976) Differential social perception and attribution of intergroup violence: Testing the lower limits of stereotyping of blacks. JOURNAL OF PERSONALITY AND SOCIAL PSYCHOLOGY, 34, 590–598

Duncan S. (1972) Some signals and rules for speaking turns in conversations. JOURNAL OF PERSONALITY AND SOCIAL PSYCHOLOGY, 23, 283–292

Dunlap R.E. and Van Liere K.D. (1984) Commitment to the dominant social paradigm and concern for environmental quality. SOCIAL SCIENCE QUARTERLY, 65, 1013–1028

Durdan C.A., Reeder G.D. and Hecht P.R. (1985) Litter in a university cafeteria: Demographic data and the use of prompts as an intervention strategy. ENVIRONMENT AND BEHAVIOR, 17, 387–404

Durm M.W., Terry C.L. and Hammonds C.R. (1986) Lunar phase and acting-out behavior. PSYCHOLOGICAL REPORTS, 59, 987–990

Dutton D.G. (1971) Reactions of restaurateurs to blacks and whites violating restaurant dress requirements. CANADIAN JOURNAL OF BEHAVIOURAL SCIENCE, 3, 298–331

Dutton D.G. (1973) The relationship of amount of perceived discrimination toward a minority group on behaviour of majority group members. CANADIAN JOURNAL OF BEHAVIOURAL SCIENCE, 5, 34–45

Dutton D.G. and Aron A. (1974) Some evidence for heightened sexual attraction under conditions of high anxiety. JOURNAL OF PERSONALITY AND SOCIAL PSYCHOLOGY, 30, 510–517

Dutton D.G. and Lake R. (1973) Threat of own prejudice and reverse discrimination in interracial situations. JOURNAL OF PERSONALITY AND SOCIAL PSYCHOLOGY, 28, 94–100

Dutton D.G. and Lennox V.I. (1974) The effect of prior "token" compliance on subsequent interracial behavior. JOURNAL OF PERSONALITY AND SOCIAL PSYCHOLOGY, 29, 65–71

Dworkin A.G., Chafetz J.S. and Dworkin R.J. (1986) The effects of tokenism on work alienation among urban public school teachers. WORK AND OCCUPATIONS, 13, 399–420

Dyer K.F. (1988) Changing patterns of marriage and mating within Australia. AUSTRALIAN JOURNAL OF SEX, MARRIAGE AND FAMILY, 9, 107–119

Eagly A.H. (1981) Recipient characteristics as determinants of responses to persuasion. In Petty R.E., Ostrom T.M. and Brock T.C. (eds) COGNITIVE RESPONSES IN PERSUASION, Erlbaum, Hillsdale, NJ

Eagly A.H. (1983) Gender and social influence: A social psychological analysis. AMERICAN PSYCHOLOGIST, 38, 971–981

Eagly A.H. (1987) SEX DIFFERENCES IN SOCIAL BEHAVIOR: A SOCIAL ROLE INTERPRETATION, Erlbaum, Hillsdale, NJ.

Eagly A.H. and Chrvala C. (1986) Sex differences in conformity: Status and gender-role interpretations. PSYCHOLOGY OF WOMEN QUARTERLY, 10, 203–220

Eagly A.H. and Crowley, M. (1986) Gender and helping behavior: A meta-analytic review of the social psychological literature. PSYCHOLOGICAL BULLETIN, 100, 283–308

Eagly A.H. and Johnson B.T. (1990) Gender and leadership style: A meta-analysis. PSYCHOLOGICAL BULLETIN, 108, 233–256

Eagly A.H. and Karav S.J. (1991) Gender and the emergence of leaders: a meta-analysis. JOURNAL OF PERSONALITY AND SOCIAL PSYCHOLOGY, 60, 685–710

Eagly A.H., Makhijani M. and Klonsky B.G. (1992) Gender and the evaluation of leaders: A meta-analysis. PSYCHOLOGICAL BULLETIN, 111, 3–22

Eagly A.H. and Steffen V.J. (1986) Gender and aggressive behavior: A meta-analytic review of the social psychological literature. PSYCHOLOGICAL BULLETIN, 100, 309–330

Eagly A.H. and Wood W. (1982) Inferred sex differences in status as a determinant of gender stereotypes about social influence. JOURNAL OF PERSONALITY AND SOCIAL PSYCHOLOGY, 43, 915–928

Eagly A.H. and Wood W. (1985) Gender and influencability: Stereotype versus behavior. In O'Leary V.E., Unger R.K. and Wallston B.J. (eds) WOMEN GENDER AND SOCIAL PSYCHOLOGY, Erlbaum, Hillsdale, NJ

Easteal P. (1992) BELIEFS ABOUT RAPE, Australian Institute of Criminology, Canberra, ACT

Eastman C.I. (1990) Natural summer and winter sunlight exposure patterns in seasonal affective disorder. PHYSIOLOGY AND BEHAVIOR, 48, 611–616

Ebbesen E., Duncan B. and Konecni V.J. (1975) Effects of content of verbal aggression on future verbal aggression: A field experiment. JOURNAL OF EXPERIMENTAL SOCIAL PSYCHOLOGY, 11, 192–204

Ebbinghaus H. (1908) ABRISS DER PSYCHOLOGIE, Viet, Leipzig

Edney J.J. (1975) Territoriality and control: A field experiment. JOURNAL OF PERSONALITY AND SOCIAL PSYCHOLOGY, 31, 1108–1115

Edney J.J. (1979) The nuts game: A concise commons dilemma analog. ENVIRONMENTAL PSYCHOLOGY AND NONVERBAL BEHAVIOR, 3, 252–254

Edney J.J. (1980) The commons problem: Alternative perspectives. AMERICAN PSYCHOLOGIST, 35, 131–150

Edwards G.R. (1989–90) A critique of creationist homophobia. JOURNAL OF HOMOSEXUALITY, 18, 95–118

Edwards V.J. and Spence J.T. (1987) Gender related traits, stereotypes and schemata. JOURNAL OF PERSONALITY AND SOCIAL PSYCHOLOGY, 53, 146–154

Efran M.G. (1974) The effect of physical appearance on the judgement of guilt, interpersonal attraction, and severity of recommended punishment in a simulated jury task. JOURNAL OF EXPERIMENTAL RESEARCH AND PERSONALITY, 8, 45–54

Eibl-Eibesfeldt I. (1975) ETHOLOGY: THE BIOLOGY OF BEHAVIOR (2nd edn), Holt, Rinehart and Winston, NY

Eisenberg-Berg N. (1979) Relationship of prosocial moral reasoning to altruism, political liberalism, and intelligence. DEVELOPMENTAL PSYCHOLOGY, 15, 87–89

Eisenberger R., Fasolo P. and Davis-LaMastro V. (1990) Perceived organizational support and employee diligence, commitment, and innovation. JOURNAL OF APPLIED PSYCHOLOGY, 75, 51–59

Ekman P. (1971) Universals and cultural differences in facial expressions of emotion. NEBRASKA SYMPOSIUM ON MOTIVATION, 207–283

Ekman P. (1985) TELLING LIES, Norton, NY

Ekman P., Davidson R.J. and Friesen W.V. (1990) The Duchenne smile: Emotional expression and brain physiology II. JOURNAL OF PERSONALITY AND SOCIAL PSYCHOLOGY, 58, 342–353

Ekman P. and Friesen W.V. (1969) Nonverbal leakage and clues to deception. PSYCHIATRY, 32, 88–106

Ekman P. and Friesen W.V. (1974) Detecting deception from the body or face. JOURNAL OF PERSONALITY AND SOCIAL PSYCHOLOGY, 29, 288–298

Ekman P. and Friesen W.V. (1975) UNMASKING THE FACE: A GUIDE TO RECOGNIZING EMOTIONS FROM FACIAL CLUES, Prentice Hall, NJ

Ekman P. and Oster H. (1979) Facial expressions of emotion. ANNUAL REVIEW OF PSYCHOLOGY, 30, 527–554

Elashoff J.R. and Snow R.E. (1971) PYGMALION RECONSIDERED, Charles A. Jones, Worthington, Ohio

Elkin R.A. and Leippe M.R. (1986) Physiological arousal, dissonance, and attitude change: Evidence for a dissonance-arousal link and a "don't remind me" effect. JOURNAL OF PERSONALITY AND SOCIAL PSYCHOLOGY, 51, 55–65

Ellis P. (1980) Review of designing for therapeutic environments. BULLETIN OF THE BRITISH PSYCHOLOGICAL SOCIETY, 33, 325–26

Ellis R.J. (1988) Self-monitoring and leadership emergence in groups. PERSONALITY AND SOCIAL PSYCHOLOGY BULLETIN, 14, 681–693

Ellsworth P.C. and Carlsmith J.M. (1973) Eye

contact and gaze aversion in aggressive encounter. JOURNAL OF PERSONALITY AND SOCIAL PSYCHOLOGY, 33, 117–122

Epstein S. (1979) The stability of behavior I: On predicting most of the people much of the time. JOURNAL OF PERSONALITY AND SOCIAL PSYCHOLOGY, 37, 1097–1126

Epstein S. (1983) Aggregation and beyond: Some basic issues on the prediction of behavior. JOURNAL OF PERSONALITY, 51, 360–392

Epstein S. and O'Brien E.J. (1985) The person-situation debate in historic and current perspective. PSYCHOLOGICAL BULLETIN, 98, 513–537

Erikson E.H. (1968) IDENTITY: YOUTH AND CRISIS, Norton, NY

Erkut S., Jaquette D.S. and Staub E. (1981) Moral judgment-situation interaction as a basis for predicting prosocial behaviour. JOURNAL OF PERSONALITY, 49, 1–14

Esses V. and Webster C. (1988) Physical attractiveness, dangerousness and the Canadian criminal code. JOURNAL OF APPLIED SOCIAL PSYCHOLOGY, 18, 1017–1031

Evans G.W. (1978) Human spatial behavior: The arousal process. In Baum A. and Epstein Y. (eds) HUMAN RESPONSE TO CROWDING, Erlbaum, Hillsdale, NJ

Evans T. (1988) A GENDER AGENDA, Allen and Unwin, Sydney

Evatt E. (1991) Valuing women's work: The role of family law. Anne Conlon Lecture, 19 July, Sydney

Fagot B.I. (1977) Consequences of moderate cross-gender behavior in pre-school children. CHILD DEVELOPMENT, 48, 902–907

Fantino E. (1973) Aversive control. In Nevin T. and Renyolds C. (eds) THE STUDY OF BEHAVIOR: LEARNING, MOTIVATION, EMOTION AND INSTINCT. Scott Foresman, Glenview, Illinois

Farr R.M. (1983) Wilhelm Wundt (1832–1920) and the origins of psychology as an experimental and social science. BRITISH JOURNAL OF SOCIAL PSYCHOLOGY, 22, 289–301

Farr R.M. (1991) The long past and the short history of social psychology. EUROPEAN JOURNAL OF SOCIAL PSYCHOLOGY, 21, 371–380

Fazio R.H. (1986) How do attitudes guide behavior? In Sorrentino R.M. and Higgins E.T. (eds) HANDBOOK OF MOTIVATION AND COGNITION: FOUNDATIONS OF SOCIAL BEHAVIOR, Guilford, NY

Fazio R.H. (1987) Self-perception theory: A current perspective. In Zanna M., Olson J.M. and Herman C.P. (eds) SOCIAL INFLU-ENCE: THE ONTARIO SYMPOSIUM (Vol. 3), Erlbaum, Hillsdale, NJ

Fazio R.H., Sherman S.J. and Herr P.M. (1982)

The feature-positive effect in the self-perception process: Does not doing matter as much as doing? JOURNAL OF PERSON-ALITY AND SOCIAL PSYCHOLOGY, 42, 404–411

Fazio R.H. and Zanna M.P. (1978) Attitudinal qualities relating to the strength of the attitude-behavior relation. JOURNAL OF EXPERIMENTAL SOCIAL PSYCHOLOGY, 14, 398–408

Fazio R.H. and Zanna M.P. (1981) Direct experience and attitude-behavior consistency. In Berkowitz L. (ed.) ADVANCES IN EXPERIMENTAL SOCIAL PSYCHOLOGY (Vol. 14), Academic Press, NY

Fazio R.H., Zanna M.P. and Cooper J. (1977) Dissonance and self-perception: An integrative view of each theory's proper domain of application. JOURNAL OF EXPERIMENTAL SOCIAL PSYCHOLOGY, 13, 464–479

Feather N.T. (1967a) Some personality correlates of external control. AUSTRALIAN JOURNAL OF PSYCHOLOGY, 19, 253–260

Feather N.T. (1967b) A structural balance approach to the analysis of communication effects. In Berkowitz L. (ed.) ADVANCES IN EXPERIMENTAL SOCIAL PSYCHOL-OGY (Vol. 3), Academic Press, NY

Feather N.T. (1982a) Reasons for entering medical school in relation to value priorities and sex of student. JOURNAL OF OCCUPATIONAL PSYCHOLOGY, 55, 119–128

Feather N.T. (1982b) EXPECTATIONS AND ACTIONS: EXPECTANCY-VALUE MODELS IN PSYCHOLOGY, Erlbaum, Hillsdale, NJ

Feather N.T. (1983) Causal attributions and beliefs about work and unemployment among adolescents in state and independent secondary schools. AUSTRALIAN JOURNAL OF PSYCHOLOGY, 35, 211–232

Feather N.T. (1985) Masculinity, femininity, self-esteem, and subclinical depression. SEX ROLES, 12, 491–500

Feather N.T. (ed.) (1985) AUSTRALIAN PSYCHOLOGY: REVIEW OF RESEARCH, Allen and Unwin, Sydney

Feather N.T. (1989) Attitudes towards the high achiever: The fall of the tall poppy. AUSTRALIAN JOURNAL OF PSYCHOLOGY, 141, 239–267

Feather N.T. (1990a) Reactions to equal reward allocations: Effects of situation, gender and values. BRITISH JOURNAL OF SOCIAL PSYCHOLOGY, 29, 315–329

Feather N.T. (1990b) THE PSYCHOLOGI-CAL IMPACT OF UNEMPLOYMENT, Springer-Verlag, Berlin

Feather N.T. (1991) Attitudes towards the high achiever: Effects of perceiver's own level of competence. AUSTRALIAN JOURNAL OF PSYCHOLOGY, 43, 121–124

Feather N.T. (1992) Australian and Japanese attitudes towards the fall of high achievers.

AUSTRALIAN JOURNAL OF PSYCHOLOGY, 44, 87–93

Feather N.T. and O'Brien G.E. (1986) A longitudinal analysis of the effects of different patterns of employment and unemployment on school-leavers. BRITISH JOURNAL OF SOCIAL PSYCHOLOGY, 77, 459–479

Feather N.T. and O'Driscoll M.P. (1980) Observers' reactions to an equal or equitable allocator in relation to allocator input, causal attributions, and value importance. EUROPEAN JOURNAL OF SOCIAL PSYCHOLOGY, 10, 107–129

Feather N.T. and Simon J.G. (1973) Fear of success and causal attribution for outcome. JOURNAL OF PERSONALITY AND SOCIAL PSYCHOLOGY, 41, 525–542

Feeney J.A. (1990) The attachment perspective on adult romantic relationships. Unpublished doctoral dissertation, University of Queensland, St Lucia

Feeney J.A. and Noller P. (1990) Attachment style as a predictor of adult romantic relationships. JOURNAL OF PERSONALITY AND SOCIAL PSYCHOLOGY, 58, 281–291

Feeney J.A. and Noller P. (1991) Attachment style and verbal descriptions of romantic partners. JOURNAL OF SOCIAL AND PERSONAL RELATIONSHIPS, 8, 187–215

Feeney J.A. and Noller P. (1992) Attachment style and romantic love: Relationship dissolution. AUSTRALIAN JOURNAL OF PSYCHOLOGY, 44, 69–74

Feingold A. (1988) Cognitive gender differences are disappearing. AMERICAN PSYCHOLOGIST, 43, 95–103

Feingold A. (1990) Gender differences in effects of physical attractiveness on romantic attraction: A comparison across five research paradigms. JOURNAL OF PERSONALITY AND SOCIAL PSYCHOLOGY, 59, 981–993

Feingold A. (1992) Sex differences in variability in intellectual abilities: A new look at an old controversy. REVIEW OF EDUCATIONAL RESEARCH, 62, 61–84

Felson R.B. and Reid M. (1986) The effects of parents on the self-appraisals of children. SOCIAL PSYCHOLOGY QUARTERLY, 49, 302–308

Ferguson C.K. and Kelley H.H. (1964) Significant factors in the overevaluation of own-group's product. JOURNAL OF ABNORMAL AND SOCIAL PSYCHOLOGY, 69, 223–228

Feshbach S. (1970) Aggression. In Mussen P.H. (ed.) CARMICHAEL MANUAL OF CHILD PSYCHOLOGY (Revised edn), Wiley, NY

Feshbach S. (1984) The catharsis hypothesis: Aggressive drive and the reduction of aggression. AGGRESSIVE BEHAVIOR, 10, 91–101

Feshbach S. (1986) Reconceptualisation of anger: Some research perspectives.

JOURNAL OF SOCIAL AND CLINICAL PSYCHOLOGY, 4, 123–132

Feshbach S., Stiles W.B. and Bitter E. (1967) The reinforcing effect of witnessing aggression. JOURNAL OF EXPERIMENTAL RESEARCH IN PERSONALITY, 2, 133–139

Festinger L. (1950) Informal social communication. PSYCHOLOGICAL REVIEW, 57, 271–282

Festinger L. (1954) A theory of social comparison processes. HUMAN RELATIONS, 2, 117–140

Festinger L. (1957) A THEORY OF COGNITIVE DISSONANCE, Stanford University Press, Stanford

Festinger L. and Carlsmith J.M. (1959) Cognitive consequences of forced compliance. JOURNAL OF ABNORMAL AND SOCIAL PSYCHOLOGY, 58, 203–210

Festinger, L., Riecken H.W. and Schachter S. (1956) WHEN PROPHESY FAILS, University of Minnesota Press, Minneapolis

Festinger L., Schachter S. and Back K. (1950) SOCIAL PRESSURES IN INFORMAL GROUPS: A STUDY OF HUMAN FACTORS IN HOUSING, Harper and Row, NY

Fiedler F.E. (1978) The contingency model and the dynamics of the leadership process. In Berkowitz L. (ed.) ADVANCES IN EXPERIMENTAL SOCIAL PSYCHOLOGY, Academic Press, NY

Fiedler F.E. (1981) Leadership effectiveness. AMERICAN BEHAVIORAL SCIENTIST, 24, 619–632

Fiedler F.E. (1986) The contribution of cognitive resources and behavior to leadership performance. In Graumann C.F. and Moscovici S. (eds) CHANGING CONCEPTIONS OF LEADERSHIP, Springer-Verlag, NY

Fielding N.G. (1988) Socialisation of police recruits into the police role. In Southgate P. (ed.) NEW DIRECTIONS IN POLICE TRAINING, H.M.S.O., Lond.

Fielding N.G. (1989) Police culture and police practice. In Weatheritt M. (ed.), POLICE RESEARCH: SOME FUTURE PROSPECTS, Gower Publishing, Aldershot, UK

Findlay B.M. and Lawrence J.A. (1991) Who does what? Gender-related distribution of household tasks for couples, their families of origin and their ideals. AUSTRALIAN JOURNAL OF SEX, MARRIAGE AND FAMILY, 12, 3–11

Findlay M. and Hogg R. (eds) (1988) UNDERSTANDING CRIME AND CRIMINAL JUSTICE, Law Book Co., North Ryde, NSW

Finighan W.R. (1980) Some empirical observations on the role of privacy in the residential environment. MAN ENVIRONMENT SYSTEMS, 10, 153–159

Finkelhor D. (1984) CHILD SEXUAL ABUSE: NEW THEMES AND RESEARCH, Free Press, NY

Firestone I.J., Lichtman C.M. and Colamosca J.V. (1975) Leader effectiveness and leadership conferral as determinants of helping in a medical emergency. JOURNAL OF PERSONALITY AND SOCIAL PSYCHOLOGY, 31, 343–348

Fish B., Karabenick S. and Heath M. (1968) The effects of observation on emotional arousal and affiliation. JOURNAL OF EXPERIMENTAL SOCIAL PSYCHOLOGY, 14, 256–265

Fishbein M. and Ajzen I. (1974) Attitudes towards objects as predictors of single and multiple behavioral criteria. PSYCHOLOGICAL REVIEW, 81, 59–74

Fishbein M. and Ajzen I. (1975) BELIEF, ATTITUDE, INTENTION, AND BEHAVIOR: AN INTRODUCTION TO THEORY AND RESEARCH. Addison-Wesley, Reading, Penn.

Fisher J.D. and Nadler A. (1976) Effect of donor resources on recipient self-esteem and self-help. JOURNAL OF EXPERIMENTAL SOCIAL PSYCHOLOGY, 12, 139–150

Fisher J.D., Nadler A. and DePaulo (eds) (1983) NEW DIRECTIONS IN HELPING: RECIPIENT REACTIONS TO AID, Academic Press NY

Fisher R. (1985) AIDS and a plague mentality. NEW SOCIETY, 71, 322–325

Fiske E.K. (1985) THE ABORIGINAL ECONOMY IN TOWN AND COUNTRY, Allen and Unwin, Sydney

Fiske S.T., Kenny D.A. and Taylor S.E. (1982) Structural models for the mediation of salience effects on attribution. JOURNAL OF EXPERIMENTAL SOCIAL PSYCHOLOGY, 18, 105–127

Fiske S.T., Kinder D.R. and Larter W.M. (1983) The novice and the expert: Knowledge-based strategies in political cognition. JOURNAL OF EXPERIMENTAL SOCIAL PSYCHOLOGY, 19, 381–400

Fiske S.T and Neuberg S.L. (1990) A continuum of impression formation, from category-based to individuating processes: Influences of information and motivation on attention and interpretation. In Zanna M.P. (ed.) ADVANCES IN EXPERIMENTAL SOCIAL PSYCHOLOGY (Vol. 23), Academic Press, NY

Fiske S.T. and Taylor S.E. (1991) SOCIAL COGNITION (2nd edn) McGraw-Hill, NY

Fitness J. and Fletcher G.J. (1990) Emotion labelling in close relationships. NEW ZEALAND JOURNAL OF PSYCHOLOGY, 19, 63–69

Flavell J.H., Botkin P.T., Fry C.L., et al. (1968) THE DEVELOPMENT OF ROLE-TAKING AND COMMUNICATION SKILLS IN CHILDREN. Wiley, NY

Fleming M.F., Bruno M., Barry K. and Fost N. (1989) Informed consent, deception, and the use of disguised alcohol questionnaires. AMERICAN JOURNAL OF DRUG AND ALCOHOL ABUSE, 15, 309–319

Fletcher G.J. (1983a) Sex differences in causal attributions for marital separation. NEW

ZEALAND JOURNAL OF PSYCHOLOGY, 12, 82–89

Fletcher G.J. (1983b) The analysis of verbal explanations for marital separation: Implications for attribution theory. JOURNAL OF APPLIED SOCIAL PSYCHOLOGY, 13, 245–258

Fletcher G.J. (1984) Psychology and commonsense. AMERICAN PSYCHO-LOGIST, 39, 203–213

Fletcher G.J. (1992) The scientific credibility of commonsense psychology. In Craik K., Hogan R. and Wolfe R. (eds) 50 YEARS OF PERSONALITY PSYCHOLOGY, Plenum Press, NY

Fletcher G.J., Bull V. and Reeder G. (1988) Bias and accuracy in trait attribution: The role of attributional complexity. Unpublished manuscript, University of Canterbury, Christchurch

Fletcher G.J. and Fincham F.D. (1991) Attribution processes in close relationships. In Fletcher G.J. and Fincham F.D. (eds) COGNITION IN CLOSE RELATIONSHIPS, Erlbaum, Hillsdale, NJ

Fletcher G.J., Fincham F.D., Cramer L. and Heron N. (1987) The role of attributions in the development of dating relationships. JOURNAL OF PERSONALITY AND SOCIAL PSYCHOLOGY, 53, 481–489

Fletcher G.J., Fitness J. and Blampied N.M. (1990) The link between attributions and happiness in close relationships: The roles of depression and explanatory style. JOURNAL OF SOCIAL AND CLINICAL PSYCHOLOGY, 9, 243–255

Fletcher G.J., Grigg F. and Bull V. (1988) The organization and accuracy of personality impressions: Neophytes versus experts in trait attribution. NEW ZEALAND JOURNAL OF PSYCHOLOGY, 17, 68–77

Fletcher G.J. and Haig B.D. (1989) An evaluation of the "naive scientist" model in social psychology. In Forgas J.P. and Innes J.M. (eds) RECENT ADVANCES IN SOCIAL PSYCHOLOGY: AN INTERNATIONAL PERSPECTIVE, Elsevier, North-Holland

Fletcher G.J., Reeder G.D. and Bull V. (1990) Bias and accuracy in attitude attribution: The role of attributional complexity. JOURNAL OF EXPERIMENTAL SOCIAL PSYCHOLOGY, 6, 68–77

Fletcher G.J., Rosanowski J., Rhodes G. and Lange C. (In press) Accuracy and speed of causal processing: Experts versus novices in social judgment. JOURNAL OF EXPERIMENTAL SOCIAL PSYCHOLOGY,

Fletcher G.J. and Ward C. (1988) Attribution theory and processes: A cross-cultural perspective. In Bond M.H. (ed.) THE CROSS-CULTURAL CHALLENGE TO SOCIAL PSYCHOLOGY, Sage, Newbury Park

Flin R., Markham R. and Davies G. (1989) Making faces: Developmental trends in the construction and recognition of photofit face composites. JOURNAL OF APPLIED

DEVELOPMENTAL PSYCHOLOGY, 10, 131–145

Foa U.G. and Foa E.B. (1974) SOCIETAL STRUCTURES OF THE MIND, Charles Thomas, Springfield, Illinois

Foder E.M. and Smith T. (1982) The power motive as an influence on group decision making. JOURNAL OF PERSONALITY AND SOCIAL PSYCHOLOGY, 42, 178–185

Foddy M.L. and Crabbe B.D. (1990) DIRECTORY OF AUSTRALIAN SOCIAL PSYCHOLOGISTS (6th edn), La Trobe University, Melbourne

Fogelman E. and Wiener V.L. (1985) The few, the brave, the noble. PSYCHOLOGY TODAY, 19, 61–65

Folger R. (1986) Rethinking equity theory: A referent cognitions model. In Bierhoff W., Cohen R.L. and Greenberg J. (eds) JUSTICE IN SOCIAL RELATIONS, Plenum, NY

Ford C.S. and Beach F.A. (1951) PATTERNS OF SEXUAL BEHAVIOR, Hoeber, NY

Forgas J.P. (1979) SOCIAL EPISODES: THE STUDY OF INTERACTION ROUTINES, Academic Press, Lond.

Forgas J.P. (1981) SOCIAL COGNITION PERSPECTIVES ON EVERYDAY UNDERSTANDING, Academic Press, Lond.

Forgas J.P. (1982) Episode cognition: Internal representations of interaction routines. In Berkowitz L. (ed.) ADVANCES IN EXPERIMENTAL SOCIAL PSYCHOL-OGY, Academic Press, NY

Forgas J.P. (1983a) The effects of prototypicality and cultural salience on perceptions of people. JOURNAL OF RESEARCH IN PERSONALITY, 17, 153–173

Forgas J.P. (1983b) What is social about social cognition? BRITISH JOURNAL OF SOCIAL PSYCHOLOGY, 22, 129–144

Forgas J.P. (1985) INTERPERSONAL BEHAVIOR: THE PSYCHOLOGY OF SOCIAL INTERACTION, Pergamon, Oxford

Forgas J.P. (1987) The role of physical attractiveness in the interpretation of facial expression cues. PERSONALITY AND SOCIAL PSYCHOLOGY BULLETIN, 13, 478–489

Forgas J.P. (ed.) (1991) EMOTION AND SOCIAL JUDGEMENTS, Pergamon, Oxford

Forgas J.P. (1992) Affect and social perception: Research evidence and an integrative theory. In Stroebe W. and Hewstone M. (eds) EUROPEAN REVIEW OF SOCIAL PSYCHOLOGY (Vol. 3), Wiley, Chichester

Forgas J.P. and Bower G.H. (1987) Mood effects on person perception judgments. JOURNAL OF PERSONALITY AND SOCIAL PSYCHOLOGY, 53, 53–60

Forgas J.P. and Bower G.H. (1988) Affect in social and personal judgements. In Fielder K. and Forgas J.P. (eds) AFFECT,

COGNITION AND SOCIAL BEHAVIOUR, Hogrefe, Toronto

Forgas J.P., Bower G.H. and Moylan S.J. (1990) Praise or blame? Affective influences on attributions for achievement. JOURNAL OF PERSONALITY AND SOCIAL PSYCHOLOGY, 59, 809–819

Forgas J.P., Burnham D. and Trimboli C. (1988) Mood, memory and social judgments in children. JOURNAL OF PERSONALITY AND SOCIAL PSYCHOLOGY, 54, 697–703

Forgas J.P. and Innes J.M. (eds) (1989) RECENT ADVANCES IN SOCIAL PSYCHOLOGY: AN INTERNATIONAL PERSPECTIVE, Elsevier, North-Holland

Forgas J.P. and Moylan S.J. (1987) After the movies: The effects of transient mood states on social judgments. PERSONALITY AND SOCIAL PSYCHOLOGY BULLETIN, 9, 587–596

Forgas J.P., O'Connor K.V. and Morris S.L. (1983) Smile and punishment: The effects of facial expression on responsibility attribution by groups and individuals. PERSONALITY AND SOCIAL PSYCHOLOGY BULLETIN, 9, 587–596

Form W.H. and Nosow S. (1958) COMMU-NITY IN DISASTER, Harper, NY

Forsterling F. (1985) Attributional retraining: A review. PSYCHOLOGICAL BULLETIN, 98, 495–512

Forsyth D. (1990) AN INTRODUCTION TO GROUP DYNAMICS (2nd edn) Brooks-Cole, Ca.

Forsyth S.J. (1978) Predicting motorists' altruism. PSYCHOLOGICAL REPORTS, 43, 567–572

Fox W.F. (1967) Human performance in the cold. HUMAN FACTORS, 9, 203–220

Frank B. (1987) Hegemonic heterosexual masculinity. STUDIES IN POLITICAL ECONOMY, 24, 159–170

Franzoi S.L. and Herzog M.E. (1987) Judging physical attractiveness: What body aspects do we use? PERSONALITY AND SOCIAL PSYCHOLOGY BULLETIN, 13, 19–33

Freedman J.L. (1972) The effects of population density on humans. In Fawcett J.T. (ed.) PSYCHOLOGICAL PERSPECTIVES ON POPULATION, Basic Books, NY

Freedman J.L. (1975) CROWDING AND BEHAVIOR, Freeman, San Francisco

Freedman J.L. and Fraser S.C. (1966) Compliance without pressure. The foot-in-the-door technique. JOURNAL OF PERSONALITY AND SOCIAL PSYCHOLOGY, 4, 195–202

Freedman J.L. and Perlick D. (1979) Crowding, contagion and laughter. JOURNAL OF EXPERIMENTAL SOCIAL PSYCHOL-OGY, 15, 295–303

Freedman J.L., Wallington S. and Bless E. (1967) Compliance without pressure: The effect of guilt. JOURNAL OF PERSONAL-ITY AND SOCIAL PSYCHOLOGY, 7, 117–124

French J.R. and Raven B. (1959) The basis of social power. In Cartwright D. (ed.)

STUDIES IN SOCIAL POWER, University of Michigan Press, Ann Arbor

Freud S. (1920) A GENERAL INTRODUCTION TO PSYCHOANALY-SIS, Boni and Liverant, New York

Freud S. (1933) Why war? In Rickman J. (ed.) (1968) CIVILISATION, WAR AND DEATH: SELECTIONS FROM FIVE WORKS BY SIGMUND FREUD, 82–97, Hogarth, Lond.

Freud S. (1933) NEW INTRODUCTORY LECTURES ON PSYCHOANALYSIS, Norton, NY

Frey D.L. and Gaertner S.L. (1986) Helping and the avoidance of inappropriate interracial behavior: A strategy that perpetuates a nonprejudiced self-image. JOURNAL OF PERSONALITY AND SOCIAL PSYCHOLOGY, 50, 1083–1090

Frey D.L., Rotton J. and Barry T. (1979) The effects of the full moon on human behavior: Yet another failure to replicate. JOURNAL OF PSYCHOLOGY, 103, 159–162

Fridlund A.J. (1990) Evolution and facial action in reflex emotion, and paralanguage. In Ackles P.K., Jennings J.R. and Coles M.G.H. (eds) ADVANCES IN PSYCHOPHYSIOLOGY, JAI Press, Greenwich, Conn.

Friedrich-Cofer L. and Huston A.C. (1986) Television violence and aggression: The debate continues. PSYCHOLOGICAL BULLETIN, 100, 364–371

Frieze I.H., Johnson P., Parsons J.E., Ruble D.N. and Zellman G.L. (eds) (1978) WOMEN AND SEX ROLES: A SOCIAL PSYCHOLOGICAL PERSPECTIVE, Norton, NY

Frieze I.H. and Weiner B. (1971) Cue utilization and attributional judgements for success and failure. JOURNAL OF PERSONALITY, 39, 591–605

Frodi A., Macauley J. and Thome R.R. (1977) Are women always less aggressive than men? A review of the experimental literature. PSYCHOLOGICAL BULLETIN, 84, 634–660

Furnham A. (1984) Unemployment, attribution theory, and mental health: A review of the British literature. INTERNA-TIONAL JOURNAL OF MENTAL HEALTH, 13, 51–67

Furnham A. and Bochner S. (1982) Social difficulty in a foreign culture: An empirical analysis of culture shock. In Bochner S. (ed.) (1982) CULTURES IN CONTACT: STUDIES IN CROSS-CULTURAL INTERACTION, Pergamon Press, Oxford

Furnham A. and Bochner S. (1989) CULTURE SHOCK: PSYCHOLOGICAL REAC-TIONS TO UNFAMILIAR ENVIRON-MENTS, Routledge, NY

Gaertner S.L. and Dovidio J.F. (1977) The subtlety of white racism, arousal, and helping behaviour. JOURNAL OF PERSONALITY AND SOCIAL PSYCHOLOGY, 35, 691–707

Gaertner S.L. and Dovidio J.F (1986) The aversive forms of racism. In Dovidio J. and

Gaertner S.L. (eds) PREJUDICE, DISCRIMINATION, AND RACISM, Academic Press, NY

Gaertner S.L., Mann J., Murrell A. and Dovidio J.F. (1989) Reducing intergroup bias: The benefits of recategorization. JOURNAL OF PERSONALITY AND SOCIAL PSYCHOLOGY, 57, 239–249

Gagnon J. and Simon W. (1973) SEXUAL CONDUCT: THE SOCIAL SOURCES OF HUMAN SEXUALITY, Aldine, Chicago

Galle O.R. and Gove W.R. (1979) Crowding and behavior in Chicago, 1940–1970. In Aiello J.R. and Baum A. (eds) RESIDENTIAL CROWDING AND DESIGN, Plenum, NY

Galton F. (1869) HEREDITY GENIUS, reprinted by Cleveland Press, Cleveland Ohio, 1962

Galton F. (1883) INQUIRIES INTO HUMAN FACULTY AND ITS DEVELOPMENT, reprinted by Dent, Lond., 1907

Ganley A. (1990) Feminist therapy with male clients. JOURNAL OF FEMINIST FAMILY THERAPY, 2, 1–23

Gavey N. (1991) Sexual victimisation prevalence among New Zealand university students. JOURNAL OF CONSULTING AND CLINICAL PSYCHOLOGY, 59, 464–466

Geen R.G. (1988) Alternative conceptions of social facilitation. In Paulus P.B. (ed.) PSYCHOLOGY OF GROUP INFLUENCE, Erlbaum, Hillsdale, NJ

Geen R.G. and Bushman B.J. (1987) Drive theory: effects of socially engendered arousal. In Mullens B. and Goethals G.R. (eds) THEORIES OF GROUP BEHAVIOR, Springer-Verlag, NY

Geen R.G. and Bushman B.J. (1989) The arousing effects of social presence. In Wagner H. and Manstead A. (eds) HANDBOOK OF PSYCHOPHYSIOLOGY, John Wiley, Chichester

Geen R.G. and Quanty M.B. (1977) The catharsis of aggression: An evaluation of a hypothesis. In Berkowitz L. (ed.) ADVANCES IN EXPERIMENTAL SOCIAL PSYCHOLOGY (Vol. 10), Academic Press, NY

Geller E.S. (1989) Applied behavior analysis and social marketing: An integration for environmental preservation. JOURNAL OF SOCIAL ISSUES, 45, 17–36

Geller E.S., Winett R.A. and Everett P.B. (1982) PRESERVING THE ENVIRONMENT: NEW STRATEGIES FOR BEHAVIOR CHANGE, Pergamon, NY

Geller E.S., Witmer J.F. and Orebaugh A.L. (1976) Instructions as a determinant of paper disposal behaviors. ENVIRONMENT AND BEHAVIOR, 8, 417–441

Geller E.S. Witmer J.F. and Tuso M.E. (1977) Environmental interventions for litter control. JOURNAL OF APPLIED PSYCHOLOGY, 62, 344–351

Gerbner G., Gross L., Morgan M. and Signorelli N. (1980) The mainstreaming of America:

Violence Profile No. 11. JOURNAL OF COMMUNICATION, 30, 10–29

Gerbner G., Gross L., Signorelli N. and Morgan M. (1980) Television violence, victimisation and power. AMERICAN BEHAVIORAL SCIENTIST, 23, 705–716

Gerbner G., Gross L., Signorelli N. and Morgan M. (1986) Television's mean world: Violence profile. Occasional papers 14–15, Annenberg School of Communications, University of Pennsylvania, Philadelphia

Gergen K.J. (1973) Social psychology as history. JOURNAL OF PERSONALITY AND SOCIAL PSYCHOLOGY, 26, 309–320

Gergen K.J., Ellsworth P., Maslach C., et al. (1975) Obligation, donor resources, and reactions to aid in three cultures. JOURNAL OF PERSONALITY AND SOCIAL PSYCHOLOGY, 31, 390–400

Gergen K.J. and Gergen M.M. (1981) SOCIAL PSYCHOLOGY, Harcourt, Brace, Jovanovich, NY

Gergen K.J., Morse S.J. and Bode K.A. (1974) Overpaid or overworked? Cognitive and behavioral reactions to inequitable rewards. JOURNAL OF APPLIED SOCIAL PSYCHOLOGY, 4, 259–274

Gibbons F.X. and Kassin S.M. (1987) Information consistency and perceptual set: Overcoming the mental retardation "schema". JOURNAL OF APPLIED SOCIAL PSYCHOLOGY, 17, 810–827

Gifford R. (1982) Children and the commons dilemma. JOURNAL OF APPLIED SOCIAL PSYCHOLOGY, 12, 269–280

Gifford R. (1987) ENVIRONMENTAL PSYCHOLOGY: PRINCIPLES AND PRACTICE, Allyn and Bacon, Boston

Gilbert D.T., Pelham B.W. and Krull D.S. (1988) On cognitive busyness: When person perceivers meet persons perceived. JOURNAL OF PERSONALITY AND SOCIAL PSYCHOLOGY, 54, 733–739

Gilbert G.M. (1951) Stereotype persistence and change among college students. JOURNAL OF ABNORMAL AND SOCIAL PSYCHOLOGY, 46, 245–254

Gilligan C. (1977) In a different voice: Women's conception of the self and of morality. HARVARD EDUCATIONAL REVIEW, 47, 481–517

Gillis A.R., Richard M.A. and Hagan J. (1986) Ethnic susceptibility to crowding: An empirical analysis. ENVIRONMENT AND BEHAVIOR, 18, 683–706

Gilmore D. (1990) MANHOOD IN THE MAKING: CULTURAL CONCEPTS OF MASCULINITY, Yale University Press, New Haven

Gilmore K. (1989) The lesson of the voices. Paper presented to the Community Action on Family Violence Seminar, October, Melbourne

Gilmour D.G. and Walkey F.H. (1981) Identifying violent offenders using a video measure of interpersonal distance. JOURNAL OF CONSULTING AND CLINICAL PSYCHOLOGY, 49, 287–291

Glaser A.N. (1982) Drive theory of social

facilitation: A critical reappraisal. BRITISH JOURNAL OF SOCIAL PSYCHOLOGY, 21, 265–282

Glazer N. (1988) The future of preferential affirmative action. In Katz P.E. and Taylor D.A. (eds) ELIMINATING RACISM: PROFILES IN CONTROVERSY, Plenum, NY

Glezer H. (1984) Changes in marriage and sex-role attitudes among young married women: 1971–1982. AUSTRALIAN FAMILY RESEARCH CONFERENCE PROCEEDINGS. VOLUME 1: FAMILY FORMATION STRUCTURE VALUES, Institute of Family Studies Melbourne, 201–255.

Glezer H. (1991) Juggling work and family commitments. FAMILY MATTERS, 28, 6–10

Glick P.C. (1977) Updating the life cycle of the family. JOURNAL OF MARRIAGE AND THE FAMILY, 39, 5–13

Goethals G.R. (1986) Fabricating and ignoring social realities: Self-serving estimates of consensus. In Olson J.M., Herman C.P. and Zanna M.P. (eds) RELATIVE DEPRIVATION AND SOCIAL COMPARISON. THE ONTARIO SYMPOSIUM (Vol. 4), Erlbaum, Hillsdale, NJ

Goethals G.R., Cooper J. and Naficy A. (1979) Role of foreseen, foreseeable and unforeseeable behavioral consequences in the arousal of cognitive dissonance. JOURNAL OF PERSONALITY AND SOCIAL PSYCHOLOGY, 37, 1179–1185

Goffman E. (1959) THE PRESENTATION OF SELF IN EVERYDAY LIFE, Doubleday, NY

Gold J.R. (1982) Territoriality and human spatial behavior. PROGRESS IN HUMAN GEOGRAPHY, 6, 44–67

Goldberg L.R. (1978) Differential attribution of trait-descriptive terms to oneself as compared to well-liked, neutral, and disliked others: A psychometric analysis. JOURNAL OF PERSONALITY AND SOCIAL PSYCHOLOGY, 36, 1012–1028

Goldberg L.R. (1981) Unconfounding situational attributions from uncertain, neutral and ambiguous ones: A psychometric analysis of descriptions of oneself and various types of others. JOURNAL OF PERSONALITY AND SOCIAL PSYCHOLOGY, 41, 517–522

Goldizen A.W. (1990) A comparative perspective on the evolution of tamarin and marmoset social systems. Special Issue: Primate socioecology, communication, and hominid evolution: I. INTERNATIONAL JOURNAL OF PRIMATOLOGY, 11, 63–83

Goldman W. and Lewis P. (1977) Beautiful is good. Evidence that the physically attractive are more socially skillful. JOURNAL OF EXPERIMENTAL SOCIAL PSYCHOLOGY, 13, 125–130

Goldstein J. and Arms R. (1971) Effects of observing athletic contests on hostility. SOCIOMETRY, 34, 83–90

Goodman G.S., Aman C. and Hirschman J.

(1987) Child sexual and physical abuse: Children's testimony. In Ceci S., Toglia M. and Ross D. (eds) CHILDREN'S EYEWITNESS TESTIMONY, Springer-Verlag, NY

Goodman M.E. (1952) RACE AWARENESS IN YOUNG CHILDREN, Addison-Wesley, Reading, Ma.

Goodman M.E. (1964) RACE AWARENESS IN YOUNG CHILDREN, (2nd edn) Crowell-Collier, NY

Goodnow J.J. (1988) Parents' ideas, actions, and feelings: Models and methods from developmental and social psychology. CHILD DEVELOPMENT, 59, 286–320

Goodnow J.J. and Warton P.M. (1991) The social bases of social cognition: Interactions about work and their implications. MERRILL PALMER QUARTERLY, 37, 27–58

Goodwin F.K., Wirz-Justice A. and Wehr T.A. (1982) Evidence that the pathophysiology of depression and the mechanisms of action of antidepressant drugs both involve alterations in circadian rhythms. In Costa E. and Racagni G. (eds) TYPICAL AND ATYPICAL ANTIDEPRESSANTS: CLINICAL PRACTICE, Raven Press, NY

Goranson R.E. and Berkowitz L. (1966) Reciprocity and responsibility reactions to prior help. JOURNAL OF PERSONALITY AND SOCIAL PSYCHOLOGY, 3, 227–232

Goranson R.E. and King D. (1970) RIOTING AND DAILY TEMPERATURE: ANALYSIS OF THE U.S. RIOTS IN 1967, York University, Toronto

Gorman P., Jones L. and Holman J. (1980) Generalising American locus of control norms to Australian populations: A warning. AUSTRALIAN PSYCHOLOGIST, 15, 125–127

Gorsuch R.L. (1988) Psychology of religion. ANNUAL REVIEW OF PSYCHOLOGY, 39, 201–222

Gould M. (1985) Teaching about men and masculinity: Method and meaning. TEACHING SOCIOLOGY, 12, 285–298

Gouldner A.W. (1960) The norm of reciprocity: A preliminary statement. AMERICAN SOCIOLOGICAL REVIEW, 25, 161–178

Gove W.R. (1972) Sex roles, marital status and suicide. JOURNAL OF HEALTH AND SOCIAL BEHAVIOR, 13, 204–213

Gove W.R. (1978) Sex differences in mental illness among adult men and women: An evaluation of four questions raised regarding the evidence on the higher rates of women. SOCIAL SCIENCE AND MEDICINE, 12, 187–198

Grabosky P. (1983) How violent is Australia? AUSTRALIAN SOCIETY, 2, 38–41

Grabosky P. (1989) Victims of violence. NATIONAL COMMITTEE ON VIOLENCE, MONOGRAPH No. 2, Australian Institute of Criminology, Canberra

Graumann C.F. (1987) History as multiple reconstruction, tributaries, and undercurrents. In Semin G. and Krahe B. (eds) ISSUES IN CONTEMPORARY GERMAN

SOCIAL PSYCHOLOGY, Sage, Lond.

Graumann C.F. (1988) Introduction to a history of social psychology. In Hewstone M., Stroebe W., Codol J. and Stephenson M. (eds) INTRODUCTION TO SOCIAL PSYCHOLOGY, Blackwell, Oxford

Grauerholz E. (1987) Balancing the power in dating relationships. SEX ROLES, 17, 563–571

Graycar R. (1991) Labouring under misconception: Legal constructions of women's work. Paper presented at the International Law and Society Conference (June), Amsterdam

Graycar R. and Morgan J. (1990) THE HIDDEN GENDER OF THE LAW, Federation Press, Annandale, NSW.

Graziano W., Brothen T. and Berscheid E. (1978) Height and attraction: Do men and women see eye-to-eye? JOURNAL OF PERSONALITY, 46, 128–145

Green A.H. (1986) True and false allegations of sexual abuse in child custody disputes. JOURNAL OF THE AMERICAN ACADEMY OF CHILD PSYCHIATRY, 25, 449–456

Green S.K., Buchanan D.R. and Heuer S.K. (1984) Winners, losers and choosers: A field investigation of dating initiation. PERSONALITY AND SOCIAL PSYCHOLOGY BULLETIN, 10, 502–511

Greenberg J. (1983) Equity and equality as clues to the relationship between exchange participants. EUROPEAN JOURNAL OF SOCIAL PSYCHOLOGY, 13, 195–196

Greenberg J. (1989) Cognitive re-evaluation of outcomes in response to underpayment inequity. ACADEMY OF MANAGEMENT JOURNAL, 32, 174–184

Greenberg J. (1990) Looking fair vs. being fair: Managing impressions of organizational justice. In Straw B.M. and Cummings L.L. (eds) RESEARCH IN ORGANIZATIONAL BEHAVIOR, JAI Press, Greenwich, Conn.

Greenberg J. and Cohen R.L. (eds) (1982) EQUITY AND JUSTICE IN SOCIAL BEHAVIOR, Academic Press NY.

Greenberg M.S. (1980) A theory of indebtedness. In Gergen J. Greenberg M.S. and Wills H. (eds) SOCIAL EXCHANGE: ADVANCES IN THEORY AND RESEARCH, Plenum Press, NY

Greene E., Flynn M.S. and Loftus E.F. (1982) Inducing resistance to misleading information. JOURNAL OF VERBAL LEARNING AND VERBAL BEHAVIOR, 21, 207–219

Greenwald A.G. (1980) The totalitarian ego: Fabrication and revision of personal history. AMERICAN PSYCHOLOGIST, 35, 603–618

Greenwald A.G., Bellezza F.S. and Banaji M.R. (1988) Is self-esteem a central ingredient of the self-concept? PERSONALITY AND SOCIAL PSYCHOLOGY BULLETIN, 14, 34–45

Grieve N. and Burns A. (1986) AUSTRALIAN WOMEN: NEW FEMINIST

PERSPECTIVES, Oxford University Press, Melbourne

Griffitt W. (1970) Environmental effects on interpersonal affective behavior: Ambient effective temperature and attraction. JOURNAL OF PERSONALITY AND SOCIAL PSYCHOLOGY, 15, 240–244

Griffitt W. and Guay P. (1969) "Object" evaluation and conditioned affect. JOURNAL OF EXPERIMENTAL RESEARCH IN PERSONALITY, 4, 1–8

Grigg F., Fletcher G.J. and Fitness J. (1989) Spontaneous attributions in happy and unhappy dating relationships. JOURNAL OF SOCIAL AND PERSONAL RELATIONSHIPS, 6, 61–68

Gross A.E. and Fleming I. (1982) Twenty years of deception in social psychology. PERSONALITY AND SOCIAL PSYCHOLOGY BULLETIN, 8, 402–408

Groth A.N. (1985) MEN WHO RAPE: THE PSYCHOLOGY OF THE OFFENDER, Plenum Press, NY

Groth A.N. and Birnbaum H.J. (1979) MEN WHO RAPE: THE PSYCHOLOGY OF THE OFFENDER, Plenum, NY

Grove J.R., Hanrahan S. and Stewart R. (1990) Attributions for rapid or slow recovery from sports injuries. CANADIAN JOURNAL OF SPORT SCIENCES, 15, 107–114

Grove J.R. and Pargman D. (1986) Attributions and performance during competition. JOURNAL OF SPORT PSYCHOLOGY, 8, 129–134

Gruder C.L. and Cook T.D. (1971) Sex, dependency and helping. JOURNAL OF PERSONALITY AND SOCIAL PSYCHOLOGY, 19, 290–294

Guerin B. (1986a) Mere presence effects in humans: A review. JOURNAL OF EXPERIMENTAL SOCIAL PSYCHOLOGY, 22, 38–77

Guerin B. (1986b) The effects of mere presence on a motor task. JOURNAL OF SOCIAL PSYCHOLOGY, 126, 399–401

Guerin B. (1989) Reducing evaluation effects in mere presence. JOURNAL OF SOCIAL PSYCHOLOGY, 129, 183–190

Gudykunst W.B. (1989) Culture and intergroup processes. In Bond M.H. (ed.) THE CROSS-CULTURAL CHALLENGE TO SOCIAL PSYCHOLOGY, Sage, Newbury Park, Ca.

Guttentag M. and Secord P.F (1983) TOO MANY WOMEN? THE SEX-RATIO QUESTION, Sage, Beverley Hills, Ca.

Hafner R.J. (1989) Health differences between married men and women: The contribution of sex-role stereotyping. AUSTRALIAN AND NEW ZEALAND JOURNAL OF FAMILY THERAPY, 10, 13–19

Hager J.C. and Ekman P. (1981) Methodological problems in Tourandgeau and Ellsworth's study of facial expression and experience of emotion. JOURNAL OF PERSONALITY AND SOCIAL PSYCHOLOGY, 40, 358–362

Haines H. (1983) Violence on television: A report on the mental health foundations.

MEDIA WATCH SURVEY, Mental Health Foundation, Auckland

Haines H. and Vaughan G.M. (1979) Was 1898 a "great date" in the history of experimental social psychology? JOURNAL OF THE HISTORY OF THE BEHAVIORAL SCIENCES, 15, 323–332

Halford G.S. and Sheehan P.W. (1991) Human response to environmental changes. Special Issue: The psychological dimensions of global change. INTERNATIONAL JOURNAL OF PSYCHOLOGY, 26, 599–611

Hall C.S. and Lindzey G. (1970) THEORIES OF PERSONALITY, John Wiley, NY

Hall D.T. and Lawler E.E. (1969) Unused potential in research and development organizations. RESEARCH MANAGE-MENT, 12, 339–354

Hall E.T. (1959) THE SILENT LANGUAGE, Doubleday, NY

Hall E.T. (1963) A system for the notation of proxemic behavior. AMERICAN ANTHROPOLOGIST, 65, 1003–1026

Hall E.T. (1966) THE HIDDEN DIMENSION, Anchor Books, NY

Hall J.A. (1984) NONVERBAL SEX DIFFERENCES: COMMUNICATION ACCURACY AND EXPRESSIVE STYLE, Johns Hopkins University Press, Baltimore

Halpern D.F. (1989) The disappearance of cognitive gender differences: What you see depends on where you look. AMERICAN PSYCHOLOGIST, 44, 1156–1158

Hamid P.N. (1989) Contact and intimacy patterns of lonely students. NEW ZEALAND JOURNAL OF PSYCHOLOGY, 18, 84–86

Hamilton D.L. and Gifford R.K. (1976) Illusory correlation in interpersonal perception: A cognitive basis of stereotypic judgments. JOURNAL OF EXPERIMENTAL SOCIAL PSYCHOLOGY, 12, 392–407

Hamilton D.L. and Sherman S.J. (1989) Illusory correlations: Implications for stereotype theory and research. In Bar-Tal D., Graumann C.F., Kruglanski A.W. and Strobe W. (eds) STEREOTYPING AND PREJUDICE: CHANGING CONCEPTIONS, Springer-Verlag, NY

Hamilton D.L. and Trollier (1986) Stereotypes and stereotyping: An overview of the cognitive approach. In Dovidio J. and Gaertner S.L. (eds) PREJUDICE, DISCRIMINATION, AND RACISM, Academic Press, NY

Hamilton V.L. (1978) Obedience and responsibility: A jury simulation. JOURNAL OF PERSONALITY AND SOCIAL PSYCHOLOGY, 36, 126–146

Haney C., Banks W.C. and Zimbardo P.G. (1973) Interpersonal dynamics in a simulated prison. INTERNATIONAL JOURNAL OF CRIMINOLOGY AND PENOLOGY, 1, 69–97

Hannson R.O. and Slade K.M. (1977) Altruism towards a deviant in city and small town. JOURNAL OF APPLIED SOCIAL PSYCHOLOGY, 7, 272–279

Hans V. and Vidmar N. (1982) Jury selection. In Kerr N. and Bray R.M. (eds) THE PSYCHOLOGY OF THE COURTROOM, Academic Press, NY

Hansen C.H. and Hansen R.D. (1988) Finding the face in the crowd: An anger superiority effect. JOURNAL OF PERSONALITY AND SOCIAL PSYCHOLOGY, 54, 917–924

Hansen R.D. and Hall C.A. (1985) Discounting and augmenting facilitative and inhibitory forces: The winner takes almost all. JOURNAL OF PERSONALITY AND SOCIAL PSYCHOLOGY, 49, 1482–1493

Hardin G. (1968) The tragedy of the commons. SCIENCE, 162, 1243–1248

Hardin G. (1977) THE LIMITS TO ALTRUISM: AN ECOLOGIST'S VIEW OF SURVIVAL, Indiana University Press, Bloomington, Indiana

Hare-Mustin R.T. (1987) The problem of gender in family therapy theory. FAMILY PROCESS, 26, 15–27

Harkins S. (1987) Social loafing and social facilitation. JOURNAL OF EXPERIMENTAL SOCIAL PSYCHOLOGY, 23, 1–18

Harkins S. and Petty R. (1982) Effects of task difficulty and task uniqueness on social loafing. JOURNAL OF PERSONALITY AND SOCIAL PSYCHOLOGY, 43, 1214–1229

Harkins S. and Szymanski K. (1988) Social loafing and self-evaluation with an objective standard. JOURNAL OF EXPERIMENTAL SOCIAL PSYCHOLOGY, 24, 354–365

Harkins S.G. and Szymanski K. (1989) Social loafing and group evaluation. JOURNAL OF PERSONALITY AND SOCIAL PSYCHOLOGY, 56, 934–941

Harre R. (1979) SOCIAL BEING, Blackwell, Oxford

Harre R. and Secord P.F. (1972) THE EXPLANATION OF SOCIAL BEHAV-IOUR, Basil Blackwell, Oxford

Harries K.D. and Stadler S.J. (1988) Heat and violence: New findings from Dallas field data 1980–1981. JOURNAL OF APPLIED SOCIAL PSYCHOLOGY, 18, 129–138

Harries K.D. and Stadler S. (1988) Heat and violence 1980–1981. JOURNAL OF APPLIED SOCIAL PSYCHOLOGY, 18, 129–138

Harris M.B., Benson S.M. and Hall C.L. (1975) The effects of confession on altruism. JOURNAL OF SOCIAL PSYCHOLOGY, 96, 187–192

Harris M.J. and Rosenthal R. (1985) Mediation of interpersonal expectancy effects: 31 meta-analyses. PSYCHOLOGICAL BULLETIN, 97, 363–386

Harris P.J. and Wilshire P. (1988) Estimating the prevalence of shyness in the "global village": Pluralistic ignorance or false consensus? JOURNAL OF PERSONALITY, 56, 405–415

Harris R.J. (1980) Equity judgements in hypothetical, four person partnerships.

JOURNAL OF EXPERIMENTAL SOCIAL PSYCHOLOGY, 16, 96–115

Harrison A.A. (1977) Mere exposure. In Berkowitz L. (ed.) ADVANCES IN EXPERIMENTAL SOCIAL PSYCHOLOGY (Vol. 10), Academic Press, NY

Harrison A.A. and Saeed L. (1977) Let's make a deal: An analysis of revelations and stipulations in lonely hearts advertise-ments. JOURNAL OF PERSONALITY AND SOCIAL PSYCHOLOGY, 35, 257–264

Hartshorne H. and May M.A (1928) STUDIES IN THE NATURE OF CHARACTER, Macmillan, NY

Harvey J.H. and Conslavi C. (1960) Status and conformity to pressure in informal groups. JOURNAL OF ABNORMAL PSYCHOLOGY, 60, 182–187

Harvey J.H., Harris B. and Barnes R.D. (1975) Actor-observer differences in the perceptions of responsibility and freedom. JOURNAL OF PERSONALITY AND SOCIAL PSYCHOLOGY, 32, 22–28

Hastie R. (1980) Memory for behavioral information that confirms or contradicts a personality impression. In Hastie R., Ostrom T.M., Ebbesen E.B., et al. (eds) PERSON MEMORY: THE COGNITIVE BASIS OF SOCIAL PERCEPTION, Erlbaum, Hillsdale, NJ

Hastie R. (1984) Causes and effects of causal attributions. JOURNAL OF PERSONALITY AND SOCIAL PSYCHOLOGY, 46, 44–56

Hastie R. and Kumar P.A. (1979) Person memory: Personality traits as organizing principles in memory for behaviors. JOURNAL OF PERSONALITY AND SOCIAL PSYCHOLOGY, 37, 25–38

Hastie R., Penrod S.D. and Pennington S. (1983) INSIDE THE JURY, Harvard University Press, Cambridge, Ma.

Hatfield E. (1988) Passionate and companion-ate love. In Sternberg R.J. and Barnes L. (eds) THE PSYCHOLOGY OF LOVE, Yale University Press, New Haven

Hatfield E. and Sprecher S. (1986) MIRROR, MIRROR... THE IMPORTANCE OF LOOKS IN EVERYDAY LIFE, University of New York Press, NY

Hatfield E., Traupmann J., et al. (1985) Equity and intimate relations: Recent research. In Eccles W. (ed.) COMPATIBLE AND INCOMPATIBLE RELATIONSHIPS, Springer-Verlag, NY

Hayes B. and Hesketh B. (1989) Attribution theory, judgmental biases, and cognitive behavior modification: Prospects and problems. COGNITIVE THERAPY AND RESEARCH, 13, 211–230

Hayes S.C., Johnson V.S. and Cone J.D. (1975) The marked item technique: A practical procedure for litter control. JOURNAL OF APPLIED BEHAVIOR ANALYSIS, 8, 381–386

Hays R.B. (1984) The development and maintenance of friendship. JOURNAL OF

SOCIAL AND PERSONAL RELATIONSHIPS, 1, 75–98

Hays R.B. (1985) A longitudinal study of friendship development. JOURNAL OF PERSONALITY AND SOCIAL PSYCHOLOGY, 48, 909–924

Hays R.B. (1989) The day-to-day functioning of close versus casual friendships. JOURNAL OF SOCIAL AND PERSONAL RELATIONSHIPS, 6, 21–37

Healy J.M. (1988) Elderly couples and the division of household tasks. AUSTRALIAN JOURNAL OF SEX, MARRIAGE AND FAMILY, 9, 204–214

Hearold S. (1986) A synthesis of 1403 effects of television on social behavior. In Comstock G. (ed.) PUBLIC COMMUNICATIONS AND BEHAVIOR (Vol. 1), Academic Press, NY

Heaven P.C. (1985) Construction and validation of a measure of authoritarian personality. JOURNAL OF PERSONALITY ASSESSMENT, 49, 545–551

Heaven P.C. (1986) Directiveness and dominance. JOURNAL OF SOCIAL PSYCHOLOGY, 126, 273–275

Heaven P.C. (1987) Authoritarianism, dominance and need for achievement. AUSTRALIAN JOURNAL OF PSYCHOLOGY, 39, 331–337

Heaven P.C. (1990) Suggestions for reducing unemployment: A study of Protestant work ethic and economic locus of control beliefs. BRITISH JOURNAL OF SOCIAL PSYCHOLOGY, 29, 55–65

Heaven P.C., Connors J.R. and Kellehear A. (1990) Structure and demographic correlates of attitudes towards AIDS sufferers. JOURNAL OF PSYCHOLOGY, 124, 245–252

Heaven P.C. and Furnham A. (1987) Race prejudice and economic beliefs. JOURNAL OF SOCIAL PSYCHOLOGY, 127, 483–489

Heaven P.C. and Rigby K. (1987) Attitudes toward authority and the EPQ. JOURNAL OF SOCIAL PSYCHOLOGY, 127, 359–360

Hebb D.O. and Thompson W.R. (1968) The social significance of animal studies. In Lindzey G. and Aronson E. (eds) THE HANDBOOK OF SOCIAL PSYCHOLOGY (2nd edn), Addison-Wesley, Reading, Ma.

Heider F. (1944) Social perception and phenomenal causality. PSYCHOLOGICAL REVIEW, 51, 358–374

Heider F. (1958) THE PSYCHOLOGY OF INTERPERSONAL RELATIONS, Wiley, NY

Heilman M.E., Simon M.C. and Repper D.P. (1987) Intentionally favored, unintentionally harmed? Impact of sex-biased preferential selection on self-perceptions and self-evaluations. JOURNAL OF APPLIED PSYCHOLOGY, 72, 62–68

Helm B., Bonoma T. and Tedeschi J.T. (1972) Reciprocity for harm done. JOURNAL OF SOCIAL PSYCHOLOGY, 87, 89–98

Helson H. (1964) ADAPTATION LEVEL THEORY, Harper and Row, NY

Hemsworth P.H., Barnett J.L., Hansen C. and Winfield C.G. (1986) Effects of social environment on welfare status and sexual behaviour of female pigs: II. Effects of space allowance. APPLIED ANIMAL BEHAVIOUR SCIENCE, 16, 259–267

Henaghan R.M., Taylor N.J. and Geddis D.C. (1990) Child sexual abuse. Part III: Child witnesses and the rules of evidence. NEW ZEALAND LAW JOURNAL, December, 425–431

Henderson A.S., Scott R. and Kay D.W. (1986) The elderly who live alone: Their mental health and social relationships. AUSTRALIAN AND NEW ZEALAND JOURNAL OF PSYCHIATRY, 20, 202–209

Hendrick C. (ed.) (1989) CLOSE RELATIONSHIPS, Sage, Newbury Park, Ca.

Hendrick C. and Hendrick S. (1986) A theory and method of love. JOURNAL OF PERSONALITY AND SOCIAL PSYCHOLOGY, 50, 392–402

Hendrick C., Hendrick S. and Adler N.L. (1988) Romantic relationships: Love, satisfaction, and staying together. JOURNAL OF PERSONALITY AND SOCIAL PSYCHOLOGY, 54, 980–988

Hendrick S.S. (1981) Self-disclosure and marital satisfaction. JOURNAL OF PERSONALITY AND SOCIAL PSYCHOLOGY, 40, 1150–1159

Hendrick S.S., Hendrick C., Slapion-Foote M.J. and Foote F.H. (1985) Gender differences in sexual attitudes. JOURNAL OF PERSONALITY AND SOCIAL PSYCHOLOGY, 48, 1630–1642

Henley N.M. (1977) BODY POLITICS: POWER, SEX AND NONVERBAL COMMUNICATION, Prentice Hall, NJ

Hennig P. and Knowles A. (1990) Factors influencing women over 40 years to take precautions against cervical cancer. JOURNAL OF APPLIED SOCIAL PSYCHOLOGY, 20, 1612–1621

Hepburn J. (1980) The objective reality of evidence and the utility of systematic jury selection. LAW AND HUMAN BEHAVIOUR, 4, 89–102

Hepworth J.T. and West S.G. (1988) Lynchings and the economy: A time-series reanalysis of Hovland and Sears (1940). JOURNAL OF PERSONALITY AND SOCIAL PSYCHOLOGY, 55, 239–247

Herr P.M. (1986) Consequences of priming: Judgment and behavior. JOURNAL OF PERSONALITY AND SOCIAL PSYCHOLOGY, 51, 1106–1115

Hersch G. (1970) MY LAI 4: A REPORT ON THE MASSACRE AND ITS AFTERMATH, Vintage Books, NY

Hesketh B. (1982) Work values of a group of potential school leavers in two New Zealand high schools. NEW ZEALAND JOURNAL OF EDUCATIONAL STUDIES, 17, 68–73

Hess E.H. (1965) Attitude and pupil size. SCIENTIFIC AMERICAN, 212, 46–54

Hess E.H. (1975) THE TELL-TALE EYE, Van Nostrand Rinehold, NY

Hewstone M. (1989) Changing stereotypes with disconfirming information. In Bar-Tal D., Graumann C.F., Kruglanski A.W. and Straube W. (eds) STEREOTYPING AND PREJUDICE: CHANGING CONCEPTIONS, Springer-Verlag, NY

Higgins E.T. (1989) Knowledge accessibility and activation: Subjectivity and suffering from unconscious sources. In Uleman J.S. and Bargh J.A. (eds) UNINTENDED THOUGHT, Guilford Press, NY

Higgins E.T. and Bargh J.A. (1987) Social cognition and social perception. ANNUAL REVIEW OF PSYCHOLOGY, 38, 369–425

Higgins E.T. and King G.A. (1981) Accessibility of social constructs: Information-processing consequences of individual and contextual variability. In Cantor N. and Kihlstrom J.F. (eds), PERSONALITY, COGNITION, AND SOCIAL INTERACTION, Erlbaum, Hillsdale, NJ

Higgins E.T., King G.A. and Mavin G.H. (1982) Individual construct accessibility and subjective impressions and recall. JOURNAL OF PERSONALITY AND SOCIAL PSYCHOLOGY, 43, 35–47

Hill C.T., Rubin Z. and Peplau L.A. (1976) Breakups before marriage: The end of 103 affairs. JOURNAL OF SOCIAL ISSUES, 32, 147–168

Hill G.J. (1989) An unwillingness to act: Behavioral appropriateness, situational constraint and self-efficacy in shyness. JOURNAL OF PERSONALITY, 57, 871–890

Hinde R.A. (1984) Why do the sexes behave differently in close relationships? JOURNAL OF SOCIAL AND PERSONAL RELATIONSHIPS, 1, 471–501

Hinsz V. (1989) Facial resemblance in engaged and married couples. JOURNAL OF PERSONAL AND SOCIAL RELATIONSHIPS, 6, 223–229

Ho R. (1987) Immigrants and immigration: A survey of attitudes. AUSTRALIAN PSYCHOLOGIST, 22, 3–16

Ho R. (1990) Multiculturalism in Australia: A survey of attitudes. HUMAN RELATIONS, 43, 259–272

Hobbes T. (1651) LEVIATHAN, OR MATTER, FORM AND POWER OF A COMMONWEALTH ECCLESIASTICAL AND CIVIL, Great Books (Vol. 23), Encyclopaedia Britannica, Chicago, 1952

Hofling C.K., Brotzman E., Dalrymple B., Graves N. and Pierce C.M. (1966) An experimental study in nurse-physician relationships. JOURNAL OF NERVOUS AND MENTAL DISORDERS, 143, 141–159

Hoffman L.W. (1977) Changes in family roles, socialisation and sex differences. AMERICAN PSYCHOLOGIST, 32, 644–657

Hoffman M.L. (1975) Sex differences in moral internalization and values. JOURNAL OF PERSONALITY AND PSYCHOLOGY, 32, 720–729

Hoffman M.L. (1981a) Is altruism part of human nature? JOURNAL OF PERSONALITY

AND SOCIAL PSYCHOLOGY, 40, 121–137

Hoffman M.L. (1981b) Moral internalization: Current theory and research. In Berkowitz L. (ed.) ADVANCES IN EXPERIMENTAL SOCIAL PSYCHOLOGY (Vol. 10), Academic Press, NY

Hogg M.A. (1992) THE SOCIAL PSYCHOLOGY OF GROUP COHESIVENESS, Harvester Wheatsheaf, Lond.

Hogg M.A. and Abrams D. (1988) SOCIAL IDENTIFICATION: A SOCIAL PSYCHOLOGY OF INTERGROUP RELATIONS AND GROUP PROCESSES, Routledge and Kegan Paul, Lond.

Hogg M.A. and Hardie E.A. (1991) Social attraction, personal attraction and self-categorisation: A field study. PERSONAL-ITY AND SOCIAL PSYCHOLOGY BULLETIN, 17, 175–180

Hogg M.A. and Sunderland J. (1991) Self-esteem and intergroup discrimination in the minimal group paradigm. BRITISH JOURNAL OF SOCIAL PSYCHOLOGY, 30, 51–62

Hogg M.A. and Turner J.C. (1987) Intergroup behaviour, self-stereotyping and the salience of social categories. BRITISH JOURNAL OF SOCIAL PSYCHOLOGY, 26, 325–340

Hogg M.A., Turner J.C. and Davidson B. (1990) Polarized norms and social frames of reference: A test of the self-categorization theory of group polarization. BASIC AND APPLIED SOCIAL PSYCHOLOGY, 11, 77–100

Hoh S.H., McLennan J. and Ho H. R. (1987) Depression-related cognition: Attribution style and self-referent importance of negative events. PSYCHOLOGICAL REPORTS, 61, 718

Hollander E.P. (1958) Conformity, status and idiosyncrasy credit. PSYCHOLOGICAL REVIEW, 65, 117–127

Hollander E.P. (1964) LEADERS, GROUPS AND INFLUENCE, Oxford University Press, NY

Hollander E.P. (1985) Leadership and power. In Lindzey G. and Aronson E. (eds) THE HANDBOOK OF SOCIAL PSYCHOLOGY (3rd edn), Random House, NY

Homans G.C. (1958) Social behavior and exchange. AMERICAN JOURNAL OF SOCIOLOGY, 63, 597–606

Homans G.C. (1974) SOCIAL BEHAVIOR: ITS ELEMENTARY FORMS, Harcourt, Brace, Jovanovich, NY

Hong S-M. (1986) Romantic love, idealistic or pragmatic: Sex differences among Australian young adults. PSYCHOLOGICAL REPORTS, 58, 922

Hong S-M. (1990) Effects of sex and church attendance on psychological reactance. PSYCHOLOGICAL REPORTS, 66, 494

Hong S-M. and Bartley C. (1986) Attitudes toward romantic love: An Australian perspective. AUSTRALIAN JOURNAL OF SEX, MARRIAGE AND FAMILY, 7, 166–170

Hong S-M. and Page S. (1989) A Psychological Reactance Scale: Development, factor structure and reliability. PSYCHOLOGI-CAL REPORTS, 64, 1323–1326

Hook E.B. (1973) Behavioral implications of the XYY genotype. SCIENCE, 179, 139–150

Hook J.G. and Cook T.D. (1979) Equity theory and the cognitive ability of children. PSYCHOLOGICAL BULLETIN, 86, 429–445

Hornstein H.A. (1976) CRUELTY AND KINDNESS: A NEW LOOK AT AGGRESSION AND ALTRUISM, Prentice Hall, NJ

Horowitz I. and Willing T.E. (1984) THE PSYCHOLOGY OF THE LAW: INTEGRATIONS AND APPLICA-TIONS, Little Brown, Boston.

House J.S. (1977) The three faces of social psychology. SOCIOMETRY, 40, 161–177

House J.S. and Wolf S. (1978) Effects of urban residence on interpersonal trust and helping behavior. JOURNAL OF PERSONALITY AND SOCIAL PSYCHOLOGY, 36, 1029–1043

House R. (1977) A 1976 theory of charismatic leadership. In Hunt J.G. and Larson L. (eds) LEADERSHIP: THE CUTTING EDGE, Southern Illinois University Press, Illinois

Hovland C.I., Harvey O.J. and Sherif M. (1957) Assimilation and contrast effects in reactions to communication and attitude change. JOURNAL OF ABNORMAL AND SOCIAL PSYCHOLOGY, 55, 244–252

Hovland C.I. and Sears R.R. (1940) Minor studies in aggression: VI. Correlation of lynchings with economic indices. JOURNAL OF PSYCHOLOGY, 9, 301–310

Howard J.W. and Rothbart M. (1980) Social categorization and memory for in-group and out-group behavior. JOURNAL OF PERSONALITY AND SOCIAL PSYCHOLOGY, 38, 301–310

Howarth E. and Hoffman M.S. (1984) A multidimensional approach to the relationship between mood and weather. BRITISH JOURNAL OF PSYCHOLOGY, 75, 15–23

Howe A (1989) Chamberlain revisited: The case against the media. Cited in Graycar R. and Morgan J. (1990) THE HIDDEN GENDER OF THE LAW, Federation Press, Annandale, NSW

Howell J.H. and Frost P.J. (1989) A laboratory study of charismatic leadership. ORGANI-SATIONAL BEHAVIOR AND HUMAN DECISION PROCESSES, 43, 243–269

Hudson J.W. and Hoyt L.L. (1981) Personal characteristics important in mate preference among college students. SOCIAL BEHAVIOR AND PERSONALITY, 9, 93–96

Huesmann L.L. and Eron L.D. (1986) The development of aggression in children of different cultures: Psychology processes and exposure to violence. In Huesmann L.R. and Eron L.D. (eds) TELEVISION AND THE AGGRESSIVE CHILD: A CROSS-NATIONAL COMPARISON, Erlbaum, Hillsdale, NJ

Huesmann L.R., Eron L.D., Lefkowitz M.M. and Walder L.O. (1984) Stability of aggression over time and generations. DEVELOPMENTAL PSYCHOLOGY, 20, 1120–1134

Huesmann L.R., Lagerspetz K. and Eron L.D. (1984) Intervening variables in the TV violence-aggression relation: Evidence from two countries. DEVELOPMENTAL PSYCHOLOGY, 20, 746–775

Hughes R. (1986) THE FATAL SHORE, William Collins, Lond.

Hull J.J. and Bond C.F. (1986) Social and behavioral consequences of alcohol consumption and expectancy: A meta-analysis. PSYCHOLOGICAL BULLETIN, 99, 347–360

Hume D. (1739) A TREATISE ON HUMAN NATURE, Noon, Lond.

Hunter M. (1990) ABUSED BOYS, THE NEGLECTED VICTIMS OF SEXUAL ABUSE, D.C. Heath and Co., NY

Huston T.L. (1973) Ambiguity of acceptance, social desirability, and dating choice. JOURNAL OF EXPERIMENTAL SOCIAL PSYCHOLOGY, 9, 32–42

Huston T.L. (1983) Power. In Kelley H.H., Berscheid E., Christensen A., Harvey J.H., et al. (eds) (1983) CLOSE RELATIONSHIPS, Freeman, NY

Huston T.L., Ruggiero M., Conner R., et al. (1981) Bystander intervention into crime: A study based on naturally occurring episodes. SOCIAL PSYCHOLOGY QUARTERLY, 44, 14–23

Hyde J.S. (1984) How large are gender differences in aggression: A developmental meta-analysis. DEVELOPMENTAL PSYCHOLOGY, 20, 722–736

Hyde J.S. (1986) Gender differences in aggression. In Hyde J.S. and Linn M.C. (eds) THE PSYCHOLOGY OF GENDER: ADVANCES THROUGH META-ANALYSIS, Johns Hopkins University Press, Baltimore

Hyde J.S. and Linn M.C. (1986) THE PSYCHOLOGY OF GENDER: AD-VANCES THROUGH META-ANALYSIS, Johns Hopkins University Press, Baltimore

Hyde J.S. and Linn M.C. (1988) Gender differences in verbal ability: A meta-analysis. PSYCHOLOGICAL BULLETIN, 104, 53–69

Hyman H.H. and Sheatsley P.B. (1954) The authoritarian personality - a methodological critique. In Christie R. and Jahoda M. (eds) STUDIES IN THE SCOPE AND METHOD OF "THE AUTHORITARIAN PERSON-ALITY", Free Press, NY

Hyman R. (1964) THE NATURE OF SCIENTIFIC INQUIRY, Prentice Hall, Englewood Cliffs, NJ

Iannotti R.J. (1978) Effect of role-taking experiences on role taking, empathy, altruism and aggression. DEVELOPMEN-TAL PSYCHOLOGY, 14, 199–224

Illich I. (1976) MEDICAL NEMESIS, Random House, NY

Imber-Black E. (1986) Women, families and larger systems. In Ault-Biche, M. (ed.) WOMEN AND FAMILY THERAPY, Aspen Press, Rochville

Innes J.M. and Thomas C. (1989) Attributional style, self-efficacy and social avoidance and inhibition among secondary school students. PERSONALITY AND INDIVIDUAL DIFFERENCES, 10, 757–762

Innes J.M. and Zeitz H. (1988) The public's view of the impact of the mass media: A test of the "third person" effect. EUROPEAN JOURNAL OF SOCIAL PSYCHOLOGY, 18, 457–463

Insko C.A. (1984) Balance theory, the Jordan paradigm, and the Wiest tetrahedron. ADVANCES IN EXPERIMENTAL SOCIAL PSYCHOLOGY, 18, 89–140

Insko C.A., Drenan S., Solomon M.R., Smith R. and Wade T.J. (1983) Conformity as a function of the consistency of positive self-evaluation with being liked and being right. JOURNAL OF EXPERIMENTAL SOCIAL PSYCHOLOGY, 14, 341–358

Insko C.A., Hoytle R.H., Pinkely R.L., et al. (1988) Individual-group discontinuity: The role of a consensus rule. JOURNAL OF EXPERIMENTAL SOCIAL PSYCHOLOGY, 24, 505–519

Insko C.A., Smith R.H., Alicke M.D., Wade J. and Taylor S. (1985) Conformity and group size: The concern with being right and the concern with being liked. PERSONALITY AND SOCIAL PSYCHOLOGY BULLETIN, 11, 41–50

Isen A.M. (1970) Success, failure, attention and reactions to others: The warm glow of success. JOURNAL OF PERSONALITY AND SOCIAL PSYCHOLOGY, 15, 294–301

Isen A.M. and Levin P.F. (1972) The effects of feeling good on helping: Cookies and kindness. JOURNAL OF PERSONALITY AND SOCIAL PSYCHOLOGY, 21, 364–388

Isen A.M. and Simmonds S.F. (1978) The effect of feeling good on a helping task that is incompatible with a good mood. SOCIAL PSYCHOLOGY, 41, 346–349

Jackson D.N. and Paunonen S.V. (1980) Personality structure and assessment. In Rosenzweig M.R. and Porter L.W. (eds) ANNUAL REVIEW OF PSYCHOLOGY (Vol. 31), Annual Reviews, Palo Alto, Ca.

Jackson D.N. and Paunonen S.V. (1985) Construct validity and the predictability of behavior. JOURNAL OF PERSONALITY AND SOCIAL PSYCHOLOGY, 49, 554–570

Jackson J.M. (1987) Social impact theory: A social forces model of influence. In Mullen B. and Goethals J.R. (eds), THEORIES OF GROUP BEHAVIOR, Springer-Verlag, NY

Jackson J.M. and Harkins S. (1985) Equity in effort: An explanation of the social loafing effects. JOURNAL OF PERSONALITY

AND SOCIAL PSYCHOLOGY, 49, 1119–1206

Jackson J. and Williams K. (1985) Social loafing on difficult tasks: Working collectively can improve performance. JOURNAL OF PERSONALITY AND SOCIAL PSYCHOLOGY, 49, 937–942

Jacobs H.E., Bailey J.S. and Crews J.I. (1984) Development and analysis of a community-based resource recovery program. JOURNAL OF APPLIED BEHAVIOR ANALYSIS, 17, 127–145

Jacobs P.A., Brunton M. and Melville M.M. (1965) Aggressive behaviour: Mental subnormality and the XYY male. NATURE, 208, 1351–1352

Jacobs R.C. and Campbell D.T. (1961) The perpetration of an arbitrary tradition through several generations of a laboratory micro-culture. JOURNAL OF ABNORMAL AND SOCIAL PSYCHOLOGY, 62, 649–658

Jahoda G. (1988) J'accuse. In Bond M.H. (ed.) THE CROSS-CULTURAL CHALLENGE TO SOCIAL PSYCHOLOGY, Sage, Newbury Park, Ca.

James K. (1984) Breaking the chains of gender: Family therapy's position. AUSTRALIAN JOURNAL OF FAMILY THERAPY, 5, 241–248

James K. and McIntyre D. (1989) A momentary gleam of enlightenment: Towards a model of feminist family therapy. JOURNAL OF FEMINIST FAMILY THERAPY, 1, 3–34

James W. (1890) THE PRINCIPLES OF PSYCHOLOGY, Great Books (Vol. 53), Encyclopaedia Britannica, Chicago, 1952

Janis, I.L. (1972) VICTIMS OF GROUPTHINK, Houghton Mifflin, Boston

Janis I.L. (1982) GROUP THINK: PSYCHOLOGICAL STUDIES OF POLICY DECISIONS AND FIASCOES (2nd edn), Houghton Mifflin, Boston

Janis I.L. and Mann L. (1977) DECISION-MAKING: A PSYCHOLOGICAL ANALYSIS OF CONFLICT, CHOICE AND COMMITMENT, Free Press, NY

Janoff-Bulman R. (1983) The aftermath of victimisation: Rebuilding shattered assumptions. In Figley C. (ed.) TRAUMA AND ITS WAKE, Brenner/Mazels, NY

Jarvik L.F., Klodin V. and Matsuyama S.S. (1973) Human aggression and the extra Y chromosome: Fact or fantasy. AMERICAN PSYCHOLOGIST, 28, 674–682

Jellett L.B. (1975) Patient compliance with drug therapy. AUSTRALIAN JOURNAL OF PHARMACY, 54, 433–436

Jellison J.M. and Green J. (1981) A self-presentational approach to the fundamental attribution error: The norm of internality. JOURNAL OF PERSONALITY AND SOCIAL PSYCHOLOGY, 40, 643–649

Jemmott J.B., Ashby K.L. and Lindenfield K. (1989) Romantic commitment and the perceived availability of opposite sex persons: On loving the one you are with. JOURNAL OF APPLIED SOCIAL PSYCHOLOGY, 19, 1198–1211

Jennings J., Geis F.L. and Brown V. (1980) Influence of television commercials on women's self-confidence and independent judgment. JOURNAL OF PERSONALITY AND SOCIAL PSYCHOLOGY, 38, 203–210

Jensen A.R. (1969) How much can we boost I.Q. and scholastic achievement? HARVARD EDUCATIONAL REVIEW, 39, 1–123

Job R.S. (1987) The effect of mood on helping behavior. JOURNAL OF SOCIAL PSYCHOLOGY, 127, 323–328

Joerges B. and Muller H. (1983) Energy conservation programs for consumers: A comparative analysis of policy conflicts and program response in eight Western countries. JOURNAL OF ECONOMIC PSYCHOLOGY, 4, 1–35

Johnson D.J. and Rusbult C.E. (1989) Resisting temptation: Devaluation of alternative partners as a means of maintaining commitment in close relationships. JOURNAL OF PERSONALITY AND SOCIAL PSYCHOLOGY, 57, 967–980

Johnson D.W. and Johnson F.P. (1975) JOINING TOGETHER: GROUP THEORY AND GROUP SKILLS, Prentice Hall, NY

Johnson J.M. (1987) Social impact theory: A social forces model of influence. In Mullen B. and Goethals G.R. (eds) THEORIES OF GROUP BEHAVIOR, Springer-Verlag, NY

Johnson M.M. (1981) Heterosexuality, male dominance, and the father image. SOCIOLOGICAL INQUIRY, 51, 129–139

Johnson P. (1974) Social power and sex-role stereotyping. Unpublished doctoral dissertation, University of California, Los Angeles

Johnson R.C., Danko G.P., Darvill T.J., et al. (1989) Cross-cultural assessment of altruism and its correlates. PERSONALITY AND INDIVIDUAL DIFFERENCES, 10, 855–868

Johnson R.N. (1972) AGGRESSION IN MAN AND ANIMALS, W.B. Saunders Co., Lond.

Jones C. and Aronson E. (1973) Attribution of fault to a rape victim as a function of respectability of the victim. JOURNAL OF PERSONALITY AND SOCIAL PSYCHOLOGY, 26, 415–419

Jones E.E. (1964) INGRATIATION, Irvington, NY

Jones E.E. and Davis K.E. (1965) From acts to dispositions: The attributional process in person perception. In Berkowitz L. (ed.) ADVANCES IN EXPERIMENTAL SOCIAL PSYCHOLOGY (Vol. 2), Academic Press, NY

Jones E.E., Davis K.E. and Gergen K. (1961) Role playing variations and their informational value for person perception. JOURNAL OF ABNORMAL AND SOCIAL PSYCHOLOGY, 63, 302–310

Jones E.E., Gergen K. and Jones R.G. (1964) Tactics of ingratiation among leaders and subordinates in a status hierarchy.

PSYCHOLOGICAL MONOGRAPHS, 77, (whole of No. 566)

Jones E.E. and McGillis D. (1976) Correspondent inferences and the attribution cube: A comparative reappraisal. In Harvey J., Ickes W.J. and Kidd R.F. (eds) NEW DIRECTIONS IN ATTRIBUTION RESEARCH (Vol. 1), Erlbaum, Hillsdale, NJ

Jones E.E. and Nisbett (1972) The actor and observer: Divergent perception of the causes of behavior. In Jones E.E., Kanouse D., Kelley H.H., et al. (eds) ATTRIBUTION: PERCEIVING THE CAUSES OF BEHAVIOR, General Learning Press, Morristown, NJ

Jones E.E. and Pittman T.S. (1982) Toward a general theory of strategic self-presentation. In Suls J. (ed.) PSYCHOLOGICAL PERSPECTIVES ON THE SELF, Erlbaum, Hillsdale, NJ

Jones E.E. and Wortman C. (1973) INGRATIATION: AN ATTRIBUTIONAL APPROACH, General Learning Press, Morristown, NJ

Jones J.W. and Bogat G.A. (1978) Air pollution and human aggression. PSYCHOLOGICAL REPORTS, 43, 721–723

Jones S. (1986) POLICE WOMEN AND EQUALITY: FORMAL POLICY VERSUS INFORMAL PRACTICE, MacMillan, Lond.

Jones W.H., Freeman J.E. and Goswick R.A. (1981) The persistence of loneliness: Self and other determinants. JOURNAL OF PERSONALITY, 49, 27–48

Jones W.H., Hobbs S.A. and Hockenbury D. (1982) Loneliness and social skill deficits. JOURNAL OF PERSONALITY AND SOCIAL PSYCHOLOGY, 42, 682–689

Josephson W.L. (1987) Television violence and children's aggression: Testing the priming, social script and disinhibition predictions. JOURNAL OF PERSONALITY AND SOCIAL PSYCHOLOGY, 53, 882–890

Joule R.V. (1987) Tobacco deprivation: The foot-in-the-door technique versus the low-ball technique. EUROPEAN JOURNAL OF SOCIAL PSYCHOLOGY, 17, 361–365

Jourard S.M. (1968) DISCLOSING MAN TO HIMSELF, Van Nostrand, Princeton, NJ

Jourard S.M. (1974) Some lethal aspects of the male role. In Pleck J. and Sawyer J. (eds), MEN AND MASCULINITY, Prentice Hall, NJ

Joy L.A., Kimball M.M. and Zabrack M.L. (1986) Television and children's aggressive behavior. In Williams T.M. (ed.) THE IMPACT OF TELEVISION: A NATIONAL EXPERIMENT IN THREE COMMUNITIES, Academic Press, Orlando, Fl.

Judd C.M. and Kulik J.A. (1980) Schematic effects of social attitudes on information processing and recall. JOURNAL OF PERSONALITY AND SOCIAL PSYCHOLOGY, 38, 569–578

Julien R.M. (1985) A PRIMER OF DRUG ACTION (4th edn), Freeman, NY

Jung J. (1982) THE EXPERIMENTER'S CHALLENGE, Macmillan NY

Jussim L. (1986) Self-fulfilling prophecies: A theoretical and integrative review. PSYCHOLOGICAL REVIEW, 93, 429–445

Jussim L. (1989) Teacher expectations: Self-fulfilling prophecies, perceptual biases, and accuracy. JOURNAL OF PERSONALITY AND SOCIAL PSYCHOLOGY, 57, 469–480

Jussim L. (1991) Social perception and social reality: A reflection-construction model. PSYCHOLOGICAL REVIEW, 98, 54–73

Kabanoff B. (1991) Equity, equality, power, and conflict. ACADEMY OF MANAGEMENT REVIEW, 16, 416–441

Kagehiro D. and Stanton W. (1985) Legal vs quantified definitions of standards of proof. LAW AND HUMAN BEHAVIOUR, 9, 159–168

Kagitcibashi C. (ed.) (1987) GROWTH AND PROGRESS IN CROSS-CULTURAL PSYCHOLOGY, Swets and Zeitlinger, Lisse, Holland

Kahle L.R. and Beatty S.E. (1987) Cognitive consequences of legislating postpurchase behavior: Growing up with the bottle bill. JOURNAL OF APPLIED SOCIAL PSYCHOLOGY, 17, 828–843

Kahn G.R. and Katz D. (1953) Leadership practices in relation to productivity and morale. In Cartwright D. and Zander A. (eds) GROUP DYNAMICS: RESEARCH AND THEORY, Row Peterson, Evanston, Illinois

Kahneman D. and Tversky A. (1972) Subjective probability: A judgement of representativeness. COGNITIVE PSYCHOLOGY, 3, 430–454

Kahneman D. and Tversky A. (1973) On the psychology of prediction. PSYCHOLOGICAL REVIEW, 80, 237–251

Kahneman D. and Tversky A. (1984) Choices, values and frames. AMERICAN PSYCHOLOGIST, 39, 341–350

Kalat J.W. (1988) BIOLOGICAL PSYCHOLOGY (3rd edn), Wadsworth and Nelson, Belmont, Ca.

Kalick S.M. and Hamilton T.E. (1986) The matching hypothesis reexamined. JOURNAL OF PERSONALITY AND SOCIAL PSYCHOLOGY, 51, 673–682

Kammann R., Thompson R. and Irwin R. (1979) Unhelpful behavior in the street: City size or immediate pedestrian density? ENVIRONMENT AND BEHAVIOR, 11, 245–250

Kandel D. (1978) Similarity in real-life adolescent friendship pairs. JOURNAL OF PERSONALITY AND SOCIAL PSYCHOLOGY, 36, 306–312

Kantola S.J., Syme G.J. and Campbell N.A. (1984) Cognitive dissonance and energy conservation. JOURNAL OF APPLIED PSYCHOLOGY, 69, 416–421

Kantola S.J., Syme G.J. and Nesdale A.R. (1983) The effects of appraised severity and efficacy in promoting water conservation: An informational analysis. JOURNAL OF

APPLIED SOCIAL PSYCHOLOGY, 68, 164–182

Kaplan S. (1987) Aesthetics, affect and cognition: Environmental preference from an evolutionary perspective. ENVIRONMENT AND BEHAVIOR, 19, 3–32

Karlins M., Coffman T.L. and Walters G. (1969) On the fading of social stereotypes: Studies in three generations of college students. JOURNAL OF PERSONALITY AND SOCIAL PSYCHOLOGY, 13, 1–16

Karlovac M. and Darley J.M. (1988) Attribution of responsibility for accidents: A negligence law analogy. SOCIAL COGNITION, 6, 287–318

Karuza J. and Brickman P. (1981) Preference for similarity in higher and lower status others. PERSONALITY AND SOCIAL PSYCHOLOGY BULLETIN, 7, 504–508

Kashima Y. and Kashima E.S. (1988) Individual differences in the predictions of behavioral intentions. JOURNAL OF SOCIAL PSYCHOLOGY, 128, 711–720

Kashima Y., Siegal M., Tanaka K. and Isaka H. (1988) Universalism in lay conceptions of distributive justice: A cross-cultural examination. INTERNATIONAL JOURNAL OF PSYCHOLOGY, 23, 51–64

Kashima Y. and Triandis H.C. (1986) The self-serving bias in attributions as a coping strategy: A cross-cultural study. JOURNAL OF CROSS CULTURAL PSYCHOLOGY, 17, 83–97

Kassarjian H.H. (1982) Consumer psychology. ANNUAL REVIEW OF PSYCHOLOGY, 33, 619–649

Kassin S.M., Ellsworth P.C. and Smith V.L. (1989) The "general acceptance" of psychological research on eye-witness testimony: A survey of the experts. AMERICAN PSYCHOLOGIST, 44, 1089–1098

Kassin S. and Juhnke, R. (1983) Juror experience and decision-making. JOURNAL OF PERSONALITY AND SOCIAL PSYCHOLOGY, 44, 1182–1191

Kassin S. and Wrightsman L. (1979) On the requirement of proof: The timing of judicial instruction and mock juror verdicts. JOURNAL OF PERSONALITY AND SOCIAL PSYCHOLOGY, 37, 1877–1887

Kassin S. and Wrightsman L. (1988) THE AMERICAN JURY ON TRIAL. PSYCHOLOGICAL PERSPECTIVES, Harper and Row, NY

Katsikitis M. and Brebner J. (1981) Individual differences in the effects of personal space invasion: A test of the Brebner-Cooper model of extraversion. PERSONALITY AND INDIVIDUAL DIFFERENCES, 2, 5–10

Katz D. and Braly K. (1933) Racial stereotypes of one hundred college students. JOURNAL OF ABNORMAL AND SOCIAL PSYCHOLOGY, 28, 280–290

Katz I. (1981) STIGMA: A SOCIAL PSYCHOLOGICAL ANALYSIS, Erlbaum, Hillsdale, NJ

Katz I. and Hass R.G. (1988) Racial ambivalence and American value conflict: Correlation and priming studies of dual cognitive structures. JOURNAL OF PERSONALITY AND SOCIAL PSYCHOLOGY, 55, 893–905

Katz J., Glucksberg S. and Krauss I. (1960) Need satisfaction and Edwards PPS scores in married couples. JOURNAL OF CONSULTING PSYCHOLOGY, 24, 205–208

Katz P.A. (1976) The acquisition of racial attitudes in children. In Katz P.A. (ed.) TOWARDS THE ELIMINATION OF RACISM, Pergamon, NY

Katz P.A. and Taylor D.A. (eds) (1988) ELIMINATING RACISM: PROFILES IN CONTROVERSY, Plenum, NY

Katzev R. and Johnson T.R. (1984) Comparing the effects of monetary incentives and foot-in-the-door strategies in promoting residential electricity conservation. JOURNAL OF APPLIED SOCIAL PSYCHOLOGY, 14, 12–27

Kaufmann H. (1970) AGGRESSION AND ALTRUISM: A PSYCHOLOGICAL ANALYSIS, Holt Rinehart and Winston, NY

Keating C.F. (1985) Gender and the physiognomy of dominance and attractiveness. SOCIAL PSYCHOLOGY QUARTERLY, 48, 61–70

Keen S. (1991) FIRE IN THE BELLY, Bantam Books, Sydney

Kelley H.H. (1950) The warm-cold variable in first impressions of persons. JOURNAL OF PERSONALITY, 18, 431–439

Kelley H.H. (1967) Attribution theory in social psychology. In Levine D. (ed.) NEBRASKA SYMPOSIUM ON MOTIVATION, University of Nebraska Press, Lincoln, Neb.

Kelley H.H. (1972) Causal schemata and the attribution process. In Jones E.E., et al. ATTRIBUTION: PERCEIVING THE CAUSES OF BEHAVIOR, General Learning Press, Morristown, NJ

Kelley H.H., Berscheid E., Christensen A., Harvey J.H., et al. (eds) (1983) CLOSE RELATIONSHIPS, Freeman, NY

Kelley H.H., Condry J.C., et al. (1965) Collective behavior in a simulated panic situation. JOURNAL OF EXPERIMENTAL SOCIAL PSYCHOLOGY, 1, 20–54

Kelley H.H. and Michela J.L. (1980) Attribution theory and research. ANNUAL REVIEW OF PSYCHOLOGY, 31, 457–501

Kelley H.H and Thibaut J.W. (1978) INTERPERSONAL RELATIONS: A THEORY OF INTERDEPENDENCE, Wiley, NY

Kelly G. (1955) THE PSYCHOLOGY OF PERSONAL CONSTRUCTS (Vol. 1–2), Norton, NY

Kelly I.W. and Rotton J. (1983) Geophysical variables and behavior: XIII. Comment on "Lunar phase and accident injuries": The dark side of the moon and lunar research. PERCEPTUAL AND MOTOR SKILLS, 57, 919–921

Kelly I.W., Saklofske D.H and Culver R. (1990) Aircraft accidents and disasters and full moon: No relationship. PSYCHOLOGY A JOURNAL OF HUMAN BEHAVIOR, 27, 30–33

Kelman H.C. (1967) Human use of human subjects: The problem of deception in social psychology experiments. PSYCHOLOGICAL BULLETIN, 67, 1–11

Kelman H.C. (1968) A TIME TO SPEAK: ON HUMAN VALUES AND SOCIAL RESEARCH, Jossey-Bass, San Francisco

Kelman H.C. and Hamilton V.L. (1989) CRIMES OF OBEDIENCE, Yale University Press, New Haven

Kenney D.A. and Zaccaro S.J. (1983) An estimate of variance due to traits in leadership. JOURNAL OF APPLIED PSYCHOLOGY, 68, 678–685

Kenrick D.T., Baumann D.J. and Cialdini R.B. (1979) A step in the socialization of altruism as hedonism: Effects of negative mood on children's generosity under public and private conditions. JOURNAL OF PERSONALITY AND SOCIAL PSYCHOLOGY, 37, 747–755

Kenrick D.T. and Cialdini R.B. (1977) Romantic attraction: Missattribution vs. reinforcement explanations. JOURNAL OF PERSONALITY AND SOCIAL PSYCHOLOGY, 35, 381–391

Kenrick D.T., Cialdini R.B. and Linder D. (1979) Misattribution under fear producing circumstances: Four failures to replicate. PERSONALITY AND SOCIAL PSYCHOLOGY BULLETIN, 5, 329–334

Kenrick D.T. and McFarlane S.W. (1986) Ambient temperature and horn honking: A field study of the heat aggression relationship. ENVIRONMENT AND BEHAVIOR, 18, 179–191

Kenrick D.T., Sadalla E.K., Groth G. and Trost M.R. (1990) Evolution, traits, and the stages of human courtship: Qualifying the parental investment model. JOURNAL OF PERSONALITY, 58, 97–116

Kenrick D.T. and Trost M.R. (1987) A biosocial model of heterosexual relationships. In Kelley H.H. (ed.) MALES, FEMALES, AND SEXUALITY: THEORY AND RESEARCH, State University of New York Press, Albany, NY

Kenrick D.T. and Trost M.R. (1989) A reproductive exchange model of heterosexual relationships: Putting proximate economics in ultimate perspective. In Hendrick C. (ed.) CLOSE RELATIONSHIPS, Sage, California

Kenrick D.T., Trost M.R., Groth G. and Sadalla E.K. (1988) Gender differences in mate selection criteria vary with different phases of courtship. Unpublished manuscript

Kerchkoff A.C. (1974) The social context of interpersonal attraction. In Huston T. (ed.) FOUNDATIONS OF INTERPERSONAL ATTRACTION, Academic Press, NY

Kerchkoff A.C. and Davis K.E. (1962) Value consensus and need complementarity in mate selection. AMERICAN SOCIOLOGICAL REVIEW, 27, 295–303

Ker Muir W. (1977) POLICE: STREETCORNER POLITICIANS, University of Chicago Press, Chicago

Kernis M.H. (1984) Need for uniqueness, self-schemas, and thought as moderators of the false-consensus effect. JOURNAL OF EXPERIMENTAL SOCIAL PSYCHOLOGY, 20, 350–362

Kernis M.H. and Wheeler L. (1981) Beautiful friends and ugly strangers: Radiation and contrast effects in perceptions of same-sex pairs. PERSONALITY AND SOCIAL PSYCHOLOGY BULLETIN, 7, 617–620

Kerr N.L. (1989) Illusions of efficacy: The effects of group size on perceived efficacy in social dilemmas. JOURNAL OF EXPERIMENTAL SOCIAL PSYCHOLOGY, 25, 287–313

Kerr N.L. and Bruun S. (1983) Dependability of member effort and group motivation loss: Free-rider effects. JOURNAL OF PERSONALITY AND SOCIAL PSYCHOLOGY, 44, 78–94

Kerr N.L. and MacCoun R. (1985) Role of expectations in social dilemmas: Sex roles and task motivation in groups. JOURNAL OF PERSONALITY AND SOCIAL PSYCHOLOGY, 49, 1547–1556

Kerr N.L. and MacCoun J. (1985) The effect of jury size and polling method on the process and product of jury deliberation. JOURNAL OF PERSONALITY AND SOCIAL PSYCHOLOGY, 48, 349–363

Khew K. and Brebner J. (1985) The role of personality in crowding research. PERSONALITY AND INDIVIDUAL DIFFERENCES, 6, 641–643

Kiddler Z.H. and Juop C.M. (1986) RESEARCH METHODS IN SOCIAL RELATIONS, Holt, Rinehart and Winston, NY

Kiesler C.A. (1971) THE PSYCHOLOGY OF COMMITMENTS: EXPERIMENTS LINKING BEHAVIOR TO BELIEF, Academic Press, NY

Kihlstrom J.F. (1987) Introduction to the special issue: Integrating personality and social psychology. JOURNAL OF PERSONALITY AND SOCIAL PSYCHOLOGY, 53, 989–992

Kilham W. and Mann L. (1974) Levels of destructive obedience as a function of transmitter and executant roles in the Milgram obedience paradigm. JOURNAL OF PERSONALITY AND SOCIAL PSYCHOLOGY, 29, 696–702

Kimball M.M. (1989) A new perspective on women's maths achievement. PSYCHOLOGICAL BULLETIN, 105, 198–214

Kimble C.E., Funk S.C. and DaPolito K.L. (1990) The effects of self-esteem certainty on behavioral self-handicapping. JOURNAL OF SOCIAL BEHAVIOR AND PERSONALITY, 5, 137–149

Kimmel A. (ed.) (1981) ETHICS OF HUMAN SUBJECT RESEARCH, Jossey-Bass, San Francisco

Kinder D.R. and Sanders L.M. (1990) Mimicking political debate with survey questions: The case of White opinion on affirmative action for Blacks. Special Issue: Thinking about politics: Comparisons of experts and novices. SOCIAL COGNITION, 8, 73–103

Kinder D.R. and Sears D.O. (1981) Prejudice and politics: Symbolic racism versus racial threats to the good life. JOURNAL OF PERSONALITY AND SOCIAL PSYCHOLOGY, 40, 414–431

Kippax S., Crawford J., Benton P. Gault U. and Noesjirwan J. (1988) Constructing emotions: weaving meaning from memories. BRITISH JOURNAL OF SOCIAL PSYCHOLOGY, 27, 19–33

Kirchler E. and Davis J.H. (1986) The influence of member status differences and task type on group consensus and member position change. JOURNAL OF PERSONALITY AND SOCIAL PSYCHOLOGY, 51, 83–91

Kirkham G.L. (1981) A professor's street lessons. In NSW POLICE NEWS, August, 22–26

Kirscht J.P. and Dillehay R.C. (1967) DIMENSIONS OF AUTHORITARIANISM, University of Kentucky Press, Lexington

Klein S.B. and Loftus J. (1988) The nature of self-referent encoding: The contributions of elaborative and organizational processes. JOURNAL OF PERSONALITY AND SOCIAL PSYCHOLOGY, 55, 5–11

Kleinke C.L. (1986) Gaze and eye contact: A research review. PSYCHOLOGICAL REVIEW, 100, 78–100

Kline S. (1988) Rationalizing attitude discrepant behavior: A case study in energy attitudes. Unpublished manuscript, York University, Toronto

Klockars C.B. (1983) THINKING ABOUT POLICE, McGraw-Hill, NY

Klockars C.B. (1985) THE IDEA OF POLICE, Sage, Ca.

Knapp M.L. (1978) NONVERBAL COMMUNICATION IN HUMAN INTERACTION (2nd edn), Rinehart and Winston, NY

Knowles E.S. (1979) The proximity of others: A critique of crowding research and integration with the social sciences. JOURNAL OF POPULATION, 2, 3–17

Knowles E.S. (1983) Social physics and the effects of others: Tests of the effects of audience size and distance on social judgements and behavior. JOURNAL OF PERSONALITY AND SOCIAL PSYCHOLOGY, 45, 1263–1279

Knox R.E. and Inkster J.A. (1968) Post decision dissonance at post time. JOURNAL OF PERSONALITY AND SOCIAL PSYCHOLOGY, 8, 319–323

Koestner R. and Wheeler L. (1988) Self-presentation in personal advertisements: The influence of implicit notions of attraction and role expectations. JOURNAL OF SOCIAL AND PERSONAL RELATIONSHIPS, 5, 149–160

Kogan N. and Wallach M.A. (1964) RISK TAKING, Holt, Rinehart and Winston, NY

Kogan N. and Wallach M.A. (1967) Risk taking as a function of the situation, the person and the group. In Mandler G., Mussen P., Kogan N. and Wallach M.A. (eds) NEW DIRECTIONS IN PSYCHOLOGY III, Holt, Rinehart and Winston, NY

Kohlberg L. (1963) Moral development and identification. In Stevenson H. (ed.) CHILD PSYCHOLOGY, University of Chicago Press, Chicago

Kohlberg L. (1969) Stage and sequence: The cognitive developmental approach to socialisation. In Goslin D.A. (ed.) HANDBOOK OF SOCIALISATION THEORY AND RESEARCH, Rand McNally, Chicago

Kohlberg L. (1976) Moral state and moralization. In Likona T. (ed.) MORAL DEVELOPMENT AND BEHAVIOR, Holt, Rinehart and Winston, NY

Kohlberg L. (1978) Revisions in the theory and practice of moral development. In Damon W. (ed.) NEW DIRECTIONS FOR CHILD DEVELOPMENT, Jossey-Bass, San Francisco

Kohlberg L. (1981) THE MEANING AND MEASUREMENT OF MORAL DEVELOPMENT, Clark University Press, Worcester, Ma.

Kohlberg L. and Ullian D.Z. (1974) Stages in the development of psychosexual concepts and attitudes. In Friedman R.C., Richart R.M. and Vande Wiele R.L. (eds) SEX DIFFERENCES IN BEHAVIOR, Wiley, NY

Kohn M.L. (1989) Social structure and personality: A quintessential sociological approach to social psychology. SOCIAL FORCES, 68, 26–33

Komisar L. (1976) Violence and the masculine mystique. In David D. and Brannon R. (eds) THE FORTY NINE PERCENT MAJORITY: THE MALE SEX ROLE, Addison-Wesley, NY

Konecni V.J. and Ebbesen E. (1982) THE CRIMINAL JUSTICE SYSTEM. A SOCIAL-PSYCHOLOGICAL ANALYSIS, W.H. Freeman, San Francisco

Konecni V.J., Libuser L., Morton H. and Ebbesen E.B. (1975) Effects of a violation of personal space on escape and helping responses. JOURNAL OF EXPERIMENTAL SOCIAL PSYCHOLOGY, 11, 288–299

Korn J.H. (1987) Judgments of acceptability of deception in psychological research. JOURNAL OF GENERAL PSYCHOLOGY, 114, 205–216

Kornhauser A., Sheppard H.L. and Mayer A.J. (1956) WHEN LABOR VOTES, University Books, NY

Korte C. (1980) Urban-nonurban differences in social behavior and social psychological models of urban impact. JOURNAL OF SOCIAL ISSUES, 36, 29–54

Korte C. (1981) Constraints on helping in an urban environment. In Rushton J.P. and Sorrentino R.M. (eds) ALTRUISM AND HELPING BEHAVIOR, Erlbaum, Hillsdale, NJ

Krafka C. and Penrod S. (1981) The effects of witness and stimulus factors on eyewitness performance. American Psychology-Law Society Biennial Convention, October

Kraus J. (1975) Ecology of juvenile delinquency in metropolitan Sydney. JOURNAL OF COMMUNITY PSYCHOLOGY, 3, 384–395

Kravitz D.A. and Martin B. (1986) Ringelmann rediscovered: The original article. JOURNAL OF PERSONALITY AND SOCIAL PSYCHOLOGY, 50, 936–941

Krebs D.L. (1970) Altruism: An examination of the concept and a review of the literature. PSYCHOLOGICAL BULLETIN, 73, 258–302

Krebs D.L. (1975) Empathy and altruism. JOURNAL OF PERSONALITY AND SOCIAL PSYCHOLOGY, 32, 1134–1146

Krebs D.L. (1978) A cognitive-developmental approach to altruism. In Wispe L. (ed.) ALTRUISM, SYMPATHY AND HELPING, Academic Press, NY

Krebs D.L. and Adinolfi A.A. (1975) Physical attractiveness, social relations, and personality style. JOURNAL OF PERSONALITY AND SOCIAL PSYCHOLOGY, 31, 245–253

Krebs D.L. and Miller D.T. (1985), Altruism and aggression. In Lindzey G. and Aronson E. (eds) HANDBOOK OF SOCIAL PSYCHOLOGY (Vol. 3), (3rd edn), Random House, NY

Krosnick J.A. and Alwin D.F. (1989) Aging and susceptibility to attitude change. JOURNAL OF PERSONALITY AND SOCIAL PSYCHOLOGY, 57, 416–425

Krueger J. and Rothbart M. (1988) Use of categorical and individuating information in making inferences about personality. JOURNAL OF PERSONALITY AND SOCIAL PSYCHOLOGY, 55, 187–195

Kruglanski A.W. (1989) LAY EPISTEMICS AND HUMAN KNOWLEDGE, Plenum Press, NY

Kuiper N.A., Olinger L.A., MacDonald M.R. and Shaw B.F. (1985) Self-schema processing of depressed and non-depressed content: The effects of vulnerability to depression. SOCIAL COGNITION, 3, 77–93

Kulik J.A. and Brown R. (1979) Frustration, attribution of blame and aggression. JOURNAL OF EXPERIMENTAL SOCIAL PSYCHOLOGY, 15, 183–194 L'Abate L. (1980) Inexpressive males or overexpressive females? A reply to Balswick. FAMILY RELATIONS, 29, 229–230

Laborde J.M., Dando W.A. and Powers M.J. (1986) Influence of weather on osteoarthritics. SOCIAL SCIENCE AND MEDICINE, 23, 549–554

Lamm H. (1988) A revision of our research on group polarisation. PSYCHOLOGICAL REPORTS, 62, 807–813

Lancaster S. and Foddy M. (1988) Self-extensions: A conceptualization. JOURNAL FOR THE THEORY OF SOCIAL BEHAVIOR, 18, 77–94

Landy D. and Aronson E. (1969) The influence of the character of the criminal and his victim on the decisions of simulated jurors. JOURNAL OF EXPERIMENTAL SOCIAL PSYCHOLOGY, 5, 141–152

Landy D. and Sigall H. (1974) Beauty is talent: Task evaluation as a function of the performer's physical attractiveness. JOURNAL OF PERSONALITY AND SOCIAL PSYCHOLOGY, 29, 299–304

Laner M.R. (1978) Media mating II: "Personal" advertisements of lesbian women. JOURNAL OF HOMOSEXUALITY, 4, 41–61

Laner M.R. and Kamel G.W. (1977) Media mating I: Newspaper "personal" ads of homosexual men. JOURNAL OF HOMOSEXUALITY, 3, 149–162

Lange R. and Tiggemann M. (1980) Changes within the Australian population to more external control beliefs. AUSTRALIAN PSYCHOLOGIST, 15, 495–497

Langer E.J. (1975) The illusion of control. JOURNAL OF PERSONALITY AND SOCIAL PSYCHOLOGY, 32, 311–328

Langlois J.H. and Downs A.C. (1979) Peer relationships as a function of physical attractiveness: The eye of the beholder or behavioral reality? CHILD DEVELOPMENT, 50, 409–418

Langlois J.H. and Stephan C.W. (1981) Beauty and the beast: The role of physical attractiveness in the development of peer relations and social behavior. In Brehm S.S., Kassin S.M. and Gibbons F.X. (eds) DEVELOPMENTAL SOCIAL PSYCHOLOGY, Oxford University Press, NY

Lanning K. (1987) Child molesters—A behavioral analysis for law enforcement. In Hazelwood R. and Burgess W. (eds) PRACTICAL ASPECTS OF RAPE INVESTIGATION: A MULTIDISCIPLINARY APPROACH, Elsevier, NY

Lantz H., Keyes J. and Schultz M. (1975) The American family in the preindustrial period: From baselines in history to change. AMERICAN SOCIOLOGICAL REVIEW, 40, 21–36

Lantz H., Schultz M. and O'Hara M. (1977) The changing American family from the preindustrial to the industrial period: A final report. AMERICAN SOCIOLOGICAL REVIEW, 42, 406–421

LaPiere R.T. (1934) Attitude and actions. SOCIAL FORCES, 13, 230–237

Larson J.H. and Bell N.J. (1988) Need for privacy and its effect upon interpersonal attraction and interaction. JOURNAL OF SOCIAL AND CLINICAL PSYCHOLOGY, 6, 1–10

Larson R., Csikszentmihalyi M. and Graef R. (1982) Time alone in daily experience: Loneliness or renewal? In Peplau L.A. and Perlman D. (eds) LONELINESS: A SOURCE BOOK OF CURRENT THEORY, RESEARCH AND THERAPY, Wiley, NY

Larzelere R. and Huston T. (1980) The dyadic trust scale: Toward understanding interpersonal trust in close relationships. JOURNAL OF MARRIAGE AND THE FAMILY, 42, 595–604

Lassiter G.D. and Briggs M.A. (1990) Effect of anticipated interaction on liking: An individual difference analysis. JOURNAL OF SOCIAL BEHAVIOR AND PERSONALITY, 5, 357–367

Latane B. (1981) The psychology of social impact. AMERICAN PSYCHOLOGIST, 36, 343–356

Latane B. and Dabbs J.M. (1975) Sex, group size and helping in three cities. SOCIOMETRY, 38, 180–194

Latane B. and Darley J. (1968) Group inhibition of bystander intervention. JOURNAL OF PERSONALITY AND SOCIAL PSYCHOLOGY, 10, 215–221

Latane B. and Darley J. (1970) THE UNRESPONSIVE BYSTANDER: WHY DOESN'T HE HELP?, Appleton Century Crofts, NY

Latane B and Nida S.A. (1981) Ten years of research on group size and helping. PSYCHOLOGICAL BULLETIN, 89, 308–324

Latane B., Williams K. and Harkins S. (1979) Many hands make light the work: The causes and consequences of social loafing. JOURNAL OF PERSONALITY AND SOCIAL PSYCHOLOGY, 37, 822–832

Latane B. and Wolf S. (1981) The social impact of majorities and minorities. PSYCHOLOGICAL REVIEW, 88, 438–453

Lavrakas P.J. (1975) Female preferences for male physiques. JOURNAL OF RESEARCH IN PERSONALITY, 9, 324–334

Lawler E.E. (1971) PSYCHOLOGY AND ORGANIZATIONAL EFFECTIVENESS: A PSYCHOLOGICAL VIEW. McGraw-Hill, NY

Lawler E.E. and O'Gara P.W. (1967) Effects of inequity produced by underpayment on work output, work quality, and attitudes toward work. JOURNAL OF APPLIED PSYCHOLOGY, 51, 403–410

Lawrence J.A. (1988) Making just decisions in magistrates' courts. SOCIAL JUSTICE RESEARCH, 2, 155–176

Lazarus R.S., Spersman J.C., Mordkoff A.M., et al. (1962) A laboratory study of psychological distress produced by a motion picture film. PSYCHOLOGICAL MONOGRAPHS, 76, (special edition).

LeBlanc J. (1975) MAN IN THE COLD, Thomas, Springfield, Il.

Lederer L. (1980) TAKE BACK THE NIGHT: WOMEN ON PORNOGRAPHY, Morrow, NY

Lee C. (1989) Perceptions of immunity to disease in adult smokers. JOURNAL OF BEHAVIORAL MEDICINE, 12, 267–277

Lee J.A. (1973) THE COLORS OF LOVE, Bantam, NY

Lee J.A. (1977) A typology of styles of loving. PERSONALITY AND SOCIAL PSYCHOLOGY BULLETIN, 3, 173–182

Lees S. and Senyard J. (1985) Taste and table manners: Class and gender in children's books in the 1950s. AUSTRALIAN AND NEW ZEALAND JOURNAL OF SOCIOLOGY, 21, 174–193

Lemyre L. and Smith P.M. (1985) Intergroup discrimination and self-esteem in the minimal group paradigm. JOURNAL OF PERSONALITY AND SOCIAL PSYCHOLOGY, 49, 660–670

Lerner M.J. (1977) The justice motive: Some hypotheses as to its origins and forms. JOURNAL OF PERSONALITY AND SOCIAL PSYCHOLOGY, 45, 1–52

Lerner M.J. (1980) THE BELIEF IN A JUST WORLD: A FUNDAMENTAL DELUSION, Plenum Press, NY

Lerner M.J. and Agar E. (1972) The consequences of perceived similarity: Attraction and rejection, approach and avoidance. JOURNAL OF EXPERIMENTAL RESEARCH IN PERSONALITY, 6, 69–75

Lerner M.J. and Matthews G. (1967) Reactions to suffering of others under conditions of indirect responsibility. JOURNAL OF PERSONALITY AND SOCIAL PSYCHOLOGY, 5, 319–325

Lerner M.J., Miller D.T. and Holmes J.G. (1976) Deserving and the emergence of forms of justice. In Berkowitz L. and Walster E. (eds) EQUITY THEORY: TOWARD A GENERAL THEORY OF SOCIAL INTERACTION. ADVANCES IN EXPERIMENTAL SOCIAL PSYCHOLOGY (Vol. 9), Academic Press, NY

Lerner R.M. and Gellert E. (1969) Body build identification, preference, and aversion in children. DEVELOPMENTAL PSYCHOLOGY, 1, 465–462

Lester D., Butler A.J., Dalley A.F., et al. (1982) Job satisfaction, cynicism and belief in an external locus of control: A study of police in four nations. POLICE STUDIES, 5, 6–9

Lester D. and Frank M.L. (1987) Beware the nones of March: Suicide at the beginning of the month. PSYCHOLOGICAL REPORTS, 61, 938

Levenson H. (1972) Distinctions with the concept of internal-external control: Development of a new scale. PROCEEDINGS OF THE 80TH ANNUAL CONFERENCE OF THE AMERICAN PSYCHOLOGICAL ASSOCIATION, American Psychological Association

Leventhal G.S. (1976) The distribution of rewards and resources in groups and organizations. In Berkowitz L. and Walster E. (eds) ADVANCES IN EXPERIMENTAL SOCIAL PSYCHOLOGY (Vol. 9), Academic Press, NY

Leventhal G.S. (1979) What should be done with equity theory? New approaches to the study of fairness in social relationships. In Gergen K.J. and Greenberg M.S. (eds) SOCIAL EXCHANGE THEORY, Wiley, NY

Leventhal G.S., Weiss T. and Long G. (1969) Equity, reciprocity, and reallocating the rewards in the dyad. JOURNAL OF PERSONALITY AND SOCIAL PSYCHOLOGY, 13, 300–305

Levine R.A. and Campbell D.T. (1972) ETHNOCENTRISM: THEORIES OF CONFLICT, ETHNIC ATTITUDES AND GROUP BEHAVIOR, Wiley, NY

Levine R.A. (1987) Waiting is a power game. PSYCHOLOGY TODAY, April, 24–33

Levinger G.S. (1964) A note on need complementarity in marriage. PSYCHOLOGICAL BULLETIN, 61, 153–157

Levinger G. (1974) A three level approach to attraction: Toward an understanding of pair relatedness. In Huston T. (ed.) FOUNDATIONS OF INTERPRESONAL ATTRACTION, Academic Press, NY

Levinger G. (1976) A social psychological perspective on marital dissolution. JOURNAL OF SOCIAL ISSUES, 32, 21–47

Levinger G. (1980) Towards the analysis of close relationships. JOURNAL OF EXPERIMENTAL SOCIAL PSYCHOLOGY, 16, 510–544

Levinger G. (1983) Development and Change. In Kelley H.H., et al. (eds) CLOSE RELATIONSHIPS, Freeman, NY

Levinger G. and Snoek J.D. (1972) ATTRACTION IN RELATIONSHIPS: A NEW LOOK AT INTERPERSONAL ATTRACTION, General Learning Press, Morristown, NJ

Lewin K. (1936) PRINCIPLES OF TOPOLOGICAL PSYCHOLOGY, McGraw-Hill, NY

Lewin K. (1951) FIELD THEORY IN SOCIAL SCIENCE, Harper and Row, NY

Lewin K., Lippitt R. and White R.K. (1939) Patterns of aggressive behavior in experimentally created "social climates". JOURNAL OF SOCIAL PSYCHOLOGY, 10, 271–299

Lewinsohn P.M., Mischel W., Chaplin W. and Barton R. (1980) Social competence and depression: The role of illusory self-perceptions. JOURNAL OF ABNORMAL PSYCHOLOGY, 89, 203–212

Lewis M. (1972) Culture and gender roles: There's no unisex in the nursery. PSYCHOLOGY TODAY, May, 54–57.

Lewis R.A. (1978) Emotional intimacy among men. JOURNAL OF SOCIAL ISSUES, 34, 108–121

Lewontin R.C. (1970) The units of selection. ANNUAL REVIEW OF ECOLOGY AND SYSTEMATICS, 1 (whole), Annual Reviews Inc, San Francisco

Lewontin R.C. (1972) The apportionment of human diversity. EVOLUTIONARY BIOLOGY, 6, 381–98

Lewy A.J., Kern H.A., Rosenthal N.E. and Wehr T.A. (1982) Bright artificial light treatment of a manic-depressive patient with a seasonal mood cycle. AMERICAN JOURNAL OF PSYCHIATRY, 139, 1496–1498

Ley P. (1978) Patient compliance - a psychologist's viewpoint. AUSTRALIAN PRESCRIBER, 2, 86–87

Ley P. (1986) Cognitive variables and noncompliance JOURNAL OF COMPLIANCE IN HEALTH CARE, 1, 171–188

Lidberg L., Tuck J., Asberg M., et al. (1985) Homicide, suicide and CSFHIAA. ACTA PSYCHIATRICA SCANDINAVIA, 71, 230–236

Liden R.C. and Mitchell T.R. (1988) Ingratiating behaviors in organisational setting. ACADEMY OF MANAGEMENT REVIEW, 13, 572–587

Lidgard C.F. (1988) Women policing in Australia. Paper presented at the Annual Conference of the Sociological Association of Australia and New Zealand. Canberra, ACT

Lieber A.L. and Sherin C.R. (1972) Homicides and the lunar cycle: Toward a theory of lunar influence on human emotional disturbance. AMERICAN JOURNAL OF PSYCHIATRY, 129, 101–106

Lieberman S. (1956) The effects of changes in roles on the attitudes of role occupants. HUMAN RELATIONS, 9, 385–402

Liebert R.M. and Baron R.A. (1972) Some immediate effects of televised violence on children's behavior. DEVELOPMENTAL PSYCHOLOGY, 6, 469–475

Liebert R.M., Sprafkin J. and Davidson E.S. (1989) THE EARLY WINDOW: THE EFFECTS OF TELEVISION ON CHILDREN AND YOUTHS (3rd edn), Pergamon, NY

Liefer A.D. and Roberts D.F. (1972) Children's responses to television violence. In Murray J.P., Rubenstein E.A. and Comstock G.A. (eds) TELEVISION AND SOCIAL LEARNING, US Government Printing Office, Washington DC

Linder D.E., Cooper J. and Jones E.E. (1967) Decison freedom as a determinant of the role of incentive magnitude in attitude change. JOURNAL OF PERSONALITY AND SOCIAL PSYCHOLOGY, 6, 245–254

Lindsay D.S. and Johnson M.K. (1989) The reversed eyewitness suggestibility effect. BULLETIN OF THE PSYCHONOMIC SOCIETY, 27, 111–113

Lindzey G. and Aronson E. (eds) (1968) THE HANDBOOK OF SOCIAL PSYCHOLOGY (2nd edn), Addison-Wesley, Reading, Ma.

Lindzey G. and Aronson E. (eds) (1985) THE HANDBOOK OF SOCIAL PSYCHOLOGY (3rd edn), Random House, NY

Ling P.A. and Thomas D.R. (1986) Imitation of television aggression among Maori and European boys and girls. NEW ZEALAND JOURNAL OF PSYCHOLOGY, 15, 47–53

Link J.M. and Pepler R.D. (1970) Associated fluctuations in daily temperature, productivity and absenteeism. ASHRAE TRANSACTIONS, 76, 326–337

Linville P.W. (1982) The complexity-extremity effect and age-based stereotyping. JOURNAL OF PERSONALITY AND SOCIAL PSYCHOLOGY, 42, 193–211

Linville P.W. and Jones E.E. (1980) Polarized appraisals of outgroup members. JOURNAL OF PERSONALITY AND SOCIAL PSYCHOLOGY, 38, 689–703

Linville P.W., Salovey P. and Fischer G.W. (1986) Stereotyping and perceived distributions of social characteristics: An application to ingroup-outgroup perception. In Dovidio J. and Gaertner S.L. (eds) PREJUDICE, DISCRIMINATION, AND RACISM, Academic Press, NY

Linz D., Donnerstein E. and Penrod S. (1984) The effects of multiple exposure to filmed violence against women. JOURNAL OF COMMUNICATION, 34, 130–137

Linz D., Donnerstein E. and Penrod S. (1987) The findings and recommendations of the Attorney General's Commission on Pornography: Do the psychological facts fit the political fury? AMERICAN PSYCHOLOGIST, 42, 946–953

Lippa R.A. (1990) INTRODUCTION TO SOCIAL PSYCHOLOGY, Wadsworth, Belmont, Ca.

Lipsey M.W. (1977) The personal antecedents and consequences of ecologically responsible behavior: A review. JSAS CATALOG OF SELECTED DOCUMENTS IN PSYCHOLOGY, 7, 70–71

Little G.L., Bowers R. and Little L.H. (1987) Geophysical variables and behavior: XLII. Lack of relationship between moon phase and incidents of disruptive behavior in inmates with psychiatric problems. PERCEPTUAL AND MOTOR SKILLS, 64, 1212

Loftus E. (1975) Leading questions and the eyewitness report. COGNITIVE PSYCHOLOGY, 6–7, 160–172

Loftus E. (1979) EYEWITNESS TESTIMONY, Harvard University Press, Cambridge, Ma.

Loftus E. (1984) Essential but unreliable. PSYCHOLOGY TODAY, February, 22–26.

Loftus E.F., Loftus G.R. and Messo J. (1987) Some facts about "weapon focus". LAW AND HUMAN BEHAVIOR, 11, 55–62

Loftus E.F. and Palmer J.C. (1974) Reconstruction of automobile destruction: An example of the interaction between language and memory. JOURNAL OF VERBAL LEARNING AND VERBAL BEHAVIOR, 13, 585–589

Lombardi W.J., Higgins E.T. and Bargh J.A. (1987) The role of consciousness in priming effects on categorization: Assimilation versus contrast as a function of awareness of the priming task. PERSONALITY AND SOCIAL PSYCHOLOGY BULLETIN, 13, 411–429

London P. (1970) The rescuers: Motivational hypotheses about Christians who saved Jews from the Nazis. In J. MacCaulay and L Berkowitz (eds) ALTRUISM AND HELPING BEHAVIOR Academic Press, NY

Lord C.G., Lepper M.R. and Mackie D. (1984) Attitude prototypes as determinants of attitude-behavior consistency. JOURNAL OF PERSONALITY AND SOCIAL PSYCHOLOGY, 47, 1254–1266

Lorenz K. (1966) ON AGGRESSION, Harcourt, Brace, Jovanovich, NY

Lorenz K. (1974) THE EIGHT DEADLY SINS

OF CIVILISED MAN, Harcourt, Brace Jovanovich, NY

Lorge I. (1936) Prestige, suggestion and attitudes. JOURNAL OF SOCIAL PSYCHOLOGY, 7, 386–402

Lortie P.C. (1968) Shared ordeals and induction to work. In Becker H.S., Greer E., Reimaux D. and Weiss R.T. (eds) INSTITUTIONS AND THE PERSON, Aldine, Chicago

Lott A. and Lott B. (1961) Group cohesiveness, communication level, and conformity. JOURNAL OF ABNORMAL AND SOCIAL PSYCHOLOGY, 62, 408–412

Lott A. and Lott B. (1985) Learning theory in contemporary social psychology. In Lindzey G. and Aronson E. (eds) HANDBOOK OF SOCIAL PSYCHOLOGY (Vol. 1), (3rd edn) Random House, NY

Lourenco O.M. (1990) From cost perception to gain-construction: Toward a Piagetian explanation of the development of altruism in children. INTERNATIONAL JOURNAL OF BEHAVIORAL DEVELOPMENT, 13, 119–132

Love A.W. (1988) Attributional style of depressed chronic low back patients. JOURNAL OF CLINICAL PSYCHOLOGY, 44, 317–321

Lovibond S.H., Mithiran and Adams W.G. (1979) The effects of three experimental prison environments on the behaviour of non-convict volunteer subjects. AUSTRALIAN PSYCHOLOGIST, 14, 273–285

Lowe R. and Wittig M.A. (1989) Comparable worth: Individual, interpersonal, and structural considerations. JOURNAL OF SOCIAL ISSUES, 45, 223–246

Luce R.D. and Raiffa H. (1957) GAMES AND DECISIONS: INTRODUCTION AND CRITICAL SURVEY, Wiley, NY

Luckmann T. (1983) LIFEWORLD AND SOCIAL REALITIES, Heinemann, Lond.

Lumby M.F. (1978) Men who advertise for sex. JOURNAL OF HOMOSEXUALITY, 4, 63–72

Lund F.H. (1925) The psychology of belief. Part IV.: The law of primacy in persuasion. JOURNAL OF ABNORMAL AND SOCIAL PSYCHOLOGY, 20, 183–191

Lundman R.G. (1980) POLICE SOCIALISATION: POLICE AND POLICING, Holt, Reinhart and Winston, NY

Lyman S.M. and Scott M.B. (1967) Territoriality: A neglected sociological dimension. SOCIAL PROBLEMS, 15, 235–249

Lynn M. and Bolig R. (1985) Personal advertisements: Sources of data about relationships. JOURNAL OF SOCIAL AND PERSONAL RELATIONSHIPS, 2, 377–383

Lynn M. and Shurgot B.A. (1984) Responses to lonely hearts advertisements: Effects of reported physical attractiveness. PERSONALITY AND SOCIAL PSYCHOLOGY BULLETIN, 10, 349–357

Lynskey M.T., Ward C. and Fletcher G.J. (1991) Stereotypes and intergroup attributions in New Zealand. PSYCHOLOGY AND DEVELOPING SOCIETIES, 3, 113–127

Maass A. and Clark R.D. (1984) Hidden impact of minorities: 15 years of minority influence research. PSYCHOLOGY BULLETIN, 95, 428–450

Maass A., Clark R.D. and Haberkorn G. (1982) The effects of differential ascribed category membership and norms on minority influence. EUROPEAN JOURNAL OF SOCIAL PSYCHOLOGY, 12, 89–104

McArthur L.Z. (1972) The how and what of why: Some determinants and consequences of causal attribution. JOURNAL OF PERSONALITY AND SOCIAL PSYCHOLOGY, 22, 171–193

McArthur L.Z. (1982) Judging a book by its cover: A cognitive analysis of the relationship between physical appearance and stereotyping. In Hastorf A.H. and Isen A.M. (eds) COGNITIVE SOCIAL PSYCHOLOGY, Elsevier, NY

McArthur L.Z. and Apatow K. (1984) Impressions of baby-faced adults. SOCIAL COGNITION, 2, 315–342

McArthur L.Z. and Baron R.M. (1983) Toward an ecological theory of social perception. PSYCHOLOGICAL REVIEW, 90, 215–238

McArthur L.Z. and Post D.L. (1977) Figural emphasis and person perception. JOURNAL OF EXPERIMENTAL SOCIAL PSYCHOLOGY, 13, 520–535

McCabe M.P. (1987) Desired and experienced levels of premarital affection and sexual intercourse during dating. JOURNAL OF SEX RESEARCH, 23, 23–33

McCann T.E. and Sheehan P.W. (1985) Violence content in Australian TV. AUSTRALIAN PSYCHOLOGIST, 20, 33–42

McCaul K.D. and Kopp J.T. (1982) Effects of goal setting and commitment on increasing metal recycling. JOURNAL OF APPLIED PSYCHOLOGY, 67, 377–379

Macaulay H. (1981–82) Achieving representative juries: A system that works. JUDICATURE, 65, 126.

McClelland D.C. (1975) POWER, Irvington, NY

McClelland D.C. (1985) HUMAN MOTIVATION, Scott Foresman, Glenview, Il.

McClelland D.C. and Apicella F.S. (1945) A functional classification of verbal reactions to experimentally induced failure. JOURNAL OF ABNORMAL AND SOCIAL PSYCHOLOGY 46, 376–390

McClelland D.C. and Boyatzis R.E. (1982) Leadership motive pattern and long term success in management. JOURNAL OF APPLIED PSYCHOLOGY, 674, 737–743

McClintock C.G. (1988) Evolution, systems of interdependence, and social values. BEHAVIORAL SCIENCE, 33, 59–76

McClintock C.G., Moskowitz J.M. and McClintock E. (1977) Variations in preferences for individualistic, competitive, and cooperative outcomes as a function of

age, game class, and tasks in nursery school children. CHILD DEVELOPMENT, 48, 1080–1085

Maccoby E.E. (ed.) (1966) THE DEVELOPMENT OF SEX DIFFERENCES, Stanford University Press, Stanford, Ca.

Maccoby E.E. (1980) SOCIAL DEVELOPMENT: PSYCHOLOGICAL GROWTH AND THE PARENT-CHILD RELATIONSHIP, Harcourt, Brace, Jovanovich, NY

Maccoby E.E. and Jacklin C.N. (1974) THE PSYCHOLOGY OF SEX DIFFERENCES, Stanford University Press, Stanford, Ca.

Maccoby E.E. and Jacklin C.N. (1980) Sex differences in aggression: A rejoinder and reprise. CHILD DEVELOPMENT, 51, 954–980

McConahay J.B. (1986) Modern racism, ambivalence, and the modern racism scale. In Dovidio J.F. and Gaertner S.L. (eds) PREJUDICE, DISCRIMINATION AND RACISM, Academic Press, NY

McCorkle L.W. and Korn R.R. (1954) Resocialization within walls. ACADEMY OF POLITICAL AND SOCIAL SCIENCE, 293, 88–98

MacCoun R.J. and Kerr N.L. (1988) Asymmetric influence on mock jury deliberation: Juror's bias for leniency. JOURNAL OF PERSONALITY AND SOCIAL PSYCHOLOGY, 54, 21–33

McCulloch B.J. (1990) The relationship of intergenerational reciprocity of aid to the morale of older parents: Equity and exchange theory comparisons. JOURNALS OF GERONTOLOGY, 45, 150–155

McCullum D.M., Harring K., Gilmore R., et al. (1985) Competition and cooperation between groups and between individuals. JOURNAL OF EXPERIMENTAL SOCIAL PSYCHOLOGY, 21, 301–320

McDavid J.W. and Sistrunk F. (1964) Personality correlates of two kinds of conformity behavior. JOURNAL OF PERSONALITY, 32, 421–435

McDougall W. (1908) AN INTRODUCTION TO SOCIAL PSYCHOLOGY, Methuen, Lond.

McFarlane A.C. (1987) Family functioning and overprotection following a natural disaster: The longitudinal effects of post-traumatic morbidity. AUSTRALIAN AND NEW ZEALAND JOURNAL OF PSYCHIATRY, 21, 210–218

McFarlane A.C. (1988a) The phenomenology of posttraumatic stress disorders following a natural disaster. JOURNAL OF NERVOUS AND MENTAL DISEASE, 176, 22–29

McFarlane A.C. (1988b) Recent life events and psychiatric disorder in children: The interaction with preceding extreme adversity. JOURNAL OF CHILD PSYCHOLOGY AND PSYCHIATRY AND ALLIED DISCIPLINES, 29, 677–690

McFarlane A.C. (1989a) The prevention and management of the psychiatric morbidity of natural disasters: An Australian experience. STRESS MEDICINE, 5, 29–36

McFarlane A.C. (1989b) The aetiology of posttraumatic morbidity: Predisposing, precipitating and perpetuating factors. BRITISH JOURNAL OF PSYCHIATRY, 154, 221–228

McFarlane A.C. (1990) An Australian disaster: The 1983 bushfires. INTERNATIONAL JOURNAL OF MENTAL HEALTH, 19, 36–47

McGinnies E., Nordholm L.A., Ward C.D. and Bhanthumnavin D.L. (1974) Sex and cultural differences in perceived locus of control among students in five countries. JOURNAL OF COUNSULTING AND CLINICAL PSYCHOLOGY, 42, 451–455

McGinnis M.D. (1986) Issue linkage and the evolution of international cooperation. JOURNAL OF CONFLICT RESOLUTION, 30, 141–170

McGrath G. (1983) Learning "the job": An examination of induction into an Australian police force. Unpublished manuscript, University of New England, Armidale, NSW

McGrath J.E. (ed.) (1970) SOCIAL AND PSYCHOLOGICAL FACTORS ON STRESS, Holt, Rinehart and Winston, NY

McGuire R.H. (1984) Recycling: Great expectations and garbage outcomes. Special Issue: Household refuse analysis-theory, method, and applications in social science. AMERICAN BEHAVIORAL SCIENTIST, 28, 93–114

McGuire W.J. (1985) Attitudes and attitude change. In Lindzey G. and Aronson E. (eds) THE HANDBOOK OF SOCIAL PSYCHOLOGY (Vol. II), (3rd edn), Random House, NY

McGuire W.J. (1986) The vicissitudes of attitudes and similar representational constructs in twentieth century psychology. EUROPEAN JOURNAL OF SOCIAL PSYCHOLOGY, 16, 89–130

McGuire W.J. and McGuire C. (1982) Significant others in self-space: Sex differences and developmental trends in the social self. in Suls J.M. (ed.) PSYCHOLOGICAL PERSPECTIVES ON THE SELF (Vol. 1), Erlbaum, Hillsdale, NJ

McGuire W.J. and Padawer-Singer A. (1976) Trait salience in the spontaneous self-concept. JOURNAL OF PERSONALITY AND SOCIAL PSYCHOLOGY, 33, 743–754

McKelvie S.J. (1990) The Asch primacy effect: Robust but not infallible. JOURNAL OF SOCIAL BEHAVIOR AND PERSONALITY, 5, 135–150

McKenna J.F. (1987) Equity/inequity, stress and employee commitment in a health care setting. STRESS MEDICINE, 3, 71–74

McKillip J. and Reidel S.L. (1983) External validity of matching on physical attractiveness for same and opposite sex couples. JOURNAL OF APPLIED SOCIAL PSYCHOLOGY, 13, 328–337

McKinnon C. (1983) Feminism, marxism, method and the state: Towards feminist jurisprudence. SIGNS, 8, 635–638

MacKinnon L.K. and Miller D. (1987) The new epistemology and the Milan approach: Feminist and sociopolitical considerations. JOURNAL OF MARITAL AND FAMILY THERAPY, 13, 139–155

McKnight J. (1990) AUSTRALIAN CHRISTIAN COMMUNES, Trojan Press, Sydney

MacRae C. and Shepherd J. (1989) Do criminal strategies mediate juridic judgements? BRITISH JOURNAL OF SOCIAL PSYCHOLOGY, 28, 189–191

Maddock R.K. (1967) Patient co-operation in taking medicine. JOURNAL OF AMERICAN MEDICAL ASSOCIATION, 199, 169–172

Major B. (1980) Information acquisition and attribution processes. JOURNAL OF PERSONALITY AND SOCIAL PSYCHOLOGY, 39, 1010–1023

Major B., Carrington P.I. and Carnevale P.J. (1984) Physical attractiveness and self esteem: Attributions for praise from an other-sex evaluator. PERSONALITY AND SOCIAL PSYCHOLOGY BULLETIN, 10, 43–50

Malamuth N.M. and Check J.V. (1981) The effects of media exposure on acceptance of violence against women: A field study. JOURNAL OF RESEARCH IN PERSONALITY, 15, 436–446

Malamuth N.M. and Check J.V. (1985) The effects of aggressive pornography on beliefs in rape myths: Individual differences. JOURNAL OF RESEARCH IN PERSONALITY, 19, 299–320

Malamuth N. and Donnerstein E. (1982) The effects of aggressive-pornographic mass media stimuli. In Berkowitz L. (ed.) ADVANCES IN EXPERIMENTAL SOCIAL PSYCHOLOGY (Vol. 15), Academic Press, NY

Malamuth N.M. and Donnerstein E. (eds) (1984) PORNOGRAPHY AND SEXUAL AGGRESSION, Academic Press, NY

Maloney M.P., Ward M.P. and Braucht G.N. (1975) A revised scale for the measurement of ecological attitudes and knowledge. AMERICAN PSYCHOLOGIST, 30, 787–790

Malthus T.R. (1798) AN ESSAY ON THE PRINCIPLES OF POPULATION (Edited and introduced by A. Flew), Penguin, Harmondsworth, 1970

Mann L. (1969) SOCIAL PSYCHOLOGY, Wiley, Sydney

Mann L. (1970) The social psychology of waiting lines. SCIENTIFIC AMERICAN, 58, 390–398

Mann L. (1977) The effect of stimulus queues on queue-joining behavior. JOURNAL OF PERSONALITY AND SOCIAL PSYCHOLOGY, 35, 437–442

Mann L. (1981) The baiting crowd in episodes of threatened suicide. JOURNAL OF PERSONALITY AND SOCIAL PSYCHOLOGY, 41, 703–709

Mann L. and Greenbaum C.W. (1987) Cross-cultural studies of children's decision rules. In Kagitcibasi C. (ed.) GROWTH AND PROGRESS IN CROSS-CULTURAL PSYCHOLOGY, Swets and Zeitlinger, Lisse, Holland

Mann L., Newton J.W. and Innes J.M. (1982) A test between deindividuation and emergent norm theories of crowd aggression. JOURNAL OF PERSONALITY AND SOCIAL PSYCHOLOGY, 42, 260–272

Mann L., Radford M. and Kanagawa, C. (1985) Cross-cultural differences in children's use of decision rules: A comparison between Japan and Australia. JOURNAL OF PERSONALITY AND SOCIAL PSYCHOLOGY (Vol. 49), 1557–1564

Mann L., Tan C., Morgan C. and Dixon A. (1984) Developmental changes in application of majority rule in group decisions. BRITISH JOURNAL OF DEVELOPMENTAL PSYCHOLOGY, 2, 275–281

Mann R. (1959) A review of the relationship between personality and performance in small groups. PSYCHOLOGICAL BULLETIN, 56, 241–270

Mannhiem K. (1972) ESSAYS ON THE SOCIOLOGY OF KNOWLEDGE, Routledge, Kegan Paul, Lond.

Manning P. (1976) Observing the police. In Neiderhoffer A. and Blumberg A.S. (eds) THE AMBIVALENT FORCE: PERSPECTIVES ON THE POLICE, Dryden Press, Hillsdale, NJ

Manning P. (1977) POLICE WORK, MIT Press, Cambridge, Ma.

Mantell D.M. (1971) The potential for violence in Germany. JOURNAL OF SOCIAL ISSUES, 27, 101–112

Manucia G.K., Baumann D.J. and Cialdini R.B. (1984) Mood influences on helping: Direct effects or side effects? JOURNAL OF PERSONALITY AND SOCIAL PSYCHOLOGY, 46, 357–364

Marjoribanks K. and Jordan D.F. (1986) Stereotyping among Aboriginal and Anglo-Australians: The uniformity, intensity, direction, and quality of auto- and heterostereotypes. JOURNAL OF CROSS CULTURAL PSYCHOLOGY, 17, 17–28

Marks G. (1984) Thinking one's abilities are unique and one's opinions are common. PERSONALITY AND SOCIAL PSYCHOLOGY BULLETIN, 10, 203–208

Marks G. and Miller N. (1987) Ten years of research on the false-consensus effect: An empirical and theoretical review. PSYCHOLOGICAL BULLETIN, 102, 72–90

Markus H. (1977) Self-schemas and processing information about the self. JOURNAL OF PERSONALITY AND SOCIAL PSYCHOLOGY, 35, 63–78

Markus H. (1978) The effects of mere presence on social facilitation: An unobtrusive test. JOURNAL OF EXPERIMENTAL SOCIAL PSYCHOLOGY, 14, 389–397

Markus H. and Nurius P. (1986) Possible selves. AMERICAN PSYCHOLOGIST, 41, 954–969

Markus H., Smith J. and Moreland R.L. (1985)

Role of the self-concept in the perception of others. JOURNAL OF PERSONALITY AND SOCIAL PSYCHOLOGY, 49, 1494–1512

Markus H. and Zajonc R.B. (1985) The cognitive perspective in social psychology. In Lindzey G. and Aronson E. (eds) HANDBOOK OF SOCIAL PSYCHOLOGY (Vol. 1), (3rd edn), Random House, NY

Marques J.M. and Yzerbyt V.Y. (1988) The black sheep effect: Judgmental extremity towards ingroup members in the inter- and intra-group situations. EUROPEAN JOURNAL OF SOCIAL PSYCHOLOGY, 18, 287–292

Marsh H.W. (1986) Self-serving effect (bias?) in academic attributions: Its relation to academic achievement and self-concept. JOURNAL OF EDUCATIONAL PSYCHOLOGY, 78, 190–200

Marsh H.W., Barnes J. and Hocevar D. (1985) Self-other agreement on multidimensional self-concept ratings: Factor analysis and multitrait-multimethod analysis. JOURNAL OF PERSONALITY AND SOCIAL PSYCHOLOGY, 49, 1360–1377

Marshall G.D. and Zimbardo P.G. (1979) Affective consequences of inadequately explained physiological arousal. JOURNAL OF PERSONALITY AND SOCIAL PSYCHOLOGY, 37, 970–988

Martens R., Kelly I.W. and Saklofske D.H. (1988) Lunar phase and birthrate: A 50–year critical review. PSYCHOLOGICAL REPORTS, 63, 923–934

Maruyama G. and Miller N. (1981) Physical attractiveness and personality. In Maher B. (ed.) ADVANCES IN EXPERIMENTAL RESEARCH IN PERSONALITY (Vol. 10), Academic Press, NY

Marwell G. and Ames R.E. (1979) Experiments on the provisions of public goods. AMERICAN JOURNAL OF SOCIOLOGY, 84, 1335–1360

Maslow A. (1971) THE FURTHER REACHES OF HUMAN NATURE, Viking, NY

Matka E. (1991) Domestic Violence in NSW. CRIME JUSTICE BULLETIN No. 12, NSW. Bureau of Crime Statistics and Research, Sydney

Matlin M.W. (1989) COGNITION (2nd edn), Holt, Rinehart and Winston, NY

Matlin M.W. and Zajonc R.B. (1968) Social facilitation of work associations. JOURNAL OF PERSONALITY AND SOCIAL PSYCHOLOGY, 10, 455–460

Matsumoto D. (1987) The role of facial response in the experience of emotion: More methodological problems and a meta-analysis. JOURNAL OF PERSONALITY AND SOCIAL PSYCHOLOGY, 52, 769–774

Maxwell G.M. (1985) The behaviour of lovers: Measuring closeness in relationships. JOURNAL OF SOCIAL AND PERSONAL RELATIONSHIPS, 2, 215–238

Maxwell G.M. and Coebergh B. (1986) Patterns of loneliness in a New Zealand population.

COMMUNITY MENTAL HEALTH IN NEW ZEALAND, 2, 48–61

May R. (1972) POWER AND INNOCENCE: A SEARCH FOR THE SOURCE OF VIOLENCE, W.W. Norton and Co., NY

Mayer F.S., Duval S., Holtz R., et al. (1985) Self-focus, helping request salience, felt responsibility, and helping behavior. PERSONALITY AND SOCIAL PSYCHOLOGY BULLETIN 11, 133–144

Mead G.H. (1934) MIND, SELF, AND SOCIETY, University of Chicago Press, Chicago

Meares R. (1984) Inner space: Its constriction in anxiety states and narcissistic personality. PSYCHIATRY, 47, 162–171

Mednick S.A., Brennan P. and Kandel E. (1988) Predisposition to violence. AGGRESSIVE BEHAVIOR, 14, 25–33

Mednick S.A. and Kandel E.S. (1988a) Congenital determinants of violence. BULLETIN OF THE AMERICAN ACADEMY OF PSYCHIATRY AND LAW, 16, 101–109

Mednick S.A. and Kandel E.S. (1988b) Genetic and perinatal factors in violence. In Moffitt T., Mednick S. (eds) BIOLOGICAL CONTRIBUTIONS TO CRIME CAUSATION, Martinus Nijhoff, Dordrecht, Netherlands

Mednick S., Pollock V., Volavka J. and Gabrielli W. (1982) Biology and violence. In Wolfgand M. and Weiner N. (eds) CRIMINAL VIOLENCE, Sage, Beverly Hills, Ca.

Meehl P.E. (1978) Theoretical risks and tabular asterisks: Sir Karl, Sir Ronald, and the slow progress of soft psychology. JOURNAL OF CONSULTING AND CLINICAL PSYCHOLOGY, 46, 806–834

Meeus W.H., Quinten A.W. and Raaijmakers Q. (1986) Administrative obedience: Carrying out orders to use psychological-administrative violence. EUROPEAN JOURNAL OF SOCIAL PSYCHOLOGY, 16, 311–322

Meindl J.R. and Lerner M.J. (1985) Exacerbation of extreme responses to an out-group. JOURNAL OF PERSONALITY AND SOCIAL PSYCHOLOGY, 47, 71–84

Mertin P. (1989) The memory of young children for eyewitness events. AUSTRALIAN JOURNAL OF SOCIAL ISSUES, 24, 23–32

Merton R. (1948) The self-fulfilling prophecy. ANTIOCH REVIEW, 8, 193–210

Merton R. (1967) Discrimination and the American Creed. In Rose P.I. (ed.) THE STUDY OF SOCIETY, Random House NY

Messe L.A. and Watts B.L. (1983) Complex nature of the sense of fairness: Internal standards and social comparison as bases for reward evaluations. JOURNAL OF EXPERIMENTAL AND SOCIAL PSYCHOLOGY, 45, 84–93

Messick D.M. and Mackie D.M. (1989) Intergroup relations. In Rosenzweig M.R. and Porter L.W. (eds) ANNUAL REVIEW OF PSYCHOLOGY, 40, 45–81

Messick D. M. and Sentis K.P. (1979) Fairness

and preference. JOURNAL OF EXPERIMENTAL SOCIAL PSYCHOLOGY, 15, 418–434

Messick D.M., Bloom S., Boldizar J.P. and Samuelson C.D. (1985) Why are we fairer than others? JOURNAL OF EXPERIMENTAL SOCIAL PSYCHOLOGY, 21, 480–500

Metalsky G.I., Halberstadt L.J. and Abramson L.Y. (1987) Vulnerability to depressive mood reactions: Toward a more powerful test of the diathesis-stress and causal mediation component reformulated theory of depression. JOURNAL OF PERSONALITY AND SOCIAL PSYCHOLOGY, 52, 386–393

Meyer J.P. and Pepper S. (1977) Need compatibility and marital adjustment in young married couples. JOURNAL OF PERSONALITY AND SOCIAL PSYCHOLOGY, 35, 331–342

Milbrath L.W. (1984) ENVIRONMENTALISTS: VANGUARD FOR A NEW SOCIETY, S.U.NY. Press, NY

Milgram S. (1963) Behavioral study of obedience. JOURNAL OF APPLIED SOCIAL PSYCHOLOGY, 67, 371–378

Milgram S. (1965) Some conditions of obedience and disobedience to authority. HUMAN RELATIONS, 18, 57–76

Milgram S. (1970) The experience of living in cities. SCIENCE, 167, 1461–1468

Milgram S. (1974) OBEDIENCE TO AUTHORITY, Harper and Row, NY

Milinski M. (1990) No alternative to tit-for-tat cooperation in sticklebacks. ANIMAL BEHAVIOUR, 39, 989–991

Miller D.J. and Romanelli R.E. (1991) From religion: Heterosexism and the golden rule. Special section: Stigma and homosexuality. JOURNAL OF GAY AND LESBIAN PSYCHOTHERAPY, 1, 45–64

Miller D.T. and Ross M. (1975) Self-serving biases in the attribution of causality: Fact or fiction? PSYCHOLOGICAL BULLETIN, 82, 213–225

Miller J. (1976) TOWARD A NEW PSYCHOLOGY OF WOMEN, Beacon Press, Boston

Miller L.E. and Grush J.E. (1986) Individual differences in attitudinal versus normative determination of behaviour. JOURNAL OF EXPERIMENTAL SOCIAL PSYCHOLOGY, 22, 190–202

Miller N. and Brewer M.B. (eds) (1984) GROUPS IN CONTACT: THE PSYCHOLOGY OF DESEGREGATION, Academic Press, NY

Miller N. and Campbell D. (1959) Recency and primacy in persuasion as a function of the timing of speeches and measurements. JOURNAL OF ABNORMAL AND SOCIAL PSYCHOLOGY, 59, 1–9

Miller N.E. (1941) The frustration-aggression hypothesis. PSYCHOLOGICAL REVIEW, 48, 337–342

Miller N.E. and Dollard J. (1941) SOCIAL LEARNING AND IMITATION, Yale University Press, New Haven

Mills R., Pedersen, J. and Grusec, J. E. (1989) Sex differences in reasoning and emotion about altruism. SEX ROLES, 20, 603–621

Minard R.D. (1952) Race relations in the Pocohontas coal field. JOURNAL OF SOCIAL ISSUES, 81, 29–44

Mintz A (1951) Nonadaptive group behavior. JOURNAL OF ABNORMAL AND SOCIAL PSYCHOLOGY, 46, 150–159

Miranda S.B., Caballero R.B., Gomez M.N. and Zamorano M.A. (1981) Obedience a la autoridad. PSIQUIS, 2, 212–221

Mischel W. (1968) PERSONALITY AND ASSESSMENT, Wiley, NY

Mischel W. (1973) Toward a cognitive social learning reconceptualization of personality. PSYCHOLOGICAL REVIEW, 80, 252–283

Mischel W. (1984) Convergences and challenges in the search for consistency. AMERICAN PSYCHOLOGIST, 39, 351–364

Mischel W. (1986) INTRODUCTION TO PERSONALITY A NEW LOOK (4th edn), CBS. Publishing, Tokyo

Mischel W. and Mischel M. (1976) A cognitive social-learning approach to morality and self-regulation. In Lickena T. (ed.) MORAL DEVELOPMENT AND BEHAVIOR, Holt, Rinehart and Winston, NY

Mischel W. and Peake P.K. (1982) In search of consistency: Measure for measure. In Zanna M.P., Higgins E.T. and Herman C.P. (eds) CONSISTENCY IN SOCIAL BEHAVIOR: THE ONTARIO SYMPOSIUM (Vol. 2), Erlbaum, Hillsdale

Mischel W. and Peake P.K. (1983) Some facets of consistency: Replies to Epstein, Funder and Bem. PSYCHOLOGICAL REVIEW, 90, 394–402

Mita T.H., Dermer M. and Knight J. (1977) Reversed facial images and the mere-exposure hypothesis. JOURNAL OF PERSONALITY AND SOCIAL PSYCHOLOGY, 35, 597–601

Mixon D. (1972) Instead of deception. JOURNAL OF THE THEORY OF SOCIAL BEHAVIOR, 2, 146–177

Mixon D. (1979) Understanding shocking and puzzling conduct. In Ginsburg G.P. (ed.) EMERGING STRATEGIES IN SOCIAL PSYCHOLOGY, Wiley, NY

Mixon D. (1986) The place of behaviour in psychological experiments. Special Issue: The rediscovery of self in social psychology. JOURNAL FOR THE THEORY OF SOCIAL BEHAVIOUR, 16, 123–137

Mixon D. (1989) OBEDIENCE AND CIVILIZATION: AUTHORISED CRIME AND THE NORMALICY OF EVIL, Pluto Press, London

Mixon D. (1990) Getting the science right is the problem, not the solution: A matter of priority. JOURNAL FOR THE THEORY OF SOCIAL BEHAVIOUR, 20, 97–110

Moghaddam F.M. (1987) Psychology in the three worlds: As reflected by the crisis in social psychology and the move toward indigenous third-world psychology.

AMERICAN PSYCHOLOGIST, 42, 912–920

Moir A. and Jessel D. (1989) BRAIN SEX: THE REAL DIFFERENCE BETWEEN MEN AND WOMEN, Michael Joseph, Lond.

Moir P. and Eijkman A. (eds) (1992) POLICING AUSTRALIA: OLD ISSUES, NEW PERSPECTIVES, Macmillan, Melbourne

Moir P. and Moir M. (1992) Community based policing and the role of community consultation. In Moir P. and Eijkman A. (eds) POLICING AUSTRALIA: OLD ISSUES, NEW PERSPECTIVES, Macmillan, Melbourne

Molm L.D. (1985) Relative effects of individual dependencies: Further tests of the relation betweeen power imbalance and power use. SOCIAL FORCES, 63, 810–837

Molm L.D. (1988) The structure and use of power: A comparison of reward and punishment power. SOCIAL PSYCHOLOGY QUARTERLY, 51, 108–122

Money J. and Tucker P. (1975) SEXUAL SIGNATURES: ON BEING A MAN OR A WOMAN, Little Brown, Boston

Montague A. (1973) MAN AND AGGRESSION (2nd edn), Oxford University Press, Lond.

Montague A. (1976) THE NATURE OF HUMAN AGGRESSION, Oxford University Press, NY

Montepare J.M. and Zebrowitz-McArthur L. (1988) Impressions of people created by age-related qualities of their gait. JOURNAL OF PERSONALITY AND SOCIAL PSYCHOLOGY, 54, 547–556

Moore J.S., Graziano W.G. and Millar M.G. (1987) Physical attractiveness, sex role orientation, and the evaluation of adults and children. PERSONALITY AND SOCIAL PSYCHOLOGY BULLETIN, 13, 95–102

Moore W.E. (1969) Occupational socialization. In Goslin D. (ed.) HANDBOOK OF SOCIALIZATION THEORY AND PRACTICE, Rand McNally, Chicago

Moreland R.L. and Zajonc R.B. (1982) Exposure effects in person perception: Familiarity, similarity and attraction. JOURNAL OF EXPERIMENTAL SOCIAL PSYCHOLOGY, 18, 395–415

Morgan D.H. (1989) Masculinity and violence. In Hanmer J. and Maynard M. (eds) WOMEN, VIOLENCE AND SOCIAL CONTROL, Humanities Press International, Atlantic Highlands, NJ

Morin S.F. and Garfinkle E.M. (1978) Male homophobia. JOURNAL OF SOCIAL ISSUES, 34, 29–47

Morris J.W. and Heaven P.C. (1986) Attitudes and behavioral intentions toward Vietnamese in Australia. JOURNAL OF SOCIAL PSYCHOLOGY, 126, 513–520

Morrison C.M. (1984) Sociological analysis of the images of British Police in the media. Unpublished doctoral thesis, University of Aberdeen, Scotland

Morton T.L. (1978) Intimacy and reciprocity of exchange: A comparison of spouses and

strangers. JOURNAL OF PERSONALITY AND SOCIAL PSYCHOLOGY, 36, 72–81

Moscovici S. (1969) Preface. In Jodelet D., Viet J. and Besnard P. (eds) UNE DISCIPLE EN MOUVEMENT LA PSYCHOLOGIE SOCIALE, Mouton-Bordas, Paris

Moscovici S. (1976) SOCIAL INFLUENCE AND SOCIAL CHANGE, Academic Press, Lond.

Moscovici S. (1980) Towards a theory of conversion behavior. In Berkowitz L. (ed.) ADVANCES IN EXPERIMENTAL SOCIAL PSYCHOLOGY, (Vol. 13), Academic Press, NY

Moscovici, S. (1985) Social influence and conformity. In Lindzey G. and Aronson E. (eds) THE HANDBOOK OF SOCIAL PSYCHOLOGY (3rd edn), Random House, NY

Moscovici S. (1989) Preconditions for explanation in social psychology. EUROPEAN JOURNAL OF SOCIAL PSYCHOLOGY, 19, 407–430

Moscovici S. (1991) Is Lenin orange or red? Imagery and social influence. EUROPEAN JOURNAL OF SOCIAL PSYCHOLOGY, 21, 101–118

Moscovici S. and Faucheux C. (1972) Social influence, conformity bias and the study of active minorities. In Berkowitz L. (ed.) ADVANCES IN EXPERIMENTAL SOCIAL PSYCHOLOGY, (Vol. 6), Academic Press, NY

Moyer K.E. (1976) THE PSYCHOLOGY OF AGGRESSION, Harper and Row, NY

Muehlenhard C.L. and Holloabaugh L.C. (1988) Do women sometimes say no when they mean yes?: The prevalence and correlates of women's token resistance to sex. JOURNAL OF PERSONALITY AND SOCIAL PSYCHOLOGY, 54, 872–879

Mugford J. (1989) Domestic violence. VIOLENCE TODAY, 2, Australian Institute of Criminology, Canberra

Mugford S. and Gronfors M. (1978) Racial and class factors in the sentencing of first offenders. AUSTRALIA AND NEW ZEALAND JOURNAL OF SOCIOLOGY, 14, 58–61

Mugny, G. (1975) Negotiations, image of the other and the process of minority influence. EUROPEAN JOURNAL OF SOCIAL PSYCHOLOGY, 5, 209–229

Mugny G. (1982) THE POWER OF MINORITIES, Academic Press, Lond.

Mukherjee S. (1981) CRIME TRENDS IN TWENTIETH CENTURY AUSTRALIA, George Allen and Unwin, Sydney

Mukherjee S.K., Scandia A., Dagger D. and Matthews W. (1989) SOURCE BOOK OF AUSTRALIAN CRIMINAL AND SOCIAL STATISTICS 1804–1988, Australian Institute of Criminology, Canberra

Mukherjee S.K. and Dagger D. (1990) THE SIZE OF THE CRIME PROBLEM IN AUSTRALIA (2nd edn) Australian Institute of Criminology, Canberra

Mullen B. (1985) Strength and immediacy of

sources: A meta-analytic evaluation of the forgotten elements of social impact theory. JOURNAL OF PERSONALITY AND SOCIAL PSYCHOLOGY, 48, 1458–1466

Mullen B., Atkins J.L., Champion D.S., et al. (1985) The false consensus effect: A meta-analysis of 115 hypothesis tests. JOURNAL OF EXPERIMENTAL SOCIAL PSYCHOLOGY, 21, 262–283

Mullen B. and Hu L. (1988) Social projection as a function of cognitive mechanisms: Two meta-analytic integrations. BRITISH JOURNAL OF SOCIAL PSYCHOLOGY, 27, 333–356

Mullen B., Salas E. and Driskell J.E. (1989) Salience, motivation and artifact as contribution to the relation between participation rate and leadership. JOURNAL OF EXPERIMENTAL SOCIAL PSYCHOLOGY, 25, 545–557

Mullins P. and Robb J.H. (1977) Residents' assessment of a New Zealand public-housing scheme. ENVIRONMENT AND BEHAVIOR, 9, 573–624

Murray H.A. (1938) EXPLORATION IN PERSONALITY, Oxford University Press, NY

Murray H.A. (1951) Towards a classification of interactions. In Parsons T. and Shils E.A. (eds) TOWARD A GENERAL THEORY OF ACTION, Harvard University Press, Cambridge Ma.

Murray J.P and Kippax S. Television diffusion and social behaviour in three communities: A field experiment AUSTRALIAN JOURNAL OF PSYCHOLOGY, 29, 31–43

Murray-Brown J. (ed.) (1979) PORTRAITS OF POWER, Times Books, NY

Murstein B.I. (1972) Physical attractiveness and marital choice. JOURNAL OF PERSONALITY AND SOCIAL PSYCHOLOGY, 22, 8–12

Murstein B.I. (1976) WHO WILL MARRY WHOM? THEORIES AND RESEARCH IN MARITAL CHOICE, Springer Verlag, NY

Murstein B.I. (1980) Mate selection in the 1970s. JOURNAL OF MARRIAGE AND THE FAMILY, 42, 777–792

Mussen P.H. and Eisenberg-Berg N. (1977) ROOTS OF CARING, SHARING AND HELPING, Freeman, San Francisco, Ca.

Myers D.G. and Kaplan M. (1976) Group-induced polarisation in simulated juries. PERSONALITY AND SOCIAL PSYCHOLOGY BULLETIN, 2, 63–66

Myers D.G. and Lamm H. (1976) The group polarisation phenomenon. PSYCHOLOGICAL BULLETIN, 83, 602–627

Nachson I. and Denno D. (1987) Violent behaviour and cerebral hemisphere dysfunction. In Mednick S.A., Moffitt T.E. and Stack S.A. (eds) CAUSES OF CRIME: NEW BIOLOGICAL APPROACHES, Cambridge University Press, Cambridge

Nadelman L. (1974) Sex identity in American children: Memory, knowledge and preference tests. DEVELOPMENTAL PSYCHOLOGY, 10, 413–417

Nadler A., Fisher J.D. and Ben-Itzhak S. (1983) With a little help from my friend: Reaction to receiving prolonged versus one-act help from a friend or stranger, as a function of centrality. JOURNAL OF PERSONALITY AND SOCIAL PSYCHOLOGY, 44, 310–321

Nagao D. and Davis J. (1980) The effects of prior experience on mock juror case judgements. SOCIAL PSYCHOLOGY QUARTERLY, 43, 190–199

Nahemow L. and Lawton M.P. (1975) Similarity and propinquity in friendship formation. JOURNAL OF PERSONALITY AND SOCIAL PSYCHOLOGY, 32, 205–213

Nalepka C.D., Jones S.L. and Jones P.K. (1983) Time variations, births, and lunar association. ISSUES IN COMPREHENSIVE PEDIATRIC NURSING, 6, 81–89

Nash M.M. (1975) Nonreactive methods and the law: Additional comments on legal liability in behavior research. AMERICAN PSYCHOLOGIST, 30, 777–780

National Committee on Violence (1990) VIOLENCE: DIRECTIONS FOR AUSTRALIA, Australian Institute of Criminology, Canberra

Neal J.H. and Slobidnik A.J. (1990) Reclaiming men's experience in couples therapy. JOURNAL OF FEMINIST FAMILY THERAPY, 2, 101–122

Neimeyer R.A. and Mitchell K. A. (1988) Similarity and attraction: A longitudinal study. JOURNAL OF SOCIAL AND PERSONAL RELATIONSHIPS, 5, 131–148

Nemeth C. (1981) Jury Trials: Psychology and the Law. In Berkowitz L. (ed.) ADVANCES IN EXPERIMENTAL SOCIAL PSYCHOLOGY, (Vol. 13), Academic Press, NY

Nesdale A.R. (1986) Distraction and the causal attribution process. JOURNAL OF SOCIAL PSYCHOLOGY, 126, 355–360

Nesdale A.R. and Dharmalingam S. (1986) Category salience, stereotyping and person memory. AUSTRALIAN JOURNAL OF PSYCHOLOGY, 38, 145–151

Nesdale A.R., Dharmalingam S. and Kerr G.K. (1987) Effect of subgroup ratio on stereotyping. EUROPEAN JOURNAL OF SOCIAL PSYCHOLOGY, 17, 353–356

Nesdale A.R. and McLaughlin K. (1987) Effects of sex stereotypes on young children's memories, predictions, and liking. BRITISH JOURNAL OF SOCIAL PSYCHOLOGY, 5, 231–241

Nesdale A.R. and Moore D. (1984) Perspective effects on causal attributions of success and failure. AUSTRALIAN JOURNAL OF PSYCHOLOGY, 36, 75–83

Nesdale A.R. and Rule B.G. (1974) The effects of an aggressor's characteristics and an observer's accountabiliy on judgements of aggression. CANADIAN JOURNAL OF BEHAVIOURAL SCIENCE, 342–350

Neuberg S.L. (1989) The goal of forming accurate impressions during social interactions: Attenuating the impact of negative expectancies. JOURNAL OF PERSONALITY AND SOCIAL PSYCHOLOGY, 56, 374–386

Newcomb T.M. (1943) PERSONALITY AND SOCIAL CHANGE, Dryden, NY

Newcomb T.M. (1961) THE AQUAINTANCE PROCESS, Holt, Rinehart, Winston, NY

Newman J. and McCauley C. (1977) Eye contact with strangers in city, suburb, and small town. ENVIRONMENT AND BEHAVIOR 9, 547–558

Newman O. (1972) DEFENSIBLE SPACE, MacMillan, NY

Newman O. (1980) COMMUNITY OF INTEREST, Anchor Press, NY

NSW Bureau of Crime Statistics and Research (1990) NSW RECORDED CRIME STATISTICS 1989/90, NSW Bureau of Crime Statistics and Research, Sydney

NSW Child Protection Council (1990) CHILD PHYSICAL ABUSE AND NEGLECT: CORE TRAINING PACKAGE, NSW Department of Family and Community Services, Sydney

NSW Department of Health (1988) SEXUAL ASSAULT SERVICES POLICY AND PROCEDURE MANUAL, State Health Publication, Sydney

NSW SEXUAL ASSAULT COMMITTEE REPORT (1985–1987)

NSW task force on services for victims of crime (1987) Report and Recommendations, Attorney General's Department, Sydney

Ng S-H. (1984) Equity and social categorization effects on intergroup allocation of rewards. BRITISH JOURNAL OF SOCIAL PSYCHOLOGY, 23, 165–172

Ng S-H. (1986) Equity, intergroup bias and interpersonal bias in reward allocation. EUROPEAN JOURNAL OF SOCIAL PSYCHOLOGY, 16, 239–255

Ng S-H. (1989) Intergroup behaviour and the self. NEW ZEALAND JOURNAL OF PSYCHOLOGY, 18, 1–12

Ng S-H. and Cram F. (1986) Complementary and antagonistic intergroup differentiations by New Zealand nurses. NEW ZEALAND JOURNAL OF PSYCHOLOGY, 15, 68–76

Ng S-H. and Wilson S. (1989) Self-categorisation theory and belief polarisation among Christian believers and atheists. BRITISH JOURNAL OF SOCIAL PSYCHOLOGY, 28, 47–56

Nieuwenhuijsen K. and de-Waal F.B. (1982) Effects of spatial crowding on social behavior in a chimpanzee colony. ZOO BIOLOGY, 1, 5–28

Nisbett R.E., Caputo C., Legant P., and Maracek J. (1973) Behavior as seen by the actor and as seen by the observer. JOURNAL OF PERSONALITY AND SOCIAL PSYCHOLOGY, 27, 154–164

Nisbett R.E. and Ross L. (1980) HUMAN INFERENCE: STRATEGIES AND SHORTCOMINGS OF HUMAN JUDGMENT, Prentice Hall, NJ

Nisbett R.E. and Schachter S. (1966) Cognitive manipulation of pain. JOURNAL OF EXPERIMENTAL SOCIAL PSYCHOLOGY, 2, 227–236

Nisbett R.E. and Wilson T.D. (1977) The halo effect: Evidence for unconscious alteration of judgments. JOURNAL OF PERSONALITY AND SOCIAL PSYCHOLOGY, 35, 250–256

Nixon C. (1991) Women as members of the Police Service. Paper presented at Women and Law Conference, Australian Institute of Criminology, Sydney

Nixon M.C. (1987) Australian psychology in the 1980s: Origins, developments and issues. In Gilgen A.R. and Gilgen C.K. (eds) INTERNATIONAL HANDBOOK OF PSYCHOLOGY, Greenwood Press, Westport, Conn.

Nixon M.C. and Taft R. (eds) (1977) PSYCHOLOGY IN AUSTRALIA: ACHIEVEMENTS AND PROSPECTS, Pergamon Press, Sydney

Noesjirwan J. (1978) A laboratory study of proxemic patterns of Indonesians and Australians. BRITISH JOURNAL OF SOCIAL AND CLINICAL PSYCHOLOGY, 17, 333–334

Noller P. (1978) Sex differences in the socialisation of affectionate affection. DEVELOPMENTAL PSYCHOLOGY, 14, 317–319

Noller P. (1984) NONVERBAL COMMUNI-CATION AND MARITAL INTERACTION, Pergamon, Oxford

Noller P. and Fitzpatrick M.A. (eds) (1988) PERSPECTIVES ON MARITAL INTERACTION, Multilingual Matters, Avon, England

Norton R.N. and Morgan M.Y. (1989) The role of alcohol in mortality and morbidity from interpersonal violence. ALCOHOL AND ALCOHOLISM, 24, 565–576

Novak W. (1981) THE GREAT AMERICAN MAN SHORTAGE AND OTHER ROADBLOCKS TO ROMANCE (AND WHAT TO DO ABOUT IT), Rawson Associates, NY

Nurcombe B. (1986) The child as witness: Competency and credibility. JOURNAL OF THE AMERICAN ACADEMY OF CHILD PSYCHIATRY, 25, 473–480

Nurius P.S. (1989) The self-concept: A social-cognitive update. SOCIAL CASEWORK, 70, 285–294

Nye F.I. (1979) Choice, exchange and the family. In Burr W.R., et al. (eds) CONTEM-PORARY THEORIES ABOUT THE FAMILY (Vol. 2), Free Press, NY

Oakes P.J. (1987) The salience of social categories. In Turner J.C., Hogg M.A., Oakes P.J., Reicher S.D. and Wetherell M.S. (eds) REDISCOVERING THE SOCIAL GROUP: A SELF-CATEGORISATION THEORY, Basil Blackwell, Oxford

Oakes P.J. and Turner J.C. (1980) Social categorization and intergroup behavior: Does minimal intergroup discrimination make social identity more positive? EUROPEAN JOURNAL OF SOCIAL PSYCHOLOGY, 10, 295–301

Oakes P.J. and Turner J.C. (1986) Distinctive-ness and the salience of social category memberships: Is there an automatic perceptual bias towards novelty? EUROPEAN JOURNAL OF SOCIAL PSYCHOLOGY, 16, 325–344

Oakes P.J., Turner J.C and Haslam S.A. (1991) Perceiving people as group members: The role of fit in the salience of social categorisa-tion. BRITISH JOURNAL OF SOCIAL PSYCHOLOGY, 30, 125–144

Oates K. (ed.) (1982) CHILD ABUSE: A COMMUNITY CONCERN, Butterworths, Lond.

Oates K. (ed.) (1990) UNDERSTANDING AND MANAGING CHILD ABUSE, Harcourt, Brace, Jovanovich, Sydney

O'Brian L. and Resnick R. (1988) THE PREVALENCE OF SELF-REPORTED RISK. FACTORS FOR ISCHAEMIC HEART DISEASE, PROBLEM DRINKING AND EMOTIONAL STRESS AMONG NSW POLICE. Department of Community Medicine, Royal Prince Alfred Hospital, Sydney

O'Brien G.E. (1981) Locus of control, previous occupation and satisfaction with retirement. AUSTRALIAN JOURNAL OF PSYCHOLOGY, 33, 305–318

O'Brien G.E. and Feather N.T. (1990) The relative effects of unemployment and quality of employment on the affect, work values and personal control of adolescents. JOURNAL OF OCCUPATIONAL PSYCHOLOGY, 63, 151–165

O'Brien G.E. and Kabanoff B. (1981) Australian norms and factor analysis of Rotter's internal-external control scale. AUSTRALIAN PSYCHOLOGIST, 16, 184–202

O'Brien G.E. and Pembroke M. (1982) Crowding, density and the job satisfaction of clerical employees. AUSTRALIAN JOURNAL OF PSYCHOLOGY, 34, 151–164

O'Callaghan G. and D'Arcy H. (1989) Use of props in questioning preschool witnesses. AUSTRALIAN JOURNAL OF PSYCHOLOGY, 41, 187–195

O'Donnell C. and Hall P. (1988) GETTING EQUAL, LABOUR MARKET REGULATION AND WOMEN'S WORK, Allen and Unwin, Sydney

O'Donnell C. and Saville H. (1982) Domestic violence and sex and class inequality. In O'Donnell C. and Craney J. (eds) FAMILY VIOLENCE IN AUSTRALIA, Longman Cheshire, Melbourne

Ohbuchi K. and Kambara T. (1985) Attacker's intent and awareness of outcome, impression management and retaliation. JOURNAL OF EXPERIMENTAL SOCIAL PSYCHOLOGY, 21, 321–330

Ohbuchi K., Kameda M. and Agarie N. (1989) Apology as aggression control: Its role in mediating appraisal of and response to harm.

JOURNAL OF PERSONALITY AND SOCIAL PSYCHOLOGY, 56, 219–227

Oliansky A. (1991) A confederate's perspective on deception. ETHICS AND BEHAVIOR, 1, 253–258

Oliner S.P. and Oliner P.M. (1988) THE ALTRUISTIC PERSONALITY: RESCUERS OF JEWS IN NAZI EUROPE, Free Press, NY

Olsen M.E. (1981) Consumers' attitudes toward energy conservation. JOURNAL OF SOCIAL ISSUES, 37, 108–131

Olson C.L. (1976) Some apparent violations of the representativeness heuristic. JOURNAL OF EXPERIMENTAL PSYCHOLOGY: HUMAN PERCEPTION AND PERFORMANCE, 2, 599–608

Olson D.H. and McCubbin H. (1990) FAMILIES: WHAT MAKES THEM WORK (2nd edn), Sage, Beverley Hills, Ca.

Olson J.M. (1988) Misattribution, preparatory information, and speech anxiety. JOURNAL OF PERSONALITY AND SOCIAL PSYCHOLOGY, 54, 758–767

Olson J.M., Herman C.P. and Zanna M.P. (eds) (1986) RELATIVE DEPRIVATION AND SOCIAL COMPARISON: THE ONTARIO SYMPOSIUM, (Vol. 4), Erlbaum, Hillsdale, NJ

Olson J.M. and Ross M. (1988) False feedback about placebo effectiveness: Consequences for the misattribution of speech anxiety. JOURNAL OF EXPERIMENTAL SOCIAL PSYCHOLOGY, 24, 275–291

Olson J.M. and Zanna M.P. (1983) Behavior change and attitude prediction. In Perlman D. and Cozby P.C. (eds) SOCIAL PSYCHOLOGY, Holt, Rinehart and Winston, NY

Olweus D. (1978) AGGRESSION IN THE SCHOOL: BULLIES AND WHIPPING BOYS, Wiley, Washington DC

Olweus D. (1979) Stability of aggressive reaction patterns in males: A review. PSYCHOLOGICAL BULLETIN, 86, 852–875

Olweus D. (1980) Familial and temperamental determinants of aggressive behavior in adoloescent boys: A causal analysis. DEVELOPMENTAL PSYCHOLOGY, 16, 646–666

Olweus D. (1984) Aggressors and their victims: Bullying at school. In Frude N. and Gault M. (eds) DISRUPTIVE BEHAVIOR IN SCHOOLS, Wiley, NY

Olweus D. (1986) Aggression and hormones: Behavioral relationships with testosterone and adrenaline. In Olweus D., Block J. and Radke-Yarrow M. (eds) DEVELOPMENT OF ANTISOCIAL AND PROSOCIAL BEHAVIORS: RESEARCH, THEORIES, AND ISSUES, Academic Press, Orlando, Florida

Olweus D. (1988) Environmental and biological factors in the development of aggressive behaviour. In Buikhuisen W. and Mednick S.A. (eds) EXPLAINING

CRIMINAL BEHAVIOUR, E.J. Brill, Leiden, Netherlands

Olweus D. (1991) Bully/victim problems among school children: Basic facts and effects of a school-based intervention program. In Rubin K. and Pepler D. (eds) THE DEVELOPMENT AND TREATMENT OF CHILDHOOD AGGRESSION, Erlbaum, Hillsdale, NJ

Olzak S. and Nagel J. (1986) COMPETITIVE ETHNIC RELATIONS, Academic Press, NY

O'Neil J.M. (1981) Patterns of gender role conflict and strain: Sexism and fear of femininity in men's lives. PERSONNEL AND GUIDANCE JOURNAL, 60, 203–209

O'Neil W.M. (1982) THE BEGINNINGS OF MODERN PSYCHOLOGY (2nd edn), The Harvester Press, Sussex

O'Neil W.M. (1987) A CENTURY OF PSYCHOLOGY IN AUSTRALIA, Sydney University Press, Sydney

O'Riordan T. (1976) Attitudes, behavior and environmental policy issues. In Altman I. and Wohlwill J.F. (eds) HUMAN BEHAVIOR AND ENVIRONMENT: ADVANCES IN THEORY AND RESEARCH (Vol. 1), Plenum, NY

Orne M.T. (1962) On the social psychology of the psychological experiment: With particular reference to demand characteristics and their implications. AMERICAN PSYCHOLOGIST, 17, 776–783

Orpen C. and Bonnici J. (1987) Effect of perceptions of pay equity on employees' motivation, involvement, satisfaction, and performance. PERCEPTUAL AND MOTOR SKILLS, 65, 601–602

Orpen C. and Bonnici J. (1990) The causes and consequences of pay satisfaction: A test of Lawler's model. PSYCHOLOGY: A JOURNAL OF HUMAN BEHAVIOR, 27, 27–29

Oskamp S. (1977) ATTITUDES AND OPINIONS, Prentice Hall, Englewood Cliffs, NJ

Oskamp S. (1983) Psychology's role in the conserving society. POPULATION AND ENVIRONMENT, BEHAVIORAL AND SOCIAL ISSUES, 6, 255–293

Oskamp S., Harrington M.J., Edwards T.C., et al. (1991) Factors influencing household recycling behavior. ENVIRONMENT AND BEHAVIOR, 23, 494–519

Ostrom T.M. (1977) Between-theory and within-theory conflict in explaining context effects in impression formation. JOURNAL OF EXPERIMENTAL SOCIAL PSYCHOLOGY, 13, 492–503

Over R. (1991a) Interest patterns of Australian psychologists. AUSTRALIAN PSYCHOLOGIST, 26, 49–53

Over R. (1991b) Membership of the Australian Psychological Society by academics in university psychology departments. AUSTRALIAN PSYCHOLOGIST, 26, 116–119

Oyserman D. and Markus R. (1990) Possible selves and delinquency. JOURNAL OF PERSONALITY AND SOCIAL PSYCHOLOGY, 59, 112–125

Page M. and Scheidt R. (1971) The elusive weapons effect: Demand awareness evaluation and slightly sophisticated subjects. JOURNAL OF PERSONALTY AND SOCIAL PSYCHOLOGY, 20, 304–318

Pagtolun-An I.G. and Clair J.M. (1986) An experimental study of attitudes toward homosexuals. DEVIANT BEHAVIOR, 7, 121–135

Pain M.D. and Sharpley C.F. (1988) Case type, anchoring errors, and counsellor education. COUNSELLOR EDUCATION AND SUPERVISION, 28, 53–58

Palinkas L.A. (1986) Health and performance of Antarctic winter-over personnel: A follow-up study. AVIATION, SPACE AND ENVIRONMENTAL MEDICINE, 57, 954–959

Pande A.C. (1985) Light-induced hypomania. AMERICAN JOURNAL OF PSYCHIATRY, 142, 1126

Park B. and Rothbart M. (1982) Perception of out-group homogeneity and levels of social categorization: Memory for the subordinate attributes of in-group and out-group members. JOURNAL OF PERSONALITY AND SOCIAL PSYCHOLOGY, 42, 1051–1068

Parke R.D., Berkowitz L., Leyes J.P., West S.G. and Sebastian R.J. (1977) Some effects of violent and nonviolent movies on the behavior of juvenile delinquents. In Berkowitz L. (ed.) ADVANCES IN EXPERIMENTAL SOCIAL PSYCHOLOGY (Vol. 10), Academic Press, NY

Parker G. (1980) Vulnerability factors to normal depression. JOURNAL OF PSYCHOSOMATIC RESEARCH, 24, 67–74

Parkinson P. (1991) The future of competency testing for child witnesses. CRIMINAL LAW JOURNAL, 15, 186–192

Parsons J.E., Kaczala C.M. and Meece J.L. (1982) Socialisation of achievement, attitudes and beliefs: Classroom influences. CHILD DEVELOPMENT, 53, 322–339

Patnoe S. (1988) A NARRATIVE HISTORY OF EXPERIMENTAL SOCIAL PSYCHOLOGY: THE LEWIN TRADITION, Springer-Verlag, NY

Patterson A.H. (1974) Hostility catharsis: A naturalistic quasi-experiment. Paper presented at the annual meeting of the American Psychological Association

Patton W. and Noller P. (1984) Unemployment and youth: A longitudinal study. AUSTRALIAN JOURNAL OF PSYCHOLOGY, 36, 399–413

Patzer G.L. (1985) THE PHYSICAL ATTRACTIVENESS PHENOMENA, Plenum Press, NY

Paulhus D. (1982) Individual differences, self-presentation, and cognitive dissonance: Their concurrent operation in forced compliance. JOURNAL OF PERSONAL-ITY AND SOCIAL PSYCHOLOGY, 43, 838–852

Paulus P.B. (1980) Crowding. In Paulus P.B. (ed.) PSYCHOLOGY OF GROUP INFLUENCE, Erlbaum, Hillsdale, NJ

Paulus P.B. (1988) PRISON CROWDING: A PSYCHOLOGICAL PERSPECTIVE, Springer-Verlag, NY

Paulus P.B. (ed.) (1989) PSYCHOLOGY OF GROUP INFLUENCE (2nd edn), Erlbaum, Hillsdale, NJ

Pearce P.L. (1980) Strangers, travellers, and Greyhound terminals: A study of small-scale helping behaviors. JOURNAL OF PERSONALITY AND SOCIAL PSYCHOLOGY 38, 935–940

Pearce P.L. and Amato P.R. (1980) A taxonomy of helping: A multidimensional scaling analysis. SOCIAL PSYCHOLOGY QUARTERLY, 43, 363–371

Pearlman M. (1963) THE CAPTURE AND TRIAL OF ADOLF EICHMANN, Simon and Schuster, NY

Peay M.Y. (1980) Changes in attitudes and beliefs in two-person interaction situations. EUROPEAN JOURNAL OF SOCIAL PSYCHOLOGY, 10, 367–377

Peay M.Y. and Peay E.R. (1983) The effects of density, group size, and crowding on behavior in an unstructured situation. BRITISH JOURNAL OF SOCIAL PSYCHOLOGY, 22, 13–18

Penner L.A. (1986) SOCIAL PSYCHOLOGY: CONCEPTS AND APPLICATIONS, West Publishing Co., NY

Pennington N. and Hastie R. (1990) Practical implications of psychological research on juror and jury decision making. PERSONALITY AND SOCIAL PSYCHOLOGY BULLETIN, 16, 90–105

Penrod S. (1986) SOCIAL PSYCHOLOGY (2nd edn), Prentice Hall, Englewood Cliffs, NJ

Pepitone A. (1981) Lessons from the history of social psychology. AMERICAN PSYCHOLOGIST, 36, 972–985

Peplau L.A., Miceli M. and Morasch B. (1982) Loneliness and self-evaluation. In Peplau L.A. and Perlman D. (eds) LONELINESS: A SOURCEBOOK OF CURRENT THEORY, RESEARCH AND THERAPY, Wiley, NY

Peplau L.A. and Perlman D. (eds) (1982) LONELINESS: A SOURCEBOOK OF CURRENT THEORY, RESEARCH AND THERAPY, Wiley, NY

Peplau L.A., Rubin Z. and Hill C.T. (1977) Sexual intimacy in dating relationships. JOURNAL OF SOCIAL ISSUES, 33, 86–109

Peplau L.A., Russell D. and Helm M. (1979) An attributional analysis of loneliness. In Frieze I.H., Bar-Tal D. and Carroll J.S. (eds) NEW APPROACHES TO SOCIAL PROBLEMS: APPLICATIONS OF ATTRIBUTION THEORY. Jossey-Bass, San Francisco, Ca.

Pepler R.D. (1972) The thermal comfort of students in climate controlled and non climate controlled schools. ASHRAE TRANSACTIONS, 78, 97–109

Pepper M. (1989) DICTIONARY OF RELIGIOUS QUOTATIONS, Andre Deutsch, Lond.

Perlman D. and Duck S. (eds) (1987) INTIMATE RELATIONSHIPS: DEVELOPMENT, DYNAMICS AND DETERIORATION, Sage, Newbury Park, Ca.

Perlman D. and Oskamp S. (1971) The effects of picture content and exposure frequency on evaluations of Negros and Whites. JOURNAL OF EXPERIMENTAL SOCIAL PSYCHOLOGY, 7, 503–514

Perry D.G. and Bussey K. (1984) SOCIAL DEVELOPMENT, Prentice Hall, NJ

Perry D.G., Kusel S.J. and Perry L.C. (1988) Victims of peer aggression. DEVELOP-MENTAL PSYCHOLOGY, 24, 807–814

Perry D.G., Perry L.C. and Weiss R.J. (1989) Sex differences in the consequences that children anticipate for aggression. DEVELOPMENTAL PSYCHOLOGY, 25, 312–319

Persinger M.A. and Nolan M. (1984) Geophysical variables and behavior: XX. Weekly numbers of mining accidents and the weather matrix: The importance of geomagnetic variation and barometric pressure. PERCEPTUAL AND MOTOR SKILLS, 59, 719–722

Peterson C. and Seligman M.E.P. (1987) Explanatory style and illness. JOURNAL OF PERSONALITY, 55, 237–265

Peterson C., Seligman M.E.P. and Vaillant G.E. (1988) Pessimistic explanatory style is a risk factor for physical illness: A thirty-five year longitudinal study. JOURNAL OF PERSONALITY AND SOCIAL PSYCHOLOGY, 55, 23–27

Peterson C.C. (1987) Need, equity, and equality in the adult family. JOURNAL OF SOCIAL PSYCHOLOGY, 127, 543–544

Peterson C.C. (1988) Older men's and women's relationships with adult kin: How equitable are they? INTERNATIONAL JOURNAL OF AGING AND HUMAN DEVELOP-MENT, 27, 221–231

Peterson C.C. (1990) Husbands' and wives' perceptions of marital fairness across the family life cycle. INTERNATIONAL JOURNAL OF AGING AND HUMAN DEVELOPMENT, 31, 179–188

Peterson C.C. and Peterson J.L. (1988) Older men's and women's relationships with adult kin: How equitable are they? INTER-NATIONAL JOURNAL OF AGING AND HUMAN DEVELOPMENT, 27, 221–231

Peterson N. (1975) Hunter-gatherer territoriality: The perspective from Australia. AMERICAN ANTHRO-POLOGIST, 77, 53–68

Pettigrew T.F. (1958) Personality and sociocultural factors in intergroup attitudes: A cross-national comparison. JOURNAL OF CONFLICT RESOLUTION, 2, 29–42

Pettigrew T.F. (1959) Regional differences in anti-Negro prejudice. JOURNAL OF ABNORMAL AND SOCIAL PSYCHOLOGY, 59, 28–36

Pettigrew T.F. (1961) Social psychology and desegregation research. AMERICAN PSYCHOLOGIST, 16, 105–112

Pettigrew T.F. (1979) The ultimate attribution error: Extending Allport's cognitive analysis of prejudice. PERSONALITY AND SOCIAL PSYCHOLOGY BULLETIN, 5, 461–476

Pettigrew T.F. (1980) Prejudice. In HARVARD ENCYCLOPEDIA OF AMERICAN ETHNIC GROUPS, Harvard University Press, Cambridge, Ma.

Pettigrew T.F. (1985) New black-white patterns: How best to conceptualize them? ANNUAL REVIEW OF SOCIOLOGY, 11, 329–346

Pettigrew T.F. and Martin J. (1987) Shaping the organizational context for black American inclusion. JOURNAL OF SOCIAL ISSUES, 43, 41–78

Petty R.E. and Cacioppo J.T. (1981) ATTITUDES AND PERSUASION: CLASSIC AND CONTEMPORARY APPROACHES, William Brown, Dubuque, Iowa

Petty R.E. and Cacioppo J.T. (1986) The elaboration likelihood model of persuasion. In Berkowitz L. (ed.) ADVANCES IN EXPERIMENTAL SOCIAL PSYCHOLOGY (Vol. 19), Academic Press, NY

Phares E.J. (1976) LOCUS OF CONTROL IN PERSONALITY, General Learning Press, Morristown, NJ

Phillips D.P. (1978) Airplane accident fatalities increase just after stories about murder and suicide. SCIENCE, 201, 748–750

Phillips D.P. (1982) The behavioural impact of violence in the mass media: A review of the evidence from laboratory and non-laboratory investigation. SOCIOLOGY AND SOCIAL RESEARCH, 66, 387–398

Phillips S. (1991) Social issues and policing: Politics and psychology. In Cochrane R. and Casrroll D. (eds) PSYCHOLOGY AND SOCIAL ISSUES, The Falmer Press, Lond.

Philpot C.L. (1991) Gender sensitive couples' therapy: A systemic definition. JOURNAL OF FAMILY PSYCHOTHERAPY, 2, 19–40

Piaget J. (1965) THE MORAL JUDGMENT OF THE CHILD, Free Press, NY

Pilger J. (1987) HEROES, Pan Books, Lond.

Piliavin J.A., Dovidio J.F., Gaertner S.L. and Clark R.D. (1981) EMERGENCY INTERVENTION, Academic Press, NY

Piliavin J.A. and Piliavin I.M. (1972) Effect of blood on reactions to a victim. JOURNAL OF PERSONALITY AND SOCIAL PSYCHOLOGY, 23, 353–361

Piliavin I.M., Piliavin J.A. and Rodin J. (1975) Costs, diffusion, and the stigmatized victim. JOURNAL OF PERSONALITY AND SOCIAL PSYCHOLOGY, 32, 429–438

Pilisuk M. and Acredolo C. (1988) Fear of technological hazards: One concern or many? SOCIAL BEHAVIOR, 3, 17–24

Pittman P. (1985) Gender myths: When does gender become pathology? THE FAMILY THERAPY NETWORKER, 9, 24–31

Place H. (1979) A biographical profile of women in management. JOURNAL OF OCCUPATIONAL PSYCHOLOGY, 52, 267–276

Platt J. (1973) Social Traps. AMERICAN PSYCHOLOGIST, 28, 641–651

Platz S.J. and Hosch H.M. (1988) Cross-racial/ethnic eye-witness identification: A field study. JOURNAL OF APPLIED SOCIAL PSYCHOLOGY, 18, 972–984

Poirier R. (1988) AIDS and traditions of homophobia. SOCIAL RESEARCH, 55, 461–475

Polk K. and Ranson D. (1989) Patterns of homicide in Victoria. Paper presented at the National Conference on Violence, 10–13 October, Canberra

Policy Studies Institute (1983) POLICE AND PEOPLE IN LONDON, London Policy Studies Institute, London

Porter A.M. (1969) Drug defaulting in general practice. BRITISH MEDICAL JOURNAL, 1, 218–222

Powers P.C. and Geen R.G. (1972) Effects of the behavior and perceived arousal of a model on instrumental aggression. JOURNAL OF PERSONALITY AND SOCIAL PSYCHOLOGY, 23, 175–184

Powling M. and Hopes W. (1988) Loneliness, self-characterisation and acquaintance in student groups. AUSTRALIAN PSY-CHOLOGIST, 23, 45–53

Prerost F.J. (1981) Positive mood-inhibiting potential of human crowding. PSYCHO-LOGICAL REPORTS, 48, 43–48

Presland P. and Antill J.K. (1987) Household division of labour: The impact of hours worked in paid employment. AUSTRAL-IAN JOURNAL OF PSYCHOLOGY, 39, 273–291

Price K.H. and Vandenberg S.G. (1979) Matching for physical attractiveness in married couples. PERSONALITY AND SOCIAL PSYCHOLOGY BULLETIN, 5, 398–400

Priest R.F. and Sawyer J (1967) Proximity and peership: Bases of balance in interpersonal attraction. AMERICAN JOURNAL OF SOCIOLOGY, 72, 633–649

Provins K.A. (1966) Environmental heat, body temperature, and behaviour: An hypothesis. AUSTRALIAN JOURNAL OF PSY-CHOLOGY, 18, 118–129

Provins K.A. and Bell C.A. (1970) Effects of heat stress on the performance of two tasks running concurrently. JOURNAL OF EXPERIMENTAL PSYCHOLOGY, 85, 40–44

Pryor J.B. and Merluzzi T.V. (1985) The role of expertise in processing social interaction scripts. JOURNAL OF EXPERIMENTAL SOCIAL PSYCHOLOGY, 21, 362–379

Przybyla D.P.J. (1985) The facilitating effects of exposure to erotica on male prosocial behavior. Doctoral thesis, State University of New York at Albany. Cited in Baron R.A. and D. Byrne, SOCIAL PSYCHOLOGY:

UNDERSTANDING HUMAN INTER-ACTION (5th edn) Allyn and Bacon, 1991

Public Policy Research Centre (1988) DOMESTIC VIOLENCE ATTITUDE SURVEY, Office for the Status of Women, Department of the Prime Minister and Cabinet, Canberra

Quattrone G.A. (1986) On the perception of a group's variability. In Worchel S. and Austin W. (eds) THE PSYCHOLOGY OF INTERGROUP RELATIONS, Nelson-Hall, Chicago

Queen C. (1987) The politics of AIDS: A review essay. INSURGENT SOCIOLO-GIST, 14, 103–124

Queensland Domestic Violence Task Force (1988) BEYOND THE WALLS, Report to the Minister for Family Services and Welfare Housing, Brisbane

Radke-Yarrow M. and Zahn-Waxler C. (1984) Roots, motives and patterns in children's prosocial behavior. In Reykowski J., et al. (eds) ORIGINS AND MAINTENANCE OF PROSOCIAL BEHAVIORS, Plenum Press, NY

Ramirez J., Bryant J. and Zillmann D. (1983) Effects of erotica on retaliatory behavior as a function of level of prior provocation. JOURNAL OF PERSONALITY AND SOCIAL PSYCHOLOGY, 43, 971–978

Rank M.R. (1982) Determinants of conjugal influence in wives' employment decision making. JOURNAL OF MARRIAGE AND THE FAMILY, 44, 591–604

Rapoport A. (1975) Toward a redefinition of density. ENVIRONMENT AND BEHAVIOR, 7, 133–158

Raskin A. (1961) Comparison of acceptors and resistors. JOURNAL OF CONSULTING PSYCHOLOGY, 25, 366

Raven B.H. and Kruglanski A.W. (1970) Conflict and power. In Swingle P. (ed.) THE STRUCTURE OF CONFLICT, Academic Press, NY

Raven B.H. and Rubin J.Z. (1983) SOCIAL PSYCHOLOGY, John Wiley, NY

Ray J.J. (1970) The development and validation of a balanced dogmatism scale. AUSTRAL-IAN JOURNAL OF PSYCHOLOGY, 22, 253–260

Ray J.J. (1972) A new balanced F Scale - and its relation to social class. AUSTRALIAN PSYCHOLOGIST, 7, 155–166

Ray J.J. (1976) Do authoritarians hold authoritarian attitudes? HUMAN RELATIONS, 29, 305–325

Ray J.J. (1980a) The psychology of environmental concern: some Australian data. PERSONALITY AND INDIVIDUAL DIFFERENCES, 1, 161–163

Ray J.J (1980b) Belief in luck and locus of control. JOURNAL OF SOCIAL PSYCHOLOGY, 111, 299–300

Ray J.J. (1981a) Are environmental activists middle class? TABLEAUS, 152, 6–7

Ray J.J. (1982a) Australia's "Deep North" and America's "Deep South": Effects of climate on conservatism, authoritarianism and attitude to love. TABLEAUS, 169, 4–7

Ray J.J. (1982b) Climate and conservatism in Australia. JOURNAL OF SOCIAL PSYCHOLOGY, 117, 297–298

Ray J.J. (1983a) Perceived deviance, personality and media exposure in Sydney. MEDIA INFORMATION AUSTRALIA, 30, 69–70

Ray J.J. (1983b) Race and climate as influences on anxiety. PERSONALITY AND INDIVIDUAL DIFFERENCES, 4, 699–701

Ray J.J. (1983c) Racial attitudes and the contact hypothesis. JOURNAL OF SOCIAL PSYCHOLOGY, 119, 3–10

Ray J.J. (1984) Authoritarianism and interpersonal spacing behavior. PERSONALITY AND INDIVIDUAL DIFFERENCES, 5, 601–602

Ray J.J. (1985) Defective validity in the Altemeyer authoritatianism scale. JOURNAL OF SOCIAL PSYCHOLOGY, 125, 271–272

Ray J.J. (1987) A participant observation study of social class among environmentalists. JOURNAL OF SOCIAL PSYCHOLOGY, 127, 99–100

Ray J.J. (1989) Authoritarianism research is alive and well - in Australia: A review. THE PSYCHOLOGICAL RECORD, 39, 555–561

Ray J.J. (1990) Enemies of Freedom: Understanding right-wing authoritarianism. AUSTRALIAN JOURNAL OF PSYCHOLOGY, 42, 87–88

Ray J.J. and Lovejoy F.H. (1984) Attitude toward the environment as a special case of attitude toward all living things. JOURNAL OF SOCIAL PSYCHOLOGY, 123, 285–286

Ray, J.J. and Najman J.M. (1988) Capitalism and compassion: A test of Milrath's environmental theory. PERSONALITY AND INDIVIDUAL DIFFERENCES, 9, 431–433

Read S.J. (1987) Constructing causal scenarios: A knowledge structure approach to causal reasoning. JOURNAL OF PERSONALITY AND SOCIAL PSYCHOLOGY, 52, 288–302

Read S.J. and Rosson M.B. (1982) Rewriting history: The biasing effects of attitude on memory. SOCIAL COGNITION, 1, 240–255

Reeder G.D. (1985) Implicit relations between dispositions and behaviors: Effects on dispositional attribution. In Harvey J.H. and Weary G. (eds) ATTRIBUTION: BASIC ISSUES AND APPLICATIONS, Academic Press, NY

Regan D.T. (1968) The effects of a favor and liking on compliance. Doctoral Dissertation, Stanford University. Cited in D.O. Sears, J.L. Freedman and L.A. Peplau, SOCIAL PSYCHOLOGY (5th edn) Prentice Hall, NJ, 1985

Regan D.T. and Totten J. (1975) Empathy and attribution: Turning observers into actors. JOURNAL OF PERSONALITY AND SOCIAL PSYCHOLOGY, 32, 850–856

Rehberg H.R. and Richman C.L. (1989) Prosocial behavior in preschool children: A look at the interaction of race, gender and

family composition. INTERNATIONAL JOURNAL OF BEHAVIORAL DEVELOPMENT, 12, 385–401

Reich J.W. and Robertson J.L. (1979) Reactance and normal appeal in anti-littering messages. JOURNAL OF APPLIED SOCIAL PSYCHOLOGY, 9, 91–101

Reiner R. (1985) THE POLITICS OF THE POLICE, Wheatsleaf, Brighton, UK

Reis H.T., et al. (1982) Physical attractiveness in social interaction II: Why does appearance affect social experience? JOURNAL OF PERSONALITY AND SOCIAL PSYCHOLOGY, 43, 979–996

Reis H.T., Nezlek J. and Wheeler L. (1980) Physical attractiveness in social interaction. JOURNAL OF PERSONALITY AND SOCIAL PSYCHOLOGY, 38, 604–617

Reis H.T. and Shaver P. (1988) Intimacy as an interpersonal process. In Duck S.W. (ed.) HANDBOOK OF PERSONAL RELA-TIONSHIPS, Wiley, NY

Reisenzein R. (1983) The Schachter theory of emotion: Two decades later. PSYCHOLOGICAL BULLETIN, 94, 239–264

Reiter L. (1991) Developmental origins of antihomosexual prejudice in heterosexual men and women. CLINICAL SOCIAL WORK JOURNAL, 19, 163–175

Relich J.D., Debus R.L. and Walker R. (1986) The mediating role of attribution and self-efficacy variables for treatment effects on achievement outcomes. CONTEMPORARY EDUCATIONAL PSYCHOLOGY, 11, 195–216

Rempel J.K., Holmes J.G. and Zanna M.P. (1985) Trust in close relationships. JOURNAL OF PERSONALITY AND SOCIAL PSYCHOLOGY, 49, 95–112

Reuss-Ianni E. and Ianni F. (1983) Street cops and management cops: The two cultures of policing. In Punch M. (ed.) CONTROL IN THE POLICE ORGANIZATION, M.I.T. Press, Mass.

Reynolds V., Flager V.S. and Vine I. (eds) (1987) THE SOCIOBIOLOGY OF ETHNOCENTRISM: EVOLUTIONARY DIMENSIONS OF XENOPHOBIA, DISCRIMINATION, RACISM AND NATIONALISM, University of Georgia Press, Athens, Georgia

Rhodewalt F. and Agustsdottir S. (1986) Effects of self-presentation on the phenomenal self. JOURNAL OF PERSONALITY AND SOCIAL PSYCHOLOGY, 50, 47–55

Rice J. (1992) (personal communication)

Richards A.D. (1964) Attitude and drug acceptance. BRITISH JOURNAL OF PSYCHIATRY, 110, 46–52

Richards M.S. and Wierzbicki M. (1990) Anchoring errors in clinical-like judgments. JOURNAL OF CLINICAL PSYCHOLOGY, 46, 358–365

Ridley M. and Dawkins R. (1981) The natural selection of altruism. In J.P. Rushton and R.M. Sorrentino (eds) ALTRUISM AND HELPING BEHAVIOR, Erlbaum, Hillsdale, NJ

Rigby K. (1984) Acceptance of authority and directiveness as indicators of authoritarianism: A new framework. JOURNAL OF SOCIAL PSYCHOLOGY, 122, 171–180

Rigby K. (1986) Acceptance of authority, self, and others. JOURNAL OF SOCIAL PSYCHOLOGY, 126, 493–501

Rigby K. (1987a) Directiveness and acceptance of authority. JOURNAL OF SOCIAL PSYCHOLOGY, 127, 235–236

Rigby K. (1987b) An authority behavior inventory. JOURNAL OF PERSONALITY ASSESSMENT, 51, 615–625

Rigby K. (1988a) Sexist attitudes and authoritarian personality characteristics among Australian adolescents. JOURNAL OF RESEARCH IN PERSONALITY, 22, 465–473

Rigby K. (1988b) Parental influence on attitudes toward institutional authority. JOURNAL OF GENETIC PSYCHOLOGY, 149, 383–391

Rigby K. (1988c) Relationships among three concepts of authoritarianism in adolescent schoolchildren. JOURNAL OF SOCIAL PSYCHOLOGY, 128, 825–832

Rigby K. and Densley T.R. (1985) Religiosity and attitude toward institutional authority among adolescents. JOURNAL OF SOCIAL PSYCHOLOGY, 125, 723–728

Rigby K., Mak A.S. and Slee P.T. (1989) Impulsiveness, orientation to institutional authority, and gender as factors in self-reported delinquency among Australian adolescents. PERSONALITY AND INDIVIDUAL DIFFERENCES, 10, 689–692

Rigby K., Metzer J.C. and Ray J.J. (1986) Working-class authoritarianism in England and Australia. JOURNAL OF SOCIAL PSYCHOLOGY, 126, 261–262

Rigby K., Schofield P. and Slee P.T. (1987) The similarity of attitudes towards personal and impersonal types of authority among adolescent schoolchildren. JOURNAL OF ADOLESCENCE, 10, 241–253

Rigby K. and Slee P.T. (1987) Eysenck's personality factors and orientation toward authority among schoolchildren. AUSTRALIAN JOURNAL OF PSYCHOLOGY, 39, 151–161

Rigby K. and Slee P.T. (1991) Bullying among Australian school children: Reported behavior and attitudes towards victims. JOURNAL OF SOCIAL PSYCHOLOGY, 131, 615–627

Riggio R.E., Tucker J. and Throckmorton B. (1987) Social skills and deception ability. PERSONALITY AND SOCIAL PSYCHOLOGY BULLETIN, 13, 568–577

Rijsman J. and Stroebe W. (1989) Introduction: The two social psychologies or whatever happened to the crisis. EUROPEAN JOURNAL OF SOCIAL PSYCHOLOGY, 19, 339–344

Ring K. (1967) Experimental social psychology: Some sober questions about frivolous values. JOURNAL OF EXPERIMENTAL SOCIAL PSYCHOLOGY, 3, 113–123

Ringelmann M. (1913) Recherches sur les monteurs animes: Travail de L'homme. ANNALES DE L'INSTITUT NATIONAL AGONOMIQUE, XII, 1–40

Robbins C.J. (1988) Attributions and Depression: Why is the literature so inconsistent? JOURNAL OF PERSONALITY AND SOCIAL PSYCHOLOGY, 54, 880–889

Roberts J.V. and Herman C.P. (1986) The psychology of height: An empirical review. In Herman C.P., Zanna M.P. and Higgins E.T. (eds) PHYSICAL APPEARANCE, STIGMA AND SOCIAL BEHAVIOR: THE ONTARIO SYMPOSIUM (Vol. 3), Erlbaum, Hillsdale, NJ

Robinson J., Young W. and Cameron N. (1988) MANAGING POLICE EFFECTIVENESS: A LITERATURE REVIEW, Institute of Criminology, Victoria University of Wellington, NZ

Robinson J.P., Shaver P.R. and Wightsman L.S. (eds) (1991) MEASURES OF PERSONALITY AND SOCIAL PSYCHOLOGICAL ATTITUDES, Academic Press, San Diego.

Roden J. (1985) The application of social psychology. In Lindzey G. and Aronson E. (eds), HANDBOOK OF SOCIAL PSYCHOLOGY (2nd edn), Random House, NY

Rofe Y. (1984) Stress and affiliation: A utility theory. PSYCHOLOGICAL REVIEW, 91, 235–250

Rogers L. (1991) New rules of evidence for the under 12's. LAW SOCIETY JOURNAL, 29, 48–49

Rogers M., Miller N., Mayer F.S., et al. (1982) Personal responsibility and salience of the request for help: Determinants of the relation between negative affect and helping behavior. JOURNAL OF PERSONALITY AND SOCIAL PSYCHOLOGY 43, 956–970

Rogers T.B., Kuiper N.A. and Kirker W.S. (1977) Self-reference and the encoding of personal information. JOURNAL OF PERSONALITY AND SOCIAL PSYCHOLOGY, 35, 677–688

Rokeach M. (1973) THE NATURE OF HUMAN VALUES, Free Press, NY

Rollins B.C. and Thomas D.L. (1979) Parental support, power and control techniques in the socialisation of children. In Burr W.R., Hill R., Nye F.I. and Reiss I.L. (eds), CONTEMPORARY THEORIES ABOUT THE FAMILY, Free Press, NY

Rosen S., Tomarelli M.M., Kidda M.L., et al. (1986) Effects of motive for helping, recipient's inability to reciprocate, and sex on devaluation of the recipient's competence. JOURNAL OF PERSONALITY AND SOCIAL PSYCHOLOGY, 50, 729–736

Rosenbaum M.E. (1986) The repulsion hypothesis: On the non-development of relationships. JOURNAL OF PERSONALITY AND SOCIAL PSYCHOLOGY, 51, 1156–1166

Rosenberg M.J. (1965) When dissonance fails: On eliminating evaluation apprehension from attitude measurement. JOURNAL OF PERSONALITY AND SOCIAL PSYCHOLOGY, 1, 28–42

Rosenberg L.A. (1961) Group size, prior experience and conformity. JOURNAL OF ABNORMAL AND SOCIAL PSYCHOLOGY, 63, 436–437

Rosenberg M.J. (1969) The conditions and consequences of evaluation apprehension. In Rosenthal R. and Rosnow R.L. (eds) ARTIFACT IN BEHAVIORAL RESEARCH, Academic Press, NY

Rosenberg S., Nelson C. and Vivekananthan P.S. (1968) A multidimensional approach to the structure of personality impressions. JOURNAL OF PERSONALITY AND SOCIAL PSYCHOLOGY, 9, 283–294

Rosenhan D.L. (1969) Some origins of concern for others. In Mussen P.M., Langer J. and Covington M. (eds) ISSUES IN DEVELOPMENTAL PSYCHOLOGY, Holt, Rinehart, Winston, NY

Rosenhan D.L. (1973) On being sane in insane places. SCIENCE, 179, 250–258

Rosenkrantz P., Vogel S., Bee H., Broverman I. and Broverman D.M. (1968) Sex-role stereotypes and self concepts in college students. JOURNAL OF CONSULTING AND CLINICAL PSYCHOLOGY, 32, 287–295

Rosenthal A.M. (1964) THIRTY-EIGHT WITNESSES, McGraw-Hill, NY

Rosenthal D.A. and Harding S.M. (1983) Intimacy, androgyny and interpersonal attraction. MELBOURNE UNIVERSITY REPORTS No. 78, Department of Psychology, The University of Melbourne, Vic.

Rosenthal N.E., Sack D.A., Carpenter C.J., et al. (1985) Antidepressant effects of light in seasonal affective disorder. AMERICAN JOURNAL OF PSYCHIATRY, 142, 163–170

Rosenthal N.E., Sack D.A., Gillen J.C., et al. (1984) Seasonal affective disorder: A description of the syndrome and preliminary findings with light therapy. ARCHIVES OF GENERAL PSYCHIATRY, 41, 72–80

Rosenthal R. (1966) EXPERIMENTER EFFECTS IN BEHAVIORAL RESEARCH, Appleton-Century-Crofts, NY

Rosenthal R. (1976) EXPERIMENTER EFFECTS IN BEHAVIORAL RESEARCH, Irvington, NY

Rosenthal R. (1985) From unconscious experimenter bias to teacher expectancy effects. In Dusek J.B., Hall V.C. and Meyer W.J. (eds) TEACHER EXPECTANCIES, Erlbaum, Hillsdale NJ

Rosenthal R. and Fode K.L. (1963) Psychology of the scientist: V. Three experiments in experimenter bias. PSYCHOLOGICAL REPORTS, 12, 491–511

Rosenthal R. and Jacobson L.F. (1968) PYGMALION IN THE CLASSROOM, Holt, Rinehart and Winston, NY

Rosenthal R. and Rubin D.B. (1978)

Interpersonal expectancy effects: The first 345 studies. THE BEHAVIOR AND BRAIN SCIENCES, 3, 377–386

Rosenhan D.L., Salovey P. and Harris K. (1981) The joys of helping: Focus of attention mediates the impact of possible affect on altruism. JOURNAL OF PERSONALITY AND SOCIAL PSYCHOLOGY 40, 899–905

Rosow I. (1958) The social effects of the physical environment. JOURNAL OF THE AMERICAN INSTITUTE OF PLANNERS 27, 127–133

Ross A. and Braband J. (1973) Effect of increased responsibility on bystander intervention. II. The cue value of a blind person. JOURNAL OF PERSONALITY AND SOCIAL PSYCHOLOGY 25, 254–258

Ross E.A. (1908) SOCIAL PSYCHOLOGY, MacMillan, NY

Ross L. (1977) The intuitive psychologist and his shortcomings: Distortions in the attribution process. In Berkowitz L. (ed.) ADVANCES IN EXPERIMENTAL SOCIAL PSYCHOLOGY (Vol. 10), Academic Press, NY

Ross L., Amabile T.M. and Steinmetz J.L. (1977) Social roles, social control, and biases in social perception processes. JOURNAL OF PERSONALITY AND SOCIAL PSYCHOLOGY, 35, 485–494

Ross L., Greene D. and House P. (1977) The "false consensus effect": An egocentric bias in social perception and attribution processes. JOURNAL OF EXPERIMENTAL SOCIAL PSYCHOLOGY, 13, 279–301

Ross M. (1975) Salience of reward and intrinsic motivation. JOURNAL OF PERSONALITY AND SOCIAL PSYCHOLOGY, 32, 245–254

Ross M. and Fletcher G.J. (1985) Attribution and social perception. In Lindzey G. and Aronson A. (eds) THE HANDBOOK OF SOCIAL PSYCHOLOGY (Vol. II), (3rd edn), Random House, NY

Ross M. and Olson J.M. (1981) An expectancy-attribution model of the effects of placebos. PSYCHOLOGICAL REVIEW, 88, 408–437

Ross M. and Sicoly F. (1979) Egocentric biases in availability and attribution. JOURNAL OF PERSONALITY AND SOCIAL PSYCHOLOGY, 37, 322–336

Ross M.W. (1988) Components and structure of attitudes toward AIDS. HOSPITAL AND COMMUNITY PSYCHIATRY, 39, 1306–1308

Ross M.W., Paulsen J.A. and Stalstrom O.W. (1988) Homosexuality and mental health: A cross-cultural review. JOURNAL OF HOMOSEXUALITY, 15, 131–152

Ross M.W. and Rosser B.S. (1989) Education and AIDS risks: A review. HEALTH EDUCATION RESEARCH, 4, 273–284

Rothbart M. and John O.P. (1985) Social categorization and behavioral episodes: A cognitive analysis and the effects of

intergroup contact. JOURNAL OF SOCIAL ISSUES, 41, 81–104

Rothblum E.D. (1990) Psychological factors in the Antarctic. JOURNAL OF PSYCHOLOGY, 124, 253–273

Rothstein S.I. and Pierotti R. (1988) Distinctions among reciprocal altruism, kin selection and cooperation and a model for the initial evolution of beneficent behavior. ETHOLOGY AND SOCIOBIOLOGY 9, 189–209

Rothstein S.I. and Pierotti R. (1989) Definitions and the genetic bases of beneficent behavior. ETHOLOGY AND SOCIOBIOLOGY 10, 453–456

Rotter J.B. (1966) Generalised expectancies for internal versus external control of reinforcement. PSYCHOLOGICAL MONOGRAPHS, 80, 1–28

Rotter J.B. (1973) Internal-external locus of control scale. In Robinson J.P. and Shaver R.P. (eds) MEASURES OF SOCIAL PSYCHOLOGICAL ATTITUDES, Institute for Social Research, Ann Arbor, Michigan

Rotter J.B. (1975) Some problems and misconceptions related to the construct of internal versus external control of reinforcement. JOURNAL OF CONSULTING AND CLINICAL PSYCHOLOGY, 40, 313–321

Rotton J., Barry T., Frey J. and Soler E. (1978) Air pollution and interpersonal attraction. JOURNAL OF APPLIED PSYCHOLOGY, 8, 57–71

Rotton J. and Frey J. (1985a) Air pollution, weather, and violent crimes: Concomitant time-series analysis of archival data. JOURNAL OF PERSONALITY AND SOCIAL PSYCHOLOGY, 49, 1207–1220

Rotton J. and Frey J. (1985b) Psychological costs of air pollution: Atmospheric conditions, seasonal trends and psychiatric emergencies. POPULATION AND ENVIRONMENT, 7, 3–16

Rotton J. and Kelly I.W. (1985a) Much ado about the full moon: A meta-analysis of lunar-lunacy research. PSYCHOLOGICAL BULLETIN, 97, 286–306

Rotton J. and Kelly I.W. (1985b) A scale for assessing belief in lunar effects: Reliability and concurrent validity. PSYCHOLOGICAL REPORTS, 57, 239–245

Rotton J. and Kelly I.W. (1987) Geophysical variables and behavior: XLVII. Comment on "The lunar-lunacy relationship": More ado about the full moon. PSYCHOLOGICAL REPORTS, 61, 733–734

Rotton J., Kelly I.W. and Elortegui P. (1986) Assessing belief in lunar effects: Known-groups validation. PSYCHOLOGICAL REPORTS, 59, 171–174

Rotton J., Kelly I.W. and Frey J. (1983) Geophysical variables and behavior: X. Detecting lunar periodicities: Something old, new, borrowed, and true. PSYCHO-LOGICAL REPORTS, 52, 111–116

Rowley K.M. and Feather N.T. (1987) The impact of unemployment in relation to age

and length of unemployment. JOURNAL OF OCCUPATIONAL PSYCHOLOGY, 60, 323–332

Ruback R.B. and Carr T.S. (1984) Crowding in a women's prison: Attitudinal and behavioral effects. JOURNAL OF APPLIED SOCIAL PSYCHOLOGY, 14, 57–68

Rubenstein C. and Shaver P. (1982) The experience of loneliness. In Peplau L.A. and Perlman D. (eds) LONELINESS: A SOURCEBOOK OF CURRENT THEORY, RESEARCH AND THERAPY, Wiley, NY

Rubin J.Z. and Brown B. (1975) THE SOCIAL PSYCHOLOGY OF BARGAINING AND NEGOTIATION, Academic Press, NY

Rubin J.Z. and Lewicki R.J. (1973) A three-factor experimental analysis of interpersonal influence. JOURNAL OF APPLIED SOCIAL PSYCHOLOGY, 3, 240–257

Rubin J.Z., Provenzano F.J. and Luria Z. (1974) The eye of the beholder: Parents' views on sex of newborns. AMERICAN JOURNAL OF ORTHOPSYCHIATRY, 44, 512–519

Rubin K.H. and Schneider, F.W. (1973) The relationship between moral judgment, egocentrism, and altruistic behavior. CHILD DEVELOPMENT, 44, 661–665

Rubin Z. (1970) Measurement of romantic love. JOURNAL OF PERSONALITY AND SOCIAL PSYCHOLOGY, 16, 265–273

Rubin Z. (1973) LIKING AND LOVING: AN INVITATION TO SOCIAL PSYCHOLOGY, Holt, Rinehart and Winston, NY

Rubin Z. and Peplau L.A. (1975) Who believes in a just world? JOURNAL OF SOCIAL ISSUES, 31, 65–89

Rubin Z., Peplau L.A. and Hill C.T. (1981) Loving and leaving: Sex differences in romantic attachments. SEX ROLES, 7, 821–835

Ruble D.N. and Feldman N.S. (1976) Order of consensus distinctiveness, and consistency information and causal attributions. JOURNAL OF PERSONALITY AND SOCIAL PSYCHOLOGY, 34, 930–937

Rule B.G., Dyck R., McAra M. and Nesdale A.R. (1975) Judgements of aggression serving personal versus prosocial purposes. SOCIAL BEHAVIOUR AND PERSONALITY: AN INTERNATIONAL JOURNAL, 3, 55–63

Rule B.G., Taylor B.R. and Dobbs A.R. (1987) Priming effects of heat on aggressive thoughts. SOCIAL COGNITION, 5, 131–143

Rusbult C.E. (1980) Commitment and satisfaction in romantic associations: A test of the investment model. JOURNAL OF EXPERIMENTAL SOCIAL PSYCHOLOGY, 16, 172–186

Rusbult C.E. and Zembrodt I.M. (1983) Response to dissatisfaction in romantic involvements: A multidimensional scaling analysis. JOURNAL OF EXPERIMENTAL SOCIAL PSYCHOLOGY, 19, 274–293

Ruse M. (1979) SOCIOBIOLOGY: SENSE OR NONSENSE? Reidel, Lond.

Rush M.C. and Russell J.E. (1988) Leader prototypes and prototype-contingent consensus in leader behavior. JOURNAL OF EXPERIMENTAL SOCIAL PSYCHOLOGY, 24, 88–104

Rushton J.P. (1980) ALTRUISM, SOCIALIZATION AND SOCIETY. Prentice Hall, NJ

Rushton J.P. (1981) The altruistic personality In J.P. Rushton and R.M. Sorrentino (eds) ALTRUISM AND HELPING BEHAVIOR, Erlbaum, NY

Rushton J.P. (1984) The altruistic personality: Evidence from laboratory, naturalistic, and self-report perspectives. In Staub E., et al. (eds) THE DEVELOPMENT AND MAINTENANCE OF PROSOCIAL BEHAVIOR: INTERNATIONAL PERSPECTIVES, Plenum Press, NY

Rushton J.P. (1987) An evolutionary theory of health, longevity, and personality: Sociobiology and R/Kr/K reproductive strategies. PSYCHOLOGICAL REPORTS, 60, 539–549

Rushton J.P. (1988) Epigenic rules in moral development: Distal-proximal approaches to altruism and aggression. AGGRESSIVE BEHAVIOR, 14, 35–40

Rushton J.P. (1989) Genetic similarity, human altruism and group selection. BEHAVIORAL AND BRAIN SCIENCES, 12, 503–559

Rushton J.P. (1991a) Racial differences: A reply to Zuckerman. AMERICAN PSYCHOLO- GIST, 46, 983–984

Rushton J.P. (1991b) Race differences: A reply to Mealey. PSYCHOLOGICAL SCIENCE, 2, 126

Rushton J.P., Fulker D.W., Neale M.C., et al. (1986) Altruism and aggression: The heritability of individual differences JOURNAL OF PERSONALITY AND SOCIAL PSYCHOLOGY, 50, 1192–1198

Rushton J.P., Russell R.J. and Wells P.A. (1984) Genetic similarity theory: Beyond kin selection. BEHAVIOR GENETICS, 14, 179–193

Russell D. and Jones W.H. (1980) When superstition fails: Reactions to disconfirmation of personal beliefs. PERSONALITY AND SOCIAL PSYCHOLOGY BULLETIN, 6, 83–88

Russell D., Peplau L.A. and Cutrona C.E. (1980) The revised UCLA Loneliness Scale: Concurrent and discriminant validity evidence. JOURNAL OF PERSONALITY AND SOCIAL PSYCHOLOGY, 39, 472–480

Russell G. (1982) Maternal employment status and fathers' involvement in child-care and play. AUSTRALIAN AND NEW ZEALAND JOURNAL OF SOCIOLOGY, 18, 172–179

Russell G. (1987) Fatherhood in Australia. In Russell G. (ed.) THE FATHER'S ROLE: CROSS-CULTURAL PERSPECTIVES, Erlbaum, Hillsdale, NJ

Russell G. and Antill J.K. (1984) An Australian sex-role scale: Additional psychometric data and correlations with self-esteem. AUSTRALIAN PSYCHOLOGIST, 19, 13–18

Russell G. and Smith J. (1979) Girls can be doctors ... can't they?: Sex differences in career aspirations. AUSTRALIAN JOURNAL OF SOCIAL ISSUES, 14, 91–102

Russell G.W. and de-Graaf J.P. (1985) Lunar cycles and human aggression: A replication. SOCIAL BEHAVIOR AND PERSONALITY, 13, 143–146

Russell R.J. and Wells P.A. (1991) Personality similarity and quality of marriage. PERSONALITY AND INDIVIDUAL DIFFERENCES, 12, 407–412

Russell R.W. (1978) Environmental stresses and the quality of life. AUSTRALIAN PSYCHOLOGIST, 13, 143–159

Russle J.A. (1980) A circumplex model of affect. JOURNAL OF PERSONALITY AND SOCIAL PSYCHOLOGY, 39, 1161–1178

Ryan W. (1971) BLAMING THE VICTIM, Random House, NY

Sackett P.R., DuBois C.L. and Noe A.W. (1991) Tokenism in performance evaluation: The effects of work group representation on male-female and White-Black differences in performance ratings. JOURNAL OF APPLIED PSYCHOLOGY, 76, 263–267

Sadalla E.K., Kenrick D.T. and Vershure B. (1987) Dominance and heterosexual attraction. JOURNAL OF PERSONALITY AND SOCIAL PSYCHOLOGY, 52, 730–738

Saegert S., Swap W. and Zajonc R.B. (1973) Exposure, context, and interpersonal attraction. JOURNAL OF PERSONALITY AND SOCIAL PSYCHOLOGY, 25, 234–242

Sagar H. and Schofield J.W. (1980) Racial and behavioral cues in black and white children's perceptions of ambiguously aggressive acts. JOURNAL OF PERSONALITY AND SOCIAL PSYCHOLOGY, 39, 590–598

Sahlins M.D. (1976) THE USE AND ABUSE OF BIOLOGY, University of Michigan, Ann Arbor, Michigan

St. George R. (1990) Legacies of empire for psychology in New Zealand. JOURNAL FOR THE HISTORY OF THE BEHAVIORAL SCIENCES, 26, 359–365

Sakurai M.M. (1975) Small group cohesiveness and detrimental conformity. SOCIOMETRY, 38, 340–359

Sales B., Elwork A. and Alfini J. (1977) Improving comprehension in jury instructions. In Sales B.D. (ed.), PERSPEC- TIVES IN LAW AND PSYCHOLOGY: THE CRIMINAL JUSTICE SYSTEM (Vol. 1), Plenum, NY

Sallman P. and Willis J. (1984) CRIMINAL JUSTICE IN AUSTRALIA, Oxford University Press, Melbourne

Sampson E.E. (1978) Scientific paradigms and social values: Wanted - a scientific revolution. JOURNAL OF PERSONALITY AND SOCIAL PSYCHOLOGY, 36, 1332–1343

Sanders G.S. and Baron R.S. (1977) Is social comparison irrelevant for producing choice shifts? JOURNAL OF EXPERIMENTAL SOCIAL PSYCHOLOGY, 13, 503–514

Sanders J.L. and Brizzolara M.S. (1982) Relationships between weather and mood. JOURNAL OF GENERAL PSYCHOLOGY, 107, 155–156

Sanna L.J. and Shotland R.L. (1990) Valence of anticipated evaluation and social facilitation. JOURNAL OF EXPERIMEN- TAL SOCIAL PSYCHOLOGY, 26, 82–92

Santrock J.W. (1986) LIFESPAN DEVELOPMENT, (2nd edn) William Brown, Dubuque, Iowa

Sarnoff I. and Zimbardo P.G. (1961) Anxiety, fear, and social affiliation. JOURNAL OF ABNORMAL AND SOCIAL PSYCHOLOGY, 62, 356–363.

Sashkin M. (1977) The structure of charismatic leadership. In Hunt J.G. and Larson L. (eds), LEADERSHIP: THE CUTTING EDGE, Southern Illinois University Press, Carbondale, Ill.

Sato K. (1988) Trust and group size in a social dilemma. JAPANESE PSYCHOLOGICAL RESEARCH, 30, 88–93

Scagliotta E.G. (1983) 2 aspirin and bedrest won't help. ACADEMIC THERAPY, 19, 93–96

Schachter S. (1959) THE PSYCHOLOGY OF AFFILIATION, Stanford University Press, Stanford, Ca.

Schachter S. (1964) The interaction of cognitive and physiological determinants of emotional state. In Berkowitz L. (ed.) ADVANCES IN EXPERIMENTAL SOCIAL PSYCHOLOGY (Vol. 1), Academic Press NY

Schachter S. (1971) EMOTION, OBESITY, AND CRIME, Academic Press, NY

Schachter S. and Singer J.E. (1962) Cognitive, social and physiological determinants of emotional state. PSYCHOLOGICAL REVIEW, 69, 379–399

Schachter S. and Singer J.E (1979) Comments on the Maslach and Marshall-Zimbardo experiments. JOURNAL OF PERSONALITY AND SOCIAL PSYCHOLOGY, 37, 989–995

Schafer R.B. (1988) Equity/inequity, and self-esteem: A reassessment. PSYCHOLOGI- CAL REPORTS, 63, 637–638

Schafer R.B. and Keith P.M. (1980) Equity and depression among married couples. SOCIAL PSYCHOLOGY QUARTERLY, 43, 430–435

Schaller M. and Maass A. (1989) Illusory correlation and social categorization: Toward an integration of motivational and cognitive factors in stereotype formation. JOURNAL OF PERSONALITY AND SOCIAL PSYCHOLOGY, 56, 709–721

Schaufeli W.B. (1988) Perceiving the causes of employment: An evaluation in a real-life situation. JOURNAL OF PERSONALITY

AND SOCIAL PSYCHOLOGY, 54, 347–356

Schein E. (1971) Organisational socialisation and the profession of management. INDUSTRIAL MANAGEMENT REVIEW, 2, 37–45

Schell R.E. and Hall E. (1983) DEVELOPMENTAL PSYCHOLOGY TODAY, Random House, NY

Scher S.J. and Cooper J. (1989) Motivational basis of dissonance: The singular role of behavioral consequences. JOURNAL OF PERSONALITY AND SOCIAL PSYCHOLOGY, 56, 899–906

Schlenker B.R. and Leary M.R. (1982) Social anxiety and self presentation: A conceptualisation and model. PSYCHOLOGICAL BULLETIN, 92, 572–587

Schmidt D.E. and Keating J.P. (1979) Human crowding and personal control: An integration of the research. PSYCHOLOGICAL BULLETIN, 86, 680–700

Schmitt B.H. (1986) Mere presence and social facilitation: One more time. JOURNAL OF EXPERIMENTAL SOCIAL PSYCHOLOGY, 22, 242–248

Schmitt B.H., Gilovich T., Goore N. and Joseph L. (1986) Mere presence and socio-facilitation: One more time. JOURNAL OF EXPERIMENTAL SOCIAL PSYCHOLOGY, 22, 242–248

Schneider D.J. (1973) Implicit personality theories: A review. PSYCHOLOGICAL BULLETIN, 79, 294–309

Schoettle V.S. (1980) Child exploitation: A study of pornography. JOURNAL AMERICAN ACADEMY CHILD PSYCHOLOGY, 19, 289–299

Schofield L.J. (1978) Withdrawal A.M.A. from an alcohol rehabilitation program. JOURNAL OF CLINICAL PSYCHOLOGY, 34, 571–573

Schopler J and Bateson N. (1962) A dependence interpretation of the effects of a severe initiation. JOURNAL OF PERSONALITY, 30, 633–649

Schopler J. and Stockdale J. (1977) An interference analysis of crowding. ENVIRONMENTAL PSYCHOLOGY AND NONVERBAL BEHAVIOR, 1, 81–88

Schumaker J.F. and Barraclough R.A. (1989) Protective self-presentation in Malaysian and Australian individuals. JOURNAL OF CROSS CULTURAL PSYCHOLOGY, 20, 54–63

Schutte J. and Light J. (1978) The relative importance of proximity and status for friendship choices in social hierarchies. SOCIAL PSYCHOLOGY, 41, 260–264

Schutz A. (1970) REFLECTIONS ON THE PROBLEMS OF RELEVANCE, University Press, New Haven, Conn.

Schutz A. (1972) THE PHENOMENOLOGY OF THE SOCIAL WORLD, Heinemann, Lond.

Schwartz S.H. (1973) Normative explanations of helping behavior: A critique, proposal, and empirical test. JOURNAL OF

EXPERIMENTAL SOCIAL PSYCHOLOGY, 9, 349–364

Schwartz S. H. (1977) Normative influences on altruism. In Berkowitz L. (ed.), ADVANCES IN EXPERIMENTAL SOCIAL PSYCHOLOGY (Vol. 10), Academic Press, NY

Schwartz S.H. and Bilsky W. (1990) Toward a theory of the universal content and structure of values: Extensions and cross-cultural replications. JOURNAL OF PERSONALITY AND SOCIAL PSYCHOLOGY, 58, 878–891

Schwartz S.H. and Clausen G.T. (1970) Responsibility, norms, and helping in an emergency. JOURNAL OF PERSONALITY AND SOCIAL PSYCHOLOGY, 16, 299–310

Schwartz S.H. and Howard J. A. (1981) A normative decision making model of altruism. In Rushton J.P. and Sorrentino R.M. (eds) ALTRUISM AND HELPING BEHAVIOR, Erlbaum, Hillsdale, NJ

Schwartz S.H. and Fleishman J.A. (1982) Effects of negative personal norms on helping behavior. PERSONALITY AND SOCIAL PSYCHOLOGY, 8, 81–86

Scott J.P. (1958) AGGRESSION, University of Chicago Press, Chicago

Scully D. (1990) UNDERSTANDING SEXUAL VIOLENCE: A STUDY OF CONVICTED RAPISTS, Unwin Hyman, Boston

Sears D.O. (1988) Symbolic racism. In Katz P.E. and Taylor D.A. (eds) ELIMINATING RACISM PROFILES IN CONTROVERSY, Plenum, NY

Sears D.O. and Allen H.M. (1984) The trajectory of local desegregation controversies and whites' opposition to busing. In Miller N. and Brewer M. (eds) GROUPS IN CONTACT: THE PSYCHOLOGY OF DESEGREGATION, Academic Press, NY

Sears D.O. and Kinder D.R. (1985) Whites' opposition to busing: On conceptualizing and operationalizing group conflict. JOURNAL OF PERSONALITY AND SOCIAL PSYCHOLOGY, 48, 1141–1147

Sears R.R., Maccoby E. and Levin H. (1957) PATTERNS OF CHILD REARING, Row Peterson, Evanston, Chicago

Sears D.O., Peplau L.A. and Taylor S.E. (1991) SOCIAL PSYCHOLOGY, Prentice Hall, NJ

Secord P.F. (1983) The imbalanced sex ratio. JOURNAL OF PERSONALITY AND SOCIAL PSYCHOLOGY, 44, 525–539

Secord P.F. and Backman C.W. (1974) SOCIAL PSYCHOLOGY, (2nd edn), McGraw-Hill, NY

Sedgwick P. (1982) PSYCHOPOLITICS, Harper and Row, NY

Segal M.W. (1974) Alphabet and attraction: An unobtrusive measure of the effect of propinquity in a field setting. JOURNAL OF PERSONALITY AND SOCIAL PSYCHOLOGY, 30, 654–657

Seligman M.E.P. (1975) HELPLESSNESS: ON

DEPRESSION, DEVELOPMENT AND DEATH, Freeman, San Francisco

Selye H. (1956) THE STRESS OF LIFE, McGraw-Hill, NY

Selye H. (1976) STRESS IN HEALTH AND DISEASE, Butterworth, Ma.

Selye H. (1978) The stress of police work. POLICE STRESS, 1, 8

Shama A. and Wisenblit J. (1984) Values of voluntary simplicity: Lifestyle and motivation. PSYCHOLOGICAL REPORTS, 55, 231–240

Shanab M.E. and Yahya K.A. (1977) A behavioral study of obedience in children. JOURNAL OF PERSONALITY AND SOCIAL PSYCHOLOGY, 35, 530–536

Shanab M.E. and Yahya K.A. (1978) A cross-cultural study of obedience. THE PSYCHONOMIC SOCIETY BULLETIN, 11, 267–269

Shanteau J. and Nagy G.F. (1979) Probability of acceptance in dating choice. JOURNAL OF PERSONALITY AND SOCIAL PSYCHOLOGY, 37, 522–533

Shaver K.G. (1985) THE ATTRIBUTION OF BLAME, Springer-Verlag, NY

Shaver K.G. and Drown D. (1986) On causality, responsibility, and self-blame: A theoretical note. JOURNAL OF PERSONALITY AND SOCIAL PSYCHOLOGY, 50, 697–702

Shaver P. and Klinnert M.D. (1982) Schachter's theories of affiliation and emotion: Implications of developmental research. In Wheeler L. (ed.) REVIEW OF PERSONALITY AND SOCIAL PSYCHOLOGY, Sage, Ca.

Shaw M.E. (1964) Communication networks. ADVANCES IN EXPERIMENTAL SOCIAL PSYCHOLOGY, 1, 111–147

Shaw M.E. (1981) GROUP DYNAMICS: THE PSYCHOLOGY OF SMALL GROUP BEHAVIOR (3rd edn), McGraw-Hill, NY

Sheehan P.W. (1986) Television viewing and its relation to aggression among children in Australia. In Huesmann L.R. and Eron L.D. (eds) TELEVISION AND THE AGGRESSIVE CHILD: A CROSS-NATIONAL COMPARISON, Erlbaum, Hillsdale, NJ

Sheehan P.W. (1987) Coping with exposure to aggression: The path from research to practice. AUSTRALIAN PSYCHOLOGIST, 22, 291–311

Sheinberg M. and Penn P. (1991) Gender dilemmas, gender questions, and the gender mantra. JOURNAL OF MARITAL AND FAMILY THERAPY, 17, 33–44

Shepherd J.W. and Bagley A. (1970) The effects of biographical information and order of presentation on the judgement of an aggressive action. JOURNAL OF SOCIAL AND CLINICAL PSYCHOLOGY, 9, 177–179

Shepperd J.A. and Arkin R.M. (1989) Determinants of self-handicapping: Task importance and the effects of preexisting handicaps on self-generated handicaps. PERSONALITY AND SOCIAL PSYCHOLOGY BULLETIN, 15, 101–112

Shepperd J.A. and Strathman A.J. (1989) Attractiveness and height: The role of stature in dating preference, frequency of dating, and perceptions of attractiveness. PERSONALITY AND SOCIAL PSYCHOLOGY BULLETIN, 15, 617–627

Sheridan C.L. and King R.G. (1972) Obedience to authority with an authentic victim. PROCEEDINGS OF THE AMERICAN PSYCHOLOGICAL ASSOCIATION, 165–166

Sherif M. (1935) A study of some social factors in perception. ARCHIVES OF PSYCHOLOGY, 27, 1–60

Sherif M. (1936) THE PSYCHOLOGY OF SOCIAL NORMS, Harper and Row, NY

Sherif M. (1966) IN COMMON PREDICAMENT: SOCIAL PSYCHOLOGY OF INTERGROUP CONFLICT AND COOPERATION, Houghton Mifflin, Boston

Sherif M., Harvey O.J., White B.J., Hood W.R. and Sherif C.W. (1961) THE ROBBER'S CAVE EXPERIMENT, University of Oklahoma Press, Norman, Okla.

Sherman L.W. (1973) A psychological view of women in policing. JOURNAL OF POLICE SCIENCE AND ADMINISTRATION, 1, 383–394

Sherman L.W. (1975) An evaluation of policewomen on patrol in a suburban police department. JOURNAL OF POLICE SCIENCE AND ADMINISTRATION, 5, 434–438

Sherman L.W. (1992) POLICING DOMESTIC VIOLENCE, The Free Press, NY

Shipley T.E. and Veroff J.A. (1952) A projective measure of need for affiliation. JOURNAL OF EXPERIMENTAL PSYCHOLOGY, 43, 349–356

Shoda Y., Mischel W. and Peake P.K. (1990) Predicting adolescent cognitive and self-regulatory competencies from preschool delay of gratification: Identifying diagnostic conditions. DEVELOPMENTAL PSYCHOLOGY, 26, 978–986

Shotland R.L. and Heinold W.D. (1985) Bystander response to arterial bleeding: Helping skills, the decision-making process, and differentiating the helping response. JOURNAL OF PERSONALITY AND SOCIAL PSYCHOLOGY, 49, 347–356

Shubik M. (1986) Cooperative game solutions: Australian, Indian, and U.S. opinions. JOURNAL OF CONFLICT RESOLUTION, 30, 63–76

Siegal M. and Shwalb D. (1985) Economic justice in adolescence: An Australian-Japanese comparison. JOURNAL OF ECONOMIC PSYCHOLOGY, 6, 313–326

Siegal M., Waters L.J. and Dinwiddy L.S. (1988) Misleading children: Causal attributions for inconsistency under repeated questioning. JOURNAL OF EXPERIMENTAL CHILD PSYCHOLOGY, 45, 438–456

Siegel P. (1979) Homophobia: Types, origins, remedies. CHRISTIANITY AND CRISIS, 39, 280–284

Siem F.M. and Spence J.T. (1986) Gender-related traits and helping behavior. JOURNAL OF PERSONALITY AND SOCIAL PSYCHOLOGY, 51, 615–621

Sigall H. and Ostrove N. (1975) Beautiful but dangerous: Effects of offender attractiveness and nature of the crime on juridic judgements. JOURNAL OF PERSONALITY AND SOCIAL PSYCHOLOGY, 31, 410–414

Sigall H. and Page R. (1971) Current stereotypes: A little fading, a little faking. JOURNAL OF PERSONALITY AND SOCIAL PSYCHOLOGY, 18, 247–255

Sigelman C.K., et al. (1986) Gender, physical attractiveness, and electability: An experimental investigation of voter biases. JOURNAL OF APPLIED SOCIAL PSYCHOLOGY, 16, 229–248

Silverman I. (1977) THE HUMAN SUBJECT IN THE PSYCHOLOGICAL LABORATORY, Pergamon, NY

Simmel G. (1957) The metropolis and mental life. In Hatt P.K and Reiss A.J. (eds) CITIES AND SOCIETIES: THE REVISED READER IN URBAN SOCIOLOGY Free Press, NY

Simpson J.A. (1987) The dissolution of romantic relationships: factors involved in relationship stability and emotional distress, JOURNAL OF PERSONALITY AND SOCIAL PSYCHOLOGY, 53, 683–692.

Simpson M. and Perry J.D. (1990) Crime and climate: A reconsideration. ENVIRONMENT AND BEHAVIOR, 22, 295–300

Singer M.S. (1990) Implicit leadership theory: Are results generalisable from student to professional samples? JOURNAL OF SOCIAL PSYCHOLOGY, 130, 407–408

Singer M.S. and Beardsley C. (1990) Attributions about effective leadership and perceptions of actual leader behavior: A comparison between managers and subordinates. JOURNAL OF SOCIAL BEHAVIOR AND PERSONALITY, 5, 115–122

Singer M.S. and Singer A.E. (1986) Relation between transformational vs transactional leadership preference and subordinates personality: An exploratory study. PERCEPTUAL AND MOTOR SKILLS, 62, 775–780

Singer P. (1987) Famine, affluence and morality. In Sher G. (ed.) MORAL PHILOSOPHY: SELECTED READINGS, Harcourt, Brace, Jovanovich, NY

Sistrunk F. and McDavid J.W. (1971) Sex variables in conformity behavior. JOURNAL OF PERSONALITY AND SOCIAL PSYCHOLOGY, 17, 200–207

Skinner B.F. (1971) BEYOND FREEDOM AND DIGNITY, Penguin, Lond.

Skolnick J. (1985) A sketch of the policeman's working personality. In Blumberg A.S. and Neiderhoffer E. (eds), THE AMBIVALENT FORCE: PERSPECTIVES ON THE POLICE, Holt, Rinehart and Winston, NY

Skrypnek B.J. and Snyder M. (1982) On the self-perpetuating nature of stereotypes about women and men. JOURNAL OF EXPERIMENTAL SOCIAL PSYCHOLOGY, 18, 277–291

Slavin R. (1983) When does cooperative learning increase student achievement? PSYCHOLOGICAL BULLETIN, 94, 429–443

Slovic P., Fischhoff B. and Lichtenstein S. (1982) Facts versus fears: Understanding perceived risk. In Kahneman D., Slovic P. and Tversky A. (eds) JUDGEMENT UNDER UNCERTAINTY: HEURISTICS AND BIASES, Cambridge University Press, Cambridge

Slusher M.P. and Anderson C.A. (1987) When reality monitoring fails: The role of imagination in stereotype maintenance. JOURNAL OF PERSONALITY AND SOCIAL PSYCHOLOGY, 52, 653–662

Smart C. (1990) Laws truth: Womens' experience. In Graycar R. (ed.) DISSENTING OPINIONS: FEMINIST EXPLORATIONS IN LAW AND SOCIETY, Allen and Unwin, Sydney

Smedslund J. (1990) A critique of Tversky and Kahneman's distinction between fallacy and misunderstanding. SCANDINAVIAN JOURNAL OF PSYCHOLOGY, 31, 110–120

Smith, D. and Gray J. (1983) POLICE AND ACTION, Policy Studies Institute, Lond.

Smith D.D. (1976) The social content of pornography. JOURNAL OF COMMUNICATION, Winter, 16–24

Smith K.D., Keating J.P. and Stotland R.L. (1989) Altruism reconsidered. The effect of denying feedback on a victim's status to empathic witnesses. JOURNAL OF PERSONALITY AND SOCIAL PSYCHOLOGY 57, 641–650

Smith L. (1989) DOMESTIC VIOLENCE: AN OVERVIEW OF THE LITERATURE, Home Office Research Study No. 107, Lond.

Smith M. (1966) Percy Forman: Defence counselor. LIFE, 94–97

Smith M. and Knowles A.D. (1991) Contributions of personality, social network, and cognitive processes to the experience of loneliness in women religious and other mature Australian women. JOURNAL OF SOCIAL PSYCHOLOGY, 131, 355–365

Smith R.E., Keating J.P., Hester R.K. and Mitchell H.E. (1976) Role and justice considerations in the attribution of responsibility to a rape victim. JOURNAL OF RESEARCH IN PERSONALITY, 10, 346–357

Smith R.J. and Knowles E.S. (1979) Affective and cognitive mediators of reactions to spatial invasions. JOURNAL OF EXPERIMENTAL SOCIAL PSYCHOLOGY, 15, 437–452

Smith S.S. and Richardson D. (1983) Amelioration of deception and harm in psychological research: The important role of debriefing. JOURNAL OF PERSONALITY AND SOCIAL PSYCHOLOGY, 44, 1075–1082

Smith V.L. and Ellsworth P.C. (1987) The

social psychology of eyewitness accuracy: Leading questions and communicator expertise. JOURNAL OF APPLIED PSYCHOLOGY, 72, 294–300

Smithson M. and Amato P.R. (1982) An unstudied region of helping: An extension of the Pearce-Amato cognitive taxonomy. SOCIAL PSYCHOLOGY QUARTERLY, 45, 67–76

Smithson M., Amato P.R. and Pearce P.L. (1983) DIMENSIONS OF HELPING BEHAVIOUR, Pergamon Press, Sydney

Snyder C.R. and Higgins R.L. (1988) Excuses: Their effective role in the negotiation of reality. PSYCHOLOGICAL BULLETIN, 104, 23–35

Snyder C.R., Higgins R.L. and Stucky R.J. (1983) EXCUSES: MASQUERADES IN SEARCH OF GRACE, Wiley/Interscience, NY

Snyder C.R., Lassegard M.A. and Ford C.E. (1986) Distancing after group success and failure: Basking in reflected glory and cutting off reflected failure. JOURNAL OF PERSONALITY AND SOCIAL PSYCHOLOGY, 51, 382–388

Snyder M. (1984) When beliefs create reality. In Berkowitz L. (ed.) ADVANCES IN EXPERIMENTAL SOCIAL PSYCHOLOGY (Vol. 18), Academic Press, NY

Snyder M. (1987) PUBLIC AND PRIVATE REALITIES: THE PSYCHOLOGY OF SELF-MONITORING, W. H. Freeman, NY

Snyder M. and Campbell B.H. (1980) Testing hypotheses about other people: The role of the hypothesis. PERSONALITY AND SOCIAL PSYCHOLOGY BULLETIN, 6, 421–426

Snyder M. and Gangestad S. (1981) Hypothesis-testing processes. In Harvey J.H., Ickes W. and Kidd R.F. (eds) NEW DIRECTIONS IN ATTRIBUTION RESEARCH (Vol. 3), Erlbaum, Hillsdale, NJ

Snyder M. and Ickes W. (1985) Personality and social behavior. In Lindzey G. and Aronson E. (eds) HANDBOOK OF SOCIAL PSYCHOLOGY (3rd. Ed), Random House, NY

Snyder M., Stephan W.G. and Rosenfield D. (1976) Egotism and attribution. JOURNAL OF PERSONALITY AND SOCIAL PSYCHOLOGY, 33, 434–441

Snyder M. and Swann W.B. (1976) When actions reflect attitudes: The politics of impression management. JOURNAL OF PERSONALITY AND SOCIAL PSYCHOLOGY, 34, 1034–1042

Snyder M. and Swann W.B. (1978a) Behavioral confirmation in social interaction: From social perception to social reality. JOURNAL OF EXPERIMENTAL SOCIAL PSYCHOLOGY, 14, 148–162

Snyder M. and Swann W.B. (1978b) Hypothesis-testing processes in social interaction. JOURNAL OF PERSONALITY AND SOCIAL PSYCHOLOGY, 36, 1202–1212

Solano C.H., Batten, P.G. and Parish E.A. (1982) Loneliness and patterns of self-disclosure. JOURNAL OF PERSONALITY AND SOCIAL PSYCHOLOGY, 43, 524–531

Solem P.E. (1978) Paid work after retirement age and mortality. AGEING INTERNATIONAL, 2, 20

Sommer R. (1966) The ecology of privacy. LIBRARY QUARTERLY, 36, 234–248

Sommer R. (1969) PERSONAL SPACE: THE BEHAVIORAL BASIS OF DESIGN, Prentice Hall, NJ

Sommer R. (1976) SOCIAL DESIGN: CREATING BUILDINGS WITH PEOPLE IN MIND, Prentice Hall, NJ

Sommer R. and Becker F.D. (1969) Territorial defense and the good neighbor. JOURNAL OF PERSONALITY AND SOCIAL PSYCHOLOGY, 11, 85–92

Sommers P. and Moos R. (1976) The weather and human behavior. In Moos R. (ed.) THE HUMAN CONTEXT: ENVIRONMENTAL DETERMINANTS OF BEHAVIOR, Wiley, NY

Sorrentino R.M. and Field N. (1986) Emergent leadership over time: The fundamental value of positive motivation. JOURNAL OF PERSONALITY AND SOCIAL PSYCHOLOGY, 50, 1091–1099

Sorrentino, R.M. and Rushton, J.P. (1981), Altruism and helping behavior: Current perspectives and future possibilities. In Rushton J.P. and Sorrentino R.M. (eds) ALTRUISM AND HELPING BEHAVIOR, Erlbaum, Hillsdale, NJ

Souetre E., Wehr T.A., Douillet P. and Darcourt G. (1990) Influence of environmental factors on suicidal behavior. PSYCHIATRY RESEARCH, 32, 253–263

South S.J. and Trent K. (1988) Sex ratios and women's roles: A cross-national analysis. AMERICAN JOURNAL OF SOCIOLOGY, 93, 1096–1115

Spence S.H. (1988) The role of social-cognitive skills in the determination of children's social competence. BEHAVIOR CHANGE, 5, 9–18

Spencer H. (1862) FIRST PRINCIPLES OF A NEW SYSTEM OF PHILOSOPHY, reprinted by the DeWitt Revolving Fund, NY (1958)

Spillane R.M. (1980) Generalising American locus of control norms to Australian populations: Managerial data. AUSTRALIAN PSYCHOLOGIST, 15, 497–499

Spinoza B. (1677) ETHICS, Reprinted in Britannica Great Books, (Vol. 31), (1952), Encyclopedia Britannica, Chicago

Sprecher S. (1986) The relationship between inequity and emotions in close relationships. SOCIAL PSYCHOLOGY QUARTERLY, 49, 309–321

Sprecher S. (1988) Investment model, equity and social support determinants of relationship commitment. SOCIAL PSYCHOLOGY QUARTERLY, 51, 318–328

Srull T.K. (1981) Person memory: Some tests of associative storage and retrieval models.

JOURNAL OF EXPERIMENTAL PSYCHOLOGY: HUMAN LEARNING AND MEMORY, 7, 440–463

Srull T.K. (1983) Organizational and retrieval processes in person memory: An examination of processing objectives, presentation format, and the possible role of self-generated retrieval cues. JOURNAL OF PERSONALITY AND SOCIAL PSYCHOLOGY, 44, 1157–1170

Stangor C., Lynch C., Duan C. and Glas B. (1992) Categorisation of individuals on the basis of multiple social features. JOURNAL OF PERSONALITY AND SOCIAL PSYCHOLOGY, 62, 207–218

Startup M.J. and Russell R.J. (1985) Lunar effects on personality tests scores: A failure to replicate. PERSONALITY AND INDIVIDUAL DIFFERENCES, 6, 267–269

Staub E. (1974) Helping a distressed person: Social, personality, and stimulus determinants. In Berkowitz L. (ed.) ADVANCES IN EXPERIMENTAL SOCIAL PSYCHOLOGY (Vol. 7), Academic Press, NY

Steblay N.M. (1987) Helping behavior in rural and urban environments: A meta analysis. PSYCHOLOGICAL BULLETIN, 102, 346–356

Steele C.M. (1988) The psychology of self-affirmation: Sustaining the integrity of the self. In Berkowitz L. (ed.) ADVANCES IN EXPERIMENTAL SOCIAL PSYCHOLOGY (Vol. 21), Academic Press, Orlando, Florida

Steele C.M. and Lui T.J. (1981) Making the dissonance act unreflective of self: Dissonance avoidance and the expectancy of a value-affirming response. PERSONALITY AND SOCIAL PSYCHOLOGY BULLETIN, 7, 393–397

Steele C.M. and Lui T.J. (1983) Dissonance process as self-affirmation. JOURNAL OF PERSONALITY AND SOCIAL PSYCHOLOGY, 45, 5–19

Steele C.M., Southwick L.L. and Critchlow B. (1981) Dissonance and alcohol: Drinking your troubles away. JOURNAL OF PERSONALITY AND SOCIAL PSYCHOLOGY, 45, 831–846

Steinman R. (1990) Social exchanges between older and younger gay male partners. JOURNAL OF HOMOSEXUALITY, 20, 179–206

Stephan C.W. and Langlois J.H. (1984) Baby beautiful: Adult attributions of infant competence as a function of infant attractiveness. CHILD DEVELOPMENT, 55, 576–585

Stephan W.G. (1987) The contact hypothesis in intergroup relations. In Hendrick C. (ed.) GROUP PROCESSES AND INTERGROUP RELATIONS, Sage, Newbury Park, Ca.

Stephan W.G., Berscheid E. and Walster E. (1971) Sexual arousal and heterosexual perception. JOURNAL OF PERSONALITY AND SOCIAL PSYCHOLOGY, 20, 93–101

Stephenson P. and Smith D. (1989) Bullying in the junior schools. In Tattum D.P. and Lane D.A. (eds) BULLYING IN SCHOOLS, Trentham Books, Stoke-on Trent, UK

Sterling B. and Gaertner S.L. (1984) The attribution of arousal and emergency helping: A bidirectional process. JOURNAL OF EXPERIMENTAL SOCIAL PSYCHOLOGY, 20, 586–596

Stern D. (1985) THE INTERPERSONAL WORLD OF THE INFANT: A VIEW FROM PSYCHOANALYSIS AND DEVELOPMENTAL PSYCHOLOGY, Basic Books, NY

Stern M. and Karraker K.H. (1989) Sex stereotyping of infants: A review of gender labeling studies. SEX ROLES, 20, 501–522

Stern P.C., Deitz T. and Black J.S. (1986) Support for environmental protection: The role of moral norms. POPULATION AND ENVIRONMENT, 8, 204–222

Stern P.C. and Gardner G.T. (1981) Psychological research and energy policy. AMERICAN PSYCHOLOGIST, 4, 329–342

Stern P.C. and Oskamp S. (1987) Managing scarce environmental resources. In Stokols D. and Altman I. (eds) HANDBOOK OF ENVIRONMENTAL PSYCHOLOGY, Wiley-Interscience, NY

Sternberg R.J. (1986) A triangular theory of love. PSYCHOLOGICAL REVIEW, 93, 119–135

Sternberg R.J. (1988) Triangulating love. In Sternberg R.J. and Barnes M.J. (eds) THE PSYCHOLOGY OF LOVE, Yale University Press, New Haven, Conn.

Sternberg R.J. and Barnes M.L. (1985) Real and ideal others in romantic relationships: Is four a crowd? JOURNAL OF PERSONALITY AND SOCIAL PSYCHOLOGY, 49, 1586–1608

Stevenson-Hinde J., Hinde R.A. and Simpson A.E. (1986) Behavior at home and friendly or hostile behavior in preschool. In Olweus D., Block J. and Radke-Yarrow M. (eds) DEVELOPMENT OF ANTISOCIAL AND PROSOCIAL BEHAVIOR: RESEARCH THEORIES AND ISSUES, Academic Press, Orlando, Florida

Stewart R.B. and Cluff L.F. (1973) Medication errors and compliance reviewed. CURRENT THERAPEUTICS, 14, 551

Stimson G.V. (1974) Obeying doctors orders: A view from the other side. SOCIAL SCIENCE AND MEDICINE, 8, 97–104

Stimson G.V. and Webb B. (1975) GOING TO SEE THE DOCTOR, Routledge, Kegan Paul, Lond.

Stockard J., Van-de-Kragt A.J. and Dodge P.J. (1988) Gender roles and behavior in social dilemmas: Are there sex differences in cooperation and in its justification? SOCIAL PSYCHOLOGY QUARTERLY, 51, 154–163

Stokes J.P. (1985) The relation of social network and individual difference variables to loneliness. JOURNAL OF

PERSONALITY AND SOCIAL PSYCHOLOGY, 48, 981–990

Stokols D. (1972) On the distinction between density and crowding: Some implications for future research. PSYCHOLOGICAL REVIEW, 79, 275–278

Stokols D. (1976) The experience of crowding in primary and secondary environments. ENVIRONMENT AND BEHAVIOR, 8, 49–86

Stokols D. and Altman I. (eds) (1987) HANDBOOK OF ENVIRONMENTAL PSYCHOLOGY, Wiley-Interscience, NY

Stone W.F., Lederer G. and Christie R. (eds) (1992) STRENGTH AND WEAKNESS: THE AUTHORITARIAN PERSONAL-ITY TODAY, Springer-Verlag, NY

Stoner J.A. (1961) A comparison of individual and group decision involving risk. Unpublished dissertation, M.I.T., Cambridge, Ma.

Storms M.D. (1973) Videotape and the attribution process: Reversing actors' and observers points of view JOURNAL OF PERSONALITY AND SOCIAL PSYCHOLOGY, 27, 165–175

Storms M.D. and Nisbett R.E. (1970) Insomnia and the attribution process. JOURNAL OF PERSONALITY AND SOCIAL PSYCHOLOGY, 16, 319–328

Straus M.A., Gelles R.J. and Steinmetz S.K. (1980) BEHIND CLOSED DOORS: VIOLENCE IN THE AMERICAN FAMILY, Doubleday, NY

Straus R. (1984) The need to drink too much, JOURNAL OF DRUG ISSUES, 14, 125–136

Strayer J. and Roberts W. (1989) Children's empathy and role-taking: Child and parental factors, and relations to prosocial behavior. JOURNAL OF APPLIED DEVELOPMEN-TAL PSYCHOLOGY, 10, 227–239

Strickland B.R. (1988) Internal-external expectancies and health-related behaviors. JOURNAL OF CONSULTING AND CLINICAL PSYCHOLOGY, 46, 1192–1211

Strickland B.R. (1989) Internal-external control expectancies: From contingency to creativity. AMERICAN PSYCHOLOGIST, 44, 1–12

Strong S.R., et al. (1988) The dynamic relations among interpersonal behaviors: A test of complementarity and anti-complementarity. JOURNAL OF PERSONALITY AND SOCIAL PSYCHOLOGY, 54, 798–810

Strongman K.T. (1982) Emotional influences on memory. CURRENT PSYCHOLOGI-CAL RESEARCH, 2, 69–74

Strongman K.T. and Russell P.N. (1986) Salience of emotion in recall. BULLETIN OF THE PSYCHONOMIC SOCIETY, 24, 25–27

Strube M.J. and Roemmele L.A. (1985) Self-enhancement, self-assessment, and self-evaluative task choice. JOURNAL OF PERSONALITY AND SOCIAL PSYCHOLOGY, 49, 981–993

Stryker S. (1977) Developments in two social psychologies. SOCIOMETRY, 40, 145–160

Stryker S. (1989) The two psychologies: Additional thoughts. SOCIAL FORCES, 68, 45–54

Stubbs J. and Powell D. (1989) DOMESTIC VIOLENCE: IMPACT OF THE LEGAL REFORM IN NSW, NSW Bureau of Crime Statistics and Research, Sydney

Stumpf W.E. and Privette T.H. (1989) Light, vitamin D and psychiatry: Role of 1,25 dihydroxyvitamin D-sub-3 (soltriol) in etiology and therapy of seasonal affective disorder and other mental processes. PSYCHOPHARMACOLOGY, 97, 285–294

Sudnow D. (1967) Dead on arrival. TRANS-ACTION, 5, 36–44

Suedfeld P. (1982) Aloneness as a healing experience. In Peplau L.A. and Perlman D. (eds) LONELINESS: A SOURCEBOOK OF CURRENT THEORY, RESEARCH AND THERAPY, Wiley, NY

Suls J.M. and Miller R.L. (eds) (1977) SOCIAL COMPARISON PROCESSES: THEORETICAL AND EMPIRICAL PERSPECTIVES, Halsted-Wiley, Washington DC

Suls J.M and Wan C.K. (1987) In search of the false uniqueness phenomenon: Fear and estimates of social consensus. JOURNAL OF PERSONALITY AND SOCIAL PSYCHOLOGY, 52, 211–217

Sundstrom E. (1978) Crowding as a sequential process: Review of research on the effects of population density on humans. In Baum A. and Epstein Y. (eds) HUMAN RESPONSE TO CROWDING, Erlbaum, Hillsdale, NJ

Sundstrom E. (1986) WORK PLACES: THE PSYCHOLOGY OF THE PHYSICAL ENVIRONMENT IN OFFICES AND FACTORIES, Cambridge University Press, NY

Sundstrom E. (1988) Interpersonal behavior and the physical environment. Invited chapter in Deaux K. and Wrightsman L.S. SOCIAL PSYCHOLOGY, (5th edn) Brooks/Cole, Ca.

Sundstrom E., Burt R. and Kamp D. (1980) Privacy at work: Architectural correlates of job satisfaction and job performance. ACADEMY OF MANAGEMENT JOURNAL, 23, 101–117

Sundstrom E., Herbert R.K. and Brown D. (1982) Privacy and communication in an open plan office: A case study. ENVIRON-MENT AND BEHAVIOR, 14, 379–392

Sundstrom E. and Sundstrom M.G. (1977) Personal space invasions: What happens when the invader asks permission? ENVIRONMENTAL PSYCHOLOGY AND NONVERBAL BEHAVIOR, 2, 76–82

Sundstrom E., Town J., Brown D., Forman A. and McGee C. (1982) Physical enclosure, type of job, and privacy in the office. ENVIRONMENT AND BEHAVIOR, 14, 543–559

Sutherland E. (1966) PRINCIPLES OF

CRIMINOLOGY, J.B. Lippincott, Philadelphia, Pa.

Sutton J.E. (1991) Violence against children: The crime in context in investigation and management of child abuse. SPECIALIST COURSE STUDY GUIDE, NSW Police Academy Publications, Goulburn, NSW

Sutton J.E. (1991) Violence against children: Denial and secrecy. In THE INVESTIGA-TION OF CRIMES AGAINST THE PERSON: THEORY AND PRACTICE, NSW Police Academy Publications, Goulburn, NSW

Sutton J.E. (1991) Sexual assault: The silent scream. In THE INVESTIGATION OF CRIMES AGAINST THE PERSON: THEORY AND PRACTICE, NSW. Police Academy Publications, Goulburn, NSW

Sutton J.E. (1991) Domestic violence in context. In THE INVESTIGATION OF CRIMES AGAINST THE PERSON: THEORY AND PRACTICE, NSW. Police Academy, Goulburn, NSW

Sutton J.E. (1992) Women in the job. In Moir P.G. and Eichmann H.S. (eds) POLICING AUSTRALIA: OLD ISSUES, NEW PERSPECTIVES, MacMillan, Melbourne

Sutton J.S. and Hatty S. (1988) POLICE INTERVENTION IN DOMESTIC VIOLENCE IN NSW, Report prepared for NSW Police Service and the National Police Research Unit, Adelaide, South Australia

Swann W.B. (1990) To be known or to be adored? The interplay of self-enhancement and self-verification. In Sorrentino R.M. and Higgins E.T. (eds) HANDBOOK OF MOTIVATION AND COGNITION: FOUNDATIONS OF SOCIAL BEHAVIOR (Vol. 2) Guilford Press, NY

Swann W.B. and Ely R.M. (1984) The battle of the wills: Self-verification versus behavioral confirmation. JOURNAL OF PERSONALITY AND SOCIAL PSYCHOLOGY, 46, 1287–1302

Swann W.B., Griffin J.J., Predmore S. and Gaines B. (1987) The cognitive-affective crossfire: When self-consistency confronts self-enhancement. JOURNAL OF PERSONALITY AND SOCIAL PSYCHOLOGY, 52, 881–889

Swann W.B., Pelham B.W. and Krull D.S. (1989) Agreeable fancy or disagreeable truth? Reconciling self-enhancement and self-verification. JOURNAL OF PERSON-ALITY AND SOCIAL PSYCHOLOGY, 57, 782–791

Swann W.B. and Read S.J. (1981) Self-verification processes: How we sustain our self-conceptions. JOURNAL OF EXPERIMENTAL SOCIAL PSYCHOL-OGY, 17, 351–372

Swap W.C. (1977) Interpersonal attraction and repeated exposure to rewarders and punishers. PERSONALITY AND SOCIAL PSYCHOLOGY BULLETIN, 3, 248–251

Sweeney P.D., Anderson K. and Bailey S. (1986) Attribution style in depression: A meta analytic review. JOURNAL OF

PERSONALITY AND SOCIAL PSYCHOLOGY, 50, 974–991

Sydney Rape Crisis Centre (1990) Surviving rape: A handbook to help women become aware of the reality of rape (2nd edn), Redfern Legal Centre Publishing Ltd, Sydney

Syme L.A. (1973) Social isolation at weaning: Some effects on two measures of activity. ANIMAL LEARNING AND BEHAVIOR, 1, 161–163

Symonds M. (1975) Victims of violence: Psychological effects and aftereffects. AMERICAN JOURNAL OF PSYCHOA-NALYSIS, 35, 19–26

Symons D. (1989) Comments on distinctions among reciprocal altruism, kin selection and cooperation and a model for the initial evolution of beneficent behavior. ETHOLOGY AND SOCIOBIOLOGY, 10, 449–451

Szwajkowski E. (1989) Lessons for the consultant from research on employee misconduct. CONSULTATION AN INTERNATIONAL JOURNAL, 8, 181–190

Taft R., Dawson J.L. and Beasley P. (eds) (1970) ATTITUDES AND SOCIAL CONDI-TIONS, Australian National University Press, Canberra

Tajfel H. (1970) Experiments in intergroup discrimination. SCIENTIFIC AMERICAN, 223, 96–102

Tajfel H. (1972) Experiments in a vacuum. In Israel J. and Tajfel H. (eds) THE CONTEXT OF SOCIAL PSYCHOLOGY: A CRITICAL ASSESSMENT, Academic Press, Lond.

Tajfel H. (ed.) (1978) DIFFERENTIATION BETWEEN SOCIAL GROUPS: STUDIES IN THE SOCIAL PSYCHOLOGY OF INTER-GROUP RELATIONS, Academic Press, NY

Tajfel H. (ed.) (1982) SOCIAL IDENTITY AND INTERGROUP RELATIONS, Cambridge University Press, Cambridge

Tajfel H., Flament C., Bilig M.G. and Bundy F.F. (1971) Social categorization and intergroup behavior. EUROPEAN JOURNAL OF SOCIAL PSYCHOLOGY, 1, 149–177

Tajfel H. and Turner J.C. (1979) An integrative theory of intergroup conflict. In Austin W.G. and Worchel S. (eds) THE SOCIAL PSYCHOLOGY OF INTERGROUP RELATIONS, Brooks/Cole, Monterey, Ca.

Tajfel H. and Turner J.C. (1986) The social identity theory of intergroup behavior. In Worchel S. and Austin W.G. (eds) THE PSYCHOLOGY OF INTERGROUP RELATIONS (2nd edn), Nelson Hall, Chicago

Tanford S. and Penrod S. (1983) Computer modelling of influence in the jury: The role of the consistent juror. SOCIAL PSYCHOLOGY QUARTERLY, 46, 200–212

Tanford S. and Penrod S. (1984) Social

influence model: A formal integration of research on majority and minority influence processes. PSYCHOLOGICAL BULLETIN, 95, 189–225

Tarde G (1898) ETUDES DE PSYCHOLOGIE SOCIALE (STUDIES ON SOCIAL PSYCHOLOGY), Giard and Briere, Paris

Tasso J. and Miller E. (1976) The effects of the full moon on human behavior. JOURNAL OF PSYCHOLOGY, 93, 81–83

Taylor A.J. (1989) Victims of crime as victims of disaster. AUSTRALIAN AND NEW ZEALAND JOURNAL OF PSYCHIATRY, 23, 403–406

Taylor A.J. and Duncum K. (1987) Some cognitive effects of wintering-over in the Antarctic. NEW ZEALAND JOURNAL OF PSYCHOLOGY, 16, 93–94

Taylor D.M. and Moghaddam F.M. (1987) THEORIES OF INTERGROUP RELA-TIONS: INTERNATIONAL SOCIAL PSYCHOLOGICAL PERSPECTIVE, Praeger, NY

Taylor J. and Riess M. (1989) "Self-serving" attributions to valenced causal factors: A field experiment. PERSONALITY AND SOCIAL PSYCHOLOGY BULLETIN, 15, 337–348

Taylor R.B. (1978) Human territoriality: A review and a model for future research. CORNELL JOURNAL OF SOCIAL RELATIONS, 13, 125–151

Taylor R.B. (1982) Neighborhood physical environment and stress. In Evans G.W. (ed.) ENVIRONMENTAL STRESS, Cambridge University Press, NY

Taylor S.E. (1981) A categorization approach to stereotyping. In Hamilton D.L. (ed.) COGNITIVE PROCESSES IN STERE-OTYPING AND INTERGROUP BEHAVIOR, Erlbaum, Hillsdale, NJ

Taylor S.E. and Brown J.D. (1988) Illusion and well-being: A social psychological perspective on mental health. PSYCHO-LOGICAL BULLETIN, 103, 193–210

Taylor S.E. and Crocker J. (1981) Schematic bases of social information processing. In Higgins E.T., Herman C. and Zanna M. (eds) SOCIAL COGNITION: THE ONTARIO SYMPOSIUM ON PERSON-ALITY AND SOCIAL PSYCHOLOGY, Erlbaum, Hillsdale, NJ

Taylor S.E. and Fiske S.T. (1975) Point of view and perceptions of causality. JOURNAL OF PERSONALITY AND SOCIAL PSYCHOLOGY, 32, 439–445

Taylor S.E., Fiske S.T., Etcoff N.L. and Ruderman A.J. (1978) Categorical and contextual bases of person memory and stereotyping. JOURNAL OF PERSONAL-ITY AND SOCIAL PSYCHOLOGY, 36, 778–793

Taylor S.E. and Koivumaki J.H. (1976) The perception of self and others: Acquaintance-ship, affect and actor-observer differences. JOURNAL OF PERSONALITY AND SOCIAL PSYCHOLOGY, 33, 403–408

Taylor S.P., Gammon C.B. and Capasso D.R. (1976) Aggression as a function of the interaction of alcohol and frustration. JOURNAL OF PERSONALITY AND SOCIAL PSYCHOLOGY, 34, 938–941

Tedeschi J.T. (ed.) (1981) IMPRESSION MANAGEMENT THEORY AND SOCIAL PSYCHOLOGICAL RESEARCH, Academic Press, NY

Tedeschi J.T., Lindskold S. and Rosenfeld P. (1985) INTRODUCTION TO SOCIAL PSYCHOLOGY, West Publishing Co., NY

Tedeschi J.T., Schlenker B.R. and Bonoma T.V. (1971) Cognitive dissonance: Private rationalization or public spectacle? AMERICAN PSYCHOLOGIST, 26, 685–695

Templer D.I., Brooner R.K. and Corgiat M.D. (1983) Geophysical variables and behavior: XIV. Lunar phase and crime: Fact or artifact. PERCEPTUAL AND MOTOR SKILLS, 57, 993–994

Templer D.I., Veleber D.M. and Brooner R.K. (1982) Geophysical variables and behavior: VI. Lunar phase and accident injuries: A difference between night and day. PERCEPTUAL AND MOTOR SKILLS, 55, 280–282

Tesser A. (1988) Toward a self-evaluation maintenance model of social behavior. In Berkowitz L. (ed.) ADVANCES IN EXPERIMENTAL SOCIAL PSYCHOLOGY, Academic Press, NY

Tesser A., Millar M. and Moore J. (1988) Some affective consequences of social comparison and reflection processes: The pain and pleasure of being close. JOURNAL OF PERSONALITY AND SOCIAL PSYCHOLOGY, 54, 49–61

Tesser A. and Shaffer D.R. (1990) Attitudes and attitude change. ANNUAL REVIEW OF PSYCHOLOGY, 41, 479–523

Tetlock P.E. and Manstead A.S. (1985) Impression management versus intrapsychic explanations in social psychology: A useful dichotomy? PSYCHOLOGICAL REVIEW, 92, 59–77

Thannhauser D. and Caird D. (1990) Politics and values in Australia: Testing Rokeach's two-value model of politics: A research note. AUSTRALIAN JOURNAL OF PSYCHOLOGY, 42, 57–61

Thayer S. and Saarni C. (1975) Demand characteristics are everywhere (anyway): A comment on the Stanford Prison Experiment. AMERICAN PSYCHOLOGIST, 30, 1015–1016

Thibaut J.W. and Kelley H.H. (1959) THE SOCIAL PSYCHOLOGY OF GROUPS, Wiley, NY

Thibaut J.W. and Walker L. (1975) PROCEDURAL JUSTICE: A PSYCHOLOGICAL ANALYSIS, Erlbaum, Hillsdale, NJ

Thomas D.R. (1974) The relationship between ethnocentrism and conservatism in an "authoritarian" culture. JOURNAL OF SOCIAL PSYCHOLOGY, 94, 179–186

Thomas D.R. (1987) Authoritarianism and child-rearing practices. AUSTRALIAN PSYCHOLOGIST, 22, 197–201

Thompson D.W. (1910) TRANSLATION OF ARISTOTLE'S HISTORIA ANIMALIUM, Oxford University Press, Lond.

Thompson J. (1989) Assessment of family interactions using Heider's balance theory. JOURNAL OF HUMAN BEHAVIOR AND LEARNING, 6, 62–70

Thompson R.A. and Hoffman M.L. (1980) Empathy and the development of guilt in children. DEVELOPMENTAL PSYCHOLOGY 16, 155–156

Thompson S.C. and Kelley H.H. (1981) Judgements of responsibility for activities in close relationships. JOURNAL OF PERSONALITY AND SOCIAL PSYCHOLOGY, 41, 469–477

Thornton B., Hogate L., Moirs K., et al. (1986) Physiological evidence of an arousal-based motivational bias in the defensive attribution of responsibility. JOURNAL OF EXPERIMENTAL SOCIAL PSYCHOLOGY, 22, 148–162

Thornton M. (1986) The equality principle and the sexual division of labour. WOMEN'S STUDIES INTERNATIONAL FORUM, 9, 13–18.

Thornton M. (1989) Hegemonic masculinity and the academy. INTERNATIONAL JOURNAL OF THE SOCIOLOGY OF LAW, 17, 115–130

Thornton M. (1991) Portia lost in the graves of academe, wondering what to do about legal education. THE AUSTRALIAN UNIVERSITIES REVIEW, 34, 26

Thurstone L.L. (1928) Attitudes can be measured. AMERICAN JOURNAL OF SOCIOLOGY, 35, 529–554

Tice D.M. and Baumeister R.F. (1985) Masculinity inhibits helping in emergencies: Personality does predict bystander effect on altruism. JOURNAL OF PERSONALITY AND SOCIAL PSYCHOLOGY, 40, 420–428

Tice D.M. and Baumeister R.F. (1990) Self-esteem, self-handicapping, and self-presentation: The strategy of inadequate practice. JOURNAL OF PERSONALITY, 58, 443–464

Tiggemann M. (1992) Body-size dissatisfaction: Individual differences in age and gender, and relationship with self-esteem. PERSONALITY AND INDIVIDUAL DIFFERENCES, 13, 39–43

Tiggemann M. and Winefield A.H. (1984) The effects of employment on mood, self-esteem, locus of control and depressive affect of school leavers. JOURNAL OF OCCUPATIONAL PSYCHOLOGY, 57, 33–42

Tindall B. and Tillett G. (1990) HIV-related discrimination. AIDS, 4, 251–256

Titchener J. and Kapp F.I. (1976) Family and character change at Buffalo Creek. AMERICAN JOURNAL OF PSYCHIATRY, 133, 295–299

Tobacyk J.J. and Wilson J.E. (1988) Paranormal beliefs and beliefs about lunar effects. PSYCHOLOGICAL REPORTS, 63, 993–994

Tooley V., Brigham J.C., Maass A. and Bothwell R.K. (1987) Facial recognition: Weapon effect and attentional focus. JOURNAL OF APPLIED SOCIAL PSYCHOLOGY, 17, 845–859

Touhey J.C. (1972) Comparison of two dimensions of attitude similarity on heterosexual attraction. JOURNAL OF PERSONALITY AND SOCIAL PSYCHOLOGY, 23, 8–10

Towler J. and Swan J.E. (1972) What do people really know about pollution? JOURNAL OF ENVIRONMENTAL EDUCATION, 4, 54–57

Traupmann J. and Hatfield E. (1981) Love and its effect on mental and physical health. In Fogel R., Hatfield E., Kiesler S. and Shanas E. (eds) AGING: STABILITY AND CHANGE IN THE FAMILY, Academic Press, NY

Triandis H.C. (1989) A strategy for cross cultural research in social psychology. In Forgas J.P. and Innes J.M. (eds) RECENT ADVANCES IN SOCIAL PSYCHOLOGY: AN INTERNATIONAL PERSPECTIVE, Elsevier, North-Holland

Trice A.D. and Ogden E.P. (1987) Informed consent: IX. Effects of the withdrawal clause in longitudinal research. PERCEPTUAL AND MOTOR SKILLS, 65, 135–138

Triplett N. (1898) The dynamogenic factors in pacemaking and competition. AMERICAN JOURNAL OF PSYCHOLOGY, 9, 507–533

Trivers R.L. (1971) The evolution of reciprocal altruism. QUARTERLY REVIEW OF BIOLOGY, 46, 35–57

Trivers R.L. (1983) The evolution of cooperation. In D.L. Bridgeman (ed.) THE NATURE OF PROSOCIAL DEVELOPMENT, Academic Press, NY

Trivers R.L. (1985) SOCIAL EVOLUTION, Benjamin-Cummings, Menlo Park, Ca.

Tromp S.W. (1980) BIOMETEOROLOGY: THE IMPACT OF WEATHER AND CLIMATE ON HUMANS AND THEIR ENVIRONMENT, Hyden, Philadelphia, Pa.

Trope Y. and Bassok M. (1982) Confirmatory and diagnosing strategies in social information gathering. JOURNAL OF PERSONALITY AND SOCIAL PSYCHOLOGY, 43, 22–34

Trope Y., Cohen O. and Moaz Y. (1988) The perceptual and inferential effects of situational inducements on dispositional attribution. JOURNAL OF PERSONALITY AND SOCIAL PSYCHOLOGY, 55, 165–177

Trope Y. and Mackie D.M. (1987) Sensitivity to alternatives in social hypothesis-testing. JOURNAL OF EXPERIMENTAL SOCIAL PSYCHOLOGY, 23, 445–459

Tucker R.K. and Byers P.Y. (1987) Factorial validity of Merzs Psychological Reactance Scale. PSYCHOLOGICAL REPORTS, 61, 811–815

Tuckman B.W. and Jensen M.A. (1977) Stages of small group development revisited. GROUP AND ORGANISATIONAL STUDIES, 2, 419–427.

Turk J. and Turk A. (1988) ENVIRONMEN-TAL SCIENCE (4th edn), Saunders, NY

Turner J.C. (1978) Social categorization and social discrimination in minimal group situation. In Tajfel H. (ed.) DIFFERENTIA-TION BETWEEN SOCIAL GROUPS, Academic Press, Lond.

Turner J.C. (1981) The experimental social psychology of intergroup behavior. In Turner J.C. and Giles H. (eds) INTERGROUP BEHAVIOR, Blackwell, Oxford

Turner J.C. (1982) Toward a cognitive redefinition of the social group. In Tajfel H. (ed.) SOCIAL IDENTITY AND INTERGROUP RELATIONS, Cambridge University Press, Cambridge

Turner J.C. (1985) Social categorisation and the self-concept: A social-cognitive theory of group behavior. In Lawler J.E. (ed.) ADVANCES IN GROUP PROCESSES (Vol. 2), JAI Press, Greenwich, UK

Turner J.C. (1987) REDISCOVERING THE SOCIAL GROUP: a SELF-CATEGORIZATION THEORY, Basil Blackwell, NY

Turner J.C. (1991) SOCIAL INFLUENCE, Open University Press, Milton Keynes, UK

Turner J.C. and Giles H. (eds) (1981) INTERGROUP BEHAVIOUR, Blackwell, Oxford

Turner J.C., Hogg M.A., Oakes P.J., Reicher S.D. and Wetherell M.S. (1987) REDISCOVERING THE SOCIAL GROUP: A SELF-CATEGORIZATION THEORY, Blackwell, Oxford

Turner J.C. and Oakes P.J. (1986) The significance of the social identity concept for social psychology with reference to individuation, interactionism and social influence. BRITISH JOURNAL OF SOCIAL PSYCHOLOGY, 25, 237–252

Turner J.C. Wetherell M.S. and Hogg M.A. (1989) Referent informational influence and group polarization. BRITISH JOURNAL OF SOCIAL PSYCHOLOGY, 28, 135–147

Turner R.H. (1975) Is there a quest for identity? SOCIOLOGICAL QUARTERLY, 16, 148–161

Turtle A.M. (1987) Psychology in the Australian context. In Blowers G.H. and Turtle A.M. (eds) PSYCHOLOGY MOVING EAST: THE STATUS OF WESTERN PSYCHOLOGY IN ASIA AND OCEANIA, Sydney University Press, Sydney

Tversky A. and Kahneman D. (1973) Availability: A heuristic for judging frequency and probability. COGNITIVE PSYCHOLOGY, 5, 207–232

Tversky A. and Kahneman D. (1974) Judgments under uncertainty: Heuristics and Biases. SCIENCE, 185, 1124–1131

Tversky A. and Kahneman D. (1982) Judgment under uncertainty: Heuristics and Biases. In Kahneman D., Slovic P. and Tversky A. (eds) JUDGMENT UNDER UNCER-TAINTY: HEURISTICS AND BIASES, Cambridge University Press, NY

Tversky A. and Kahneman D. (1983) Extensional versus intuitive reasoning: The conjunction fallacy in probability judgement. PSYCHOLOGICAL REVIEW, 90, 293–315

Tversky B. and Tuchin M. (1989) A reconcilia-tion of the evidence on eyewitness testimony: Comments on McCloskey and Zaragoza. JOURNAL OF EXPERIMENTAL PSYCHOLOGY, 118, 86–91

Tyler T.R., and Sears D.O. (1977) Coming to like obnoxious people when we must live with them. JOURNAL OF PERSONALITY AND SOCIAL PSYCHOLOGY, 15, 200–211

Underwood B. and Moore B. (1982) Perspec-tive-taking and altruism. PSYCHOLOGI-CAL BULLETIN, 91, 143–173

Valins S. (1966) Cognitive effects of false heart-rate feedback. JOURNAL OF PERSONALITY AND SOCIAL PSYCHOLOGY, 4, 400–408

Valins S. (1970) The perception and labeling of bodily changes as determinants of emotional behavior. In Black P. (ed.) PHYSIOLOGI-CAL CORRELATES OF EMOTION, Academic Press, NY

Vallerand R.J., Deshaies P., Cuerrier J-P., Pelletier L.G. and Mongeau C. (1992) Ajzen and Fishbein's theory of reasoned action as applied to moral behavior: A confirmatory analysis. JOURNAL OF PERSONALITY AND SOCIAL PSYCHOLOGY, 62, 98–109

Vanbeselaere N. (1987) The effects of dichotomous and crossed social categoriza-tion upon intergroup discrimination. EUROPEAN JOURNAL OF SOCIAL PSYCHOLOGY, 17, 143–156

Van der Pligt J. (1984) Attributions, false concensus, and valence: Two field studies. JOURNAL OF PERSONALITY AND SOCIAL PSYCHOLOGY, 46, 57–68

Van Fossen T. (1988) How do movements survive failures of prophecy? RESEARCH IN SOCIAL MOVEMENTS, CONFLICT AND CHANGE, 10, 193–212.

Van Maanen J. (1972) Working the street: A developmental view of police behavior. In Jacob J. (ed.), THE POTENTIAL FOR REFORMS OF CRIMINAL JUSTICE, Sage, Beverly Hills, Ca.

Van Maanen J. (1985) Observations on the making of policemen. In Blumberg A.S. and Niederhoffer E. (eds) THE AMBIVALENT FORCE (3rd edn), Holt Rinehart and Winston, NY

Van-Yperen N. and Buunk B.P. (1990) A longitudinal study of equity and satisfaction in intimate relationships. EUROPEAN JOURNAL OF SOCIAL PSYCHOLOGY, 20, 287–309

Vaughan G.M. (1963) Concept formation and the development of ethnic awareness. JOURNAL OF GENETIC PSYCHOLOGY, 103, 93–103

Vaughan G.M. (1964) The development of ethnic attitudes in New Zealand school children. GENETIC PSYCHOLOGY MONOGRAPHS, 70, 135–175

Vaughan G.M. (1978) Social change and intergroup preferences in New Zealand. EUROPEAN JOURNAL OF SOCIAL PSYCHOLOGY, 8, 297–314

Vaughan G.M. (1986) Social change and racial identity: Issues in the use of picture and doll measures. Special Issue: Contributions to cross-cultural psychology. AUSTRALIAN JOURNAL OF PSYCHOLOGY, 38, 359–370

Vaughan G.M. (1988) The psychology of intergroup discrimination. NEW ZEALAND JOURNAL OF PSYCHOLOGY, 17, 1–14

Veitch R. and Griffitt W. (1976) Good news, bad news: Affective and interpersonal effects. JOURNAL OF APPLIED SOCIAL PSYCHOLOGY, 6, 69–75

Veno A. (1976) Response to approach: A preliminary process oriented study of human spacing. SOCIAL SCIENCE INFORMATION, 15, 93–115

Ventimiglia J.C. (1982) Sex roles and chivalry: Some conditions of gratitude to altruism. SEX ROLES, 8, 1107–1122

Verdieck M.J., Shields J.J. and Hoge D.R. (1988) Role commitment processes revisited: American Catholic priests 1970 and 1985. JOURNAL FOR THE SCIEN-TIFIC STUDY OF RELIGION, 27, 524–535

Vinacke W.E., Mogy R., et al. (1974) Accommodative strategy and communica-tion in a three person matrix game. JOURNAL OF PERSONALITY AND SOCIAL PSYCHOLOGY, 29, 509–525

Vining J. and Ebreo A. (1990) What makes a recycler?: A comparison of recyclers and non recyclers. ENVIRONMENT AND BEHAVIOR, 22, 55–73

Violante J.M. (1982) Police stress: A conceptual definition. POLICE STRESS, February, 22–23

Von Neumann J. and Morgenstern O. (1944) THEORY OF GAMES AND ECONOMIC BEHAVIOR, Princeton University Press, NJ

Voyce M. (1991) Women and the acquisition of property. Paper presented at the Interna-tional Law and Society Conference, June, Amsterdam

Waber D.P. (1977) Sex differences in mental abilities, hemispheric lateralization and rate of physical growth at adolescence. DEVELOPMENTAL PSYCHOLOGY, 13, 29–38

Wagner M.W. and Almeida L. (1987) Geophysical variables and behavior: XXXVII. Lunar phase, "no;" weekend, "yes;" month, "sometimes." PERCEPTUAL AND MOTOR SKILLS, 64, 949–950

Wagner U., Hewstone M. and Machleit U. (1989) Contact and prejudice between Germans and Turks: A correlational study. HUMAN RELATIONS, 42, 561–574

Wakil S.P (1973) Campus mate selection preferences: A cross-national comparison. SOCIAL FORCES, 51, 471–476

Walker C., Bonner B. and Kaufman K. (1988) THE PHYSICALLY AND SEXUALLY ABUSED CHILD, Pergamon Press, NY

Walker I. and Mann L (1987) Unemployment, relative deprivation, and social protest. PERSONALITY AND SOCIAL PSYCHOLOGY BULLETIN, 13, 275–283

Walker L.E. (1979) THE BATTERED WOMAN, Harper and Row, NY

Walker L.E. (1984) THE BATTERED WOMAN SYNDROME, Springer-Verlag, NY

Walkey F.H. and Gilmour D.R. (1979) Comparative evaluation of a videotaped measure of interpersonal distance. JOURNAL OF CONSULTING AND CLINICAL PSYCHOLOGY, 47, 575–580

Walkey F.H. and Gilmour D.R. (1984) The relationship between interpersonal distance and violence in imprisoned offenders. CRIMINAL JUSTICE AND BEHAVIOR, 11, 331–340

Wallace A. (1986) HOMICIDE: THE SOCIAL REALITY, NSW Bureau of Crime Statistics and Research, Sydney

Wallach M.A., Kogan N. and Bem D.J. (1964) Diffusion of responsibility and levels of risk taking in groups. JOURNAL OF ABNORMAL AND SOCIAL PSYCHOLOGY, 68, 263–274

Wallschutzky I.G. (1984) Possible causes of tax evasion. JOURNAL OF ECONOMIC PSYCHOLOGY, 5, 371–384

Walmsley D.J. and Lewis G.J. (1989) The pace of pedestrian flows in cities. ENVIRONMENT AND BEHAVIOR, 21, 123–150

Walster E. (1966) Assignment of responsibility for an accident. JOURNAL OF PERSONALITY AND SOCIAL PSYCHOLOGY, 3, 73–79

Walster E., et al. (1966) Importance of physical attractiveness in dating behavior. JOURNAL OF PERSONALITY AND SOCIAL PSYCHOLOGY, 4, 508–516

Walster E. and Walster G. (1978) LOVE, Addison-Wesley, Ma.

Walster E., Walster G.W. and Berscheid E., (1978) EQUITY: THEORY AND RESEARCH, Allyn and Bacon, Boston

Wambaugh J. (1987) ECHOES IN THE DARKNESS, Bantam, NY

Wang T.H. and Katzev R.D. (1990) Group commitment and resource conservation: Two field experiments on promoting recycling. JOURNAL OF APPLIED SOCIAL PSYCHOLOGY, 20, 265–275

Waters B. (1989) Mediation of children's TV video and film viewing in the home. Unpublished paper, presented at the Office of Film and Literature Classification Seminar: Media Violence Censorship and the Community, Sydney

Watkins D. (1979) Prediction of university success: A follow-up study of the 1977 internal intake to the University of New England. AUSTRALIAN JOURNAL OF EDUCATION, 23, 301–303

Watkins D. (1980) Rotter's internal-external locus of control scale: Some further Australian data. AUSTRALIAN PSYCHOLOGIST, 15, 494–495

Watkins W.G. and Bentovim A. (1992) The sexual abuse of male children and adolescents: A review of current research. JOURNAL OF CHILD PSYCHOLOGY AND PSYCHIATRY AND ALLIED DISCIPLINES, 33, 197–248

Watson D. (1982) The actor and the observer: How are their perceptions of causality divergent? PSYCHOLOGICAL BULLETIN, 92, 682–700

Watson J. (1986) Parental attributions of emotional disturbance and their relation to the outcome of therapy: Preliminary findings. AUSTRALIAN PSYCHOLOGIST, 21, 271–282

Weber M. (1947) THE THEORY OF SOCIAL AND ECONOMIC ORGANISATION, Free Press, Glencoe, Illinois

Weber R. and Crocker J. (1983) Cognitive process in the revision of stereotypic beliefs. JOURNAL OF PERSONALITY AND SOCIAL PSYCHOLOGY, 45, 961–977

Wedell D.H., Parducci A. and Geiselman R.E. (1987) A formal analysis of ratings of physical attractiveness: Successive contrast and simultaneous assimilation. JOURNAL OF EXPERIMENTAL SOCIAL PSYCHOLOGY, 23, 230–249

Wehr T.A., Jacobsen F.M., Sack D., et al. (1986) Phototherapy of seasonal affective disorder. ARCHIVES OF GENERAL PSYCHIATRY, 43, 870–875

Weiner B. (1982) The emotional consequences of causal attributions. In Clark M.S. and Fiske S.T. (eds) AFFECT AND COGNITION, Erlbaum, Hillsdale, NJ

Weiner B. (1986) AN ATTRIBUTIONAL THEORY OF MOTIVATION AND EMOTION, Springer-Verlag, NY

Weiner B., Amirkhan J., Folkes V.S. and Verette J.A. (1987) An attributional analysis of excuse giving: Studies of a naive theory of emotion. JOURNAL OF PERSONALITY AND SOCIAL PSYCHOLOGY, 52, 316–324

Weiner B., Frieze I., Kukla A., Reed L., Rest S. and Rosenbaum R.M. (1972) Perceiving the causes of success and failure. In Jones E., Kanouse D., Kelley H., Nisbett R., Valins S. and Weiner B. (eds) ATTRIBUTION: PERCEIVING THE CAUSES OF BEHAVIOR, General Learning Press, Morristown, NJ

Weiner F.H. (1976) Altruism, ambience and action: The effects of rural and urban rearing on helping behavior. JOURNAL OF PERSONALITY AND SOCIAL PSYCHOLOGY, 34, 112–124

Weir A.J. (1983) Notes for a prehistory of cognitive balance theory. BRITISH JOURNAL OF SOCIAL PSYCHOLOGY, 22, 351–362

Weisbrot D. (1990) AUSTRALIAN LAWYERS, Longman Cheshire, Melb.

Weiss R.S. (1973) LONELINESS: THE EXPERIENCE OF EMOTIONAL AND SOCIAL ISOLATION, M.I.T. Press, Ma.

Weiss R.S. (1974) The provisions of social relationships. In Rubin Z. (ed.) DOING UNTO OTHERS, Prentice Hall, NJ

Welford A.T. (1973) Stress and performance. ERGONOMICS, 16, 567–580

Wells G.L. and Loftus E.F. (eds) (1984) EYEWITNESS TESTIMONY, Cambridge University Press, Cambridge

Wells G.L. and Luus C.A. (1990) Police lineups as experiments: Social methodology as a framework for properly conducted lineups. PERSONALITY AND SOCIAL PSYCHOLOGY BULLETIN, 16, 106–117

Wells G.L. and Murray D.M. (1984) Eyewitness confidence. In Wells G.L. and Loftus E.F. (eds) EYEWITNESS TESTIMONY, Cambridge University Press, Cambridge

Wells J.Z. and Murray D.M. (1983) What can psychologists say about the Neil v Biggers criteria for judging eye-witness accuracy? JOURNAL OF APPLIED PSYCHOLOGY, 68, 347–362

Werner C. and Parmalee P. (1979) Similarity of activity preferences among friends: Those who play together stay together. SOCIAL PSYCHOLOGY QUARTERLY, 42, 62–66

Werner C.M., Strube M.J., Cole A.M. and Kagehiro D.K (1985) The impact of case characteristics and prior jury experience on jury verdicts. JOURNAL OF APPLIED SOCIAL PSYCHOLOGY, 15, 409–427

West S.G. and Brown T.J. (1975) Physical attractiveness, the severity of the emergency and helping: A field experiment and interpersonal simulation. JOURNAL OF EXPERIMENTAL SOCIAL PSYCHOLOGY, 11, 531–538

West S.G., Whitney G. and Schnedler R. (1975) Helping a motorist in distress: The effects of sex, race and neighborhood. JOURNAL OF PERSONALITY AND SOCIAL PSYCHOLOGY 31, 691–698

Westbrook M.T. and Nordholm L.A. (1987) Medical handmaidens: Changing self-image. AUSTRALIAN JOURNAL OF SOCIAL ISSUES, 22, 561–572

Westin A. (1967) PRIVACY AND FREEDOM, Atheneum, NY

Wetzel C.G. and Walton M.D. (1985) Developing biased social judgments: The false-consensus effect. JOURNAL OF PERSONALITY AND SOCIAL PSYCHOLOGY, 43, 197–209

Wexler G. and Logan D. (1983) Sources of stress among women police officers. JOURNAL OF POLICE SCIENCE AND ADMINISTRATION, 11, 46–53

Wexler M.N. (1990) Prediction dilemmas and the applied behavioral sciences. HUMBOLDT JOURNAL OF SOCIAL RELATIONS, 16, 95–123

Wheeler L. and Caggiula A.R. (1966) The contagion of aggression. JOURNAL OF EXPERIMENTAL SOCIAL PSYCHOLOGY, 2, 1–10

Wheeler L. and Reis H. (1988) On titles, citations, and outlets: What do mainstreamers want? In Bond M.H. (ed.) THE CROSS-CULTURAL CHALLENGE TO SOCIAL PSYCHOLOGY, Sage, Newbury Park

White G.L., Fishbein S. and Rutstein J. (1981)

Passionate love and the misattribution of arousal. JOURNAL OF PERSONALITY AND SOCIAL PSYCHOLOGY, 41, 56–62

White G.L. and Knight T.D. (1984) Misattribution of arousal and attraction: Effects of salience of explanations for arousal. JOURNAL OF EXPERIMENTAL SOCIAL PSYCHOLOGY, 20, 55–64

White J.D. and Carlston D.E. (1983) Consequences of schemata for attention, impressions, and recall in complex social interactions. JOURNAL OF PERSONALITY AND SOCIAL PSYCHOLOGY, 45, 538–549

White P.A. (1984) A model of the layperson as pragmatist. PERSONALITY AND SOCIAL PSYCHOLOGY BULLETIN, 10, 333–348

White P.A. and Younger D.P. (1988) Differences in the ascription of transient internal states to self and other. JOURNAL OF EXPERIMENTAL SOCIAL PSYCHOLOGY, 24, 292–309

White R.K. (1977) Misperception in the Arab-Israeli conflict. JOURNAL OF SOCIAL ISSUES, 33, 190–221

Whiting B.B. and Edwards C.P. (1973) A crosscultural analysis of sex differences in the behavior of children aged three through eleven. JOURNAL OF SOCIAL PSYCHOLOGY, 91, 171–188

Whiting B.B. and Whiting J.W. (1975) CHILDREN OF SIX CULTURES, Harvard University Press, Cambridge, Ma.

Whitton J.L., Kramer P.M. and Eastwood M.R. (1982) Weather and infradian rhythms in self-reports of health, sleep and mood measures. JOURNAL OF PSYCHOSOMATIC RESEARCH, 26, 231–235

Wicker A.W. (1969) Attitudes versus actions: The relationship of verbal and overt behavioral responses to attitude objects. JOURNAL OF SOCIAL ISSUES, 25, 41–78

Wicker A.W. (1979) AN INTRODUCTION TO ECOLOGICAL PSYCHOLOGY, Brooks/Cole Monterey, Ca.

Wicklund R.A. and Brehm J.W. (1976) PERSPECTIVES ON COGNITIVE DISSONANCE, Erlbaum, Hillsdale, NJ

Wiggins J.S., Wiggins N. and Conger J.C. (1968) Corrrelates of heterosexual somatic preference. JOURNAL OF PERSONALITY AND SOCIAL PSYCHOLOGY, 10, 82–90

Wilder D.A. (1977) Perceptions of groups, size of opposition and social influence. JOURNAL OF EXPERIMENTAL AND SOCIAL PSYCHOLOGY, 13, 253–262

Wilder D.A. (1986) Social categorization: Implications for creation and reduction of intergroup bias. In Berkowitz L. (ed.) ADVANCES IN EXPERIMENTAL SOCIAL PSYCHOLOGY, Academic Press, Orlando, Florida

Wilke H. and Lanzetta J.T. (1970) The obligation to help: The effects of the amount of prior help on subsequent helping behavior. JOURNAL OF EXPERIMENTAL SOCIAL PSYCHOLOGY, 6, 253–258

Wilkie M. (1987) Composition of juries. In Zdenkowski G., Ronalds C. and Richardson M. (eds) THE CRIMINAL INJUSTICE SYSTEM, Pluto Press, Sydney

Williams E. (1991) College students and recycling: Their attitudes and behaviors. JOURNAL OF COLLEGE STUDENT DEVELOPMENT, 32, 86–88

Williams G.C. (1966) ADAPTATION AND NATURAL SELECTION: A CRITIQUE OF SOME CURRENT EVOLUTIONARY THOUGHT, Princeton University Press, Princeton

Williams K., Harkins S. and Latane B. (1981) Identifiability as a deterrent to social loafing: Two cheering experiments. JOURNAL OF PERSONALITY AND SOCIAL PSYCHOLOGY, 40, 303–311

Williams J.A. (1984) Gender and intergroup behaviour: Towards an integration. BRITISH JOURNAL OF SOCIAL PSYCHOLOGY, 23, 311–316.

Wilson E.O. (1975) SOCIOBIOLOGY: THE NEW SYNTHESIS, Harvard University Press, Cambridge, Ma.

Wilson E.O. (1978) The genetic evolution of altruism. In Wispe L. (ed.), ALTRUISM, SYMPATHY AND HELPING: PSYCHOLOGICAL AND SOCIOLOGICAL PRINCIPLES, Academic Press, NY

Wilson E.O. (1984) BIOPHILIA, Harvard University Press, Cambridge, Ma.

Wilson J.E. and Tobacyk J.J. (1990) Lunar phases and crisis center telephone calls. JOURNAL OF SOCIAL PSYCHOLOGY, 130, 47–51

Wilson P.R. (1968) The perceptual distortion of height as a function of ascribed academic status. JOURNAL OF SOCIAL PSYCHOLOGY, 74, 97–102

Wilson P.R. (1989a) Sexual and violent crime in Australia: Rhetoric and reality. CURRENT AFFAIRS BULLETIN, 65, 11–17

Wilson P.R. (1989b) The police and the future. In Chappell D. and Wilson P. (eds) AUSTRALIAN POLICING: CONTEMPORARY ISSUES, Butterworths, Sydney

Wilson P.R. and Nugent S. (1987) Sexually explicit and violent media material: Research and policy implications. TRENDS AND ISSUES IN CRIME AND CRIMINAL JUSTICE (No. 9), Australian Institute of Criminology, Canberra

Wilson T.D. and Dunn D.S. (1986) Effects of introspection on attitude-behavior consistency: Analyzing reasons versus focusing on feelings. JOURNAL OF EXPERIMENTAL SOCIAL PSYCHOLOGY, 22, 249–263

Winch R. (1958) MATE-SELECTION: A STUDY OF COMPLEMENTARY NEEDS, Harper and Row, NY

Winefield A.H. (1982) Methodological difficulties in demonstrating learned helplessness in humans. JOURNAL OF GENERAL PSYCHOLOGY, 107, 255–266

Winefield A.H. and Tiggemann M. (1990) Employment status and psychological well-being: A longitudinal study. JOURNAL OF APPLIED PSYCHOLOGY, 75, 455–459

Winefield A.H., Tiggemann M. and Goldney R.D. (1988) Psychological concomitants of satisfactory employment and unemployment in young people. SOCIAL PSYCHIATRY AND PSYCHIATRIC EPIDEMIOLOGY, 23, 149–157

Winefield A.H., Tiggemann M. and Smith S. (1987) Unemployment, attributional style and psychological well-being. PERSONALITY AND INDIVIDUAL DIFFERENCES, 8, 659–665

Winett R.A., Neale M.S. and Grier H.C. (1979) Effects of self-monitoring and feedback on residential electricity consumption. JOURNAL OF APPLIED BEHAVIOR ANALYSIS, 12, 173–184

Winkler R.C. and Winett R.A. (1982) Behavioral interventions in resource management: A systems approach based on behavioral economics. AMERCIAN PSYCHOLOGIST, 37, 421–435

Winsborough H. (1965) The social consequences of high population density. LAW AND CONTEMPORARY PROBLEMS, 30, 120–126

Winton W.M. (1990) Jamesian aspects of misattribution research. Special Issue: Centennial celebration of The Principles of Psychology. PERSONALITY AND SOCIAL PSYCHOLOGY BULLETIN, 16, 652–664

Wirth I. (1938) Urbanism as a way of life. AMERICAN JOURNAL OF SOCIOLOGY, 44, 1–24

Witkin H.A., Mednick S.A., Schulsinger F., et al. (1976) Criminality in XYY and XXY men. SCIENCE, 196, 547–555

Witmer J.F. and Geller E.S. (1976) Facilitating paper recycling: Effects of prompts, raffles, and contests. JOURNAL OF APPLIED BEHAVIOR ANALYSIS, 9, 315–322

Witt A.L. (1989) Urban-nonurban differences in social cognition: Locus of control and perceptions of a just world. JOURNAL OF SOCIAL PSYCHOLOGY, 129, 715–717

Wolf S. (1979) Behavioural style and group cohesiveness as sources of minority influence. EUROPEAN JOURNAL OF SOCIAL PSYCHOLOGY, 9, 381–395

Wolf S. (1985) Manifest and latent influences of majorities and minorities. JOURNAL OF PERSONALITY AND SOCIAL PSYCHOLOGY, 48, 899–908

Wolf S. and Bugaj A. (1990) The social impact of courtroom witnesses. SOCIAL BEHAVIOR, 5, 1–13

Woll S. (1986) So many to choose from: Decision strategies in videodating. JOURNAL OF SOCIAL AND PERSONALITY RELATIONSHIPS, 3, 43–52

Won-Doornink M.J. (1985) Self-disclosure and reciprocity in conversation: A cross-national study. SOCIAL PSYCHOLOGY QUARTERLY, 48, 97–107

Worchel S. (1974) The effects of three types of arbitrary thwarting on the instigation to aggression. JOURNAL OF PERSONALITY, 42, 301–318

Worchel S. and Teddie C. (1976) The experience of crowding: A two-factor theory. JOURNAL OF PERSONALITY AND SOCIAL PSYCHOLOGY, 34, 36–40

Word C.O., Zanna M.P. and Cooper J. (1974) The nonverbal mediation of self-fulfilling prophecies in interracial interaction. JOURNAL OF EXPERIMENTAL SOCIAL PSYCHOLOGY, 10, 109–120

Worsley A. (1988) A study of South Australian shopping and cooking habits. JOURNAL OF THE HOME ECONOMICS ASSOCIATION OF AUSTRALIA, 20, 7–10

Wortman C.B. (1975) Some determinants of perceived control. JOURNAL OF PERSONALITY AND SOCIAL PSYCHOLOGY, 31, 282–294

Wright S.C., Taylor D.M. and Moghaddam F.M. (1990) Responding to membership in a disadvantaged group: From acceptance to collective protest. JOURNAL OF PERSONALITY AND SOCIAL PSYCHOLOGY, 58, 994–1003

Wyer R.S. and Carlston D.E. (1979) SOCIAL COGNITION, INFERENCE, AND ATTRIBUTION, Erlbaum, Hillsdale, NJ

Wyer R.S. and Srull T.K. (1980) The processing of social stimulus information: A conceptual integration. In Hastie R., Ostrom E.B., Ebbesen R.S., et al. (eds) PERSON MEMORY: THE COGNITIVE BASIS OF SOCIAL PERCEPTION, Erlbaum, Hillsdale, NJ

Wynne-Edwards V.C. (1962) ANIMAL DISPERSION IN RELATION TO SOCIAL BEHAVIOUR, Oliver and Boyd, Edinburgh

Yamagishi T. (1988) Seriousness of social dilemmas and the provision of a sanctioning system. SOCIAL PSYCHOLOGY QUARTERLY, 51, 32–42

Yarmey A.D. (1986) Verbal, visual and voice identification of a rape suspect under different laws of illumination. JOURNAL OF APPLIED SOCIAL PSYCHOLOGY, 71, 363–370

Yarmey A.D. (1990) UNDERSTANDING POLICE AND POLICE WORK: PSYCHOLOGICAL ISSUES, Columbia University Press, Irvington, NY

Yarmey A.D. and Jones H.P. (1983) Accuracy of memory of male and female eyewitnesses to a criminal assault and rape. BULLETIN OF THE PSYCHONOMIC SOCIETY, 21, 89–92

Yarmey A.D. and Jones H.P. (1983) Is the psychology of eyewitness identification a matter of common sense? In Lloyd-Bostock S. and Clifford B.R. (eds) EVALUATING EYEWITNESS EVIDENCE, Wiley, Lond.

Yarmey A.D. and Jones H.P. (1985) Is the psychology of eyewitness identification a matter of commonsense? In Lloyd-Bostock S. and Clifford B.R. (eds), EVALUATING EYEWITNESS EVIDENCE, Wiley, Lond.

Yarwood A.J. and Knowling M.J. (1982)

RACE RELATIONS IN AUSTRALIA: A HISTORY, Methuen, Lond.

Yinon Y., Sharon I., Gonen Y., et al. (1982) Escape from responsibility and help in emergencies among persons alone or within groups. EUROPEAN JOURNAL OF SOCIAL PSYCHOLOGY, 12, 301–305

Yoder J.D. (1991) Rethinking tokenism: Looking beyond numbers. GENDER AND SOCIETY, 5, 178–192

Young L. and Brooks R. (1988) THE PROFILE OF CHILD ABUSE IN NSW, Department of Family and Community Services, Parramatta, Sydney

Yourell A.M. and McCabe M.P. (1988) The motivations underlying male rape of women. AUSTRALIAN JOURNAL OF SEX, MARRIAGE AND THE FAMILY, 9, 215–224

Yuille J.C. and Cutshall J.Z. (1986) A case study of eye witness memory of a crime. JOURNAL OF APPLIED PSYCHOLOGY, 71, 291–301

Yukl G.A. (1981) LEADERSHIP IN ORGANISATIONS, Prentice Hall, Lond.

Zaccaro S.J. (1984) Social loafing: The role of task attractiveness. PERSONALITY AND SOCIAL PSYCHOLOGY BULLETIN, 10, 99–106

Zahn-Waxler C., Radke-Yarrow M. and King R.A. (1979) Child rearing and children's prosocial initiations towards victims of distress. CHILD DEVELOPMENT, 50, 319–330

Zajonc R.B. (1965) Social Facilitation. SCIENCE, 149, 260–274

Zajonc R.B. (1968a) Attitudinal effects of mere exposure. JOURNAL OF PERSONALITY AND SOCIAL PSYCHOLOGY, 9, 1–27

Zajonc R.B. (1968b) Cognitive theories in social psychology. In Lindzey G. and Aronson E. (eds) THE HANDBOOK OF SOCIAL PSYCHOLOGY (Vol 1.), (2nd edn), Addison-Wesley, Ma.

Zajonc R.B. (1980a) Feeling and thinking: Preferences need no inferences. AMERICAN PSYCHOLOGIST, 35, 151–175

Zajonc R.B (1980b) Compresence. In Paulus P.B. (ed.) PSYCHOLOGY OF GROUP INFLUENCE, Erlbaum, Hillsdale, NJ

Zajonc. R.B. (1989) Styles of explanation in social psychology. EUROPEAN JOURNAL OF SOCIAL PSYCHOLOGY, 19, 345–368

Zajonc R.B., Adelmann P., Murphy S.T. and Niedenthal P.M. (1987) Convergence in the physical appearance of spouses. MOTIVATION AND EMOTION, 11, 335–346

Zajonc R.B., Heingartner A. and Herman E. (1969) Social enhancement and impairment of performance in the cockroach. JOURNAL OF PERSONALITY AND SOCIAL PSYCHOLOGY, 13, 83–92

Zajonc R.B. and Sales S.M. (1966) Social facilitation of dominant and subordinate responses. JOURNAL OF EXPERIMENTAL SOCIAL PSYCHOLOGY, 2, 160–168

Zanna M.P. and Cooper J. (1974) Dissonance and the pill An attributional approach to studying the arousal properties of dissonance. JOURNAL OF PERSONALITY AND SOCIAL PSYCHOLOGY, 29, 703–709

Zanna M.P. and Fazio R.H. (1982) The attitude-behavior relation: Moving toward a third generation of research. In Zanna M.P., Higgins E.T. and Herman C.P. (eds) CONSISTENCY IN SOCIAL BEHAVIOR: THE ONTARIO SYMPOSIUM (Vol. 2), Erlbaum, Hillsdale, NJ

Zanna M.P., Olson J.M. and Fazio R.H. (1980) Attitude-behavior consistency: An individual difference perspective. JOURNAL OF PERSONALITY AND SOCIAL PSYCHOLOGY, 38, 432–440

Zaragoza M.S. and McCloskey M. (1989) Misleading post event information and the memory impairment hypothesis: Comment on Belli and reply to Tversky and Tuchin. JOURNAL OF EXPERIMENTAL PSYCHOLOGY: GENERAL, 118, 92–99

Zillmann D. (1978) Attribution and misattributions of excitatory reactions. In Harvey J.H., Icles W.J. and Kidd R.F. (eds) NEW DIRECTIONS IN ATTRIBUTION RESEARCH (Vol. 2), Erlbaum, Hillsdale, NJ

Zillmann D. (1979) HOSTILITY AND AGGRESSION, Erlbaum, Hillsdale, NJ

Zillmann D. and Bryant J. (1984) Effects of massive exposure to pornography. In Malamuth N. and Donnerstein E. (eds) PORNOGRAPHY AND SEXUAL AGGRESSION, Academic Press, NY

Zillmann D. and Bryant J. (1984) PORNOGRAPHY AND SEXUAL AGGRESSION, Academic Press, NY

Zillmann D. and Bryant J. (1988) Pornography's impact on sexual satisfaction. JOURNAL OF APPLIED SOCIAL PSYCHOLOGY, 18, 438–453

Zillmann D. and Bryant J. (eds) (1989) PORNOGRAPHY: RESEARCH ADVANCES AND POLICY CONSIDERATIONS, Erlbaum, Hillsdale, NJ

Zillmann D., Johnson R.C. and Day K.D. (1974) Attribution of apparent arousal and proficiency of recovery from sympathetic activation affecting activation transfer to aggressive behavior. JOURNAL OF EXPERIMENTAL SOCIAL PSYCHOLOGY, 10, 503–515

Zimbardo P.G. (1965) The effect of effort and improvisation on self-persuasion produced by role playing. JOURNAL OF EXPERIMENTAL SOCIAL PSYCHOLOGY, 1, 103–120

Zimbardo P., Haney C., Banks W. and Jaffe D. (1972) The psychology of imprisonment: Privation, power and pathology. Unpublished paper, Stanford University, Stanford, Ca.

Zimbardo P.G., Weisenberg M., Firestone L. and Levy B. (1965) Communicator effectiveness in producing public conformity and private attitude change. JOURNAL OF PERSONALITY, 33, 233–255

Zuckerman M., DePaulo B.M. and Rosenthal R. (1981) Verbal and nonverbal communication of deception. In Berkowitz L. (ed.) ADVANCES IN EXPERIMENTAL SOCIAL PSYCHOLOGY (Vol. 14), Academic Press, NY

Zuckerman M., Lazzaro M.M. and Waldgeir D. (1979) Undermining the effects of the foot-in-the-door technique with extrinsic rewards. JOURNAL OF APPLIED SOCIAL PSYCHOLOGY, 9, 292–296

Zukier H. (1982) The role of the correlation and the dispersion of predictor variables in the use of nondiagnostic information. JOURNAL OF PERSONALITY AND SOCIAL PSYCHOLOGY, 43, 1163–1175

Zukier H. and Jennings D.L. (1983–84) Nondiagnosticity and typicality effects in prediction. SOCIAL COGNITION, 2, 187–198

NAMES INDEX

Page numbers in *italics* indicate photographs

SUBJECT INDEX

Page numbers in *italics* indicate illustrations